SPSS® 10.0
Syntax Reference Guide

For more information about SPSS® software products, please visit our WWW site at *http://www.spss.com* or contact

Marketing Department
SPSS Inc.
233 South Wacker Drive, 11th Floor
Chicago, IL 60606-6307
Tel: (312) 651-3000
Fax: (312) 651-3668

Preface

This manual is a reference to the command syntax for the SPSS Base system and the Regression Models and Advanced Models options. This reference guide does *not* provide an overview of SPSS, teach you how to create jobs and interpret results, or show you how to run SPSS on your computer and operating system. This information is supplied in a separate *SPSS Base User's Guide*.

Manuals for the Base System. Documentation for SPSS Release 10.0 consists of:

- The *SPSS Base User's Guide* provides detailed information on how to run SPSS on your computer's operating system, including complete documentation of the user interface provided for your system. It also explains many of the statistical concepts involved, how to use the statistical procedures correctly, and how to interpret the results.

- A companion book, the *SPSS Base Applications Guide*, provides examples of statistical procedures and related data transformations, with advice on screening data, using appropriate procedures, and interpreting the output.

- *SPSS Interactive Graphics* documents interactive charts, an important feature in the SPSS Base system. Once you have created a chart, you can make many modifications dynamically, such as insert or delete graphical elements, change colors and textures, rotate 3-D graphs smoothly, and adjust fit lines and surfaces.

- The *SPSS Syntax Reference Guide* documents and provides examples of the command syntax. On some computer operating systems, the user interface makes it possible to obtain most of the features of SPSS without ever looking at command syntax. There are, however, some features that can be obtained only by entering and running SPSS commands.

Contacting SPSS

If you would like to be on our mailing list, contact one of our offices, listed on page iv, or visit our WWW site at *http://www.spss.com*. We will send you a copy of our newsletter and let you know about SPSS Inc. activities in your area.

SPSS Inc.
Chicago, Illinois, U.S.A.
Tel: 1.312.651.3000
www.spss.com/corpinfo
Customer Service:
1.800.521.1337
Sales:
1.800.543.2185
sales@spss.com
Training:
1.800.543.6607
Technical Support:
1.312.651.3410
support@spss.com

SPSS Federal Systems
Tel: 1.703.527.6777
www.spss.com

SPSS Argentina srl
Tel: +5411.4814.5030
www.spss.com

SPSS Asia Pacific Pte. Ltd.
Tel: +65.245.9110
www.spss.com

SPSS Australasia Pty. Ltd.
Tel: +61.2.9954.5660
www.spss.com

SPSS Belgium
Tel: +32.163.170.70
www.spss.com

SPSS Benelux BV
Tel: +31.183.651777
www.spss.com

SPSS Brasil Ltda
Tel: +55.11.5505.3644
www.spss.com

SPSS Czech Republic
Tel: +420.2.24813839
www.spss.cz

SPSS Denmark A/S
Tel: +45.45.46.02.00
www.spss.com

SPSS Finland Oy
Tel: +358.9.524.801
www.spss.com

SPSS France SARL
Tel: +01.55.35.27.00 x03
www.spss.com

SPSS Germany
Tel: +49.89.4890740
www.spss.com

SPSS Hellas SA
Tel: +30.1.72.51.925/72.51.950
www.spss.com

SPSS Hispanoportuguesa S.L.
Tel: +34.91.447.37.00
www.spss.com

SPSS Hong Kong Ltd.
Tel: +852.2.811.9662
www.spss.com

SPSS India
Tel: +91.80.225.0260
www.spss.com

SPSS Ireland
Tel: +353.1.496.9007
www.spss.com

SPSS Israel Ltd.
Tel: +972.9.9526700
www.spss.com

SPSS Italia srl
Tel: +39.51.252573
www.spss.it

SPSS Japan Inc.
Tel: +81.3.5466.5511
www.spss.com

SPSS Kenya Limited
Tel: +254.2.577.262/3
www.spss.com

SPSS Korea KIC Co., Ltd.
Tel: +82.2.3446.7651
www.spss.co.kr

SPSS Latin America
Tel: +1.312.651.3539
www.spss.com

SPSS Malaysia Sdn Bhd
Tel: +60.3.7873.6477
www.spss.com

SPSS Mexico SA de CV
Tel: +52.5.682.87.68
www.spss.com

SPSS Norway
Tel: +47.22.40.20.60
www.spss.com

SPSS Polska
Tel: +48.12.6369680
www.spss.pl

SPSS Russia
Tel: +7.095.125.0069
www.spss.com

SPSS Schweiz AG
Tel: +41.1.266.90.30
www.spss.com

SPSS Sweden AB
Tel: +46.8.506.105.68
www.spss.com

SPSS BI (Singapore) Pte. Ltd.
Tel: +65.324.5150
www.spss.com

SPSS South Africa
Tel: +27.11.807.3189
www.spss.com

SPSS Taiwan Corp.
Taipei, Republic of China
Tel: +886.2.25771100
www.sinter.com.tw/spss/

SPSS (Thailand) Co., Ltd.
Tel: +66.2.260.7070, +66.2.260.7080
www.spss.com

SPSS UK Ltd.
Tel: +44.1483.719200
www.spss.com

Contents

Introduction: A Guide to SPSS Command Syntax   1

Universals   11

Commands   11

Files   19

Variables   29

Transformation Expressions   43

Date and Time   60

Commands   75

ACF   75

ADD FILES   82

ADD VALUE LABELS   89

AGGREGATE   92

ALSCAL   102

ANOVA   119

APPLY DICTIONARY   128

AUTORECODE   132

BEGIN DATA—END DATA   137

BREAK   139

CACHE   140

CASEPLOT   141

CCF   152

CLEAR TRANSFORMATIONS   158

CLUSTER   159

COMMENT   178

COMPUTE   179

CORRELATIONS   191

COUNT   197

COXREG   199

CREATE   212

CROSSTABS   221

CURVEFIT   234

DATA LIST   241

DATE   259

DEFINE—!ENDDEFINE   268

DESCRIPTIVES   286

DISCRIMINANT   292

DISPLAY   312

DOCUMENT   315

DO IF   317

DO REPEAT—END REPEAT   326

DROP DOCUMENTS   331

EDIT   332

END CASE   334

END FILE   342

ERASE   344

EXAMINE   345

EXECUTE   354

EXPORT   355

FACTOR   361

FILE HANDLE   378

FILE LABEL   380

FILE TYPE—END FILE TYPE   381

FILTER   396

FINISH   398

FIT   400

FLIP   403

FORMATS   407

FREQUENCIES   411

GENLOG   420

GET   431

GET CAPTURE   435

GET DATA   438

GET SAS   445

GET TRANSLATE   453

GLM: Overview   461

GLM: Univariate   469

GLM: Multivariate   490

GLM: Repeated Measures   495

GRAPH   504

HILOGLINEAR   535

IF   544

IGRAPH   550

IMPORT   574

INCLUDE   578

INFO   580

INPUT PROGRAM—END INPUT
PROGRAM   584

KEYED DATA LIST   588

KM   594

LEAVE   603

LIST   605

LOGISTIC REGRESSION   609

LOGLINEAR   623

LOOP—END LOOP   637

MANOVA: Overview   646

MANOVA: Univariate   650

MANOVA: Multivariate   675

MANOVA: Repeated Measures   688

MATCH FILES   697

MATRIX—END MATRIX   705

MATRIX DATA   750

MCONVERT   769

MEANS   772

MISSING VALUES   777

MULT RESPONSE   780

NEW FILE   790

NLR   791

N OF CASES   808

NOMREG   810

NONPAR CORR   817

NPAR TESTS   823

NUMBERED and UNNUMBERED   843

NUMERIC   844

OLAP CUBE   846

ONEWAY   850

PACF   860

PARTIAL CORR   866

PLOT   875

PLUM   880

POINT   888

PPLOT   892

PREDICT   902

PRESERVE   906

PRINT   907

PRINT EJECT   913

PRINT FORMATS   916

PRINT SPACE   919

PROBIT   922

PROCEDURE OUTPUT   931

PROXIMITIES   933

QUICK CLUSTER   951

RANK   958

RECODE   964

RECORD TYPE   970

REFORMAT   979

REGRESSION   981

REGRESSION: Residuals   997

RELIABILITY   1006

RENAME VARIABLES   1016

REPEATING DATA   1018

REPORT   1032

REREAD   1061

RESTORE   1068

RMV   1069

ROC   1073

SAMPLE   1077

SAVE   1079

SAVE TRANSLATE   1085

SCRIPT   1094

SELECT IF   1095

SET   1100

SHOW   1113

SORT CASES   1117

SPCHART   1119

SPLIT FILE   1137

STRING   1140

SUBTITLE   1142

SUMMARIZE   1144

SURVIVAL   1150

SYSFILE INFO   1163

TEMPORARY   1164

TITLE   1167

TSET   1169

TSHOW   1172

TSPLOT   1173

T-TEST   1183

2SLS   1188

UNIANOVA   1193

UPDATE   1214

USE   1221

VALUE LABELS   1224

VARCOMP   1227

VARIABLE ALIGNMENT   1234

VARIABLE LABELS   1235

VARIABLE LEVEL   1237

VARIABLE WIDTH   1238

VECTOR   1239

VERIFY   1245

WEIGHT   1247

WLS   1249

WRITE   1255

WRITE FORMATS   1260

XSAVE   1263

Appendix A
Commands and Program
States   1269

Program States   1269

Determining Command Order   1271

Appendix B
IMPORT/EXPORT Character
Sets   1279

Appendix C
Defining Complex Files   1287

A Rectangular File   1287

Nested Files   1288

Grouped Data   1291

Mixed Files   1294

Repeating Data   1297

Appendix D
Using the Macro Facility   1301

Example 1: Automating a File-Matching
Task   1302

Example 2: Testing Correlation
Coefficients   1308

Example 3: Generating Random
Data   1312

Subject Index   1317

Syntax Index   1353

Introduction: A Guide to SPSS Command Syntax

Overview

The *SPSS Syntax Reference Guide* is arranged alphabetically by command name to provide quick access to detailed information on each command in the SPSS command language. This introduction is intended to help you determine which commands are best for the job at hand.

Most SPSS commands can be classified according to what they do to the **working data file**, which is simply the rectangular array of cases and variables with which SPSS is currently working. Operations with the working data file include:

- **Defining a working data file**. Data-definition commands define a new data file or read a previously defined data file and make it available for analysis.

- **Describing the working data file**. These commands add labels or other optional information to the data in the file.

- **Modifying data values**. The SPSS transformation language allows you to specify calculations, simple or elaborate, to be carried out with your data.

- **Defining complex data files**. More powerful "programming" commands let you take control of the process by which SPSS builds the working data file.

- **Selecting cases for processing**. Capabilities for logical case selection and random sampling are essential in data analysis.

- **Modifying the structure of the working data file**. You can easily rearrange, combine, or split up your data files.

- **Saving the working data file**. Save in SPSS format for efficiency or another format for portability.

- **Displaying data values**. Take a look at the data in your working data file.

- **Statistical analysis, tabulation, and graphics**. The analytical commands in SPSS calculate and display statistics, graphics, or tabulations. They are probably the reason you are using SPSS.

- **Other utilities**. This group includes utility commands that do not affect the working data file but that enhance or simplify the operation of SPSS itself.

The remainder of this introduction provides overviews of the commands that perform these functions. For details on the operation of any command, consult the appropriate section of this guide.

Defining a Working Data File

SPSS can read data files created in a wide variety of spreadsheet and database formats. Commands are also available for defining and reading data from simple, unformatted text files.

Data Files in SPSS, Spreadsheet, or Database Format

The easiest way to define a working data file is to open a data file that has already been defined, either in SPSS or in some other software. If you have data in such a file, use one of the following commands:

GET. Reads data files in SPSS format as created by the SAVE command in SPSS running under the same operating system or a compatible one. GET is the fastest way to define a working data file. Labels and missing-value definitions that were in effect when the file was saved are preserved.

IMPORT. Reads data files as created by the EXPORT command in SPSS on any machine under any operating system. IMPORT is noticeably slower than GET but preserves labels and missing-value definitions.

GET TRANSLATE. Reads data files created by popular spreadsheet and database software. Field names may be preserved as SPSS variable names. (Other GET commands for other software formats are available under some operating systems. Consult the appropriate sections of this guide for details.)

Unformatted Text Files

If your data are in an unformatted "text" file such as the ASCII files that can be saved by text editors or word processors, you must tell SPSS exactly where and how to read the variables in the file. Do this with:

DATA LIST. Specifies names, formats, and locations of variables to be read from a text file.

MATRIX DATA. Defines an SPSS matrix file to be read from a text or ASCII file. An SPSS matrix-format file can contain correlation, covariance, or other kinds of matrices. Statistical procedures are sometimes able to analyze a matrix-format file more efficiently than a case-oriented data file. The MCONVERT command converts between correlation and covariance matrix files.

Other Data Definition Commands

A utility command that can be useful in defining a data file is:

APPLY DICTIONARY. Applies labels, formats, and missing-value definitions to the working data file from a data file saved in SPSS format, when some or all of the variables in the two files have the same names.

If you are running SPSS under a suitable operating system, you can use:

KEYED DATA LIST and POINT. These commands read keyed (indexed sequential) or direct-access (VSAM) data files under certain operating systems.

Describing the Working Data File

Once you have defined a working data file, you can add other information to its dictionary. With the exception of the MISSING VALUES command, these commands are basically cosmetic and affect the appearance rather than the content of SPSS output.

MISSING VALUES. Specifies that certain values should be excluded from the analysis. These are typically codes used to represent absent or irrelevant data.

FORMATS. Specifies the format (numeric, date, dollar, etc.) by which data values should be displayed. You can also use PRINT FORMATS to specify one format for displayed values and WRITE FORMATS to specify another format (possibly nonprintable) for use with the WRITE command.

VARIABLE LABELS. Provides extended descriptive labels for variables. SPSS automatically uses variable labels to annotate its output.

VALUE LABELS. Provides extended descriptive labels for individual values of variables. These labels are particularly useful if you use numeric codes to represent categorical information, such as gender or race. SPSS automatically uses value labels to annotate its output.

ADD VALUE LABELS. Adds value labels without replacing those previously defined for a variable.

RENAME VARIABLES. Changes the names of variables in the working data file.

Related utilities include:

DISPLAY. Displays information on variables, documents, or macros defined in the working data file.

DOCUMENT. Adds documentary information to the working data file. Documents are preserved by the SAVE command.

Modifying Data Values

The SPSS transformation language makes it easy to change the values of your variables in almost any systematic way. (*Ad hoc* changes in individual values can be made in the Data Editor, available in some operating environments.)

Transformation commands are not executed immediately. Instead, they are stored in the computer's memory until a command that needs the data is processed. At that time, SPSS executes all transformation commands that are pending since the last time it read the data file. (See EXECUTE to override this behavior.)

COMPUTE. Evaluates an expression and assigns the result to the values of a new or existing variable. The expression can involve constants, variables in the working data file, arithmetic or logical operators, and any of several dozen functions.

IF. Evaluates an expression conditionally (depending on whether a logical expression is true for a particular case) and assigns the result of the expression to a new or existing variable.

DO IF and related commands (ELSE IF, ELSE, END IF). Delimit a block of transformation commands that are to be executed conditionally, depending on whether a logical expression is true for each particular case.

RECODE. Reassigns the values of individual variables or collapses ranges of values into single values, according to your specifications. This command can also create a new variable to contain the recoded or collapsed values.

AUTORECODE. Recodes values automatically into consecutive integers. This command works for both numeric and string (alphanumeric) variables.

COUNT. Counts how many of a set of variables have any of a set of specified values and sets a variable equal to the count.

DO REPEAT. Replicates a block of transformation commands, substituting different variables or constants into each copy.

RANK. Assigns rank orders to cases, based on a variable in the working data file. Unlike other commands listed here, RANK requires SPSS to process the data file immediately.

TEMPORARY. Indicates that a group of transformation commands should modify the working data file only temporarily.

Two utility commands do nothing but add variable names to the dictionary:

NUMERIC. Adds a list of numeric variables to the dictionary. Since new variables are numeric by default, the main use of this command is to specify in advance the order of a group of new variables.

STRING. Adds a string (alphanumeric) variable or a list of string variables to the dictionary. Since new variables are numeric by default, this command is required before any transformation command that uses a new string variable.

Defining Complex Data Files

The above commands all read or modify rectangular data files in ways that handle typical situations. When your data are not arranged in one of these typical ways, you can use the more powerful programming facilities of SPSS to take control of building the working data file. With these facilities, you can read a data file of almost any shape, or you can generate deterministic or random data in a file of your own creation.

INPUT PROGRAM. Marks the beginning of a program to define or create a working data file. The program usually includes control structures (such as LOOP or DO IF), one or more DATA LIST commands, and transformation commands (such as COMPUTE).

The following special-purpose commands are available within an input program:

END CASE. Sends a case to the working data file.

END FILE. Closes the working data file explicitly rather than waiting for the end of a data file being read by SPSS.

REREAD. Causes the next DATA LIST command executed to read the same record as the previously executed DATA LIST command. This lets you use part of a data record to determine the way in which the rest of the record is read.

REPEATING DATA. Allows more than one case to be defined by a single input record. This command can also be used in a FILE TYPE structure, described below.

LOOP. Marks the beginning of a group of transformation commands to be executed repeatedly. Loop termination can be controlled by a logical criterion, an index variable, or explicitly with the BREAK command. The LOOP command can also be used as a part of the transformation language, outside of an input program.

Certain commonly encountered data structures, where a data value on each record determines how that record should be treated, are handled automatically by the FILE TYPE and RECORD TYPE commands. Each variety of FILE TYPE provides "canned" logic for rereading data records, with automatic checks for such problems as invalid record types, missing or out-of-order records, and duplicate records. Subsequent RECORD TYPE commands provide the details for each record type.

FILE TYPE MIXED. Builds a case from each record that is read. Unwanted record types can be skipped, and each record type can be treated differently, but one case is built from each record processed.

FILE TYPE GROUPED. Builds a single case from a group of records.

FILE TYPE NESTED. Builds cases from hierarchical data files, spreading data values from higher-level (aggregated) records to lower-level records.

Utility commands that are particularly helpful in defining complex files include:

LEAVE. Retains the values of specified variables from one case to another, rather than reinitializing them between cases.

VECTOR. Defines a group of consecutive variables as a pseudo-vector. Transformation commands can then refer to individual variables by means of an index variable that is evaluated at run time. This facility is particularly helpful within a loop structure, since the loop index can also be used within the vector.

Selecting Cases for Processing

The following commands specify that subsequent processing should be based on selected cases only:

SELECT IF. Lets you specify a logical criterion for case selection.

FILTER. Lets you specify a logical criterion for temporary case selection.

SAMPLE. Lets you select a sample of the cases in the working data file, based on a pseudo-random number generated by SPSS.

N OF CASES. Specifies that only a certain number of cases from the beginning of the data file should be used.

Modifying the Structure of the Working Data File

The following commands, used singly or in combination, let you reorganize the working data file in almost any way you could want:

SORT CASES. Sorts the cases in the working data file into ascending or descending order of the values of one or more variables.

FLIP. Transposes the data matrix so that each variable becomes a case and each case becomes a variable.

WEIGHT. Simulates the replication of individual cases in statistical calculations and tables.

AGGREGATE. Combines groups of cases into single aggregated cases. Variables in the aggregated file contain statistical functions (such as sums or means) of the original variables, computed across a group of cases in the original, unaggregated file.

UPDATE. Replaces data values in a master file with values from one or more transaction files.

ADD FILES. Combines the cases in two or more data files, normally files containing many of the same variables.

MATCH FILES. Combines the variables in two or more data files, normally files containing many of the same cases. Can also perform table lookups, in which the value of a key variable is used to extract data from a table file.

SPLIT FILE. Specifies that analysis should be performed separately for each group of cases, as defined by one or more grouping variables.

Saving the Working Data File

A working data file exists only during the course of an SPSS session. The following commands save a copy of the working data file on any available storage device:

SAVE. Saves the working data file in native SPSS format, which can be read by the GET command under the same operating system or a compatible one. This is the best format in which to save data files that you will analyze repeatedly with SPSS. All dictionary information is preserved. SPSS reads and writes files much faster in its own format. Files in this format can be used only within SPSS.

XSAVE. Saves the working data file in native SPSS format while carrying out the next SPSS procedure, thus saving the processing time required to read the data file (provided that there is another SPSS procedure within the session).

EXPORT. Saves the working data file in SPSS portable format, which can be read by the SPSS Import command, on any machine under any operating system. EXPORT is noticeably slower than SAVE or XSAVE.

SAVE TRANSLATE. Saves the working data file in one of several formats that can be read by popular spreadsheet and database software.

WRITE. Saves the data values in the working data file in text (typically ASCII) format, with no dictionary information.

Displaying Data Values

The simplest thing that SPSS can do to the working data file is display it. The Data Editor (where available) provides the quickest and easiest way to view the contents of the working data file. The following commands display data in increasingly elaborate ways:

LIST. Displays the data in the working data file. This command offers minimal control over the data displayed or its format.

PRINT. Displays data values, or calculated values or constants, while carrying out the next SPSS procedure. This is an efficient and flexible way of displaying data, provided that there will be another procedure. It requires you to specify the format and to calculate any summary statistics using the transformation language.

REPORT. Produces reports containing summary statistics, listings of individual cases, or both. This is usually the easiest way to obtain reports more complex than simple case listings.

Statistical Analysis, Tabulation, and Graphics

The procedures performing these tasks are probably why you are using SPSS. Consult the *SPSS Base User's Guide* for your version of SPSS for assistance in choosing the right procedure and interpreting the results.

Analytical procedures read the working data file. As they do so, SPSS carries out any transformation commands that have been specified since the data file was last read. If the working data file has been modified, a new copy is written for subsequent use.

Summary Measures, Frequency Tables, and Crosstabulation

CROSSTABS. Builds cross-classification tables and calculates tests of independence and measures of association for categorical variables.

DESCRIPTIVES. Efficiently calculates univariate statistics, such as means and variances, that do not require tabulation.

EXAMINE. Displays exploratory plots and statistics.

FREQUENCIES. Displays frequency tables, as well as univariate statistics and plots.

MULT RESPONSE. Displays frequency tables and crosstabulations for multiple-response and multiple-dichotomy variables.

Comparing Means and Analysis of Variance

ANOVA. Performs factorial analysis of variance for single dependent variables and multiple factors.

MEANS. Displays subgroup means based on one or more grouping variables.

ONEWAY. Performs analysis of variance with one factor, allowing user-specified contrasts and displaying any of several multiple-comparison tests. See also ANOVA.

T-TEST. Performs the *t* test for a difference between two means, for either independent or paired samples.

Correlation and Linear Regression

CORRELATIONS. Calculates Pearson correlation coefficients.

REGRESSION. Performs least-squares regression analysis, displaying coefficients, significance tests, and a variety of diagnostic plots, statistics, and listings.

PARTIAL CORR. Calculates matrices of partial correlation coefficients.

Nonparametric Measures

NONPAR CORR. Calculates Spearman and Kendall nonparametric correlation coefficients.

NPAR TESTS. Calculates a variety of significance tests and measures of association for ordinal and nominal variables.

Graphical Display

GRAPH. Produces high-resolution charts and plots. This facility varies greatly from one operating environment to another.

PLOT. Displays high- or low-resolution (character-based) scatterplots.

Other Utilities

The following commands perform miscellaneous useful tasks whose implementation often differs widely from one operating environment to another. Such differences are noted, where possible, in the reference section for each command.

SET. Controls any of numerous settings that can be used to tailor the behavior or output of SPSS.

SHOW. Displays the current settings of the specifications controlled by SET.

PRESERVE and RESTORE. Allow you to "remember" the current settings of the SET specifications and restore them later. They are chiefly used in macros.

DEFINE (macro). The DEFINE command lets you define a macro, which is a block of SPSS command syntax (a command, part of a command, or multiple commands) that can be invoked by name. You can pass parameters to a macro when invoking it. See Appendix D for examples of how to use the macro facility.

HELP. The basic HELP facility described in this guide is replaced by a more powerful Help system in some environments. Consult the *SPSS Base User's Guide* for your version of SPSS.

EXECUTE. Causes SPSS to read the working data file and execute any commands that are pending, such as transformation commands. This is sometimes useful after commands that act like transformations (such as PRINT and XSAVE), carrying out their function during the next data pass.

INCLUDE. Reads and executes SPSS command syntax from a file.

HOST. Gives you access to native operating-system commands during an SPSS session, in operating systems where this facility is implemented.

ERASE. Deletes files during an SPSS session, in operating systems where this facility is implemented.

SYSFILE INFO. Displays information such as variable names from data files saved in SPSS format without disturbing the working data file.

TITLE and SUBTITLE. Include titles of your choice on each page of SPSS output.

COMMENT. Lets you annotate the listing of SPSS commands executed in a session. To save comments with a data file, use DOCUMENT.

Example

The following commands could be used in SPSS either as part of an SPSS session or as a complete batch job:

```
GET FILE=WEATHER.SAV.
COMPUTE AVTEMP=MEAN.2(TEMP1,TEMP2,TEMP3).
VARIABLE LABELS AVTEMP 'Average Daily Temperature'.
REGRESSION
 /DEPENDENT=NEWTEMP
 /ENTER=AVTEMP HUMID PRESSURE WINDDIR WINDSPD
 /SAVE=PRED(PREDICT).
SAVE OUTFILE=FORECAST.SAV.
```

- The GET command reads the SPSS data file *WEATHER.SAV* and uses it as the working data file.

- The COMPUTE command uses a statistical function to create a new variable, *AVTEMP*.

- The statistical function MEAN.2 indicates that the value of *AVTEMP* should be the mean of the three variables (*TEMP1, TEMP2, TEMP3*) and that at least two of the variables must have nonmissing values.

- The VARIABLE LABELS command supplies a descriptive label for the new variable.

- The REGRESSION command initiates a statistical procedure.

- The SAVE subcommand saves the predicted values generated by the REGRESSION procedure and assigns the variable name *PREDICT* to these values.

- The SAVE command creates a new SPSS data file, *FORECAST.SAV*, which contains all of the variables from *WEATHER.SAV* plus the two new variables, *AVTEMP* and *PREDICT*.

Universals

This part of the *SPSS Syntax Reference Guide* discusses general topics pertinent to using command syntax. The topics are divided into five sections:

- *Commands* explains command syntax, including command specification, command order, and running commands in different modes. In this section, you will learn how to read syntax charts, which summarize command syntax in diagrams and provide an easy reference. Discussions of individual commands are found in an alphabetical reference in the next part of this manual.

- *Files* discusses different types of files used by the program. Terms frequently mentioned in this manual are defined. This section provides an overview of how files are handled.

- *Variables* contains important information on general rules and conventions concerning variables and variable definition. In this section, you will find detailed information on variable formats.

- *Transformation Expressions* describes expressions that can be used in data transformation. Functions and operators are defined and illustrated. In this section, you will find a complete list of available functions and how to use them.

- *Date and Time* deals with functions and formats used with date and time expressions. In this section, you will find ways to read and convert date and time, use them in analysis, and display them in output.

Commands

Commands are the instructions that you give the program to initiate an action. For the program to interpret your commands correctly, you must follow certain rules.

Syntax Diagrams

Each command described in this manual includes a syntax diagram that shows all the subcommands, keywords, and specifications allowed for that command. By recognizing symbols and different type fonts, you can use the syntax diagram as a quick reference for any command. Figure 1 is an example.

- Lines of text in italics indicate limitation or operation mode of the command.

- Elements shown in upper case are keywords defined by SPSS to identify commands, subcommands, functions, operators, and other specifications. In Figure 1, T-TEST is the command and GROUPS is a subcommand.

- Elements in lower case describe specifications you supply. For example, varlist indicates that you need to supply a list of variables.

- Elements in bold are defaults. SPSS supports two types of defaults. When the default is followed by **, as ANALYSIS** is in Figure 1, the default (ANALYSIS) is in effect if the subcommand (MISSING) is not specified. If a default is not followed by **, it is in effect when the subcommand (or keyword) is specified by itself.

Figure 1   Syntax diagram

```
                                                           → Subgrouping (in italics)
Independent samples:
                                                           → Keywords (in all upper case)
T-TEST GROUPS=varname ({1,2**      }) /VARIABLES=varlist
                       {value     }          → User specification (in lower case)
                       {value,value}
                                                           → Default (in bold)
   [/MISSING={ANALYSIS**}  [INCLUDE]]
            {LISTWISE  }
                                                           → Alternatives (in aligned { })
   [/FORMAT={LABELS**}]
           {NOLABELS}
                                                           → Optional specification (in [ ])
Paired samples:

T-TEST PAIRS=varlist [WITH varlist [(PAIRED)]] [/varlist ...]

   [/MISSING={ANALYSIS**}  [INCLUDE]]         → Repeatable elements (with ...)
            {LISTWISE  }

   [/FORMAT={LABELS**}]                        → Parentheses (cannot be omitted)
           {NOLABELS}
```

**Default if the subcommand is omitted.   → Note

- Parentheses, apostrophes, and quotation marks are required where indicated.
- Elements enclosed in square brackets ([ ]) are optional. Wherever brackets would confuse the format, they are omitted. The command description explains which specifications are required and which are optional.
- Braces ({ }) indicate a choice between elements. You can specify any one of the elements enclosed within the aligned braces.
- Ellipses indicate that you can repeat an element in the specification. The specification

  T-TEST PAIRS=varlist [WITH varlist [(PAIRED)]] [/varlist ...]

  means that you can specify multiple variable lists with optional WITH variables and the keyword PAIRED in parentheses.
- Most abbreviations are obvious; for example, varname stands for variable name and varlist stands for a variable list.
- The command terminator is not shown in the syntax diagram.

Command Specification

The following rules apply to all commands:

- Commands begin with a keyword that is the name of the command and often have additional specifications, such as subcommands and user specifications. Refer to the discussion of each command to see which subcommands and additional specifications are required.
- Commands and any command specifications can be entered in upper and lower case. Commands, subcommands, keywords, and variable names are translated to upper case

before processing. All user specifications, including labels and data values, preserve upper and lower case.

- Spaces can be added between specifications at any point where a single blank is allowed. In addition, lines can be broken at any point where a single blank is allowed. There are two exceptions: the END DATA command can have only one space between words, and string specifications on commands such as TITLE, SUBTITLE, VARIABLE LABELS, and VALUE LABELS can be broken across two lines only by specifying a + between string segments (see "String Values in Command Specifications" on p. 15).

- The first word of a command can be abbreviated to a minimum of three letters provided no duplicates result. For example, AGGREGATE can be abbreviated to AGG, but COMPUTE can only be abbreviated to COMP to avoid confusion with COMMENT. A very small number of commands can duplicate an internal command when abbreviated to three characters (for example, LIST) and at least four characters should be used. For internal command structure, DATA LIST cannot be abbreviated.

- If the first word of a multiple-word command has a duplicate (for example, FILE LABEL and FILE TYPE), the first word cannot be abbreviated.

- All keywords after the first command word can be abbreviated to three characters. For example, ADD VAL LAB is a valid abbreviation for ADD VALUE LABELS, and EXA VAR=varlist is valid for EXAMINE VARIABLES=varlist. END DATA is an exception. You must spell both command keywords in full; END DAT is *not* a valid abbreviation for END DATA.

- Three-character truncation does not apply to INFO command specifications. Spell out all keywords in full. For procedure names specified on INFO, spell out the first word in full and subsequent words through at least the first three characters.

Running Commands

You can run commands in either batch (production) or interactive mode. In batch mode, commands are read and acted upon as a batch, so the system knows that a command is complete when it encounters a new command. In interactive mode, commands are executed immediately, and you must use a command terminator to tell SPSS when a command is complete.

Interactive Mode

The following rules apply to command specifications in interactive mode:

- Each command ends with a command terminator. The default command terminator is a period. It is best to omit the terminator on BEGIN DATA, however, so that inline data is treated as one continuous specification.

- The command terminator must be the last nonblank character in a command.

- Commands can begin in any column of a command line and continue for as many lines as needed. The exception is the END DATA command, which must begin in the first column of the first line after the end of data.

- The maximum length of any command line is 80 characters, including the prompt and the command terminator.

You should observe interactive rules when you:

- Submit commands from a syntax window or with an SPSS Manager, either one command at a time or as a group.
- Enter commands at a command prompt on those systems that run prompted sessions.

See the *SPSS Base User's Guide* for your version of SPSS for more information.

Batch (Production) Mode

The following rules apply to command specifications in batch or production mode:

- All commands in the command file must begin in column 1. You can use plus (+) or minus (−) signs in the first column if you want to indent the command specification to make the command file more readable.
- If multiple lines are used for a command, column 1 of each continuation line must be blank.
- Command terminators are optional.
- An asterisk (*) in the first column indicates a comment line (see the COMMENT command).

You should observe batch rules when you:

- Construct a command file for use with the Production Facility.
- Construct a command file that will be submitted to your operating system for execution.
- Construct a command file that will be included using the INCLUDE command. You can include a command file when you are working in interactive mode. The included command file, however, must follow batch rules.

The way you submit a command file for execution varies from operating system to operating system. Command files do not necessarily need to be submitted to a batch queue, although they can be on operating systems that have a batch queue. In batch mode, the commands in the file are executed one after the other, and output is displayed when all commands are executed.

The following is a sample command file:

```
GET FILE=BANK.SAV /KEEP ID TIME SEX JOBCAT SALBEG SALNOW
       /RENAME SALNOW = SAL90.

DO IF TIME LT 82.
+   COMPUTE RATE=0.05.
ELSE.
+   COMPUTE RATE=0.04.
END IF.

COMPUTE SALNOW=(1+RATE)*SAL90.

EXAMINE VARIABLES=SALNOW BY SEX /PLOT=NONE.
```

Subcommands

Many commands include additional specifications called *subcommands* for locating data, handling data, and formatting the output.

- Subcommands begin with a keyword that is the name of the subcommand. Some subcommands include additional specifications.

- A subcommand keyword is separated from its specifications, if any, by an equals sign. The equals sign is usually optional but is required where ambiguity is possible in the specification. To avoid ambiguity, it is best to use the equals signs as shown in the syntax diagrams in this manual.

- Most subcommands can be named in any order. However, some commands require a specific subcommand order. The description of each command includes a section on subcommand order.

- Subcommands are separated from each other by a slash. To avoid ambiguity, it is best to use the slashes as shown in the syntax diagrams in this manual.

Keywords

Keywords identify commands, subcommands, functions, operators, and other specifications in SPSS.

- Keywords, including commands and subcommands, can often be truncated to the first three characters of each word. An exception is the keyword WITH, which must be spelled in full. See "Command Specification" on p. 12 for additional rules for three-character truncation of commands.

- Keywords identifying logical operators (AND, OR, and NOT), relational operators (EQ, GE, GT, LE, LT, and NE), and ALL, BY, TO, and WITH are reserved words and cannot be used as variable names.

Values in Command Specifications

The following rules apply to values specified in commands:

- A single lowercase character in the syntax diagram, such as n, w, or d, indicates a user-specified value.

- The value can be an integer or a real number within a restricted range, as required by the specific command or subcommand. For exact restrictions, read the individual command description.

- A number specified as an argument to a subcommand can be entered with or without leading zeros.

String Values in Command Specifications

- Each string specified in a command should be enclosed in a set of apostrophes or quotation marks.

- To specify an apostrophe within a string, either use quotation marks to enclose the string or specify double apostrophes. Both of the following specifications are valid:

```
'Client''s Satisfaction'
```

```
"Client's Satisfaction"
```

- To specify quotation marks within a string, use apostrophes to enclose the string:

```
'Categories Labeled "UNSTANDARD" in the Report'
```

- String specifications can be broken across command lines by specifying each string segment within apostrophes or quotation marks and using a + sign to join segments. For example,

```
'One, Two'
```

can be specified as

```
'One,'
+ ' Two'
```

The plus sign can be specified on either the first or the second line of the broken string. Any blanks separating the two segments must be enclosed within one or the other string segment.

- Blanks within apostrophes or quotation marks are significant.

Delimiters

Delimiters are used to separate data values, keywords, arguments, and specifications.

- A blank is usually used to separate one specification from another, except when another delimiter serves the same purpose or when a comma is required.
- Commas are required to separate arguments to functions. Otherwise, blanks are generally valid substitutes for commas.
- Arithmetic operators (+, −, *, and /) serve as delimiters in expressions.
- Blanks can be used before and after operators or equals signs to improve readability, but commas cannot.
- Special delimiters include parentheses, apostrophes, quotation marks, the slash, and the equals sign. Blanks before and after special delimiters are optional.
- The slash is used primarily to separate subcommands and lists of variables. Although slashes are sometimes optional, it is best to enter them as shown in the syntax diagrams.
- The equals sign is used between a subcommand and its specifications, as in STATISTICS= MEAN, and to show equivalence, as in COMPUTE target variable=expression. Equals signs following subcommands are frequently optional, but it is best to enter them for clarity.

Command Order

Command order is more often than not a matter of common sense and follows this logical sequence: variable definition, data transformation, and statistical analysis. For example, you cannot label, transform, analyze, or use a variable in any way before it exists. The following general rules apply:

- Commands that define variables for a session (DATA LIST, GET, MATRIX DATA, etc.) must precede commands that assign labels or missing values to those variables; they must also precede transformation and procedure commands that use those variables.

- Transformation commands (IF, COUNT, COMPUTE, etc.) that are used to create and modify variables must precede commands that assign labels or missing values to those variables, and they must also precede the procedures that use those variables.
- Generally, the logical outcome of command processing determines command order. For example, a procedure that creates new variables in the working data file must precede a procedure that uses those new variables.
- Some commands, such as REREAD and END CASE, can appear only in an *input program* where the cases are created. Other commands, such as SELECT IF, can appear only in a *transformation program* after cases have been created. Still other commands, such as COMPUTE, can appear in an input or transformation program. For a discussion of these program states and command order, see Appendix A.

In addition to observing the rules above, it is important to distinguish between commands that cause the data to be read and those that do not. Table 1 shows the commands that cause the data to be read. Most of the remaining commands (those that do not cause the data to be read) do not take effect immediately; they are read but are not executed until a command that causes the data to be read is encountered in the command sequence. This avoids unnecessary passes through the data.

Table 1   Commands that cause the data to be read[*]

AGGREGATE	FREQUENCIES	PARTIAL CORR
ALSCAL	GRAPH	PLOT
ANOVA	HILOGLINEAR	PROBIT
AUTORECODE	IMPORT	PROXIMITIES
BEGIN DATA	LIST	QUICK CLUSTER
CLUSTER	LOGISTIC REGRESSION	RANK
CNLR	LOGLINEAR	REGRESSION
CORRELATIONS	MANOVA	RELIABILITY
CROSSTABS	MATRIX	REPORT
DESCRIPTIVES	MCONVERT	SAVE
DISCRIMINANT	MEANS	SAVE SCSS
EXAMINE	MULTIPLE RESPONSE	SAVE TRANSLATE
EXECUTE	NLR	SORT
EXPORT	NONPAR CORR	SURVIVAL
FACTOR	NPAR TESTS	T-TEST
FLIP	ONEWAY	

* This table shows the procedures in the SPSS Base system and the Regression Models and Advanced Models options; it does not show commands in other SPSS options, such as SPSS Tables or SPSS Trends.

Transformation commands that alter the dictionary of the working data file, such as MISSING VALUES, and commands that do not affect the working data, such as SET, SHOW, and DISPLAY, take effect as soon as they are encountered in the command sequence, regardless of conditional statements that precede them. Table 2 lists all transformation commands that take effect immediately.

Table 2   Transformation commands that take effect immediately

ADD VALUE LABELS	PRINT FORMATS
DOCUMENT	SPLIT FILE
DROP DOCUMENTS	STRING
FORMATS	VALUE LABELS
LEAVE	VARIABLE LABELS
MISSING VALUES	VECTOR
N OF CASES	WEIGHT
NUMERIC	WRITE FORMATS

Since these transformations take effect regardless of the conditional statements that precede them, they cannot be applied selectively to individual cases, as shown in the following example:

```
DO IF AGE>69.
MISSING VALUES INCOME EXPENSES (0).
ELSE.
COMPUTE PROFIT=INCOME-EXPENSES.
END IF.
LIST.
```

The MISSING VALUES command is in effect when COMPUTE is executed, even if the condition defined on DO IF is false. To treat 0 income and expenses as missing only for those older than 69, use RECODE in the DO IF—END IF structure to selectively recode 0 to a negative number and declare the negative number as missing:

```
MISSING VALUES INCOME EXPENSES (-1).
DO IF (AGE>69).
RECODE INCOME EXPENSES (0=-1).
END IF.
COMPUTE PROFILE=INCOME-EXPENSES.
LIST.
```

In addition, the order of transformations that take effect immediately in the command sequence can be misleading. Consider the following:

```
COMPUTE PROFIT=INCOME-EXPENSES.
MISSING VALUES INCOME EXPENSES (0).
LIST.
```

- COMPUTE precedes MISSING VALUES and is processed first; however, execution is delayed until the data are being read.

- MISSING VALUES takes effect as soon as it is encountered.

- LIST causes the data to be read; thus, SPSS executes both COMPUTE and LIST during the same data pass. Because MISSING VALUES is already in effect by this time, all cases with the value 0 for either *INCOME* or *EXPENSES* return a missing value for *PROFIT*.

To prevent the MISSING VALUES command from taking effect before COMPUTE is executed, you must position MISSING VALUES after the LIST command. Alternatively, place an EXECUTE command between COMPUTE and MISSING VALUES.

Files

SPSS reads, creates, and writes different types of files. This section provides an overview of the types of files used in SPSS and discusses concepts and rules that apply to all files. Conventions for naming, printing, deleting, or permanently saving files, and for submitting command files for processing, differ from one computer and operating system to another. For specific information, consult the *SPSS Base User's Guide* for your version of SPSS.

Command File

Command files contain commands, sometimes with inline data. They can be created by a text editor. Wherever SPSS allows you to paste commands, either in a syntax window or with an SPSS manager, the resulting file is a command file. You can also edit a journal file to produce a command file (see "Journal File" below). The following is an example of a simple command file that contains both commands and inline data:

```
DATA LIST /ID 1-3 SEX 4 (A) AGE 5-6 OPINION1 TO OPINION5 7-11.
BEGIN DATA
001F2621221
002M5611122
003F3422212
329M2121212
END DATA.
LIST.
```

- Case does not matter for commands but is significant for inline data. If you specified *f* for female and *m* for male in column 4 of the data line, the value of *SEX* would be *f* or *m*, instead of *F* or *M* as it is now.
- Commands can be in upper or lower case. Uppercase characters are used for all commands throughout this manual only to distinguish them from other text.

Journal File

SPSS keeps a journal file to record all commands either entered in the syntax window or generated from a dialog box during a session. You can retrieve this file with any text editor and review it to learn how the session went. You can also edit the file to build a new command file and use it in another run. An edited and tested journal file can be saved and used later for repeated tasks. The journal file also records any error or warning messages generated by commands. You can rerun these commands after making corrections and removing the messages.

The default name for the journal file is *SPSS.JNL* on most operating systems. You can turn off the journal or assign a different name to it (see SET). SPSS erases an existing journal file with the default name when it starts a new session. If you want to save a journal file for future use, rename it before you start another session. On some operating systems, SPSS allows you to overwrite or append to journals from a previous session. Consult the *SPSS Base User's Guide* for your version of SPSS for specific information. Figure 2 is a journal file for a short session with a warning message.

Figure 2   Records from a journal file

```
DATA LIST /ID 1-3 SEX 4 (A) AGE 5-6 OPINION1 TO OPINION5 7-11.
BEGIN DATA
001F2621221
002M5611122
003F3422212
004F45112L2
>Warning # 1102
>An invalid numeric field has been found.  The result has been set to the
>system-missing value.
END DATA.
LIST.
```

- The warning message, marked by the > symbol, tells you that an invalid numeric field has been found. Checking the last data line, you will notice that column 10 is *L*, which is probably a typographic error. You can correct the typo (for example, by changing the *L* to 1), delete the warning message, and submit the file again.

Data Files

SPSS is capable of reading and writing a wide variety of data file formats, including raw data files created by a data entry device or a text editor, formatted data files produced by a data management program, data files generated by other software packages, and SPSS-format data files.

Raw Data File

Raw data files contain only data, either generated by a programming language, such as COBOL, FORTRAN, and Assembler, or entered with a data entry device or a text editor. SPSS can read raw data arranged in almost any format, including raw matrix materials and nonprintable codes. User-entered data can be embedded within a command file as inline data or saved on tape or disk as an external file. Nonprintable machine codes are usually stored in an external file.

Raw data must be defined before they can be used by procedures. Data definition commands such as DATA LIST, KEYED DATA LIST, and MATRIX DATA can be used to read in raw data. Appropriate input formats must be specified on these commands (see "Variable Formats" on p. 31). If for some reason you need to write a raw data file, use the WRITE command or specify WRITE on a procedure with that subcommand. On most operating systems, the default extension of a raw data file produced by SPSS is *.DAT*.

Files from Other Software Applications

You can read files from a variety of other software applications, including dBASE, Lotus, SYLK, and Excel. You can also read simple tab-delimited spreadsheet files. Use GET TRANSLATE with different TYPE specifications to read files from common spreadsheet and database programs. To produce data files for these programs, use SAVE TRANSLATE.

Consult the *SPSS Base User's Guide* for your version of SPSS for the types of files (if any) that your system can read and write.

SPSS-Format Data File

An SPSS-format data file is a file specifically formatted for use by SPSS, containing both data and the dictionary that defines the data. The **dictionary** contains names for the variables, formats for reading and displaying values, and optional variable and value labels and missing-value specifications. SPSS-format data files are created by using a SAVE or XSAVE command during a session. On most operating systems, the default extension of a saved SPSS-format data file is *.SAV*. An SPSS-format data file can also be a matrix file created with the MATRIX=OUT subcommand on procedures that write matrices.

To retrieve an SPSS-format data file, use GET. SPSS-format data files speed processing and are required as input for combining files during a session. For a discussion of the structure of SPSS-format data files, see "SPSS Data File Structure" below.

SPSS Portable File

A portable file contains all of the data and dictionary information stored in the working data file but is specially formatted for transporting files between installations with different versions of SPSS (such as the PRIME, VAX, or HONEYWELL GCOS computers) or for transporting files between SPSS, SPSS/PC+, and other software using the same portable file format. Use IMPORT to read a portable file and EXPORT to save the working data file as a portable file. On most operating systems, the default extension of a saved portable file is *.POR*. Since a portable file needs conversion, it is always simpler to transport a file as an SPSS-format data file whenever possible.

Working Data File

The working data file is the data file you build to use in the current session. You can retrieve an SPSS-format data file using GET, which in effect makes a working copy of the specified file. You can also build a new file with DATA LIST or other data definition commands.

The working data file is not created until SPSS encounters a command (usually a procedure) that causes it to read the data (see Table 1 on p. 17). At that point, SPSS executes all of the preceding data definition and transformation commands and the command that causes the data to be read. The working data file is then available for further transformations and procedures, and it remains available until replaced by a new working data file or until the end of the session.

Some procedures can add variables to the working data file. Others, such as AGGREGATE and procedures that write matrix materials, can replace the working data file.

Any transformations and statistical analyses that you request during a session are performed on the working data file. Transformations performed during a session apply to the working data file only. Changes to the file are lost if the working data file is erased or replaced before you have saved it. See SAVE and XSAVE.

SPSS Data File Structure

An SPSS-format data file is a self-documented file containing data and descriptive information. The descriptive information is called the **dictionary**. It contains variable names and locations, variable and value labels, print and write formats, and missing-value indicators. To use an SPSS-format data file, you must retrieve it with GET, which creates a working data file from the SPSS-format data file. Only a few commands can use an SPSS-format data file directly without first specifying GET; they include MATCH FILES, ADD FILES, and procedures that can read SPSS matrix data files.

To view the contents of an SPSS-format data file, retrieve it with GET and then use LIST to display the variables in the working data file. Figure 3 shows a partial listing of a working file. The values are displayed using their print format, which is different from the way they are internally stored.

Figure 3   Part of a listed working data file

```
  ID SALBEG SEX TIME    AGE SALNOW EDLEVEL   WORK JOBCAT MINORITY   SEXRACE

 628   8400  0   81   28.50  16080    16      .25    4      0        1.00
 630  24000  0   73   40.33  41400    16    12.50    5      0        1.00
 632  10200  0   83   31.08  21960    15     4.08    5      0        1.00
 633   8700  0   93   31.17  19200    16     1.83    4      0        1.00
 635  17400  0   83   41.92  28350    19    13.00    5      0        1.00
 637  12996  0   80   29.50  27250    18     2.42    4      0        1.00
 641   6900  0   79   28.00  16080    15     3.17    1      0        1.00
 649   5400  0   67   28.75  14100    15      .50    1      0        1.00
 650   5040  0   96   27.42  12420    15     1.17    1      0        1.00
 652   6300  0   77   52.92  12300    12    26.42    3      0        1.00
 653   6300  0   84   33.50  15720    15     6.00    1      0        1.00
 656   6000  0   88   54.33   8880    12    27.00    1      0        1.00
 657  10500  0   93   32.33  22000    17     2.67    4      0        1.00
 658  10800  0   98   41.17  22800    15    12.00    5      0        1.00
```

The dictionary is created when an SPSS-format data file is built. You can display or modify the dictionary of a working file. Use DISPLAY DICTIONARY to view the dictionary, and use commands such as VARIABLE LABELS, VALUE LABELS, and MISSING VALUES to modify specific information contained in the dictionary. Figure 4 shows part of the displayed dictionary information of the working data file displayed in Figure 3.

Figure 4   Displayed dictionary information

```
               List of variables on the active file

Name                                                            Position

ID        Employee Code                                            1
          Print Format: F4
          Write Format: F4

SALBEG    Beginning Salary                                         2
          Print Format: F5
          Write Format: F5
          Missing Values: 0

SEX       Sex of Employee                                          3
          Print Format: F1
          Write Format: F1
          Missing Values: 9

          Value     Label

             0      Males
             1      Females
TIME      Job Seniority                                            4
          Print Format: F2
          Write Format: F2
          Missing Values: 0
```

SPSS Matrix Data Files

An SPSS matrix data file is similar to any SPSS-format data file. It is a self-documented file containing data and descriptive information. The descriptive information, stored in the file dictionary, includes variable names, variable print and write formats, and optional variable and value labels. You can assign or change the names, labels, and formats of the variables in a matrix data file, just as you can in any SPSS-format data file. Many procedures can read raw matrix data and write a representative matrix of the data values to an SPSS matrix data file, which can be used as input for subsequent analysis.

Table 3 shows the types of matrix materials written by SPSS procedures. The *ROWTYPE_* values (discussed below) of each matrix are also included so that you can see which procedure matrices are readable by other procedures. If a procedure produces more than one type of matrix, the subcommands required for each type of matrix are listed.

Table 3   Types of matrices and their contents

Command	Subcommands/Notes	ROWTYPE_ values
ALSCAL		PROX
CLUSTER		PROX
CORRELATIONS		MEAN STDDEV N CORR
DISCRIMINANT	/CLASSIFY=POOLED	N (1 per cell) COUNT (1 per cell) MEAN (1 per cell) STDDEV (pooled) CORR (pooled)
	/CLASSIFY=SEPARATE, /STATISTICS=BOXM, or /STATISTICS=GCOV	N (1 per cell) COUNT (1 per cell) MEAN (1 per cell) STDDEV (1 per cell) CORR (1 per cell)
FACTOR	/MATRIX=OUT(CORR=file) /MATRIX=IN(CORR=file)	CORR
	/MATRIX=OUT(FAC=file) /MATRIX=IN(FAC=file)	FACTOR
MANOVA		N (cell and pooled) MEAN (1 per cell) STDDEV (pooled) CORR (pooled)
NONPAR CORR	/PRINT=SPEARMAN	N RHO
	/PRINT=KENDALL	N TAUB

Table 3   Types of matrices and their contents (Continued)

Command	Subcommands/Notes	ROWTYPE_ values
ONEWAY	Separate variance Can be input and output	MEAN (1 per cell) STDDEV (1 per cell) N (1 per cell)
	Pooled variance Can be input only	MEAN (1 per cell) N (1 per cell) MSE (pooled) DFE (pooled)
PARTIAL CORR		N CORR
PROXIMITIES		PROX
REGRESSION		MEAN STDDEV N CORR
RELIABILITY		N MEAN STDDEV CORR

- All SPSS procedures that handle matrix materials use the MATRIX subcommand. The MATRIX subcommand specifies the file from which the input matrix is read and/or the file to which the output matrix is written.
- Matrix materials can be read from an external file as long as a working data file has been created. The working file does not have to be the matrix data file.
- The procedures that read matrix materials cannot read every type of SPSS matrix data file. For example, REGRESSION cannot read a matrix data file written by NONPAR CORR.

Figure 5 lists the structure of a matrix file and Figure 6 shows the dictionary information for the same file.

Variable Order. The following variable order is standard for all SPSS matrix data files:

1. Split variables, if any. In Figure 5, the split variable is *SEX*.

2. *ROWTYPE_* variable. The values of the *ROWTYPE_* variable describe the contents of the matrix data file, such as *MEAN*, *STDDEV*, *N*, and *CORR*.

3. Factor or grouping variables, if any.

4. *VARNAME_* variable (or *FACTOR_* variable for factor-loading matrices). The values of the *VARNAME_* variable are the names of the variable used to form the matrix.

5. Continuous variables used to form the matrix.

Figure 5   A matrix data file (LIST output)

```
FILE:      MATRIX FILE
SEX:   1   FEMALE

SEX ROWTYPE_ VARNAME_       FOOD       RENT    PUBTRANS    TEACHER       COOK    ENGINEER

   1 MEAN              73.3750000 134.500000 53.5000000 46.8000000 72.4375000 59.8125000
   1 STDDEV            15.4483009 115.534699 25.8173069 19.4209018 29.5746936 21.5196616
   1 N        FOOD     16.0000000 16.0000000 16.0000000 15.0000000 16.0000000 16.0000000
   1 N        RENT     16.0000000 16.0000000 16.0000000 15.0000000 16.0000000 16.0000000
   1 N        PUBTRANS 16.0000000 16.0000000 16.0000000 15.0000000 16.0000000 16.0000000
   1 N        TEACHER  15.0000000 15.0000000 15.0000000 15.0000000 15.0000000 15.0000000
   1 N        COOK     16.0000000 16.0000000 16.0000000 15.0000000 16.0000000 16.0000000
   1 N        ENGINEER 16.0000000 16.0000000 16.0000000 15.0000000 16.0000000 16.0000000
   1 CORR     FOOD      1.0000000   .3658643   .5372333   .1733358   .1378010   .3778351
   1 CORR     RENT       .3658643  1.0000000   .1045105  -.0735708   .2026299   .1237062
   1 CORR     PUBTRANS   .5372333   .1045105  1.0000000   .6097397   .3877995   .6413121
   1 CORR     TEACHER    .1733358  -.0735708   .6097397  1.0000000   .4314755   .7312415
   1 CORR     COOK       .1378010   .2026299   .3877995   .4314755  1.0000000   .7807327
   1 CORR     ENGINEER   .3778351   .1237062   .6413121   .7312415   .7807327  1.0000000


NUMBER OF CASES READ =     14    NUMBER OF CASES LISTED =      14



FILE:      MATRIX FILE
SEX:   2   MALE

SEX ROWTYPE_ VARNAME_       FOOD       RENT    PUBTRANS    TEACHER       COOK    ENGINEER

   2 MEAN              68.8620690 112.137931 45.1379310 33.9310345 60.2142857 60.1785714
   2 STDDEV            20.4148478 81.3430672 24.1819356 26.9588722 30.2952840 28.8752792
   2 N        FOOD     29.0000000 29.0000000 29.0000000 29.0000000 28.0000000 28.0000000
   2 N        RENT     29.0000000 29.0000000 29.0000000 29.0000000 28.0000000 28.0000000
   2 N        PUBTRANS 29.0000000 29.0000000 29.0000000 29.0000000 28.0000000 28.0000000
   2 N        TEACHER  29.0000000 29.0000000 29.0000000 29.0000000 28.0000000 28.0000000
   2 N        COOK     28.0000000 28.0000000 28.0000000 28.0000000 28.0000000 28.0000000
   2 N        ENGINEER 28.0000000 28.0000000 28.0000000 28.0000000 28.0000000 28.0000000
   2 CORR     FOOD      1.0000000   .2012077   .5977491   .6417034   .4898941   .5190702
   2 CORR     RENT       .2012077  1.0000000  -.1405952  -.0540657   .0727153   .3508598
   2 CORR     PUBTRANS   .5977491  -.1405952  1.0000000   .7172945   .7170419   .6580408
   2 CORR     TEACHER    .6417034  -.0540657   .7172945  1.0000000   .6711871   .6650047
   2 CORR     COOK       .4898941   .0727153   .7170419   .6711871  1.0000000   .7688210
   2 CORR     ENGINEER   .5190702   .3508598   .6580408   .6650047   .7688210  1.0000000


NUMBER OF CASES READ =     14    NUMBER OF CASES LISTED =      14
```

Split Files. When split-file processing is in effect, a full set of matrix materials is written for each split-file group defined by the split variables.

- A split variable cannot have the same variable name as any other variable written to the matrix data file. Not all procedures allow split-file variables in their matrices.

- If split-file processing is in effect when a matrix is written, the same split file must be in effect when that matrix is read by any procedure.

Additional Statistics. Some procedures include statistics with their matrix materials. For example, CORRELATION matrices always include the mean, standard deviation, and number of cases used to compute each coefficient, as shown in Figure 5. Other procedures, for example PROXIMITIES and FACTOR, include no statistics with their matrices. See Table 3 for a list of the statistics written by each procedure. Refer to the description of each command for its requirements for a matrix input file.

Missing Values. The treatment of missing values in a procedure affects the matrix materials written to the data file. With pairwise treatment of missing values, the matrix of N's used to compute each coefficient is included in the matrix. With any other missing-value treatment, the single N used to calculate all coefficients in the matrix is included in the form of a vector. Figure 5 includes the matrix of N's written by CORRELATIONS when missing values are excluded pairwise from the analysis. Figure 7 shows the single N written by CORRELATIONS when missing values are excluded listwise.

The missing-value treatment that was in effect when the matrix was written must be compatible with the missing-value treatment in effect when the matrix is read. For example, REGRESSION can read a matrix written by CORRELATIONS but only if the missing-value treatment of both procedures is consistent. Either both must refer to a matrix of N's or both must refer to a single N. For all procedures, pairwise treatment of missing values generates a matrix of N's; any other treatment of missing values generates a single vector of N's.

Matrix File Dictionaries. As shown in Figure 6, print and write formats of A8 are assigned to the matrix variables that SPSS creates (for example, *ROWTYPE_*, *VARNAME_*, and *FACTOR_*). No labels are assigned to these variables. Print and write formats of F10.7 are assigned to all of the continuous variables in the matrix analysis; the names and variable labels defined for these variables in the original data file are retained, but their original values and value labels are dropped because they do not apply to the matrix data file. When split-file processing is in effect, the variable names, variable and value labels, and print and write formats of the split-file variables are read from the dictionary of the original data file.

Procedures read and write matrices in which each row corresponds to a single case in the matrix data file. For example, the matrix shown in Figure 7 has nine cases. The first three cases with the *ROWTYPE_* values of *MEAN*, *STDDEV*, and *N* have no values for *VARNAME_* but do have values for all the variables from *FOOD* to *ENGINEER*. The fourth case, *CORR*, in the matrix generated for the first split-file group has a value of *FOOD* for *VARNAME_*, a value of 0.3652366 when correlated with variable *RENT*, a value of 0.5371597 when correlated with variable *PUBTRANS*, and so on.

Figure 6   Dictionary of a matrix system file (DISPLAY output)

```
FILE:       MATRIX FILE

            LIST OF VARIABLES ON THE ACTIVE FILE

NAME                                                              POSITION

SEX                                                                  1
                    PRINT FORMAT: F2
                    WRITE FORMAT: F2

            VALUE    LABEL

               1     FEMALE
               2     MALE

ROWTYPE_                                                             2
                    PRINT FORMAT: A8
                    WRITE FORMAT: A8

VARNAME_                                                             3
                    PRINT FORMAT: A8
                    WRITE FORMAT: A8

FOOD        AVG FOOD PRICES                                          4
                    PRINT FORMAT: F10.7
                    WRITE FORMAT: F10.7

RENT        NORMAL RENT                                              5
                    PRINT FORMAT: F10.7
                    WRITE FORMAT: F10.7

PUBTRANS    PRICE FOR PUBLIC TRANSPORT                               6
                    PRINT FORMAT: F10.7
                    WRITE FORMAT: F10.7

TEACHER     NET TEACHER'S SALARY                                     7
                    PRINT FORMAT: F10.7
                    WRITE FORMAT: F10.7

COOK        NET COOK'S SALARY                                        8
                    PRINT FORMAT: F10.7
                    WRITE FORMAT: F10.7

ENGINEER    NET ENGINEER'S SALARY                                    9
                    PRINT FORMAT: F10.7
                    WRITE FORMAT: F10.7
```

Figure 7   Single N in the matrix system file

```
FILE:      MATRIX FILE
SEX:   1   FEMALE

SEX ROWTYPE_ VARNAME_      FOOD       RENT    PUBTRANS    TEACHER       COOK    ENGINEER

  1 MEAN               73.4666667 136.800000 54.0000000 46.8000000 73.8666667 60.0000000
  1 STDDEV             15.9860058 119.210019 26.6431444 19.4209018 30.0353760 22.2614337
  1 N                  15.0000000 15.0000000 15.0000000 15.0000000 15.0000000 15.0000000
  1 CORR    FOOD        1.0000000   .3652366   .5371597   .1733358   .1358120   .3773434
  1 CORR    RENT         .3652366  1.0000000   .0989524  -.0735708   .1914448   .1213899
  1 CORR    PUBTRANS     .5371597   .0989524  1.0000000   .6097397   .3811372   .6409265
  1 CORR    TEACHER      .1733358  -.0735708   .6097397  1.0000000   .4314755   .7312415
  1 CORR    COOK         .1358120   .1914448   .3811372   .4314755  1.0000000   .7893533
  1 CORR    ENGINEER     .3773434   .1213899   .6409265   .7312415   .7893533  1.0000000


NUMBER OF CASES READ =      9   NUMBER OF CASES LISTED =       9

                                                                      2

FILE:      MATRIX FILE
SEX:   2   MALE

SEX ROWTYPE_ VARNAME_      FOOD       RENT    PUBTRANS    TEACHER       COOK    ENGINEER

  2 MEAN               69.6428571 114.464286 46.1428571 33.7500000 60.2142857 60.1785714
  2 STDDEV             20.3437392 81.8474109 24.0011023 27.4356149 30.2952840 28.8752792
  2 N                  28.0000000 28.0000000 28.0000000 28.0000000 28.0000000 28.0000000
  2 CORR    FOOD        1.0000000   .1752920   .5784136   .6638084   .4898941   .5190702
  2 CORR    RENT         .1752920  1.0000000  -.1817862  -.0491139   .0727153   .3508598
  2 CORR    PUBTRANS     .5784136  -.1817862  1.0000000   .7447511   .7170419   .6580408
  2 CORR    TEACHER      .6638084  -.0491139   .7447511  1.0000000   .6711871   .6650047
  2 CORR    COOK         .4898941   .0727153   .7170419   .6711871  1.0000000   .7688210
  2 CORR    ENGINEER     .5190702   .3508598   .6580408   .6650047   .7688210  1.0000000


NUMBER OF CASES READ =      9   NUMBER OF CASES LISTED =       9
```

Variables

To prepare data for processing, you must define variables by assigning variable names and formats. You can also specify variable labels, value labels, and missing values, but they are optional. This section discusses the two essential components of variable definition: variable names and formats.

Variable Names

Each variable must have a unique name. Variable names are stored in the dictionary of an SPSS-format data file or working data file. Observe the following rules when establishing variable names or referring to variables by their names on commands:

- Variable names can contain up to eight characters, the first of which must be a letter or one of the characters @, #, or $.

- A # character in the first position of a variable name defines a scratch variable (see "Scratch Variables" on p. 31).

- A $ sign in the first position indicates that the variable is a system variable (see "System Variables" on p. 30). The $ sign is not allowed as the initial character of a user-defined variable.

- The period, underscore, and the characters $, #, and @ can be used within variable names. For example, A._$@#1 is a valid variable name.

- Variable names ending with a period should be avoided, since the period may be interpreted as a command terminator.

- Variable names ending in underscores should be avoided, since such names may conflict with names of variables automatically created by a number of commands—for example, YEAR_ and DATE_ created by the DATE command.

- Variable names can be established on the DATA LIST, KEYED DATA LIST, MATRIX DATA, NUMERIC, STRING, COMPUTE, RECODE, and COUNT commands. They can be changed with the RENAME VARIABLES command.

- Reserved keywords cannot be used as variable names. Reserved keywords are

ALL	AND	BY	EQ	GE	GT	LE
LT	NE	NOT	OR	TO	WITH	

Keyword TO

You can establish names for a set of variables or to refer to any number of consecutive variables by specifying the beginning and the ending variables joined by the keyword TO.

To establish names for a set of variables with the keyword TO, use a character prefix with a numeric suffix.

- The prefix can be any valid name. Both the beginning and ending variables must use the same prefix.

- The numeric suffix can be any integer, but the first number must be smaller than the second. For example, ITEM1 TO ITEM5 establishes five variables named *ITEM1*, *ITEM2*, *ITEM3*, *ITEM4*, and *ITEM5*.

- Each variable name, including the number, must not exceed eight characters.

- Leading zeros used in numeric suffixes are included in the variable name. For example, V001 TO V100 establishes 100 variables, *V001*, *V002*, *V003*, ..., *V100*. V1 TO V100 establishes 100 variables, *V1*, *V2*, *V3*, ..., *V100*.

The keyword TO can also be used on procedures and other commands to refer to consecutive variables on the working data file. For example, AVAR TO VARB refers to the variables *AVAR* and all subsequent variables up to and including *VARB*.

- In most cases, the TO specification uses the variable order on the working data file. Use the DISPLAY command to see the order of variables on the working data file.

- On some subcommands, the order in which variables are named on a previous subcommand, usually the VARIABLES subcommand, is used to determine which variables are consecutive and therefore are implied by the TO specification. This is noted in the description of individual commands.

Keyword ALL

The keyword ALL can be used in many commands to specify all the variables in the working data file. For example:

```
FREQUENCIES /VARIABLES = ALL.
```

or

```
OLAP CUBES income by ALL.
```

In the second example, a separate table will be created for every variable in the data file, including a table of *income* by *income*.

System Variables

System variables are special variables created during a working session to keep system-required information, such as the number of cases read by the system, the system-missing value, and the current date. System variables can be used in data transformations.

- The names of system variables begin with a dollar sign ($).

- You cannot modify a system variable or alter its print or write format. Except for these restrictions, you can use system variables anywhere a normal variable is used in the transformation language.

- System variables are not available for procedures.

$CASENUM   *Permanent case sequence number.* For each case, *$CASENUM* is the number of permanent cases read up to and including that case. The format is F8.0. The value of *$CASENUM* is not necessarily the row number in a Data Editor window (available in windowed environments).

$SYSMIS   *System-missing value.* The system-missing value displays as a period (.) or whatever is used as the decimal point.

$JDATE   *Current date in number of days from October 14, 1582* (day 1 of the Gregorian calendar). The format is F6.0.

$DATE   *Current date in international date format with two-digit year.* The format is A9 in the form dd-mmm-yy.

$DATE11   *Current date in international date format with four-digit year.* The format is A11 in the form dd-mmm-yyyy.

$TIME   *Current date and time. $TIME* represents the number of seconds from midnight, October 14, 1582, to the date and time when the transformation command is executed. The format is F20.

$LENGTH   *The current page length.* The format is F11.0. For more information, see SET.

$WIDTH   *The current page width.* The format is F3.0. For more information, see SET.

Scratch Variables

Scratch variables are variables created for the sole purpose of facilitating operations during a session.

- To create a scratch variable, specify a variable name that begins with the # character—for example, *#ID*. Scratch variables can be either numeric or string.
- Scratch variables are initialized to 0 for numeric variables or blank for string variables.
- SPSS does not reinitialize scratch variables when reading a new case. Their values are always carried across cases. Therefore, a scratch variable is a good choice for a looping index.
- Do not use LEAVE with a scratch variable.
- Scratch variables cannot be used in procedures and cannot be saved in a data file.
- Scratch variables cannot be assigned missing values, variable labels, or value labels.
- Scratch variables can be created between procedures but are always discarded as the next procedure begins.
- Scratch variables are discarded once a TEMPORARY command is specified.
- The keyword TO cannot refer to scratch variables and permanent variables at the same time.
- Scratch variables cannot be named on a WEIGHT command.

Variable Formats

SPSS accepts two variable types: numeric and string (also referred to as alphanumeric). Numeric values are stored internally as double-precision floating-point numbers and string values as codes listed in the SPSS character set (see Appendix B). Variable formats determine how SPSS reads raw data into storage and how it displays and writes values out.

Input and Output Formats

Values are read according to their *input* format and displayed on your terminal or written to a file according to their *output* format. The input and output formats differ in several ways.

- The input format is either specified or implied on the DATA LIST, KEYED DATA LIST, or other data definition commands. It is in effect only when SPSS builds cases in a working data file. Figure 8 shows the command printback for DATA LIST, which includes input format specifications.

Figure 8   Output showing input formats

```
  1   0   DATA LIST   /ID 1-4 SCORE 6-9 (F,2).

This command will read 1 records from the command file

Variable   Rec   Start    End        Format

ID           1     1       4          F4.0
SCORE        1     6       9          F4.2
```

- DATA LIST or any other data definition command automatically generates an output format from the input format and expands the output format to include punctuation characters such as decimal points, commas, dollar signs, and percent signs. To see the current output formats of variables in the working data file, use DISPLAY VARIABLES. The variables defined by the above DATA LIST command are displayed in Figure 9. Note that the output format for *SCORE* has been expanded one space to allow the display of the decimal point (the F4.2 input format indicates a four-character variable with two implied decimal places; the F5.2 output format includes one space for the decimal point).

Figure 9   Output showing output formats

```
List of variables on the active file

Name      Pos   Print Fmt    Write Fmt    Missing Values

ID         1    F4           F4
SCORE      2    F5.2         F5.2
```

- The formats (specified or default) on NUMERIC, COMPUTE, or other commands that create new variables are output formats. You must specify adequate widths to accommodate all punctuation characters.
- The output format is in effect during the entire working session (unless explicitly changed) and is saved in the dictionary of an SPSS-format data file.
- Output formats for numeric variables can be changed with the FORMATS, PRINT FORMATS, or WRITE FORMATS command.
- Output formats (widths) for string variables cannot be changed with command syntax. However, you can use STRING to declare a new variable with the desired format and then use COMPUTE to copy values from the existing string variable into the new variable.
- The format type cannot be changed from string to numeric, or vice versa, with command syntax. However, you can use RECODE to recode values from one variable into another variable of a different type.

See DATA LIST for information on specifying input data formats. See FORMATS, PRINT FORMATS, and WRITE FORMATS for information on specifying output data formats. See STRING for information on declaring new string variables.

Numeric Variable Formats

- The formats used in this manual use FORTRAN-like syntax—for example, Fw.d, where F denotes the format type (numeric), w represents the variable width, and d represents the number of decimal places.
- By default, the DATA LIST and KEYED DATA LIST commands assume that variables are numeric with an F format type. The default width depends on whether the data are in fixed or freefield format. For discussion of fixed data and freefield data, see DATA LIST.
- Numeric variables created by COMPUTE, COUNT, or other commands that create numeric variables are assigned a format type F8.2 (or the default format defined on SET FORMAT).
- If a data value exceeds its width specification, SPSS makes an attempt to display some value nevertheless. It first rounds the decimals, then takes out punctuation characters, then tries scientific notation, and if there is still not enough space, produces asterisks (***), indicating that a value is present but cannot be displayed in the assigned width.
- The output format does not affect the value stored in the file. A numeric value is always stored in double precision.

F, N, and E Formats

Table 4 lists the formats most commonly used to read in and write out numeric data.

Table 4   Common numeric formats

Format type	Description	Sample format	Sample input	Output for fixed input Format	Output for fixed input Value	Output for freefield input Format	Output for freefield input Value
Fw.d	Standard numeric	F5.0	1234	F5.0	1234	F5.0	1234
			1.234		1		1[*]
		F5.2	1234	F6.2	12.34	F6.2	1234.0
			1.234		1.23		1.23
Nw.d	Restricted numeric	N5.0	00123	F5.0	123	F5.0	123
			1.234		. [†]		1
		N5.2	12345	F6.2	123.45	F6.2	12345
			12.34		.		12.34
Ew.d	Scientific notation	E8.0	1234E3	E10.3	1.234E+06	E10.3	1.234E+06[**]
			1234		1.234E+03		1.234E+03

* Only the display is truncated. The value is stored in full precision.
† System-missing value. In this case, the value entered contains an illegal decimal point.
** Scientific notation is accepted in input data with F, COMMA, DOLLAR, DOT, and PCT formats. The same rules apply as specified below.

For fixed data:

- If a value has no coded decimal point but the input format specifies decimal positions, the rightmost positions are interpreted as implied decimal digits. For example, if the input F format specifies two decimal digits, the value 1234 is interpreted as 12.34; however, the value 123.4 is still interpreted as 123.4.

- With the N format, decimal places are always implied. Only unsigned integers are allowed. Values not padded with leading zeros to the specified width or those containing decimal points are assigned the system-missing value. This format is useful for reading and checking values that should be integers containing leading zeros.

- The E format reads all forms of scientific notation. If the sign is omitted, + is assumed. If the sign (+ or −) is specified before the exponent, the E or D can be omitted. A single space is permitted after the E or D and/or after the sign. If both the sign and the letter E or D are omitted, implied decimal places are assumed. For example, 1.234E3, 1.234+3, 1.234E+3, 1.234D3, 1.234D+3, 1.234E 3, and 1234 are all legitimate values. Only the last value can imply decimal places.

- E format input values can be up to 40 characters wide and include up to 15 decimal positions.

- The default output width (w) for the E format is either the specified input width or the number of specified decimal positions plus 7 ($d+7$), whichever is greater. The minimum width is 10 and the minimum decimal places are 3.

For freefield data:

- F format w and d specifications do not affect how data are read. They only determine the output formats (expanded, if necessary). 1234 is always read as 1234 in freefield data, but a specified F5.2 format will be expanded to F6.2 and the value will be displayed as 1234.0 (the last decimal place is rounded because of lack of space).

- The N format, when used for freefield data, is treated as the F format.

- The E format for freefield data follows the same rules as for fixed data except that no blank space is permitted in the value. Thus, 1.234E3 and 1.234+3 are allowed, but the value 1.234 3 will cause mistakes when the data are read.

- The default output E format and the width and decimal place limitations are the same as with fixed data.

COMMA, DOT, DOLLAR, and PCT Formats

Table 5 lists the formats that read and write data with embedded punctuation characters and symbols, such as commas, dots, and dollar and percent signs. The input data may or may not contain such characters. The data values read in are stored as numbers but displayed using the appropriate formats. Other formats that use punctuation characters and symbols are date and time formats and currency formats. Date and time are discussed in "Date and Time" on p. 60. Currency formats are output formats only. (See SET and FORMATS.)

Table 5   Numeric formats with punctuation and symbols

Format type	Description	Sample format	Sample input	Default output format	Displayed value
COMMAw.d	Commas in numbers	COMMA6.0	12345	COMMA7.0	12,345
			12,345		12,345
			123,45		12,345
		COMMA6.3	12345	COMMA7.3	12.345
			123,45		12.345
			1.2345		1.234
			1234.5		1234.50[*]
DOTw.d	Dots in numbers	DOT6.0	12345	DOT7.0	12.345
			123.45		12.345
			123.45		12.345
		DOT6.3	12345	DOT7.3	12,345
			123.45		12,345
			1,2345		1,234
			1234,5		1234,50*
DOLLARw.d	Dollar sign and comma in numbers	DOLLAR7.0	1234	DOLLAR10.0	$1,234
			1,234		$1,234
			$1234		$1,234
			$1,234		$1,234
		DOLLAR7.3	1234	DOLLAR10.3	$1.234
			1,234		$1.234
			$1,23.4		$123.400
			12345.6		$12345.600*
PCTw.d	Percent sign after numbers	PCT7.0	1234	PCT8.0	1234%
			12.34		12%
		PCT7.2	1234	PCT9.3	1.234%
			12.3		12.340%
			1234		12.34%

* When the decimal point is coded in input, SPSS displays all specified decimal places whether recorded in the data or not. When the width is inadequate, thousands separators are dropped before decimal places.

- Formats listed in Table 5 cannot be used to read freefield data.
- Data values can appear anywhere within the column specification. Both leading and trailing blanks are allowed.
- The sign (for example, "$" for DOLLAR format) or punctuation mark (for example, "." for DOT format) is ignored in the input data. Its position does not affect the value read into storage.
- The default output format expands the width of the input format by the number of the required signs or punctuation marks plus the decimal point if d is not 0. For example, COMMA9.2 is expanded to COMMA12.2 to accommodate two possible commas and one decimal point.
- DOT format is similar to COMMA format but reverses the symbols used for the thousands separator and the decimal point. For example, in DOT format, 1.234 has the value of one thousand, two hundred and thirty-four.

Binary and Hexadecimal Formats

SPSS is capable of reading and writing data in formats used by a number of programming languages such as PL/I, COBOL, FORTRAN, and Assembler. The data can be binary, hexadecimal, or zoned decimal. Formats described in this section can be used both as input formats and output formats, but with fixed data only. The described formats are not available on all systems. Consult the *SPSS Base User's Guide* for your version of SPSS for details.

The default output format for all formats described in this section is an equivalent F format, allowing the maximum number of columns for values with symbols and punctuation. To change the default, use FORMATS or WRITE FORMATS.

IBw.d (integer binary):

The IB format reads fields that contain fixed-point binary (integer) data. The data might be generated by COBOL using COMPUTATIONAL data items, by FORTRAN using INTEGER*2 or INTEGER*4, or by Assembler using fullword and halfword items. The general format is a signed binary number that is 16 or 32 bits in length.

The general syntax for the IB format is IBw.d, where w is the field width in bytes (omitted for column-style specifications) and d is the number of digits to the right of the decimal point. Since the width is expressed in bytes and the number of decimal positions is expressed in digits, d can be greater than w. For example, both of the following commands are valid:

```
DATA LIST FIXED /VAR1 (IB4.8).
DATA LIST FIXED /VAR1 1-4 (IB,8).
```

Widths of 2 and 4 represent standard 16-bit and 32-bit integers, respectively. Fields read with the IB format are treated as signed. For example, the one-byte binary value 11111111 would be read as −1.

PIBw.d (positive integer binary):

The PIB format is essentially the same as IB except that negative numbers are not allowed. This restriction allows one additional bit of magnitude. The same one-byte value 11111111 would be read as 255.

PIBHEXw (hexadecimal of PIB):

The PIBHEX format reads hexadecimal numbers as unsigned integers and writes positive integers as hexadecimal numbers. The general syntax for the PIBHEX format is PIBHEXw, where w indicates the total number of hexadecimal characters. The w specification must be an even number, with a maximum of 16.

   For input data, each hexadecimal number must consist of the exact number of characters. No signs, decimal points, or leading and trailing blanks are allowed. For some operating systems (such as IBM CMS), hexadecimal characters must be upper case. The following example illustrates the kind of data the PIBHEX format can read:

```
DATA LIST FIXED
 /VAR1 1-4 (PIBHEX) VAR2 6-9 (PIBHEX) VAR3 11-14 (PIBHEX).
BEGIN DATA
0001 0002 0003
0004 0005 0006
0007 0008 0009
000A 000B 000C
000D 000E 000F
00F0 0B2C FFFF
END DATA.
LIST.
```

The values for *VAR1*, *VAR2*, and *VAR3* are listed in Figure 10. The PIBHEX format can also be used to write decimal values as hexadecimal numbers, which may be useful for programmers.

Figure 10   Output displaying values read in PIBHEX format

```
VAR1    VAR2    VAR3

   1       2       3
   4       5       6
   7       8       9
  10      11      12
  13      14      15
 240    2860   65535
```

Zw.d (zoned decimal):

The Z format reads data values that contain zoned decimal data. Such numbers may be generated by COBOL systems using DISPLAY data items, by PL/I systems using PICTURE data items, or by Assembler using zoned decimal data items.

   In zoned decimal format, one digit is represented by one byte, generally hexadecimal F1 representing 1, F2 representing 2, and so on. The last byte, however, combines the sign for the number with the last digit. In the last byte, hexadecimal A, F, or C assigns +, and B, D, or E assigns −. For example, hexadecimal D1 represents 1 for the last digit and assigns the minus sign (−) to the number.

   The general syntax of the Z format is Zw.d, where w is the total number of bytes (which is the same as columns) and d is the number of decimals. For input data, values can appear anywhere within the column specifications. Both leading and trailing blanks are allowed. Decimals can be implied by the input format specification or explicitly coded in the data. Explicitly coded decimals override the input format specifications.

The following example illustrates how the Z format reads zoned decimals in their printed forms on IBM mainframe and PC systems. The printed form for the sign zone (A to I for +1 to +9, and so on) may vary from system to system.

```
DATA LIST FIXED /VAR1 1-5 (Z) VAR2 7-11 (Z,2) VAR3 13-17 (Z)
 VAR4 19-23 (Z,2) VAR5 25-29 (Z) VAR6 31-35 (Z,2).
BEGIN DATA
1234A 1234A 1234B 1234B 1234C 1234C
1234D 1234D 1234E 1234E 1234F 1234F
1234G 1234G 1234H 1234H 1234I 1234I
1234J 1234J 1234K 1234K 1234L 1234L
1234M 1234M 1234N 1234N 1234O 1234O
1234P 1234P 1234Q 1234Q 1234R 1234R
1234{ 1234{ 1234} 1234} 1.23M 1.23M
END DATA.
LIST.
```

The values for *VAR1* to *VAR6* are listed in Figure 11.

Figure 11   Output displaying values read in Z format

```
VAR1     VAR2     VAR3     VAR4     VAR5     VAR6

 12341   123.41    12342   123.42    12343   123.43
 12344   123.44    12345   123.45    12346   123.46
 12347   123.47    12348   123.48    12349   123.49
-12341  -123.41   -12342  -123.42   -12343  -123.43
-12344  -123.44   -12345  -123.45   -12346  -123.46
-12347  -123.47   -12348  -123.48   -12349  -123.49
 12340   123.40   -12340  -123.40       -1    -1.23
```

The default output format for the Z format is the equivalent F format, as shown in Figure 11. The default output width is based on the input width specification plus one column for the sign and one column for the implied decimal point (if specified). For example, an input format of Z4.0 generates an output format of F5.0 and an input format of Z4.2 generates an output format of F6.2.

Pw.d (packed decimal):

The P format is used to read fields with packed decimal numbers. Such numbers are generated by COBOL using COMPUTATIONAL–3 data items and by Assembler using packed decimal data items. The general format of a packed decimal field is two four-bit digits in each byte of the field except the last. The last byte contains a single digit in its four leftmost bits and a four-bit sign in its rightmost bits. If the last four bits are 1111 (hexadecimal F), the value is positive; if they are 1101 (hexadecimal D), the value is negative. One byte under the P format can represent numbers from −9 to 9.

The general syntax of the P format is Pw.d, where w is the number of bytes (not digits) and d is the number of digits to the right of the implied decimal point. The number of digits in a field is (2*w−1).

PKw.d (unsigned packed decimal):

The PK format is essentially the same as P except that there is no sign. That is, even the right-most byte contains two digits, and negative data cannot be represented. One byte under the PK format can represent numbers from 0 to 99. The number of digits in a field is 2*w.

RBw (real binary):

The RB format is used to read data values that contain internal format floating-point numbers. Such numbers are generated by COBOL using COMPUTATIONAL–1 or COMPUTATIONAL–2 data items, by PL/I using FLOATING DECIMAL data items, by FORTRAN using REAL or REAL*8 data items, or by Assembler using floating-point data items.

    The general syntax of the RB format is RBw, where w is the total number of bytes. The width specification must be an even number between 2 and 8. Normally, a width specification of 8 is used to read double-precision values, and a width of 4 is used to read single-precision values.

RBHEXw (hexadecimal of RB):

The RBHEX format interprets a series of hexadecimal characters as a number that represents a floating-point number. This representation is system-specific. If the field width is less than twice the width of a floating-point number, the value is right-padded with binary zeros. For some operating systems (for example, IBM CMS), letters in hexadecimal values must be upper case.

    The general syntax of the RBHEX format is RBHEXw, where w indicates the total number of columns. The width must be an even number. The values are real (floating-point) numbers. Leading and trailing blanks are not allowed. Any data values shorter than the specified input width must be padded with leading zeros.

String Variable Formats

- The values of string variables can contain numbers, letters, and special characters and can be up to 255 characters long.

- SPSS differentiates between long strings and short strings. Long strings can be displayed by some procedures and by the PRINT command, and they can be used as break variables to define subgroups in REPORT. They cannot, however, be tabulated in procedures such as CROSSTABS, and they cannot have user-missing values. Short strings, on the other hand, can be tabulated and can have user-missing values. The maximum length of a short string depends on the computer and operating system; it is typically 8 characters.

- System-missing values cannot be generated for string variables, since any character is a legal string value.

- When a transformation command that creates or modifies a string variable yields a missing or undefined result, a null string is assigned. The variable displays as blanks and is not treated as missing.

- String formats are used to read and write string variables. The input values can be alphanumeric characters (A format) or the hexadecimal representation of alphanumeric characters (AHEX format).

- For fixed data, the width can be explicitly specified on DATA LIST or KEYED DATA LIST or implied if column-style specifications are used. For freefield data, the default width is 1; if the input string may be longer, *w* must be explicitly specified. Input strings shorter than the specified width are right-padded with blanks.

- The output format for a string variable is always A. The width is determined by the input format or the format assigned on the STRING command. String formats can be displayed with DISPLAY VARIABLES but cannot be changed.

Aw (Standard Characters)

The A format is used to read standard characters. Characters can include letters, numbers, punctuation marks, blanks, and most other characters on your keyboard. Numbers entered as values for string variables cannot be used in calculations unless you convert them to numeric format with the NUMBER function (see "String Functions" on p. 51).

Fixed data:

With fixed-format input data, any punctuation—including leading, trailing, and embedded blanks—within the column specifications is included in the string value. For example, a string value of "Mr. Ed" (with one embedded blank) is distinguished from a value of "Mr. Ed" (with two embedded blanks). It is also distinguished from a string value of "MR. ED" (all upper case), and all three are treated as separate values. These can be important considerations for any procedures, transformations, or data selection commands involving string variables. Consider the following example:

```
DATA LIST FIXED /ALPHAVAR 1-10 (A).
BEGIN DATA
Mr. Ed
Mr. Ed
MR. ED
Mr.   Ed
 Mr. Ed
END DATA.
AUTORECODE ALPHAVAR /INTO NUMVAR.
LIST.
```

AUTORECODE recodes the values into consecutive integers. Figure 12 shows the recoded values.

Figure 12   Different string values illustrated

```
ALPHAVAR    NUMVAR

Mr. Ed         4
Mr. Ed         4
MR. ED         2
Mr.   Ed       3
 Mr. Ed        1
```

Freefield data:

With freefield data, blanks and commas are treated as delimiters for A format variables unless the value is enclosed in apostrophes or quotation marks. For example,

```
Ed, Mr.
```

is read as two separate values (Ed and Mr.). To include blanks and/or commas in a string value, enclose the value in apostrophes or quotation marks. For example, the following command file will generate a list of values as shown in Figure 13:

```
DATA LIST FREE /ALPHAVAR (A10).
BEGIN DATA
Mr.   Ed
Ed,Mr.
'Mr.   Ed'
'Ed, Mr.'
END DATA.
LIST.
```

Figure 13   Blanks and commas in freefield string input

```
ALPHAVAR

Mr.
Ed
Ed
Mr.
Mr.   Ed
Ed, Mr.
```

AHEXw (Hexadecimal Characters)

The AHEX format is used to read the hexadecimal representation of standard characters. Each set of two hexadecimal characters represents one standard character. For codes used on different operating systems, see Appendix B.

- The w specification refers to columns of the hexadecimal representation and must be an even number. Leading, trailing, and embedded blanks are not allowed, and only valid hexadecimal characters can be used in input values.

- For some operating systems (for example, IBM CMS), letters in hexadecimal values must be upper case.

- The default output format for variables read with the AHEX input format is the A format. The default width is half the specified input width. For example, an input format of AHEX14 generates an output format of A7.

- Used as an output format, the AHEX format displays the printable characters in the hexadecimal characters specific to your system. The following commands run on a UNIX system (where A=41 (decimal 65), a=61 (decimal 97), and so on) produce the output shown in Figure 14:

```
DATA LIST FIXED
   /A,B,C,D,E,F,G,H,I,J,K,L,M,N,O,P,Q,R,S,T,U,V,W,X,Y,Z 1-26 (A).
FORMATS ALL (AHEX2).
BEGIN DATA
ABCDEFGHIJKLMNOPQRSTUVWXYZ
abcdefghijklmnopqrstuvwxyz
END DATA.
LIST.
```

Figure 14   Display of hexadecimal representation of the character set with AHEX format

```
A  B  C  D  E  F  G  H  I  J  K  L  M  N  O  P  Q  R  S  T  U  V  W  X  Y  Z

41 42 43 44 45 46 47 48 49 4A 4B 4C 4D 4E 4F 50 51 52 53 54 55 56 57 58 59 5A
61 62 63 64 65 66 67 68 69 6A 6B 6C 6D 6E 6F 70 71 72 73 74 75 76 77 78 79 7A
```

FORTRAN-like Format Specifications

You can use FORTRAN-like format specifications to define formats for a set of variables, as in the following example:

```
DATA LIST FILE=HUBDATA RECORDS=3
     /MOHIRED, YRHIRED, DEPT1 TO DEPT4 (T12, 2F2.0, 4(1X,F1.0)).
```

- The specification T12 in parentheses tabs to the 12th column. The first variable (*MOHIRED*) will be read beginning from column 12.

- The specification 2F2.0 assigns the format F2.0 to two adjacent variables (*MOHIRED* and *YRHIRED*).

- The next four variables (*DEPT1* to *DEPT4*) are each assigned the format F1.0. The 4 in 4(1X,F1.0) distributes the same format to four consecutive variables. 1X skips one column before each variable. (The column-skipping specification placed within the parentheses is distributed to each variable.)

Transformation Expressions

Transformation expressions are used in commands like COMPUTE, IF, DO IF, LOOP IF, and SELECT IF. This section describes the three types of expressions: numeric, string, and logical, as well as available operators. For date and time functions, see "Date and Time" on p. 60.

Numeric Expressions

Numeric expressions can be used with the COMPUTE and IF command and as part of a logical expression for commands such as IF, DO IF, LOOP IF, and SELECT IF. Arithmetic expressions can also appear in the index portion of a LOOP command, on the REPEATING DATA command, and on the PRINT SPACES command.

Arithmetic Operations

The following arithmetic operators are available:

+   *Addition.*

–   *Subtraction.*

*   *Multiplication.*

/   *Division.*

**   *Exponentiation.*

- No two operators can appear consecutively.
- Arithmetic operators cannot be implied. For example, (VAR1)(VAR2) is not a legal specification; you must specify VAR1*VAR2.
- Arithmetic operators and parentheses serve as delimiters. To improve readability, blanks (not commas) can be inserted before and after an operator.
- To form complex expressions, you can use variables, constants, and functions with arithmetic operators.
- The order of execution is functions first, then exponentiation, then multiplication, division, and unary –, and then addition and subtraction.
- Operators at the same level are executed from left to right.
- To override the order of operation, use parentheses. Execution begins with the innermost set of parentheses and progresses out.

Numeric Constants

- Constants used in numeric expressions or as arguments to functions can be integer or non-integer, depending on the application or function.

- You can specify as many digits in a constant as needed, as long as you understand the precision restrictions of your computer.
- Numeric constants can be signed (+ or –) but cannot contain any other special characters such as the comma or dollar sign.
- Numeric constants can be expressed with scientific notation. Thus, the exponent for a constant in scientific notation is limited to two digits. The range of values allowed for exponents in scientific notation is from –99 to +99.

Complex Numeric Arguments

- Except where explicitly restricted, complex expressions can be formed by nesting functions and arithmetic operators as arguments to functions.
- The order of execution for complex numeric arguments is functions first, then exponentiation, then multiplication, division, and unary –, and then addition and subtraction.
- To control the order of execution in complex numeric arguments, use parentheses.

Numeric Functions

Numeric functions can be used in any numeric expression on IF, SELECT IF, DO IF, ELSE IF, LOOP IF, END LOOP IF, and COMPUTE commands. Numeric functions always return numbers (or the system-missing value whenever the result is indeterminate). The expression to be transformed by a function is called the *argument*. Most functions have a variable or a list of variables as arguments.

- In numeric functions with two or more arguments, each argument must be separated by a comma. Blanks alone cannot be used to separate variable names, expressions, or constants in transformation expressions.
- Arguments should be enclosed in parentheses, as in TRUNC(INCOME), where the TRUNC function returns the integer portion of the variable *INCOME*.
- Multiple arguments should be separated by commas, as in MEAN(Q1,Q2,Q3), where the MEAN function returns the mean of variables *Q1*, *Q2*, and *Q3*.

Arithmetic Functions

- All arithmetic functions except MOD have single arguments; MOD has two. The arguments to MOD must be separated by a comma.
- Arguments can be numeric expressions, as in RND(A**2/B).

ABS(arg)   *Absolute value.* ABS(SCALE) is 4.7 when *SCALE* equals 4.7 or –4.7.

RND(arg)   *Round the absolute value to an integer and reaffix the sign.* RND(SCALE) is –5 when *SCALE* equals –4.7.

TRUNC(arg)   *Truncate to an integer.* TRUNC(SCALE) is –4 when *SCALE* equals –4.7.

MOD(arg,arg)   *Remainder (modulo) of the first argument divided by the second.* When *YEAR* equals 1983, MOD(YEAR,100) is 83.

SQRT(arg)	*Square root.* SQRT(SIBS) is 1.41 when *SIBS* equals 2.
EXP(arg)	*Exponential. e* is raised to the power of the argument. EXP(VARA) is 7.39 when *VARA* equals 2.
LG10(arg)	*Base 10 logarithm.* LG10(VARB) is 0.48 when *VARB* equals 3.
LN(arg)	*Natural or Naperian logarithm (base* e). LN(VARC) is 2.30 when *VARC* equals 10.
ARSIN(arg)	*Arcsine.* (Alias ASIN.) The result is given in radians. ARSIN(ANG) is 1.57 when *ANG* equals 1.
ARTAN(arg)	*Arctangent.* (Alias ATAN.) The result is given in radians. ARTAN(ANG2) is 0.79 when *ANG2* equals 1.
SIN(arg)	*Sine.* The argument must be specified in radians. SIN(VARD) is 0.84 when *VARD* equals 1.
COS(arg)	*Cosine.* The argument must be specified in radians. COS(VARE) is 0.54 when *VARE* equals 1.

Statistical Functions

- Each argument to a statistical function (expression, variable name, or constant) must be separated by a comma.
- The *.n* suffix can be used with all statistical functions to specify the number of valid arguments. For example, MEAN.2(A,B,C,D) returns the mean of the valid values for variables *A*, *B*, *C*, and *D* only if at least two of the variables have valid values. The default for *n* is 2 for SD, VARIANCE, and CFVAR, and 1 for other statistical functions.
- The keyword TO can be used to refer to a set of variables in the argument list.

SUM(arg list)	*Sum of the nonmissing values across the argument list.*
MEAN(arg list)	*Mean of the nonmissing values across the argument list.*
SD(arg list)	*Standard deviation of the nonmissing values across the argument list.*
VARIANCE(arg list)	*Variance of the nonmissing values across the argument list.*
CFVAR(arg list)	*Coefficient of variation of the nonmissing values across the argument list.* The coefficient of variation is the standard deviation divided by the mean.
MIN(arg list)	*Minimum nonmissing value across the argument list.*
MAX(arg list)	*Maximum nonmissing value across the argument list.*

Random Variable and Distribution Functions

- Random variable and distribution functions take both constants and variables for arguments.

- A function argument, if required, must come first and is denoted by q (quantile) for cumulative distribution functions and p (probability) for inverse distribution functions.

- All random variable and distribution functions must specify distribution parameters, denoted by a, b, and/or c, according to the number required.

- All arguments are real numbers.

- Cumulative distribution functions take the prefix CDF. A cumulative distribution function CDF.d_spec(q,a,...) returns a probability (p) that a variate with the specified distribution (d_spec) falls below q for continuous functions and at or below q for discrete functions.

- Inverse distribution functions take the prefix IDF. Inverse distribution functions are not available for discrete distributions. An inverse distribution function IDF.d_spec(p,a,...) returns a value q such that CDF.d_spec(q,a,...)=p with the specified distribution (d_spec).

- Random number generation functions take the prefix RV. A random number generation function RV.d_spec(a,...) generates an independent observation with the specified distribution (d_spec).

- Noncentral cumulative distribution functions take the prefix NCDF. A noncentral distribution function NCDF.d_spec(q,a,b,...) returns a probability (p) that a variate with the specified noncentral distribution falls below q. It is available only for beta, chi-square, F, and Student's t.

- Restrictions to distribution parameters a, b, and c apply to all functions for that distribution. Restrictions for the function parameter p or q apply to that particular distribution function. The program issues a warning and returns system missing when it encounters an out-of-range value for an argument.

The following are continuous distributions:

BETA　　*Beta distribution.* The beta distribution takes two shape parameters a and b; both must be positive. The functions are CDF.BETA(q,a,b), IDF.BETA(p,a,b), and RV.BETA(a,b), where both q and p must be between 0 and 1 inclusive. The noncentral beta distribution takes an extra noncentrality parameter c, which must be greater than or equal to 0. The noncentral cumulative distribution function is NCDF.BETA(q,a,b,c). The beta distribution is used in Bayesian analyses as a conjugate to the binomial distribution.

CAUCHY　　*Cauchy distribution.* The Cauchy distribution takes one location parameter (a) and one scale parameter (b); b must be positive. The functions are CDF.CAUCHY(q,a,b), IDF.CAUCHY(p,a,b), and RV.CAUCHY(a,b), where $0<p<1$. The Cauchy distribution is symmetric about the location parameter a and has slowly decaying tails that the expectation does not exist. The harmonic mean of variates that have positive density at 0 is typically distributed as Cauchy.

CHI-SQUARE　　*Chi-square distribution.* The chi-square distribution takes one shape parameter (a), which is the degrees of freedom and must be positive. The functions are CDF.CHISQ(q,a), IDF.CHISQ(p,a), and RV.CHISQ(a), where $q\geq0$ and $0\leq p<1$. The noncentral chi-square distribution takes an extra noncentrality parameter c, which must be greater than or equal to 0. The noncentral cumulative distribution function is NCDF.CHISQ(q,a,c). Chi-square is a special case of the gamma distribution and is commonly used to test quadratic forms under the Gaussian assumption.

EXPONENTIAL   *Exponential distribution.* The exponential distribution takes one scale parameter (a), which can represent the rate of decay and must be positive. The functions are CDF.EXP(q,a), IDF.EXP(p,a), and RV.EXP(a), where $q \geq 0$ and $0 \leq p < 1$. The exponential distribution is a special case of the gamma distribution. A major use of this distribution is life testing.

F   *F distribution.* The F distribution takes two shape parameters a and b, which are the degrees of freedom and must be positive. The F distribution functions are CDF.F(q,a,b), IDF.F(p,a,b), and RV.F(a,b), where $q \geq 0$ and $0 \leq p < 1$. The noncentral F distribution takes an extra noncentrality parameter c, which must be greater than or equal to 0. The noncentral cumulative distribution function is NCDF.F(q,a,b,c). The F distribution is commonly used to test hypotheses under the Gaussian assumption.

GAMMA   *Gamma distribution.* The gamma distribution takes one shape parameter (a) and one scale parameter (b). Both parameters must be positive. The functions are CDF.GAMMA(q,a,b), IDF.GAMMA(p,a,b), and RV.GAMMA(a,b), where $q \geq 0$ and $0 \leq p < 1$. The gamma distribution is commonly used in queuing theory, inventory control, and precipitation processes. If a is an integer and $b=1$, it is the Erlang distribution.

LAPLACE   *Laplace or double exponential distribution.* The Laplace distribution takes one location parameter (a) and one scale parameter (b). Parameter b must be positive. The Laplace functions are CDF.LAPLACE(q,a,b), IDF.LAPLACE(p,a,b), and RV.LAPLACE(a,b), where $0 < p < 1$. The Laplace distribution is symmetric about 0 and has exponentially decaying tails on both ends.

LOGISTIC   *Logistic distribution.* The logistic distribution takes one location parameter (a) and one scale parameter (b). Parameter b must be positive. The logistic functions are CDF.LOGISTIC(q,a,b), IDF.LOGISTIC(p,a,b), and RV.LOGISTIC(a,b), where $0 < p < 1$. The logistic distribution is a unimodal, symmetric distribution with tails that are longer than the Gaussian distribution. It is used to model growth curves.

LOGNORMAL   *Lognormal distribution.* This distribution takes two parameters a and b. Both parameters must be positive. The functions are CDF.LOGNORMAL(q,a,b), IDF.LOGNORMAL(p,a,b), and RV.LOGNORMAL(a,b), where $q \geq 0$ and $0 \leq p < 1$. Lognormal is used in the distribution of particle sizes in aggregates, flood flows, concentrations of air contaminants, and failure time.

NORMAL   *Normal distribution.* The normal distribution takes one location parameter (a) and one scale parameter (b). Parameter b must be positive. The normal functions are CDF.NORMAL(q,a,b), IDF.NORMAL(p,a,b), and RV.NORMAL(a,b), where $0 < p < 1$. Three functions in SPSS releases earlier than 6.0 are special cases of the normal distribution functions:
CDFNORM(arg)=CDF.NORMAL(q,0,1)
where arg is q;
PROBIT(srg)=IDF.NORMAL(p,0,1)
where arg is p; and
NORMAL(arg)=RV.NORMAL(0,b)

where arg is *b*. The normal or Gaussian distribution is symmetric about the mean and is the most widely used in statistics.

PARETO   *Pareto distribution.* The Pareto distribution takes a threshold parameter (*a*) and a shape parameter (*b*). Both parameters must be positive. The functions are CDF.PARETO(q,a,b), IDF.PARETO(p,a,b), and RV.PARETO(a,b), where $q \geq a$ and $0 \leq p < 1$. Pareto is commonly used in economics as a model for a density function with a slowly decaying tail.

STUDENT T   *Student* t *distribution.* The Student *t* distribution takes one shape parameter (*a*), which is the degrees of freedom and must be positive. The functions are CDF.T(q,a), IDF.T(p,a), and RV.T(a), where $0 < p < 1$. The Student *t* distribution is symmetric about 0 and approaches the Gaussian distribution as *a* approaches infinity. The noncentral Student *t* distribution takes an extra non-centrality parameter *b*. The noncentral cumulative distribution function is NCDF.T(q,a,b). The major use of the Student *t* distribution is to test hypotheses and construct confidence intervals for means of Gaussian data.

UNIFORM   *Uniform distribution.* The uniform distribution takes two parameters *a* and *b*. The first parameter *a* must be less than or equal to the second parameter *b*. The functions are CDF.UNIFORM(q,a,b), IDF.UNIFORM(p,a,b), and RV.UNIFORM(a,b), where $a \leq q \leq b$ and $0 \leq p \leq 1$. The uniform random number function in SPSS releases earlier than 6.0 is a special case:
UNIFORM(arg)=RV.UNIFORM(0,b)
where arg is parameter *b*. Among other uses, the uniform distribution commonly models the round-off error.

WEIBULL   *Weibull distribution.* The Weibull distribution takes two parameters *a* and *b*, both of which must be positive. The functions are CDF.WEIBULL(q,a,b), IDF.WEIBULL(p,a,b), and RV.WEIBULL(a,b), where $q \geq 0$ and $0 \leq p < 1$. The Weibull distribution is commonly used in survival analysis.

The following are discrete distributions:

BERNOULLI   *Bernoulli distribution.* The Bernoulli distribution takes one probability parameter *a*, which must be between 0 and 1 inclusive. The functions are CDF.BERNOULLI(q,a) and RV.BERNOULLI(a), where *a* is the probability of obtaining a success. The Bernoulli distribution is a special case of the binomial distribution and is used in simple success-failure experiments.

BINOMIAL   *Binomial distribution.* The binomial distribution takes one trial parameter (*a*) and one probability parameter (*b*). Parameter *a* must be a positive integer and parameter *b* must be between 0 and 1 inclusive. The functions are CDF.BINOM(q,a,b) and RV.BINOM(a,b), where *a* is the number of trials, *b* is the probability of obtaining a success in any single trial, and *q* is the number of successes in *a* trials. When *a*=1, it is the Bernoulli distribution. The binomial distribution is used in independently replicated success-failure experiments.

GEOMETRIC   *Geometric distribution.* The geometric distribution takes one probability parameter (*a*), which must be greater than 0 and less than or equal to 1. The functions are CDF.GEOM(q,a) and RV.GEOM(a), where q is the number of trials needed (including the last trial) before a success is observed and a is the probability of obtaining a success in a single trial.

HYPERGEOMETRIC   *Hypergeometric distribution.* The hypergeometric distribution takes three parameters a, b, and c. All three parameters are positive integers, and both b and c must be less than or equal to a. The functions are CDF.HYPER(q,a,b,c) and RV.HYPER(a,b,c), where a is the total number of objects in an urn model, b is the number of objects randomly drawn without replacement from the urn, c is the number of objects with distinct characteristics, and q is the number of objects with these distinct characteristics observed out of the withdrawn objects.

NEGATIVE BINOMIAL   *Negative binomial distribution.* The negative binomial distribution takes one threshold parameter (a) and one probability parameter (b). Parameter a must be an integer and parameter b must be greater than 0 and less than or equal to 1. The functions are CDF.NEGBIN(q,a,b) and RV.NEGBIN(a,b), where q is the number of trials needed (including the last trial) before a successes are observed and b is the probability of obtaining a success in a single trial. If $a=1$, it is a geometric distribution.

POISSON   *Poisson distribution.* The Poisson distribution takes one rate or mean parameter (a). Parameter a must be positive. The functions are CDF.POISSON(q,a) and RV.POISSON(a). The Poisson distribution is used in modeling the distribution of counts, such as traffic counts and insect counts.

Missing Values in Numeric Expressions

- Most numeric expressions receive the system-missing value when any one of the values in the expression is missing.

- Some arithmetic operations involving 0 can be evaluated even when the variables have missing values. These operations are:

Expression	Result
0 * missing	0
0 / missing	0
MOD(0,missing)	0

- The *n* suffix can be used with the statistical functions SUM, MEAN, MIN, MAX, SD, VARIANCE, and CFVAR to specify the number of valid arguments you consider acceptable. The default of n is 2 for SD, VARIANCE, and CFVAR, and 1 for other statistical functions. For example,

```
COMPUTE FACTOR = SUM.2(SCORE1 TO SCORE3).
```

computes the variable *FACTOR* only if a case has valid information for at least two scores. *FACTOR* is assigned the system-missing value if a case has valid values for fewer than two scores.

Domain Errors

Domain errors occur when numeric expressions are mathematically undefined or cannot be represented numerically on the computer for reasons other than missing data. Two common examples are division by zero and the square root of a negative number. When SPSS detects a domain error, it issues a warning and assigns the system-missing value to the expression. For example, the command COMPUTE TESTVAR = TRUNC(SQRT(X/Y) * .5) returns system-missing if *X/Y* is negative or if *Y* is 0.

The following are domain errors in numeric expressions:

**   *A negative number to a non-integer power.*

/   *A divisor of 0.*

MOD   *A divisor of 0.*

SQRT   *A negative argument.*

EXP   *An argument that produces a result too large to be represented on the computer.*

LG10   *A negative or 0 argument.*

LN   *A negative or 0 argument.*

ARSIN   *An argument whose absolute value exceeds 1.*

NORMAL *A negative or 0 argument.*

PROBIT   *A negative or 0 argument, or an argument 1 or greater.*

String Expressions

Expressions involving string variables can be used on COMPUTE and IF commands and in logical expressions on commands such as IF, DO IF, LOOP IF, and SELECT IF.

- A string expression can be a constant enclosed in apostrophes (for example, 'IL'), a string function (see "String Functions" below), or a string variable.
- An expression must return a string if the target variable is a string.
- The string returned by a string expression does not have to be the same length as the target variable; no warning messages are issued if the lengths are not the same. If the target variable produced by a COMPUTE command is shorter, the result is right-trimmed. If the target variable is longer, the result is right-padded.

String Functions

- The target variable for each string function must be a string and *must have already been declared* (see STRING).
- Multiple arguments in a list must be separated by commas.
- When two strings are compared, the case in which they are entered is significant. The LOWER and UPCASE functions are useful for making comparisons of strings regardless of case.
- For certain functions (for example, MIN, MAX, ANY, and RANGE), the outcome will be affected by case and by whether the string includes numbers or special characters. The character set in use varies by system. With the ASCII character set, lower case follows upper case in the sort order. Therefore, if *NAME1* is in upper case and *NAME2* is in lower case, MIN(NAME1,NAME2) will return *NAME1* as the minimum. The reverse is true with the EBCDIC character set, which sorts lower case before upper case.

CONCAT(arg list)	*Concatenate the arguments into a string.* String variables and strings can be intermixed as arguments. For example, CONCAT(A,'**') creates the string ABCD** for a case with the value *ABCD* for the string variable *A*.
LOWER(arg)	*Convert upper case to lower case.* All other characters remain unchanged. The argument can be a string variable or value. For example, LOWER(NAME1) returns charles if the value of *NAME1* is *CHARLES*.
LPAD(a1, a2, a3)	*Left-pad.* The variable a1 is left-padded up to the length specified by a2 using the optional single character a3 as the pad character. a2 must be a positive integer from 1 to 255. The default pad character is a blank. For example, LPAD(ALPHA1,10) adds four leading blanks to the target variable if *ALPHA1* has an A6 format. a3 can be any character enclosed in apostrophes or any expression that yields a single character.
LTRIM(a1, a2)	*Left-trim.* The character a2 is trimmed from the beginning of a1. For example, LTRIM(ALPHA2,'0') trims leading zeros from the variable *ALPHA2*. a2 can be any character enclosed in apostrophes or any expression that yields a single character. The default for a2 is a blank.
RPAD(a1, a2, a3)	*Right-pad.* The variable a1 is right-padded up to the length of a2 using the optional single character a3 as the pad character. a2 must be a positive integer from 1 to 255. The default pad character is a blank. For example, RPAD(ALPHA3,8,'*') adds two trailing asterisks to the target variable if *ALPHA3* has an A6 format. a3 can be any character enclosed in apostrophes or any expression that yields a single character.
RTRIM(a1, a2)	*Right-trim.* The character a2 is trimmed from the end of a1. For example, RTRIM(ALPHA4,'*') trims trailing asterisks from variable *ALPHA4*. a2 can be any character enclosed in apostrophes or any expression that yields a single character. The default for a2 is a blank.
SUBSTR(a1, a2, a3)	*Substring.* This function returns the substring within a1 beginning with the position specified by a2 and optionally for a length of a3. a2 can be a positive integer from 1 to the length of a1. a3, when added to a2, should not exceed the length of a1. If a3 is not specified, the substring is re-

turned up to the end of a1. For example, if the variable *ALPHA5* has an A6 format, SUBSTR(ALPHA5,3) returns the last four characters of *ALPHA5*. SUBSTR (ALPHA5,3,1) returns the third character of *ALPHA5*.

When used on the left side of an equals sign, the substring is replaced by the string specified on the right side of the equals sign. The rest of the original string remains intact. For example, SUBSTR(ALPHA6,3,1)='*' changes the third character of all values for *ALPHA6* to *. If the replacement string is longer or shorter than the substring, the replacement is truncated or padded with blanks on the right to an equal length.

UPCASE(arg)   *Convert lower case to upper case.* The argument can be a string variable or a string. For example, UPCASE(NAME1) returns CHARLES if the value of *NAME1* is *Charles*.

MBLEN.BYTE(arg,a1)   *Return the number of bytes in the character at the specified position.* The argument is a string expression and a1 indicates the beginning byte of the character in the specified string.

Search Functions

- The values returned by INDEX and/or RINDEX can be used as arguments to SUBSTR to pull out substrings with the same beginning or ending character but with varying position and length.

INDEX(a1, a2, a3)   *Return a number that indicates the position of the first occurrence of a2 in a1.* a1 is the string that is searched. a2 is the string variable or string that is used in the search. If a3 is not specified, all of a2 is used. For example, INDEX(ALPHA8,'*X*') returns 2 for a case with the value $X**X**X*$ for the variable *ALPHA8*. The optional a3 is the number of characters used to divide a2 into separate strings. Each substring is used for searching and the function returns the first occurrence of any of the substrings. With the same value $X**X**X*$ for *ALPHA8*, both INDEX(ALPHA8, '*X*', 2) and INDEX(ALPHA8, '*X*', 1) return 1. a3 must be a positive integer and must divide evenly into the length of a2. The target variable must be numeric. If a2 is not found within a1, the value 0 is returned.

LENGTH(arg)   *Return the length of the specified string.* The argument can be a string variable or a string. For example, LENGTH(LNAME) always returns 6 if *LNAME* has an A6 format. The target variable must be numeric.

MAX(arg list)   *Return the maximum value across the argument list.* For example, MAX(LNAME,FNAME) selects the name that comes last in the sort order, the first or the last name. MAX is also available as a numeric function.

MIN(arg list)   *Return the minimum value across the argument list.* For example, MIN(LNAME,FNAME) selects the name that comes first in the sort order, the first or the last name. MIN is also available as a numeric function.

RINDEX(a1,a2,a3)   *Return a number indicating the position of the last occurrence of a2 in a1.* a1 is the string that is searched. a2 is the string variable or string that is used in the search. If a3 is not specified, all of a2 is used. For example, RINDEX(ALPHA8,'**X*') returns 5 for a case with the value $X**X**X*$ for the variable *ALPHA8.* The optional a3 is the number of characters used to divide a2 into separate strings. Each substring is used for searching, and the function returns the last occurrence of any of the substrings. With the same value $X**X**X*$ for *ALPHA8,* RINDEX (ALPHA8, '**X*', 2) returns 7, and RINDEX (ALPHA8, '**X*', 1) returns 8. a3 must be a positive integer and must divide evenly into the length of a2. The target variable must be numeric. If a2 is not found within a1, the value 0 is returned.

Conversion Functions

NUMBER(arg,format)   *Convert the argument into a number using the specified format.* The argument is string, the format is a numeric format, and the result is numeric. The string is essentially reread using the format and returned as a number. For example, NUMBER (XALPHA,F3.1) converts all values for *XALPHA* to numbers using the F3.1 format. The function returns the system-missing value if the conversion is invalid.

STRING(arg,format)   *Converts the argument into a string using the specified format.* The argument is numeric, the format is a numeric format, and the result is a string. The number is converted from internal representation according to the format and then stored as a string. For example, STRING (INCOME, DOLLAR8) converts the numeric values for *INCOME* to the dollar format and returns it as a string value. If the result is shorter than the string variable that receives the values, it is right-justified. If the result is longer, it is right-trimmed.

Missing Values in String Expressions

- If the numeric argument (which can be an expression) for functions LPAD and RPAD is illegal or missing, the result is a null string. If the padding or trimming is the only operation, the string is then padded to its entire length with blanks. If the operation is nested, the null string is passed to the next nested level.

- If a numeric argument to SUBSTR is illegal or missing, the result is a null string. If SUBSTR is the only operation, the string is blank. If the operation is nested, the null string is passed to the next nested level.

- If a numeric argument to INDEX or RINDEX is illegal or missing, the result is system-missing.

Logical Expressions

Logical expressions can appear on the IF, SELECT IF, DO IF, ELSE IF, LOOP IF, and END LOOP IF commands. SPSS evaluates a logical expression as true or false, or as missing if it is indeterminate. A logical expression returns 1 if the expression is true, 0 if it is false, or system-missing if it is missing. Thus, logical expressions can be any expressions that yield this three-value logic.

- The simplest logical expression is a logical variable. A logical variable is any numeric variable that has values 1, 0, or system-missing. Logical variables cannot be strings.
- Logical expressions can be simple logical variables or relations, or they can be complex logical tests involving variables, constants, functions, relational operators, logical operators, and parentheses to control the order of evaluation.
- On an IF command, a logical expression that is true causes the assignment expression to be executed. A logical expression that returns missing has the same effect as one that is false: the assignment expression is not executed and the value of the target variable is not altered.
- On a DO IF command, a logical expression that is true causes SPSS to execute the commands immediately following the DO IF, up to the next ELSE IF, ELSE, or END IF. If it is false, SPSS looks for the next ELSE IF or ELSE command. If the logical expression returns missing for each of these, the entire structure is skipped.
- On a SELECT IF command, a logical expression that is true causes the case to be selected. A logical expression that returns missing has the same effect as one that is false: the case is not selected.
- On a LOOP IF command, a logical expression that is true causes looping to begin (or continue). A logical expression that returns missing has the same effect as one that is false: the structure is skipped.
- On an END LOOP IF command, a logical expression that is false returns control to the LOOP command for that structure and looping continues. If it is true, looping stops and the structure is terminated. A logical expression that returns a missing value has the same effect as one that is true: the structure is terminated.

String Variables in Logical Expressions

String variables, like numeric variables, can be tested in logical expressions.

- String variables must be declared before they can be used in a string expression.
- String variables cannot be compared to numeric variables.
- If strings of different lengths are compared, the shorter string is right-padded with blanks to equal the length of the longer.
- The magnitude of strings can be compared using LT, GT, and so on, but the outcome depends on the sorting sequence of the computer. Use with caution.

Logical Functions

- Each argument to a logical function (expression, variable name, or constant) must be separated by a comma.
- The target variable for a logical function must be numeric.

- The functions RANGE and ANY can be useful shortcuts to more complicated specifications on the IF, DO IF, and other conditional commands. For example, the command

```
SELECT IF ANY(REGION,'NW','NE','SE').
```

is equivalent to

```
SELECT IF (REGION EQ 'NW' OR REGION EQ 'NE' OR REGION EQ
'SE').
```

RANGE(arg,arg list) *Return 1 or true if the value of the first argument is in the inclusive ranges; return 0 or false if not.* The first argument is usually a variable, and the second argument is a list of one or more pairs of values. The variable can be either numeric or string. For example, RANGE (AGE,1,17,62,99) returns 1 for ages 1 through 17 and 62 through 99, inclusive, and 0 for any other ages. RANGE (LNAME,'A','MZZZZZZ') returns 1 for last names that begin with a letter between A and M, inclusive, and 0 for last names beginning with other letters.

ANY(arg,arg list) *Return 1 or true if the value of the first argument matches one of the arguments in the list; return 0 or false if not.* The first argument is usually a variable, either numeric or string. For example, ANY(PROJECT,3,4,7,9) returns 1 if the value for variable *PROJECT* is 3, 4, 7, or 9, and 0 for other values of *PROJECT*. Similarly, ANY (LNAME,'MARTIN','JONES','EVANS') returns 1 for people whose last names are *MARTIN*, *JONES*, or *EVANS*, and 0 for all other last names.

Relational Operators

A relation is a logical expression that compares two values using a *relational operator*. In the command

```
IF (X EQ 0) Y=1
```

the variable *X* and 0 are expressions that yield the values to be compared by the EQ relational operator. Relational operators are

EQ or =   *Equal to.*

NE or ~= ¬ = or <>   *Not equal to.*

LT or <   *Less than.*

LE or <=   *Less than or equal to.*

GT or >   *Greater than.*

GE or >=   *Greater than or equal to.*

- The symbols representing NE (~= or ¬=) are system dependent (see "NOT Logical Operator" below).

- The expressions in a relation can be variables, constants, or more complicated arithmetic expressions.

- Blanks (not commas) must be used to separate the relational operator from the expressions. To make the command more readable, use extra blanks or parentheses.

NOT Logical Operator

The NOT logical operator reverses the true/false outcome of the expression that immediately follows.

- The NOT operator affects only the expression that immediately follows, unless a more complex logical expression is enclosed in parentheses.
- The valid substitute for NOT varies from operating system to operating system. In general, the tilde (~) is valid for ASCII systems, while ¬ (or the symbol over number 6 on the keyboard) is valid for IBM EBCDIC systems. See the *SPSS Base User's Guide* for your version of SPSS.
- NOT can be used to check whether a numeric variable has the value 0, 1, or any other value. For example, all scratch variables are initialized to 0. Therefore, NOT (#ID) returns false or missing when *#ID* has been assigned a value other than 0.

AND and OR Logical Operators

Two or more relations can be logically joined using the logical operators AND and OR. Logical operators combine relations according to the following rules:

- The ampersand (&) symbol is a valid substitute for the logical operator AND. The vertical bar (|) is a valid substitute for the logical operator OR.
- Only one logical operator can be used to combine two relations. However, multiple relations can be combined into a complex logical expression.
- Regardless of the number of relations and logical operators used to build a logical expression, the result is either true, false, or indeterminate because of missing values.
- Operators or expressions cannot be implied. For example, X EQ 1 OR 2 is illegal; you must specify X EQ 1 OR X EQ 2.
- The ANY and RANGE functions can be used to simplify complex expressions.

AND   *Both relations must be true for the complex expression to be true.*

OR   *If either relation is true, the complex expression is true.*

Table 6 lists the outcome for AND and OR combinations.

Table 6   Outcome for AND and OR combinations

Expression	Outcome	Expression	Outcome
true AND true	= true	true OR true	= true
true AND false	= false	true OR false	= true
false AND false	= false	false OR false	= false
true AND missing	= missing	true OR missing	= true[*]
missing AND missing	= missing	missing OR missing	= missing

[*] Expressions where SPSS can evaluate the outcome with incomplete information. See "Missing Values in Logical Expressions" below.

Order of Evaluation

- When arithmetic operators and functions are used in a logical expression, the order of operations is functions and arithmetic operations first, then relational operators, and then logical operators.
- When more than one logical operator is used, NOT is evaluated first, then AND, and then OR.
- To change the order of evaluation, use parentheses.

Missing Values in Logical Expressions

In a simple relation, the logic is indeterminate if the expression on either side of the relational operator is missing. When two or more relations are joined by logical operators AND and OR, SPSS always returns a missing value if all of the relations in the expression are missing. However, if any one of the relations can be determined, SPSS tries to return true or false according to the logical outcomes shown in Table 6.

- When two relations are joined with the AND operator, the logical expression can never be true if one of the relations is indeterminate. The expression can, however, be false.
- When two relations are joined with the OR operator, the logical expression can never be false if one relation returns missing. The expression, however, can be true.

Other Functions

SPSS also includes a lag function and several missing-value functions.

LAG Function

LAG(arg,n)   *The value of the variable* n *cases before.* The first argument is a variable. The second argument, if specified, is a constant and must be a positive integer; the default is 1. For example, PREV4=LAG(GNP,4) returns the value of *GNP* for the fourth case before the current one. The first four cases have system-missing values for *PREV4*.

- The result is of the same type (numeric or string) as the variable specified as the first argument.
- The first *n* cases for string variables are set to blanks. For example, if PREV2=LAG (LNAME,2) is specified, blanks will be assigned to the first two cases for *PREV2*.
- When LAG is used with commands that select cases (for example, SELECT IF and SAMPLE), LAG counts cases *after* case selection, even if specified before these commands (see "Command Order" on p. 16).

Missing-Value Functions

- Each argument to a missing-value function (expression, variable name, or constant) must be separated by a comma.
- Only numeric values can be used as arguments in missing-value functions.
- The keyword TO can be used to refer to a set of variables in the argument list for functions NMISS and NVALID.
- The functions MISSING and SYSMIS are logical functions and can be useful shortcuts to more complicated specifications on the IF, DO IF, and other conditional commands.

VALUE(arg)	*Ignore user-defined missing values.* The value is treated as is. The argument must be a variable name.
MISSING(arg)	*True or 1 if the value is user-missing or system-missing; false or 0 otherwise.*
SYSMIS(arg)	*True or 1 if the value is system-missing; false or 0 otherwise.*
NMISS(arg list)	*Number of system-missing values in the argument list.*
NVALID(arg list)	*Number of valid values in the argument list.*

Treatment of Missing Values in Arguments

If the logic of an expression is indeterminate because of missing values, the expression returns a missing value, and the command is not executed. Table 7 summarizes how missing values are handled in arguments to various functions.

Table 7   Missing values in arguments

Function	Returns system-missing if
MOD (x1,x2)	x1 is missing, or x2 is missing and x1 is not 0
MAX.n (x1,x2,...xk) MEAN.n (x1,x2,...xk) MIN.n (x1,x2,...x1) SUM.n (x1,x2,...xk)	fewer than *n* arguments are valid; the default *n* is 1

Table 7   Missing values in arguments (Continued)

Function	Returns system-missing if
CFVAR.n (x1,x2,...xk) SD.n (x1,x2,...xk) VARIANCE.n (x1,x2,...xk)	fewer than *n* arguments are valid; the default *n* is 2
LPAD(x1,x2,x3) LTRIM(x1,x2) RTRIM(x1,x2) RPAD(x1,x2,x3)	x1 or x2 is illegal or missing
SUBSTR(x1,x2,x3)	x2 or x3 is illegal or missing
NUMBER(x,format) STRING(x,format)	the conversion is invalid
INDEX(x1,x2,x3) RINDEX(x1,x2,x3)	x3 is invalid or missing
LAG (x,n)	x is missing *n* cases previously (and always for the first *n* cases); the default *n* is 1
ANY (x,x1,x2,...xk) RANGE (x,x1,x2,...xk)	x or all of x1, x2, ..., xk are missing
VALUE (x)	x is system-missing
MISSING (x) NMISS (x1,x2,...xk) NVALID (x1,x2,...xk) SYSMIS (x)	never

- Any function that is not listed in Table 7 returns the system-missing value when the argument is missing.
- The system-missing value is a displayed as a period (.) for numeric variables.
- String variables do not have system-missing values. An invalid string expression nested within a complex transformation yields a null string, which is passed to the next level of operation and treated as missing. However, an invalid string expression that is not nested is displayed as a blank string and is *not* treated as missing.

Date and Time

SPSS reads and writes date and time in many different formats but stores them as floating-point numbers. You can perform arithmetic operations on them, use them in statistical procedures, and display or print them in a format of your choice. This section discusses the input and output formats for date and time, arithmetic operations using date and time variables, and date and time functions.

Date and Time Formats

Date and time formats are both input and output formats. They can be used on DATA LIST and other variable definition commands to read in values representing dates or times or date-time combinations. Like numeric formats, each input format generates a default output format, automatically expanded (if necessary) to accommodate display width. In addition, you can assign or modify output formats using FORMATS, WRITE FORMATS, and PRINT FORMATS commands. The output formats are effective only with LIST, REPORT, and TABLES procedures and the PRINT and WRITE transformation commands. Other procedures use the F format and display the values as numbers.

- All date and time formats have a minimum input width, and some have a different minimum output. Wherever the input minimum width is less than the output minimum, SPSS expands the width automatically when displaying or printing values. However, when you specify output formats, you must allow enough space for displaying the date and time in the format you choose.

- Input data shorter than the specified width are correctly evaluated as long as all the necessary elements are present. For example, with the TIME format, 1:2, 01 2, and 01:02 are all correctly evaluated even though the minimum width is 5. However, if only one element (hours or minutes) is present, you must use a time function to aggregate or convert the data (see "Date and Time Functions" on p. 67).

- If a date or time value cannot be completely displayed in the specified width, values are truncated in the output. For example, an input time value of 1:20:59 (1 hour, 20 minutes, 59 seconds) displayed with a width of 5 will generate an output value of 01:20, not 01:21. The truncation of output does not affect the numeric value stored in the working file.

Table 8 shows all available date and time formats, where w indicates the total number of columns and d (if present), the number of decimal places for fractional seconds. The example shows the output format with the minimum width and default decimal positions (if applicable). The format allowed in the input data is much less restrictive (see "Input Data Specification" on p. 62).

Table 8   Date and time formats

Format type	Description	Min w		Max w	Max d	General form	Example
		In	**Out**				
DATEw	International date	8	9	40		dd-mmm-yy	28-OCT-90
		10	11			dd-mmm-yyyy	28-OCT-1990
ADATEw	American date	8	8	40		mm/dd/yy	10/28/90
		10	10			mm/dd/yyyy	10/28/1990
EDATEw	European date	8	8	40		dd.mm.yy	28.10.90
		10	10			dd.mm.yyyy	28.10.1990
JDATEw	Julian date	5	5	40		yyddd	90301
		7	7			yyyyddd	1990301
SDATEw	Sortable date*	8	8	40		yy/mm/dd	90/10/28
		10	10			yyyy/mm/dd	1990/10/28
QYRw	Quarter and year	4	6	40		q Q yy	4 Q 90
		6	8			q Q yyyy	4 Q 1990
MOYRw	Month and year	6	6	40		mmm yy	OCT 90
		8	8			mmm yyyy	OCT 1990
WKYRw	Week and year	6	8	40		ww WK yy	43 WK 90
		8	10			ww WK yyyy	43 WK 1990
WKDAYw	Day of the week	2	2	40		(name of the day)	SU
MONTHw	Month	3	3	40		(name of the month)	JAN
TIMEw	Time	5	5	40		hh:mm	01:02
TIMEw.d		10	10	40	16	hh:mm:ss.s	01:02:34.75
DTIMEw	Days and time	8	8	40		dd hh:mm	20 08:03
DTIMEw.d		13	13	40	16	dd hh:mm:ss.s	20 08:03:00
DATETIMEw	Date and time	17	17	40		dd-mmm-yyyy hh:mm	20-JUN-1990 08:03
DATETIMEw.d		22	22	40	16	dd-mmm-yyyy hh:mm:ss.s	20-JUN-1990 08:03:00

* All date and time formats produce sortable data. SDATE, a date format used in a number of Asian countries, can be sorted in its character form and is used as a sortable format by many programmers.

Input Data Specification

The following general rules apply to date and time input formats:

- Input data must be fixed. Data can appear anywhere within the specified columns. Leading and trailing blanks are allowed. If column-style specifications are used, the width specification can be omitted (see DATA LIST). For example,

```
DATA LIST /BIRTHDAY 1-8 (DATE).
```

is equivalent to

```
DATA LIST /BIRTHDAY (DATE8).
```

- You cannot use date and time formats to read freefield data.

- The century value for two-digit years is defined by the *SET EPOCH* value. By default, the century range begins 69 years prior to the current year and end 30 years after the current year. Whether all four digits or only two digits are displayed in output depends on the width specification on the format.

- Dashes, periods, commas, slashes, or blanks can be used as delimiters in the date-month-year input. For example, with the DATE format, the following input forms are all acceptable:

```
28-10-90      28/10/1990      28.OCT.90      October 28, 1990
```

The displayed values, however, will be the same: *28-OCT-90* or *28-OCT-1990*, depending on whether the specified width allows 11 characters in output.

- The JDATE format does not allow internal delimiters and requires leading zeros for day values less than 100 and two-digit year values less than 10. For example, for January 1, 1990, the following two specifications are acceptable:

```
90001          1990001
```

However, neither of the following is acceptable:

```
90 1           90/1
```

- Months can be represented in digits, Roman numerals, or three-character abbreviations, and they can be fully spelled out. For example, all of the following specifications are acceptable for October:

```
10      X      OCT      October
```

- The quarter in QYR format is expressed as 1, 2, 3, or 4. It must be separated from the year by the letter *Q*. Blanks can be used as additional delimiters. For example, for the fourth quarter of 1990, all of the following specifications are acceptable:

```
4Q90      4Q1990      4 Q 90      4 Q 1990
```

On some operating systems, such as IBM CMS, *Q* must be upper case. The displayed output is *4 Q 90* or *4 Q 1990*, depending on whether the width specified allows all four digits of the year.

- The week in the WKYR format is expressed as a number from 1 to 53. Week 1 begins on January 1, week 2 on January 8, and so on. The value may be different from the number of the calendar week. The week and year must be separated by the string WK. Blanks can be used as additional delimiters. For example, for the 43rd week of 1990, all of the following specifications are acceptable:

```
43WK90      43WK1990      43 WK 90      43 WK 1990
```

On some operating systems, such as IBM CMS, WK must be upper case. The displayed output is *43 WK 90* or *43 WK 1990*, depending on whether the specified width allows enough space for all four digits of the year.

- In time specifications, colons can be used as delimiters between hours, minutes, and seconds. Hours and minutes are required but seconds are optional. A period is required to separate seconds from fractional seconds. Hours can be of unlimited magnitude, but the maximum value for minutes is 59 and for seconds 59.999. . . .

- Data values can contain a sign (+ or −) in TIME and DTIME formats to represent time intervals before or after a point in time.

Example

```
DATA LIST FIXED
 /VAR1 1-17 (DATE) VAR2 21-37 (ADATE) VAR3 41-47 (JDATE).
BEGIN DATA
28-10-90            10/28/90            90301
28.OCT.1990         X 28 1990           1990301
28 October, 2001    Oct. 28, 2001       2001301
END DATA.
LIST.
```

- Internally, all date format variables are stored as the number of seconds from 0 hours, 0 minutes, and 0 seconds of Oct. 14, 1582.

The LIST output from these commands is shown in Figure 15.

Figure 15   Output illustrating DATE, ADATE, and JDATE formats

```
      VAR1            VAR2            VAR3

28-OCT-1990      10/28/1990      1990301
28-OCT-1990      10/28/1990      1990301
28-OCT-2001      10/28/2001      2001301
```

Example

```
DATA LIST FIXED /VAR1 1-10 (QYR) VAR2 12-25 (MOYR) VAR3 28-37 (WKYR).
BEGIN DATA
4Q90        10/90           43WK90
4 Q 90      Oct-1990        43 WK 1990
4 Q 2001    October, 2001   43 WK 2001
END DATA.
LIST.
```

- Internally, the value of a QYR variable is stored as midnight of the first day of the first month of the specified quarter, the value of a MOYR variable is stored as midnight of the first day of the specified month, and the value of a WKYR format variable is stored as midnight of the first day of the specified week. Thus, *4Q90* and *10/90* are both equivalent to October 1, 1990, and *43WK90* is equivalent to October 22, 1990.

The LIST output from these commands is shown in Figure 16.

Figure 16   Output illustrating QYR, MOYR, and WKYR formats

```
      VAR1        VAR2           VAR3

4 Q 1990     OCT 1990      43 WK 1990
4 Q 1990     OCT 1990      43 WK 1990
4 Q 2001     OCT 2001      43 WK 2001
```

Example

```
DATA LIST FIXED
 /VAR1 1-11 (TIME,2) VAR2 13-21 (TIME) VAR3 23-28 (TIME).
BEGIN DATA
1:2:34.75    1:2:34.75 1:2:34
END DATA.
LIST.
```

- TIME reads and writes time of the day or a time interval.
- Internally, the TIME values are stored as the number of seconds from midnight of the day or of the time interval.

The LIST output from these commands is shown in Figure 17.

Figure 17   Output illustrating TIME format

```
        VAR1      VAR2     VAR3

  1:02:34.75   1:02:34   1:02
```

Example

```
DATA LIST FIXED
 /VAR1 1-9 (WKDAY) VAR2 10-18 (WKDAY)
  VAR3 20-29 (MONTH) VAR4 30-32 (MONTH) VAR5 35-37 (MONTH).
BEGIN DATA
Sunday   Sunday    January   1    Jan
Monday   Monday    February  2    Feb
Tues     Tues      March     3    Mar
Wed      Wed       April     4    Apr
Th       Th        Oct       10   Oct
Fr       Fr        Nov       11   Nov
Sa       Sa        Dec       12   Dec
END DATA.
FORMATS VAR2 VAR5 (F2).
LIST.
```

- WKDAY reads and writes the day of the week; MONTH reads and writes the month of the year.
- Values for WKDAY are entered as strings but stored as numbers. They can be used in arithmetic operations but not in string functions.
- Values for MONTH can be entered either as strings or as numbers, but are stored as numbers. They can be used in arithmetic operations but not in string functions.
- To display the values as numbers, assign an F format to the variable, as was done for *VAR2* and *VAR5* in the above example.

The LIST output from these commands is shown in Figure 18.

Figure 18   Output illustrating WKDAY and MONTH formats

```
       VAR1 VAR2          VAR3 VAR4 VAR5

   SUNDAY       1   JANUARY     JAN   1
   MONDAY       2   FEBRUARY    FEB   2
   TUESDAY      3   MARCH       MAR   3
   WEDNESDAY    4   APRIL       APR   4
   THURSDAY     5   OCTOBER     OCT  10
   FRIDAY       6   NOVEMBER    NOV  11
   SATURDAY     7   DECEMBER    DEC  12
```

Example

```
DATA LIST FIXED /VAR1 1-14 (DTIME) VAR2 18-42 (DATETIME).
BEGIN DATA
20 8:3             20-6-90 8:3
20:8:03:46         20/JUN/1990 8:03:46
20 08 03 46.75     20 June, 2001 08 03 46.75
END DATA.
LIST.
```

- DTIME and DATETIME read and write time intervals.

- The decimal point explicitly coded in the input data for fractional seconds.

- The DTIME format allows a − or + sign in the data value to indicate a time interval before or after a point in time.

- Internally, values for a DTIME variable are stored as the number of seconds of the time interval while those for a DATETIME variable are stored as the number of seconds from 0 hours, 0 minutes, and 0 seconds of Oct. 14, 1582.

The LIST output from these commands is shown in Figure 19.

Figure 19   Output illustrating DTIME and DATETIME formats

```
          VAR1                    VAR2

   20 08:03:00      20-JUN-1990 08:03:00
   20 08:03:46      20-JUN-1990 08:03:46
   20 08:03:46      20-JUN-2001 08:03:46
```

Arithmetic Operations with Date and Time Variables

Most date and time variables are stored internally as the number of seconds from a particular date or as a time interval and therefore can be used in arithmetic operations:

- A *date* is a floating-point number representing the number of seconds from midnight, October 14, 1582. Dates, which represent a particular point in time, are stored as the number of seconds to that date. For example, November 8, 1957, is stored as 1.2E+10.

- A date includes the time of day, which is the time interval past midnight. When time of day is not given, it is taken as 00:00 and the date is an even multiple of 86,400 (the number of seconds in a day).

- A *time interval* is a floating-point number representing the number of seconds in a time period, for example, an hour, minute, or day. For example, the value representing 5.5 days is 475,200; the value representing the time interval 14:08:17 is 50,897.

- QYR, MOYR, and WKYR variables are stored as midnight of the first day of the respective quarter, month, and week of the year. Therefore, *1 Q 90*, *1/90*, and *1 WK 90* are all equivalents of January 1, 1990 0:0:00. See "Date and Time Functions" on p. 67 for information on how to determine the quarter, month, or week of a year for a certain date.

- WKDAY variables are stored as 1 to 7, and MONTH variables as 1 to 12. For information on how to determine the day of the week or the month of the year for a certain date, see "Date and Time Functions" on p. 67.

- Both dates and time intervals can be used in arithmetic expressions. The results are stored as the number of seconds or days (see Table 9).

- Do not mix time variables (TIME and DTIME) with date variables (DATE, ADATE, EDATE, and so on) in computations. Since date variables have an implicit time value of 00:00:00, calculations involving time values that are not multiples of a whole day (for example, 24 hours, 0 minutes, 0 seconds) will yield unreliable results.

- Mixing a DATETIME variable with a date variable may yield an unreliable result. Operations involving date variables are accurate only to the days. To avoid possible misinterpretation, use the DTIME format and ignore the hours and minutes portion of the resulting value.

You can perform virtually any arithmetic operation with them. Of course, not all of these operations are particularly useful. You can calculate the number of days between two dates by subtracting one date from the other—but adding two dates does not produce a very meaningful result.

By default, any new numeric variables you compute are displayed in F format. In the case of calculations involving time and date variables, this means that the default output is expressed as a number of seconds or days. Use the FORMATS (or PRINT FORMATS) command to specify an appropriate format for the computed variable. Table 9 shows the recommended output formats for some of the calculations possible with date and time variables.

Table 9   Recommended output formats for date and time calculations

Arithmetic operation	Result	Recommended output format
time ± time[*]	time	TIME, DTIME
date – date [†]	time	DTIME
DATETIME – DATETIME	time	TIME, DTIME
DATETIME ± time	date	DATETIME

[*] Including TIME and DTIME formats.
[†] Including DATE, ADATE, EDATE, JDATE, and SDATE formats.

Example

```
DATA LIST RECORDS=2
 /TIME 1-8 (TIME) DTIME 10-19 (DTIME) DATE 21-29 (DATE)
  ADATE 31-38 (ADATE)
 /DATTIME1 1-18 (DATETIME) DATTIME2 20-37 (DATETIME).
BEGIN DATA
1:10:15   1 0:25:10    13-8-90   10/21/90
28-OCT-90 9:15:17   29/OCT/90 10:30:22
END DATA.
COMPUTE ADDTIME=TIME+DTIME.
COMPUTE DATEDIF1=ADATE-DATE.
COMPUTE DATEDIF2=DATTIME2-DATTIME1.
COMPUTE DATETIME=DATTIME2+DTIME.
LIST VARIABLES=ADDTIME DATEDIF1 DATEDIF2 DATETIME.
FORMATS ADDTIME DATEDIF2 (TIME15) DATEDIF1 (DTIME15)
 DATETIME (DATETIME25).
LIST VARIABLES=ADDTIME DATEDIF1 DATEDIF2 DATETIME.
```

The results of these commands are shown in Figure 20.

Figure 20   Results of arithmetic operations with date and time variables

ADDTIME	DATEDIF1	DATEDIF2	DATETIME
25:35:25	69 00:00:00	25:15:05	30-OCT-1990 10:55:32

Date and Time Functions

Date and time functions provide aggregation, conversion, and extraction routines for dates and time intervals. Each function transforms an expression consisting of one or more arguments. Arguments can be complex expressions, variable names, or constants. Date and time expressions and variables are legitimate arguments.

All date functions that accept the argument of day—for example, DATE.DMY(d,m,y), DATE.MDY(m,d,y), and DATE.YRDAY(y,d)—check the validity of the argument. The value for day must be an integer between 1 and 31. If an invalid value is encountered, a warning is displayed and the value is set to system-missing. However, if the day value is invalid for a particular month—for example, 31 in September, April, June, and November or 29 through 31 for February in non-leap years—the resulting date is placed in the next month (for example, if you enter 2 for *MONTH*, 31 for *DAY*, and 91 for *YEAR*, the result becomes 03/02/91).

Aggregation Functions

Aggregation functions generate dates and time intervals from values that were not read by date and time input formats.

- All aggregation functions begin with DATE or TIME, depending on whether a date or a time interval is requested. This is followed by a subfunction that corresponds to the type of values found in the data.
- The subfunctions are separated from the function by a period (.) and are followed by an argument list specified in parentheses.
- The arguments to the DATE and TIME functions must be separated by commas and must contain integer values.

DATE.DMY(d,m,y)   *Combine day, month, and year.* The value of the argument for day must be expressed as an integer between 1 and 31. The value of the argument for month must be expressed as an integer between 1 and 13 (13 returns January of the following year). Years should be expressed in four digits. For example, the command

```
COMPUTE BIRTHDAY=DATE.DMY(DAY,MONTH,YEAR).
```

stores the value of approximately *1.184E+10* in *BIRTHDAY* when *DAY* is 8, *MONTH* is 11, and *YEAR* is 57. This value can be displayed with a DATE9 format as *08-NOV-57*.

DATE.MDY(m,d,y)   *Combine month, day, and year.* This function follows the same rules as DATE.DMY, except for the order of the arguments. For example, the command

```
COMPUTE BIRTHDAY=DATE.MDY(MONTH,DAY,YEAR).
```

stores the same value as the previous example in *BIRTHDAY* for the same values of *MONTH*, *DAY*, and *YEAR*. The value can be displayed as *11/08/57* with an ADATE8 format.

DATE.YRDAY(y,d)   *Combine year and day of the year.* The year can be expressed as either two or four digits. Years should be expressed in four digits. The day can be expressed as any integer between and including 1 and 366. For example, the command

```
COMPUTE BIRTHDAY=DATE.YRDAY(1688,301).
```

when combined with a DATE11 print format produces the date *27-OCT-1688* for *BIRTHDAY*.

DATE.QYR(q,y)   *Combine quarter and year.* The quarter must be expressed as a single digit between and including 1 and 4. The year can contain two or four digits. Years should be expressed in four digits. For example, the command

```
COMPUTE QUART=DATE.QYR(QTR,YEAR).
```

with a QDATE6 print format produces a value of *4 Q 57* for *QUART* when *QTR* is 4 and *YEAR* is 57. Since each quarter is assumed to begin on the first day of the first month of the quarter, a DATE9 print format for the same value is displayed as *01-OCT-57*.

DATE.MOYR(m,y) *Combine month and year.* The value of the month must be expressed as an integer between and including 1 and 12. The year can be expressed as two or four digits. For example, the command

```
COMPUTE START=DATE.MOYR(MONTH,YEAR).
```

displays *NOV 57* for *START* when *MONTH* is 11 and *YEAR* is 57 and the print format is MOYR.

DATE.WKYR(w,y) *Combine week and year.* The week must be an integer between and including 1 and 53. The year can be represented by two or four digits. For example, the command

```
COMPUTE WEEK=DATE.WKYR(WK,YEAR).
```

displays *26-NOV-57* for *WEEK* when *WK* is 48 and *YEAR* is 57 and the print format is DATE9. The number of the week in the WKYR format is calculated beginning with the first day of the year. It may be different from the number of the calendar week.

TIME.HMS(h,m,s) *Combine hour, minute, and second into a time interval.* For example, the command

```
COMPUTE PERIOD1= TIME.HMS (HR,MIN,SEC).
```

produces an interval of 45,030 seconds for *PERIOD1* when *HR* equals 12, *MIN* equals 30, and *SEC* equals 30. The value can be displayed as *12:30:30* with a TIME8 print format.

You can supply one, two, or three arguments. Trailing arguments can be omitted and default to 0. The value of the first nonzero argument can spill over into the next higher argument. For example, the command

```
COMPUTE PERIOD2=TIME.HMS(HR,MIN).
```

produces an interval of 5400 seconds for *PERIOD2* when *HR* is 0 and *MIN* is 90. The value can be displayed as 01:30 with a TIME5 print format.

You can have a non-integer value for the last argument. For example, the command

```
COMPUTE PERIOD3=TIME.HMS(HR).
```

produces an interval of 5400 seconds for *PERIOD3* when *HR* equals 1.5 and is displayed as *01:30* with a TIME5 format. When you supply a nonzero argument to a function, each of the lower-level units must be within the range of −60 to +60.

TIME.DAYS(d) *Aggregate days into a time interval.* The argument can be expressed as any numeric value. For example, the command

```
COMPUTE NDAYS=TIME.DAYS(SPELL).
```

with a value of 2.5 for *SPELL* generates a value for *NDAYS* that is displayed as *2 12:00* with a DTIME7 format.

Conversion Functions

The conversion functions convert time intervals from one unit of time to another. Time intervals are stored as the number of seconds in the interval; the conversion functions provide a means for calculating more appropriate units, for example, converting seconds to days.

Each conversion function consists of the CTIME function followed by a period (.), the target time unit, and an argument. The argument can consist of expressions, variable names, or constants. The argument must already be a time interval (see "Aggregation Functions" on p. 68). Time conversions produce non-integer results with a default format of F8.2.

Since time and dates are stored internally as seconds, a function that converts to seconds is not necessary.

CTIME.DAYS(arg)   *Convert a time interval to the number of days.* For example, the command

COMPUTE NDAYS=CTIME.DAYS(TIME.HMS(HR,MIN,SEC)).

with 12 for *HR*, 30 for *MIN*, and 30 for *SEC* yields a value of 0.52 for *NDAYS*. CTIME.DAYS(45030) yields the same result.

CTIME.HOURS(arg)   *Convert a time interval to the number of hours.* For example, the command

COMPUTE NHOURS=CTIME.HOURS(TIME.HMS(HR,MIN,SEC)).

using the same values as the previous example produces a value of 12.51 for *NHOURS*.

CTIME.MINUTES(arg)   *Convert a time interval to the number of minutes.* Using the same values as the previous example for *HR*, *MIN*, and, *SEC*, the command

COMPUTE NMINS=CTIME.MINUTES(TIME.HMS(HR,MIN,SEC)).

converts the interval to minutes and produces a value of 750.50 for *NMINS*.

YRMODA Function

YRMODA(arg list)   *Convert year, month, and day to a day number.* The number returned is the number of days since October 14, 1582 (day 0 of the Gregorian calendar).

- Arguments for YRMODA can be variables, constants, or any other type of numeric expression but must yield integers.
- Year, month, and day must be specified in that order.
- The first argument can be any year between 0 and 99, or between 1582 to 47516.
- If the first argument yields a number between 00 and 99, 1900 through 1999 is assumed.
- The month can range from 1 through 13. Month 13 with day 0 yields the last day of the year. For example, YRMODA(1990,13,0) produces the day number for December 31, 1990. Month 13 with any other day yields the day of the first month of the coming year, for example, YRMODA(1990,13,1) produces the day number for January 1, 1991.

- The day can range from 0 through 31. Day 0 is the last day of the previous month regardless of whether it is 28, 29, 30, or 31. For example, YRMODA(1990,3,0) yields 148791.00, the day number for February 28, 1990.
- The function returns the system-missing value if any of the three arguments is missing or if the arguments do not form a valid date *after* October 14, 1582.
- Since YRMODA yields the number of days instead of seconds, you can not display it in date format unless you convert it to the number of seconds.

Extraction Functions

The extraction functions extract subfields from dates or time intervals, targeting the day or a time from a date value. This permits you to classify events by day of the week, season, shift, and so forth.

- Each extraction function begins with XDATE, followed by a period, the subfunction name (what you want to extract), and an argument.
- The argument can be an expression, a variable name, or a constant, provided the argument is already in date form.
- In the following examples, the value for the variable *BIRTHDAY* is *05-DEC-1954 5:30:15*, read with a DATE20 input format.

XDATE.MDAY(arg)   *Return day number in a month from a date.* The result is an integer between 1 and 31. The date must have occurred after October 14, 1582. For example, you can extract the day number from *BIRTHDAY*, as in

```
COMPUTE DAYNUM=XDATE.MDAY(BIRTHDAY).
```

When the value for *BIRTHDAY* is *05-DEC-1954 5:30:15*, *DAYNUM* is 5.

XDATE.MONTH(arg)   *Return month number from a date.* The result is an integer between 1 and 12. The date must have occurred after October 14, 1582. For example, you can extract the month number from *BIRTHDAY*, as in

```
COMPUTE MONTHNUM=XDATE.MONTH(BIRTHDAY).
```

When the value for *BIRTHDAY* is *05-DEC-1954 5:30:15*, this command yields 12 for *MONTHNUM*. If you provide a print format of MONTH12, as in

```
PRINT FORMAT MONTHNUM(MONTH12).
```

the value would be displayed as *DECEMBER*.

XDATE.YEAR(arg)   *Return a four-digit year from a date.* The date must have occurred after October 14, 1582. For example, you can extract the year from *BIRTHDAY*, as in

```
COMPUTE YEAR=XDATE.YEAR(BIRTHDAY).
```

When the value for *BIRTHDAY* is *05-DEC-1954 5:30:15*, this command returns 1954 for *YEAR*.

XDATE.HOUR(arg) *Return the hour from a date or time of day.* The result is an integer between 0 and 23. For example, you can extract the hour from *BIRTHDAY*, as in

```
COMPUTE HOUR=XDATE.HOUR(BIRTHDAY).
```

When the value for *BIRTHDAY* is *05-DEC-1954 5:30:15*, this command returns 5 for *HOUR*.

XDATE.MINUTE(arg) *Return the minute of the hour from a date or time of day.* The result is an integer from 0 through 59. For example, you can extract the minute of the hour from *BIRTHDAY*, as in

```
COMPUTE MIN=XDATE.MINUTE(BIRTHDAY).
```

When the value for *BIRTHDAY* is *05-DEC-1954 5:30:15*, this command returns 30 for *MIN*.

XDATE.SECOND(arg) *Return the second of the minute from a date or time of day.* The result is an integer or, if there are fractional seconds, a value with decimals. For example, you can extract the second of the minute from *BIRTHDAY*, as in

```
COMPUTE SEC=XDATE.SECOND(BIRTHDAY).
```

When the value for *BIRTHDAY* is *05-DEC-1954 5:30:15*, this command returns a value of 15.00 for *SEC*.

XDATE.WKDAY(arg) *Return the day within a week from a date.* The result is an integer between and including 1 and 7, with Sunday being 1 and Saturday being 7. The date must have occurred after October 14, 1582. For example, you can extract the day of the week from *BIRTHDAY*, as in

```
COMPUTE DAYNAME=XDATE.WKDAY(BIRTHDAY).
```

When the value for *BIRTHDAY* is *05-DEC-1954 5:30:15*, this command returns the value 1 for *DAYNAME*. If you provide an output format of WKDAY, as in

```
PRINT FORMAT DAYNAME (WKDAY9).
```

the value for *DAYNAME* would display as *SUNDAY*.

XDATE.JDAY(arg) *Return the day of the year from the date.* The result is an integer between 1 and 366 inclusive. The date must have occurred after October 14, 1582. For example, you can extract the day of the year from *BIRTHDAY*, as in

```
COMPUTE DAYNUM=XDATE.JDAY(BIRTHDAY).
```

When the value for *BIRTHDAY* is *05-DEC-1954 5:30:15*, this command returns the value 339 for *DAYNUM*.

XDATE.QUARTER(arg) *Return quarter number within a year for a date.* The result is 1, 2, 3, or 4. The date must have occurred after October 14, 1582. To extract the quarter in which *BIRTHDAY* occurred, use the command

```
COMPUTE Q=XDATE.QUARTER(BIRTHDAY).
```

When *BIRTHDAY* equals *5-DEC-1954 05:30:15*, the value of *Q* is 4.

XDATE.WEEK(arg)   *Return the week number of a date.* The result is an integer between 1 and 53. The date must have occurred after October 14, 1582. For example, you can extract the week number from *BIRTHDAY*, as in

```
COMPUTE WEEKNUM=XDATE.WEEK(BIRTHDAY).
```

When the value for *BIRTHDAY* is *5-DEC-1954 05:30:15*, this command returns the value 49 for *WEEKNUM*.

XDATE.TDAY(arg)   *Return number of days in a time interval or from October 14, 1582.* The value returned is an integer (the fractional portion of a day is ignored). For example, the command

```
COMPUTE NDAYS=XDATE.TDAY(BIRTHDAY).
```

returns the value 135922 when the value for *BIRTHDAY* is *05-DEC-1954 5:30:15*, indicating the number of days between October 14, 1582 and December 5, 1954. The hours, minutes, and seconds are ignored.

XDATE.TIME(arg)   *Return time of day from a date.* The result is expressed as the number of elapsed seconds since midnight of that date. For example, when the value for *BIRTHDAY* is *05-DEC-1954 5:30:15*, the command

```
COMPUTE ELSEC=XDATE.TIME(BIRTHDAY).
```

returns the value 19815 for *ELSEC*. If you provide a TIME print format, as in

```
PRINT FORMAT ELSEC(TIME8).
```

the value is displayed as *5:30:15*.

XDATE.DATE(arg)   *Return the date portion of a date.* The result is the integral date portion of a date, which is the number of elapsed seconds between midnight October 14, 1582 and midnight of the date in question. The date must have occurred after October 14, 1582. To extract the date from variable *BIRTHDAY*, use

```
COMPUTE BRTHDATE=XDATE.DATE(BIRTHDAY).
```

The value for *BIRTHDATE* can then be displayed as *12/05/54* using ADATE8 format.

Precautions with Date and Time Variables

Dates and times are represented internally as seconds. The numbers for dates are very large, and arithmetic overflows can result. For example, dates in the 20th century are on the order of 10 to the 10th power (11 digits). For that reason, a few precautions are in order:

- Some machine environments cannot accommodate the computation of higher powers of date and time variables. For example, computations higher than the sixth power may cause overflows on some machines.
- The magnitude of the values may cause inaccuracies in some statistical procedures. It is advisable to subtract a fixed date if you want to keep seconds as the unit, or to convert

days using the XDATE.TDAYS function. REGRESSION, CORRELATIONS, ANOVA, and ONEWAY use an adaptive centering method, so their accuracy will not be affected.

- LIST, REPORT, and TABLES are the only procedures that display values in date and time formats. The PRINT and WRITE transformation commands can also display and write date and time formats. However, some summary variables in REPORT and calculated variables in TABLES display in F format, regardless of the print formats of variables used as arguments.

- All other procedures use F format in all cases. The default width and number of decimal places is taken from the print format, but the format type is ignored. For example, in a frequency table, the date 1/09/57 with a print format of DATE9 will be displayed as *11830147200*, not *01-SEP-57*.

- Changing the print format in no way alters the values that are stored. For example, if you assign a print format of DATE9 for a variable read with DATETIME format, the time of day will not display but continues to be part of the value. This means that seemingly identical values can be displayed as separate entries within procedures.

Commands

ACF

```
ACF [VARIABLES=] series names

 [/DIFF={1}]
       {n}

 [/SDIFF={1}]
        {n}

 [/PERIOD=n]

 [/{NOLOG**}]
   {LN     }

 [/SEASONAL]

 [/MXAUTO={16**}]
          {n   }

 [/SERROR={IND**}]
          {MA   }

 [/PACF]

 [/APPLY [='model name']]
```

**Default if the subcommand is omitted and there is no corresponding specification on the TSET command.

Example
```
ACF TICKETS
  /LN
  /DIFF=1
  /SDIFF=1
  /PER=12
  /MXAUTO=50.
```

Overview

ACF displays and plots the sample autocorrelation function of one or more time series. You can also display and plot the autocorrelations of transformed series by requesting natural log and differencing transformations within the procedure.

Options

Modifying the Series. You can request a natural log transformation of the series using the LN subcommand and seasonal and nonseasonal differencing to any degree using the

SDIFF and DIFF subcommands. With seasonal differencing, you can specify the periodicity on the PERIOD subcommand.

Statistical Output. With the MXAUTO subcommand, you can specify the number of lags for which you want autocorrelations displayed and plotted, overriding the maximum specified on TSET. You can also display and plot values only at periodic lags using the SEASONAL subcommand. In addition to autocorrelations, you can display and plot partial autocorrelations using the PACF subcommand.

Method of Calculating Standard Errors. You can specify one of two methods of calculating the standard errors for the autocorrelations on the SERROR subcommand.

Basic Specification

The basic specification is one or more series names.

- For each series specified, ACF automatically displays the autocorrelation value, standard error, Box-Ljung statistic, and probability for each lag.
- ACF plots the autocorrelations and marks the bounds of two standard errors on the plot. By default, ACF displays and plots autocorrelations for up to 16 lags or the number of lags specified on TSET.
- If a method has not been specified on TSET, the default method of calculating the standard error (IND) assumes the process is white noise.

Subcommand Order

- Subcommands can be specified in any order.

Syntax Rules

- VARIABLES can be specified only once.
- Other subcommands can be specified more than once, but only the last specification of each one is executed.

Operations

- Subcommand specifications apply to all series named on the ACF command.
- If the LN subcommand is specified, any differencing requested on that ACF command is done on the log-transformed series.
- Confidence limits are displayed in the plot, marking the bounds of two standard errors at each lag.

Limitations

- Maximum 1 VARIABLES subcommand. There is no limit on the number of series named on the list.

Example

```
ACF TICKETS
  /LN
  /DIFF=1
  /SDIFF=1
  /PER=12
  /MXAUTO=50.
```

- This example produces a plot of the autocorrelation function for the series *TICKETS* after a natural log transformation, differencing, and seasonal differencing have been applied. Along with the plot, the autocorrelation value, standard error, Box-Ljung statistic, and probability are displayed for each lag.
- LN transforms the data using the natural logarithm (base *e*) of the series.
- DIFF differences the series once.
- SDIFF and PERIOD apply one degree of seasonal differencing with a period of 12.
- MXAUTO specifies that the maximum number of lags for which output is to be produced is 50.

VARIABLES Subcommand

VARIABLES specifies the series names and is the only required subcommand. The actual keyword VARIABLES can be omitted.

DIFF Subcommand

DIFF specifies the degree of differencing used to convert a nonstationary series to a stationary one with a constant mean and variance before the autocorrelations are computed.

- You can specify any positive integer on DIFF.
- If DIFF is specified without a value, the default is 1.
- The number of values used in the calculations decreases by 1 for each degree-1 of differencing.

Example

```
ACF SALES
  /DIFF=1.
```

- In this example, the series *SALES* will be differenced once before the autocorrelations are computed and plotted.

SDIFF Subcommand

If the series exhibits a seasonal or periodic pattern, you can use the SDIFF subcommand to seasonally difference the series before obtaining autocorrelations.

- The specification on SDIFF indicates the degree of seasonal differencing and can be any positive integer.
- If SDIFF is specified without a value, the degree of seasonal differencing defaults to 1.
- The number of seasons used in the calculations decreases by 1 for each degree of seasonal differencing.
- The length of the period used by SDIFF is specified on the PERIOD subcommand. If the PERIOD subcommand is not specified, the periodicity established on the TSET or DATE command is used (see the PERIOD subcommand below).

PERIOD Subcommand

PERIOD indicates the length of the period to be used by the SDIFF or SEASONAL subcommands.

- The specification on PERIOD indicates how many observations are in one period or season and can be any positive integer.
- The PERIOD subcommand is ignored if it is used without the SDIFF or SEASONAL subcommands.
- If PERIOD is not specified, the periodicity established on TSET PERIOD is in effect. If TSET PERIOD is not specified, the periodicity established on the DATE command is used. If periodicity was not established anywhere, the SDIFF and SEASONAL subcommands will not be executed.

Example

```
ACF SALES
  /SDIFF=1M
  /PERIOD=12.
```

- This command applies one degree of seasonal differencing with a periodicity (season) of 12 to the series *SALES* before autocorrelations are computed.

LN and NOLOG Subcommands

LN transforms the data using the natural logarithm (base *e*) of the series and is used to remove varying amplitude over time. NOLOG indicates that the data should not be log transformed. NOLOG is the default.

- If you specify LN on an ACF command, any differencing requested on that command will be done on the log-transformed series.
- There are no additional specifications on LN or NOLOG.
- Only the last LN or NOLOG subcommand on an ACF command is executed.

- If a natural log transformation is requested when there are values in the series that are less than or equal to zero, the ACF will not be produced for that series because nonpositive values cannot be log transformed.
- NOLOG is generally used with an APPLY subcommand to turn off a previous LN specification.

Example

```
ACF SALES
  /LN.
```

- This command transforms the series *SALES* using the natural log transformation and then computes and plots autocorrelations.

SEASONAL Subcommand

Use the SEASONAL subcommand to focus attention on the seasonal component by displaying and plotting autocorrelations only at periodic lags.

- There are no additional specifications on SEASONAL.
- If SEASONAL is specified, values are displayed and plotted at the periodic lags indicated on the PERIOD subcommand. If PERIOD is not specified, the periodicity established on the TSET or DATE command is used (see the PERIOD subcommand on p. 78).
- If SEASONAL is not specified, autocorrelations for all lags up to the maximum are displayed and plotted.

Example

```
ACF SALES
  /SEASONAL
  /PERIOD=12.
```

- In this example, autocorrelations are displayed only at every 12th lag.

MXAUTO Subcommand

MXAUTO specifies the maximum number of lags for a series.

- The specification on MXAUTO must be a positive integer.
- If MXAUTO is not specified, the default number of lags is the value set on TSET MXAUTO. If TSET MXAUTO is not specified, the default is 16.
- The value on MXAUTO overrides the value set on TSET MXAUTO.

Example

```
ACF SALES
  /MXAUTO=14.
```

- This command sets the maximum number of autocorrelations to be displayed for series *SALES* to 14.

SERROR Subcommand

SERROR specifies the method of calculating the standard errors for the autocorrelations.

- You must specify either keyword IND or MA on SERROR.
- The method on SERROR overrides the method specified on the TSET ACFSE command.
- If SERROR is not specified, the method indicated on TSET ACFSE is used. If TSET ACFSE is not specified, the default is IND.

IND   *Independence model.* The method of calculating the standard errors assumes the underlying process is white noise.

MA   *MA model.* The method of calculating the standard errors is based on Bartlett's approximation. With this method, appropriate where the true MA order of the process is $k-1$, standard errors grow at increased lags (Pankratz, 1983).

Example

```
ACF SALES
  /SERROR=MA.
```

- In this example, the standard errors of the autocorrelations are computed using the MA method.

PACF Subcommand

Use the PACF subcommand to display and plot sample partial autocorrelations as well as autocorrelations for each series named on the ACF command.

- There are no additional specifications on PACF.
- PACF also displays the standard errors of the partial autocorrelations and indicates the bounds of two standard errors on the plot.
- With the exception of SERROR, all other subcommands specified on that ACF command apply to both the partial autocorrelations and the autocorrelations.

Example

```
ACF SALES
  /DIFFERENCE=1
  /PACF.
```

- This command requests both autocorrelations and partial autocorrelations for the series *SALES* after it has been differenced once.

APPLY Subcommand

APPLY allows you to use a previously defined ACF model without having to repeat the specifications.

- The only specification on APPLY is the name of a previous model in quotes. If a model name is not specified, the model specified on the previous ACF command is used.

- To change one or more model specifications, specify the subcommands of only those portions you want to change after the APPLY subcommand.
- If no series are specified on the ACF command, the series that were originally specified with the model being reapplied are used.
- To change the series used with the model, enter new series names before or after the APPLY subcommand.

Example

```
ACF TICKETS
  /LN
  /DIFF=1
  /SDIFF=1
  /PERIOD=12
  /MXAUTO=50.
ACF ROUNDTRP
  /APPLY.
ACF APPLY
  /NOLOG.
ACF APPLY 'MOD_2'
  /PERIOD=6.
```

- The first command requests a maximum of 50 autocorrelations for the series *TICKETS* after it has been natural log transformed, differenced once, and had one degree of seasonal differencing with a periodicity of 12 applied to it. This model is assigned the default name *MOD_1*.
- The second command displays and plots the autocorrelation function for the series *ROUNDTRP* using the same model that was used for the series *TICKETS*. This model is assigned the name *MOD_2*.
- The third command requests another autocorrelation function of the series *ROUNDTRP* using the same model but without the natural log transformation. Note that when APPLY is the first specification after the ACF command, the slash (/) before it is not necessary. This model is assigned the name *MOD_3*.
- The fourth command reapplies *MOD_2*, autocorrelations for the series *ROUNDTRP* with the natural log and differencing specifications, but this time with a periodicity of 6. This model is assigned the name *MOD_4*. It differs from *MOD_2* only in the periodicity.

References

Box, G. E. P., and G. M. Jenkins. 1976. *Time series analysis: Forecasting and control.* San Francisco: Holden-Day.

Pankratz, A. 1983. *Forecasting with univariate Box-Jenkins models: Concepts and cases.* New York: John Wiley and Sons.

ADD FILES

```
ADD FILES FILE={file}
              {*    }

 [/RENAME=(old varnames=new varnames)...]

 [/IN=varname]

 /FILE=... [/RENAME=...] [/IN=...]

 [/BY varlist]

 [/MAP]

 [/KEEP={ALL**  }] [/DROP=varlist]
        {varlist}

 [/FIRST=varname]  [/LAST=varname]
```

**Default if the subcommand is omitted.

Example

```
ADD FILES FILE=SCHOOL1 /FILE=SCHOOL2.
```

Overview

ADD FILES combines cases from 2 up to 50 SPSS-format data files by concatenating or interleaving cases. When cases are **concatenated,** all cases from one file are added to the end of all cases from another file. When cases are **interleaved,** cases in the resulting file are ordered according to the values of one or more key variables.

The files specified on ADD FILES can be SPSS-format data files created by the SAVE or XSAVE commands or the working data file. The combined file becomes the new working file. Statistical procedures following ADD FILES use this combined file unless you replace it by building another working file. You must use the SAVE or XSAVE commands if you want to save the combined file as an SPSS-format data file.

In general, ADD FILES is used to combine files containing the same variables but different cases. To combine files containing the same cases but different variables, use MATCH FILES. To update existing SPSS-format data files, use UPDATE. ADD FILES cannot concatenate raw data files. To concatenate raw data files, use DATA LIST within an INPUT PROGRAM structure (see p. 251 for an example). Alternatively, convert the raw data files to SPSS-format data files with the SAVE or XSAVE commands and then use ADD FILES to combine them.

Options

Variable Selection. You can specify which variables from each input file are included in the new working file using the DROP and KEEP subcommands.

Variable Names. You can rename variables in each input file before combining the files using the RENAME subcommand. This permits you to combine variables that are the same but whose names differ in different input files, or to separate variables that are different but have the same name.

Variable Flag. You can create a variable that indicates whether a case came from a particular input file using IN. When interleaving cases, you can use the FIRST or LAST subcommands to create a variable that flags the first or last case of a group of cases with the same value for the key variable.

Variable Map. You can request a map showing all variables in the new working file, their order, and the input files from which they came using the MAP subcommand.

Basic Specification

- The basic specification is two or more FILE subcommands, each of which specifies a file to be combined. If cases are to be interleaved, the BY subcommand specifying the key variables is also required.
- All variables from all input files are included in the new working file unless DROP or KEEP is specified.

Subcommand Order

- RENAME and IN must immediately follow the FILE subcommand to which they apply.
- BY, FIRST, and LAST must follow all FILE subcommands and their associated RENAME and IN subcommands.

Syntax Rules

- RENAME can be repeated after each FILE subcommand. RENAME applies only to variables in the file named on the FILE subcommand immediately preceding it.
- BY can be specified only once. However, multiple key variables can be specified on BY. When BY is used, all files must be sorted in ascending order by the key variables (see SORT CASES).
- FIRST and LAST can be used only when files are interleaved (when BY is used).
- MAP can be repeated as often as desired.

Operations

- ADD FILES reads all input files named on FILE and builds a new working data file that replaces any working file created earlier in the session. ADD FILES is executed when the data are read by one of the procedure commands or the EXECUTE, SAVE, or SORT CASES commands.

- The resulting file contains complete dictionary information from the input files, including variable names, labels, print and write formats, and missing-value indicators. It also contains the documents from each input file. See DROP DOCUMENTS for information on deleting documents.

- Variables are copied in order from the first file specified, then from the second file specified, and so on. Variables that are not contained in all files receive the system-missing value for cases that do not have values for those variables.

- If the same variable name exists in more than one file but the format type (numeric or string) does not match, the command is not executed.

- If a numeric variable has the same name but different formats (for example, F8.0 and F8.2) in different input files, the format of the variable in the first-named file is used.

- If a string variable has the same name but different formats (for example, A24 and A16) in different input files, the command is not executed.

- If the working file is named as an input file, any N and SAMPLE commands that have been specified are applied to the working file before files are combined.

- If only one of the files is weighted, the program turns weighting off when combining cases from the two files. To weight the cases, use the WEIGHT command again.

Limitations

- Maximum 50 files can be combined on one ADD FILES command.
- The TEMPORARY command cannot be in effect if the working data file is used as an input file.

Examples

```
ADD FILES FILE=SCHOOL1 /FILE=SCHOOL2.
```

- ADD FILES concatenates cases from the SPSS-format data files *SCHOOL*1 and SCHOOL2. All cases from *SCHOOL1* precede all cases from *SCHOOL2* in the resulting file.

```
SORT CASES BY LOCATN DEPT.
ADD FILES  FILE=SOURCE /FILE=* /BY LOCATN DEPT
 /KEEP AVGHOUR AVGRAISE LOCATN DEPT SEX HOURLY RAISE /MAP.
SAVE OUTFILE=PRSNNL.
```

- SORT CASES sorts cases in the working file in ascending order of their values for *LOCATN* and *DEPT*.

- ADD FILES combines two files: the SPSS-format data file *SOURCE* and the sorted working file. The file *SOURCE* must also be sorted by *LOCATN* and *DEPT*.

- BY indicates that the keys for interleaving cases are *LOCATN* and *DEPT*, the same variables used on SORT CASES.

- KEEP specifies the variables to be retained in the resulting file.

- MAP produces a list of variables in the resulting file and the two input files.

- SAVE saves the resulting file as a new SPSS-format data file named *PRSNNL*.

FILE Subcommand

FILE identifies the files to be combined. A separate FILE subcommand must be used for each input file.

- An asterisk may be specified on FILE to indicate the working data file.
- The order in which files are named determines the order of cases in the resulting file.

Raw Data Files

To add cases from a raw data file, you must first define the file as the working data file using the DATA LIST command. ADD FILES can then combine the working file with an SPSS-format data file.

Example

```
DATA LIST FILE=GASDATA/1 OZONE 10-12 CO 20-22 SULFUR 30-32.
ADD FILES   FILE=PARTICLE /FILE=*.
SAVE   OUTFILE=POLLUTE.
```

- The *GASDATA* file is a raw data file and is defined on the DATA LIST command.
- The *PARTICLE* file is a previously saved SPSS-format data file.
- FILE=* on ADD FILES specifies the working data file, which contains the gas data. FILE=PARTICLE specifies the SPSS-format data file *PARTICLE*.
- SAVE saves the resulting file as an SPSS-format data file with the filename *POLLUTE*. Cases from the *GASDATA* file follow cases from the *PARTICLE* file.

RENAME Subcommand

RENAME renames variables in input files *before* they are processed by ADD FILES. RENAME follows the FILE subcommand that specifies the file containing the variables to be renamed.

- RENAME applies only to the FILE subcommand immediately preceding it. To rename variables from more than one input file, enter a RENAME subcommand after each FILE subcommand that specifies a file with variables to be renamed.
- Specifications for RENAME consist of a left parenthesis, a list of old variable names, an equals sign, a list of new variable names, and a right parenthesis. The two variable lists must name or imply the same number of variables. If only one variable is renamed, the parentheses are optional.
- More than one such specification can be entered on a single RENAME subcommand, each enclosed in parentheses.
- The TO keyword can be used to refer to consecutive variables in the file and to generate new variable names (see "Keyword TO" on p. 29).
- RENAME takes effect immediately. KEEP and DROP subcommands entered prior to RENAME must use the old names, while those entered after RENAME must use the new names.
- All specifications within a single set of parentheses take effect simultaneously. For example, the specification RENAME (A,B = B,A) swaps the names of the two variables.
- Variables cannot be renamed to scratch variables.

- Input data files are not changed on disk; only the copy of the file being combined is affected.

Example

```
ADD FILES FILE=CLIENTS /RENAME=(TEL_NO, ID_NO = PHONE, ID)
 /FILE=MASTER /BY ID.
```

- ADD FILES adds new client cases from the file *CLIENTS* to existing client cases in the file *MASTER*.
- Two variables on *CLIENTS* are renamed prior to the match. *TEL_NO* is renamed *PHONE* to match the name used for phone numbers in the master file. *ID_NO* is renamed *ID* so that it will have the same name as the identification variable in the master file and can be used on the BY subcommand.
- The BY subcommand orders the resulting file according to client ID number.

BY Subcommand

BY specifies one or more key variables that determine the order of cases in the resulting file. When BY is specified, cases from the input files are interleaved according to their values for the key variables.

- BY must follow the FILE subcommands and any associated RENAME and IN subcommands.
- The key variables specified on BY must be present and have the same names in all input files.
- Key variables can be long or short string variables or numerics.
- All input files must be sorted in ascending order of the key variables. If necessary, use SORT CASES before ADD FILES.
- Cases in the resulting file are ordered by the values of the key variables. All cases from the first file with the first value for the key variable are first, followed by all cases from the second file with the same value, followed by all cases from the third file with the same value, and so forth. These cases are followed by all cases from the first file with the next value for the key variable, and so on.
- Cases with system-missing values are first in the resulting file. User-missing values are interleaved with other values.

DROP and KEEP Subcommands

DROP and KEEP are used to include only a subset of variables in the resulting file. DROP specifies a set of variables to exclude and KEEP specifies a set of variables to retain.

- DROP and KEEP do not affect the input files on disk.
- DROP and KEEP must follow all FILE and RENAME subcommands.
- DROP and KEEP must specify one or more variables. If RENAME is used to rename variables, specify the new names on DROP and KEEP.
- DROP and KEEP take effect immediately. If a variable specified on DROP or KEEP does not exist in the input files, was dropped by a previous DROP subcommand, or was not retained by a previous KEEP subcommand, the program displays an error message and does not execute the ADD FILES command.

- DROP cannot be used with variables created by the IN, FIRST, or LAST subcommands.
- KEEP can be used to change the order of variables in the resulting file. With KEEP, variables are kept in the order they are listed on the subcommand. If a variable is named more than once on KEEP, only the first mention of the variable is in effect; all subsequent references to that variable name are ignored.
- The keyword ALL can be specified on KEEP. ALL must be the last specification on KEEP, and it refers to all variables not previously named on that subcommand. It is useful when you want to arrange the first few variables in a specific order.

Example

```
ADD FILES FILE=PARTICLE /RENAME=(PARTIC=POLLUTE1)
/FILE=GAS /RENAME=(OZONE TO SULFUR=POLLUTE2 TO POLLUTE4)
/KEEP=POLLUTE1 POLLUTE2 POLLUTE3 POLLUTE4.
```

- The renamed variables are retained in the resulting file. KEEP is specified after all the FILE and RENAME subcommands, and it refers to the variables by their new names.

IN Subcommand

IN creates a new variable in the resulting file that indicates whether a case came from the input file named on the preceding FILE subcommand. IN applies only to the file specified on the immediately preceding FILE subcommand.

- IN has only one specification, the name of the flag variable.
- The variable created by IN has value 1 for every case that came from the associated input file and value 0 for every case that came from a different input file.
- Variables created by IN are automatically attached to the end of the resulting file and cannot be dropped. If FIRST or LAST are used, the variable created by IN precedes the variables created by FIRST or LAST.

Example

```
ADD FILES  FILE=WEEK10 /FILE=WEEK11 /IN=INWEEK11 /BY=EMPID.
```

- IN creates the variable *INWEEK11*, which has value 1 for all cases in the resulting file that came from the input file *WEEK11* and value 0 for those cases that were not in the file *WEEK11*.

Example

```
ADD FILES  FILE=WEEK10 /FILE=WEEK11 /IN=INWEEK11 /BY=EMPID.
IF  (NOT INWEEK11) SALARY1=0.
```

- The variable created by IN is used to screen partially missing cases for subsequent analyses.
- Since IN variables have either value 1 or 0, they can be used as logical expressions, where 1=true and 0=false. The IF command sets variable *SALARY1* equal to 0 for all cases that came from the file *INWEEK11*.

FIRST and LAST Subcommands

FIRST and LAST create logical variables that flag the first or last case of a group of cases with the same value on the BY variables. FIRST and LAST must follow all FILE subcommands and their associated RENAME and IN subcommands.

- FIRST and LAST have only one specification, the name of the flag variable.
- FIRST creates a variable with value 1 for the first case of each group and value 0 for all other cases.
- LAST creates a variable with value 1 for the last case of each group and value 0 for all other cases.
- Variables created by FIRST and LAST are automatically attached to the end of the resulting file and cannot be dropped.

Example

```
ADD FILES  FILE=SCHOOL1 /FILE=SCHOOL2
 /BY=GRADE /FIRST=HISCORE.
```

- The variable *HISCORE* contains value 1 for the first case in each grade in the resulting file and value 0 for all other cases.

MAP Subcommand

MAP produces a list of the variables included in the new working file and the file or files from which they came. Variables are listed in the order in which they exist in the resulting file. MAP has no specifications and must follow after all FILE and RENAME subcommands.

- Multiple MAP subcommands can be used. Each MAP subcommand shows the current status of the working file and reflects only the subcommands that precede the MAP subcommand.
- To obtain a map of the working data file in its final state, specify MAP last.
- If a variable is renamed, its original and new names are listed. Variables created by IN, FIRST, and LAST are not included in the map, since they are automatically attached to the end of the file and cannot be dropped.

ADD VALUE LABELS

```
ADD VALUE LABELS varlist value 'label' value 'label'...[/varlist...]
```

Example

```
ADD VALUE LABELS JOBGRADE 'P' 'Parttime Employee'
                          'C' 'Customer Support'.
```

Overview

ADD VALUE LABELS adds or alters value labels without affecting other value labels already defined for that variable. In contrast, VALUE LABELS adds or alters value labels but deletes all existing value labels for that variable when it does so.

Basic Specification

The basic specification is a variable name and individual values with associated labels.

Syntax Rules

- Labels can be assigned to values of any previously defined variable. It is not necessary to enter value labels for all of a variable's values.
- Each value label must be enclosed in apostrophes or quotation marks.
- When an apostrophe occurs as part of a label, enclose the label in quotation marks or enter the internal apostrophe twice with no intervening space.
- Value labels can contain any characters, including blanks.
- The same labels can be assigned to the same values of different variables by specifying a list of variable names. For string variables, the variables on the list must have the same defined width (for example, A8).
- Multiple sets of variable names and value labels can be specified on one ADD VALUE LABELS command as long as each set is separated from the previous one by a slash.
- To continue a label from one command line to the next, specify a plus sign (+) before the continuation of the label and enclose each segment of the label, including the blank between them, in apostrophes or quotes.

Operations

- Unlike most transformations, ADD VALUE LABELS takes effect as soon as it is encountered in the command sequence. Thus, special attention should be paid to its position among commands. See "Command Order" on p. 16 for more information.

- The added value labels are stored in the working file dictionary.
- ADD VALUE LABELS can be used for variables that have no previously assigned value labels.
- Adding labels to some values does not affect labels previously assigned to other values.

Limitations

- Value labels cannot exceed 60 characters. Most procedures display only 20 characters.
- Value labels cannot be assigned to long string variables.

Example

```
ADD VALUE LABELS V1 TO V3 1 'Officials & Managers'
                          6 'Service Workers'
                /V4 'N' 'New Employee'.
```

- Labels are assigned to the values 1 and 6 of the variables between and including *V1* and *V3* in the working data file.
- Following the required slash, a label for value N for variable *V4* is specified. N is a string value and must be enclosed in apostrophes or quotation marks.
- If labels already exist for these values, they are changed in the dictionary. If labels do not exist for these values, new labels are added to the dictionary.
- Existing labels for other values for these variables are not affected.

Example

```
ADD VALUE LABELS OFFICE88 1 "EMPLOYEE'S OFFICE ASSIGNMENT PRIOR"
  + " TO 1988".
```

- The label for value 1 for *OFFICE88* is specified on two command lines. The plus sign concatenates the two string segments and a blank is included at the beginning of the second string in order to maintain correct spacing in the label.

Value Labels for String Variables

- For short string variables, the values and the labels must be enclosed in apostrophes or quotation marks.
- If a specified value is longer than the defined width of the variable, the program displays a warning and truncates the value. The added label will be associated with the truncated value.
- If a specified value is shorter than the defined width of the variable, the program adds blanks to right-pad the value without warning. The added label will be associated with the padded value.
- If a single set of labels is to be assigned to a list of string variables, the variables must have the same defined width (for example, A8).

Example

```
ADD VALUE LABELS  STATE 'TEX' 'TEXAS' 'TEN' 'TENNESSEE'
                        'MIN' 'MINNESOTA'.
```

- ADD VALUE LABELS assigns labels to three values of the variable *STATE*. Each value and each label is specified in apostrophes.
- Assuming that the variable *STATE* is defined as three characters wide, the labels *TEXAS*, *TENNESSEE*, and *MINNESOTA* will be appropriately associated with values TEX, TEN, and MIN. However, if *STATE* were defined as two characters wide, the program would truncate the specified values to two characters and would not be able to associate the labels correctly. Both TEX and TEN would be truncated to TE and would first be assigned the label *TEXAS*, which would then be changed to *TENNESSEE* by the second specification.

Example

```
ADD VALUE LABELS=STATE REGION "U" "UNKNOWN".
```

- The label *UNKNOWN* is assigned to value U for both *STATE* and *REGION*.
- *STATE* and *REGION* must have the same defined width. If they do not, a separate specification must be made for each, as in the following:

```
ADD VALUE LABELS STATE "U" "UNKNOWN" / REGION "U" "UNKNOWN".
```

AGGREGATE

```
AGGREGATE OUTFILE={file} [/MISSING=COLUMNWISE] [/DOCUMENT]
                 {*    }

[/PRESORTED] /BREAK=varlist[({A})][varlist...]
                           {D}

/aggvar['label']aggvar['label']...=function(arguments)

[/aggvar ...]
```

Available functions:

SUM	Sum	MEAN	Mean
SD	Standard deviation	MAX	Maximum
MIN	Minimum	PGT	% of cases greater than value
PLT	% of cases less than value	PIN	% of cases between values
POUT	% of cases not in range	FGT	Fraction greater than value
FLT	Fraction less than value	FIN	Fraction between values
FOUT	Fraction not in range	N	Weighted number of cases
NU	Unweighted number of cases	NMISS	Weighted number of missing cases
NUMISS	Unweighted number of missing cases	FIRST	First nonmissing value
LAST	Last nonmissing value		

Example

```
AGGREGATE OUTFILE=AGGEMP /BREAK=LOCATN DEPT /COUNT=N
  /AVGSAL AVGRAISE = MEAN(SALARY RAISE)
  /SUMSAL SUMRAISE = SUM(SALARY RAISE)
  /BLACKPCT 'Percentage Black' = PIN(RACE,1,1)
  /WHITEPCT 'Percentage White' = PIN(RACE,5,5).
```

Overview

AGGREGATE aggregates groups of cases in the working data file into single cases and creates a new, aggregated file. The values of one or more variables in the working file define the case groups. These variables are called **break variables.** A set of cases with identical values for each break variable is called a **break group.** A series of aggregate functions are applied to **source variables** in the working file to create new, aggregated variables that have one value for each break group.

AGGREGATE is often used with MATCH FILES to add variables with summary measures (sum, mean, etc.) to a file. Transformations performed on the combined file can create composite summary measures. With the REPORT procedure, the composite variables can be used to write reports with nested composite information.

Options

Aggregated File. You can produce either an SPSS-format data file or a new working file.

Documentary Text. You can copy documentary text from the original file into the aggregated file using the DOCUMENT subcommand. By default, documentary text is dropped.

Sorting. By default, cases in the aggregated file are sorted in ascending order of the values of each break variable. Alternatively, you can specify descending order. If the working file is already sorted by the break variables, you can skip this final sorting pass through the file using the PRESORTED subcommand.

Aggregated Variables. You can create aggregated variables using any of 19 aggregate functions. The functions SUM, MEAN, and SD can aggregate only numeric variables. All other functions can use both numeric and string variables.

Labels and Formats. You can specify variable labels for the aggregated variables. Variables created with the functions MAX, MIN, FIRST, and LAST assume the formats and value labels of their source variables. All other variables assume the default formats described under "Aggregate Functions" on p. 96.

Basic Specification

The basic specification is OUTFILE, BREAK, and at least one aggregate function and source variable. OUTFILE specifies a name for the aggregated file. BREAK names the case grouping (break) variables. The aggregate function creates a new aggregated variable.

Subcommand Order

- OUTFILE must be specified first.
- If specified, DOCUMENT and PRESORTED must precede BREAK. No other subcommand can be specified between these two subcommands.
- MISSING, if specified, must immediately follow OUTFILE.
- The aggregate functions must be specified last.

Operations

- When AGGREGATE produces an SPSS-format data file, the working file remains unchanged and is still available for analysis. When AGGREGATE creates a new working file, it replaces the old working file. Only the new working file is available for analysis.
- The aggregated file contains the break variables plus the variables created by the aggregate functions.
- AGGREGATE excludes cases with missing values from all aggregate calculations except those involving functions N, NU, NMISS, and NUMISS.
- Unless otherwise specified, AGGREGATE sorts cases in the aggregated file in ascending order of the values of the grouping variables.

- If PRESORTED is specified, a new aggregate case is created each time a different value or combination of values is encountered on variables named on the BREAK subcommand.
- AGGREGATE ignores split-file processing. To achieve the same effect, name the variable or variables used to split the file as break variables before any other break variables. AGGREGATE produces one file, but the aggregated cases are in the same order as the split files.

Example

```
AGGREGATE OUTFILE=AGGEMP /BREAK=LOCATN DEPT
 /COUNT=N
 /AVGSAL AVGRAISE = MEAN(SALARY RAISE)
 /SUMSAL SUMRAISE = SUM(SALARY RAISE)
 /BLACKPCT 'Percentage Black' = PIN(RACE,1,1)
 /WHITEPCT 'Percentage White' = PIN(RACE,5,5).
```

- AGGREGATE creates a new SPSS-format data file *AGGEMP*. *AGGEMP* contains two break variables (*LOCATN* and *DEPT*) and all the new aggregate variables (*COUNT, AVGSAL, AVGRAISE, SUMSAL, SUMRAISE, BLACKPCT,* and *WHITEPCT*).
- BREAK specifies *LOCATN* and *DEPT* as the break variables. In the aggregated file, cases are sorted in ascending order of *LOCATN* and in ascending order of *DEPT* within *LOCATN*. The working data file remains unsorted.
- Variable *COUNT* is created as the weighted number of cases in each break group. *AVGSAL* is the mean of *SALARY* and *AVGRAISE* is the mean of *RAISE*. *SUMSAL* is the sum of *SALARY* and *SUMRAISE* is the sum of *RAISE*. *BLACKPCT* is the percentage of cases with value 1 for *RACE*. *WHITEPCT* is the percentage of cases with value 5 for *RACE*.

Example

```
GET FILE=HUBEMPL /KEEP=LOCATN DEPT HOURLY RAISE SEX.
AGGREGATE OUTFILE=AGGFILE /BREAK=LOCATN DEPT
 /AVGHOUR AVGRAISE=MEAN(HOURLY RAISE).
SORT CASES BY LOCATN DEPT.
MATCH FILES  TABLE=AGGFILE /FILE=* /BY LOCATN DEPT
 /KEEP AVGHOUR AVGRAISE LOCATN DEPT SEX HOURLY RAISE /MAP.

COMPUTE HOURDIF=HOURLY/AVGHOUR.
COMPUTE RAISEDIF=RAISE/AVGRAISE.
LIST.
```

- GET reads the SPSS-format data file *HUBEMPL* and keeps a subset of variables.
- AGGREGATE creates a file aggregated by *LOCATN* and *DEPT* with the two new variables *AVGHOUR* and *AVGRAISE*, containing the means by location and department for *HOURLY* and *RAISE*. The aggregated file is saved as an SPSS-format data file named *AGGFILE*. Only the aggregated data file *AGGFILE* is sorted by *LOCATN* and *DEPT*; the working data file remains unchanged.
- SORT CASES sorts the working data file in ascending order of *LOCATN* and *DEPT*, the same variables used as AGGREGATE break variables.

- MATCH FILES specifies a table lookup match with *AGGFILE* as the table file and the sorted working data file as the case file.
- BY indicates that the keys for the match are *LOCATN* and *DEPT.*
- KEEP specifies the subset and order of variables to be retained in the resulting file.
- MAP provides a listing of the variables in the resulting file and the two input files.
- The COMPUTE commands calculate the ratios of each employee's hourly wage and raise to the department averages for wage and raise. The results are stored in the variables *HOURDIF* and *RAISEDIF.*
- LIST displays the resulting file.

OUTFILE Subcommand

OUTFILE specifies a name for the file created by AGGREGATE. If an asterisk is specified on OUTFILE, the aggregated file replaces the working file. OUTFILE must be the first subcommand specified on AGGREGATE.

- If the aggregated file replaces the working file, the file is not automatically saved on disk. To save the file, use the SAVE command.

Example

```
AGGREGATE OUTFILE=AGGEMP
 /BREAK=LOCATN
 /AVGSAL = MEAN(SALARY).
```

- OUTFILE creates an SPSS-format data file named *AGGEMP.* The working file remains unchanged and is available for further analysis.
- The file *AGGEMP* contains two variables, *LOCATN* and *AVGSAL.*

BREAK Subcommand

BREAK lists the grouping variables, also called break variables. Each unique combination of values of the break variables defines one break group.

- The variables named on BREAK can be any combination of variables in the working data file.
- Unless PRESORTED is specified, AGGREGATE sorts cases after aggregating. By default, cases are sorted in ascending order of the values of the break variables. AGGREGATE sorts first on the first break variable, then on the second break variable within the groups created by the first, and so on.
- Sort order can be controlled by specifying an A (for ascending) or D (for descending) in parentheses after any break variables.
- The designations A and D apply to all preceding undesignated variables.
- The subcommand PRESORTED overrides all sorting specifications.

Example

```
AGGREGATE OUTFILE=AGGEMP
 /BREAK=LOCATN DEPT (A) TENURE (D)
 /AVGSAL = MEAN(SALARY).
```

- BREAK names the variables *LOCATN*, *DEPT*, and *TENURE* as the break variables.
- Cases in the aggregated file are sorted in ascending order of *LOCATN*, in ascending order of *DEPT* within *LOCATN*, and in descending order of *TENURE* within *LOCATN* and *DEPT*. For each group defined by these variables, *AVGSAL* is computed as the mean of salary.

DOCUMENT Subcommand

DOCUMENT copies documentation from the original file into the aggregated file. By default, documents are dropped from the aggregated file, whether the file is the working file or an SPSS-format data file. DOCUMENT must appear after OUTFILE but before BREAK.

PRESORTED Subcommand

PRESORTED indicates that cases in the working data file are sorted according to the values of the break variables. This prevents AGGREGATE from sorting cases that have already been sorted and can save a considerable amount of processing time.

- If specified, PRESORTED must precede BREAK. The only specification is the keyword PRESORTED. PRESORTED has no additional specifications.
- When PRESORTED is specified, the program forms an aggregate case out of each group of *adjacent* cases with the same values for the break variables.
- If the working file is not sorted by the break variables in ascending order and PRESORTED is specified, a warning message is generated but the procedure is executed. Each group of adjacent cases with the same values for break variables forms a case in the aggregated file, which may produce multiple cases with the same values for the break variables.

Example

```
AGGREGATE OUTFILE=AGGEMP
 /PRESORTED
 /BREAK=LOCATN DEPT
 /AVGSAL = MEAN(SALARY).
```

- PRESORTED indicates that cases are already sorted by the variables *LOCATN* and *DEPT*.
- AGGREGATE does not make an extra data pass to sort the cases.

Aggregate Functions

An aggregated variable is created by applying an aggregate function to a variable in the working file. The variable in the working file is called the **source** variable, and the new aggregated variable is the **target** variable.

- The aggregate functions must be specified last on AGGREGATE.

- The simplest specification is a target variable list, followed by an equals sign, a function name, and a list of source variables.

- The number of target variables named must match the number of source variables.

- When several aggregate variables are defined at once, the first-named target variable is based on the first-named source variable, the second-named target is based on the second-named source, and so on.

- Only the functions MAX, MIN, FIRST, and LAST copy complete dictionary information from the source variable. For all other functions, new variables do not have labels and are assigned default dictionary print and write formats. The default format for a variable depends on the function used to create it (see the list of available functions below).

- You can provide a variable label for a new variable by specifying the label in apostrophes immediately following the new variable name. Value labels cannot be assigned in AGGREGATE.

- To change formats or add value labels to a working data file created by AGGREGATE, use the PRINT FORMATS, WRITE FORMATS, FORMATS, or VALUE LABELS commands. If the aggregate file is written to disk, first retrieve the file using GET, specify the new labels and formats, and resave the file.

The following is a list of available functions:

SUM(varlist)
Sum across cases. Default formats are F8.2.

MEAN(varlist)
Mean across cases. Default formats are F8.2.

SD(varlist)
Standard deviation across cases. Default formats are F8.2.

MAX(varlist)
Maximum value across cases. Complete dictionary information is copied from the source variables to the target variables.

MIN(varlist)
Minimum value across cases. Complete dictionary information is copied from the source variables to the target variables.

PGT(varlist,value)
Percentage of cases greater than the specified value. Default formats are F5.1.

PLT(varlist,value)
Percentage of cases less than the specified value. Default formats are F5.1.

PIN(varlist,value1,value2)
Percentage of cases between value1 and value2, inclusive. Default formats are F5.1.

POUT(varlist,value1,value2)
Percentage of cases not between value1 and value2. Cases where the source variable equals value1 or value2 are not counted. Default formats are F5.1.

FGT(varlist,value)
Fraction of cases greater than the specified value. Default formats are F5.3.

FLT(varlist,value)
Fraction of cases less than the specified value. Default formats are F5.3.

FIN(varlist,value1,value2)	*Fraction of cases between value1 and value2, inclusive.* Default formats are F5.3.
FOUT(varlist,value1,value2)	*Fraction of cases not between value1 and value2.* Cases where the source variable equals value1 or value2 are not counted. Default formats are F5.3.
N(varlist)	*Weighted number of cases in break group.* Default formats are F7.0 for unweighted files and F8.2 for weighted files.
NU(varlist)	*Unweighted number of cases in break group.* Default formats are F7.0.
NMISS(varlist)	*Weighted number of missing cases.* Default formats are F7.0 for unweighted files and F8.2 for weighted files.
NUMISS(varlist)	*Unweighted number of missing cases.* Default formats are F7.0.
FIRST(varlist)	*First nonmissing observed value in break group.* Complete dictionary information is copied from the source variables to the target variables.
LAST(varlist)	*Last nonmissing observed value in break group.* Complete dictionary information is copied from the source variables to the target variables.

- The functions SUM, MEAN, and SD can be applied only to numeric source variables. All other functions can use short and long string variables as well as numeric ones.

- The N and NU functions do not require arguments. Without arguments, they return the number of weighted and unweighted valid cases in a break group. If you supply a variable list, they return the number of weighted and unweighted valid cases for the variables specified.

- For several functions, the argument includes values as well as a source variable designation. Either blanks or commas can be used to separate the components of an argument list.

- For PIN, POUT, FIN, and FOUT, the first value should be less than or equal to the second. If the first is greater, AGGREGATE automatically reverses them and prints a warning message. If the two values are equal, PIN and FIN calculate the percentages and fractions of values equal to the argument. POUT and FOUT calculate the percentages and fractions of values not equal to the argument.

- String values specified in an argument should be enclosed in apostrophes. They are evaluated in alphabetical order.

Example

```
AGGREGATE OUTFILE=AGGEMP /BREAK=LOCATN
 /AVGSAL 'Average Salary' AVGRAISE = MEAN(SALARY RAISE).
```

- AGGREGATE defines two aggregate variables, *AVGSAL* and *AVGRAISE*.

- *AVGSAL* is the mean of *SALARY* for each break group, and *AVGRAISE* is the mean of *RAISE*.

- The label *Average Salary* is assigned to *AVGSAL*.

Example

```
AGGREGATE OUTFILE=* /BREAK=DEPT
 /LOWVAC,LOWSICK = PLT (VACDAY SICKDAY,10).
```

- AGGREGATE creates two aggregated variables: *LOWVAC* and *LOWSICK. LOWVAC* is the percentage of cases with values less than 10 for *VACDAY* and *LOWSICK* is the percentage of cases with values less than 10 for *SICKDAY*.

Example

```
AGGREGATE OUTFILE=GROUPS /BREAK=OCCGROUP
 /COLLEGE = FIN(EDUC,13,16).
```

- AGGREGATE creates the variable *COLLEGE*, which is the fraction of cases with 13 to 16 years of education (variable *EDUC*).

Example

```
AGGREGATE OUTFILE=* /BREAK=CLASS
 /LOCAL = PIN(STATE,'IL','IO').
```

- AGGREGATE creates the variable *LOCAL*, which is the percentage of cases in each break group whose two-letter state code represents Illinois, Indiana, or Iowa. (The abbreviation for Indiana, IN, is between IL and IO in an alphabetical sort sequence.)

MISSING Subcommand

By default, AGGREGATE uses all nonmissing values of the source variable to calculate aggregated variables. An aggregated variable will have a missing value only if the source variable is missing for every case in the break group. You can alter the default missing-value treatment by using the MISSING subcommand. You can also specify the inclusion of user-missing values on any function.

- MISSING must immediately follow OUTFILE.
- COLUMNWISE is the only specification available for MISSING.
- If COLUMNWISE is specified, the value of an aggregated variable is missing for a break group if the source variable is missing for any case in the group.
- COLUMNWISE does not affect the calculation of the N, NU, NMISS, or NUMISS functions.
- COLUMNWISE does not apply to break variables. If a break variable has a missing value, cases in that group are processed and the break variable is saved in the file with the missing value. Use SELECT IF if you want to eliminate cases with missing values for the break variables.

Including Missing Values

You can force a function to include user-missing values in its calculations by specifying a period after the function name.

- AGGREGATE ignores periods used with functions N, NU, NMISS, and NUMISS if these functions have no argument.

- User-missing values are treated as valid when these four functions are followed by a period and have a variable as an argument. NMISS.(AGE) treats user-missing values as valid and thus gives the number of cases for which *AGE* has the system-missing value only.

The effect of specifying a period with N, NU, NMISS, and NUMISS is illustrated by the following:

N = N. = N(AGE) + NMISS(AGE) = N.(AGE) + NMISS.(AGE)

NU = NU. = NU(AGE) + NUMISS(AGE) = NU.(AGE) + NUMISS.(AGE)

- The function N (the same as N. with no argument) yields a value for each break group that equals the number of cases with valid values (N(AGE)) plus the number of cases with user- or system-missing values (NMISS(AGE)).
- This in turn equals the number of cases with either valid or user-missing values (N.(AGE)) plus the number with system-missing values (NMISS.(AGE)).
- The same identities hold for the NU, NMISS, and NUMISS functions.

Example

```
AGGREGATE OUTFILE=AGGEMP /MISSING=COLUMNWISE /BREAK=LOCATN
 /AVGSAL = MEAN(SALARY).
```

- *AVGSAL* is missing for an aggregated case if *SALARY* is missing for any case in the break group.

Example

```
AGGREGATE OUTFILE=* /BREAK=DEPT
 /LOVAC = PLT.(VACDAY,10).
```

- *LOVAC* is the percentage of cases within each break group with values less than 10 for *VACDAY*, even if some of those values are defined as user-missing.

Example

```
AGGREGATE OUTFILE=CLASS /BREAK=GRADE
 /FIRSTAGE = FIRST.(AGE).
```

- The first value of *AGE* in each break group is assigned to the variable *FIRSTAGE*.
- If the first value of *AGE* in a break group is user missing, that value will be assigned to *FIRSTAGE*. However, the value will retain its missing-value status, since variables created with FIRST take dictionary information from their source variables.

Comparing Missing-Value Treatments

Table 1 demonstrates the effects of specifying the MISSING subcommand and a period after the function name. Each entry in the table is the number of cases used to compute the specified function for the variable *EDUC*, which has 10 nonmissing cases, 5 user-missing cases, and 2 system-missing cases for the group. Note that columnwise treatment produces the same results as the default for every function except the MEAN function.

Table 1   Default versus columnwise missing-value treatments

Function	Default	Columnwise
N	17	17
N.	17	17
N(EDUC)	10	10
N.(EDUC)	15	15
MEAN(EDUC)	10	0
MEAN.(EDUC)	15	0
NMISS(EDUC)	7	7
NMISS.(EDUC)	2	2

ALSCAL

```
ALSCAL   VARIABLES=varlist

[/FILE=file]   [CONFIG  [({INITIAL})]]   [ROWCONF [({INITIAL})]]
                        {FIXED  }                 {FIXED  }

              [COLCONF [({INITIAL})]]   [SUBJWGHT[({INITIAL})]]
                       {FIXED  }                 {FIXED  }

              [STIMWGHT[({INITIAL})]]
                       {FIXED  }

[/INPUT=ROWS ({ALL**})]
             { n   }

[/SHAPE={SYMMETRIC**}]
        {ASYMMETRIC }
        {RECTANGULAR}

[/LEVEL={ORDINAL**  [([UNTIE] [SIMILAR])]}]
        {INTERVAL[({1})]                 }
        {        {n}                      }
        {RATIO[({1})]                     }
        {       {n}                       }
        {NOMINAL                          }

[/CONDITION={MATRIX**      }]
            {ROW          }
            {UNCONDITIONAL}

[/{MODEL }={EUCLID**}]
   {METHOD} {INDSCAL }
            {ASCAL   }
            {AINDS   }
            {GEMSCAL }

[/CRITERIA=[NEGATIVE] [CUTOFF({0**})] [CONVERGE({.001})]
                             { n }              { n  }

          [ITER({30})] [STRESSMIN({.005})] [NOULB]
                {n }              { n  }

          [DIMENS({2**       })] [DIRECTIONS(n)]
                  {min[,max]}

          [CONSTRAIN]  [TIESTORE(n)]]

[/PRINT=[DATA] [HEADER]]     [/PLOT=[DEFAULT] [ALL]]

[/OUTFILE=file]

[/MATRIX=IN({file})]
            {*  }
```

**Default if the subcommand or keyword is omitted.

Example

```
ALSCAL VARIABLES=ATLANTA TO TAMPA.
```

ALSCAL was originally designed and programmed by Forrest W. Young, Yoshio Takane, and Rostyslaw J. Lewyckyj of the Psychometric Laboratory, University of North Carolina.

Overview

ALSCAL uses an alternating least-squares algorithm to perform multidimensional scaling (MDS) and multidimensional unfolding (MDU). You can select one of the five models to obtain stimulus coordinates and/or weights in multidimensional space.

Options

Data Input. You can read inline data matrices, including all types of two- or three-way data, such as a single matrix or a matrix for each of several subjects, using the INPUT subcommand. You can read square (symmetrical or asymmetrical) or rectangular matrices of proximities with the SHAPE subcommand and proximity matrices created by PROXIMITIES and CLUSTER with the MATRIX subcommand. You can also read a file of coordinates and/or weights to provide initial or fixed values for the scaling process with the FILE subcommand.

Methodological Assumptions. You can specify data as matrix-conditional, row-conditional, or unconditional on the CONDITION subcommand. You can treat data as nonmetric (nominal or ordinal) or as metric (interval or ratio) using the LEVEL subcommand. You can also use LEVEL to identify ordinal-level proximity data as measures of similarity or dissimilarity and can specify tied observations as untied (continuous) or leave them tied (discrete).

Model Selection. You can specify most commonly used multidimensional scaling models by selecting the correct combination of ALSCAL subcommands, keywords, and criteria. In addition to the default Euclidean distance model, the MODEL subcommand offers the individual differences (weighted) Euclidean distance model (INDSCAL), the asymmetric Euclidean distance model (ASCAL), the asymmetric individual differences Euclidean distance model (AINDS), and the generalized Euclidean metric individual differences model (GEMSCAL).

Output. You can produce output that includes raw and scaled input data, missing-value patterns, normalized data with means, squared data with additive constants, each subject's scalar product and individual weight space, plots of linear or nonlinear fit, and plots of the data transformations using the PRINT and PLOT subcommands.

Basic Specification

The basic specification is VARIABLES followed by a variable list. By default, ALSCAL produces a two-dimensional nonmetric Euclidean multidimensional scaling solution. Input is assumed to be one or more square symmetric matrices with data elements that are dissimilarities at the ordinal level of measurement. Ties are not untied, and conditionality is by subject. Values less than 0 are treated as missing. The default output includes the improvement in Young's S-stress for successive iterations, two measures of fit for each input matrix (Kruskal's stress and the squared correlation, RSQ), and the derived configurations for each of the dimensions.

Subcommand Order

Subcommands can be named in any order.

Operations

- ALSCAL calculates the number of input matrices by dividing the total number of observations in the data set by the number of rows in each matrix. All matrices must contain the same number of rows. This number is determined by the settings on SHAPE and INPUT (if used). For square matrix data, the number of rows in the matrix equals the number of variables. For rectangular matrix data, it equals the number of rows specified or implied. For additional information, see the INPUT and SHAPE subcommands below.

- ALSCAL ignores user-missing specifications in all variables in the configuration/weights file (see the FILE subcommand on p. 107). The system-missing value is converted to 0.

- With split-file data, ALSCAL reads initial or fixed configurations from the configuration/weights file for each split-file group (see the FILE subcommand on p. 107). If there is only one initial configuration in the file, ALSCAL rereads these initial or fixed values for successive split-file groups.

- By default, ALSCAL estimates upper and lower bounds on missing values in the working data file in order to compute the initial configuration. To prevent this, specify CRITERIA=NOULB. Missing values are always ignored during the iterative process.

Limitations

- Maximum 100 variables on the VARIABLES subcommand.
- Maximum six dimensions can be scaled.
- ALSCAL does not recognize data weights created by the WEIGHT command.
- ALSCAL analyses can include no more than 32,767 values in each of the input matrices. Large analyses may require significant computing time.

Example

```
* Air distances among U.S. cities.
* Data are from Johnson and Wichern (1982), page 563.
DATA LIST
 /ATLANTA BOSTON CINCNATI COLUMBUS DALLAS INDNPLIS
   LITTROCK LOSANGEL MEMPHIS STLOUIS SPOKANE TAMPA 1-60.
BEGIN DATA
    0
1068    0
 461   867    0
 549   769   107    0
 805  1819   943  1050    0
 508   941   108   172   882    0
 505  1494   618   725   325   562    0
2197  3052  2186  2245  1403  2080  1701    0
 366  1355   502   586   464   436   137  1831    0
 558  1178   338   409   645   234   353  1848   294    0
2467  2747  2067  2131  1891  1959  1988  1227  2042  1820    0
 467  1379   928   985  1077   975   912  2480   779  1016  2821    0
END DATA.

ALSCAL VARIABLES=ATLANTA TO TAMPA
 /PLOT.
```

- By default, ALSCAL assumes a symmetric matrix of dissimilarities for ordinal-level variables. Only values below the diagonal are used. The upper triangle can be left blank. The 12 cities form the rows and columns of the matrix.
- The result is a classical MDS analysis that reproduces a map of the United States when the output is rotated to a north-south by east-west orientation.

VARIABLES Subcommand

VARIABLES identifies the columns in the proximity matrix or matrices that ALSCAL reads.

- VARIABLES is required and can name only numeric variables.
- Each matrix must have at least four rows and four columns.

INPUT Subcommand

ALSCAL reads data row by row, with each case in the working data file representing a single row in the data matrix. (VARIABLES specifies the columns.) Use INPUT when reading rectangular data matrices to specify how many rows are in each matrix.

- The specification on INPUT is ROWS. If INPUT is not specified or is specified without ROWS, the default is ROWS(ALL). ALSCAL assumes that each case in the working data file represents one row of a single input matrix, and the result is a square matrix.
- You can specify the number of rows (n) in each matrix in parentheses after the keyword ROWS. The number of matrices equals the number of observations divided by the number specified.
- The number specified on ROWS must be at least 4 and must divide evenly into the total number of rows in the data.
- With split-file data, n refers to the number of cases in each split-file group. All split-file groups must have the same number of rows.

Example

```
ALSCAL VARIABLES=V1 to V7 /INPUT=ROWS(8).
```

- INPUT indicates that there are eight rows per matrix, with each case in the working data file representing one row.
- The total number of cases must be divisible by 8.

SHAPE Subcommand

Use SHAPE to specify the structure of the input data matrix or matrices.

- You can specify one of the three keywords listed below.
- Both SYMMETRIC and ASYMMETRIC refer to square matrix data.

SYMMETRIC   *Symmetric data matrix or matrices.* For a symmetric matrix, ALSCAL looks only at the values below the diagonal. Values on and above the diagonal can be omitted. This is the default.

ASYMMETRIC	*Asymmetric data matrix or matrices.* The corresponding values in the upper and lower triangles are not all equal. The diagonal is ignored.
RECTANGULAR	*Rectangular data matrix or matrices.* The rows and columns represent different sets of items.

Example

```
ALSCAL VAR=V1 TO V8 /SHAPE=RECTANGULAR.
```

• ALSCAL performs a classical MDU analysis, treating the rows and columns as separate sets of items.

LEVEL Subcommand

LEVEL identifies the level of measurement for the values in the data matrix or matrices. You can specify one of the keywords defined below.

ORDINAL	*Ordinal-level data.* This specification is the default. It treats the data as ordinal, using Kruskal's (1964) least-squares monotonic transformation. The analysis is nonmetric. By default, the data are treated as discrete dissimilarities. Ties in the data remain tied throughout the analysis. To change the default, specify UNTIE and/or SIMILAR in parentheses. UNTIE treats the data as continuous and resolves ties in an optimal fashion; SIMILAR treats the data as similarities. UNTIE and SIMILAR cannot be used with the other levels of measurement.
INTERVAL(n)	*Interval-level data.* This specification produces a metric analysis of the data using classical regression techniques. You can specify any integer from 1 to 4 in parentheses for the degree of polynomial transformation to be fit to the data. The default is 1.
RATIO(n)	*Ratio-level data.* This specification produces a metric analysis. You can specify an integer from 1 to 4 in parentheses for the degree of polynomial transformation. The default is 1.
NOMINAL	*Nominal-level data.* This specification treats the data as nominal by using a least-squares categorical transformation (Takane et al., 1977). This option produces a nonmetric analysis of nominal data. It is useful when there are few observed categories, when there are many observations in each category, and when the order of the categories is not known.

Example

```
ALSCAL VAR=ATLANTA TO TAMPA /LEVEL=INTERVAL(2).
```

• This example identifies the distances between U.S. cities as interval-level data. The 2 in parentheses indicates a polynomial transformation with linear and quadratic terms.

CONDITION Subcommand

CONDITION specifies which numbers in a data set are comparable.

MATRIX   *Only numbers within each matrix are comparable.* If each matrix represents a different subject, this specification makes comparisons conditional by subject. This is the default.

ROW   *Only numbers within the same row are comparable.* This specification is appropriate only for asymmetric or rectangular data. They cannot be used when ASCAL or AINDS is specified on MODEL.

UNCONDITIONAL   *All numbers are comparable.* Comparisons can be made among any values in the input matrix or matrices.

Example

```
ALSCAL VAR=V1 TO V8 /SHAPE=RECTANGULAR /CONDITION=ROW.
```

- ALSCAL performs a Euclidean MDU analysis conditional on comparisons within rows.

FILE Subcommand

ALSCAL can read proximity data from the working data file or, with the MATRIX subcommand, from a matrix data file created by PROXIMITIES or CLUSTER. The FILE subcommand reads a file containing additional data: an initial or fixed configuration for the coordinates of the stimuli and/or weights for the matrices being scaled. This file can be created with the OUTFILE subcommand on ALSCAL or with an SPSS input program.

- The minimum specification is the file that contains the configurations and/or weights.
- FILE can include additional specifications that define the structure of the configuration/weights file.
- The variables in the configuration/weights file that correspond to successive ALSCAL dimensions must have the names *DIM1*, *DIM2*,...*DIMr*, where *r* is the maximum number of ALSCAL dimensions. The file must also contain the short string variable *TYPE_* to identify the types of values in all rows.
- Values for the variable *TYPE_* can be CONFIG, ROWCONF, COLCONF, SUBJWGHT, and STIMWGHT, in that order. Each value can be truncated to the first three letters. Stimulus coordinate values are specified as CONFIG; row stimulus coordinates as ROWCONF; column stimulus coordinates as COLCONF; and subject and stimulus weights as SUBJWGHT and STIMWGHT, respectively. ALSCAL accepts CONFIG and ROWCONF interchangeably.
- ALSCAL skips unneeded types as long as they appear in the file in their proper order. Generalized weights (GEM) and flattened subject weights (FLA) cannot be initialized or fixed and will always be skipped. (These weights can be generated by ALSCAL but cannot be used as input.)

The following list summarizes the optional specifications that can be used on FILE to define the structure of the configuration/weights file:

- Each specification can be further identified with option INITIAL or FIXED in parentheses.

- INITIAL is the default. INITIAL indicates that the external configuration or weights are to be used as initial coordinates and are to be modified during each iteration.
- FIXED forces ALSCAL to use the externally defined structure without modification to calculate the best values for all unfixed portions of the structure.

CONFIG　　　*Read stimulus configuration.* The configuration/weights file contains initial stimulus coordinates. Input of this type is appropriate when SHAPE=SYMMETRIC or SHAPE=ASYMMETRIC, or when the number of variables in a matrix equals the number of variables on the ALSCAL command. The value of the *TYPE_* variable must be either CON or ROW for all stimulus coordinates for the configuration.

ROWCONF　　*Read row stimulus configuration.* The configuration/weights file contains initial row stimulus coordinates. This specification is appropriate if SHAPE=RECTANGULAR and if the number of ROWCONF rows in the matrix equals the number of rows specified on the INPUT subcommand (or, if INPUT is omitted, the number of cases in the working data file). The value of *TYPE_* must be either ROW or CON for the set of coordinates for each row.

COLCONF　　*Read column stimulus configuration.* The configuration/weights file contains initial column stimulus coordinates. This kind of file can be used only if SHAPE=RECTANGULAR and if the number of COLCONF rows in the matrix equals the number of variables on the ALSCAL command. The value of *TYPE_* must be COL for the set of coordinates for each column.

SUBJWGHT　*Read subject (matrix) weights.* The configuration/weights file contains subject weights. The number of observations in a subject-weights matrix must equal the number of matrices in the proximity file. Subject weights can be used only if the model is INDSCAL, AINDS, or GEMSCAL. The value of *TYPE_* for each set of weights must be SUB.

STIMWGHT　*Read stimulus weights.* The configuration/weights file contains stimulus weights. The number of observations in the configuration/weights file must equal the number of matrices in the proximity file. Stimulus weights can be used only if the model is AINDS or ASCAL. The value of *TYPE_* for each set of weights must be STI.

If the optional specifications for the configuration/weights file are not specified on FILE, ALSCAL sequentially reads the *TYPE_* values appropriate to the model and shape according to the defaults in Table 1.

Example

```
ALSCAL VAR=V1 TO V8 /FILE=ONE CON(FIXED) STI(INITIAL).
```

- ALSCAL reads the configuration/weights file *ONE*.
- The stimulus coordinates are read as fixed values, and the stimulus weights are read as initial values.

Table 1   Default specifications for the FILE subcommand

Shape	Model	Default specifications
SYMMETRIC	EUCLID	CONFIG (or ROWCONF)
	INDSCAL	CONFIG (or ROWCONF) SUBJWGHT
	GEMSCAL	CONFIG (or ROWCONF) SUBJWGHT
ASYMMETRIC	EUCLID	CONFIG (or ROWCONF)
	INDSCAL	CONFIG (or ROWCONF) SUBJWGHT
	GEMSCAL	CONFIG (or ROWCONF) SUBJWGHT
	ASCAL	CONFIG (or ROWCONF) STIMWGHT
	AINDS	CONFIG (or ROWCONF) SUBJWGHT STIMWGHT
RECTANGULAR	EUCLID	ROWCONF (or CONFIG) COLCONF
	INDSCAL	ROWCONF (or CONFIG) COLCONF SUBJWGHT
	GEMSCAL	ROWCONF (or CONFIG) COLCONF SUBJWGHT

MODEL Subcommand

MODEL (alias METHOD) defines the scaling model for the analysis. The only specification is MODEL (or METHOD) and any one of the five scaling and unfolding model types. EUCLID is the default.

EUCLID   *Euclidean distance model.* This model can be used with any type of proximity matrix and is the default.

INDSCAL   *Individual differences (weighted) Euclidean distance model.* ALSCAL scales the data using the weighted individual differences Euclidean distance model proposed by Carroll and Chang (1970). This type of analysis can be specified only if the analysis involves more than one data matrix and more than one dimension is specified on CRITERIA.

ASCAL   *Asymmetric Euclidean distance model.* This model (Young, 1975) can be used only if SHAPE=ASYMMETRIC and more than one dimension is requested on CRITERIA.

AINDS   *Asymmetric individual differences Euclidean distance model.* This option combines Young's (1975) asymmetric Euclidean model with the individual differences model proposed by Carroll and Chang (1970). This model can be used only when SHAPE=ASYMMETRIC, the analysis involves more than one data matrix, and more than one dimension is specified on CRITERIA.

GEMSCAL   *Generalized Euclidean metric individual differences model.* The number of directions for this model is set with the DIRECTIONS option on CRITERIA. The number of directions specified can be equal to but cannot exceed the group space dimensionality. By default, the number of directions equals the number of dimensions in the solution.

Example

```
ALSCAL VARIABLES = V1 TO V6
 /SHAPE = ASYMMETRIC
 /CONDITION = ROW
 /MODEL = GEMSCAL
 /CRITERIA = DIM(4) DIRECTIONS(4).
```

• In this example, the number of directions in the GEMSCAL model is set to 4.

CRITERIA Subcommand

Use CRITERIA to control features of the scaling model and to set convergence criteria for the solution. You can specify one or more of the following:

CONVERGE(n)   *Stop iterations if the change in S-stress is less than* n. S-stress is a goodness-of-fit index. By default, $n=0.001$. To increase the precision of a solution, specify a smaller value, for example, 0.0001. To obtain a less precise solution (perhaps to reduce computing time), specify a larger value, for example, 0.05. Negative values are not allowed. If $n=0$, the algorithm will iterate 30 times unless a value is specified with the ITER option.

ITER(n)   *Set the maximum number of iterations to* n. The default value is 30. A higher value will give a more precise solution but will take longer to compute.

STRESSMIN(n)   *Set the minimum stress value to* n. By default, ALSCAL stops iterating when the value of S-stress is 0.005 or less. STRESSMIN can be assigned any value from 0 to 1.

NEGATIVE   *Allow negative weights in individual differences models.* By default, ALSCAL does not permit the weights to be negative. Weighted models include INDSCAL, ASCAL, AINDS, and GEMSCAL. The NEGATIVE option is ignored if the model is EUCLID.

CUTOFF(n)   *Set the cutoff value for treating distances as missing to* n. By default, ALSCAL treats all negative similarities (or dissimilarities) as missing, and 0 and positive similarities as nonmissing ($n=0$). Changing the CUTOFF value causes ALSCAL to treat similarities greater than or equal to that value as nonmissing. User- and system-missing values are considered missing regardless of the CUTOFF specification.

NOULB	*Do not estimate upper and lower bounds on missing values.* By default, ALSCAL estimates the upper and lower bounds on missing values in order to compute the initial configuration. This specification has no effect during the iterative process, when missing values are ignored.
DIMENS(min[,max])	*Set the minimum and maximum number of dimensions in the scaling solution.* By default, ALSCAL calculates a solution with two dimensions. To obtain solutions for more than two dimensions, specify the minimum and the maximum number of dimensions in parentheses after DIMENS. The minimum and maximum can be integers between 2 and 6. A single value represents both the minimum and the maximum. For example, DIMENS(3) is equivalent to DIMENS(3,3). The minimum number of dimensions can be set to 1 only if MODEL=EUCLID.
DIRECTIONS(n)	*Set the number of principal directions in the generalized Euclidean model to* n. This option has no effect for models other than GEMSCAL. The number of principal directions can be any positive integer between 1 and the number of dimensions specified on the DIMENS option. By default, the number of directions equals the number of dimensions.
TIESTORE(n)	*Set the amount of storage needed for ties to* n. This option estimates the amount of storage needed to deal with ties in ordinal data. By default, the amount of storage is set to 1000 or the number of cells in a matrix, whichever is smaller. Should this be insufficient, ALSCAL terminates and displays a message that more space is needed.
CONSTRAIN	*Constrain multidimensional unfolding solution.* This option can be used to keep the initial constraints throughout the analysis.

PRINT Subcommand

PRINT requests output not available by default. You can specify the following:

DATA	*Display input data.* The display includes both the initial data and the scaled data for each subject according to the structure specified on SHAPE.
HEADER	*Display a header page.* The header includes the model, output, algorithmic, and data options in effect for the analysis.

- Data options listed by PRINT=HEADER include the number of rows and columns, number of matrices, measurement level, shape of the data matrix, type of data (similarity or dissimilarity), whether ties are tied or untied, conditionality, and data cutoff value.

- Model options listed by PRINT=HEADER are the type of model specified (EUCLID, INDSCAL, ASCAL, AINDS, or GEMSCAL), minimum and maximum dimensionality, and whether or not negative weights are permitted.

- Output options listed by PRINT=HEADER indicate whether the output includes the header page and input data, whether ALSCAL plotted configurations and transformations, whether an output data set was created, and whether initial stimulus coordinates, initial column stimulus coordinates, initial subject weights, and initial stimulus weights were computed.

- Algorithmic options listed by PRINT=HEADER include the maximum number of iterations permitted, the convergence criterion, the maximum S-stress value, whether or not missing data are estimated by upper and lower bounds, and the amount of storage allotted for ties in ordinal data.

Example

```
ALSCAL VAR=ATLANTA TO TAMPA /PRINT=DATA.
```

- In addition to scaled data, ALSCAL will display initial data.

PLOT Subcommand

PLOT controls the display of plots. The minimum specification is simply PLOT to produce the defaults.

DEFAULT   *Default plots.* Default plots include plots of stimulus coordinates, matrix weights (if the model is INDSCAL, AINDS, or GEMSCAL), and stimulus weights (if the model is AINDS or ASCAL). The default also includes a scatterplot of the linear fit between the data and the model and, for certain types of data, scatterplots of the nonlinear fit and the data transformation.

ALL   *Transformation plots in addition to the default plots.* SPSS produces a separate plot for each subject if CONDITION=MATRIX and a separate plot for each row if CONDITION=ROW. For interval and ratio data, PLOT=ALL has the same effect as PLOT=DEFAULT. This option can generate voluminous output, particularly when CONDITION=ROW.

Example

```
ALSCAL VAR=V1 TO V8 /INPUT=ROWS(8) /PLOT=ALL.
```

- This command produces all the default plots. It also produces a separate plot for each subject's data transformation and a plot of *V1* through *V8* in a two-dimensional space for each subject.

OUTFILE Subcommand

OUTFILE saves coordinate and weight matrices to an SPSS data file. The only specification is a name for the output file.

- The output data file has an alphanumeric (short string) variable named *TYPE_* that identifies the kind of values in each row, a numeric variable *DIMENS* that specifies the number of dimensions, a numeric variable *MATNUM* that indicates the subject (matrix) to which each set of coordinates corresponds, and variables *DIM1, DIM2,...DIMn* that correspond to the *n* dimensions in the model.
- The values of any split-file variables are also included in the output file.
- The file created by OUTFILE can be used by subsequent ALSCAL commands as initial data.

The following are the types of configurations and weights that can be included in the output file:

CONFIG   *Stimulus configuration coordinates.*

ROWCONF   *Row stimulus configuration coordinates.*

COLCONF   *Column stimulus configuration coordinates.*

SUBJWGHT   *Subject (matrix) weights.*

FLATWGHT   *Flattened subject (matrix) weights.*

GEMWGHT   *Generalized weights.*

STIMWGHT   *Stimulus weights.*

Only the first three characters of each identifier are written to variable *TYPE_* in the file. For example, CONFIG becomes CON. The structure of the file is determined by the SHAPE and MODEL subcommands, as shown in Table 2.

Table 2   Types of configurations and/or weights in output files

Shape	Model	TYPE_
SYMMETRIC	EUCLID	CON
	INDSCAL	CON SUB FLA
	GEMSCAL	CON SUB FLA GEM
ASYMMETRIC	EUCLID	CON
	INDSCAL	CON SUB FLA
	GEMSCAL	CON SUB FLA GEM
	ASCAL	CON STI
	AINDS	CON SUB FLA STI
RECTANGULAR	EUCLID	ROW COL
	INDSCAL	ROW COL SUB FLA
	GEMSCAL	ROW COL SUB FLA GEM

Example

```
ALSCAL VAR=ATLANTA TO TAMPA /OUTFILE=ONE.
```

• OUTFILE creates the SPSS configuration/weights file *ONE* from the example of air distances between cities.

MATRIX Subcommand

MATRIX reads SPSS matrix data files. It can read a matrix written by either PROXIMITIES or CLUSTER.

- Generally, data read by ALSCAL are already in matrix form. If the matrix materials are in the working data file, you do not need to use MATRIX to read them. Simply use the VARIABLES subcommand to indicate the variables (or columns) to be used. However, if the matrix materials are not in the working data file, MATRIX must be used to specify the matrix data file that contains the matrix.

- The proximity matrices ALSCAL reads have *ROWTYPE_* values of PROX. No additional statistics should be included with these matrix materials.

- ALSCAL ignores unrecognized *ROWTYPE_* values in the matrix file. In addition, it ignores variables present in the matrix file that are not specified on the VARIABLES subcommand in ALSCAL. The order of rows and columns in the matrix is unimportant.

- Since ALSCAL does not support case labeling, it ignores values for the *ID* variable (if present) in a CLUSTER or PROXIMITIES matrix.

- If split-file processing was in effect when the matrix was written, the same split file must be in effect when ALSCAL reads that matrix.

- The specification on MATRIX is the keyword IN and the matrix file in parentheses.

- MATRIX=IN cannot be used unless a working data file has already been defined. To read an existing matrix data file at the beginning of a session, first use GET to retrieve the matrix file and then specify IN(*) on MATRIX.

IN (filename)   *Read a matrix data file.* If the matrix data file is the working data file, specify an asterisk in parentheses (*). If the matrix data file is another file, specify the filename in parentheses. A matrix file read from an external file does not replace the working data file.

Example

```
PROXIMITIES V1 TO V8 /ID=NAMEVAR /MATRIX=OUT(*).
ALSCAL VAR=CASE1 TO CASE10 /MATRIX=IN(*).
```

- PROXIMITIES uses *V1* through *V8* in the working data file to generate a matrix file of Euclidean distances between each pair of cases based on the eight variables. The number of rows and columns in the resulting matrix equals the number of cases. MATRIX=OUT then replaces the working data file with this new matrix data file.

- MATRIX=IN on ALSCAL reads the matrix data file, which is the new working data file. In this instance, MATRIX is optional because the matrix materials are in the working data file.

- If there were 10 cases in the original working data file, ALSCAL performs a multidimensional scaling analysis in two dimensions on *CASE1* through *CASE10*.

Example

```
GET FILE PROXMTX.
ALSCAL VAR=CASE1 TO CASE10 /MATRIX=IN(*).
```

- GET retrieves the matrix data file *PROXMTX*.

- MATRIX=IN specifies an asterisk because the working data file is the matrix. MATRIX is optional, however, since the matrix materials are in the working data file.

Example

```
GET FILE PRSNNL.
FREQUENCIES VARIABLE=AGE.
ALSCAL VAR=CASE1 TO CASE10 /MATRIX=IN(PROXMTX).
```

- This example performs a frequencies analysis on file *PRSNNL* and then uses a different file containing matrix data for ALSCAL. The file is an existing matrix data file.
- MATRIX=IN is required because the matrix data file, *PROXMTX*, is not the working data file. *PROXMTX* does not replace *PRSNNL* as the working data file.

Specification of Analyses

Table 3 summarizes the analyses that can be performed for the major types of proximity matrices you can use with ALSCAL, Table 4 lists the specifications needed to produce these analyses for nonmetric models, and Table 5 lists the specifications for metric models. You can include additional specifications to control the precision of your analysis with CRITERIA.

Table 3   Models for types of matrix input

Matrix mode	Matrix form	Model class	Single matrix	Replications of single matrix	Two or more individual matrices
Object by object	Symmetric	Multi-dimensional scaling	CMDS Classical multi-dimensional scaling	RMDS Replicated multi-dimensional scaling	WMDS(INDSCAL) Weighted multi-dimensional scaling
	Asymmetric single process	Multi-dimensional scaling	CMDS(row conditional) Classical row conditional multi-dimensional scaling	RMDS(row conditional) Replicated row conditional multi-dimensional scaling	WMDS(row conditional) Weighted row conditional multi-dimensional scaling
	Asymmetric multiple process	Internal asymmetric multi-dimensional scaling	CAMDS Classical asymmetric multidimensional scaling	RAMDS Replicated asymmetric multidimensional scaling	WAMDS Weighted asymmetric multidimensional scaling
		External asymmetric multi-dimensional scaling	CAMDS(external) Classical external asymmetric multidimensional scaling	RAMDS(external) Replicated external asymmetric multi-dimensional scaling	WAMDS(external) Weighted external asymmetric multi-dimensional scaling
Object by attribute	Rectangular	Internal unfolding	CMDU Classical internal multidimensional unfolding	RMDU Replicated internal multidimensional unfolding	WMDU Weighted internal multi-dimensional unfolding
		External unfolding	CMDU(external) Classical external multidimensional unfolding	RMDU(external) Replicated external multidimensional unfolding	WMDU(external) Weighted external multi-dimensional unfolding

Table 4   ALSCAL specifications for nonmetric models

Matrix mode	Matrix form	Model class	Single matrix	Replications of single matrix	Two or more individual matrices
Object by object	Symmetric	Multi-dimensional scaling	ALSCAL VAR= varlist.	ALSCAL VAR= varlist.	ALSCAL VAR= varlist /MODEL=INDSCAL.
	Asymmetric single process	Multi-dimensional scaling	ALSCAL VAR= varlist /SHAPE=ASYMMETRIC /CONDITION=ROW.	ALSCAL VAR= varlist /SHAPE=ASYMMETRIC /CONDITION=ROW.	ALSCAL VAR= varlist /SHAPE=ASYMMETRIC /CONDITION=ROW /MODEL=INDSCAL.
	Asymmetric multiple process	Internal asymmetric multi-dimensional scaling	ALSCAL VAR= varlist /SHAPE=ASYMMETRIC /MODEL=ASCAL.	ALSCAL VAR= varlist /SHAPE=ASYMMETRIC /MODEL=ASCAL.	ALSCAL VAR= varlist /SHAPE=ASYMMETRIC /MODEL=AINDS.
		External asymmetric multi-dimensional scaling	ALSCAL VAR= varlist /SHAPE=ASYMMETRIC /MODEL=ASCAL /FILE=file COLCONF(FIX).	ALSCAL VAR= varlist /SHAPE=ASYMMETRIC /MODEL=ASCAL /FILE=file COLCONF(FIX).	ALSCAL VAR= varlist /SHAPE=ASYMMETRIC /MODEL=AINDS /FILE=file COLCONF(FIX).
Object by attribute	Rectangular	Internal unfolding	ALSCAL VAR= varlist /SHAPE=REC /INP=ROWS /CONDITION=ROW.	ALSCAL VAR= varlist /SHAPE=REC /INP=ROWS /CONDITION(ROW).	ALSCAL VAR= varlist /SHAPE=REC /INP=ROWS /CONDITION=ROW /MODEL=INDSCAL.
		External unfolding	ALSCAL VAR= varlist /SHAPE=REC /INP=ROWS /CONDITION=ROW /FILE=file ROWCONF(FIX).	ALSCAL VAR= varlist /SHAPE=REC /INP=ROWS /CONDITION=ROW /FILE=file ROWCONF(FIX).	ALSCAL VAR= varlist /SHAPE=REC /INP=ROWS /CONDITION=ROW /FILE=file ROWCONF(FIX) /MODEL=INDSCAL.

Table 5   ALSCAL specifications for metric models

Matrix mode	Matrix form	Model class	Single matrix	Replications of single matrix	Two or more individual matrices
Object by object	Symmetric	Multi-dimensional scaling	ALSCAL VAR= varlist /LEVEL=INT.	ALSCAL VAR= varlist /LEVEL=INT.	ALSCAL VAR= varlist /LEVEL=INT /MODEL=INDSCAL.
	Asymmetric single process	Multi-dimensional scaling	ALSCAL VAR= varlist /SHAPE=ASYMMETRIC /CONDITION=ROW /LEVEL=INT.	ALSCAL VAR= varlist /SHAPE=ASYMMETRIC /CONDITION=ROW /LEVEL=INT.	ALSCAL VAR= varlist /SHAPE=ASYMMETRIC /CONDITION=ROW /LEVEL=INT /MODEL=INDSCAL.
	Asymmetric multiple process	Internal asymmetric multi-dimensional scaling	ALSCAL VAR= varlist /SHAPE=ASYMMETRIC /LEVEL=INT /MODEL=ASCAL.	ALSCAL VAR= varlist /SHAPE=ASYMMETRIC /LEVEL=INT /MODEL=ASCAL.	ALSCAL VAR= varlist /SHAPE=ASYMMETRIC /LEVEL=INT /MODEL=AINDS.
		External asymmetric multi-dimensional scaling	ALSCAL VAR= varlist /SHAPE=ASYMMETRIC /LEVEL=INT /MODEL=ASCAL /FILE=file COLCONF(FIX).	ALSCAL VAR= varlist /SHAPE=ASYMMETRIC /LEVEL=INT /MODEL=ASCAL /FILE=file COLCONF(FIX).	ALSCAL VAR= varlist /SHAPE=ASYMMETRIC /LEVEL=INT /MODEL=AINDS /FILE=file COLCONF(FIX).
Object by attribute	Rectangular	Internal unfolding	ALSCAL VAR= varlist /SHAPE=REC /INP=ROWS /CONDITION=ROW /LEVEL=INT.	ALSCAL VAR= varlist /SHAPE=REC /INP=ROWS /CONDITION=ROW /LEVEL=INT.	ALSCAL VAR= varlist /SHAPE=REC /INP=ROWS /CONDITION=ROW /LEVEL=INT /MODEL=INDSCAL.
		External unfolding	ALSCAL VAR= varlist /SHAPE=REC /INP=ROWS /CONDITION=ROW /LEVEL=INT /FILE=file ROWCONF(FIX).	ALSCAL VAR= varlist /SHAPE=REC /INP=ROWS /CONDITION=ROW /LEVEL=INT /FILE=file ROWCONF(FIX).	ALSCAL VAR= varlist /SHAPE=REC /INP=ROWS /CONDITION=ROW /LEVEL=INT /FILE=file ROWCONF(FIX) /MODEL=INDSCAL.

ANOVA

```
ANOVA [VARIABLES=] varlist BY varlist(min,max)...varlist(min,max)
 [WITH varlist] [/VARIABLES=...]

[/COVARIATES={FIRST**}]
            {WITH   }
            {AFTER  }

[/MAXORDERS={ALL** }]
            {n     }
            {NONE  }

[/METHOD={UNIQUE**     }]
         {EXPERIMENTAL}
         {HIERARCHICAL}

[/STATISTICS=[MCA] [REG†] [MEAN] [ALL] [NONE]]

[/MISSING={EXCLUDE**}]
          {INCLUDE  }
```

**Default if the subcommand is omitted.
†REG (table of regression coefficients) is displayed only if the design is relevant.

Example

```
ANOVA VARIABLES=PRESTIGE BY REGION(1,9) SEX,RACE(1,2)
 /MAXORDERS=2
 /STATISTICS=MEAN.
```

Overview

ANOVA performs analysis of variance for factorial designs. The default is the full factorial model if there are five or fewer factors. Analysis of variance tests the hypothesis that the group means of the dependent variable are equal. The dependent variable is interval level, and one or more categorical variables define the groups. These categorical variables are termed **factors**. ANOVA also allows you to include continuous explanatory variables, termed **covariates**. Other procedures that perform analysis of variance are ONEWAY, SUMMARIZE, and GLM. To perform a comparison of two means, use TTEST.

Options

Specifying Covariates. You can introduce covariates into the model using the WITH keyword on the VARIABLES subcommand.

Order of Entry of Covariates. By default, covariates are processed before main effects for factors. You can process covariates with or after main effects for factors using the COVARIATES subcommand.

Suppressing Interaction Effects. You can suppress the effects of various orders of interaction using the MAXORDERS subcommand.

119

Methods for Decomposing Sums of Squares. By default, the regression approach (keyword UNIQUE) is used. You can request the classic experimental or hierarchical approach using the METHOD subcommand.

Statistical Display. Using the STATISTICS subcommand, you can request means and counts for each dependent variable for groups defined by each factor and each combination of factors up to the fifth level. You also can request unstandardized regression coefficients for covariates and multiple classification analysis (MCA) results, which include the MCA table, the Factor Summary table, and the Model Goodness of Fit table. The MCA table shows **treatment effects** as deviations from the grand mean and includes a listing of unadjusted category effects for each factor, category effects adjusted for other factors, and category effects adjusted for all factors and covariates. The Factor Summary table displays eta and beta values. The Goodness of Fit table shows R and R^2 for each model.

Basic Specification

- The basic specification is a single VARIABLES subcommand with an analysis list. The minimum analysis list specifies a list of dependent variables, the keyword BY, a list of factor variables, and the minimum and maximum integer values of the factors in parentheses.
- By default, the model includes all interaction terms up to five-way interactions. The sums of squares are decomposed using the regression approach, in which all effects are assessed simultaneously, with each effect adjusted for all other effects in the model. A case that has a missing value for any variable in an analysis list is omitted from the analysis.

Subcommand Order

- The analysis list must be first if the keyword VARIABLES is omitted from the specification.
- The remaining subcommands can be named in any order.

Operations

A separate analysis of variance is performed for each dependent variable in an analysis list, using the same factors and covariates.

Limitations

- Maximum 5 analysis lists.
- Maximum 5 dependent variables per analysis list.
- Maximum 10 factor variables per analysis list.
- Maximum 10 covariates per analysis list.
- Maximum 5 interaction levels.
- Maximum 25 value labels per variable displayed in the MCA table.
- The combined number of categories for all factors in an analysis list plus the number of covariates must be less than the sample size.

Example

```
ANOVA VARIABLES=PRESTIGE BY REGION(1,9) SEX, RACE(1,2)
 /MAXORDERS=2
 /STATISTICS=MEAN.
```

- VARIABLES specifies a three-way analysis of variance—*PRESTIGE* by *REGION*, *SEX*, and *RACE*.
- The variables *SEX* and *RACE* each have two categories, with values 1 and 2 included in the analysis. *REGION* has nine categories, valued 1 through 9.
- MAXORDERS examines interaction effects up to and including the second order. All three-way interaction terms are pooled into the error sum of squares.
- STATISTICS requests a table of means of *PRESTIGE* within the combined categories of *REGION*, *SEX*, and *RACE*.

Example

```
ANOVA VARIABLES=PRESTIGE BY REGION(1,9) SEX,RACE(1,2)
 /RINCOME BY SEX,RACE(1,2).
```

- ANOVA specifies a three-way analysis of variance of *PRESTIGE* by *REGION*, *SEX*, and *RACE*, and a two-way analysis of variance of *RINCOME* by *SEX* and *RACE*.

VARIABLES Subcommand

VARIABLES specifies the analysis list. The actual keyword VARIABLES can be omitted.

- More than one design can be specified on the same ANOVA command by separating the analysis lists with a slash.
- Variables named before keyword BY are dependent variables. Value ranges are not specified for dependent variables.
- Variables named after BY are factor (independent) variables.
- Every factor variable must have a value range indicating its minimum and maximum values. The values must be separated by a space or a comma and enclosed in parentheses.
- Factor variables must have integer values. Noninteger values for factors are truncated.
- Cases with values outside the range specified for a factor are excluded from the analysis.
- If two or more factors have the same value range, you can specify the value range once following the last factor to which it applies. You can specify a single range that encompasses the ranges of all factors on the list. For example, if you have two factors, one with values 1 and 2 and the other with values 1 through 4, you can specify the range for both as 1,4. However, this may reduce performance and cause memory problems if the specified range is larger than some of the actual ranges.
- Variables named after the keyword WITH are covariates.
- Each analysis list can include only one BY and one WITH keyword.

COVARIATES Subcommand

COVARIATES specifies the order for assessing blocks of covariates and factor main effects.

• The order of entry is irrelevant when METHOD=UNIQUE.

FIRST   *Process covariates before factor main effects.* This is the default.

WITH   *Process covariates concurrently with factor main effects.*

AFTER   *Process covariates after factor main effects.*

MAXORDERS Subcommand

MAXORDERS suppresses the effects of various orders of interaction.

ALL   *Examine all interaction effects up to and including the fifth order.* This is the default.

n   *Examine all interaction effects up to and including the nth order.* For example, MAXORDERS=3 examines all interaction effects up to and including the third order. All higher-order interaction sums of squares are pooled into the error term.

NONE   *Delete all interaction terms from the model.* All interaction sums of squares are pooled into the error sum of squares. Only main and covariate effects appear in the ANOVA table.

METHOD Subcommand

METHOD controls the method for decomposing sums of squares.

UNIQUE   *Regression approach.* UNIQUE overrides any keywords on the COVARIATES subcommand. All effects are assessed simultaneously for their partial contribution. The MCA and MEAN specifications on the STATISTICS subcommand are not available with the regression approach. This is the default if METHOD is omitted.

EXPERIMENTAL   *Classic experimental approach.* Covariates, main effects, and ascending orders of interaction are assessed separately in that order.

HIERARCHICAL   *Hierarchical approach.*

Regression Approach

All effects are assessed simultaneously, with each effect adjusted for all other effects in the model. This is the default when the METHOD subcommand is omitted. Since MCA tables cannot be produced when the regression approach is used, specifying MCA or ALL on STATISTICS with the default method triggers a warning.

Some restrictions apply to the use of the regression approach:

- The lowest specified categories of all the independent variables must have a marginal frequency of at least 1, since the lowest specified category is used as the reference category. If this rule is violated, no ANOVA table is produced and a message identifying the first offending variable is displayed.

- Given an *n*-way crosstabulation of the independent variables, there must be no empty cells defined by the lowest specified category of any of the independent variables. If this restriction is violated, one or more levels of interaction effects are suppressed and a warning message is issued. However, this constraint does not apply to categories defined for an independent variable but not occurring in the data. For example, given two independent variables, each with categories of 1, 2, and 4, the (1,1), (1,2), (1,4), (2,1), and (4,1) cells must not be empty. The (1,3) and (3,1) cells will be empty but the restriction on empty cells will not be violated. The (2,2), (2,4), (4,2), and (4,4) cells may be empty, although the degrees of freedom will be reduced accordingly.

To comply with these restrictions, specify precisely the lowest nonempty category of each independent variable. Specifying a value range of (0,9) for a variable that actually has values of 1 through 9 results in an error, and no ANOVA table is produced.

Classic Experimental Approach

Each type of effect is assessed separately in the following order (unless WITH or AFTER is specified on the COVARIATES subcommand):

- Effects of covariates
- Main effects of factors
- Two-way interaction effects
- Three-way interaction effects
- Four-way interaction effects
- Five-way interaction effects

The effects within each type are adjusted for all other effects of that type and also for the effects of all prior types (see Table 1).

Hierarchical Approach

The hierarchical approach differs from the classic experimental approach only in the way it handles covariate and factor main effects. In the hierarchical approach, factor main effects and covariate effects are assessed hierarchically—factor main effects are adjusted only for the factor main effects already assessed, and covariate effects are adjusted only for the covariates already assessed (see Table 1). The order in which factors are listed on the ANOVA command determines the order in which they are assessed.

Example

The following analysis list specifies three factor variables named *A*, *B*, and *C*:

```
ANOVA VARIABLES=Y BY A,B,C(0,3).
```

Table 1 summarizes the three methods for decomposing sums of squares for this example.

- With the default *regression* approach, each factor or interaction is assessed with all other factors and interactions held constant.
- With the *classic experimental* approach, each main effect is assessed with the two other main effects held constant, and two-way interactions are assessed with all main effects and other two-way interactions held constant. The three-way interaction is assessed with all main effects and two-way interactions held constant.
- With the *hierarchical* approach, the factor main effects A, B, and C are assessed with all prior main effects held constant. The order in which the factors and covariates are listed on the ANOVA command determines the order in which they are assessed in the hierarchical analysis. The interaction effects are assessed the same way as in the experimental approach.

Table 1   Terms adjusted for under each option

Effect	Regression (UNIQUE)	Experimental	Hierarchical
A	All others	B,C	None
B	All others	A,C	A
C	All others	A,B	A,B
AB	All others	A,B,C,AC,BC	A,B,C,AC,BC
AC	All others	A,B,C,AB,BC	A,B,C,AB,BC
BC	All others	A,B,C,AB,AC	A,B,C,AB,AC
ABC	All others	A,B,C,AB,AC,BC	A,B,C,AB,AC,BC

Summary of Analysis Methods

Table 2 describes the results obtained with various combinations of methods for controlling entry of covariates and decomposing the sums of squares.

Table 2   Combinations of COVARIATES and METHOD subcommands

	Assessments between types of effects	Assessments within the same type of effect
METHOD=UNIQUE	**Covariates, Factors,** and **Interactions** simultaneously	**Covariates**: adjust for factors, interactions, and all other covariates **Factors**: adjust for covariates, interactions, and all other factors **Interactions**: adjust for covariates, factors, and all other interactions
METHOD=EXPERIMENTAL	**Covariates** then **Factors** then **Interactions**	**Covariates:** adjust for all other covariates **Factors:** adjust for covariates and all other factors **Interactions**: adjust for covariates, factors, and all other interactions of the same and lower orders
METHOD=HIERARCHICAL	**Covariates** then **Factors** then **Interactions**	**Covariates**: adjust for covariates that are preceding in the list **Factors**: adjust for covariates and factors preceding in the list **Interactions**: adjust for covariates, factors, and all other interactions of the same and lower orders
COVARIATES=WITH and METHOD=EXPERIMENTAL	**Factors** and **Covariates** concurrently then **Interactions**	**Covariates**: adjust for factors and all other covariates **Factors**: adjust for covariates and all other factors **Interactions**: adjust for covariates, factors, and all other interactions of the same and lower orders
COVARIATES=WITH and METHOD=HIERARCHICAL	**Factors** and **Covariates** concurrently then **Interactions**	**Factors**: adjust only for preceding factors **Covariates**: adjust for factors and preceding covariates **Interactions**: adjust for covariates, factors, and all other interactions of the same and lower orders
COVARIATES=AFTER and METHOD=EXPERIMENTAL	**Factors** then **Covariates** then **Interactions**	**Factors**: adjust for all other factors **Covariates**: adjust for factors and all other covariates **Interactions**: adjust for covariates, factors, and all other interactions of the same and lower orders
COVARIATES=AFTER and METHOD=HIERARCHICAL	**Factors** then **Covariates** then **Interactions**	**Factors**: adjust only for preceding factors **Covariates**: adjust factors and preceding covariates **Interactions**: adjust for covariates, factors, and all other interactions of the same and lower orders

STATISTICS Subcommand

STATISTICS requests additional statistics. STATISTICS can be specified by itself or with one or more keywords.

- If you specify STATISTICS without keywords, ANOVA calculates MEAN and REG (each defined below).
- If you specify a keyword or keywords on the STATISTICS subcommand, ANOVA calculates only the additional statistics you request.

MEAN   *Means and counts table.* This statistic is not available when METHOD is omitted or when METHOD=UNIQUE. See "Cell Means" below.

REG   *Unstandardized regression coefficients.* Displays unstandardized regression coefficients for the covariates. See "Regression Coefficients for the Covariates" below.

MCA   *Multiple classification analysis.* The MCA, the Factor Summary, and the Goodness of Fit tables are not produced when METHOD is omitted or when METHOD=UNIQUE. See "Multiple Classification Analysis" on p. 127.

ALL   *Means and counts table, unstandardized regression coefficients, and multiple classification analysis.*

NONE   *No additional statistics.* ANOVA calculates only the statistics needed for analysis of variance. This is the default if the STATISTICS subcommand is omitted.

Cell Means

STATISTICS=MEAN displays the Cell Means table.

- This statistic is not available with METHOD=UNIQUE.
- The Cell Means table shows means and counts of each dependent variable for each cell defined by the factors and combinations of factors. Dependent variables and factors appear in their order on the VARIABLES subcommand.
- If MAXORDERS is used to suppress higher-order interactions, cell means corresponding to suppressed interaction terms are not displayed.
- The means displayed are the observed means in each cell, and they are produced only for dependent variables, not for covariates.

Regression Coefficients for the Covariates

STATISTICS=REG requests the unstandardized regression coefficients for the covariates.

- The regression coefficients are computed at the point where the covariates are entered into the equation. Thus, their values depend on the type of design specified by the COVARIATES or METHOD subcommands.
- The coefficients are displayed in the ANOVA table.

Multiple Classification Analysis

STATISTICS=MCA displays the MCA, the Factor Summary, and the Model Goodness of Fit tables.

- The MCA table presents counts, predicted means, and deviations of predicted means from the grand mean for each level of each factor. The predicted and deviation means each appear in up to three forms: unadjusted, adjusted for other factors, and adjusted for other factors and covariates.

- The Factor Summary table displays the correlation ratio (eta) with the unadjusted deviations (the square of eta indicates the proportion of variance explained by all categories of the factor), a partial beta equivalent to the standardized partial regression coefficient that would be obtained by assigning the unadjusted deviations to each factor category and regressing the dependent variable on the resulting variables, and the parallel partial betas from a regression that includes covariates in addition to the factors.

- The Model Goodness of Fit table shows R and R^2 for each model.

- The tables cannot be produced if METHOD is omitted or if METHOD=UNIQUE. When produced, the MCA table does not display values adjusted for factors if COVARIATES is omitted, if COVARIATES=FIRST, or if COVARIATES=WITH and METHOD=EXPERIMENTAL. A full MCA table is produced only if METHOD=HIERARCHICAL or if METHOD=EXPERIMENTAL and COVARIATES=AFTER.

MISSING Subcommand

By default, a case that has a missing value for any variable named in the analysis list is deleted for all analyses specified by that list. Use MISSING to include cases with user-missing data.

EXCLUDE   *Exclude cases with missing data.* This is the default.

INCLUDE   *Include cases with user-defined missing data.*

References

Andrews, F., J. Morgan, J. Sonquist, and L. Klein. 1973. *Multiple classification analysis.* 2nd ed. Ann Arbor: University of Michigan.

APPLY DICTIONARY

```
APPLY DICTIONARY FROM=file
```

Example

```
APPLY DICTIONARY FROM = 'MASTER.SAV'.
```

Overview

APPLY DICTIONARY applies dictionary information from an external SPSS-format data file to the working data file. The applied dictionary information includes variable and value labels, missing-value flags, print and write formats, and weight. APPLY DICTIONARY does not add or remove variables, and it cannot apply dictionary information selectively to individual variables.

Basic Specification

The basic specification is the FROM subcommand and the name of an SPSS-format data file. The file specification may vary from operating system to operating system, but enclosing the filename in apostrophes generally works.

Syntax Rules

- The equals sign after FROM is optional.
- The file containing the dictionary information to be applied (the **source file**) must be an SPSS-format data file.
- The file to which the dictionary information is applied (the **target file**) must be the working data file. You cannot specify another file.

Operation

- APPLY DICTIONARY adds or replaces dictionary information variable by variable by matching variables that have the same name and the same type (string or numeric) in both files. Variables in the working data file that do not have a match in the source file are not changed.
- APPLY DICTIONARY does not add or remove variables from the working data file.
- If no matched variables are found, the program displays a warning message.
- Variables that have the same name but different types are not considered matching. The program displays a warning message and lists the variables with nonmatching types.

Variable Labels

APPLY DICTIONARY adds labels or replaces old labels with new ones. It cannot be used to remove a defined variable label in the working data file.

- If the variable label in the source file is blank, it will not replace an existing variable label, even if the blanks are in quotes.

Table 1 shows how variable labels are replaced between matched variables.

Table 1   Variable label replacement

Variable	Label in working file (target file)	Label in external file (source file)	Label in resulting file
VAR1	"AGE 86"	"AGE 91"	"AGE 91"
VAR2		"JOBCAT91"	"JOBCAT91"
VAR3	"WORK ID"		"WORK ID"
VAR4	"RACE"	" "	"RACE"

Value Labels

APPLY DICTIONARY treats the value labels of a variable as a set. It adds or replaces the entire set of value labels for a matched variable in the working data file. You cannot remove the defined value label set from a variable or selectively add or replace individual value labels.

- APPLY DICTIONARY does not merge the set of value labels for a variable in the SPSS-format data file with the labels for a matched variable in the working data file. The variable in the resulting file uses the labels from the SPSS-format data file only.
- If the variable in the SPSS-format data file does not have any defined value labels, the matching variable in the working data file keeps its original value labels.
- If the matched variable in the working data file is a long string, value labels are not applied even if the source variable is a short string and has value labels defined. The program displays a message when this occurs.
- If the matched variables are both short strings but the target variable is longer than the source variable, the values for the source variable are right-padded before their labels are applied to the target variable.
- If the matched variables are both short strings but the source variable is longer, the values for the source variable are right-trimmed if there are enough blank spaces on the right. If any one of the values that has labels defined does not have enough blank spaces to be trimmed, the entire set of value labels is not applied and the variable in the working data file maintains its original value label specifications.

Missing Values

APPLY DICTIONARY treats the missing-value specifications of a variable as a set. It adds or replaces the entire set of missing values for a matched variable in the working data file. You can remove the entire set of missing-value specifications from a variable but cannot selectively add or replace individual missing-value specifications.

- APPLY DICTIONARY does not merge the set of missing values for a variable in the SPSS-format data file with the missing-value specifications for a matched variable in the working data file. The variable in the resulting file uses the missing values defined in the SPSS-format data file only.
- If the variable in the SPSS-format data file does not define any missing values, the variable in the working data file keeps its missing-value specifications.
- If the matched variable in the working data file is a long string, missing-value specifications are not applied even if the source variable is a short string and has missing values defined. The program displays a message specifying the missing value and information about the length of the matched variables.
- If the matched variables are both short strings but the target variable is longer than the source variable, the missing values from the source variable are right-padded.
- If the matched variables are both short strings but the source variable is longer, the missing values from the source variable are right-trimmed if there are enough blank spaces on the right. If any one of the defined missing values does not have enough blank spaces to be trimmed, the entire set will not be applied. The variable in the working data file maintains its original missing-value specifications.

Print and Write Formats

APPLY DICTIONARY always replaces the print and write formats of matched numeric variables in the working data file.

- The print and write formats of string variables are not changed. They keep the original length defined on the DATA LIST or STRING command. To change the length of a string variable, define a new variable using STRING and then use the COMPUTE command.

Weight

APPLY DICTIONARY adds or replaces the weighting information in the working data file. Table 2 summarizes how weighting information is applied. In the table, *WTWORK* refers to the weight variable in the working file and *WTSPSS* to the weight variable in the SPSS-format data file.

- A message is displayed when either the weight status or the weight variable is changed.

Table 2   Weight information

Working file		External file		Resulting file	
Status	**Weight**	**Status**	**Weight**	**Status**	**Weight**
Weighted	*WTWORK*	Unweighted	N/A	Weighted	*WTWORK*
		Weighted	*WTSPSS*	Weighted	*WTSPSS** *WTWORK*†
Unweighted	N/A	Weighted	*WTSPSS*	Weighted	*WTSPSS**
				Unweighted†	N/A

*If *WTSPSS* exists in the working file.
†If *WTSPSS* does not exist in the working file.

FROM Subcommand

FROM specifies an SPSS-format data file as the source file whose dictionary information is to be applied to the working file.

- FROM is required.
- Only one SPSS-format data file can be specified on FROM.
- The SPSS-format data file from which the current working file was built can be specified on FROM. This will restore dictionary information from the most recently saved version of the file.

AUTORECODE

```
AUTORECODE VARIABLES=varlist

 /INTO new varlist

 [/DESCENDING]

 [/PRINT]
```

Example

```
AUTORECODE VARIABLES=COMPANY /INTO RCOMPANY.
```

Overview

AUTORECODE recodes the values of string and numeric variables to consecutive integers and puts the recoded values into a new variable called a **target variable**. The value labels or values of the original variable are used as value labels for the target variable. AUTORECODE is useful for creating numeric independent (grouping) variables from string variables for procedures like ONEWAY, ANOVA, MANOVA, and DISCRIMINANT. AUTORECODE can also recode the values of factor variables to consecutive integers, which is required by MANOVA and which reduces the amount of workspace needed by other statistical procedures like ANOVA. AUTORECODE is also useful with the TABLES procedure, where string values are truncated to eight characters but value labels can be displayed in full. (See the *SPSS Tables* manual for more information.)

AUTORECODE is similar to the RECODE command. The main difference is that AUTORECODE automatically generates the values. In RECODE, you must specify the new values.

Options

Displaying Recoded Variables. You can display the values of the original and recoded variables using the PRINT subcommand.

Ordering of Values. By default, values are recoded in ascending order (lowest to highest). You can recode values in descending order (highest to lowest) using the DESCENDING subcommand.

Basic Specification

The basic specification is VARIABLES, and INTO. VARIABLES specifies the variables to be recoded. INTO provides names for the target variables that store the new values. VARIABLES and INTO must name or imply the same number of variables.

Subcommand Order

- VARIABLES must be specified first.
- INTO must immediately follow VARIABLES.

Syntax Rules

A variable cannot be recoded into itself. More generally, target variable names cannot duplicate any variable names already in the working file.

Operations

- The values of each variable to be recoded are sorted and then assigned numeric values. By default, the values are assigned in ascending order: 1 is assigned to the lowest nonmissing value of the original variable, 2 to the second-lowest nonmissing value, and so on for each value of the original variable.
- Values of the original variables are unchanged.
- Missing values are recoded into values higher than any nonmissing values, with their order preserved. For example, if the original variable has 10 nonmissing values, the first missing value is recoded as 11 and retains its user-missing status. System-missing values remain system-missing.
- AUTORECODE does not sort the cases in the working file. As a result, the consecutive numbers assigned to the target variables may not be in order in the file.
- Target variables are assigned the same variable labels as the original source variables. To change the variable labels, use the VARIABLE LABELS command after AUTORECODE.
- Value labels are automatically generated for each value of the target variables. If the original value had a label, that label is used for the corresponding new value. If the original value did not have a label, the old value itself is used as the value label for the new value. The defined print format of the old value is used to create the new value label.
- AUTORECODE ignores SPLIT FILE specifications. However, any SELECT IF specifications are in effect for AUTORECODE.

Example

```
DATA LIST / COMPANY 1-21 (A) SALES 24-28.
BEGIN DATA
CATFOOD JOY              10000
OLD FASHIONED CATFOOD   11200
 . . .
PRIME CATFOOD            10900
CHOICE CATFOOD          14600
END DATA.

AUTORECODE VARIABLES=COMPANY /INTO=RCOMPANY /PRINT.

TABLES TABLE = SALES BY RCOMPANY
  /TTITLE='CATFOOD SALES BY COMPANY'.
```

- Because TABLES truncates string variables to eight characters, AUTORECODE is used to recode the string variable *COMPANY*, which contains the names of various hypothetical cat food companies.
- AUTORECODE recodes *COMPANY* into a numeric variable *RCOMPANY*. Values of *RCOMPANY* are consecutive integers beginning with 1 and ending with the number of different values entered for *COMPANY*. The values of *COMPANY* are used as value labels for *RCOMPANY*'s numeric values. The *PRINT* subcommand displays a table of the original and recoded values.
- The variable *RCOMPANY* is used as the banner variable in the TABLES procedure to produce a table of sales figures for each cat food company. The value labels for *RCOMPANY* are used as column headings. Since TABLES does not truncate value labels, the full company names appear.

Example

```
AUTORECODE VARIABLES=REGION /INTO=RREGION /PRINT.
ANOVA Y BY RREGION (1,5).
```

- In statistical procedures, empty cells can reduce performance and increase memory requirements. In this example, assume that the factor *REGION* has only five nonempty categories, represented by the numeric codes 1, 4, 6, 14, and 20. AUTORECODE recodes those values into 1, 2, 3, 4, and 5 for target variable *RREGION*.
- The variable *RREGION* is used in ANOVA. If the original variable *REGION* were used, the amount of memory required by ANOVA would be 4429 bytes. Using variable *RREGION*, ANOVA requires only 449 bytes of memory.

Example

```
DATA LIST / RELIGION 1-8 (A) Y 10-13.
MISSING VALUES RELIGION (' ').
BEGIN DATA
CATHOLIC 2013
PROTEST  3234
JEWISH   5169
NONE      714
OTHER    2321
  . . .
END DATA.
AUTORECODE VARIABLES=RELIGION /INTO=NRELIG /PRINT /DESCENDING.
MANOVA Y BY NRELIG(1,5).
```

- Because MANOVA requires consecutive integer values for factor levels, the string variable *RELIGION* is recoded into a numeric variable. The five values for *RELIGION* are first sorted in descending order (Z to A) and are then assigned values 1, 2, 3, 4, and 5 in target variable *NRELIG*.
- Since a blank space is specified as a user-missing value, it is assigned the value 6. In the table produced by PRINT, the value 6 is displayed as 6M for the variable *NRELIG* to flag it as a user-missing value.
- The values of *RELIGION* are used as value labels for the corresponding new values in *NRELIG*.
- Target variable *NRELIG* is used as a factor variable in MANOVA.

VARIABLES Subcommand

VARIABLES specifies the variables to be recoded. VARIABLES is required and must be specified first. The actual keyword VARIABLES is optional.

- Values from the specified variables are recoded and stored in the target variables listed on INTO. Values of the original variables are unchanged.

INTO Subcommand

INTO provides names for the target variables that store the new values. INTO is required and must immediately follow VARIABLES.

- The number of target variables named or implied on INTO must equal the number of source variables listed on VARIABLES.

Example

```
AUTORECODE VARIABLES=V1 V2 V3 /INTO=NEWV1 TO NEWV3 /PRINT.
```

- AUTORECODE stores the recoded values of *V1*, *V2*, and *V3* into target variables named *NEWV1*, *NEWV2*, and *NEWV3*.

PRINT Subcommand

PRINT displays a correspondence table of the original values of the source variables and the new values of the target variables. The new value labels are also displayed.

- The only specification is keyword PRINT. There are no additional specifications.

DESCENDING Subcommand

By default, values for the source variable are recoded in ascending order (from lowest to highest). DESCENDING assigns the values to new variables in descending order (from highest to lowest). The largest value is assigned 1, the second-largest, 2, and so on.

- The only specification is keyword DESCENDING. There are no additional specifications.

BEGIN DATA—END DATA

```
BEGIN DATA
data records
END DATA
```

Example

```
BEGIN DATA
1   3424   274 ABU DHABI 2
2 39932    86 AMSTERDAM 4
3   8889  232 ATHENS
4   3424  294 BOGOTA      3
END DATA.
```

Overview

BEGIN DATA and END DATA are used when data are entered within the command sequence (inline data). BEGIN DATA and END DATA are also used for inline matrix data. BEGIN DATA signals the beginning of data lines and END DATA signals the end of data lines.

Basic Specification

The basic specification is BEGIN DATA, the data lines, and END DATA. BEGIN DATA must be specified by itself on the line that immediately precedes the first data line. END DATA is specified by itself on the line that immediately follows the last data line.

Syntax Rules

- BEGIN DATA, the data, and END DATA must precede the first procedure.
- The command terminator after BEGIN DATA is optional. It is best to leave it out so that the program will treat inline data as one continuous specification.
- END DATA must always begin in column 1. It must be spelled out in full and can have only one space between the words END and DATA. Procedures and additional transformations can follow the END DATA command.
- Data lines must *not* have a command terminator. For inline data formats, see DATA LIST.
- Inline data records are limited to a maximum of 80 columns. (On some systems, the maximum may be fewer than 80 columns.) If data records exceed 80 columns, they must be stored in an external file that is specified on the FILE subcommand of the DATA LIST (or similar) command.

Operations

- When the program encounters BEGIN DATA, it begins to read and process data on the next input line. All preceding transformation commands are processed as the working file is built.

- The program continues to evaluate input lines as data until it encounters END DATA, at which point it begins evaluating input lines as commands.

- No other commands are recognized between BEGIN DATA and END DATA.

- The INCLUDE command can specify a file that contains BEGIN DATA, data lines, and END DATA. The data in such a file are treated as inline data. Thus, the FILE subcommand should be omitted from the DATA LIST (or similar) command.

- When running the program from prompts, the prompt DATA> appears immediately after BEGIN DATA is specified. After END DATA is specified, the command line prompt returns.

Example

```
DATA LIST /XVAR 1 YVAR ZVAR 3-12 CVAR 14-22(A) JVAR 24.
BEGIN DATA
1  3424   274 ABU DHABI  2
2 39932    86 AMSTERDAM  4
3  8889   232 ATHENS
4  3424   294 BOGOTA     3
5 11323   332 HONG KONG  3
6   323   232 MANILA     1
7  3234   899 CHICAGO    4
8 78998  2344 VIENNA     3
9  8870   983 ZURICH     5
END DATA.
MEANS XVAR BY JVAR.
```

- DATA LIST defines the names and column locations of the variables. The FILE subcommand is omitted because the data are inline.

- There are nine cases in the inline data. Each line of data completes a case.

- END DATA signals the end of data lines. It begins in column 1 and has only a single space between END and DATA.

BREAK

BREAK

Overview

BREAK controls looping that cannot be fully controlled with IF clauses. Generally, BREAK is used within a DO IF—END IF structure. The expression on the DO IF command specifies the condition in which BREAK is executed.

Basic Specification

- The only specification is keyword BREAK. There are no additional specifications.
- BREAK must be specified within a loop structure. Otherwise, an error results.

Operations

- A BREAK command inside a loop structure but not inside a DO IF—END IF structure terminates the first iteration of the loop for all cases, since no conditions for BREAK are specified.
- A BREAK command within an inner loop terminates only iterations in that structure, not in any outer loop structures.

Example

```
VECTOR          #X(10).
LOOP            #I = 1 TO #NREC.
+   DATA LIST      NOTABLE/ #X1 TO #X10 1-20.
+   LOOP           #J = 1 TO 10.
+     DO IF          SYSMIS(#X(#J)).
+       BREAK.
+     END IF.
+     COMPUTE        X = #X(#J).
+     END CASE.
+   END LOOP.
END LOOP.
```

- The inner loop terminates when there is a system-missing value for any of the variables *#X1* to *#X10*.
- The outer loop continues until all records are read.

CACHE

CACHE.

Although the virtual active file can vastly reduce the amount of temporary disk space required, the absence of a temporary copy of the "active" file means that the original data source has to be re-read for each procedure. For data tables read from a database source this means the SQL query that reads the information from the database must be re-executed for any command or procedure that needs to read the data. Since virtually all statistical analysis procedures and charting procedures need to read the data, the SQL query is re-executed for each procedure you run, which can result in a significant increase in processing time if you run a large number of procedures.

If you have sufficient disk space on the computer performing the analysis (either your local computer or a remote server), you can eliminate multiple SQL queries and improve processing time by creating a data cache of the active file with the CACHE command. The CACHE command tells SPSS to copy all the data to a temporary disk file the next time the data are passed to run a procedure. If you want the cache written immediately, use the EXECUTE command after the CACHE command.

- The only specification is the command name CACHE.
- A cache file will not be written during a procedure which uses temporary variables.
- A cache file will not be written if the data are already in a temporary disk file and that file has not been modified since it was written.

Example

```
CACHE.
TEMPORARY.
RECODE alcohol(0 thru .04 = 'sober') (.04 thru .08 = 'tipsy')
  (else = 'drunk') into state.
FREQUENCIES var=state.
GRAPH...
```

No cache file will be written during the FREQUENCIES procedure. It will be written during the GRAPH procedure.

CASEPLOT

```
CASEPLOT [VARIABLES=]varlist

 [/DIFF={1}]
        {n}

 [/SDIFF={1}]
        {n}

 [/PERIOD=n]

 [/{NOLOG**}]
   {LN   }

 [/ID=varname]

 [/MARK={varname           }]
        {date specification}

 [/SPLIT {UNIFORM**}]
         {SCALE    }

 [/APPLY [='model name']]
```

For plots with one variable:

```
 [/FORMAT=[{NOFILL**}]   [{NOREFERENCE**}]
           {LEFT    }     {REFERENCE    }
           {RIGHT   }
```

For plots with multiple variables:

```
 [/FORMAT={NOJOIN**}]
          {JOIN    }
          {HILO    }
```

**Default if the subcommand is omitted.

Example

```
CASEPLOT TICKETS
  /LN
  /DIFF
  /SDIFF
  /PERIOD=12
  /FORMAT=REFERENCE
  /MARK=Y 55 M 6.
```

Overview

CASEPLOT produces a plot of one or more time series or sequence variables. You can request natural log and differencing transformations to produce plots of transformed variables. There are several plot formats available.

Options

Modifying the Variables. You can request a natural log transformation of the variable using the LN subcommand and seasonal and nonseasonal differencing to any degree using the SDIFF and DIFF subcommands. With seasonal differencing, you can also specify the periodicity on the PERIOD subcommand.

Plot Format. With the FORMAT subcommand, you can fill in the area on one side of the plotted values on plots with one variable. You can also plot a reference line indicating the variable mean. For plots with two or more variables, you can specify whether you want to join the values for each case with a horizontal line. With the ID subcommand, you can label the vertical axis with the values of a specified variable. You can mark the onset of an intervention variable on the plot with the MARK subcommand.

Split-File Processing. You can control how to plot data that have been divided into subgroups by a SPLIT FILE command using the SPLIT subcommand.

Basic Specification

The basic specification is one or more variable names.

- If the DATE command has been specified, the vertical axis is labeled with the *DATE_* variable at periodic intervals. Otherwise, sequence numbers are used. The horizontal axis is labeled with the value scale determined by the plotted variables.

Figure 1 shows a default high-resolution plot with DATE=YEAR 1900. Figure 2 shows the same default plot in low resolution.

Figure 1   CASEPLOT=PRICE (in high resolution)

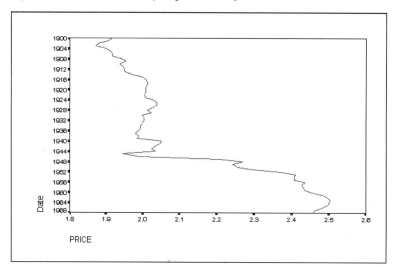

Figure 2   CASEPLOT=PRICE (low resolution)

The following plot symbols are used:
P - Variable PRICE
M - Missing Data (placed left of the vertical axis)

```
       1.7        1.9        2.1        2.3        2.5        2.7
YYYY  œ¡fffffffff¡fffffffff¡fffffffff¡fffffffff¡fffffffff¡ø         PRICE
1900   £         P                                          £      1.9176
1901   £          P                                         £      1.9059
1902   £        P                                           £      1.8798
1903   £        P                                           £      1.8727
1904   £         P                                          £      1.8984
1905   £          P                                         £      1.9137
1906   £          P                                         £      1.9176
1907   £          P                                         £      1.9176
1908   £           P                                        £      1.9420
1909  f£            P                                       £f     1.9547
1910   £           P                                        £      1.9379
1911   £           P                                        £      1.9462
1912   £            P                                       £      1.9504
1913   £            P                                       £      1.9504
1914   £             P                                      £      1.9723
1915   £              P                                     £      2.0000
1916   £              P                                     £      2.0097
1917   £               P                                    £      2.0146
1918   £               P                                    £      2.0146
1919  f£              P                                     £f     2.0097
1920   £              P                                     £      2.0097
1921   £              P                                     £      2.0097
1922   £              P                                     £      2.0048
1923   £              P                                     £      2.0097
1924   £               P                                    £      2.0296
1925   £                P                                   £      2.0399
1926   £                P                                   £      2.0399
1927   £               P                                    £      2.0296
1928   £               P                                    £      2.0146
1929  f£               P                                    £f     2.0245
1930   £              P                                     £      2.0000
1931   £              P                                     £      2.0048
1932   £              P                                     £      2.0048
1933   £              P                                     £      2.0000
1934   £              P                                     £      1.9952
1935   £              P                                     £      1.9952
1936   £              P                                     £      1.9905
1937   £             P                                      £      1.9813
1938   £              P                                     £      1.9905
1939  f£             P                                      £f     1.9859
1940   £                 P                                  £      2.0518
1941   £                P                                   £      2.0474
1942   £                P                                   £      2.0341
1943   £               P                                    £      2.0255
1944   £                P                                   £      2.0341
1945   £           P                                        £      1.9445
1946   £            P                                       £      1.9939
1947   £                    P                               £      2.2082
1948   £                      P                             £      2.2700
1949  f£                     P                              £f     2.2430
1950   £                      P                             £      2.2567
1951   £                        P                           £      2.2988
1952   £                           P                        £      2.3723
1953   £                             P                      £      2.4105
1954   £                             P                      £      2.4081
1955   £                             P                      £      2.4081
1956   £                              P                     £      2.4367
1957   £                              P                     £      2.4284
1958   £                              P                     £      2.4310
1959  f£                              P                     £f     2.4363
1960   £                               P                    £      2.4552
1961   £                                P                   £      2.4838
1962   £                                P                   £      2.4958
1963   £                                P                   £      2.5048
1964   £                                P                   £      2.5017
1965   £                                P                   £      2.4958
1966   £                               P                    £      2.4838
1967   £                              P                     £      2.4636
1968   £                              P                     £      2.4580
YYYY  ¿¶fffffffff¶fffffffff¶fffffffff¶fffffffff¶fffffffff¶¶Ŷ       PRICE
       1.7        1.9        2.1        2.3        2.5        2.7
```

Subcommand Order

- Subcommands can be specified in any order.

Syntax Rules

- VARIABLES can be specified only once.
- Other subcommands can be specified more than once, but only the last specification of each one is executed.

Operations

- Subcommand specifications apply to all variables named on the CASEPLOT command.
- If the LN subcommand is specified, any differencing requested on that CASEPLOT command is done on the log-transformed variables.
- In high-resolution plots, split-file information is displayed as part of the subtitle and transformation information is displayed as part of the footnote.
- In low-resolution plots, values of plotted variables are displayed along the right axis. A wider page specification on SET allows you to display the values of more variables but does not change the plot frame size.

Limitations

- Maximum 1 VARIABLES subcommand. There is no limit on the number of variables named on the list.

Example

```
CASEPLOT TICKETS
  /LN
  /DIFF
  /SDIFF
  /PERIOD=12
  /FORMAT=REFERENCE
  /MARK=Y 55 M 6.
```

- This example produces a plot of *TICKETS* after a natural log transformation, differencing, and seasonal differencing have been applied.
- LN transforms the data using the natural logarithm (base e) of the variable.
- DIFF differences the variable once.
- SDIFF and PERIOD apply one degree of seasonal differencing with a period of 12.
- FORMAT=REFERENCE adds a reference line at the variable mean. In a low-resolution plot, the area between the plotted values and the mean is filled with the plotting symbol (*T*).

- MARK provides a marker on the plot at June 1955. The marker is displayed as a horizontal reference line in a high-resolution plot.

VARIABLES Subcommand

VARIABLES specifies the names of the variables to be plotted and is the only required subcommand. The actual keyword VARIABLES can be omitted.

DIFF Subcommand

DIFF specifies the degree of differencing used to convert a nonstationary variable to a stationary one with a constant mean and variance before plotting.

- You can specify any positive integer on DIFF.
- If DIFF is specified without a value, the default is 1.
- The number of values displayed decreases by 1 for each degree of differencing.

Example

```
CASEPLOT TICKETS
  /DIFF=2.
```

- In this example, TICKETS is differenced twice before plotting.

SDIFF Subcommand

If the variable exhibits a seasonal or periodic pattern, you can use the SDIFF subcommand to seasonally difference a variable before plotting.

- The specification on SDIFF indicates the degree of seasonal differencing and can be any positive integer.
- If SDIFF is specified without a value, the degree of seasonal differencing defaults to 1.
- The number of seasons displayed decreases by 1 for each degree of seasonal differencing.
- The length of the period used by SDIFF is specified on the PERIOD subcommand. If the PERIOD subcommand is not specified, the periodicity established on the TSET or DATE command is used (see the PERIOD subcommand below).

PERIOD Subcommand

PERIOD indicates the length of the period to be used by the SDIFF subcommand.

- The specification on PERIOD indicates how many observations are in one period or season and can be any positive integer.
- PERIOD is ignored if it is used without the SDIFF subcommand.
- If PERIOD is not specified, the periodicity established on TSET PERIOD is in effect. If TSET PERIOD is not specified either, the periodicity established on the DATE command

is used. If periodicity is not established anywhere, the SDIFF subcommand will not be executed.

Example

```
CASEPLOT TICKETS
  /SDIFF=1
  /PERIOD=12.
```

- This command applies one degree of seasonal differencing with 12 observations per season to *TICKETS* before plotting.

LN and NOLOG Subcommands

LN transforms the data using the natural logarithm (base e) of the variable and is used to remove varying amplitude over time. NOLOG indicates that the data should not be log transformed. NOLOG is the default.

- If you specify LN on CASEPLOT, any differencing requested on that command will be done on the log-transformed variable.
- There are no additional specifications on LN or NOLOG.
- Only the last LN or NOLOG subcommand on a CASEPLOT command is executed.
- If a natural log transformation is requested, any value less than or equal to zero is set to system-missing.
- NOLOG is generally used with an APPLY subcommand to turn off a previous LN specification.

Example

```
CASEPLOT TICKETS
  /LN.
```

- In this example, *TICKETS* is transformed using the natural logarithm before plotting.

ID Subcommand

ID names a variable whose values will be used as the left-axis labels.

- The only specification on ID is a variable name. If you have a variable named *ID* in your working data file, the equals sign after the subcommand is required.
- ID overrides the specification on TSET ID.
- If ID or TSET ID is not specified, the left vertical axis is labeled with the *DATE_* variable created by the DATE command. If the *DATE_* variable has not been created, the observation or sequence number is used as the label.

Example

```
CASEPLOT VARA
  /ID=VARB.
```

- In this example, the values of variable *VARB* will be used to label the left axis of the plot of *VARA*.

FORMAT Subcommand

FORMAT controls the plot format.

- The specification on FORMAT is one of the keywords listed below.
- Keywords NOFILL, LEFT, RIGHT, NOREFERENCE, and REFERENCE apply to plots with one variable. NOFILL, LEFT, and RIGHT are alternatives and indicate how the plot is filled. NOREFERENCE and REFERENCE are alternatives and specify whether a reference line is displayed. For low-resolution plots, only one keyword can be specified. One keyword *from each set* can be specified for high-resolution plots. NOFILL and NOREFERENCE are the defaults.
- Keywords JOIN, NOJOIN, and HILO apply to plots with multiple variables and are alternatives. NOJOIN is the default. Only one keyword can be specified on a FORMAT subcommand for plots with two variables.

The following formats are available for plots of one variable:

NOFILL   *Plot only the values for the variable with no fill.* NOFILL produces a plot with no fill to the left or right of the plotted values. This is the default format when one variable is specified.

LEFT   *Plot the values for the variable and fill in the area to the left.* For high-resolution plots, if the plotted variable has missing or negative values, keyword LEFT is ignored and the default NOFILL is used instead. Figure 3 contains a left-filled high-resolution plot. In low-resolution plots, the area to the left of the plotted curve is filled in with the first character of the variable name.

RIGHT   *Plot the values for the variable and fill in the area to the right.* In low-resolution plots, the area to the right of the plotted curve is filled in with the first character of the variable name. For high-resolution plots, RIGHT is ignored; if specified, the default NOFILL is used instead.

Figure 3   FORMAT=LEFT

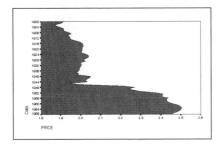

NOREFERENCE   *Do not plot a reference line.* This is the default when one variable is specified.

REFERENCE   *Plot a reference line indicating the variable mean.* In low resolution, the area between the plotted curve and the reference line is filled in with the plotting character (the first character of the variable name). For low-resolution plots, you cannot specify REFERENCE together with either LEFT or RIGHT. In high resolution, a fill chart is displayed as an area chart with a reference line and a nofill chart is a line chart with a reference line. Figure 4 shows a high-resolution plot with a reference line indicating the mean of the variable.

Figure 4   FORMAT=REFERENCE

The following formats are available for plots of multiple variables:

NOJOIN *Plot the values of each variable named.* In high-resolution plots, different colors or line patterns are used for multiple variables. In low-resolution plots, the plotting character for each variable is the first character of the variable name. Multiple occurrences of the same value for a single observation are plotted using a dollar sign ($). This is the default format for plots of multiple variables.

JOIN *Plot the values of each variable and join the values for each case.* Values are plotted as described for NOJOIN and the values for each case are joined together by a line. Figure 5 contains a plot in this format with three variables (*PRICE, INCOME,* and *CONSUMP*).

HILO *Plot the highest and lowest values across variables for each case and join the two values together.* The high and low values are plotted as a pair of vertical bars and are joined with a dashed line. For high-resolution plots, HILO is ignored if more than three variables are specified and the default NOJOIN is used instead. Figure 6 contains a plot in this format with three variables (*PRICE, INCOME,* and *CONSUMP*).

Figure 5   FORMAT=JOIN

Figure 6   FORMAT=HILO

MARK Subcommand

Use MARK to indicate the onset of an intervention variable. Figure 7 shows a high-resolution plot with a reference line indicating the year 1945.

- In high resolution, the onset date is indicated by a horizontal reference line. In low resolution it is indicated by a tick mark on the left axis.

- The specification on MARK can be either a variable name or an onset date if the *DATE_* variable exists.

- If a variable is named, the reference line indicates where the values of that variable change.

- A date specification follows the same format as the DATE command, that is, a keyword followed by a value. For example, the specification for June 1955 is Y 1955 M 6 (or Y 55 M 6 if only the last two digits of the year are used on DATE).

Figure 7   MARK=Y 1945

SPLIT Subcommand

SPLIT specifies how to plot data that have been divided into subgroups by a SPLIT FILE command. The specification on SPLIT is either SCALE or UNIFORM.

- If FORMAT=REFERENCE is specified when SPLIT=SCALE, the reference line is placed at the mean of the subgroup. If FORMAT=REFERENCE is specified when SPLIT=UNIFORM, the reference line is placed at the overall mean.

UNIFORM *Uniform scale.* The horizontal axis is scaled according to the values of the entire data set. This is the default if SPLIT is not specified.

SCALE *Individual scale.* The horizontal axis is scaled according to the values of each individual subgroup.

Example

```
SPLIT FILE BY REGION.
CASEPLOT TICKETS / SPLIT=SCALE.
```

- This example produces one plot for each *REGION* subgroup.
- The horizontal axis for each plot is scaled according to the values of *TICKETS* for each particular region.

APPLY Subcommand

APPLY allows you to produce a caseplot using previously defined specifications without having to repeat the CASEPLOT subcommands.

- The only specification on APPLY is the name of a previous model in quotes. If a model name is not specified, the specifications from the previous CASEPLOT command are used.

- If no variables are specified, the variables that were specified for the original plot are used.
- To change one or more plot specifications, specify the subcommands of only those portions you want to change after the APPLY subcommand.
- To plot different variables, enter new variable names before or after the APPLY subcommand.

Example

```
CASEPLOT TICKETS
  /LN
  /DIFF=1
  /SDIFF=1
  /PER=12.
CASEPLOT ROUNDTRP
  /APPLY.
CASEPLOT APPLY
  /NOLOG.
```

- The first command produces a plot of *TICKETS* after a natural log transformation, differencing, and seasonal differencing.
- The second command plots *ROUNDTRP* using the same transformations specified for *TICKETS*.
- The third command produces a plot of *ROUNDTRP*, but this time without any natural log transformation. The variable is still differenced once and seasonally differenced with a periodicity of 12.

CCF

```
CCF [VARIABLES=] series names [WITH series names]

[/DIFF={1}]
       {n}

[/SDIFF={1}]
        {n}

[/PERIOD=n]

[/{NOLOG**}]
  {LN     }

[/SEASONAL]

[/MXCROSS={7**}]
          {n  }

[/APPLY[='model name']]
```

**Default if the subcommand is omitted and there is no corresponding specification on the TSET command.

Example

```
CCF VARX VARY
  /LN
  /DIFF=1
  /SDIFF=1
  /PERIOD=12
  /MXCROSS=25.
```

Overview

CCF displays and plots the cross-correlation functions of two or more time series. You can also display and plot the cross-correlations of transformed series by requesting natural log and differencing transformations within the procedure.

Options

Modifying the Series. You can request a natural log transformation of the series using the LN subcommand and seasonal and nonseasonal differencing to any degree using the SDIFF and DIFF subcommands. With seasonal differencing, you can also specify the periodicity on the PERIOD subcommand.

Statistical Display. You can control which series are paired by using the keyword WITH. You can specify the range of lags for which you want values displayed and plotted with the MXCROSS subcommand, overriding the maximum specified on TSET. You can also display and plot values only at periodic lags using the SEASONAL subcommand.

Basic Specification

The basic specification is two or more series names. By default, CCF automatically displays the cross-correlation coefficient and standard error for the negative lags (second series leading), the positive lags (first series leading), and the 0 lag for all possible pair combinations in the series list. It also plots the cross-correlations and marks the bounds of two standard errors on the plot. By default, CCF displays and plots values up to 7 lags (lags −7 to +7), or the range specified on TSET.

Subcommand Order

- Subcommands can be specified in any order.

Syntax Rules

- The VARIABLES subcommand can be specified only once.
- Other subcommands can be specified more than once, but only the last specification of each one is executed.

Operations

- Subcommand specifications apply to all series named on the CCF command.
- If the LN subcommand is specified, any differencing requested on that CCF command is done on the log transformed series.
- Confidence limits are displayed in the plot, marking the bounds of two standard errors at each lag.

Limitations

- Maximum 1 VARIABLES subcommand. There is no limit on the number of series named on the list.

Example

```
CCF VARX VARY
  /LN
  /DIFF=1
  /SDIFF=1
  /PERIOD=12
  /MXCROSS=25.
```

- This example produces a plot of the cross-correlation function for *VARX* and *VARY* after a natural log transformation, differencing, and seasonal differencing have been applied to both series. Along with the plot, the cross-correlation coefficients and standard errors are displayed for each lag.

- LN transforms the data using the natural logarithm (base e) of each series.
- DIFF differences each series once.
- SDIFF and PERIOD apply one degree of seasonal differencing with a period of 12.
- MXCROSS specifies 25 for the maximum range of positive and negative lags for which output is to be produced (lags −25 to +25).

VARIABLES Subcommand

VARIABLES specifies the series to be plotted and is the only required subcommand. The actual keyword VARIABLES can be omitted.

- The minimum VARIABLES specification is a pair of series names.
- If you do not use keyword WITH, each series is paired with every other series in the list.
- If you specify keyword WITH, every series named before WITH is paired with every series named after WITH.

Example

```
CCF VARIABLES=VARA VARB WITH VARC VARD.
```

- This example displays and plots the cross-correlation functions for the following pairs of series: *VARA* with *VARC*, *VARA* with *VARD*, *VARB* with *VARC*, and *VARB* with *VARD*.
- *VARA* is not paired with *VARB*, and *VARC* is not paired with *VARD*.

DIFF Subcommand

DIFF specifies the degree of differencing used to convert a nonstationary series to a stationary one with a constant mean and variance before obtaining cross-correlations.

- You can specify any positive integer on DIFF.
- If DIFF is specified without a value, the default is 1.
- The number of values used in the calculations decreases by 1 for each degree of differencing.

Example

```
CCF VARX VARY
  /DIFF=1.
```

- This command differences series *VARX* and *VARY* before calculating and plotting the cross-correlation function.

SDIFF Subcommand

If the series exhibits seasonal or periodic patterns, you can use SDIFF to seasonally difference the series before obtaining cross-correlations.

- The specification on SDIFF indicates the degree of seasonal differencing and can be any positive integer.
- If SDIFF is specified without a value, the degree of seasonal differencing defaults to 1.
- The number of seasons used in the calculations decreases by 1 for each degree of seasonal differencing.
- The length of the period used by SDIFF is specified on the PERIOD subcommand. If the PERIOD subcommand is not specified, the periodicity established on the TSET or DATE command is used (see the PERIOD subcommand below).

Example

```
CCF VAR01 WITH VAR02 VAR03
 /SDIFF=1.
```

- In this example, one degree of seasonal differencing using the periodicity established on the TSET or DATE command is applied to the three series.
- Two cross-correlation functions are then plotted, one for the pair *VAR01* and *VAR02*, and one for the pair *VAR01* and *VAR03*.

PERIOD Subcommand

PERIOD indicates the length of the period to be used by the SDIFF or SEASONAL subcommands.

- The specification on PERIOD indicates how many observations are in one period or season and can be any positive integer.
- PERIOD is ignored if it is used without the SDIFF or SEASONAL subcommands.
- If PERIOD is not specified, the periodicity established on TSET PERIOD is in effect. If TSET PERIOD is not specified, the periodicity established on the DATE command is used. If periodicity was not established anywhere, the SDIFF and SEASONAL subcommands will not be executed.

Example

```
CCF VARX WITH VARY
 /SDIFF=1
 /PERIOD=6.
```

- This command applies one degree of seasonal differencing with a periodicity of 6 to both series and computes and plots the cross-correlation function.

LN and NOLOG Subcommands

LN transforms the data using the natural logarithm (base *e*) of each series and is used to remove varying amplitude over time. NOLOG indicates that the data should not be log transformed. NOLOG is the default.

- There are no additional specifications on LN or NOLOG.
- Only the last LN or NOLOG subcommand on a CCF command is executed.
- LN and NOLOG apply to all series named on the CCF command.

- If a natural log transformation is requested and any values in either series in a pair are less than or equal to 0, the CCF for that pair will not be produced because nonpositive values cannot be log transformed.
- NOLOG is generally used with an APPLY subcommand to turn off a previous LN specification.

Example

```
CCF VAR01 VAR02
  /LN.
```

- This command transforms the series *VAR01* and *VAR02* using the natural log before computing cross-correlations.

SEASONAL Subcommand

Use SEASONAL to focus attention on the seasonal component by displaying and plotting cross-correlations only at periodic lags.

- There are no additional specifications on SEASONAL.
- If SEASONAL is specified, values are displayed and plotted at the periodic lags indicated on the PERIOD subcommand. If no PERIOD subcommand is specified, the periodicity first defaults to the TSET PERIOD specification and then to the DATE command periodicity. If periodicity is not established anywhere, SEASONAL is ignored (see the PERIOD subcommand on p. 155).
- If SEASONAL is not used, cross-correlations for all lags up to the maximum are displayed and plotted.

Example

```
CCF VAR01 VAR02 VAR03
  /SEASONAL.
```

- This command plots and displays cross-correlations at periodic lags.
- By default, the periodicity established on TSET PERIOD (or the DATE command) is used. If no periodicity is established, cross-correlations for all lags are displayed and plotted.

MXCROSS Subcommand

MXCROSS specifies the maximum range of lags for a series.

- The specification on MXCROSS must be a positive integer.
- If MXCROSS is not specified, the default range is the value set on TSET MXCROSS. If TSET MXCROSS is not specified, the default is 7 (lags −7 to +7).
- The value specified on the MXCROSS subcommand overrides the value set on TSET MXCROSS.

Example

```
CCF VARX VARY
  /MXCROSS=5.
```

- The maximum number of cross-correlations can range from lag −5 to lag +5.

APPLY Subcommand

APPLY allows you to use a previously defined CCF model without having to repeat the specifications.

- The only specification on APPLY is the name of a previous model enclosed in apostrophes. If a model name is not specified, the model specified on the previous CCF command is used.
- To change one or more model specifications, specify the subcommands of only those portions you want to change after the APPLY subcommand.
- If no series are specified on the command, the series that were originally specified with the model being applied are used.
- To change the series used with the model, enter new series names before or after the APPLY subcommand.

Example

```
CCF VARX VARY
   /LN
   /DIFF=1
   /MXCROSS=25.
CCF VARX VARY
   /LN
   /DIFF=1
   /SDIFF=1
   /PERIOD=12
   /MXCROSS=25.
CCF VARX VAR01
   /APPLY.
CCF VARX VAR01
   /APPLY='MOD_1'.
```

- The first command displays and plots the cross-correlation function for *VARX* and *VARY* after each series is log transformed and differenced. The maximum range is set to 25 lags. This model is assigned the name *MOD_1* as soon as the command is executed.
- The second command displays and plots the cross-correlation function for *VARX* and *VARY* after each series is log transformed, differenced, and seasonally differenced with a periodicity of 12. The maximum range is again set to 25 lags. This model is assigned the name *MOD_2*.
- The third command requests the cross-correlation function for the series *VARX* and *VAR01* using the same model and the same range of lags as used for *MOD_2*.
- The fourth command applies *MOD_1* (from the first command) to the series *VARX* and *VAR01*.

References

Box, G. E. P., and G. M. Jenkins. 1976. *Time series analysis: Forecasting and control.* San Francisco: Holden-Day.

CLEAR TRANSFORMATIONS

```
CLEAR TRANSFORMATIONS
```

Overview

CLEAR TRANSFORMATIONS discards previous data transformation commands.

Basic Specification

The only specification is the command itself. CLEAR TRANSFORMATIONS has no additional specifications.

Operations

- CLEAR TRANSFORMATIONS discards all data transformation commands that have accumulated since the last procedure.
- CLEAR TRANSFORMATIONS has no effect if a command file is submitted to your operating system for execution. It generates a warning when a command file is present.
- Be sure to delete CLEAR TRANSFORMATIONS and any unwanted transformation commands from the journal file if you plan to submit the file to the operating system for batch-mode execution. Otherwise, the unwanted transformations will cause problems.

Example

```
GET FILE=QUERY.
FREQUENCIES=ITEM1 ITEM2 ITEM3.
RECODE ITEM1, ITEM2, ITEM3 (0=1) (1=0) (2=-1).
COMPUTE INDEXQ=(ITEM1 + ITEM2 + ITEM3)/3.
VARIABLE LABELS INDEXQ 'SUMMARY INDEX OF QUESTIONS'.
CLEAR TRANSFORMATIONS.
DISPLAY DICTIONARY.
```

- The GET and FREQUENCIES commands are executed.
- The RECODE, COMPUTE, and VARIABLE LABELS commands are transformations. They do not affect the data until the next procedure is executed.
- The CLEAR TRANSFORMATIONS command discards the RECODE, COMPUTE, and VARIABLE LABELS commands.
- The DISPLAY command displays the working file dictionary. Data values and labels are exactly as they were when the FREQUENCIES command was executed. Variable *INDEXQ* does not exist because CLEAR TRANSFORMATIONS discarded the COMPUTE command.

CLUSTER

```
CLUSTER varlist [/MISSING=LISTWISE**] [INCLUDE]

[/MEASURE=[{SEUCLID**             }]
           {EUCLID               }
           {COSINE               }
           {CORRELATION          }
           {BLOCK                }
           {CHEBYCHEV            }
           {POWER(p,r)           }
           {MINKOWSKI(p)         }
           {CHISQ                }
           {PH2                  }
           {RR[(p[,np])]         }
           {SM[(p[,np])]         }
           {JACCARD[(p[,np])]    }
           {DICE[(p[,np])]       }
           {SS1[(p[,np])]        }
           {RT[(p[,np])]         }
           {SS2[(p[,np])]        }
           {K1[(p[,np])]         }
           {SS3[(p[,np])]        }
           {K2[(p[,np])]         }
           {SS4[(p[,np])]        }
           {HAMANN[(p[,np])]     }
           {OCHIAI[(p[,np])]     }
           {SS5[(p[,np])]        }
           {PHI[(p[,np])]        }
           {LAMBDA[(p[,np])]     }
           {D[(p[,np])]          }
           {Y[(p[,np])]          }
           {Q[(p[,np])]          }
           {BEUCLID[(p[,np])]    }
           {SIZE[(p[,np])]       }
           {PATTERN[(p[,np])]    }
           {BSEUCLID[(p[,np])]   }
           {BSHAPE[(p[,np])]     }
           {DISPER[(p[,np])]     }
           {VARIANCE[(p[,np])]   }
           {BLWMN[(p[,np])]      }


[/METHOD={BAVERAGE**}[(rootname)] [...]]
         {WAVERAGE  }
         {SINGLE    }
         {COMPLETE  }
         {CENTROID  }
         {MEDIAN    }
         {WARD      }
         {DEFAULT** }

[/SAVE=CLUSTER({level   })]  [/ID=varname]
              {min,max}

[/PRINT=[CLUSTER({level   })] [DISTANCE] [SCHEDULE**] [NONE]]
                {min,max}

[/PLOT=[VICICLE**[(min[,max[,inc]])]]] [DENDROGRAM] [NONE]]
       [HICICLE[(min[,max[,inc]])]]]

[/MATRIX=[IN({file})] [OUT({file})]]
            {*   }        {*   }
```

** Default if subcommand or keyword is omitted.

Example

```
CLUSTER V1 TO V4
 /PLOT=DENDROGRAM
 /PRINT=CLUSTER (2,4).
```

Overview

CLUSTER produces hierarchical clusters of items based on distance measures of dissimilarity or similarity. The items being clustered are usually cases from the working data file, and the distance measures are computed from their values for one or more variables. You can also cluster variables if you read in a matrix measuring distances between variables. Cluster analysis is discussed in Anderberg (1973).

Options

Cluster Measures and Methods. You can specify one of 37 similarity or distance measures on the MEASURE subcommand and any of the seven methods on the METHOD subcommand.

New Variables. You can save cluster membership for specified solutions as new variables in the working data file using the SAVE subcommand.

Display and Plots. You can display cluster membership, the distance or similarity matrix used to cluster variables or cases, and the agglomeration schedule for the cluster solution with the PRINT subcommand. You can request either a horizontal or vertical icicle plot or a dendrogram of the cluster solution and control the cluster levels displayed in the icicle plot with the PLOT subcommand. You can also specify a variable to be used as a case identifier in the display on the ID subcommand.

Matrix Input and Output. You can write out the distance matrix and use it in subsequent CLUSTER, PROXIMITIES, or ALSCAL analyses or read in matrices produced by other CLUSTER or PROXIMITIES procedures using the MATRIX subcommand.

Basic Specification

The basic specification is a variable list. CLUSTER assumes that the items being clustered are cases and uses the squared Euclidean distances between cases on the variables in the analysis as the measure of distance.

Subcommand Order

- The variable list must be specified first.
- The remaining subcommands can be specified in any order.

Syntax Rules

- The variable list and subcommands can each be specified once.

- More than one clustering method can be specified on the METHOD subcommand.

Operations

The CLUSTER procedure involves four steps:

- First, CLUSTER obtains distance measures of similarities between or distances separating initial clusters (individual cases or individual variables if the input is a matrix measuring distances between variables).
- Second, it combines the two nearest clusters to form a new cluster.
- Third, it recomputes similarities or distances of existing clusters to the new cluster.
- It then returns to the second step until all items are combined in one cluster.

This process yields a hierarchy of cluster solutions, ranging from one overall cluster to as many clusters as there are items being clustered. Clusters at a higher level can contain several lower-level clusters. Within each level, the clusters are disjoint (each item belongs to only one cluster).

- CLUSTER identifies clusters in solutions by sequential integers (1, 2, 3, and so on).

Limitations

- CLUSTER stores cases and a lower-triangular matrix of proximities in memory. Storage requirements increase rapidly with the number of cases. You should be able to cluster 100 cases using a small number of variables in an 80K workspace.
- CLUSTER does not honor weights.

Example

```
CLUSTER V1 TO V4
  /PLOT=DENDROGRAM
  /PRINT=CLUSTER (2 4).
```

- This example clusters cases based on their values for all variables between and including *V1* and *V4* in the working data file.
- The analysis uses the default measure of distance (squared Euclidean) and the default clustering method (average linkage between groups).
- PLOT requests a dendrogram.
- PRINT displays a table of the cluster membership of each case for the two-, three-, and four-cluster solutions.

Variable List

The variable list identifies the variables used to compute similarities or distances between cases.

- The variable list is required except when matrix input is used. It must be specified before the optional subcommands.
- If matrix input is used, the variable list can be omitted. The names for the items in the matrix are used to compute similarities or distances.
- You can specify a variable list to override the names for the items in the matrix. This allows you to read in a subset of cases for analysis. Specifying a variable that does not exist in the matrix results in an error.

MEASURE Subcommand

MEASURE specifies the distance or similarity measure used to cluster cases.

- If the MEASURE subcommand is omitted or included without specifications, squared Euclidean distances are used.
- Only one measure can be specified.

Measures for Interval Data

For interval data, use any one of the following keywords on MEASURE:

SEUCLID   *Squared Euclidean distance.* The distance between two items, x and y, is the sum of the squared differences between the values for the items. SEUCLID is the measure commonly used with centroid, median, and Ward's methods of clustering. SEUCLID is the default and can also be requested with keyword DEFAULT.

$$\text{SEUCLID}(x, y) = \Sigma_i (x_i - y_i)^2$$

EUCLID   *Euclidean distance.* This is the default specification for MEASURE. The distance between two items, x and y, is the square root of the sum of the squared differences between the values for the items.

$$\text{EUCLID}(x, y) = \sqrt{\Sigma_i (x_i - y_i)^2}$$

CORRELATION *Correlation between vectors of values.* This is a pattern similarity measure.

$$\text{CORRELATION}(x, y) = \frac{\Sigma_i (Z_{xi} Z_{yi})}{N - 1}$$

where Z_{xi} is the Z-score (standardized) value of x for the ith case or variable, and N is the number of cases or variables.

COSINE   *Cosine of vectors of values.* This is a pattern similarity measure.

$$\text{COSINE}(x, y) = \frac{\Sigma_i (x_i y_i)}{\sqrt{(\Sigma_i x_i^2)(\Sigma_i y_i^2)}}$$

CHEBYCHEV   *Chebychev distance metric.* The distance between two items is the maximum absolute difference between the values for the items.

$$\text{CHEBYCHEV}(x, y) = \max_i |x_i - y_i|$$

BLOCK   *City-block or Manhattan distance.* The distance between two items is the sum of the absolute differences between the values for the items.

$$\text{BLOCK}(x, y) = \Sigma_i |x_i - y_i|$$

MINKOWSKI(p)   *Distance in an absolute Minkowski power metric.* The distance between two items is the *p*th root of the sum of the absolute differences to the *p*th power between the values for the items. Appropriate selection of the integer parameter *p* yields Euclidean and many other distance metrics.

$$\text{MINKOWSKI}(x, y) = (\Sigma_i |x_i - y_i|^p)^{1/p}$$

POWER(p,r)   *Distance in an absolute power metric.* The distance between two items is the *r*th root of the sum of the absolute differences to the *p*th power between the values for the items. Appropriate selection of the integer parameters *p* and *r* yields Euclidean, squared Euclidean, Minkowski, city-block, and many other distance metrics.

$$\text{POWER}(x, y) = (\Sigma_i |x_i - y_i|^p)^{1/r}$$

Measures for Frequency Count Data

For frequency count data, use any one of the following keywords on MEASURE:

CHISQ   *Based on the chi-square test of equality for two sets of frequencies.* The magnitude of this dissimilarity measure depends on the total frequencies of the two cases or variables whose dissimilarity is computed. Expected values are from the model of independence of cases or variables *x* and *y*.

$$\text{CHISQ}(x, y) = \sqrt{\frac{\Sigma_i (x_i - E(x_i))^2}{E(x_i)} + \frac{\Sigma_i (y_i - E(y_i))^2}{E(y_i)}}$$

PH2   *Phi-square between sets of frequencies.* This is the CHISQ measure normalized by the square root of the combined frequency. Therefore, its value does not depend on the total frequencies of the two cases or variables whose dissimilarity is computed.

$$\text{PH2}(x, y) = \sqrt{\frac{\dfrac{\Sigma_i (x_i - E(x_i))^2}{E(x_i)} + \dfrac{\Sigma_i (y_i - E(y_i))^2}{E(y_i)}}{N}}$$

Measures for Binary Data

Different binary measures emphasize different aspects of the relationship between sets of binary values. However, all the measures are specified in the same way. Each measure has two optional integer-valued parameters, *p* (present) and *np* (not present).

- If both parameters are specified, CLUSTER uses the value of the first as an indicator that a characteristic is present and the value of the second as an indicator that a characteristic is absent. CLUSTER skips all other values.

- If only the first parameter is specified, CLUSTER uses that value to indicate presence and all other values to indicate absence.

- If no parameters are specified, CLUSTER assumes that 1 indicates presence and 0 indicates absence.

Using the indicators for presence and absence within each item (case or variable), CLUSTER constructs a 2×2 contingency table for each pair of items in turn. It uses this table to compute a proximity measure for the pair.

	Item 2 characteristics	
	Present	**Absent**
Item 1 characteristics		
Present	*a*	*b*
Absent	*c*	*d*

CLUSTER computes all binary measures from the values of *a*, *b*, *c*, and *d*. These values are tallied across variables (when the items are cases) or across cases (when the items are variables). For example, if variables *V, W, X, Y, Z* have values 0, 1, 1, 0, 1 for case 1 and values 0, 1, 1, 0, 0 for case 2 (where 1 indicates presence and 0 indicates absence), the contingency table is as follows:

	Case 2 characteristics	
	Present	**Absent**
Case 1 characteristics		
Present	2	1
Absent	0	2

The contingency table indicates that both cases are present for two variables (*W* and *X*), both cases are absent for two variables (*V* and *Y*), and case 1 is present and case 2 is absent for one variable (*Z*). There are no variables for which case 1 is absent and case 2 is present.

The available binary measures include matching coefficients, conditional probabilities, predictability measures, and others.

Matching Coefficients. Table 1 shows a classification scheme for matching coefficients. In this scheme, *matches* are joint presences (value *a* in the contingency table) or joint absences (value *d*). *Nonmatches* are equal in number to value *b* plus value *c*. Matches and nonmatches may be weighted equally or not. The three coefficients JACCARD, DICE, and SS2 are related monotonically, as are SM, SS1, and RT. All coefficients in Table 1 are similarity measures, and all except two (K1 and SS3) range from 0 to 1. K1 and SS3 have a minimum value of 0 and no upper limit.

Table 1   Binary matching coefficients in CLUSTER

	Joint absences excluded from numerator	Joint absences included in numerator
All matches included in denominator		
Equal weight for matches and nonmatches	RR	SM
Double weight for matches		SS1
Double weight for nonmatches		RT
Joint absences excluded from denominator		
Equal weight for matches and nonmatches	JACCARD	
Double weight for matches	DICE	
Double weight for nonmatches	SS2	
All matches excluded from denominator		
Equal weight for matches and nonmatches	K1	SS3

RR[(p[,np])]

Russell and Rao similarity measure. This is the binary dot product.

$$RR(x, y) = \frac{a}{a + b + c + d}$$

SM[(p[,np])]

Simple matching similarity measure. This is the ratio of the number of matches to the total number of characteristics.

$$SM(x, y) = \frac{a + d}{a + b + c + d}$$

JACCARD[(p[,np])]

Jaccard similarity measure. This is also known as the *similarity ratio.*

$$JACCARD(x, y) = \frac{a}{a + b + c}$$

DICE[(p[,np])]

Dice (or Czekanowski or Sorenson) similarity measure.

$$\text{DICE}(x, y) = \frac{2a}{2a + b + c}$$

SS1[(p[,np])]

Sokal and Sneath similarity measure 1.

$$\text{SS1}(x, y) = \frac{2(a + d)}{2(a + d) + b + c}$$

RT[(p[,np])]

Rogers and Tanimoto similarity measure.

$$\text{RT}(x, y) = \frac{a + d}{a + d + 2(b + c)}$$

SS2[(p[,np])]

Sokal and Sneath similarity measure 2.

$$\text{SS2}(x, y) = \frac{a}{a + 2(b + c)}$$

K1[(p[,np])]

Kulczynski similarity measure 1. This measure has a minimum value of 0 and no upper limit. It is undefined when there are no nonmatches ($b=0$ and $c=0$). PROXIMITIES assigns an artificial upper limit of 10,000 to K1 when it is undefined or exceeds this value.

$$\text{K1}(x, y) = \frac{a}{b + c}$$

SS3[(p[,np])]

Sokal and Sneath similarity measure 3. This measure has a minimum value of 0 and no upper limit. It is undefined when there are no non-matches ($b=0$ and $c=0$). PROXIMITIES assigns an artificial upper limit of 10,000 to SS3 when it is undefined or exceeds this value.

$$\text{SS3}(x, y) = \frac{a + d}{b + c}$$

Conditional Probabilities. The following binary measures yield values that can be interpreted in terms of conditional probability. All three are similarity measures.

K2[(p[,np])]

Kulczynski similarity measure 2. This yields the average conditional probability that a characteristic is present in one item given that the characteristic is present in the other item. The measure is an average over both items acting as predictors. It has a range of 0 to 1.

$$\text{K2}(x, y) = \frac{a/(a + b) + a/(a + c)}{2}$$

SS4[(p[,np])]

Sokal and Sneath similarity measure 4. This yields the conditional probability that a characteristic of one item is in the same state (presence or absence) as the characteristic of the other item. The measure is an average over both items acting as predictors. It has a range of 0 to 1.

$$SS4(x, y) = \frac{a/(a+b) + a/(a+c) + d/(b+d) + d/(c+d)}{4}$$

HAMANN[(p[,np])]   *Hamann similarity measure.* This measure gives the probability that a characteristic has the same state in both items (present in both or absent from both) minus the probability that a characteristic has different states in the two items (present in one and absent from the other). HAMANN has a range of -1 to $+1$ and is monotonically related to SM, SS1, and RT.

$$HAMANN(x, y) = \frac{(a+d)-(b+c)}{a+b+c+d}$$

Predictability Measures. The following four binary measures assess the association between items as the predictability of one given the other. All four measures yield similarities.

LAMBDA[(p[,np])]   *Goodman and Kruskal's lambda (similarity).* This coefficient assesses the predictability of the state of a characteristic on one item (present or absent) given the state on the other item. Specifically, LAMBDA measures the proportional reduction in error using one item to predict the other when the directions of prediction are of equal importance. LAMBDA has a range of 0 to 1.

$$LAMBDA(x, y) = \frac{t_1 - t_2}{2(a+b+c+d) - t_2}$$

where
$t_1 = \max(a,b) + \max(c,d) + \max(a,c) + \max(b,d)$
$t_2 = \max(a + c, b + d) + \max(a + d, c + d).$

D[(p[,np])]   *Anderberg's D (similarity).* This coefficient assesses the predictability of the state of a characteristic on one item (present or absent) given the state on the other. D measures the actual reduction in the error probability when one item is used to predict the other. The range of D is 0 to 1.

$$D(x, y) = \frac{t_1 - t_2}{2(a+b+c+d)}$$

where
$t_1 = \max(a,b) + \max(c,d) + \max(a,c) + \max(b,d)$
$t_2 = \max(a + c, b + d) + \max(a + d, c + d)$

Y[(p[,np])]   *Yule's Y coefficient of colligation (similarity).* This is a function of the cross ratio for a 2×2 table. It has a range of -1 to $+1$.

$$Y(x, y) = \frac{\sqrt{ad} - \sqrt{bc}}{\sqrt{ad} + \sqrt{bc}}$$

Q[(p[,np])]   *Yule's* Q *(similarity).* This is the 2×2 version of Goodman and Kruskal's ordinal measure *gamma.* Like Yule's Y, Q is a function of the cross ratio for a 2×2 table and has a range of -1 to $+1$.

$$Q(x, y) = \frac{ad - bc}{ad + bc}$$

Other Binary Measures. The remaining binary measures available in CLUSTER are either binary equivalents of association measures for continuous variables or measures of special properties of the relationship between items.

OCHIAI[(p[,np])]   *Ochiai similarity measure.* This is the binary form of the cosine. It has a range of 0 to 1.

$$OCHIAI(x, y) = \sqrt{\frac{a}{a + b} \cdot \frac{a}{a + c}}$$

SS5[(p[,np])]   *Sokal and Sneath similarity measure 5.* The range is 0 to 1.

$$SS5(x, y) = \frac{ad}{\sqrt{(a + b)(a + c)(b + d)(c + d)}}$$

PHI[(p[,np])]   *Fourfold point correlation (similarity).* This is the binary form of the Pearson product-moment correlation coefficient.

$$PHI(x, y) = \frac{ad - bc}{\sqrt{(a + b)(a + c)(b + d)(c + d)}}$$

BEUCLID[(p[,np])]   *Binary Euclidean distance.* This is a distance measure. Its minimum value is 0, and it has no upper limit.

$$BEUCLID(x, y) = \sqrt{b + c}$$

BSEUCLID[(p[,np])]   *Binary squared Euclidean distance.* This is a distance measure. Its minimum value is 0, and it has no upper limit.

$$BSEUCLID(x, y) = b + c$$

SIZE[(p[,np])]   *Size difference.* This is a dissimilarity measure with a minimum value of 0 and no upper limit.

$$SIZE(x, y) = \frac{(b - c)^2}{(a + b + c + d)^2}$$

PATTERN[(p[,np])]   *Pattern difference.* This is a dissimilarity measure. The range is 0 to 1.

$$\text{PATTERN}(x, y) \; = \; \frac{bc}{(a + b + c + d)^2}$$

BSHAPE[(p[,np])]   *Binary shape difference.* This dissimilarity measure has no upper or lower limit.

$$\text{BSHAPE}(x, y) \; = \; \frac{(a + b + c + d)(b + c) - (b - c)^2}{(a + b + c + d)^2}$$

DISPER[(p[,np])]   *Dispersion similarity measure.* The range is -1 to $+1$.

$$\text{DISPER}(x, y) \; = \; \frac{ad - bc}{(a + b + c + d)^2}$$

VARIANCE[(p[,np])]   *Variance dissimilarity measure.* This measure has a minimum value of 0 and no upper limit.

$$\text{VARIANCE}(x, y) \; = \; \frac{b + c}{4(a + b + c + d)}$$

BLWMN[(p[,np])]   *Binary Lance-and-Williams nonmetric dissimilarity measure.* This measure is also known as the Bray-Curtis nonmetric coefficient. The range is 0 to 1.

$$\text{BLWMN}(x, y) \; = \; \frac{b + c}{2a + b + c}$$

METHOD Subcommand

METHOD specifies one or more clustering methods.

- If the METHOD subcommand is omitted or included without specifications, the method of average linkage between groups is used.
- Only one METHOD subcommand can be used, but more than one method can be specified on it.
- When the number of items is large, CENTROID and MEDIAN require significantly more CPU time than other methods.

BAVERAGE   *Average linkage between groups (UPGMA).* BAVERAGE is the default and can also be requested with keyword DEFAULT.

WAVERAGE   *Average linkage within groups.*

SINGLE   *Single linkage or nearest neighbor.*

COMPLETE   *Complete linkage or furthest neighbor.*

CENTROID   *Centroid clustering (UPGMC).* Squared Euclidean distances are commonly used with this method.

MEDIAN   *Median clustering (WPGMC).* Squared Euclidean distances are commonly used with this method.

WARD   *Ward's method.* Squared Euclidean distances are commonly used with this method.

Example

```
CLUSTER V1 V2 V3
 /METHOD=SINGLE COMPLETE WARDS.
```

- This example clusters cases based on their values for variables *V1*, *V2*, and *V3*, and uses three clustering methods: single linkage, complete linkage, and Ward's method.

SAVE Subcommand

SAVE allows you to save cluster membership at specified solution levels as new variables in the working data file.

- The specification on SAVE is the CLUSTER keyword, followed by either a single number indicating the level (number of clusters) of the cluster solution or a range separated by a comma indicating the minimum and maximum numbers of clusters when membership of more than one solution is to be saved. The number or range must be enclosed in parentheses and applies to all methods specified on METHOD.

- You can specify a rootname in parentheses after each method specification on the METHOD subcommand. CLUSTER forms new variable names by appending the number of the cluster solution to the rootname.

- If no rootname is specified, CLUSTER forms variable names using the formula *CLUn_m*, where *m* increments to create a unique rootname for the set of variables saved for one method and *n* is the number of the cluster solution.

- As *n* and *m* increase, the prefix *CLU* is truncated to keep names within eight characters.

- The names and descriptive labels of the new variables are displayed in the procedure information notes.

- You cannot use the SAVE subcommand if you are replacing the working data file with matrix materials (see "Matrix Output" on p. 173).

Example

```
CLUSTER A B C
 /METHOD=BAVERAGE SINGLE (SINMEM) WARD
 /SAVE=CLUSTERS(3,5).
```

- This command creates nine new variables: *CLU5_1*, *CLU4_1*, and *CLU3_1* for BAVERAGE, *SINMEM5*, *SINMEM4*, and *SINMEM3* for SINGLE, and *CLU5_2*, *CLU4_2*, and *CLU3_2* for WARD. The variables contain the cluster membership for each case at the five-, four-, and three-cluster solutions using the three clustering methods. Ward's method is the third specification on METHOD but uses the second set of default names since it is the second method specified without a rootname.

- The order of the new variables in the working data file is the same as listed above, since the solutions are obtained in the order from 5 to 3.

- New variables are listed in the procedure information notes.

ID Subcommand

ID names a string variable to be used as the case identifier in cluster membership tables, icicle plots, and dendrograms. If the ID subcommand is omitted, cases are identified by case numbers alone.

PRINT Subcommand

PRINT controls the display of cluster output (except plots, which are controlled by the PLOT subcommand).

- If the PRINT subcommand is omitted or included without specifications, an agglomeration schedule is displayed. If any keywords are specified on PRINT, the agglomeration schedule is displayed only if explicitly requested.
- CLUSTER automatically displays summary information (the method and measure used, the number of cases) for each method named on the METHOD subcommand. This summary is displayed regardless of specifications on PRINT.

You can specify any or all of the following on the PRINT subcommand:

SCHEDULE — *Agglomeration schedule.* The agglomeration schedule shows the order and distances at which items and clusters combine to form new clusters. It also shows the cluster level at which an item joins a cluster. SCHEDULE is the default and can also be requested with keyword DEFAULT.

CLUSTER(min,max) — *Cluster membership.* For each item, the display includes the value of the case identifier (or the variable name if matrix input is used), the case sequence number, and a value (1, 2, 3, and so on) identifying the cluster to which that case belongs in a given cluster solution. Specify either a single integer value in parentheses indicating the level of a single solution or a minimum value and a maximum value indicating a range of solutions for which display is desired. If the number of clusters specified exceeds the number produced, the largest number of clusters is used (the number of items minus 1). If CLUSTER is specified more than once, the last specification is used.

DISTANCE — *Proximities matrix.* The proximities matrix table displays the distances or similarities between items computed by CLUSTER or obtained from an input matrix. DISTANCE produces a large volume of output and uses significant CPU time when the number of cases is large.

NONE — *None of the above.* NONE overrides any other keywords specified on PRINT.

Example

```
CLUSTER V1 V2 V3 /PRINT=CLUSTER(3,5).
```

- This example displays cluster membership for each case for the three-, four-, and five-cluster solutions.

PLOT Subcommand

PLOT controls the plots produced for each method specified on the METHOD subcommand. For icicle plots, PLOT allows you to control the cluster solution at which the plot begins and ends and the increment for displaying intermediate cluster solutions.

- If the PLOT subcommand is omitted or included without specifications, a vertical icicle plot is produced.
- If any keywords are specified on PLOT, only those plots requested are produced.
- The icicle plots are generated as pivot tables and the dendrogram is generated as text output.
- If there is not enough memory for a dendrogram or an icicle plot, the plot is skipped and a warning is issued.
- The size of an icicle plot can be controlled by specifying range values or an increment for VICICLE or HICICLE. Smaller plots require significantly less workspace and time.

VICICLE(min,max,inc) *Vertical icicle plot.* This is the default. The range specifications are optional. If used, they must be integer and must be enclosed in parentheses. The specification *min* is the cluster solution at which to start the display (the default is 1), and the specification *max* is the cluster solution at which to end the display (the default is the number of cases minus 1). If *max* is greater than the number of cases minus 1, the default is used. The increment to use between cluster solutions is *inc* (the default is 1). If *max* is specified, *min* must be specified, and if *inc* is specified, both *min* and *max* must be specified. If VICICLE is specified more than once, only the last range specification is used.

HICICLE(min,max,inc) *Horizontal icicle plot.* The range specifications are the same as for VICICLE. If both VICICLE and HICICLE are specified, the last range specified is used for both. If a range is not specified on the last instance of VICICLE or HICICLE, the defaults are used even if a range is specified earlier.

DENDROGRAM *Tree diagram.* The dendrogram is scaled by the joining distances of the clusters.

NONE *No plots.*

Example

```
CLUSTER V1 V2 V3 /PLOT=VICICLE(1,20).
```

- This example produces a vertical icicle plot for the one-cluster through the twenty-cluster solution.

Example

```
CLUSTER V1 V2 V3 /PLOT=VICICLE(1,151,5).
```

- This example produces a vertical icicle plot for every fifth cluster solution starting with 1 and ending with 151 (1 cluster, 6 clusters, 11 clusters, and so on).

MISSING Subcommand

MISSING controls the treatment of cases with missing values. By default, a case that has a missing value for any variable on the variable list is omitted from the analysis.

LISTWISE *Delete cases with missing values listwise.* Only cases with nonmissing values for all variables on the variable list are used. LISTWISE is the default and can also be requested with keyword DEFAULT.

INCLUDE *Include cases with user-missing values.* Only cases with system-missing values are excluded.

MATRIX Subcommand

MATRIX reads and writes SPSS-format matrix data files.

- Either IN or OUT and a matrix file in parentheses are required. When both IN and OUT are used on the same CLUSTER procedure, they can be specified on separate MATRIX subcommands or on the same subcommand.
- The input or output matrix information is displayed in the procedure information notes.

OUT (filename) *Write a matrix data file.* Specify either a filename or an asterisk in parentheses (*). If you specify a filename, the file is stored on disk and can be retrieved at any time. If you specify an asterisk (*), the matrix data file replaces the working data file but is not stored on disk unless you use SAVE or XSAVE.

IN (filename) *Read a matrix data file.* If the matrix data file is the current working data file, specify an asterisk (*) in parentheses. If the matrix data file is another file, specify the filename in parentheses. A matrix file read from an external file does not replace the working data file.

Matrix Output

- CLUSTER writes proximity-type matrices with *ROWTYPE_* values of PROX. CLUSTER neither reads nor writes additional statistics with its matrix materials. See "Format of the Matrix Data File" on p. 174 for a description of the file.
- The matrices produced by CLUSTER can be used by subsequent CLUSTER procedures or by procedures PROXIMITIES and ALSCAL.

- Any documents contained in the working data file are not transferred to the matrix file.

Matrix Input

- CLUSTER can read matrices written by a previous CLUSTER command or by PROXIMITIES, or created by MATRIX DATA. When the input matrix contains distances between variables, CLUSTER clusters all or a subset of the variables.
- The order among rows and cases in the input matrix file is unimportant, as long as values for split-file variables precede values for *ROWTYPE_*.
- CLUSTER ignores unrecognized *ROWTYPE_* values.
- When you are reading a matrix created with MATRIX DATA, you should supply a value label for PROX of either *SIMILARITY* or *DISSIMILARITY* so the matrix is correctly identified. If you do not supply a label, CLUSTER assumes *DISSIMILARITY*. (See "Format of the Matrix Data File" below.)
- The program reads variable names, variable and value labels, and print and write formats from the dictionary of the matrix data file.
- MATRIX=IN cannot be specified unless a working data file has already been defined. To read an existing matrix data file at the beginning of a session, use GET to retrieve the matrix file and then specify IN(*) on MATRIX.
- The variable list on CLUSTER can be omitted when a matrix data file is used as input. By default, all cases or variables in the matrix data file are used in the analysis. Specify a variable list when you want to read in a subset of items for analysis.

Format of the Matrix Data File

- The matrix data file can include three special variables created by the program: *ROWTYPE_*, *ID*, and *VARNAME_*.
- Variable *ROWTYPE_* is a string variable with value PROX (for proximity measure). PROX is assigned value labels containing the distance measure used to create the matrix and either *SIMILARITY* or *DISSIMILARITY* as an identifier.
- *ID* is included only when an identifying variable is not specified on the ID subcommand. *ID* is a short string and takes the value CASE m, where m is the actual number of each case. Note that m may not be consecutive if cases have been selected.
- If an identifying variable is specified on the ID subcommand, it takes the place of *ID* between *ROWTYPE_* and *VARNAME_*. Up to 20 characters can be displayed for the identifying variable.
- *VARNAME_* is a string variable that takes the values VAR1, VAR2 ...VARn, to correspond to the names of the distance variables in the matrix (*VAR1, VAR2 ... VARn*, where n is the number of cases in the largest split file). The numeric suffix for the variable names is consecutive and may not be the same as the actual case number.
- The remaining variables in the matrix file are the distance variables used to form the matrix. The distance variables are assigned variable labels in the form of CASE m to identify the actual number of each case.

Split Files

- When split-file processing is in effect, the first variables in the matrix data file are the split variables, followed by *ROWTYPE_*, the case-identifier variable or *ID*, *VARNAME_*, and the distance variables.

- A full set of matrix materials is written for each split-file group defined by the split variables.

- A split variable cannot have the same name as any other variable written to the matrix data file.

- If split-file processing is in effect when a matrix is written, the same split file must be in effect when that matrix is read by any procedure.

Missing Values

Missing-value treatment affects the values written to a matrix data file. When reading a matrix data file, be sure to specify a missing-value treatment on CLUSTER that is compatible with the treatment that was in effect when the matrix materials were generated.

Example

```
DATA LIST FILE=ALMANAC1 RECORDS=3
  /1 CITY 6-18(A) POP80 53-60
  /2 CHURCHES 10-13 PARKS 14-17 PHONES 18-25 TVS 26-32
     RADIOST 33-35 TVST 36-38 TAXRATE 52-57(2).
N OF CASES 8.

CLUSTER CHURCHES TO TAXRATE
  /ID=CITY
  /MEASURE=EUCLID
  /MATRIX=OUT(CLUSMTX).
```

- CLUSTER reads raw data from file *ALMANAC1* and writes one set of matrix materials to file *CLUSMTX*.

- The working data file is still the *ALMANAC1* file defined on DATA LIST. Subsequent commands are executed on *ALMANAC1*.

Example

```
DATA LIST FILE=ALMANAC1 RECORDS=3
  /1 CITY 6-18(A) POP80 53-60
  /2 CHURCHES 10-13 PARKS 14-17 PHONES 18-25 TVS 26-32
     RADIOST 33-35 TVST 36-38 TAXRATE 52-57(2).
N OF CASES 8.

CLUSTER CHURCHES TO TAXRATE
  /ID=CITY
  /MEASURE=EUCLID
  /MATRIX=OUT(*).
LIST.
```

- CLUSTER writes the same matrix as in the previous example. However, the matrix data file replaces the working data file. The LIST command is executed on the matrix file, not on *ALMANAC1*.

Example

```
GET FILE=CLUSMTX.
CLUSTER
   /ID=CITY
   /MATRIX=IN(*).
```

- This example starts a new session and reads an existing matrix data file. GET retrieves the matrix data file *CLUSMTX*.
- MATRIX=IN specifies an asterisk because the matrix data file is the working data file. If MATRIX=IN(CLUSMTX) is specified, the program issues an error message.
- If the GET command is omitted, the program issues an error message.

Example

```
GET FILE=PRSNNL.
FREQUENCIES VARIABLE=AGE.

CLUSTER
   /ID=CITY
   /MATRIX=IN(CLUSMTX).
```

- This example performs a frequencies analysis on file *PRSNNL* and then uses a different file for CLUSTER. The file is an existing matrix data file.
- The variable list is omitted on the CLUSTER command. By default, all cases in the matrix file are used in the analysis.
- MATRIX=IN specifies the matrix data file *CLUSMTX*.
- *CLUSMTX* does not replace *PRSNNL* as the working data file.

Example

```
GET FILE=CRIME.
PROXIMITIES MURDER TO MOTOR
   /VIEW=VARIABLE
   /MEASURE=PH2
   /MATRIX=OUT(*).
CLUSTER
   /MATRIX=IN(*).
```

- GET retrieves an SPSS-format data file.
- PROXIMITIES uses the data from the *CRIME* file, which is now the working data file. The VIEW subcommand specifies computation of proximity values between variables. The MATRIX subcommand writes the matrix to the working data file.
- MATRIX=IN(*) on the CLUSTER command reads the matrix materials from the working data file. Since the matrix contains distances between variables, CLUSTER clusters vari-

ables based on distance measures in the input. The variable list is omitted on the CLUSTER command, so all variables are used in the analysis. The slash preceding the MATRIX subcommand is required because there is an implied variable list. Without the slash, CLUSTER would attempt to interpret MATRIX as a variable name rather than a subcommand name.

COMMENT

```
{COMMENT} text
{   *   }
```

Overview

COMMENT inserts explanatory text within the command sequence. Comments are included among the commands printed back in the output; they do not become part of the information saved in an SPSS-format data file. To include commentary in the dictionary of a data file, use the DOCUMENT command.

Syntax Rules

- The first line of a comment can begin with the keyword COMMENT or with an asterisk (*). Comment text can extend for multiple lines and can contain any characters. A period is required at the end of the last line to terminate the comment.

- Use /* and */ to set off a comment within a command. The comment can be placed wherever a blank is valid (except within strings) and should be preceded by a blank. Comments within a command cannot be continued onto the next line.

- The closing */ is optional when the comment is at the end of the line. The command can continue onto the next line just as if the inserted comment was a blank.

- Comments cannot be inserted within data lines.

Example

```
* Create a new variable as a combination of two old variables;
  the new variable is a scratch variable used later in the
  session;  it will not be saved with the data file.

COMPUTE #XYVAR=0.
IF (XVAR EQ 1 AND YVAR EQ 1) #XYVAR=1.
```

- The three-line comment will be included in the display file but will not be part of the data file if the working data file is saved.

Example

```
IF (RACE EQ 1 AND SEX EQ 1) SEXRACE = 1.   /*White males.
```

- The comment is entered on a command line. The closing */ is not needed because the comment is at the end of the line.

COMPUTE

```
COMPUTE target variable=expression
```

Arithmetic operators:

+	Addition	–	Subtraction
*	Multiplication	/	Division
**	Exponentiation		

Arithmetic functions:

ABS(arg)	Absolute value
RND(arg)	Round
TRUNC(arg)	Truncate
MOD(arg)	Modulus
SQRT(arg)	Square root
EXP(arg)	Exponential
LG10(arg)	Base 10 logarithm
LN(arg)	Natural logarithm
ARSIN(arg)	Arcsine
ARTAN(arg)	Arctangent
SIN(arg)	Sine
COS(arg)	Cosine

Statistical functions:

SUM[.n](arg list)	Sum of values across argument list
MEAN[.n](arg list)	Mean value across argument list
SD[.n](arg list)	Standard deviation of values across list
VAR[.n](arg list)	Variance of values across list
CFVAR[.n](arg list)	Coefficient of variation of values across list
MIN[.n](arg list)	Minimum value across list
MAX[.n](arg list)	Maximum value across list

Cumulative distribution functions (continuous):

CDF.BETA(q,a,b)	Return probability that the beta random variate falls below q ($0 \le q \le 1$; a>0; b>0).
CDF.CAUCHY(q,a,b)	Return probability that the Cauchy random variate falls below q ($q \ge 0$; b>0).
CDF.CHISQ (q,a)	Return probability that the chi-square random variate falls below q ($q \ge 0$; a>0).
CDF.EXP(q,a)	Return probability that the exponential random variate falls below q ($q \ge 0$; a>0).
CDF.F(q,a,b)	Return probability that the F random variate falls below q ($q \ge 0$; a>0; b>0).
CDF.GAMMA(q,a,b)	Return probability that the gamma random variate falls below q ($q \ge 0$; a>0; b>0).
CDF.LAPLACE(q,a,b)	Return probability that the Laplace random variate falls below q (b>0).
CDF.LOGISTIC(q,a,b)	Return probability that the logistic random variate falls below q (b>0).
CDF.LNORMAL(q,a,b)	Return probability that the lognormal random variate falls below q ($q \ge 0$; b>0).
CDF.NORMAL(q,a,b)	Return probability that the normal random variate falls below q (b>0). When $a=0$, $b=1$, alias CDFNORM(q).
CDF.PARETO(q,a,b)	Return probability that the Pareto random variate falls below q ($q \ge a > 0$; b>0).
CDF.T(q,a)	Return probability that the Student t random variate falls below q (a>0).
CDF.UNIFORM(q,a,b)	Return probability that the uniform random variate falls below q ($a \le q \le b$).
CDF.WEIBULL(q,a,b)	Return probability that the Weibull random variate falls below q ($q \ge 0$; a>0; b>0).

Inverse distribution functions (continuous):

IDF.BETA(p,a,b)	Return value q such that CDF.BETA(q,a,b)=p ($0 \le p \le 1$; a>0; b>0).
IDF.CAUCHY(p,a,b)	Return value q such that CDF.CAUCHY(q,a,b)=p ($0 < p < 1$; b>0).
IDF.CHISQ(p,a)	Return value q such that CDF.CHISQ(q,a)=p ($0 \le p < 1$; a>0).
IDF.EXP(p,a)	Return value q such that CDF.EXP(q,a)=p ($0 \le p < 1$; a>0).
IDF.F(p,a,b)	Return value q such that CDF.F(q,a,b)=p ($0 \le p < 1$; a>0; b>0).
IDF.GAMMA(p,a,b)	Return value q such that CDF.GAMMA(q,a,b)=p ($0 \le p < 1$; a>0; b>0).
IDF.LAPLACE(p,a,b)	Return value q such that CDF.LAPLACE(q,a,b)=p ($0 < p < 1$; b>0).
IDF.LOGISTIC(p,a,b)	Return value q such that CDF.LOGISTIC(q,a,b)=p ($0 < p < 1$; b>0).
IDF.LNORMAL(p,a,b)	Return value q such that CDF.LNORMAL(q,a,b)=p ($0 \le p \le 1$; b>0).
IDF.NORMAL(p,a,b)	Return value q such that CDF.NORMAL(q,a,b)=p ($0 < p < 1$; b>0). When $a=0$, $b=1$, alias PROBIT(p).
IDF.PARETO(p,a,b)	Return value q such that CDF.PARETO(q,a,b)=p ($0 \le p < 1$; a>0; b>0).
IDF.T(p,a)	Return value q such that CDF.T(q,a)=p ($0 < p < 1$; a>0).
IDF.UNIFORM(p,a,b)	Return value q such that CDF.UNIFORM(q,a,b)=p ($0 \le p \le 1$; $a \le b$).
IDF.WEIBULL(p,a,b)	Return value q such that CDF.WEIBULL(q,a,b)=p ($0 \le p < 1$; a>0; b>0).

Random variable functions (continuous distributions):

RV.BETA(a,b)	Generate a random variable of the beta distribution (a>0; b>0).
RV.CAUCHY(a,b)	Generate a random variable of the Cauchy distribution (b>0).
RV.CHISQ(a)	Generate a random variable of the chi-square distribution (a>0).
RV.EXP(a)	Generate a random variable of the exponential distribution (a>0).
RV.F(a,b)	Generate a random variable of the F distribution (a>0; b>0).
RV.GAMMA(a,b)	Generate a random variable of the gamma distribution (a>0; b>0).
RV.LAPLACE(a,b)	Generate a random variable of the Laplace distribution (b>0).

RV.LOGISTIC(a,b)	Generate a random variable of the logistic distribution (b>0).
RV.LNORMAL(a,b)	Generate a random variable of the lognormal distribution (b>0).
RV.NORMAL(a,b)	Generate a random variable of the normal distribution (b>0). When a=0, alias NORMAL(b).
RV.PARETO(x,a,b)	Generate a random variable of the Pareto distribution (b>0).
RV.T(a)	Generate a random variable of the Student t distribution (b>0).
RV.UNIFORM(a,b)	Generate a random variable of the uniform distribution. When a=0, alias UNIFORM(b).
RV.WEIBULL(a,b)	Generate a random variable of the Weibull distribution (a>0; b>0).

Cumulative distribution functions (discrete):

CDF.BERNOULLI(q,a)	Return probability that the Bernoulli distributed variate is less than or equal to q (q=0 or 1 only, $0 \le a \le 1$).
CDF.BINOM(q,a,b)	Return probability that the binomially distributed variate is less than or equal to q ($0 \le q \le a$ integer, $0 \le b \le 1$).
CDF.GEOM(q,a)	Return probability that the geometrically distributed variate is less than or equal to q (q>0 integer; $0 < a \le 1$).
CDF.HYPER(q,a,b,c)	Return probability that the hypergeometrically distributed variate is less than or equal to q (a>0 integer, $0 \le c \le a$, $0 \le b \le a$; $\max(0,b-a+c) \le q \le \min(c,b)$).
CDF.NEGBIN(q,a,b)	Return probability that the negative binomially distributed variate is less than or equal to q (a>0 integer, $0 \le b \le 1$; $q \ge a$ integer).
CDF.POISSON(q,a)	Return probability that the Poisson distributed variate is less than or equal to q (a>0; $q \ge 0$ integer).

Random variable functions (discrete distributions):

RV.BERNOULLI(a)	Generate a random variable from the Bernoulli distribution.
RV.BINOM(a,b)	Generate a random variable from the binomial distribution.
RV.GEOM(a)	Generate a random variable from the geometric distribution.
RV.HYPER(a,b,c)	Generate a random variable from the hypergeometric distribution (a>0 integer, $0 \le c \le a$, $0 \le b \le a$).
RV.NEGBIN(a,b)	Generate a random variable from the negative binomial distribution (a>0 integer, $0 \le b \le 1$).
RV.POISSON(a)	Generate a random variable from the Poisson distribution (a>0).

Noncentral distribution functions:

NCDF.BETA(x,a,b,c)	Return probability that the noncentral beta distributed variate falls below x (a>0,b>0,$c \ge 0$; $0 \le x \le 1$).
NCDF.CHISQ(x,a,c)	Return probability that the noncentral chi-square distributed variate falls below x (a>0, $c \ge 0$; $x \ge 0$).
NCDF.F(x,a,b,c)	Return probability that the noncentral F distributed variate falls below x (a>0, b>0, $c \ge 0$; $x \ge 0$).
NCDF.T(x,a,c)	Return probability that the noncentral Student t distributed variate falls below x (a>0, $c \ge 0$).

Missing-value functions:

VALUE(varname)	Ignore user-missing.
MISSING(varname)	True if missing.
SYSMIS(varname)	True if system-missing.
NMISS(arg list)	Number of missing values across list.
NVALID(arg list)	Number of valid values across list.

Cross-case function:

LAG(varname,n)	Value of variable *n* cases before.

Logical functions:

RANGE(varname,range)	True if value of variable is in range.
ANY(arg,arg list)	True if value of first argument is included on argument list.

Other functions:

UNIFORM(arg)	Uniform pseudo-random number between 0 and *n*.
NORMAL(arg)	Normal pseudo-random number with mean of 0 and standard deviation of *n*.
CDFNORM(arg)	Probability that random variable falls below *n*.
PROBIT(arg)	Inverse of CDFNORM.

Date and time aggregation functions:

DATE.DMY(d,m,y)	Read day, month, year, and return date.
DATE.MDY(m,d,y)	Read month, day, year, and return date.
DATE.YRDAY(y,d)	Read year, day, and return date.
DATE.QYR(q,y)	Read quarter, year, and return quarter start date.
DATE.MOYR(m,y)	Read month, year, and return month start date.
DATE.WKYR(w,y)	Read week, year, and return week start date.
TIME.HMS(h,m,s)	Read hour, minutes, seconds, and return time interval.
TIME.DAYS(d)	Read days and return time interval.

Date and time conversion functions:

YRMODA(yr,mo,da)	Convert year, month, day to day number.
CTIME.DAYS(arg)	Convert time interval to days.
CTIME.HOURS(arg)	Convert time interval to hours.
CTIME.MINUTES(arg)	Convert time interval to minutes.

Date and time extraction functions:

XDATE.MDAY(arg)	Return day of the month.
XDATE.MONTH(arg)	Return month of the year.
XDATE.YEAR(arg)	Return four-digit year.
XDATE.HOUR(arg)	Return hour of a day.
XDATE.MINUTE(arg)	Return minute of an hour.
XDATE.SECOND(arg)	Return second of a minute.
XDATE.WKDAY(arg)	Return weekday number.
XDATE.JDAY(arg)	Return day number of day in given year.
XDATE.QUARTER(arg)	Return quarter of date in given year.
XDATE.WEEK(arg)	Return week number of date in given year.
XDATE.TDAY(arg)	Return number of days in time interval.
XDATE.TIME(arg)	Return time portion of given date and time.
XDATE.DATE(arg)	Return integral portion of date.

String functions:

ANY(arg,arg list)	Return 1 if value of argument is included on argument list.
CONCAT(arg list)	Join the arguments into a string.
INDEX(a1,a2,a3)	Return number indicating position of first occurrence of $a2$ in $a1$; optionally, $a2$ in $a3$ evenly divided substrings of $a1$.
LAG(arg,n)	Return value of argument n cases before.
LENGTH(arg)	Return length of argument.
LOWER(arg list)	Convert upper case to lower case.
LPAD(a1,a2,a3)	Left-pad beginning of $a1$ to length $a2$ with character $a3$.
LTRIM(a1,a2)	Trim character $a2$ from beginning of $a1$.
MAX(arg list)	Return maximum value of argument list.
MIN(arg list)	Return minimum value of argument list.
NUMBER(arg,format)	Convert argument into number using format.
RANGE(arg,arg list)	Return 1 if value of argument is in inclusive range of argument list.
RINDEX(a1,a2,a3)	Return number indicating rightmost occurrence of $a2$ in $a1$; optionally, $a2$ in $a3$ evenly divided substrings of $a1$.
RPAD(a1,a2,a3)	Right-pad end of $a1$ to length $a2$ with character $a3$.
RTRIM(a1,a2)	Trim character $a2$ from end of $a1$.
STRING(arg,format)	Convert argument into string using format.
SUBSTR(a1,a2,a3)	Return substring of $a1$ beginning with position $a2$ for length $a3$.
UPCASE(arg list)	Convert lower case to upper case.
MBLEN.BYTE(arg,a1)	Return the number of bytes for the character beginning at position $a1$ in the string argument. If $a1$ is not specified, it defaults to 1.

Example

```
COMPUTE NEWVAR=RND((V1/V2)*100).
STRING DEPT(A20).
COMPUTE DEPT='PERSONNEL DEPARTMENT'.
```

Overview

COMPUTE creates new numeric variables or modifies the values of existing string or numeric variables. The variable named on the left of the equals sign is the **target variable**. The variables, constants, and functions on the right side of the equals sign form an **assignment expression**. For a complete discussion of functions, see "Transformation Expressions" on p. 43.

Numeric Transformations

Numeric variables can be created or modified with COMPUTE. The assignment expression for numeric transformations can include combinations of constants, variables, numeric operators, and functions.

String Transformations

String variables can be modified but cannot be created with COMPUTE. However, a new string variable can be declared and assigned a width with the STRING command and then assigned values by COMPUTE. The assignment expression can include string constants, string variables, and any of the string functions. All other functions are available for numeric transformations only.

Basic Specification

The basic specification is a target variable, an equals sign (required), and an assignment expression.

Syntax Rules

- The target variable must be named first, and the equals sign is required. Only one target variable is allowed per COMPUTE command.
- Numeric and string variables cannot be mixed in an expression. In addition, if the target variable is numeric, the expression must yield a numeric value; if the target variable is a string, the expression must yield a string value.
- Each function must specify at least one argument enclosed in parentheses. If a function has two or more arguments, the arguments must be separated by commas. For a complete discussion of the functions and their arguments, see "Transformation Expressions" on p. 43.
- You can use the TO keyword to refer to a set of variables where the argument is a list of variables.

Numeric Variables

- Parentheses are used to indicate the order of execution and to set off the arguments to a function.
- Numeric functions use simple or complex expressions as arguments. Expressions must be enclosed in parentheses.

String Variables

- String values and constants must be enclosed in apostrophes or quotation marks.
- When strings of different lengths are compared using the ANY or RANGE functions, the shorter string is right-padded with blanks so that its length equals that of the longer string.

Operations

- If the target variable already exists, its values are replaced.
- If the target variable does not exist and the assignment expression is numeric, the program creates a new variable.
- If the target variable does not exist and the assignment expression is a string, the program displays an error message and does not execute the command.
- COMPUTE is not executed if it contains invalid syntax. New variables are not created and existing target variables remain unchanged.

Numeric Variables

- New numeric variables created with COMPUTE are assigned a dictionary format of F8.2 and are initialized to the system-missing value for each case (unless the LEAVE command is used). Existing numeric variables transformed with COMPUTE retain their original dictionary formats. The format of a numeric variable can be changed with the FORMATS command.
- All expressions are evaluated in the following order: first functions, then exponentiation, and then arithmetic operations. The order of operations can be changed with parentheses.
- COMPUTE returns the system-missing value when it doesn't have enough information to evaluate a function properly. Arithmetic functions that take only one argument cannot be evaluated if that argument is missing. The date and time functions cannot be evaluated if any argument is missing. Statistical functions are evaluated if a sufficient number of arguments is valid. For example, in the command

```
COMPUTE FACTOR = SCORE1 + SCORE2 + SCORE3
```

FACTOR is assigned the system-missing value for a case if any of the three score values is missing. It is assigned a valid value only when all score values are valid. In the command

```
COMPUTE FACTOR = SUM(SCORE1 TO SCORE3).
```

FACTOR is assigned a valid value if at least one score value is valid. It is system-missing only when all three score values are missing.

String Variables

- String variables can be modified but not created on COMPUTE. However, a new string variable can be created and assigned a width with the STRING command and then assigned new values with COMPUTE.
- Existing string variables transformed with COMPUTE retain their original dictionary formats. String variables declared on STRING and transformed with COMPUTE retain the formats assigned to them on STRING.
- The format of string variables cannot be changed with FORMATS. Instead, use STRING to create a new variable with the desired width and then use COMPUTE to set the values of the new string equal to the values of the original.
- The string returned by a string expression does not have to be the same width as the target variable. If the target variable is shorter, the result is right-trimmed. If the target variable is longer, the result is right-padded. The program displays no warning messages when trimming or padding.
- To control the width of strings, use the functions that are available for padding (LPAD, RPAD), trimming (LTRIM, RTRIM), and selecting a portion of strings (SUBSTR).
- To determine whether a character in a string is single-byte or double-byte, use the MBLEN.BYTE function. Specify the string and, optionally, its beginning byte position. If the position is not specified, it defaults to 1.

Examples

The following examples illustrate the use of COMPUTE. For a complete discussion of each function, see "Transformation Expressions" on p. 43.

Arithmetic Operations

```
COMPUTE V1=25-V2.
COMPUTE V3=(V2/V4)*100.

DO IF TENURE GT 5.
COMPUTE RAISE=SALARY*.12.
ELSE IF TENURE GT 1.
COMPUTE RAISE=SALARY*.1.
ELSE.
COMPUTE RAISE=0.
END IF.
```

- *V1* is 25 minus *V2* for all cases. *V3* is *V2* expressed as a percentage of *V4*.
- *RAISE* is 12% of *SALARY* if *TENURE* is greater than 5. For remaining cases, *RAISE* is 10% of *SALARY* if *TENURE* is greater than 1. For all other cases, *RAISE* is 0.

Arithmetic Functions

```
COMPUTE WTCHANGE=ABS(WEIGHT1-WEIGHT2).
COMPUTE NEWVAR=RND((V1/V2)*100).
COMPUTE INCOME=TRUNC(INCOME).
COMPUTE MINSQRT=SQRT(MIN(V1,V2,V3,V4)).

COMPUTE TEST = TRUNC(SQRT(X/Y)) * .5.
COMPUTE PARENS = TRUNC(SQRT(X/Y) * .5).
```

- *WTCHANGE* is the absolute value of *WEIGHT1* minus *WEIGHT2*.

- *NEWVAR* is the percentage *V1* is of *V2*, rounded to an integer.

- *INCOME* is truncated to an integer.

- *MINSQRT* is the square root of the minimum value of the four variables *V1* to *V4*. MIN determines the minimum value of the four variables, and SQRT computes the square root.

- The last two examples above illustrate the use of parentheses to control the order of execution. For a case with value 2 for *X* and *Y*, *TEST* equals 0.5, since 2 divided by 2 (*X/Y*) is 1, the square root of 1 is 1, truncating 1 returns 1, and 1 times 0.5 is 0.5. However, *PARENS* equals 0 for the same case, since SQRT(*X/Y*) is 1, 1 times 0.5 is 0.5, and truncating 0.5 returns 0.

Statistical Functions

```
COMPUTE NEWSAL = SUM(SALARY,RAISE).
COMPUTE MINVAL = MIN(V1,V2,V3,V4).
COMPUTE MEANVAL = MEAN(V1,V2,V3,V4).
COMPUTE NEWMEAN = MEAN.3(V1,V2,V3,V4).
```

- *NEWSAL* is the sum of *SALARY* plus *RAISE*.

- *MINVAL* is the minimum of the values for *V1* to *V4*.

- *MEANVAL* is the mean of the values for *V1* to *V4*. Since the mean can be computed for one, two, three, or four values, *MEANVAL* is assigned a valid value as long as any one of the four variables has a valid value for that case.

- In the last example above, the .3 suffix specifies the minimum number of valid arguments required. *NEWMEAN* is the mean of variables *V1* to *V4* *only* if at least three of these variables have valid values. Otherwise, *NEWMEAN* is system-missing for that case.

Missing-Value Functions

```
MISSING VALUE V1 V2 V3 (0).
COMPUTE ALLVALID=V1 + V2 + V3.
COMPUTE UM=VALUE(V1) + VALUE(V2) + VALUE(V3).
COMPUTE SM=SYSMIS(V1) + SYSMIS(V2) + SYSMIS(V3).
COMPUTE M=MISSING(V1) + MISSING(V2) + MISSING(V3).
```

- The MISSING VALUE command declares value 0 as missing for *V1*, *V2*, and *V3*.

- *ALLVALID* is the sum of three variables only for cases with valid values for all three variables. *ALLVALID* is assigned the system-missing value for a case if any variable in the assignment expression has a system- or user-missing value.

- The VALUE function overrides user-missing value status. Thus, *UM* is the sum of *V1*, *V2*, and *V3* for each case, including cases with value 0 (the user-missing value) for any of the three variables. Cases with the system-missing value for *V1*, *V2*, and *V3* are system-missing.
- The SYSMIS function on the third COMPUTE returns the value 1 if the variable is system-missing. Thus, *SM* ranges from 0 to 3 for each case, depending on whether variables *V1*, *V2*, and *V3* are system-missing for that case.
- The MISSING function on the fourth COMPUTE returns the value 1 if the variable named is system- or user-missing. Thus, *M* ranges from 0 to 3 for each case, depending on whether variables *V1*, *V2*, and *V3* are user- or system-missing for that case.
- Alternatively, you could use the COUNT command to create variables *SM* and *M*.

```
* Test for listwise deletion of missing values.

DATA LIST /V1 TO V6 1-6.
BEGIN DATA
213 56
123457
123457
9234 6
END DATA.
MISSING VALUES V1 TO V6(6,9).

COMPUTE NOTVALID=NMISS(V1 TO V6).
FREQUENCIES VAR=NOTVALID.
```

- COMPUTE determines the number of missing values for each case. For each case without missing values, the value of *NOTVALID* is 0. For each case with one missing value, the value of *NOTVALID* is 1, and so on. Both system- and user-missing values are counted.
- FREQUENCIES generates a frequency table for *NOTVALID*. The table gives a count of how many cases have all valid values, how many cases have one missing value, how many cases have two missing values, and so on, for variables *V1* to *V6*. This table can be used to determine how many cases would be dropped in an analysis that uses listwise deletion of missing values. See p. 322 and p. 548 for other ways to check listwise deletion.

Cross-Case Operations

```
COMPUTE LV1=LAG(V1).
COMPUTE LV2=LAG(V2,3).
```

- *LV1* is the value of *V1* for the previous case.
- *LV2* is the value of *V2* for three cases previous. The first three cases of *LV2* receive the system-missing value.

Logical Functions

```
COMPUTE WORKERS=RANGE(AGE,18,65).
COMPUTE QSAME=ANY(Q1,Q2).
```

- *WORKERS* is 1 for cases where *AGE* is from 18 through 65, 0 for all other valid values of *AGE*, and system-missing for cases with a missing value for *AGE*.
- *QSAME* is 1 whenever *Q1* equals *Q2* and 0 whenever they are different.

Other Functions

```
COMPUTE V1=UNIFORM(10).
COMPUTE V2=NORMAL(1.5).
```

- *V1* is a pseudo-random number from a distribution with values ranging between 0 and the specified value of 10.

- *V2* is a pseudo-random number from a distribution with a mean of 0 and a standard deviation of the specified value of 1.5.

- You can change the seed value of the pseudo-random-number generator with the SEED specification on SET.

Date and Time Aggregation Functions

```
COMPUTE OCTDAY=DATE.YRDAY(1688,301).
COMPUTE QUART=DATE.QYR(QTR,YEAR).
COMPUTE WEEK=DATE.WKYR(WK,YEAR).
```

- *OCTDAY* is the 301st day of the year 1688. With a DATE format, *OCTDAY* displays as 27-OCT-1688.

- *QUART* reads values for the quarter from the variable *QTR* and values for the year from the variable *YEAR*. If *QTR* is 3 and *YEAR* is 88, *QUART* with a QDATE format displays as 3 Q 88.

- *WEEK* takes the value for the week from the variable *WK* and the value for the year from the variable *YEAR*. If *WK* is 48 and *YEAR* is 57, *WEEK* with a DATE format displays as 26-NOV-57.

Date and Time Conversion Functions

```
COMPUTE NMINS=CTIME.MINUTES(TIME.HMS(HR,MIN,SEC)).
COMPUTE AGER=(YRMODA(1992,10,01)-
              YRMODA(YRBIRTH,MOBIRTH,DABIRTH))/365.25.
```

- The CTIME.MINUTES function converts a time interval to number of minutes. If *HR* equals 12, *MIN* equals 30, and *SEC* equals 30, the TIME.HMS function returns an interval of 45,030, which CTIME.MINUTES converts to minutes. *NMINS* equals 750.50.

- The YRMODA function converts the current date (in this example, October 1, 1992) and birthdate to a number of days. The birthdate is subtracted from the current date and the remainder is divided by the number of days in a year to yield the age in years.

Date and Time Extraction Functions

```
COMPUTE MONTHNUM=XDATE.MONTH(BIRTHDAY).
COMPUTE DAYNUM=XDATE.JDAY(BIRTHDAY).
```

- The XDATE.MONTH function reads a date and returns the month number expressed as an integer from 1 to 12. If *BIRTHDAY* is formatted as DATETIME20 and contains the value 05-DEC-1954 5:30:15, *MONTHNUM* equals 12.

- The XDATE.JDAY function returns the day of the year, expressed as an integer between 1 and 366. For the value *BIRTHDAY* used by the first COMPUTE, *DAYNUM* equals 339.

Equivalence

```
STRING DEPT(A20).
COMPUTE DEPT='Personnel Department'.
COMPUTE OLDVAR=NEWVAL.
```

- *DEPT* is a new string variable and must be specified on STRING before it can be specified on COMPUTE. STRING assigns *DEPT* a width of 20 characters, and COMPUTE assigns the value *Personnel Department* to *DEPT* for each case.
- *OLDVAR* must already exist; otherwise, it would have to be declared on STRING. The values of *OLDVAR* are modified to equal the values of *NEWVAL*. *NEWVAL* must be an existing string variable. If the dictionary width of *NEWVAL* is longer than the dictionary width of *OLDVAR*, the modified values of *OLDVAR* are truncated.

String Functions

```
STRING NEWSTR(A7) / DATE(A8) / #MO #DA #YR (A2).
COMPUTE NEWSTR=LAG(OLDSTR,2).

COMPUTE #MO=STRING(MONTH,F2.0).
COMPUTE #DA=STRING(DAY,F2.0).
COMPUTE #YR=STRING(YEAR,F2.0).
COMPUTE DATE=CONCAT(#MO,'/',#DA,'/',#YR).

COMPUTE LNAME=UPCASE(LNAME).
```

- STRING declares *NEWSTR* as a new string variable with a width of seven characters, *DATE* with a width of eight characters, and scratch variables *#MO, #DA, and #YR* with a width of two characters each.
- The first COMPUTE sets *NEWSTR* equal to the value of *OLDSTR* for two cases previous. The first two cases receive the system-missing value for *NEWSTR*.
- The next three COMPUTE commands convert the existing numeric variables *MONTH*, *DAY*, and *YEAR* to the temporary string variables *#MO, #DA, and #YR* so that they can be used with the CONCAT function. The next COMPUTE assigns the concatenated value of *#MO, #DA, and #YR*, separated by slashes, to *DATE*. If *#MO* is 10, *#DA* is 16, and *#YR* is 49, *DATE* is 10/16/49.
- The final COMPUTE converts lowercase letters for the existing string variable *LNAME* to uppercase letters.

CORRELATIONS

```
CORRELATIONS [VARIABLES=] varlist [WITH varlist] [/varlist...]

[/MISSING={PAIRWISE**}   [{INCLUDE}]]
          {LISTWISE }    {EXCLUDE}

[/PRINT={TWOTAIL**}  {SIG**}]
        {ONETAIL  }  {NOSIG}

[/MATRIX=OUT({*   })]
            {file}

[/STATISTICS=[DESCRIPTIVES] [XPROD] [ALL]]
```

**Default if the subcommand is omitted.

Example

```
CORRELATIONS VARIABLES=FOOD RENT PUBTRANS TEACHER COOK ENGINEER
  /MISSING=INCLUDE.
```

Overview

CORRELATIONS (alias PEARSON CORR) produces Pearson product-moment correlations with significance levels and, optionally, univariate statistics, covariances, and cross-product deviations. Other procedures that produce correlation matrices are PARTIAL CORR, REGRESSION, DISCRIMINANT, and FACTOR.

Options

Types of Matrices. A simple variable list on the VARIABLES subcommand produces a square matrix. You can also request a rectangular matrix of correlations between specific pairs of variables or between variable lists using the keyword WITH on VARIABLES.

Significance Levels. By default, CORRELATIONS displays the number of cases and significance levels for each coefficient. Significance levels are based on a two-tailed test. You can request a one-tailed test, and you can display the significance level for each coefficient as an annotation using the PRINT subcommand.

Additional Statistics. You can obtain the mean, standard deviation, and number of nonmissing cases for each variable, and the cross-product deviations and covariance for each pair of variables using the STATISTICS subcommand.

Matrix Output. You can write matrix materials to a data file using the MATRIX subcommand. The matrix materials include the mean, standard deviation, number of cases used to compute each coefficient, and Pearson correlation coefficient for each variable. The matrix data file can be read by several other procedures.

Basic Specification

- The basic specification is the VARIABLES subcommand, which specifies the variables to be analyzed. The actual keyword VARIABLES can be omitted.
- By default, CORRELATIONS produces a matrix of correlation coefficients. The number of cases and the significance level are displayed for each coefficient. The significance level is based on a two-tailed test.

Subcommand Order

- The VARIABLES subcommand must be first.
- The remaining subcommands can be specified in any order.

Operations

- The correlation of a variable with itself is displayed as 1.0000.
- A correlation that cannot be computed is displayed as a period (.).
- CORRELATIONS does not execute if long or short string variables are specified on the variable list.

Limitations

- Maximum 40 variable lists.
- Maximum 500 variables total per command.
- Maximum 250 syntax elements. Each individual occurrence of a variable name, keyword, or special delimiter counts as 1 toward this total. Variables implied by the TO keyword do not count toward this total.

Example

```
CORRELATIONS VARIABLES=FOOD RENT PUBTRANS TEACHER COOK ENGINEER
 /VARIABLES=FOOD RENT WITH COOK TEACHER MANAGER ENGINEER
 /MISSING=INCLUDE.
```

- The first VARIABLES subcommand requests a square matrix of correlation coefficients among variables *FOOD*, *RENT*, *PUBTRANS*, *TEACHER*, *COOK*, and *ENGINEER*.
- The second VARIABLES subcommand requests a rectangular correlation matrix in which *FOOD* and *RENT* are the row variables and *COOK*, *TEACHER*, *MANAGER*, and *ENGINEER* are the column variables.
- MISSING requests that user-missing values be included in the computation of each coefficient.

VARIABLES Subcommand

VARIABLES specifies the variable list. The actual keyword VARIABLES is optional.

- A simple variable list produces a square matrix of correlations of each variable with every other variable.
- Variable lists joined by the keyword WITH produce a rectangular correlation matrix. Variables before WITH define the rows of the matrix and variables after WITH define the columns.
- The keyword ALL can be used on the variable list to refer to all user-defined variables.
- You can specify multiple VARIABLES subcommands on a single CORRELATIONS command. The slash between the subcommands is required; the keyword VARIABLES is not.

PRINT Subcommand

PRINT controls whether the significance level is based on a one- or two-tailed test and whether the number of cases and the significance level for each correlation coefficient are displayed.

TWOTAIL   *Two-tailed test of significance.* This test is appropriate when the direction of the relationship cannot be determined in advance, as is often the case in exploratory data analysis. This is the default.

ONETAIL   *One-tailed test of significance.* This test is appropriate when the direction of the relationship between a pair of variables can be specified in advance of the analysis.

SIG   *Do not flag significant values.* SIG is the default.

NOSIG   *Flag significant values.* Values significant at the 0.05 level are flagged with a single asterisk; those that are significant at the 0.01 level are flagged with two asterisks.

STATISTICS Subcommand

The correlation coefficients are automatically displayed in the Correlations table for an analysis specified by a VARIABLES list. STATISTICS requests additional statistics.

DESCRIPTIVES   *Display mean, standard deviation, and number of nonmissing cases for each variable on the Variables list in the Descriptive Statistics table.* This table precedes all Correlations tables. Variables specified on more than one VARIABLES lists are displayed only once. Missing values are handled on a variable-by-variable basis regardless of the missing-value option in effect for the correlations.

XPROD   *Display cross-product deviations and covariance for each pair of variables in the Correlations table(s).*

ALL   *All additional statistics.* This produces the same statistics as DESCRIPTIVES and XPROD together.

MISSING Subcommand

MISSING controls the treatment of missing values.

- The PAIRWISE and LISTWISE keywords are alternatives; however, each can be specified with INCLUDE or EXCLUDE.
- The default is LISTWISE and EXCLUDE.

PAIRWISE   *Exclude missing values pairwise.* Cases that have missing values for one or both of a pair of variables for a specific correlation coefficient are excluded from the computation of that coefficient. Since each coefficient is based on all cases that have valid values for that particular pair of variables, this can result in a set of coefficients based on a varying number of cases. The valid number of cases is displayed in the Correlations table. This is the default.

LISTWISE   *Exclude missing values listwise.* Cases that have missing values for any variable named on any VARIABLES list are excluded from the computation of all coefficients across lists. The valid number of cases is the same for all analyses and is displayed in a single annotation.

INCLUDE   *Include user-missing values.* User-missing values are included in the analysis.

EXCLUDE   *Exclude all missing values.* Both user- and system-missing values are excluded from the analysis.

MATRIX Subcommand

MATRIX writes matrix materials to a data file. The matrix materials include the mean and standard deviation for each variable, the number of cases used to compute each coefficient, and the Pearson correlation coefficients. Several procedures can read matrix materials produced by CORRELATIONS, including PARTIAL CORR, REGRESSION, FACTOR, and CLUSTER (see "SPSS Matrix Data Files" on p. 23).

- CORRELATIONS cannot write rectangular matrices (those specified with the keyword WITH) to a file.
- If you specify more than one variable list on CORRELATIONS, only the last list that does not use the keyword WITH is written to the matrix data file.
- The keyword OUT specifies the file to which the matrix is written. The filename must be specified in parentheses.
- Documents from the original file will not be included in the matrix file and will not be present if the matrix file becomes the working data file.

OUT (filename)   *Write a matrix data file.* Specify either a file or an asterisk (*), enclosed in parentheses. If you specify a file, the file is stored on disk and can be retrieved at any time. If you specify an asterisk, the matrix data file replaces the working file but is not stored on disk unless you use SAVE or XSAVE.

Format of the Matrix Data File

- The matrix data file has two special variables created by the program: *ROWTYPE_* and *VARNAME_*. The variable *ROWTYPE_* is a short string variable with values *MEAN*, *STDDEV*, *N*, and *CORR* (for Pearson correlation coefficient). The next variable, *VARNAME_*, is a short string variable whose values are the names of the variables used to form the correlation matrix. When *ROWTYPE_* is *CORR*, *VARNAME_* gives the variable associated with that row of the correlation matrix.
- The remaining variables in the file are the variables used to form the correlation matrix.

Split Files

- When split-file processing is in effect, the first variables in the matrix file will be split variables, followed by *ROWTYPE_*, *VARNAME_*, and the variables used to form the correlation matrix.
- A full set of matrix materials is written for each subgroup defined by the split variables.
- A split variable cannot have the same name as any other variable written to the matrix data file.
- If split-file processing is in effect when a matrix is written, the same split-file specifications must be in effect when that matrix is read by another procedure.

Missing Values

- With pairwise treatment of missing values (the default), a matrix of the number of cases used to compute each coefficient is included with the matrix materials.
- With listwise treatment, a single number indicating the number of cases used to calculate all coefficients is included.

Example

```
GET FILE=CITY /KEEP FOOD RENT PUBTRANS TEACHER COOK ENGINEER.
CORRELATIONS VARIABLES=FOOD TO ENGINEER
 /MATRIX OUT(CORRMAT).
```

- CORRELATIONS reads data from the file *CITY* and writes one set of matrix materials to the file *CORRMAT*. The working file is still *CITY*. Subsequent commands are executed on *CITY*.

Example

```
GET FILE=CITY /KEEP FOOD RENT PUBTRANS TEACHER COOK ENGINEER.
CORRELATIONS VARIABLES=FOOD TO ENGINEER
 /MATRIX OUT(*).
LIST.
DISPLAY DICTIONARY.
```

- CORRELATIONS writes the same matrix as in the example above. However, the matrix data file replaces the working file. The LIST and DISPLAY commands are executed on the matrix file, not on the *CITY* file.

Example

```
CORRELATIONS VARIABLES=FOOD RENT COOK TEACHER MANAGER ENGINEER
 /FOOD TO TEACHER /PUBTRANS WITH MECHANIC
 /MATRIX OUT(*).
```

- Only the matrix for *FOOD* TO *TEACHER* is written to the matrix data file because it is the last variable list that does not use the keyword WITH.

COUNT

```
COUNT varname=varlist(value list) [/varname=...]
```

Keywords for numeric value lists:

LOWEST, LO, HIGHEST, HI, THRU, MISSING, SYSMIS

Example

```
COUNT TARGET=V1 V2 V3 (2).
```

Overview

COUNT creates a numeric variable that, for each case, counts the occurrences of the same value (or list of values) across a list of variables. The new variable is called the *target* variable. The variables and values that are counted are the *criterion* variables and values. Criterion variables can be either numeric or string.

Basic Specification

The basic specification is the target variable, an equals sign, the criterion variable(s), and the criterion value(s) enclosed in parentheses.

Syntax Rules

- Use a slash to separate the specifications for each target variable.
- The criterion variables specified for a single target variable must be either all numeric or all string.
- Each value on a list of criterion values must be separated by a comma or space. String values must be enclosed in apostrophes.
- The keywords THRU, LOWEST (LO), HIGHEST (HI), SYSMIS, and MISSING can be used only with numeric criterion variables.
- A variable can be specified on more than one criterion variable list.
- You can use the keyword TO to specify consecutive criterion variables that have the same criterion value or values.
- You can specify multiple variable lists for a single target variable to count different values for different variables.

Operations

- Target variables are always numeric and are initialized to 0 for each case. They are assigned a dictionary format of F8.2.
- If the target variable already exists, its previous values are replaced.
- COUNT ignores the missing-value status of user-missing values. It counts a value even if that value has been previously declared as missing.
- The target variable is never system-missing. To define user-missing values for target variables, use the RECODE or MISSING VALUES command.
- SYSMIS counts system-missing values for numeric variables.
- MISSING counts both user- and system-missing values for numeric variables.

Example

```
COUNT TARGET=V1 V2 V3 (2).
```

- The value of *TARGET* for each case will be either 0, 1, 2, or 3, depending on the number of times the value 2 occurs across the three variables for each case.
- *TARGET* is a numeric variable with an F8.2 format.

Example

```
COUNT QLOW=Q1 TO Q10 (LO THRU 0)
  /QSYSMIS=Q1 TO Q10 (SYSMIS).
```

- Assuming that there are 10 variables between and including *Q1* and *Q10* in the working data file, *QLOW* ranges from 0 to 10, depending on the number of times a case has a negative or 0 value across the variables *Q1* to *Q10*.
- *QSYSMIS* ranges from 0 to 10, depending on how many system-missing values are encountered for *Q1* to *Q10* for each case. User-missing values are not counted.
- Both *QLOW* and *QSYSMIS* are numeric variables and have F8.2 formats.

Example

```
COUNT SVAR=V1 V2 ('male  ') V3 V4 V5 ('female').
```

- *SVAR* ranges from 0 to 5, depending on the number of times a case has a value of male for *V1* and *V2* and a value of female for *V3*, *V4*, and *V5*.
- *SVAR* is a numeric variable with an F8.2 format.

COXREG

COXREG is available in the Advanced Models option.

```
[TIME PROGRAM]*
[commands to compute time dependent covariates]

[CLEAR TIME PROGRAM]

COXREG [VARIABLES =] survival varname [WITH varlist]
    / STATUS = varname [EVENT] (vallist) [LOST (vallist)]
    [/STRATA  = varname]
    [/CATEGORICAL = varname]
    [/CONTRAST (varname) = {DEVIATION (refcat)}]
                          {SIMPLE (refcat)    }
                          {DIFFERENCE         }
                          {HELMERT            }
                          {REPEATED           }
                          {POLYNOMIAL(metric) }
                          {SPECIAL (matrix)   }
                          {INDICATOR (refcat) }

    [/METHOD = {ENTER**      }   [{varlist}]]
               {BSTEP [{COND}]}  {ALL      }
                      {LR  }
                      {WALD}
               {FSTEP [{COND}]}
                      {LR  }
                      {WALD}

    [/MISSING = {EXCLUDE**}]
                {INCLUDE  }

    [/PRINT = [{DEFAULT**}]  [CI ({95})]]]
               {SUMMARY  }       {n }
               {BASELINE }
               {CORR     }
               {ALL      }

    [/CRITERIA = [{BCON}({1E-4**})]]  [LCON({1E-5**})]
                  {PCON} { n     }          { n     }
                 [ITERATE({20**})]
                         { n  }
                 [PIN({0.05**})]]      [POUT({0.1**})]]]
                     { n   }                { n  }

    [/PLOT = [NONE**] [SURVIVAL] [HAZARD] [LML] [OMS]]
    [/PATTERN = [varname(value)...] [BY varname]]
    [/OUTFILE = [COEFF(file)] [TABLE(file)]]
    [/SAVE = tempvar [(newvarname)],tempvar ...]
    [/EXTERNAL]
```

* **TIME PROGRAM** is required to generate time-dependent covariates.

**Default if subcommand or keyword is omitted.

Temporary variables created by COXREG are:

SURVIVAL
SE
HAZARD
RESID
LML
DFBETA

PRESID
XBETA

Example

```
TIME PROGRAM.
COMPUTE Z=AGE + T_.

COXREG SURVIVAL WITH Z
  /STATUS SURVSTA EVENT(1).
```

Overview

COXREG applies Cox proportional hazards regression to analysis of survival times—that is, the length of time before the occurrence of an event. COXREG supports continuous and categorical independent variables (covariates), which can be time-dependent. Unlike SURVIVAL and KM, which compare only distinct subgroups of cases, COXREG provides an easy way of considering differences in subgroups as well as analyzing effects of a set of covariates.

Options

Processing of Independent Variables. You can specify which of the independent variables are categorical with the CATEGORICAL subcommand and control treatment of these variables with the CONTRAST subcommand. You can select one of seven methods for entering independent variables into the model using the METHOD subcommand. You can also indicate interaction terms using the keyword BY between variable names on either the VARIABLES subcommand or the METHOD subcommand.

Specifying Termination and Model-Building Criteria. You can specify the criteria for termination of iteration and control variable entry and removal with the CRITERIA subcommand.

Adding New Variables to Working Data File. You can use the SAVE subcommand to save the cumulative survival, standard error, cumulative hazard, log-minus-log-of-survival function, residuals, XBeta, and, wherever available, partial residuals and DfBeta.

Output. You can print optional output using the PRINT subcommand, suppress or request plots with the PLOT subcommand, and, with the OUTFILE subcommand, write SPSS data files containing coefficients from the final model or a survival table. When only time-constant covariates are used, you can use the PATTERN subcommand to specify a pattern of covariate values in addition to the covariate means to use for the plots and the survival table.

Basic Specification

- The minimum specification on COXREG is a dependent variable with the STATUS subcommand.
- To analyze the influence of time-constant covariates on the survival times, the minimum specification requires either the WITH keyword followed by at least one covariate (independent variable) on the VARIABLES subcommand or a METHOD subcommand with at least one independent variable.

- To analyze the influence of time-dependent covariates on the survival times, the TIME PROGRAM command and transformation language are required to define the functions for the time-dependent covariate(s).

Subcommand Order

- The VARIABLES subcommand must be specified first; the subcommand keyword is optional.
- Remaining subcommands can be named in any order.

Syntax Rules

- Only one dependent variable can be specified for each COXREG command.
- Any number of covariates (independent variables) can be specified. The dependent variable cannot appear on the covariate list.
- The covariate list is required if any of the METHOD subcommands are used without a variable list or if the METHOD subcommand is not used.
- Only one status variable can be specified on the STATUS subcommand. If multiple STATUS subcommands are specified, only the last specification is in effect.
- You can use the BY keyword to specify interaction between covariates.

Operations

- TIME PROGRAM computes the values for time-dependent covariates.
- COXREG replaces covariates specified on CATEGORICAL with sets of contrast variables. In stepwise analyses, the set of contrast variables associated with one categorical variable is entered or removed from the model as a block.
- Covariates are screened to detect and eliminate redundancies.
- COXREG deletes all cases that have negative values for the dependent variable.

Limitations

- Only one dependent variable is allowed.
- Maximum 100 covariates in a single interaction term.
- Maximum 35 levels for a BY variable on PATTERN.

Example

```
TIME PROGRAM.
COMPUTE Z=AGE + T_.

COXREG SURVIVAL WITH Z
  /STATUS SURVSTA EVENT (1).
```

- TIME PROGRAM defines the time-dependent covariate *Z* as the current age. *Z* is then specified as a covariate.
- The dependent variable *SURVIVAL* contains the length of time to the terminal event or to censoring.
- A value of 1 on the variable *SURVSTA* indicates an event.

TIME PROGRAM Command

TIME PROGRAM is required to define time-dependent covariates. These are covariates whose values change during the course of the study.

- TIME PROGRAM and the transformations that define the time-dependent covariate(s) must precede the COXREG command.
- A time-dependent covariate is a function of the current time, which is represented by the special variable *T_*.
- The working data file must not have a variable named *T_*. If it does, rename the variable before you run the COXREG command. Otherwise, you will trigger an error.
- *T_* cannot be specified as a covariate. Any other variable in the TIME PROGRAM can be specified on the covariate list.
- For every time-dependent covariate, values are generated for each valid case for all uncensored times in the same stratum that occur before the observed time. If no STRATA subcommand is specified, all cases are considered to belong to one stratum.
- If any function defined by the time program results in a missing value for a case that has no missing values for any other variable used in the procedure, COXREG terminates with an error.

CLEAR TIME PROGRAM Command

CLEAR TIME PROGRAM deletes all time-dependent covariates created in the previous time program. It is primarily used in interactive mode to remove temporary variables associated with the time program so that you can redefine time-dependent covariates for the Cox Regression procedure. It is not necessary to use this command if you have already executed COXREG. All temporary variables created by the time program are automatically deleted.

VARIABLES Subcommand

VARIABLES identifies the dependent variable and the covariates to be included in the analysis.

- The minimum specification is the dependent variable. The subcommand keyword is optional.
- You must specify the keyword WITH and a list of all covariates if no METHOD subcommand is specified or if a METHOD subcommand is specified without naming the variables to be used.
- If the covariate list is not specified on VARIABLES but one or more METHOD subcommands are used, the covariate list is assumed to be the union of the sets of variables listed on all the METHOD subcommands.

- You can specify an interaction of two or more covariates using the keyword BY. For example, A B BY C D specifies the three terms *A*, *B*C*, and *D*.
- The keyword TO can be used to specify a list of covariates. The implied variable order is the same as in the working data file.

STATUS Subcommand

To determine whether the event has occurred for a particular observation, COXREG checks the value of a status variable. STATUS lists the status variable and the code for the occurrence of the event.

- Only one status variable can be specified. If multiple STATUS subcommands are specified, COXREG uses the last specification and displays a warning.
- The keyword EVENT is optional, but the value list in parentheses must be specified.
- The value list must be enclosed in parentheses. All cases with non-negative times that do not have a code within the range specified after EVENT are classified as **censored cases**— that is, cases for which the event has not yet occurred.
- The value list can be one value, a list of values separated by blanks or commas, a range of values using the keyword THRU, or a combination.
- If missing values occur within the specified ranges, they are ignored if MISSING=EXCLUDE (the default) is specified, but they are treated as valid values for the range if MISSING=INCLUDE is specified.
- The status variable can be either numeric or string. If a string variable is specified, the EVENT values must be enclosed in apostrophes and the keyword THRU cannot be used.

Example

```
COXREG SURVIVAL WITH GROUP
  /STATUS SURVSTA (3 THRU 5, 8 THRU 10).
```

- STATUS specifies that *SURVSTA* is the status variable.
- A value between either 3 and 5, or 8 and 10, inclusive, means that the terminal event occurred.
- Values outside the specified ranges indicate censored cases.

STRATA Subcommand

STRATA identifies a stratification variable. A different baseline survival function is computed for each stratum.

- The only specification is the subcommand keyword with one, and only one, variable name.
- If you have more than one stratification variable, create a new variable that corresponds to the combination of categories of the individual variables before invoking the COXREG command.
- There is no limit to the number of levels for the strata variable.

Example

```
COXREG SURVIVAL WITH GROUP
 /STATUS SURVSTA (1)
 /STRATA=LOCATION.
```

- STRATA specifies *LOCATION* as the strata variable.
- Different baseline survival functions are computed for each value of *LOCATION*.

CATEGORICAL Subcommand

CATEGORICAL identifies covariates that are nominal or ordinal. Variables that are declared to be categorical are automatically transformed to a set of contrast variables (see "CONTRAST Subcommand" below). If a variable coded as 0 – 1 is declared as categorical, by default, its coding scheme will be changed to deviation contrasts.

- Covariates not specified on CATEGORICAL are assumed to be at least interval, except for strings.
- Variables specified on CATEGORICAL but not on VARIABLES or any METHOD subcommand are ignored.
- Variables specified on CATEGORICAL are replaced by sets of contrast variables. If the categorical variable has n distinct values, there will be $n - 1$ contrast variables generated. The set of contrast variables associated with one categorical variable are entered or removed from the model together.
- If any one of the variables in an interaction term is specified on CATEGORICAL, the interaction term is replaced by contrast variables.
- All string variables are categorical. Only the first eight characters of each value of a string variable are used in distinguishing among values. Thus, if two values of a string variable are identical for the first eight characters, the values are treated as though they were the same.

CONTRAST Subcommand

CONTRAST specifies the type of contrast used for categorical covariates. The interpretation of the regression coefficients for categorical covariates depends on the contrasts used. The default is DEVIATION. For illustration of contrast types, see the appendix.

- The categorical covariate is specified in parentheses following CONTRAST.
- If the categorical variable has n values, there will be $n - 1$ rows in the contrast matrix. Each contrast matrix is treated as a set of independent variables in the analysis.
- Only one variable can be specified per CONTRAST subcommand, but multiple CONTRAST subcommands can be specified.
- You can specify one of the contrast keywords in the parentheses after the variable specification to request a specific contrast type.

The following contrast types are available:

DEVIATION(refcat)   *Deviations from the overall effect.* This is the default. The effect for each category of the independent variable except one is compared to the overall effect. Refcat is the category for which parameter estimates are not displayed (they must be calculated from the others). By default, refcat is the last category. To omit a category other than the last, specify the sequence number of the omitted category (which is not necessarily the same as its value) in parentheses after the keyword DEVIATION.

SIMPLE(refcat) *Each category of the independent variable except the last is compared to the last category.* To use a category other than the last as the omitted reference category, specify its sequence number (which is not necessarily the same as its value) in parentheses following the keyword SIMPLE.

DIFFERENCE *Difference or reverse Helmert contrasts.* The effects for each category of the covariate except the first are compared to the mean effect of the previous categories.

HELMERT *Helmert contrasts.* The effects for each category of the independent variable except the last are compared to the mean effects of subsequent categories.

POLYNOMIAL(metric) *Polynomial contrasts.* The first degree of freedom contains the linear effect across the categories of the independent variable, the second contains the quadratic effect, and so on. By default, the categories are assumed to be equally spaced; unequal spacing can be specified by entering a metric consisting of one integer for each category of the independent variable in parentheses after the keyword POLYNOMIAL. For example, CONTRAST (STIMULUS) = POLYNOMIAL(1,2,4) indicates that the three levels of *STIMULUS* are actually in the proportion 1:2:4. The default metric is always $(1,2,...,k)$, where k categories are involved. Only the relative differences between the terms of the metric matter: (1,2,4) is the same metric as (2,3,5) or (20,30,50) because, in each instance, the difference between the second and third numbers is twice the difference between the first and second.

REPEATED *Comparison of adjacent categories.* Each category of the independent variable except the first is compared to the previous category.

SPECIAL(matrix) *A user-defined contrast.* After this keyword, a matrix is entered in parentheses with $k - 1$ rows and k columns, where k is the number of categories of the independent variable. The rows of the contrast matrix contain the special contrasts indicating the desired comparisons between categories. If the special contrasts are linear combinations of each other, COXREG reports the linear dependency and stops processing. If k rows are entered, the first row is discarded and only the last $k - 1$ rows are used as the contrast matrix in the analysis.

INDICATOR(refcat) *Indicator variables.* Contrasts indicate the presence or absence of category membership. By default, refcat is the last category (represented in the contrast matrix as a row of zeros). To omit a category other than the last, specify the sequence number of the category (which is not necessarily the same as its value) in parentheses after keyword INDICATOR.

Example

```
COXREG SURVIVAL WITH GROUP
 /STATUS SURVSTA (1)
 /STRATA=LOCATION
 /CATEGORICAL = GROUP
 /CONTRAST(GROUP)=SPECIAL(2 -1 -1
                         0  1 -1).
```

- The specification of *GROUP* on CATEGORICAL replaces the variable with a set of contrast variables.
- *GROUP* identifies whether a case is in one of the three treatment groups.
- A SPECIAL type contrast is requested. A three-column, two-row contrast matrix is entered in parentheses.

METHOD Subcommand

METHOD specifies the order of processing and the manner in which the covariates enter the model. If no METHOD subcommand is specified, the default method is ENTER.

- The subcommand keyword METHOD can be omitted.
- You can list all covariates to be used for the method on a variable list. If no variable list is specified, the default is ALL: all covariates named after WITH on the VARIABLES subcommand are used for the method.
- The keyword BY can be used between two variable names to specify an interaction term.
- Variables specified on CATEGORICAL are replaced by sets of contrast variables. The contrast variables associated with a categorical variable are entered or removed from the model together.

Three keywords are available to specify how the model is to be built:

ENTER   *Forced entry.* All variables are entered in a single step. This is the default if the METHOD subcommand is omitted.

FSTEP   *Forward stepwise.* The covariates specified on FSTEP are tested for entry into the model one by one based on the significance level of the score statistic. The variable with the smallest significance less than PIN is entered into the model. After each entry, variables that are already in the model are tested for possible removal based on the significance of the Wald statistic, likelihood ratio, or conditional criterion. The variable with the largest probability greater than the specified POUT value is removed and the model is reestimated. Variables in the model are then again evaluated for removal. Once no more variables satisfy the removal criteria, covariates not in the model are evaluated for entry. Model building stops when no more variables meet entry or removal criteria, or when the current model is the same as a previous one.

BSTEP   *Backward stepwise.* As a first step, the covariates specified on BSTEP are entered into the model together and are tested for removal one by one. Stepwise removal and entry then follow the same process as described for FSTEP until no more variables meet entry and removal criteria, or when the current model is the same as a previous one.

- Multiple METHOD subcommands are allowed and are processed in the order in which they are specified. Each method starts with the results from the previous method. If BSTEP is used, all eligible variables are entered at the first step. All variables are then eligible for entry and removal unless they have been excluded from the METHOD variable list.

The statistic used in the test for removal can be specified by an additional keyword in parentheses following FSTEP or BSTEP. If FSTEP or BSTEP is specified by itself, the default is COND.

COND   *Conditional statistic.* This is the default if FSTEP or BSTEP is specified by itself.

WALD   *Wald statistic.* The removal of a covariate from the model is based on the significance of the Wald statistic.

LR   *Likelihood ratio.* The removal of a covariate from the model is based on the significance of the change in the log-likelihood. If LR is specified, the model must be reestimated without each of the variables in the model. This can substantially increase computational time. However, the likelihood-ratio statistic is better than the Wald statistic for deciding which variables are to be removed.

Example

```
COXREG SURVIVAL WITH GROUP SMOKE DRINK
 /STATUS SURVSTA (1)
 /CATEGORICAL = GROUP SMOKE DRINK
 /METHOD ENTER GROUP
 /METHOD BSTEP (LR) SMOKE DRINK SMOKE BY DRINK.
```

- *GROUP*, *SMOKE*, and *DRINK* are specified as covariates and as categorical variables.
- The first METHOD subcommand enters GROUP into the model.
- Variables in the model at the termination of the first METHOD subcommand are included in the model at the beginning of the second METHOD subcommand.
- The second METHOD subcommand adds *SMOKE*, *DRINK*, and the interaction of *SMOKE* with *DRINK* to the previous model.
- Backward stepwise regression analysis is then done using the likelihood-ratio statistic as the removal criterion. The variable *GROUP* is not eligible for removal because it was not specified on the BSTEP subcommand.
- The procedure continues until the removal of a variable will result in a decrease in the log-likelihood with a probability smaller than POUT.

MISSING Subcommand

MISSING controls missing value treatments. If MISSING is omitted, the default is EXCLUDE.

- Cases with negative values on the dependent variable are automatically treated as missing and are excluded.
- To be included in the model, a case must have nonmissing values for the dependent, status, strata, and all independent variables specified on the COXREG command.

EXCLUDE   *Exclude user-missing values.* User-missing values are treated as missing. This is the default if MISSING is omitted.

INCLUDE   *Include user-missing values.* User-missing values are included in the analysis.

PRINT Subcommand

By default, COXREG prints a full regression report for each step. You can use the PRINT subcommand to request specific output. If PRINT is not specified, the default is DEFAULT.

DEFAULT   *Full regression output including overall model statistics and statistics for variables in the equation and variables not in the equation.* This is the default when PRINT is omitted.

SUMMARY   *Summary information.* The output includes –2 log-likelihood for the initial model, one line of summary for each step, and the final model printed with full detail.

CORR   *Correlation/covariance matrix of parameter estimates for the variables in the model.*

BASELINE   *Baseline table.* For each stratum, a table is displayed showing the baseline cumulative hazard, as well as survival, standard error, and cumulative hazard evaluated at the covariate means for each observed time point in that stratum.

CI (value)   *Confidence intervals for e^{β}.* Specify the confidence level in parentheses. The requested intervals are displayed whenever a variables-in-equation table is printed. The default is 95%.

ALL   *All available output.*

- Estimation histories showing the last 10 iterations are printed if the solution fails to converge.

Example

```
COXREG SURVIVAL WITH GROUP
 /STATUS = SURVSTA (1)
 /STRATA = LOCATION
 /CATEGORICAL = GROUP
 /METHOD = ENTER
 /PRINT ALL.
```

- PRINT requests summary information, a correlation matrix for parameter estimates, a baseline survival table for each stratum, and confidence intervals for e^{β} with each variables-in-equation table, in addition to the default output.

CRITERIA Subcommand

CRITERIA controls the statistical criteria used in building the Cox Regression models. The way in which these criteria are used depends on the method specified on the METHOD subcommand. The default criteria are noted in the description of each keyword below. Iterations will stop if any of the criteria for BCON, LCON, or ITERATE are satisfied.

BCON(value) *Change in parameter estimates for terminating iteration.* Alias PCON. Iteration terminates when the parameters change by less than the specified value. BCON defaults to $1E - 4$. To eliminate this criteria, specify a value of 0.

ITERATE(value) *Maximum number of iterations.* If a solution fails to converge after the maximum number of iterations has been reached, COXREG displays an iteration history showing the last 10 iterations and terminates the procedure. The default for ITERATE is 20.

LCON(value) *Percentage change in the log-likelihood ratio for terminating iteration.* If the log-likelihood decreases by less than the specified value, iteration terminates. LCON defaults to $1E-5$. To eliminate this criterion, specify a value of 0.

PIN(value) *Probability of score statistic for variable entry.* A variable whose significance level is greater than PIN cannot enter the model. The default for PIN is 0.05.

POUT(value) *Probability of Wald, LR, or conditional LR statistic to remove a variable.* A variable whose significance is less than POUT cannot be removed. The default for POUT is 0.1.

Example

```
COXREG SURVIVAL WITH GROUP AGE BP TMRSZ
 /STATUS = SURVSTA (1)
 /STRATA = LOCATION
 /CATEGORICAL = GROUP
 /METHOD BSTEP
 /CRITERIA BCON(0) ITERATE(10) PIN(0.01) POUT(0.05).
```

- A backward stepwise Cox Regression analysis is performed.
- CRITERIA alters four of the default statistical criteria that control the building of a model.
- Zero specified on BCON indicates that change in parameter estimates is not a criterion for termination. BCON can be set to 0 if only LCON and ITER are to be used.
- ITERATE specifies that the maximum number of iterations is 10. LCON is not changed and the default remains in effect. If either ITERATE or LCON is met, iterations will terminate.
- POUT requires that the probability of the statistic used to test whether a variable should remain in the model be smaller than 0.05. This is more stringent than the default value of 0.1.
- PIN requires that the probability of the score statistic used to test whether a variable should be included be smaller than 0.01. This makes it more difficult for variables to be included in the model than does the default PIN, which has a value of 0.05.

PLOT Subcommand

You can request specific plots to be produced with the PLOT subcommand. Each requested plot is produced once for each pattern specified on the PATTERN subcommand. If PLOT is not specified, the default is NONE (no plots are printed). Requested plots are displayed at the end of the final model.

- The set of plots requested is displayed for the functions at the mean of the covariates and at each combination of covariate values specified on PATTERN.
- If time-dependent covariates are included in the model, no plots are produced.
- Lines on a plot are connected as step functions.

NONE   *Do not display plots.*

SURVIVAL   *Plot the cumulative survival distribution.*

HAZARD   *Plot the cumulative hazard function.*

LML   *Plot the log-minus-log-of-survival function.*

OMS   *Plot the one-minus-survival function.*

PATTERN Subcommand

PATTERN specifies the pattern of covariate values to be used for the requested plots and coefficient tables.

- A value must be specified for each variable specified on PATTERN.
- Continuous variables that are included in the model but not named on PATTERN are evaluated at their means.
- Categorical variables that are included in the model but not named on PATTERN are evaluated at the means of the set of contrasts generated to replace them.
- You can request separate lines for each category of a variable that is in the model. Specify the name of the categorical variable after the keyword BY. The BY variable must be a categorical covariate. You cannot specify a value for the BY covariate.
- Multiple PATTERN subcommands can be specified. COXREG produces a set of requested plots for each specified pattern.
- PATTERN cannot be used when time-dependent covariates are included in the model.

OUTFILE Subcommand

OUTFILE writes an external SPSS data file. COXREG writes two types of data files. You can specify the file type to be created with one of the two keywords, followed by the file specification in parentheses.

COEFF   *Write an SPSS data file containing the coefficients from the final model.*

TABLE   *Write the survival table to an SPSS data file.* The file contains cumulative survival, standard error, and cumulative hazard statistics for each uncensored time within each stratum evaluated at the baseline and at the mean of the covariates. Additional covariate patterns can be requested on PATTERN.

- The specified SPSS data file must be an external file. You cannot specify an asterisk (*) to identify the working data file.
- The variables saved in the external file are listed in the output.

SAVE Subcommand

SAVE saves the temporary variables created by COXREG. The temporary variables include:

SURVIVAL   *Survival function evaluated at the current case.*

SE	*Standard error of the survival function.*
HAZARD	*Cumulative hazard function evaluated at the current case.* Alias RESID.
LML	*Log-minus-log-of-survival function.*
DFBETA	*Change in the coefficient if the current case is removed.* There is one *DFBETA* for each covariate in the final model. If there are time-dependent covariates, only *DFBETA* can be requested. Requests for any other temporary variable are ignored.
PRESID	*Partial residuals.* There is one residual variable for each covariate in the final model. If a covariate is not in the final model, the corresponding new variable has the system-missing value.
XBETA	*Linear combination of mean corrected covariates times regression coefficients from the final model.*

- To specify variable names for the new variables, assign the new names in parentheses following each temporary variable name.
- Assigned variable names must be unique in the working data file. Scratch or system variable names cannot be used (that is, the variable names cannot begin with # or $).
- If new variable names are not specified, COXREG generates default names. The default name is composed of the first three characters of the name of the temporary variable (two for *SE*), followed by an underscore and a number to make it unique.
- A temporary variable can be saved only once on the same SAVE subcommand.

Example

```
COXREG SURVIVAL WITH GROUP
 /STATUS = SURVSTA (1)
 /STRATA = LOCATION
 /CATEGORICAL = GROUP
 /METHOD = ENTER
 /SAVE SURVIVAL HAZARD.
```

- COXREG saves cumulative survival and hazard in two new variables, *SUR_1* and *HAZ_1*, provided that neither of the two names exists in the working data file. If one does, the numeric suffixes will be incremented to make a distinction.

EXTERNAL Subcommand

EXTERNAL specifies that the data for each split-file group should be held in an external scratch file during processing. This helps conserve working space when running analyses with large data sets.

- The EXTERNAL subcommand takes no other keyword and is specified by itself.
- If time-dependent covariates exist, external data storage is unavailable, and EXTERNAL is ignored.

CREATE

```
CREATE new series={CSUM (series)                         }
                  {DIFF (series, order)                   }
                  {FFT (series)                           }
                  {IFFT (series)                          }
                  {LAG (series, order [,order ])          }
                  {LEAD (series, order [,order ])         }
                  {MA (series, span [,minimum span])      }
                  {PMA (series, span)                     }
                  {RMED (series, span [,minimum span])    }
                  {SDIFF (series, order [,periodicity])}  }
                  {T4253H (series)                        }

[/new series=function (series {,span  {,minimum span}})]
                              {,order {,order         }}
                                      {,periodicity   }
```

Function keywords:

CSUM	Cumulative sum
DIFF	Difference
FFT	Fast Fourier transform
IFFT	Inverse fast Fourier transform
LAG	Lag
LEAD	Lead
MA	Centered moving averages
PMA	Prior moving averages
RMED	Running medians
SDIFF	Seasonal difference
T4253H	Smoothing

Example

```
CREATE NEWVAR1 NEWVAR2 = CSUM(TICKETS RNDTRP).
```

Overview

CREATE produces new series as a function of existing series. You can also use CREATE to replace the values of existing series. The new or revised series can be used in any procedure and can be saved in an SPSS-format data file.

CREATE displays a list of the new series, the case numbers of the first and last nonmissing cases, the number of valid cases, and the functions used to create the variables.

Basic Specification

The basic specification is a new series name, an equals sign, a function, and the existing series, along with any additional specifications needed.

Syntax Rules

- The existing series together with any additional specifications (order, span, or periodicity) must be enclosed in parentheses.
- The equals sign is required.
- Series names and additional specifications must be separated by commas or spaces.
- You can specify only one function per equation.
- You can create more than one new series per equation by specifying more than one new series name on the left side of the equation and either multiple existing series names or multiple orders on the right.
- The number of new series named on the left side of the equation must equal the number of series created on the right. Note that the FFT function creates two new series for each existing series, and IFFT creates one series from two existing series.
- You can specify more than one equation on a CREATE command. Equations are separated by slashes.
- A newly created series can be specified in subsequent equations on the same CREATE command.

Operations

- Each new series created is added to the working data file.
- If the new series named already exist, their values are replaced.
- If the new series named do not already exist, they are created.
- Series are created in the order in which they are specified on the CREATE command.
- If multiple series are created by a single equation, the first new series named is assigned the values of the first series created, the second series named is assigned the values of the second series created, and so on.
- CREATE automatically generates a variable label for each new series describing the function and series used to create it.
- The format of the new series is based on the function specified and the format of the existing series.
- CREATE honors the TSET MISSING setting that is currently in effect.
- CREATE does not honor the USE command.
- When an even-length span is specified for functions MA and RMED, the centering algorithm uses an average of two spans of the specified length. The first span ranges from span/2 cases before the current observation to the span length. The second span ranges from (span/2)−1 cases before the current observation to the span length.

Limitations

- Maximum 1 function per equation.
- There is no limit on the number of series created by an equation.
- There is no limit on the number of equations.

Example

```
CREATE NEWVAR1 = DIFF(OLDVAR,1).
```

- In this example, the series *NEWVAR1* is created by taking the first-order difference of *OLDVAR*.

CSUM Function

CSUM produces new series based on the cumulative sums of the existing series. Cumulative sums are the inverse of first-order differencing.

- The only specification on CSUM is the name or names of the existing series in parentheses.
- Cases with missing values in the existing series are not used to compute values for the new series. The values of these cases are system-missing in the new series.

Example

```
CREATE NEWVAR1 NEWVAR2 = CSUM(TICKETS RNDTRP).
```

- This example produces a new series called *NEWVAR1*, which is the cumulative sum of the series *TICKETS*, and a new series called *NEWVAR2*, which is the cumulative sum of the series *RNDTRP*.

DIFF Function

DIFF produces new series based on nonseasonal differences of existing series.

- The specification on DIFF is the name or names of the existing series and the degree of differencing, in parentheses.
- The degree of differencing must be specified; there is no default.
- Since one observation is lost for each order of differencing, system-missing values will appear at the beginning of the new series.
- You can specify only one degree of differencing per DIFF function.
- If either of the pair of values involved in a difference computation is missing, the result is set to system-missing in the new series.

Example

```
CREATE ADIF2 = DIFF(VARA,2) /
       YDIF1 ZDIF1 = DIFF(VARY VARZ,1).
```

- The series *ADIF2* is created by differencing *VARA* twice.
- The series *YDIF1* is created by differencing *VARY* once.
- The series *ZDIF1* is created by differencing *VARZ* once.

FFT Function

FFT produces new series based on fast Fourier transformations of existing series (Brigham, 1974).

- The only specification on FFT is the name or names of the existing series in parentheses.

- FFT creates two series, the cosine and sine parts (also called real and imaginary parts), for each existing series named. Thus, you must specify two new series names on the left side of the equation for each existing series specified on the right side.

- The first new series named becomes the real series, and the second new series named becomes the imaginary series.

- The existing series cannot have imbedded missing values.

- The existing series must be of even length. If an odd-length series is specified, FFT pads it with a 0 to make it even. Alternatively, you can make the series even by adding or dropping an observation.

- The new series will be only half as long as the existing series. The remaining cases are assigned the system-missing value.

Example

```
CREATE A B = FFT(C).
```

- Two series, A (real) and B (imaginary), are created by applying a fast Fourier transformation to series C.

IFFT Function

IFFT produces new series based on the inverse Fourier transformation of existing series.

- The only specification on IFFT is the name or names of the existing series in parentheses.

- IFFT needs two existing series to compute each new series. Thus, you must specify two existing series names on the right side of the equation for each new series specified on the left.

- The first existing series specified is the real series and the second series is the imaginary.

- The existing series cannot have imbedded missing values.

- The new series will be twice as long as the existing series. Thus, the last half of each existing series must be system-missing to allow enough room to create the new series.

Example

```
CREATE C = IFFT(A B).
```

- This command creates one new series, C, from the series A (real) and B (imaginary).

LAG Function

LAG creates new series by copying the values of the existing series and moving them forward the specified number of observations. This number is called the **lag order**. Table 1 shows a first-order lag for a hypothetical data set.

- The specification on LAG is the name or names of the existing series and one or two lag orders, in parentheses.
- At least one lag order must be specified; there is no default.
- Two lag orders indicate a range. For example, 2,6 indicates lag orders two through six. A new series is created for each lag order in the range.
- The number of new series specified must equal the number of existing series specified times the number of lag orders in the range.
- The first *n* cases at the beginning of the new series, where *n* is the lag order, are assigned the system-missing value.
- Missing values in the existing series are lagged and are assigned the system-missing value in the new series.
- A first-order lagged series can also be created using COMPUTE. COMPUTE does not cause a data pass (see COMPUTE).

Table 1   First-order lag and lead of series X

X	Lag	Lead
198	.	220
220	198	305
305	220	470
470	305	.

Example

```
CREATE LAGVAR2 TO LAGVAR5 = LAG(VARA,2,5).
```

- Four new variables are created based on lags on *VARA*. *LAGVAR2* is *VARA* lagged two steps, *LAGVAR3* is *VARA* lagged three steps, *LAGVAR4* is *VARA* lagged four steps, and *LAGVAR5* is *VARA* lagged five steps.

LEAD Function

LEAD creates new series by copying the values of the existing series and moving them back the specified number of observations. This number is called the lead order. Table 1 shows a first-order lead for a hypothetical data set.

- The specification on LEAD is the name or names of the existing series and one or two lead orders, in parentheses.
- At least one lead order must be specified; there is no default.

- Two lead orders indicate a range. For example, 1,5 indicates lead orders one through five. A new series is created for each lead order in the range.
- The number of new series must equal the number of existing series specified times the number of lead orders in the range.
- The last *n* cases at the end of the new series, where *n* equals the lead order, are assigned the system-missing value.
- Missing values in the existing series are moved back and are assigned the system-missing value in the new series.

Example

```
CREATE LEAD1 TO LEAD4 = LEAD(VARA,1,4).
```

- Four new series are created based on leads of *VARA*. *LEAD1* is *VARA* led one step, *LEAD2* is *VARA* led two steps, *LEAD3* is *VARA* led three steps, and *LEAD4* is *VARA* led four steps.

MA Function

MA produces new series based on the centered moving averages of existing series.

- The specification on MA is the name or names of the existing series and the span to be used in averaging, in parentheses.
- A span must be specified; there is no default.
- If the specified span is odd, the MA is naturally associated with the middle term. If the specified span is even, the MA is centered by averaging each pair of uncentered means (Velleman and Hoaglin, 1981).
- After the initial span, a second span can be specified to indicate the minimum number of values to use in averaging when the number specified for the initial span is unavailable. This makes it possible to produce nonmissing values at or near the ends of the new series.
- The second span must be greater than or equal to 1 and less than or equal to the first span.
- The second span should be even (or 1) if the first span is even; it should be odd if the first span is odd. Otherwise, the next higher span value will be used.
- If no second span is specified, the minimum span is simply the value of the first span.
- If the number of values specified for the span or the minimum span is not available, the case in the new series is set to system-missing. Thus, unless a minimum span of 1 is specified, the endpoints of the new series will contain system-missing values.
- When MA encounters an imbedded missing value in the existing series, it creates two subsets, one containing cases before the missing value and one containing cases after the missing value. Each subset is treated as a separate series for computational purposes.
- The endpoints of these subset series will have missing values according to the rules described above for the endpoints of the entire series. Thus, if the minimum span is 1, the endpoints of the subsets will be nonmissing; the only cases that will be missing in the new series are cases that were missing in the original series.

Example

```
CREATE TICKMA = MA(TICKETS,4,2).
```

- This example creates the series *TICKMA* based on centered moving average values of the series *TICKETS*.

- A span of 4 is used for computing averages. At the endpoints, where four values are not available, the average is based on the specified minimum of two values.

PMA Function

PMA creates new series based on the prior moving averages of existing series. The prior moving average for each case in the original series is computed by averaging the values of a span of cases preceding it.

- The specification on PMA is the name or names of the existing series and the span to be used, in parentheses.

- Only one span can be specified and it is required. There is no default span.

- If the number of values specified for the span is not available, the case is set to system-missing. Thus, the number of cases with system-missing values at the beginning of the new series equals the number specified for the span.

- When PMA encounters an imbedded missing value in the existing series, it creates two subsets, one containing cases before the missing value and one containing cases after the missing value. Each subset is treated as a separate series for computational purposes. The first n cases in the second subset will be system-missing, where n is the span.

Example

```
CREATE PRIORA = PMA(VARA,3).
```

- This command creates series *PRIORA* by computing prior moving averages for series *VARA*. Since the span is 3, the first three cases in series *PRIORA* are system-missing. The fourth case equals the average of cases 1, 2, and 3 of *VARA*, the fifth case equals the average of cases 2, 3, and 4 of *VARA*, and so on.

RMED Function

RMED produces new series based on the centered running medians of existing series.

- The specification on RMED is the name or names of the existing series and the span to be used in finding the median, in parentheses.

- A span must be specified; there is no default.

- If the specified span is odd, RMED is naturally the middle term. If the specified span is even, the RMED is centered by averaging each pair of uncentered medians (Velleman and Hoaglin, 1981).

- After the initial span, a second span can be specified to indicate the minimum number of values to use in finding the median when the number specified for the initial span is unavailable. This makes it possible to produce nonmissing values at or near the ends of the new series.

- The second span must be greater than or equal to 1 and less than or equal to the first span.
- The second span should be even (or 1) if the first span is even; it should be odd if the first span is odd. Otherwise, the next higher span value will be used.
- If no second span is specified, the minimum span is simply the value of the first span.
- If the number of values specified for the span or the minimum span is not available, the case in the new series is set to system-missing. Thus, unless a minimum span of 1 is specified, the endpoints of the new series will contain system-missing values.
- When RMED encounters an imbedded missing value in the existing series, it creates two subsets, one containing cases before the missing value and one containing cases after the missing value. Each subset is treated as a separate series for computational purposes.
- The endpoints of these subset series will have missing values according to the rules described above for the endpoints of the entire series. Thus, if the minimum span is 1, the endpoints of the subsets will be nonmissing; the only cases that will be missing in the new series are cases that were missing in the original series.

Example

```
CREATE TICKRMED = RMED(TICKETS,4,2).
```

- This example creates the series *TICKRMED* using centered running median values of the series *TICKETS*.
- A span of 4 is used for computing medians. At the endpoints, where four values are not available, the median is based on the specified minimum of two values.

SDIFF Function

SDIFF produces new series based on seasonal differences of existing series.
- The specification on SDIFF is the name or names of the existing series, the degree of differencing, and, optionally, the periodicity, all in parentheses.
- The degree of differencing must be specified; there is no default.
- Since the number of seasons used in the calculations decreases by 1 for each order of differencing, system-missing values will appear at the beginning of the new series.
- You can specify only one degree of differencing per SDIFF function.
- If no periodicity is specified, the periodicity established on TSET PERIOD is in effect. If TSET PERIOD has not been specified, the periodicity established on the DATE command is used. If periodicity was not established anywhere, the SDIFF function cannot be executed.
- If either of the pair of values involved in a seasonal difference computation is missing, the result is set to system-missing in the new series.

Example

```
CREATE SDVAR = SDIFF(VARA,1,12).
```

- The series *SDVAR* is created by applying one seasonal difference with a periodicity of 12 to the series *VARA*.

T4253H Function

T4253H produces new series by applying a compound data smoother to the original series. The smoother starts with a running median of 4, which is centered by a running median of 2. It then resmooths these values by applying a running median of 5, a running median of 3, and hanning (running weighted averages). Residuals are computed by subtracting the smoothed series from the original series. This whole process is then repeated on the computed residuals. Finally, the smoothed residuals are added to the smoothed values obtained the first time through the process (Velleman and Hoaglin, 1981).

- The only specification on T4253H is the name or names of the existing series in parentheses.
- The existing series cannot contain imbedded missing values.
- Endpoints are smoothed through extrapolation and are not system-missing.

Example

```
CREATE SMOOTHA = T4253H(VARA).
```

- The series *SMOOTHA* is a smoothed version of the series *VARA*.

References

Box, G. E. P., and G. M. Jenkins. 1976. *Time series analysis: Forecasting and control.* San Francisco: Holden-Day.

Brigham, E. O. 1974. *The fast Fourier transform.* Englewood Cliffs, N.J.: Prentice-Hall.

Cryer, J. D. 1986. *Time series analysis.* Boston: Duxbury Press.

Makridakis, S., S. C. Wheelwright, and V. E. McGee. 1983. *Forecasting: Methods and applications.* New York: John Wiley and Sons.

Monro, D. M. 1975. Algorithm AS 83: Complex discrete fast Fourier transform. *Applied Statistics*, 24: 153–160.

Monro, D. M., and J. L. Branch. 1977. Algorithm AS 117: The Chirp discrete Fourier transform of general length. *Applied Statistics*, 26: 351–361.

Velleman, P. F., and D. C. Hoaglin. 1981. *Applications, basics, and computing of exploratory data analysis.* Boston: Duxbury Press.

CROSSTABS

General mode:

```
CROSSTABS [TABLES=]varlist BY varlist [BY...] [/varlist...]

 [/MISSING={TABLE**}]
          {INCLUDE}

 [/WRITE[={NONE**}]]
         {CELLS }
```

Integer mode:

```
CROSSTABS VARIABLES=varlist(min,max) [varlist...]

 /TABLES=varlist BY varlist [BY...] [/varlist...]

 [/MISSING={TABLE**}]
          {INCLUDE}
          {REPORT }

 [/WRITE[={NONE**}]]
         {CELLS }
         {ALL   }
```

Both modes:

```
 [/FORMAT= {AVALUE**}  {TABLES**}]
           {DVALUE  }  {NOTABLES}

 [/CELLS=[{COUNT**}]  [ROW    ] [EXPECTED] [SRESID ]]
         {NONE   }    [COLUMN] [RESID  ] [ASRESID]
                      [TOTAL ]            [ALL    ]

 [/STATISTICS=[CHISQ] [LAMBDA] [BTAU ] [GAMMA  ] [ETA    ]]
              [PHI  ] [UC    ] [CTAU ] [D      ] [CORR   ]
              [CC   ] [RISK  ] [KAPPA] [MCNEMAR] [CMH(1*)]
              [ALL  ] [NONE  ]

 [/METHOD={MC [CIN({99.0 })] [SAMPLES({10000})]}]††
              {value}            {value}
          {EXACT [TIMER({5    })]              }
                       {value}

 [/BARCHART]
```

**Default if the subcommand is omitted.

†† The **METHOD** subcommand is available only if the Exact Tests option is installed.

Example

```
CROSSTABS TABLES=FEAR BY SEX
 /CELLS=ROW COLUMN EXPECTED RESIDUALS
 /STATISTICS=CHISQ.
```

Overview

CROSSTABS produces contingency tables showing the joint distribution of two or more variables that have a limited number of distinct values. The frequency distribution of one variable is subdivided according to the values of one or more variables. The unique combination of values for two or more variables defines a cell.

CROSSTABS can operate in two different modes: *general* and *integer*. Integer mode builds some tables more efficiently but requires more specifications than general mode. Some subcommand specifications and statistics are available only in integer mode.

Options

Methods for building tables. To build tables in general mode, use the TABLES subcommand. Integer mode requires the TABLES and VARIABLES subcommands and minimum and maximum values for the variables.

Cell contents. By default, CROSSTABS displays only the number of cases in each cell. You can request row, column, and total percentages, and also expected values and residuals by using the CELLS subcommand.

Statistics. In addition to the tables, you can obtain measures of association and tests of hypotheses for each subtable using the STATISTICS subcommand.

Formatting options. With the FORMAT subcommand, you can control the display order for categories in rows and columns of subtables and suppress crosstabulation.

Writing and reproducing tables. You can write cell frequencies to a file and reproduce the original tables with the WRITE subcommand.

Basic Specification

In general mode, the basic specification is TABLES with a table list. The actual keyword TABLES can be omitted. In integer mode, the minimum specification is the VARIABLES subcommand, specifying the variables to be used and their value ranges, and the TABLES subcommand with a table list.

- The minimum table list specifies a list of row variables, the keyword BY, and a list of column variables.

- In integer mode, all variables must be numeric with integer values. In general mode, variables can be numeric (integer or non-integer) or string.

- The default table shows cell counts.

Subcommand Order

- In general mode, the table list must be first if the keyword TABLES is omitted. If the keyword TABLES is explicitly used, subcommands can be specified in any order.

- In integer mode, VARIABLES must precede TABLES. The keyword TABLES must be explicitly specified.

Operations

- Integer mode builds tables more quickly but requires more workspace if a table has many empty cells.
- If a long string variable is used in general mode, only the short string portion (first eight characters) is tabulated.
- Statistics are calculated separately for each two-way table or two-way subtable. Missing values are reported for the table as a whole.
- In general mode, the keyword TO on the TABLES subcommand refers to the order of variables in the working file. ALL refers to all variables in the working file. In integer mode, TO and ALL refer to the position and subset of variables specified on the VARIABLES subcommand.

Limitations

The following limitations apply to CROSSTABS in *general mode*:
- Maximum 200 variables named or implied on the TABLES subcommand
- Maximum 1000 non-empty rows or columns for each table
- Maximum 20 table lists per CROSSTABS command
- Maximum 10 dimensions (9 BY keywords) per table
- Maximum 400 value labels displayed on any single table

The following limitations apply to CROSSTABS in *integer mode*:
- Maximum 100 variables named or implied on the VARIABLES subcommand
- Maximum 100 variables named or implied on the TABLES subcommand
- Maximum 1000 non-empty rows or columns for each table
- Maximum 20 table lists per CROSSTABS command
- Maximum 8 dimensions (7 BY keywords) per table
- Maximum 20 rows or columns of missing values when REPORT is specified on MISSING
- Minimum value that can be specified is –99,999
- Maximum value that can be specified is 999,999

Example

```
CROSSTABS TABLES=FEAR BY SEX
 /CELLS=ROW COLUMN EXPECTED RESIDUALS
 /STATISTICS=CHISQ.
```

- CROSSTABS generates a Case Processing Summary table, a Crosstabulation table, and a Chi-Square Tests table.
- The variable *FEAR* defines the rows and the variable *SEX* defines the columns of the Crosstabulation table. CELLS requests row and column percentages, expected cell frequencies, and residuals.

- STATISTICS requests the chi-square statistics displayed in the Chi-Square Tests table.

Example

```
CROSSTABS TABLES=JOBCAT BY EDCAT BY SEX BY INCOME3.
```

- This table list produces a subtable of *JOBCAT* by *EDCAT* for each combination of values of *SEX* and *INCOME3*.

VARIABLES Subcommand

The VARIABLES subcommand is required for integer mode. VARIABLES specifies a list of variables to be used in the crosstabulations and the lowest and highest values for each variable. Values are specified in parentheses and must be integers. Non-integer values are truncated.

- Variables can be specified in any order. However, the order in which they are named on VARIABLES determines their implied order on TABLES (see the TABLES subcommand below).
- A range must be specified for each variable. If several variables can have the same range, it can be specified once after the last variable to which it applies.
- CROSSTABS uses the specified ranges to allocate tables. One cell is allocated for each possible combination of values of the row and column variables before the data are read. Thus, if the specified ranges are larger than the actual ranges, workspace will be wasted.
- Cases with values outside the specified range are considered missing and are not used in the computation of the table. This allows you to select a subset of values within CROSSTABS.
- If the table is sparse because the variables do not have values throughout the specified range, consider using general mode or recoding the variables.

Example

```
CROSSTABS VARIABLES=FEAR SEX RACE (1,2) MOBILE16 (1,3)
    /TABLES=FEAR BY SEX MOBILE16 BY RACE.
```

- VARIABLES defines values 1 and 2 for *FEAR*, *SEX*, and *RACE*, and values 1, 2, and 3 for *MOBILE16*.

TABLES Subcommand

TABLES specifies the table lists and is required in both integer mode and general mode. The following rules apply to both modes:

- You can specify multiple TABLES subcommands on a single CROSSTABS command. The slash between the subcommands is required; the keyword TABLES is required only in integer mode.
- Variables named before the first BY on a table list are row variables, and variables named after the first BY on a table list are column variables.

- When the table list specifies two dimensions (one BY keyword), the first variable before BY is crosstabulated with each variable after BY, then the second variable before BY with each variable after BY, and so on.

- Each subsequent use of the keyword BY on a table list adds a new dimension to the tables requested. Variables named after the second (or subsequent) BY are control variables.

- When the table list specifies more than two dimensions, a two-way subtable is produced for each combination of values of control variables. The value of the last specified control variable changes the most slowly in determining the order in which tables are displayed.

- You can name more than one variable in each dimension.

General Mode

- The actual keyword TABLES can be omitted in general mode.

- In general mode, both numeric and string variables can be specified. Long strings are truncated to short strings for defining categories.

- The keywords ALL and TO can be specified in any dimension. In general mode, TO refers to the order of variables in the working data file and ALL refers to all variables defined in the working data file.

Example

```
CROSSTABS   TABLES=FEAR BY SEX BY RACE.
```

- This example crosstabulates *FEAR* by *SEX* controlling for *RACE*. In each subtable, *FEAR* is the row variable and *SEX* is the column variable.

- A subtable is produced for each value of the control variable *RACE*.

Example

```
CROSSTABS   TABLES=CONFINAN TO CONARMY BY SEX TO REGION.
```

- This command produces crosstabulations of all variables in the working data file between and including *CONFINAN* and *CONARMY* by all variables between and including *SEX* and *REGION*.

Integer Mode

- In integer mode, variables specified on TABLES must first be named on VARIABLES.

- The keywords TO and ALL can be specified in any dimension. In integer mode, TO and ALL refer to the position and subset of variables specified on the VARIABLES subcommand, not to the variables in the working data file.

Example

```
CROSSTABS   VARIABLES=FEAR (1,2) MOBILE16 (1,3)
   /TABLES=FEAR BY MOBILE16.
```

- VARIABLES names two variables, *FEAR* and *MOBILE16*. Values 1 and 2 for *FEAR* are used in the tables, and values 1, 2, and 3 are used for the variable *MOBILE16*.

- TABLES specifies a Crosstabulation table with two rows (values 1 and 2 for *FEAR*) and three columns (values 1, 2, and 3 for *MOBILE16*). *FEAR* and *MOBILE16* can be named on TABLES because they were named on the previous VARIABLES subcommand.

Example

```
CROSSTABS  VARIABLES=FEAR SEX RACE DEGREE (1,2)
   /TABLES=FEAR BY SEX BY RACE BY DEGREE.
```

- This command produces four subtables. The first subtable crosstabulates *FEAR* by *SEX*, controlling for the first value of *RACE* and the first value of *DEGREE*; the second subtable controls for the second value of *RACE* and the first value of *DEGREE*; the third subtable controls for the first value of *RACE* and the second value of *DEGREE*; and the fourth subtable controls for the second value of *RACE* and the second value of *DEGREE*.

CELLS Subcommand

By default, CROSSTABS displays only the number of cases in each cell of the Crosstabulation table. Use CELLS to display row, column, or total percentages, expected counts, or residuals. These are calculated separately for each Crosstabulation table or subtable.

- CELLS specified without keywords displays cell counts plus row, column, and total percentages for each cell.
- If CELLS is specified with keywords, CROSSTABS displays only the requested cell information.
- Scientific notation is used for cell contents when necessary.

COUNT *Observed cell counts.* This is the default if CELLS is omitted.

ROW *Row percentages.* The number of cases in each cell in a row is expressed as a percentage of all cases in that row.

COLUMN *Column percentages.* The number of cases in each cell in a column is expressed as a percentage of all cases in that column.

TOTAL *Two-way table total percentages.* The number of cases in each cell of a subtable is expressed as a percentage of all cases in that subtable.

EXPECTED *Expected counts.* Expected counts are the number of cases expected in each cell if the two variables in the subtable are statistically independent.

RESID *Residuals.* Residuals are the difference between the observed and expected cell counts.

SRESID *Standardized residuals* (Haberman, 1978).

ASRESID *Adjusted standardized residuals* (Haberman, 1978).

ALL *All cell information.* This includes cell counts; row, column, and total percentages; expected counts; residuals; standardized residuals; and adjusted standardized residuals.

NONE   *No cell information.* Use NONE when you want to write tables to a procedure output file without displaying them (see the WRITE subcommand on p. 230). This is the same as specifying NOTABLES on FORMAT.

STATISTICS Subcommand

STATISTICS requests measures of association and related statistics. By default, CROSSTABS does not display any additional statistics.

- STATISTICS without keywords displays the chi-square test.
- If STATISTICS is specified with keywords, CROSSTABS calculates only the requested statistics.
- In integer mode, values that are not included in the specified range are *not* used in the calculation of the statistics, even if these values exist in the data.
- If user-missing values are included with MISSING, cases with user-missing values are included in the calculation of statistics as well as in the tables.

CHISQ   *Display the Chi-Square Test table.* Chi-square statistics include Pearson chi-square, likelihood-ratio chi-square, and Mantel-Haenszel chi-square (linear-by-linear association). Mantel-Haenszel is valid only if both variables are numeric. Fisher's exact test and Yates' corrected chi-square are computed for all 2×2 tables. This is the default if STATISTICS is specified with no keywords.

PHI   *Display phi and Cramér's V in the Symmetric Measures table.*

CC   *Display contingency coefficient in the Symmetric Measures table.*

LAMBDA   *Display lambda (symmetric and asymmetric) and Goodman and Kruskal's tau in the Directional Measures table.*

UC   *Display uncertainty coefficient (symmetric and asymmetric) in the Directional Measures table.*

BTAU   *Display Kendall's tau-b in the Symmetric Measures table.*

CTAU   *Display Kendall's tau-c in the Symmetric Measures table.*

GAMMA   *Display gamma in the Symmetric Measures table or Zero-Order and Partial Gammas table.* The Zero-Order and Partial Gammas table is produced only for tables with more than two variable dimensions in integer mode.

D   *Display Somers' d (symmetric and asymmetric) in the Directional Measures table.*

ETA   *Display eta in the Directional Measures table.* Available for numeric data only.

CORR   *Display Pearson's r and Spearman's correlation coefficient in the Symmetric Measures table.* This is available for numeric data only.

KAPPA   *Display kappa coefficient* (Kraemer, 1982) *in the Symmetric Measures table.* Kappa can be computed only for square tables in which the row and column values are identical.

RISK   *Display relative risk* (Bishop et al., 1975) *in the Risk Estimate table.* Relative risk can be calculated only for 2×2 tables.

MCNEMAR   *Display a Crosstabulation table for each pair of related dichotomous variables and a Test Statistics table for all pairs showing the number of valid cases, chi-square, and probability for each pair.* Useful for detecting changes in responses due to experimental intervention in "before-and-after" designs.

CMH(1*)   *Conditional independence and homogeneity tests.* Cochran's and the Mantel-Haenszel statistics are computed for the test for conditional independence. The Breslow-Day and Taron's statistics are computed for the test for homogeneity. For each test, the chi-squared statistic with its degrees of freedom and asymptotic *p* value are computed. *Mantel-Haenszel relative risk (common odds ratio) estimate.* The Mantel-Haenszel relative risk (common odds ratio) estimate, the natural log of the estimate, the standard error of the natural log of the estimate, the asymptotic *p* value, and the asymptotic confidence intervals for common odds ratio and for the natural log of the common odds ratio are computed. The user can specify the null hypothesis for the common odds ratio in parentheses after the keyword. The passive default is 1. (The parameter value must be positive.)

ALL   *All statistics available.*

NONE   *No summary statistics.* This is the default if STATISTICS is omitted.

METHOD Subcommand

METHOD displays additional results for each statistic requested. If no METHOD subcommand is specified, the standard asymptotic results are displayed. If fractional weights have been specified, results for all methods will be calculated on the weight rounded to the nearest integer.

MC   Displays an unbiased point estimate and confidence interval based on the Monte Carlo sampling method, for all statistics. Asymptotic results are also displayed. When exact results can be calculated, they will be provided instead of the Monte Carlo results.

CIN(n)   Controls the confidence level for the Monte Carlo estimate. CIN is available only when /METHOD=MC is specified. CIN has a default value of 99.0. You can specify a confidence interval between 0.01 and 99.9, inclusive.

SAMPLES   Specifies the number of tables sampled from the reference set when calculating the Monte Carlo estimate of the exact *p* value. Larger sample sizes lead to narrower confidence limits but also take longer to calculate. You can specify any integer between 1 and 1,000,000,000 as the sample size. SAMPLES has a default value of 10,000.

EXACT   Computes the exact significance level for all statistics in addition to the asymptotic results. If both the EXACT and MC keywords are specified, only exact results are provided. Calculating the exact *p* value can be memory-intensive. If you have specified /METHOD=EXACT and find that you have insufficient memory to calculate results, you should first close any other applications that are currently running in order to make more memory available. You can also enlarge the size of your swap file (see your Windows manual for more information). If you still cannot obtain exact results, specify /METHOD=MC to obtain the Monte Carlo estimate of the exact *p* value. An optional TIMER keyword is available if you choose /METHOD=EXACT.

TIMER(n)   Specifies the maximum number of minutes allowed to run the exact analysis for each statistic. If the time limit is reached, the test is terminated, no exact results are provided, and the program begins to calculate the next test in the analysis. TIMER is available only when /METHOD=EXACT is specified. You can specify any integer value for TIMER. Specifying a value of 0 for TIMER turns the timer off completely. TIMER has a default value of 5 minutes. If a test exceeds a time limit of 30 minutes, it is recommended that you use the Monte Carlo, rather than the exact, method.

Example

```
CROSSTABS TABLES=FEAR BY SEX
 /CELLS=ROW COLUMN EXPECTED RESIDUALS
 /STATISTICS=CHISQ
 /METHOD=MC SAMPLES(10000) CIN(95).
```

- This example requests chi-square statistics.
- An unbiased point estimate and confidence interval based on the Monte Carlo sampling method are displayed with the asymptotic results.

MISSING Subcommand

By default, CROSSTABS deletes cases with missing values on a table-by-table basis. Cases with missing values for any variable specified for a table are not used in the table or in the calculation of statistics. Use MISSING to specify alternative missing-value treatments.

- The only specification is a single keyword.
- The number of missing cases is always displayed in the Case Processing Summary table.
- If the missing values are not included in the range specified on VARIABLES, they are excluded from the table regardless of the keyword you specify on MISSING.

TABLE   *Delete cases with missing values on a table-by-table basis.* When multiple table lists are specified, missing values are handled separately for each list. This is the default.

INCLUDE   *Include user-missing values.* Available in integer mode only.

REPORT   *Report missing values in the tables.* This option includes missing values in tables but not in the calculation of percentages or statistics. The missing status is indicated on the categorical label. REPORT is available only in integer mode.

FORMAT Subcommand

By default, CROSSTABS displays tables and subtables. The values for the row and column variables are displayed in order from lowest to highest. Use FORMAT to modify the default table display.

AVALUE   *Display row and column variables from lowest to highest value.* This is the default.

DVALUE   *Display row and column variables from highest to lowest.*

TABLES   *Display tables.* This is the default.

NOTABLES   *Suppress Crosstabulation tables.* NOTABLES is useful when you want to write tables to a file without displaying them or when you want only the Statistics table. This is the same as specifying NONE on CELLS.

BARCHART Subcommand

BARCHART produces a clustered bar chart where bars represent categories defined by the first variable in a crosstabulation while clusters represent categories defined by the second variable in a crosstabulation. Any controlling variables in a crosstabulation are collapsed over before the clustered bar chart is created.

- BARCHART takes no further specification.
- If integer mode is in effect and MISSING=REPORT, BARCHART displays valid and user-missing values. Otherwise only valid values are used.

WRITE Subcommand

Use the WRITE subcommand to write cell frequencies to a file for subsequent use by the current program or another program. CROSSTABS can also use these cell frequencies as input to reproduce tables and compute statistics. When WRITE is specified, an Output File Summary table is displayed before all other tables.

- The only specification is a single keyword.
- The name of the file must be specified on the PROCEDURE OUTPUT command preceding CROSSTABS.
- If both CELLS and ALL are specified, CELLS is in effect and only the contents of non-empty cells are written to the file.
- If you include missing values with INCLUDE or REPORT on MISSING, no values are considered missing and all non-empty cells, including those with missing values, are written, even if CELLS is specified.
- If you exclude missing values on a table-by-table basis (the default), no records are written for combinations of values that include a missing value.
- If multiple tables are specified, the tables are written in the same order as they are displayed.

NONE   *Do not write cell counts to a file.* This is the default.

CELLS	*Write cell counts for non-empty and nonmissing cells to a file.* Combinations of values that include a missing value are not written to the file.
ALL	*Write cell counts for all cells to a file.* A record for each combination of values defined by VARIABLES and TABLES is written to the file. ALL is available only in integer mode.

The file contains one record for each cell. Each record contains the following:

Columns	Contents
1–4	*Split-file group number, numbered consecutively from 1.* Note that this is not the value of the variable or variables used to define the splits.
5–8	*Table number.* Tables are defined by the TABLES subcommand.
9–16	*Cell frequency.* The number of times this combination of variable values occurred in the data, or, if case weights are used, the sum of case weights for cases having this combination of values.
17–24	*The value of the row variable* (the one named before the first BY).
25–32	*The value of the column variable* (the one named after the first BY).
33–40	*The value of the first control variable* (the one named after the second BY).
41–48	*The value of the second control variable* (the one named after the third BY).
49–56	*The value of the third control variable* (the one named after the fourth BY).
57–64	*The value of the fourth control variable* (the one named after the fifth BY).
65–72	*The value of the fifth control variable* (the one named after the sixth BY).
73–80	*The value of the sixth control variable* (the one named after the seventh BY).

- The split-file group number, table number, and frequency are written as integers.
- In integer mode, the values of variables are also written as integers. In general mode, the values are written according to the print format specified for each variable. Alphanumeric values are written at the left end of any field in which they occur.
- Within each table, records are written from one column of the table at a time, and the value of the last control variable changes the most slowly.

Example
```
PROCEDURE OUTPUT  OUTFILE=CELLDATA.
CROSSTABS VARIABLES=FEAR SEX (1,2)
 /TABLES=FEAR BY SEX
 /WRITE=ALL.
```

- CROSSTABS writes a record for each cell in the table *FEAR* by *SEX* to the file *CELLDATA*. Figure 1 shows the contents of the *CELLDATA* file.

Figure 1   Cell records

```
1   1       55      1       1
1   1      172      2       1
1   1      180      1       2
1   1       89      2       2
```

Example

```
PROCEDURE OUTPUT   OUTFILE=XTABDATA.
CROSSTABS   TABLES=V1 TO V3 BY V4 BY V10 TO V15
  /WRITE=CELLS.
```

- CROSSTABS writes a set of records for each table to file *XTABDATA*.

- Records for the table *V1* by *V4* by *V10* are written first, followed by records for *V1* by *V4* by *V11*, and so on. The records for *V3* by *V4* by *V15* are written last.

Reading a CROSSTABS Procedure Output File

You can use the file created by WRITE in a subsequent session to reproduce a table and compute statistics for it. Each record in the file contains all the information used to build the original table. The cell frequency information can be used as a weight variable on the WEIGHT command to replicate the original cases.

Example

```
DATA LIST FILE=CELLDATA
  /WGHT 9-16 FEAR 17-24 SEX 25-32.
VARIABLE LABELS FEAR 'AFRAID TO WALK AT NIGHT IN NEIGHBORHOODS'.
VALUE LABELS   FEAR 1 'YES' 2 'NO'/ SEX 1 'MALE' 2 'FEMALE'.
WEIGHT BY WGHT.
CROSSTABS TABLES=FEAR BY SEX
  /STATISTICS=ALL.
```

- DATA LIST reads the cell frequencies and row and column values from the *CELLDATA* file shown in Figure 1. The cell frequency is read as a weighting factor (variable *WGHT*). The values for the rows are read as *FEAR*, and the values for the columns are read as *SEX*, the two original variables.

- The WEIGHT command recreates the sample size by weighting each of the four cases (cells) by the cell frequency.

If you do not have the original data or the CROSSTABS procedure output file, you can reproduce a crosstabulation and compute statistics simply by entering the values from the table:

```
DATA LIST   /FEAR 1 SEX 3 WGHT 5-7.
VARIABLE LABELS   FEAR 'AFRAID TO WALK AT NIGHT IN NEIGHBORHOOD'.
VALUE LABELS   FEAR 1 'YES' 2 'NO'/ SEX 1 'MALE' 2 'FEMALE'.
 WEIGHT   BY WGHT.
BEGIN DATA
1 1  55
2 1 172
1 2 180
2 2  89
END DATA.
CROSSTABS   TABLES=FEAR BY SEX
/STATISTICS=ALL.
```

References

Bishop, Y. M. M., S. E. Feinberg, and P. W. Holland. 1975. *Discrete multivariate analysis: Theory and practice.* Cambridge, Mass.: MIT Press.

Haberman, S. J. 1978. *Analysis of qualitative data.* Vol. 1. London: Academic Press.

Kraemer, H. C. 1982. Kappa coefficient. In: *Encyclopedia of Statistical Sciences*, S. Katz and N. L. Johnson, eds. New York: John Wiley and Sons.

CURVEFIT

```
CURVEFIT [VARIABLES=] varname [WITH varname]

 [/MODEL= [LINEAR**] [LOGARITHMIC] [INVERSE]

          [QUADRATIC] [CUBIC] [COMPOUND]

          [POWER] [S] [GROWTH] [EXPONENTIAL]

          [LGSTIC] [ALL]]

 [/CIN={95** }]
       {value}

 [/UPPERBOUND={NO**}]
             {n   }

 [/{CONSTANT† }
   {NOCONSTANT}

 [/PLOT={FIT**}]
        {NONE }

 [/ID = varname]

 [/PRINT=ANOVA]

 [/SAVE=[PRED] [RESID] [CIN]]

 [/APPLY [='model name'] [{SPECIFICATIONS}]]
                         {FIT            }
```

**Default if the subcommand is omitted.
†Default if the subcommand is omitted and there is no corresponding specification on the TSET command.

Example

```
CURVEFIT VARY
  /MODEL=CUBIC.
```

Overview

CURVEFIT fits selected curves to a line plot, allowing you to examine the relationship between one or more dependent variables and one independent variable. CURVEFIT also fits
curves to time series and produces forecasts, forecast errors, lower confidence limits, and
upper confidence limits. You can choose curves from a variety of regression models.

Options

Model Specification. There are 11 regression models available on the MODEL subcommand.
You can fit any or all of these to the data. The keyword ALL is available to fit all 11 models.
You can control whether the regression equation includes a constant term using the
CONSTANT or NOCONSTANT subcommand.

Upperbound Value. You can specify the upperbound value for the logistic model using the UPPERBOUND subcommand.

Output. You can produce an analysis-of-variance summary table using the PRINT subcommand. You can suppress the display of the curve-fitting plot using the PLOT subcommand.

New Variables. To evaluate the regression statistics without saving predicted and residual variables, specify TSET NEWVAR=NONE prior to CURVEFIT. To save the new variables and replace the variables saved earlier, use TSET NEWVAR=CURRENT (the default). To save the new variables without erasing variables saved earlier, use TSET NEWVAR=ALL or the SAVE subcommand on CURVEFIT.

Forecasting. When used with the PREDICT command, CURVEFIT can produce forecasts and confidence limits beyond the end of the series (see PREDICT).

Basic Specification

The basic specification is one or more dependent variables. If the variables are not time series, you must also specify the keyword WITH and an independent variable.

- By default, the LINEAR model is fit.
- A 95% confidence interval is used unless it is changed by a TSET CIN command prior to the procedure.
- CURVEFIT produces a plot of the curve, a regression summary table displaying the type of curve used, the R^2 coefficient, degrees of freedom, overall F test and significance level, and the regression coefficients.
- For each variable and model combination, CURVEFIT creates four variables: fit/forecast values, residuals, lower confidence limits, and upper confidence limits. These variables are automatically labeled and added to the working data file unless TSET NEWVAR=NONE is specified prior to CURVEFIT. For the new variable names, see the SAVE subcommand on p. 239.

Subcommand Order

- Subcommands can be specified in any order.

Syntax Rules

- VARIABLES can be specified only once.
- Other subcommands can be specified more than once, but only the last specification of each one is executed.

Operations

- When CURVEFIT is used with the PREDICT command to forecast values beyond the end of a time series, the original and residual series are assigned the system-missing value after the last case in the original series.
- If a model requiring a log transformation (COMPOUND, POWER, S, GROWTH, EXPONENTIAL, or LGSTIC) is requested and there are values in the dependent variable(s) less than or equal to 0, the model cannot be fit because nonpositive values cannot be log-transformed.
- CURVEFIT uses listwise deletion of missing values. Whenever one dependent variable is missing a value for a particular case or observation, that case or observation will not be included in any computations.
- For models QUADRATIC and CUBIC, a message is issued if the tolerance criterion is not met. (See TSET for information on changing the tolerance criterion.)
- Since CURVEFIT automatically generates four variables for each dependent variable and model combination, the ALL specification after MODEL should be used cautiously to avoid creating and adding to the working data file many more variables than are necessary.
- The residual variable is always reported in the original metric. To compute the logged residual (which should be used for diagnostic checks) for the models COMPOUND, POWER, S, GROWTH, and EXPONENTIAL, specify

```
COMPUTE NEWVAR = LN(VAR) - LN(FIT#n).
```

  where *NEWVAR* is the logged residual, *VAR* is the name of the dependent variable or observed series, and *FIT#n* is the name of the fitted variable generated by CURVEFIT.

  For the LGSTIC (logistic) model, the logged residual can be obtained by

```
COMPUTE NEWERR = LN(VAR) - LN(1/FIT#n).
```

  or, if upperbound value *u* is specified on the UPPERBOUND subcommand, by

```
COMPUTE NEWVAR = LN(1/VAR - 1/u) - LN(1/FIT#n).
```

- CURVEFIT obeys the WEIGHT command when there is an independent variable. The WEIGHT specification is ignored if no independent variable is specified.

Limitations

- Maximum 1 VARIABLES subcommand. There is no limit on the number of dependent variables or series named on the subcommand.
- Maximum 1 independent variable can be specified after the keyword WITH.

Example

```
CURVEFIT VARY
   /MODEL=CUBIC.
```

- This example fits a cubic curve to the series *VARY*.

VARIABLES Subcommand

VARIABLES specifies the variables and is the only required subcommand. The actual keyword VARIABLES can be omitted.

- If the dependent variables specified are not time series, you must also specify the keyword WITH and an independent variable.

MODEL Subcommand

MODEL specifies the model or models to be fit to the data. The default model is LINEAR.

- You can fit any or all of the 11 available models.
- Model name keywords can be abbreviated to the first three characters.
- You can use the keyword ALL to fit all models.
- When the LGSTIC model is specified, the upperbound value is included in the output.

The following table lists the available models and their regression equations. The linear transformations for the last six models are also shown.

Keyword	Equation	Linear equation
LINEAR	$Y = b_0 + b_1 t$	
LOGARITHMIC	$Y = b_0 + b_1 \ln(t)$	
INVERSE	$Y = b_0 + b_1/t$	
QUADRATIC	$Y = b_0 + b_1 t + b_2 t^2$	
CUBIC	$Y = b_0 + b_1 t + b_2 t^2 + b_3 t^3$	
COMPOUND	$Y = b_0 b_1{}^t$	$\ln(Y) = \ln(b_0) + t \ln(b_1)$
POWER	$Y = b_0(t^{b_1})$	$\ln(Y) = \ln(b_0) + b_1 \ln(t)$
S	$Y = e^{b_0 + b_1/t}$	$\ln(Y) = b_0 + b_1/t$
GROWTH	$Y = e^{b_0 + b_1 t}$	$\ln(Y) = b_0 + b_1 t$
EXPONENTIAL	$Y = b_0(e^{b_1 t})$	$\ln(Y) = \ln(b_0) + b_1 t$
LGSTIC (logistic)	$Y = (1/u + b_0 b_1{}^t)_{-1}$	$\ln(1/Y - 1/u) = \ln(b_0) + t \ln(b_1)$

where

b_0 = a constant
b_n = regression coefficient
t = independent variable or time value
$\ln$ = the natural log base
e = base e logs
u = upperbound value for LGSTIC

Example

```
CURVEFIT VARX.
```

- This command fits a curve to *VARX* using the linear regression model (the default).

Example

```
CURVEFIT VARY
  /MODEL=GROWTH EXPONENTIAL.
```

- This command fits two curves to *VARY*, one using the growth model and the other using the exponential model.

UPPERBOUND Subcommand

UPPERBOUND is used with the logistic model (keyword LGSTIC) to specify an upper boundary value to be used in the regression equation.

- The specification on UPPERBOUND must be a positive number and must be greater than the largest data value in any of the specified dependent variables.
- The default UPPERBOUND value is infinity, so that $1/u = 0$ and is dropped from the equation.
- You can specify UPPERBOUND NO to reset the value to infinity when applying a previous model.
- If you specify UPPERBOUND without LGSTIC, it is ignored.
- Note that UPPERBOUND is a subcommand and cannot be used within a MODEL subcommand. For example, the following specification is *not* valid:

```
  /MODEL=CUBIC LGSTIC   /UPPER=99 LINEAR
```

The correct specification is:

```
  /MODEL=CUBIC LGSTIC LINEAR
  /UPPER=99
```

CONSTANT and NOCONSTANT Subcommands

CONSTANT and NOCONSTANT indicate whether a constant term should be estimated in the regression equation. The specification overrides the corresponding setting on the TSET command.

- CONSTANT indicates that a constant should be estimated. It is the default unless changed by TSET NOCONSTANT prior to the current procedure.
- NOCONSTANT eliminates the constant term from the model.

Example

```
CURVEFIT Y1
  /MODEL=COMPOUND
  /NOCONSTANT.
```

- In this example, a compound curve is fit to *Y1* with no constant term in the model.

CIN Subcommand

CIN controls the size of the confidence interval.

- The specification on CIN must be greater than 0 and less than 100.
- The default confidence interval is 95.
- The CIN subcommand overrides the TSET CIN setting.

PLOT Subcommand

PLOT specifies whether the curve-fitting plot is displayed. If PLOT is not specified, the default is FIT. The curve-fitting plot is displayed. PLOT=FIT is generally used with an APPLY subcommand to turn off a PLOT=NONE specification in the applied model.

FIT   *Display the curve-fitting plot.*

NONE   *Do not display the plot.*

ID Subcommand

ID specifies an identification variable. When in point selection mode, you can click on an individual chart point to display the value of the ID variable for the selected case.

SAVE Subcommand

SAVE saves the values of predicted, residual, and/or confidence interval variables generated during the current session in the working data file.

- SAVE saves the specified variables with default names: *PRED_n* for predicted values *RESID_n* for residuals, *LCL_n* for the lower confidence limit, and *UCL_n* for the upper confidence limit, where *n* increments each time any variable is saved for a model.
- SAVE overrides the CURRENT or NONE setting on TSET NEWVARS (see TSET).

PRED   *Predicted variable.*

RESID   *Residual variable.*

CIN   *Confidence interval.*

PRINT Subcommand

PRINT is used to produce an additional analysis-of-variance table for each model and variable.

- The only specification on PRINT is the keyword ANOVA.

APPLY Subcommand

APPLY allows you to use a previously defined CURVEFIT model without having to repeat the specifications.

- The specifications on APPLY can include the name of a previous model in quotes and one of two keywords. All of these specifications are optional.
- If a model name is not specified, the model specified on the previous CURVEFIT command is used.
- To change one or more of the specifications of the model, specify the subcommands of only those portions you want to change after the subcommand APPLY.
- If no variables or series are specified on the CURVEFIT command, the dependent variables that were originally specified with the model being reapplied are used.
- To change the dependent variables used with the model, enter new variable names before or after the APPLY subcommand.

The keywords available for APPLY on CURVEFIT are:

SPECIFICATIONS   *Use only the specifications from the original model.* This is the default.

FIT   *Use the coefficients estimated for the original model in the equation.*

Example

```
CURVEFIT X1
   /MODEL=QUADRATIC.
CURVEFIT Z1
   /APPLY.
```

- The first command fits a quadratic curve to *X1*.
- The second command fits the same type of curve to *Z1*.

Example

```
CURVEFIT X1 Y1 Z1
   /MODEL=QUADRATIC.
CURVEFIT APPLY
   /MODEL=CUBIC.
```

- The first command fits quadratic curves to *X1*, *Y1*, and *Z1*.
- The second command fits curves to the same three series using the cubic model.

References

Abraham, B., and J. Ledolter. 1983. *Statistical methods of forecasting.* New York: John Wiley and Sons.

Draper, N. R., and H. Smith. 1981. *Applied regression analysis.* New York: John Wiley and Sons.

Montgomery, D. C., and E. A. Peck. 1982. *Introduction to linear regression analysis.* New York: John Wiley and Sons.

DATA LIST

```
DATA LIST [FILE=file] [{FIXED}] [RECORDS={1}] [SKIP={n}] [{TABLE  }]
                                           {n}            {NOTABLE}

                  {FREE}  [{("delimiter", "delimiter,..., TAB)}]
                  {LIST}

/{1    } varname {col location [(format)]} [varname ...]
 {rec #}         {(FORTRAN-like format)  }

[/{2    } ...] [/ ...]
  {rec #}
```

Numeric and string input formats:

Type	Column-style format	FORTRAN-like format
Numeric (default)	d or F,d	Fw.d
Restricted numeric	N,d	Nw.d
Scientific notation	E,d	Ew.d
Numeric with commas	COMMA,d	COMMAw.d
Numeric with dots	DOT,d	DOTw.d
Numeric with commas and dollar sign	DOLLAR,d	DOLLARw.d
Numeric with percent sign	PCT,d	PCTw.d
Zoned decimal	Z,d	Zw.d
String	A	Aw

Format elements to skip columns:
Some formats are not available on all implementations of the program.

Type	Column-style format	FORTRAN-like format
Tab to column *n*		Tn
Skip *n* columns		nX

Date and time input formats:

Type	Data input	Format	FORTRAN-like format
International date	dd-mmm-yyyy	DATE	DATEw
American date	mm/dd/yyyy	ADATE	ADATEw
European date	dd/mm/yy	EDATE	EDATEw
Julian date	yyddd	JDATE	JDATEw
Sorted date	yy/mm/dd	SDATE	SDATEw
Quarter and year	qQyyyy	QYR	QYRw

Month and year	mm/yyyy	MOYR	MOYRw
Week and year	wkWKyyyy	WKYR	WKYRw
Date and time	dd-mmm-yyyy hh:mm:ss.ss	DATETIME	DATETIMEw.d
Time	hh:mm:ss.ss	TIME	TIMEw.d
Days and time	ddd hh:mm:ss.ss	DTIME	DTIMEw.d
Day of the week	string	WKDAY	WKDAYw
Month	string	MONTH	MONTHw

Example

```
DATA LIST /ID 1-3 SEX 5 (A) AGE 7-8 OPINION1 TO OPINION5 10-14 .
```

Overview

DATA LIST defines a raw data file (a raw data file contains numbers and other alphanumeric characters) by assigning names and formats to each variable in the file. Raw data can be inline (entered with your commands between BEGIN DATA and END DATA) or stored in an external file. They can be in fixed format (values for the same variable are always entered in the same location on the same record for each case) or in freefield format (values for consecutive variables are not in particular columns but are entered one after the other, separated by blanks or commas).

For information on defining matrix materials, see MATRIX DATA. For information on defining complex data files that cannot be defined with DATA LIST, see FILE TYPE and REPEATING DATA. For information on reading SPSS-format data files and SPSS-format portable files, see GET and IMPORT.

The program can also read data files created by other software applications. Commands that read these files include GET CAPTURE and GET TRANSLATE.

Options

Data Source. You can use inline data or data from an external file.

Data Formats. You can define numeric (with or without decimal places) and string variables using an array of input formats (percent, dollar, date and time, and so forth). You can also specify column binary and unaligned positive integer binary formats (available only if used with the MODE=MULTIPUNCH setting on the FILE HANDLE command). For a complete list of available formats, see "Variable Formats" on p. 31.

Data Organization. You can define data that are in fixed format (values in the same location on the same record for each case), in freefield format with multiple cases per record, or in freefield format with one case on each record using the FIXED, FREE, and LIST keywords.

Multiple Records. For fixed-format data, you can indicate the number of records per case on the RECORDS subcommand. You can specify which records to read in the variable definition portion of DATA LIST.

Summary Table. For fixed-format data, you can display a table that summarizes the variable definitions using the TABLE subcommand. You can suppress this table using NOTABLE.

Value Delimiter. For freefield-format data (keywords FREE and LIST), you can specify the character(s) that separate data values, or you can use the keyword TAB to specify the tab character as the delimiter. Any delimiter other than the TAB keyword must be enclosed in quotation marks, and the specification must be enclosed in parentheses, as in DATA LIST FREE(",").

End-of-File Processing. You can specify a logical variable that indicates the end of the data using the END subcommand. This logical variable can be used to invoke special processing after all the cases from the data file have been read.

Basic Specification

- The basic specification is the FIXED, LIST, or FREE keyword, followed by a slash that signals the beginning of variable definition.
- FIXED is the default.
- If the data are in an external file, the FILE subcommand must be used.
- If the data are inline, the FILE subcommand is omitted and the data are specified between the BEGIN DATA and END DATA commands.
- Variable definition for fixed-format data includes a variable name, a column location, and a format (unless the default numeric format is used). The column location is not specified if FORTRAN-like formats are used, since these formats include the variable width.
- Variable definition for freefield data includes a variable name and, optionally, a delimiter specification and a FORTRAN-like format specification. If format specifications include a width and number of decimal positions (for example, F8.2), the width and decimal specifications are not used to read the data but are assigned as print and write formats for the variables.

Subcommand Order

Subcommands can be named in any order. However, all subcommands must precede the first slash, which signals the beginning of variable definition.

Syntax Rules

Subcommands on DATA LIST are separated by spaces or commas, not by slashes.

Operations

- DATA LIST clears the working data file and defines a new working file.
- Variable names are stored in the working file dictionary.
- Formats are stored in the working file dictionary and are used to display and write the values. To change output formats of numeric variables defined on DATA LIST, use the FORMATS command.

Fixed-Format Data

- The order of the variables in the working file dictionary is the order in which they are defined on DATA LIST, not their sequence in the input data file. This order is important if you later use the TO keyword to refer to variables on subsequent commands.
- In numeric format, blanks to the left or right of a number are ignored; imbedded blanks are invalid. When the program encounters a field that contains one or more blanks interspersed among the numbers, it issues a warning message and assigns the system-missing value to that case.
- Alphabetical and special characters, except the decimal point and leading plus and minus signs, are not valid in numeric variables and are set to system-missing if encountered in the data.
- The system-missing value is assigned to a completely blank field for numeric variables. The value assigned to blanks can be changed using the BLANKS specification on the SET command.
- The program ignores data contained in columns and records that are not specified in the variable definition.

Freefield Data

FREE can read freefield data with multiple cases recorded on one record or with one case recorded on more than one record. LIST can read freefield data with one case on each record.

- Line endings are read as delimiters between values.
- If you use FORTRAN-like format specifications (for example, DOLLAR12.2), width and decimal specifications are not used to read the data but are assigned as print and write formats for the variable.

For freefield data *without* explicitly specified value delimiters:

- Commas and blanks are interpreted as delimiters between values.
- Extra blanks are ignored.
- Multiple commas with or without blank space between them can be used to specify missing data.
- If a valid value contains commas or blank spaces, enclose the values in quotation marks or apostrophes.

For data with explicitly specified value delimiters (for example, DATA LIST FREE (",")):

- Multiple delimiters without any intervening space can be used to specify missing data.
- The specified delimiters cannot occur within a data value, even if you enclose the value in quotation marks or apostrophes.

Note: Freefield format with specified value delimiters is typically used to read data in text format written by a computer program, not for data manually entered in a text editor.

Example

```
* Column-style format specifications.

DATA LIST /ID 1-3 SEX 5 (A) AGE 7-8 OPINION1 TO OPINION5 10-14.
BEGIN DATA
001 m 28 12212
002 f 29 21212
003 f 45 32145
  . . .
128 m 17 11194
END DATA.
```

- The data are inline between the BEGIN DATA and END DATA commands, so the FILE subcommand is not specified. The data are in fixed format. The keyword FIXED is not specified because it is the default.

- Variable definition begins after the slash. Variable *ID* is in columns 1 through 3. Because no format is specified, numeric format is assumed. Variable *ID* is therefore a numeric variable that is three characters wide.

- Variable *SEX* is a short string variable in column 5. Variable *SEX* is one character wide.

- *AGE* is a two-column numeric variable in columns 7 and 8.

- Variables *OPINION1*, *OPINION2*, *OPINION3*, *OPINION4*, and *OPINION5* are named using the TO keyword (see "Keyword TO" on p. 29). Each is a one-column numeric variable, with *OPINION1* located in column 10 and *OPINION5* located in column 14.

- The BEGIN DATA and END DATA commands enclose the inline data. Note that the values of *SEX* are lowercase letters and must be specified as such on subsequent commands.

FILE Subcommand

FILE specifies the raw data file. FILE is required when data are stored in an external data file. FILE must not be used when the data are stored in a file that is included with the INCLUDE command or when the data are inline (see INCLUDE and BEGIN DATA—END DATA).

- FILE must be separated from other DATA LIST subcommands by at least one blank or comma.

- FILE must precede the first slash, which signals the beginning of variable definition.

FIXED, FREE, and LIST Keywords

FIXED, FREE, or LIST indicates the format of the data. Only one of these keywords can be used on each DATA LIST. The default is FIXED.

FIXED *Fixed-format data.* Each variable is recorded in the same column location on the same record for each case in the data. FIXED is the default.

FREE *Freefield data.* The variables are recorded in the same order for each case but not necessarily in the same column locations. More than one case can be entered on the same record. By default, values are separated by blanks or commas. You can also specify different value delimiters.

LIST   *Freefield data with one case on each record.* The variables are recorded in freefield format as described for the keyword FREE except that the variables for each case must be recorded on one record.

- FIXED, FREE, or LIST must be separated from other DATA LIST subcommands by at least one blank or comma.

- FIXED, FREE, or LIST must precede the first slash, which signals the beginning of data definition.

- For fixed-format data, you can use column-style or FORTRAN-like formats, or a combination of both. For freefield data, you can use only FORTRAN-like formats.

- For fixed-format data, the program reads values according to the column locations specified or implied by the FORTRAN-like format. Values in the data do *not* have to be in the same order as the variables named on DATA LIST and do *not* have to be separated by a space or column.

- For freefield data, the program reads values sequentially in the order in which the variables are named on DATA LIST. Values in the data *must* be in the order in which the variables are named on DATA LIST and *must* be separated by at least one valid delimiter.

- For freefield data, multiple blank spaces can be used to indicate missing information only if a blank space is explicitly specified as the delimiter. In general, it is better to use multiple non-blank delimiters (for example, two commas with no intervening space) to specify missing data.

- In freefield format, a value cannot be split across records.

Example

```
* Data in fixed format.

DATA LIST FILE=HUBDATA FIXED RECORDS=3
 /1 YRHIRED 14-15 DEPT 19 SEX 20.
```

- FIXED indicates explicitly that the *HUBDATA* file is in fixed format. Because FIXED is the default, the keyword FIXED could have been omitted.

- Variable definition begins after the slash. Column locations are specified after each variable. Since formats are not specified, the default numeric format is used. Variable widths are determined by the column specifications: *YRHIRED* is two characters wide, and *DEPT* and *SEX* are each one character wide.

Example

```
* Data in freefield format.
DATA LIST FREE / POSTPOS NWINS.
BEGIN DATA
2, 19, 7, 5, 10, 25, 5, 17, 8, 11, 3,, 6, 8, 1, 29
END DATA.
```

- Data are inline, so FILE is omitted. The keyword FREE is used because data are in freefield format with multiple cases on a single record. Two variables, *POSTPOS* and *NWINS*, are defined. Since formats are not specified, both variables receive the default F8.2 format.

- All of the data are recorded on one record. The first two values build the first case in the working data file. For the first case, *POSTPOS* has value 2 and *NWINS* has value 19. For the second case, *POSTPOS* has value 7 and *NWINS* has value 5, and so on. The working data file will contain eight cases.

- The two commas without intervening space after the data value 3 indicate a missing data value.

Example

```
* Data in list format.

DATA LIST LIST (",")/ POSTPOS NWINS.
BEGIN DATA
2,19
7,5
10,25
5,17
8,11
3,
6,8
1,29
END DATA.
```

- This example defines the same data as the previous example, but LIST is used because each case is recorded on a separate record. FREE could also be used. However, LIST is less prone to errors in data entry. If you leave out a value in the data with FREE format, all values after the missing value are assigned to the wrong variable. Since LIST format reads a case from each record, a missing value will affect only one case.
- A comma is specified as the delimiter between values.
- Since line endings are interpreted as delimiters between values, the second comma after the value 3 (in the sixth line of data) is not necessary to indicate that the value of *NWINS* is missing for that case.

TABLE and NOTABLE Subcommands

TABLE displays a table summarizing the variable definitions supplied on DATA LIST. NOTABLE suppresses the summary table. TABLE is the default.

- TABLE and NOTABLE can be used only for fixed-format data.
- TABLE and NOTABLE must be separated from other DATA LIST subcommands by at least one blank or comma.
- TABLE and NOTABLE must precede the first slash, which signals the beginning of variable definition.

RECORDS Subcommand

RECORDS indicates the number of records per case for fixed-format data. In the variable definition portion of DATA LIST, each record is preceded by a slash. By default, DATA LIST reads one record per case.

- The only specification on RECORDS is a single integer indicating the *total* number of records for each case (even if the DATA LIST command does not define all the records).

- RECORDS can be used only for fixed-format data and must be separated from other DATA LIST subcommands by at least one blank or comma. RECORDS must precede the first slash, which signals the beginning of variable definition.
- Each slash in the variable definition portion of DATA LIST indicates the beginning of a new record. The first slash indicates the first (or only) record. The second and any subsequent slashes tell the program to go to a new record.
- To skip a record, specify a slash without any variables for that record.
- The number of slashes in the variable definition cannot exceed the value of the integer specified on RECORDS.
- The sequence number of the record being defined can be specified after each slash. DATA LIST reads the number to determine which record to read. If the sequence number is used, you *do not* have to use a slash for any skipped records. However, the records to be read must be in their sequential order.
- The slashes for the second and subsequent records can be specified within the variable list, or they can be specified on a format list following the variable list (see the example below).
- All variables to be read from one record should be defined before you proceed to the next record.
- Since RECORDS can be used only with fixed format, it is not necessary to define all the variables on a given record or to follow their order in the input data file.

Example

```
DATA LIST FILE=HUBDATA RECORDS=3
 /2 YRHIRED 14-15 DEPT 19 SEX 20.
```

- DATA LIST defines fixed-format data. RECORDS can be used only for fixed-format data.
- RECORDS indicates that there are three records per case in the data. Only one record per case is defined in the data definition.
- The sequence number (2) before the first variable definition indicates that the variables being defined are on the second record. Because the sequence number is provided, a slash is not required for the first record, which is skipped.
- The variables *YRHIRED*, *DEPT*, and *SEX* are defined and will be included in the working data file. Any other variables on the second record or on the other records are not defined and are not included in the working file.

Example

```
DATA LIST FILE=HUBDATA RECORDS=3
 / /YRHIRED 14-15 DEPT 19 SEX 20.
```

- This command is equivalent to the one in the previous example. Because the record sequence number is omitted, a slash is required to skip the first record.

Example

```
DATA LIST FILE=HUBDATA RECORDS=3
 /YRHIRED (T14,F2.0) /  /NAME (T25,A24) .
```

- RECORDS indicates there are three records for each case in the data.

- *YRHIRED* is the only variable defined on the first record. The FORTRAN-like format specification T14 means tab over 14 columns. Thus, *YRHIRED* begins in column 14 and has format F2.0.

- The second record is skipped. Because the record sequence numbers are not specified, a slash must be used to skip the second record.

- *NAME* is the only variable defined for the third record. *NAME* begins in column 25 and is a string variable with a width of 24 characters (format A24).

Example

```
DATA LIST FILE=HUBDATA RECORDS=3
  /YRHIRED NAME (T14,F2.0 /  / T25,A24).
```

- This command is equivalent to the one in the previous example. *YRHIRED* is located on the first record, and *NAME* is located on the third record.

- The slashes that indicate the second and third records are specified within the format specifications. The format specifications follow the complete variable list.

END Subcommand

END provides control of end-of-file processing by specifying a variable that is set to a value of 0 until the end of the data file is encountered, at which point the variable is set to 1. The values of all variables named on DATA LIST are left unchanged. The logical variable created with END can then be used on DO IF and LOOP commands to invoke special processing after all the cases from a particular input file have been built.

- DATA LIST and the entire set of commands used to define the cases must be enclosed within an INPUT PROGRAM—END INPUT PROGRAM structure. The END FILE command must also be used to signal the end of case generation.

- END can be used only with fixed-format data. An error is generated if the END subcommand is used with FREE or LIST.

Example

```
INPUT PROGRAM.
NUMERIC      .      TINCOME (DOLLAR8.0).                    /* Total income
LEAVE               TINCOME.
DO IF               $CASENUM EQ 1.
+  PRINT            EJECT.
+  PRINT            / 'Name          Income'.
END IF
DATA LIST           FILE=INCOME END=#EOF NOTABLE / NAME 1-10(A)
                                                   INCOME 16-20(F).
DO IF               #EOF.
+  PRINT            / 'TOTAL       ', TINCOME.
+  END FILE.
ELSE.
+  PRINT            / NAME, INCOME (A10,COMMA8).
+  COMPUTE          TINCOME = TINCOME+INCOME.  /* Accumulate total income
END IF.
END INPUT PROGRAM.

EXECUTE.
```

- The data definition commands are enclosed within an INPUT PROGRAM—END INPUT PROGRAM structure.

- NUMERIC indicates that a new numeric variable, *TINCOME*, will be created.

- LEAVE tells the program to leave variable *TINCOME* at its value for the previous case as each new case is read, so that it can be used to accumulate totals across cases.

- The first DO IF structure, enclosing the PRINT EJECT and PRINT commands, tells the program to display the headings *Name* and *Income* at the top of the display (when *$CASE-NUM* equals 1).

- DATA LIST defines variables *NAME* and *INCOME*, and it specifies the scratch variable *#EOF* on the END subcommand.

- The second DO IF prints the values for *NAME* and *INCOME* and accumulates the variable *INCOME* into *TINCOME* by passing control to ELSE as long as *#EOF* is not equal to 1. At the end of the file, *#EOF* equals 1, and the expression on DO IF is true. The label *TOTAL* and the value for *TINCOME* are displayed, and control is passed to END FILE.

Example

```
* Concatenate three raw data files.

INPUT PROGRAM.
NUMERIC #EOF1 TO #EOF3.   /*These will be used as the END variables.

DO IF #EOF1 & #EOF2 & #EOF3.
+    END FILE.
ELSE IF #EOF1 & #EOF2.
+      DATA LIST  FILE=THREE END=#EOF3 NOTABLE / NAME 1-20(A)
              AGE 25-26 SEX 29(A).
+      DO IF NOT #EOF3.
+         END CASE.
+      END IF.
ELSE IF #EOF1.
+      DATA LIST  FILE=TWO END=#EOF2 NOTABLE / NAME 1-20(A)
              AGE 21-22 SEX 24(A).
+      DO IF NOT #EOF2.
+         END CASE.
+      END IF.
ELSE.
+      DATA LIST  FILE=ONE END=#EOF1 NOTABLE /1 NAME 1-20(A)
              AGE 21-22 SEX 24 (A).
+      DO IF NOT #EOF1.
+         END CASE.
+      END IF.
END IF.
END INPUT PROGRAM.

REPORT FORMAT AUTOMATIC LIST /VARS=NAME AGE SEX.
```

- The input program contains a DO IF—ELSE IF—END IF structure.

- Scratch variables are used on each END subcommand so the value will not be reinitialized to the system-missing value after each case is built.

- Three data files are read, two of which contain data in the same format. The third requires a slightly different format for the data items. All three DATA LIST commands are placed within the DO IF structure.

- END CASE builds cases from each record of the three files. END FILE is used to trigger end-of-file processing once all data records have been read.

- This application can also be handled by creating three separate SPSS-format data files and using ADD FILES to put them together. The advantage of using the input program is that additional files are not required to store the separate data files prior to performing ADD FILES.

Variable Definition

The variable definition portion of DATA LIST assigns names and formats to the variables in the data. Depending on the format of the file, you may also need to specify record and column location. The following sections describe variable names, location, and formats.

Variable Names

- Variable names can contain up to eight characters. All variable names must begin with a letter or the @ or # character. A # symbol as the first character of the variable name defines the variable as a scratch variable. System variables (beginning with a $) cannot be defined on DATA LIST. An underscore can be used within a variable name, provided the underscore is not the first character.
- The keyword TO can be used to generate names for consecutive variables in the data. Leading zeros in the number are preserved in the name. *X1* TO *X100* and *X001* TO *X100* both generate 100 variable names, but the first 99 names are not the same in the two lists. *X01* TO *X9* is not a valid specification. For more information on the TO keyword and other variable-naming rules, see "Variable Names" on p. 29.
- The order in which variables are named on DATA LIST determines their order in the working data file. If the working file is saved as an SPSS-format data file, the variables are saved in this order unless they are explicitly reordered on the SAVE or XSAVE command.

Example

```
DATA LIST FREE / ID SALARY #V1 TO #V4.
```

- The FREE keyword indicates that the data are in freefield format. Six variables are defined: *ID*, *SALARY*, *#V1*, *#V2*, *#V3*, and *#V4*. *#V1* to *#V4* are scratch variables that are not stored in the working data file. Their values can be used in transformations but not in procedure commands.

Variable Location

For fixed-format data, variable locations are specified either explicitly using column locations or implicitly using FORTRAN-like formats. For freefield data, variable locations are not specified. Values are read sequentially in the order in which variables are named on the variable list.

Fixed-Format Data

- If column-style formats are used, you must specify the column location of each variable after the variable name. If the variable is one column wide, specify the column number. Otherwise, specify the first column number followed by a dash (–) and the last column number.
- If several adjacent variables on the same record have the same width and format type, you can use one column specification after the last variable name. Specify the beginning column location of the first variable, a dash, and the ending column location of the last variable. the program divides the total number of columns specified equally among the variables. If the number of columns does not divide equally, an error message is issued.
- The same column locations can be used to define multiple variables.
- For FORTRAN-like formats, column locations are implied by the width specified on the formats (see "Variable Formats" on p. 254). To skip columns, use the Tn or nX format specifications.

- With fixed format, column-style and FORTRAN-like specifications can be mixed on the same DATA LIST command.
- Record location is indicated by a slash or a slash and record number before the names of the variables on that record. See the RECORDS subcommand on p. 247 for information on specifying record location.
- The program ignores data in columns and on records that are not specified on DATA LIST.
- In the data, values do not have to be separated by a space or comma.

Example

```
DATA LIST  FILE=HUBDATA RECORDS=3
 /1 YRHIRED 14-15 DEPT 19 SEX 20
 /2 SALARY 21-25.
```

- The data are in fixed format (the default) and are read from the file *HUBDATA*.
- Three variables, *YRHIRED*, *DEPT*, and *SEX*, are defined on the first record of the *HUBDA-TA* file. One variable, *SALARY*, is read from columns 21 through 25 on the second record. The total number of records per case is specified as 3 even though no variables are defined on the third record. The third record is simply skipped in data definition.

Example

```
DATA LIST  FILE=HUBDATA RECORDS=3
 /1 DEPT 19 SEX 20 YRHIRED 14-15 MOHIRED 12-13 HIRED 12-15
 /2 SALARY 21-25.
```

- The first two defined variables are *DEPT* and *SEX*, located in columns 19 and 20 on record 1. The next three variables, *YRHIRED*, *MOHIRED*, and *HIRED*, are also located on the first record.
- *YRHIRED* is read from columns 14 and 15, *MOHIRED* from columns 12 and 13, and *HIRED* from columns 12 through 15. The variable *HIRED* is a four-column variable with the first two columns representing the month when an employee was hired (the same as *MO-HIRED*) and the last two columns representing the year of employment (the same as *YRHIRED*).
- The order of the variables in the dictionary is the order in which they are defined on DATA LIST, not their sequence in the *HUBDATA* file.

Example

```
DATA LIST  FILE=HUBDATA RECORDS=3
 /1 DEPT 19 SEX 20 MOHIRED YRHIRED 12-15
 /2 SALARY 21-25.
```

- A single column specification follows *MOHIRED* and *YRHIRED*. DATA LIST divides the total number of columns specified equally between the two variables. Thus, each variable has a width of two columns.

Example

```
* Mixing column-style and FORTRAN-like format specifications.

DATA LIST FILE=PRSNL / LNAME M_INIT STREET (A20,A1,1X,A10)
    AGE 35-36.
```

- FORTRAN-like format specifications are used for string variables *LNAME*, *M_INIT*, and *STREET*. These variables must be adjacent in the data file. *LNAME* is 20 characters wide and is located in columns 1–20. *M_INIT* is one character wide and is located in column 21. The 1X specification defines a blank column between *M_INIT* and *STREET*. *STREET* is 10 characters wide and is located in columns 23–32.

- A column-style format is used for the variable *AGE*. *AGE* begins in column 35, ends in column 36, and by default has numeric format.

Freefield Data

- In freefield data, column location is irrelevant, since values are not in fixed column positions. Instead, values are simply separated from each other by blanks or by commas or a specified delimiter. Any number of consecutive blanks are interpreted as one delimiter unless a blank space is explicitly specified as the value delimiter. A value cannot be split across records.

- If there are not enough values to complete the last case, a warning is issued and the incomplete case is dropped.

- The specified delimiter can only be used within data values if the value is enclosed in quotations marks or apostrophes.

- To include an apostrophe in a string value, enclose the value in quotation marks. To include quotation marks in a value, enclose the value in apostrophes (see "String Values in Command Specifications" on p. 15).

Variable Formats

Two types of format specifications are available: column-style and FORTRAN-like. With each type, you can specify both numeric and string formats. The difference between the two types is that FORTRAN-like formats include the width of the variable and column-style formats do not.

- Column-style formats are available only for fixed-format data.

- Column-style and FORTRAN-like formats can be mixed on the same DATA LIST to define fixed-format data.

- A value that cannot be read according to the format type specified is assigned the system-missing value and a warning message is issued.

The following sections discuss the rules for specifying column-style and FORTRAN-like formats, followed by additional considerations for numeric and string formats. See p. 241 for a partial list of available formats. For a complete discussion of formats, see "Variable Formats" on p. 31.

Column-Style Format Specifications

The following rules apply to column-style formats:

- Data must be in a fixed format.
- Column locations must be specified after variable names. The width of a variable is determined by the number of specified columns. See "Fixed-Format Data" on p. 252 for information on specifying column location.
- Following the column location, specify the format type in parentheses. The format type applies only to the variable or the list of variables associated with the column location specification immediately before it. If no format type is specified, numeric (F) format is used.
- To include decimal positions in the format, specify the format type followed by a comma and the number of decimal positions. For example, (DOLLAR) specifies only whole dollar amounts; (DOLLAR,2) specifies DOLLAR format with two decimal positions.
- Since column positions are explicitly specified, the variables can be named in any order.

FORTRAN-like Format Specifications

The following rules apply to FORTRAN-like formats:

- Data can be in either fixed or freefield format.
- Column locations cannot be specified. The width of a variable is determined by the width portion (w) of the format specification. The width must specify the number of characters in the widest value.
- One format specification applies to only one variable. The format is specified in parentheses after the variable to which it applies. Alternatively, a variable list can be followed by an equal number of format specifications contained in one set of parentheses. When a number of consecutive variables have the same format, the number can be used as a multiplying factor preceding the format. For example, (3F5.2) assigns the format F5.2 to three consecutive variables.
- For fixed data, the number of formats specified (either explicitly or implied by the multiplication factor) must be the same as the number of variables. Otherwise, the program issues an error message. If no formats are specified, all variables have the default format F8.2.
- For freefield data, variables with no specified formats take the default F8.2 format. However, an asterisk (*) must be used to indicate where the default format stops. Otherwise, the program tries to apply the next specified format to every variable before it and issues an error message if the number of formats specified is less than the number of variables.
- For freefield data, width and decimal specifications are not used to read the data but are assigned as print and write formats for the variable.
- For fixed data, Tn can be used before a format to indicate that the variable begins at the nth column, and nX can be used to skip n columns before reading the variable. When Tn is specified, variables named do not have to follow the order of the variables in the data.
- For freefield data, variables are located according to the sequence in which they are named on DATA LIST. The order of variables on DATA LIST must correspond to the order of variables in the data.

- To include decimal positions in the format for fixed-format data, specify the total width followed by a decimal point and the number of decimal positions. For example, (DOLLAR5) specifies a five-column DOLLAR format without decimal positions; (DOLLAR5.2) specifies a five-column DOLLAR format, two columns of which are decimal positions.

Numeric Formats

- Format specifications on DATA LIST are input formats. Based on the width specification and format type, the program generates output (print and write) formats for each variable. The program automatically expands the output format to accommodate punctuation characters such as decimal points, commas, dollar signs, or date and time delimiters. (The program does not automatically expand the output formats you assign on the FORMATS, PRINT FORMATS, and WRITE FORMATS commands. For information on assigning output formats, refer to these commands.)
- Scientific notation is accepted in input data with F, COMMA, DOLLAR, DOT, and PCT formats. The same rules apply to these formats as to E format. The values 1.234E3, 1.234+3, and 1.234E 3 are all legitimate. The last value (with a blank space) will cause freefield data to be misread and therefore should be avoided when LIST or FREE is specified.

Implied Decimal Positions

- For fixed-format data, decimal positions can be coded in the data or implied by the format. If decimal positions are implied but are not entered in the data, the program interprets the rightmost digits in each value as the decimal digits. A coded decimal point in a value overrides the number of implied decimal places. For example, (DOLLAR,2) specifies two decimal positions. The value 123 is interpreted as 1.23; however, the value 12.3 is interpreted as 12.3 because the coded decimal position overrides the number of implied decimal positions.
- For freefield data, decimal positions cannot be implied but must be coded in the data. If decimal positions are specified in the format but a data value does not include a decimal point, the program fills the decimal places with zeros. For example, with F3.1 format (three columns with one decimal place), the value 22 is displayed as 22.0. If a value in the data has more decimal digits than are specified in the format, the additional decimals are truncated in displayed output (but not in calculations). For example, with F3.1 format, the value 2.22 is displayed as 2.2 even though in calculations it remains 2.22.

Table 1 compares how values are interpreted for fixed and freefield formats. Values in the table are for a four-column numeric variable.

Table 1   Interpretation of values in fixed and freefield format

	Fixed		Freefield	
Values	Default	Two defined decimal places	Default	Two defined decimal places
2001	2001	20.01	2001.00	2001.00
201	201	2.01	201.00	201.00
–201	–201	–2.01	–201.00	–201.00

Table 1   Interpretation of values in fixed and freefield format (Continued)

2	2	.02	2.00	2.00
20	20	.20	20.00	20.00
2.2	2.2	2.2	2.20	2.20
.201	.201	.201	.201	.201
2 01	Undefined	Undefined	Two values	Two values

Example

```
DATA LIST
  /MODEL 1 RATE 2-6(PCT,2) COST 7-11(DOLLAR) READY 12-21(ADATE).
BEGIN DATA
1935   7878811-07-1988
2 16754654606-08-1989
3 17684783612-09-1989
END DATA.
```

- Data are inline and in fixed format (the default).
- Each variable is followed by its column location. After the column location, a column-style format is specified in parentheses.
- *MODEL* begins in column 1, is one column wide, and receives the default numeric F format.
- *RATE* begins in column 2 and ends in column 6. The PCT format is specified with two decimal places. A comma is used to separate the format type from the number of decimal places. Decimal points are not coded in the data. Thus, the program reads the rightmost digits of each value as decimal digits. The value 935 for the first case in the data is interpreted as 9.35. Note that it does not matter where numbers are entered within the column width.
- *COST* begins in column 7 and ends in column 11. DOLLAR format is specified.
- *READY* begins in column 12 and ends in column 21. ADATE format is specified.

Example

```
DATA LIST FILE=DATA1
  /MODEL (F1) RATE (PCT5.2) COST (DOLLAR5) READY (ADATE10).
```

- In this example, the FILE subcommand is used because the data are in an external file.
- The variable definition is the same as in the preceding example except that FORTRAN-like format specifications are used rather than column-style. Column locations are not specified. Instead, the format specifications include a width for each format type.
- The width (w) portion of each format must specify the total number of characters in the widest value. DOLLAR5 format for *COST* accepts the five-digit value 78788, which displays as $78,788. Thus, the specified input format DOLLAR5 generates an output format DOLLAR7. The program automatically expands the width of the output format to accommodate the dollar sign and comma in displayed output.

String Formats

String (alphanumeric) variables can contain any numbers, letters, or characters, including special characters and imbedded blanks. Numbers entered as values for string variables cannot be used in calculations unless you convert them to numeric format (see RECODE). On DATA LIST, a string variable is defined with an A format if data are in standard character form or an AHEX format if data are in hexadecimal form. For further discussion of string formats, see "String Variable Formats" on p. 39.

- For fixed-format data, the width of a string variable is either implied by the column location specification or specified by the *w* on the FORTRAN-like format. For freefield data, the width must be specified on the FORTRAN-like format.

- The string formats defined on DATA LIST are both input and output formats. You cannot change the format of a defined string variable in this program. However, you can use the STRING command to define a new string variable and COMPUTE to copy the values from the old variable (see COMPUTE).

- AHEX format is available only for fixed-format data. Since each set of two hexadecimal characters represents one standard character, the width specification must be an even number. The output format for a variable in AHEX format is A format with half the specified width.

- If a string in the data is longer than its specified width, the string is truncated and a warning message is displayed. If the string in the data is shorter, it is right-padded with blanks and no warning message is displayed.

- For fixed-format data, all characters within the specified or implied columns, including leading, trailing, and imbedded blanks and punctuation marks, are read as the value of the string.

- For freefield data without a specified delimiter, string values in the data must be enclosed in apostrophes or quotation marks if the string contains a blank or a comma. Otherwise, the blank or comma is treated as a delimiter between values. Apostrophes can be included in a string by enclosing the string in quotation marks. Quotation marks can be included in a string by enclosing the string in apostrophes.

Example

```
DATA LIST FILE=WINS FREE /POSTPOS NWINS * POSNAME (A24).
```

- *POSNAME* is specified as a 24-character string. The asterisk preceding *POSNAME* indicates that *POSTPOS* and *NWINS* are read with the default format. If the asterisk was not specified, the program would apply the A24 format to *POSNAME* and then issue an error message indicating that there are more variables than specified formats.

Example

```
DATA LIST FILE=WINS FREE /POSTPOS * NWINS (A5) POSWINS.
```

- Both *POSTPOS* and *POSWINS* receive the default numeric format F8.2.
- *NWINS* receives the specified format of A5.

DATE

```
DATE  keyword [starting value [periodicity]]

     [keyword [starting value [periodicity]]]

     [BY increment]
```

Keywords for long time periods:

Keyword	Abbreviation	Default starting value	Default periodicity
YEAR	Y	1	none
QUARTER	Q	1	4
MONTH	M	1	12

Keywords for short time periods:

Keyword	Abbreviation	Default starting value	Default periodicity
WEEK	W	1	none
DAY	D	1	7
HOUR	H	0	24
MINUTE	MI	0	60
SECOND	S	0	60

Keywords for any time periods:

Keyword	Abbreviation	Default starting value	Default periodicity
CYCLE	C	1	none
OBS	O	none	none

Example

```
DATE Y 1960 M.
```

Overview

DATE generates date identification variables. You can use these variables to label plots and other output, establish periodicity, and distinguish between historical, validation, and forecasting periods.

Options

You can specify the starting value and periodicity. You can also specify an increment for the lowest-order keyword specified.

Basic Specification

The basic specification on DATE is a single keyword.

- For each keyword specified, DATE creates a numeric variable whose name is the keyword with an underscore as a suffix. Values for this variable are assigned to observations sequentially, beginning with the specified starting value. DATE also creates a string variable named *DATE_*, which combines the information from the numeric date variables and is used for labeling.
- If no starting value is specified, either the default is used or the value is inferred from the starting value of another DATE keyword.
- All variables created by DATE are automatically assigned variable labels that describe periodicity and associated formats. DATE produces a list of the names of the variables it creates and their variable labels.

Subcommand Order

- Keywords can be specified in any order.

Syntax Rules

- You can specify more than one keyword per command.
- If a keyword is specified more than once, only the last one is executed.
- Keywords that describe long time periods (YEAR, QUARTER, MONTH) cannot be used on the same command with keywords that describe short time periods (WEEK, DAY, HOUR, MINUTE, SECOND).
- Keywords CYCLE and OBS can be used with any other keyword.
- The lowest-order keyword specified should correspond to the level at which observations occur. For example, if observations are daily, the lowest-order keyword should be DAY.
- Keywords (except MINUTE) can be abbreviated down to the first character. MINUTE must have at least two characters (MI) to distinguish it from keyword MONTH.
- Keywords and additional specifications are separated by commas or spaces.

Starting Value and Periodicity

- A starting value and periodicity can be entered for any keyword except CYCLE. CYCLE can have only a starting value.
- Starting value and periodicity *must* be specified for keyword OBS.

- The starting value is specified first, followed by the periodicity, if any.
- You cannot specify a periodicity without first specifying a starting value.
- Starting values for HOUR, MINUTE, and SECOND can range from 0 to the periodicity minus 1 (for example, 0 to 59). For all other keywords, the range is 1 to the periodicity.
- If both MONTH and QUARTER are specified, DATE can infer the starting value of one from the other (see "Example 5" on p. 265).
- Specifying conflicting starting values for MONTH and QUARTER, such as Q 1 M 4, results in an error.
- For keyword YEAR, the starting value can be specified as the last two digits (93) instead of the whole year (1993) when the series and any forecasting are all within the same century. The same format (2 digits or 4 digits) must be used in all other commands that use year values.
- If you specify keywords that describe short time periods and skip over a level of measurement (for example, if you specify HOUR and SECOND but not MINUTE), you must specify the starting value and periodicity of the keyword after the skipped keywords. Otherwise, inappropriate periodicities will be generated (see "Example 7" on p. 266).

BY Keyword

- Keyword BY and a positive integer can be specified after the lowest-order keyword on the command to indicate an increment value. This value indicates how much to increment values of the lowest-order date variable as they are assigned to observations (see "Example 4" on p. 264).
- The increment value must divide evenly into the periodicity of the lowest-order DATE variable specified.

Operations

- DATE creates a numeric variable for every keyword specified, plus a string variable *DATE_*, which combines information from all the specified keywords.
- DATE automatically creates variable labels for each keyword specified indicating the variable name and its periodicity. For the *DATE_* variable, the label indicates the variable name and format.
- If the highest-order DATE variable specified has a periodicity, the *CYCLE_* variable will automatically be created. *CYCLE_* cannot have a periodicity (see "Example 3" on p. 263).
- Default periodicities are not used for the highest-order keyword specified. The exception is QUARTER, which will always have a default periodicity.
- The periodicity of the lowest-order variable is the default periodicity used by the procedures when periodicity is not defined either within the procedure or by the TSET command.
- The keyword name with an underscore is always used as the new variable name, even if keyword abbreviations are used in the specifications.
- Each time the DATE command is used, any DATE variables already in the working data file are deleted.

- The DATE command invalidates any previous USE and PREDICT commands specified. The USE and PREDICT periods must be respecified after DATE.

Limitations

- There is no limit on the number of keywords on the DATE command. However, keywords that describe long time periods (YEAR, QUARTER, MONTH) cannot be used on the same command with keywords that describe short time periods (WEEK, DAY, HOUR, MINUTE, SECOND).
- User-defined variable names must not conflict with DATE variable names.

Example 1

```
DATE Y 1960 M.
```

- This command generates variables *DATE_*, *YEAR_*, and *MONTH_*.
- *YEAR_* has a starting value of 1960. *MONTH_* starts at the default value of 1.
- By default, *YEAR_* has no periodicity, and *MONTH_* has a periodicity of 12.

DATE reports the following:

```
Name        Label

YEAR_       YEAR, not periodic
MONTH_      MONTH, period 12
DATE_       DATE.  FORMAT:  "MMM YYYY"
```

The following is a partial listing of the new variables:

```
YEAR_ MONTH_ DATE_

 1960     1   JAN 1960
 1960     2   FEB 1960
 1960     3   MAR 1960
 1960     4   APR 1960
 ...
 1960    10   OCT 1960
 1960    11   NOV 1960
 1960    12   DEC 1960
 1961     1   JAN 1961
 1961     2   FEB 1961
 ...
 1999     4   APR 1999
 1999     5   MAY 1999
 1999     6   JUN 1999
```

Example 2

```
DATE WEEK DAY 1 5 HOUR 1 8.
```

- This command creates four variables (*DATE_*, *WEEK_*, *DAY_*, and *HOUR_*) in a file where observations occur hourly in a 5-day, 40-hour week.
- For *WEEK_*, the default starting value is 1 and the default periodicity is none.

- For *DAY_*, the starting value has to be specified, even though it is the same as the default, because a periodicity is specified. The periodicity of 5 means that observations are measured in a 5-day week.

- For *HOUR_*, a starting value of 1 is specified. The periodicity of 8 means that observations occur in an 8-hour day.

DATE reports the following:

```
Name        Label

WEEK_       WEEK, not periodic
DAY_        DAY, period 5
HOUR_       HOUR, period 24
DATE_       DATE.  FORMAT:   "WWW D HH"
```

The following is a partial listing of the new variables:

```
WEEK_ DAY_ HOUR_ DATE_

    1    1     1    1 1  1
    1    1     2    1 1  2
    1    1     3    1 1  3
    1    1     4    1 1  4
    1    1     5    1 1  5
  ...
    1    1    22    1 1 22
    1    1    23    1 1 23
    1    2     0    1 2  0
    1    2     1    1 2  1
    1    2     2    1 2  2
  ...
    4    5    16    4 5 16
    4    5    17    4 5 17
    4    5    18    4 5 18
```

Example 3

```
DATE DAY 1 5 HOUR 3 8.
```

- This command creates four variables (*DATE_*, *CYCLE_*, *DAY_*, and *HOUR_*) in a file where observations occur hourly.

- For *HOUR_*, the starting value is 3 and the periodicity is 8.

- For *DAY_*, the starting value is 1 and the periodicity is 5. Since *DAY_* is the highest-order variable and it has a periodicity assigned, variable *CYCLE_* is automatically created.

DATE reports the following:

```
Name        Label

CYCLE_      CYCLE, not periodic
DAY_        DAY, period 5
HOUR_       HOUR, period 8
DATE_       DATE.  FORMAT:   "CCCC D H"
```

The following is a partial listing of the new variables:

```
CYCLE_ DAY_ HOUR_ DATE_
   1    1     3     1 1 3
   1    1     4     1 1 4
   1    1     5     1 1 5
   1    1     6     1 1 6
   1    1     7     1 1 7
   1    2     0     1 2 0
   1    2     1     1 2 1
 ...
  12    4     6    12 4 6
  12    4     7    12 4 7
  12    5     0    12 5 0
  12    5     1    12 5 1
  12    5     2    12 5 2
  12    5     3    12 5 3
  12    5     4    12 5 4
```

Example 4

```
DATE DAY HOUR 1 24 BY 2.
```

- This command creates three variables (*DATE_*, *DAY_*, and *HOUR_*) in a file where observations occur every two hours in a 24-hour day.
- *DAY_* uses the default starting value of 1. It has no periodicity, since none is specified, and it is the highest-order keyword on the command.
- *HOUR_* starts with a value of 1 and has a periodicity of 24.
- Keyword BY specifies an increment of 2 to use in assigning hour values.

DATE reports the following:

```
Name       Label

DAY_       DAY, not periodic
HOUR_      HOUR, period 24 by 2
DATE_      DATE. FORMAT:  "DDDD HH"
```

The following is a partial listing of the new variables:

```
DAY_ HOUR_ DATE_
   1    1     1  1
   1    3     1  3
   1    5     1  5
 ...
  39   17    39 17
  39   19    39 19
  39   21    39 21
  39   23    39 23
  40    1    40  1
  40    3    40  3
  40    5    40  5
  40    7    40  7
  40    9    40  9
  40   11    40 11
```

Example 5

```
DATE Y 1950 Q 2 M.
```

- This example creates four variables (*DATE_*, *YEAR_*, *QUARTER_*, and *MONTH_*) in a file where observations are quarterly, starting with April 1950.
- The starting value for *MONTH_* is inferred from *QUARTER_*.
- This specification is equivalent to DATE Y 1950 Q M 4. Here, the starting value for *QUARTER_* (2) would be inferred from MONTH.

DATE reports the following:

```
Name          Label

YEAR_         YEAR, not periodic
QUARTER_      QUARTER, period 4
MONTH_        MONTH, period 12
DATE_         DATE.  FORMAT:  "MMM YYYY"
```

The following is a partial listing of the new variables:

```
YEAR_ QUARTER_ MONTH_ DATE_

 1950      2        4    APR 1950
 1950      2        5    MAY 1950
 1950      2        6    JUN 1950
 1950      3        7    JUL 1950
 1950      3        8    AUG 1950
 ...
 1988      4       11    NOV 1988
 1988      4       12    DEC 1988
 1989      1        1    JAN 1989
 1989      1        2    FEB 1989
 1989      1        3    MAR 1989
 1989      2        4    APR 1989
 1989      2        5    MAY 1989
 1989      2        6    JUN 1989
 1989      3        7    JUL 1989
 1989      3        8    AUG 1989
 1989      3        9    SEP 1989
```

Example 6

```
DATE OBS 9 17.
```

- This command creates variables *DATE_*, *CYCLE_*, and *OBS_* and assigns values to observations sequentially, starting with value 9. The periodicity is 17.

DATE reports the following:

```
Name          Label

CYCLE_        CYCLE, not periodic
OBS_          OBS, period 17
DATE_         DATE.  FORMAT:  "CCCC OO"
```

The following is a partial listing of the new variables:

```
CYCLE_ OBS_ DATE_

    1    9     1   9
    1   10     1  10
    1   11     1  11
    1   12     1  12
    1   13     1  13
    1   14     1  14
    1   15     1  15
    1   16     1  16
    1   17     1  17
    2    1     2   1
    2    2     2   2
   ...
   28   15    28  15
   28   16    28  16
   28   17    28  17
   29    1    29   1
   29    2    29   2
   29    3    29   3
   29    4    29   4
   29    5    29   5
   29    6    29   6
```

Example 7

```
DATE W H 1 168
```

- This example creates three variables (*DATE_*, *WEEK_*, and *HOUR_*) in a file where observations occur hourly.
- Since the DAY keyword is not specified, a periodicity must be specified for HOUR. The value 168 indicates that there are 168 hours in a week.
- The starting value of HOUR is specified as 1.

DATE reports the following:

```
Name        Label

WEEK_       WEEK, not periodic
HOUR_       HOUR, period 168
DATE_       DATE.  FORMAT:  "WWWW HHH"
```

The following is a partial listing of the new variables:

```
WEEK_  HOUR_  DATE_
     1      1     1     1
     1      2     1     2
     1      3     1     3
     1      4     1     4
     1      5     1     5
     1      6     1     6
. . .
     1    161     1   161
     1    162     1   162
     1    163     1   163
     1    164     1   164
     1    165     1   165
     1    166     1   166
     1    167     1   167
     2      0     2     0
     2      1     2     1
     2      2     2     2
     2      3     2     3
     2      4     2     4
     2      5     2     5
. . .
     3    131     3   131
     3    132     3   132
     3    133     3   133
     3    134     3   134
     3    135     3   135
     3    136     3   136
     3    137     3   137
     3    138     3   138
```

DEFINE—!ENDDEFINE

```
DEFINE macro name

 ([{argument name=} [!DEFAULT (string)] [!NOEXPAND] {!TOKENS  (n)              }]
    {!POSITIONAL= }                               {!CHAREND ('char')           }
                                                  {!ENCLOSE ('char', 'char')}
                                                  {!CMDEND                     }


 [/{argument name=} ...])
    {!POSITIONAL= }

 macro body

 !ENDDEFINE
```

SET command controls:

```
PRESERVE
RESTORE
```

Assignment:

```
!LET var=expression
```

Conditional processing:

```
!IF (expression) !THEN statements
    [!ELSE statements]
!IFEND
```

Looping constructs:

```
!DO !varname=start !TO finish [BY step]
    statements  [!BREAK]
!DOEND

!DO !varname !IN (list)
    statements  [!BREAK]
!DOEND
```

Macro directives:

```
!OFFEXPAND
!ONEXPAND
```

String manipulation functions:

```
!LENGTH (string)
!CONCAT (string1,string2)
!SUBSTR (string,from,[length])
!INDEX (string1,string2)
!HEAD (string)
!TAIL (string)
!QUOTE (string)
!UNQUOTE (string)
!UPCASE (string)
!BLANKS (n)
!NULL
!EVAL (string)
```

Example

```
DEFINE sesvars ()
  age sex educ religion.
!ENDDEFINE.
```

Overview

DEFINE—!ENDDEFINE defines a program macro, which can then be used within a command sequence. A macro can be useful in several different contexts. For example, it can be used to:

- Issue a series of the same or similar commands repeatedly, using looping constructs rather than redundant specifications.
- Specify a set of variables.
- Produce output from several program procedures with a single command.
- Create complex input programs, procedure specifications, or whole sessions that can then be executed.

A macro is defined by specifying any part of a valid command and giving it a macro name. This name is then specified in a macro call within a command sequence. When the program encounters the macro name, it expands the macro.

In the examples of macro definition throughout this reference, the macro name, body, and arguments are shown in lower case for readability. Macro keywords, which are always preceded by an exclamation point (!), are shown in upper case. For additional examples of the macro facility, see Appendix D.

Options

Macro Arguments. You can declare and use arguments in the macro definition and then assign specific values to these arguments in the macro call. You can define defaults for the arguments and indicate whether an argument should be expanded when the macro is called. (See pp. 272–279.)

Macro Directives. You can turn macro expansion on and off (see p. 279).

String Manipulation Functions. You can process one or more character strings and produce either a new character string or a character representation of a numeric result (see pp. 279–281).

Conditional Processing. You can build conditional and looping constructs (see p. 283).

Macro Variables. You can directly assign values to macro variables (see p. 285).

Basic Specification

All macros must start with the DEFINE command and end with the macro command !ENDDEFINE. These commands identify the beginning and end of a macro definition and are used to separate the macro definition from the rest of the command sequence.

- Immediately after DEFINE, specify the **macro name**. All macros must have a name. The name is used in the macro call to refer to the macro. Macro names can begin with an exclamation point (!), but other than this, follow the usual naming conventions. Starting a name with an ! ensures that it will not conflict with the other text or variables in the session.

- Immediately after the macro name, specify an optional **argument** definition in parentheses. This specification indicates the arguments that will be read when the macro is called. If you do not want to include arguments, specify just the parentheses; *the parentheses are required, whether or not they enclose an argument.*

- Next specify the body of the macro. The **macro body** can include commands, parts of commands, or macro statements (macro directives, string manipulation statements, and looping and conditional processing statements).

- At the end of the macro body, specify the !ENDDEFINE command.

To invoke the macro, issue a **macro call** in the command sequence. To call a macro, specify the macro name and any necessary arguments. If there are no arguments, only the macro name is required.

Operations

- When macros are used in a prompted session, the command line prompt changes to DEFINE> between the DEFINE and !ENDDEFINE commands.

- When the program reads the macro definition, it translates into upper case all text (except arguments) not enclosed in quotation marks. Arguments are read in upper and lower case.

- The macro facility does not build and execute commands; rather, it expands strings in a process called **macro expansion**. A macro call initiates macro expansion. After the strings are expanded, the commands (or parts of commands) that contain the expanded strings are executed as part of the command sequence.

- Any elements on the macro call that are not used in the macro expansion are read and combined with the expanded strings.

- The expanded strings and the remaining elements from the macro call, if any, must conform to the syntax rules for the program. If not, the program generates either a warning or an error message, depending on the nature of the syntax problem.

Limitations

- The BEGIN DATA—END DATA commands are not allowed within a macro.
- The DEFINE command is not allowed within a macro.

Example

```
* Macro without arguments: Specify a group of variables.

DEFINE sesvars ()
   age sex educ religion.
!ENDDEFINE.

FREQUENCIES VARIABLES=sesvars.
```

- The macro name is **sesvars**. Because the parentheses are empty, **sesvars** has no arguments. The macro body defines four variables: *AGE*, *SEX*, *EDUC*, and *RELIGION*.
- The macro call is specified on FREQUENCIES. When the call is executed, **sesvars** is expanded into the variables *AGE*, *SEX*, *EDUC*, and *RELIGION*.
- After the macro expansion, FREQUENCIES is executed.

Example

```
* Macro without arguments: Repeat a sequence of commands.

DATA LIST FILE = MAC4D /GROUP 1   REACTIME 3-5 ACCURACY 7-9.
VALUE LABELS GROUP    1'normal'
                      2'learning disabled'.
* Macro definition.
DEFINE check ().
split file by group.
frequencies variables = reactime accuracy
  /histogram.
descriptives reactime accuracy.
list.
split file off.
regression variables = group reactime accuracy
  /dependent = accuracy
  /enter
  /scatterplot (reactime, accuracy).
!ENDDEFINE.

check.                      /* First call of defined macro check

COMPUTE REACTIME = SQRT (REACTIME).
COMPUTE ACCURACY = SQRT (ACCURACY).

check.                      /* Second call of defined macro check

COMPUTE REACTIME = lg10 (REACTIME * REACTIME).
COMPUTE ACCURACY = lg10 (ACCURACY * ACCURACY).

check.                      /* Third call of defined macro check
```

- The name of the macro is *CHECK*. The empty parentheses indicate that there are no arguments to the macro.
- The macro definition (between DEFINE and !ENDDEFINE) contains the command sequence to be repeated: SPLIT FILE, FREQUENCIES, DESCRIPTIVES, LIST, SPLIT FILE, and REGRESSION.

- The macro is called three times. Every time check is encountered, it is replaced with the command sequence SPLIT FILE, FREQUENCIES, DESCRIPTIVES, LIST, SPLIT FILE OFF, and REGRESSION. The command sequence using the macro facility is identical to the command sequence in which the specified commands are explicitly stated three separate times.

Example

```
* Macro with an argument.

DEFINE myfreq (vars = !CHAREND('/')).
frequencies variables = !vars
  /format = notable
  /hbar = normal
  /statistics = default skewness kurtosis.
!ENDDEFINE.

myfreq vars = AGE SEX EDUC RELIGION /.
```

- The macro definition defines vars as the macro argument. In the macro call, four variables are specified as the argument to the macro myfreq. When the program expands the myfreq macro, it substitutes the argument, AGE, SEX, EDUC, and RELIGION, for !vars and executes the resulting commands.

Macro Arguments

The macro definition can include macro arguments, which can be assigned specific values in the macro call. There are two types of arguments: keyword and positional. Keyword arguments are assigned names in the macro definition; in the macro call, they are identified by name. Positional arguments are defined after the keyword !POSITIONAL in the macro definition; in the macro call, they are identified by their relative position within the macro definition.

- There is no limit to the number of arguments that can be specified in a macro.
- All arguments are specified in parentheses and must be separated by slashes.
- If both keyword and positional arguments are defined in the same definition, the positional arguments must be defined, used in the macro body, and invoked in the macro call before the keyword arguments.

Example

```
* A keyword argument.

DEFINE macname (arg1 = !TOKENS(1)).
frequencies variables = !arg1.
!ENDDEFINE.

macname arg1 = V1.
```

- The macro definition defines macname as the macro name and arg1 as the argument. The argument arg1 has one token and can be assigned any value in the macro call.

- The macro call expands the macname macro. The argument is identified by its name, arg1, and is assigned the value V1. V1 is substituted wherever !arg1 appears in the macro body. The macro body in this example is the FREQUENCIES command.

Example

```
* A positional argument.

DEFINE macname (!POSITIONAL !TOKENS(1)
               /!POSITIONAL !TOKENS(2)).
frequencies variables = !1 !2.
!ENDDEFINE.

macname V1 V2 V3.
```

- The macro definition defines macname as the macro name with two positional arguments. The first argument has one token and the second argument has two tokens. The tokens can be assigned any values in the macro call.
- The macro call expands the macname macro. The arguments are identified by their positions. V1 is substituted for !1 wherever !1 appears in the macro body. V2 and V3 are substituted for !2 wherever !2 appears in the macro body. The macro body in this example is the FREQUENCIES command.

Keyword Arguments

Keyword arguments are called with user-defined keywords that can be specified in any order. In the macro body, the argument name is preceded by an exclamation point. On the macro call, the argument is specified without the exclamation point.

- Keyword argument definitions contain the argument name, an equals sign, and the !TOKENS, !ENCLOSE, !CHAREND, or !CMDEND keyword (see "Assigning Tokens to Arguments" on p. 275).
- Argument names are limited to seven characters and cannot match the character portion of a macro keyword, such as DEFINE, TOKENS, CHAREND, and so forth. See the syntax chart on p. 268 for a list of macro keywords for the program.
- The keyword !POSITIONAL cannot be used in keyword argument definitions.
- Keyword arguments do not have to be called in the order they were defined.

Example

```
DATA LIST FILE=MAC / V1 1-2 V2 4-5 V3 7-8.

* Macro definition.
DEFINE macdef2 (arg1 = !TOKENS(1)
               /arg2 = !TOKENS(1)
               /arg3 = !TOKENS(1)).
frequencies  variables = !arg1 !arg2 !arg3.
!ENDDEFINE.

* Macro call.
macdef2 arg1=V1  arg2=V2  arg3=V3.
macdef2 arg3=V3  arg1=V1  arg2=V2.
```

- Three arguments are defined: arg1, arg2, and arg3, each with one token. In the first macro call, arg1 is assigned the value V1, arg2 is assigned the value V2, and arg3 is assigned the value V3. V1, V2, and V3 are then used as the variables in the FREQUENCIES command.
- The second macro call yields the same results as the first one. With keyword arguments, you do not need to call the arguments in the order in which they were defined.

Positional Arguments

Positional arguments must be defined in the order in which they will be specified on the macro call. In the macro body, the first positional argument is referred to by !1, the second positional argument defined is referred to by !2, and so on. Similarly, the value of the first argument in the macro call is assigned to !1, the value of the second argument is assigned to !2, and so on.

- Positional arguments can be collectively referred to in the macro body by specifying !*. The !* specification concatenates arguments, separating individual arguments with a blank.

Example

```
DATA LIST FILE=MAC / V1 1-2 V2 4-5 V3 7-8.

* Macro definition.
DEFINE macdef (!POS !TOKENS(1).
              /!POS !TOKENS(1).
              /!POS !TOKENS(1)).
frequencies variables = !1 !2 !3.
!ENDDEFINE.

* Macro call.
macdef  V1    V2    V3.
macdef  V3    V1    V2.
```

- Three positional arguments with one token each are defined. The first positional argument is referred to by !1 on the FREQUENCIES command, the second by !2, and the third by !3.
- When the first call expands the macro, the first positional argument (!1) is assigned the value V1, the second positional argument (!2) is assigned the value V2, and the third positional argument (!3) is assigned the value V3.
- In the second call, the first positional argument is assigned the value V3, the second positional argument is assigned the value V1, and the third positional argument is assigned the value V2.

Example

```
DEFINE macdef (!POS !TOKENS(3)).
frequencies variables = !1.
!ENDDEFINE.

macdef  V1    V2    V3.
```

- This example is the same as the previous one, except that it assigns three tokens to one argument instead of assigning one token to each of three arguments. The result is the same.

Example

```
DEFINE macdef (!POS !TOKENS(1)
               /!POS !TOKENS(1)
               /!POS !TOKENS(1)).
frequencies variables = !*.
!ENDDEFINE.

macdef  V1   V2   V3.
```

- This is a third alternative for achieving the macro expansion shown in the previous two examples. It specifies three arguments but then joins them all together on one FREQUENCIES command using the symbol !*.

Assigning Tokens to Arguments

A **token** is a character or group of characters that has a predefined function in a specified context. The argument definition must include a keyword that indicates which tokens following the macro name are associated with each argument.

- Any program keyword, variable name, or delimiter (a slash, comma, etc.) is a valid token.
- The arguments for a given macro can use a combination of the token keywords.

!TOKENS (n)   *Assign the next* n *tokens to the argument.* The value *n* can be any positive integer and must be enclosed in parentheses. !TOKENS allows you to specify exactly how many tokens are desired.

!CHAREND ('char')   *Assign all tokens up to the specified character to the argument.* The character must be a one-character string specified in apostrophes and enclosed in parentheses. !CHAREND specifies the character that ends the argument assignment. This is useful when the number of assigned tokens is arbitrary or not known in advance.

!ENCLOSE ('char','char') *Assign all tokens between the indicated characters to the argument.* The starting and ending characters can be any one-character strings, and they do not need to be the same. The characters are each enclosed in apostrophes and separated by a comma. The entire specification is enclosed in parentheses. !ENCLOSE allows you to group multiple tokens within a specified pair of symbols. This is useful when the number of tokens to be assigned to an argument is indeterminate, or when the use of an ending character is not sufficient.

!CMDEND   *Assign to the argument all of the remaining text on the macro call, up to the start of the next command.* !CMDEND is useful for changing the defaults on an existing command. Since !CMDEND reads up to the next command, only the last argument on the argument list can be specified with !CMDEND. If !CMDEND is not the final argument, the arguments following !CMDEND are read as text.

Example

```
* Keyword !TOKENS.

DEFINE macname (!POSITIONAL !TOKENS (3)).
frequencies variables = !1.
!ENDDEFINE.

macname ABC DEFG HI.
```

- The three tokens following macname (ABC, DEFG, and HI) are assigned to the positional argument !1, and FREQUENCIES is then executed.

Example

```
* Keyword !TOKENS.

* Macro definition.
DEFINE earnrep (varrep = !TOKENS (1)).
sort cases by !varrep.
report variables = earnings
  /break = !varrep
  /summary = mean.
!ENDDEFINE.

* Call the macro three times.
earnrep varrep= SALESMAN.   /*First macro call
earnrep varrep = REGION.    /*Second macro call
earnrep varrep = MONTH.     /*Third macro call
```

- This macro runs a REPORT command three times, each time with a different break variable.
- The macro name is earnrep, and there is one keyword argument, varrep, which has one token.
- In the first macro call, the token SALESMAN is substituted for !varrep when the macro is expanded. REGION and MONTH are substituted for !varrep when the macro is expanded in the second and third calls.

Example

```
* Keyword !CHAREND'.

DEFINE macname (!POSITIONAL !CHAREND ('/')
               /!POSITIONAL !TOKENS(2)).
frequencies variables = !1.
correlations variables= !2.
!ENDDEFINE.

macname A B C D / E F.
```

- When the macro is called, all tokens up to the slash (A, B, C, and D) are assigned to the positional argument !1. E and F are assigned to the positional argument !2.

Example

```
* Keyword !CHAREND.

DEFINE macname (!POSITIONAL !CHAREND ('/')).
frequencies variables = !1.
!ENDDEFINE.

macname A B C D / E F.
```

- Although E and F are not part of the positional argument and are not used in the macro expansion, the program still reads them as text and interprets them in relation to where the macro definition ends. In this example, macro definition ends after the expanded variable list (D). E and F are names of variables. Thus, E and F are added to the variable list and FREQUENCIES is executed with six variables: *A, B, C, D, E,* and *F.*

Example

```
* Keyword !ENCLOSE.

DEFINE macname (!POSITIONAL !ENCLOSE('(',')')).
frequencies variables = !1
  /statistics = default skewness.
!ENDDEFINE.

macname (A B C) D E.
```

- When the macro is called, the three tokens enclosed in parentheses, A, B, and C, are assigned to the positional argument !1 in the macro body.

- After macro expansion is complete, the program reads the remaining characters on the macro call as text. In this instance, the macro definition ends with keyword SKEWNESS on the STATISTICS subcommand. Adding variable names to the STATISTICS subcommand is not valid syntax. The program generates a warning message but is still able to execute the frequencies command. Frequency tables and the specified statistics are generated for the variables *A, B,* and *C.*

Example

```
* Keyword !CMDEND'.

DEFINE macname (!POSITIONAL !TOKENS(2)
                /!POSITIONAL !CMDEND).
frequencies variables = !1.
correlations variables= !2.
!ENDDEFINE.

macname A B C D E.
```

- When the macro is called, the first two tokens following macname (A and B) are assigned to the positional argument !1. C, D, and E are assigned to the positional argument !2. Thus, the variables used for FREQUENCIES are *A* and *B,* and the variables used for CORRELATION are *C, D,* and *E.*

Example

```
* Incorrect order for !CMDEND.

DEFINE macname  (!POSITIONAL !CMDEND
                 /!POSITIONAL !tokens(2)).
frequencies variables = !1.
correlations variables= !2.
!ENDDEFINE.

macname  A B C D E.
```

- When the macro is called, all five tokens, A, B, C, D, and E, are assigned to the first positional argument. No variables are included on the variable list for CORRELATIONS, causing the program to generate an error message. The previous example declares the arguments in the correct order.

Example

```
* Using !CMDEND.
SUBTITLE 'CHANGING DEFAULTS ON A COMMAND'.

DEFINE myfreq (!POSITIONAL !CMDEND ).
frequencies !1
  /statistics=default skewness  /* Modify default statistics.
!ENDDEFINE.

myfreq VARIABLES = A B /HIST.
```

- The macro myfreq contains options for the FREQUENCIES command. When the macro is called, myfreq is expanded to perform a FREQUENCIES analysis on the variables *A* and *B*. The analysis produces default statistics and the skewness statistic, plus a histogram, as requested on the macro call.

Example

```
* Keyword arguments: Using a combination of token keywords.

DATA LIST FREE / A B C D E.
DEFINE macdef3 (arg1 = !TOKENS(1)
                /arg2 = !ENCLOSE ('(',')')
                /arg3 = !CHAREND('%')).
frequencies variables = !arg1  !arg2 !arg3.
!ENDDEFINE.
macdef arg1 = A  arg2=(B C)  arg3=DE %.
```

- Because arg1 is defined with the !TOKENS keyword, the value for arg1 is simply specified as A. The value for arg2 is specified in parentheses, as indicated by !ENCLOSE. The value for arg3 is followed by a percent sign, as indicated by !CHAREND.

Defining Defaults

The optional !DEFAULT keyword in the macro definition establishes default settings for arguments.

!DEFAULT   *Default argument.* After !DEFAULT, specify the value you want to use as a default for that argument. A default can be specified for each argument.

Example

```
DEFINE macdef (arg1 = !DEFAULT (V1) !TOKENS(1)
               /arg2 = !TOKENS(1)
               /arg3 = !TOKENS(1)).
frequencies variables = !arg1 !arg2 !arg3.
!ENDDEFINE.

macdef arg2=V2  arg3=V3.
```

- V1 is defined as the default value for argument arg1. Since arg1 is not specified on the macro call, it is set to V1.

- If !DEFAULT (V1) were not specified, the value of arg1 would be set to a null string.

Controlling Expansion

!NOEXPAND indicates that an argument should not be expanded when the macro is called.

!NOEXPAND   *Do not expand the specified argument.* !NOEXPAND applies to a single argument and is useful only when a macro calls another macro (imbedded macros).

Macro Directives

!ONEXPAND and !OFFEXPAND determine whether macro expansion is on or off. !ONEXPAND activates macro expansion and !OFFEXPAND stops macro expansion. All symbols between !OFFEXPAND and !ONEXPAND in the macro definition will not be expanded when the macro is called.

!ONEXPAND   *Turn macro expansion on.*

!OFFEXPAND   *Turn macro expansion off.* !OFFEXPAND is effective only when SET MEXPAND is ON (the default).

Macro Expansion in Comments

When macro expansion is on, a macro is expanded when its name is specified in a comment line beginning with *. To use a macro name in a comment, specify the comment within slashes and asterisks (/*...*/) to avoid unwanted macro expansion. (See COMMENT.)

String Manipulation Functions

String manipulation functions process one or more character strings and produce either a new character string or a character representation of a numeric result.

- The result of any string manipulation function is treated as a character string.

- The arguments to string manipulation functions can be strings, variables, or even other macros. A macro argument or another function can be used in place of a string.
- The strings within string manipulation functions must be either single tokens, such as ABC, or delimited by apostrophes or quotation marks, as in 'A B C'. See Table 1 for a set of expressions and their results.

Table 1   Expressions and results

Expression	Result
!UPCASE(abc)	ABC
!UPCASE('abc')	ABC
!UPCASE(a b c)	error
!UPCASE('a b c')	A B C
!UPCASE(a/b/c)	error
!UPCASE('a/b/c')	A/B/C
!UPCASE(!CONCAT(a,b,c))	ABC
!UPCASE(!CONCAT('a','b','c'))	ABC
!UPCASE(!CONCAT(a, b, c))	ABC
!UPCASE(!CONCAT('a ','b ','c '))	A B C
!UPCASE(!CONCAT('a,b,c'))	A,B,C
!QUOTE(abc)	'ABC'
!QUOTE('abc')	abc
!QUOTE('Bill''s')	'Bill''s'
!QUOTE("Bill's")	"Bill's"
!QUOTE(Bill's)	error
!QUOTE(!UNQUOTE('Bill''s'))	'Bill''s'

!LENGTH (str)

Return the length of the specified string. The result is a character representation of the string length. !LENGTH(abcdef) returns 6. If the string is specified with apostrophes around it, each apostrophe adds 1 to the length. !LENGTH ('abcdef') returns 8. If an argument is used in place of a string and it is set to null, this function will return 0.

!CONCAT(str1,str2 . . .)

Return a string that is the concatenation of the strings. For example, !CONCAT (abc,def) returns abcdef.

!SUBSTR (str,from,[length])

Return a substring of the specified string. The substring starts at the *from* position and continues for the specified *length*. If the length is not specified, the substring ends at the end of the input string. For example, !SUBSTR (abcdef, 3, 2) returns cd.

!INDEX (haystack,needle)

Return the position of the first occurrence of the needle in the haystack. If the needle is not found in the haystack, the function returns 0. !INDEX (abcdef,def) returns 4.

!HEAD (str)	*Return the first token within a string.* The input string is not changed. !HEAD ('a b c') returns a.
!TAIL (str)	*Return all tokens except the head token.* The input string is not changed. !TAIL('a b c') returns b c.
!QUOTE (str)	*Put apostrophes around the argument.* !QUOTE replicates any imbedded apostrophe. !QUOTE(abc) returns 'abc'. If !1 equals Bill's, !QUOTE(!1) returns 'Bill''s'.
!UNQUOTE (str)	*Remove quotation marks and apostrophes from the enclosed string.* If !1 equals 'abc', !UNQUOTE(!1) is abc. Internal paired quotation marks are unpaired; if !1 equals 'Bill''s', !UNQUOTE(!1) is Bill's. The specification !UNQUOTE(!QUOTE(Bill)) returns Bill.
!UPCASE (str)	*Convert all lowercase characters in the argument to upper case.* !UPCASE('abc def') returns ABC DEF.
!BLANKS (n)	*Generate a string containing the specified number of blanks.* The *n* specification must be a positive integer. !BLANKS(5) returns a string of five blank spaces. Unless the blanks are quoted, they cannot be processed, since the macro facility compresses blanks.
!NULL	*Generate a string of length 0.* This can help determine whether an argument was ever assigned a value, as in !IF (!1 !EQ !NULL) !THEN. . . .
!EVAL (str)	*Scan the argument for macro calls.* During macro definition, an argument to a function or an operand in an expression is not scanned for possible macro calls unless the !EVAL function is used. It returns a string that is the expansion of its argument. For example, if mac1 is a macro, then !EVAL(mac1) returns the expansion of mac1. If mac1 is not a macro, !EVAL(mac1) returns mac1.

SET Subcommands for Use with Macro

Four subcommands on the SET command were designed for use with the macro facility.

MPRINT	*Display a list of commands after macro expansion.* The specification on MPRINT is YES or NO (alias ON or OFF). By default, the output does not include a list of commands after macro expansion (MPRINT NO). The MPRINT subcommand on SET is independent of the PRINTBACK command.
MEXPAND	*Macro expansion.* The specification on MEXPAND is YES or NO (alias ON or OFF). By default, MEXPAND is on. SET MEXPAND OFF prevents macro expansion. Specifying SET MEXPAND ON reestablishes macro expansion.
MNEST	*Maximum nesting level for macros.* The default number of levels that can be nested is 50. The maximum number of levels depends on storage capacity.

MITERATE   *Maximum loop iterations permitted in macro expansions.* The default number of iterations is 1000.

Restoring SET Specifications

The PRESERVE and RESTORE commands bring more flexibility and control over SET. PRESERVE and RESTORE are available generally within the program but are especially useful with macros.

- The settings of all SET subcommands—those set explicitly and those set by default (except MEXPAND)—are saved with PRESERVE. PRESERVE has no further specifications.
- With RESTORE, all SET subcommands are changed to what they were when the PRESERVE command was executed. RESTORE has no further specifications.
- PRESERVE...RESTORE sequences can be nested up to five levels.

PRESERVE   *Store the SET specifications that are in effect at this point in the session.*

RESTORE   *Restore the SET specifications to what they were when PRESERVE was specified.*

Example

```
* Two nested levels of preserve and restore'.

DEFINE macdef ().
preserve.
set format F5.3.
descriptives v1 v2.
+ preserve.
set format F3.0 blanks=999.
descriptives v3 v4.
+ restore.
descriptives v5 v6.
restore.
!ENDDEFINE.
```

- The first PRESERVE command saves all of the current SET conditions. If none have been specified, the default settings are saved.
- Next, the format is set to F5.3 and descriptive statistics for *V1* and *V2* are obtained.
- The second PRESERVE command saves the F5.3 format setting and all other settings in effect.
- The second SET command changes the format to F3.0 and sets BLANKS to 999 (the default is SYSMIS). Descriptive statistics are then obtained for *V3* and *V4*.
- The first RESTORE command restores the format to F5.3 and BLANKS to the default, the setting in effect at the second PRESERVE. Descriptive statistics are then obtained for *V5* and *V6*.
- The last RESTORE restores the settings in effect when the first PRESERVE was specified.

Conditional Processing

The !IF construct specifies conditions for processing. The syntax is as follows:

```
!IF (expression) !THEN statements
                 [!ELSE statements]
!IFEND
```

- !IF, !THEN, and !IFEND are all required. !ELSE is optional.
- If the result of the expression is true, the statements following !THEN are executed. If the result of the expression is false and !ELSE is specified, the statements following !ELSE are executed. Otherwise, the program continues.
- Valid operators for the expressions include !EQ, !NE, !GT, !LT, !GE, !LE, !OR, !NOT, and !AND, or =, ~= (¬=), >, <, >=, <=, |, ~ (¬), and & (see "Relational Operators" on p. 55).
- When a macro is expanded, conditional processing constructs are interpreted after arguments are substituted and functions are executed.
- !IF statements can be nested whenever necessary. Parentheses can be used to specify the order of evaluation. The default order is the same as for transformations: !NOT has precedence over !AND, which has precedence over !OR.

Looping Constructs

Looping constructs accomplish repetitive tasks. Loops can be nested to whatever depth is required, but loops cannot be crossed. The macro facility has two looping constructs: the index loop (DO loop) and the list-processing loop (DO IN loop).

- When a macro is expanded, looping constructs are interpreted after arguments are substituted and functions are executed.

Index Loop

The syntax of an index loop is as follows:

```
!DO !var = start !TO finish [ !BY step ]
    statements
!BREAK
!DOEND
```

- The indexing variable is *!var* and must begin with an exclamation point.
- The start, finish, and step values must be numbers or expressions that evaluate to numbers.
- The loop begins at the start value and continues until it reaches the finish value (unless a !BREAK statement is encountered). The step value is optional and can be used to specify a subset of iterations. If start is set to 1, finish to 10, and step to 3, the loop will be executed four times with the index variable assigned values 1, 4, 7, and 10.
- The statements can be any valid commands or macro keywords. !DOEND specifies the end of the loop.
- !BREAK is an optional specification. It can be used in conjunction with conditional processing to exit the loop.

Example

```
DEFINE macdef (arg1 = !TOKENS(1)
               /arg2 = !TOKENS(1)).
!DO !i = !arg1 !TO !arg2.
frequencies variables = !CONCAT(var,!i).
!DOEND.
!ENDDEFINE.
macdef arg1 = 1 arg2 = 3.
```

- The variable *!i* is initially assigned the value 1 (arg1) and is incremented until it equals 3 (arg2), at which point the loop ends.

- The first loop concatenates var and the value for *!I*, which is 1 in the first loop. The second loop concatenates var and 2, and the third concatenates var and 3. The result is that FREQUENCIES is executed three times, with variables *VAR1*, *VAR2*, and *VAR3*, respectively.

List-processing Loop

The syntax of a list-processing loop is as follows:

```
!DO !var !IN (list)
    statements
!BREAK
!DOEND
```

- The !DO and !DOEND statements begin and end the loop. !BREAK is used to exit the loop.

- The !IN function requires one argument, which must be a list of items. The number of items on the list determines the number of iterations. At each iteration, the index variable *!var* is set to each item on the list.

- The list can be any expression, although it is usually a string. Only one list can be specified in each list-processing loop.

Example

```
DEFINE macdef (!POS !CHAREND('/') ).
!DO !i !IN ( !1).
frequencies variables = !i.
!DOEND.
!ENDDEFINE.
macdef VAR1 VAR2 VAR3   /.
```

- The macro call assigns three variables, *VAR1*, *VAR2*, and *VAR3*, to the positional argument !1. Thus, the loop completes three iterations.

- In the first iteration, *!i* is set to value *VAR1*. In the second and third iterations, *!I* is set to *VAR2* and *VAR3*, respectively. Thus, FREQUENCIES is executed three times, respectively with *VAR1*, *VAR2*, and *VAR3*.

Example

```
DEFINE macdef (!POS !CHAREND('/') ).
!DO !i !IN ( !1).
sort cases by !i.
report var = earnings
  /break = !i
  /summary = mean.
!DOEND.
!ENDDEFINE.

macdef SALESMAN REGION MONTH /.
```

- The positional argument !1 is assigned the three variables *SALESMAN*, *REGION*, and *MONTH*. The loop is executed three times and the index variable *!i* is set to each of the variables in succession. The macro creates three reports.

Direct Assignment of Macro Variables

The macro command !LET assigns values to macro variables. The syntax is as follows:

```
!LET !var = expression
```

- The expression must be either a single token or enclosed in parentheses.
- The macro variable *!var* cannot be a macro keyword (see the syntax chart on p. 268 for a list of macro keywords), and it cannot be the name of one of the arguments within the macro definition. Thus, !LET cannot be used to change the value of an argument.
- The macro variable *!var* can be a new variable or one previously assigned by a !DO command or another !LET command.

Example

```
!LET !a = 1.
!LET !b = !CONCAT(ABC,!SUBSTR(!1,3,1),DEF).
!LET !c = (!2 ~= !NULL).
```

- The first !LET sets *!a* equal to 1.
- The second !LET sets *!b* equal to ABC followed by 1 character taken from the third position of !1 followed by DEF.
- The last !LET sets *!c* equal to 0 (false) if !2 is a null string or to 1 (true) if !2 is not a null string.

DESCRIPTIVES

```
DESCRIPTIVES [VARIABLES=] varname[(zname)] [varname...]

 [/MISSING={VARIABLE**}  [INCLUDE]]
           {LISTWISE  }

 [/SAVE]

 [/STATISTICS=[DEFAULT**]  [MEAN**]  [MIN**]  [SKEWNESS]]
              [STDDEV** ]  [SEMEAN]  [MAX**]  [KURTOSIS]
              [VARIANCE ]  [SUM   ]  [RANGE]  [ALL]

 [/SORT=[{MEAN    }] [{(A)}]]
         {SMEAN   }   {(D)}
         {STDDEV  }
         {VARIANCE}
         {KURTOSIS}
         {SKEWNESS}
         {RANGE   }
         {MIN     }
         {MAX     }
         {SUM     }
         {NAME    }
```

**Default if the subcommand is omitted.

Example

```
DESCRIPTIVES VARIABLES=FOOD RENT, APPL TO COOK, TELLER, TEACHER
  /STATISTICS=VARIANCE DEFAULT
  /MISSING=LISTWISE.
```

Overview

DESCRIPTIVES computes univariate statistics, including the mean, standard deviation, minimum, and maximum, for numeric variables. Because it does not sort values into a frequency table, DESCRIPTIVES is an efficient means of computing descriptive statistics for continuous variables. Other procedures that display descriptive statistics include FREQUENCIES, MEANS, and EXAMINE.

Options

Z Scores. You can create new variables that contain z scores (standardized deviation scores from the mean) and add them to the working data file by specifying z-score names on the VARIABLES subcommand or by using the SAVE subcommand.

Statistical Display. Optional statistics available with the STATISTICS subcommand include the standard error of the mean, variance, kurtosis, skewness, range, and sum. DESCRIPTIVES does not compute the median or mode (see FREQUENCIES or EXAMINE).

Display Order. You can list variables in ascending or descending alphabetical order or by the numerical value of any of the available statistics using the SORT subcommand.

Basic Specification

The basic specification is the VARIABLES subcommand with a list of variables. The actual keyword VARIABLES can be omitted. All cases with valid values for a variable are included in the calculation of statistics for that variable. Statistics include the mean, standard deviation, minimum, maximum, and number of cases with valid values.

Subcommand Order

- Subcommands can be used in any order.

Operations

- If a string variable is specified on the variable list, no statistics are displayed for that variable.
- If there is insufficient memory available to calculate statistics for all variables requested, DESCRIPTIVES truncates the variable list.

Example

```
DESCRIPTIVES VARIABLES=FOOD RENT, APPL TO COOK, TELLER, TEACHER
 /STATISTICS=VARIANCE DEFAULT
 /MISSING=LISTWISE.
```

- DESCRIPTIVES requests statistics for the variables *FOOD*, *RENT*, *TELLER*, *TEACHER*, and all of the variables between and including *APPL* and *COOK* in the working data file.
- STATISTICS requests the variance and the default statistics: mean, standard deviation, minimum, and maximum.
- MISSING specifies that cases with missing values for any variable on the variable list will be omitted from the calculation of statistics for all variables.

Example

```
DESCRIPTIVES VARS=ALL.
```

- DESCRIPTIVES requests statistics for all variables in the working file.
- Because no STATISTICS subcommand is included, only the mean, standard deviation, minimum, and maximum are displayed.

VARIABLES Subcommand

VARIABLES names the variables for which you want to compute statistics. The actual keyword VARIABLES can be omitted.

- The keyword ALL can be used to refer to all user-defined variables in the working data file.
- Only one variable list can be specified.

Z Scores

The *z*-score transformation standardizes variables to the same scale, producing new variables with a mean of 0 and a standard deviation of 1. These variables are added to the working data file.

- To obtain *z* scores for all specified variables, use the SAVE subcommand.
- To obtain *z* scores for a subset of variables, name the new variable in parentheses following the source variable on the VARIABLES subcommand and do not use the SAVE subcommand.
- Specify new names individually; a list in parentheses is not recognized.
- The new variable name can be any acceptable eight-character name that is not already part of the working data file.

Example

```
DESCRIPTIVES VARIABLES=NTCSAL NTCPUR (PURCHZ) NTCPRI (PRICEZ).
```

- DESCRIPTIVES creates *z*-score variables named *PURCHZ* and *PRICEZ* for *NTCPUR* and *NTCPRI*, respectively. No *z*-score variable is created for *NTCSAL*.

SAVE Subcommand

SAVE creates a *z*-score variable for each variable specified on the VARIABLES subcommand. The new variables are added to the working data file.

- When DESCRIPTIVES creates new *z*-score variables, it displays the source variable names, the new variable names, and their labels in the Notes table.
- DESCRIPTIVES automatically supplies variable names for the new variables. The new variable name is created by prefixing the letter *Z* to the first seven characters of the source variable name. For example, *ZNTCPRI* is the *z*-score variable for *NTCPRI*.
- If the default naming convention duplicates variable names in the working data file, DESCRIPTIVES uses an alternative naming convention: first *ZSC001* through *ZSC099*, then *STDZ01* through *STDZ09*, then *ZZZZ01* through *ZZZZ09*, and then *ZQZQ01* through *ZQZQ09*.
- Variable labels are created by prefixing *ZSCORE* to the first 31 characters of the source variable label. If the alternative naming convention is used, DESCRIPTIVES prefixes *ZSCORE(varname)* to the first 31 characters of the label. If the source variable does not have a label, DESCRIPTIVES uses *ZSCORE(varname)* for the label.
- If you specify new names on the VARIABLES subcommand *and* use the SAVE subcommand, DESCRIPTIVES creates one new variable for each variable on the VARIABLES subcommand, using default names for variables not assigned names on VARIABLES.
- If at any time you want to change any of the variable names, whether those DESCRIPTIVES created or those you previously assigned, you can do so with the RENAME VARIABLES command.

Example

```
DESCRIPTIVES VARIABLES=ALL
  /SAVE.
```

- SAVE creates a *z*-score variable for all variables in the working file. All *z*-score variables receive the default name.

Example

```
DESCRIPTIVES VARIABLES=NTCSAL NTCPUR (PURCHZ) NTCPRI (PRICEZ)
  /SAVE.
```

- DESCRIPTIVES creates three *z*-score variables named *ZNTCSAL* (the default name), *PURCHZ*, and *PRICEZ*.

Example

```
DESCRIPTIVES VARIABLES=SALARY86 SALARY87 SALARY88
  /SAVE.
```

- In this example, the default naming convention would produce duplicate names. Thus, the names of the three *z*-score variables are *ZSALARY8*, *ZSC001*, and *ZSC002*.

STATISTICS Subcommand

By default, DESCRIPTIVES displays the mean, standard deviation, minimum, and maximum. Use the STATISTICS subcommand to request other statistics.

- When you use STATISTICS, DESCRIPTIVES displays *only* those statistics you request.
- The keyword ALL obtains all statistics.
- You can specify the keyword DEFAULT to obtain the default statistics without having to name MEAN, STDDEV, MIN, and MAX.
- The median and mode, which are available in FREQUENCIES and EXAMINE, are not available in DESCRIPTIVES. These statistics require that values be sorted, and DESCRIPTIVES does not sort values (the SORT subcommand does not sort values, it simply lists variables in the order you request).
- If you request a statistic that is not available, DESCRIPTIVES issues an error message and the command is not executed.

MEAN	*Mean.*
SEMEAN	*Standard error of the mean.*
STDDEV	*Standard deviation.*
VARIANCE	*Variance.*
KURTOSIS	*Kurtosis and standard error of kurtosis.*
SKEWNESS	*Skewness and standard error of skewness.*
RANGE	*Range.*
MIN	*Minimum observed value.*

MAX　　　　*Maximum observed value.*

SUM　　　　*Sum.*

DEFAULT　　*Mean, standard deviation, minimum, and maximum.* These are the default statistics.

ALL　　　　*All statistics available in DESCRIPTIVES.*

SORT Subcommand

By default, DESCRIPTIVES lists variables in the order in which they are specified on VARIABLES. Use SORT to list variables in ascending or descending alphabetical order of variable name or in ascending or descending order of numeric value of any of the statistics.

- If you specify SORT without any keywords, variables are sorted in ascending order of the mean.
- SORT can sort variables by the value of any of the statistics available with DESCRIPTIVES, but only those statistics specified on STATISTICS (or the default statistics) are displayed.

Only one of the following keywords can be specified on SORT:

MEAN　　　*Sort by mean.* This is the default when SORT is specified without a keyword.

SEMEAN　　*Sort by standard error of the mean.*

STDDEV　　*Sort by standard deviation.*

VARIANCE　*Sort by variance.*

KURTOSIS　*Sort by kurtosis.*

SKEWNESS　*Sort by skewness.*

RANGE　　　*Sort by range.*

MIN　　　　*Sort by minimum observed value.*

MAX　　　　*Sort by maximum observed value.*

SUM　　　　*Sort by sum.*

NAME　　　*Sort by variable name.*

Sort order can be specified in parentheses following the specified keyword:

A　　　*Sort in ascending order.* This is the default when SORT is specified without keywords.

D　　　*Sort in descending order.*

Example

```
DESCRIPTIVES VARIABLES=A B C
 /STATISTICS=DEFAULT RANGE
 /SORT=RANGE (D).
```

- DESCRIPTIVES sorts variables *A*, *B*, and *C* in descending order of range and displays the mean, standard deviation, minimum and maximum values, range, and the number of valid cases.

MISSING Subcommand

MISSING controls missing values.

- By default, DESCRIPTIVES deletes cases with missing values on a variable-by-variable basis. A case with a missing value for a variable will not be included in the summary statistics for that variable, but the case *will* be included for variables where it is not missing.
- The VARIABLE and LISTWISE keywords are alternatives; however, each can be specified with INCLUDE.
- When either the keyword VARIABLE or the default missing-value treatment is used, DESCRIPTIVES reports the number of valid cases for each variable. It always displays the number of cases that would be available if listwise deletion of missing values had been selected.

VARIABLE   *Exclude cases with missing values on a variable-by-variable basis.* This is the default.

LISTWISE   *Exclude cases with missing values listwise.* Cases with missing values for any variable named are excluded from the computation of statistics for all variables.

INCLUDE   *Include user-missing values.*

DISCRIMINANT

```
DISCRIMINANT GROUPS=varname(min,max) /VARIABLES=varlist

 [/SELECT=varname(value)]

 [/ANALYSIS=varlist[(level)] [varlist...]]

 [/METHOD={DIRECT**}] [/TOLERANCE={0.001}]
          {WILKS   }              {  n  }
          {MAHAL   }
          {MAXMINF }
          {MINRESID}
          {RAO     }

 [/MAXSTEPS={n}]

 [/FIN={3.84**}] [/FOUT={2.71**}] [/PIN={n}]
       {  n   }        {  n   }

 [/POUT={n}] [/VIN={0**}]
                   { n }

 [/FUNCTIONS={g-1,100.0,1.0**}] [/PRIORS={EQUAL**     }]
             {n1 , n2 ,n3     }          {SIZE        }
                                         {value list}
 [/SAVE=[CLASS[=varname]] [PROBS[=rootname]]

         [SCORES[=rootname]]]

 [/ANALYSIS=...]

 [/MISSING={EXCLUDE**}]
           {INCLUDE  }

 [/MATRIX=[OUT({*    })] [IN({*    })]]
              {file}        {file}

 [/HISTORY={STEP**} ]
           {NONE  }

 [/ROTATE={NONE**   }]
          {COEFF    }
          {STRUCTURE}

 [/CLASSIFY={NONMISSING  } {POOLED  }  [MEANSUB]]
            {UNSELECTED  } {SEPARATE}
            {UNCLASSIFIED}

 [/STATISTICS=[MEAN]  [COV ]  [FPAIR]  [RAW ]  [STDDEV]
              [GCOV]  [UNIVF] [COEFF]  [CORR]  [TCOV ]
              [BOXM]  [TABLE] [CROSSVALID]
              [ALL]]

 [/PLOT=[MAP]  [SEPARATE]  [COMBINED]  [CASES[(n)]]  [ALL]]

 [/OUTFILE MODEL(filename)]
```

**Default if subcommand or keyword is omitted.

Example

```
DISCRIMINANT GROUPS=OUTCOME (1,4)
  /VARIABLES=V1 TO V7
  /SAVE CLASS=PREDOUT.
```

Overview

DISCRIMINANT performs linear discriminant analysis for two or more groups. The goal of discriminant analysis is to classify cases into one of several mutually exclusive groups based on their values for a set of predictor variables. In the analysis phase, a classification rule is developed using cases for which group membership is known. In the classification phase, the rule is used to classify cases for which group membership is not known. The grouping variable must be categorical, and the independent (predictor) variables must be interval or dichotomous, since they will be used in a regression-type equation.

Options

Variable Selection Method. In addition to the direct-entry method, you can specify any of several stepwise methods for entering variables into the discriminant analysis using the METHOD subcommand. You can set the values for the statistical criteria used to enter variables into the equation using the TOLERANCE, FIN, PIN, FOUT, POUT, and VIN subcommands, and you can specify inclusion levels on the ANALYSIS subcommand. You can also specify the maximum number of steps in a stepwise analysis using the MAXSTEPS subcommand.

Case Selection. You can select a subset of cases for the analysis phase using the SELECT subcommand.

Prior Probabilities. You can specify prior probabilities for membership in a group using the PRIORS subcommand. Prior probabilities are used in classifying cases.

New Variables. You can add new variables to the working data file containing the predicted group membership, the probability of membership in each group, and discriminant function scores using the SAVE subcommand.

Classification Options. With the CLASSIFY subcommand, you can classify only those cases that were not selected for inclusion in the discriminant analysis, or only those cases whose value for the grouping variable was missing or fell outside the range analyzed. In addition, you can classify cases based on the separate-group covariance matrices of the functions instead of the pooled within-groups covariance matrix.

Statistical Display. You can request any of a variety of statistics on the STATISTICS subcommand. You can rotate the pattern or structure matrices using the ROTATE subcommand. You can compare actual with predicted group membership using a classification results table requested with the STATISTICS subcommand or compare any of several types of plots or histograms using the PLOT subcommand.

Basic Specification

The basic specification requires two subcommands:

- GROUPS specifies the variable used to group cases.
- VARIABLES specifies the predictor variables.

By default, DISCRIMINANT enters all variables simultaneously into the discriminant equation (the DIRECT method), provided that they are not so highly correlated that multicollinearity problems arise. Default output includes analysis case processing summary, valid numbers of cases in group statistics, variables failing tolerance test, a summary of canonical discriminant functions, standardized canonical discriminant function coefficients, a structure matrix showing pooled within-groups correlations between the discriminant functions and the predictor variables, and functions at group centroids.

Subcommand Order

- The GROUPS, VARIABLES, and SELECT subcommands must precede all other subcommands and may be entered in any order.
- The analysis block follows, which may include ANALYSIS, METHOD, TOLERANCE, MAXSTEPS, FIN, FOUT, PIN, POUT, VIN, FUNCTIONS, PRIORS, and SAVE. Each analysis block performs a single analysis. To do multiple analyses, specify multiple analysis blocks.
- The keyword ANALYSIS is optional for the first analysis block. Each new analysis block must begin with an ANALYSIS subcommand. Remaining subcommands in the block may be used in any order and apply only to the analysis defined within the same block.
- No analysis block subcommands can be specified after any of the global subcommands, which apply to all analysis blocks. The global subcommands are MISSING, MATRIX, HISTORY, ROTATE, CLASSIFY, STATISTICS, and PLOT. If an analysis block subcommand appears after a global subcommand, the program displays a warning and ignores it.

Syntax Rules

- Only one GROUPS, one SELECT, and one VARIABLES subcommand can be specified per DISCRIMINANT command.

Operations

- DISCRIMINANT first estimates one or more discriminant functions that best distinguish among the groups.
- Using these functions, DISCRIMINANT then classifies cases into groups (if classification output is requested).
- If more than one analysis block is specified, the above steps are repeated for each block.

Limitations

- Pairwise deletion of missing data is not available.

Example

```
DISCRIMINANT GROUPS=OUTCOME (1,4)
  /VARIABLES=V1 TO V7
  /SAVE CLASS=PREDOUT
  /STATISTICS=COV GCOV TCOV.
```

- Only cases with values 1, 2, 3, or 4 for the grouping variable *GROUPS* will be used in computing the discriminant functions.
- The variables in the working data file between and including *V1* and *V7* will be used to compute the discriminant functions and to classify cases.
- Predicted group membership will be saved in the variable *PREDOUT*.
- In addition to the default output, the STATISTICS subcommand requests the pooled within-groups covariance matrix and the group and total covariance matrices.
- Since SAVE is specified, DISCRIMINANT also displays a classification processing summary table and a priori probabilities for groups table.

GROUPS Subcommand

GROUPS specifies the name of the grouping variable, which defines the categories or groups, and a range of categories.

- GROUPS is required and can be specified only once.
- The specification consists of a variable name followed by a range of values in parentheses.
- Only one grouping variable may be specified; its values must be integers. To use a string variable as the grouping variable, first use AUTORECODE to convert the string values to integers and then specify the recoded variable as the grouping variable.
- Empty groups are ignored and do not affect calculations. For example, if there are no cases in group 2, the value range (1, 5) will define only four groups.
- Cases with values outside the value range or missing are ignored during the analysis phase but are classified during the classification phase.

VARIABLES Subcommand

VARIABLES identifies the predictor variables, which are used to classify cases into the groups defined on the GROUPS subcommand. The list of variables follows the usual conventions for variable lists.

- VARIABLES is required and can be specified only once. Use the ANALYSIS subcommand to obtain multiple analyses.
- Only numeric variables can be used.

- Variables should be suitable for use in a regression-type equation, either measured at the interval level or dichotomous.

SELECT Subcommand

SELECT limits cases used in the analysis phase to those with a specified value for any one variable.

- Only one SELECT subcommand is allowed. It can follow the GROUPS and VARIABLES subcommands but must precede all other subcommands.
- The specification is a variable name and a single integer value in parentheses. Multiple variables or values are not permitted.
- The selection variable does not have to be specified on the VARIABLES subcommand.
- Only cases with the specified value for the selection variable are used in the analysis phase.
- All cases, whether selected or not, are classified by default. Use CLASSIFY=UNSELECTED to classify only the unselected cases.
- When SELECT is used, classification statistics are reported separately for selected and unselected cases, unless CLASSIFY=UNSELECTED is used to restrict classification.

Example

```
DISCRIMINANT GROUPS=APPROVAL(1,5)
  /VARS=Q1 TO Q10
  /SELECT=COMPLETE(1)
  /CLASSIFY=UNSELECTED.
```

- Using only cases with the value 1 for the variable *COMPLETE*, DISCRIMINANT estimates a function of *Q1* to *Q10* that discriminates between the categories 1 to 5 of the grouping variable *APPROVAL*.
- Because CLASSIFY=UNSELECTED is specified, the discriminant function will be used to classify only the unselected cases (cases for which *COMPLETE* does not equal 1).

ANALYSIS Subcommand

ANALYSIS is used to request several different discriminant analyses using the same grouping variable, or to control the order in which variables are entered into a stepwise analysis.

- ANALYSIS is optional for the first analysis block. By default, all variables specified on the VARIABLES subcommand are included in the analysis.
- The variables named on ANALYSIS must first be specified on the VARIABLES subcommand.
- The keyword ALL includes all variables on the VARIABLES subcommand.
- If the keyword TO is used to specify a list of variables on an ANALYSIS subcommand, it refers to the order of variables on the VARIABLES subcommand, which is not necessarily the order of variables in the working data file.

Example

```
DISCRIMINANT GROUPS=SUCCESS(0,1)
  /VARIABLES=V10 TO V15, AGE, V5
  /ANALYSIS=V15 TO V5
  /ANALYSIS=ALL.
```

- The first analysis will use the variables *V15*, *AGE*, and *V5* to discriminate between cases where *SUCCESS* equals 0 and *SUCCESS* equals 1.
- The second analysis will use all variables named on the VARIABLES subcommand.

Inclusion Levels

When you specify a stepwise method on the METHOD subcommand (any method other than the default direct-entry method), you can control the order in which variables are considered for entry or removal by specifying inclusion levels on the ANALYSIS subcommand. By default, all variables in the analysis are entered according to the criterion requested on the METHOD subcommand.

- An **inclusion level** is an integer between 0 and 99, specified in parentheses after a variable or list of variables on the ANALYSIS subcommand.
- The default inclusion level is 1.
- Variables with higher inclusion levels are considered for entry before variables with lower inclusion levels.
- Variables with even inclusion levels are entered as a group.
- Variables with odd inclusion levels are entered individually, according to the stepwise method specified on the METHOD subcommand.
- Only variables with an inclusion level of 1 are considered for removal. To make a variable with a higher inclusion level eligible for removal, name it twice on the ANALYSIS subcommand, first specifying the desired inclusion level and then an inclusion level of 1.
- Variables with an inclusion level of 0 are never entered. However, the statistical criterion for entry is computed and displayed.
- Variables that fail the tolerance criterion are not entered regardless of their inclusion level.

The following are some common methods of entering variables and the inclusion levels that could be used to achieve them. These examples assume that one of the stepwise methods is specified on the METHOD subcommand (otherwise, inclusion levels have no effect).

Direct. ANALYSIS=ALL(2) forces all variables into the equation. (This is the default and can be requested with METHOD=DIRECT or simply by omitting the METHOD subcommand.)

Stepwise. ANALYSIS=ALL(1) yields a stepwise solution in which variables are entered and removed in stepwise fashion. (This is the default when anything other than DIRECT is specified on the METHOD subcommand.)

Forward. ANALYSIS=ALL(3) enters variables into the equation stepwise but does not remove variables.

Backward. ANALYSIS=ALL(2) ALL(1) forces all variables into the equation and then allows them to be removed stepwise if they satisfy the criterion for removal.

Example

```
DISCRIMINANT GROUPS=SUCCESS(0,1)
  /VARIABLES=A, B, C, D, E
  /ANALYSIS=A TO C (2) D, E (1)
  /METHOD=WILKS.
```

- *A*, *B*, and *C* are entered into the analysis first, assuming that they pass the tolerance criterion. Since their inclusion level is even, they are entered together.

- *D* and *E* are then entered stepwise. The one that minimizes the overall value of Wilks' lambda is entered first.

- After entering *D* and *E*, the program checks whether the partial *F* for either one justifies removal from the equation (see the FOUT and POUT subcommands on p. 299).

Example

```
DISCRIMINANT GROUPS=SUCCESS(0,1)
  /VARIABLES=A, B, C, D, E
  /ANALYSIS=A TO C (2) D, E (1).
```

- Since no stepwise method is specified, inclusion levels have no effect and all variables are entered into the model at once.

METHOD Subcommand

METHOD is used to select a method for entering variables into an analysis.

- A variable will never be entered into the analysis if it does not pass the tolerance criterion specified on the TOLERANCE subcommand (or the default).

- A METHOD subcommand applies only to the *preceding* ANALYSIS subcommand, or to an analysis using all predictor variables if no ANALYSIS subcommand has been specified before it.

- If more than one METHOD subcommand is specified within one analysis block, the last is used.

Any one of the following methods can be specified on the METHOD subcommand:

DIRECT   *All variables passing the tolerance criteria are entered simultaneously. This is the default method.*

WILKS   *At each step, the variable that minimizes the overall Wilks' lambda is entered.*

MAHAL   *At each step, the variable that maximizes the Mahalanobis distance between the two closest groups is entered.*

MAXMINF   *At each step, the variable that maximizes the smallest* F *ratio between pairs of groups is entered.*

MINRESID   *At each step, the variable that minimizes the sum of the unexplained variation for all pairs of groups is entered.*

RAO　　　　*At each step, the variable that produces the largest increase in Rao's V is entered.*

OUTFILE subcommand

OUTFILE writes model information to an XML file. *SmartScore* and future releases of *WhatIf?* will be able to use this file.

- The minimum specification is the keyword MODEL and a file name enclosed in parentheses.
- The OUTFILE subcommand cannot be used if split file processing is on (SPLIT FILE command).

TOLERANCE Subcommand

TOLERANCE specifies the minimum tolerance a variable can have and still be entered into the analysis. The tolerance of a variable that is a candidate for inclusion in the analysis is the proportion of its within-groups variance not accounted for by other variables in the analysis. A variable with very low tolerance is nearly a linear function of the other variables; its inclusion in the analysis would make the calculations unstable.

- The default tolerance is 0.001.
- You can specify any decimal value between 0 and 1 as the minimum tolerance.

PIN and POUT Subcommands

PIN specifies the minimum probability of F that a variable can have to enter the analysis and POUT specifies the maximum probability of F that a variable can have and not be removed from the model.

- PIN and POUT take precedence over FIN and FOUT. That is, if all are specified, PIN and POUT values are used.
- If PIN and POUT are omitted, FIN and FOUT are used by default.
- You can set PIN and POUT to any decimal value between 0 and 1. However, POUT should be greater than PIN if PIN is also specified.
- PIN and POUT apply only to the stepwise methods and are ignored if the METHOD subcommand is omitted or if DIRECT is specified on METHOD.

FIN and FOUT Subcommands

FIN specifies the minimum partial F value that a variable must have to enter the analysis. As additional variables are entered into the analysis, the partial F for variables already in the equation changes. FOUT specifies the smallest partial F that a variable can have and not be removed from the model.

- PIN and POUT take precedence over FIN and FOUT. That is, if all are specified, PIN and POUT values are used.
- If PIN and POUT are omitted, FIN and FOUT are used by default. If FOUT is specified but FIN is omitted, the default value for FIN is 3.84. If FIN is specified, the default value for FOUT is 2.71.
- You can set FIN and FOUT to any non-negative number. However, FOUT should be less than FIN if FIN is also specified.
- FIN and FOUT apply only to the stepwise methods and are ignored if the METHOD subcommand is omitted or if DIRECT is specified on METHOD.

VIN Subcommand

VIN specifies the minimum Rao's V that a variable must have to enter the analysis. When you use METHOD=RAO, variables satisfying one of the other criteria for entering the equation may actually cause a decrease in Rao's V for the equation. The default VIN prevents this but does not prevent the addition of variables that provide no additional separation between groups.

- You can specify any value for VIN. The default is 0.
- VIN should be used only when you have specified METHOD=RAO. Otherwise, it is ignored.

MAXSTEPS Subcommand

MAXSTEPS is used to decrease the maximum number of steps allowed. By default, the maximum number of steps allowed in a stepwise analysis is the number of variables with inclusion levels greater than 1 plus twice the number of variables with inclusion levels equal to 1. This is the maximum number of steps possible without producing a loop in which a variable is repeatedly cycled in and out.

- MAXSTEPS applies only to the stepwise methods (all except DIRECT).
- MAXSTEPS applies only to the preceding METHOD subcommand.
- The format is MAX=n, where n is the maximum number of steps desired.
- If multiple MAXSTEPS subcommands are specified, the last is used.

FUNCTIONS Subcommand

By default, DISCRIMINANT computes all possible functions. This is either the number of groups minus 1 or the number of predictor variables, whichever is less. Use FUNCTIONS to set more restrictive criteria for the extraction of functions.

FUNCTIONS has three parameters:

n_1 *Maximum number of functions.* The default is the number of groups minus 1 or the number of predictor variables, whichever is less.

n_2 *Cumulative percentage of the sum of the eigenvalues.* The default is 100.

n_3 *Significance level of function.* The default is 1.0.

- The parameters must always be specified in sequential order (n_1, n_2, n_3). To specify n_2, you must explicitly specify the default for n_1. Similarly, to specify n_3, you must specify the defaults for n_1 and n_2.
- If more than one restriction is specified, the program stops extracting functions when any one of the restrictions is met.
- When multiple FUNCTIONS subcommands are specified, the program uses the last; however, if n_2 or n_3 are omitted on the last FUNCTIONS subcommand, the corresponding specifications on the previous FUNCTIONS subcommands will remain in effect.

Example

```
DISCRIMINANT  GROUPS=CLASS(1,5)
   /VARIABLES = SCORE1 TO SCORE20
   /FUNCTIONS=4,100,.80.
```

- The first two parameters on the FUNCTIONS subcommand are defaults: the default for n_1 is 4 (the number of groups minus 1), and the default for n_2 is 100.
- The third parameter tells DISCRIMINANT to use fewer than four discriminant functions if the significance level of a function is greater than 0.80.

PRIORS Subcommand

By default, DISCRIMINANT assumes equal prior probabilities for groups when classifying cases. You can provide different prior probabilities with the PRIORS subcommand.

- Prior probabilities are used only during classification.
- If you provide unequal prior probabilities, DISCRIMINANT adjusts the classification coefficients to reflect this.
- If adjacent groups have the same prior probability, you can use the notation $n*c$ on the value list to indicate that n adjacent groups have the same prior probability c.
- You can specify a prior probability of 0. No cases are classified into such a group.
- If the sum of the prior probabilities is not 1, the program rescales the probabilities to sum to 1 and issues a warning.

EQUAL *Equal prior probabilities.* This is the default.

SIZE *Proportion of the cases analyzed that fall into each group.* If 50% of the cases included in the analysis fall into the first group, 25% in the second, and 25% in the third, the prior probabilities are 0.5, 0.25, and 0.25, respectively. Group size is determined after cases with missing values for the predictor variables are deleted.

Value list *User-specified prior probabilities.* The list of probabilities must sum to 1.0. The number of prior probabilities named or implied must equal the number of groups.

Example

```
DISCRIMINANT  GROUPS=TYPE(1,5)
  /VARIABLES=A TO H
  /PRIORS = 4*.15,.4.
```

- The PRIORS subcommand establishes prior probabilities of 0.15 for the first four groups and 0.4 for the fifth group.

SAVE Subcommand

SAVE allows you to save casewise information as new variables in the working data file.

- SAVE applies only to the current analysis block. To save casewise results from more than one analysis, specify a SAVE subcommand in each analysis block.
- You can specify a variable name for CLASS and rootnames for SCORES and PROBS to obtain descriptive names for the new variables.
- If you do not specify a variable name for CLASS, the program forms variable names using the formula *DSC_m*, where *m* increments to distinguish group membership variables saved on different SAVE subcommands for different analysis blocks.
- If you do not specify a rootname for SCORES or PROBS, the program forms new variable names using the formula *DSCn_m*, where *m* increments to create unique rootnames and *n* increments to create unique variable names. For example, the first set of default names assigned to discriminant scores or probabilities are *DSC1_1*, *DSC2_1*, *DSC3_1*, and so on. The next set of default names assigned will be *DSC1_2*, *DSC2_2*, *DSC3_2*, and so on, regardless of whether discriminant scores or probabilities are being saved or whether they are saved by the same SAVE subcommand.
- As *m* and/or *n* increase, the prefix *DSC* is truncated to keep variable names within eight characters. For example, *DS999_12* increases to *D1000_12*. The initial character *D* is required.
- The keywords CLASS, SCORES, and PROBS can be used in any order, but the new variables are always added to the end of the working data file in the following order: first the predicted group, then the discriminant scores, and finally probabilities of group membership.
- Appropriate variable labels are automatically generated. The labels describe whether the variables contain predictor group membership, discriminant scores, or probabilities, and for which analysis they are generated.
- The CLASS variable will use the value labels (if any) from the grouping variable specified for the analysis.
- When SAVE is specified with any keyword, DISCRIMINANT displays a classification processing summary table and a prior probabilities for groups table.
- You cannot use the SAVE subcommand if you are replacing the working data file with matrix materials (see "Matrix Output" on p. 307).

CLASS [(varname)]   *Predicted group membership.*

SCORES [(rootname)]   *Discriminant scores.* One score is saved for each discriminant function derived. If a rootname is specified, DISCRIMINANT will append a sequential number to the name to form new variable names for the discriminant scores.

PROBS [(rootname)]   *For each case, the probabilities of membership in each group.* As many variables are added to each case as there are groups. If a rootname is specified, DISCRIMINANT will append a sequential number to the name to form new variable names.

Example

```
DISCRIMINANT GROUPS=WORLD(1,3)
 /VARIABLES=FOOD TO FSALES
 /SAVE CLASS=PRDCLASS SCORES=SCORE PROBS=PRB
 /ANALYSIS=FOOD SERVICE COOK MANAGER FSALES
 /SAVE CLASS SCORES PROBS.
```

- Two analyses are specified. The first uses all variables named on the VARIABLES subcommand and the second narrows down to five variables. For each analysis, a SAVE subcommand is specified.

- For each analysis, DISCRIMINANT displays a classification processing summary table and a prior probabilities for groups table.

- On the first SAVE subcommand, a variable name and two rootnames are provided. With three groups, the following variables are added to each case:

Name	Variable label	Description
PRDCLASS	Predicted group for analysis 1	Predicted group membership
SCORE1	Function 1 for analysis 1	Discriminant score for function 1
SCORE2	Function 2 for analysis 1	Discriminant score for function 2
PRB1	Probability 1 for analysis 1	Probability of being in group 1
PRB2	Probability 2 for analysis 1	Probability of being in group 2
PRB3	Probability 3 for analysis 1	Probability of being in group 3

- Since no variable name or rootnames are provided on the second SAVE subcommand, DISCRIMINANT uses default names. Note that *m* serves only to distinguish variables saved as a set and does not correspond to the sequential number of an analysis. To find out what information a new variable holds, read the variable label, as shown in the following table:

Name	Variable label	Description
DSC_1	Predicted group for analysis 2	Predicted group membership
DSC1_1	Function 1 for analysis 2	Discriminant score for function 1
DSC2_1	Function 2 for analysis 2	Discriminant score for function 2
DSC1_2	Probability 1 for analysis 2	Probability of being in group 1
DSC2_2	Probability 2 for analysis 2	Probability of being in group 2
DSC3_2	Probability 3 for analysis 2	Probability of being in group 3

STATISTICS Subcommand

By default, DISCRIMINANT produces the following statistics for each analysis: analysis case processing summary, valid numbers of cases in group statistics, variables failing tolerance test, a summary of canonical discriminant functions, standardized canonical discriminant function coefficients, a structure matrix showing pooled within-groups correlations between the discriminant functions and the predictor variables, and functions at group centroids.

- *Group statistics.* Only valid number of cases is reported.
- *Summary of canonical discriminant functions.* Displayed in two tables: an eigenvalues table with percentage of variance, cumulative percentage of variance, and canonical correlations and a Wilks' lambda table with Wilks' lambda, chi-square, degrees of freedom, and significance.
- *Stepwise statistics.* Wilks' lambda, equivalent *F*, degrees of freedom, significance of *F* and number of variables are reported for each step. Tolerance, *F*-to-remove, and the value of the statistic used for variable selection are reported for each variable in the equation. Tolerance, minimum tolerance, *F*-to-enter, and the value of the statistic used for variable selection are reported for each variable not in the equation. (These statistics can be suppressed with HISTORY=NONE.)
- *Final statistics.* Standardized canonical discriminant function coefficients, the structure matrix of discriminant functions and all variables named in the analysis (whether they were entered into the equation or not), and functions evaluated at group means are reported following the last step.

In addition, you can request optional statistics on the STATISTICS subcommand. STATISTICS can be specified by itself or with one or more keywords.

- STATISTICS without keywords displays MEAN, STDDEV, and UNIVF. If you include a keyword or keywords on STATISTICS, only the statistics you request are displayed.

MEAN	*Means.* Total and group means for all variables named on the ANALYSIS subcommand are displayed.
STDDEV	*Standard deviations.* Total and group standard deviations for all variables named on the ANALYSIS subcommand are displayed.
UNIVF	*Univariate* F *ratios.* The analysis-of-variance *F* statistic for equality of group means for each predictor variable is displayed. This is a one-way analysis-of-variance test for equality of group means on a single discriminating variable.
COV	*Pooled within-groups covariance matrix.*
CORR	*Pooled within-groups correlation matrix.*
FPAIR	*Matrix of pairwise* F *ratios.* The *F* ratio for each pair of groups is displayed. This *F* is the significance test for the Mahalanobis distance between groups. This statistic is available only with stepwise methods.
BOXM	*Box's* M *test.* This is a test for equality of group covariance matrices.
GCOV	*Group covariance matrices.*
TCOV	*Total covariance matrix.*

RAW   *Unstandardized canonical discriminant functions.*

COEFF   *Classification function coefficients.* Although DISCRIMINANT does not
                    directly use these coefficients to classify cases, you can use them to classify
                    other samples (see the CLASSIFY subcommand below).

TABLE   *Classification results.* If both selected and unselected cases are classified, the
                    results are reported separately. To obtain cross-validated results for selected
                    cases, specify CROSSVALID.

CROSSVALID   *Cross-validated classification results.* The cross-validation is done by treating
                    $n-1$ out of n observations as the training data set to determine the discrimi-
                    nation rule and using the rule to classify the one observation left out. The
                    results are displayed only for selected cases.

ALL   *All optional statistics.*

ROTATE Subcommand

The coefficient and correlation matrices can be rotated to facilitate interpretation of results.
To control varimax rotation, use the ROTATE subcommand.

- Neither COEFF nor STRUCTURE affects the classification of cases.

COEFF   *Rotate pattern matrix.* DISCRIMINANT displays a varimax transformation
                    matrix, a rotated standardized canonical discriminant function coefficients
                    table, and a correlations between variables and rotated functions table.

STRUCTURE   *Rotate structure matrix.* DISCRIMINANT displays a varimax transformation
                    matrix, a rotated structure matrix, and a rotated standardized canonical dis-
                    criminant function coefficients table.

NONE   *Do not rotate.* This is the default.

HISTORY Subcommand

HISTORY controls the display of stepwise and summary output.

- By default, HISTORY displays both the step-by-step output and the summary table (keyword STEP, alias END).

STEP   *Display step-by-step and summary output.* Alias END. This is the default. See
                    Stepwise statistics in "STATISTICS Subcommand" on p. 304.

NONE   *Suppress the step-by-step and summary table.* Alias NOSTEP, NOEND.

CLASSIFY Subcommand

CLASSIFY determines how cases are handled during classification.

- By default, all cases with nonmissing values for all predictors are classified, and the
  pooled within-groups covariance matrix is used to classify cases.

- The default keywords for CLASSIFY are NONMISSING and POOLED.

NONMISSING   *Classify all cases that do not have missing values on any predictor variables.* Two sets of classification results are produced, one for selected cases (those specified on the SELECT subcommand) and one for unselected cases. This is the default.

UNSELECTED   *Classify only unselected cases.* The classification phase is suppressed for cases selected via the SELECT subcommand. If all cases are selected (when the SELECT subcommand is omitted), the classification phase is suppressed for all cases and no classification results are produced.

UNCLASSIFIED   *Classify only unclassified cases.* The classification phase is suppressed for cases that fall within the range specified on the GROUPS subcommand.

POOLED   *Use the pooled within-groups covariance matrix to classify cases.* This is the default.

SEPARATE   *Use separate-groups covariance matrices of the discriminant functions for classification.* DISCRIMINANT displays the group covariances of canonical discriminant functions and Box's test of equality of covariance matrices of canonical discriminant functions. Since classification is based on the discriminant functions and not the original variables, this option is not necessarily equivalent to quadratic discrimination.

MEANSUB   *Substitute means for missing predictor values during classification.* During classification, means are substituted for missing values and cases with missing values are classified. Cases with missing values are not used during analysis.

PLOT Subcommand

PLOT requests additional output to help you examine the effectiveness of the discriminant analysis.

- If PLOT is specified without keywords, the default is COMBINED and CASES.
- If any keywords are requested on PLOT, only the requested plots are displayed.
- If PLOT is specified with any keyword except MAP, DISCRIMINANT displays a classification processing summary table and a prior probabilities for groups table.

COMBINED   *All-groups plot.* For each case, the first two function values are plotted.

CASES(n)   *Casewise statistics.* For each case, classification information, squared Mahalanobis distance to centroid for the highest and second highest groups, and discriminant scores of all functions are plotted. Validated statistics are displayed for selected cases if CROSSVALID is specified on STATISTICS. If *n* is specified, DISCRIMINANT displays the first *n* cases only.

MAP   *Territorial map.* A plot of group centroids and boundaries used for classifying groups.

SEPARATE   *Separate-groups plots.* These are the same types of plots produced by the keyword COMBINED, except that a separate plot is produced for each group. If only one function is used, a histogram is displayed.

ALL   *All available plots.*

MISSING Subcommand

MISSING controls the treatment of cases with missing values in the analysis phase. By default, cases with missing values for any variable named on the VARIABLES subcommand are not used in the analysis phase but are used in classification.

- The keyword INCLUDE includes cases with user-missing values in the analysis phase.
- Cases with missing or out-of-range values for the grouping variable are always excluded.

EXCLUDE   *Exclude all cases with missing values.* Cases with user- or system-missing values are excluded from the analysis. This is the default.

INCLUDE   *Include cases with user-missing values.* User-missing values are treated as valid values. Only the system-missing value is treated as missing.

MATRIX Subcommand

MATRIX reads and writes SPSS-format matrix data files.

- Either IN or OUT and the matrix file in parentheses are required. When both IN and OUT are used in the same DISCRIMINANT procedure, they can be specified on separate MATRIX subcommands or on the same subcommand.

OUT (filename)   *Write a matrix data file.* Specify either a filename or an asterisk in parentheses (*). If you specify a filename, the file is stored on disk and can be retrieved at any time. If you specify an asterisk (*), the matrix data file replaces the working data file but is not stored on disk unless you use SAVE or XSAVE.

IN (filename)   *Read a matrix data file.* If the matrix data file is the working data file, specify an asterisk (*) in parentheses. If the matrix file is another file, specify the filename in parentheses. A matrix file read from an external file does not replace the working data file.

Matrix Output

- In addition to Pearson correlation coefficients, the matrix materials written by DISCRIMINANT include weighted and unweighted numbers of cases, means, and standard deviations. (See "Format of the Matrix Data File" on p. 308 for a description of the file.) These materials can be used in subsequent DISCRIMINANT procedures.
- Any documents contained in the working data file are not transferred to the matrix file.
- If BOXM or GCOV is specified on the STATISTICS subcommand or SEPARATE is specified on the CLASSIFY subcommand when a matrix file is written, the *STDDEV* and *CORR* records in the matrix materials represent within-cell data, and separate covariance

matrices are written to the file. When the matrix file is used as input for a subsequent DISCRIMINANT procedure, at least one of these specifications must be used on that DISCRIMINANT command.

Matrix Input

- DISCRIMINANT can read correlation matrices written by a previous DISCRIMINANT command or by other procedures. Matrix materials read by DISCRIMINANT must contain records with *ROWTYPE_* values *MEAN*, *N* or *COUNT* (or both), *STDDEV*, and *CORR*.

- If the data do not include records with *ROWTYPE_* value *COUNT* (unweighted number of cases), DISCRIMINANT uses information from records with *ROWTYPE_* value *N* (weighted number of cases). Conversely, if the data do not have *N* values, DISCRIMINANT uses the *COUNT* values. These records can appear in any order in the matrix input file with the following exceptions: the order of split-file groups cannot be violated and all *CORR* vectors must appear consecutively within each split-file group.

- If you want to use a covariance-type matrix as input to DISCRIMINANT, you must first use the MCONVERT command to change the covariance matrix to a correlation matrix.

- DISCRIMINANT can use a matrix from a previous data set to classify data in the working data file. The program checks to make sure that the grouping variable (specified on GROUPS) and the predictor variables (specified on VARIABLES) are the same in the working data file as in the matrix file. If they are not, the program displays an error message and the classification will not be executed.

- MATRIX=IN cannot be used unless a working data file has already been defined. To read an existing matrix data file at the beginning of a session, first use GET to retrieve the matrix file and then specify IN(*) on MATRIX.

Format of the Matrix Data File

- The matrix data file has two special variables created by the program: *ROWTYPE_* and *VARNAME_*. Variable *ROWTYPE_* is a short string variable having values *N*, *COUNT*, *MEAN*, *STDDEV*, and *CORR* (for Pearson correlation coefficient). The variable *VARNAME_* is a short string variable whose values are the names of the variables used to form the correlation matrix.

- When *ROWTYPE_* is *CORR*, *VARNAME_* gives the variable associated with that row of the correlation matrix.

- Between *ROWTYPE_* and *VARNAME_* is the grouping variable, which is specified on the GROUPS subcommand of DISCRIMINANT.

- The remaining variables are the variables used to form the correlation matrix.

Split Files

- When split-file processing is in effect, the first variables in the matrix data file will be split variables, followed by *ROWTYPE_*, the grouping variable, *VARNAME_*, and then the variables used to form the correlation matrix.

- A full set of matrix materials is written for each subgroup defined by the split variables.
- A split variable cannot have the same variable name as any other variable written to the matrix data file.
- If split-file processing is in effect when a matrix is written, the same split file must be in effect when that matrix is read by another procedure.

STDDEV and CORR Records

Records written with *ROWTYPE_* values *STDDEV* and *CORR* are influenced by specifications on the STATISTICS and CLASSIFY subcommands.

- If BOXM or GCOV is specified on STATISTICS or SEPARATE is specified on CLASSIFY, the *STDDEV* and *CORR* records represent within-cell data and receive values for the grouping variable.
- If none of the above specifications is in effect, the *STDDEV* and *CORR* records represent pooled values. The *STDDEV* vector contains the square root of the mean square error for each variable, and *STDDEV* and *CORR* records receive the system-missing value for the grouping variable.

Missing Values

Missing-value treatment affects the values written to a matrix data file. When reading a matrix data file, be sure to specify a missing-value treatment on DISCRIMINANT that is compatible with the treatment that was in effect when the matrix materials were generated.

Example

```
GET FILE=UNIONBK /KEEP WORLD FOOD SERVICE BUS MECHANIC
                 CONSTRUC COOK MANAGER FSALES APPL RENT.
DISCRIMINANT  GROUPS=WORLD(1,3)
 /VARIABLES=FOOD SERVICE BUS MECHANIC CONSTRUC COOK MANAGER FSALES
 /METHOD=WILKS
 /PRIORS=SIZE
 /MATRIX=OUT(DISCMTX).
```

- DISCRIMINANT reads data from the SPSS-format data file *UNIONBK* and writes one set of matrix materials to the file *DISCMTX*.
- The working data file is still *UNIONBK*. Subsequent commands are executed on this file.

Example

```
* Use matrix output to classify data in a different file.

GET FILE=UB2 /KEEP WORLD FOOD SERVICE BUS MECHANIC
                CONSTRUC COOK MANAGER FSALES APPL RENT.
DISCRIMINANT  GROUPS=WORLD(1,3)
 /VARIABLES=FOOD SERVICE BUS MECHANIC CONSTRUC COOK MANAGER FSALES
 /METHOD=WILKS
 /PRIORS=SIZE
 /MATRIX=IN(DISCMTX).
```

- The matrix data file created in the previous example is used to classify data from the file *UB2*.

Example

```
GET FILE=UNIONBK /KEEP WORLD FOOD SERVICE BUS MECHANIC
                 CONSTRUC COOK MANAGER FSALES APPL RENT.
DISCRIMINANT  GROUPS=WORLD(1,3)
 /VARIABLES=FOOD SERVICE BUS MECHANIC CONSTRUC COOK MANAGER FSALES
 /METHOD=WILKS
 /PRIORS=SIZE
 /MATRIX=OUT(*).
LIST.
```

- DISCRIMINANT writes the same matrix as in the first example. However, the matrix data file replaces the working data file.
- The LIST command is executed on the matrix file, not on the *UNIONBK* file.

Example

```
GET FILE=DISCMTX.
DISCRIMINANT  GROUPS=WORLD(1,3)
 /VARIABLES=FOOD SERVICE BUS MECHANIC CONSTRUC COOK MANAGER FSALES
 /METHOD=RAO
 /MATRIX=IN(*).
```

- This example assumes that you are starting a new session and want to read an existing matrix data file. GET retrieves the matrix data file *DISCMTX*.
- MATRIX=IN specifies an asterisk because the matrix data file is the working data file. If MATRIX=IN(DISCMTX) is specified, the program issues an error message.
- If the GET command is omitted, the program issues an error message.

Example

```
GET FILE=UNIONBK /KEEP WORLD FOOD SERVICE BUS MECHANIC
                      CONSTRUC COOK MANAGER FSALES APPL RENT.
DISCRIMINANT  GROUPS=WORLD(1,3)
 /VARIABLES=FOOD SERVICE BUS MECHANIC CONSTRUC COOK MANAGER FSALES
 /CLASSIFY=SEPARATE
 /MATRIX=OUT(*).
DISCRIMINANT  GROUPS=WORLD(1,3)
 /VARIABLES=FOOD SERVICE BUS MECHANIC CONSTRUC COOK MANAGER FSALES
 /STATISTICS=BOXM
 /MATRIX=IN(*).
```

- The first DISCRIMINANT command creates a matrix with CLASSIFY=SEPARATE in effect. To read this matrix, the second DISCRIMINANT command must specify either BOXM or GCOV on STATISTICS or SEPARATE on CLASSIFY. STATISTICS=BOXM is used.

DISPLAY

```
DISPLAY [SORTED] [{NAMES**   }] [/VARIABLES=varlist]
                  {INDEX      }
                  {VARIABLES  }
                  {LABELS     }
                  {DICTIONARY}

         {[SCRATCH]   }
         {[VECTOR]    }
         {[MACROS]    }
         {[DOCUMENTS]}
```

**Default if the subcommand is omitted.

Example

```
DISPLAY SORTED DICTIONARY /VARIABLES=DEPT SALARY SEX TO JOBCAT.
```

Overview

DISPLAY exhibits information from the dictionary of the working data file. The information can be sorted, and it can be limited to selected variables.

Basic Specification

The basic specification is simply the command keyword, which displays an unsorted list of the variables in the working data file.

Syntax Rules

DISPLAY can be specified by itself or with one of the keywords defined below. NAMES is the default. To specify two or more keywords, use multiple DISPLAY commands.

NAMES   *Variable names.* A list of the variables in the working data file is displayed. The names are not sorted and display in a compressed format, about eight names across the page. This is the default.

DOCUMENTS   *Documentary text.* Documentary text is provided on the DOCUMENT command. No error message is issued if there is no documentary information in the working data file.

DICTIONARY   *Complete dictionary information for variables.* Information includes variable names, labels, sequential position of each variable in the file, print and write formats, missing values, and value labels. Up to 60 characters can be displayed for variable and value labels.

INDEX   *Variable names and positions.*

VARIABLES	*Variable names, positions, print and write formats, and missing values.*
LABELS	*Variable names, positions, and variable labels.*
SCRATCH	*Scratch variable names.*
VECTOR	*Vector names.*
MACROS	*Currently defined macros.* The macro names are always sorted.

Operations

- DISPLAY directs information to the output.
- If SORTED is not specified, information is displayed according to the order of variables in the working data file.
- DISPLAY is executed as soon as it is encountered in the command sequence, as long as a dictionary has been defined.

Example

```
GET FILE=HUB.
DISPLAY DOCUMENTS.
DISPLAY DICTIONARY.
```

- Each DISPLAY command specifies only one keyword. The first requests documentary text and the second requests complete dictionary information for the *HUB* file.

SORTED Keyword

SORTED alphabetizes the display by variable name. SORTED can precede the keywords NAMES, DICTIONARY, INDEX, VARIABLES, LABELS, SCRATCH, or VECTOR.

Example

```
DISPLAY SORTED DICTIONARY.
```

- This command displays complete dictionary information for variables in the working data file, sorted alphabetically by variable name.

VARIABLES Subcommand

VARIABLES (alias NAMES) limits the displayed information to a set of specified variables. VARIABLES must be the last specification on DISPLAY and can follow any specification that requests information about variables (all except VECTOR, SCRATCH, DOCUMENTS, and MACROS).

- The only specification is a slash followed by a list of variables. The slash is optional.

- If the keyword SORTED is not specified, information is displayed in the order in which variables are stored in the working data file, regardless of the order in which variables are named on VARIABLES.

Example

```
DISPLAY SORTED DICTIONARY
 /VARIABLES=DEPT, SALARY, SEX TO JOBCAT.
```

- DISPLAY exhibits dictionary information only for the variables named and implied by the keyword TO on the VARIABLES subcommand, sorted alphabetically by variable name.

DOCUMENT

```
DOCUMENT text
```

Example

```
DOCUMENT    This file contains a subset of variables from the
            General Social Survey data.  For each case it records
            only the age, sex, education level, marital status,
            number of children, and type of medical insurance
            coverage.
```

Overview

DOCUMENT saves a block of text of any length in an SPSS-format data file. The documentation can be displayed with the DISPLAY command.

When GET retrieves a data file, or when ADD FILES, MATCH FILES, or UPDATE is used to combine data files, all documents from each specified file are copied into the working file. DROP DOCUMENTS can be used to drop those documents from the working file. Whether or not DROP DOCUMENTS is used, new documents can be added to the working file with the DOCUMENT command.

Basic Specification

The basic specification is DOCUMENT followed by any length of text. The text is stored in the file dictionary when the data are saved in an SPSS-format data file.

Syntax Rules

- The text can be entered on as many lines as needed.
- Blank lines can be used to separate paragraphs.
- A period at the end of a line terminates the command, so you should not place a period at the end of any line but the last.
- Multiple DOCUMENT commands can be used within the command sequence. However, the DISPLAY command cannot be used to exhibit the text from a particular DOCUMENT command. DISPLAY shows all existing documentation.

Operations

- The documentation and the date it was entered are saved in the data file's dictionary. New documentation is saved along with any documentation already in the working data file.

- If a DROP DOCUMENTS command *follows* a DOCUMENT command anywhere in the command sequence, the documentation added by that DOCUMENT command is dropped from the working file along with all other documentation.

Example

```
GET FILE=GENSOC /KEEP=AGE SEX EDUC MARITAL CHILDRN MED_INS.
FILE LABEL   General Social Survey subset.

DOCUMENT     This file contains a subset of variables from the
             General Social Survey data.  For each case it records
             only the age, sex, education level, marital status,
             number of children, and type of medical insurance
             coverage.

SAVE OUTFILE=SUBSOC.
```

- GET keeps only a subset of variables from the file *GENSOC*. All documentation from the file *GENSOC* is copied into the working file.
- FILE LABEL creates a label for the new working file.
- DOCUMENT specifies the new document text. Both existing documents from the file *GENSOC* and the new document text are saved in the file *SUBSOC*.

Example

```
GET FILE=GENSOC /KEEP=AGE SEX EDUC MARITAL CHILDRN MED_INS.

DROP DOCUMENTS.

FILE LABEL   General Social Survey subset.

DOCUMENT     This file contains a subset of variables from the
             General Social Survey data.  For each case it records
             only the age, sex, education level, marital status,
             number of children, and type of medical insurance
             coverage.

SAVE OUTFILE=SUBSOC.
```

- DROP DOCUMENTS drops the documentation from the file *GENSOC* as data are copied into the working file. Only the new documentation specified on DOCUMENT is saved in the file *SUBSOC*.

DO IF

```
DO IF [(]logical expression[)]

transformation commands

[ELSE IF [(]logical expression[)]]

transformation commands

[ELSE IF [(]logical expression[)]]
    .
    .
    .
[ELSE]

transformation commands

END IF
```

The following relational operators can be used in logical expressions:

Symbol	Definition	Symbol	Definition
EQ or =	Equal to	NE or <>*	Not equal to
LT or <	Less than	LE or <=	Less than or equal to
GT or >	Greater than	GE or >=	Greater than or equal to

* On ASCII systems (for example, UNIX, VAX, and all PC's), you can also use ~=; on IBM EBCDIC systems (for example, IBM 360 and IBM 370), you can also use ¬=.

The following logical operators can be used in logical expressions:

Symbol	Definition
AND or &	Both relations must be true
OR or |	Either relation can be true
NOT*	Reverses the outcome of an expression

* On ASCII systems, you can also use ~; on IBM EBCDIC systems, you can also use ¬ (or the symbol above number 6).

Example

```
DO IF (YRHIRED GT 87).
COMPUTE            BONUS = 0.
ELSE IF (DEPT87 EQ 3).
COMPUTE            BONUS = .1*SALARY87.
ELSE IF (DEPT87 EQ 1).
COMPUTE            BONUS = .12*SALARY87.
ELSE IF (DEPT87 EQ 4).
COMPUTE            BONUS = .08*SALARY87.
ELSE IF (DEPT87 EQ 2).
COMPUTE            BONUS = .14*SALARY87.
END IF.
```

Overview

The DO IF—END IF structure conditionally executes one or more transformations on subsets of cases based on one or more logical expressions. The ELSE command can be used within the structure to execute one or more transformations when the logical expression on DO IF is not true. The ELSE IF command within the structure provides further control.

The DO IF—END IF structure is best used for conditionally executing multiple transformation commands, such as COMPUTE, RECODE, and COUNT. IF is more efficient for executing a single conditional COMPUTE-like transformation. DO IF—END IF transforms data for subsets of cases defined by logical expressions. To perform repeated transformations on the same case, use LOOP—END LOOP.

A DO IF—END IF structure can be used within an input program to define complex files that cannot be handled by standard file definition facilities. See "Complex File Structures" on p. 324 for an example.

See END FILE for information on using DO IF—END IF to instruct the program to stop reading data before it encounters the end of the file or to signal the end of the file when creating data. See p. 251 for an example of using DO IF—END IF with END FILE to concatenate raw data files.

Basic Specification

The basic specification is DO IF followed by a logical expression, a transformation command, and the END IF command, which has no specifications.

Syntax Rules

- The ELSE IF command is optional and can be repeated as many times as needed.
- The ELSE command is optional. It can be used only once and must follow any ELSE IF commands.
- The END IF command must follow any ELSE IF and ELSE commands.
- A logical expression must be specified on the DO IF and ELSE IF commands. Logical expressions are not used on the ELSE and END IF commands.
- String values used in expressions must be specified in quotation marks and must include any leading or trailing blanks. Lowercase letters are distinguished from uppercase letters.
- To create a new string variable within a DO IF—END IF structure, you must first declare the variable on the STRING command.
- DO IF—END IF structures can be nested to any level permitted by available memory. They can be nested within LOOP—END LOOP structures, and loop structures can be nested within DO IF structures.

Logical Expressions

- Logical expressions can be simple logical variables or relations, or they can be complex logical tests involving variables, constants, functions, relational operators, and logical operators. Logical expressions can use any of the numeric or string functions allowed in COMPUTE transformations (see COMPUTE).

- Parentheses can be used to enclose the logical expression itself and to specify the order of operations within a logical expression. Extra blanks or parentheses can be used to make the expression easier to read.

- Blanks (*not* commas) are used to separate relational operators from expressions.

- A relation can include variables, constants, or more complicated arithmetic expressions. Relations cannot be abbreviated. For example, the first relation below is valid; the second is not:

    Valid: (A EQ 2 OR A EQ 5)
    Not valid: (A EQ 2 OR 5)

- A relation cannot compare a string variable to a numeric value or variable, or vice versa. A relation cannot compare the result of a logical function (SYSMIS, MISSING, ANY, or RANGE) to a number.

Operations

- DO IF marks the beginning of the control structure and END IF marks the end. Control for a case is passed out of the structure as soon as a logical condition is met on a DO IF, ELSE IF, or ELSE command.

- A logical expression is evaluated as true, false, or missing. A transformation specified for a logical expression is executed only if the expression is true.

- Logical expressions are evaluated in the following order: functions, exponentiation, arithmetic operations, relations, and finally, logical operators. (For strings, the order is functions, relations, and then logical operators.) When more than one logical operator is used, NOT is evaluated first, followed by AND and then OR. You can change the order of operations using parentheses.

- Numeric variables created within a DO IF structure are initially set to the system-missing value. By default, they are assigned an F8.2 format.

- New string variables created within a DO IF structure are initially set to a blank value and are assigned the format specified on the STRING command that creates them.

- If the transformed value of a string variable exceeds the variable's defined format, the value is truncated. If the value is shorter than the format, the value is right-padded with blanks.

- If WEIGHT is specified within a DO IF structure, it takes effect unconditionally.

- Commands like SET, DISPLAY, SHOW, and so forth specified within a DO IF structure are executed when they are encountered in the command file.

- The DO IF—END IF structure (like LOOP—END LOOP) can include commands such as DATA LIST, END CASE, END FILE, and REREAD, which define complex file structures.

Flow of Control

- If the logical expression on DO IF is true, the commands immediately following DO IF are executed up to the next ELSE IF, ELSE, or END IF command. Control then passes to the first statement following END IF.

- If the expression on DO IF is false, control passes to the following ELSE IF command. Multiple ELSE IF commands are evaluated in the order in which they are specified until the logical expression on one of them is true. Commands following that ELSE IF command are executed up to the ELSE or END IF command, and control passes to the first statement following END IF.

- If none of the expressions are true on the DO IF or any of the ELSE IF commands, the commands following ELSE are executed and control passes out of the structure. If there is no ELSE command, a case goes through the entire structure with no change.

- Missing values returned by the logical expression on DO IF or on any ELSE IF cause control to pass to the END IF command at that point.

Missing Values and Logical Operators

When two or more relations are joined by logical operators AND and OR, the program always returns missing if all of the relations in the expression are missing. However, if any one of the relations can be determined, the program tries to return true or false according to the logical outcomes shown in Table 1. The asterisk indicates situations where the program can evaluate the outcome with incomplete information.

Table 1   Logical outcome

Expression	Outcome	Expression	Outcome
true AND true	= true	true OR true	= true
true AND false	= false	true OR false	= true
false AND false	= false	false OR false	= false
true AND missing	= missing	true OR missing	= true*
missing AND missing	= missing	missing OR missing	= missing
false AND missing	= false*	false OR missing	= missing

Example

```
DO IF (YRHIRED LT 87).
RECODE RACE(1=5)(2=4)(4=2)(5=1).
END IF.
```

- The RECODE command recodes RACE for those individuals hired before 1987 (YRHIRED is less than 87). The RACE variable is not recoded for individuals hired in 1987 or later.

- The RECODE command is skipped for any case with a missing value for YRHIRED.

Example

```
DATA LIST        FREE / X(F1).
NUMERIC          #QINIT.
DO IF            NOT #QINIT.
+   PRINT EJECT.
+   COMPUTE      #QINIT = 1.
END IF.
PRINT            / X.

BEGIN DATA
1 2 3  4  5
END DATA.
EXECUTE.
```

- This example shows how to execute a command only once.

- The NUMERIC command creates scratch variable *#QINIT*, which is initialized to 0.

- The NOT logical operator on DO IF reverses the outcome of a logical expression. In this example, the logical expression is a numeric variable that takes only 0 (false) or 1 (true) as its values. The PRINT EJECT command is executed only once, when the value of scratch variable *#QINIT* equals 0. After the COMPUTE command sets *#QINIT* to 1, the DO IF structure is skipped for all subsequent cases. A scratch variable is used because it is initialized to 0 and is not reinitialized after each case.

ELSE Command

ELSE executes one or more transformations when none of the logical expressions on DO IF or any ELSE IF commands is true.

- Only one ELSE command is allowed within a DO IF—END IF structure.

- ELSE must follow all ELSE IF commands (if any) in the structure.

- If the logical expression on DO IF or any ELSE IF command is true, the program ignores the commands following ELSE.

Example

```
DO IF (X EQ 0).
COMPUTE Y=1.
ELSE.
COMPUTE Y=2.
END IF.
```

- *Y* is set to 1 for all cases with value 0 for *X*, and *Y* is 2 for all cases with any other valid value for *X*.

- The value of *Y* is not changed by this structure if *X* is missing.

Example

```
DO IF  (YRHIRED GT 87).
COMPUTE          BONUS = 0.
ELSE.
IF  (DEPT87 EQ 1) BONUS = .12*SALARY87.
IF  (DEPT87 EQ 2) BONUS = .14*SALARY87.
IF  (DEPT87 EQ 3) BONUS = .1*SALARY87.
IF  (DEPT87 EQ 4) BONUS = .08*SALARY87.
END IF.
```

- If an individual was hired after 1987 (*YRHIRED* is greater than 87), *BONUS* is set to 0 and control passes out of the structure. Otherwise, control passes to the IF commands following ELSE.

- Each IF command evaluates every case. The value of *BONUS* is transformed only when the case meets the criteria specified on IF. Compare this structure with ELSE IF in the second example on p. 323, which performs the same task more efficiently.

Example

```
* Test for listwise deletion of missing values.

DATA LIST / V1 TO V6 1-6.
BEGIN DATA
123456
    56
1 3456
123456
123456
END DATA.

DO IF NMISS(V1 TO V6)=0.
+  COMPUTE SELECT='V'.
ELSE
+  COMPUTE SELECT='M'.
END IF.

FREQUENCIES VAR=SELECT.
```

- If there are no missing values for any of the variables *V1* to *V6*, COMPUTE sets the value of *SELECT* equal to V (for valid). Otherwise, COMPUTE sets the value of *SELECT* equal to M (for missing).

- FREQUENCIES generates a frequency table for *SELECT*. The table gives a count of how many cases have missing values for one or more variables, and how many cases have valid values for all variables. Commands in this example can be used to determine how many cases are dropped from an analysis that uses listwise deletion of missing values. See pp. 188 and 548 for alternative ways to check listwise deletion of missing values.

ELSE IF Command

ELSE IF executes one or more transformations when the logical expression on DO IF is not true.

- Multiple ELSE IF commands are allowed within the DO IF—END IF structure.

- If the logical expression on DO IF is true, the program executes the commands immediately following DO IF up to the first ELSE IF. Then control passes to the command following the END IF command.

- If the result of the logical expression on DO IF is false, control passes to ELSE IF.

Example

```
STRING STOCK(A9).
DO IF (ITEM EQ 0).
COMPUTE STOCK='New'.
ELSE IF (ITEM LE 9).
COMPUTE STOCK='Old'.
ELSE.
COMPUTE STOCK='Cancelled'.
END IF.
```

- STRING declares string variable *STOCK* and assigns it a width of nine characters.

- The first COMPUTE is executed for cases with value 0 for *ITEM*, and then control passes out of the structure. Such cases are not reevaluated by ELSE IF, even though 0 is less than 9.

- When the logical expression on DO IF is false, control passes to the ELSE IF command, where the second COMPUTE is executed only for cases with *ITEM* less than or equal to 9. Then control passes out of the structure.

- If the logical expressions on both the DO IF and ELSE IF commands are false, control passes to ELSE, where the third COMPUTE is executed.

- The DO IF—END IF structure sets *STOCK* equal to New when *ITEM* equals 0, to Old when *ITEM* is less than or equal to 9 but not equal to 0 (including negative numbers if they are valid), and to Cancelled for all valid values of *ITEM* greater than 9. The value of *STOCK* remains blank if *ITEM* is missing.

Example

```
DO IF (YRHIRED GT 87).
COMPUTE           BONUS = 0.
ELSE IF (DEPT87 EQ 3).
COMPUTE           BONUS = .1*SALARY87.
ELSE IF (DEPT87 EQ 1).
COMPUTE           BONUS = .12*SALARY87.
ELSE IF (DEPT87 EQ 4).
COMPUTE           BONUS = .08*SALARY87.
ELSE IF (DEPT87 EQ 2).
COMPUTE           BONUS = .14*SALARY87.
END IF.
```

- For cases hired after 1987, *BONUS* is set to 0 and control passes out of the structure. For a case that was hired before 1987 with value 3 for *DEPT87*, *BONUS* equals 10% of salary. Control then passes out of the structure. The other three ELSE IF commands are not evaluated for that case. This differs from the example on p. 322, where the IF command is evaluated for every case. The DO IF—ELSE IF structure shown here is more efficient.

- If Department 3 is the largest, Department 1 the next largest, and so forth, control passes out of the structure quickly for many cases. For a large number of cases or a command file that will be executed frequently, these efficiency considerations can be important.

Nested DO IF Structures

To perform transformations involving logical tests on two variables, you can use nested DO IF—END IF structures.

- There must be an END IF command for every DO IF command in the structure.

Example

```
DO IF (RACE EQ 5).          /*Do whites
+   DO IF (SEX EQ 2).       /*White female
+   COMPUTE SEXRACE=3.
+   ELSE.                   /*White male
+   COMPUTE SEXRACE=1.
+   END IF.                 /*Whites done
ELSE IF (SEX EQ 2).         /*Nonwhite female
COMPUTE SEXRACE=4.
ELSE.                       /*Nonwhite male
COMPUTE SEXRACE=2.
END IF.                     /*Nonwhites done
```

- This structure creates variable *SEXRACE*, which indicates both the sex and minority status of an individual.
- An optional plus sign, minus sign, or period in the first column allows you to indent commands so you can easily see the nested structures.

Complex File Structures

Some complex file structures may require you to imbed more than one DATA LIST command inside a DO IF—END IF structure. For example, consider a data file that has been collected from various sources. The information from each source is basically the same, but it is in different places on the records:

```
111295100FORD         CHAPMAN AUTO SALES
121199005VW       MIDWEST VOLKSWAGEN SALES
11 395025FORD         BETTER USED CARS
11        CHEVY 195005         HUFFMAN SALES & SERVICE
11        VW    595020         MIDWEST VOLKSWAGEN SALES
11        CHEVY 295015         SAM'S AUTO REPAIR
12        CHEVY 210 20         LONGFELLOW CHEVROLET
 9555032 VW                    HYDE PARK IMPORTS
```

In the above file, an automobile part number always appears in columns 1 and 2, and the automobile manufacturer always appears in columns 10 through 14. The location of other information, such as price and quantity, depends on both the part number and the type of automobile. The DO IF—END IF structure in the following example reads records for part type 11.

Example

```
INPUT PROGRAM.
DATA LIST FILE=CARPARTS /PARTNO 1-2 KIND 10-14 (A).

DO IF (PARTNO EQ 11 AND KIND EQ 'FORD').
+ REREAD.
+ DATA LIST /PRICE 3-6 (2) QUANTITY 7-9 BUYER 20-43 (A).
+ END CASE.

ELSE IF (PARTNO EQ 11 AND (KIND EQ 'CHEVY' OR KIND EQ 'VW')).
+ REREAD.
+ DATA LIST /PRICE 15-18 (2) QUANTITY 19-21 BUYER 30-53 (A).
+ END CASE.
END IF.
END INPUT PROGRAM.

PRINT FORMATS PRICE (DOLLAR6.2).
PRINT /PARTNO TO BUYER.
WEIGHT BY QUANTITY.
DESCRIPTIVES PRICE.
```

- The first DATA LIST extracts the part number and the type of automobile.

- Depending on the information from the first DATA LIST, the records are reread, pulling the price, quantity, and buyer from different places.

- The two END CASE commands limit the working file to only those cases with Part 11 and automobile type Ford, Chevrolet, or Volkswagen. Without the END CASE commands, cases would be created in the working file for other part numbers and automobile types with missing values for price, quantity, and buyer.

- The results of the PRINT command are shown in Figure 1.

Figure 1   Printed information for part 11

```
11 FORD   $12.95 100 CHAPMAN AUTO SALES
11 FORD   $3.95   25 BETTER USED CARS
11 CHEVY  $1.95    5 HUFFMAN SALES & SERVICE
11 VW     $5.95   20 MIDWEST VOLKSWAGEN SALES
11 CHEVY  $2.95   15 SAM'S AUTO REPAIR
```

DO REPEAT—END REPEAT

```
DO REPEAT stand-in var={varlist  } [/stand-in var=...]
                      {value list}

transformation commands

END REPEAT [PRINT]
```

Example

```
DO REPEAT R=REGION1 TO REGION5.
COMPUTE R=0.
END REPEAT.
```

Overview

The DO REPEAT—END REPEAT structure repeats the same transformations on a specified set of variables, reducing the number of commands you must enter to accomplish a task. This utility does not reduce the number of commands the program executes, just the number of commands you enter. To display the expanded set of commands the program generates, specify PRINT on END REPEAT.

DO REPEAT uses a *stand-in variable* to represent a *replacement list* of variables or values. The stand-in variable is specified as a place holder on one or more transformation commands within the structure. When the program repeats the transformation commands, the stand-in variable is replaced, in turn, by each variable or value specified on the replacement list.

The following commands can be used within a DO REPEAT—END REPEAT structure:

- Data transformations: COMPUTE, RECODE, IF, COUNT, and SELECT IF
- Data declarations: VECTOR, STRING, NUMERIC, and LEAVE
- Data definition: DATA LIST, MISSING VALUES (but not VARIABLE LABELS or VALUE LABELS)
- Loop structure commands: LOOP, END LOOP, and BREAK
- Do-if structure commands: DO IF, ELSE IF, ELSE, and END IF
- Print and write commands: PRINT, PRINT EJECT, PRINT SPACE, and WRITE
- Format commands: PRINT FORMATS, WRITE FORMATS, and FORMATS

Basic Specification

The basic specification is DO REPEAT, a stand-in variable followed by a required equals sign and a replacement list of variables or values, and at least one transformation command. The structure must end with the END REPEAT command. On the transformation commands, a single stand-in variable represents every variable or value specified on the replacement list.

Syntax Rules

- Multiple stand-in variables can be specified on a DO REPEAT command. Each stand-in variable must have its own equals sign and associated variable or value list and must be separated from other stand-in variables by a slash. All lists must name or generate the same number of items.

- Stand-in variables can be assigned any valid variable names: permanent, temporary, scratch, system, and so forth. A stand-in variable does not exist outside the DO REPEAT—END REPEAT structure and has no effect on variables with the same name that exist outside the structure. However, two stand-in variables cannot have the same name within the same DO REPEAT structure.

- A replacement variable list can include new or existing variables, and they can be string or numeric. Keyword TO can be used to name consecutive existing variables and to create a set of new variables. New string variables must be declared on the STRING command either before DO REPEAT or within the DO REPEAT structure. All replacement variable and value lists must have the same number of items.

- A replacement value list can be a list of strings or numeric values, or it can be of the form n_1 TO n_2, where n_1 is less than n_2 and both are integers. (Note that the keyword is TO, not THRU.)

Operations

- DO REPEAT marks the beginning of the control structure and END REPEAT marks the end. Once control passes out of the structure, all stand-in variables defined within the structure cease to exist.

- The program repeats the commands between DO REPEAT and END REPEAT once for each variable or value on the replacement list.

- Numeric variables created within the structure are initially set to the system-missing value. By default, they are assigned an F8.2 format.

- New string variables declared within the structure are initially set to a blank value and are assigned the format specified on the STRING command that creates them.

- If DO REPEAT is used to create new variables, the order in which they are created depends on how the transformation commands are specified. Variables created by specifying the TO keyword (for example, *V1* TO *V5*) are not necessarily consecutive in the working data file. See the PRINT subcommand on p. 329 for examples.

Example

```
DO REPEAT R=REGION1 TO REGION5.
COMPUTE R=0.
END REPEAT.
```

- DO REPEAT defines the stand-in variable *R*, which represents five new numeric variables: *REGION1, REGION2, REGION3, REGION4,* and *REGION5*.

- The five variables are initialized to 0 by a single COMPUTE specification that is repeated for each variable on the replacement list. Thus, the program generates five COMPUTE commands from the one specified.

- Stand-in variable *R* ceases to exist once control passes out of the DO REPEAT structure.

Example

```
* This example shows a typical application of INPUT PROGRAM, LOOP,
    and DO REPEAT. A data file containing random numbers is generated.

INPUT PROGRAM.
+   LOOP #I = 1 TO 1000.
+      DO REPEAT RESPONSE = R1 TO R400.
+         COMPUTE RESPONSE = UNIFORM(1) > 0.5.
+      END REPEAT.
+      COMPUTE AVG = MEAN(R1 TO R400).
+      END CASE.
+   END LOOP.
+   END FILE.
END INPUT PROGRAM.

FREQUENCIES VARIABLE=AVG
 /FORMAT=CONDENSE
 /HISTOGRAM
 /STATISTICS=MEAN MEDIAN MODE STDDEV MIN MAX.
```

- The INPUT PROGRAM—END INPUT PROGRAM structure encloses an input program that builds cases from transformation commands.

- The indexing variable (*#I*) on LOOP—END LOOP indicates that the loop should be executed 1000 times.

- The DO REPEAT—END REPEAT structure generates 400 variables, each with a 50% chance of being 0 and a 50% chance of being 1. This is accomplished by specifying a logical expression on COMPUTE that compares the values returned by UNIFORM(1) to the value 0.5. (UNIFORM(1) generates random numbers between 0 and 1.) Logical expressions are evaluated as false (0), true (1), or missing. Thus, each random number returned by UNIFORM that is 0.5 or less is evaluated as false and assigned the value 0, and each random number returned by UNIFORM that is greater than 0.5 is evaluated as true and assigned the value 1.

- The second COMPUTE creates variable *AVG*, which is the mean of *R1* to *R400* for each case.

- END CASE builds a case with the variables created within each loop. Thus, the loop structure creates 1000 cases, each with 401 variables (*R1* to *R400*, and *AVG*).

- END FILE signals the end of the data file generated by the input program. If END FILE were not specified in this example, the input program would go into an infinite loop. No working file would be built, and the program would display an error message for every procedure that follows the input program.

- FREQUENCIES produces a condensed frequency table, histogram, and statistics for *AVG*. The histogram for *AVG* shows a normal distribution.

PRINT Subcommand

The PRINT subcommand on END REPEAT displays the commands generated by the DO REPEAT—END REPEAT structure. PRINT can be used to verify the order in which commands are executed.

Example

```
DO REPEAT Q=Q1 TO Q5/ R=R1 TO R5.
COMPUTE Q=0.
COMPUTE R=1.
END REPEAT PRINT.
```

- The DO REPEAT—END REPEAT structure initializes one set of variables to 0 and another set to 1.

- The output from the PRINT subcommand is shown in Figure 1. The generated commands are preceded by plus signs.

- The COMPUTE commands are generated in such a way that variables are created in alternating order: *Q1*, *R1*, *Q2*, *R2*, and so forth. If you plan to use the TO keyword to refer to *Q1* to *Q5* later, you should use two separate DO REPEAT utilities; otherwise, *Q1* to *Q5* will include four of the five *R* variables. Alternatively, use the NUMERIC command to predetermine the order in which variables are added to the working file, or specify the replacement value lists as shown in the next example.

Figure 1   Output from the PRINT subcommand

```
 2   0        DO REPEAT Q=Q1 TO Q5/ R=R1 TO R5
 3   0        COMPUTE Q=0
 4   0        COMPUTE R=1
 5   0        END REPEAT PRINT

 6   0        +COMPUTE Q1=0
 7   0        +COMPUTE R1=1
 8   0        +COMPUTE Q2=0
 9   0        +COMPUTE R2=1
10   0        +COMPUTE Q3=0
11   0        +COMPUTE R3=1
12   0        +COMPUTE Q4=0
13   0        +COMPUTE R4=1
14   0        +COMPUTE Q5=0
15   0        +COMPUTE R5=1
```

Example

```
DO REPEAT Q=Q1 TO Q5,R1 TO R5/ N=0,0,0,0,0,1,1,1,1,1.
COMPUTE Q=N.
END REPEAT PRINT.
```

- In this example, a series of constants is specified as a stand-in value list for *N*. All the *Q* variables are initialized first, and then all the *R* variables, as shown in Figure 2.

Figure 2   Output from the PRINT subcommand

```
2   0              DO REPEAT Q=Q1 TO Q5,R1 TO R5/ N=0,0,0,0,0,1,1,1,1,1
3   0              COMPUTE Q=N
4   0              END REPEAT PRINT

5   0              +COMPUTE  Q1=0
6   0              +COMPUTE  Q2=0
7   0              +COMPUTE  Q3=0
8   0              +COMPUTE  Q4=0
9   0              +COMPUTE  Q5=0
10  0              +COMPUTE  R1=1
11  0              +COMPUTE  R2=1
12  0              +COMPUTE  R3=1
13  0              +COMPUTE  R4=1
14  0              +COMPUTE  R5=1
```

Example

```
DO REPEAT R=REGION1 TO REGION5/ X=1 TO 5.
COMPUTE R=REGION EQ X.
END REPEAT PRINT.
```

- In this example, stand-in variable *R* represents the variable list *REGION1* to *REGION5*. Stand-in variable *X* represents the value list 1 to 5.

- The DO REPEAT—END REPEAT structure creates dummy variables *REGION1* to *REGION5* that equal 0 or 1 for each of 5 regions, depending on whether variable *REGION* equals the current value of stand-in variable *X*.

- PRINT on END REPEAT causes the program to display the commands generated by the structure, as shown in Figure 3.

Figure 3   Commands generated by DO REPEAT

```
2  0  DO REPEAT R=REGION1 TO REGION5/ X=1 TO 5
3  0  COMPUTE R=REGION EQ X
4  0  END REPEAT PRINT

5  0  +COMPUTE REGION1=REGION EQ 1
6  0  +COMPUTE REGION2=REGION EQ 2
7  0  +COMPUTE REGION3=REGION EQ 3
8  0  +COMPUTE REGION4=REGION EQ 4
9  0  +COMPUTE REGION5=REGION EQ 5
```

DROP DOCUMENTS

```
DROP DOCUMENTS
```

Overview

When GET retrieves an SPSS-format data file, or when ADD FILES, MATCH FILES, or UPDATE are used to combine SPSS-format data files, all documents from each specified file are copied into the working file. DROP DOCUMENTS is used to drop these or any documents added with the DOCUMENT command from the working file. Whether or not DROP DOCUMENTS is used, new documents can be added to the working file with the DOCUMENT command.

Basic Specification

The only specification is DROP DOCUMENTS. There are no additional specifications.

Operations

- Documents are dropped from the working data file only. The original data file is unchanged, unless it is resaved.
- DROP DOCUMENTS drops all documentation, including documentation added by any DOCUMENT commands specified prior to the DROP DOCUMENTS command.

Example

```
GET FILE=GENSOC /KEEP=AGE SEX EDUC MARITAL CHILDRN MED_INS.

DROP DOCUMENTS.

FILE LABEL  General Social Survey Subset.
DOCUMENT    This file contains a subset of variables from the
            General Social Survey data.  For each case it records
            only the age, sex, education level, marital status,
            number of children, and type of medical insurance
            coverage.

SAVE OUTFILE=SUBSOC.
```

- DROP DOCUMENTS drops the documentation text from file *GENSOC*. Only the new documentation added with the DOCUMENT command is saved in file *SUBSOC*.
- The original file *GENSOC* is unchanged.

EDIT

This command is not available on all operating systems.

```
EDIT
```

Example

```
EDIT.
GET FILE=QUERY.
RECODE ITEM1, ITEM2, ITEM3 (0=1) (1=0) (2=-1).
COMPUTE INDEXQ=(ITEM1 + ITEM2 + ITEM3)/3.
VARIABLE LABELS INDEXQ 'Summary Index of Questions'.
FREQUENCIES=ITEM1 ITEM2 ITEM3.
```

Overview

EDIT causes the program to evaluate a sequence of commands without actually running the commands. EDIT is available only for batch mode.

Syntax Rules

The minimum specification is simply the command keyword. EDIT has no additional specifications.

- EDIT can be positioned anywhere within the sequence of commands and checks all the commands that follow it.

Operations

- EDIT checks for syntax errors, and it checks to see if all variables used in the commands have been defined. EDIT will look for variable definitions in a specified SPSS-format data file, on a DATA LIST command, and on any commands that create variables.
- EDIT cannot determine whether a DATA LIST command correctly defines the data. It can only determine whether the syntax is correct.
- If the variable definitions are contained in an SPSS-format data file that is not available to the program for checking, you can replicate data definitions in the EDIT session by using the DATA LIST, NUMERIC, or STRING commands. The DATA LIST does not need to correspond exactly with the data, but it must name all the variables to be used in the remainder of the session in the same order and with the same format as the variables in the data file.
- If data are inline, the BEGIN DATA and END DATA commands must be in their appropriate positions within the sequence of commands. However, EDIT does not check the data records.

- EDIT reports when a string variable is used where a numeric variable is required and vice versa.
- Some program procedures create variables such as standard scores and residuals and add them to the working data file. EDIT does not know about these variables and issues error messages when it encounters them in subsequent commands.
- EDIT *does not* detect every possible error. For example, it will not recognize that a computation is impossible.

Example

```
EDIT.
DATA LIST   FILE=HUBDATA RECORDS=3
 /1 EMPLOYID 1-5 MOHIRED YRHIRED 12-15 DEPT79 TO DEPT82 SEX 16-20
 /2 SALARY79 TO SALARY82 6-25 HOURLY81 HOURLY82 40-53(2)
    PROMO81 72 AGE 54-55 RAISE82 66-70
 /3 JOBCAT 6 NAME 25-48 (A).
LIST VARIABLES=MOHIRED YRHIRED DEPT82
    SALARY79 TO SALARY82 NAME /FORMAT=NUMBERED.
```

- EDIT ensures that syntax on DATA LIST and LIST is correct and that all variables specified on LIST have been defined.
- The DATA LIST and LIST commands are not executed and the data are not read.

Example

```
EDIT.
GET FILE=HUBDATA.
COMPUTE   CASESEQ2=CASESEQ+1.
LEAVE CASESEQ2.
PRINT FORMATS CASESEQ2 (F3).

SELECT IF DEPT82 EQ 4.
LIST VARIABLES=CASESEQ2 MOHIRED YRHIRED DEPT82
    SALARY79 TO SALARY82 NAME /FORMAT=NUMBERED.
```

- All commands following EDIT are checked for syntax and variable names.
- The program reads the dictionary of the *HUBDATA* data file (specified on the GET command) so that it can check variables used throughout the session.
- EDIT is able to recognize *CASESEQ2* when it is specified on the LIST command because *CASESEQ2* is defined on the COMPUTE command. However, *CASESEQ2* is not created.
- The commands in this session are not executed and the data are not read.

END CASE

```
END CASE
```

Example

```
* Restructure a data file to make each data item into a single case.

INPUT PROGRAM.
DATA LIST /#X1 TO #X3 (3(F1,1X)).

VECTOR V=#X1 TO #X3.

LOOP #I=1 TO 3.
- COMPUTE X=V(#I).
- END CASE.
END LOOP.
END INPUT PROGRAM.
```

Overview

END CASE is used in an INPUT PROGRAM—END INPUT PROGRAM structure to signal that a case is complete. Control then passes to the commands immediately following the input program. After these commands are executed for the newly created case, the program returns to the input program and continues building cases by processing the commands immediately after the last END CASE command that was executed. For more information about the flow control in an input program, see INPUT PROGRAM—END INPUT PROGRAM.

END CASE is especially useful for restructuring files, either building a single case from several cases or building several cases from a single case. It can also be used to generate data without any data input (see p. 328 for an example).

Basic Specification

The basic specification is simply END CASE. There are no additional specifications.

Syntax Rules

- END CASE is available only within an input program and is generally specified within a loop.
- Multiple END CASE commands can be used within an input program. Each builds a case from the transformation and data definition commands executed since the last END CASE command.
- If no END CASE is explicitly specified, an END CASE command is implied immediately before END INPUT PROGRAM and the input program loops until an end-of-file is encountered or specified (see END FILE).

Operations

- When an END CASE command is encountered, the program suspends execution of the rest of the commands before the END INPUT PROGRAM command and passes control to the commands after the input program. After these commands are executed for the new case, control returns to the input program. The program continues building cases by processing the commands immediately after the most recent END CASE command. Use a loop to build cases from the same set of transformation and data definition commands.

- When multiple END CASE commands are specified, the program follows the flow of the input program and builds a case whenever it encounters an END CASE command, using the set of commands executed since the last END CASE.

- Unless LEAVE is specified, all variables are reinitialized each time the input program is resumed.

- When transformations such as COMPUTE, definitions such as VARIABLE LABELS, and utilities such as PRINT are specified between the last END CASE command and END INPUT PROGRAM, they are executed while a case is being initialized, not when it is complete. This may produce undesirable results (see the example beginning on p. 340).

Example

```
* Restructuring a data file to make each data item a single case.

INPUT PROGRAM.
DATA LIST /#X1 TO #X3 (3(F1,1X)).

VECTOR V=#X1 TO #X3.

LOOP #I=1 TO 3.
- COMPUTE X=V(#I).
- END CASE.
END LOOP.
END INPUT PROGRAM.

BEGIN DATA
2 1 1
3 5 1
END DATA.
FORMAT X(F1.0).
PRINT / X.
EXECUTE.
```

- The input program encloses the commands that build cases from the input file. An input program is required because END CASE is used to create multiple cases from single input records.

- DATA LIST defines three variables. In the format specification, the number 3 is a repetition factor that repeats the format in parentheses three times, once for each variable. The specified format is F1 and the 1X specification skips 1 column.

- VECTOR creates the vector V with the original scratch variables as its three elements. The indexing expression on the LOOP command increments the variable $\#I$ three times to control the number of iterations per input case and to provide the index for the vector V.

- COMPUTE sets *X* equal to each of the scratch variables. END CASE tells the program to build a case. Thus, the first loop (for the first case) sets *X* equal to the first element of vector *V*. Since *V(1)* references *#X1*, and *#X1* is 2, the value of *X* is 2. Variable *X* is then formatted and printed before control returns to the command END LOOP. The loop continues, since indexing is not complete. Thus, the program then sets *X* to *#X2*, which is 1, builds the second case, and passes it to the FORMAT and PRINT commands. After the third iteration, which sets *X* equal to 1, the program formats and prints the case and terminates the loop. Since the end of the file has not been encountered, END INPUT PROGRAM passes control to the first command in the input program, DATA LIST, to read the next input case. After the second loop, however, the program encounters END DATA and completes building the working data file.

- The six new cases are shown in Figure 1.

Figure 1   Outcome for multiple cases read from a single case

```
2
1
1
3
5
1
```

Example

```
*Restructuring a data file to create a separate case for
 each book order.

INPUT PROGRAM.
DATA LIST  /ORDER 1-4 #X1 TO #X22 (1X,11(F3.0,F2.0,1X)).

LEAVE ORDER.
VECTOR BOOKS=#X1 TO #X22.

LOOP #I=1 TO 21 BY 2 IF NOT SYSMIS(BOOKS(#I)).
- COMPUTE ISBN=BOOKS(#I).
- COMPUTE QUANTITY=BOOKS(#I+1).
- END CASE.
END LOOP.
END INPUT PROGRAM.
BEGIN DATA
1045 182 2 155 1 134 1 153 5
1046 155 3 153 5 163 1
1047 161 5 182 2 163 4 186 6
1048 186 2
1049 155 2 163 2 153 2 074 1 161 1
END DATA.

SORT CASES ISBN.
DO IF $CASENUM EQ 1.
- PRINT EJECT /'Order ISBN Quantity'.
- PRINT SPACE.
END IF.

FORMATS ISBN (F3)/ QUANTITY (F2).
PRINT /' ' ORDER ' ' ISBN '  ' QUANTITY.

EXECUTE.
```

- Data are extracted from a file whose records store values for an invoice number and a series of book codes and quantities ordered. For example, invoice 1045 is for four different titles and a total of nine books: two copies of book 182, one copy each of 155 and 134, and five copies of book 153. The task is to break each individual book order into a record, preserving the order number on each new case.

- The input program encloses the commands that build cases from the input file. They are required because the END CASE command is used to create multiple cases from single input records.

- DATA LIST specifies *ORDER* as a permanent variable and defines 22 scratch variables to hold the book numbers and quantities (this is the maximum number of numbers and quantities that will fit in 72 columns). In the format specification, the first element skips one space after the value for the variable *ORDER*. The number 11 repeats the formats that follow it 11 times: once for each book number and quantity pair. The specified format is F3.0 for book numbers and F2.0 for quantities. The 1X specification skips 1 column after each quantity value.

- LEAVE preserves the value of the variable *ORDER* across the new cases to be generated.

- VECTOR sets up the vector *BOOKS* with the 22 scratch variables as its elements. The first element is *#X1*, the second is *#X2*, and so on.

- If the element for the vector *BOOKS* is not system-missing, LOOP initiates the loop structure that moves through the vector *BOOKS*, picking off the book numbers and quantities. The indexing clause initiates the indexing variable *#I* at 1, to be increased by 2 to a maximum of 21.

- The first COMPUTE command sets the variable *ISBN* equal to the element in the vector *BOOKS* indexed by *#I*, which is the current book number. The second COMPUTE sets the variable *QUANTITY* equal to the next element in the vector *BOOKS*, *#I* +1, which is the quantity associated with the book number in *BOOKS(#I)*.

- END CASE tells the program to write out a case with the current values of the three variables: *ORDER*, *ISBN*, and *QUANTITY*.

- END LOOP terminates the loop structure and control is returned to the LOOP command, where *#I* is increased by 2 and looping continues until the entire input case is read or until *#I* exceeds the maximum value of 21.

- SORT CASES sorts the new cases by book number.

- The DO IF structure encloses a PRINT EJECT command and a PRINT SPACE command to set up titles for the output.

- FORMATS establishes dictionary formats for the new variables *ISBN* and *QUANTITY*. PRINT displays the new cases.

- EXECUTE runs the commands. The output is shown in Figure 2.

Figure 2   PRINT output showing new cases

```
Order ISBN Quantity
1049   74   1
1045  134   1
1045  153   5
1046  153   5
1049  153   2
1045  155   1
1046  155   3
1049  155   2
1047  161   5
1049  161   1
1046  163   1
1047  163   4
1049  163   2
1045  182   2
1047  182   2
1047  186   6
1048  186   2
```

Example

```
* Create variable that approximates a log-normal distribution.

SET FORMAT=F8.0.

INPUT PROGRAM.
LOOP I=1 TO 1000.
+ COMPUTE SCORE=EXP(NORMAL(1)).
+ END CASE.
END LOOP.
END FILE.
END INPUT PROGRAM.

FREQUENCIES VARIABLES=SCORE /FORMAT=NOTABLE /HISTOGRAM
  /PERCENTILES=1 10 20 30 40 50 60 70 80 90 99
  /STATISTICS=ALL.
```

- The input program creates 1000 cases with a single variable *SCORE*. Values for *SCORE* approximate a log-normal distribution.

Example

```
* Restructure a data file to create a separate case for each
    individual.
INPUT PROGRAM.
DATA LIST  /#RECS 1 HEAD1 HEAD2 3-4(A).    /*Read header info
LEAVE  HEAD1 HEAD2.

LOOP  #I=1 TO #RECS.
DATA LIST  /INDIV 1-2(1).                   /*Read individual info
PRINT  /#RECS HEAD1 HEAD2 INDIV.
END CASE.                                   /*Create combined case
END LOOP.
END INPUT PROGRAM.
```

```
BEGIN DATA
1 AC
91
2 CC
35
43
0 XX
1 BA
34
3 BB
42
96
37
END DATA.
LIST.
```

- Data are in a file with header records that indicate the type of record and the number of individual records that follow. The number of records following each header record varies. For example, the 1 in the first column of the first header record (AC) says that only one individual record (91) follows. The 2 in the first column of the second header record (CC) says that two individual records (35 and 43) follow. The next header record has no individual records, indicated by the 0 in column 1, and so on.

- The first DATA LIST reads the expected number of individual records for each header record into temporary variable *#RECS*. *#RECS* is then used as the terminal value in the indexing variable to read the correct number of individual records using the second DATA LIST.

- The variables *HEAD1* and *HEAD2* contain the information in columns 3 and 4, respectively, in the header records. The LEAVE command retains *HEAD1* and *HEAD2* so that this information can be spread to the individual records.

- The variable *INDIV* is the information from the individual record. *INDIV* is combined with *#RECS*, *HEAD1*, and *HEAD2* to create the new case. Notice in the output from the PRINT command in Figure 3 that no case is created for the header record with 0 for *#RECS*.

- END CASE passes each case out of the input program to the LIST command. Without END CASE, the PRINT command would still display the cases as shown in Figure 3 because it is inside the loop. However, only one (the last) case per header record would pass out of the input program. The outcome for LIST will be quite different (compare Figure 4 with Figure 5).

Figure 3   PRINT output

```
1 A C 9.1
2 C C 3.5
2 C C 4.3
1 B A 3.4
3 B B 4.2
3 B B 9.6
3 B B 3.7
```

Figure 4   LIST output when END CASE is specified

```
HEAD1 HEAD2 INDIV

A       C      9.1
C       C      3.5
C       C      4.3
B       A      3.4
B       B      4.2
B       B      9.6
B       B      3.7
```

Figure 5   LIST output when END CASE is not specified

```
HEAD1 HEAD2 INDIV

A       C      9.1
C       C      4.3
X       X       .
B       A      3.4
B       B      3.7
```

Example

```
* Note: the following is an erroneous program! The COMPUTE and
  PRINT commands that follow END CASE are misplaced. They should
  be specified after the END INPUT PROGRAM command.

INPUT PROGRAM.
DATA LIST  /#X1 TO #X3 (3(F1,1X)).

VECTOR V=#X1 TO #X3.

LOOP #I=1 TO 3.
COMPUTE X=V(#I).
END CASE.
END LOOP.

COMPUTE Y=X**2.    /* This should be specified after the input program
VARIABLE LABELS X 'TEST VARIABLE' Y 'SQUARE OF X'.
PRINT FORMATS X Y (F2).
END INPUT PROGRAM.

BEGIN DATA
2 1 1
3 5 1
END DATA.

FREQUENCIES VARIABLES=X Y.
```

- No error or warning is issued for these commands, but the result is not what was intended. The computed value for X is passed out of the input program when the END CASE command is encountered. Thus, Y is computed from the initialized value of X, which is the system-missing value. As Figure 6 shows, all six cases computed for Y within the input program have the system-missing value, represented by a period (.).

- The frequencies table for *X* is as expected, because *X* is computed from inline data and no computation is done between END CASE and END INPUT PROGRM.

- The VARIABLE LABELS and PRINT FORMATS commands have their desired effects even though they are executed with the COMPUTE command, because they do not act on any data read in.

- Moving COMPUTE before END CASE will solve the problem, but the preferred solution is to specify END INPUT PROGRAM before all commands in the transformation program, since they operate on the cases created by the input program.

Figure 6   FREQUENCIES output

```
X        TEST VARIABLE

                                         VALID    CUM
    VALUE LABEL          VALUE  FREQUENCY  PERCENT  PERCENT  PERCENT

                           1        3      50.0     50.0     50.0
                           2        1      16.7     16.7     66.7
                           3        1      16.7     16.7     83.3
                           5        1      16.7     16.7    100.0
                                 -------  -------  -------
                        TOTAL       6     100.0    100.0

VALID CASES      6   MISSING CASES     0
- - - - - - - - - - - - - - - - - - - - - - - - - - - - - - - - - -


Y        SQUARE OF X

                                         VALID    CUM
    VALUE LABEL          VALUE  FREQUENCY  PERCENT  PERCENT  PERCENT

                           .        6     100.0   MISSING
                                 -------  -------  -------
                        TOTAL       6     100.0    100.0
```

END FILE

```
END FILE
```

Example

```
INPUT PROGRAM.
DATA LIST FILE=PRICES /YEAR 1-4 QUARTER 6 PRICE 8-12(2).
DO IF (YEAR GE 1881).  /*Stop reading before 1881
END FILE.
END IF.
END INPUT PROGRAM.
```

Overview

END FILE is used in an INPUT PROGRAM—END INPUT PROGRAM structure to tell the program to stop reading data before it actually encounters the end of the file. END FILE can be used with END CASE to concatenate raw data files by causing the program to delay end-of-file processing until it has read multiple data files (see p. 251 for an example). END FILE can also be used with LOOP and END CASE to generate data without any data input (see p. 328 for an example).

Basic Specification

The basic specification is simply END FILE. There are no additional specifications. The end of file is defined according to the conditions specified for END FILE in the input program.

Syntax Rules

- END FILE is available only within an INPUT PROGRAM structure.
- Only one END FILE command can be executed per input program. However, multiple END FILE commands can be specified within a conditional structure in the input program.

Operations

- When END FILE is encountered, the program stops reading data and puts an end of file in the working data file it was building. The case that causes the execution of END FILE is not read. To include this case, use the END CASE command before END FILE (see the examples below).
- END FILE has the same effect as the end of the input data file. It terminates the input program (see INPUT PROGRAM—END INPUT PROGRAM).

Example

```
*Select cases.

INPUT PROGRAM.
DATA LIST FILE=PRICES /YEAR 1-4 QUARTER 6 PRICE 8-12(2).

DO IF (YEAR GE 1881).  /*Stop reading before 1881
END FILE.
END IF.

END INPUT PROGRAM.

LIST.
```

- This example assumes that data records are entered chronologically by year. The DO IF—END IF structure specifies an end of file when the first case with a value of 1881 or later for *YEAR* is reached.
- LIST executes the input program and lists cases in the working data file. The case that causes the end of the file is not included in the working data file.
- As an alternative to an input program with END FILE, you can use N OF CASES to select cases if you know the exact number of cases. Another alternative is to use SELECT IF to select cases before 1881, but then the program would unnecessarily read the entire input file.

Example

```
Select cases but retain the case that causes end-of-file processing.

INPUT PROGRAM.
DATA LIST FILE=PRICES /YEAR 1-4 QUARTER 6 PRICE 8-12(2).

DO IF (YEAR GE 1881).   /*Stop reading before 1881 (or at end of file)
END CASE.               /*Create case 1881
END FILE.

ELSE.
END CASE.               /*Create all other cases
END IF.
END INPUT PROGRAM.

LIST.
```

- The first END CASE command forces the program to retain the case that causes end-of-file processing.
- The second END CASE indicates the end of case for all other cases and passes them out of the input program one at a time. It is required because the first END CASE command causes the program to abandon default end-of-case processing (see END CASE).

ERASE

```
ERASE FILE='file'
```

Example

```
ERASE FILE='PRSNL.DAT'.
```

Overview

ERASE removes a file from a disk.

Basic Specification

The basic specification is the keyword FILE followed by a file specification. The specified file is erased from the disk. The file specification may vary from operating system to operating system, but enclosing the filename in apostrophes generally works.

Syntax Rules

- The keyword FILE is required but the equals sign is optional.
- ERASE allows one file specification only and does not accept wildcard characters. To erase more than one file, specify multiple ERASE commands.
- The file to be erased must be specified in full. ERASE does not recognize any default file extension.

Operations

ERASE deletes the specified file regardless of its type. No message is displayed unless the command cannot be executed. Use ERASE with caution.

Example

```
ERASE FILE 'PRSNL.DAT'.
```

- The file *PRSNL.SAV* is deleted from the current directory. Whether it is an SPSS-format data file or a file of any other type makes no difference.

EXAMINE

```
EXAMINE VARIABLES=varlist [[BY varlist] [varname BY varname]]

[/COMPARE={GROUPS** }]
          {VARIABLES}

[/{TOTAL**}]
  {NOTOTAL}

[/ID={case number**}]
     {varname        }

[/PERCENTILES [[({5,10,25,50,75,90,95})=[{HAVERAGE  }] [NONE]]
                {value list            }  {WAVERAGE  }
                                          {ROUND     }
                                          {AEMPIRICAL}
                                          {EMPIRICAL }

[/PLOT=[STEMLEAF**] [BOXPLOT**] [NPPLOT] [SPREADLEVEL(n)] [HISTOGRAM]]

       [{ALL }]
        {NONE}

[/STATISTICS=[DESCRIPTIVES**] [EXTREME({5})]]
                                      {n}
             [{ALL }]
              {NONE}

[/CINTERVAL {95**}]
            {n   }

[/MESTIMATOR=[{NONE**}]]
             {ALL    }

             [HUBER({1.339})] [ANDREW({1.34}]
                   {c     }           {c    }

             [HAMPEL({1.7,3.4,8.5})]
                    {a  ,b  ,c  }

             [TUKEY({4.685})]
                   {c     }

[/MISSING=[{LISTWISE**}] [{EXCLUDE**}] [{NOREPORT**}]]
           {PAIRWISE  }   {INCLUDE  }   {REPORT    }
```

**Default if the subcommand is omitted.

Examples

```
EXAMINE VARIABLES=ENGSIZE,COST.

EXAMINE VARIABLES=MIPERGAL BY MODEL,MODEL BY CYLINDERS.
```

Overview

EXAMINE provides stem-and-leaf plots, histograms, boxplots, normal plots, robust estimates of location, tests of normality, and other descriptive statistics. Separate analyses can be obtained for subgroups of cases.

345

Options

Cells. You can subdivide cases into cells based on their values for grouping (factor) variables using the BY keyword on the VARIABLES subcommand.

Output. You can control the display of output using the COMPARE subcommand. You can specify the computational method and break points for percentiles with the PERCENTILES subcommand, and you can assign a variable to be used for labeling outliers on the ID subcommand.

Plots. You can request stem-and-leaf plots, histograms, vertical boxplots, spread-versus-level plots with Levene tests for homogeneity of variance, and normal and detrended probability plots with tests for normality. These plots are available through the PLOT subcommand.

Statistics. You can request univariate statistical output with the STATISTICS subcommand and maximum-likelihood estimators with the MESTIMATORS subcommand.

Basic Specification

- The basic specification is VARIABLES and at least one dependent variable.
- The default output includes a Descriptives table displaying univariate statistics (mean, median, standard deviation, standard error, variance, kurtosis, kurtosis standard error, skewness, skewness standard error, sum, interquartile range (IQR), range, minimum, maximum, and 5% trimmed mean), a vertical boxplot and a stem-and-leaf plot. Outliers are labeled on the boxplot with the system variable *$CASENUM*.

Subcommand Order

Subcommands can be named in any order.

Limitations

- When string variables are used as factors, only the first eight characters are used to form cells. String variables cannot be specified as dependent variables.
- When more than eight crossed factors (for example, A, B, . . . in the specification Y by A by B by . . .) are specified, the command is not executed.

Example

```
EXAMINE VARIABLES=ENGSIZE,COST.
```

- *ENGSIZE* and *COST* are the dependent variables.
- EXAMINE produces univariate statistics for *ENGSIZE* and *COST* in the Descriptives table and a vertical boxplot and a stem-and-leaf plot for each variable.

Example

```
EXAMINE VARIABLES=MIPERGAL BY MODEL,MODEL BY CYLINDERS.
```

- *MIPERGAL* is the dependent variable. The cell specification follows the first BY keyword. Cases are subdivided based on values of *MODEL* and also based on the combination of values of *MODEL* and *CYLINDERS*.
- Assuming that there are three values for *MODEL* and two values for *CYLINDERS*, this example produces a Descriptives table, a stem-and-leaf plot, and a boxplot for the total sample, a Descriptives table and a boxplot for each factor defined by the first BY (*MIPERGAL* by *MODEL* and *MIPERGAL* by *MODEL* by *CYLINDERS*), and a stem-and-leaf plot for each of the nine cells (three defined by *MODEL* and six defined by *MODEL* and *CYLINDERS* together).

VARIABLES Subcommand

VARIABLES specifies the dependent variables and the cells. The dependent variables are specified first, followed by the keyword BY and the variables that define the cells. Repeated models on the same EXAMINE are discarded.

- To create cells defined by the combination of values of two or more factors, specify the factor names separated by the keyword BY.

Caution. Large amounts of output can be produced if many cells are specified. If there are many factors or if the factors have many values, EXAMINE will produce a large number of separate analyses.

Example

```
EXAMINE VARIABLES=SALARY,YRSEDUC BY RACE,SEX,DEPT,RACE BY SEX.
```

- *SALARY* and *YRSEDUC* are dependent variables.
- Cells are formed first for the values of *SALARY* and *YRSEDUC* individually, and then each by values for *RACE*, *SEX*, *DEPT*, and the combination of *RACE* and *SEX*.
- By default, EXAMINE produces Descriptives tables, stem-and-leaf plots, and boxplots.

COMPARE Subcommand

COMPARE controls how boxplots are displayed. This subcommand is most useful if there is more than one dependent variable and at least one factor in the design.

GROUPS   *For each dependent variable, boxplots for all cells are displayed together.* With this display, comparisons across cells for a single dependent variable are easily made. This is the default.

VARIABLES   *For each cell, boxplots for all dependent variables are displayed together.* With this display, comparisons of several dependent variables are easily made. This is useful in situations where the dependent variables are repeated measures of the same variable (see the following example) or have similar scales, or when the dependent variable has very different values for different cells, and plotting all cells on the same scale would cause information to be lost.

Example

```
EXAMINE VARIABLES=GPA1 GPA2 GPA3 GPA4 BY MAJOR    /COMPARE=VARIABLES.
```

- The four GPA variables are summarized for each value of *MAJOR*.
- COMPARE=VARIABLES groups the boxplots for the four GPA variables together for each value of *MAJOR*.

Example

```
EXAMINE VARIABLES=GPA1 GPA2 GPA3 GPA4 BY MAJOR /COMPARE=GROUPS.
```

- COMPARE=GROUPS groups the boxplots for *GPA1* for all majors together, followed by boxplots for *GPA2* for all majors, and so on.

TOTAL and NOTOTAL Subcommands

TOTAL and NOTOTAL control the amount of output produced by EXAMINE when factor variables are specified.

- TOTAL is the default. By default, or when TOTAL is specified, EXAMINE produces statistics and plots for each dependent variable overall and for each cell specified by the factor variables.
- NOTOTAL suppresses overall statistics and plots.
- TOTAL and NOTOTAL are alternatives.
- NOTOTAL is ignored when the VARIABLES subcommand does not specify factor variables.

ID Subcommand

ID assigns a variable from the working data file to identify the cases in the output. By default the case number is used for labeling outliers and extreme cases in boxplots.

- The identification variable can be either string or numeric. If it is numeric, value labels are used to label cases. If no value labels exist, the values are used.
- Only one identification variable can be specified.

Example

```
EXAMINE VARIABLES=SALARY BY RACE BY SEX /ID=LASTNAME.
```

- ID displays the value of *LASTNAME* for outliers and extreme cases in the boxplots.

PERCENTILES Subcommand

PERCENTILES displays the Percentiles table. If PERCENTILES is omitted, no percentiles are produced. If PERCENTILES is specified without keywords, HAVERAGE is used with default break points of 5, 10, 25, 50, 75, 90, and 95.

- Values for break points are specified in parentheses following the subcommand. EXAMINE displays up to six decimal places for user-specified percentile values.

- The method keywords follow the specifications for break points.

In the following formulas, cases are assumed to be ranked in ascending order. The following notation is used: w is the sum of the weights for all nonmissing cases, p is the specified percentile divided by 100, i is the rank of each case, and X_i is the value of the ith case.

HAVERAGE   *Weighted average at* $X_{(w+1)p}$. The percentile value is the weighted average of X_i and X_{i+1} using the formula $(1-f)X_i + fX_{i+1}$, where $(w+1)p$ is decomposed into an integer part i and a fractional part f. This is the default if PERCENTILES is specified without a keyword.

WAVERAGE   *Weighted average at* X_{wp}. The percentile value is the weighted average of X_i and $X_{(i+1)}$ using the formula $(1-f)X_i + fX_{i+1}$, where i is the integer part of wp and f is the fractional part of wp.

ROUND   *Observation closest to* wp. The percentile value is X_i, where i is the integer part of $(wp + 0.5)$.

EMPIRICAL   *Empirical distribution function.* The percentile value is X_i when the fractional part of wp is equal to 0. The percentile value is X_{i+1} when the fractional part of wp is greater than 0.

AEMPIRICAL   *Empirical distribution with averaging.* The percentile value is $(X_i + X_{i+1})/2$ when the fractional part of wp equals 0. The percentile value is X_{i+1} when the fractional part of wp is greater than 0.

NONE   *Suppress percentile output.* This is the default if PERCENTILES is omitted.

Example

```
EXAMINE VARIABLE=SALARY /PERCENTILES(10,50,90)=EMPIRICAL.
```

- PERCENTILES produces the 10th, 50th, and 90th percentiles for the dependent variable *SALARY* using the EMPIRICAL distribution function.

PLOT Subcommand

PLOT controls plot output. The default is a vertical boxplot and a stem-and-leaf plot for each dependent variable for each cell in the model.

- Spread-versus-level plots can be produced only if there is at least one factor variable on the VARIABLES subcommand. If you request a spread-versus-level plot and there are no factor variables, the program issues a warning and no spread-versus-level plot is produced.
- If you specify the PLOT subcommand, only those plots explicitly requested are produced.

BOXPLOT   *Vertical boxplot.* The boundaries of the box are Tukey's hinges. The median is identified by an asterisk. The length of the box is the interquartile range (IQR) computed from Tukey's hinges. Values more than three IQR's from the end of a box are labeled as extreme (E). Values more than 1.5 IQR's but less than 3 IQR's from the end of the box are labeled as outliers (O).

STEMLEAF	*Stem-and-leaf plot.* In a stem-and-leaf plot, each observed value is divided into two components—leading digits (stem) and trailing digits (leaf).
HISTOGRAM	*Histogram.*
SPREADLEVEL(n)	*Spread-versus-level plot with the Test of Homogeneity of Variance table.* If the keyword appears alone, the natural logs of the interquartile ranges are plotted against the natural logs of the medians for all cells. If a power for transforming the data (n) is given, the IQR and median of the transformed data are plotted. If 0 is specified for n, a natural log transformation of the data is done. The slope of the regression line and Levene tests for homogeneity of variance are also displayed. The Levene tests are based on the original data if no transformation is specified and on the transformed data if a transformation is requested.
NPPLOT	*Normal and detrended Q-Q plots with the Tests of Normality table presenting Shapiro-Wilk's statistic and a Kolmogorov-Smirnov statistic with a Lilliefors significance level for testing normality.* Shapiro-Wilk's statistic is not calculated when the sample size exceeds 50.
ALL	*All available plots.*
NONE	*No plots.*

Example

```
EXAMINE VARIABLES=CYCLE BY TREATMNT /PLOT=NPPLOT.
```

- PLOT produces normal and detrended Q-Q plots for each value of *TREATMNT* and a Tests of Normality table.

Example

```
EXAMINE VARIABLES=CYCLE BY TREATMNT /PLOT=SPREADLEVEL(.5).
```

- PLOT produces a spread-versus-level plot of the medians and interquartile ranges of the square root of *CYCLE*. Each point on the plot represents one of the *TREATMNT* groups.
- A Test of Homogeneity of Variance table displays Levene statistics.

Example

```
EXAMINE VARIABLES=CYCLE BY TREATMNT /PLOT=SPREADLEVEL(0).
```

- PLOT generates a spread-versus-level plot of the medians and interquartile ranges of the natural logs of *CYCLE* for each *TREATMENT* group.
- A Test of Homogeneity of Variance table displays Levene statistics.

Example

```
EXAMINE VARIABLES=CYCLE BY TREATMNT /PLOT=SPREADLEVEL.
```

- PLOT generates a spread-versus-level plot of the natural logs of the medians and interquartile ranges of *CYCLE* for each *TREATMNT* group.
- A Test of Homogeneity of Variance table displays Levene statistics.

STATISTICS Subcommand

STATISTICS requests univariate statistics and determines how many extreme values are displayed. DESCRIPTIVES is the default. If you specify keywords on STATISTICS, only the requested statistics are displayed.

DESCRIPTIVES   *Display the Descriptives table showing univariate statistics (the mean, median, 5% trimmed mean, standard error, variance, standard deviation, minimum, maximum, range, interquartile range, skewness, skewness standard error, kurtosis, and kurtosis standard error).* This is the default.

EXTREME(n)   *Display the Extreme Values table presenting cases with the* n *largest and* n *smallest values.* If *n* is omitted, the five largest and five smallest values are displayed. Extreme cases are labeled with their values for the identification variable if the ID subcommand is used or with their values for the system variable *$CASENUM* if ID is not specified.

ALL   *Display the Descriptives and Extreme Values tables.*

NONE   *Display neither the Descriptives nor the Extreme Values tables.*

Example

```
EXAMINE VARIABLE=FAILTIME /ID=BRAND
   /STATISTICS=EXTREME(10) /PLOT=NONE.
```

- STATISTICS identifies the cases with the 10 lowest and 10 highest values for *FAILTIME*. These cases are labeled with the first characters of their values for the variable *BRAND*. The Descriptives table is not displayed.

CINTERVAL Subcommand

CINTERVAL controls the confidence level when the default DESCRIPTIVES statistics is displayed. CINTERVAL has a default value of 95.

- You can specify a CINTERVAL value (*n*) between 50 and 99.99 inclusive. If the value you specify is out of range, the program issues a warning and uses the default 95% intervals.
- If you specify a keyword on STATISTICS subcommand that turns off the default DESCRIPTIVES, the CINTERVAL subcommand is ignored.
- The confidence interval appears in the output with the label *n% CI for Mean*, followed by the confidence interval in parentheses. For example,

```
95% CI for Mean (.0001,.00013)
```

The *n* in the label shows up to six decimal places. That is, input `/CINTERVAL 95` displays as *95% CI* while input `/CINTERVAL 95.975` displays as *95.975% CI.*

MESTIMATORS Subcommand

M-estimators are robust maximum-likelihood estimators of location. Four M-estimators are available for display in the M-Estimators table. They differ in the weights they apply to the cases. MESTIMATORS with no keywords produces Huber's M-estimator with $c=1.339$; Andrews' wave with $c=1.34\pi$; Hampel's M-estimator with $a=1.7$, $b=3.4$, and $c=8.5$; and Tukey's biweight with $c=4.685$.

HUBER(c)   *Huber's M-estimator.* The value of weighting constant c can be specified in parentheses following the keyword. The default is $c=1.339$.

ANDREW(c)   *Andrews' wave estimator.* The value of weighting constant c can be specified in parentheses following the keyword. Constants are multiplied by π. The default is 1.34π.

HAMPEL(a,b,c)   *Hampel's M-estimator.* The values of weighting constants a, b, and c can be specified in order in parentheses following the keyword. The default values are $a=1.7$, $b=3.4$, and $c=8.5$.

TUKEY(c)   *Tukey's biweight estimator.* The value of weighting constant c can be specified in parentheses following the keyword. The default is $c=4.685$.

ALL   *All four above M-estimators.* This is the default when MESTIMATORS is specified with no keyword. The default values for weighting constants are used.

NONE   *No M-estimators.* This is the default if MESTIMATORS is omitted.

Example

```
EXAMINE VARIABLE=CASTTEST /MESTIMATORS.
```

- MESTIMATORS generates all four M-estimators computed with the default constants.

Example

```
EXAMINE VARIABLE=CASTTEST /MESTIMATORS=HAMPELS(2,4,8).
```

- MESTIMATOR produces Hampel's M-estimator with weighting constants $a=2$, $b=4$, and $c=8$.

MISSING Subcommand

MISSING controls the processing of missing values in the analysis. The default is LISTWISE, EXCLUDE, and NOREPORT.

- LISTWISE and PAIRWISE are alternatives and apply to all variables. They are modified for dependent variables by INCLUDE/EXCLUDE and for factor variables by REPORT/NOREPORT.
- INCLUDE and EXCLUDE are alternatives; they apply only to dependent variables.
- REPORT and NOREPORT are alternatives; they determine if missing values for factor variables are treated as valid categories.

LISTWISE   *Delete cases with missing values listwise.* A case with missing values for any dependent variable or any factor in the model specification is excluded from statistics and plots unless modified by INCLUDE or REPORT. This is the default.

PAIRWISE	*Delete cases with missing values pairwise.* A case is deleted from the analysis only if it has a missing value for the dependent variable or factor being analyzed.
EXCLUDE	*Exclude user-missing values.* User-missing values and system-missing values for dependent variables are excluded. This is the default.
INCLUDE	*Include user-missing values.* Only system-missing values for dependent variables are excluded from the analysis.
NOREPORT	*Exclude user- and system-missing values for factor variables.* This is the default.
REPORT	*Include user- and system-missing values for factor variables.* User- and system-missing values for factors are treated as valid categories and are labeled as missing.

Example

```
EXAMINE VARIABLES=RAINFALL MEANTEMP BY REGION.
```

- MISSING is not specified and the default is used. Any case with a user- or system-missing value for *RAINFALL*, *MEANTEMP*, or *REGION* is excluded from the analysis and display.

Example

```
EXAMINE VARIABLES=RAINFALL MEANTEMP BY REGION
  /MISSING=PAIRWISE.
```

- Only cases with missing values for *RAINFALL* are excluded from the analysis of *RAINFALL*, and only cases with missing values for *MEANTEMP* are excluded from the analysis of *MEANTEMP*. Missing values for *REGION* are not used.

Example

```
EXAMINE VARIABLES=RAINFALL MEANTEMP BY REGION
  /MISSING=REPORT.
```

- Missing values for *REGION* are considered valid categories and are labeled as missing.

References

Frigge, M., D. C. Hoaglin, and B. Iglewicz. 1987. Some implementations of the boxplot. In: *Computer Science and Statistics Proceedings of the 19th Symposium on the Interface,* R. M. Heiberger and M. Martin, eds. Alexandria, Virginia: American Statistical Association.

Hoaglin, D. C., F. Mosteller, and J. W. Tukey. 1983. *Understanding robust and exploratory data analysis.* New York: John Wiley and Sons.

_____. 1985. *Exploring data tables, trends, and shapes.* New York: John Wiley and Sons.

Tukey, J. W. 1977. *Exploratory data analysis.* Reading, Mass.: Addison-Wesley.

Velleman, P. F., and D. C. Hoaglin. 1981. *Applications, basics, and computing of exploratory data analysis.* Boston: Duxbury Press.

EXECUTE

```
EXECUTE
```

Overview

EXECUTE forces the data to be read and executes the transformations that precede it in the command sequence.

Basic Specification

The basic specification is simply the command keyword. EXECUTE has no additional specifications.

Operations

- EXECUTE causes the data to be read but has no other influence on the session.
- EXECUTE is designed for use with transformation commands and facilities such as ADD FILES, MATCH FILES, UPDATE, PRINT, and WRITE, which do not read data and are not executed unless followed by a data-reading procedure.

Example

```
DATA LIST  FILE=RAWDATA / 1 LNAME 1-13 (A) FNAME 15-24 (A)
  MMAIDENL 40-55.
VAR LABELS  MMAIDENL 'MOTHER''S MAIDEN NAME'.
DO IF (MMAIDENL EQ 'Smith').
WRITE OUTFILE=SMITHS/LNAME FNAME.
END IF.
EXECUTE.
```

- This example writes the last and first names of all people whose mother's maiden name was Smith to the data file *SMITHS*.
- DO IF—END IF and WRITE do not read data and are executed only when data are read for a procedure. Because there is no procedure in this session, EXECUTE is used to read the data and execute all of the preceding transformation commands. Otherwise, the commands would not be executed.

EXPORT

```
EXPORT OUTFILE=file

 [/TYPE={COMM**}]
       {TAPE  }

 [/UNSELECTED=[{RETAIN}]
              {DELETE}

 [/KEEP={ALL** }] [/DROP=varlist]
        {varlist}

 [/RENAME=(old varnames=new varnames)...]

 [/MAP]

 [/DIGITS=n]
```

**Default if the subcommand is omitted.

Example

```
EXPORT OUTFILE=NEWDATA /RENAME=(V1 TO V3=ID, SEX, AGE) /MAP.
```

Overview

EXPORT produces a portable data file. A portable data file is a data file created used to transport data between different types of computers and operating systems (such as between IBM CMS and Digital VAX/VMS) or between SPSS, SPSS/PC+, or other software using the same portable file format. Like an SPSS-format data file, a portable file contains all of the data and dictionary information stored in the working data file from which it was created. (To send data to a computer and operating system the same as your own, send an SPSS-format data file, which is easier and faster to process than a portable file.)

EXPORT is similar to the SAVE command. It can occur in the same position in the command sequence as the SAVE command and saves the working data file. The file includes the results of all permanent transformations and any temporary transformations made just prior to the EXPORT command. The working data file is unchanged after the EXPORT command.

Options

Format. You can control the format of the portable file using the TYPE subcommand.

Variables. You can save a subset of variables from the working file and rename the variables using the DROP, KEEP, and RENAME subcommands. You can also produce a record of all variables and their names on the exported file with the MAP subcommand.

Precision. You can specify the number of decimal digits of precision for the values of all numeric variables on the DIGITS subcommand.

Basic Specification

The basic specification is the OUTFILE subcommand with a file specification. All variables from the working data file are written to the portable file, with variable names, variable and value labels, missing-value flags, and print and write formats.

Subcommand Order

Subcommands can be named in any order.

Operations

- Portable files are written with 80-character record lengths.
- Portable files may contain some unprintable characters.
- The working data file is still available for transformations and procedures after the portable file is created.
- The system variables *$CASENUM* and *$DATE* are assigned when the file is read by IMPORT.
- If the WEIGHT command is used before EXPORT, the weighting variable is included in the portable file.

Example

```
EXPORT OUTFILE=NEWDATA /RENAME=(V1 TO V3=ID,SEX,AGE) /MAP.
```

- The portable file is written to *NEWDATA*.
- The variables *V1*, *V2*, and *V3* are renamed *ID*, *SEX*, and *AGE* in the portable file. Their names remain *V1*, *V2*, and *V3* in the working file. None of the other variables written to the portable file are renamed.
- MAP requests a display of the variables in the portable file.

Methods of Transporting Portable Files

Portable files can be transported on magnetic tape or by a communications program.

Magnetic Tape

Before transporting files on a magnetic tape, make sure the receiving computer can read the tape being sent. The following tape specifications must be known before you write the portable file on the tape:

- Number of tracks—either 7 or 9.
- Tape density—200, 556, 800, 1600, or 6250 bits per inch (BPI).
- Parity—even or odd. This must be known only when writing a 7-track tape.

- Tape labeling—labeled or unlabeled. Check whether the site can use tape labels. Also make sure that the site has the ability to read multivolume tape files if the file being written uses more than one tape.

- Blocksize—the maximum blocksize the receiving computer can accept.

A tape written with the following characteristics can be read by most computers: 9 track, 1600 BPI, unlabeled, and a blocksize of 3200 characters. However, there is no guarantee that a tape written with these characteristics can be read successfully. The best policy is to know the requirements of the receiving computer ahead of time.

The following advice may help ensure successful file transfers by magnetic tape:

- Unless you are certain that the receiving computer can read labels, prepare an unlabeled tape.

- Make sure the record length of 80 is not changed.

- Do not use a separate character translation program, especially ASCII/EBCDIC translations. EXPORT/IMPORT takes care of this for you.

- Make sure the same blocking factor is used when writing and reading the tape. A blocksize of 3200 is frequently a good choice.

- If possible, write the portable file directly to tape to avoid possible interference from copy programs. Read the file directly from the tape for the same reason.

- Use the INFO LOCAL command to find out about using the program on your particular computer and operating system. INFO LOCAL generally includes additional information about reading and writing portable files.

Communications Programs

Transmission of a portable file by a communications program may not be possible if the program misinterprets any characters in the file as control characters (for example, as a line feed, carriage return, or end of transmission). This can be prevented by specifying TYPE=COMM on EXPORT. This specification replaces each control character with the character 0. The affected control characters are in positions 0–60 of the IMPORT/EXPORT character set (see Appendix B).

The line length that the communications program uses must be set to 80 to match the 80-character record length of portable files. A transmitted file must be checked for blank lines or special characters inserted by the communications program. These must be edited out prior to reading the file with the IMPORT command.

Character Translation

Portable files are character files, not binary files, and they have 80-character records so they can be transmitted over data links. A receiving computer may not use the same character set as the computer where the portable file was written. When it imports a portable file, the program translates characters in the file to the character set used by the receiving computer. Depending on the character set in use, some characters in labels and in string data may be lost in the translation. For example, if a file is transported from a computer using a seven-bit ASCII character set to a computer using a six-bit ASCII character set, some characters in the file may have no matching characters in six-bit ASCII. For a character that has no match, the program generates an appropriate nonprintable character (the null character in most cases).

For a table of the character-set translations available with IMPORT and EXPORT, refer to Appendix B. A blank in a column of the table means that there is no matching character for that character set and an appropriate nonprintable character will be generated when you import a file.

OUTFILE Subcommand

OUTFILE specifies the portable file. OUTFILE is the only required subcommand on EXPORT.

TYPE Subcommand

TYPE indicates whether the portable file should be formatted for magnetic tape or for a communications program. You can specify either COMM or TAPE. See "Methods of Transporting Portable Files" on p. 356 for more information on magnetic tapes and communications programs.

COMM   *Transport portable files by a communications program.* When COMM is specified on TYPE, the program removes all control characters and replaces them with the character 0. This is the default.

TAPE   *Transport portable files on magnetic tape.*

Example

```
EXPORT TYPE=TAPE /OUTFILE=HUBOUT.
```

- File *HUBOUT* is saved as a tape-formatted portable file.

UNSELECTED Subcommand

UNSELECTED determines whether cases excluded on a previous FILTER or USE command are to be retained or deleted in the SPSS-format data file. The default is RETAIN. The UNSELECTED subcommand has no effect when the working data file does not contain unselected cases.

RETAIN   *Retain the unselected cases.* All cases in the working data file are saved. This is the default when UNSELECTED is specified by itself.

DELETE   *Delete the unselected cases.* Only cases that meet the FILTER or USE criteria are saved in the SPSS-format data file.

DROP and KEEP Subcommands

DROP and KEEP save a subset of variables in the portable file.

- DROP excludes a variable or list of variables from the portable file. All variables not named are included in the portable file.

- KEEP includes a variable or list of variables in the portable file. All variables not named are excluded.

- Variables can be specified on DROP and KEEP in any order. With the DROP subcommand, the order of variables in the portable file is the same as their order in the working file. With the KEEP subcommand, the order of variables in the portable file is the order in which they are named on KEEP. Thus, KEEP can be used to reorder variables in the portable file.

- Both DROP and KEEP can be used on the same EXPORT command; the effect is cumulative. If you specify a variable already named on a previous DROP or one not named on a previous KEEP, the variable is considered nonexistent and the program displays an error message. The command is aborted and no portable file is saved.

Example

```
EXPORT OUTFILE=NEWSUM /DROP=DEPT TO DIVISION.
```

- The portable file is written to file *NEWSUM*. Variables between and including *DEPT* and *DIVISION* in the working file are excluded from the portable file.

- All other variables are saved in the portable file.

RENAME Subcommand

RENAME renames variables being written to the portable file. The renamed variables retain their original variable and value labels, missing-value flags, and print formats. The names of the variables are not changed in the working data file.

- To rename a variable, specify the name of the variable in the working data file, an equals sign, and the new name.

- A variable list can be specified on both sides of the equals sign. The number of variables on both sides must be the same, and the entire specification must be enclosed in parentheses.

- The keyword TO can be used for both variable lists (see "Keyword TO" on p. 29).

- If you specify a renamed variable on a subsequent DROP or KEEP subcommand, the new variable name must be used.

Example

```
EXPORT OUTFILE=NEWSUM /DROP=DEPT TO DIVISION
  /RENAME=(NAME,WAGE=LNAME,SALARY).
```

- RENAME renames *NAME* and *WAGE* to *LNAME* and *SALARY*.

- *LNAME* and *SALARY* retain the variable and value labels, missing-value flags, and print formats assigned to *NAME* and *WAGE*.

MAP Subcommand

MAP displays any changes that have been specified by the RENAME, DROP, or KEEP subcommands.

- MAP can be specified as often as desired.
- Each MAP subcommand maps the results of subcommands that precede it; results of subcommands that follow it are not mapped.When MAP is specified last, it also produces a description of the portable file.

Example

```
EXPORT OUTFILE=NEWSUM /DROP=DEPT TO DIVISION /MAP
  /RENAME NAME=LNAME WAGE=SALARY /MAP.
```

- The first MAP subcommand produces a listing of the variables in the file after DROP has dropped the specified variables.
- RENAME renames *NAME* and *WAGE*.
- The second MAP subcommand shows the variables in the file after renaming. Since this is the last subcommand, the listing will show the variables as they are written in the portable file.

DIGITS Subcommand

DIGITS specifies the degree of precision for all noninteger numeric values written to the portable file.

- DIGITS has the general form DIGITS=n, where n is the number of digits of precision.
- DIGITS applies to all numbers for which rounding is required.
- Different degrees of precision *cannot* be specified for different variables. Thus, DIGITS should be set according to the requirements of the variable that needs the most precision.
- Default precision methods used by EXPORT work perfectly for integers that are not too large and for fractions whose denominators are products of 2, 3, and 5 (all decimals, quarters, eighths, sixteenths, thirds, thirtieths, sixtieths, and so forth.) For other fractions and for integers too large to be represented exactly in the working data file (usually more than 9 digits, often 15 or more), the representation used in the working file contains some error already, so no exact way of sending these numbers is possible. The program sends enough digits to get very close. The number of digits sent in these cases depends on the originating computer: on mainframe IBM versions of the program, it is the equivalent of 13 decimal digits (integer and fractional parts combined). If many numbers on a file require this level of precision, the file can grow quite large. If you do not need the full default precision, you can save some space in the portable file by using the DIGITS subcommand.

Example

```
EXPORT OUTFILE=NEWSUM /DROP=DEPT TO DIVISION /MAP /DIGITS=4.
```

- DIGITS guarantees the accuracy of values to four significant digits. For example, 12.34567890876 will be rounded to 12.35.

FACTOR

```
FACTOR VARIABLES=varlist† [/MISSING=[{LISTWISE**}] [INCLUDE]]
                                     {PAIRWISE  }
                                     {MEANSUB   }
                                     {DEFAULT** }

[/MATRIX=[IN({COR=file})]  [OUT({COR=file})]]
            {COR=*   }          {COR=*   }
            {COV=file}          {COV=file}
            {COV=*   }          {COV=*   }
            {FAC=file}          {FAC=file}
            {FAC=*   }          {FAC=*   }

[/METHOD = {CORRELATION**}]
           {COVARIANCE   }

[/SELECT=varname(value)]

[/ANALYSIS=varlist...]

[/PRINT=[DEFAULT**] [INITIAL**] [EXTRACTION**] [ROTATION**]
        [UNIVARIATE] [CORRELATION] [COVARIANCE] [DET] [INV]
        [REPR] [AIC] [KMO] [FSCORE] [SIG] [ALL]]

[/PLOT=[EIGEN] [ROTATION [(n1,n2)]]]

[/DIAGONAL={value list}]
           {DEFAULT** }

[/FORMAT=[SORT] [BLANK(n)] [DEFAULT**]]

[/CRITERIA=[FACTORS(n)] [MINEIGEN({1.0**})] [ITERATE({25**})]
                                  {n    }            {n   }

           [RCONVERGE({0.0001**})] [{KAISER**}]
                      {n        }   {NOKAISER}

           [ECONVERGE({0.001**})] [DEFAULT**]]
                      {n       }

[/EXTRACTION={PC**    }] [/ROTATION={VARIMAX**   }]
             {PA1**   }             {EQUAMAX     }
             {PAF     }             {QUARTIMAX   }
             {ALPHA   }             {OBLIMIN({0})}
             {IMAGE   }                     {n}
             {ULS     }             {PROMAX({4} }
             {GLS     }                    {n}
             {ML      }             {NOROTATE    }
             {DEFAULT**}            {DEFAULT**   }

[/SAVE=[{REG    } ({ALL}[rootname])]]]
        {BART   } {n  }
        {AR     }
        {DEFAULT}
```

† Omit VARIABLES with matrix input.
**Default if subcommand or keyword is omitted.

Example

```
FACTOR VARIABLES=V1 TO V12.
```

Overview

FACTOR performs factor analysis based either on correlations or covariances and using one of the seven extraction methods. FACTOR also accepts matrix input in the form of correlation matrices, covariance matrices, or factor loading matrices and can write the matrix materials to a matrix data file.

Options

Analysis Phase Options. You can choose to analyze a correlation or covariance matrix using the METHOD subcommand. You can select a subset of cases for the analysis phase using the SELECT subcommand. You can tailor the statistical display for an analysis using the PRINT subcommand. You can sort the output in the factor pattern and structure matrices with the FORMAT subcommand. You can also request scree plots and plots of the variables in factor space on the PLOT subcommand.

Extraction Phase Options. With the EXTRACTION subcommand you can specify one of six extraction methods in addition to the default principal components extraction: principal axis factoring, alpha factoring, image factoring, unweighted least squares, generalized least squares, and maximum likelihood. You can supply initial diagonal values for principal axis factoring on the DIAGONAL subcommand. On the CRITERIA subcommand, you can alter the default statistical criteria used in the extraction.

Rotation Phase Options. You can control the criteria for factor rotation with the CRITERIA subcommand. On the ROTATION subcommand you can choose among four rotation methods (equamax, quartimax, promax, and oblimin) in addition to the default varimax rotation, or you can specify no rotation.

Factor Scores. You can save factor scores as new variables in the working data file using any of the three methods available on the SAVE subcommand.

Matrix Input and Output. With the MATRIX subcommand, you can write a correlation matrix, a covariance matrix, or a factor loading matrix. You can also read matrix materials written either by a previous FACTOR procedure or by a procedure that writes correlation or covariance matrices.

Basic Specification

The basic specification is the VARIABLES subcommand with a variable list. FACTOR performs principal components analysis with a varimax rotation on all variables in the analysis using default criteria.

- When matrix materials are used as input, do not specify VARIABLES. Use the ANALYSIS subcommand to specify a subset of the variables in the matrix.

Subcommand Order

- METHOD and SELECT can be specified anywhere. VARIABLES must be specified before any other subcommands, unless an input matrix is specified. MISSING must be specified before ANALYSIS.

- The ANALYSIS, EXTRACTION, ROTATION, and SAVE subcommands must be specified in the order they are listed here. If you specify these subcommands out of order, you may get unpracticed results. For example, if you specify EXTRACTION before ANALYSIS and SAVE before ROTATION, EXTRACTION and SAVE are ignored. If no EXTRACTION and SAVE subcommands are specified in proper order, the default will be used, that is, PC for EXTRACTION and no SAVE.

- The FORMAT subcommand can be specified anywhere after the VARIABLES subcommand.

- If an ANALYSIS subcommand is present, the statistical display options on PRINT, PLOT, or DIAGONAL must be specified after. it. PRINT, PLOT, and DIAGONAL subcommands specified before the ANALYSIS subcommand are ignored. If no such commands are specified after the ANALYSIS subcommand, the default is used.

- The CRITERIA subcommand can be specified anywhere, but applies only to the subcommands that follow. If no CRITERIA subcommand is specified before EXTRACTION or ROTATION, the default criteria for the respective subcommand are used.

Example

```
FACTOR VAR=V1 TO V12
  /ANALYSIS=V1 TO V8
  /CRITERIA=FACTORS(3)
  /EXTRACTION=PAF
  /ROTATION=QUARTIMAX.
```

- The default CORRELATION method is used. FACTOR performs a factor analysis of the correlation matrix based on the first eight variables in the working data file (*V1* to *V8*).

- The procedure extracts three factors using the principal axis method and quartimax rotation.

- LISTWISE (the default for MISSING) is in effect. Cases with missing values for any one of the variables from *V1* to *V12* are omitted from the analysis. As a result, if you ask for the factor analysis using VAR=V1 TO V8 and ANALYSIS=ALL, the results may be different even though the variables used in the analysis are the same.

Syntax Rules

- Each FACTOR procedure performs only one analysis with one extraction and one rotation. Use multiple FACTOR commands to perform multiple analyses.

- VARIABLES or MATRIX=IN can be specified only once. Any other subcommands can be specified multiple times but only the last in proper order takes effect.

Operations

- VARIABLES calculates a correlation and a covariance matrix. If SELECT is specified, only the selected cases are used.
- The correlation or covariance matrix (either calculated from the data or read in) is the basis for the factor analysis.
- Factor scores are calculated for all cases (selected and unselected).

Example

```
FACTOR VARIABLES=V1 TO V12.
```

- This example uses the default CORRELATION method.
- It produces the default principal components analysis of 12 variables. Those with eigenvalues greater than 1 (the default criterion for extraction) are rotated using varimax rotation (the default).

VARIABLES Subcommand

VARIABLES names all the variables to be used in the FACTOR procedure.

- VARIABLES is required except when matrix input is used. When FACTOR reads a matrix data file, the VARIABLES subcommand cannot be used.
- The specification on VARIABLES is a list of numeric variables.
- Keyword ALL on VARIABLES refers to all variables in the working data file.
- Only one VARIABLES subcommand can be specified, and it must be specified first.

MISSING Subcommand

MISSING controls the treatment of cases with missing values.

- If MISSING is omitted or included without specifications, listwise deletion is in effect.
- MISSING must precede the ANALYSIS subcommand.
- The LISTWISE, PAIRWISE, and MEANSUB keywords are alternatives, but any one of them can be used with INCLUDE.

LISTWISE   *Delete cases with missing values listwise.* Only cases with nonmissing values for all variables named on the VARIABLES subcommand are used. Cases are deleted even if they have missing values only for variables listed on VARIABLES and have valid values for all variables listed on ANALYSIS. Alias DEFAULT.

PAIRWISE   *Delete cases with missing values pairwise.* All cases with nonmissing values for each pair of variables correlated are used to compute that correlation, regardless of whether the cases have missing values for any other variable.

MEANSUB   *Replace missing values with the variable mean.* All cases are used after the substitution is made. If INCLUDE is also specified, user-missing values are included in the computation of the means, and means are substituted only for the system-missing value. If SELECT is in effect, only the values of selected cases are used in calculating the means used to replace missing values for selected cases in analysis and for all cases in computing factor scores.

INCLUDE   *Include user-missing values.* Cases with user-missing values are treated as valid.

METHOD Subcommand

METHOD specifies whether the factor analysis is performed on a correlation matrix or a covariance matrix.

- Only one METHOD subcommand is allowed. If more than one is specified, the last is in effect.

CORRELATION   *Perform a correlation matrix analysis.* This is the default.

COVARIANCE   *Perform a covariance matrix analysis.* Valid only with principal components, principal axis factoring, or image factoring methods of extraction. The program issues an error if this keyword is specified when the input is a factor loading matrix or a correlation matrix that does not contain standard deviations (STDDEV or SD).

SELECT Subcommand

SELECT limits cases used in the analysis phase to those with a specified value for any one variable.

- Only one SELECT subcommand is allowed. If more than one is specified, the last is in effect.
- The specification is a variable name and a valid value in parentheses. A string value must be specified within quotes. Multiple variables or values are not permitted.
- The selection variable does not have to be specified on the VARIABLES subcommand.
- Only cases with the specified value for the selection variable are used in computing the correlation or covariance matrix. You can compute and save factor scores for the unselected cases as well as the selected cases.
- SELECT is not valid if MATRIX = IN is specified.

Example

```
FACTOR VARIABLES = V1 TO V10
  /SELECT=COMPLETE(1)
  /SAVE (4).
```

- FACTOR analyzes all ten variables named on VARIABLES, using only cases with a value of 1 for the variable *COMPLETE*.

- By default, FACTOR uses the CORRELATION method and performs the principal components analysis of the selected cases. Those with eigenvalues greater than 1 are rotated using varimax rotation.
- Four factor scores, for both selected and unselected cases, are computed using the default regression method and four new variables are saved in the working data file.

ANALYSIS Subcommand

The ANALYSIS subcommand specifies a subset of the variables named on VARIABLES for use in an analysis.

- The specification on ANALYSIS is a list of variables, all of which must have been named on the VARIABLES subcommand. For matrix input, ANALYSIS can specify a subset of the variables in a correlation or covariance matrix.
- Only one ANALYSIS subcommand is allowed. When multiple ANALYSIS subcommands are specified, the last is in effect.
- If no ANALYSIS is specified, all variables named on the VARIABLES subcommand (or included in the matrix input file) are used.
- Keyword TO in a variable list on ANALYSIS refers to the order in which variables are named on the VARIABLES subcommand, not to their order in the working data file.
- Keyword ALL refers to all variables named on the VARIABLES subcommand.

Example

```
FACTOR VARIABLES=V1 V2 V3 V4 V5 V6
    /ANALYSIS=V4 TO V6.
```

- This example requests a factor analysis of *V4*, *V5*, and *V6*. Keyword TO on ANALYSIS refers to the order of variables on VARIABLES, not the order in the working data file.
- Cases with missing values for all variables specified on VARIABLES are omitted from the analysis. (The default setting for MISSING.)
- By default, the CORRELATION method is used and a principal components analysis with a varimax rotation is performed.

FORMAT Subcommand

FORMAT modifies the format of factor pattern and structure matrices.

- FORMAT can be specified anywhere after VARIABLES and MISSING. If more than one FORMAT is specified, the last is in effect.
- If FORMAT is omitted or included without specifications, variables appear in the order in which they are named on ANALYSIS and all matrix entries are displayed.

SORT   *Order the factor loadings in descending order.*

BLANK(n)   *Suppress coefficients lower than n in absolute value.*

DEFAULT   *Turn off keywords SORT and BLANK.*

Example

```
FACTOR VARIABLES=V1 TO V12
  /MISSING=MEANSUB
  /FORMAT=SORT BLANK(.3)
  /EXTRACTION=ULS
  /ROTATION=NOROTATE.
```

- This example specifies an analysis of all variables between and including *V1* and *V12* in the working data file.
- The default CORRELATION method is used.
- The MISSING subcommand substitutes variable means for missing values.
- The FORMAT subcommand orders variables in factor pattern matrices by descending value of loadings. Factor loadings with an absolute value less than 0.3 are omitted.
- Factors are extracted using unweighted least squares and are not rotated.

PRINT Subcommand

PRINT controls the statistical display in the output.

- Keywords INITIAL, EXTRACTION, and ROTATION are the defaults if PRINT is omitted or specified without keywords.
- If any keywords are specified, only the output specifically requested is produced.
- The requested statistics are displayed only for variables specified on the last ANALYSIS subcommand.
- If more than one PRINT subcommand is specified, the last is in effect.
- If any ANALYSIS subcommand is explicitly specified, all PRINT subcommands specified before the last ANALYSIS subcommand are ignored. If no PRINT subcommand is specified after the last ANALYSIS subcommand, the default takes effect.

INITIAL	*Initial communalities for each variable, eigenvalues of the unreduced correlation matrix, and percentage of variance for each factor.*
EXTRACTION	*Factor pattern matrix, revised communalities, the eigenvalue of each factor retained, and the percentage of variance each eigenvalue represents.*
ROTATION	*Rotated factor pattern matrix, factor transformation matrix, factor correlation matrix, and the post-rotation sums of squared loadings.*
UNIVARIATE	*Valid number of cases, means, and standard deviations.* (Not available with matrix input.) If MISSING=MEANSUB or PAIRWISE, the output also includes the number of missing cases.
CORRELATION	*Correlation matrix.* Ignored if the input is a factor loading matrix.
COVARIANCE	*Covariance matrix.* Ignored if the input is a factor loading matrix or a correlation matrix that does not contain standard deviations (STDDEV or SD).
SIG	*Matrix of significance levels of correlations.*

DET	*Determinant of the correlation or covariance matrix, depending on the specification on* METHOD.
INV	*Inverse of the correlation or covariance matrix, depending on the specification on* METHOD.
AIC	*Anti-image covariance and correlation matrices* (Kaiser, 1970). The measure of sampling adequacy for the individual variable is displayed on the diagonal of the anti-image correlation matrix.
KMO	*Kaiser-Meyer-Olkin measure of sampling adequacy and Bartlett's test of sphericity.* Always based on the correlation matrix. Not computed for an input matrix when it does not contain *N* values.
REPR	*Reproduced correlations and residuals or reproduced covariance and residuals, depending on the specification on* METHOD.
FSCORE	*Factor score coefficient matrix.* Factor score coefficients are calculated using the method requested on the SAVE subcommand. The default is the regression method.
ALL	*All available statistics.*
DEFAULT	INITIAL, EXTRACTION, *and* ROTATION.

Example

```
FACTOR VARS=V1 TO V12
  /SELECT=COMPLETE ('yes')
  /MISS=MEANSUB
  /PRINT=DEF AIC KMO REPR
  /EXTRACT=ULS
  /ROTATE=VARIMAX.
```

- This example specifies a factor analysis that includes all variables between and including *V1* and *V12* in the working data file.
- Only cases with the value "yes" on *COMPLETE* are used.
- Variable means are substituted for missing values. Only values for the selected cases are used in computing the mean. This mean is used to substitute missing values in analyzing the selected cases and in computing factor scores for all cases.
- The output includes the anti-image correlation and covariance matrices, the Kaiser-Meyer-Olkin measure of sampling adequacy, the reproduced correlation and residual matrix, as well as the default statistics.
- Factors are extracted using unweighted least squares.
- The factor pattern matrix is rotated using the varimax rotation.

PLOT Subcommand

Use PLOT to request scree plots or plots of variables in rotated factor space.

- If PLOT is omitted, no plots are produced. If PLOT is used without specifications, it is ignored.

- If more than one PLOT subcommand is specified, only the last one is in effect.
- If any ANALYSIS subcommand is explicitly specified, all PLOT subcommands specified before the last ANALYSIS subcommand are ignored. If no PLOT subcommand is specified after the last ANALYSIS subcommand, no plot is produced.

EIGEN *Scree plot* (Cattell, 1966). The eigenvalues from each extraction are plotted in descending order.

ROTATION *Plots of variables in factor space.* When used without any additional specifications, ROTATION can produce only high-resolution graphics. If three or more factors are extracted, a 3-D plot is produced with the factor space defined by the first three factors. You can request two-dimensional plots by specifying pairs of factor numbers in parentheses; for example, PLOT ROTATION(1,2)(1,3)(2,3) requests three plots, each defined by two factors. The ROTATION subcommand must be explicitly specified when you enter the keyword ROTATION on the PLOT subcommand.

DIAGONAL Subcommand

DIAGONAL specifies values for the diagonal in conjunction with principal axis factoring.

- If DIAGONAL is omitted or included without specifications, FACTOR uses the default method for specifying the diagonal.
- DIAGONAL is ignored with extraction methods other than PAF. The values are automatically adjusted by corresponding variances if METHOD=COVARIANCE.
- If more than one DIAGONAL subcommand is specified, only the last one is in effect.
- If any ANALYSIS subcommand is explicitly specified, DIAGONAL subcommands specified before the last ANALYSIS subcommand are ignored. If no DIAGONAL is specified after the last ANALYSIS subcommand, the default is used.
- Default communality estimates for PAF are squared multiple correlations. If these cannot be computed, the maximum absolute correlation between the variable and any other variable in the analysis is used.

valuelist *Diagonal values.* The number of values supplied must equal the number of variables in the analysis block. Use the notation n* before a value to indicate that the value is repeated *n* times.

DEFAULT *Initial communality estimates.*

Example

```
FACTOR VARIABLES=V1 TO V12
  /DIAGONAL=.56 .55 .74 2*.56 .70 3*.65 .76 .64 .63
  /EXTRACTION=PAF
  /ROTATION=VARIMAX.
```

- The factor analysis includes all variables between and including *V1* and *V12* in the working data file.
- DIAGONAL specifies 12 values to use as initial estimates of communalities in principal axis factoring.

- The factor pattern matrix is rotated using varimax rotation.

CRITERIA Subcommand

CRITERIA controls extraction and rotation criteria.

- CRITERIA can be specified anywhere after VARIABLES and MISSING.
- Only explicitly specified criteria are changed. Unspecified criteria keep their defaults.
- Multiple CRITERIA subcommands are allowed. Changes made by a previous CRITERIA subcommand are overwritten by a later CRITERIA subcommand.
- Any CRITERIA subcommands specified after the last EXTRACTION subcommand have no effect on extraction.
- Any CRITERIA subcommands specified after the last ROTATION subcommand have no effect on rotation.

The following keywords on CRITERIA apply to extractions:

FACTORS(n)   *Number of factors extracted.* The default is the number of eigenvalues greater than MINEIGEN. When specified, FACTORS overrides MINEIGEN.

MINEIGEN(n)   *Minimum eigenvalue used to control the number of factors extracted.* If METHOD=CORRELATION, the default is 1. If METHOD=COVARIANCE, the default is computed as *(Total Variance/Number of Variables)*n*, where *Total Variance* is the total weighted variance principal components or principal axis factoring extraction and the total image variance for image factoring extraction.

ECONVERGE(n)   *Convergence criterion for extraction.* The default is 0.001.

The following keywords on CRITERIA apply to rotations:

RCONVERGE(n)   *Convergence criterion for rotation.* The default is 0.0001.

KAISER   *Kaiser normalization in the rotation phase.* This is the default. The alternative is NOKAISER.

NOKAISER   *No Kaiser normalization.*

The following keywords on CRITERIA apply to both extractions and rotations:

ITERATE(n)   *Maximum number of iterations for solutions in the extraction or rotation phases.* The default is 25.

DEFAULT   *Reestablish default values for all criteria.*

Example

```
FACTOR VARIABLES=V1 TO V12
  /CRITERIA=FACTORS(6)
  /EXTRACTION=PC
  /ROTATION=NOROTATE
  /PLOT=ROTATION.
```

- This example analyzes all variables between and including *V1* and *V12* in the working data file.
- Six factors are extracted using the default principal components method, and the factor pattern matrix is not rotated.
- PLOT sends all extracted factors to the graphics editor and shows a 3-D plot of the first three factors.

EXTRACTION Subcommand

EXTRACTION specifies the factor extraction technique.

- Only one EXTRACTION subcommand is allowed. If multiple EXTRACTION subcommands are specified, only the last is performed.
- If any ANALYSIS subcommand is explicitly specified, all EXTRACTION subcommands before the last ANALYSIS subcommand are ignored. If no EXTRACTION subcommand is specified after the last ANALYSIS subcommand, the default extraction is performed.
- If EXTRACTION is not specified or is included without specifications, principal components extraction is used.
- If you specify criteria for EXTRACTION, the CRITERIA subcommand must precede the EXTRACTION subcommand.
- When you specify EXTRACTION, you should always explicitly specify the ROTATION subcommand. If ROTATION is not specified, the factors are not rotated.

PC   *Principal components analysis* (Harman, 1967). This is the default. PC can also be requested with keyword PA1 or DEFAULT.

PAF   *Principal axis factoring.* PAF can also be requested with keyword PA2.

ALPHA   *Alpha factoring* (Kaiser & Caffry, 1965). Invalid if METHOD=COVARIANCE.

IMAGE   *Image factoring* (Kaiser, 1963).

ULS   *Unweighted least squares* (Harman & Jones, 1966). Invalid if METHOD=COVARIANCE.

GLS   *Generalized least squares.* Invalid if METHOD=COVARIANCE.

ML   *Maximum likelihood* (Jöreskog & Lawley, 1968). Invalid if METHOD=VARIANCE.

Example

```
FACTOR VARIABLES=V1 TO V12
  /ANALYSIS=V1 TO V6
  /EXTRACTION=ULS
  /ROTATE=NOROTATE.
```

- This example analyzes variables *V1* through *V6* with an unweighted least-squares extraction. No rotation is performed.

ROTATION Subcommand

ROTATION specifies the factor rotation method. It can also be used to suppress the rotation phase entirely.

- Only one ROTATION subcommand is allowed. If multiple ROTATION subcommands are specified, only the last is performed.
- If any ANALYSIS subcommand is explicitly specified, all ROTATION subcommands before the last ANALYSIS subcommand are ignored. If any EXTRACTION subcommand is explicitly specified, all ROTATION subcommands before the last EXTRACTION subcommand are ignored.
- If ROTATION is omitted together with EXTRACTION, varimax rotation is used.
- If ROTATION is omitted but EXTRACTION is not, factors are not rotated.
- Keyword NOROTATE on the ROTATION subcommand produces a plot of variables in unrotated factor space if the PLOT subcommand is also included for the analysis.

VARIMAX   *Varimax rotation.* This is the default if ROTATION is entered without specifications or if EXTRACTION and ROTATION are both omitted. Varimax rotation can also be requested with keyword DEFAULT.

EQUAMAX   *Equamax rotation.*

QUARTIMAX   *Quartimax rotation.*

OBLIMIN(n)   *Direct oblimin rotation.* This is a nonorthogonal rotation; thus, a factor correlation matrix will also be displayed. You can specify a delta ($n \leq 0.8$) in parentheses. The value must be less than or equal to 0.8. The default is 0.

PROMAX(n)   *Promax rotation.* This is a nonorthogonal rotation; thus, a factor correlation matrix will also be displayed. For this method, you can specify a real-number value greater than 1. The default is 4.

NOROTATE   *No rotation.*

Example
```
FACTOR VARIABLES=V1 TO V12
  /EXTRACTION=ULS
  /ROTATION
  /ROTATION=OBLIMIN.
```

- The first ROTATION subcommand specifies the default varimax rotation.
- The second ROTATION subcommand specifies an oblimin rotation based on the same extraction of factors.

SAVE Subcommand

SAVE allows you to save factor scores from any rotated or unrotated extraction as new variables in the working data file. You can use any of the three methods for computing the factor scores.

- Only one SAVE subcommand is executed. If you specify multiple SAVE subcommands, only the last is executed.
- SAVE must follow the last ROTATION subcommand.
- If no ROTATION subcommand is specified after the last EXTRACTION subcommand, SAVE must follow the last EXTRACTION subcommand and no rotation is used.
- If neither ROTATION nor EXTRACTION is specified, SAVE must follow the last ANALYSIS subcommand and the default extraction and rotation are used to compute the factor scores.
- SAVE subcommands before any explicitly specified ANALYSIS, EXTRACTION, or ROTATION subcommands are ignored.
- You cannot use the SAVE subcommand if you are replacing the working data file with matrix materials (see "Matrix Output" on p. 374).
- The new variables are added to the end of the working data file.

Keywords to specify the method of computing factor scores are:

REG   *Regression method.* This is the default.

BART   *Bartlett method.*

AR   *Anderson-Rubin method.*

DEFAULT   *The same as REG.*

- After one of the above keywords, specify in parentheses the number of scores to save and a rootname to use in naming the variables.
- You can specify either an integer or the keyword ALL. The maximum number of scores you can specify is the number of factors in the solution.
- FACTOR forms variable names by appending sequential numbers to the rootname you specify. The rootname must begin with a letter and conform to the rules for variable names. It must be short enough that the variable names formed will not exceed eight characters.
- If you do not specify a rootname, FACTOR forms unique variable names using the formula *FACn_m*, where *m* increments to create a new rootname and *n* increments to create a unique variable name. For example, *FAC1_1, FAC2_1, FAC3_1*, and so on will be generated for the first set of saved scores and *FAC1_2, FAC2_2, FAC3_2*, and so on for the second set. As *m* and *n* increase, the prefix *FAC* is truncated to keep the variable names within eight characters. For example, *FAC999_12* is increased to *F1000_12*. The initial *F* is required.
- FACTOR automatically generates variable labels for the new variables. Each label contains information about the method of computing the factor score, its sequential number, and the sequential number of the analysis.

Example

```
FACTOR VARIABLES=V1 TO V12
  /CRITERIA FACTORS(4)
  /ROTATION
  /SAVE REG (4,PCOMP).
```

- Since there is no EXTRACTION subcommand before the ROTATION subcommand, the default principal components extraction is performed.

- The CRITERIA subcommand specifies that four principal components should be extracted.
- The ROTATION subcommand requests the default varimax rotation for the principal components.
- The SAVE subcommand calculates scores using the regression method. Four scores will be added to the file: *PCOMP1*, *PCOMP2*, *PCOMP3*, and *PCOMP4*.

MATRIX Subcommand

MATRIX reads and writes SPSS-format matrix data files.

- MATRIX must always be specified first.
- Only one IN and one OUT keyword can be specified on the MATRIX subcommand. If either IN or OUT is specified more than once, the FACTOR procedure is not executed.
- The matrix type must be indicated on IN or OUT. The types are COR for a correlation matrix, COV for a covariance matrix, and FAC for a factor loading matrix. Indicate the matrix type within parentheses immediately before you identify the matrix file.
- If you use both IN and OUT on MATRIX, you can specify them in either order. You cannot write a covariance matrix if the input matrix is a factor loading matrix or a correlation matrix that does not contain standard deviations (STDDEV or SD).
- If you read in a covariance matrix and write out a factor loading matrix, the output factor loadings are rescaled.

OUT (filename)   *Write a matrix data file.* Specify the matrix type (COR, COV, or FAC) and the matrix file in parentheses. For the matrix data file, specify a filename to store the matrix materials on disk or an asterisk to replace the working data file. If you specify an asterisk, the matrix data file is not stored on disk unless you use SAVE or XSAVE.

IN (filename)   *Read a matrix data file.* Specify the matrix type (COR, COV, or FAC) and the matrix file in parentheses. For the matrix data file, specify an asterisk if the matrix data file is the working data file. If the matrix file is another file, specify the filename in parentheses. A matrix file read from an external file does not replace the working data file.

Matrix Output

- FACTOR can write matrix materials in the form of a correlation matrix, a covariance matrix, or a factor loading matrix. The correlation and covariance matrix materials include counts, means, and standard deviations in addition to correlations or covariances. The factor loading matrix materials contain only factor values and no additional statistics. See "Format of the Matrix Data File" below for a description of the file.
- FACTOR generates one matrix per split file.
- Any documents contained in the working data file are not transferred to the matrix file.

Matrix Input

- FACTOR can read matrix materials written either by a previous FACTOR procedure or by a procedure that writes correlation or covariance matrices. For more information, see Universals on p. 11.
- MATRIX=IN cannot be used unless a working data file has already been defined. To read an existing matrix data file at the beginning of a session, first use GET to retrieve the matrix file and then specify IN(COR=*), IN(COV=*) or IN(FAC=*) on MATRIX.
- The VARIABLES subcommand cannot be used with matrix input.
- For correlation and covariance matrix input, the ANALYSIS subcommand can specify a subset of the variables in the matrix. You cannot specify a subset of variables for factor loading matrix input. By default, the ANALYSIS subcommand uses all variables in the matrix.

Format of the Matrix Data File

- For correlation or covariance matrices, the matrix data file has two special variables created by the program: ROWTYPE_ and VARNAME_. Variable ROWTYPE_ is a short string variable with the value CORR (for Pearson correlation coefficient) or COV (for covariance) for each matrix row. Variable VARNAME_ is a short string variable whose values are the names of the variables used to form the correlation matrix.
- For factor loading matrices, the program generates two special variables named ROWTYPE_ and FACTOR_. The value for ROWTYPE_ is always FACTOR. The values for FACTOR_ are the ordinal numbers of the factors.
- The remaining variables are the variables used to form the matrix.

Split Files

- FACTOR can read or write split-file matrices.
- When split-file processing is in effect, the first variables in the matrix data file are the split variables, followed by ROWTYPE_, VARNAME_ (or FACTOR_), and then the variables used to form the matrix.
- A full set of matrix materials is written for each split-file group defined by the split variables.
- A split variable cannot have the same variable name as any other variable written to the matrix data file.
- If split-file processing is in effect when a matrix is written, the same split file must be in effect when that matrix is read by any other procedure.

Example

```
GET FILE=GSS80 /KEEP ABDEFECT TO ABSINGLE.
FACTOR VARIABLES=ABDEFECT TO ABSINGLE
  /MATRIX OUT(COR=CORMTX).
```

- FACTOR retrieves the *GSS80* file and writes a factor correlation matrix to the file *CORMTX*.
- The working data file is still *GSS80*. Subsequent commands will be executed on this file.

Example

```
GET FILE=GSS80 /KEEP ABDEFECT TO ABSINGLE.
FACTOR VARIABLES=ABDEFECT TO ABSINGLE
  /MATRIX OUT(COR=*).
LIST.
```

- FACTOR writes the same matrix as in the previous example.
- The working data file is replaced with the correlation matrix. The LIST command is executed on the matrix file, not on *GSS80*.

Example

```
GET FILE=GSS80 /KEEP ABDEFECT TO ABSINGLE.
FACTOR VARIABLES=ABDEFECT TO ABSINGLE
  /MATRIX OUT(FAC=*).
```

- FACTOR generates a factor loading matrix that replaces the working data file.

Example

```
GET FILE=COUNTRY /KEEP SAVINGS POP15 POP75 INCOME GROWTH.
REGRESSION MATRIX OUT(*)
  /VARS=SAVINGS TO GROWTH
  /MISS=PAIRWISE
  /DEP=SAVINGS /ENTER.
FACTOR MATRIX IN(COR=*) /MISSING=PAIRWISE.
```

- The GET command retrieves the *COUNTRY* file and selects the variables needed for the analysis.
- The REGRESSION command computes correlations among five variables with pairwise deletion. MATRIX=OUT writes a matrix data file, which replaces the working data file.
- MATRIX IN(COR=*) on FACTOR reads the matrix materials REGRESSION has written to the working data file. An asterisk is specified because the matrix materials are in the working data file. FACTOR uses pairwise deletion, since this is what was in effect when the matrix was built.

Example

```
GET FILE=COUNTRY /KEEP SAVINGS POP15 POP75 INCOME GROWTH.
REGRESSION
  /VARS=SAVINGS TO GROWTH
  /MISS=PAIRWISE
  /DEP=SAVINGS /ENTER.
FACTOR MATRIX IN(COR=CORMTX).
```

- This example performs a regression analysis on file *COUNTRY* and then uses a different file for FACTOR. The file is an existing matrix data file.
- MATRIX=IN specifies the matrix data file *CORMTX*.
- *CORMTX* does not replace *COUNTRY* as the working data file.

Example

```
GET FILE=CORMTX.
FACTOR MATRIX IN(COR=*).
```

- This example starts a new session and reads an existing matrix data file. GET retrieves the matrix data file *CORMTX*.
- MATRIX=IN specifies an asterisk because the matrix data file is the working data file. If MATRIX=IN(CORMTX) is specified, the program issues an error message.
- If the GET command is omitted, the program issues an error message.

FILE HANDLE

```
FILE HANDLE handle /NAME=file specifications
                  [/MODE={CHARACTER }] [/RECFORM \={FIXED    } [/LRECL=n]
                         {BINARY    }                {VARIABLE}
                         {MULTIPUNCH}                {SPANNED }
                         {IMAGE     }
                         {360       }
```

Overview

FILE HANDLE assigns a unique *file handle* to a file and supplies operating system specifications for the file. A defined file handle can be specified on any subsequent FILE, OUTFILE, MATRIX, or WRITE subcommands of various procedures.

Syntax Rules

- A file handle cannot exceed eight characters and must begin with an alphabetical character (A–Z) or a $, #, or @. It can contain numeric digits (0–9) but not imbedded blanks.
- FILE HANDLE is required for reading IBM VSAM data sets, EBCDIC data files, binary data files, and character data files that are not delimited by ASCII line feeds.
- If you specify 360 on the MODE subcommand, you must specify RECFORM.
- If you specify IMAGE on the MODE subcommand, you must specify LRECL.

Operations

A file handle is used only during the current work session. The handle is never saved as part of an SPSS-format data file.

NAME Subcommand

NAME specifies the file you want to refer to by the file handle. The file specifications must conform to the file naming convention for the type of computer and operating system on which the program is run. See the documentation for your system for specific information about the file naming convention.

MODE Subcommand

MODE specifies the type of file you want to refer to by the file handle.

CHARACTER   *Character file whose logical records are delimited by ASCII line feeds.*

BINARY	*Unformatted binary file generated by Microsoft FORTRAN.*
MULTIPUNCH	*Column binary file.*
IMAGE	*Binary file consisting of fixed-length records.*
360	*EBCDIC data file.*

Example

```
FILE HANDLE ELE48 /NAME='OSPS:[SPSSUSER]ELE48.DAT' /MODE=MULTIPUNCH.
DATA LIST FILE=ELE48.
```

- FILE HANDLE defines *ELE48* as the handle for the file.
- The MODE subcommand indicates that the file contains multipunch data.
- The file specification on NAME conforms to VMS convention: the file *ELE48.DAT* is located in the directory *OSPS:[SPSSUSER]*.
- The FILE subcommand on DATA LIST refers to the handle defined on the FILE HANDLE command.

RECFORM Subcommand

RECFORM specifies the record format and is necessary when you specify 360 on MODE. RECFORM has no effect with other specifications on MODE.

FIXED	*Fixed-length record.* All records have the same length. Alias F. When FIXED is specified, the record length must be specified on the LRECL subcommand.
VARIABLE	*Variable-length record.* No logical record is larger than one physical block. Alias V.
SPANNED	*Spanned record.* Records may be larger than fixed-length physical blocks. Alias VS.

LRECL Subcommand

LRECL specifies the length of each record in the file. When you specify IMAGE under UNIX, OS/2, or Microsoft Windows, or 360 for IBM360 EBCDIC data files, you must specify LRECL. You can specify a record length greater than the default (8192) for an image file, a character file, or a binary file. Do not use LRECL with MULTIPUNCH.

Example

```
FILE HANDLE TRGT1 /NAME='OSPS:RGT.DAT'
                  /MODE=IMAGE LRECL=16.
DATA LIST FILE=TRGT1.
```

- IMAGE is specified on the MODE subcommand. Subcommand LRECL must be specified.
- The file handle is used on the DATA LIST command.

FILE LABEL

```
FILE LABEL label
```

Overview

FILE LABEL provides a descriptive label for a data file.

Syntax Rules

The only specification is a label up to 60 characters long.

Operations

- The file label is printed on the first line of each page of output displayed by the program.
- If the specified label is longer than 60 characters, the program truncates the label to 60 characters without warning.
- If the file is saved, the label is included in the dictionary of the SPSS-format data file.

Example

```
FILE LABEL  Hubbard Industrial Consultants Inc. employee data.
SAVE OUTFILE=HUBEMPL
  /RENAME=(AGE JOBCAT=AGE80 JOBCAT82) /MAP.
```

- FILE LABEL assigns a file label to the Hubbard Consultants Inc. employee data.
- The SAVE command saves the file as an SPSS-format data file, renaming two variables and mapping the results to check the renamed variables.

FILE TYPE—END FILE TYPE

For mixed file types:

```
FILE TYPE MIXED [FILE=file] RECORD=[varname] column location [(format)]

                  [WILD={NOWARN}]
                        {WARN  }
```

For grouped file types:

```
FILE TYPE GROUPED [FILE=file] RECORD=[varname] column location [(format)]

 CASE=[varname] column location [(format)]

 [WILD={WARN  }] [DUPLICATE={WARN  }]
       {NOWARN}             {NOWARN}

 [MISSING={WARN  }] [ORDERED={YES}]
          {NOWARN}           {NO }
```

For nested file types:

```
FILE TYPE NESTED [FILE=file] RECORD=[varname] column location [(format)]

 [CASE=[varname] column location [(format)]]

 [WILD={NOWARN}] [DUPLICATE={NOWARN}]
       {WARN  }             {WARN  }
                            {CASE  }

 [MISSING={NOWARN}]
          {WARN  }

END FILE TYPE
```

Example

```
FILE TYPE  MIXED RECORD=RECID 1-2.
RECORD TYPE 23.
DATA LIST   /SEX 5 AGE 6-7 DOSAGE 8-10 RESULT 12.
END FILE TYPE.

BEGIN DATA
21   145010 1
22   257200 2
25   235   250  2
35   167            300      3
24   125150 1
23   272075 1
21   149050 2
25   134   035  3
30   138            300      3
32   229            500      3
END DATA.
```

Overview

The FILE TYPE—END FILE TYPE structure defines data for any one of the three types of complex raw data files: *mixed files,* which contain several types of records that define different types of cases; *hierarchical* or *nested files,* which contain several types of records with a defined relationship among the record types; or *grouped files,* which contain several records for each case with some records missing or duplicated. A fourth type of complex file, files with *repeating groups* of information, can be defined with the REPEATING DATA command.

FILE TYPE must be followed by at least one RECORD TYPE command and one DATA LIST command. Each pair of RECORD TYPE and DATA LIST commands defines one type of record in the data. END FILE TYPE signals the end of file definition.

Within the FILE TYPE structure, the lowest-level record in a nested file can be read with a REPEATING DATA command rather than a DATA LIST command. In addition, any record in a mixed file can be read with REPEATING DATA.

Basic Specification

The basic specification on FILE TYPE is one of the three file type keywords (MIXED, GROUPED, or NESTED) and the RECORD subcommand. RECORD names the record identification variable and specifies its column location. If keyword GROUPED is specified, the CASE subcommand is also required. CASE names the case identification variable and specifies its column location.

The FILE TYPE—END FILE TYPE structure must enclose at least one RECORD TYPE and one DATA LIST command. END FILE TYPE is required to signal the end of file definition.

- RECORD TYPE specifies the values of the record type identifier (see RECORD TYPE).

- DATA LIST defines variables for the record type specified on the preceding RECORD TYPE command (see DATA LIST).

- Separate pairs of RECORD TYPE and DATA LIST commands must be used to define each different record type.

The resulting working data file is always a rectangular file, regardless of the structure of the original data file.

Specification Order

- FILE TYPE must be the first command in the FILE TYPE—END FILE TYPE structure. FILE TYPE subcommands can be named in any order.

- Each RECORD TYPE command must precede its corresponding DATA LIST command.

- END FILE TYPE must be the last command in the structure.

Syntax Rules

- For mixed files, if the record types have different variables or if they have the same variables recorded in different locations, separate RECORD TYPE and DATA LIST commands are required for each record type.

- For mixed files, the same variable name can be used on different DATA LIST commands, since each record type defines a separate case.

- For mixed files, if the same variable is defined for more than one record type, the format type and length of the variable should be the same on all DATA LIST commands. The program refers to the *first* DATA LIST command that defines a variable for the print and write formats to include in the dictionary of the working data file.

- For grouped and nested files, the variable names on each DATA LIST must be unique, since a case is built by combining all record types together into a single record.

- For nested files, the order of the RECORD TYPE commands defines the hierarchical structure of the file. The first RECORD TYPE defines the highest-level record type, the next RECORD TYPE defines the next highest-level record, and so forth. The last RECORD TYPE command defines a case in the working data file. By default, variables from higher-level records are spread to the lowest-level record.

- For nested files, the SPREAD subcommand on RECORD TYPE can be used to spread the values in a record type only to the *first* case built from each record of that type. All other cases associated with that record are assigned the system-missing value for the variables defined on that type. See RECORD TYPE for more information.

- String values specified on the RECORD TYPE command must be enclosed in apostrophes or quotation marks.

Operations

- For mixed file types, the program skips all records that are not specified on one of the RECORD TYPE commands.

- If different variables are defined for different record types in mixed files, the variables are assigned the system-missing value for those record types on which they are not defined.

- For nested files, the first record in the file should be the type specified on the first RECORD TYPE command—the highest level of the hierarchy. If the first record in the file is not the highest-level type, the program skips all records until it encounters a record of the highest-level type. If MISSING or DUPLICATE has been specified, these records may produce warning messages but will not be used to build a case in the working file.

- When defining complex files, you are effectively building an input program and can use only commands that are allowed in the input state. See Appendix A for information on program states.

Example

```
* Reading multiple record types from a mixed file.

FILE TYPE  MIXED FILE=TREATMNT RECORD=RECID 1-2.
+ RECORD TYPE 21,22,23,24.
+ DATA LIST    /SEX 5 AGE 6-7 DOSAGE 8-10 RESULT 12.
+ RECORD TYPE 25.
+ DATA LIST    /SEX 5 AGE 6-7 DOSAGE 10-12 RESULT 15.
END FILE TYPE.
```

- Variable *DOSAGE* is read from columns 8–10 for record types 21, 22, 23, and 24 and from columns 10–12 for record type 25. *RESULT* is read from column 12 for record types 21, 22, 23, and 24, and from column 15 for record type 25.

- The working data file contains values for all variables defined on the DATA LIST commands for record types 21 through 25. All other record types are skipped.

Example

```
* Reading only one record type from a mixed file.

FILE TYPE  MIXED RECORD=RECID 1-2.
RECORD TYPE 23.
DATA LIST    /SEX 5 AGE 6-7 DOSAGE 8-10 RESULT 12.
END FILE TYPE.

BEGIN DATA
21  145010 1
22  257200 2
25  235  250  2
35  167          300      3
24  125150 1
23  272075 1
21  149050 2
25  134  035  3
30  138          300      3
32  229          500      3
END DATA.
```

- FILE TYPE begins the file definition and END FILE TYPE indicates the end of file definition. FILE TYPE specifies a mixed file type. Since the data are included between BEGIN DATA—END DATA, the FILE subcommand is omitted. The record identification variable *RECID* is located in columns 1 and 2.

- RECORD TYPE indicates that records with value 23 for variable *RECID* will be copied into the working data file. All other records are skipped. the program does not issue a warning when it skips records in mixed files.

- DATA LIST defines variables on records with the value 23 for variable *RECID*.

Example

```
* A grouped file of student test scores.

FILE TYPE GROUPED RECORD=#TEST 6 CASE=STUDENT 1-4.
RECORD TYPE 1.
DATA LIST  /ENGLISH 8-9 (A).
RECORD TYPE 2.
DATA LIST /READING 8-10.
RECORD TYPE 3.
DATA LIST /MATH 8-10.
END FILE TYPE.

BEGIN DATA
0001 1 B+
0001 2  74
0001 3  83
0002 1 A
0002 2 100
0002 3  71
0003 1 B-
0003 2  88
0003 3  81
0004 1 C
0004 2  94
0004 3  91
END DATA.
```

- FILE TYPE identifies the file as a grouped file. As required for grouped files, all records for a single case are together in the data. The record identification variable *#TEST* is located in column 6. A scratch variable is specified so it won't be saved in the working data file. The case identification variable *STUDENT* is located in columns 1–4.

- Because there are three record types, there are three RECORD TYPE commands. For each RECORD TYPE, there is a DATA LIST to define variables on that record type.

- END FILE TYPE signals the end of file definition.

- The program builds four cases—one for each student. Each case includes the case identification variable plus the variables defined for each record type (the test scores). The values for *#TEST* are not saved in the working data file. Thus, each case in the working file has four variables: *STUDENT*, *ENGLISH*, *READING*, and *MATH*.

Example

```
* A nested file of accident records.

FILE TYPE NESTED RECORD=6 CASE=ACCID 1-4.
RECORD TYPE 1.
DATA LIST /ACC_ID 9-11 WEATHER 12-13 STATE 15-16 (A) DATE 18-24 (A).
RECORD TYPE 2.
DATA LIST /STYLE 11 MAKE 13 OLD 14 LICENSE 15-16(A) INSURNCE 18-21 (A).
RECORD TYPE 3.
DATA LIST /PSNGR_NO 11 AGE 13-14 SEX 16 (A) INJURY 18 SEAT 20-21 (A)
          COST 23-24.
END FILE TYPE.

BEGIN DATA
0001 1   322 1 IL 3/13/88   /* Type 1:  accident record
0001 2     1 44MI 134M      /* Type 2:    vehicle record
0001 3     1 34 M 1 FR   3  /* Type 3:      person record
0001 2     2 16IL 322F      /*              vehicle record
0001 3     1 22 F 1 FR 11   /*                person record
0001 3     2 35 M 1 FR   5  /*                person record
0001 3     3 59 M 1 BK   7  /*                person record
0001 2     3 21IN 146M      /*              vehicle record
0001 3     1 46 M 0 FR   0  /*                person record
END DATA.
```

- FILE TYPE specifies a nested file type. The record identifier, located in column 6, is not assigned a variable name, so the default scratch variable name *####RECD* is used. The case identification variable *ACCID* is located in columns 1–4.

- Because there are three record types, there are three RECORD TYPE commands. For each RECORD TYPE, there is a DATA LIST command to define variables on that record type. The order of the RECORD TYPE commands defines the hierarchical structure of the file.

- END FILE TYPE signals the end of file definition.

- The program builds a case for each lowest-level (type 3) record, representing each person in the file. There can be only one type 1 record for each type 2 record, and one type 2 record for each type 3 record. Each vehicle can be in only one accident, and each person can be in only one vehicle. The variables from the type 1 and type 2 records are spread to their corresponding type 3 records.

Types of Files

The first specification on FILE TYPE is a file type keyword, which defines the structure of the data file. There are three file type keywords: MIXED, GROUPED, and NESTED. Only one of the three types can be specified on FILE TYPE.

MIXED *Mixed file type.* MIXED specifies a file in which each record type named on a RECORD TYPE command defines a case. You do not need to define all types of records in the file. In fact, FILE TYPE MIXED is useful for reading only one type of record because the program can decide whether to execute the DATA LIST for a record by simply reading the variable that identifies the record type.

GROUPED   *Grouped file type.* GROUPED defines a file in which cases are defined by grouping together record types with the same identification number. Each case usually has one record of each type. All records for a single case must be together in the file. By default, the program assumes that the records are in the same sequence within each case.

NESTED   *Nested file type.* NESTED defines a file in which the record types are related to each other hierarchically. The record types are grouped together by a case identification number that identifies the highest level—the first record type—of the hierarchy. Usually, the last record type specified—the lowest level of the hierarchy—defines a case. For example, in a file containing household records and records for each person living in the household, each person record defines a case. Information from higher record types may be *spread* to each case. For example, the value for a variable on the household record, such as *CITY*, can be spread to the records for each person in the household.

Subcommands and Their Defaults for Each File Type

The specifications on the FILE TYPE differ for each type of file. Table 1 shows whether each subcommand is required or optional and, where applicable, what the default specification is for each file type. N/A indicates that the subcommand is not applicable to that type of file.

Table 1   Summary of FILE TYPE subcommands for different file types

Subcommand	Mixed	Grouped	Nested
FILE	Conditional	Conditional	Conditional
RECORD	Required	Required	Required
CASE	Not Applicable	Required	Optional
WILD	NOWARN	WARN	NOWARN
DUPLICATE	N/A	WARN	NOWARN
MISSING	N/A	WARN	NOWARN
ORDERED	N/A	YES	N/A

- FILE is required unless data are inline (included between BEGIN DATA—END DATA).
- RECORD is always required.
- CASE is required for grouped files.
- The subcommands CASE, DUPLICATE, and MISSING can also be specified on the associated RECORD TYPE commands for grouped files. However, `DUPLICATE=CASE` is invalid.
- For nested files, CASE and MISSING can be specified on the associated RECORD TYPE commands.
- If the subcommands CASE, DUPLICATE, or MISSING are specified on a RECORD TYPE command, the specification on the FILE TYPE command (or the default) is overridden only for the record types listed on that RECORD TYPE command. The FILE TYPE specification or default applies to all other record types.

FILE Subcommand

FILE specifies a text file containing the data. FILE is not used when the data are inline.

Example

```
FILE TYPE  MIXED FILE=TREATMNT RECORD=RECID 1-2.
```

- Data are in file *TREATMNT*. The file type is mixed. The record identification variable *RECID* is located in columns 1 and 2 of each record.

RECORD Subcommand

RECORD specifies the name and column location of the record identification variable.

- The column location of the record identifier is required. The variable name is optional.
- If you do not want to save the record type variable, you can assign a scratch variable name by using the # character as the first character of the name. If a variable name is not specified on RECORD, the record identifier is defined as the scratch variable *####RECD*.
- The value of the identifier for each record type must be unique and must be in the same location on all records. However, records do not have to be sorted according to type.
- A column-style format can be specified for the record identifier. For example, the following two specifications are valid:

```
RECORD=V1  1-2(N)
RECORD=V1  1-2(F,1)
```

FORTRAN-like formats cannot be used because the column location must be specified explicitly.

- Specify A in parentheses after the column location to define the record type variable as a string variable.

Example

```
FILE TYPE  MIXED FILE=TREATMNT RECORD=RECID 1-2.
```

- The record identifier is variable *RECID*, located in columns 1 and 2 of the hospital treatment data file.

CASE Subcommand

CASE specifies a name and column location for the case identification variable. CASE is required for grouped files and optional for nested files. It cannot be used with mixed files.

- For grouped files, each unique value for the case identification variable defines a case in the working data file.
- For nested files, the case identification variable identifies the highest-level record of the hierarchy. The program issues a warning message for each record with a case identification number not equal to the case identification number on the last highest-level record. However, the record with the invalid case number is used to build the case.

- The column location of the case identifier is required. The variable name is optional.

- If you do not want to save the case identification variable, you can assign a scratch variable name by using the # character as the first character of the name. If a variable name is not specified on CASE, the case identifier is defined as the scratch variable *####CASE*.

- A column-style format can be specified for the case identifier. For example, the following two specifications are valid:

```
CASE=V1  1-2(N)
CASE=V1  1-2(F,1)
```

FORTRAN-like formats cannot be used because the column location must be specified explicitly.

- Specify A in parentheses after the column location to define the case identification variable as a string variable.

- If the case identification number is not in the same columns on all record types, use the CASE subcommand on the RECORD TYPE commands as well as on the FILE TYPE command (see RECORD TYPE).

Example

```
* A grouped file of student test scores.

FILE TYPE GROUPED RECORD=#TEST 6 CASE=STUDENT 1-4.
RECORD TYPE 1.
DATA LIST  /ENGLISH 8-9 (A).
RECORD TYPE 2.
DATA LIST /READING 8-10.
RECORD TYPE 3.
DATA LIST /MATH 8-10.
END FILE TYPE.

BEGIN DATA
0001 1 B+
0001 2  74
0001 3  83
0002 1 A
0002 2 100
0002 3  71
0003 1 B-
0003 2  88
0003 3  81
0004 1 C
0004 2  94
0004 3  91
END DATA.
```

- CASE is required for grouped files. CASE specifies variable *STUDENT*, located in columns 1–4, as the case identification variable.

- The data contain four different values for *STUDENT*. The working data file therefore has four cases, one for each value of *STUDENT*. In a grouped file, each unique value for the case identification variable defines a case in the working file.

- Each case includes the case identification variable plus the variables defined for each record type. The values for *#TEST* are not saved in the working data file. Thus, each case in the working file has four variables: *STUDENT*, *ENGLISH*, *READING*, and *MATH*.

Example

```
* A nested file of accident records.

FILE TYPE NESTED RECORD=6 CASE=ACCID 1-4.
RECORD TYPE 1.
DATA LIST   /ACC_ID 9-11 WEATHER 12-13 STATE 15-16 (A) DATE 18-24 (A).
RECORD TYPE 2.
DATA LIST /STYLE 11 MAKE 13 OLD 14 LICENSE 15-16 (A) INSURNCE 18-21 (A).
RECORD TYPE 3.
DATA LIST /PSNGR_NO 11 AGE 13-14 SEX 16 (A) INJURY 18 SEAT 20-21 (A)
          COST 23-24.
END FILE TYPE.

BEGIN DATA
0001 1   322 1 IL 3/13/88   /* Type 1:  accident record
0001 2     1 44MI 134M      /* Type 2:   vehicle record
0001 3     1 34 M 1 FR  3   /* Type 3:    person record
0001 2     2 16IL 322F      /*            vehicle record
0001 3     1 22 F 1 FR 11   /*             person record
0001 3     2 35 M 1 FR  5   /*             person record
0001 3     3 59 M 1 BK  7   /*             person record
0001 2     3 21IN 146M      /*            vehicle record
0001 3     1 46 M 0 FR  0   /*             person record
END DATA.
```

- CASE specifies variable *ACCID*, located in columns 1–4, as the case identification variable. *ACCID* identifies the highest level of the hierarchy: the level for the accident records.

- As each case is built, the value of the variable *ACCID* is checked against the value of *ACCID* on the last highest-level record (record type 1). If the values do not match, a warning message is issued. However, the record is used to build the case.

- The data in this example contain only one value for *ACCID*, which is spread across all cases. In a nested file, the lowest-level record type determines the number of cases in the working data file. In this example, the working file has five cases because there are five person records.

Example

```
* Specifying case on the RECORD TYPE command.

FILE TYPE GROUPED FILE=HUBDATA RECORD=#RECID 80 CASE=ID 1-5.
RECORD TYPE 1.
DATA LIST   /MOHIRED YRHIRED 12-15 DEPT79 TO DEPT82 SEX 16-20.
RECORD TYPE 2.
DATA LIST   /SALARY79 TO SALARY82 6-25 HOURLY81 HOURLY82 40-53 (2)
            PROMO81 72  AGE 54-55 RAISE82 66-70.
RECORD TYPE 3   CASE=75-79.
DATA LIST   /JOBCAT 6 NAME 25-48 (A).
END FILE TYPE.
```

- The CASE subcommand on FILE TYPE indicates that the case identification number is located in columns 1–5. However, for type 3 records, the case identification number is located in columns 75–79. The CASE subcommand is therefore specified on the third RECORD TYPE command to override the case setting for type 3 records.

- The format of the case identification variable must be the same on all records. If the case identification variable is defined as a string on the FILE TYPE command, it cannot be defined as a numeric variable on the RECORD TYPE command, and vice versa.

WILD Subcommand

WILD determines whether the program issues a warning when it encounters undefined record types in the data file. Regardless of whether the warning is issued, undefined records are not included in the working data file.

- The only specification on WILD is keyword WARN or NOWARN.
- WARN cannot be specified if keyword OTHER is specified on the last RECORD TYPE command to indicate all other record types (see RECORD TYPE).

WARN   *Issue warning messages.* The program displays a warning message and the first 80 characters of the record for each record type that is not mentioned on a RECORD TYPE command. This is the default for grouped file types.

NOWARN   *Suppress warning messages.* The program simply skips all record types not mentioned on a RECORD TYPE command and does not display warning messages. This is the default for mixed and nested file types.

Example

```
FILE TYPE  MIXED FILE=TREATMNT RECORD=RECID 1-2 WILD=WARN.
```

- WARN is specified on the WILD subcommand. The program displays a warning message and the first 80 characters of the record for each record type that is not mentioned on a RECORD TYPE command.

DUPLICATE Subcommand

DUPLICATE determines how the program responds when it encounters more than one record of each type for a single case. DUPLICATE is optional for grouped and nested files. DUPLICATE cannot be used with mixed files.

- The only specification on DUPLICATE is keyword WARN, NOWARN, or CASE.

WARN   *Issue warning messages.* The program displays a warning message and the first 80 characters of the last record of the duplicate set of record types. Only the *last* record from a set of duplicates is included in the working data file. This is the default for grouped files.

NOWARN   *Suppress warning messages.* The program does not display warning messages when it encounters duplicate record types. Only the *last* record from a set of duplicates is included in the working data file. This is the default for nested files.

CASE   *Build a case in the working data file for each duplicate record.* The program builds one case in the working file for each duplicate record, spreading information from any higher-level records and assigning system-missing values to the variables defined on lower-level records. This option is available only for nested files.

Example

```
* A nested file of accident records.
* Issue a warning for duplicate record types.

FILE TYPE NESTED RECORD=6 CASE=ACCID 1-4 DUPLICATE=WARN.
RECORD TYPE 1.
DATA LIST   /ACC_ID 9-11 WEATHER 12-13 STATE 15-16 (A) DATE 18-24 (A).
RECORD TYPE 2.
DATA LIST /STYLE 11 MAKE 13 OLD 14 LICENSE 15-16 (A) INSURNCE 18-21 (A).
RECORD TYPE 3.
DATA LIST /PSNGR_NO 11 AGE 13-14 SEX 16 (A) INJURY 18 SEAT 20-21 (A)
          COST 23-24.
END FILE TYPE.

BEGIN DATA
0001 1  322 1 IL 3/13/88   /*          accident record
0001 2    1 44MI 134M      /*          vehicle record
0001 3    1 34 M 1 FR  3   /*          person record
0001 2    1 31IL 134M      /*   duplicate vehicle record
0001 2    2 16IL 322F      /*          vehicle record
0001 3    1 22 F 1 FR 11   /*          person record
0001 3    2 35 M 1 FR  5   /*          person record
0001 3    3 59 M 1 BK  7   /*          person record
0001 2    3 21IN 146M      /*          vehicle record
0001 3    1 46 M 0 FR  0   /*          person record
END DATA.
```

- In the data, there are two vehicle (type 2) records above the second set of person (type 3) records. This implies that an empty (for example, parked) vehicle was involved, or that each of the three persons was in two vehicles, which is impossible.

- DUPLICATE specifies keyword WARN. The program displays a warning message and the first 80 characters of the second of the duplicate set of type 2 records. The first duplicate record is skipped, and only the second is included in the working data file. This assumes that no empty vehicles were involved in the accident.

- If the duplicate record represents an empty vehicle, it can be included in the working data file by specifying keyword CASE on DUPLICATE. The program builds one case in the working data file for the first duplicate record, spreading information to that case from the previous type 1 record and assigning system-missing values to the variables defined for type 3 records. The second record from the duplicate set is used to build the three cases for the associated type 3 records.

MISSING Subcommand

MISSING determines whether the program issues a warning when it encounters a missing record type for a case. Regardless of whether the program issues the warning, it builds the case in the working file with system-missing values for the variables defined on the missing record. MISSING is optional for grouped and nested files.

- MISSING cannot be used with mixed files and is optional for grouped and nested files.

- For grouped and nested files, the program verifies that each defined case includes one record of each type.

- The only specification is keyword WARN or NOWARN.

WARN   *Issue a warning message when a record type is missing for a case.* This is the default for grouped files.

NOWARN   *Suppress the warning message when a record type is missing for a case.* This is the default for nested files.

Example

```
* A grouped file with missing records.

FILE TYPE GROUPED RECORD=#TEST 6 CASE=STUDENT 1-4 MISSING=NOWARN.
RECORD TYPE 1.
DATA LIST  /ENGLISH 8-9 (A).
RECORD TYPE 2.
DATA LIST /READING 8-10.
RECORD TYPE 3.
DATA LIST /MATH 8-10.
END FILE TYPE.

BEGIN DATA
0001 1 B+
0001 2  74
0002 1 A
0002 2 100
0002 3  71
0003 3  81
0004 1 C
0004 2  94
0004 3  91
END DATA.
```

- The data contain records for three tests administered to four students. However, not all students took all tests. The first student took only the English and reading tests. The third student took only the math test.

- One case in the working data file is built for each of the four students. If a student did not take a test, the system-missing value is assigned in the working file to the variable for the missing test. Thus, the first student has the system-missing value for the math test, and the third student has missing values for the English and reading tests.

- Keyword NOWARN is specified on MISSING. Therefore, no warning messages are issued for the missing records.

Example

```
* A nested file with missing records.

FILE TYPE NESTED RECORD=6 CASE=ACCID 1-4 MISSING=WARN.
RECORD TYPE 1.
DATA LIST   /ACC_ID 9-11 WEATHER 12-13 STATE 15-16 (A) DATE 18-24 (A).
RECORD TYPE 2.
DATA LIST /STYLE 11 MAKE 13 OLD 14 LICENSE 15-16 (A) INSURNCE 18-21 (A).
RECORD TYPE 3.
DATA LIST /PSNGR_NO 11 AGE 13-14 SEX 16 (A) INJURY 18 SEAT 20-21 (A)
          COST 23-24.
END FILE TYPE.
```

```
BEGIN DATA
0001 1   322 1 IL 3/13/88    /*              accident record
0001 3     1 34 M 1 FR   3   /*               person record
0001 2     2 16IL 322F       /*              vehicle record
0001 3     1 22 F 1 FR  11   /*               person record
0001 3     2 35 M 1 FR   5   /*               person record
0001 3     3 59 M 1 BK   7   /*               person record
0001 2     3 21IN 146M       /*              vehicle record
0001 3     1 46 M 0 FR   0   /*               person record
END DATA.
```

- The data contain records for one accident. The first record is a type 1 (accident) record, and the second record is a type 3 (person) record. However, there is no type 2 record, and therefore no vehicle associated with the first person. The person may have been a pedestrian, but it is also possible that the vehicle record is missing.

- One case is built for each person record. The first case has missing values for the variables specified on the vehicle record.

- Keyword WARN is specified on MISSING. A warning message is issued for the missing record.

ORDERED Subcommand

ORDERED indicates whether the records are in the same order as they are defined on the RECORD TYPE commands. Regardless of the order of the records in the data file and the specification on ORDERED, the program builds cases in the working data file with records in the order defined on the RECORD TYPE commands.

- ORDERED can be used only for grouped files.

- The only specification is keyword YES or NO.

- If YES is in effect but the records are not in the order defined on the RECORD TYPE commands, the program issues a warning for each record that is out of order. The program still uses these records to build cases.

YES   *Records for each case are in the same order as they are defined on the RECORD TYPE commands.* This is the default.

NO   *Records are not in the same order within each case.*

Example

```
* A grouped file with records out of order.

FILE TYPE GROUPED RECORD=#TEST 6 CASE=STUDENT 1-4  MISSING=NOWARN
   ORDERED=NO.
RECORD TYPE 1.
DATA LIST   /ENGLISH 8-9 (A).
RECORD TYPE 2.
DATA LIST /READING 8-10.
RECORD TYPE 3.
DATA LIST /MATH 8-10.
END FILE TYPE.
```

```
BEGIN DATA
0001 2  74
0001 1  B+
0002 3  71
0002 2 100
0002 1 A
0003 2  81
0004 2  94
0004 1 C
0004 3  91
END DATA.
```

- The first RECORD TYPE command specifies record type 1, the second specifies record type 2, and the third specifies record type 3. However, records for each case are not always ordered type 1, type 2, and type 3.

- NO is specified on ORDERED. The program builds cases without issuing a warning that they are out of order in the data.

- Regardless of whether YES or NO is in effect for ORDERED, the program builds cases in the working data file in the same order specified on the RECORD TYPE commands.

FILTER

```
FILTER  {BY var}
        {OFF   }
```

Example

```
FILTER BY SEX.
FREQUENCIES BONUS.
```

Overview

FILTER is used to exclude cases from program procedures without deleting them from the working data file. When FILTER is in effect, cases with a zero or missing value for the specified variable are not used in program procedures. Those cases are not actually deleted and are available again if the filter is turned off. To see the current filter status, use the SHOW command.

Basic Specification

The basic specification is keyword BY followed by a variable name. Cases that have a zero or missing value for the filter variable are excluded from subsequent procedures.

Syntax Rules

- Only one numeric variable can be specified. The variable can be one of the original variables in the data file or a variable computed with transformation commands.
- Keyword OFF turns off the filter. All cases in the working data file become available to subsequent procedures.
- If FILTER is specified without a keyword, FILTER OFF is assumed but the program displays a warning message.
- FILTER can be specified anywhere in the command sequence. Unlike SELECT IF, FILTER has the same effect within an input program as it does outside an input program. Attention must be paid to the placement of any transformation command used to compute values for the filter variable (see INPUT PROGRAM).

Operations

- FILTER performs case selection without changing the working data file. Cases that have a zero or missing value are excluded from subsequent procedures but are not deleted from the file.

- Both system-missing and user-missing values are treated as missing. The FILTER command does not offer options for changing selection criteria. To set up different criteria for exclusion, create a numeric variable and conditionally compute its values before specifying it on FILTER.

- If FILTER is specified after TEMPORARY, FILTER affects the next procedure only. After that procedure, the filter status reverts to whatever it was before the TEMPORARY command.

- The filter status does not change until another FILTER command is specified or the working data file is replaced.

- If the specified filter variable is renamed, it is still in effect. The SHOW command will display the new name of the filter variable. However, the filter is turned off if the filter variable is recoded into a string variable or is deleted from the file.

- If the working data file is replaced after a MATCH FILES, ADD FILES, or UPDATE command and the working file is one of the input files, the filter remains in effect if the new working file has a numeric variable with the name of the filter variable. If the working data file does not have a numeric variable with that name (for example, if the filter variable was dropped or renamed), the filter is turned off.

- If the working data file is replaced by an entirely new data file (for example, by a DATA LIST, GET, and IMPORT command), the filter is turned off.

- The FILTER command changes the filter status and takes effect when a procedure is executed or an EXECUTE command is encountered.

Example

```
FILTER BY SEX.
FREQUENCIES BONUS.
```

- This example assumes that *SEX* is a numeric variable, with male and female coded as 0 and 1, respectively. The FILTER command excludes males and cases with missing values for *SEX* from the subsequent procedures. The FREQUENCIES command generates a frequency table of *BONUS* for females only.

Example

```
RECODE SEX (1=0)(0=1).
FILTER BY SEX.
FREQUENCIES BONUS.
```

- This example assumes the same coding scheme for *SEX* as the previous example. Before FILTER is specified, variable *SEX* is recoded. The FILTER command then excludes females and cases with missing values for *SEX*. The FREQUENCIES command generates a frequency table of *BONUS* for males only.

FINISH

```
FINISH
```

Overview

FINISH causes the program to stop reading commands.

Basic Specification

The basic specification is keyword FINISH. There are no additional specifications.

Command Files

- FINISH is optional in a command file and is used to mark the end of a session.
- FINISH causes the program to stop reading commands. Anything following FINISH in the command file is ignored. Any commands following FINISH in an INCLUDE file are ignored.
- FINISH cannot be used within a DO IF structure to end a session conditionally. FINISH within a DO IF structure will end the session unconditionally.

Prompted Sessions

- FINISH is required in a prompted session to terminate the session.
- Because FINISH is a program command, it can be used only after the command line prompt for the program, which expects a procedure name. FINISH cannot be used to end a prompted session from a DATA>, CONTINUE>, HELP>, or DEFINE> prompt.

Operations

- FINISH immediately causes the program to stop reading commands.
- The appearance of FINISH on the printback of commands in the display file indicates that the session has been completed.
- When issued within the SPSS Manager (not available on all systems), FINISH terminates command processing and causes the program to query whether you want to continue working. If you answer *yes*, you can continue creating and editing files in both the input window and the output window; however, you can no longer run commands.

Example

```
* A command file.

DATA LIST FILE=RAWDATA /NAME 1-15(A) V1 TO V15 16-30.
LIST.
FINISH.
REPORT FORMAT=AUTO LIST /VARS=NAME V1 TO V10.
```

- FINISH causes the program to stop reading commands after LIST is executed. The REPORT command is not executed.

Example

```
SPSS> * A prompted session.

SPSS> DATA LIST FILE=RAWDATA /NAME 1-15(A) V1 TO V15 16-30.
SPSS> LIST.
SPSS> FINISH.
```

- FINISH terminates the prompted session.

FIT

```
FIT [[ERRORS=] residual series names]

  [/OBS=observed series names]

  [/{DFE=error degrees of freedom       }]
    {DFH=hypothesis degrees of freedom}
```

Example

```
FIT ERR_4  ERR_8.
```

Overview

FIT displays a variety of descriptive statistics computed from the residual series as an aid in evaluating the goodness of fit of one or more models.

Options

Statistical Output. You can produce statistics for a particular residual series by specifying the names of the series after FIT. You can also obtain percent error statistics for specified residual series by specifying observed series on the OBS subcommand.

Degrees of Freedom. You can specify the degrees of freedom for the residual series using the DFE or DFH subcommands.

Basic Specification

The basic specification is simply the command keyword FIT. All other specifications are optional.

- By default, FIT calculates the mean error, mean percent error, mean absolute error, mean absolute percent error, sum of squared errors, mean square error, root mean square error, and the Durbin-Watson statistic for the last *ERR_n* (residual) series generated and the corresponding observed series in the working data file.
- If neither residual nor observed series are specified, percent error statistics for the default residual and observed series are included.

Syntax Rules

- If OBS is specified, the ERRORS subcommand naming the residual series is required.

Operations

- Observed series and degrees of freedom are matched with residual series according to the order in which they are specified.
- If residual series are explicitly specified but observed series are not, percent error statistics are not included in the output. If neither residual nor observed series are specified, percent error statistics for the default residual and observed series are included.
- If subcommand DFH is specified, FIT calculates the DFE (error degrees of freedom) by subtracting the DFH (hypothesis degrees of freedom) from the number of valid cases in the series.
- If a PREDICT period (validation period) starts before the end of the observed series, statistics are reported separately for the USE period (historical period) and the PREDICT period.

Limitations

- There is no limit on the number of residual series specified. However, the number of observed series must equal the number of residual series.

Example

```
FIT ERR_4 ERR_5 ERR_6.
```

- This command requests goodness-of-fit statistics for the residual series *ERR_4*, *ERR_5*, and *ERR_6*, which were generated by previous procedures. Percent error statistics are not included in the output, since only residual series are named.

ERRORS Subcommand

ERRORS specifies the residual (error) series.
- The actual keyword ERRORS can be omitted. VARIABLES is an alias for ERRORS.
- The minimum specification on ERRORS is a residual series name.
- The ERRORS subcommand is required if the OBS subcommand is specified.

OBS Subcommand

OBS specifies the observed series to use for calculating the mean percentage error and mean absolute percentage error.
- OBS can be used only when the residual series are explicitly specified.
- The number and order of observed series must be the same as that of the residual series.

- If more than one residual series was calculated from a single observed series, the observed series is specified once for each residual series that is based on it.

Example

```
FIT ERRORS=ERR#1 ERR#2
  /OBS=VAR1 VAR1.
```

- This command requests FIT statistics for two residual series, *ERR#1* and *ERR#2*, which were computed from the same observed series, *VAR1*.

DFE and DFH Subcommands

DFE and DFH specify the degrees of freedom for each residual series. With DFE, error degrees of freedom are entered directly. DFH specifies hypothesis degrees of freedom so FIT can compute the DFE.

- Only one DFE or DFH subcommand should be specified. If both are specified, only the last one is in effect.
- The specification on DFE or DFH is a list of numeric values. The order of these values should correspond to the order of the residual series list.
- The error degrees of freedom specified on DFE are used to compute the mean square error (MSE) and root mean square (RMS).
- The value specified for DFH should equal the number of parameters in the model (including the constant if it is present). Differencing is not considered in calculating DFH, since any observations lost due to differencing are system-missing.
- If neither DFE or DFH are specified, FIT sets DFE equal to the number of observations.

Example

```
FIT ERR#1 ERR#2
  /OBS=VAR1 VAR2
  /DFE=47 46.
```

- In this example, the error degrees of freedom for the first residual series, *ERR#1*, is 47. The error degrees of freedom for the second residual series, *ERR#2*, is 46.

Output Considerations for SSE

The sum of squared errors (SSE) reported by FIT may not be the same as the SSE reported by the estimation procedure. The SSE from the procedure is an estimate of sigma squared for that model. The SSE from FIT is simply the sum of the squared residuals.

References

Makridakis, S., S. C. Wheelwright, and V. E. McGee. 1983. *Forecasting: Methods and applications*. New York: John Wiley and Sons.

McLaughlin, R. L. 1984. *Forecasting techniques for decision making*. Rockville, Md.: Control Data Management Institute.

FLIP

```
FLIP [[VARIABLES=] {ALL     }]
                  {varlist}

     [/NEWNAMES=variable]
```

Example

```
FLIP VARIABLES=WEEK1 TO WEEK52 /NEWNAMES=DEPT.
```

Overview

The program requires a file structure in which the variables are the columns and observations (cases) are the rows. If a file is organized such that variables are in rows and observations are in columns, you need to use FLIP to reorganize it. FLIP transposes the rows and columns of the data in the working data file so that, for example, row 1, column 2 becomes row 2, column 1, and so forth.

Options

Variable Subsets. You can transpose specific variables (columns) from the original file using the VARIABLES subcommand.

Variable Names. You can use the values of one of the variables from the original file as the variable names in the new file, using the NEWNAMES subcommand.

Basic Specification

The basic specification is the command keyword FLIP, which transposes all rows and columns.

- By default, FLIP assigns variable names *VAR001* to *VARn* to the variables in the new file. It also creates the new variable *CASE_LBL*, whose values are the variable names that existed before transposition.

Subcommand Order

VARIABLES must precede NEWNAMES.

Operations

- FLIP replaces the working data file with the transposed file and displays a list of variable names in the transposed file.

403

- FLIP discards any previous VARIABLE LABELS, VALUE LABELS, and WEIGHT settings. Values defined as user-missing in the original file are translated to system-missing in the transposed file.
- FLIP obeys any SELECT IF, N, and SAMPLE commands in effect.
- FLIP does not obey the TEMPORARY command. Any transformations become permanent when followed by FLIP.
- String variables in the original file are assigned system-missing values after transposition.
- Numeric variables are assigned a default format of F8.2 after transposition (with the exceptions of *CASE_LBL* and the variable specified on NEWNAMES).
- The variable *CASE_LBL* is created and added to the working data file each time FLIP is executed.
- If *CASE_LBL* already exists as the result of a previous FLIP, its current values are used as the names of variables in the new file (if NEWNAMES is not specified).

Example

The following is the LIST output for a data file arranged in a typical spreadsheet format, with variables in rows and observations in columns:

```
A              B         C         D

Income      22.00     31.00     43.00
Price       34.00     29.00     50.00
Year      1970.00   1971.00   1972.00
```

The command

```
FLIP.
```

transposes all variables in the file. The LIST output for the transposed file is as follows:

```
CASE_LBL    VAR001    VAR002    VAR003

A              .         .         .
B           22.00     34.00   1970.00
C           31.00     29.00   1971.00
D           43.00     50.00   1972.00
```

- The values for the new variable *CASE_LBL* are the variable names from the original file.
- Case *A* has system-missing values, since variable *A* had the string values Income, Price, and Year.
- The names of the variables in the new file are *CASE_LBL, VAR001, VAR002,* and *VAR003*.

VARIABLES Subcommand

VARIABLES names one or more variables (columns) to be transposed. The specified variables become observations (rows) in the new working file.

- The VARIABLES subcommand is optional. If it is not used, all variables are transposed.
- The actual keyword VARIABLES can be omitted.
- If the VARIABLES subcommand is specified, variables that are not named are discarded.

Example

Using the untransposed file from the previous example, the command

```
FLIP VARIABLES=A TO C.
```

transposes only variables *A* through *C*. Variable *D* is not transposed and is discarded from the working data file. The LIST output for the transposed file is as follows:

```
CASE_LBL    VAR001    VAR002    VAR003

A              .         .         .
B            22.00     34.00    1970.00
C            31.00     29.00    1971.00
```

NEWNAMES Subcommand

NEWNAMES specifies a variable whose values are used as the new variable names.

- The NEWNAMES subcommand is optional. If it is not used, the new variable names are either *VAR001* to *VARn*, or the values of *CASE_LBL* if it exists.
- Only one variable can be specified on NEWNAMES.
- The variable specified on NEWNAMES does not become an observation (case) in the new working data file, regardless of whether it is specified on the VARIABLES subcommand.
- If the variable specified is numeric, its values become a character string beginning with the letter *V*.
- If the variable specified is a long string, only the first eight characters are used.
- Lowercase character values of a string variable are converted to upper case, and any bad character values, such as blank spaces, are replaced with underscore (_) characters.
- If the variable's values are not unique, a numeric extension *n* is added to the end of a value after its first occurrence, with *n* increasing by 1 at each subsequent occurrence.

Example

Using the untransposed file from the first example, the command

```
FLIP NEWNAMES=A.
```

uses the values for variable *A* as variable names in the new file. The LIST output for the transposed file is as follows:

```
CASE_LBL    INCOME    PRICE     YEAR

B            22.00     34.00    1970.00
C            31.00     29.00    1971.00
D            43.00     50.00    1972.00
```

- Variable *A* does not become an observation in the new file. The string values for *A* are converted to upper case.

The following command transposes this file back to a form resembling its original structure:

```
FLIP.
```

The LIST output for the transposed file is as follows:

```
CASE_LBL        B           C           D

INCOME       22.00       31.00       43.00
PRICE        34.00       29.00       50.00
YEAR       1970.00     1971.00     1972.00
```

- Since the NEWNAMES subcommand is not used, the values of *CASE_LBL* from the previous FLIP (*B, C,* and *D*) are used as variable names in the new file.

- The values of *CASE_LBL* are now INCOME, PRICE, and YEAR.

FORMATS

```
FORMATS varlist(format) [varlist...]
```

Example

```
FORMATS SALARY (DOLLAR8) / HOURLY (DOLLAR7.2) / RAISE BONUS (PCT2).
```

Overview

FORMATS changes variable print and write formats. In this program, print and write formats are *output* formats. Print formats, also called display formats, control the form in which values are displayed by a procedure or by the PRINT command; write formats control the form in which values are written by the WRITE command.

FORMATS changes both print and write formats. To change only print formats, use PRINT FORMATS. To change only write formats, use WRITE FORMATS. For information on assigning input formats during data definition, see DATA LIST.

Table 1 shows the output formats that can be assigned with the FORMATS, PRINT FORMATS, and WRITE FORMATS commands. For additional information on formats, see "Variable Formats" on p. 31.

Basic Specification

The basic specification is a variable list followed by a format specification in parentheses. All variables on the list receive the new format.

Syntax Rules

- You can specify more than one variable or variable list, followed by a format in parentheses. Only one format can be specified after each variable list. For clarity, each set of specifications can be separated by a slash.
- You can use keyword TO to refer to consecutive variables in the working data file.
- The specified width of a format must include enough positions to accommodate any punctuation characters such as decimal points, commas, dollar signs, or date and time delimiters. (This differs from assigning an *input* format on DATA LIST, where the program automatically expands the input format to accommodate punctuation characters in output.)
- Custom currency formats (CCw, CCw.d) must first be defined on the SET command before they can be used on FORMATS.
- FORMATS cannot be used with string variables. To change the length of a string variable, declare a new variable of the desired length with the STRING command and then use COMPUTE to copy values from the existing string into the new variable.
- To save the new print and write formats, you must save the working data file as an SPSS-format data file with the SAVE or XSAVE command.

Table 1 shows the formats that can be assigned by FORMATS, PRINT FORMATS, or WRITE FORMATS. The first column of the table lists the FORTRAN-like specification. The column labeled *PRINT* indicates whether the format can be used to display values. The columns labeled *Min w* and *Max w* refer to the minimum and maximum widths allowed for the format type. The column labeled *Max d* refers to the maximum decimal places.

Table 1   Output data formats

Type	PRINT	Min w	Max w	Max d	
Numeric					
Fw, Fw.d	yes	1*	40	16	
COMMAw, COMMAw.d	yes	1*	40	16	
DOTw, DOTw.d	yes	1*	40	16	
DOLLARw, DOLLARw.d	yes	2*	40	16	
CCw, CCw.d	yes	2*	40	16	
PCTw, PCTw.d	yes	1*	40	16	
PIBHEXw	yes	2†	16†		
RBHEXw	yes	4†	16†		
Zw, Zw.d	yes	1	40	16	
IBw, IBw.d	no	1	8	16	
PIBw, PIBw.d	no	1	8	16	
Nw.d	yes	1	40	16	
Pw, Pw.d	no	1	16	16	
Ew, Ew.d	yes	6	40		
PKw, PKw.d	no	1	16	16	
RBw	no	2	8		
String					
Aw	yes	1	254		
AHEXw	yes	2†	510		
Date and time					Resulting form
DATEw	yes	9	40		dd-mmm-yy
		11			dd-mmm-yyyy
ADATEw	yes	8	40		mm/dd/yy
		10			mm/dd/yyyy
EDATEw	yes	8	40		dd/mm/yy
		10			dd/mm/yyyy
JDATEw	yes	5	40		yyddd
		7			yyyyddd
SDATEw	yes	8	40		yy/mm/dd
		10			yyyy/mm/dd
QYRw	yes	6	40		q Q yy

Table 1   Output data formats (Continued)

Type	PRINT	Min w	Max w	Max d	
		8			q Q yyyy
MOYRw	yes	6	40		mmm yy
		8			mmm yyyy
WKYRw	yes	8	40		ww WK yy
		10			ww WK yyyy
WKDAYw	yes	2**	40		
MONTHw	yes	3**	40		
TIMEw	yes	5††	40		hh:mm
TIMEw.d	yes	10	40	16	hh:mm:ss.s
DTIMEw	yes	8††	40		dd hh:mm
DTIMEw.d	yes	13	40	16	dd hh:mm:ss.s
DATETIMEw	yes	17††	40		dd-mmm-yyyy hh:mm
DATETIMEw.d	yes	22	40	16	dd-mmm-yyyy hh:mm:ss.s

*Add number of decimals plus 1 if number of decimals is more than 0. Total width cannot exceed 40 characters.
†Must be a multiple of 2.
**As the field width is expanded, the output string is expanded until the entire name of the day or month is produced.
††Add 3 to display seconds.

Operations

- Unlike most transformations, FORMATS takes effect as soon as it is encountered in the command sequence. Special attention should be paid to its position among commands. For more information, see "Command Order" on p. 16.

- Variables not specified on FORMATS retain their current print and write formats in the working file. To see the current formats, use the DISPLAY command.

- The new formats are changed only in the working file and are in effect for the duration of the current session or until changed again with a FORMATS, PRINT FORMATS, or WRITE FORMATS command. Formats in the original data file (if one exists) are not changed unless the file is resaved with the SAVE or XSAVE command.

- New numeric variables created with transformation commands are assigned default print and write formats of F8.2 (or the format specified on the FORMAT subcommand of SET). The FORMATS command can be used to change the new variable's print and write formats.

- New string variables created with transformation commands are assigned the format specified on the STRING command that declares the variable. FORMATS cannot be used to change the format of a new string variable.

- If a numeric data value exceeds its width specification, the program attempts to display some value nevertheless. The program first rounds decimal values, then removes punctuation characters, then tries scientific notation, and finally, if there is still not enough space, produces asterisks indicating that a value is present but cannot be displayed in the assigned width.

Example

```
FORMATS SALARY (DOLLAR8) /HOURLY (DOLLAR7.2)
        /RAISE BONUS (PCT2).
```

- The print and write formats for *SALARY* are changed to DOLLAR format with eight positions, including the dollar sign and comma when appropriate. The value 11550 is displayed as $11,550. An eight-digit number would require a DOLLAR11 format: eight characters for the digits, two characters for commas, and one character for the dollar sign.

- The print and write formats for *HOURLY* are changed to DOLLAR format with seven positions, including the dollar sign, decimal point, and two decimal places. The value 115 is displayed as $115.00. If DOLLAR6.2 had been specified, the value 115 would be displayed as $115.0. The program would truncate the last 0 because a width of 6 is not enough to display the full value.

- The print and write formats for both *RAISE* and *BONUS* are changed to PCT with two positions: one position for the percentage and one position for the percent sign. The value 9 is displayed as 9%. Since the width allows for only two positions, the value 10 is displayed as 10, since the percent sign is truncated.

Example

```
COMPUTE V3=V1 + V2.
FORMATS V3 (F3.1).
```

- COMPUTE creates the new numeric variable *V3*. By default, *V3* is assigned an F8.2 format (or the default format specified on SET).

- FORMATS changes both the print and write formats for *V3* to F3.1.

Example

```
SET CCA='-/-.Dfl ..-'.
FORMATS COST (CCA14.2).
```

- SET defines a European currency format for the custom currency format type CCA.

- FORMATS assigns format CCA to variable *COST*. With the format defined for CCA on SET, the value 37419 is displayed as Dfl 37.419,00. See the SET command for more information on custom currency formats.

FREQUENCIES

```
FREQUENCIES [VARIABLES=]varlist [varlist...]

[/FORMAT= [{NOTABLE }] [{AVALUE}]
          {LIMIT(n)}   {DVALUE}
                       {AFREQ }
                       {DFREQ }

[/MISSING=INCLUDE]

[/BARCHART=[MINIMUM(n)] [MAXIMUM(n)] [{FREQ(n)    }]]
                                     {PERCENT(n)}

[/PIECHART=[MINIMUM(n)] [MAXIMUM(n)] [{FREQ    }] [{MISSING  }]]
                                     {PERCENT}    {NOMISSING}

[/HISTOGRAM=[MINIMUM(n)] [MAXIMUM(n)] [{FREQ(n)   }] [{NONORMAL}] ]
                                                     {NORMAL   }

[/GROUPED=varlist [{(width)        }]]
                  {(boundary list)}

[/NTILES=n]

[/PERCENTILES=value list]

[/STATISTICS=[DEFAULT] [MEAN] [STDDEV] [MINIMUM] [MAXIMUM]
             [SEMEAN] [VARIANCE] [SKEWNESS] [SESKEW] [RANGE]
             [MODE] [KURTOSIS] [SEKURT] [MEDIAN] [SUM] [ALL]
             [NONE]]

[/ORDER=[{ANALYSIS}] [{VARIABLE}]
```

Example

```
FREQUENCIES VAR=RACE /STATISTICS=ALL.
```

Overview

FREQUENCIES produces Frequency tables showing frequency counts and percentages of the values of individual variables. You can also use FREQUENCIES to obtain Statistics tables for categorical variables and to obtain Statistics tables and graphical displays for continuous variables.

Options

Display Format. You can suppress tables and alter the order of values within tables using the FORMAT subcommand.

Statistical Display. Percentiles and ntiles are available for numeric variables with the PERCENTILES and NTILES subcommands. The following statistics are available with the STATISTICS subcommand: mean, median, mode, standard deviation, variance, skewness, kurtosis, and sum.

411

Plots. Histograms can be specified for numeric variables on the HISTOGRAM subcommand. Bar charts can be specified for numeric or string variables on the BARCHART subcommand.

Input Data. On the GROUPED subcommand, you can indicate whether the input data are grouped (or collapsed) so that a better estimate can be made of percentiles.

Basic Specification

The basic specification is the VARIABLES subcommand and the name of at least one variable. By default, FREQUENCIES produces a Frequency table.

Subcommand Order

Subcommands can be named in any order.

Syntax Rules

- You can specify multiple NTILES subcommands.
- BARCHART and HISTOGRAM are mutually exclusive.
- You can specify numeric variables (with or without decimal values) or string variables. Only the short-string portion of long string variables are tabulated.
- Keyword ALL can be used on VARIABLES to refer to all user-defined variables in the working data file.

Operations

- Variables are tabulated in the order they are mentioned on the VARIABLES subcommand.
- If a requested ntile or percentile cannot be calculated, a period (.) is displayed.
- FREQUENCIES dynamically builds the table, setting up one cell for each unique value encountered in the data.

Limitations

- Maximum 500 variables total per FREQUENCIES command.
- Maximum of 32,767 observed values over all variables.

Example

```
FREQUENCIES VAR=RACE /STATISTICS=ALL.
```

- FREQUENCIES requests a Frequency table and a Statistics table showing all statistics for the categorical variable *RACE*.

Example

```
FREQUENCIES STATISTICS=ALL /HISTOGRAM
 /VARIABLES=SEX TVHOURS SCALE1 TO SCALE5
 /FORMAT=NOTABLE.
```

- FREQUENCIES requests statistics and histograms for *SEX, TVHOURS,* and all variables between and including *SCALE1* and *SCALE5* in the working data file.
- FORMAT suppresses the Frequency tables, which are not useful for continuous variables.

VARIABLES Subcommand

VARIABLES names the variables to be tabulated and is the only required subcommand. The actual keyword VARIABLES can be omitted.

FORMAT Subcommand

FORMAT controls various features of the output, including order of categories and suppression of tables.

- The minimum specification is a single keyword.
- By default, FREQUENCIES displays the Frequency table and sort categories in ascending order of values for numeric variables and in alphabetical order for string variables.

Table Order

AVALUE   *Sort categories in ascending order of values (numeric variables) or in alphabetical order (string variables).* This is the default.

DVALUE   *Sort categories in descending order of values (numeric variables) or in reverse alphabetical order (string variables).* This is ignored when HISTOGRAM, NTILES, or PERCENTILES is requested.

AFREQ   *Sort categories in ascending order of frequency.* This is ignored when HISTOGRAM, NTILES, or PERCENTILES is requested.

DFREQ   *Sort categories in descending order of frequency.* This is ignored when HISTOGRAM, NTILES, or PERCENTILES is requested.

Table Suppression

LIMIT(n)   *Suppress frequency tables with more than* n *categories.* The number of missing and valid cases and requested statistics are displayed for suppressed tables.

NOTABLE   *Suppress all frequency tables.* The number of missing and valid cases are displayed for suppressed tables. NOTABLE overrides LIMIT.

BARCHART Subcommand

BARCHART produces a bar chart for each variable named on the VARIABLES subcommand. By default, the horizontal axis for each bar chart is scaled in frequencies, and the interval width is determined by the largest frequency count for the variable being plotted. Bar charts are labeled with value labels or with the value if no label is defined.

- The minimum specification is the BARCHART keyword, which generates default bar charts.
- BARCHART cannot be used with HISTOGRAM.

MIN(n)	*Lower bound below which values are not plotted.*
MAX(n)	*Upper bound above which values are not plotted.*
FREQ(n)	*Vertical axis scaled in frequencies, where optional* n *is the maximum.* If *n* is not specified or if it is too small, FREQUENCIES chooses 5, 10, 20, 50, 100, 200, 500, 1000, 2000, and so forth, depending on the largest category. This is the default.
PERCENT(n)	*Vertical axis scaled in percentages, where optional* n *is the maximum.* If *n* is not specified or if it is too small, FREQUENCIES chooses 5, 10, 25, 50, or 100, depending on the frequency count for the largest category.

Example

```
FREQUENCIES VAR=RACE /BARCHART.
```

- FREQUENCIES produces a frequency table and the default bar chart for variable *RACE*.

Example

```
FREQUENCIES VAR=V1 V2 /BAR=MAX(10).
```

- FREQUENCIES produces a frequency table and bar chart with values through 10 for each of variables *V1* and *V2*.

PIECHART Subcommand

PIECHART produces a pie chart for each variable named on the VARIABLES subcommand. By default, one slice corresponds to each category defined by the variable with one slice representing all missing values. Pie charts are labeled with value labels or with the value if no label is defined.

- The minimum specification is the PIECHART keyword, which generates default pie charts.
- PIECHART can be requested together with either BARCHART or HISTOGRAM.
- FREQ and PERCENT are mutually exclusive. If both are specified, only the first specification is in effect.
- MISSING and NOMISSING are mutually exclusive. If both are specified, only the first specification is in effect.

MIN(n)	*Lower bound below which values are not plotted.*
MAX(n)	*Upper bound above which values are not plotted.*

FREQ   *The pie charts are based on frequencies.* Frequencies are displayed when you request values in the Chart Editor. This is the default.

PERCENT   *The pie charts are based on percentage.* Percentage is displayed when you request values in the Chart Editor.

MISSING   *User-missing and system-missing values are treated as one category.* This is the default. Specify INCLUDE on the MISSING subcommand to display system-missing and user-missing values as separate slices.

NOMISSING   *Missing values are excluded from the chart.* If you specify INCLUDE on the MISSING subcommand, each user-missing value is represented by one slice.

Example

```
FREQUENCIES VAR=RACE /PIECHART.
```

- FREQUENCIES produces a frequency table and the default pie chart for variable *RACE*.

Example

```
FREQUENCIES VAR=V1 V2 /PIE=MAX(10).
```

- For each variable *V1* and *V2*, FREQUENCIES produces a frequency table and a pie chart with values through 10.

HISTOGRAM Subcommand

HISTOGRAM displays a plot for each numeric variable named on the VARIABLES subcommand. By default, the horizontal axis of each histogram is scaled in frequencies and the interval width is determined by the largest frequency count of the variable being plotted.

- The minimum specification is the HISTOGRAM keyword, which generates default histograms.
- HISTOGRAM cannot be used with BARCHART.

MIN(n)   *Lower bound below which values are not plotted.*

MAX(n)   *Upper bound above which values are not plotted.*

FREQ(n)   *Vertical axis scaled in frequencies, where optional* n *is the scale.* If *n* is not specified or if it is too small, FREQUENCIES chooses 5, 10, 20, 50, 100, 200, 500, 1000, 2000, and so forth, depending on the largest category. This is the default.

NORMAL   *Superimpose a normal curve.* The curve is based on all valid values for the variable, including values excluded by MIN and MAX.

NONORMAL   *Suppress the normal curve.* This is the default.

Example

```
FREQUENCIES VAR=V1 /HIST=NORMAL.
```

- FREQUENCIES requests a histogram with a superimposed normal curve.

GROUPED Subcommand

When the values of a variable represent grouped or collapsed data, it is possible to estimate percentiles for the original, ungrouped data from the grouped data. The GROUPED subcommand specifies which variables have been grouped. It affects only the output from the PERCENTILES and NTILES subcommands and the MEDIAN statistic from the STATISTICS subcommand.

- Multiple GROUPED subcommands can be used on a single FREQUENCIES command. Multiple variable lists, separated by slashes, can appear on a single GROUPED subcommand.

- The variables named on GROUPED must have been named on the VARIABLES subcommand.

- The value or value list in the parentheses is optional. When it is omitted, the program treats the values of the variables listed on GROUPED as midpoints. If the values are not midpoints, they must first be recoded with the RECODE command.

- A single value in parentheses specifies the width of each grouped interval. The data values must be group midpoints, but there can be empty categories. For example, if you have data values of 10, 20, and 30 and specify an interval width of 5, the categories are 10 ± 2.5, 20 ± 2.5, and 30 ± 2.5. The categories 15 ± 2.5 and 25 ± 2.5 are empty.

- A value list in the parentheses specifies interval boundaries. The data values do not have to represent midpoints, but the lowest boundary must be lower than any value in the data. If any data values exceed the highest boundary specified (the last value within the parentheses), they will be assigned to an open-ended interval. In this case, some percentiles cannot be calculated.

Example

```
RECODE AGE (1=15) (2=25) (3=35) (4=45) (5=55)
           (6=65) (7=75) (8=85) (9=95)
   /INCOME (1=5)  (2=15) (3=25) (4=35) (5=45)
           (6=55) (7=65) (8=75) (9=100).

FREQUENCIES VARIABLES=AGE, SEX, RACE, INCOME
   /GROUPED=AGE, INCOME
   /PERCENTILES=5,25,50,75,95.
```

- The *AGE* and *INCOME* categories of 1, 2, 3, and so forth are recoded to category midpoints. Note that data can be recoded to category midpoints on any scale; here *AGE* is recoded in years, but *INCOME* is recoded in thousands of dollars.

- The GROUPED subcommand on FREQUENCIES allows more accurate estimates of the requested percentiles.

Example

```
FREQUENCIES VARIABLES=TEMP
   /GROUPED=TEMP (0.5)
   /NTILES=10.
```

- The values of *TEMP* (temperature) in this example were recorded using an inexpensive thermometer whose readings are precise only to the nearest half degree.

- The observed values of 97.5, 98, 98.5, 99, and so on, are treated as group midpoints, smoothing out the discrete distribution. This yields more accurate estimates of the deciles.

Example

```
FREQUENCIES VARIABLES=AGE
  /GROUPED=AGE (17.5, 22.5, 27.5, 32.5, 37.5, 42.5, 47.5
               52.5, 57.5, 62.5, 67.5, 72.5, 77.5, 82.5)
  /PERCENTILES=5, 10, 25, 50, 75, 90, 95.
```

- The values of *AGE* in this example have been estimated to the nearest five years. The first category is 17.5 to 22.5, the second is 22.5 to 27.5, and so forth. The artificial clustering of age estimates at multiples of five years is smoothed out by treating *AGE* as grouped data.
- It is not necessary to recode the ages to category midpoints, since the interval boundaries are explicitly given.

PERCENTILES Subcommand

PERCENTILES displays the value below which the specified percentage of cases falls. The desired percentiles must be explicitly requested. There are no defaults.

Example

```
FREQUENCIES VAR=V1 /PERCENTILES=10 25 33.3 66.7 75.
```

- FREQUENCIES requests the values for percentiles 10, 25, 33.3, 66.7, and 75 for *V1*.

NTILES Subcommand

NTILES calculates the percentages that divide the distribution into the specified number of categories and displays the values below which the requested percentages of cases fall. There are no default ntiles.

- Multiple NTILES subcommands are allowed. Each NTILES subcommand generates separate percentiles. Any duplicate percentiles generated by different NTILES subcommands are consolidated in the output.

Example

```
FREQUENCIES VARIABLE=V1 /NTILES=4.
```

- FREQUENCIES requests quartiles (percentiles 25, 50, and 75) for *V1*.

Example

```
FREQUENCIES VARIABLE=V1 /NTILES=4 /NTILES=10.
```

- The first NTILES subcommand requests percentiles 25, 50, and 75.
- The second NTILES subcommand requests percentiles 10 through 90 in increments of 10.
- The 50th percentile is produced by both specifications but is displayed only once in the output.

STATISTICS Subcommand

STATISTICS controls the display of statistics. By default, cases with missing values are excluded from the calculation of statistics.

- The minimum specification is the keyword STATISTICS, which generates the mean, standard deviation, minimum, and maximum (these statistics are also produced by keyword DEFAULT).

MEAN	*Mean.*
SEMEAN	*Standard error of the mean.*
MEDIAN	*Median.* Ignored when AFREQ or DFREQ are specified on the FORMAT subcommand.
MODE	*Mode.* If there is more than one mode, only the first mode is displayed.
STDDEV	*Standard deviation.*
VARIANCE	*Variance.*
SKEWNESS	*Skewness.*
SESKEW	*Standard error of the skewness statistic.*
KURTOSIS	*Kurtosis.*
SEKURT	*Standard error of the kurtosis statistic.*
RANGE	*Range.*
MINIMUM	*Minimum.*
MAXIMUM	*Maximum.*
SUM	*Sum.*
DEFAULT	*Mean, standard deviation, minimum, and maximum.*
ALL	*All available statistics.*
NONE	*No statistics.*

Example

```
FREQUENCIES VAR=AGE /STATS=MODE.
```

- STATISTICS requests the mode of *AGE*.

Example

```
FREQUENCIES VAR=AGE /STATS=DEF MODE.
```

- STATISTICS requests the default statistics (mean, standard deviation, minimum, and maximum) plus the mode of *AGE*.

MISSING Subcommand

By default, both user-missing and system-missing values are labeled as missing in the table but are not included in the valid and cumulative percentages, in the calculation of descriptive statistics, or in charts and histograms.

INCLUDE   *Include cases with user-missing values.* Cases with user-missing values are included in statistics and plots.

ORDER Subcommand

You can organize your output by variable or by analysis. Frequencies output that is organized by analysis has a single statistics table for all variables. Output organized by variable has a statistics table and a frequency table for each variable.

ANALYSIS   *Organize output by analysis.* Displays a single statistics table for all variables. This is the default.

VARIABLE   *Organize output by variable.* Displays a statistics table and a frequency table for each variable.

GENLOG

GENLOG is available in the Advanced Models option.

```
GENLOG varlist[BY] varlist [WITH covariate varlist]

[/CSTRUCTURE=varname]

[/GRESID=varlist]

[/GLOR=varlist]

[/MODEL={POISSON**  }]
        {MULTINOMIAL}

[/CRITERIA=[CONVERGE({0.001**})][ITERATE({20**})][DELTA({0.5**})]
                    {n      }          {n   }         {n      }

          [CIN({95**})] [EPS({1E-8**})]
              {n   }        {n       }

          [DEFAULT]

[/PRINT=[FREQ**][RESID**][ADJRESID**][DEV**]
        [ZRESID][ITERATE][COV][DESIGN][ESTIM][COR]
        [ALL] [NONE]
        [DEFAULT]]

[/PLOT={DEFAULT**                }]
       {RESID([ADJRESID][DEV])   }
       {NORMPROB([ADJRESID][DEV]) }
       {NONE                     }

[/SAVE=tempvar (newvar)[tempvar (newvar)...]]

[/MISSING=[{EXCLUDE**}]]
          {INCLUDE  }

[/DESIGN=effect[(n)] effect[(n)]... effect {BY} effect...]
                                           {*  }
```

**Default if subcommand or keyword is omitted.

Overview

GENLOG is a general procedure for model fitting, hypothesis testing, and parameter estimation for any model that has categorical variables as its major components. As such, GENLOG subsumes a variety of related techniques, including general models of multiway contingency tables, logit models, logistic regression on categorical variables, and quasi-independence models.

GENLOG, following the regression approach, uses dummy coding to construct a design matrix for estimation and produces maximum likelihood estimates of parameters by means of the Newton-Raphson algorithm. Since the regression approach uses the original parameter spaces, the parameter estimates correspond to the original levels of the categories and are therefore easier to interpret.

HILOGLINEAR, which uses an iterative proportional-fitting algorithm, is more efficient for hierarchical models and useful in model building, but it cannot produce parameter estimates for unsaturated models, does not permit specification of contrasts for parameters, and does not display a correlation matrix of the parameter estimates.

The General Loglinear Analysis and Logit Loglinear Analysis dialog boxes are both associated with the GENLOG command. In previous releases of SPSS, these dialog boxes were associated with the LOGLINEAR command. The LOGLINEAR command is now available only as a syntax command. The differences are described in the discussion of the LOGLINEAR command.

Options

Cell Weights. You can specify cell weights (such as structural zero indicators) for the model with the CSTRUCTURE subcommand.

Linear Combinations. You can compute linear combinations of observed cell frequencies, expected cell frequencies, and adjusted residuals using the GRESID subcommand.

Generalized Log-Odds Ratios. You can specify contrast variables on the GLOR subcommand and test whether the generalized log-odds ratio equals 0.

Model Assumption. You can specify POISSON or MULTINOMIAL on the MODEL subcommand to request the Poisson loglinear model or the product multinomial loglinear model.

Tuning the Algorithm. You can control the values of algorithm-tuning parameters with the CRITERIA subcommand.

Output Display. You can control the output display with the PRINT subcommand.

Optional Plots. You can request plots of adjusted or deviance residuals against observed and expected counts, or normal plots and detrended normal plots of adjusted or deviance residuals using the PLOT subcommand.

Basic Specification

The basic specification is one or more factor variables that define the tabulation. By default, GENLOG assumes a Poisson distribution and estimates the saturated model. Default output includes the factors or effects, their levels, and any labels; observed and expected frequencies and percentages for each factor and code; and residuals, adjusted residuals, and deviance residuals.

Limitations

- Maximum 10 factor variables (dependent *and* independent).
- Maximum 200 covariates.

Subcommand Order

- The variable specification must come first.
- Subcommands can be specified in any order.
- When multiple subcommands are specified, only the last specification takes effect.

Example

```
GENLOG DPREF RACE CAMP.
```

- *DPREF*, *RACE*, and *CAMP* are categorical variables.
- This is a general loglinear model because no BY keyword appears.
- The design defaults to a saturated model that includes all main effects and two-way and three-way interaction effects.

Example

```
GENLOG GSLEVEL EDUC SEX
  /DESIGN=GSLEVEL EDUC SEX.
```

- *GSLEVEL*, *EDUC*, and *SEX* are categorical variables.
- DESIGN specifies a model with main effects only.

Variable List

The variable list specifies the variables to be included in the model. GENLOG analyzes two classes of variables—categorical and continuous. Categorical variables are used to define the cells of the table. Continuous variables are used as cell covariates.

- The list of categorical variables must be specified first. Categorical variables must be numeric.
- Continuous variables can be specified only after the WITH keyword following the list of categorical variables.
- To specify a logit model, use the keyword BY (see "Logit Model" below). A variable list without the keyword BY generates a general loglinear model.
- A variable can be specified only once in the variable list—as a dependent variable immediately following GENLOG, as an independent variable following the keyword BY, or as a covariate following the keyword WITH.
- No range needs to be specified for categorical variables.

Logit Model

The logit model examines the relationships between dependent and independent factor variables.

- To separate the independent variables from the dependent variables in a logit model, use the keyword BY. The categorical variables preceding BY are the dependent variables; the categorical variables following BY are the independent variables.
- Up to 10 variables can be specified, including both dependent and independent variables.
- For the logit model, you must specify MULTINOMIAL on the MODEL subcommand.
- GENLOG displays an analysis of dispersion and two measures of association—entropy and concentration. These measures are discussed in Haberman (1982) and can be used to quantify the magnitude of association among the variables. Both are proportional-reduction-in-error measures. The entropy statistic is analogous to Theil's entropy measure, while the concentration statistic is analogous to Goodman and Kruskal's tau-*b*. Both statistics measure the strength of association between the dependent variable and the independent variable set.

Example

```
GENLOG  GSLEVEL BY EDUC SEX
 /MODEL=MULTINOMIAL
 /DESIGN=GSLEVEL, GSLEVEL BY EDUC, GSLEVEL BY SEX.
```

- The keyword BY on the variable list specifies a logit model in which *GSLEVEL* is the dependent variable and *EDUC* and *SEX* are the independent variables.
- A logit model is multinomial.
- DESIGN specifies a model that can test for the absence of the joint effect of *SEX* and *EDUC* on *GSLEVEL*.

Cell Covariates

- Continuous variables can be used as covariates. When used, the covariates must be specified after the WITH keyword following the list of categorical variables.
- A variable cannot be named as both a categorical variable and a cell covariate.
- To enter cell covariates into a model, the covariates must be specified on the DESIGN subcommand.
- Cell covariates are not applied on a case-by-case basis. The weighted covariate mean for a cell is applied to that cell.

Example

```
GENLOG DPREF RACE CAMP WITH X
 /DESIGN=DPREF RACE CAMP X.
```

- The variable *X* is a continuous variable specified as a cell covariate. Cell covariates must be specified after the keyword WITH following the variable list. No range is defined for cell covariates.
- To include the cell covariate in the model, the variable *X* is specified on DESIGN.

CSTRUCTURE Subcommand

CSTRUCTURE specifies the variable that contains values for computing cell weights, such as structural zero indicators. By default, cell weights are equal to 1.

- The specification must be a numeric variable.
- Variables specified as dependent or independent variables in the variable list cannot be specified on CSTRUCTURE.
- Cell weights are not applied on a case-by-case basis. The weighted mean for a cell is applied to that cell.
- CSTRUCTURE can be used to impose structural, or *a priori*, zeros on the model. This feature is useful in specifying a quasi-symmetry model and in excluding cells from entering into estimation.
- If multiple CSTRUCTURE subcommands are specified, the last specification takes effect.

Example

```
COMPUTE  CWT=(HUSED NE WIFED).
GENLOG HUSED WIFED WITH DISTANCE
  /CSTRUCTURE=CWT
  /DESIGN=HUSED WIFED DISTANCE.
```

- The Boolean expression assigns *CWT* the value of 1 when *HUSED* is not equal to *WIFED*, and the value of 0 otherwise.
- CSTRUCTURE imposes structural zeros on the diagonal of the symmetric crosstabulation.

GRESID Subcommand

GRESID (Generalized Residual) calculates linear combinations of observed and expected cell frequencies as well as simple, standardized, and adjusted residuals.

- The variables specified must be numeric, and they must contain coefficients of the desired linear combinations.
- Variables specified as dependent or independent variables in the variable list cannot be specified on GRESID.
- The generalized residual coefficient is not applied on a case-by-case basis. The weighted coefficient mean of the value for all cases in a cell is applied to that cell.
- Each variable specified on the GRESID subcommand contains a single linear combination.
- If multiple GRESID subcommands are specified, the last specification takes effect.

Example

```
COMPUTE GR_1=(MONTH LE 6).
COMPUTE GR_2=(MONTH GE 7).
GENLOG  MONTH WITH Z
 /GRESID=GR_1 GR_2
 /DESIGN=Z.
```

- The first variable, *GR_1*, combines the first six months into a single effect; the second variable, *GR_2*, combines the rest of the months.

- For each effect, GENLOG displays the observed and expected counts as well as the simple, standardized, and adjusted residuals.

GLOR Subcommand

GLOR (Generalized Log-Odds Ratio) specifies the population contrast variable(s). For each variable specified, GENLOG tests the null hypothesis that the generalized log-odds ratio equals 0 and displays the Wald statistic and the confidence interval. You can specify the level of the confidence interval using the CIN significance level keyword on CRITERIA. By default, the confidence level is 95%.

- The variable sum is 0 for the loglinear model and for each combined level of independent variables for the logit model.
- Variables specified as dependent or independent variables in the variable list cannot be specified on GLOR.
- The coefficient is not applied on a case-by-case basis. The weighted mean for a cell is applied to that cell.
- If multiple GLOR subcommands are specified, the last specification takes effect.

Example

```
GENLOG A B
 /GLOR=COEFF
 /DESIGN=A B.
```

- Variable *COEFF* contains the coefficients of two dichotomous factors *A* and *B*.
- If the weighted cell mean for *COEFF* is 1 when *A* equals *B* and −1 otherwise, this example tests whether the log-odds ratio equals 0, or in this case, whether variables *A* and *B* are independent.

MODEL Subcommand

MODEL specifies the assumed distribution of your data.

- You can specify only one keyword on MODEL. The default is POISSON.
- If more than one MODEL subcommand is specified, the last specification takes effect.

POISSON   *The Poisson distribution.* This is the default.

MULTINOMIAL   *The multinomial distribution.* For the logit model, you must specify MULTINOMIAL.

CRITERIA Subcommand

CRITERIA specifies the values used in tuning the parameters for the Newton-Raphson algorithm.

- If multiple CRITERIA subcommands are specified, the last specification takes effect.

CONVERGE(n)   *Convergence criterion.* Specify a positive value for the convergence criterion. The default is 0.001.

ITERATE(n)   *Maximum number of iterations.* Specify an integer. The default number is 20.

DELTA(n)   *Cell delta value.* Specify a non-negative value to add to each cell frequency for the first iteration. (For the saturated model, the delta value is added for all iterations.) The default is 0.5. The delta value is used to solve mathematical problems created by 0 observations; if all of your observations are greater than 0, we recommend that you set DELTA to 0.

CIN(n)   *Level of confidence interval.* Specify the percentage interval used in the test of generalized log-odds ratios and parameter estimates. The value must be between 50 and 99.99, inclusive. The default is 95.

EPS(n)   *Epsilon value used for redundancy checking in design matrix.* Specify a positive value. The default is 0.00000001.

DEFAULT   *Default values are used.* DEFAULT can be used to reset all criteria to default values.

Example

```
GENLOG  DPREF BY RACE ORIGIN CAMP
 /MODEL=MULTINOMIAL
 /CRITERIA=ITERATION(50) CONVERGE(.0001).
```

- ITERATION increases the maximum number of iterations to 50.
- CONVERGE lowers the convergence criterion to 0.0001.

PRINT Subcommand

PRINT controls the display of statistics.

- By default, GENLOG displays the frequency table and simple, adjusted, and deviance residuals.
- When PRINT is specified with one or more keywords, only the statistics requested by these keywords are displayed.
- When multiple PRINT subcommands are specified, the last specification takes effect.

The following keywords can be used on PRINT:

FREQ   *Observed and expected cell frequencies and percentages.* This is displayed by default.

RESID   *Simple residuals.* This is displayed by default.

ZRESID   *Standardized residuals.*

ADJRESID   *Adjusted residuals.* This is displayed by default.

DEV   *Deviance residuals.* This is displayed by default.

DESIGN   *The design matrix of the model.* The design matrix corresponding to the specified model is displayed.

ESTIM   *The parameter estimates of the model.* The parameter estimates refer to the original categories.

COR   *The correlation matrix of the parameter estimates.*

COV   *The covariance matrix of the parameter estimates.*

ALL   *All available output.*

DEFAULT   *FREQ, RESID, ADJRESID, and DEV.* This keyword can be used to reset PRINT to its default setting.

NONE   *The design and model information with goodness-of-fit statistics only.* This option overrides all other specifications on the PRINT subcommand.

Example

```
GENLOG A B
 /PRINT=ALL
 /DESIGN=A B.
```

- The DESIGN subcommand specifies a main-effects model, which tests the hypothesis of no interaction. The PRINT subcommand displays all available output for this model.

PLOT Subcommand

PLOT specifies what plots you want displayed. Plots of adjusted residuals against observed and expected counts, and normal and detrended normal plots of the adjusted residuals are displayed if PLOT is not specified or is specified without a keyword. When multiple PLOT subcommands are specified, only the last specification is executed.

DEFAULT   *RESID (ADJRESID) and NORMPROB (ADJRESID).* This is the default if PLOT is not specified or is specified with no keyword.

RESID (type)   *Plots of residuals against observed and expected counts.* You can specify the type of residuals to plot. ADJRESID plots adjusted residuals; DEV plots deviance residuals. ADJRESID is the default if you do not specify a type.

NORMPROB (type)   *Normal and detrended normal plots of the residuals.* You can specify the type of residuals to plot. ADJRESID plots adjusted residuals; DEV plots deviance residuals. ADJRESID is the default if you do not specify a type.

NONE   *No plots.*

Example

```
GENLOG  RESPONSE BY SEASON
  /MODEL=MULTINOMIAL
  /PLOT=RESID(ADJRESID,DEV)
  /DESIGN=RESPONSE SEASON(1) BY RESPONSE.
```

- This example requests plots of adjusted and deviance residuals against observed and expected counts.

- Note that if you specify `/PLOT=RESID(ADJRESID) RESID(DEV)`, only the deviance residuals are plotted. The first keyword specification, `RESID(ADJRESID)`, is ignored.

MISSING Subcommand

MISSING controls missing values. By default, GENLOG excludes all cases with system- or user-missing values for any variable. You can specify INCLUDE to include user-missing values.

EXCLUDE   *Delete cases with user-missing values.* This is the default if the subcommand is omitted. You can also specify the keyword DEFAULT.

INCLUDE   *Include cases with user-missing values.* Only cases with system-missing values are deleted.

Example

```
MISSING VALUES A(0).
GENLOG A B
  /MISSING=INCLUDE
  /DESIGN=B.
```

- Even though 0 was specified as missing, it is treated as a nonmissing category of *A* in this analysis.

SAVE Subcommand

SAVE saves specified temporary variables into the working data file. You can assign a new name to each temporary variable saved.

- The temporary variables you can save include *RESID* (raw residual), *ZRESID* (standardized residual), *ADJRESID* (adjusted residual), *DEV* (deviance residual), and *PRED* (predicted cell frequency). An explanatory label is assigned to each saved variable.

- A temporary variable can be saved only once on a SAVE subcommand.

- To assign a name to a saved temporary variable, specify the new name in parentheses following that temporary variable. The new name must conform to SPSS naming conventions and must be unique in the working data file. The names cannot begin with # or $.

- If you do not specify a variable name in parentheses, GENLOG assigns default names to the saved temporary variables. A default name starts with the first three characters of the name of the saved temporary variable, followed by an underscore and a unique number. For example, *RESID* will be saved as *RES_n*, where *n* is a number incremented each time a default name is assigned to a saved *RESID*.

- The saved variables are pertinent to cells in the contingency table, *not* to individual observations. In the Data Editor, all cases that define one cell receive the same value. To make sense of these values, you need to aggregate the data to obtain cell counts.

Example

```
GENLOG A B
 /SAVE PRED (PREDA_B)
 /DESIGN = A, B.
```

- SAVE saves the predicted values for two independent variables *A* and *B*.
- The saved variable is renamed *PREDA_B* and added to the working data file.

DESIGN Subcommand

DESIGN specifies the model to be fit. If DESIGN is omitted or used with no specifications, the saturated model is produced. The saturated model fits all main effects and all interaction effects.

- Only one design can be specified on the subcommand.
- To obtain main-effects models, name all of the variables listed on the variables specification.
- To obtain interactions, use the keyword BY or an asterisk (*) to specify each interaction, for example, A BY B or C*D. To obtain the single-degree-of-freedom partition of a specified factor, specify the partition in parentheses following the factor (see the example below).
- To include cell covariates in the model, first identify them on the variable list by naming them after the keyword WITH, and then specify the variable names on DESIGN.
- Effects that involve only independent variables result in redundancy. GENLOG removes these effects from the model.
- If your variable list includes a cell covariate (identified by the keyword WITH), you cannot imply the saturated model by omitting DESIGN or specifying it alone. You need to request the model explicitly by specifying all main effects and interactions on DESIGN.

Example

```
COMPUTE X=MONTH.
GENLOG MONTH WITH X
  /DESIGN X.
```

- This example tests the linear effect of the dependent variable.
- The variable specification identifies *MONTH* as a categorical variable. The keyword WITH identifies *X* as a covariate.
- DESIGN tests the linear effect of *MONTH*.

Example

```
GENLOG A B
  /DESIGN=A.

GENLOG A B
  /DESIGN=A,B.
```

- Both designs specify main-effects models.
- The first design tests the homogeneity of category probabilities for *B*; it fits the marginal frequencies on *A* but assumes that membership in any of the categories of *B* is equiprobable.
- The second design tests the independence of *A* and *B*. It fits the marginals on both *A* and *B*.

Example

```
GENLOG A   B   C
  /DESIGN=A,B,C, A BY B.
```

- This design consists of the *A* main effect, the *B* main effect, the *C* main effect, and the interaction of *A* and *B*.

Example

```
GENLOG A BY B
  /MODEL=MULTINOMIAL
  /DESIGN=A,A BY B(1).
```

- This example specifies single-degree-of-freedom partitions.
- The value 1 following *B* refers to the first category of *B*.

Example

```
GENLOG HUSED WIFED WITH DISTANCE
  /DESIGN=HUSED WIFED DISTANCE.
```

- The continuous variable *DISTANCE* is identified as a cell covariate by the keyword WITH. The cell covariate is then included in the model by naming it on DESIGN.

Example

```
COMPUTE  X=1.
GENLOG  MONTH WITH X
  /DESIGN=X.
```

- This example specifies an equiprobability model.
- The design tests whether the frequencies in the table are equal by using a constant of 1 as a cell covariate.

GET

```
GET FILE=file

  [/KEEP={ALL**  }] [/DROP=varlist]
        {varlist}

  [/RENAME=(old varnames=new varnames)...]

  [/MAP]
```

**Default if the subcommand is omitted.

Example

```
GET FILE=EMPL.
```

Overview

GET reads an SPSS-format data file that was created by the SAVE or XSAVE command. An SPSS-format data file contains data plus a dictionary. The dictionary contains a name for each variable in the data file, plus any assigned variable and value labels, missing-value flags, and variable print and write formats. The dictionary also contains document text created with the DOCUMENTS command.

GET is used only for reading SPSS-format data files. See DATA LIST for information on reading and defining data in a text data file. See MATRIX DATA for information on defining matrix materials in a text data file. For information on defining complex data files that cannot be defined with DATA LIST alone, see FILE TYPE and REPEATING DATA.

The program can also read data files created for other software applications. See IMPORT for information on reading *portable files* created with EXPORT. See commands such as GET TRANSLATE and GET SAS for information on reading files created by other software programs.

Options

Variable Subsets and Order. You can read a subset of variables and reorder the variables that are copied into the working data file using the DROP and KEEP subcommands.

Variable Names. You can rename variables as they are copied into the working data file with the RENAME subcommand.

Variable Map. To confirm the names and order of variables in the working data file, use the MAP subcommand. MAP displays the variables in the working file next to their corresponding names in the SPSS-format data file.

Basic Specification

- The basic specification is the FILE subcommand, which specifies the SPSS-format data file to be read.
- By default, GET copies all variables from the SPSS-format data file into the working data file. Variables in the working file are in the same order and have the same names as variables in the SPSS-format data file. Documentary text from the SPSS-format data file is copied into the dictionary of the working file.

Subcommand Order

- FILE must be specified first.
- The remaining subcommands can be specified in any order.

Syntax Rules

- FILE is required and can be specified only once.
- KEEP, DROP, RENAME, and MAP can be used as many times as needed.
- Documentary text copied from the SPSS-format data file can be dropped from the working data file with the DROP DOCUMENTS command.
- GET cannot be used inside a DO IF—END IF or LOOP—END LOOP structure.

Operations

- GET reads the dictionary of the SPSS-format data file.
- If KEEP is not specified, variables in the working data file are in the same order as variables in the SPSS-format data file.
- A file saved with weighting in effect maintains the values of the variable $WEIGHT. For a discussion of turning off weights, see WEIGHT.
- The order of cases in the working data file is the same as their order in the SPSS-format data file. The values of $CASENUM are those from the original text data file before any selecting (see SELECT IF) or sorting (see SORT). The value of $CASENUM may differ from the actual number of a case after selecting or sorting.

FILE Subcommand

FILE specifies the SPSS-format data file to be read. FILE is required and can be specified only once. It must be the first specification on GET.

DROP and KEEP Subcommands

DROP and KEEP are used to copy a subset of variables into the working data file. DROP specifies variables that should not be copied into the working file. KEEP specifies variables that should be copied. Variables not specified on KEEP are dropped.

- Variables can be specified in any order. The order of variables on KEEP determines the order of variables in the working file. The order of variables on DROP does not affect the order of variables in the working file.

- The keyword ALL on KEEP refers to all remaining variables not previously specified on KEEP. ALL must be the last specification on KEEP.

- If a variable is specified twice on the same subcommand, only the first mention is recognized.

- Multiple DROP and KEEP subcommands are allowed. However, specifying a variable named on a previous DROP or not named on a previous KEEP results in an error, and the GET command is not executed.

- The keyword TO can be used to specify a group of consecutive variables in the SPSS-format data file.

Example

```
GET FILE=HUBTEMP /DROP=DEPT79 TO DEPT84 SALARY79.
```

- The working data file is copied from SPSS-format data file *HUBTEMP*. All variables between and including *DEPT79* and *DEPT84*, as well as *SALARY79*, are excluded from the working file. All other variables are copied into the working file.

- Variables in the working data file are in the same order as the variables in the *HUBTEMP* file.

Example

```
GET FILE=PRSNL /DROP=GRADE STORE
               /KEEP=LNAME NAME TENURE JTENURE ALL.
```

- The variables *GRADE* and *STORE* are dropped when the file *PRSNL* is copied into the working data file.

- KEEP specifies that *LNAME*, *NAME*, *TENURE*, and *JTENURE* are the first four variables in the working file, followed by all remaining variables (except those dropped by the previous DROP). These remaining variables are copied into the working file in the same sequence in which they appear in the *PRSNL* file.

RENAME Subcommand

RENAME changes the names of variables as they are copied into the working data file.

- The specification on RENAME is a list of old variable names followed by an equals sign and a list of new variable names. The same number of variables must be specified on both lists. The keyword TO can be used on the first list to refer to consecutive variables in the SPSS-format data file and on the second list to generate new variable names (see "Keyword TO" on p. 29). The entire specification must be enclosed in parentheses.

- Alternatively, you can specify each old variable name individually, followed by an equals sign and the new variable name. Multiple sets of variable specifications are allowed. The parentheses around each set of specifications are optional.
- Old variable names do not need to be specified according to their order in the SPSS-format data file.
- Name changes take place in one operation. Therefore, variable names can be exchanged between two variables.
- Variables cannot be renamed to scratch variables.
- Multiple RENAME subcommands are allowed.
- On a subsequent DROP or KEEP subcommand, variables are referred to by their new names.

Example

```
GET FILE=EMPL88 /RENAME  AGE=AGE88 JOBCAT=JOBCAT88.
```

- RENAME specifies two name changes for the working data file. *AGE* is renamed to *AGE88* and *JOBCAT* is renamed to *JOBCAT88*.

Example

```
GET FILE=EMPL88 /RENAME (AGE JOBCAT=AGE88 JOBCAT88).
```

- The name changes are identical to those in the previous example. *AGE* is renamed to *AGE88* and *JOBCAT* is renamed to *JOBCAT88*. The parentheses are required with this method.

MAP Subcommand

MAP displays a list of the variables in the working data file and their corresponding names in the SPSS-format data file.

- The only specification is the keyword MAP. There are no additional specifications.
- Multiple MAP subcommands are allowed. Each MAP subcommand maps the results of subcommands that precede it; results of subcommands that follow it are not mapped.

Example

```
GET FILE=EMPL88 /RENAME=(AGE=AGE88) (JOBCAT=JOBCAT88)
/KEEP=LNAME NAME JOBCAT88 ALL /MAP.
```

- MAP is specified to confirm the new names for the variables *AGE* and *JOBCAT* and the order of variables in the working data file (*LNAME*, *NAME*, and *JOBCAT88*, followed by all remaining variables in the SPSS-format data file).

GET CAPTURE

```
GET CAPTURE {ODBC   }*

[/CONNECT='connection string']
[/LOGIN=login] [/PASSWORD=password]
[/SERVER=host] [/DATABASE=database name]†

/SQL 'select statement'
    ['continuation of select statement']
```

* You can import data from any database for which you have an ODBC driver installed.

† Optional subcommands are database-specific. See "Syntax Rules" below for the subcommand(s) required by a database type.

Example

```
GET CAPTURE ODBC
  /CONNECT='DSN=sales.mdb;DBQ=C:\spss10\saledata.mdb;DriverId=281;FIL=MS'+
  ' Access;MaxBufferSize=2048;PageTimeout=5;'
  /SQL = 'SELECT  T0.ID AS ID`,  T0.JOBCAT AS JOBCAT,  '
  '`T0`.`REGION` AS `REGION`,  `T0`.`DIVISION` AS `DIVISION`,`T0`.`TRAVEL`'
  ' AS `TRAVEL`,  `T0`.`SALES` AS `SALES`,  `T0`.`VOLUME96` AS `VOLUME96`, '
  '`T1`.`REGION` AS `REGION1`,  `T1`.`AVGINC` AS `AVGINC`,`T1`.`AVGAGE` AS'
  ' `AVGAGE`,  `T1`.`POPULAT` AS `POPULAT` FROM { oj `Regions` `T1` LEFT '
  'OUTER JOIN `EmployeeSales` `T0` ON `T1`.`REGION` = `T0`.`REGION` } '.
```

Overview

GET CAPTURE retrieves data from a database and converts them to a format that can be used by program procedures. GET CAPTURE retrieves data and data information and builds a working data file for the current session.

Basic Specification

The basic specification is one of the subcommands specifying the database type followed by the SQL subcommand and any select statement in quotation marks or apostrophes. Each line of the select statement should be enclosed in quotation marks or apostrophes, and no quoted string should exceed 255 characters.

Subcommand Order

The subcommand specifying the type of database must be the first specification. The SQL subcommand must be the last.

Syntax Rules

- Only one subcommand specifying the database type can be used.

- The CONNECT subcommand must be specified if you use the Microsoft ODBC (Open Database Connectivity) driver.

Operations

- GET CAPTURE retrieves the data specified on SQL.
- The variables are in the same order in which they are specified on the SQL subcommand.
- The data definition information captured from the database is stored in the working data file dictionary.

Limitations

- Maximum 3800 characters (approximately) can be specified on the SQL subcommand. This translates to 76 lines of 50 characters. Characters beyond the limit are ignored.

CONNECT Subcommand

CONNECT is required to access any database that has an installed Microsoft ODBC driver.

- You cannot specify the connection string directly in the syntax window, but you can paste it with the rest of the command from the Results dialog box, which is the last of the series of dialog boxes opened with the Database Wizard.

SQL Subcommand

SQL specifies any SQL select statement accepted by the database you access. With ODBC, you can now select columns from more than one related table in an ODBC data source using either the inner join or the outer join.

Data Conversion

GET CAPTURE converts variable names, labels, missing values, and data types, wherever necessary, to a format that conforms to SPSS-format conventions.

Variable Names and Labels

Database columns are read as variables.

- A column name is converted to a variable name if it conforms to SPSS-format naming conventions and is different from all other names created for the working data file. If not, GET CAPTURE gives the column a name formed from the first few letters of the column and its column number. If this is not possible, the letters COL followed by the column number are used. For example, the seventh column specified in the select statement could be *COL7*.
- GET CAPTURE labels each variable with its full column name specified in the original database.

- You can display a table of variable names with their original database column names using the DISPLAY LABELS command.

Missing Values

Null values in the database are transformed into the system-missing value in numeric variables or into blanks in string variables.

GET DATA

```
GET DATA
  /TYPE = {ODBC}
          {XLS }
          {TXT }

  /FILE = 'filename'

Subcommands for TYPE = ODBC
  /CONNECT='connection string'
  /SQL 'select statement'
       ['select statement continued']

Subcommands for TYPE = XLS*
  [/SHEET = {INDEX**} {sheet number}]
            {NAME   } {'sheet name'}
  [/CELLRANGE = {RANGE }  {'start point:end point' }]
                {FULL**}
  [/READNAMES = {on** }]
                {off  }

Subcommands for TYPE = TXT
  [/ARRANGEMENT = {FIXED     }]
                  {DELIMITED**}
  [/FIRSTCASE = {n}]
  [/DELCASE = {LINE**      }]¹
              {VARIABLES n}

  [/FIXCASE = n]²
  [/IMPORTCASE = {ALL**    }]
                 {FIRST n  }
                 {PERCENT n}
  [/DELIMITERS = {"delimiters"}]


VARIABLES subcommand for ARRANGEMENT = DELIMITED
  /VARIABLES = varname  {format}

VARIABLES subcommand for ARRANGEMENT = FIXED
  /VARIABLES varname {startcol - endcol} {format}
     {/rec#} varname {startcol - endcol} {format}
```

*Valid only for Excel 5 or later. For earlier Excel files, use GET TRANSLATE.

**Default if subcommand omitted

[1]Valid only with ARRANGEMENT = DELIMTED

[2] Valid only with ARRANGEMENT = FIXED

Example
```
GET DATA
   /TYPE=XLS
   /FILE='c:\PlanningDocs\files10.xls'
   /SHEET=name 'First Quarter'
   /CELLRANGE=full
   /READNAMES=on.
```

Overview

GET DATA reads data from ODBC data sources (databases), Excel files (release 5 or later), and text data files. It contains functionality and syntax similar to GET CAPTURE, GET TRANSLATE, and DATA LIST.

- GET DATA /TYPE=ODBC is almost identical to GET CAPTURE ODBC in both syntax and functionality.
- GET DATA /TYPE=XLS reads Excel 5 or later files, whereas GET TRANSLATE reads Excel 4 or earlier, Lotus, and dBASE files.
- GET DATA /TYPE=TXT is similar to DATA LIST but does not create a temporary copy of the data file, significantly reducing temporary file space requirements for large data files.

TYPE Subcommand

The TYPE subcommand is required and must be the first subcommand specified.

ODBC   *Data sources accessed with ODBC drivers.*

XLS   *Excel 5 or later files.* For earlier versions of Excel files, Lotus 1-2-3 files, and dBASE files, see the GET TRANSLATE command.

TXT   *Simple (ASCII) text data files.*

FILE Subcommand

The FILE subcommand is required for TYPE=XLS and TYPE=TXT and must immediately follow the TYPE subcommand. It specifies the file to read.

- File specifications should be enclosed in quotes or apostrophes.
- UNC file specifications are recommended for distributed analysis mode (available with the server version of SPSS).

Subcommands for TYPE=ODBC

The CONNECT and SQL subcommands are both required, and SQL must be the last subcommand.

CONNECT Subcommand

The recommended method for generating a valid CONNECT specification is to initially use the Database Wizard and paste the resulting syntax to a syntax window in the last step of the wizard.

SQL Subcommand

SQL specifies any SQL select statement accepted by the database you access. You can select columns from more than one related table in an ODBC data source using either the inner join or the outer join. Each line of the SQL select statement should be enclosed in quotation marks or apostrophes, and no quoted string should exceed 255 characters.

Example

```
GET DATA /TYPE=ODBC
  /CONNECT='DSN=saledata.mdb;DBQ=saledata.mdb;DriverId=281;FIL=MS'+
 ' Access;MaxBufferSize=2048;PageTimeout=5;'
  /SQL='SELECT  `T0`.`DIV` AS `DIV`,  `T0`.`REGION` AS `REGION`,  '
 '`T1`.`AVGAGE` AS `AVGAGE`,  `T1`.`REGION` AS `REGION1` FROM  '
 '`saledata`.`EmployeeSales` `T0`, ``.`Regions`'
 ' `T1` WHERE `T1`.`REGION` = `T0`.`REGION` '.
```

Subcommands for TYPE=XLS

For Excel files, you can specify a spreadsheet within the workbook, a range of cells to read, and the contents of the first row of the spreadsheet (variable names or data).

SHEET Subcommand

The SHEET subcommand indicates the worksheet in the Excel file that will be read. Only one sheet can be specified. If no sheet is specified, the first sheet will be read.

INDEX n   *Read the specified sheet number.* The number represents the sequential order of the sheet within the workbook.

NAME 'name'   *Read the specified sheet name.* If the name contains spaces, it must be enclosed in quotes or apostrophes.

CELLRANGE Subcommand

The CELLRANGE subcommand specifies a range of cells to read within the specified worksheet. By default, the entire worksheet is read.

FULL   *Read the entire worksheet.* This is the default.

RANGE 'start:end'   *Read the specified range of cells.* Specify the beginning column letter and row number, a colon, and the ending column letter and row number, as in A1:K14. The cell range must be enclosed in quotes or apostrophes.

READNAMES Subcommand

ON *Read the first row of the sheet or specified range as variable names.* This is the default. Values longer than eight characters are truncated. Values that contain invalid characters for variable names are converted to valid variable names.

OFF *Read the first row of the sheet or specified range as data.* SPSS assigns default variable names and reads all rows as data.

Example

```
GET DATA /TYPE=XLS
  /FILE='\\hqdev01\public\sales.xls'
  /SHEET=name 'June Sales'
  /CELLRANGE=range 'A1:C3'
  /READNAMES=on.
```

Subcommands for TYPE=TXT

The VARIABLES subcommand is required and must be the last GET DATA subcommand.

ARRANGEMENT Subcommand

The ARRANGEMENT subcommand specifies the data format.

DELIMITED *Spaces, commas, tabs, or other characters are used to separate variables. The variables are recorded in the same order for each case but not necessarily in the same column locations.* This is the default.

FIXED *Each variable is recorded in the same column location for every case.*

FIRSTCASE Subcommand

FIRSTCASE specifies the first line (row) to read for the first case of data. This allows you to bypass information in the first *n* lines of the file that either don't contain data or contain data you don't want to read. This subcommand applies to both fixed and delimited file formats.

The only specification for this subcommand is an integer greater than zero that indicates the number of lines to skip. The default is 1.

DELCASE Subcommand

The DELCASE subcommand applies to delimited data (ARRANGEMENT=DELIMITED) only.

LINE *Each case is contained on a single line (row).* This is the default.

VARIABLES *n* *Each case contains n variables.* Multiple cases can be contained on the same line, and data for one case can span more than one line. A case is defined by the number of variables.

FIXCASE Subcommand

The FIXCASE subcommand applies to fixed data (ARRANGEMENT=FIXED) only. It specifies the number of lines (records) to read for each case.

The only specification for this subcommand is an integer greater than zero that indicates the number of lines (records) per case. The default is 1.

IMPORTCASES Subcommand

The IMPORTCASES subcommand allows you to specify the number of cases to read.

ALL   *Read all cases in the file.* This is the default.

FIRST *n*   *Read the first n cases.* The value of *n* must be a positive integer.

PERCENT *n* *Read approximately the first n percent of cases.* The value of *n* must be a positive integer less than 100. The percentage of cases actually selected only approximates the specified percentage. The more cases there are in the data file, the closer the percentage of cases selected is to the specified percentage.

DELIMITERS Subcommand

The DELIMITERS subcommand applies to delimited data (ARRANGEMENT=DELIMITED) only. It specifies the characters to read as delimiters between data values.

- Each delimiter can only be a single character, except for the specification of a tab or a backslash as a delimiter (see below).
- The list of delimiters must be enclosed in quotes or apostrophes.
- There should be no spaces or other delimiters between delimiter specifications, except for a space that indicates a space as a delimiter.
- To specify a tab as a delimiter use "\t". This must be the first delimiter specified.
- To specify a backslash as a delimiter, use two backslashes ("\\"). This must be the first delimiter specified unless you also specify a tab as a delimiter, in which case the backslash specification should come second—immediately after the tab specification.

Missing data with delimited data. Multiple consecutive spaces in a data file are treated as a single space and cannot be used to indicate missing data. For any other delimiter, multiple delimiters without any intervening data indicate missing data.

Example

```
DELIMITERS "\t\\ ,;"
```

In this example, tabs, backslashes, spaces, commas, and semicolons will be read as delimiters between data values.

VARIABLES Subcommand for ARRANGEMENT = DELIMITED

For delimited files, the VARIABLES subcommand specifies the variable names and variable formats.

- Variable names must begin with a letter and cannot exceed eight characters (see "Variables" on p. 29).
- Each variable name must be followed by a format specification (see "Variable Format Specifications for TYPE = TXT" below).

VARIABLES Subcommand for ARRANGEMENT = FIXED

For fixed-format files, the VARIABLES subcommand specifies variable names, start and end column locations, and variable formats.

- Variable names must begin with a letter and cannot exceed eight characters.
- Each variable name must be followed by column specifications. Start and end columns must be separated by a dash, as in: 1-10.
- Each column specification must be followed by a format specification.

Multiple records. If each case spans more than one record (as specified with the FIXCASE subcommand), delimit variable specifications for each record with a slash (/) followed by the record number, as in:

```
VARIABLES = /1 var1 1-10 F var2 11-20 DATE
/2 var3 1-5 A var4 6-10 F
/3 var5 1-20 A var6 21-30 DOLLAR
```

Variable Format Specifications for TYPE = TXT

For both fixed and delimited files, available formats include:

F*n.d*   *Numeric*. Specification of the total number of characters (*n*) and decimals (*d*) are optional.

A*n*   *String (alphanumeric)*. Specification of the maximum string length (*n*) is optional.

DATE*n*   *Dates of the general format dd-mmm-yyyy*. Specification of the maximum length (*n*) is optional but must be eight or greater if specified.

ADATE*n*   *Dates of the general format mm/dd/yyyy*. Specification of the maximum length (*n*) is optional but must be eight or greater if specified.

DOLLAR*n.d*   *Currency with or without a leading dollar sign ($)*. Input values can include a leading dollar sign, but it is not required. Specification of the total number of characters (*n*) and decimals (*d*) are optional.

For comprehensive lists of available formats, see "Variables" on p. 29 and "Date and Time" on p. 60.

Example

```
GET DATA  /TYPE = TXT
  /FILE = 'D:\Program Files\SPSS\textdata.dat'
  /DELCASE = LINE
  /DELIMITERS = "\t ,"
  /ARRANGEMENT = DELIMITED
  /FIRSTCASE = 2
  /IMPORTCASE = FIRST 200
  /VARIABLES = id F3.2 gender A1 bdate DATE10 educ F2.2
   jobcat F1.2 salary DOLLAR8 salbegin DOLLAR8
   jobtime F2.2 prevexp F3.2 minority F1.2.
```

GET SAS

GET SAS had not yet been implemented when SPSS for Windows 10.0 was first shipped. See http://www.spss.com/tech/utilities/spss10-getsas.htm for information on how to acquire this facility.

```
GET SAS DATA=file [DSET(data set)]

 [/FORMATS=file [FSET(data set)]]
```

Example

```
GET SAS DATA='ELECT' DSET(Y1948).
```

Overview

GET SAS builds an SPSS-format working data file from a data set contained in a SAS transport file. A SAS transport file is a sequential file written in SAS transport format and can be created by the SAS export engine available in SAS Release 6.06 or higher or by the EXPORT option on the COPY or XCOPY procedure in earlier versions. (See "Tips for Creating and Moving a SAS Transport File" on p. 451.) In most instances, GET SAS retrieves data and data definition items stored in the SAS transport file, including variable labels, print and write formats, missing values, and, optionally, value labels. GET SAS automatically modifies these data definition items where necessary to conform with SPSS conventions.

Note that the terms "file" and "data set" used to describe GET SAS follow the SAS convention. A SAS data set is approximately equivalent to an SPSS data file that contains both the data values and the descriptor information.

Options

Retrieving User-defined Formats in SAS. You can specify a SAS transport file on the FORMATS subcommand to retrieve user-defined formats associated with the data being read. GET SAS retrieves user-defined formats from a data set contained in the file, either applying them as output formats or using them as value labels.

Specifying the Data Set. You can name a data set contained in a specified SAS transport file, using DSET on the DATA subcommand or FSET on the FORMATS subcommand. GET SAS reads the specified data set from the SAS transport file.

Basic Specification

The basic specification is the DATA subcommand followed by the name of the SAS transport file to read. By default, the first SAS data set is copied into the working data file and any necessary data conversions are made (see "SAS to SPSS Data Conversion" on p. 447).

Syntax Rules

- The subcommand DATA and the SAS transport file are required and must be specified first.
- The subcommand FORMATS is optional. When specified, it requires a file specification whether it is the same as or different from the file specification on the DATA subcommand.
- GET SAS does not allow KEEP, DROP, RENAME, and MAP subcommands. To use a subset of the variables, rename them, or display the file content, you can specify the appropriate commands after the SPSS working data file is created.

Operations

- GET SAS reads data from the specified or default data set contained in the SAS transport file named on the DATA subcommand.
- When GET SAS encounters an unknown format name, it inspects the data set specified on FSET. If the format exists, it is applied after any necessary modifications are made (see "SAS to SPSS Data Conversion" on p. 447); otherwise, GET SAS applies the default format for the SPSS session (see SET).
- Value labels retrieved from a SAS user-defined format are used for variables associated with that format, becoming part of the SPSS dictionary.
- All variables from the SAS data set are included in the working data file, and they are in the same order as in the SAS data set.

DATA Subcommand

DATA specifies the transport file that contains the SAS data set to be read.

- DATA is required and must be the first specification on GET SAS.
- The file specification varies from operating system to operating system. Enclosing the filename within apostrophes always works.
- The optional DSET keyword on DATA determines which data set within the specified SAS transport file is to be read. The default is the first data set.

DSET (data set)   *Data set to be read.* Specify the name of the data set in parentheses. If the specified data set does not exist in the SAS transport file, GET SAS displays a message informing you that the data set was not found. Names of the data sets in the file are then listed.

Example

```
GET SAS DATA='ELECT' DSET(Y1948).
```

- The SAS transport file *ELECT* is opened and the data set named *Y1948* is used to build the working file for the SPSS session.

FORMATS Subcommand

FORMATS specifies the SAS transport file with the data set containing user-defined formats to be applied to the retrieved data. User-defined formats in SAS may contain value labels and/or user-defined output formats. In most cases, SPSS reads in value labels, if specified, and sets user-defined output formats to SPSS defaults.

- The file specification varies from operating system to operating system. Enclosing the filename within apostrophes always works.
- FORMATS is optional. If the user-defined formats reside in the same transport file as the data, you can specify FSET directly on the DATA subcommand. The data set named on FSET must be different from that named on DSET.
- If FORMATS is omitted and FSET is not specified on DATA either, no value labels are available and all user-defined formats used in the data are set to the default for the session.

The optional keyword FSET specifies the data set containing the formats. The default is the first data set in the specified transport file.

FSET (data set)   *Data set containing formats.* Specify the data set from which user-defined formats and value labels are to be obtained. The data set name must be enclosed in parentheses. If the specified data set does not exist in the SAS transport file, GET SAS displays a message informing you that the data set was not found. Names of the data sets in the file are then listed.

Example

```
GET SAS /DATA='ELECT' DSET(Y1948)
 /FORMATS='ELECTFM' FSET(F1948).
```

- The user-defined formats reside in a different transport file. The FORMATS subcommand is required.
- FSET specifies *F1948* as the data set to read for user-specified formats.
- Value labels and formats read from the SAS transport file *ELECTFM* are converted to conform to SPSS conventions.

Example

```
GET SAS /DATA='ELECT' DSET(Y1948) FSET(F1948).
```

- The SAS transport file *ELECT* contains both the data and the user-defined formats.
- DSET specifies *Y1948* as the data set to read for input data.
- FSET specifies *F1948* as the data set to read for user-specified formats.

SAS to SPSS Data Conversion

Although SAS and SPSS data files have similar attributes, they are not identical. SPSS makes the following conversions to force SAS data sets to comply with SPSS conventions.

File Label

The file label for the SPSS file is obtained from the name specified on the LABEL option of the SAS DATA statement.

Variable Names

- Like SPSS, SAS allows variable names up to eight characters long, but the SAS naming conventions are different from those in SPSS. A SAS variable name must begin with a letter or an underscore. The underscore can be used within SPSS variable names but not at the beginning of a name. All leading underscores in SAS files are changed to the @ symbol.
- If an SPSS reserved keyword is used as a SAS variable name, SPSS appends the # symbol to the name and issues a warning message. The SPSS reserved keywords are ALL, AND, BY, GE, GT, LE, LT, NE, NOT, OR, TO, and WITH. A SAS variable named *AND*, for example, would be converted to *AND#*.

Variable Labels

SAS variable labels specified on the LABEL statement in the DATA step are used as variable labels in SPSS.

Value Labels

SAS value formats that assign value labels are read from the data set specified on the FORMATS subcommand. The SAS value labels are then converted to SPSS value labels in the following manner:

- Labels assigned to single values are retained.
- Labels assigned to a range of values are assigned to the beginning and end points of the range. For example, if SAS assigns the label *LOW* to values 1–3, in the resulting SPSS working data file the label *LOW* is assigned only to values 1 and 3.
- Labels assigned to SAS keywords LOW, HIGH, and OTHER are ignored.
- Labels assigned to long string variables are ignored.
- Labels over 60 characters long are truncated.

Missing Values

Since SAS has no user-defined missing values, all SAS missing codes are converted to SPSS system-missing values.

Variable Types

- Both SAS and SPSS allow two types of variables: numeric and character string. During conversion, SAS numeric variables become SPSS numeric variables, and SAS string variables become SPSS string variables of the same length.

- Values for SAS variables that can be identified in date format are converted to the number of seconds from October 15, 1582, to the given date. Similarly, values for any SAS variables that are clearly in date-time format are converted to the number of seconds from October 15, 1582, to the given date and time.

Print and Write Formats

SAS formats are converted to their closest representation within SPSS. Esoteric formats are converted to the default print format and the closest write format. If a numeric variable does not have a SAS format, the default SPSS format is used for both print and write formats. (The default numeric format for an SPSS session can be specified on SET FORMAT. If SET FORMAT is not specified for the session, the default numeric format is F8.2.)

Table 1 shows the correspondence between SPSS and SAS formats.

Table 1   Output format correspondence

SAS	SPSS print format	SPSS write format	Notes
BEST	default	default	
BINARYw.d	PIBHEXk	IBw.d	k=ceil(w/4)
Fw.d	Fw.d	Fw.d	
NEGPARENw.d	Fw.d	Fw.d	Prints negative numbers in parentheses in SAS
COMMAw.d	COMMAw.d	COMMAw.d	
COMMAXw.d	DOTw.d	DOTw.d	
DOLLARw.d	DOLLARw.d	DOLLARw.d	
DOLLARXw.d	DOTw.d	DOTw.d	Prints dollar format with comma as decimal delimiter in SAS
Ew.d	Ew.d	Ew.d	
FRACT	default	default	Prints n/m format in SAS
HEXw	PIBHEXw	PIBHEXw	
IBw	Fk.0	IBw	k=2w+1
OCTALw	PIBHEXk.d	PIBHEXk.d	k=3/4w
PDw	Fk.d	PW	k=2w+1
PERCENTw.d	PCTw.d	PCTw.d	
PIBw.d	default	PIBw.d	
PKw.d	Fk.d	PKw.d	k=2w+1
RBw	default	RBw	
ROMAN	F8.0	F8.0	

Table 1   Output format correspondence (Continued)

SAS	SPSS print format	SPSS write format	Notes
SSNw	Fw.0	Fw.0	
WORDFw.d	Fw.d	Fw.d	Prints numeric values as words in SAS
WORDSw.d	Fw.d	Fw.d	Prints numeric values as words and decimals as fractions in SAS
Zw	Nw	Nw	
ZDw	Zw	Zw	
$w	Aw	Aw	
$CHARw	Aw	Aw	
$ASCIIw	Aw	Aw	
$EBCDIC	Aw	Aw	
$HEXw	AHEXw	AHEXw	
$OCTALw	AHEXk	AHEXk	k=2/3w
$BINARYw	AHEXk	AHEXk	k=w/4
$VARYINGw	Aw	Aw	
DATEw	DATEw	DATEw	Minimum width for SPSS is 9
DATETIMEw	DATETIMEw	DATETIMEw	Minimum width for SPSS is 17
DAYw	DATE9	DATE9	Prints day of month in SAS
DDMMYYw	EDATEw	EDATEw	Minimum width for SPSS is 9
DOWNAMEw	WKDAYw	WKDAYw	
HHMMw.d	TIMEw+d	TIMEw+d	Minimum width for SPSS is 5
HOURw.d	TIME5.0	TIME5.0	No equivalent format for fractions of an hour in SPSS
JULIANw	JDATEw	JDATEw	
JULDAYw	JDATEw	JDATEW	
MMDDYYw	ADATEw	ADATEw	Minimum width for SPSS is 8
MMSSw.d	TIMEw.d	TIMEw.d	
MMYYw	MOYRw+1	MOYRw+1	
MONNAMEw	MONTHw	MONTHw	Prints name of the month in SAS
MONTH	MONTHw	MONTHw	
MONYYw	MOYRw+1	MOYRw+1	
NENGOw	JDATEw	JDATEw	Prints Japanese date format in SAS
QTRw	QYR8	QYR8	SPSS assumes the current year
QTRRw	QYR8	QYR8	Prints quarter in Roman numerals in SAS
TIMEw.d	TIMEw.d	TIMEw.d	Minimum width for SPSS is 5
TODw	DATETIMEw	DATETIMEw	Minimum width for SPSS is 21
WEEKDATEw	DATE12	DATE12	Prints day of week and date in SAS (day-of-week, month-name dd yy)
WEEKDATEXw	EDATE12	EDATE12	Prints day of week and date in SAS (day-of-week, dd month-name yy)

Table 1   Output format correspondence (Continued)

SAS	SPSS print format	SPSS write format	Notes
WEEKDAYw	WKDAYw	WKDAYw	
WORDDATEw	ADATE12	ADATE12	
WORDDATXw	DATE12	DATE12	
YEARw	SDATE10	SDATE10	
YYMMXw	MOYR8	MOYR8	
YYMONw	MOYR8	MOYR8	
YYMMDDw	MOYR6	MOYR6	SDATE10 if width is 6 or more
YYQXw	QYRw+2	QYRw+2	
YYQRw	QYRw+2	QYRw+2	Prints quarter in Roman numerals in SAS

Tips for Creating and Moving a SAS Transport File

Most versions of SAS are capable of creating a transport file using a machine-independent portable format. Here are some tips for creating and moving a SAS transport file with a data set containing either data or user-defined formats, or both:

- Use the SAS export engine available in SAS Release 6.06 and higher to create a transport file containing two data sets, one of data and the other of formats:

```
LIBNAME OUTLIB XPORT 'dir/filename';
PROC FORMAT CNTLOUT=format_set_name;
VALUE format_name 1='value label' 2='value label' ... ;

DATA data_set_name; INPUT var1 ...;
ATTRIB var1 FORMAT=format_name.;
CARDS;
1 ...
2 ...
...
;
PROC COPY IN=WORK OUT=OUTLIB;
SELECT data_set_name format_set_name;
RUN;
```

where `filename` is the name of the transport file, `dir` is the directory to save the transport file to, `format_set_name` is the name of the data set that will contain your formats, `format_name` is the name of a format defined on **PROC FORMAT** and later to be associated with *var1* in the data set, `value label` stands for the labels specified for numeric values 1 and so on, and `data_set_name` is the name of the data set created from the input. Note that the SAS export engine on PCs is **SASV5XPT**. Use `SASV5XPT` in place of `XPORT` if you are on a PC.

- Use the SAS export engine to write a SAS data set (either with data or with user-defined formats) into a transport format:

```
LIBNAME TRANFILE XPORT 'dir/filename';
LIBNAME OLDLIB 'dir';

PROC COPY IN=OLDLIB OUT=TRANFILE;
SELECT data_set_name;
RUN;
```

where `filename` is the name of the transport file, `dir` is the directory containing the data set file, and `data_set_name` is the name of the data set to be written into the transport file. Note that the SAS export engine on PCs is **SASV5XPT**. Use `SASV5XPT` in place of `XPORT` if you are on a PC.

- If the user-defined formats have been stored in a format library, you must create a SAS data set first:

```
LIBNAME=libref;
PROC FORMAT LIBRARY=LIBRARY CNTLOUT=libname.data_set_name;
RUN;
```

where `libref` is the name of the format library you want to convert to a data set and `libname.data_set_name` is the name of the data set containing the formats. You can now write it to a transport file.

- The SAS transport file is a binary file. When you move it through your network or to a different platform, transport it in binary mode. For example, you can FTP it with the binary switch on.

GET TRANSLATE

```
GET TRANSLATE FILE=file

[/TYPE={WK }]
       {WK1}
       {WKS}
       {WR1}
       {WRK}
       {SLK}
       {XLS}¹
       {DBF}
       {TAB}
       {SYS}

[/FIELDNAMES]*

[/RANGE={range name }]*
        {start..stop}
        {start:stop }

[/KEEP={ALL** }] [/DROP=varlist]
       {varlist}

[/MAP]
```

[1]Excel 4 or earlier. For Excel 5 or later, use the **GET DATA** command.
*Available only for spreadsheet and tab-delimited ASCII files.
**Default if the subcommand is omitted.

Keyword	Type of file
WK	Any Lotus 1-2-3 or Symphony file
WK1	1-2-3 Release 2.0
WKS	1-2-3 Release 1A
WR1	Symphony Release 2.0
WRK	Symphony Release 1.0
SLK	Microsoft Excel and Multiplan in SYLK (symbolic link) format
XLS	Microsoft Excel
DBF	All dBASE files
TAB	Tab-delimited ASCII file
SYS	Systat data file

Example

```
GET TRANSLATE FILE='PROJECT.WKS'
 /FIELDNAMES
 /RANGE=D3..J279.
```

Overview

GET TRANSLATE creates a working data file from files produced by other software applications. Supported formats are 1-2-3, Symphony, Multiplan, Excel, dBASE II, dBASE III, dBASE IV, and tab-delimited ASCII files.

Options

Variable Subsets. You can use the DROP and KEEP subcommands to specify variables to omit or retain in the resulting working data file.

Variable Names. You can rename variables as they are translated using the RENAME subcommand.

Variable Map. To confirm the names and order of the variables in the working data file, use the MAP subcommand. MAP displays the variables in the working data file and their corresponding names in the other application.

Spreadsheet Files. You can use the RANGE subcommand to translate a subset of cells from a spreadsheet file. You can use the FIELDNAMES subcommand to translate field names in the spreadsheet file to variable names.

Basic Specification

- The basic specification is FILE with a file specification enclosed in apostrophes.
- If the file's extension is not the default for the type of file you are reading, TYPE must also be specified.

Subcommand Order

Subcommands can be named in any order.

Operations

GET TRANSLATE replaces an existing working data file.

Spreadsheets

A spreadsheet file suitable for this program should be arranged so that each row represents a case and each column a variable.

- By default, the new working data file contains all rows and up to 256 columns from Lotus 1-2-3, Symphony, or Excel, or up to 255 columns from Multiplan.
- By default, GET TRANSLATE uses the column letters as variable names in the working data file.

- The first row of a spreadsheet or specified range may contain field labels immediately followed by rows of data. These names can be transferred as SPSS variable names (see the FIELDNAMES subcommand on p. 458).

- The current value of a formula is translated to the working data file.

- Blank, ERR, and NA values in 1-2-3 and Symphony and error values such as #N/A in Excel are translated as system-missing values in the working data file.

- Hidden columns and cells in 1-2-3 Release 2 and Symphony files are translated and copied into the working data file.

- Column width and format type are transferred to the dictionary of the working data file.

- The format type is assigned from values in the first data row. By default, the first data row is row 1. If RANGE is specified, the first data row is the first row in the range. If FIELDNAMES is specified, the first data row follows immediately after the single row containing field names.

- If a cell in the first data row is empty, the variable is assigned the global default format from the spreadsheet.

The formats from 1-2-3, Symphony, Excel, and Multiplan are translated as follows:

1-2-3/Symphony	Excel	SYLK	SPSS
Fixed	0.00; #,##0.00	Fixed	F
	0; #,##0	Integer	F
Scientific	0.00E+00	Exponent	E
Currency	$#,##0_);...	$ (dollar)	DOLLAR
, (comma)			COMMA
General	General	General	F
+/ -		* (bargraph)	F
Percent	0%; 0.00%	Percent	PCT
Date	m/d/yy;d-mmm-yy...		DATE
Time	h:mm; h:mm:ss...		TIME
Text/Literal			F
Label		Alpha	String

- If a string is encountered in a column with numeric format, it is converted to the system-missing value in the working data file.

- If a numeric value is encountered in a column with string format, it is converted to a blank in the working data file.

- Blank lines are translated as cases containing the system-missing value for numeric variables and blanks for string variables.

- 1-2-3 and Symphony date and time indicators (shown at the bottom of the screen) are not transferred from *WKS*, *WK1*, *WRK*, or *WR1* files.

Databases

Database files are logically very similar to SPSS-format data files.

- By default, all fields and records from dBASE II, dBASE III, or dBASE IV files are included in the working data file.
- Field names are automatically translated into variable names. If the FIELDNAMES subcommand is used with database files, it is ignored.
- Field names to be translated should comply with SPSS-format variable naming conventions. Names longer than eight characters are truncated. If a field name is not unique in the first eight characters, the field will be dropped.
- Colons used in dBASE II field names are translated to underscores.
- Records in dBASE II, dBASE III, or dBASE IV that have been marked for deletion but that have not actually been purged are included in the working data file. To differentiate these cases, GET TRANSLATE creates a new string variable D_R, which contains an asterisk for cases marked for deletion. Other cases contain a blank for D_R.
- Character, floating, and numeric fields are transferred directly to variables. Logical fields are converted into string variables. Memo fields are ignored.

dBASE formats are translated as follows:

dBASE	SPSS
Character	String
Logical	String
Date	Date
Numeric	Number
Floating	Number
Memo	Ignored

Tab-delimited ASCII Files

Tab-delimited ASCII files are simple spreadsheets produced by a text editor, with the columns delimited by tabs and rows by carriage returns. The first row is usually occupied by column headings.

- By default all columns of all rows are treated as data. Default variable names VAR1, VAR2, and so on are assigned to each column. The data type (numeric or string) for each variable is determined by the first data value in the column.
- If FIELDNAMES is specified, the program reads in the first row as variable names and determines data type by the values in from the second row.
- Any value that contains non-numeric characters is considered a string value. Dollar and date formats are not recognized and are treated as strings. When string values are encountered for a numeric variable, they are converted to the system-missing value.
- For numeric variables, the assigned format is F8.2 or the format of the first data value in the column, whichever is wider. Values that exceed the defined width are rounded for display, but the entire value is stored internally.

- For string variables, the assigned format is A8 or the format of the first data value in the column, whichever is wider. Values that exceed the defined width are truncated.
- ASCII data files delimited by space (instead of tabs) or in fixed format should be read by DATA LIST.

Limitations

The maximum number of variables that can be translated into the working data file depends on the maximum number of variables the other software application can handle:

Application	Maximum variables
1-2-3	256
Symphony	256
Multiplan	255
Excel	256
dBASE IV	255
dBASE III	128
dBASE II	32

FILE Subcommand

FILE names the file to read. The only specification is the name of the file.

- On some systems, file specifications should be enclosed in quotation marks or apostrophes.

Example

```
GET TRANSLATE FILE='PROJECT.WKS'.
```

- GET TRANSLATE creates a working data file from the 1-2-3 Release 1.0 spreadsheet with the name *PROJECT.WKS*.
- The working file contains all rows and columns and uses the column letters as variable names.
- The format for each variable is determined by the format of the value in the first row of each column.

TYPE Subcommand

TYPE indicates the format of the file.

- TYPE can be omitted if the file extension named on FILE is the default for the type of file you are reading.
- The TYPE subcommand takes precedence over the file extension.
- You can create a Lotus format file in Multiplan and translate it to an working data file by specifying WKS on TYPE.

WK	*Any Lotus 1-2-3 or Symphony file.*
WK1	*1-2-3 Release 2.0.*
WKS	*1-2-3 Release 1A.*
WR1	*Symphony Release 2.0.*
WRK	*Symphony Release 1.0.*
SLK	*Microsoft Excel and Multiplan saved in SYLK (symbolic link) format.*
XLS	*Microsoft Excel, Release 4.0 or earlier. (For Excel 5 or later, use* GET CAPTURE.*)*
DBF	*All dBASE files.*
TAB	*Tab-delimited ASCII data file.*

Example

```
GET TRANSLATE FILE='PROJECT.OCT' /TYPE=SLK.
```

- GET TRANSLATE creates a working data file from the Multiplan file *PROJECT.OCT*.

FIELDNAMES Subcommand

FIELDNAMES translates spreadsheet field names into variable names.

- FIELDNAMES can be used with spreadsheet and tab-delimited ASCII files only. FIELDNAMES is ignored when used with database files.
- Each cell in the first row of the spreadsheet file (or the specified range) must contain a field name. If a column does not contain a name, the column is dropped.
- Field names to be translated should conform to SPSS-format naming conventions. They must be unique in the first eight characters and cannot have leading blanks.
- Field names that exceed eight characters are truncated.
- If two or more columns in the spreadsheet have the same field name, digits are appended to all field names after the first, making them unique.
- Illegal characters in field names are changed to underscores in this program.
- If the spreadsheet file uses reserved words (ALL, AND, BY, EQ, GE, GT, LE, LT, NE, NOT, OR, TO, or WITH) as field names, GET TRANSLATE appends a dollar sign ($) to the variable name. For example, columns named *GE, GT, EQ,* and *BY* will be renamed *GE$, GT$, EQ$,* and *BY$* in the working data file.

Example

```
GET TRANSLATE FILE='MONTHLY.WRK' /FIELDNAMES.
```

- GET TRANSLATE creates a working data file from a Symphony 1.0 spreadsheet. The first row in the spreadsheet contains field names that are used as variable names in the working file.

RANGE Subcommand

RANGE translates a specified set of cells from a spreadsheet file.

- RANGE cannot be used for translating database files.
- For 1-2-3 or Symphony, specify the beginning of the range with a column letter and row number followed by two periods and the end of the range with a column letter and row number, as in A1..K14.
- For Multiplan spreadsheets, specify the beginning and ending cells of the range separated by a colon, as in R1C1:R14C11.
- For Excel files, specify the beginning column letter and row number, a colon, and the ending column letter and row number, as in A1:K14.
- You can also specify the range using range names supplied in Symphony, 1-2-3, or Multiplan.
- If you specify FIELDNAMES with RANGE, the first row of the range must contain field names.

Example

```
GET TRANSLATE FILE='PROJECT.WKS' /FIELDNAMES /RANGE=D3..J279.
```

- GET TRANSLATE creates an SPSS working data file from the 1-2-3 Release 1A file *PROJECT.WKS*.
- The field names in the first row of the range (row 3) are used as variable names.
- Data from cells D4 through J279 are transferred to the working data file.

DROP and KEEP Subcommands

DROP and KEEP are used to copy a subset of variables into the working data file. DROP specifies the variables not to copy into the working file. KEEP specifies variables to copy. Variables not specified on KEEP are dropped.

- DROP and KEEP cannot precede the FILE or TYPE subcommands.
- DROP and KEEP specifications use variable names. By default, this program uses the column letters from spreadsheets and the field names from databases as variable names.
- If FIELDNAMES is specified when translating from a spreadsheet, the DROP and KEEP subcommands must refer to the field names, not the default column letters.
- Variables can be specified in any order. Neither DROP nor KEEP affects the order of variables in the resulting file. Variables are kept in their original order.
- If a variable is referred to twice on the same subcommand, only the first mention of the variable is recognized.
- Multiple DROP and KEEP subcommands are allowed; the effect is cumulative. Specifying a variable named on a previous DROP or not named on a previous KEEP results in an error and the command is not executed.
- If you specify both RANGE and KEEP, the resulting file contains only variables that are both within the range and specified on KEEP.
- If you specify both RANGE and DROP, the resulting file contains only variables within the range and excludes those mentioned on DROP, even if they are within the range.

Example

```
GET TRANSLATE FILE='ADDRESS.DBF' /DROP=PHONENO, ENTRY.
```

- GET TRANSLATE creates an SPSS working data file from the dBASE file *ADDRESS.DBF*, omitting the fields named *PHONENO* and *ENTRY*.

Example

```
GET TRANSLATE FILE='PROJECT.OCT' /TYPE=WK1 /FIELDNAMES
 /KEEP=NETINC, REP, QUANTITY, REGION, MONTH, DAY, YEAR.
```

- GET TRANSLATE creates a working data file from the 1-2-3 Release 2.0 file called *PROJECT.OCT*.
- The subcommand FIELDNAMES indicates that the first row of the spreadsheet contains field names, which will be translated into variable names in the working file.
- The subcommand KEEP translates columns with the field names *NETINC*, *REP*, *QUANTITY*, *REGION*, *MONTH*, *DAY*, and *YEAR* to the working file.

MAP Subcommand

MAP displays a list of the variables in the working data file and their corresponding names in the other application.

- The only specification is the keyword MAP. There are no additional specifications.
- Multiple MAP subcommands are allowed. Each MAP subcommand maps the results of subcommands that precede it; results of subcommands that follow it are not mapped.

Example

```
GET TRANSLATE FILE='ADDRESS.DBF' /DROP=PHONENO, ENTRY /MAP.
```

- MAP is specified to confirm that variables *PHONENO* and *ENTRY* have been dropped.

GLM: Overview

GLM is available in the Advanced Models option.

```
GLM dependent varlist [BY factor list [WITH covariate list]]

[/WSFACTOR=name levels [{DEVIATION [(refcat)]      }] name...
                        {SIMPLE [(refcat)]          }
                        {DIFFERENCE                 }
                        {HELMERT                    }
                        {REPEATED                   }
                        {POLYNOMIAL [({1,2,3...})]**}
                        {            {metric }      }
                        {SPECIAL (matrix)           }

[/MEASURE=newname newname...]

[/WSDESIGN=effect effect...]†

[/RANDOM=factor factor...]

[/REGWGT=varname]

[/METHOD=SSTYPE({1  })]
               {2  }
               {3**}
               {4  }

[/INTERCEPT=[INCLUDE**] [EXCLUDE]]

[/MISSING=[INCLUDE] [EXCLUDE**]]

[/CRITERIA=[EPS({1E-8**})][ALPHA({0.05**})]
               {a      }        {a      }

[/PRINT  = [DESCRIPTIVE] [HOMOGENEITY] [PARAMETER][ETASQ] [RSSCP]
           [GEF] [LOF] [OPOWER] [TEST [([SSCP] [LMATRIX] [MMATRIX])]]

[/PLOT=[SPREADLEVEL] [RESIDUALS]
       [PROFILE (factor factor*factor factor*factor*factor ...)]

[/TEST=effect VS {linear combination [DF(df)]}]
                 {value DF (df)               }

[/LMATRIX={["label"] effect list effect list ...;...}]
          {["label"] effect list effect list ...     }
          {["label"] ALL list; ALL...                 }
          {["label"] ALL list                         }

[/CONTRAST (factor name)={DEVIATION[(refcat)]**‡  }]
                         {SIMPLE [(refcat)]        }
                         {DIFFERENCE               }
                         {HELMERT                  }
                         {REPEATED                 }
                         {POLYNOMIAL  [({1,2,3...})]}
                         {            {metric }    }
                         {SPECIAL (matrix)         }

[/MMATRIX= {["label"] depvar value depvar value ...;["label"]...}]
           {["label"] depvar value depvar value ...             }
           {["label"] ALL list; ["label"] ...                   }
           {["label"] ALL list                                  }
```

```
[/KMATRIX= {list of numbers    }]
           {list of numbers;...}

[/POSTHOC = effect [effect...]
           ([SNK] [TUKEY] [BTUKEY][DUNCAN]
            [SCHEFFE] [DUNNETT(refcat)] [DUNNETTL(refcat)]
            [DUNNETTR(refcat)] [BONFERRONI] [LSD] [SIDAK]
            [GT2] [GABRIEL] [FREGW] [QREGW]  [T2] [T3] [GH][C]
            [WALLER ({100** })])]
                     {kratio}
           [VS effect]

[/EMMEANS=TABLES({OVERALL          })] [COMPARE ADJ(LSD(none)) (BONFERRONI) (SIDAK)]
                {factor            }
                {factor*factor...  }
                {wsfactor          }
                {wsfactor*wsfactor ... }
                {factor*...wsfactor*...}

[/SAVE=[tempvar [(list of names)]] [tempvar [(list of names)]]...]
       [DESIGN]

[/OUTFILE= [{COVB (filename)}] [EFFECT(filename)] [DESIGN(filename)]
            {CORB (filename)}

[/DESIGN={[INTERCEPT...]    }]
         {[effect effect...]}
```

† **WSDESIGN** uses the same specification as **DESIGN**, with only within-subjects factors.

‡ **DEVIATION** is the default for between-subjects factors, while **POLYNOMIAL** is the default for within-subjects factors.

** Default if subcommand or keyword is omitted.

Temporary variables (tempvar) are:

PRED, WPRED, RESID, WRESID, DRESID, ZRESID, SRESID, SEPRED, COOK, LEVER

Overview

GLM (general linear model) is a general procedure for analysis of variance and covariance, as well as regression. GLM is the most versatile of the analysis-of-variance procedures in SPSS and can be used for both univariate and multivariate designs. GLM allows you to:

- Include interaction and nested effects in your design model. Multiple nesting is allowed; for example, A within B within C is specified as $A(B(C))$.

- Include covariates in your design model. GLM also allows covariate-by-covariate and covariate-by-factor interactions such as X by X (or $X*X$), X by A (or $X*A$), and X by A within B (or $X*A(B)$). Thus, polynomial regression or a test of the homogeneity of regressions can be performed.

- Select appropriate sums-of-squares hypothesis tests for effects in balanced design models, unbalanced all-cells-filled design models, and some-cells-empty design models. The estimable functions corresponding to the hypothesis test for each effect in the model can also be displayed.

- Display the general form of estimable functions.

- Display expected mean squares, automatically detecting and using the appropriate error term for testing each effect in mixed- and random-effects models.

- Select commonly used contrasts or specify custom contrasts to perform hypothesis tests.

- Customize hypothesis testing, based on the null hypothesis **LBM = K**, where **B** is the parameter vector or matrix.

- Display a variety of post hoc tests for multiple comparisons.

- Display estimates of population marginal cell means for both between-subjects factors and within-subjects factors, adjusted for covariates.

- Perform multivariate analysis of variance and covariance.

- Estimate parameters using the method of weighted least squares and a generalized inverse technique.

- Compare graphically the levels in a model by displaying plots of estimated marginal cell means for each level of a factor, with separate lines for each level of another factor in the model.

- Display a variety of estimates and measures useful for diagnostic checking. All of these estimates and measures can be saved in a data file for use by another SPSS procedure.

- Perform repeated measures analysis of variance.

- Display homogeneity tests for testing underlying assumptions in multivariate and univariate analyses.

General Linear Model (GLM) and MANOVA

MANOVA, the other generalized procedure for analysis of variance and covariance in SPSS, is available only in syntax. The major distinction between GLM and MANOVA in terms of statistical design and functionality is that GLM uses a non-full-rank, or overparameterized, indicator variable approach to parameterization of linear models, instead of the full-rank reparameterization approach used in MANOVA. The generalized inverse approach and the aliasing of redundant parameters to zero employed by GLM allow greater flexibility in handling a variety of messy data situations, particularly those involving empty cells. GLM offers a variety of features unavailable in MANOVA:

- Identification of the general forms of estimable functions.

- Identification of forms of estimable functions specific to four types of sums of squares (Types I–IV).

- Tests using the four types of sums of squares, including Type IV, specifically designed for situations involving empty cells.

- Flexible specification of general comparisons among parameters, using the syntax subcommands LMATRIX, MMATRIX and KMATRIX; sets of contrasts can be specified that involve any number of orthogonal or nonorthogonal linear combinations.

- Nonorthogonal contrasts for within-subjects factors (using the syntax subcommand WSFACTORS).

- Tests against nonzero null hypotheses can be specified using the syntax subcommand KMATRIX.

- Estimated marginal means (EMMEANS) and standard errors adjusted for other factors and covariates are available for all between- and within-subjects factor combinations in the original variable metrics.

- Uncorrected pairwise comparisons among estimated marginal means for any main effect in the model, for both between- and within-subjects factors.

- Post hoc or multiple comparison tests for unadjusted one-way factor means are available for between-subjects factors in ANOVA designs; 20 different types of comparisons are offered.

- Weighted least squares (WLS) estimation, including saving of weighted predicted values and residuals.

- Automatic handling of random effects in random-effects models and mixed models, including generation of expected mean squares and automatic assignment of proper error terms.

- Specification of several types of nested models via dialog boxes with proper use of the interaction operator (*), due to the nonreparameterized approach.

- Univariate homogeneity-of-variance assumption tested using the Levene test.

- Between-subjects factors do not require specification of levels.

- Profile (interaction) plots of estimated marginal means for visual exploration of interactions involving combinations of between- and/or within-subjects factors.

- Saving of casewise temporary variables for model diagnosis:

  - Predicted values—unstandardized (raw), weighted unstandardized.

  - Residuals—unstandardized, weighted unstandardized, standardized, Studentized, deleted.

  - Standard error of prediction.

  - Cook's distance.

  - Leverage.

- Saving of an SPSS file with parameter estimates and their degrees of freedom, significance level.

To simplify the presentation, reference material on GLM is divided into three sections: *univariate* designs with one dependent variable, *multivariate* designs with several interrelated dependent variables, and *repeated measures* designs, in which the dependent variables represent the same types of measurements taken at more than one time.

The full syntax diagram for GLM is presented here. The GLM sections that follow include partial syntax diagrams showing the subcommands and specifications discussed in that section. Individually, those diagrams are incomplete. Subcommands listed for univariate designs are available for any analysis, and subcommands listed for multivariate designs can be used in any multivariate analysis, including repeated measures.

Models

The following are examples of models that can be specified using GLM:

Model 1: Univariate or multivariate simple and multiple regression

```
GLM Y WITH X1 X2.
GLM Y1 Y2 WITH X1 X2 X3.
```

Model 2: Fixed-effects ANOVA and MANOVA

```
GLM Y1 Y2 by B.
```

Model 3: ANCOVA and multivariate ANCOVA (MANCOVA)

```
GLM Y1 Y2 BY B WITH X1 X2 X3.
```

Model 4: Random-effects ANOVA and ANCOVA

```
GLM Y1 BY C WITH X1 X2
 /RANDOM = C.
```

Model 5: Mixed-model ANOVA and ANCOVA

```
GLM Y1 BY B, C WITH X1 X2
 /RANDOM = C.
```

Model 6: Repeated measures analysis using a split-plot design

```
(Univariate mixed models approach with subject as a random effect)
```

If *drug* is a between-subjects factor and *time* is a within-subjects factor,

```
GLM Y BY DRUG SUBJECT TIME
 /RANDOM = SUBJECT
 /DESIGN = DRUG SUBJECT*DRUG TIME DRUG*TIME.
```

Model 7: Repeated measures using the WSFACTOR subcommand

Use this model only when there is no random between-subjects effect in the model. For example, if *Y1*, *Y2*, *Y3*, and *Y4* are the dependent variables measured at times 1 to 4,

```
GLM Y1 Y2 Y3 Y4 BY DRUG
 /WSFACTOR = TIME 4
 /DESIGN.
```

Model 8: Repeated measures doubly multivariate model

Repeated measures fixed-effects MANOVA is also called a doubly multivariate model. Varying or time-dependent covariates are not available. This model can be used only when there is no random between-subjects effect in the model.

```
GLM X11 X12 X13 X21 X22 X23
    Y11 Y12 Y13 Y21 Y22 Y23 BY C D
/MEASURE = X Y
/WSFACTOR = A 2 B 3
/WSDESIGN = A B A*B
/DESIGN = C D.
```

Model 9: Means model for ANOVA and MANOVA

This model takes only fixed-effect factors (no random effects and covariates) and always assumes the highest order of the interactions among the factors. For example, *B*, *D*, and *E* are fixed factors, and *Y1* and *Y2* are two dependent variables. You can specify a means model by suppressing the intercept effect and specifying the highest order of interaction on the DESIGN subcommand.

```
GLM Y1 Y2 BY B, D, E
/INTERCEPT = EXCLUDE
/DESIGN = B*D*E.
```

Custom Hypothesis Specifications

GLM provides a flexible way for you to customize hypothesis testing based on the general linear hypothesis **LBM** = **K**, where **B** is the parameter vector or matrix. You can specify a customized linear hypothesis by using one or a combination of the subcommands LMATRIX, MMATRIX, KMATRIX, and CONTRAST.

LMATRIX, MMATRIX, and KMATRIX Subcommands

- The **L** matrix is called the **contrast coefficients matrix**. This matrix specifies coefficients of contrasts, which can be used for studying the between-subjects effects in the model. One way to define the **L** matrix is by specifying the CONTRAST subcommand, on which you select a type of contrast. Another way is to specify your own **L** matrix directly by using the LMATRIX subcommand. For details, see the syntax rules for these two subcommands in GLM: Univariate.

- The **M** matrix is called the **transformation coefficients matrix**. This matrix provides a transformation for the dependent variables. This transformation can be used to construct contrasts among the dependent variables in the model. The **M** matrix can be specified on the MMATRIX subcommand. For details, see the syntax rule for this subcommand in GLM: Multivariate.

- The **K** matrix is called the **contrast results matrix**. This matrix specifies the results matrix in the general linear hypothesis. To define your own **K** matrix, the KMATRIX subcommand can be used. For details, see the syntax rules for this subcommand in GLM: Univariate.

For univariate and multivariate models, you can specify one, two, or all three of the **L**, **M**, and **K** matrices. If only one or two types are specified, the unspecified matrices use the defaults shown in Table 1 (read across the rows).

Table 1   Default matrices for univariate and multivariate models if one matrix is specified

L matrix	M matrix	K matrix
If LMATRIX is used to specify the **L** matrix	Default = identity matrix*	Default = zero matrix
Default = intercept matrix†	If MMATRIX is used to specify the **M** matrix	Default = zero matrix
Default = intercept matrix†	Default = identity matrix*	If KMATRIX is used to specify the **K** matrix

* The dimension of the identity matrix is the same as the number of dependent variables being studied.

† The intercept matrix is the matrix corresponding to the estimable function for the intercept term in the model, provided that the intercept term is included in the model. If the intercept term is not included in the model, the **L** matrix is not defined and this custom hypothesis test cannot be performed.

Example

```
GLM Y1 Y2 BY A B
 /LMATRIX = A 1 -1
 /DESIGN A B.
```

Assume that factor *A* has two levels.

- Since there are two dependent variables, this is a multivariate model with two main factor effects, *A* and *B*.
- A custom hypothesis test is requested by the LMATRIX subcommand.
- Since no MMATRIX or KMATRIX is specified. The **M** matrix is the default two-dimensional identity matrix, and the **K** matrix is a zero-row vector (0, 0).

For a repeated measures model, you can specify one, two, or all three of the **L**, **M**, and **K** matrices. If only one or two types are specified, the unspecified matrices use the defaults shown in Table 2 (read across the rows).

Table 2   Default matrices for repeated measures models if only one matrix is specified

L matrix	M matrix	K matrix
If LMATRIX is used to specify the **L** matrix	Default = average matrix[*]	Default = zero matrix
Default = intercept matrix[†]	If MMATRIX is used to specify the **M** matrix	Default = zero matrix
Default = intercept matrix[†]	Default = average matrix[*]	If KMATRIX is used to specify the **K** matrix

[*] The average matrix is the transformation matrix that corresponds to the transformation for the between-subjects test. The dimension is the number of measures.

[†] The intercept matrix is the matrix corresponding to the estimable function for the intercept term in the model, provided that the intercept term is included in the model. If the intercept term is not included in the model, the **L** matrix is not defined and this custom hypothesis test cannot be performed.

Example

```
GLM Y1 Y2 BY A B
 /WSFACTOR TIME (2)
 /MMATRIX Y1 1 Y2 1; Y1 1 Y2 -1
 /DESIGN A B.
```

- Since WSFACTOR is specified, this is a repeated measures model with two between-subjects factors *A* and *B*, and a within-subjects factor, *TIME*.

- A custom hypothesis is requested by the MMATRIX subcommand. The **M** matrix is a 2×2 matrix:

  1   1
  1   −1

- Since the **L** matrix and the **K** matrix are not specified, their defaults are used. The default for the **L** matrix is the matrix corresponding to the estimable function for the intercept term in the between-subjects model, and the default for the **K** matrix is a zero-row vector $(0, 0)$.

CONTRAST Subcommand

When the CONTRAST subcommand is used, an **L** matrix, which is used in custom hypothesis testing, is generated according to the contrast chosen. The **K** matrix is always taken to be the zero matrix. If the model is univariate or multivariate, the **M** matrix is always the identity matrix and its dimension is equal to the number of dependent variables. For a repeated measures model, the **M** matrix is always the average matrix that corresponds to the average transformation for the dependent variable.

GLM: Univariate

GLM is available in the Advanced Models option.

```
GLM dependent var [BY factor list [WITH covariate list]]

[/RANDOM=factor factor...]

[/REGWGT=varname]

[/METHOD=SSTYPE({1  })]
                {2  }
                {3**}
                {4  }

[/INTERCEPT=[INCLUDE**] [EXCLUDE]]

[/MISSING=[INCLUDE] [EXCLUDE**]]

[/CRITERIA=[EPS({1E-8**})][ALPHA({0.05**})]
               {a     }         {a      }

[/PRINT = [DESCRIPTIVE] [HOMOGENEITY] [PARAMETER][ETASQ]
          [GEF] [LOF] [OPOWER] [TEST(LMATRIX)]]

[/PLOT=[SPREADLEVEL] [RESIDUALS]
       [PROFILE (factor factor*factor factor*factor*factor ...)]

[/TEST=effect VS {linear combination [DF(df)]}]
                 {value DF (df)                }

[/LMATRIX={["label"] effect list effect list ...;...}]
          {["label"] effect list effect list ...     }
          {["label"] ALL list; ALL...                 }
          {["label"] ALL list                         }

[/KMATRIX= {number    }]
           {number;...}

[/CONTRAST (factor name)={DEVIATION[(refcat)]**       }]
                         {SIMPLE [(refcat)]           }
                         {DIFFERENCE                  }
                         {HELMERT                     }
                         {REPEATED                    }
                         {POLYNOMIAL   [({1,2,3...})]]}
                                        {metric  }
                         {SPECIAL (matrix)           }

[/POSTHOC =effect [effect...]
          ([SNK] [TUKEY] [BTUKEY][DUNCAN]
          [SCHEFFE] [DUNNETT(refcat)] [DUNNETTL(refcat)]
          [DUNNETTR(refcat)] [BONFERRONI] [LSD] [SIDAK]
          [GT2] [GABRIEL] [FREGW] [QREGW]  [T2] [T3] [GH] [C]
          [WALLER ({100** })])]
                   {kratio}
          [VS effect]

[/EMMEANS=TABLES({OVERALL          })]  [COMPARE ADJ(LSD(none)) (BONFERRONI) (SIDAK)]
                 {factor           }
                 {factor*factor...}

[/SAVE=[tempvar [(name)]] [tempvar [(name)]]...]

[/OUTFILE= [{COVB (filename)}] [EFFECT(filename)] [DESIGN(filename)]
            {CORB (filename)}
```

```
[/DESIGN={[INTERCEPT...]    }]
         {[effect effect...]}
```

** Default if subcommand or keyword is omitted.

Temporary variables (tempvar) are:

PRED, WPRED, RESID, WRESID, DRESID, ZRESID, SRESID, SEPRED, COOK, LEVER

Example

```
GLM YIELD BY SEED FERT
  /DESIGN.
```

Overview

This section describes the use of GLM for univariate analyses. However, most of the subcommands described here can be used in any type of analysis with GLM. For additional subcommands used in those types of analysis, see GLM: Multivariate and GLM: Repeated Measures. For basic specification, syntax rules, and limitations of the GLM procedures, see GLM: Overview. For examples, see the *SPSS Base Applications Guide*.

Options

Design Specification. You can specify which terms to include in the design on the DESIGN subcommand. This allows you to estimate a model other than the default full factorial model, incorporate factor-by-covariate interactions or covariate-by-covariate interactions, and indicate nesting of effects.

Contrast Types. You can specify contrasts other than the default deviation contrasts on the CONTRAST subcommand.

Optional Output. You can choose from a wide variety of optional output on the PRINT subcommand. Output appropriate to univariate designs includes descriptive statistics for each cell, parameter estimates, Levene's test for equality of variance across cells, partial eta-squared for each effect and each parameter estimate, the general estimable function matrix, and a contrast coefficients table (**L'** matrix). The OUTFILE subcommand allows you to write out the covariance or correlation matrix, the design matrix, or the statistics from the between-subjects ANOVA table into a separate SPSS data file.

Using the EMMEANS subcommand, you can request tables of estimated marginal means of the dependent variable and their standard deviations. The SAVE subcommand allows you to save predicted values and residuals in weighted or unweighted and standardized or unstandardized forms. You can specify different means comparison tests for comparing all possible pairs of cell means using the POSTHOC subcommand. In addition, you can specify your own hypothesis tests by specifying an **L** matrix and a **K** matrix to test the univariate hypothesis **LB = K**.

Basic Specification

- The basic specification is a variable list identifying the dependent variable, the factors (if any), and the covariates (if any).
- By default, GLM uses a model that includes the intercept term, the covariate (if any), and the full factorial model, which includes all main effects and all possible interactions among factors. The intercept term is excluded if it is excluded in the model by specifying the keyword EXCLUDE on the INTERCEPT subcommand. Sums of squares are calculated and hypothesis tests are performed using type-specific estimable functions. Parameters are estimated using the normal equation and a generalized inverse of the SSCP matrix.

Subcommand Order

- The variable list must be specified first.
- Subcommands can be used in any order.

Syntax Rules

- For many analyses, the GLM variable list and the DESIGN subcommand are the only specifications needed.
- If you do not enter a DESIGN subcommand, GLM will use a full factorial model, with main effects of covariates, if any.
- Minimum syntax—at least one dependent variable must be specified, and at least one of the following must be specified: INTERCEPT, a between-subjects factor, or a covariate. The design contains the intercept by default.
- If more than one DESIGN subcommand is specified, only the last one is in effect.
- Dependent variables and covariates must be numeric, but factors can be numeric or string variables.
- If a string variable is specified as a factor, only the first eight characters of each value are used in distinguishing among values.
- If more than one MISSING subcommand is specified, only the last one is in effect.
- The following words are reserved as keywords or internal commands in the GLM procedure:
  INTERCEPT, BY, WITH, ALL, OVERALL, WITHIN

  Variable names that duplicate these words should be changed before you run GLM.

Limitations

- Any number of factors can be specified, but if the number of between-subjects factors plus the number of split variables exceeds 18, the Descriptive Statistics table is not printed even when you request it.

- Memory requirements depend primarily on the number of cells in the design. For the default full factorial model, this equals the product of the number of levels or categories in each factor.

Example

```
GLM YIELD BY SEED FERT WITH RAINFALL
  /PRINT=DESCRIPTIVE PARAMETER
  /DESIGN.
```

- *YIELD* is the dependent variable; *SEED* and *FERT* are factors; *RAINFALL* is a covariate.
- The PRINT subcommand requests the descriptive statistics for the dependent variable for each cell and the parameter estimates, in addition to the default tables Between-Subjects Factors and Univariate Tests.
- The DESIGN subcommand requests the default design, a full factorial model with a covariate. This subcommand could have been omitted or could have been specified in full as

```
/DESIGN = INTERCEPT RAINFALL, SEED, FERT, SEED BY FERT.
```

GLM Variable List

The variable list specifies the dependent variable, the factors, and the covariates in the model.
- The dependent variable must be the first specification on GLM.
- The names of the factors follow the dependent variable. Use the keyword BY to separate the factors from the dependent variable.
- Enter the covariates, if any, following the factors. Use the keyword WITH to separate covariates from factors (if any) and the dependent variable.

Example

```
GLM DEPENDNT BY FACTOR1 FACTOR2, FACTOR3.
```

- In this example, three factors are specified.
- A default full factorial model is used for the analysis.

Example

```
GLM Y BY A WITH X
  /DESIGN.
```

- In this example, the DESIGN subcommand requests the default design, which includes the intercept term, the covariate *X* and the factor *A*.

RANDOM Subcommand

RANDOM allows you to specify which effects in your design are random. When the RANDOM subcommand is used, a table of expected mean squares for all effects in the design is displayed, and an appropriate error term for testing each effect is calculated and used automatically.
- Random always implies a univariate mixed-model analysis.

- If you specify an effect on RANDOM, higher-order effects containing the specified effect (excluding any effects containing covariates) are automatically treated as random effects.
- The keyword INTERCEPT and effects containing covariates are not allowed on this subcommand.
- The RANDOM subcommand cannot be used if there is any within-subjects factor in the model (that is, RANDOM cannot be specified if WSFACTOR is specified).
- When the RANDOM subcommand is used, the appropriate error terms for the hypothesis testing of all effects in the model are automatically computed and used.
- More than one RANDOM subcommand is allowed. The specifications are accumulated.

Example

```
GLM DEP BY A B
  /RANDOM = B
  /DESIGN = A,B, A*B.
```

- In the example, effects *B* and *A*B* are considered as random effects. Notice that if only effect *B* is specified in the RANDOM subcommand, *A*B* is automatically considered as a random effect.
- The hypothesis testing for each effect (*A*, *B*, and *A*B*) in the design will be carried out using the appropriate error term, which is calculated automatically.

REGWGT Subcommand

The only specification on REGWGT is the name of the variable containing the weights to be used in estimating a weighted least-squares model.

- Specify a numeric weight variable name following the REGWGT subcommand. Only observations with positive values in the weight variable will be used in the analysis.
- If more than one REGWGT subcommand is specified, only the last one is in effect.

Example

```
GLM OUTCOME BY TREATMNT
  /REGWGT WT.
```

- The procedure performs a weighted least-squares analysis. The variable *WT* is used as the weight variable.

METHOD Subcommand

METHOD controls the computational aspects of the GLM analysis. You can specify one of four different methods for partitioning the sums of squares. If more than one METHOD subcommand is specified, only the last one is in effect.

SSTYPE(1)   *Type I sum-of-squares method.* The Type I sum-of-squares method is also known as the hierarchical decomposition of the sum-of-squares method. Each term is adjusted only for the terms that precede it on the DESIGN subcommand. Under a balanced design, it is an orthogonal decomposition, and the sums of squares in the model add up to the total sum of squares.

SSTYPE(2)   *Type II sum-of-squares method.* This method calculates the sum of squares of an effect in the model adjusted for all other "appropriate" effects. An appropriate effect is one that corresponds to all effects that do not *contain* the effect being examined.

For any two effects *F1* and *F2* in the model, *F1* is said to be **contained** in *F2* under the following three conditions:
- Both effects *F1* and *F2* have the same covariate, if any.
- *F2* consists of more factors than *F1*.
- All factors in *F1* also appear in *F2*.

The intercept effect is treated as contained in all the pure factor effects. However, it is not contained in any effect involving a covariate. No effect is contained in the intercept effect. Thus, for any one effect *F* of interest, all other effects in the model can be classified as in one of the following two groups: the effects that do not contain *F* or the effects that contain *F*.

If the model is a main-effects design (that is, only main effects are in the model), the Type II sum-of-squares method is equivalent to the regression approach sums of squares. This means that each main effect is adjusted for every other term in the model.

SSTYPE(3)   *Type III sum-of-squares method.* This is the default. This method calculates the sum of squares of an effect *F* in the design as the sum of squares adjusted for any other effects that do not contain it, and *orthogonal* to any effects (if any) that contain it. The Type III sums of squares have one major advantage—they are invariant with respect to the cell frequencies as long as the general form of estimability remains constant. Hence, this type of sums of squares is often used for an unbalanced model with no missing cells. In a factorial design with no missing cells, this method is equivalent to the Yates' weighted squares of means technique, and it also coincides with the overparameterized Σ-restricted model.

SSTYPE(4)   *Type IV sum-of-squares method.* This method is designed for a situation in which there are missing cells. For any effect *F* in the design, if *F* is not contained in any other effect, then Type IV = Type III = Type II. When *F* is contained in other effects, then Type IV distributes the contrasts being made among the parameters in *F* to all higher-level effects equitably.

Example

```
GLM DEP BY A B C
  /METHOD=SSTYPE(3)
  /DESIGN=A, B, C.
```

- The design is a main-effects model.

- The METHOD subcommand requests that the model be fitted with Type III sums of squares.

INTERCEPT Subcommand

INTERCEPT controls whether an intercept term is included in the model. If more than one IN-TERCEPT subcommand is specified, only the last one is in effect.

INCLUDE   *Include the intercept term.* The intercept (constant) term is included in the model. This is the default.

EXCLUDE   *Exclude the intercept term.* The intercept term is excluded from the model. Specification of the keyword INTERCEPT on the DESIGN subcommand overrides INTERCEPT = EXCLUDE.

MISSING Subcommand

By default, cases with missing values for any of the variables on the GLM variable list are excluded from the analysis. The MISSING subcommand allows you to include cases with user-missing values.

- If MISSING is not specified, the default is EXCLUDE.
- Pairwise deletion of missing data is not available in GLM.
- Keywords INCLUDE and EXCLUDE are mutually exclusive.
- If more than one MISSING subcommand is specified, only the last one is in effect.

EXCLUDE   *Exclude both user-missing and system-missing values.* This is the default when MISSING is not specified.

INCLUDE   *User-missing values are treated as valid.* System-missing values cannot be included in the analysis.

CRITERIA Subcommand

CRITERIA controls the statistical criteria used to build the models.

- More than one CRITERIA subcommand is allowed. The specifications are accumulated. Conflicts across CRITERIA subcommands are resolved using the conflicting specification given on the last CRITERIA subcommand.
- The keyword must be followed by a positive number in parentheses.

EPS(n)   *The tolerance level in redundancy detection.* This value is used for redundancy checking in the design matrix. The default value is 1E-8.

ALPHA(n)   *The alpha level.* This keyword has two functions. First, it gives the alpha level at which the power is calculated for the F test. Once the noncentrality parameter for the alternative hypothesis is estimated from the data, then the power is the probability that the test statistic is greater than the critical value under the alternative hypothesis. (The observed power is displayed by default for GLM.) The second function of alpha is to specify the level of the confidence interval. If the alpha level specified is n, the value $(1 - n) \times 100$ indicates the level of confidence for all individual and simultaneous confidence intervals generated for the specified model. The value of n must be between 0 and 1, exclusive. The default value of alpha is 0.05. This means that the default power calculation is at the 0.05 level, and the default level of the confidence intervals is 95%, since $(1 - 0.05) \times 100 = 95$.

PRINT Subcommand

PRINT controls the display of optional output.

- Some PRINT output applies to the entire GLM procedure and is displayed only once.
- Additional output can be obtained on the EMMEANS, PLOT, and SAVE subcommands.
- Some optional output may greatly increase the processing time. Request only the output you want to see.
- If no PRINT command is specified, default output for a univariate analysis includes a factor information table and a Univariate Tests table (ANOVA) for all effects in the model.
- If more than one PRINT subcommand is specified, only the last one is in effect.

The following keywords are available for GLM univariate analyses. For information on PRINT specifications appropriate for other GLM models, see GLM: Multivariate and GLM: Repeated Measures.

DESCRIPTIVES
Basic information about each cell in the design. Observed means, standard deviations, and counts for the dependent variable in all cells. The cells are constructed from the highest-order crossing of the between-subjects factors. For a multivariate model, statistics are given for each dependent variable. If the number of between-subjects factors plus the number of split variables exceeds 18, the Descriptive Statistics table is not printed.

HOMOGENEITY
Tests of homogeneity of variance. Levene's test for equality of variances for the dependent variable across all level combinations of the between-subjects factors. If there are no between-subjects factors, this keyword is not valid. For a multivariate model, tests are displayed for each dependent variable.

PARAMETER
Parameter estimates. Parameter estimates, standard errors, t tests, and confidence intervals.

ETASQ
Partial eta-squared (η^2). This value is an overestimate of the actual effect size in an F test. It is defined as

$$\text{partial eta-squared} = \frac{dfh \times F}{dfh \times F + dfe}$$

where F is the test statistic and dfh and dfe are its degrees of freedom and degrees of freedom for error. The keyword EFSIZE can be used in place of ETASQ.

GEF
General estimable function table. This table shows the general form of the estimable functions.

LOF   *Perform a lack-of-fit test (which requires at least one cell to have multiple observations).* If the test is rejected, it implies that the current model cannot adequately account for the relationship between the response variable and the predictors. Either a variable is omitted or extra terms are needed in the model.

OPOWER   *Observed power for each test.* The observed power gives the probability that the F test would detect a population difference between groups equal to that implied by the sample difference.

TEST(LMATRIX)   *Set of contrast coefficients (L) matrices.* The transpose of the **L** matrix (**L'**) is displayed. This set always includes one matrix displaying the estimable function for each between-subjects effect appearing or implied in the DESIGN subcommand. Also, any **L** matrices generated by the LMATRIX or CONTRAST subcommands are displayed. TEST(ESTIMABLE) can be used in place of TEST(LMATRIX).

Example

```
GLM DEP BY A B WITH COV
  /PRINT=DESCRIPTIVE, TEST(LMATRIX), PARAMETER
  /DESIGN.
```

- Since the design in the DESIGN subcommand is not specified, the default design is used. In this case, the design includes the intercept term, the covariate *COV*, and the full factorial terms of *A* and *B*, which are *A*, *B*, and *A*B*.

- For each combination of levels of *A* and *B*, SPSS displays the descriptive statistics of *DEP*.

- The set of **L** matrices that generates the sums of squares for testing each effect in the design is displayed.

- The parameter estimates, their standard errors, *t* tests, confidence intervals, and the observed power for each test are displayed.

PLOT Subcommand

PLOT provides a variety of plots useful in checking the assumptions needed in the analysis. The PLOT subcommand can be specified more than once. All of the plots requested on each PLOT subcommand are produced.

Use the following keywords on the PLOT subcommand to request plots:

SPREADLEVEL   *Spread-versus-level plots.* Plots of observed cell means versus standard deviations, and versus variances.

RESIDUALS   *Observed by predicted by standardized residuals plot.* A plot is produced for each dependent variable. In a univariate analysis, a plot is produced for the single dependent variable.

PROFILE   *Line plots of dependent variable means for one-way, two-way, or three-way crossed factors.* The PROFILE keyword must be followed by parentheses containing a list of one or more factor combinations. All factors specified (either individual or crossed) must be made up of only valid factors on the factor list. Factor combinations on the PROFILE keyword may use an asterisk

(*) or the keyword BY to specify crossed factors. A factor cannot occur in a single factor combination more than once.

The order of factors in a factor combination is important, and there is no restriction on the order of factors. If a single factor is specified after the PROFILE keyword, a line plot of estimated means at each level of the factor is produced. If a two-way crossed factor combination is specified, the output includes a multiple-line plot of estimated means at each level of the first specified factor, with a separate line drawn for each level of the second specified factor. If a three-way crossed factor combination is specified, the output includes multiple-line plots of estimated means at each level of the first specified factor, with separate lines for each level of the second factor, and separate plots for each level of the third factor.

Example

```
GLM DEP BY A B
  /PLOT = SPREADLEVEL PROFILE(A A*B A*B*C)
  /DESIGN.
```

Assume each of the factors A, B, and C has three levels.

- Spread-versus-level plots are produced showing observed cell means versus standard deviations and observed cell means versus variances.

- Five profile plots are produced. For factor A, a line plot of estimated means at each level of A is produced (one plot). For the two-way crossed factor combination A*B, a multiple-line plot of estimated means at each level of A, with a separate line for each level of B, is produced (one plot). For the three-way crossed factor combination A*B*C, a multiple-line plot of estimated means at each level of A, with a separate line for each level of B, is produced for each of the three levels of C (three plots).

TEST Subcommand

The TEST subcommand allows you to test a hypothesis term against a specified error term.

- TEST is valid only for univariate analyses. Multiple TEST subcommands are allowed, each executed independently.

- You must specify both the hypothesis term and the error term. There is no default.

- The hypothesis term is specified before the keyword VS. It must be a valid effect specified or implied on the DESIGN subcommand.

- The error term is specified after the keyword VS. You can specify either a linear combination or a value. The linear combination of effects takes the general form: coefficient*effect +/- coefficient*effect ...

- All effects in the linear combination must be specified or implied on the DESIGN subcommand. Effects specified or implied on DESIGN but not listed after VS are assumed to have a coefficient of 0.

- Duplicate effects are allowed. GLM adds coefficients associated with the same effect before performing the test. For example, the linear combination 5*A-0.9*B-A will be combined to 4*A-0.9B.

- A coefficient can be specified as a fraction with a positive denominator—for example, 1/3 or –1/3, but 1/–3 is invalid.
- If you specify a value for the error term, you must specify the degrees of freedom after the keyword DF. The degrees of freedom must be a positive real number. DF and the degrees of freedom are optional for a linear combination.

Example

```
GLM DEP BY A B
  /TEST = A VS B + A*B
  /DESIGN = A, B, A*B.
```

- *A* is tested against the pooled effect of *B + A*B*.

LMATRIX Subcommand

The LMATRIX subcommand allows you to customize your hypotheses tests by specifying the **L** matrix (contrast coefficients matrix) in the general form of the linear hypothesis **LB = K**, where **K = 0** if it is not specified on the KMATRIX subcommand. The vector **B** is the parameter vector in the linear model.

- The basic format for the LMATRIX subcommand is an optional label in quotes, an effect name or the keyword ALL, and a list of real numbers. There can be multiple effect names (or the keyword ALL) and number lists.
- The optional label is a string with a maximum length of 255 characters. Only one label can be specified.
- Only valid effects appearing or implied on the DESIGN subcommand can be specified on the LMATRIX subcommand.
- The length of the list of real numbers must be equal to the number of parameters (including the redundant ones) corresponding to that effect. For example, if the effect *A*B* takes up six columns in the design matrix, then the list after *A*B* must contain exactly six numbers.
- A number can be specified as a fraction with a positive denominator—for example, 1/3 or –1/3, but 1/–3 is invalid.
- A semicolon (;) indicates the end of a row in the **L** matrix.
- When ALL is specified, the length of the list that follows ALL is equal to the total number of parameters (including the redundant ones) in the model.
- Effects appearing or implied on the DESIGN subcommand but not specified here are assumed to have entries of 0 in the corresponding columns of the **L** matrix.
- Multiple LMATRIX subcommands are allowed. Each is treated independently.

Example

```
GLM DEP BY A B
  /LMATRIX = "B1 vs B2 at A1"
             B 1 -1 0 A*B 1 -1
  /LMATRIX = "Effect A"
             A 1 0 -1
             A*B 1/3   1/3   1/3
                  0     0     0
                -1/3 -1/3 -1/3;
             A 0 1 -1
```

```
         A*B  0    0    0
              1/3  1/3  1/3
             -1/3 -1/3 -1/3
/LMATRIX = "B1 vs B2 at A2"
         ALL  0
              0  0  0
              1 -1  0
              0  0  0  1 -1  0  0  0  0
/DESIGN = A, B, A*B.
```

Assume that factors *A* and *B* each have three levels. There are three LMATRIX subcommands; each is treated independently.

- **B1 versus B2 at A1.** In the first LMATRIX subcommand, the difference is tested between levels 1 and 2 of effect *B* when effect *A* is fixed at level 1. Since there are three levels each in effects *A* and *B*, the interaction effect *A*B* should take up nine columns in the design matrix. Notice that only the first two columns of *A*B* are specified with values 1 and –1; the rest are all assumed to be 0. Columns corresponding to effect *B* are all assumed to be 0.

- **Effect A.** In the second LMATRIX subcommand, effect *A* is tested. Since there are three levels in effect *A*, at most two independent contrasts can be formed; thus, there are two rows in the **L** matrix, which are separated by a semicolon (;). The first row tests the difference between levels 1 and 3 of effect *A*, while the second row tests the difference between levels 2 and 3 of effect *A*.

- **B1 versus B2 at A2.** In the last LMATRIX subcommand, the keyword ALL is used. The first 0 corresponds to the intercept effect; the next three zeros correspond to effect *A*.

KMATRIX Subcommand

The KMATRIX subcommand allows you to customize your hypothesis tests by specifying the **K** matrix (contrast results matrix) in the general form of the linear hypothesis **LB** = **K**. The vector **B** is the parameter vector in the linear model.

- The default **K** matrix is a zero matrix; that is, **LB** = 0 is assumed.

- For the KMATRIX subcommand to be valid, at least one of the following subcommands must be specified: the LMATRIX subcommand or the INTERCEPT = INCLUDE subcommand.

- If KMATRIX is specified but LMATRIX is not specified, the LMATRIX is assumed to take the row vector corresponding to the intercept in the estimable function, provided the subcommand INTERCEPT = INCLUDE is specified. In this case, the **K** matrix can be only a scalar matrix.

- If KMATRIX and LMATRIX are specified, then the number of rows in the requested **K** and **L** matrices must be equal. If there are multiple LMATRIX subcommands, then all requested **L** matrices must have the same number of rows, and **K** must have the same number of rows as these **L** matrices.

- A semicolon (;) can be used to indicate the end of a row in the **K** matrix.

- If more than one KMATRIX subcommand is specified, only the last one is in effect.

Example

```
GLM DEP BY A B
  /LMATRIX = "Effect A"
                A 1  0 -1; A 1 -1  0
  /LMATRIX = "Effect B"
                B 1  0 -1; B 1 -1  0
  /KMATRIX = 0; 0
  /DESIGN = A B.
```

In this example, assume that factors *A* and *B* each have three levels.

- There are two LMATRIX subcommands; both have two rows.
- The first LMATRIX subcommand tests whether the effect of *A* is 0, while the second LMATRIX subcommand tests whether the effect of *B* is 0.
- The KMATRIX subcommand specifies that the **K** matrix also has two rows, each with value 0.

CONTRAST Subcommand

CONTRAST specifies the type of contrast desired among the levels of a factor. For a factor with *k* levels or values, the contrast type determines the meaning of its $k - 1$ degrees of freedom.

- Specify the factor name in parentheses following the subcommand CONTRAST.
- You can specify only one factor per CONTRAST subcommand, but you can enter multiple CONTRAST subcommands.
- After closing the parentheses, enter an equals sign followed by one of the contrast keywords.
- This subcommand creates an **L** matrix such that the columns corresponding to the factor match the contrast given. The other columns are adjusted so that the **L** matrix is estimable.

The following contrast types are available:

DEVIATION *Deviations from the grand mean.* This is the default for between-subjects factors. Each level of the factor except one is compared to the grand mean. One category (by default, the last) must be omitted so that the effects will be independent of one another. To omit a category other than the last, specify the number of the omitted category (which is not necessarily the same as its value) in parentheses after the keyword DEVIATION. For example,

```
GLM Y BY B
  /CONTRAST(B)=DEVIATION(1).
```

Suppose factor *B* has three levels, with values 2, 4, and 6. The specified contrast omits the first category, in which *B* has the value 2. Deviation contrasts are not orthogonal.

POLYNOMIAL *Polynomial contrasts.* This is the default for within-subjects factors. The first degree of freedom contains the linear effect across the levels of the factor, the second contains the quadratic effect, and so on. In a balanced design, polynomial contrasts are orthogonal. By default, the levels are assumed to be equally spaced; you can specify unequal spacing by entering a metric consisting of one integer for each level of the factor in parentheses after the keyword POLYNOMIAL. (All metrics specified cannot be equal; thus, $(1, 1, \ldots 1)$ is not valid.) For example,

```
GLM RESPONSE BY STIMULUS
   /CONTRAST(STIMULUS) = POLYNOMIAL(1,2,4).
```

Suppose that factor *STIMULUS* has three levels. The specified contrast indicates that the three levels of *STIMULUS* are actually in the proportion 1:2:4. The default metric is always $(1, 2, \ldots k)$, where k levels are involved. Only the relative differences between the terms of the metric matter $(1, 2, 4)$ is the same metric as $(2, 3, 5)$ or $(20, 30, 50)$ because, in each instance, the difference between the second and third numbers is twice the difference between the first and second.

DIFFERENCE   *Difference or reverse Helmert contrasts.* Each level of the factor except the first is compared to the mean of the previous levels. In a balanced design, difference contrasts are orthogonal.

HELMERT   *Helmert contrasts.* Each level of the factor except the last is compared to the mean of subsequent levels. In a balanced design, Helmert contrasts are orthogonal.

SIMPLE   *Each level of the factor except the last is compared to the last level.* To use a category other than the last as the omitted reference category, specify its number (which is not necessarily the same as its value) in parentheses following the keyword SIMPLE. For example,

```
GLM Y BY B
   /CONTRAST(B)=SIMPLE(1).
```

Suppose that factor *B* has three levels with values 2, 4, and 6. The specified contrast compares the other levels to the first level of *B*, in which *B* has the value 2. Simple contrasts are not orthogonal.

REPEATED   *Comparison of adjacent levels.* Each level of the factor except the first is compared to the previous level. Repeated contrasts are not orthogonal.

SPECIAL   *A user-defined contrast.* Values specified after this keyword are stored in a matrix in column major order. For example, if factor *A* has three levels, then CONTRAST(A)= SPECIAL(1 1 1 -1 0 0 1 -1) produces the following contrast matrix:

$$
\begin{matrix}
1 & 1 & 0 \\
1 & -1 & 1 \\
1 & 0 & -1
\end{matrix}
$$

Orthogonal contrasts are particularly useful. In a balanced design, contrasts are orthogonal if the sum of the coefficients in each contrast row is 0 and if, for any pair of contrast rows, the products of corresponding coefficients sum to 0. DIFFERENCE, HELMERT, and POLYNOMIAL contrasts always meet these criteria in balanced designs.

Example

```
GLM DEP BY FAC
  /CONTRAST(FAC)=DIFFERENCE
  /DESIGN.
```

- Suppose that the factor *FAC* has five categories and therefore four degrees of freedom.
- CONTRAST requests DIFFERENCE contrasts, which compare each level (except the first) with the mean of the previous levels.

POSTHOC Subcommand

POSTHOC allows you to produce multiple comparisons between means of a factor. These comparisons are usually not planned at the beginning of the study but are suggested by the data in the course of study.

- Post hoc tests are computed for the dependent variable. The alpha value used in the tests can be specified by using the keyword ALPHA on the CRITERIA subcommand. The default alpha value is 0.05. The confidence level for any confidence interval constructed is $(1 - \alpha) \times 100$. The default confidence level is 95. For a multivariate model, tests are computed for all dependent variables specified.
- Only between-subjects factors appearing in the factor list are valid in this subcommand. Individual factors can be specified.
- You can specify one or more effects to be tested. Only fixed main effects appearing or implied on the DESIGN subcommand are valid test effects.
- Optionally, you can specify an effect defining the error term following the keyword VS after the test specification. The error effect can be any single effect in the design that is not the intercept or a main effect named on a POSTHOC subcommand.
- A variety of multiple comparison tests are available. Some tests are designed for detecting homogeneity subsets among the groups of means, some are designed for pairwise comparisons among all means, and some can be used for both purposes.
- For tests that are used for detecting homogeneity subsets of means, non-empty group means are sorted in ascending order. Means that are not significantly different are included together to form a homogeneity subset. The significance for each homogeneity subset of means is displayed. In a case where the numbers of valid cases are not equal in all groups, for most post hoc tests, the harmonic mean of the group sizes is used as the sample size in the calculation. For QREGW or FREGW, individual sample sizes are used.
- For tests that are used for pairwise comparisons, the display includes the difference between each pair of compared means, the confidence interval for the difference, and the significance. The sample sizes of the two groups being compared are used in the calculation.
- Output for tests specified on the POSTHOC subcommand are available according to their statistical purposes. The following table illustrates the statistical purpose of the post hoc tests:

Post Hoc Tests	Statistical Purpose	
Keyword	Homogeneity Subsets Detection	Pairwise Comparison and Confidence Interval
LSD		Yes
SIDAK		Yes
BONFERRONI		Yes
GH		Yes
T2		Yes
T3		Yes
C		Yes
DUNNETT		Yes*
DUNNETTL		Yes*
DUNNETTR		Yes*
SNK	Yes	
BTUKEY	Yes	
DUNCAN	Yes	
QREGW	Yes	
FREGW	Yes	
WALLER	Yes†	
TUKEY	Yes	Yes
SCHEFFE	Yes	Yes
GT2	Yes	Yes
GABRIEL	Yes	Yes

* Only C.I.'s for differences between test group means and control group means are given.

† No significance for Waller test is given.

- Tests that are designed for homogeneity subset detection display the detected homogeneity subsets and their corresponding significances.
- Tests that are designed for both homogeneity subset detection and pairwise comparisons display both kinds of output.
- For the DUNNETT, DUNNETTL, and DUNNETTR keywords, only individual factors can be specified.
- The default reference category for DUNNETT, DUNNETTL, and DUNNETTR is the last category. An integer greater than 0 within parentheses can be used to specify a different reference category. For example, POSTHOC = A (DUNNETT(2)) requests a DUNNETT test for factor A, using the second level of A as the reference category.
- The keywords DUNCAN, DUNNETT, DUNNETTL, and DUNNETTR must be spelled out in full; using the first three characters alone is not sufficient.
- If the REGWGT subcommand is specified, weighted means are used in performing post hoc tests.

- Multiple POSTHOC subcommands are allowed. Each specification is executed independently so that you can test different effects against different error terms.

SNK	*Student-Newman-Keuls procedure based on the Studentized range test.*
TUKEY	*Tukey's honestly significant difference.* This test uses the Studentized range statistic to make all pairwise comparisons between groups.
BTUKEY	*Tukey's b.* Multiple comparison procedure based on the average of Studentized range tests.
DUNCAN	*Duncan's multiple comparison procedure based on the Studentized range test.*
SCHEFFE	*Scheffé's multiple comparison t test.*
DUNNETT(refcat)	*Dunnett's two-tailed t test.* Each level of the factor is compared to a reference category. A reference category can be specified in parentheses. The default reference category is the last category. This keyword must be spelled out in full.
DUNNETTL(refcat)	*Dunnett's one-tailed t test.* This test indicates whether the mean at any level (except the reference category) of the factor is *smaller* than that of the reference category. A reference category can be specified in parentheses. The default reference category is the last category. This keyword must be spelled out in full.
DUNNETTR(refcat)	*Dunnett's one-tailed t test.* This test indicates whether the mean at any level (except the reference category) of the factor is *larger* than that of the reference category. A reference category can be specified in parentheses. The default reference category is the last category. This keyword must be spelled out in full.
BONFERRONI	*Bonferroni t test.* This test is based on Student's *t* statistic and adjusts the observed significance level for the fact that multiple comparisons are made.
LSD	*Least significant difference t test.* Equivalent to multiple *t* tests between all pairs of groups. This test does not control the overall probability of rejecting the hypotheses that some pairs of means are different, while in fact they are equal.
SIDAK	*Sidak t test.* This test provides tighter bounds than the Bonferroni test.
GT2	*Hochberg's GT2.* Pairwise comparisons test based on the Studentized maximum modulus test. Unless the cell sizes are extremely unbalanced, this test is fairly robust even for unequal variances.
GABRIEL	*Gabriel's pairwise comparisons test based on the Studentized maximum modulus test.*
FREGW	*Ryan-Einot-Gabriel-Welsch's multiple stepdown procedure based on an F test.*

QREGW	*Ryan-Einot-Gabriel-Welsch's multiple stepdown procedure based on the Studentized range test.*
T2	*Tamhane's T2.* Tamhane's pairwise comparisons test based on a *t* test. This test can be applied in situations where the variances are unequal.
T3	*Dunnett's T3.* Pairwise comparisons test based on the Studentized maximum modulus. This test is appropriate when the variances are unequal.
GH	*Games and Howell's pairwise comparisons test based on the Studentized range test.* This test can be applied in situations where the variances are unequal.
C	*Dunnett's C.* Pairwise comparisons based on the weighted average of Studentized ranges. This test can be applied in situations where the variances are unequal.
WALLER(kratio)	*Waller-Duncan t test.* This test uses a Bayesian approach. It is restricted to cases with equal sample sizes. For cases with unequal sample sizes, the harmonic mean of the sample size is used. The kratio is the Type 1/Type 2 error seriousness ratio. The default value is 100. You can specify an integer greater than 1 within parentheses.

EMMEANS Subcommand

EMMEANS displays estimated marginal means of the dependent variable in the cells (with covariates held at their overall mean value) and their standard errors for the specified factors. Note that these are predicted, not observed, means. The estimated marginal means are calculated using a modified definition by Searle, Speed, and Milliken (1980).

- TABLES, followed by an option in parentheses, is required. COMPARE is optional; if specified, it must follow TABLES.

- Multiple EMMEANS subcommands are allowed. Each is treated independently.

- If redundant EMMEANS subcommands are specified, only the last redundant subcommand is in effect. EMMEANS subcommands are redundant if the option specified on TABLES is the same (including redundant crossed factor combinations—for example, *A*B* and *B*A*).

TABLES(option)	*Table specification.* Valid options are the keyword OVERALL, factors appearing on the factor list, and crossed factors constructed of factors on the factor list. Crossed factors can be specified using an asterisk (*) or the keyword BY. All factors in a crossed factor specification must be unique.
	If OVERALL is specified, the estimated marginal means of the dependent variable are displayed, collapsing over between-subjects factors.
	If a between-subjects factor, or a crossing of between-subjects factors, is specified on the TABLES keyword, GLM collapses over any other between-subjects factors before computing the estimated marginal

means for the dependent variable. For a multivariate model, GLM collapses over any other between- or within-subjects factors.

COMPARE(factor) ADJ(method)

Main- or simple-main-effects omnibus tests and pairwise comparisons of the dependent variable. This option gives the mean difference, standard error, significance, and confidence interval for each pair of levels for the effect specified in the TABLES command, as well as an omnibus test for that effect. If only one factor is specified on TABLES, COMPARE can be specified by itself; otherwise, the factor specification is required. In this case, levels of the specified factor are compared with each other for each level of the other factors in the interaction.

The optional ADJ keyword allows you to apply an adjustment to the confidence intervals and significance values to account for multiple comparisons. Methods available are LSD (no adjustment), BONFERRONI, or SIDAK.

Example

```
GLM DEP BY A B
  /EMMEANS = TABLES(A*B) COMPARE(A)
  /DESIGN.
```

- The output of this analysis includes a pairwise comparisons table for the dependent variable *DEP*.
- Assume that *A* has three levels and *B* has two levels. The first level of *A* is compared with the second and third levels, the second level with the first and third levels, and the third level with the first and second levels. The pairwise comparison is repeated for the two levels of *B*.

SAVE Subcommand

Use SAVE to add one or more residual or fit values to the working data file.

- Specify one or more temporary variables, each followed by an optional new name in parentheses. For a multivariate model, you can optionally specify a new name for the temporary variable related to each dependent variable.
- WPRED and WRESID can be saved only if REGWGT has been specified.
- Specifying a temporary variable on this subcommand results in a variable being added to the active data file for each dependent variable.
- You can specify variable names for the temporary variables. These names must be unique, valid variable names. For a multivariate model, there should be as many variable names specified as there are dependent variables, listed in the order of the dependent variables as specified on the GLM command. If you do not specify enough variable names, default variable names are used for any remaining variables.
- If new names are not specified, GLM generates a rootname using a shortened form of the temporary variable name with a suffix. For a multivariate model, the suffix _*n* is added to

the temporary variable name, where n is the ordinal number of the dependent variable as specified on the GLM command.

- If more than one SAVE subcommand is specified, only the last one is in effect.

PRED   *Unstandardized predicted values.*

WPRED   *Weighted unstandardized predicted values.* Available only if REGWGT has been specified.

RESID   *Unstandardized residuals.*

WRESID   *Weighted unstandardized residuals.* Available only if REGWGT has been specified.

DRESID   *Deleted residuals.*

ZRESID   *Standardized residuals.*

SRESID   *Studentized residuals.*

SEPRED   *Standard errors of predicted value.*

COOK   *Cook's distances.*

LEVER   *Uncentered leverage values.*

OUTFILE Subcommand

The OUTFILE subcommand writes an SPSS data file that can be used in other procedures.

- You must specify a keyword on OUTFILE. There is no default.
- You must specify a filename in parentheses after a keyword. A filename with a path must be enclosed within quotation marks. The asterisk (*) is not allowed.
- If you specify more than one keyword, a different filename is required for each.
- If more than one OUTFILE subcommand is specified, only the last one is in effect.
- For COVB or CORB, the output will contain, in addition to the covariance or correlation matrix, three rows for each dependent variable: a row of parameter estimates, a row of residual degrees of freedom, and a row of significance values for the t statistics corresponding to the parameter estimates. All statistics are displayed separately by split.

COVB (filename)   *Writes the parameter covariance matrix.*

CORB (filename)   *Writes the parameter correlation matrix.*

EFFECT (filename)   *Writes the statistics from the between-subjects ANOVA table.* Invalid for repeated measures analyses.

DESIGN (filename)   *Writes the design matrix.* The number of rows equals the number of cases, and the number of columns equals the number of parameters. The variable names are *DES_1, DES_2, ..., DES_p*, where p is the number of the parameters.

DESIGN Subcommand

DESIGN specifies the effects included in a specific model. The cells in a design are defined by all of the possible combinations of levels of the factors in that design. The number of cells equals the product of the number of levels of all the factors. A design is *balanced* if each cell contains the same number of cases. GLM can analyze both balanced and unbalanced designs.

- Specify a list of terms to be included in the model, separated by spaces or commas.

- The default design, if the DESIGN subcommand is omitted or is specified by itself, is a design consisting of the following terms in order: the intercept term (if INTERCEPT=INCLUDE is specified), next the covariates given in the covariate list, and then the full factorial model defined by all factors on the factor list and excluding the intercept.

- To include a term for the main effect of a factor, enter the name of the factor on the DESIGN subcommand.

- To include the intercept term in the design, use the keyword INTERCEPT on the DESIGN subcommand. If INTERCEPT is specified on the DESIGN subcommand, the subcommand INTERCEPT=EXCLUDE is overridden.

- To include a term for an interaction between factors, use the keyword BY or the asterisk (*) to join the factors involved in the interaction. For example, *A*B* means a two-way interaction effect of *A* and *B*, where *A* and *B* are factors. *A*A* is not allowed because factors inside an interaction effect must be distinct.

- To include a term for nesting one effect within another, use the keyword WITHIN or a pair of parentheses on the DESIGN subcommand. For example, *A(B)* means that *A* is nested within *B*. The expression *A(B)* is equivalent to the expression *A WITHIN B*. When more than one pair of parentheses is present, each pair of parentheses must be enclosed or nested within another pair of parentheses. Thus, *A(B)(C)* is not valid.

- Multiple nesting is allowed. For example, *A(B(C))* means that *B* is nested within *C*, and *A* is nested within *B(C)*.

- Interactions between nested effects are not valid. For example, neither *A(C)*B(C)* nor *A(C)*B(D)* is valid.

- To include a covariate term in the design, enter the name of the covariate on the DESIGN subcommand.

- Covariates can be connected, but not nested, through the * operator to form another covariate effect. Therefore, interactions among covariates such as *X1*X1* and *X1*X2* are valid, but not *X1(X2)*. Using covariate effects such as *X1*X1*, *X1*X1*X1*, *X1*X2*, and *X1*X1*X2*X2* makes fitting a polynomial regression model easy in GLM.

- Factor and covariate effects can be connected only by the * operator. Suppose *A* and *B* are factors, and *X1* and *X2* are covariates. Examples of valid factor-by-covariate interaction effects are *A*X1*, *A*B*X1*, *X1*A(B)*, *A*X1*X1*, and *B*X1*X2*.

- If more than one DESIGN subcommand is specified, only the last one is in effect.

Example

```
GLM Y BY A B C WITH X
   /DESIGN A B(A) X*A.
```

- In this example, the design consists of a main effect *A*, a nested effect *B* within *A*, and an interaction effect of a covariate *X* with a factor *A*.

GLM: Multivariate

GLM is available in the Advanced Models option.

```
GLM dependent varlist [BY factor list [WITH covariate list]]

[/REGWGT=varname]

[/METHOD=SSTYPE({1  })]
               {2  }
               {3**}
               {4  }

[/INTERCEPT=[INCLUDE**] [EXCLUDE]]

[/MISSING=[INCLUDE] [EXCLUDE**]]

[/CRITERIA=[EPS({1E-8**})] [ALPHA({0.05**})]
               {a     }          {a      }

[/PRINT  = [DESCRIPTIVE] [HOMOGENEITY] [PARAMETER][ETASQ] [RSSCP]
           [GEF] [LOF] [OPOWER] [TEST [([SSCP] [LMATRIX] [MMATRIX])]]

[/PLOT=[SPREADLEVEL] [RESIDUALS]
       [PROFILE (factor factor*factor factor*factor*factor ...)]

[/LMATRIX={["label"] effect list effect list ...;...}]
          {["label"] effect list effect list ...     }
          {["label"] ALL list; ALL...                 }
          {["label"] ALL list                         }

[/MMATRIX= {["label"] depvar value depvar value ...;["label"]...}]
           {["label"] depvar value depvar value ...              }
           {["label"] ALL list; ["label"] ...                    }
           {["label"] ALL list                                   }

[/KMATRIX= {list of numbers    }]
           {list of numbers;...}

[/SAVE=[tempvar [(list of names)]] [tempvar [(list of names)]]...]
       [DESIGN]

[/OUTFILE= [{COVB (filename)}] [EFFECT(filename)] [DESIGN(filename)]
            {CORB (filename)}

[/DESIGN={[INTERCEPT...]     }]
         {[effect effect...]}
```

** Default if subcommand or keyword is omitted.

Temporary variables (tempvar) are:

PRED, WPRED, RESID, WRESID, DRESID, ZRESID, SRESID, SEPRED, COOK, LEVER

Example

```
GLM SCORE1 TO SCORE4 BY METHOD(1,3).
```

Overview

This section discusses the subcommands that are used in multivariate general linear models and covariance designs with several interrelated dependent variables. The discussion focuses on subcommands and keywords that do not apply, or apply in different manners, to univariate analyses. It does not contain information on all of the subcommands you will need to specify the design. For subcommands not covered here, see GLM: Univariate.

Options

Optional Output. In addition to the output described in GLM: Univariate, you can have both multivariate and univariate F tests. Using the PRINT subcommand, you can request the hypothesis and error sums-of-squares and cross-product matrices for each effect in the design, the transformation coefficient table (**M** matrix), Box's M test for equality of covariance matrices, and Bartlett's test of sphericity.

Basic Specification

- The basic specification is a variable list identifying the dependent variables, with the factors (if any) named after BY and the covariates (if any) named after WITH.
- By default, GLM uses a model that includes the intercept term, the covariates (if any), and the full factorial model, which includes all main effects and all possible interactions among factors. The intercept term is excluded if it is excluded in the model by specifying EXCLUDE on the INTERCEPT subcommand. GLM produces multivariate and univariate F tests for each effect in the model. It also calculates the power for each test based on the default alpha value.

Subcommand Order

- The variable list must be specified first.
- Subcommands can be used in any order.

Syntax Rules

- The syntax rules applicable to univariate analysis, in "Syntax Rules" on p. 471 in GLM: Univariate, also apply to multivariate analysis.
- If you enter one of the multivariate specifications in a univariate analysis, GLM ignores it.

Limitations

- Any number of factors can be specified, but if the number of between-subjects factors plus the number of split variables exceeds 18, the Descriptive Statistics table is not printed even when you request it.

- Memory requirements depend primarily on the number of cells in the design. For the default full factorial model, this equals the product of the number of levels or categories in each factor.

GLM Variable List

- Multivariate GLM calculates statistical tests that are valid for analyses of dependent variables that are correlated with one another. The dependent variables must be specified first.
- The factor and covariate lists follow the same rules as in univariate analyses.
- If the dependent variables are uncorrelated, the univariate significance tests have greater statistical power.

PRINT Subcommand

By default, if no PRINT subcommand is specified, multivariate GLM produces multivariate tests (MANOVA) and univariate tests (ANOVA) for all effects in the model. All of the PRINT specifications described in GLM: Univariate are available in multivariate analyses. The following additional output can be requested:

TEST(SSCP)   *Sums-of-squares and cross-product matrices.* Hypothesis (HSSCP) and error (ESSCP) sums-of-squares and cross-product matrices for each effect in the design are displayed. Each between-subjects effect has a different HSSCP matrix, but there is a single ESSCP matrix for all between-subjects effects. For a repeated measures design, each within-subjects effect has an HSSCP matrix and an ESSCP matrix. If there are no within-subjects effects, the ESSCP matrix for the between-subjects effects is the same as the RSSCP matrix.

TEST(MMATRIX)   *Set of transformation coefficients (M) matrices.* Any **M** matrices generated by the MMATRIX subcommand are displayed. If no **M** matrix is specified on the MMATRIX subcommand, this specification will be skipped, unless you are using a repeated measures design. In a repeated measures design, this set always includes the **M** matrix determined by the WSFACTOR subcommand. The specification TEST(TRANSFORM) is equivalent to TEST(MMATRIX).

HOMOGENEITY   *Tests of homogeneity of variance.* In addition to Levene's test for equality of variances for each dependent variable, the display includes Box's *M* test of homogeneity of the covariance matrices of the dependent variables across all level combinations of the between-subjects factors.

RSSCP   *Sums-of-squares and cross-products of residuals.* Three matrices are displayed:

Residual SSCP matrix. A square matrix of sums of squares and cross-products of residuals. The dimension of this matrix is the same as the number of dependent variables in the model.

Residual covariance matrix. The residual SSCP matrix divided by the degrees of freedom of the residual.

Residual correlation matrix. The standardized form of the residual covariance matrix.

Example

```
GLM Y1 Y2 Y3 BY A B
 /PRINT = HOMOGENEITY RSSCP
 /DESIGN.
```

- Since there are three dependent variables, this is a multivariate model.
- The keyword RSSCP produces three matrices of sums of squares and cross-products of residuals. The output also contains the result of Bartlett's test of the sphericity of the residual covariance matrix.
- In addition to the Levene test for each dependent variable, the keyword HOMOGENEITY produces the result of Box's M test of homogeneity in the multivariate model.

MMATRIX Subcommand

The MMATRIX subcommand allows you to customize your hypothesis tests by specifying the **M** matrix (transformation coefficients matrix) in the general form of the linear hypothesis **LBM = K**, where **K = 0** if it is not specified on the KMATRIX subcommand. The vector **B** is the parameter vector in the linear model.

- Specify an optional label in quotes. Then either list dependent variable names, each followed by a real number, or specify the keyword ALL followed by a list of real numbers. Only variable names that appear on the dependent variable list can be specified on the MMATRIX subcommand.
- You can specify one label for each column in the **M** matrix.
- If you specify ALL, the length of the list that follows ALL should be equal to the number of dependent variables.
- There is no limit on the length of the label.
- For the MMATRIX subcommand to be valid, at least one of the following must be specified: the LMATRIX subcommand or INTERCEPT=INCLUDE. (Either of these specifications defines an **L** matrix.)
- If both LMATRIX and MMATRIX are specified, the **L** matrix is defined by the LMATRIX subcommand.
- If MMATRIX or KMATRIX is specified but LMATRIX is not specified, the **L** matrix is defined by the estimable function for the intercept effect, provided that the intercept effect is included in the model.
- If LMATRIX is specified, but MMATRIX is not specified, the **M** matrix is assumed to be an $r \times r$ identity matrix, where r is the number of dependent variables.
- A semicolon (;) indicates the end of a column in the **M** matrix.
- Dependent variables not appearing on a list of dependent variable names and real numbers are assigned a value of 0.

- Dependent variables not appearing in the MMATRIX subcommand will have a row of zeros in the **M** matrix.
- A number can be specified as a fraction with a positive denominator—for example, 1/3 or –1/3, but 1/–3 is invalid.
- The number of columns must be greater than 0. You can specify as many columns as you need.
- If more than one MMATRIX subcommand is specified, only the last one is in effect.

Example

```
GLM Y1 Y2 Y3 BY A B
 /MMATRIX = "Y1-Y2" Y1 1 Y2 -1; "Y1-Y3" Y1 1 Y3 -1
            "Y2-Y3" Y2 1 Y3 -1
 /DESIGN.
```

- In the above example, *Y1*, *Y2*, and *Y3* are the dependent variables.
- The MMATRIX subcommand requests all pairwise comparisons among the dependent variables.
- Since LMATRIX was not specified, the **L** matrix is defined by the estimable function for the intercept effect.

GLM: Repeated Measures

GLM is available in the Advanced Models option.

```
GLM dependent varlist [BY factor list [WITH covariate list]]

/WSFACTOR=name levels [{DEVIATION [(refcat)]      }] name...
                       {SIMPLE [(refcat)]          }
                       {DIFFERENCE                 }
                       {HELMERT                    }
                       {REPEATED                   }
                       {POLYNOMIAL [({1,2,3...})]**}
                       {            {metric }      }
                       {SPECIAL (matrix)           }

[/MEASURE=newname newname...]

[/WSDESIGN=effect effect...]

[/REGWGT=varname]

[/METHOD=SSTYPE({1  })]
               {2  }
               {3**}
               {4  }

[/INTERCEPT=[INCLUDE**] [EXCLUDE]]

[/MISSING=[INCLUDE] [EXCLUDE**]]

[/PRINT = [DESCRIPTIVE] [HOMOGENEITY] [PARAMETER][ETASQ] [RSSCP]
          [GEF] [LOF] [OPOWER] [TEST [([SSCP] [LMATRIX] [MMATRIX])]]

[/SAVE=[tempvar [(list of names)]] [tempvar [(list of names)]]...]
       [DESIGN]

[/EMMEANS=TABLES({OVERALL               }] [COMPARE ADJ(LSD(none)(BONFERRONI)(SIDAK))]
                 {factor                }
                 {factor*factor...      }
                 {wsfactor              }
                 {wsfactor*wsfactor...  }
                 {factor*...wsfactor*...]
                 {factor*factor...      }

[/DESIGN={[INTERCEPT...]    }]*
         {[effect effect...]}
```

* The DESIGN subcommand has the same syntax as is described in GLM: Univariate.

** Default if subcommand or keyword is omitted.

Example

```
GLM Y1 TO Y4 BY GROUP
  /WSFACTOR=YEAR 4.
```

Overview

This section discusses the subcommands that are used in repeated measures designs, in which the dependent variables represent measurements of the same variable (or variables) taken repeatedly. This section does not contain information on all of the subcommands that you will need to specify the design. For some subcommands or keywords not covered here, such as DESIGN, see GLM: Univariate. For information on optional output and the multivariate significance tests available, see GLM: Multivariate.

- In a simple repeated measures analysis, all dependent variables represent different measurements of the same variable for different values (or levels) of a within-subjects factor. Between-subjects factors and covariates can also be included in the model, just as in analyses not involving repeated measures.

- A **within-subjects factor** is simply a factor that distinguishes measurements made on the same subject or case, rather than distinguishing different subjects or cases.

- GLM permits more complex analyses, in which the dependent variables represent levels of two or more within-subjects factors.

- GLM also permits analyses in which the dependent variables represent measurements of several variables for the different levels of the within-subjects factors. These are known as **doubly multivariate designs**.

- A repeated measures analysis includes a within-subjects design describing the model to be tested with the within-subjects factors, as well as the usual between-subjects design describing the effects to be tested with between-subjects factors. The default for the within-subjects factors design is a full factorial model which includes the main within-subjects factor effects and all their interaction effects.

- If a custom hypothesis test is required (defined by the CONTRAST, LMATRIX, or KMATRIX subcommands), the default transformation matrix (**M** matrix) is taken to be the average transformation matrix, which can be displayed by using the keyword TEST(MMATRIX) on the PRINT subcommand. The default contrast result matrix (**K** matrix) is the zero matrix.

- If the contrast coefficient matrix (**L** matrix) is not specified, but a custom hypothesis test is required by the MMATRIX or the KMATRIX subcommand, the contrast coefficient matrix (**L** matrix) is taken to be the **L** matrix which corresponds to the estimable function for the intercept in the between-subjects model. This matrix can be displayed by using the keyword TEST(LMATRIX) on the PRINT subcommand.

Basic Specification

- The basic specification is a variable list followed by the WSFACTOR subcommand.

- Whenever WSFACTOR is specified, GLM performs special repeated measures processing. The multivariate and univariate tests are provided. In addition, for any within-subjects effect involving more than one transformed variable, the Mauchly test of sphericity is displayed to test the assumption that the covariance matrix of the transformed variables is constant on the diagonal and zero off the diagonal. The Greenhouse-Geisser epsilon and the Huynh-Feldt epsilon are also displayed for use in correcting the significance tests in the event that the assumption of sphericity is violated.

Subcommand Order

- The list of dependent variables, factors, and covariates must be first.

Syntax Rules

- The WSFACTOR (within-subjects factors), WSDESIGN (within-subjects design), and MEASURE subcommands are used only in repeated measures analysis.
- WSFACTOR is required for any repeated measures analysis.
- If WSDESIGN is not specified, a full factorial within-subjects design consisting of all main effects and all interactions among within-subjects factors is used by default.
- The MEASURE subcommand is used for doubly multivariate designs, in which the dependent variables represent repeated measurements of more than one variable.

Limitations

- Any number of factors can be specified, but if the number of between-subjects factors plus the number of split variables exceeds 18, the Descriptive Statistics table is not printed even when you request it.
- Maximum 18 within-subjects factors.
- Memory requirements depend primarily on the number of cells in the design. For the default full factorial model, this equals the product of the number of levels or categories in each factor.

Example

```
GLM Y1 TO Y4 BY GROUP
 /WSFACTOR=YEAR 4 POLYNOMIAL
 /WSDESIGN=YEAR
 /PRINT=PARAMETER
 /DESIGN=GROUP.
```

- WSFACTOR specifies a repeated measures analysis in which the four dependent variables represent a single variable measured at four levels of the within-subjects factor. The within-subjects factor is called *YEAR* for the duration of the GLM procedure.
- POLYNOMIAL requests polynomial contrasts for the levels of *YEAR*. Because the four variables, *Y1*, *Y2*, *Y3*, and *Y4*, in the working data file represent the four levels of *YEAR*, the effect is to perform an orthonormal polynomial transformation of these variables.
- PRINT requests that the parameter estimates be displayed.
- WSDESIGN specifies a within-subjects design that includes only the effect of the *YEAR* within-subjects factor. Because *YEAR* is the only within-subjects factor specified, this is the default design, and WSDESIGN could have been omitted.
- DESIGN specifies a between-subjects design that includes only the effect of the *GROUP* between-subjects factor. This subcommand could have been omitted.

GLM Variable List

The list of dependent variables, factors, and covariates must be specified first.

- WSFACTOR determines how the dependent variables on the GLM variable list will be interpreted.

- The number of dependent variables on the GLM variable list must be a multiple of the number of cells in the within-subjects design. If there are six cells in the within-subjects design, each group of six dependent variables represents a single within-subjects variable that has been measured in each of the six cells.

- Normally, the number of dependent variables should equal the number of cells in the within-subjects design multiplied by the number of variables named on the MEASURE subcommand (if one is used). If you have more groups of dependent variables than are accounted for by the MEASURE subcommand, GLM will choose variable names to label the output, which may be difficult to interpret.

- Covariates are specified after keyword WITH. You can specify constant covariates. Constant covariates represent variables whose values remain the same at each within-subjects level.

Example

```
GLM MATH1 TO MATH4 BY METHOD WITH SES
  /WSFACTOR=SEMESTER 4.
```

- The four dependent variables represent a score measured four times (corresponding to the four levels of *SEMESTER*).

- *SES* is a constant covariate. Its value does not change over the time covered by the four levels of *SEMESTER*.

- Default contrast (POLYNOMIAL) is used.

WSFACTOR Subcommand

WSFACTOR names the within-subjects factors, specifies the number of levels for each, and specifies the contrast for each.

- Presence of the WSFACTOR subcommand implies that the repeated measures model is being used.

- Mauchly's test of sphericity is automatically performed when WSFACTOR is specified.

- Names and number levels for the within-subjects factors are specified on the WSFACTOR subcommand. Factor names must not duplicate any of the dependent variables, factors, or covariates named on the GLM variable list. A type of contrast can also be specified for each within-subjects factor in order to perform comparisons among its levels. This contrast amounts to a transformation on the dependent variables.

- If there are more than one within-subjects factors, they must be named in the order corresponding to the order of the dependent variables on the GLM variable list. GLM varies the levels of the last-named within-subjects factor most rapidly when assigning dependent variables to within-subjects cells (see the example below).

- The number of cells in the within-subjects design is the product of the number of levels for all within-subjects factors.

- Levels of the factors must be represented in the data by the dependent variables named on the GLM variable list.

- The number of levels of each factor must be at least two. Enter an integer equal to or greater than 2 after each factor to indicate how many levels the factor has. Optionally, you can enclose the number of levels in parentheses.

- Enter only the *number of levels* for within-subjects factors, not a range of values.

- If more than one WSFACTOR subcommand is specified, only the last one is in effect.

Contrasts for WSFACTOR

The levels of a within-subjects factor are represented by different dependent variables. Therefore, contrasts between levels of such a factor compare these dependent variables. Specifying the type of contrast amounts to specifying a transformation to be performed on the dependent variables.

- In testing the within-subjects effects, an orthonormal transformation is automatically performed on the dependent variables in a repeated measures analysis.

- The contrast for each within-subjects factor is entered after the number of levels. If no contrast keyword is specified, POLYNOMIAL(1,2,3...) is the default. This contrast is used in comparing the levels of the within-subjects factors. Intrinsically orthogonal contrast types are recommended for within-subjects factors if you wish to examine each degree-of-freedom test, provided compound symmetry is assumed within each within-subjects factor. Other orthogonal contrast types are DIFFERENCE and HELMERT.

- If there are more than one within-subjects factors, the transformation matrix (**M** matrix) is computed as the Kronecker product of the matrices generated by the contrasts specified.

- The transformation matrix (**M** matrix) generated by the specified contrasts can be displayed by using the keyword TEST(MMATRIX) on the subcommand PRINT.

- The contrast types available for within-subjects factors are the same as those on the CONTRAST subcommand for between-subjects factors, described in "CONTRAST Subcommand" on p. 481 in GLM: Univariate.

The following contrast types are available:

DEVIATION   *Deviations from the grand mean.* This is the default for between-subjects factors. Each level of the factor except one is compared to the grand mean. One category (by default the last) must be omitted so that the effects will be independent of one another. To omit a category other than the last, specify the number of the omitted category in parentheses after the keyword DEVIATION. For example,

```
GLM Y1 Y2 Y3 BY GROUP
 /WSFACTOR = Y 3 DEVIATION (1)
```

Deviation contrasts are not orthogonal.

POLYNOMIAL   *Polynomial contrasts.* This is the default for within-subjects factors. The first degree of freedom contains the linear effect across the levels of the factor, the second contains the quadratic effect, and so on. In a balanced design, polynomial contrasts are orthogonal. By default, the levels are assumed to be equally spaced; you can specify unequal spacing by entering a metric consisting of one integer for each level of the factor in parentheses after the keyword POLYNOMIAL. (All metrics specified cannot be equal; thus (1, 1, ..., 1) is not valid.) For example,

```
/WSFACTOR=D 3 POLYNOMIAL(1,2,4).
```

Suppose that factor D has three levels. The specified contrast indicates that the three levels of D are actually in the proportion 1:2:4. The default metric is always $(1,2,...,k)$, where k levels are involved. Only the relative differences between the terms of the metric matter (1,2,4) is the same metric as (2,3,5) or (20,30,50) because, in each instance, the difference between the second and third numbers is twice the difference between the first and second.

DIFFERENCE   *Difference or reverse Helmert contrasts.* Each level of the factor except the first is compared to the mean of the previous levels. In a balanced design, difference contrasts are orthogonal.

HELMERT   *Helmert contrasts.* Each level of the factor except the last is compared to the mean of subsequent levels. In a balanced design, Helmert contrasts are orthogonal.

SIMPLE   *Each level of the factor except the last is compared to the last level.* To use a category other than the last as the omitted reference category, specify its number in parentheses following keyword SIMPLE. For example,

```
/WSFACTOR=B 3 SIMPLE (1).
```

Simple contrasts are not orthogonal.

REPEATED   *Comparison of adjacent levels.* Each level of the factor except the first is compared to the previous level. Repeated contrasts are not orthogonal.

SPECIAL   *A user-defined contrast.* Values specified after this keyword are stored in a matrix in column major order. For example, if factor A has three levels, then WSFACTOR(A)= SPECIAL(1 1 1 -1 0 0 1 -1) produces the following contrast matrix:

$$
\begin{array}{rrr}
1 & 1 & 0 \\
1 & -1 & 1 \\
1 & 0 & -1
\end{array}
$$

Example

```
GLM X1Y1 X1Y2 X2Y1 X2Y2 X3Y1 X3Y2 BY TREATMNT GROUP
  /WSFACTOR=X 3 Y 2
  /DESIGN.
```

- The GLM variable list names six dependent variables and two between-subjects factors, *TREATMNT* and *GROUP*.

- WSFACTOR identifies two within-subjects factors whose levels distinguish the six dependent variables. *X* has three levels and *Y* has two. Thus, there are $3 \times 2 = 6$ cells in the within-subjects design, corresponding to the six dependent variables.

- Variable *X1Y1* corresponds to levels 1,1 of the two within-subjects factors; variable *X1Y2* corresponds to levels 1,2; *X2Y1* to levels 2,1; and so on up to *X3Y2*, which corresponds to levels 3,2. The first within-subjects factor named, *X*, varies most slowly, and the last within-subjects factor named, *Y*, varies most rapidly on the list of dependent variables.

- Because there is no WSDESIGN subcommand, the within-subjects design will include all main effects and interactions: *X*, *Y*, and *X* by *Y*.

- Likewise, the between-subjects design includes all main effects and interactions (*TREATMNT*, *GROUP*, and *TREATMNT* by *GROUP*) plus the intercept.

- In addition, a repeated measures analysis always includes interactions between the within-subjects factors and the between-subjects factors. There are three such interactions for each of the three within-subjects effects.

Example

```
GLM SCORE1 SCORE2 SCORE3 BY GROUP
  /WSFACTOR=ROUND 3 DIFFERENCE
  /CONTRAST(GROUP)=DEVIATION
  /PRINT=PARAMETER TEST(LMATRIX).
```

- This analysis has one between-subjects factor, *GROUP*, and one within-subjects factor, *ROUND*, with three levels that are represented by the three dependent variables.

- The WSFACTOR subcommand also specifies difference contrasts for *ROUND*, the within-subjects factor.

- There is no WSDESIGN subcommand, so a default full factorial within-subjects design is assumed. This could also have been specified as WSDESIGN=ROUND, or simply WSDESIGN.

- The CONTRAST subcommand specifies deviation contrasts for *GROUP*, the between-subjects factor. This subcommand could have been omitted because deviation contrasts are the default.

- PRINT requests the display of the parameter estimates for the model and the **L** matrix.

- There is no DESIGN subcommand, so a default full factorial between-subjects design is assumed. This could also have been specified as DESIGN=GROUP, or simply DESIGN.

WSDESIGN Subcommand

WSDESIGN specifies the design for within-subjects factors. Its specifications are like those of the DESIGN subcommand, but it uses the within-subjects factors rather than the between-subjects factors.

- The default WSDESIGN is a full factorial design, which includes all main effects and all interactions for within-subjects factors. The default is in effect whenever a design is processed without a preceding WSDESIGN or when the preceding WSDESIGN subcommand has no specifications.

- A WSDESIGN specification cannot include between-subjects factors or terms based on them, nor does it accept interval-level variables.

- The keyword INTERCEPT is not allowed on WSDESIGN.

- Nested effects are not allowed. Therefore, the symbols ( ) are not allowed here.
- If more than one WSDESIGN subcommand is specified, only the last one is in effect.

Example

```
GLM JANLO,JANHI,FEBLO,FEBHI,MARLO,MARHI BY SEX
  /WSFACTOR MONTH 3 STIMULUS 2
  /WSDESIGN MONTH, STIMULUS
  /DESIGN SEX.
```

- There are six dependent variables, corresponding to three months and two different levels of stimulus.
- The dependent variables are named on the GLM variable list in an order such that the level of stimulus varies more rapidly than the month. Thus, *STIMULUS* is named last on the WSFACTOR subcommand.
- The WSDESIGN subcommand specifies only the main effects for within-subjects factors. There is no *MONTH* by *STIMULUS* interaction term.

MEASURE Subcommand

In a doubly multivariate analysis, the dependent variables represent multiple variables measured under the different levels of the within-subjects factors. Use MEASURE to assign names to the variables that you have measured for the different levels of within-subjects factors.

- Specify a list of one or more variable names to be used in labeling the averaged results. If no within-subjects factor has more than two levels, MEASURE has no effect. You can use up to 255 characters for each name.
- The number of dependent variables in the dependent variables list should equal the product of the number of cells in the within-subjects design and the number of names on MEASURE.
- If you do not enter a MEASURE subcommand and there are more dependent variables than cells in the within-subjects design, GLM assigns names (normally *MEASURE_1*, *MEASURE_2*, etc.) to the different measures.
- All of the dependent variables corresponding to each measure should be listed together and ordered so that the within-subjects factor named last on the WSFACTORS subcommand varies most rapidly.

Example

```
GLM TEMP11 TEMP12 TEMP21 TEMP22 TEMP31 TEMP32,
  WEIGHT11 WEIGHT12 WEIGHT21 WEIGHT22 WEIGHT31 WEIGHT32 BY GROUP
  /WSFACTOR=DAY 3 AMPM 2
  /MEASURE=TEMP WEIGHT
  /WSDESIGN=DAY, AMPM, DAY BY AMPM
  /DESIGN.
```

- There are 12 dependent variables: 6 temperatures and 6 weights, corresponding to morning and afternoon measurements on three days.
- WSFACTOR identifies the two factors (*DAY* and *AMPM*) that distinguish the temperature and weight measurements for each subject. These factors define six within-subjects cells.
- MEASURE indicates that the first group of six dependent variables correspond to *TEMP* and the second group of six dependent variables correspond to *WEIGHT*.

- These labels, *TEMP* and *WEIGHT*, are used on the output as the measure labels.
- WSDESIGN requests a full factorial within-subjects model. Because this is the default, WSDESIGN could have been omitted.

EMMEANS Subcommand

EMMEANS displays estimated marginal means of the dependent variables in the cells, adjusted for the effects of covariates at their overall means, for the specified factors. Note that these are predicted, not observed, means. The standard errors are also displayed. For a detailed description of the EMMEANS subcommand, see "EMMEANS Subcommand" on p. 486 in GLM: Univariate.

- For the TABLES and COMPARE keywords, valid options include the within-subjects factors specified in the WSFACTOR subcommand, crossings among them, and crossings among factors specified in the factor list and factors specified on the WSFACTOR subcommand.
- All factors in a crossed-factors specification must be unique.
- If a between- or within-subjects factor, or a crossing of between- or within-subjects factors, is specified on the TABLES keyword, then GLM will collapse over any other between- or within-subjects factors before computing the estimated marginal means for the dependent variables.

GRAPH

This command is available only on systems with high-resolution graphics capabilities.

```
GRAPH

  [/TITLE='line 1' ['line 2']]
  [/SUBTITLE='line 1']
  [/FOOTNOTE='line 1' ['line 2']]

  {/BAR [{(SIMPLE)       }]=function/variable specification†        }
       {(GROUPED)       }
       {(STACKED)       }
       {(RANGE)         }

  {/LINE [{(SIMPLE)    }]=function/variable specification†          }
        {(MULTIPLE)   }
        {(DROP)       }
        {(AREA)       }
        {(DIFFERENCE) }

  {/PIE                                                             }

  {/PARETO[{(CUM)  }][{(SIMPLE) }]=function/variable specification†}
          {(NOCUM) }  {(STACKED)}

  {/HILO[{(SIMPLE) }]=function/variable specification††             }
        {(GROUPED)}

  {/HISTOGRAM [(NORMAL)]=var                                        }

  {/SCATTERPLOT[{(BIVARIATE)}]=variable specification†††            }
               {(OVERLAY)  }
               {(MATRIX)   }
               {(XYZ)      }

  {/ERRORBAR[{(CI[{95}])      }]={var [var var ...][BY var]}        }
            {n }                {var BY var BY var        }
          {(STERRIR[{12}])}
                  {n }
          {(STDDEV[{2}])  }
                  {n}

  [/TEMPLATE=file]

  [/MISSING=[{LISTWISE**}][{NOREPORT**}][{EXCLUDE**}]]
            {VARIABLE  }] {REPORT    } {INCLUDE  }
```

** Default if the subcommand is omitted.

GRAPH   505

The following table shows all possible function/variable specifications for BAR, LINE, PIE, BLOCK, and PARETO subcommands. For special restrictions, see individual subcommands. In the table, valuef refers to the value function, countf refers to the count functions, and sumf refers to the summary functions.

	Simple Bar, Simple or Area Line, Pie, Simple High-Low, and Simple Pareto Charts	**Grouped or Stacked Bar, Multiple, Drop or Difference Line, and Stacked Pareto Charts**
Categorical Charts	[countf BY] var	[countf BY] var BY var
	sumf(var) BY var	sumf(var) BY var BY var
	sumf(varlist)	sumf(varlist) BY var
	sumf(var) sumf(var)...	sumf(var) sumf(var)... BY var
Noncategorical Charts	valuef(var) [BY var]	valuef(varlist) [BY var]

The following table shows all possible function/variable specifications for the HILO subcommand. Categorical variables for simple high-low-close charts must be dichotomous or trichotomous.

Simple Range Bar and Simple High-Low-Close Charts	**Clustered Range Bar and Clustered High-Low-Close Charts**
[countf BY] var	(sumf(var) sumf(var) [sumf(var)]) (...) ...BY var
sumf(var) sumf(var) sumf(var) BY var	sumf(var) sumf(var) [sumf(var)] BY var BY var
sumf(var) BY var BY var	
valuef(varlist) [BY var]	valuef(varlist) (...) ... [BY var]

Variable specification is required on all types of scatterplots. The following table shows all possible specifications:

BIVARIATE	var WITH var [BY var] [BY var ({NAME })] {IDENTIFY}
OVERLAY	varlist WITH varlist [(PAIR)] [BY var ({NAME })] {IDENTIFY}
MATRIX	varlist [BY var] [BY var ({NAME })] {IDENTIFY}
XYZ	var WITH var WITH var [BY var] [BY var ({NAME })] {IDENTIFY}

Value function:

The VALUE function yields the value of the specified variable for each case. It always produces one bar, point, or slice for each case. The VALUE(X) specification implies the value of *X* by *n*, where *n* is the number of each case. You can specify multiple variables, as in:

```
GRAPH /BAR = VALUE(SALARY BONUS BENEFIT).
```

This command draws a bar chart with the values of *SALARY, BONUS*, and *BENEFIT* for each employee (case). A BY variable can be used to supply case labels, but it does not affect the layout of the chart, even if values of the BY variable are the same for multiple cases.

Aggregation functions:

Two groups of aggregation functions are available: count functions and summary functions.

Count functions:

COUNT   *Frequency of cases in each category.*

PCT   *Frequency of cases in each category expressed as a percentage of the whole.*

CUPCT   *Cumulative percentage sorted by category value.*

CUFREQ   *Cumulative frequency sorted by category value.*

- Count functions yield the count or percentage of valid cases within categories determined by one or more BY variables, as in

```
GRAPH /BAR (SIMPLE) = PCT BY REGION.
```

- Count functions do not have any arguments.
- You can omit the keyword COUNT and subsequent keyword BY and specify just a variable, as in

```
GRAPH /BAR = DEPT.
```

This command is interpreted as

```
GRAPH /BAR = COUNT BY DEPT.
```

Summary functions:

MINIMUM   *Minimum value of the variable.*

MAXIMUM   *Maximum value of the variable.*

N   *Number of cases for which the variable has a nonmissing value.*

SUM   *Sum of the values of the variable.*

CUSUM   *Sum of the summary variable accumulated across values of the category variable.*

MEAN   *Mean.*

STDDEV   *Standard deviation.*

VARIANCE   *Variance.*

MEDIAN   *Median.*

GMEDIAN   *Group median.*

MODE   *Mode.*

PTILE(x)   *Xth percentile value of the variable. X must be greater than 0 and less than 100.*

PLT(x)   *Percentage of cases for which the value of the variable is less than* x.

PGT(x)   *Percentage of cases for which the value of the variable is greater than* x.

NLT(x)   *Number of cases for which the value of the variable is less than* x.

GRAPH   507

NGT(x)   *Number of cases for which the value of the variable is greater than* x.

PIN(x1,x2)   *Percentage of cases for which the value of the variable is greater than or equal to* x1 *and less than or equal to* x2. x1 *cannot exceed* x2.

NIN(x1,x2)   *Number of cases for which the value of the variable is greater than or equal to* x1 *and less than or equal to* x2. x1 *cannot exceed* x2.

- Summary functions are usually used with summary variables (variables that record continuous values, like age or expenses). To use a summary function, specify the name of one or more variables in parentheses after the name of the function, as in

```
GRAPH /BAR = SUM(SALARY) BY DEPT.
```

- You can specify multiple summary functions for more chart types. For example, the same function can be applied to a list of variables, as in

```
GRAPH /BAR = SUM(SALARY BONUS BENEFIT) BY DEPT.
```

This syntax is equivalent to

```
GRAPH /BAR = SUM(SALARY) SUM(BONUS) SUM(BENEFIT) BY DEPT.
```

Different functions can be applied to the same variable, as in

```
GRAPH /BAR = MEAN(SALARY) MEDIAN(SALARY) BY DEPT.
```

Different functions and variables can be combined, as in

```
GRAPH /BAR = MIN(SALARY81) MAX(SALARY81)
             MIN(SALARY82) MAX(SALARY82) BY JOBCAT.
```

The effect of multiple summary functions on the structure of the charts is illustrated under the discussion of specific chart types.

Overview

GRAPH generates a high-resolution chart by computing statistics from variables in the working data file and constructing the chart according to your specification. The chart can be a bar chart, pie chart, line chart, error bar chart, high-low-close histogram, scatterplot, or Pareto chart. The chart is displayed where high-resolution display is available and can be edited with a chart editor and saved as a chart file.

Options

Titles and Footnotes. You can specify a title, subtitle, and footnote for the chart using the TITLE, SUBTITLE, and FOOTNOTE subcommands.

Chart Type. You can request a specific type of chart using the BAR, LINE, PIE, ERRORBAR, HILO, HISTOGRAM, SCATTERPLOT, or PARETO subcommand.

Chart Content. You can specify an aggregated categorical chart using various aggregation functions or a nonaggregated categorical chart using the VALUE function (see pp. 505–507 for a list of available functions).

Templates. You can specify a template, using the TEMPLATE subcommand, to override the default chart attribute settings on your system.

Basic Specification

The basic specification is a chart type subcommand. By default, the generated chart will have no title, subtitle, or footnote.

Subcommand Order

Subcommands can be specified in any order.

Syntax Rules

- Only one chart type subcommand can be specified.
- The function/variable specification is required for all subtypes of bar, line, error bar, hilo, and Pareto charts; the variable specification is required for histograms and all subtypes of scatterplots.
- The function/variable or variable specifications should match the subtype keywords. If there is a discrepancy, GRAPH produces the default chart for the function/variable or variable specification regardless of the specified keyword.

Operations

- GRAPH computes aggregated functions to obtain the values needed for the requested chart and calculates an optimal scale for charting.
- The chart title, subtitle, and footnote are assigned as they are specified on TITLE, SUBTITLE, and FOOTNOTE subcommands. If you do not use these subcommands, the chart title, subtitle, and footnote are null. The split-file information is displayed as a subtitle if split-file is in effect.
- GRAPH creates labels that provide information on the source of the values being plotted. Labeling conventions vary for different subtypes. Where variable or value labels are defined in the working data file, GRAPH uses the labels; otherwise, variable names or values are used.

Limitations

Categorical charts cannot display fewer than 2 or more than 3000 categories.

Example

```
GRAPH /BAR=SUM (MURDER) BY CITY.
```

- This command generates a simple (default) bar chart showing the number of murders in each city.
- The category axis (*x* axis) labels are defined by the value labels (or values if no value labels exit) of the variable *CITY.*

GRAPH   509

- The default span (2) and sigma value (3) are used.
- Since no BY variable is specified, the *x* axis is labeled by sequence numbers.

TITLE, SUBTITLE, and FOOTNOTE Subcommands

TITLE, SUBTITLE, and FOOTNOTE specify lines of text placed at the top or bottom of the chart.

- One or two lines of text can be specified for TITLE or FOOTNOTE, and one line of text can be specified for SUBTITLE.
- Each line of text must be enclosed in apostrophes or quotation marks. The maximum length of any line is 72 characters.
- The default font sizes and types are used for the title, subtitle, and footnote.
- By default, the title, subtitle, and footnote are left-aligned with the *y* axis.
- If you do not specify TITLE, the default title, subtitle, and footnote are null, which leaves more space for the chart. If split-file processing is in effect, the split-file information is provided as a default subtitle.

Example

```
GRAPH TITLE = 'Murder in Major U.S. Cities'
 /SUBTITLE='per 100,000 people'
 /FOOTNOTE='The above data was reported on August 26, 1987'
 /BAR=SUM(MURDER) BY CITY.
```

BAR Subcommand

BAR creates one of five types of bar charts using keywords SIMPLE, COMPOSITIONAL, GROUPED, STACKED, or RANGE.

- Only one keyword can be specified, and it must be specified in the parentheses.
- When no keyword is specified, the default is either SIMPLE or GROUPED, depending on the type of function/variable specification.

SIMPLE   *Simple bar chart.* This is the default if no keyword is specified on the BAR subcommand and the variables define a simple bar chart. A simple bar chart can be defined by a single summary or count function and a single BY variable, or by multiple summary functions and no BY variable (see Figure 1 to Figure 4).

GROUPED   *Clustered bar chart.* A clustered bar chart is defined by a single function and two BY variables, or by multiple functions and a single BY variable. This is the default if no keyword is specified on the BAR subcommand and the variables define a clustered bar chart (see Figure 5 to Figure 8).

STACKED   *Stacked bar chart.* A stacked bar chart displays a series of bars, each divided into segments stacked one on top of the other. The height of each segment represents the value of the category. Like a clustered bar chart, it is defined by a single function and two BY variables or by multiple functions and a single BY variable (see Figure 9 to Figure 11).

RANGE   *Range bar chart.* A range bar chart displays a series of floating bars. The height of each bar represents the range of the category and its position in the chart indicates the minimum and maximum values. A range bar chart can be defined by a single function and two BY variables or by multiple functions and a single BY variable. If a variable list is used as the argument for a function, the list must be of an even number. If a second BY variable is used to define the range, the variable must be dichotomous (see Figure 12 to Figure 14).

Figure 1   /BAR=COUNT BY JOBCAT

Specification: count_function BY var
or: sum_function(var) BY var

y-axis title:	fn name [+fn var label]
y-axis labels:	fn value scale
x-axis title:	BY var label
x-axis labels:	BY var value labels

Each bar shows the number of cases in the indicated job categories.

Figure 2   /BAR=MEAN(SALBEG, SALNOW)

Specification: sum_function (varlist)

y-axis title:	fn name
y-axis labels:	fn value scale
x-axis title:	none
x-axis labels:	fn var labels

One bar is produced for each variable, representing the summary function of that variable across all cases.

GRAPH   511

Figure 3   /BAR=MEAN(SALBEG) MEDIAN(SALBEG) MEAN(SALNOW) MEDIAN(SALNOW)

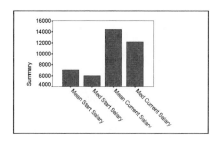

Specification: sum_function list

y-axis title:	Summary
y-axis labels:	fn value scale
x-axis title:	none
x-axis labels:	fn names +var names

One bar is produced for each summary function. The arguments can be the same or different.

Figure 4   /BAR=VALUE(SALNOW) BY ID

Specification: value_function(var) [BY var]

y-axis title:	value + var label
y-axis labels:	fn value scale
x-axis title:	BY var value labels
x-axis labels:	BY var label

Each bar shows the value of a single case. If no BY variable is specified, the *x*-axis title will be Case Number and the *x*-axis labels will be case numbers.

Figure 5   /BAR=COUNT BY JOBCAT BY SEX

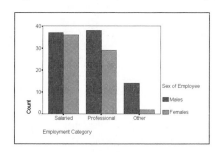

Specification: count_function BY var1 BY var2
        or: sum_function(var) BY var1 BY var2

Legend title:	2nd BY var label
Legend labels:	2nd BY var value labels
y-axis title:	fn name [+var label]
y-axis labels:	fn value scale
x-axis title:	1st BY var label
x-axis labels:	1st BY value labels

Cases are broken down into categories by *VAR1* and then by *VAR2*. Each bar shows the valid number of cases or the summary function value within each subcategory.

Figure 6   /BAR=MEAN(SALBEG SALNOW) BY JOBCAT

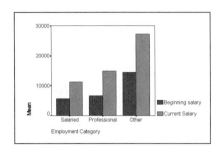

Specification: sum_function (varlist) BY var

Legend title:	none
Legend labels:	fn var labels
y-axis title:	fn name
y-axis labels:	fn value scale
x-axis title:	var label
x-axis labels:	BY value labels

The variables are broken down into categories. Within a category, each bar shows the value of the function for each variable.

Figure 7   /BAR=MEDIAN(SALNOW) MEAN(SALNOW) BY SEX

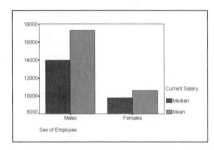

Specification: sum_function list BY var

Legend title:	fn var label (if only one fn var)
Legend labels:	fn name
y-axis title:	none
y-axis labels:	fn value scale
x-axis title:	BY var label
x-axis labels:	BY var value label

The variable is broken down into categories. Within a category, each bar shows a different function of the same variable.

Figure 8   /BAR=VALUE(SALBEG SALNOW) BY ID

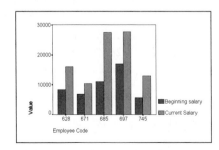

Specification: value_function(varlist) [BY var]

Legend title:	none
Legend labels:	fn var name
y-axis title:	value
y-axis labels:	values
x-axis title:	BY var label
x-axis labels:	BY var value label

Each group shows one case identified by the category variable following BY. Each bar within the case shows the value of one variable for that case.

GRAPH   513

Figure 9   /BAR(STACKED)=COUNT BY JOBCAT BY SEX

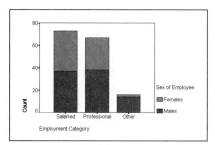

Specification: count_function BY var1 BY var2
            or: sum_function(var) BY var1 BY var2

Legend title:	2nd BY var label
Legend labels:	2nd BY var value labels
y-axis title:	fn name [+fn var label]
y-axis labels:	fn value scale
x-axis title:	1st BY var label
x-axis labels:	1st BY var value labels

Each bar represents one subcategory defined by the two category variables. The bars are stacked within each category defined by the first category variable.

Figure 10   /BAR(STACKED)=SUM(THEFT AUTO BURGLARY) BY YEAR

Specification: sum_function (varlist) BY var

Legend title:	none
Legend labels:	fn var labels
y-axis title:	fn name
y-axis labels:	fn value scale
x-axis title:	BY var label
x-axis labels:	BY var value labels

Each bar represents the function value of one variable broken down into categories. Bars within each category are stacked.

Figure 11   /BAR(STACKED)=VALUE(SALNOW FRINGE) BY ID

Specification: value_function(varlist)[BY var]

Legend title:	none
Legend labels:	var labels
y-axis title:	fn name
y-axis labels:	fn value scale
x-axis title:	BY var label
x-axis labels:	BY var value labels

Each bar shows the value of each variable for the indicated case. If no BY variable is specified, the *x* axis is labeled by case numbers and its title is **Case Number**.

Figure 12   /BAR(RANGE)=COUNT BY JOBCAT BY RACE

Specification: count_function BY var1 BY var2

Legend title:	var2 label
Legend labels:	var2 value labels
y-axis title:	fn name
y-axis labels:	fn value scale
x-axis title:	var1 label
x-axis labels:	var1 value labels

The height of each bar represents the difference between the two categories defined by *var2*, which must be dichotomous. The direction of difference, that is, whether nonwhite employees in each category defined by *var1* are more or less, is not shown.

Figure 13   /BAR(RANGE)=VALUE(SWI_HI SWI_LO) BY DAY

Specification: value_function(var1 var2)[BY var]

Legend title:	none
Legend labels:	var1 label–var2 label
y-axis title:	none
y-axis labels:	fn value scale
x-axis title:	BY var label
x-axis labels:	BY var value labels

The height of each bar represents the difference between the high and the low values of the day. The position of each bar shows the fluctuation over the two-week period.

Figure 14   /BAR(RANGE)=MEAN(SWI_HI SWI_LO GER_HI GER_LO CAN_HI CAN_LO) BY WEEK

Specification: sum_function (varlist) BY var

Legend title:	fn name
Legend labels:	pairs of var labels
y-axis title:	none
y-axis labels:	fn value scale
x-axis title:	BY var label
x-axis labels:	BY var value labels

The variable list must contain an even number of variables. Each pair of variables is plotted as a separate series.

GRAPH   515

LINE Subcommand

LINE creates one of five types of line charts using keywords SIMPLE, MULTIPLE, DROP, AREA, or DIFFERENCE.

- Only one keyword can be specified, and it must be specified in the parentheses.
- When no keyword is specified, the default is either SIMPLE or MULTIPLE, depending on the type of function/variable specification.

SIMPLE *Simple line chart.* A simple line chart is defined by a single function and a single BY variable or by multiple functions and no BY keyword. This is the default if no keyword is specified on LINE and the data define a simple line (see Figure 15 to Figure 17).

MULTIPLE *Multiple line chart.* A multiple line chart is defined by a single function and two BY variables or by multiple functions and a single BY variable. This is the default if no keyword is specified on LINE and the data define a multiple line (see Figure 18 to Figure 20).

DROP *Drop-line chart.* A drop-line chart shows the difference between two or more fluctuating variables. It is defined by a single function and two BY variables or by multiple functions and a single BY variable (see Figure 21 to Figure 24).

AREA *Area line chart.* An area line chart fills the area beneath each line with a color or pattern. When multiple lines are specified, the second line is the sum of the first and second variables, the third line is the sum of the first, second, and third variables, and so on. The specification is the same as that for a simple or multiple line chart. Figure 25 to Figure 27 show area line charts with multiple lines.

DIFFERENCE *Difference line chart.* A difference line chart fills the area between a pair of lines. It highlights the difference between two variables or two groups. A difference line chart is defined by a single function and two BY variables or by two summary functions and a single BY variable. If a second BY variable is used to define the two groups, the variable must be dichotomous (see Figure 28 to Figure 31).

Figure 15 /LINE=COUNT BY TIME

Specification: count_function BY var
   or: sum_function(var) BY var

y-axis title: fn name [+fn var label]

y-axis labels: fn value scale

x-axis title: BY var label

x-axis labels: BY var value labels

Each point on the line represents the number of valid cases for one category.

Figure 16   /LINE=MEAN(SPRING SUMMER FALL WINTER)

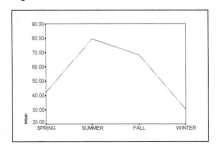

Specification: sum_function (varlist)

y-axis title:	fn name
y-axis labels:	fn value scale
x-axis title:	none
x-axis labels:	fn var labels

Each point on the line shows the function value for one variable across all valid cases.

Figure 17   /LINE=VALUE(POUND) BY DAY

Specification: value_function (var) [BY var]

y-axis title:	value + var name
y-axis labels:	value labels
x-axis title:	BY var label
x-axis label:	BY var value labels

Each point on the line shows the value of a single case. If a BY variable is not specified, the *x*-axis title will be Case Number and the *x*-axis labels will be the number of each case.

Figure 18   /LINE=COUNT BY TIME BY SEX

Specification: count_function BY var1 BY var2
or: sum_function(var) BY var1 BY var2

Legend title:	2nd BY var label
Legend labels:	2nd BY var value labels
y-axis title:	fn name [+fn var label]
y-axis labels:	fn value scale
x-axis title:	1st BY var label
x-axis labels:	1st BY var value labels

Each line represents one category defined by the second BY variable. Each point on the line shows the number of valid cases for one category defined by the first BY variable. Missing values are indicated by unconnected lines.

GRAPH 517

Figure 19 /LINE=MEAN(THEFT AUTO BURGLARY) BY YEAR

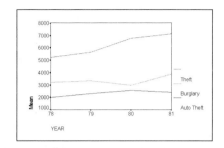

Specification: sum_function (varlist) BY var

Legend title:	none
Legend labels:	fn var labels
y-axis title:	fn name
y-axis labels:	fn value scale
x-axis title:	BY var label
x-axis labels:	BY var value labels

Each line represents one variable. Each point on the line shows the value for one category.

Figure 20 /LINE=VALUE(SALBEG SALNOW) BY ID

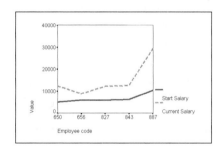

Specification: value_function (varlist) [BY var]

Legend title:	none
Legend labels:	var labels
y-axis title:	value
y-axis labels:	values
x-axis title:	BY var label
x-axis labels:	BY var value labels

Each line represents one variable. Each point shows the value of each case for the variable. If no BY variable is specified, the *x*-axis title will be Case Number and the *x*-axis labels will be the number of each individual case.

Figure 21 LINE(DROP)=NEAN (SALBEG SALNOW) BY SEXRACE

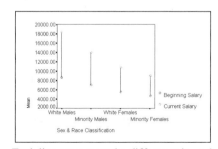

Specification: sum_function (varlist) BY var

Legend title:	none
Legend labels:	var labels
y-axis title:	fn name
y-axis labels:	fn value scale
x-axis title:	BY var label
x-axis labels:	BY var value labels

Each line represents the difference in each sex and race category between summary function values computed from the two variables. If more variables are specified, each will be represented by a symbol on the lines.

Figure 22   LINE(DROP)=MEAN(SALNOW) BY SEXRACE BY JOBCAT

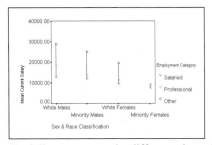

Specification: sum_function BY var BY var

Legend title:	2nd BY var label
Legend labels:	2nd BY var value labels
y-axis title:	fn name[+var label]
y-axis labels:	fn value scale
x-axis title:	1st BY var label
x-axis labels:	1st BY var value labels

Each line represents the difference in each sex and race category between job categories.

Figure 23   LINE(DROP)=COUNT BY JOBCAT BY SEX

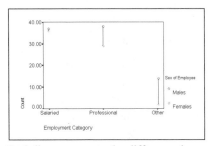

Specification: count_function BY var1 BY var2

Legend title:	2nd BY var label
Legend labels:	2nd BY var value labels
y-axis title:	fn name
y-axis labels:	fn value scale
x-axis title:	1st BY var label
x-axis labels:	1st BY var value labels

Each line represents the difference in number of valid cases in each job category between male and female.

Figure 24   LINE(DROP)=VALUE(SALBEG SALNOW) BY ID

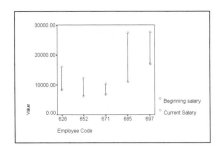

Specification: value_function (varlist) [BY var]

Legend title:	none
Legend labels:	var labels
y-axis title:	fn name
y-axis labels:	value scale
x-axis title:	BY var label
x-axis labels:	BY var value labels

If no BY variable is specified, the x-axis title is Case Number and the x-axis labels are the numbers of cases.

GRAPH   519

Figure 25   /LINE(AREA)=COUNT BY TIME

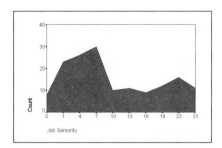

Specification: count_function BY var
or: sum_function(var) BY var

y-axis title:	fn name [+fn var label]
y-axis labels:	fn value scale
x-axis title:	BY var label
x-axis labels:	BY var value labels

The area shows the number of valid cases for categories defined by the BY variable.

Figure 26   /LINE(AREA)=COUNT BY TIME BY SEX

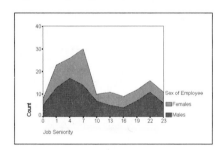

Specification: count_function BY var1 BY var2
or: sum_function(var) BY var1 BY var2

Legend title:	2nd BY var label
Legend labels:	2nd BY var value labels
y-axis title:	fn name [+fn var label]
y-axis labels:	fn value scale
x-axis title:	1st BY var label
x-axis labels:	1st BY var value labels

The two areas respectively represent the categories defined by the second BY variable.

Figure 27   /LINE(AREA)=SUM(VIOLENT PROPERTY) BY YEAR

Specification: sum_function (varlist) BY var

Legend title:	none
Legend labels:	fn var labels
y-axis title:	fn name
y-axis labels:	fn value scale
x-axis title:	BY var label
x-axis labels:	BY var value labels

Each area represents one function variable.

Figure 28   LINE(DIFFERENCE)=MEAN(SALBEG SALNOW) BY TIME

Specification: sum_function (varlist) BY var

Legend title:	fn name
Legend labels:	fn var labels
y-axis title:	none
y-axis labels:	fn value scale
x-axis title:	BY var label
x-axis labels:	BY var value labels

Figure 29   LINE(DIFFERENCE)=MEAN(SALNOW) BY TIME BY SEX

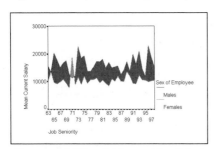

Specification: sum_function(var) BY var BY var

Legend title:	2nd BY var label
Legend labels:	2nd BY var value labels
y-axis title:	fn name [+var label]
y-axis labels:	fn value scale
x-axis title:	1st BY var label
x-axis labels:	1st BY var value labels

The second BY variable must be dichotomous.

Figure 30   LINE(DIFFERENCE)=COUNT BY TIME BY SEX

Specification: count_function BY var BY var

Legend title:	2nd BY var label
Legend labels:	2nd BY var value labels
y-axis title:	fn name
y-axis labels:	fn value scale
x-axis title:	1st BY var label
x-axis labels:	1st BY var value labels

The second BY variable must be dichotomous.

GRAPH 521

Figure 31 LINE(DIFFERENCE)=VALUE(SALBEG SALNOW) BY TIME

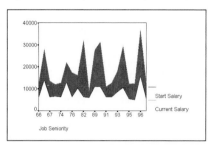

Specification: value_function(var1 var2 [BY var]

Legend title:	2nd BY var label
Legend labels:	2nd BY var value labels
y-axis title:	fn name
y-axis labels:	fn value scale
x-axis title:	1st BY var label
x-axis labels:	1st BY var value labels

If no BY variable is specified, the *x*-axis title is Case Number and *x*-axis labels are the case numbers.

PIE Subcommand

PIE creates pie charts. A pie chart can be defined by a single function and a single BY variable or by multiple summary functions and no BY variable. A pie chart divides a circle into slices. The size of each slice indicates the value of the category relative to the whole (see Figure 32 to Figure 34). Cumulative functions (CUPCT, CUFREQ, and CUSUM) are inappropriate for pie charts but are not prohibited. When specified, all cases except those in the last category are counted more than once in the resulting pie.

Figure 32 /PIE=COUNT BY JOBCAT

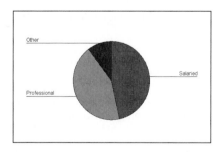

Specification: count_function BY var

Labels: BY var value labels

Each pie slice shows proportionally the number of cases in each category defined by the BY variable.

Figure 33   /PIE=SUM(THEFT AUTO BURGLARY)

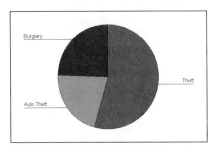

Specification: summary_function(varlist)

Labels: fn var labels

Each pie slice proportionally shows the function value for one variable.

Figure 34   /PIE=VALUE(SALNOW) BY ID

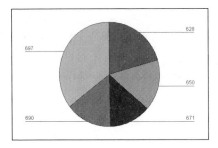

Specification: value_function (var) [BY var]

Labels: BY variable value labels

Each pie slice shows the value of one case. If no BY variable is specified, the number of each case is used as the label.

HILO Subcommand

HILO creates one of two types of high-low-close charts using keywords SIMPLE or GROUPED. High-low-close charts show the range and the closing (or average) value of a series.

- Only one keyword can be specified.
- When a keyword is specified, it must be specified in the parentheses.
- When no keyword is specified, the default is either SIMPLE or GROUPED, depending on the type of function/variable specification.

SIMPLE   *Simple high-low-close chart.* A simple high-low-close chart can be defined by a single summary or count function and two BY variables, by three summary functions and one BY variable, or by three values with one or no BY variable. When a second BY variable is used to define a high-low-close chart, the

GRAPH   523

variable must be dichotomous or trichotomous. If dichotomous, the first value defines low and the second value defines high; if trichotomous, the first value defines high, the second defines low and the third defines close (see Figure 35 to Figure 37).

GROUPED   *Grouped high-low-close chart.* A grouped high-low-close chart is defined by a single function and two BY variables or by multiple functions and a single BY variable. When a variable list is used for a single function, the list must contain two or three variables. If it contains two variables, the first defines the high value, and the second defines the low value. If it contains three variables, the first defines the high value, the second defines the low value, and the third defines the close value. Likewise, if multiple functions are specified, they must be either in groups of two or in groups of three. The first function defines the high value, the second defines the low value, and the third, if specified, defines the close value (see Figure 38 and Figure 39).

Figure 35   HILO=MEAN(HIGH LOW CLOSE) BY DATE

Specification: sum_function(varlist) BY var

Legend title:	fn name
Legend labels:	fn var labels
y-axis title:	none
y-axis labels:	fn value scale
x-axis title:	BY var label
x-axis labels:	BY var value labels

You can specify three variables with one summary function or three summary functions each with one variable. The line represents the close or average series defined by the function. If you specify only two, they are used as high and low values.

Figure 36   HILO=MEAN(VALUE) BY DATE BY HILO

Specification: sum_function(var) BY var BY var

Legend title:	2nd BY var label
Legend labels:	2nd BY var value labels
y-axis title:	fn name+fn var label
y-axis labels:	fn value scale
x-axis title:	1st BY var label
x-axis labels:	1st BY var value labels

The second BY variable must be dichotomous or trichotomous. If dichotomous, the first value defines the high and the second value defines the low value. If trichotomous, the first value defines the high value, the second value defines the low, and the last value defines the close.

Figure 37   HILO=VALUE(HIGH LOW CLOSE) BY TIME

Specification: value_function(varlist) BY var

Legend title:	none
Legend labels:	var labels
y-axis title:	none
y-axis labels:	value scale
x-axis title:	BY var label
x-axis labels:	BY var value labels

The first variable represents the high value, the second, the low value, and the third, the close value.

Figure 38   HILO=MEAN(HIGH) MEAN(LOW) MEAN(CLOSE) BY DATE BY COMPANY

Specification: sum_function list BY var BY var

Legend title:	2nd BY var label
Legend labels:	2nd BY var value labels
	3rd fn name + var label
y-axis title:	1st 2 fn names+var labels
y-axis labels:	fn value scale
x-axis title:	1st BY var label
x-axis labels:	1st BY var value labels

The function-variable specification automatically produces a clustered high-low-close chart. The function list must consist of two or three functions. If two functions are specified, they represent the high and the low; if three functions are specified, they represent the high, the low, and the close.

Figure 39   HILO=VALUE(RH RL RA) VALUE(FH HL HA)   VALUE(GH GL HA) BY WEEK

Specification: value_function list BY var

Legend title:	none
Legend labels:	var labels
y-axis title:	none
y-axis labels:	value scale
x-axis title:	BY var label
x-axis labels:	BY var value labels

Each function must have two or three variables to represent high and low values or high, low, and close values. If no BY variable is specified, case numbers are used as *x*-axis labels.

GRAPH   525

ERRORBAR Subcommand

ERRORBAR creates either a simple or a clustered error bar chart, depending on the variable specification on the subcommand. A simple error bar chart is defined by one numeric variable with or without a BY variable or a variable list. A clustered error bar chart is defined by one numeric variable with two BY variables or a variable list with a BY variable (see Figure 40 to Figure 43).

Error bar charts can display confidence intervals, standard deviations, or standard errors of the mean. To specify the statistics to be displayed, one of the following keywords is required:

CI value   *Display confidence intervals for mean.* You can specify a confidence level between 50 and 99.9. The default is 95.

STERROR *n*   *Display standard errors of mean.* You can specify any positive number for *n*. The default is 2.

STDDEV *n*   *Display standard deviations.* You can specify any positive number for *n*. The default is 2.

Figure 40   ERRORBAR=SALNOW BY SEXRACE

Specification: var by var

Legend title:	none
Legend labels:	none
y-axis title:	display + var label
y-axis labels:	value scale
x-axis title:	BY var label
x-axis labels:	BY var value labels

CI(95) is the default. Error bars can also display standard errors of the mean or standard deviations if you specify the appropriate keyword in the parentheses.

Figure 41   ERRORBAR=FRINGE SALBEG SALNOW

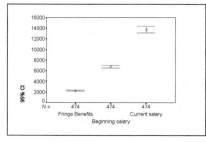

Specification: varlist

Legend title:	none
Legend labels:	none
y-axis title:	displayed statistics
y-axis labels:	value scale
x-axis title:	none
x-axis labels:	var labels

CI(95) is the default. Error bars can also display standard errors of the mean or standard deviations if you specify the appropriate keyword in the parentheses. Numbers of valid cases for each variable are displayed.

Figure 42   ERRORBAR=SALNOW BY JOBCAT BY SEXRACE

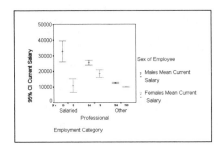

Specification: var1 BY var2 BY var3

Legend title:	var3 label
Legend labels:	var3 value labels+Mean +var1 label
y-axis title:	display+var1 label
y-axis labels:	value scale
x-axis title:	var2 label
x-axis labels:	var2 value labels

Figure 43   ERRORBAR=FRINGE SALBEG SALNOW BY SEX

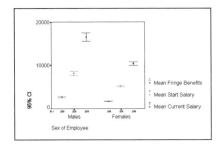

Specification: varlist BY var

Legend title:	none
Legend labels:	Mean+var labels
y-axis title:	displayed statistics
y-axis labels:	values
x-axis title:	BY var label
x-axis labels:	BY var value labels

SCATTERPLOT Subcommand

SCATTERPLOT produces two- or three-dimensional scatterplots. Multiple two-dimensional plots can be plotted within the same frame or as a scatterplot matrix. Only variables can be specified; aggregated functions cannot be plotted. When SCATTERPLOT is specified without keywords, the default is BIVARIATE.

BIVARIATE   *One two-dimensional scatterplot.* A basic scatterplot is defined by two variables separated by the keyword WITH (see Figure 44 to Figure 46). This is the default when SCATTERPLOT is specified without keywords.

OVERLAY   *Multiple plots drawn within the same frame.* Specify a variable list on both sides of WITH. By default, one scatterplot is drawn for each combination of variables on the left of WITH with variables on the right (see Figure 47). You can specify PAIR in parentheses to indicate that the first variable on the left is paired with the first variable on the right, the second variable on the left with the second variable on the right, and so on. All plots are drawn within the same frame and are differentiated by color or pattern. The axes are scaled to accommodate the minimum and maximum values across all variables.

GRAPH 527

MATRIX   *Scatterplot matrix.* Specify at least two variables. One scatterplot is drawn for each combination of the specified variables above the diagonal and a second below the diagonal in a square matrix (see Figure 48).

XYZ   *One three-dimensional plot.* Specify three variables, each separated from the next with the keyword WITH (see Figure 49).

- If you specify a control variable using BY, GRAPH produces a control scatterplot where values of the BY variable are indicated by different colors or patterns. A control variable cannot be specified for overlay plots.

- You can display the value label of an identification variable at the plotting position for each case by adding BY *var* (NAME) or BY *var* (IDENTIFY) to the end of any valid scatterplot specification. When the chart is created, NAME turns the labels on while IDENTIFY turns the labels off. You can use the Point Selection tool to turn individual labels off or on in the scatterplot. Figure 46 shows a simple scatterplot with labels turned on.

Figure 44   /SCATTERPLOT=PROFITS WITH COMPS

Specification: var1 WITH var2
                [BY var] [BY var (NAME)]

y-axis title:	var2 var label
y-axis labels:	scaled values
x-axis title:	var1 var label
x-axis labels:	scaled values

Figure 45   /SCATTERPLOT=SALBEG WITH SALNOW BY SEX

Specification: var1 WITH var2 BY var3*

Legend title	marker var (var3) label
Legend labels:	marker var value [label]
y-axis title:	var2 var label
y-axis labels:	scaled values
x-axis title:	var1 var label
x-axis labels:	scaled values

*VAR3 is a marker variable. For specification of a label variable, see Figure 46.

Figure 46   /SCATTERPLOT=JOBCAT WITH SALNOW BY ID (NAME)

Specification: var1 WITH var2 BY var3(NAME)*

Point labels: Label var (*VAR3)* value labels
y-axis title: var2 var label
y-axis labels: scaled values
x-axis title: var1 var label
x-axis labels: scaled values

*When keyword NAME is specified, *VAR3* serves as a label variable. For the specification of a marker variable, see Figure 45. You can specify both a marker variable and a label variable for a simple scatterplot.

Figure 47   /SCATTERPLOT(OVERLAY)=VERBAL MATH WITH AARATIO)

Specification: varlist WITH varlist [BY var(NAME)]*

Legend title: none
Legend labels: pairs of var names
y-axis title: none
y-axis labels: scaled values**
x-axis title: none
x-axis labels: scaled values**

*You can specify only a label variable after BY for an overlay scatterplot. The keyword NAME is required if a BY variable is specified.
**Values are scaled to accommodate the maximum and minimum values of each pair.

Figure 48   /SCATTERPLOT(MATRIX)=SCORE COST SFRATIO

Specification: varlist [BY var] [BY var(NAME)]*

Legend title: marker var name
Legend labels: marker var value labels
Point labels: label value labels
Diagonal titles: var labels

*Matrix scatterplots can have both marker variable and label variable specifications.

GRAPH   529

Figure 49   /SCATTERPLOT(XYZ)=JOBCAT WITH SALARY WITH EDLEVEL BY SEX BY ID (NAME)

Specification:
xvar WITH yvar WITH zvar [BY var] [BY var(NAME)]

Legend title:	1st BY var label
Legend labels:	1st BY var value labels
Point labels:	2nd BY var value labels
x-axis title:	xvar label
y-axis title:	yvar label
z-axis title:	zvar label

*3-D scatterplots allow both marker variable and label variable specifications.

HISTOGRAM Subcommand

HISTOGRAM creates a histogram (see Figure 50 and Figure 51).

- Only one variable can be specified on this subcommand.
- GRAPH divides the values of the variable into several evenly spaced intervals and produces a bar chart showing the number of times the values for the variable fall within each interval.
- You can request a normal distribution line by specifying the keyword NORMAL in parentheses (see Figure 51).

Figure 50   /HISTOGRAM=RATIO

Specification: var

y-axis title:	none
y-axis label:	number of valid cases
x-axis title:	var label
x-axis label:	scaled values

The standard deviation, mean, and number of valid cases are displayed.

Figure 51   /HISTOGRAM(NORMAL)=VERBAL

Specification: var

y-axis title:	none
y-axis labels:	number of valid cases
x-axis title:	var label
x-axis labels:	scaled values

The normal distribution line as well as the standard deviation, mean, and number of valid cases are displayed.

PARETO Subcommand

PARETO creates one of two types of Pareto charts. A Pareto chart is used in quality control to identify the few problems that create the majority of nonconformities. Only SUM, VALUE, and COUNT can be used with the PARETO subcommand.

Before plotting, PARETO sorts the plotted values in descending order by category. The right axis is always labeled by the cumulative percentage from 0 to 100. By default, a cumulative line is displayed. You can eliminate the cumulative line or explicitly request it by specifying one of the following keywords:

CUM   *Display the cumulative line.* This is the default.

NOCUM   *Do not display the cumulative line.*

You can request a simple or a stacked Pareto chart by specifying one of the following keywords and define it with appropriate function/variable specifications:

SIMPLE   *Simple Pareto chart.* Each bar represents one type of nonconformity. A simple Pareto chart can be defined by a single variable, a single VALUE function, a single SUM function with a BY variable, or a SUM function with a variable list as an argument with no BY variable (see Figure 52 and Figure 53).

STACKED   *Stacked Pareto chart.* Each bar represents one or more types of nonconformity within the category. A stacked Pareto chart can be defined by a single SUM function with two BY variables, a single variable with a BY variable, a VALUE function with a variable list as an argument, or a SUM function with a variable list as an argument and a BY variable (see Figure 54 and Figure 55).

GRAPH   531

Figure 52   PARETO(CUM SIMPLE)=SUM(DEF1 TO DEF7)

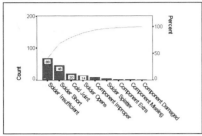

Specification: sum_fun (varlist)

Right axis title:	Percent
Right axis labels:	Cumulative percentage
y-axis title:	Count
y-axis labels:	defect count
x-axis title:	none
x-axis labels:	var labels

The data are sorted in descending order. The cumulative line is displayed. The first two defects account for over 75% of the returned products.

Figure 53   PARETO(CUM SIMPLE)=SUM(DEFECTS) BY SHIFT

Specification: sum_fun (var) BY var

Right axis title:	Percent
Right axis labels:	Cumulative percentage
y-axis title:	fn var label
y-axis labels:	defect count
x-axis title:	BY var label
x-axis labels:	var labels

The data are sorted in descending order. The cumulative line is displayed. The work shifts 7, 3, and 9 account for 60% of the defective products.

Figure 54   PARETO(CUM STACKED)=SUM(DEF1 TO DEF5) BY SHIFT

Specification: sum_fn(varlist) BY var

Legend title:	none
Legend labels:	fn variable labels
y-axis title:	Count
y-axis labels:	defect count
x-axis title:	BY var label
x-axis labels:	BY var value labels

The Pareto chart shows the work shifts that are responsible for most of the defects. It also shows the type of defects each work shift produces.

Figure 55   PARETO(CUM STACKED)=SUM(DEFECTS) BY SHIFT BY TYPE

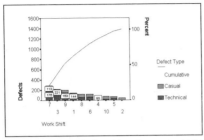

Specification: sum_fn(var1) BY var2 BY var3

Legend title:	var3 label
Legend labels:	var3 value labels
y-axis title:	var1 label
y-axis labels:	defect count
x-axis title:	var2 label
x-axis labels:	var2 value labels

The stacks are defined by the second BY variable (*TYPE*); the categories are defined by the first BY variable (*SHIFT*).

TEMPLATE Subcommand

TEMPLATE uses an existing chart as a template and applies it to the chart requested by the current GRAPH command.

- The specification on TEMPLATE is a chart file saved during a previous session.
- The general rule of application is that the template overrides the default setting, but the specifications on the current GRAPH command override the template. Nonapplicable elements and attributes are ignored.
- Three types of elements and attributes can be applied from a chart template: those dependent on data, those dependent on the chart type, and those dependent on neither.

Elements and Attributes Independent of Chart Types or Data

Elements and attributes common to all chart types are always applied unless overridden by the specifications on the current GRAPH command.

- The title, subtitle, and footnote, including text, color, font type and size, and line alignment are always applied. To give your chart a new title, subtitle, or footnote, specify the text on the TITLE, SUBTITLE, or FOOTNOTE subcommand. You cannot change other attributes.
- The outer frame of the chart, including line style, color, and fill pattern, is always applied. The inner frame is applied except for those charts that do not have an inner frame. The template overrides the system default.
- Label formats are applied wherever applicable. The template overrides the system default. Label text, however, is not applied. GRAPH automatically provides axis labels according to the function/variable specification.
- Legends and the legend title attributes, including color, font type and size, and alignment, are applied provided the current chart requires legends. The legend title text, however, is not applied. GRAPH provides the legend title according to the function/variable specification.

GRAPH   533

Elements and Attributes Dependent on Chart Type

Elements and attributes dependent on the chart type are those that exist only in a specific chart type. They include bars (in bar charts), lines and areas (in line charts), markers (in scatterplots), boxes (in boxplots), and pie sectors (in pie charts). These elements and their attributes are usually applied only when the template chart and the requested chart are of the same type. Some elements or their attributes may override the default settings across chart type.

- Color and pattern are always applied except for pie charts. The template overrides the system default.

- Scale axis lines are applied across chart types. Scale axis range is never applied.

- Interval axis lines are applied from interval axis to interval axis. Interval axis bins are never applied.

- If the template is a 3-D bar chart and you request a chart with one category axis, attributes of the first axis are applied from the template. If you request a 3-D bar chart and the template is not a 3-D chart, no category axis attributes are applied.

Elements and Attributes Dependent on Data

Data-dependent elements and attributes are applied only when the template and the requested chart are of the same type and the template has at least as many series assigned to the same types of chart elements as the requested chart.

- Category attributes and elements, including fill, border, color, pattern, line style, weight of pie sectors, pie sector explosion, reference lines, projection lines, and annotations, are applied only when category values in the requested chart match those in the template.

- The attributes of data-related elements with on/off states are always applied. For example, the line style, weight, and color of a quadratic fit in a simple bivariate scatterplot are applied if the requested chart is also a simple bivariate scatterplot. The specification on the GRAPH command, for example, HISTOGRAM(NORMAL), overrides the applied on/off status; in this case, a normal curve is displayed regardless of whether the template displays a normal curve.

- In bar, line, and area charts, the assignment of series to bars, lines, and areas is not applied.

- Case weighting status for histograms and scatterplots is not applied. You must turn weighting on or off before specifying the GRAPH command.

MISSING Subcommand

MISSING controls the treatment of missing values in the chart drawn by GRAPH.

- The default is LISTWISE.

- The MISSING subcommand has no effect on variables used with the VALUE function to create nonaggregated charts. User-missing and system-missing values create empty cells.

- LISTWISE and VARIABLE are alternatives and apply to variables used in summary functions for a chart or to variables being plotted in a scatterplot.

- REPORT and NOREPORT are alternatives and apply only to category variables. They control whether categories and series with missing values are created. NOREPORT is the default.
- INCLUDE and EXCLUDE are alternatives and apply to both summary and category variables. EXCLUDE is the default.
- When a case has a missing value for the name variable but contains valid values for the dependent variable in a scatterplot, the case is always included. User-missing values are displayed as point labels; system-missing values are not displayed.
- For an aggregated categorical chart, if every aggregated series is empty in a category, the empty category is excluded.
- A nonaggregated categorical chart created with the VALUE function can contain completely empty categories. There are always as many categories as rows of data. However, at least one nonempty cell must be present; otherwise the chart is not created.

LISTWISE	*Listwise deletion of cases with missing values.* A case with a missing value for any dependent variable is excluded from computations and graphs.
VARIABLE	*Variable-wise deletion.* A case is deleted from the analysis only if it has a missing value for the dependent variable being analyzed.
NOREPORT	*Suppress missing-value categories.* This is the default.
REPORT	*Report and graph missing-value categories.*
EXCLUDE	*Exclude user-missing values.* Both user- and system-missing values for dependent variables are excluded from computations and graphs. This is the default.
INCLUDE	*Include user-missing values.* Only system-missing values for dependent variables are excluded from computations and graphs.

HILOGLINEAR

HILOGLINEAR is available in the Advanced Models option.

```
HILOGLINEAR {varlist} (min,max) [varlist ...]
            {ALL     }

 [/METHOD [= BACKWARD]]

 [/MAXORDER = k]

 [/CRITERIA = [CONVERGE({0.25**})] [ITERATE({20**})] [P({0.05**})]
                        {n     }             {n   }      {prob  }
               [DELTA({0.5**})] [MAXSTEPS({10**})]
                      {d    }            {n   }
               [DEFAULT] ]

 [/CWEIGHT = {varname }]
             {(matrix)}

 [/PRINT = {[FREQ**]  [RESID**]  [ESTIM**] [ASSOCIATION**]}]
           {DEFAULT**                                     }
           {ALL                                           }
           {NONE                                          }

 [/PLOT = [{NONE**              } ]
           {DEFAULT             }
           {[RESID] [NORMPROB]}
           {ALL                 }

 [/MISSING = [{EXCLUDE**}]]]
             {INCLUDE  }

 [/DESIGN = effectname effectname*effectname ...]
```

** Default if subcommand or keyword is omitted.

Example

```
HILOGLINEAR V1(1,2) V2(1,2)
  /DESIGN=V1*V2.
```

Overview

HILOGLINEAR fits hierarchical loglinear models to multidimensional contingency tables using an iterative proportional-fitting algorithm. HILOGLINEAR also estimates parameters for saturated models. These techniques are described in Everitt (1977), Bishop et al. (1975), and Goodman (1978). HILOGLINEAR is much more efficient for these models than the LOGLINEAR procedure because HILOGLINEAR uses an iterative proportional-fitting algorithm rather than the Newton-Raphson method used in LOGLINEAR.

Options

Design Specification. You can request automatic model selection using backward elimination with the METHOD subcommand. You can also specify any hierarchical design and request multiple designs using the DESIGN subcommand.

Design Control. You can control the criteria used in the iterative proportional-fitting and model-selection routines with the CRITERIA subcommand. You can also limit the order of effects in the model with the MAXORDER subcommand and specify structural zeros for cells in the tables you analyze with the CWEIGHT subcommand.

Display and Plots. You can select the display for each design with the PRINT subcommand. For saturated models, you can request tests for different orders of effects as well. With the PLOT subcommand, you can request residuals plots or normal probability plots of residuals.

Basic Specification

- The basic specification is a variable list with at least two variables followed by their minimum and maximum values.
- HILOGLINEAR estimates a saturated model for all variables in the analysis.
- By default, HILOGLINEAR displays parameter estimates, measures of partial association, goodness of fit, and frequencies for the saturated model.

Subcommand Order

- The variable list must be specified first.
- Subcommands affecting a given DESIGN must appear before the DESIGN subcommand. Otherwise, subcommands can appear in any order.
- MISSING can be placed anywhere after the variable list.

Syntax Rules

- DESIGN is optional. If DESIGN is omitted or the last specification is not a DESIGN subcommand, a default saturated model is estimated.
- You can specify multiple PRINT, PLOT, CRITERIA, MAXORDER, and CWEIGHT subcommands. The last of each type specified is in effect for subsequent designs.
- PRINT, PLOT, CRITERIA, MAXORDER, and CWEIGHT specifications remain in effect until they are overridden by new specifications on these subcommands.
- You can specify multiple METHOD subcommands, but each one affects only the next design.
- MISSING can be specified only once.

Operations

- HILOGLINEAR builds a contingency table using all variables on the variable list. The table contains a cell for each possible combination of values within the range specified for each variable.
- HILOGLINEAR assumes that there is a category for every integer value in the range of each variable. Empty categories waste space and can cause computational problems. If there are empty categories, use the RECODE command to create consecutive integer values for categories.
- Cases with values outside the range specified for a variable are excluded.
- If the last subcommand is not a DESIGN subcommand, HILOGLINEAR displays a warning and generates the default model. This is the saturated model unless MAXORDER is specified. This model is in addition to any that are explicitly requested.
- If the model is not saturated (for example, when MAXORDER is less than the number of factors), only the goodness of fit and the observed and expected frequencies are given.
- The display uses the WIDTH subcommand defined on the SET command. If the defined width is less than 132, some portions of the display may be deleted.

Limitations

The HILOGLINEAR procedure cannot estimate all possible frequency models, and it produces limited output for unsaturated models.

- It can estimate only hierarchical loglinear models.
- It treats all table variables as nominal. (You can use LOGLINEAR to fit nonhierarchical models to tables involving variables that are ordinal.)
- It can produce parameter estimates for saturated models only (those with all possible main-effect and interaction terms).
- It can estimate partial associations for saturated models only.
- It can handle tables with no more than 10 factors.

Example

```
HILOGLINEAR V1(1,2) V2(1,2) V3(1,3) V4(1,3)
   /DESIGN=V1*V2*V3, V4.
```

- HILOGLINEAR builds a $2 \times 2 \times 3 \times 3$ contingency table for analysis.
- DESIGN specifies the generating class for a hierarchical model. This model consists of main effects for all four variables, two-way interactions among *V1*, *V2*, and *V3*, and the three-way interaction term *V1* by *V2* by *V3*.

Variable List

The required variable list specifies the variables in the analysis. The variable list must precede all other subcommands.

- Variables must be numeric and have integer values. If a variable has a fractional value, the fractional portion is truncated.
- Keyword ALL can be used to refer to all user-defined variables in the working data file.
- A range must be specified for each variable, with the minimum and maximum values separated by a comma and enclosed in parentheses.
- If the same range applies to several variables, the range can be specified once after the last variable to which it applies.
- If ALL is specified, all variables must have the same range.

METHOD Subcommand

By default, HILOGLINEAR tests the model specified on the DESIGN subcommand (or the default model) and does not perform any model selection. All variables are entered and none are removed. Use METHOD to specify automatic model selection using backward elimination for the next design specified.

- You can specify METHOD alone or with the keyword BACKWARD for an explicit specification.
- When the backward-elimination method is requested, a step-by-step output is displayed regardless of the specification on the PRINT subcommand.
- METHOD affects only the next design.

BACKWARD   *Backward elimination.* Perform backward elimination of terms in the model. All terms are entered. Those that do not meet the P criterion specified on the CRITERIA subcommand (or the default P) are removed one at a time.

MAXORDER Subcommand

MAXORDER controls the maximum order of terms in the model estimated for subsequent designs. If MAXORDER is specified, HILOGLINEAR tests a model only with terms of that order or less.

- MAXORDER specifies the highest-order term that will be considered for the next design. MAXORDER can thus be used to abbreviate computations for the BACKWARD method.
- If the integer on MAXORDER is less than the number of factors, parameter estimates and measures of partial association are not available. Only the goodness of fit and the observed and expected frequencies are displayed.
- You can use MAXORDER with backward elimination to find the best model with terms of a certain order or less. This is computationally much more efficient than eliminating terms from the saturated model.

Example

```
HILOGLINEAR V1 V2 V3(1,2)
  /MAXORDER=2
  /DESIGN=V1 V2 V3
  /DESIGN=V1*V2*V3.
```

- HILOGLINEAR builds a $2 \times 2 \times 2$ contingency table for *V1*, *V2*, and *V3*.
- MAXORDER has no effect on the first DESIGN subcommand because the design requested considers only main effects.
- MAXORDER restricts the terms in the model specified on the second DESIGN subcommand to two-way interactions and main effects.

CRITERIA Subcommand

Use the CRITERIA subcommand to change the values of constants in the iterative proportional-fitting and model-selection routines for subsequent designs.

- The default criteria are in effect if the CRITERIA subcommand is omitted (see below).
- You cannot specify the CRITERIA subcommand without any keywords.
- Specify each CRITERIA keyword followed by a criterion value in parentheses. Only those criteria specifically altered are changed.
- You can specify more than one keyword on CRITERIA, and they can be in any order.

DEFAULT   *Reset parameters to their default values.* If you have specified criteria other than the defaults for a design, use this keyword to restore the defaults for subsequent designs.

CONVERGE(n)   *Convergence criterion.* The default is 10^{-3} times the largest cell size, or 0.25, whichever is larger.

ITERATE(n)   *Maximum number of iterations.* The default is 20.

P(n)   *Probability for change in chi-square if term is removed.* Specify a value between (but not including) 0 and 1 for the significance level. The default is 0.05. P is in effect only when you request BACKWARD on the METHOD subcommand.

MAXSTEPS(n)   *Maximum number of steps for model selection.* Specify an integer between 1 and 99, inclusive. The default is 10.

DELTA(d)   *Cell delta value.* The value of delta is added to each cell frequency for the first iteration. It is left in the cells for saturated models only. The default value is 0.5. You can specify any decimal value between 0 and 1 for *d*. HILOGLINEAR does not display parameter estimates or the covariance matrix of parameter estimates if any zero cells (either structural or sampling) exist in the expected table after delta is added.

CWEIGHT Subcommand

CWEIGHT specifies cell weights for a model. CWEIGHT is typically used to specify structural zeros in the table. You can also use CWEIGHT to adjust tables to fit new margins.

- You can specify the name of a variable whose values are cell weights, or provide a matrix of cell weights enclosed in parentheses.
- If you use a variable to specify cell weights, you are allowed only one CWEIGHT subcommand.
- If you specify a matrix, you must provide a weight for every cell in the contingency table, where the number of cells equals the product of the number of values of all variables.
- Cell weights are indexed by the values of the variables in the order in which they are specified on the variable list. The index values of the rightmost variable change the most quickly.
- You can use the notation $n*cw$ to indicate that cell weight cw is repeated n times in the matrix.

Example

```
HILOGLINEAR V1(1,2) V2(1,2) V3(1,3)
  /CWEIGHT=CELLWGT
  /DESIGN=V1*V2, V2*V3, V1*V3.
```

- This example uses the variable *CELLWGT* to assign cell weights for the table. Only one CWEIGHT subcommand is allowed.

Example

```
HILOGLINEAR V4(1,3) V5(1,3)
  /CWEIGHT=(0 1 1  1 0 1  1 1 0)
  /DESIGN=V4, V5.
```

- The HILOGLINEAR command sets the diagonal cells in the model to structural zeros. This type of model is known as a **quasi-independence model**.
- Because both *V4* and *V5* have three values, weights must be specified for nine cells.
- The first cell weight is applied to the cell in which *V4* is 1 and *V5* is 1; the second weight is applied to the cell in which *V4* is 1 and *V5* is 2; and so on.

Example

```
HILOGLINEAR V4(1,3) V5(1,3)
  /CWEIGHT=(0 3*1 0 3*1 0)
  /DESIGN=V4,V5.
```

- This example is the same as the previous example except that the $n*cw$ notation is used.

Example

```
* An Incomplete Rectangular Table

DATA LIST FREE / LOCULAR RADIAL FREQ.
WEIGHT BY FREQ.
BEGIN DATA
1 1 462
1 2 130
1 3 2
1 4 1
2 1 103
2 2 35
2 3 1
2 4 0
3 5 614
3 6 138
3 7 21
3 8 14
3 9 1
4 5 443
4 6 95
4 7 22
4 8 8
4 9 5
END DATA.
HILOGLINEAR LOCULAR (1,4) RADIAL (1,9)
  /CWEIGHT=(4*1 5*0   4*1 5*0   4*0 5*1   4*0 5*1)
  /DESIGN LOCULAR RADIAL.
```

- This example uses aggregated table data as input.

- The DATA LIST command defines three variables. The values of *LOCULAR* and *RADIAL* index the levels of those variables, so that each case defines a cell in the table. The values of *FREQ* are the cell frequencies.

- The WEIGHT command weights each case by the value of the variable *FREQ*. Because each case represents a cell in this example, the WEIGHT command assigns the frequencies for each cell.

- The BEGIN DATA and END DATA commands enclose the inline data.

- The HILOGLINEAR variable list specifies two variables. *LOCULAR* has values 1, 2, 3, and 4. *RADIAL* has integer values 1 through 9.

- The CWEIGHT subcommand identifies a block rectangular pattern of cells that are logically empty. There is one weight specified for each cell of the 36-cell table.

- In this example, the matrix form needs to be used in CWEIGHT because the structural zeros do not appear in the actual data. (For example, there is no case corresponding to *LOCULAR*=1, *RADIAL*=5.)

- The DESIGN subcommand specifies main effects only for *LOCULAR* and *RADIAL*. Lack of fit for this model indicates an interaction of the two variables.

- Because there is no PRINT or PLOT subcommand, HILOGLINEAR produces the default output for an unsaturated model.

PRINT Subcommand

PRINT controls the display produced for the subsequent designs.

- If PRINT is omitted or included with no specifications, the default display is produced.
- If any keywords are specified on PRINT, only output specifically requested is displayed.
- HILOGLINEAR displays Pearson and likelihood-ratio chi-square goodness-of-fit tests for models. For saturated models, it also provides tests that the k-way effects and the k-way and higher-order effects are 0.
- Both adjusted and unadjusted degrees of freedom are displayed for tables with sampling or structural zeros. K-way and higher-order tests use the unadjusted degrees of freedom.
- The unadjusted degrees of freedom are not adjusted for zero cells, and they estimate the upper bound of the true degrees of freedom. These are the same degrees of freedom you would get if all cells were filled.
- The adjusted degrees of freedom are calculated from the number of non-zero-fitted cells minus the number of parameters that would be estimated if all cells were filled (that is, unadjusted degrees of freedom minus the number of zero-fitted cells). This estimate of degrees of freedom may be too low if some parameters do not exist because of zeros.

DEFAULT   *Default displays.* This option includes FREQ and RESID output for nonsaturated models, and FREQ, RESID, ESTIM, and ASSOCIATION output for saturated models. For saturated models, the observed and expected frequencies are equal, and the residuals are zeros.

FREQ   *Observed and expected cell frequencies.*

RESID   *Raw and standardized residuals.*

ESTIM   *Parameter estimates for a saturated model.*

ASSOCIATION   *Partial associations.* You can request partial associations of effects only when you specify a saturated model. This option is computationally expensive for tables with many factors.

ALL   *All available output.*

NONE   *Design information and goodness-of-fit statistics only.* Use of this option overrides all other specifications on PRINT.

PLOT Subcommand

Use PLOT to request residuals plots.

- If PLOT is included without specifications, standardized residuals and normal probability plots are produced.
- No plots are displayed for saturated models.
- If PLOT is omitted, no plots are produced.

RESID   *Standardized residuals by observed and expected counts.*

NORMPLOT   *Normal probability plots of adjusted residuals.*

NONE   *No plots.* Specify NONE to suppress plots requested on a previous PLOT sub-command. This is the default if PLOT is omitted.

DEFAULT   *Default plots.* Includes RESID and NORMPLOT. This is the default when PLOT is specified without keywords.

ALL   *All available plots.*

MISSING Subcommand

By default, a case with either system-missing or user-missing values for any variable named on the HILOGLINEAR variable list is omitted from the analysis. Use MISSING to change the treatment of cases with user-missing values.

- MISSING can be named only once and can be placed anywhere following the variable list.
- MISSING cannot be used without specifications.
- A case with a system-missing value for any variable named on the variable list is always excluded from the analysis.

EXCLUDE   *Delete cases with missing values.* This is the default if the subcommand is omitted. You can also specify keyword DEFAULT.

INCLUDE   *Include user-missing values as valid.* Only cases with system-missing values are deleted.

DESIGN Subcommand

By default, HILOGLINEAR uses a saturated model that includes all variables on the variable list. The model contains all main effects and interactions for those variables. Use DESIGN to specify a different generating class for the model.

- If DESIGN is omitted or included without specifications, the default model is estimated. When DESIGN is omitted, SPSS issues a warning message.
- To specify a design, list the highest-order terms, using variable names and asterisks (*) to indicate interaction effects.
- In a hierarchical model, higher-order interaction effects imply lower-order interaction and main effects. V1*V2*V3 implies the three-way interaction *V1* by *V2* by *V3*, two-way interactions *V1* by *V2*, *V1* by *V3*, and *V2* by *V3*, and main effects for *V1*, *V2*, and *V3*. The highest-order effects to be estimated are the generating class.
- Any PRINT, PLOT, CRITERIA, METHOD, and MAXORDER subcommands that apply to a DESIGN subcommand must appear before it.
- All variables named on DESIGN must be named or implied on the variable list.
- You can specify more than one DESIGN subcommand. One model is estimated for each DESIGN subcommand.
- If the last subcommand on HILOGLINEAR is not DESIGN, the default model will be estimated in addition to models explicitly requested. SPSS issues a warning message for a missing DESIGN subcommand.

IF

```
IF [(]logical expression[)] target variable=expression
```

The following relational operators can be used in logical expressions:

Symbol	Definition	Symbol	Definition
EQ or =	Equal to	NE or <>[*]	Not equal to
LT or <	Less than	LE or <=	Less than or equal to
GT or >	Greater than	GE or >=	Greater than or equal to

* On ASCII systems (for example, UNIX, VAX, and all PC's) you can also use ~=; on IBM EBCDIC systems (for example, IBM 360 and IBM 370) you can also use ¬=.

The following logical operators can be used in logical expressions:

Symbol	Definition
AND or &	Both relations must be true
Or or I	Either relation can be true
Not*	Reverses the outcome of an expression[*]

* On ASCII systems you can also use ~; on IBM EBCDIC systems you can also use ¬ (or the symbol above number 6).

Example

```
IF (AGE > 20 AND SEX = 1) GROUP=2.
```

Overview

IF conditionally executes a single transformation command based upon logical conditions found in the data. The transformation can create a new variable or modify the values of an existing variable for each case in the working data file. You can create or modify the values of both numeric and string variables. If you create a new string variable, you must first declare it on the STRING command.

IF has three components: a *logical expression* (see "Logical Expressions" on p. 53) that sets up the logical criteria, a *target variable* (the one to be modified or created), and an *assignment expression*. The target variable's values are modified according to the assignment expression.

IF is most efficient when used to execute a single, conditional, COMPUTE-like transformation. If you need multiple IF statements to define the condition, it is usually more efficient to use the RECODE command or a DO IF—END IF structure.

Basic Specification

The basic specification is a logical expression followed by a target variable, a required equals sign, and the assignment expression. The assignment is executed only if the logical expression is true.

Syntax Rules

- Logical expressions can be simple logical variables or relations, or complex logical tests involving variables, constants, functions, relational operators, and logical operators. Both the logical expression and the assignment expression can use any of the numeric or string functions allowed in COMPUTE transformations (see COMPUTE and "Transformation Expressions" on p. 43).
- Parentheses can be used to enclose the logical expression. Parentheses can also be used within the logical expression to specify the order of operations. Extra blanks or parentheses can be used to make the expression easier to read.
- A relation can compare variables, constants, or more complicated arithmetic expressions. Relations cannot be abbreviated. For example, (A EQ 2 OR A EQ 5) is valid, while (A EQ 2 OR 5) is not. Blanks (not commas) must be used to separate relational operators from the expressions being compared.
- A relation cannot compare a string variable to a numeric value or variable, or vice versa. A relation cannot compare the result of the logical functions SYSMIS, MISSING, ANY, or RANGE to a number.
- String values used in expressions must be specified in quotes and must include any leading or trailing blanks. Lowercase letters are considered distinct from uppercase letters.
- String variables that are used as target variables must already exist. To declare a new string variable, first create the variable with the STRING command and then specify the new variable as the target variable on IF.

Operations

- Each IF command evaluates every case in the data. Compare IF with DO IF, which passes control for a case out of the DO IF—END IF structure as soon as a logical condition is met.
- The logical expression is evaluated as true, false, or missing. The assignment is executed only if the logical expression is true. If the logical expression is false or missing, the assignment is not made. Existing target variables remain unchanged; new numeric variables retain their initial (system-missing) values.
- In general, a logical expression is evaluated as missing if any one of the variables used in the logical expression is system- or user-missing. However, when relations are joined by the logical operators AND or OR, the expression can sometimes be evaluated as true or false even when variables have missing values (see "Missing Values and Logical Operators" on p. 546).

Numeric Variables

- Numeric variables created with IF are initially set to the system-missing value. By default, they are assigned an F8.2 format.

- Logical expressions are evaluated in the following order: functions, followed by exponentiation, arithmetic operations, relations, and logical operators. When more than one logical operator is used, NOT is evaluated first, followed by AND and then OR. You can change the order of operations using parentheses.

- Assignment expressions are evaluated in the following order: functions, then exponentiation, and then arithmetic operators.

String Variables

- New string variables declared on IF are initially set to a blank value and are assigned the format specified on the STRING command that creates them.

- Logical expressions are evaluated in the following order: string functions, then relations, and then logical operators. When more than one logical operator is used, NOT is evaluated first, followed by AND and then OR. You can change the order of operations using parentheses.

- If the transformed value of a string variable exceeds the variable's defined width, the transformed value is truncated. If the transformed value is shorter than the defined width, the string is right-padded with blanks.

Missing Values and Logical Operators

When two or more relations are joined by logical operators AND or OR, the program always returns a missing value if all of the relations in the expression are missing. However, if any one of the relations can be determined, the program interprets the expression as true or false according to the logical outcomes shown in Table 1. The asterisk flags expressions where the program can evaluate the outcome with incomplete information.

Table 1   Logical outcome

Expression	Outcome	Expression	Outcome
true AND true	= true	true OR true	= true
true AND false	= false	true OR false	= true
false AND false	= false	false OR false	= false
true AND missing	= missing	true OR missing	= true*
missing AND missing	= missing	missing OR missing	= missing
false AND missing	= false*	false OR missing	= missing

Example

```
IF (AGE > 20 AND SEX = 1) GROUP=2.
```

- The numeric variable *GROUP* is set to 2 for cases where *AGE* is greater than 20 *and SEX* is equal to 1.
- When the expression is false or missing, the value of *GROUP* remains unchanged. If *GROUP* has not been previously defined, it contains the system-missing value.

Example

```
IF (SEX EQ 'F') EEO=QUOTA+GAIN.
```

- The logical expression tests the string variable *SEX* for the value *F*.
- When the expression is true (when *SEX* equals *F*), the value of the numeric variable *EEO* is assigned the value of *QUOTA* plus *GAIN*. Both *QUOTA* and *GAIN* must be previously defined numeric variables.
- When the expression is false or missing (for example, if *SEX* equals *F*), the value of *EEO* remains unchanged. If *EEO* has not been previously defined, it contains the system-missing value.

Example

```
COMPUTE V3=0.
IF ((V1-V2) LE 7) V3=V1**2.
```

- COMPUTE assigns *V3* the value 0.
- The logical expression tests whether *V1* minus *V2* is less than or equal to 7. If it is, the value of *V3* is assigned the value of *V1* squared. Otherwise, the value of *V3* remains at 0.

Example

```
IF (ABS(A-C) LT 100) INT=100.
```

- IF tests whether the absolute value of the variable *A* minus the variable *C* is less than 100. If it is, *INT* is assigned the value 100. Otherwise, the value is unchanged. If *INT* has not been previously defined, it is system-missing.

Example

```
IF (MEAN(V1 TO V5) LE 7) INDEX=1.
```

- If the mean of variables *V1* through *V5* is less than or equal to 7, *INDEX* equals 1.

Example

```
* Test for listwise deletion of missing values.

DATA LIST  /V1 TO V6 1-6.
STRING SELECT(A1).
COMPUTE SELECT='V'.
VECTOR V=V1 TO V6.

LOOP #I=1 TO 6.
IF MISSING(V(#I)) SELECT='M'.
END LOOP.

BEGIN DATA
123456
    56
1 3456
123456
123456
END DATA.

FREQUENCIES VAR=SELECT.
```

- STRING creates the string variable *SELECT* with an A1 format and COMPUTE sets the value of *SELECT* to *V*.

- VECTOR defines the vector *V* as the original variables *V1* to *V6*. Variables on a single vector must be all numeric or all string variables. In this example, because the vector *V* is used as an argument on the MISSING function of IF, the variables must be numeric (MISSING is not available for string variables).

- The loop structure executes six times: once for each VECTOR element. If a value is missing for any element, SELECT is set equal to *M*. In effect, if any case has a missing value for any of the variables *V1* to *V6*, SELECT is set to *M*.

- FREQUENCIES generates a frequency table for SELECT. The table gives a count of how many cases have missing values for at least one variable and how many cases have valid values for all variables. This table can be used to determine how many cases would be dropped from an analysis that uses listwise deletion of missing values. See pp. 188 and 322 for alternative ways to test for listwise deletion of missing values.

Example

```
IF YRHIRED LT 1980 RATE=0.02.
IF DEPT='SALES' DIVISION='TRANSFERRED'.
```

- The logical expression on the first IF command tests whether *YRHIRED* is less than 1980 (hired before 1980). If so, the variable *RATE* is set to 0.02.

- The logical expression on the second IF command tests whether *DEPT* equals *SALES*. When the condtion is true, the value for the string variable *DIVISION* is changed to *TRANSFERRED* but is truncated if the format for *DIVISION* is not at least 11 characters wide. For any other value of *DEPT*, the value of *DIVISION* remains unchanged.

- Although there are two IF statements, each defines a separate and independent condition. The IF command is used rather than the DO IF—END IF structure in order to test both conditions on every case. If DO IF—END IF is used, control passes out of the structure as soon as the first logical condition is met.

Example

```
IF (STATE EQ 'IL' AND CITY EQ 13) COST=1.07 * COST.
```

- The logical expression tests whether *STATE* equals *IL* and *CITY* equals 13.
- If the logical expression is true, the numeric variable *COST* is increased by 7%.
- For any other value of *STATE* or *CITY*, the value of *COST* remains unchanged.

Example

```
STRING GROUP (A18).
IF (HIRED GE 1988) GROUP='Hired after merger'.
```

- STRING declares the string variable *GROUP* and assigns it a width of 18 characters.
- When *HIRED* is greater than or equal to 1988, *GROUP* is assigned the value *Hired after merger*. When *HIRED* is less than 1988, *GROUP* remains blank.

Example

```
IF (RECV GT DUE OR (REVNUES GE EXPNS AND BALNCE GT 0))STATUS='SOLVENT.
```

- First, the program tests whether *REVNUES* is greater than or equal to *EXPNS* and whether *BALNCE* is greater than 0.
- Second, the program evaluates if *RECV* is greater than *DUE*.
- If either of these expressions is true, *STATUS* is assigned the value *SOLVENT*.
- If both expressions are false, *STATUS* remains unchanged.
- *STATUS* is an existing string variable in the working data file. Otherwise, it would have to be declared on a preceding STRING command.

IGRAPH

```
IGRAPH

[/Y=[VAR(varname1)]
    [TYPE={SCALE ([MIN=value] [MAX=value])}]
          {CATEGORICAL                        }
    [TITLE='string']]

[/X1=[VAR(varname2)]]
     [TYPE={SCALE([MIN=value] [MAX=value])}]
           {CATEGORICAL                        }
     [TITLE='string']]

[/X2=[VAR(varname3)]]
     [TYPE={SCALE([MIN=value] [MAX=value])}]
           {CATEGORICAL                        }
     [TITLE='string']]

[/YLENGTH=value]

[/X1LENGTH=value]

[/X2LENGTH=value]

[/CATORDER VAR(varname)
   ({COUNT     }   [{ASCENDING }]  [{SHOWEMPTY}])]
    {OCCURRENCE}    {DESCENDING}    {OMITEMPTY}
    {LABEL}
    {VALUE}

[/COLOR=varname
    [TYPE={SCALE([MIN=value] [MAX=value])}]
          {CATEGORICAL                        }
    [LEGEND={ON|OFF}]
    [TITLE='string']]
    [{CLUSTER}]]
     {STACK   }

[/REFLINE varname value [LABEL={ON|OFF}]
                        [SPIKE = {ON|OFF}]]
                        [COLOR={ON|OFF}]
                        [STYLE={ON|OFF}]

[/STYLE=varname
    [LEGEND={ON|OFF}]
    [TITLE='string']]
    [{CLUSTER}]
     {STACK   }

[/NORMALIZE]

[/SIZE=varname
    [TYPE={SCALE([MIN=value] [MAX=value])}]
          {CATEGORICAL                        }
    [LEGEND={ON|OFF}]
    [TITLE='string']]

[/CLUSTER=varname]

[/SUMMARYVAR=varname]

[/PANEL varlist]

[/POINTLABEL=varname]

[/COORDINATE={HORIZONTAL}]
```

```
                      {VERTICAL  }
                      {THREE     }

[/EFFECT={NONE }]
         {THREE}

[/TITLE='string']

[/SUBTITLE='string']

[/CAPTION='string']

[/VIEWNAME='line 1']

[/CHARTLOOK='filename']

[/SCATTER
    [COINCIDENT={NONE              }]
                {JITTER[(amount)]}]

[/BAR [(summary function)]
    [LABEL {INSIDE }[VAL][N]]
           {OUTSIDE}
    [SHAPE={RECTANGLE}]
           {PYRAMID  }
           {OBELISK  }
    [BARBASE={SQUARE}]
             {ROUND }
    [BASELINE (value)]]

[/PIE [(summary function)]
     [START value]
     [{CW|CCW}]
     [SLICE={INSIDE } [LABEL] [PCT] [VAL] [N]]
            {OUTSIDE}
            {TEXTIN }
            {NUMIN  }
     [CLUSTER={URIGHT} [LABEL] [PCT] [VAL] [N]]]
              {LRIGHT}
              {ULEFT }
              {LLEFT }

[/BOX [OUTLIERS={ON|OFF}] [EXTREME={ON|OFF}]
     [MEDIAN={ON|OFF}]
     [LABEL=[N]]
     [BOXBASE={SQUARE}]
              {ROUND }
     [WHISKER={T    }]
              {FANCY}
              {LINE }
     [CAPWIDTH (pct)]]

[/LINE [(summary function)]
    STYLE={DOTLINE}
          {LINE   }
          {DOT    }
          {NONE   }
    [DROPLINE={ON|OFF}]
    [LABEL=[VAL] [N] [PCT]]
    [LINELABEL=[CAT] [N] [PCT]]
    [INTERPOLATE={STRAIGHT}]
                 {LSTEP    }
                 {CSTEP    }
                 {RSTEP    }
                 {LJUMP    }
                 {RJUMP    }
                 {CJUMP    }
                 {SPLINE   }
                 {LAGRANGE3}
                 {LAGRANGE5}
```

```
                      [BREAK={MISSING}]]
                             {NONE   }

          [/ERRORBAR [{CI(pctvalue)}]
                      {SD(sdval)    }
                      {SE(seval)    }
                     [LABEL [VAL][N]]
                     [DIRECTION={BOTH|UP|DOWN|SIGN}
                     [CAPWIDTH (pct)]
                     [CAPSTYLE {NONE }]
                               {T    }
                               {FANCY}
                     [SYMBOL={ON|OFF}]
                     [BASELINE value]]

          [/HISTOGRAM [CUM]
                      [SHAPE={HISTOGRAM}]
                      [X1INTERVAL={AUTO    }]
                                  {NUM=n   }
                                  {WIDTH=n}
                      [X2INTERVAL={AUTO    }]
                                  {NUM=n   }
                                  {WIDTH=n}
                      [X1START=n]
                      [X2START=n]
                      [CURVE={OFF|ON}]
                      [SURFACE={OFF|ON}]]

          [/FITLINE [METHOD={NONE                }]
                            {REGRESSION LINEAR}
                            {ORIGIN LINEAR     }
                            {MEAN              }
                            {LLR [(NORMAL|EPANECHNIKOV|UNIFORM)]
                                 [BANDWIDTH={FAST|CONSTRAINED}]
                                 [X1MULTIPLIER=multiplier]
                                 [X2MULTIPLIER=multiplier]}
                     [INTERVAL[(cval)]=[MEAN] [INDIVIDUAL]]
                     [LINE=[TOTAL] [MEFFECT]]]

          [/SPIKE   {X1                          }]
                    {X2                          }
                    {Y                           }
                    {CORNER                      }
                    {ORIGIN                      }
                    {FLOOR                       }
                    {CENTROID [TOTAL] [MEFFECT]}

           [/FORMAT [ SPIKE [COLOR={ON|OFF}] [STYLE={ON|OFF}]]
```

Summary function names are found beginning on p. 572.

Example

```
IGRAPH
 /VIEWNAME='Scatterplot'
 /X1=VAR(trial1) TYPE=SCALE
 /Y=VAR(trial3) TYPE=SCALE
 /X2=VAR(trial2) TYPE=SCALE
 /COORDINATE=THREE
 /X1LENGTH=3.0
 /YLENGTH=3.0
 /X2LENGTH=3.0
 /SCATTER COINCIDENT=NONE
 /FITLINE METHOD=REGRESSION LINEAR INTERVAL(90.0)=MEAN  LINE=TOTAL.
```

Overview

The interactive Chart Editor is designed to emulate the experience of drawing a statistical chart with a pencil and paper. The Chart Editor is a highly interactive, direct manipulation environment that automates the data manipulation and drawing tasks required to draw a chart by hand, such as determining data ranges for axes; drawing ticks and labels; aggregating and summarizing data; drawing data representations such as bars, boxes, or clouds; and incorporating data dimensions as legends when the supply of dependent axes is exhausted.

The IGRAPH command creates a chart in an interactive environment. The interactive Chart Editor allows you to make extensive and fundamental changes to this chart instead of creating a new chart. The Chart Editor allows you to replace data, add new data, change dimensionality, create separate chart panels for different groups, or change the way data are represented in a chart (that is, change a bar chart into a boxplot). The Chart Editor is not a "typed" chart system. You can use chart elements in any combination, and you are not limited by "types" that the application recognizes.

To create a chart, you assign data dimensions to the domain (independent) and range (dependent) axes to create a "data region." You also add data representations such as bars or clouds to the data region. Data representations automatically position themselves according to the data dimensions assigned to the data region.

There is no required order for assigning data dimensions or adding data representations; you can add the data dimensions first or add the data representations first. When defining the data region, you can define the range axis first or the domain axis first.

Options

Titles and Captions. You can specify a title, subtitle, and caption for the chart.

Chart Type. You can request a specific type of chart using the BAR, PIE, BOX, LINE, ERRORBAR, HISTOGRAM, and SCATTERPLOT subcommands.

Chart Content. You can combine elements in a single chart. For example, you can add error bars to a bar chart.

Chart Legends. You can specify either scale legends or categorical legends. Moreover, you can define which properties of the chart reflect the legend variables.

Chart Appearance. You can specify a template, using the CHARTLOOK subcommand, to override the default chart attribute settings.

Basic Specification

The minimum syntax to create a graph is simply the IGRAPH command, without any variable assignment. This will create an empty graph. To create an element in a chart, a dependent variable must be assigned and a chart element specified.

Subcommand Order

- Subcommands can be used in any order.

Syntax Rules

- EFFECT=THREE and COORDINATE=THREE cannot be specified together. If they are, the EFFECT keyword will be ignored.

Operations

- The chart title, subtitle, and caption are assigned as they are specified on the TITLE, SUBTITLE, and CAPTION subcommands. In the absence of any of these subcommands, the missing title, subtitle, or caption are null.

General Syntax

Following are the most general-purpose subcommands. Even so, not all plots will use all subcommands. For example, if the only element in a chart is a bar, the SIZE subcommand will not be shown in the graph.

Each general subcommand may be specified only once. If one of these subcommands appears more than once, the last one is used.

X1, Y, and X2 Subcommands

X1, Y, and X2 assign variables to the *X1*, *Y*, and *X2* dimensions of the chart.

- The variable must be enclosed in parentheses after the VAR keyword.
- Each of these subcommands can include the TITLE keyword, specifying a string with which to title the corresponding axis.
- Each variable must be either a scale variable, a categorical variable, or a built-in data dimension. If a type is not specified, a default type is used from the variable's definition.

SCALE   A scale dimension is interpreted as a measurement on some continuous scale for each case. Optionally, the minimum (MIN) and maximum (MAX) scale values can be specified. In the absence of MIN and MAX, the entire data range is used.

CATEGORICAL   A categorical dimension partitions cases into exclusive groups (each case is a member of exactly one group). The categories are represented by evenly spaced ticks.

A built-in dimension is a user interface object used to create a chart of counts or percentages and to make a casewise chart of elements that usually aggregate data like bars or lines. The built-in dimensions are **count** ($COUNT), **percentage** ($PCT), and **case** ($CASE).

- To create a chart that displays counts or percentages, one of the built-in data dimensions is assigned to the range (*Y*) axis. The VAR keyword is not used for built-in dimensions.
- Built in count and percentage data dimensions cannot be assigned to a domain axis (*X1* or *X2*) or to a legend subcommand.
- The count and percentage data dimensions are all scales and cannot be changed into categorizations.

CATORDER Subcommand

The CATORDER subcommand defines the order in which categories are displayed in a chart and controls the display of empty categories, based on the characteristics of a variable specified in parenthesis after the subcommand name.

- You can display categories in ascending or descending order based on category values, category value labels, counts, or values of a summary variable.
- You can either show or hide empty categories (categories with no cases).

Keywords for the CATORDER subcommand include:

ASCENDING   *Display categories in ascending order of the specified order keyword.*

DESCENDING   *Display categories in descending order of the specified order keyword.*

SHOWEMPTY   *Include empty categories in the chart.*

OMITEMPTY   *Do not include empty categories in the chart.*

ASCENDING and DESCENDING are mutually exclusive. SHOWEMPTY and OMITEMPTY are mutually exclusive.

Order keywords include:

COUNT   *Sort categories based on the number of observations in each category.*

OCCURRENCE   *Sort categories based on the first occurrence of each unique value in the data file.*

LABEL   *Sort categories based on defined value labels for each category.* For categories without defined value labels, the category value is used.

VALUE   *Sort categories based on the values of the categories or the values of a specified summary function for the specified variable.* Summary functions are defined on p. 572.

Order keywords are mutually exclusive. You can specify only one order keyword on each CATORDER subcommand.

X1LENGTH, YLENGTH, and X2LENGTH Subcommands

X1LENGTH, YLENGTH, and X2LENGTH define the length in inches of the corresponding axis.

Example

```
IGRAPH
 /VIEWNAME='Scatterplot'
 /Y=VAR(sales96) TYPE=SCALE
 /X1=VAR(sales95) TYPE=SCALE
 /X2=VAR(region) TYPE=CATEGORICAL
 /X1LENGTH=2.39
 /YLENGTH=2.42
 /X2LENGTH=2.47
 /SCATTER.
```

- Y assigns *sales96* to the dependent axis, defining it to be continuous.
- X1 assigns *sales95* to the *X1* axis, defining it to be a scale variable (continuous).
- X2 assigns *region* to the *X2* axis, defining it to be categorical.
- X1LENGTH, YLENGTH, and X2LENGTH define the length of each axis in inches.

COLOR, STYLE, and SIZE Subcommands

COLOR, STYLE, and SIZE specify variables used to create a legend. Each value of these variables corresponds to a unique property of the chart. The effect of these variables depends on the type of chart.

- Most charts use color in a similar fashion; casewise elements draw each case representation using the color value for the case, and summary elements draw each group representation in the color that represents a summarized value in the color data dimension.
- For dot-line charts, dot charts, and scatterplots, symbol shape is used for style variables and symbol size is used for size variables.
- For line charts and lines in a scatterplot, dash patterns encode style variables and line thickness encodes size variables.
- For bar charts, pie charts, boxplots, histograms, and error bars, fill pattern encodes style variables. Typically, these charts are not sensitive to size variables.

CATEGORICAL legend variables split the elements in the chart into categories. A categorical legend shows the reader which color, style, or size is associated with which category of the variable. The colors, styles, or sizes are assigned according to the discrete categories of the variable.

SCALE legend variables apply color or size to the elements by the value or a summary value of the legend variable, creating a continuum across the values. COLOR and SIZE can create either scale legends or categorical legends. STYLE can create categorical legends only.

Scale variables have the following keywords:

MIN   *Defines the minimum value of the scale.*

MAX   *Defines the maximum value of the scale.*

- The keywords MIN and MAX and their assigned values must be enclosed in parentheses.

In addition, the following keywords are available for COLOR, STYLE, and SIZE:

LEGEND   *Determines if the legend is displayed or not.* The legend explains how to decode color, size, or style in a chart.

TITLE   *Specifies a string used to title the legend.*

The following keywords are available for COLOR and STYLE:

CLUSTER   *Creates clustered charts based on color or size variables.*

STACK   *Creates stacked charts based on color or size variables.*

CLUSTER and STACK are mutually exclusive. Only one can be specified.

Example

```
IGRAPH
 /VIEWNAME='Scatterplot'
 /Y=VAR(sales96) TYPE=SCALE
 /X1=VAR(sales95) TYPE=SCALE
 /X2=VAR(region) TYPE=CATEGORICAL
 /COLOR=VAR(tenure) TYPE=SCALE
 /STYLE=VAR(vol94)
 /SCATTER.
```

- The chart contains a three-dimensional scatterplot.
- COLOR defines a scale legend corresponding to the variable *TENURE*. Points appear in a continuum of colors, with the point color reflecting the value of *TENURE*.
- STYLE defines a categorical legend. Points appear with different shapes, with the point shape reflecting the value of *VOL94*.

CLUSTER Subcommand

CLUSTER defines the variable used to create clustered pie charts. The variable specified must be categorical. The cluster will contain as many pies as there are categories in the cluster variable.

SUMMARYVAR Subcommand

SUMMARYVAR specifies the variable or function for summarizing a pie element. It can only have the built-in variables $COUNT or $PCT or a user-defined variable name.

Specifying a user-defined variable on SUMMARYVAR requires specifying a summary function on the PIE subcommand. Valid summary functions include SUM, SUMAV, SUMSQ, NLT(x), NLE(x), NEQ(x), NGT(x), and NGE(x). The slices of the pie represent categories defined by the values of the summary function applied to SUMMARYVAR.

PANEL Subcommand

PANEL specifies a categorical variable or variables for which separate charts will be created.

- Specifying a single panel variable results in a separate chart for each level of the panel variable.
- Specifying multiple panel variables results in a separate chart for each combination of levels of the panel variables.

POINTLABEL Subcommand

POINTLABEL specifies a variable used to label points in a boxplot or scatterplot.

- If a label variable is specified without ALL or NONE, no labels are turned on (NONE).
- The keyword NONE turns all labels off.

COORDINATE Subcommand

COORDINATE specifies the orientation of the chart. Three-dimensional charts (THREE) have a default orientation that cannot be altered. Keywords available for two-dimensional charts include:

HORIZONTAL   *The* Y *variable appears along the horizontal axis and the* X1 *variable appears along the vertical axis.*

VERTICAL   *The* Y *variable appears along the vertical axis and the* X1 *variable appears along the horizontal axis.*

Example

```
IGRAPH
 /VIEWNAME='Scatterplot'
 /Y=VAR(sales96) TYPE=SCALE
 /X1=VAR(region) TYPE=CATEGORICAL
 /COORDINATE=HORIZONTAL
 /BAR (mean).
```

- The COORDINATE subcommand defines the bar chart as horizontal with *region* on the vertical dimension and means of *sales96* on the horizontal dimension.

EFFECT Subcommand

EFFECT displays a two-dimensional chart with additional depth along a third dimension. Two-dimensional objects are displayed as three-dimensional solids.
- EFFECT is unavailable for three-dimensional charts.

TITLE, SUBTITLE, and CAPTION Subcommands

TITLE, SUBTITLE, and CAPTION specify lines of text placed at the top or bottom of a chart.
- Multiple lines of text can be entered using the carriage control character (\n).
- Each title, subtitle, or caption must be enclosed in apostrophes or quotation marks.
- The maximum length of a title, subtitle, or caption is 255 characters.
- The font, point size, color, alignment, and orientation of the title, subtitle, and caption text is determined by the ChartLook.

VIEWNAME Subcommand

VIEWNAME assigns a name to the chart, which will appear in the outline pane of the Viewer. The name can have a maximum of 255 characters.

CHARTLOOK Subcommand

CHARTLOOK identifies a file containing specifications concerning the initial visual properties of a chart, such as fill, color, font, style, and symbol. By specifying a ChartLook, you can control cosmetic properties that are not explicitly available as syntax keywords.

Valid ChartLook files have a *.clo* extension. Files designated on CHARTLOOK must either be included with the software or created using the Chart Properties and ChartLooks options on the Format menu.

A ChartLook contains values for the following properties:

- Color sequence for categorical color legends
- Color range for scale color legends
- Line style sequence for categorical style legends
- Symbol style sequence for categorical style legends
- Categorical legend fill styles
- Categorical symbol size sequence for categorical size legends
- Symbol size sequence for scale size sequences
- Categorical line weight sequence for categorical size legends
- Font, size, alignment, bold, and italic properties for text objects
- Fill and border for filled objects
- Style, weight, and color for line objects
- Font, shape, size, and color for symbol objects
- Style, weight, and color for visual connectors
- Axis properties: axis line style, color, weight; major tick shape, location, color, size.

Example

```
IGRAPH
/VIEWNAME='Slide 1'
/X1=VAR(sales95) TYPE=SCALE
/Y=VAR(sales96) TYPE=SCALE
/X2=VAR(region) TYPE=CATEGORICAL
/COORDINATE=THREE
/POINTLABEL=VAR(division) NONE
/TITLE='Scatterplot Comparing Regions'
/SUBTITLE='Predicting 1996 Sales\nfrom 1995 Sales'
/CHARTLOOK='Classic.clo'
/SCATTER.
```

- VIEWNAME assigns the name *Slide 1* to the chart. The outline pane of the Viewer uses this name for the chart.
- Points in the chart are labeled with the values of *division*. Initially, all labels are off. Labels for individual points can be turned on interactively after creating the chart.
- TITLE and SUBTITLE define text to appear of the plot. The subtitle contains a carriage return between *Sales* and *from*.
- The appearance of the chart is defined in the Classic ChartLook.

REFLINE Subcommand

The REFLINE subcommand inserts a reference line for the specified variable at the specified value. Optional keywords are:

LABEL={ON|OFF} *Display a label for the reference line.* For variables with defined value labels, the value label for the specified value is displayed. If there is no defined value label for the specified value, the specified value is displayed.

SPIKE={ON|OFF} *Display spikes from the reference line to individual data points.*

Example

```
IGRAPH
  /X1 = VAR(gender) TYPE = CATEGORICAL
  /Y = VAR(salary) TYPE = SCALE
  /BAR(MEAN)
  /REFLINE salary 30000 LABEL=ON.
```

SPIKE Subcommand

The SPIKE subcommand inserts spikes from individual data points to the specified location. Keywords for location include:

X1 *Display spikes to the X1 axis.*

X2 *Display spikes to the X2 axis.*

Y *Display spikes to the Y axis.*

CORNER *Display spikes to the corner defined by the lowest displayed values of the X1, X2, and Y axes.*

ORIGIN *Display spikes to the origin. The origin is the point defined by the 0 values for the X1, X2, and Y axes.*

FLOOR *Display spikes to the "floor" defined by the X1 and X2 axes.*

CENTROID *Display spikes to the point defined by the mean values of the X1, X2, and Y variables.* CENTROID=TOTAL displays spikes to the overall mean. CENTROID=MEFFECT displays spikes to subgroup means defined by color and/or style variables.

Example:

```
IGRAPH
  /X1 = VAR(salbegin) TYPE = SCALE
  /Y = VAR(salary) TYPE = SCALE
  /COLOR = VAR(gender) TYPE = CATEGORICAL
  /SPIKE CENTROID=MEFFECT.
```

FORMAT Subcommand

For charts with color or style variables, the FORMAT subcommand controls the color and style attributes of spikes. The keywords are:

SPIKE
: *Applies color and style specifications to spikes.* This keyword is required.

COLOR{ON|OFF}
: *Controls use of color in spikes as defined by color variable.* The default is ON.

STYLE {ON|OFF}
: *Controls use of line style in spikes as defined by style variable.* The default is ON.

Example

```
IGRAPH
  /X1 = VAR(salbegin) TYPE = SCALE
  /Y = VAR(salary) TYPE = SCALE
  /COLOR = VAR(gender) TYPE = CATEGORICAL
  /SPIKE CENTROID=MEFFECT
  /FORMAT COLOR=OFF.
```

KEY Keyword

All interactive chart types except histograms include a key element that identifies the summary measures displayed in the chart (for example, counts, means, medians). The KEY keyword controls the display of the key in the chart. The default is ON, which displays the key. The OFF specification hides the key. The KEY specification is part of the subcommand that defines the chart type.

Example

```
IGRAPH
  /X1 = VAR(jobcat) TYPE = CATEGORICAL
  /Y = $count
  /BAR KEY=OFF.
```

Element Syntax

The following subcommands add elements to a chart. The same subcommand can be specified more than once. Each subcommand adds another element to the chart.

SCATTER Subcommand

SCATTER produces two- or three-dimensional scatterplots. Scatterplots can use either categorical or scale dimensions to create color or size legends. Categorical dimensions are required to create style legends.

The keyword COINCIDENT controls the placement of markers that have identical values on all axes. COINCIDENT can have one of the following two values:

NONE   *Places coincident markers on top of one another.* This is the default value.

JITTER(amount)   *Adds a small amount of random noise to all scale axis dimensions.* Amount indicates the percentage of noise added and ranges from 0 to 10.

Example

```
IGRAPH
 /Y=VAR(sales96) TYPE=SCALE
 /X1=VAR(sales95) TYPE=SCALE
 /COORDINATE=VERTICAL
 /SCATTER COINCIDENT=JITTER(5).
```

- COORDINATE defines the chart as two-dimensional with *sales96* on the vertical dimension.
- SCATTER creates a scatterplot of *sales96* and *sales95*.
- The scale axes have 5% random noise added by the JITTER keyword allowing separation of coincident points.

AREA Subcommand

AREA creates area charts. These charts summarize categories of one or more variables. The following keywords are available:

summary function   *Defines a function used to summarize the variable defined on the* Y *subcommand.* If the *Y* axis assignment is $COUNT or $PCT, the AREA subcommand cannot have a summary function. If the Y subcommand specifies TYPE=CATEGORICAL, then AREA can only specify MODE as the summary function. Otherwise, all summary functions described on p. 572 are available.

POINTLABEL   *Labels points with the actual values corresponding to the dependent axis (*VAL*), the percentage of cases (*PCT*), and the number of cases included in each data point (*N*).* The default is no labels.

AREALABEL   *Labels area with category labels (*CAT*), the percentage of cases (*PCT*), and the number of cases included in each line (*N*).* The default is no labels.

BREAK   *Indicates whether the lines break at missing values (*MISSING*) or not (*NONE*).*

BASELINE   *The baseline value determines the location from which the areas will hang (vertical) or extend (horizontal).* The default value is 0.

The INTERPOLATE keyword determines how the lines connecting the points are drawn. Options include:

STRAIGHT   *Straight lines.*

LSTEP   *A horizontal line extends from each data point.* A vertical riser connects the line to the next data point.

CSTEP	*Each data point is centered on a horizontal line that extends half of the distance between consecutive points.* Vertical risers connect the line to the next horizontal line.
RSTEP	*A horizontal line terminates at each data point.* A vertical riser extends from each data point, connecting to the next horizontal line.

BAR Subcommand

BAR creates a bar element in a chart, corresponding to the *X1*, *X2*, and *Y* axis assignments. Bars can by clustered by assigning variables to COLOR or STYLE. Horizontal or vertical orientation is specified by the COORDINATE subcommand.

summary function	*Defines a function used to summarize the variable defined on the* Y *subcommand.* If the *Y* axis assignment is $COUNT or $PCT, the BAR subcommand cannot have a summary function. If the Y subcommand specifies TYPE=CATEGORICAL, then BAR can specify only MODE as the summary function. Otherwise, all summary functions described on p. 572 are available.
LABEL	*Bars can be labeled with the actual values corresponding to the dependent axis* (VAL) *or with the number of cases included in each bar* (N). The default is no labels. The placement of the labels is inside the bars (INSIDE) or outside the bars (OUTSIDE).
SHAPE	*Determines whether the bars are drawn as rectangles* (RECTANGLE), *pyramids* (PYRAMID), *or obelisks* (OBELISK). The default is rectangular bars.
BARBASE	*For three-dimensional bars, the base can be round* (ROUND) *or square* (SQUARE). The default is square.
BASELINE	*The baseline value determines the location from which the bars will hang (vertical) or extend (horizontal).* The default value is 0.

Example

```
IGRAPH
 /X1=VAR(volume96) TYPE=CATEGORICAL
 /Y=$count
 /COORDINATE=VERTICAL
 /EFFECT=THREE
 /BAR LABEL INSIDE N SHAPE=RECTANGLE.
```

- X1 assigns the categorical variable *volume96* to the *X1* axis.
- Y assigns the built-in dimension *$count* to the range axis.
- VERTICAL defines the counts to appear along the vertical dimension.
- BAR adds a bar element to the chart.
- LABEL labels the bars in the chart with the number of cases included in the bars. These labels appear inside the bars.

- SHAPE indicates that the bars are rectangles. However, EFFECT adds a third dimension to the chart, yielding three-dimensional solids.

Example

```
IGRAPH
 /X1=VAR(volume94) TYPE=CATEGORICAL
 /Y=VAR(sales96) TYPE=SCALE
 /COORDINATE=HORIZONTAL
 /EFFECT=NONE
 /BAR (MEAN) LABEL OUTSIDE VAL SHAPE=PYRAMID BASELINE=370.00.
```

- X1 assigns the categorical variable *volume94* to the *X1* axis.
- Y assigns the scale variable *sales96* to the range axis.
- HORIZONTAL defines *sales96* to appear along the horizontal dimension.
- EFFECT defines the chart as two-dimensional.
- BAR adds a bar element to the chart.
- MEAN defines the summary function to apply to *sales96*. Each bar represents the mean *sales96* value for the corresponding category of *volume94*.
- LABEL labels the bars in the chart with the mean *sales96* value. These labels appear outside the bars.
- SHAPE indicates that the bars are pyramids.
- BASELINE indicates that bars should extend from 370. Any bar with a mean value above 370 extends to the right. Any bar with a mean value below 370 extends to the left.

PIE Subcommand

A simple pie chart summarizes categories defined by a single variable or by a group of related variables. A clustered pie chart contains a cluster of simple pies, all of which are stacked into categories by the same variable. The pies are of different sizes and appear to be stacked on top of one another. The cluster contains as many pies as there are categories in the cluster variable. For both simple and clustered pie charts, the size of each slice represents the count, the percentage, or a summary function of a variable.

The following keywords are available:

summary function *Defines a function used to summarize the variable defined on the* SUMMARYVAR *subcommand. If the* SUMMARYVAR *assignment is* $COUNT *or* $PCT, *the* PIE *subcommand cannot have a summary function. Otherwise, of the summary functions described on p. 572,* SUM, SUMAV, SUMSQ, NGT(x), NLE(x), NEQ(x), NGE(x), NGT(x), *and* NIN(x1,x2) *are available.*

START num *Indicates the starting position of the smallest slice of the pie chart. Any integer can be specified for num. The value is converted to a number between 0 and 360, which represents the degree of rotation of the smallest slice.*

CW I CCW   *Sets the positive rotation of the pie to either clockwise (CW) or counterclockwise (CCW). The default rotation is clockwise.*

SLICE   *Sets the labeling characteristics for the slices of the pie.* The pie slices can be labeled with the category labels (LABEL), the category percentages (PCT), the number of cases (N), and the category values (VAL). Label position is either all labels inside the pie (INSIDE), all labels outside the pie (OUTSIDE), text labels inside the pie with numeric labels outside (TEXTIN), or numeric labels inside the pie with text labels outside (NUMIN).

CLUSTER   *Sets the labeling characteristics for the pies from clusters.* The pies can be labeled with the category labels (LABEL), the category percentages (PCT), the number of cases (N), and the category values (VAL). Label position is either upper left (ULEFT), upper right (URIGHT), lower left (LLEFT), or lower right (LRIGHT) of the figure.

Example

```
IGRAPH
/SUMMARYVAR=$count
/COLOR=VAR(volume96) TYPE=CATEGORICAL
/EFFECT=THREE
/PIE START 180 CW SLICE=TEXTIN LABEL PCT N.
```

- The pie slices represent the number of cases (SUMMARYVAR=$count) in each category of *volume96* (specified on the COLOR subcommand).
- EFFECT yields a pie chart with an additional third dimension.
- PIE creates a pie chart.
- The first slice begins at 180 degrees and the rotation of the pie is clockwise.
- SLICE labels the slices with category labels, the percentage in each category, and the number of cases in each category. TEXTIN places the text labels (category labels) inside the pie slices and the numeric labels outside.

Example

```
IGRAPH
/SUMMARYVAR=VAR(sales96)
/COLOR=VAR(volume95) TYPE=CATEGORICAL
/X1=VAR(region) TYPE=CATEGORICAL
/Y=VAR(division) TYPE=CATEGORICAL
/COORDINATE=VERTICAL
/PIE (SUM) START 0 CW SLICE=INSIDE VAL.
```

- The pie slices represent the sums of *sales96* values for each category of *volume95* (specified on the COLOR subcommand).
- X1 and Y define two axes representing *region* and *division*. A pie chart is created for each combination of these variables.
- The first slice in each pie begins at 0 degrees and the rotation of the pie is clockwise.
- SUM indicates the summary function applied to the summary variable, *sales96*. The pie slices represent the sum of the *sales96* values.

- SLICE labels the slices with the value of the summary function. INSIDE places the labels inside the pie slices.

BOX Subcommand

BOX creates a boxplot, sometimes called a box-and-whiskers plot, showing the median, quartiles, and outlier and extreme values for a scale variable. The interquartile range (IQR) is the difference between the 75th and 25th percentiles and corresponds to the length of the box.

The following keywords are available:

OUTLIERS	*Indicates whether outliers should be displayed.* Outliers are values between 1.5 IQR's and 3 IQR's from the end of a box. By default, the boxplot displays outliers (ON).
EXTREME	*Indicates whether extreme values should be displayed.* Values more than 3 IQR's from the end of a box are defined as extreme. By default, the boxplot displays extreme values (ON).
MEDIAN	*Indicates whether a line representing the median should be included in the box.* By default, the boxplot displays the median line (ON).
LABEL	*Displays the number of cases (*N*) represented by each box.*
BOXBASE	*Controls the shape of the box for three dimensional plots.* SQUARE results in rectangular solids. ROUND yields cylinders.
WHISKER	*Controls the appearance of the whiskers.* Whiskers can be straight lines (LINE), end in a *T*-shape (T), or end in a fancy *T*-shape (FANCY). Fancy whiskers are unavailable for three-dimensional boxplots.
CAPWIDTH(pct)	*Controls the width of the whisker cap relative to the corresponding box.* Pct equals the percentage of the box width. The default value for pct is 45.

Example

```
IGRAPH
 /X1=VAR(region) TYPE=CATEGORICAL
 /Y=VAR(sales96) TYPE=SCALE
 /COORDINATE=HORIZONTAL
 /BOX OUTLIERS=ON EXTREME=ON MEDIAN=ON WHISKER=FANCY.
```

- X1 assigns the variable *region* to the *X1* axis.
- Y assigns the variable *sales96* to the range axis.
- COORDINATE positions the range axis along the horizontal dimension.
- BOX creates a boxplot. The outliers and extreme vales are shown. In addition, a line representing the median is added to the box.
- WHISKER yields whiskers ending in a fancy *T*.

Example

```
IGRAPH
 /X1=VAR(region) TYPE=CATEGORICAL
 /Y=VAR(sales96) TYPE=SCALE
 /X2=VAR(division) TYPE=CATEGORICAL
 /COORDINATE=THREE
 /BOX OUTLIERS=OFF EXTREME=ON MEDIAN=OFF LABEL=N BOXBASE=ROUND WHISKER=T.
```

- X2 adds a third dimension, corresponding to *division*, to the boxplot in the previous example.
- COORDINATE indicates that the chart displays the third dimension.
- BOX creates a boxplot without outliers or a median line. Extreme values are shown.
- LABEL labels each box with the number of cases represented by each box.
- BOXBASE defines the three-dimensional representation of the boxes to be cylindrical.

LINE Subcommand

LINE creates line charts, dot charts, and ribbon charts. These charts summarize categories of one or more variables. Line charts tend to emphasize flow or movement instead of individual values. They are commonly used to display data over time and therefore can be used to give a good sense of trends. A ribbon chart is similar to a line chart, with the lines displayed as ribbons in a third dimension. Ribbon charts can either have two dimensions displayed with a 3-D effect, or they can have three dimensions.

The following keywords are available:

summary function   *Defines a function used to summarize the variable defined on the* Y *subcommand.* If the Y axis assignment is $COUNT or $PCT, the LINE subcommand cannot have a summary function. If the Y subcommand specifies TYPE=CATEGORICAL, then LINE can specify only MODE as the summary function. Otherwise, all summary functions described on p. 572 are available.

STYLE   *Chart can include dots and lines (*DOTLINE*), lines only (*LINE*), or dots only (*DOT*).* The keyword NONE creates an empty chart.

DROPLINE   *Indicates whether drop lines between points having the same value of a variable are included in the chart (*ON*) or not (*OFF*).* To include drop lines, specify a categorical variable on the STYLE, COLOR, or SIZE subcommands.

LABEL   *Labels points with the actual values corresponding to the dependent axis (*VAL*), the percentage of cases (*PCT*), and the number of cases included in each data point (*N*).* The default is no labels.

LINELABEL   *Labels lines with category labels (*CAT*), the percentage of cases (*PCT*), and the number of cases included in each line (*N*).* The default is no labels.

BREAK   *Indicates whether the lines break at missing values (*MISSING*) or not (*NONE*).*

The INTERPOLATE keyword determines how the lines connecting the points are drawn. Options include:

STRAIGHT   *Straight lines.*

LSTEP   *A horizontal line extends from each data point.* A vertical riser connects the line to the next data point.

CSTEP   *Each data point is centered on a horizontal line that extends half of the distance between consecutive points.* Vertical risers connect the line to the next horizontal line.

RSTEP   *A horizontal line terminates at each data point.* A vertical riser extends from each data point, connecting to the next horizontal line.

LJUMP   *A horizontal line extends from each data point.* No vertical risers connect the lines to the points.

RJUMP   *A horizontal line terminates at each data point.* No vertical risers connect the points to the next horizontal line.

CJUMP   *A horizontal line is centered at each data point, extending half of the distance between consecutive points.* No vertical risers connect the lines.

SPLINE   *Connects data points with a cubic spline.*

LAGRANGE3   *Connects data points with third-order Lagrange interpolations, in which a third-order polynomial is fit to the nearest four points.*

LAGRANGE5   *Connects data points with fifth-order Lagrange interpolations, in which a fifth-order polynomial is fit to the nearest six points.*

Example

```
IGRAPH
/X1=VAR(volume95) TYPE=CATEGORICAL
/Y=VAR(sales96) TYPE=SCALE
/COLOR=VAR(volume94) TYPE=CATEGORICAL
/COORDINATE=VERTICAL
/LINE (MEAN) STYLE=LINE DROPLINE=ON LABEL VAL
       INTERPOLATE=STRAIGHT BREAK=MISSING.
```

- LINE creates a line chart. The lines represent the mean value of *sales96* for each category of *volume95*.

- The chart contains a line for each category of *volume94*, with droplines connecting the lines at each category of *volume95*.

- LABEL labels the lines with the mean *sales96* value for each category of *volume95*.

- INTERPOLATE specifies that straight lines connect the mean *sales96* values across the *volume95* categories.

- BREAK indicates that the lines will break at any missing values.

ERRORBAR Subcommand

Error bars help you to visualize distributions and dispersion by indicating the variability of the measure being displayed. The mean of a scale variable is plotted for a set of categories, and the length of an error bar on either side of the mean value indicates a confidence interval or a specified number of standard errors or standard deviations. Error bars can extend in one direction or in both directions from the mean. Error bars are sometimes displayed in the same chart with other chart elements, such as bars.

One of the following three keywords indicating the statistic and percentage/multiplier applied to the error bars must be specified:

CI(Pct)	*Error bars represent confidence intervals.* Pct indicates the level of confidence and varies from 0 to 100.
SD(sdval)	*Error bars represent standard deviations.* Sdval indicates how many standard deviations above and below the mean the error bars extend. Sdval must between 0 and 6.
SE(seval)	*Error bars represent standard errors.* Seval indicates how many standard errors above and below the mean the error bars extend. Seval must between 0 and 6.

In addition, the following keywords can be specified:

LABEL	*Labels error bars with means (VAL) and the number of cases (N).*
DIRECTION	*Error bars can extend both above and below the mean values (BOTH), only above the mean values (UP), only below the mean values (DOWN), or above for error bars above the baseline and below for error bars below the baseline (SIGN).*
CAPSTYLE	*For error bars, the style can be T-shaped (T), no cap (NONE), or a cap with end pieces (FANCY). The default style is T-shaped.*
SYMBOL	*Displays the mean marker (ON). For no symbol, specify OFF.*
BASELINE val	*Defines the value (val) above which the error bars extend above the bars and below which the error bars extend below the bars.*
CAPWIDTH(pct)	*Controls the width of the cap relative to the distance between categories. Pct equals the percent of the distance. The default value for pct is 45.*

Example

```
IGRAPH
/X1=VAR(volume94) TYPE=CATEGORICAL
/Y=VAR(sales96) TYPE=SCALE
/BAR (MEAN) LABEL INSIDE VAL SHAPE=RECTANGLE BASELINE=0.00
/ERRORBAR SE(2.0) DIRECTION=BOTH CAPWIDTH (45) CAPSTYLE=FANCY.
```

- BAR creates a bar chart with rectangular bars. The bars represent the mean *sales96* values for the *volume94* categories.

- ERRORBAR adds error bars to the bar chart. The error bars extend two standard errors above and below the mean.

HISTOGRAM Subcommand

HISTOGRAM creates a histogram element in a chart, corresponding to the *X1*, *X2*, and *Y* axis assignments. Horizontal or vertical orientation is specified by the COORDINATE subcommand. A histogram groups the values of a variable into evenly spaced groups (intervals or bins) and plots a count of the number of cases in each group. The count can be expressed as a percentage. Percentages are useful for comparing data sets of different sizes. The count or percentage can also be accumulated across the groups.

- $COUNT or $PCT must be specified on the Y subcommand.

The following keywords are available:

SHAPE	*Defines the shape of the histogram.* Currently, the only value for SHAPE is HISTOGRAM.
CUM	*Specifies a cumulative histogram.* Counts or percentages are aggregated across the values of the domain variables.
X1INTERVAL	*Intervals on the* X1 *axis can be set automatically, or you can specify the number of intervals (1 to 250) along the axis* (NUM) *or the width of an interval* (WIDTH).
X2INTERVAL	*Intervals on the* X2 *axis can be set automatically, or you can specify the number of intervals (1 to 250) along the axis* (NUM) *or the width of an interval* (WIDTH).
CURVE	*Superimposes a normal curve on a 2-D histogram.* The normal curve has the same mean and variance as the data.
X1START	*The starting point along the* X1 *axis.* Indicates the percentage of an interval width above the minimum value along the *X1* axis at which to begin the histogram. The value can range from 0 to 99.
X2START	*The starting point along the* X2 *axis.* Indicates the percentage of an interval width above the minimum value along the *X2* axis at which to begin the histogram. The value can range from 0 to 99.

Example

```
IGRAPH
 /X1=VAR(sales96) TYPE=SCALE
 /Y=$count
 /Histogram SHAPE=HISTOGRAM CURVE=ON X1INTERVAL WIDTH=100.
```

- Histogram creates a histogram of *sales96*. The *sales96* intervals are 100 units wide.
- CURVE superimposes a normal curve on the histogram.

FITLINE Subcommand

FITLINE adds a line or surface to a scatterplot to help you discern the relationship shown in the plot. The following general methods are available:

NONE	*No line is fit.*

REGRESSION   *Fits a straight line (or surface) using ordinary least squares.* Must be followed by the keyword LINEAR.

ORIGIN   *Fits a straight line (or surface) through the origin.* Must be followed by the keyword LINEAR.

MEAN   *For a 2-D chart, fits a line at the mean of the dependent (Y) variable.* For a 3-D chart, the *Y* mean is shown as a plane.

LLR   *Fits a local linear regression curve or surface.* A normal (NORMAL) kernel is the default. With EPANECHNIKOV, the curve is not as smooth as with a normal kernel and is smoother than with a uniform (UNIFORM) kernel. (For more information, see Simonoff, J. S. 1966. *Smoothing methods in statistics.* New York: Springer-Verlag.)

The keyword LINE indicates the number of fit lines. TOTAL fits the line to all of the cases. MEFFECT fits a separate line to the data for each value of a legend variable.

The REGRESSION, ORIGIN, and MEAN methods offer the option of including prediction intervals with the following keyword:

INTERVAL[(cval)]   *The intervals are based on the mean* (MEAN) *or on the individual cases* (INDIVIDUAL). Cval indicates the size of the interval and ranges from 50 to 100.

The local linear regression (LLR) smoother offers the following controls for the smoothing process:

BANDWIDTH   *Constrains the bandwidth to be constant across subgroups or panels* (CONSTRAINED). The default is unconstrained (FAST).

X1MULTIPLIER   *Specifies the bandwidth multiplier for the* X1 *axis.* The bandwidth multiplier changes the amount of data that is included in each calculation of a small part of the smoother. The multiplier can be adjusted to emphasize specific features of the plot that are of interest. Any positive multiplier (including fractions) is allowed. The larger the multiplier, the smoother the curve. The range between 0 and 10 should suffice in most applications.

X2MULTIPLIER   *Specifies the bandwidth multiplier for the* X2 *axis.* The bandwidth multiplier changes the amount of data that is included in each calculation of a small part of the smoother. The multiplier can be adjusted to emphasize specific features of the plot that are of interest. Any positive multiplier (including fractions) is allowed. The larger the multiplier, the smoother the curve. The range between 0 and 10 should suffice in most applications.

Example

```
IGRAPH
 /X1=VAR(sales95) TYPE=SCALE
 /Y=VAR(sales96) TYPE=SCALE
 /COLOR=VAR(region) TYPE=CATEGORICAL
 /SCATTER
 /FITLINE METHOD=LLR EPANECHNIKOV BANDWIDTH=CONSTRAINED
       X1MULTIPLIER=2.00 LINE=MEFFECT.
```

- SCATTER creates a scatterplot of *sales95* and *sales96*.
- FITLINE adds a local linear regression smoother to the scatterplot. The Epanechnikov smoother is used with an *X1* multiplier of 2. A separate line is fit for each category of region and the bandwidth is constrained to be equal across region categories.

Summary Functions

Summary functions apply to scale variables selected for a dependent axis or a slice summary. Percentages are based on the specified percent base. For a slice summary, only summary functions appropriate for the type of chart are available.

The following summary functions are available:

First Values (FIRST). The value found in the first case for each category in the data file at the time the summary was defined.

Kurtosis (KURTOSIS). A measure of the extent to which observations cluster around a central point. For a normal distribution, the value of the kurtosis statistic is 0. Positive kurtosis indicates that the observations cluster more and have longer tails than those in the normal distribution, and negative kurtosis indicates the observations cluster less and have shorter tails.

Last Values (LAST). The value found in the last case for each category in the data file at the time the summary was defined.

Maximum Values (MAXIMUM). The largest value for each category.

Minimum Values (MINIMUM). The smallest value within the category.

Means (MEAN). The arithmetic average for each category.

Medians (MEDIAN). The values below which half of the cases fall in each category.

Modes (MODE). The most frequently occurring value within each category.

Number of Cases Above (NGT(x)). The number of cases having values above the specified value.

Number of Cases Between (NIN(x1,x2)). The number of cases between two specified values.

Number of Cases Equal to (NEQ(x)). The number of cases equal to the specified value.

Number of Cases Greater Than or Equal to (NGE(x)). The number of cases having values above or equal to the specified value.

Number of Cases Less Than (NLT(x)). The number of cases below the specified value.

Number of Cases Less Than or Equal to (NLE(x)). The number of cases below or equal to the specified value.

Percentage of Cases Above (PGT(x)). The percentage of cases having values above the specified value.

Percentage of Cases Between (PIN(x1,x2)). The percentage of cases between two specified values.

Percentage of Cases Equal to (PEQ(x)). The percentage of cases equal to the specified value.

Percentage of Cases Greater Than or Equal to (PGE(x)). The percentage of cases having values above or equal to the specified value.

Percentage of Cases Less Than (PLT(x)). The percentage of cases having values below the specified value.

Percentage of Cases Less Than or Equal to (PLE(x)). The percentage of cases having values below or equal to the specified value.

Percentiles (PTILE(x)). The data value below which the specified percentage of values fall within each category.

Skewness (SKEW). A measure of the asymmetry of a distribution. The normal distribution is symmetric and has a skewness value of 0. A distribution with a significant positive skewness has a long right tail. A distribution with a significant negative skewness has a long left tail.

Standard Deviations (STDDEV). A measure of dispersion around the mean, expressed in the same units of measurement as the observations, equal to the square root of the variance. In a normal distribution, 68% of cases fall within one SD of the mean and 95% of cases fall within two SD's.

Standard Errors of Kurtosis (SEKURT). The ratio of kurtosis to its standard error can be used as a test of normality (that is, you can reject normality if the ratio is less than -2 or greater than $+2$). A large positive value for kurtosis indicates that the tails of the distribution are longer than those of a normal distribution; a negative value for kurtosis indicates shorter tails (becoming like those of a box-shaped uniform distribution).

Standard Errors of the Mean (SEMEAN). A measure of how much the value of the mean may vary from sample to sample taken from the same distribution. It can be used to roughly compare the observed mean to a hypothesized value (that is, you can conclude the two values are different if the ratio of the difference to the standard error is less than -2 or greater than $+2$).

Standard Errors of Skewness (SESKEW). The ratio of skewness to its standard error can be used as a test of normality (that is, you can reject normality if the ratio is less than -2 or greater than $+2$). A large positive value for skewness indicates a long right tail; an extreme negative value, a long left tail.

Sums (SUM). The sums of the values within each category.

Sums of Absolute Values (SUMAV). The sums of the absolute values within each category.

Sums of Squares (SUMSQ). The sums of the squares of the values within each category.

Variances (VARIANCE). A measure of how much observations vary from the mean, expressed in squared units.

IMPORT

```
IMPORT FILE=file

 [/TYPE={COMM}]
        {TAPE}

 [/KEEP={ALL** }] [/DROP=varlist]
        {varlist}

 [/RENAME=(old varnames=new varnames)...]

 [/MAP]
```

**Default if the subcommand is omitted.

Example

```
IMPORT FILE=NEWDATA /RENAME=(V1 TO V3=ID, SEX, AGE) /MAP.
```

Overview

IMPORT reads SPSS-format portable data files created with the EXPORT command. A portable data file is a data file created by the program and used to transport data between different types of computers and operating systems (such as between IBM CMS and Digital VAX/VMS) or between SPSS, SPSS/PC+, or other software using the same portable file format. Like an SPSS-format data file, a portable file contains all of the data and dictionary information stored in the working data file from which it was created.

The program can also read data files created by other software programs. See GET TRANSLATE for information on reading files created by spreadsheet and database programs such as dBASE, Lotus, and Excel.

Options

Format. You can specify the format of the portable file (magnetic tape or communications program) on the TYPE subcommand. For more information on magnetic tapes and communications programs, see "Methods of Transporting Portable Files" on p. 356.

Variables. You can read a subset of variables from the working data file with the DROP and KEEP subcommands. You can rename variables using RENAME. You can also produce a record of all variables and their names in the working file with the MAP subcommand.

Basic Specification

The basic specification is the FILE subcommand with a file specification. All variables from the portable file are copied into the working data file with their original names, variable and value labels, missing-value flags, and print and write formats.

Subcommand Order

- FILE and TYPE must precede all other subcommands.
- No specific order is required between FILE and TYPE or among other subcommands.

Operations

- The portable data file and dictionary become the working data file and dictionary.
- A file saved with weighting in effect (using the WEIGHT command) automatically uses the case weights when the file is read.

Example

```
IMPORT FILE=NEWDATA /RENAME=(V1 TO V3=ID,SEX,AGE) /MAP.
```

- The working data file is generated from the portable file *NEWDATA*.
- Variables *V1*, *V2*, and *V3* are renamed *ID*, *SEX*, and *AGE* in the working file. Their names remain *V1*, *V2*, and *V3* in the portable file. None of the other variables copied into the working file are renamed.
- MAP requests a display of the variables in the working data file.

FILE Subcommand

FILE specifies the portable file. FILE is the only required subcommand on IMPORT.

TYPE Subcommand

TYPE indicates whether the portable file is formatted for magnetic tape or for a communications program. TYPE can specify either COMM or TAPE. For more information on magnetic tapes and communications programs, see EXPORT.

COMM   *Communications-formatted file.* This is the default.

TAPE   *Tape-formatted file.*

Example

```
IMPORT TYPE=TAPE /FILE=HUBOUT.
```

- The file *HUBOUT* is read as a tape-formatted portable file.

DROP and KEEP Subcommands

DROP and KEEP are used to read a subset of variables from the portable file.

- DROP excludes a variable or list of variables from the working data file. All variables not named are included in the file.
- KEEP includes a variable or list of variables in the working file. All variables not specified on KEEP are excluded.
- DROP and KEEP cannot precede the FILE or TYPE subcommands.
- Variables can be specified in any order. The order of variables on KEEP determines the order of variables in the working file. The order on DROP does not affect the order of variables in the working file.
- If a variable is referred to twice on the same subcommand, only the first mention is recognized.
- Multiple DROP and KEEP subcommands are allowed; the effect is cumulative. Specifying a variable named on a previous DROP or not named on a previous KEEP results in an error and the command is not executed.
- The keyword TO can be used to specify a group of consecutive variables in the portable file.
- The portable file is not affected by DROP or KEEP.

Example

```
IMPORT FILE=NEWSUM /DROP=DEPT TO DIVISION.
```

- The working data file is generated from the portable file *NEWSUM*. Variables between and including *DEPT* and *DIVISION* in the portable file are excluded from the working file.
- All other variables are copied into the working file.

RENAME Subcommand

RENAME renames variables being read from the portable file. The renamed variables retain the variable and value labels, missing-value flags, and print formats contained in the portable file.

- To rename a variable, specify the name of the variable in the portable file, a required equals sign, and the new name.
- A variable list can be specified on both sides of the equals sign. The number of variables on both sides must be the same, and the entire specification must be enclosed in parentheses.
- The keyword TO can be used for both variable lists (see "Keyword TO" on p. 29).
- Any DROP or KEEP subcommand after RENAME must use the new variable names.

Example

```
IMPORT FILE=NEWSUM /DROP=DEPT TO DIVISION
  /RENAME=(NAME,WAGE=LNAME,SALARY).
```

- RENAME renames *NAME* and *WAGE* to *LNAME* and *SALARY*.
- *LNAME* and *SALARY* retain the variable and value labels, missing-value flags, and print formats assigned to *NAME* and *WAGE*.

MAP Subcommand

MAP displays a list of variables in the working data file, showing all changes that have been specified on the RENAME, DROP, or KEEP subcommands.

- MAP can be specified as often as desired.
- MAP confirms only the changes specified on the subcommands that precede the MAP request.
- Results of subcommands that follow MAP are not mapped. When MAP is specified last, it also produces a description of the file.

Example

```
IMPORT FILE=NEWSUM /DROP=DEPT TO DIVISION /MAP
  /RENAME NAME=LNAME WAGE=SALARY /MAP.
```

- The first MAP subcommand produces a listing of the variables in the file after DROP has dropped the specified variables.
- RENAME renames *NAME* and *WAGE*.
- The second MAP subcommand shows the variables in the file after renaming.

INCLUDE

```
INCLUDE FILE=file
```

Example
```
INCLUDE FILE=GSSLABS.
```

Overview

INCLUDE includes a file of commands in a session. INCLUDE is especially useful for including a long series of data definition statements or transformations. Another use for INCLUDE is to set up a library of commonly used commands and include them in the command sequence as they are needed.

INCLUDE allows you to run multiple commands together during a session and can save time. Complex or repetitive commands can be stored in a command file and included in the session, while simpler commands or commands unique to the current analysis can be entered during the session, before and after the included file.

Basic Specification

The only specification is the FILE subcommand, which specifies the file to include. When INCLUDE is executed, the commands in the specified file are processed.

Syntax Rules

- Commands in an included file must begin in column 1, and continuation lines for each command must be indented at least one column.
- A raw data file can be used as an include file if the first line of the included file contains the BEGIN DATA command and the last line contains the END DATA command. However, because the data are specified between BEGIN DATA and END DATA, they are limited to a maximum of 80 columns (the maximum may be fewer than 80 columns on some systems).
- As many INCLUDE commands as needed can be used in a session.
- INCLUDE commands can be nested so that one set of included commands includes another set of commands. This nesting can go to five levels. However, a file cannot be included that is still open from a previous step.

Operations

- If an included file contains a FINISH command, the session ends and no further commands are processed.

- If a journal file is created for the session, INCLUDE is copied to the journal file. Commands from the included file are also copied to the journal file but are treated like printed messages. Thus, INCLUDE can be executed from the journal file if the journal file is later used as a command file. Commands from the included file are executed only once.

FILE Subcommand

FILE identifies the file containing commands. FILE is the only specification on INCLUDE and is required.

Example

```
INCLUDE FILE=GSSLABS.
```

- INCLUDE includes the file *GSSLABS* in the prompted session. When INCLUDE is executed, the commands in *GSSLABS* are processed.
- Assume that the include file *GSSLABS* contains the following:

```
DATA LIST FILE=DATA52
  /RELIGION 5 OCCUPAT 7 SES 12 ETHNIC 15
   PARTY 19 VOTE48 33 VOTE52 41.
```

The working data file will be defined and ready for analysis after INCLUDE is executed.

INFO

This command is not available on all operating systems.

```
INFO [OUTFILE = file]
     [OVERVIEW]
     [LOCAL]
     [ERRORS]
     [FACILITIES]
     [PROCEDURES]
     [ALL]
     [procedure name] [/procedure name...]
     [SINCE release number]
```

Example

```
INFO LOCAL.
```

Overview

INFO makes available two kinds of online documentation: local and update.

Local Documentation

Local documentation concerns the environment in which the program is run. It includes some or all of the following, depending on the operating system:

- Commands or job control language for running the program.
- Conventions for referring to files. These include instructions on how your computer's operating system accesses or creates a particular file.
- Conventions for handling tapes and other input/output devices.
- Data formats. The formats the program reads and writes may differ from one computer and operating system to another.
- Default values for parameters controlled by the SET command. Many defaults for these parameters are set at the individual installation. The SHOW command displays the values that are currently in effect. Local documentation may contain information on why one setting is preferred over another.
- Information about your computer and operating system or your individual installation.

Update Documentation

Update documentation includes changes to existing procedures and facilities made after publication of this manual, new procedures and facilities, and corrections to this manual. Update documentation can be requested for all available releases, or for releases after a particular release.

Basic Specification

- The minimum specification is the command name. When specified by itself, the program displays an overview of available documents.

Syntax Rules

- Multiple keywords and/or procedure names can be specified on a single INFO command.
- Multiple procedure names must be separated by slashes.
- The order of specifications is unimportant and does not affect the order in which the documentation is printed.
- Three- or four-character truncation does *not* apply to INFO command specifications. Spell all keywords in full. For procedure names, spell the first word in full and subsequent words through at least the first three characters.

Operations

- By default, the INFO command produces update information only for the current release. Documentation for earlier releases may also be available; read the INFO overview to find out whether it is available on your system.
- If overlapping sets of information are requested, only one copy is printed.
- If there is no available documentation for the requested information, only a copyright page is printed.
- If information is requested for an unrecognized topic, the program prints an error message.
- The characteristics of the output produced by the INFO command may vary by computer type. As implemented at SPSS Inc., the output includes carriage control, with the maximum length of a page determined by the LENGTH subcommand on SET. A printer width of 132 characters is assumed for some examples, although the text is generally much narrower.
- The program requires more computer resources than most printing utilities. Your installation may therefore provide an alternative method for printing INFO documentation. In this case, the INFO command may simply provide instructions for using the alternative method.

Example

```
INFO   OVERVIEW FACILITIES FREQUENCIES / CROSSTABS.
```

- INFO produces an overview and documentation for any changes made to system facilities and to the FREQUENCIES and CROSSTABS procedures.
- Because the keyword SINCE is not specified, INFO prints only documentation for the current release.

Types of Information

The following types of information can be requested on INFO:

OVERVIEW   *Overview of available documentation.* This includes a table of contents for the documentation available with INFO, along with information about SPSS manuals.

LOCAL   *Local documentation.* See "Local Documentation" on p. 580.

ERRORS   *List of known unfixed errors.* This lists the known unfixed errors in the current release of the program. Since ERRORS applies only to the current release, the SINCE keyword (described below) has no effect with ERRORS.

FACILITIES   *Update information for system facilities.* This covers all differences, except in procedures, between the system as documented in this manual and the system as installed on your computer—whether those differences result from updates to the system, revisions required for conversions to particular operating systems, or errors in this manual. Only updates for the most current release are printed unless keyword SINCE is specified.

PROCEDURES   *Update information for procedures.* This includes full documentation for procedures new in the current release and update information for procedures that existed prior to the current release.

PROCEDURE   *Documentation for the procedure named.* This is the same information as that printed by the PROCEDURES keyword, but limited to the procedure named. You can specify multiple procedures, separating each from the other with a slash.

ALL   *All available documentation.* ALL includes OVERVIEW, LOCAL, ERRORS, FACILITIES, and PROCEDURES.

SINCE Keyword

Releases of SPSS are numbered by integers, with decimal digits indicating maintenance releases between major releases. The release number appears in the default heading for SPSS output. Each SPSS manual is identified in the preface by the number of the release it documents.

The keyword SINCE obtains information for earlier releases or limits the information to maintenance releases since the last major release.

- The minimum specification is the keyword SINCE followed by a release number.

- SINCE is not inclusive. Specifying 3.0 does not include changes made to the system in release 3.0.

- To identify a maintenance release, enter the exact number, with decimal, as in 3.1.

- Information for some earlier releases may not be available. For example, information for release 2.2 and earlier is not available if INFO is run with SPSS release 5.0 or later.

Example

```
INFO  OVERVIEW FACILITIES FREQUENCIES / CROSSTABS SINCE 3.
```

- INFO prints documentation for all changes to system facilities and to procedures FREQUENCIES and CROSSTABS since release 3.0.

OUTFILE Subcommand

By default, the information generated by INFO is part of the output. OUTFILE sends INFO output to a separate file.

Example

```
INFO OUTFILE=SPSSDOC ALL SINCE 3.
```

- INFO creates a text file that includes an overview, local documentation, error, and update information for facilities and procedures since release 3.0.
- The OUTFILE subcommand sends the documentation to the file *SPSSDOC*.

INPUT PROGRAM—END INPUT PROGRAM

```
INPUT PROGRAM

commands to create or define cases

END INPUT PROGRAM
```

Example

```
INPUT PROGRAM.
DATA LIST FILE=PRICES /YEAR 1-4 QUARTER 6 PRICE 8-12(2).

DO IF (YEAR GE 1881).   /*Stop reading before 1881
END FILE.
END IF.
END INPUT PROGRAM.
```

Overview

The INPUT PROGRAM and END INPUT PROGRAM commands enclose data definition and transformation commands that build cases from input records. The input program often encloses one or more DO IF—END IF or LOOP—END LOOP structures, and it must include at least one file definition command, such as DATA LIST. One of the following utility commands is also usually used:

END CASE   *Build cases from the commands within the input program and pass the cases to the commands immediately following the input program.*

END FILE   *Terminate processing of a data file before the actual end of the file or define the end of the file when the input program is used to read raw data.*

REREAD   *Reread the current record using a different* DATA LIST.

REPEATING DATA   *Read repeating groups of data from the same input record.*

For more information on the commands used in an input program, see the discussion of each command.

Input programs create a dictionary and data for a working file from raw data files; they cannot be used to read SPSS-format data files. They can be used to process direct-access and keyed data files. For details, see KEYED DATA LIST.

Input Programs

The program builds the working data file dictionary when it encounters commands that create and define variables. At the same time, the program builds an *input program* that constructs cases and an optional *transformation program* that modifies cases prior to analysis or display. By the time the program encounters a procedure command that tells it to read the data, the working file dictionary is ready, and the programs that construct and modify the cases in the working file are built.

The internal input program is usually built from either a single DATA LIST command or from any of the commands that read or combine SPSS-format data files (for example, GET, ADD FILES, MATCH FILES, UPDATE, and so on). The input program can also be built from the FILE TYPE—END FILE TYPE structure used to define nested, mixed, or grouped files. The third type of input program is specified with the INPUT PROGRAM—END INPUT PROGRAM commands.

With INPUT PROGRAM—END INPUT PROGRAM, you can create your own input program to perform many different operations on raw data. You can use transformation commands to build cases. You can read nonrectangular files, concatenate raw data files, and build cases selectively. You can also create a working data file without reading any data at all.

Input State

There are four program states in the program: the *initial state,* in which there is no working file dictionary; the *input state,* in which cases are created from the input file; the *transformation state,* in which cases are transformed; and the *procedure state,* in which procedures are executed. When you specify INPUT PROGRAM—END INPUT PROGRAM, you must pay attention to which commands are allowed within the input state, which commands can appear only within the input state, and which are not allowed within the input state. See Appendix A for a discussion of program states, command order, and a table that describes what happens to each command when it is encountered in each of the four states.

Basic Specification

The basic specification is INPUT PROGRAM, the commands used to create cases and define the working data file, and END INPUT PROGRAM.

- INPUT PROGRAM and END INPUT PROGRAM each must be specified on a separate line and have no additional specifications.
- To define a working data file, the input program must include at least one DATA LIST or END FILE command.

Operations

- The INPUT PROGRAM—END INPUT PROGRAM structure defines a working data file and is not executed until the program encounters a procedure or the EXECUTE command.
- INPUT PROGRAM clears the current working data file.

Example

```
* Select cases with an input program.

INPUT PROGRAM.
DATA LIST FILE=PRICES /YEAR 1-4 QUARTER 6 PRICE 8-12(2).

DO IF (YEAR GE 1881).  /*Stop reading when reaching 1881
END FILE.
END IF.
END INPUT PROGRAM.

LIST.
```

- The input program is defined between the INPUT PROGRAM and END INPUT PROGRAM commands.
- This example assumes that data records are entered chronologically by year. The DO IF— END IF structure specifies an end of file when the first case with a value of 1881 or later for *YEAR* is reached.
- LIST executes the input program and lists cases in the working data file. The case that causes the end of the file is not included in the working file generated by the input program.
- As an alternative to this input program, you can use N OF CASES to select cases if you know the exact number of cases. Another alternative is to use SELECT IF to select cases before 1881, but then the program would unnecessarily read the entire input file.

Example

```
* Skip the first n records in a file.

INPUT PROGRAM.
NUMERIC         #INIT.
DO IF           NOT (#INIT).
+   LOOP          #I = 1 TO 5.
+     DATA LIST     NOTABLE/.   /* No data - just skip record
+   END LOOP.
+   COMPUTE       #INIT = 1.
END IF.
DATA LIST        NOTABLE/ X 1.
END INPUT PROGRAM.

BEGIN DATA
A                          /* The first 5 records are skipped
B
C
D
E
1
2
3
4
5
END DATA.
LIST.
```

- NUMERIC declares the scratch variable *#INIT*, which is initialized to system-missing.
- The DO IF structure is executed as long as *#INIT* does not equal 1.
- LOOP is executed five times. Within the loop, DATA LIST is specified without variable names, causing the program to read records in the data file without copying them into the working file. LOOP is executed five times, so the program reads five records in this manner. END LOOP terminates this loop.
- COMPUTE creates the scratch variable *#INIT* and sets it equal to 1. The DO IF structure is therefore not executed again.
- END IF terminates the DO IF structure.
- The second DATA LIST specifies numeric variable *X*, which is located in column 1 of each record. Because the program has already read five records, the first value for *X* that is copied into the working file is read from record 6.

More Examples

For additional examples of input programs, refer to DATA LIST (p. 251), DO IF (p. 325), DO REPEAT (p. 328), END CASE, END FILE, LOOP, NUMERIC (p. 845), POINT (p. 889), REPEATING DATA, REREAD, and VECTOR (p. 1242).

KEYED DATA LIST

```
KEYED DATA LIST KEY=varname IN=varname

 FILE=file [{TABLE  }]
           {NOTABLE}

 /varname {col location [(format)]} [varname ..]
          {(FORTRAN-like format)  }
```

Example

```
FILE HANDLE EMPL/ file specifications.
KEYED DATA LIST FILE=EMPL KEY=#NXTCASE IN=#FOUND
        /YRHIRED 1-2 SEX 3 JOBCLASS 4.
```

Overview

KEYED DATA LIST reads raw data from two types of nonsequential files: direct-access files, which provide direct access by a record number, and keyed files, which provide access by a record key. An example of a direct-access file is a file of 50 records, each corresponding to one of the United States. If you know the relationship between the states and the record numbers, you can retrieve the data for any specific state. An example of a keyed file is a file containing social security numbers and other information about a firm's employees. The social security number can be used to identify the records in the file.

Direct-Access Files

There are various types of direct-access files. This program's concept of a direct-access file, however, is very specific. The file must be one from which individual records can be selected according to their number. The records in a 100-record direct-access file, for example, are numbered from 1 to 100.

Although the concept of record number applies to almost any file, not all files can be treated by this program as direct-access files. In fact, some operating systems provide no direct-access capabilities at all, and others permit only a narrowly defined subset of all files to be treated as direct access.

Very few files turn out to be good candidates for direct-access organization. In the case of an inventory file, for example, the usual large gaps in the part numbering sequence would result in large amounts of wasted file space. Gaps are not a problem, however, if they are predictable. For example, if you recognize that telephone area codes have first digits of 2 through 9, second digits of 0 or 1, and third digits of 0 through 9, you can transform an area code into a record number by using the following COMPUTE statement:

```
COMPUTE RECNUM = 20*(DIGIT1-2) + 10*DIGIT2 + DIGIT3 + 1.
```

where *DIGIT1*, *DIGIT2*, and *DIGIT3* are variables corresponding to the respective digits in the area code, and *RECNUM* is the resulting record number. The record numbers would range from 1, for the non-existent area code 200, through 160, for area code 919. The file would then have a manageable number of unused records.

Keyed Files

Of the many kinds of keyed files, the ones to which the program can provide access are generally known as *indexed sequential files*. A file of this kind is basically a sequential file in which an index is maintained so that the file can be processed either sequentially or selectively. In effect, there is an underlying data file that is accessed through a file of index entries. The file of index entries may, for example, contain the fact that data record 797 is associated with social security number 476-77-1359. Depending on the implementation, the underlying data may or may not be maintained in sequential order.

The key for each record in the file generally comprises one or more pieces of information found within the record. An example of a complex key is a customer's last name and house number, plus the consonants in the street name, plus the zip code, plus a unique digit in case there are duplicates. Regardless of the information contained in the key, the program treats it as a character string.

On some systems, more than one key is associated with each record. That is, the records in a file can be identified according to different types of information. Although the primary key for a file normally must be unique, sometimes the secondary keys need not be. For example, the records in an employee file might be identified by social security number and job classification.

Options

Data Source. You can specify the name of the keyed file on the FILE subcommand. By default, the last file that was specified on an input command, such as DATA LIST or REPEATING DATA, is read.

Summary Table. You can display a table that summarizes the variable definitions.

Basic Specification

- The basic specification requires FILE, KEY, and IN, each of which specifies one variable, followed by a slash and variable definitions.
- FILE specifies the direct-access or keyed file. The file must have a file handle already defined.
- KEY specifies the variable whose value will be used to read a record. For direct-access files, the variable must be numeric; for keyed files, it must be string.
- IN creates a logical variable that flags whether a record was successfully read.
- Variable definitions follow all subcommands; the slash preceding them is required. Variable definitions are similar to those specified on DATA LIST.

Subcommand Order

- Subcommands can be named in any order.
- Variable definitions must follow all specified subcommands.

Syntax Rules

- Specifications for the variable definitions are the same as those described for DATA LIST. The only difference is that only one record can be defined per case.

- The FILE HANDLE command must be used if the FILE subcommand is specified on KEYED DATA LIST.

- KEYED DATA LIST can be specified in an input program, or it can be used as a transformation language to change an existing working data file. This differs from all other input commands, such as GET and DATA LIST, which create new working files.

Operations

- Variable names are stored in the working file dictionary.

- Formats are stored in the working file dictionary and are used to display and write the values. To change output formats of numeric variables, use the FORMATS command.

Example

```
FILE HANDLE EMPL/ file specifications.
KEYED DATA LIST FILE=EMPL KEY=#NXTCASE IN=#FOUND
        /YRHIRED 1-2 SEX 3 JOBCLASS 4.
```

- FILE HANDLE defines the handle for the data file to be read by KEYED DATA LIST. The handle is specified on the FILE subcommand of KEYED DATA LIST.

- KEY on KEYED DATA LIST specifies the variable to be used as the access key. For a direct-access file, the value of the variable must be between 1 and the number of records in the file. For a keyed file, the value must be a string.

- IN creates the logical scratch variable *#FOUND*, whose value will be 1 if the record is successfully read, or 0 if the record is not found.

- The variable definitions are the same as those used for DATA LIST.

Example

```
* Reading a direct-access file: sampling 1 out of every 25 records.

FILE HANDLE     EMPL/ file specifications.
INPUT PROGRAM.
COMPUTE #INTRVL = TRUNC(UNIF(48))+1. /* Mean interval = 25
COMPUTE #NXTCASE = #NXTCASE+#INTRVL. /* Next record number
COMPUTE #EOF = #NXTCASE > 1000.      /* End of file check
DO IF   #EOF.
+ END FILE.
ELSE.
+ KEYED DATA LIST  FILE=EMPL, KEY=#NXTCASE, IN=#FOUND, NOTABLE
                   /YRHIRED 1-2 SEX 3 JOBCLASS 4.
+ DO IF       #FOUND.
+    END CASE.                       /* Return a case
+ ELSE.
+    PRINT / 'Oops. #NXTCASE=' #NXTCASE.
+ END IF.
END IF.
END INPUT PROGRAM.
EXECUTE.
```

- FILE HANDLE defines the handle for the data file to be read by the KEYED DATA LIST command. The record numbers for this example are generated by the transformation language; they are not based on data taken from another file.

- The INPUT PROGRAM and END INPUT PROGRAM commands begin and end the block of commands that build cases from the input file. Since the session generates cases, an input program is required.

- The first two COMPUTE statements determine the number of the next record to be selected. This is done in two steps. First, the integer portion is taken from the sum of 1 and a uniform pseudo-random number between 1 and 49. The result is a mean interval of 25. Second, the variable *#NXTCASE* is added to this number to generate the next record number. This record number, *#NXTCASE*, will be used for the key variable on the KEYED DATA LIST command. The third COMPUTE creates a logical scratch variable, *#EOF*, that has a value of 0 if the record number is less than or equal to 1000, or 1 if the value of the record number is greater than 1000.

- The DO IF—END IF structure controls the building of cases. If the record number is greater than 1000, *#EOF* equals 1, and the END FILE command tells the program to stop reading data and end the file.

- If the record number is less than or equal to 1000, the record is read via KEYED DATA LIST using the value of *#NXTCASE*. A case is generated if the record exists (*#FOUND* equals 1). If not, the program displays the record number and continues to the next case. The sample will have about 40 records.

- EXECUTE causes the transformations to be executed.

- This example illustrates the difference between DATA LIST, which always reads the next record in a file, and KEYED DATA LIST, which reads only specified records. The record numbers must be generated by another command or be contained in the working data file.

Example

```
* Reading a keyed file: reading selected records.

GET FILE=STUDENTS/KEEP=AGE,SEX,COURSE.
FILE HANDLE COURSES/ file specifications.
STRING #KEY(A4).
COMPUTE #KEY = STRING(COURSE,N4). /* Create a string key
KEYED DATA LIST FILE=COURSES KEY=#KEY IN=#FOUND NOTABLE
     /PERIOD 13 CREDITS 16.
SELECT IF #FOUND.
LIST.
```

- GET reads the *STUDENTS* file, which contains information on students, including a course identification for each student. The course identification will be used as the key for selecting one record from a file of courses.

- The FILE HANDLE command defines a file handle for the file of courses.

- The STRING and COMPUTE commands transform the course identification from numeric to string for use as a key. For keyed files, the key variable must be a string.

- KEYED DATA LIST uses the value of the newly created string variable *#KEY* as the key to search the course file. If a record that matches the value of *#KEY* is found, *#FOUND* is set to 1; otherwise, it is set to 0. Note that KEYED DATA LIST appears outside an input program in this example.

- If the course file contains the requested record, *#FOUND* equals 1. The variables *PERIOD* and *CREDITS* are added to the case and the case is selected via the SELECT IF command; otherwise, the case is dropped.

- LIST lists the values of the selected cases.

- This example shows how existing cases can be updated on the basis of information read from a keyed file.

- This task could also be accomplished by reading the entire course file with DATA LIST and combining it with the student file via the MATCH FILES command. The technique you should use depends on the percentage of the records in the course file that need to be accessed. If fewer than 10% of the course file records are read, KEYED DATA LIST is probably more efficient. As the percentage of the records that are read increases, reading the entire course file and using MATCH makes more sense.

FILE Subcommand

FILE specifies the handle for the direct-access or keyed data file. The file handle must have been defined on a previous FILE HANDLE command (or, in the case of the IBM OS environment, on a DD statement in the JCL).

KEY Subcommand

KEY specifies the variable whose value will be used as the key. This variable must already exist as the result of a prior DATA LIST, KEYED DATA LIST, GET, or transformation command.

- KEY is required. Its only specification is a single variable. The variable can be a permanent variable or a scratch variable.
- For direct-access files, the key variable must be numeric, and its value must be between 1 and the number of records in the file.
- For keyed files, the key variable must be string. If the keys are numbers, such as social security numbers, the STRING function can be used to convert the numbers to strings. For example, the following might be required to get the value of a numeric key into exactly the same format as used on the keyed file:

```
COMPUTE #KEY=STRING(123,IB4).
```

IN Subcommand

IN creates a numeric variable whose value indicates whether or not the specified record is found.

- IN is required. Its only specification is a single numeric variable. The variable can be a permanent variable or a scratch variable.
- The value of the variable is 1 if the record is successfully read or 0 if the record is not found. The IN variable can be used to select all cases that have been updated by KEYED DATA LIST.

Example

```
FILE HANDLE EMPL/ file specifications.
KEYED DATA LIST FILE=EMPL KEY=#NXTCASE IN=#FOUND
        /YRHIRED 1-2 SEX 3 JOBCLASS 4.
```

- IN creates the logical scratch variable *#FOUND*. The values of *#FOUND* will be 1 if the record indicated by the key value in *#NXTCASE* is found or 0 if the record does not exist.

TABLE and NOTABLE Subcommands

TABLE and NOTABLE determine whether the program displays a table that summarizes the variable definitions. TABLE, the default, displays the table. NOTABLE suppresses the table.

- TABLE and NOTABLE are optional and mutually exclusive.
- The only specification for TABLE or NOTABLE is the subcommand keyword. Neither subcommand has additional specifications.

KM

KM is available in the Advanced Models option.

```
KM varname [BY factor varname]

   /STATUS = varname [EVENT](vallist) [LOST(vallist)]

   [/STRATA = varname]

   [/PLOT = {NONE**                          }]
            {[SURVIVAL][LOGSURV][HAZARD][OMS]}

   [/ID  = varname]

   [/PRINT = [TABLE**][MEAN**][NONE]]

   [/PERCENTILE = [(]{25, 50, 75 }[)]]
                     {value list }

   [/TEST = [LOGRANK**][BRESLOW][TARONE]]

   [/COMPARE = [{OVERALL**}][{POOLED**}]]
               {PAIRWISE }  {STRATA  }

   [/TREND = [(METRIC)]]

   [/SAVE = tempvar[(newvar)],...]
```

**Default if subcommand or keyword is omitted.

Temporary variables created by Kaplan-Meier are:

SURVIVAL
HAZARD
SE
CUMEVENT

Example

```
KM LENGTH BY SEXRACE
 /STATUS=EMPLOY  EVENT (1) LOST (2)
 /STRATA=LOCATION.
```

Overview

KM (alias K-M) uses the Kaplan-Meier (product-limit) technique to describe and analyze the length of time to the occurrence of an event, often known as **survival time**. KM is similar to SURVIVAL in that it produces nonparametric estimates of the survival functions. However, instead of dividing the period of time under examination into arbitrary intervals, KM evaluates the survival function at the observed event times. For analysis of survival times with covariates, including time-dependent covariates, see the COXREG command.

Options

KM Tables. You can include one factor variable on the KM command. A KM table is produced for each level of the factor variable. You can also suppress the KM tables in the output with the PRINT subcommand.

Survival Status. You can specify the code(s) indicating that an event has occurred as well as code(s) for cases lost to follow-up using the STATUS subcommand.

Plots. You can plot the survival functions on a linear or log scale or plot the hazard function for each combination of factor and stratum with the PLOT subcommand.

Test Statistics. When a factor variable is specified, you can specify one or more tests of equality of survival distributions for the different levels of the factor using the TEST subcommand. You can also specify a trend metric for the requested tests with the TREND subcommand.

Display ID and Percentiles. You can specify an ID variable on the ID subcommand to identify each case. You can also request display of percentiles in the output with the PERCENTILES subcommand.

Comparisons. When a factor variable is specified, you can use the COMPARE subcommand to compare the different levels of the factor, either pairwise or across all levels, and either pooled across all strata or within a stratum.

Add New Variables to Working Data File. You can save new variables appended to the end of the working data file with the SAVE subcommand.

Basic Specification

- The basic specification requires a survival variable and the STATUS subcommand naming a variable that indicates whether the event occurred.
- The basic specification prints one survival table followed by the mean and median survival time with standard errors and 95% confidence intervals.

Subcommand Order

- The survival variable and the factor variable (if there is one) must be specified first.
- Remaining subcommands can be specified in any order.

Syntax Rules

- Only one survival variable can be specified. To analyze multiple survival variables, use multiple KM commands.
- Only one factor variable can be specified following the BY keyword. If you have multiple factors, use the transformation language to create a single factor variable before invoking KM.

- Only one status variable can be listed on the STATUS subcommand. You must specify the value(s) indicating that the event occurred.
- Only one variable can be specified on the STRATA subcommand. If you have more than one stratum, use the transformation language to create a single variable to specify on the STRATA subcommand.

Operations

- KM deletes all cases that have negative values for the survival variable.
- KM estimates the survival function and associated statistics for each combination of factor and stratum.
- Three statistics can be computed to test the equality of survival functions across factor levels within a stratum or across all factor levels while controlling for strata. The statistics are the log rank (Mantel-Cox), the generalized Wilcoxon (Breslow), and the Tarone-Ware tests.
- When the PLOTS subcommand is specified, KM produces one plot of survival functions for each stratum, with all factor levels represented by different symbols or colors.

Limitations

- Maximum 35 factor levels (symbols) can appear in a plot.

Example

```
KM LENGTH BY SEXRACE
 /STATUS=EMPLOY EVENT (1) LOST (2)
 /STRATA=LOCATION.
```

- Survival analysis is used to examine the length of unemployment. The survival variable *LENGTH* contains the number of months a subject is unemployed. The factor variable *SEXRACE* combines sex and race factors.
- A value of 1 on the variable *EMPLOY* indicates the occurrence of the event (employment). All other observed cases are censored. A value of 2 on *EMPLOY* indicates cases lost to follow-up. Cases with other values for *EMPLOY* are known to have remained unemployed during the course of the study. KM separates the two types of censored cases in the KM table if LOST is specified.
- For each combination of *SEXRACE* and *LOCATION,* one KM table is produced, followed by the mean and median survival time with standard errors and confidence intervals.

Survival and Factor Variables

You must identify the survival and factor variables for the analysis.
- The minimum specification is one, and only one, survival variable.
- Only one factor variable can be specified using the BY keyword. If you have more than one factor, create a new variable combining all factors. There is no limit to the factor levels.

Example

```
DO IF SEX = 1.
+ COMPUTE SEXRACE = RACE.
ELSE.
+ COMPUTE SEXRACE = RACE + SEX.
END IF.
KM LENGTH BY SEXRACE
 /STATUS=EMPLOY EVENT (1) LOST (2).
```

- The two control variables, *SEX* and *RACE*, each with two values, 1 and 2, are combined into one factor variable, *SEXRACE*, with four values, 1 to 4.

- KM specifies *LENGTH* as the survival variable and *SEXRACE* as the factor variable.

- One KM table is produced for each factor level.

STATUS Subcommand

To determine whether the terminal event has occurred for a particular observation, KM checks the value of a status variable. STATUS lists the status variable and the code(s) for the occurrence of the event. The code(s) for cases lost to follow-up can also be specified.

- Only one status variable can be specified. If multiple STATUS subcommands are specified, KM uses the last specification and displays a warning.

- The keyword EVENT is optional, but the value list in parentheses must be specified. Use EVENT for clarity's sake, especially when LOST is specified.

- The value list must be enclosed in parentheses. All cases with non-negative times that do not have a code within the range specified after EVENT are classified as **censored cases**— that is, cases for which the event has not yet occurred.

- The keyword LOST and the following value list are optional. LOST cannot be omitted if the value list for lost cases is specified.

- When LOST is specified, all cases with non-negative times that have a code within the specified value range are classified as lost to follow-up. Cases lost to follow-up are treated as censored in the analysis, and the statistics do not change, but the two types of censored cases are listed separately in the KM table.

- The value lists on EVENT or LOST can be one value, a list of values separated by blanks or commas, a range of values using the keyword THRU, or a combination.

- The status variable can be either numeric or string. If a string variable is specified, the EVENT or LOST values must be enclosed in apostrophes, and the keyword THRU cannot be used.

Example

```
KM LENGTH BY SEXRACE
 /STATUS=EMPLOY  EVENT (1) LOST (3,5 THRU 8).
```

- STATUS specifies that *EMPLOY* is the status variable.

- A value of 1 for *EMPLOY* means that the event (employment) occurred for the case.

- Values of 3 and 5 through 8 for *EMPLOY* mean that contact was lost with the case. The different values code different causes for the loss of contact.

- The summary table in the output includes columns for number lost and percentage lost, as well as for number censored and percentage censored.

STRATA Subcommand

STRATA identifies a **stratification variable**—that is, a variable whose values are used to form subgroups (strata) within the categories of the factor variable. Analysis is done within each level of the strata variable for each factor level, and estimates are pooled over strata for an overall comparison of factor levels.

- The minimum specification is the subcommand keyword with one, and only one, variable name.
- If you have more than one strata variable, create a new variable to combine the levels on separate variables before invoking the KM command.
- There is no limit to the number of levels for the strata variable.

Example

```
KM LENGTH BY SEXRACE
 /STATUS=EMPLOY EVENT (1) LOST (3,5 THRU 8)
 /STRATA=LOCATION.
```

- STRATA specifies *LOCATION* as the stratification variable. Analysis of the length of unemployment is done for each location within each sex and race subgroup.

PLOT Subcommand

PLOT plots the cumulative survival distribution on a linear or logarithmic scale or plots the cumulative hazard function. A separate plot with all factor levels is produced for each stratum. Each factor level is represented by a different symbol or color. Censored cases are indicated by markers.

- When PLOT is omitted, no plots are produced. The default is NONE.
- When PLOT is specified without a keyword, the default is SURVIVAL. A plot of survival functions for each stratum is produced.
- To request specific plots, specify, following the PLOT subcommand, any combination of the keywords defined below.
- Multiple keywords can be used on the PLOT subcommand, each requesting a different plot. The effect is cumulative.

NONE   *Suppress all plots.* NONE is the default if PLOT is omitted.

SURVIVAL   *Plot the cumulative survival distribution on a linear scale.* SURVIVAL is the default when PLOT is specified without a keyword.

LOGSURV   *Plot the cumulative survival distribution on a logarithmic scale.*

HAZARD   *Plot the cumulative hazard function.*

OMS   *Plot the one-minus-survival function.*

Example

```
KM LENGTH BY SEXRACE
 /STATUS=EMPLOY EVENT (1) LOST (3,5 THRU 8)
 /STRATA=LOCATION
 /PLOT = SURVIVAL HAZARD.
```

- PLOT produces one plot of the cumulative survival distribution on a linear scale and one plot of the cumulative hazard rate for each value of *LOCATION*.

ID Subcommand

ID specifies a variable used for labeling cases. If the ID variable is a string, KM uses the string values as case identifiers in the KM table. If the ID variable is numeric, KM uses value labels or numeric values if value labels are not defined.

- ID is the first column of the KM table displayed for each combination of factor and stratum.
- If a string value or a value label exceeds 20 characters in width, KM truncates the case identifier and displays a warning.

PRINT Subcommand

By default, KM prints survival tables and the mean and median survival time with standard errors and confidence intervals if PRINT is omitted. If PRINT is specified, only the specified keyword is in effect. Use PRINT to suppress tables or the mean statistics.

TABLE *Print the KM tables.* If PRINT is not specified, TABLE, together with MEAN, is the default. Specify TABLE on PRINT to suppress the mean statistics.

MEAN *Print the mean statistics.* KM prints the mean and median survival time with standard errors and confidence intervals. If PRINT is not specified, MEAN, together with TABLE, is the default. Specify MEAN on PRINT to suppress the KM tables.

NONE *Suppress both the KM tables and the mean statistics.* Only plots and comparisons are printed.

Example

```
KM LENGTH BY SEXRACE
 /STATUS=EMPLOY EVENT (1) LOST (3,5 THRU 8)
 /STRATA=LOCATION
 /PLOT=SURVIVAL HAZARD
 /PRINT=NONE.
```

- PRINT=NONE suppresses both the KM tables and the mean statistics.

PERCENTILES Subcommand

PERCENTILES displays percentiles for each combination of factor and stratum. Percentiles are not displayed without the PERCENTILES subcommand. If the subcommand is specified without a value list, the default is 25, 50, and 75 for quartile display. You can specify any values between 0 and 100.

TEST Subcommand

TEST specifies the test statistic to use for testing the equality of survival distributions for the different levels of the factor.

- TEST is valid only when a factor variable is specified. If no factor variable is specified, KM issues a warning and TEST is not executed.
- If TEST is specified without a keyword, the default is LOGRANK. If a keyword is specified on TEST, only the specified test is performed.
- Each of the test statistics has a chi-square distribution with one degree of freedom.

LOGRANK   *Perform the log rank (Mantel-Cox) test.*

BRESLOW   *Perform the Breslow (generalized Wilcoxon) test.*

TARONE   *Perform the Tarone-Ware test.*

COMPARE Subcommand

COMPARE compares the survival distributions for the different levels of the factor. Each of the keywords specifies a different method of comparison.

- COMPARE is valid only when a factor variable is specified. If no factor variable is specified, KM issues a warning and COMPARE is not executed.
- COMPARE uses whatever tests are specified on the TEST subcommand. If no TEST subcommand is specified, the log rank test is used.
- If COMPARE is not specified, the default is OVERALL and POOLED. All factor levels are compared across strata in a single test. The test statistics are displayed after the summary table at the end of output.
- Multiple COMPARE subcommands can be specified to request different comparisons.

OVERALL   *Compare all factor levels in a single test.* OVERALL, together with POOLED, is the default when COMPARE is not specified.

PAIRWISE   *Compare each pair of factor levels.* KM compares all distinct pairs of factor levels.

POOLED   *Pool the test statistics across all strata.* The test statistics are displayed after the summary table for all strata. POOLED, together with OVERALL, is the default when COMPARE is not specified.

STRATA   *Compare the factor levels for each stratum.* The test statistics are displayed for each stratum separately.

- If a factor variable has different levels across strata, you cannot request a pooled comparison. If you specify POOLED on COMPARE, KM displays a warning and ignores the request.

Example

```
KM LENGTH BY SEXRACE
 /STATUS=EMPLOY EVENT (1) LOST (3,5 THRU 8)
 /STRATA=LOCATION
 /TEST = BRESLOW
 /COMPARE = PAIRWISE.
```

- TEST specifies the Breslow test.
- COMPARE uses the Breslow test statistic to compare all distinct pairs of *SEXRACE* values and pools the test results over all strata defined by *LOCATION*.
- Test statistics are displayed at the end of output for all strata.

TREND Subcommand

TREND specifies that there is a trend across factor levels. This information is used when computing the tests for equality of survival functions specified on the TEST subcommand.

- The minimum specification is the subcommand keyword by itself. The default metric is chosen as follows:

  if *g* is even,

  $$(-(g-1), ..., -3, -1, 1, 3, ..., (g-1))$$

  otherwise,

  $$\left(-\frac{(g-1)}{2}, ..., -1, 0, 1, ..., \frac{(g-1)}{2}\right)$$

  where *g* is the number of levels for the factor variable.

- If TREND is specified but COMPARE is not, KM performs the default log rank test with the trend metric for an OVERALL POOLED comparison.
- If the metric specified on TREND is longer than required by the factor levels, KM displays a warning and ignores extra values.

Example

```
KM LENGTH BY SEXRACE
 /STATUS=EMPLOY EVENT (1) LOST (3,5 THRU 8)
 /STRATA=LOCATION
 /TREND.
```

- TREND is specified by itself. KM uses the default metric. Since *SEXRACE* has four levels, the default is (−3,−1, 1, 3).
- Even though no TEST or COMPARE subcommand is specified, KM performs the default log rank test with the trend metric and does a default OVERALL POOLED comparison.

SAVE Subcommand

SAVE saves the temporary variables created by KM. The following temporary variables can be saved:

SURVIVAL *Survival function evaluated at current case.*

SE *Standard error of the survival function.*

HAZARD *Cumulative hazard function evaluated at current case.*

CUMEVENT *Cumulative number of events.*

- To specify variable names for the new variables, assign the new names in parentheses following each temporary variable name.
- Assigned variable names must be unique in the working data file. Scratch or system variable names cannot be used (that is, variable names cannot begin with # or $).
- If new variable names are not specified, KM generates default names. The default name is composed of the first three characters of the name of the temporary variable (two for *SE*), followed by an underscore and a number to make it unique.
- A temporary variable can be saved only once on the same SAVE subcommand.

Example

```
KM LENGTH BY SEXRACE
 /STATUS=EMPLOY EVENT (1) LOST (3,5 THRU 8)
 /STRATA=LOCATION
 /SAVE SURVIVAL HAZARD.
```

- KM saves cumulative survival and cumulative hazard rates in two new variables, *SUR_1* and *HAZ_1*, provided that neither name exists in the working data file. If one does, the numeric suffixes will be incremented to make a distinction.

LEAVE

```
LEAVE varlist
```

Example
```
COMPUTE TSALARY=TSALARY+SALARY.
LEAVE TSALARY.
FORMAT TSALARY (DOLLAR8)/ SALARY (DOLLAR7).
EXECUTE.
```

Overview

Normally, the program reinitializes variables each time it prepares to read a new case. LEAVE suppresses reinitialization and retains the current value of the specified variable or variables when the program reads the next case. It also sets the initial value received by a numeric variable to 0 instead of system-missing. LEAVE is frequently used with COMPUTE to create a variable to store an accumulating sum. LEAVE is also used to spread a variable's values across multiple cases when VECTOR is used within an input program to restructure a data file (see p. 336 for an example).

LEAVE cannot be used with scratch variables. For information on using scratch variables, see "Scratch Variables" on p. 31.

Basic Specification

The basic specification is the variable(s) whose values are not to be reinitialized as each new case is read.

Syntax Rules

- Variables named on LEAVE must already exist and cannot be scratch variables.
- Multiple variables can be named. The keyword TO can be used to refer to a list of consecutive variables.
- String and numeric variables can be specified on the same LEAVE command.

Operations

- Unlike most transformations, which do not take effect until the data are read, LEAVE takes effect as soon as it is encountered in the command sequence. Thus, special attention should be paid to its position among commands. For more information, see "Command Order" on p. 16.

- Numeric variables named on LEAVE are initialized to 0 for the first case, and string variables are initialized to blanks. These variables are not reinitialized when new cases are read.

Example

```
COMPUTE TSALARY=TSALARY+SALARY.
LEAVE TSALARY.
FORMAT TSALARY (DOLLAR8)/ SALARY (DOLLAR7).
```

- These commands keep a running total of salaries across all cases. *SALARY* is the variable containing the employee's salary, and *TSALARY* is the new variable containing the cumulative salaries for all previous cases.
- For the first case, *TSALARY* is initialized to 0, and *TSALARY* equals *SALARY*. For the rest of the cases, *TSALARY* stores the cumulative totals for *SALARY*.
- LEAVE follows COMPUTE because *TSALARY* must first be defined before it can be specified on LEAVE.
- If LEAVE were not specified for this computation, *TSALARY* would be initialized to system-missing for all cases. *TSALARY* would remain system-missing because its value would be missing for every computation.

Example

```
SORT CASES DEPT.
IF DEPT NE LAG(DEPT,1) TSALARY=0.    /*Initialize for new dept
COMPUTE TSALARY=TSALARY+SALARY.      /*Sum salaries
LEAVE TSALARY.                /*Prevent  initialization
each case
FORMAT TSALARY (DOLLAR8)/ SALARY (DOLLAR7).
```

- These commands accumulate a sum across cases for each department.
- SORT first sorts cases by the values of variable *DEPT*.
- IF specifies that if the value of *DEPT* for the current case is not equal to the value of *DEPT* for the previous case, *TSALARY* equals 0. Thus, *TSALARY* is reset to 0 each time the value of *DEPT* changes. (For the first case in the file, the logical expression on IF is missing. However, the desired effect is obtained because LEAVE initializes *TSALARY* to 0 for the first case, independent of the IF statement.)
- LEAVE prevents *TSALARY* from being initialized for cases within the same department.

LIST

```
LIST [[VARIABLES=]{ALL**  }] [/FORMAT=[{WRAP**}] [{UNNUMBERED**}]]
                 {varlist}           {SINGLE}   {NUMBERED    }

[/CASES=[FROM {1**}] [TO {eof**}] [BY {1**}]]
              {n  }       {n   }       {n  }
```

**Default if the subcommand is omitted.

Example

```
LIST VARIABLES=V1 V2 /CASES=FROM 10 TO 100 BY 2.
```

Overview

LIST displays case values for variables in the working data file. The output is similar to the output produced by the PRINT command. However, LIST is a procedure and reads data, whereas PRINT is a transformation and requires a procedure (or the EXECUTE command) to execute it.

Options

Selecting and Ordering Variables. You can specify a list of variables to be listed using the VARIABLES subcommand.

Format. You can limit each case listing to a single line, and you can display the case number for each listed case with the FORMAT subcommand.

Selecting Cases. You can limit the listing to a particular sequence of cases using the CASES subcommand.

Basic Specification

- The basic specification is simply LIST, which displays the values for all variables in the working data file.
- By default, cases wrap to multiple lines if all the values do not fit within the page width (the page width is determined by the SET WIDTH command). Case numbers are not displayed for the listed cases.

Subcommand Order

All subcommands are optional and can be named in any order.

Operations

- If VARIABLES is not specified, variables are listed in the order in which they appear in the working file.
- LIST does not display values for scratch or system variables.
- LIST uses print formats contained in the dictionary of the working data file. Alternative formats cannot be specified on LIST. See FORMATS or PRINT FORMATS for information on changing print formats.
- LIST output uses the width specified on SET.
- If a numeric value is longer than its defined width, the program first attempts to list the value by removing punctuation characters, then uses scientific notation, and finally prints asterisks.
- If a long string variable cannot be listed within the output width, it is truncated.
- Values of the variables listed for a case are always separated by at least one blank.
- System-missing values are displayed as a period for numeric variables and a blank for string variables.
- If cases fit on one line, the column width for each variable is determined by the length of the variable name or the format, whichever is greater. If the variable names do not fit on one line, they are printed vertically.
- If cases do not fit on one line within the output width specified on SET, they are wrapped. LIST displays a table illustrating the location of the variables in the output and prints the name of the first variable in each line at the beginning of the line.
- Each execution of LIST begins at the top of a new page. If SPLIT FILE is in effect, each split also begins at the top of a new page.

Example

```
LIST.
```

- LIST by itself requests a display of the values for all variables in the working file.

Example

```
LIST VARIABLES=V1 V2 /CASES=FROM 10 TO 100 BY 2.
```

- LIST produces a list of every second case for variables *V1* and *V2*, starting with case 10 and stopping at case 100.

VARIABLES Subcommand

VARIABLES specifies the variables to be listed. The actual keyword VARIABLES can be omitted.

- The variables must already exist, and they cannot be scratch or system variables.
- If VARIABLES is used, only the specified variables are listed.

- Variables are listed in the order in which they are named on VARIABLES.
- If a variable is named more than once, it is listed more than once.
- The keyword ALL (the default) can be used to request all variables. ALL can also be used with a variable list (see example below).

ALL   *List all user-defined variables.* Variables are listed in the order in which they appear in the working data file. This is the default if VARIABLES is omitted.

Example

```
LIST VARIABLES=V15 V31 ALL.
```

- VARIABLES is used to list values for *V15* and *V31* before all other variables. The keyword ALL then lists all variables, including *V15* and *V31*, in the order in which they appear in the working data file. Values for *V15* and *V31* are therefore listed twice.

FORMAT Subcommand

FORMAT controls whether cases wrap if they cannot fit on a single line and whether the case number is displayed for each listed case. The default display uses more than one line per case (if necessary) and does not number cases.

- The minimum specification is a single keyword.
- WRAP and SINGLE are alternatives, as are NUMBERED and UNNUMBERED. Only one of each pair can be specified.
- If SPLIT FILE is in effect for NUMBERED, case numbering restarts at each split. To get sequential numbering regardless of splits, create a variable and set it equal to the system variable *$CASENUM* and then name this variable as the first variable on the VARIABLES subcommand. An appropriate format should be specified for the new variable before it is used on LIST.

WRAP   *Wrap cases if they do not fit on a single line.* Page width is determined by the SET WIDTH command. This is the default.

SINGLE   *Limit each case to one line.* Only variables that fit on a single line are displayed.

UNNUMBERED   *Do not include the sequence number of each case.* This is the default.

NUMBERED   *Include the sequence number of each case.* The sequence number is displayed to the left of the listed values.

CASES Subcommand

CASES limits the number of cases listed. By default, all cases in the working data file are listed.

- Any or all of the keywords below can be used. Defaults that are not changed remain in effect.
- If LIST is preceded by a SAMPLE or SELECT IF command, case selections specified by CASES are taken from those cases that were selected by SAMPLE or SELECT IF.

- If SPLIT FILE is in effect, case selections specified by CASES are restarted for each split.

FROM n   *Number of the first case to be listed.* The default is 1.

TO n   *Number of the last case to be listed.* The default is the end of the working file. CASES 100 is interpreted as CASES TO 100.

BY n   *Increment used to choose cases for listing.* The default is 1.

Example

```
LIST CASES BY 3 /FORMAT=NUMBERED.
```

- Every third case is listed for all variables in the working data file. The listing begins with the first case and includes every third case up to the end of the file.
- FORMAT displays the case number of each listed case.

Example

```
LIST CASES FROM 10 TO 20.
```

- Cases from case 10 through case 20 are listed for all variables in the working file.

LOGISTIC REGRESSION

LOGISTIC REGRESSION is available in the Regression Models option.

```
LOGISTIC REGRESSION [VARIABLES =] dependent var
        [WITH independent varlist [BY var [BY var] ... ]]

[/CATEGORICAL = var1, var2, ... ]

[/CONTRAST (categorical var) = [{INDICATOR [(refcat)]    }]]
                                {DEVIATION [(refcat)]    }
                                {SIMPLE [(refcat)]        }
                                {DIFFERENCE               }
                                {HELMERT                  }
                                {REPEATED                 }
                                {POLYNOMIAL[({1,2,3...})]}]
                                            {metric }
                                {SPECIAL (matrix)         }

[/METHOD = {ENTER**      }   [{ALL    }]]
           {BSTEP [{COND}]}   {varlist}
                  {LR  }
                  {WALD}
           {FSTEP [{COND}]}
                  {LR  }
                  {WALD}

[/SELECT = {ALL**                    }]
           {varname relation value}

[/{NOORIGIN**}]
  {ORIGIN    }

[/ID = [variable]]

[/PRINT = [DEFAULT**] [SUMMARY] [CORR] [ALL] [ITER [({1})]] [GOODFIT]]
                                                      {n}
          [CI(level)]

[/CRITERIA = [BCON ({0.001**})] [ITERATE({20**})] [LCON({0.01**})]
                   {value  }            {n   }          {value }

             [PIN({0.05**})] [POUT({0.10**})] [EPS({.00000001**})]]
                 {value }         {value }        {value       }

             [CUT[{0.5**  }]]
                 [value  }

[/CLASSPLOT]

[/MISSING = {EXCLUDE **}]
            {INCLUDE   }

[/CASEWISE = [tempvarlist]  [OUTLIER({2**  })]]
                                    {value}

[/SAVE = tempvar[(newname)] tempvar[(newname)]...]

[/EXTERNAL]
```

** Default if the subcommand or keyword is omitted.

Temporary variables created by LOGISTIC REGRESSION are:

PRED	LEVER	COOK
PGROUP	LRESID	DFBETA
RESID	SRESID	
DEV	ZRESID	

Example

```
LOGISTIC REGRESSION PROMOTED WITH AGE, JOBTIME, JOBRATE.
```

Overview

LOGISTIC REGRESSION regresses a dichotomous dependent variable on a set of independent variables (Aldrich and Nelson, 1984; Fox, 1984; Hosmer and Lemeshow, 1989; McCullagh and Nelder, 1989; Agresti, 1990). Categorical independent variables are replaced by sets of contrast variables, each set entering and leaving the model in a single step.

Options

Processing of Independent Variables. You can specify which independent variables are categorical in nature on the CATEGORICAL subcommand. You can control treatment of categorical independent variables by the CONTRAST subcommand. Seven methods are available for entering independent variables into the model. You can specify any one of them on the METHOD subcommand. You can also use the keyword BY between variable names to enter interaction terms.

Selecting Cases. You can use the SELECT subcommand to define subsets of cases to be used in estimating a model.

Regression through the Origin. You can use the ORIGIN subcommand to exclude a constant term from a model.

Specifying Termination and Model-Building Criteria. You can further control computations when building the model by specifying criteria on the CRITERIA subcommand.

Adding New Variables to the Working Data File. You can save the residuals, predicted values, and diagnostics generated by LOGISTIC REGRESSION in the working data file.

Output. You can use the PRINT subcommand to print optional output, use the CASEWISE subcommand to request analysis of residuals, and use the ID subcommand to specify a variable whose values or value labels identify cases in output. You can request plots of the actual and predicted values for each case with the CLASSPLOT subcommand.

Basic Specification

- The minimum specification is the VARIABLES subcommand with one dichotomous dependent variable. You must specify a list of independent variables either following the keyword WITH on the VARIABLES subcommand or on a METHOD subcommand.

- The default output includes goodness-of-fit tests for the model (−2 log-likelihood, goodness-of-fit statistic, Cox and Snell R^2, and NagelKerke R^2) and a classification table for the predicted and observed group memberships. The regression coefficient, standard error of the regression coefficient, Wald statistic and its significance level, and a multiple correlation coefficient adjusted for the number of parameters (Atkinson, 1980) are displayed for each variable in the equation.

Subcommand Order

- Subcommands can be named in any order. If the VARIABLES subcommand is not specified first, a slash (/) must precede it.
- The ordering of METHOD subcommands determines the order in which models are estimated. Different sequences may result in different models.

Syntax Rules

- Only one dependent variable can be specified for each LOGISTIC REGRESSION.
- Any number of independent variables may be listed. The dependent variable may not appear on this list.
- The independent variable list is required if any of the METHOD subcommands are used without a variable list or if the METHOD subcommand is not used. The keyword TO cannot be used on any variable list.
- If you specify the keyword WITH on the VARIABLES subcommand, all independent variables must be listed.
- If the keyword WITH is used on the VARIABLES subcommand, interaction terms do not have to be specified on the variable list, but the individual variables that make up the interactions must be listed.
- Multiple METHOD subcommands are allowed.
- The minimum truncation for this command is LOGI REG.

Operations

- Independent variables specified on the CATEGORICAL subcommand are replaced by sets of contrast variables. In stepwise analyses, the set of contrast variables associated with a categorical variable is entered or removed from the model as a single step.
- Independent variables are screened to detect and eliminate redundancies.
- If the linearly dependent variable is one of a set of contrast variables, the set will be reduced by the redundant variable or variables. A warning will be issued, and the reduced set will be used.
- For the forward stepwise method, redundancy checking is done when a variable is to be entered into the model.
- When backward stepwise or direct-entry methods are requested, all variables for each METHOD subcommand are checked for redundancy before that analysis begins.

Limitations

- The dependent variable must be dichotomous for each split-file group. Specifying a dependent variable with more or less than two nonmissing values per split-file group will result in an error.

Example

```
LOGISTIC REGRESSION PASS WITH GPA, MAT, GRE.
```

- *PASS* is specified as the dependent variable.
- *GPA*, *MAT*, and *GRE* are specified as independent variables.
- LOGISTIC REGRESSION produces the default output for the logistic regression of *PASS* on *GPA*, *MAT*, and *GRE*.

VARIABLES Subcommand

VARIABLES specifies the dependent variable and, optionally, all independent variables in the model. The dependent variable appears first on the list and is separated from the independent variables by the keyword WITH.

- One VARIABLES subcommand is allowed for each Logistic Regression procedure.
- The dependent variable must be dichotomous—that is, it must have exactly two values other than system-missing and user-missing values for each split-file group.
- The dependent variable may be a string variable if its two values can be differentiated by their first eight characters.
- You can indicate an interaction term on the variable list by using the keyword BY to separate the individual variables.
- If all METHOD subcommands are accompanied by independent variable lists, the keyword WITH and the list of independent variables may be omitted.
- If the keyword WITH is used, *all* independent variables must be specified. For interaction terms, only the individual variable names that make up the interaction (for example, X1, X2) need to be specified. Specifying the actual interaction term (for example, X1 BY X2) on the VARIABLES subcommand is optional if you specify it on a METHOD subcommand.

Example

```
LOGISTIC REGRESSION PROMOTED WITH AGE,JOBTIME,JOBRATE,
    AGE BY JOBTIME.
```

- *PROMOTED* is specified as the dependent variable.
- *AGE*, *JOBTIME*, *JOBRATE*, and the interaction *AGE* by *JOBTIME* are specified as the independent variables.
- Because no METHOD is specified, all three single independent variables and the interaction term are entered into the model.
- LOGISTIC REGRESSION produces the default output.

CATEGORICAL Subcommand

CATEGORICAL identifies independent variables that are nominal or ordinal. Variables that are declared to be categorical are automatically transformed to a set of contrast variables as specified on the CONTRAST subcommand. If a variable coded as $0 - 1$ is declared as categorical, its coding scheme will be changed to deviation contrasts by default.

- Independent variables not specified on CATEGORICAL are assumed to be at least interval level, except for string variables.
- Any variable specified on CATEGORICAL is ignored if it does not appear either after WITH on the VARIABLES subcommand or on any METHOD subcommand.
- Variables specified on CATEGORICAL are replaced by sets of contrast variables. If the categorical variable has n distinct values, there will be $n - 1$ contrast variables generated. The set of contrast variables associated with a categorical variable is entered or removed from the model as a step.
- If any one of the variables in an interaction term is specified on CATEGORICAL, the interaction term is replaced by contrast variables.
- All string variables are categorical. Only the first eight characters of each value of a string variable are used in distinguishing between values. Thus, if two values of a string variable are identical for the first eight characters, the values are treated as though they were the same.

Example

```
LOGISTIC REGRESSION PASS WITH GPA, GRE, MAT, CLASS, TEACHER
/CATEGORICAL = CLASS,TEACHER.
```

- The dichotomous dependent variable *PASS* is regressed on the interval-level independent variables *GPA*, *GRE*, and *MAT* and the categorical variables *CLASS* and *TEACHER*.

CONTRAST Subcommand

CONTRAST specifies the type of contrast used for categorical independent variables. The interpretation of the regression coefficients for categorical variables depends on the contrasts used. The default is INDICATOR. The categorical independent variable is specified in parentheses following CONTRAST. The closing parenthesis is followed by one of the contrast-type keywords.

- If the categorical variable has n values, there will be $n - 1$ rows in the contrast matrix. Each contrast matrix is treated as a set of independent variables in the analysis.
- Only one categorical independent variable can be specified per CONTRAST subcommand, but multiple CONTRAST subcommands can be specified.

The following contrast types are available. See Finn (1974) and Kirk (1982) for further information on a specific type.

INDICATOR(refcat)   *Indicator variables.* Contrasts indicate the presence or absence of category membership. By default, refcat is the last category (represented in the contrast matrix as a row of zeros). To omit a category other than the last, specify the sequence number of the omitted category (which is not necessarily the same as its value) in parentheses after the keyword INDICATOR.

DEVIATION(refcat)   *Deviations from the overall effect.* This is the default. The effect for each category of the independent variable except one is compared to the overall effect. Refcat is the category for which parameter estimates are not displayed (they must be calculated from the others). By default, refcat is the last category. To omit a category other than the last, specify the sequence number of the omitted category (which is not necessarily the same as its value) in parentheses after the keyword DEVIATION.

SIMPLE(refcat)   *Each category of the independent variable except the last is compared to the last category.* To use a category other than the last as the omitted reference category, specify its sequence number (which is not necessarily the same as its value) in parentheses following the keyword SIMPLE.

DIFFERENCE   *Difference or reverse Helmert contrasts.* The effects for each category of the independent variable except the first are compared to the mean effects of the previous categories.

HELMERT   *Helmert contrasts.* The effects for each category of the independent variable except the last are compared to the mean effects of subsequent categories.

POLYNOMIAL(metric)   *Polynomial contrasts.* The first degree of freedom contains the linear effect across the categories of the independent variable, the second contains the quadratic effect, and so on. By default, the categories are assumed to be equally spaced; unequal spacing can be specified by entering a metric consisting of one integer for each category of the independent variable in parentheses after the keyword POLYNOMIAL. For example, `CONTRAST(STIMULUS)=POLYNOMIAL(1,2,4)` indicates that the three levels of STIMULUS are actually in the proportion 1:2:4. The default metric is always $(1,2,...,k)$, where k categories are involved. Only the relative differences between the terms of the metric matter: (1,2,4) is the same metric as (2,3,5) or (20,30,50) because the difference between the second and third numbers is twice the difference between the first and second in each instance.

REPEATED   *Comparison of adjacent categories.* Each category of the independent variable except the first is compared to the previous category.

SPECIAL(matrix)   *A user-defined contrast.* After this keyword, a matrix is entered in parentheses with $k - 1$ rows and k columns (where k is the number of categories of the independent variable). The rows of the contrast matrix contain the special contrasts indicating the desired comparisons between categories. If the special contrasts are linear combinations of each other, LOGISTIC REGRESSION reports the linear dependency and stops processing. If k rows are entered, the first row is discarded and only the last $k - 1$ rows are used as the contrast matrix in the analysis.

Example

```
LOGISTIC REGRESSION PASS WITH GRE, CLASS
 /CATEGORICAL = CLASS
 /CONTRAST(CLASS)=HELMERT.
```

- A logistic regression analysis of the dependent variable *PASS* is performed on the interval independent variable *GRE* and the categorical independent variable *CLASS*.

- *PASS* is a dichotomous variable representing course pass/fail status and *CLASS* identifies whether a student is in one of three classrooms. A HELMERT contrast is requested.

Example

```
LOGISTIC REGRESSION PASS WITH GRE, CLASS
 /CATEGORICAL = CLASS
 /CONTRAST(CLASS)=SPECIAL(2 -1 -1
                          0  1 -1).
```

- In this example, the contrasts are specified with the keyword SPECIAL.

METHOD Subcommand

METHOD indicates how the independent variables enter the model. The specification is the METHOD subcommand followed by a single method keyword. The keyword METHOD can be omitted. Optionally, specify the independent variables and interactions for which the method is to be used. Use the keyword BY between variable names of an interaction term.

- If no variable list is specified or if the keyword ALL is used, all of the independent variables following the keyword WITH on the VARIABLES subcommand are eligible for inclusion in the model.

- If no METHOD subcommand is specified, the default method is ENTER.

- Variables specified on CATEGORICAL are replaced by sets of contrast variables. The set of contrast variables associated with a categorical variable is entered or removed from the model as a single step.

- Any number of METHOD subcommands can appear in a Logistic Regression procedure. METHOD subcommands are processed in the order in which they are specified. Each method starts with the results from the previous method. If BSTEP is used, all remaining eligible variables are entered at the first step. All variables are then eligible for entry and removal unless they have been excluded from the METHOD variable list.

- The beginning model for the first METHOD subcommand is either the constant variable (by default or if NOORIGIN is specified) or an empty model (if ORIGIN is specified).

The available METHOD keywords are:

ENTER *Forced entry.* All variables are entered in a single step. This is the default if the METHOD subcommand is omitted.

FSTEP *Forward stepwise.* The variables (or interaction terms) specified on FSTEP are tested for entry into the model one by one, based on the significance level of the score statistic. The variable with the smallest significance less than PIN is entered into the model. After each entry, variables that are already in the model are tested for possible removal, based on the significance of the conditional statistic, the Wald statistic, or the likelihood-ratio criterion. The variable with the largest probability greater than the specified POUT value is removed and the model is reestimated. Variables in the model are then evaluated again for removal. Once no more variables satisfy the removal criterion, covariates not in the model are evaluated for entry. Model building stops when no more variables meet entry or removal criteria, or when the current model is the same as a previous one.

BSTEP   *Backward stepwise.* As a first step, the variables (or interaction terms) specified on BSTEP are entered into the model together and are tested for removal one by one. Stepwise removal and entry then follow the same process as described for FSTEP until no more variables meet entry or removal criteria, or when the current model is the same as a previous one.

The statistic used in the test for removal can be specified by an additional keyword in parentheses following FSTEP or BSTEP. If FSTEP or BSTEP is specified by itself, the default is COND.

COND   *Conditional statistic.* This is the default if FSTEP or BSTEP is specified by itself.

WALD   *Wald statistic.* The removal of a variable from the model is based on the significance of the Wald statistic.

LR   *Likelihood ratio.* The removal of a variable from the model is based on the significance of the change in the log-likelihood. If LR is specified, the model must be reestimated without each of the variables in the model. This can substantially increase computational time. However, the likelihood-ratio statistic is the best criterion for deciding which variables are to be removed.

Example

```
LOGISTIC REGRESSION PROMOTED WITH AGE JOBTIME JOBRATE RACE SEX AGENCY
 /CATEGORICAL RACE SEX AGENCY
 /METHOD ENTER AGE  JOBTIME
 /METHOD BSTEP (LR) RACE SEX JOBRATE AGENCY.
```

- *AGE*, *JOBTIME*, *JOBRATE*, *RACE*, *SEX*, and *AGENCY* are specified as independent variables. *RACE*, *SEX*, and *AGENCY* are specified as categorical independent variables.

- The first METHOD subcommand enters *AGE* and *JOBTIME* into the model.

- Variables in the model at the termination of the first METHOD subcommand are included in the model at the beginning of the second METHOD subcommand.

- The second METHOD subcommand adds the variables *RACE*, *SEX*, *JOBRATE*, and *AGENCY* to the previous model.

- Backward stepwise logistic regression analysis is then done with only the variables on the BSTEP variable list tested for removal using the LR statistic.

- The procedure continues until all variables from the BSTEP variable list have been removed or the removal of a variable will not result in a decrease in the log-likelihood with a probability larger than POUT.

SELECT Subcommand

By default, all cases in the working data file are considered for inclusion in LOGISTIC REGRESSION. Use the optional SELECT subcommand to include a subset of cases in the analysis.

- The specification is either a logical expression or keyword ALL. ALL is the default. Variables named on VARIABLES, CATEGORICAL, or METHOD subcommands cannot appear on SELECT.

- In the logical expression on SELECT, the relation can be EQ, NE, LT, LE, GT, or GE. The variable must be numeric and the value can be any number.

- Only cases for which the logical expression on SELECT is true are included in calculations. All other cases, including those with missing values for the variable named on SELECT, are unselected.

- Diagnostic statistics and classification statistics are reported for both selected and unselected cases.

- Cases deleted from the working data file with the SELECT IF or SAMPLE command are not included among either the selected or unselected cases.

Example

```
LOGISTIC REGRESSION VARIABLES=GRADE WITH GPA,TUCE,PSI
 /SELECT SEX EQ 1 /CASEWISE=RESID.
```

- Only cases with the value 1 for *SEX* are included in the logistic regression analysis.

- Residual values generated by CASEWISE are displayed for both selected and unselected cases.

ORIGIN and NOORIGIN Subcommands

ORIGIN and NOORIGIN control whether or not the constant is included. NOORIGIN (the default) includes a constant term (intercept) in all equations. ORIGIN suppresses the constant term and requests regression through the origin. (NOCONST can be used as an alias for ORIGIN.)

- The only specification is either ORIGIN or NOORIGIN.

- ORIGIN or NOORIGIN can be specified only once per Logistic Regression procedure, and it affects all METHOD subcommands.

Example

```
LOGISTIC REGRESSION VARIABLES=PASS WITH GPA,GRE,MAT /ORIGIN.
```

- ORIGIN suppresses the automatic generation of a constant term.

ID Subcommand

ID specifies a variable whose values or value labels identify the casewise listing. By default, cases are labeled by their case number.

- The only specification is the name of a single variable that exists in the working data file.
- Only the first eight characters of the variable's value labels are used to label cases. If the variable has no value labels, the values are used.
- Only the first eight characters of a string variable are used to label cases.

PRINT Subcommand

PRINT controls the display of optional output. If PRINT is omitted, DEFAULT output (defined below) is displayed.

- The minimum specification is PRINT followed by a single keyword.
- If PRINT is used, only the requested output is displayed.

DEFAULT *Goodness-of-fit tests for the model, classification tables, and statistics for the variables in and not in the equation at each step.* Tables and statistics are displayed for each split file and METHOD subcommand.

SUMMARY *Summary information.* Same output as DEFAULT, except that the output for each step is not displayed.

CORR *Correlation matrix of parameter estimates for the variables in the model.*

ITER(value) *Iterations at which parameter estimates are to be displayed.* The value in parentheses controls the spacing of iteration reports. If the value is *n*, the parameter estimates are displayed for every *n*th iteration starting at 0. If a value is not supplied, intermediate estimates are displayed at each iteration.

GOODFIT *Hosmer-Lemeshow goodness-of-fit statistic* (Hosmer and Lemeshow, 1989).

CI(level) *Confidence interval for exp(B).* The value in parentheses must be an integer between 1 and 99.

ALL *All available output.*

Example

```
LOGISTIC REGRESSION VARIABLES=PASS WITH GPA,GRE,MAT
 /METHOD FSTEP
 /PRINT CORR SUMMARY ITER(2).
```

- A forward stepwise logistic regression analysis of *PASS* on *GPA*, *GRE*, and *MAT* is specified.
- The PRINT subcommand requests the display of the correlation matrix of parameter estimates for the variables in the model (CORR), classification tables and statistics for the variables in and not in the equation for the final model (SUMMARY), and parameter estimates at every second iteration (ITER(2)).

CRITERIA Subcommand

CRITERIA controls the statistical criteria used in building the logistic regression models. The way in which these criteria are used depends on the method specified on the METHOD subcommand. The default criteria are noted in the description of each keyword below. Iterations will stop if the criterion for BCON, LCON, or ITERATE is satisfied.

BCON(value)   *Change in parameter estimates to terminate iteration.* Iteration terminates when the parameters change by less than the specified value. The default is 0.001. To eliminate this criterion, specify a value of 0.

ITERATE   *Maximum number of iterations.* The default is 20.

LCON(value)   *Percentage change in the log-likelihood ratio for termination of iterations.* If the log-likelihood decreases by less than the specified value, iteration terminates. The default is 0.01. To eliminate this criterion, specify a value of 0.

PIN(value)   *Probability of score statistic for variable entry.* The default is 0.05. The larger the specified probability, the easier it is for a variable to enter the model.

POUT(value)   *Probability of conditional, Wald, or LR statistic to remove a variable.* The default is 0.1. The larger the specified probability, the easier it is for a variable to remain in the model.

EPS(value)   *Epsilon value used for redundancy checking.* The specified value must be less than or equal to 0.05 and greater than or equal to 10^{-12}. The default is 10^{-8}. Larger values make it harder for variables to pass the redundancy check—that is, they are more likely to be removed from the analysis.

CUT(value)   *Cutoff value for classification.* A case is assigned to a group when the predicted event probability is greater than or equal to the cutoff value. The cutoff value affects the value of the dichotomous derived variable in the classification table, the predicted group (PGROUP on CASEWISE), and the classification plot (CLASSPLOT). The default cutoff value is 0.5. You can specify a value between 0 and 1 ($0 <$ value < 1).

Example

```
LOGISTIC REGRESSION PROMOTED WITH AGE JOBTIME RACE
 /CATEGORICAL RACE
 /METHOD BSTEP
 /CRITERIA BCON(0.01) PIN(0.01) POUT(0.05).
```

- A backward stepwise logistic regression analysis is performed for the dependent variable *PROMOTED* and the independent variables *AGE*, *JOBTIME*, and *RACE*.

- CRITERIA alters four of the statistical criteria that control the building of a model.

- BCON specifies that if the change in the absolute value of all of the parameter estimates is less than 0.01, the iterative estimation process should stop. Larger values lower the number of iterations required. Notice that the ITER and LCON criteria remain unchanged and that if either of them is met before BCON, iterations will terminate. (LCON can be set to 0 if only BCON and ITER are to be used.)

- POUT requires that the probability of the statistic used to test whether a variable should remain in the model be smaller than 0.05. This is more stringent than the default value of 0.1.

- PIN requires that the probability of the score statistic used to test whether a variable should be included be smaller than 0.01. This makes it more difficult for variables to be included in the model than the default value of 0.05.

CLASSPLOT Subcommand

CLASSPLOT generates a classification plot of the actual and predicted values of the dichotomous dependent variable at each step.

- Keyword CLASSPLOT is the only specification.
- If CLASSPLOT is not specified, plots are not generated.

Example

```
LOGISTIC REGRESSION PROMOTED WITH JOBTIME RACE
 /CATEGORICAL RACE
 /CLASSPLOT.
```

- A logistic regression model is constructed for the dichotomous dependent variable *PROMOTED* and the independent variables *JOBTIME* and *RACE*.
- CLASSPLOT produces a classification plot for the dependent variable *PROMOTED*. The vertical axis of the plot is the frequency of the variable *PROMOTED*. The horizontal axis is the predicted probability of membership in the second of the two levels of *PROMOTED*.

CASEWISE Subcommand

CASEWISE produces a casewise listing of the values of the temporary variables created by LOGISTIC REGRESSION.

The following keywords are available for specifying temporary variables (see Fox, 1984). When CASEWISE is specified by itself, the default lists *PRED*, *PGROUP*, *RESID*, and *ZRESID*. If a list of variable names is given, only those named temporary variables are displayed.

PRED *Predicted probability.* For each case, the predicted probability of having the second of the two values of the dichotomous dependent variable.

PGROUP *Predicted group.* The group to which a case is assigned based on the predicted probability.

RESID *Difference between observed and predicted probabilities.*

DEV *Deviance values.* For each case, a log-likelihood-ratio statistic, which measures how well the model fits the case, is computed.

LRESID *Logit residual.* Residual divided by the product of *PRED* and 1–š̌*PRED*.

SRESID *Studentized residual.*

ZRESID *Normalized residual.* Residual divided by the square root of the product of *PRED* and 1–š̌*PRED*.

LEVER *Leverage value.* A measure of the relative influence of each observation on the model's fit.

COOK *Analog of Cook's influence statistic.*

DFBETA *Difference in beta.* The difference in the estimated coefficients for each independent variable if the case is omitted.

The following keyword is available for restricting the cases to be displayed, based on the absolute value of *SRESID*:

OUTLIER (value)   *Cases with absolute values of SRESID greater than or equal to the specified value are displayed.* If OUTLIER is specified with no value, the default is 2.

Example

```
LOGISTIC REGRESSION PROMOTED WITH JOBTIME SEX RACE
 /CATEGORICAL SEX RACE
 /METHOD ENTER
 /CASEWISE SRESID LEVER DFBETA.
```

- CASEWISE produces a casewise listing of the temporary variables *SRESID*, *LEVER*, and *DFBETA*.

- There will be one *DFBETA* value for each parameter in the model. The continuous variable *JOBTIME*, the two-level categorical variable *SEX*, and the constant each require one parameter while the four-level categorical variable *RACE* requires three parameters. Thus, six values of *DFBETA* will be produced for each case.

MISSING Subcommand

LOGISTIC REGRESSION excludes all cases with missing values on any of the independent variables. For a case with a missing value on the dependent variable, predicted values are calculated if it has nonmissing values on all independent variables. The MISSING subcommand controls the processing of user-missing values. If the subcommand is not specified, the default is EXCLUDE.

EXCLUDE   *Delete cases with user-missing values as well as system-missing values.* This is the default.

INCLUDE   *Include user-missing values in the analysis.*

SAVE Subcommand

SAVE saves the temporary variables created by LOGISTIC REGRESSION. To specify variable names for the new variables, assign the new names in parentheses following each temporary variable name. If new variable names are not specified, LOGISTIC REGRESSION generates default names.

- Assigned variable names must be unique in the working data file. Scratch or system variable names (that is, names that begin with # or $) cannot be used.

- A temporary variable can be saved only once on the same SAVE subcommand.

Example

```
LOGISTIC REGRESSION PROMOTED WITH JOBTIME AGE
 /SAVE PRED (PREDPRO) DFBETA (DF).
```

- A logistic regression analysis of *PROMOTED* on the independent variables *JOBTIME* and *AGE* is performed.
- SAVE adds four variables to the working data file: one variable named *PREDPRO*, containing the predicted value from the specified model for each case, and three variables named *DF0*, *DF1*, and *DF2*, containing, respectively, the *DFBETA* values for each case of the constant, the independent variable *JOBTIME*, and the independent variable *AGE*.

EXTERNAL Subcommand

EXTERNAL indicates that the data for each split-file group should be held in an external scratch file during processing. This can help conserve memory resources when running complex analyses or analyses with large data sets.

- The keyword EXTERNAL is the only specification.
- Specifying EXTERNAL may result in slightly longer processing time.
- If EXTERNAL is not specified, all data are held internally and no scratch file is written.

LOGLINEAR

LOGLINEAR is available in the Advanced Models option.

The syntax for LOGLINEAR is available only in a syntax window, not from the dialog box interface. See GENLOG for information on the LOGLINEAR command available from the dialog box interface.

```
LOGLINEAR varlist(min,max)...[BY] varlist(min,max)

        [WITH covariate varlist]

 [/CWEIGHT={varname }] [/CWEIGHT=(matrix)...]
          {(matrix)}

 [/GRESID={varlist }]  [/GRESID=(matrix)...]
          {(matrix)}

 [/CONTRAST (varname)={DEVIATION [(refcat)]      } [/CONTRAST...]]
                      {DIFFERENCE                 }
                      {HELMERT                    }
                      {SIMPLE [(refcat)]          }
                      {REPEATED                   }
                      {POLYNOMIAL [({1,2,3,...})]}}
                      {            {metric  }   }
                      {[BASIS] SPECIAL(matrix)    }

 [/CRITERIA=[CONVERGE({0.001**})] [ITERATE({20**})] [DELTA({0.5**})]
                      {n       }            {n    }          {n    }
             [DEFAULT]]

 [/PRINT={[FREQ**][RESID**][DESIGN][ESTIM][COR]}]
         {DEFAULT                              }
         {ALL                                  }
         {NONE                                 }

 [/PLOT={NONE**   }]
        {DEFAULT }
        {RESID   }
        {NORMPROB}

 [/MISSING=[{EXCLUDE**}]]
            {INCLUDE  }

 [/DESIGN=effect[(n)] effect[(n)]... effect BY effect...] [/DESIGN...]
```

**Default if subcommand or keyword is omitted.

Example
```
LOGLINEAR JOBSAT (1,2) ZODIAC (1,12) /DESIGN=JOBSAT.
```

Overview

LOGLINEAR is a general procedure for model fitting, hypothesis testing, and parameter estimation for any model that has categorical variables as its major components. As such, LOGLINEAR subsumes a variety of related techniques, including general models of multiway contingency tables, logit models, logistic regression on categorical variables, and quasi-independence models.

LOGLINEAR models cell frequencies using the multinomial response model and produces maximum likelihood estimates of parameters by means of the Newton-Raphson algorithm (Haberman, 1978). HILOGLINEAR, which uses an iterative proportional-fitting algorithm, is more efficient for hierarchical models, but it cannot produce parameter estimates for unsaturated models, does not permit specification of contrasts for parameters, and does not display a correlation matrix of the parameter estimates.

Comparison of the GENLOG and LOGLINEAR Commands

The General Loglinear Analysis and Logit Loglinear Analysis dialog boxes are both associated with the GENLOG command. In previous releases of SPSS, these dialog boxes were associated with the LOGLINEAR command. The LOGLINEAR command is now available only as a syntax command. The differences are described below.

Distribution assumptions

- GENLOG can handle both Poisson and multinomial distribution assumptions for observed cell counts.

- LOGLINEAR assumes only multinomial distribution.

Approach

- GENLOG uses a regression approach to parameterize a categorical variable in a design matrix.

- LOGLINEAR uses contrasts to reparameterize a categorical variable. The major disadvantage of the reparameterization approach is in the interpretation of the results when there is a redundancy in the corresponding design matrix. Also, the reparameterization approach may result in incorrect degrees of freedom for an incomplete table, leading to incorrect analysis results.

Contrasts and generalized log-odds ratios (GLOR)

- GENLOG doesn't provide contrasts to reparameterize the categories of a factor. However, it offers generalized log-odds ratios (GLOR) for cell combinations. Often, comparisons among categories of factors can be derived from GLOR.

- LOGLINEAR offers contrasts to reparameterize the categories of a factor.

Deviance residual

- GENLOG calculates and displays the deviance residual and its normal probability plot, in addition to the other residuals.

- LOGLINEAR does not calculate the deviance residual.

Factor-by-covariate design

- When there is a factor-by-covariate term in the design, GENLOG generates one regression coefficient of the covariate for each combination of factor values. The estimates of these regression coefficients are calculated and displayed.

- LOGLINEAR estimates and displays the contrasts of these regression coefficients.

Partition effect

- In GENLOG, the term *partition effect* refers to the category of a factor.
- In LOGLINEAR, the term *partition effect* refers to a particular contrast.

Options

Model Specification. You can specify the model or models to be fit using the DESIGN subcommand.

Cell Weights. You can specify cell weights, such as structural zeros, for the model with the CWEIGHT subcommand.

Output Display. You can control the output display with the PRINT subcommand.

Optional Plots. You can produce plots of adjusted residuals against observed and expected counts, normal plots, and detrended normal plots with the PLOT subcommand.

Linear Combinations. You can calculate linear combinations of observed cell frequencies, expected cell frequencies, and adjusted residuals using the GRESID subcommand.

Contrasts. You can indicate the type of contrast desired for a factor using the CONTRAST subcommand.

Criteria for Algorithm. You can control the values of algorithm-tuning parameters with the CRITERIA subcommand.

Basic Specification

The basic specification is two or more variables that define the crosstabulation. The minimum and maximum values for each variable must be specified in parentheses after the variable name.

By default, LOGLINEAR estimates the saturated model for a multidimensional table. Output includes the factors or effects, their levels, and any labels; observed and expected frequencies and percentages for each factor and code; residuals, standardized residuals, and adjusted residuals; two goodness-of-fit statistics (the likelihood-ratio chi-square and Pearson's chi-square); and estimates of the parameters with accompanying z values and 95% confidence intervals.

Limitations

- Maximum 10 independent (factor) variables.
- Maximum 200 covariates.

Subcommand Order

- The variables specification must come first.
- The subcommands that affect a specific model must be placed before the DESIGN subcommand specifying the model.

- All subcommands can be used more than once and, with the exception of the DESIGN subcommand, are carried from model to model unless explicitly overridden.
- If the last subcommand is not DESIGN, LOGLINEAR generates a saturated model in addition to the explicitly requested model(s).

Example

```
LOGLINEAR JOBSAT (1,2) ZODIAC (1,12) /DESIGN=JOBSAT, ZODIAC.
```

- The variable list specifies two categorical variables, *JOBSAT* and *ZODIAC*. *JOBSAT* has values 1 and 2. *ZODIAC* has values 1 through 12.
- DESIGN specifies a model with main effects only.

Example

```
LOGLINEAR DPREF (2,3) RACE CAMP (1,2).
```

- *DPREF* is a categorical variable with values 2 and 3. *RACE* and *CAMP* are categorical variables with values 1 and 2.
- This is a general loglinear model because no BY keyword appears. The design defaults to a saturated model that includes all main effects and interaction effects.

Example

```
LOGLINEAR GSLEVEL (4,8) EDUC (1,4) SEX (1,2)
    /DESIGN=GSLEVEL EDUC SEX.
```

- *GSLEVEL* is a categorical variable with values 4 through 8. *EDUC* is a categorical variable with values 1 through 4. *SEX* has values 1 and 2.
- DESIGN specifies a model with main effects only.

Example

```
LOGLINEAR GSLEVEL (4,8) BY EDUC (1,4) SEX (1,2)
    /DESIGN=GSLEVEL, GSLEVEL BY EDUC, GSLEVEL BY SEX.
```

- The keyword BY on the variable list specifies a logit model in which *GSLEVEL* is the dependent variable and *EDUC* and *SEX* are the independent variables.
- DESIGN specifies a model that can test for the absence of joint effect of *SEX* and *EDUC* on *GSLEVEL*.

Variable List

The variable list specifies the variables to be included in the model. LOGLINEAR analyzes two classes of variables: categorical and continuous. Categorical variables are used to define the cells of the table. Continuous variables are used as cell covariates. Continuous variables can be specified only after the keyword WITH following the list of categorical variables.

- The list of categorical variables must be specified first. Categorical variables must be numeric and integer.

- A range must be defined for each categorical variable by specifying, in parentheses after each variable name, the minimum and maximum values for that variable. Separate the two values with at least one space or a comma.

- To specify the same range for a list of variables, specify the list of variables followed by a single range. The range applies to all variables on the list.

- To specify a logit model, use the keyword BY (see "Logit Model" below). A variable list without the keyword BY generates a general loglinear model.

- Cases with values outside the specified range are excluded from the analysis. Non-integer values within the range are truncated for the purpose of building the table.

Logit Model

- To segregate the independent (factor) variables from the dependent variables in a logit model, use the keyword BY. The categorical variables preceding BY are the dependent variables; the categorical variables following BY are the independent variables.

- A total of 10 categorical variables can be specified. In most cases, one of them is dependent.

- A DESIGN subcommand should be used to request the desired logit model.

- LOGLINEAR displays an analysis of dispersion and two measures of association: entropy and concentration. These measures are discussed in Haberman (1982) and can be used to quantify the magnitude of association among the variables. Both are proportional reduction in error measures. The entropy statistic is analogous to Theil's entropy measure, while the concentration statistic is analogous to Goodman and Kruskal's tau-*b*. Both statistics measure the strength of association between the dependent variable and the predictor variable set.

Cell Covariates

- Continuous variables can be used as covariates. When used, the covariates must be specified after the keyword WITH following the list of categorical variables. Ranges are not specified for the continuous variables.

- A variable cannot be named as both a categorical variable and a cell covariate.

- To enter cell covariates into a model, the covariates must be specified on the DESIGN subcommand.

- Cell covariates are not applied on a case-by-case basis. The mean covariate value for a cell in the contingency table is applied to that cell.

Example

```
LOGLINEAR DPREF(2,3) RACE CAMP (1,2) WITH CONSTANT
  /DESIGN=DPREF RACE CAMP CONSTANT.
```

- Variable *CONSTANT* is a continuous variable specified as a cell covariate. Cell covariates must be specified after the keyword WITH following the variable list. No range is defined for cell covariates.
- To include the cell covariate in the model, variable *CONSTANT* is specified on DESIGN.

CWEIGHT Subcommand

CWEIGHT specifies cell weights, such as structural zeros, for a model. By default, cell weights are equal to 1.

- The specification is either one numeric variable or a matrix of weights enclosed in parentheses.
- If a matrix of weights is specified, the matrix must contain the same number of elements as the product of the levels of the categorical variables. An asterisk can be used to signify repetitions of the same value.
- If weights are specified for a multiple-factor model, the index value of the rightmost factor increments the most rapidly.
- If a numeric variable is specified, only one CWEIGHT subcommand can be used on LOGLINEAR.
- To use multiple cell weights on the same LOGLINEAR command, specify all weights in matrix format. Each matrix must be specified on a separate CWEIGHT subcommand, and each CWEIGHT specification remains in effect until explicitly overridden by another CWEIGHT subcommand.
- CWEIGHT can be used to impose structural, or *a priori*, zeros on the model. This feature is useful in the analysis of symmetric tables.

Example

```
COMPUTE  CWT=1.
IF (HUSED EQ WIFED) CWT=0.
LOGLINEAR HUSED WIFED(1,4) WITH DISTANCE
  /CWEIGHT=CWT
  /DESIGN=HUSED WIFED DISTANCE.
```

- COMPUTE initially assigns *CWT* the value 1 for all cases.
- IF assigns *CWT* the value 0 when *HUSED* equals *WIFED*.
- CWEIGHT imposes structural zeros on the diagonal of the symmetric crosstabulation. Because a variable name is specified, only one CWEIGHT can be used.

Example

```
LOGLINEAR  HUSED WIFED(1,4) WITH DISTANCE
  /CWEIGHT=(0, 4*1, 0, 4*1, 0, 4*1, 0)
  /DESIGN=HUSED WIFED DISTANCE
  /CWEIGHT=(16*1)
  /DESIGN=HUSED WIFED DISTANCE.
```

- The first CWEIGHT matrix specifies the same values as variable *CWT* provided in the first example. The specified matrix is as follows:

```
0 1 1 1
1 0 1 1
1 1 0 1
1 1 1 0
```

- The same matrix can be specified in full as (0 1 1 1 1 0 1 1 1 1 0 1 1 1 1 0).

- By using the matrix format on CWEIGHT rather than a variable name, a different CWEIGHT subcommand can be used for the second model.

GRESID Subcommand

GRESID (Generalized Residual) calculates linear combinations of observed cell frequencies, expected cell frequencies, and adjusted residuals.

- The specification is either a numeric variable or a matrix whose contents are coefficients of the desired linear combinations.

- If a matrix of coefficients is specified, the matrix must contain the same number of elements as the number of cells implied by the variables specification. An asterisk can be used to signify repetitions of the same value.

- Each GRESID subcommand specifies a single linear combination. Each matrix or variable must be specified on a separate GRESID subcommand. All GRESID subcommands specified are displayed for each design.

Example

```
LOGLINEAR  MONTH(1,18) WITH Z
 /GRESID=(6*1,12*0)
 /GRESID=(6*0,6*1,6*0)
 /GRESID=(12*0,6*1)
 /DESIGN=Z.
```

- The first GRESID subcommand combines the first six months into a single effect. The second GRESID subcommand combines the second six months, and the third GRESID subcommand combines the last six months.

- For each effect, LOGLINEAR displays the observed and expected counts, the residual, and the adjusted residual.

CONTRAST Subcommand

CONTRAST indicates the type of contrast desired for a factor, where a factor is any categorical dependent or independent variable. The default contrast is DEVIATION for each factor.

- The specification is CONTRAST, which is followed by a variable name in parentheses and the contrast-type keyword.

- To specify a contrast for more than one factor, use a separate CONTRAST subcommand for each specified factor. Only one contrast can be in effect for each factor on each DESIGN.

- A contrast specification remains in effect for subsequent designs until explicitly overridden by another CONTRAST subcommand.

- The design matrix used for the contrasts can be displayed by specifying keyword DESIGN on the PRINT subcommand. However, this matrix is the basis matrix that is used to determine contrasts; it is not the contrast matrix itself.

- CONTRAST can be used for a multinomial logit model, in which the dependent variable has more than two categories.

- CONTRAST can be used for fitting linear logit models. The keyword BASIS is not appropriate for such models.

- In a logit model, CONTRAST is used to transform the independent variable into a metric variable. Again, the keyword BASIS is not appropriate.

The following contrast types are available:

DEVIATION(refcat) *Deviations from the overall effect.* DEVIATION is the default contrast if the CONTRAST subcommand is not used. Refcat is the category for which parameter estimates are not displayed (they are the negative of the sum of the others). By default, refcat is the last category of the variable.

DIFFERENCE *Levels of a factor with the average effect of previous levels of a factor.* Also known as reverse Helmert contrasts.

HELMERT *Levels of a factor with the average effect of subsequent levels of a factor.*

SIMPLE(refcat) *Each level of a factor to the reference level.* By default, LOGLINEAR uses the last category of the factor variable as the reference category. Optionally, any level can be specified as the reference category enclosed in parentheses after the keyword SIMPLE. The sequence of the level, not the actual value, must be specified.

REPEATED *Adjacent comparisons across levels of a factor.*

POLYNOMIAL(metric) *Orthogonal polynomial contrasts.* The default is equal spacing. Optionally, the coefficients of the linear polynomial can be specified in parentheses, indicating the spacing between levels of the treatment measured by the given factor.

[BASIS]SPECIAL(matrix) *User-defined contrast.* As many elements as the number of categories squared must be specified. If BASIS is specified before SPECIAL, a basis matrix is generated for the special contrast, which makes the coefficients of the contrast equal to the special matrix. Otherwise, the matrix specified is transposed and then used as the basis matrix to determine coefficients for the contrast matrix.

Example

```
LOGLINEAR  A(1,4) BY B(1,4)
 /CONTRAST(B)=POLYNOMIAL
 /DESIGN=A A BY B(1)
 /CONTRAST(B)=SIMPLE
 /DESIGN=A A BY B(1).
```

- The first CONTRAST subcommand requests polynomial contrasts of *B* for the first design.

- The second CONTRAST subcommand requests the simple contrast of *B*, with the last category (value 4) used as the reference category for the second DESIGN subcommand.

Example

```
* Multinomial logit model

LOGLINEAR  PREF(1,5) BY RACE ORIGIN CAMP(1,2)
 /CONTRAST(PREF)=SPECIAL(5*1, 1 1 1 1 -4, 3 -1 -1 -1 0,
      0 1 1 -2 0, 0 1 -1 0 0).
```

- LOGLINEAR builds special contrasts among the five categories of the dependent variable *PREF*, which measures preference for training camps among Army recruits. For *PREF*, 1=stay, 2=move to north, 3=move to south, 4=move to unnamed camp, and 5=undecided.

- The four contrasts are: (1) move or stay versus undecided, (2) stay versus move, (3) named camp versus unnamed, and (4) northern camp versus southern. Because these contrasts are orthogonal, SPECIAL and BASIS SPECIAL produce equivalent results.

Example

```
* Contrasts for a linear logit model

LOGLINEAR RESPONSE(1,2) BY YEAR(0,20)
 /PRINT=DEFAULT ESTIM
 /CONTRAST(YEAR)=SPECIAL(21*1,  -10, -9, -8, -7, -6, -5, -4,
                          -3, -2, -1, 0, 1, 2, 3, 4, 5, 6, 7,
                          8, 9, 10, 399*1)
 /DESIGN=RESPONSE RESPONSE BY YEAR(1).
```

- *YEAR* measures years of education and ranges from 0 through 20. Therefore, allowing for the constant effect, *YEAR* has 20 estimable parameters associated with it.

- The SPECIAL contrast specifies the constant—that is, 21*1—and the linear effect of *YEAR*—that is, –10 to 10. The other 399 1's fill out the 21*21 matrix.

Example

```
* Contrasts for a logistic regression model

LOGLINEAR RESPONSE(1,2) BY TIME(1,4)
  /CONTRAST(TIME) = SPECIAL(4*1, 7 14 27 51, 8*1)
  /PRINT=ALL /PLOT=DEFAULT
  /DESIGN=RESPONSE, TIME(1) BY RESPONSE.
```

- CONTRAST is used to transform the independent variable into a metric variable.

- *TIME* represents elapsed time in days. Therefore, the weights in the contrast represent the metric of the passage of time.

CRITERIA Subcommand

CRITERIA specifies the values of some constants in the Newton-Raphson algorithm. Defaults or specifications remain in effect until overridden with another CRITERIA subcommand.

CONVERGE(n)   *Convergence criterion.* Specify a value for the convergence criterion. The default is 0.001.

ITERATE(n)   *Maximum number of iterations.* Specify the maximum number of iterations for the algorithm. The default number is 20.

DELTA(n)   *Cell delta value.* The value of delta is added to each cell frequency for the first iteration. For saturated models, it remains in the cell. The default value is 0.5. LOGLINEAR does not display parameter estimates or correlation matrices of parameter estimates if any sampling zero cells exist in the expected table after delta is added. Parameter estimates and correlation matrices can be displayed in the presence of structural zeros.

DEFAULT   *Default values are used.* DEFAULT can be used to reset the parameters to the default.

Example

```
LOGLINEAR  DPREF(2,3) BY RACE ORIGIN CAMP(1,2)
  /CRITERIA=ITERATION(50) CONVERGE(.0001).
```

- ITERATION increases the maximum number of iterations to 50.
- CONVERGE lowers the convergence criterion to 0.0001.

PRINT Subcommand

PRINT requests statistics that are not produced by default.

- By default, LOGLINEAR displays the frequency table and residuals. The parameter estimates of the model are also displayed if DESIGN is not used.

- Multiple PRINT subcommands are permitted. The specifications are cumulative.

The following keywords can be used on PRINT:

FREQ   *Observed and expected cell frequencies and percentages.* This is displayed by default.

RESID   *Raw, standardized, and adjusted residuals.* This is displayed by default.

DESIGN   *The design matrix of the model, showing the basis matrix corresponding to the contrasts used.*

ESTIM   *The parameter estimates of the model.* If you do not specify a design on the DESIGN subcommand, LOGLINEAR generates a saturated model and displays the parameter estimates for the saturated model. LOGLINEAR does not display parameter estimates or correlation matrices of parameter estimates if any sampling zero cells exist in the expected table after delta is added. Parameter estimates and a correlation matrix are displayed when structural zeros are present.

COR   *The correlation matrix of the parameter estimates.* Alias COV.

ALL   *All available output.*

DEFAULT   *FREQ and RESID.* ESTIM is also displayed by default if the DESIGN subcommand is not used.

NONE   *The design information and goodness-of-fit statistics only.* This option overrides all other specifications on the PRINT subcommand. The NONE option applies only to the PRINT subcommand.

Example

```
LOGLINEAR A(1,2) B(1,2)
 /PRINT=ESTIM
 /DESIGN=A,B,A BY B
 /PRINT=ALL
 /DESIGN=A,B.
```

- The first design is the saturated model. The parameter estimates are displayed with ESTIM specified on PRINT.

- The second design is the main-effects model, which tests the hypothesis of no interaction. The second PRINT subcommand displays all available display output for this model.

PLOT Subcommand

PLOT produces optional plots. No plots are displayed if PLOT is not specified or is specified without any keyword. Multiple PLOT subcommands can be used. The specifications are cumulative.

RESID   *Plots of adjusted residuals against observed and expected counts.*

NORMPROB   *Normal and detrended normal plots of the adjusted residuals.*

NONE   *No plots.*

DEFAULT   *RESID and NORMPROB.* Alias ALL.

Example

```
LOGLINEAR  RESPONSE(1,2) BY TIME(1,4)
  /CONTRAST(TIME)=SPECIAL(4*1, 7 14 27 51, 8*1)
  /PLOT=DEFAULT
  /DESIGN=RESPONSE TIME(1) BY RESPONSE
  /PLOT=NONE
  /DESIGN.
```

- RESID and NORMPROB plots are displayed for the first design.

- No plots are displayed for the second design.

MISSING Subcommand

MISSING controls missing values. By default, LOGLINEAR excludes all cases with system- or user-missing values on any variable. You can specify INCLUDE to include user-missing values. If INCLUDE is specified, user-missing values must also be included in the value range specification.

EXCLUDE   *Delete cases with user-missing values.* This is the default if the subcommand is omitted. You can also specify the keyword DEFAULT.

INCLUDE   *Include user-missing values.* Only cases with system-missing values are deleted.

Example

```
MISSING VALUES A(0).
LOGLINEAR A(0,2) B(1,2) /MISSING=INCLUDE
  /DESIGN=B.
```

- Even though 0 was specified as missing, it is treated as a nonmissing category of *A* in this analysis.

DESIGN Subcommand

DESIGN specifies the model or models to be fit. If DESIGN is omitted or used with no specifications, the saturated model is produced. The saturated model fits all main effects and all interaction effects.

- To specify more than one model, use more than one DESIGN subcommand. Each DESIGN specifies one model.

- To obtain main-effects models, name all the variables listed on the variables specification.

- To obtain interactions, use the keyword BY to specify each interaction, as in A BY B and C BY D. To obtain the single-degree-of-freedom partition of a specified contrast, specify the partition in parentheses following the factor (see the example below).

- To include cell covariates in the model, first identify them on the variable list by naming them after the keyword WITH, and then specify the variable names on DESIGN.

- To specify an equiprobability model, name a cell covariate that is actually a constant of 1.

Example

```
* Testing the linear effect of the dependent variable

COMPUTE X=MONTH.
LOGLINEAR MONTH (1,12) WITH X
  /DESIGN X.
```

- The variable specification identifies *MONTH* as a categorical variable with values 1 through 12. The keyword WITH identifies *X* as a covariate.
- DESIGN tests the linear effect of *MONTH*.

Example

```
* Specifying main effects models

LOGLINEAR A(1,4) B(1,5)
  /DESIGN=A
  /DESIGN=A,B.
```

- The first design tests the homogeneity of category probabilities for *B*; it fits the marginal frequencies on *A*, but assumes that membership in any of the categories of *B* is equiprobable.
- The second design tests the independence of *A* and *B*. It fits the marginals on both *A* and *B*.

Example

```
* Specifying interactions

LOGLINEAR A(1,4) B(1,5) C(1,3)
  /DESIGN=A,B,C, A BY B.
```

- This design consists of the *A* main effect, the *B* main effect, the *C* main effect, and the interaction of *A* and *B*.

Example

```
* Single-degree-of-freedom partitions

LOGLINEAR A(1,4) BY B(1,5)
  /CONTRAST(B)=POLYNOMIAL
  /DESIGN=A,A BY B(1).
```

- The value 1 following *B* refers to the first partition of *B*, which is the linear effect of *B*; this follows from the contrast specified on the CONTRAST subcommand.

Example

```
* Specifying cell covariates

LOGLINEAR HUSED WIFED(1,4) WITH DISTANCE
   /DESIGN=HUSED WIFED DISTANCE.
```

- The continuous variable *DISTANCE* is identified as a cell covariate by specifying it after WITH on the variable list. The cell covariate is then included in the model by naming it on DESIGN.

Example

```
* Equiprobability model

COMPUTE  X=1.
LOGLINEAR  MONTH(1,18) WITH X
  /DESIGN=X.
```

- This model tests whether the frequencies in the 18-cell table are equal by using a cell covariate that is a constant of 1.

LOOP—END LOOP

```
LOOP [varname=n TO m [BY {1**}]]   [IF [(]logical expression[)]]
                        {n  }

transformation commands

END LOOP [IF [(]logical expression[)]]
```

**Default if the subcommand is omitted.

Examples

```
SET MXLOOPS=10.     /*Maximum number of loops allowed
LOOP.               /*Loop with no limit other than MXLOOPS
COMPUTE X=X+1.
END LOOP.

LOOP #I=1 TO 5.     /*Loop five times
COMPUTE X=X+1.
END LOOP.
```

Overview

The LOOP—END LOOP structure performs repeated transformations specified by the commands within the loop until they reach a specified cutoff. The cutoff can be specified by an indexing clause on the LOOP command, an IF clause on the END LOOP command, or a BREAK command within the loop structure (see BREAK). In addition, the maximum number of iterations within a loop can be specified on the MXLOOPS subcommand on SET. The default MXLOOPS is 40.

The IF clause on the LOOP command can be used to perform repeated transformations on a subset of cases. The effect is similar to nesting the LOOP—END LOOP structure within a DO IF—END IF structure, but using IF on LOOP is simpler and more efficient. You have to use the DO IF—END IF structure, however, if you want to perform different transformations on different subsets of cases. You can also use IF on LOOP to specify the cutoff, especially when the cutoff may be reached before the first iteration.

LOOP and END LOOP are usually used within an input program or with the VECTOR command. Since the loop structure repeats transformations on a single case or on a single input record containing information on multiple cases, it allows you to read complex data files or to generate data for a working data file. For more information, see INPUT PROGRAM—END INPUT PROGRAM and VECTOR.

The loop structure repeats transformations on single cases across variables. It is different from the DO REPEAT—END REPEAT structure, which replicates transformations on a specified set of variables. When both can be used to accomplish a task, such as selectively transforming data for some cases on some variables, LOOP and END LOOP are generally more efficient and more flexible, but DO REPEAT allows selection of nonadjacent variables and use of replacement values with different intervals.

Options

Missing Values. You can prevent cases with missing values for any of the variables used in the loop structure from entering the loop (see "Missing Values" on p. 644).

Creating Data. A loop structure within an input program can be used to generate data (see "Creating Data" on p. 645).

Defining Complex File Structures. A loop structure within an input program can be used to define complex files that cannot be handled by standard file definition facilities (see pp. 335, 336, and 338 for examples).

Basic Specification

The basic specification is LOOP followed by at least one transformation command. The structure must end with the END LOOP command. Commands within the loop are executed until the cutoff is reached.

Syntax Rules

- If LOOP and END LOOP are specified before a working data file exists, they must be specified within an input program.
- If both an indexing and an IF clause are used on LOOP, the indexing clause must be first.
- Loop structures can be nested within other loop structures or within DO IF structures, and vice versa.

Operations

- The LOOP command defines the beginning of a loop structure and the END LOOP command defines its end. The END LOOP command returns control to LOOP unless the cutoff has been reached. When the cutoff has been reached, control passes to the command immediately following END LOOP.
- When specified within a loop structure, definition commands (such as MISSING VALUES and VARIABLE LABELS) and utility commands (such as SET and SHOW) are invoked only once, when they are encountered for the first time within the loop.

Example

```
SET MXLOOPS=10.
LOOP.    /*Loop with no limit other than MXLOOPS
COMPUTE X=X+1.
END LOOP.
```

- This and the following examples assume that a working data file and all of the variables mentioned in the loop exist.

- The SET MXLOOPS command limits the number of times the loop is executed to 10. The function of MXLOOPS is to prevent infinite loops when there is no iteration clause.
- Within the loop structure, each iteration increments X by 1. After 10 iterations, the value of X for all cases is increased by 10, and, as specified on the SET command, the loop is terminated.

IF Keyword

The keyword IF and a logical expression can be specified on LOOP or on END LOOP to control iterations through the loop.

- The specification on IF is a logical expression enclosed in parentheses. For more information, see "Logical Expressions" on p. 53.

Example

```
LOOP.
COMPUTE X=X+1.
END LOOP IF (X EQ 5).        /*Loop until X is 5
```

- Iterations continue until the logical expression on END LOOP is true, which for every case is when X equals 5. Each case does not go through the same number of iterations.
- This corresponds to the programming notion of DO UNTIL. The loop is always executed at least once.

Example

```
LOOP IF (X LT 5).           /*Loop while X is less than 5
COMPUTE X=X+1.
END LOOP.
```

- The IF clause is evaluated each trip through the structure, so looping stops once X equals 5.
- This corresponds to the programming notion of DO WHILE. The loop may not be executed at all.

Example

```
LOOP IF (Y GT 10).          /*Loop only for cases with Y GT 10
COMPUTE X=X+1.
END LOOP IF (X EQ 5).       /*Loop until X IS 5
```

- The IF clause on LOOP allows transformations to be performed on a subset of cases. X is increased by 5 only for cases with values greater than 10 for Y. X is not changed for all other cases.

Indexing Clause

The indexing clause limits the number of iterations for a loop by specifying the number of times the program should execute commands within the loop structure. The indexing clause is specified on the LOOP command and includes an indexing variable followed by initial and terminal values.

- The program sets the *indexing variable* to the *initial value* and increases it by the specified increment each time the loop is executed for a case. When the indexing variable reaches the specified *terminal value*, the loop is terminated for that case.

- By default, the program increases the indexing variable by 1 for each iteration. The keyword BY overrides this increment.

- The indexing variable can have any valid variable name. Unless you specify a scratch variable, the indexing variable is treated as a permanent variable and is saved on the working data file. If the indexing variable is assigned the same name as an existing variable, the values of the existing variable are altered by the LOOP structure as it is executed, and the original values are lost.

- The indexing clause overrides the maximum number of loops specified by SET MXLOOPS.

- The initial and terminal values of the indexing clause can be numeric expressions. Non-integer and negative expressions are allowed.

- If the expression for the initial value is greater than the terminal value, the loop is not executed. For example, #J=X TO Y is a zero-trip loop if X is 0 and Y is -1.

- If the expressions for the initial and terminal values are equal, the loop is executed once. #J=0 TO Y is a one-trip loop when Y is 0.

- If the loop is exited via BREAK or a conditional clause on the END LOOP statement, the iteration variable is not updated. If the LOOP statement contains both an indexing clause and a conditional clause, the indexing clause is executed first, and the iteration variable is updated regardless of which clause causes the loop to terminate.

Example

```
LOOP #I=1 TO 5.              /*LOOP FIVE TIMES
COMPUTE X=X+1.
END LOOP.
```

- The scratch variable *#I* (the indexing variable) is set to the initial value of 1 and increased by 1 each time the loop is executed for a case. When *#I* increases beyond the terminal value 5, no further loops are executed. Thus, the value of X will be increased by 5 for every case.

Example

```
LOOP #I=1 TO 5 IF (Y GT 10). /*Loop to X=5 only if Y GT 10
COMPUTE X=X+1.
END LOOP.
```

- Both an indexing clause and an IF clause are specified on LOOP. X is increased by 5 for all cases where Y is greater than 10.

Example

```
LOOP #I=1 TO Y.              /*Loop to the value of Y
COMPUTE X=X+1.
END LOOP.
```

- The number of iterations for a case depends on the value of the variable Y for that case. For a case with value 0 for the variable Y, the loop is not executed and X is unchanged. For a case with value 1 for the variable Y, the loop is executed once and X is increased by 1.

Example

```
* Factorial routine.

DATA LIST FREE / X.
BEGIN DATA
1 2 3 4 5 6 7
END DATA.

COMPUTE FACTOR=1.
LOOP #I=1 TO X.
COMPUTE FACTOR=FACTOR * #I.
END LOOP.
LIST.
```

- The loop structure computes *FACTOR* as the factorial value of *X*.

Example

```
* Example of nested loops: compute every possible combination of values
  for each variable.

INPUT PROGRAM.
-LOOP #I=1 TO 4.        /* LOOP TO NUMBER OF VALUES FOR I
+    LOOP #J=1 TO 3.        /* LOOP TO NUMBER OF VALUES FOR J
@        LOOP #K=1 TO 4.        /* LOOP TO NUMBER OF VALUES FOR K

@              COMPUTE I=#I.
@              COMPUTE J=#J.
@              COMPUTE K=#K.
@              END CASE.

@        END LOOP.
+    END LOOP.
-END LOOP.
END FILE.
END INPUT PROGRAM.
LIST.
```

- The first loop iterates four times. The first iteration sets the indexing variable $\#I$ equal to 1 and then passes control to the second loop. $\#I$ remains 1 until the second loop has completed all of its iterations.
- The second loop is executed 12 times, three times for each value of $\#I$. The first iteration sets the indexing variable $\#J$ equal to 1 and then passes control to the third loop. $\#J$ remains 1 until the third loop has completed all of its iterations.
- The third loop results in 48 iterations ($4 \times 3 \times 4$). The first iteration sets $\#K$ equal to 1. The COMPUTE statements set the variables *I, J,* and *K* each to 1, and END CASE creates a case. The third loop iterates a second time, setting $\#K$ equal to 2. Variables *I, J,* and *K* are then computed with values 1, 1, 2, respectively, and a second case is created. The third and fourth iterations of the third loop produce cases with *I, J,* and *K,* equal to 1, 1, 3 and 1, 1, 4, respectively. After the fourth iteration within the third loop, control passes back to the second loop.
- The second loop is executed again. $\#I$ remains 1, while $\#J$ increases to 2, and control returns to the third loop. The third loop completes its iterations, resulting in four more cases with *I* equal to 1, *J* to 2, and *K* increasing from 1 to 4. The second loop is executed a third

time, resulting in cases with I=1, J=3, and K increasing from 1 to 4. Once the second loop has completed three iterations, control passes back to the first loop, and the entire cycle is repeated for the next increment of #I.

- Once the first loop completes four iterations, control passes out of the looping structures to END FILE. END FILE defines the resulting cases as a data file, the input program terminates, and the LIST command is executed.

- This example does not require a LEAVE command because the iteration variables are scratch variables. If the iteration variables were I, J, and K, LEAVE would be required because the variables would be reinitialized after each END CASE command.

Example

```
* Modifying the loop iteration variable.
INPUT PROGRAM.
PRINT SPACE      2.
LOOP             A = 1 TO 3.              /*Simple iteration
+   PRINT            /'A WITHIN LOOP: ' A(F1).
+   COMPUTE          A = 0.
END LOOP
PRINT             /'A AFTER LOOP:  ' A(F1).

NUMERIC          #B.
LOOP             B = 1 TO 3.              /*Iteration + UNTIL
+   PRINT            /'B WITHIN LOOP: ' B(F1).
+   COMPUTE          B = 0.
+   COMPUTE          #B = #B+1.
END LOOP         IF #B = 3.
PRINT             /'B AFTER LOOP:  ' B(F1).

NUMERIC          #C.
LOOP             C = 1 TO 3 IF #C NE 3.   /*Iteration + WHILE
+   PRINT            /'C WITHIN LOOP: ' C(F1).
+   COMPUTE          C = 0.
+   COMPUTE          #C = #C+1.
END LOOP.
PRINT             /'C AFTER LOOP:  ' C(F1).

NUMERIC          #D.
LOOP             D = 1 TO 3.              /*Iteration + BREAK
+   PRINT            /'D WITHIN LOOP: ' D(F1).
+   COMPUTE          D = 0.
+   COMPUTE          #D = #D+1.
+   DO IF            #D = 3.
+      BREAK.
+   END IF.
END LOOP.
PRINT             /'D AFTER LOOP:  ' D(F1).

LOOP             E = 3 TO 1.              /*Zero-trip iteration
+   PRINT            /'E WITHIN LOOP: ' E(F1).
+   COMPUTE          E = 0.
END LOOP.
PRINT             /'E AFTER LOOP:  ' E(F1).
END FILE.
END INPUT PROGRAM.
EXECUTE.
```

- If a loop is exited via BREAK or a conditional clause on the END LOOP statement, the iteration variable is not updated.
- If the LOOP statement contains both an iteration clause and a conditional clause, the iteration clause is executed first, and the actual iteration variable will be updated regardless of which clause causes termination of the loop.

Figure 1 shows the output from this example.

Figure 1   Modify the loop iteration variable

```
A WITHIN LOOP: 1
A WITHIN LOOP: 2
A WITHIN LOOP: 3
A AFTER LOOP:  4
B WITHIN LOOP: 1
B WITHIN LOOP: 2
B WITHIN LOOP: 3
B AFTER LOOP:  0
C WITHIN LOOP: 1
C WITHIN LOOP: 2
C WITHIN LOOP: 3
C AFTER LOOP:  4
D WITHIN LOOP: 1
D WITHIN LOOP: 2
D WITHIN LOOP: 3
D AFTER LOOP:  0
E AFTER LOOP:  3
```

BY Keyword

By default, the program increases the indexing variable by 1 for each iteration. The keyword BY overrides this increment.

- The *increment value* can be a numeric expression and can therefore be non-integer or negative. Zero causes a warning and results in a zero-trip loop.
- If the initial value is greater than the terminal value and the increment is positive, the loop is never entered. #I=1 TO 0 BY 2 results in a zero-trip loop.
- If the initial value is less than the terminal value and the increment is negative, the loop is never entered. #I=1 TO 2 BY −1 also results in a zero-trip loop.
- Order is unimportant: 2 BY 2 TO 10 is equivalent to 2 TO 10 BY 2.

Example

```
LOOP #I=2 TO 10 BY 2.          /*Loop five times by 2'S
COMPUTE X=X+1.
END LOOP.
```

- The scratch variable #I starts at 2 and increases by 2 for each of five iterations until it equals 10 for the last iteration.

Example

```
LOOP #I=1 TO Y BY Z.          /*Loop to Y incrementing by Z
COMPUTE X=X+1.
END LOOP.
```

- The loop is executed once for a case with *Y* equal to 2 and *Z* equal to 2 but twice for a case with *Y* equal to 3 and *Z* equal to 2.

Example

```
* Repeating data using LOOP.

INPUT PROGRAM.
DATA LIST        NOTABLE/ ORDER 1-4(N) #BKINFO 6-71(A).
LEAVE ORDER.
LOOP             #I = 1 TO 66 BY 6 IF SUBSTR(#BKINFO,#I,6) <> ' '.
+  REREAD           COLUMN = #I+5.
+  DATA LIST        NOTABLE/ ISBN 1-3(N) QUANTITY 4-5.
+  END CASE.
END LOOP.
END INPUT PROGRAM.
SORT CASES       BY ISBN ORDER.
BEGIN DATA
1045 182 2 155 1 134 1 153 5
1046 155 3 153 5 163 1
1047 161 5 182 2 163 4 186 6
1048 186 2
1049 155 2 163 2 153 2 074 1 161 1
END DATA.

DO IF            $CASENUM = 1.
+  PRINT EJECT   /'Order' 1  'ISBN' 7  'Quantity' 13.
END IF.
PRINT            /ORDER 2-5(N) ISBN 8-10(N) QUANTITY 13-17.
EXECUTE.
```

- This example uses LOOP to simulate a REPEATING DATA command.
- DATA LIST specifies the scratch variable *#BKINFO* as a string variable (format A) to allow blanks in the data.
- LOOP is executed if the SUBSTR function returns anything other than a blank or null value. SUBSTR returns a six-character substring of *#BKINFO*, beginning with the character in the position specified by the value of the indexing variable *#I*. As specified on the indexing clause, *#I* begins with a value of 1 and is increased by 6 for each iteration of LOOP, up to a maximum *#I* value of 61 ($1 + 10 \times 6 = 61$). The next iteration would exceed the maximum *#I* value ($1 + 11 \times 6 = 67$).

Missing Values

- If the program encounters a case with a missing value for the initial, terminal, or increment value or expression, or if the conditional expression on the LOOP command returns missing, a zero-trip loop results and control is passed to the first command after the END LOOP command.
- If a case has a missing value for the conditional expression on an END LOOP command, the loop is terminated after the first iteration.
- To prevent cases with missing values for any variable used in the loop structure from entering the loop, use the IF clause on the LOOP command (see third example below).

Example

```
LOOP #I=1 TO Z   IF (Y GT 10). /*Loop to X=Z for cases with Y GT 10
COMPUTE X=X+1.
END LOOP.
```

- The value of *X* remains unchanged for cases with a missing value for *Y* or a missing value for *Z* (or if *Z* is less than 1).

Example

```
MISSING VALUES X(5).
LOOP.
COMPUTE X=X+1.
END LOOP IF (X GE 10). /*Loop until X is at least 10 or missing
```

- Looping is terminated when the value of *X* is 5 because 5 is defined as missing for *X*.

Example

```
LOOP IF NOT MISSING(Y).      /*Loop only when Y isn't missing
COMPUTE X=X+Y.
END LOOP IF (X GE 10).       /*Loop until X is at least 10
```

- The variable *X* is unchanged for cases with a missing value for *Y*, since the loop is never entered.

Creating Data

A loop structure and an END CASE command within an input program can be used to create data without any data input. The END FILE command must be used outside the loop (but within the input program) to terminate processing.

Example

```
INPUT PROGRAM.
LOOP #I=1 TO 20.
COMPUTE AMOUNT=RND(UNIFORM(5000))/100.
END CASE.
END LOOP.
END FILE.
END INPUT PROGRAM.

PRINT FORMATS AMOUNT (DOLLAR6.2).
PRINT /AMOUNT.
EXECUTE.
```

- This example creates 20 cases with a single variable, *AMOUNT*. *AMOUNT* is a uniformly distributed number between 0 and 5000, rounded to an integer and divided by 100 to provide a variable in dollars and cents.
- The END FILE command is required to terminate processing once the loop structure is complete.

See pp. 328 and 338 for other examples of creating data without any data input.

MANOVA: Overview

MANOVA is available in the Advanced Models option.

```
MANOVA dependent varlist [BY factor list (min,max)[factor list...]
                          [WITH covariate list]]

[/WSFACTORS=varname (levels) [varname...] ]

[/WSDESIGN]*

[/TRANSFORM [(dependent varlist [/dependent varlist])]=
                    [ORTHONORM] [{CONTRAST}] {DEVIATION (refcat)   } ]
                               {BASIS   } {DIFFERENCE            }
                                          {HELMERT               }
                                          {SIMPLE (refcat)       }
                                          {REPEATED              }
                                          {POLYNOMIAL [({1,2,3...})]]}
                                          {            {metric  }  }
                                          {SPECIAL (matrix)      }

[/MEASURE=newname newname...]

[/RENAME={newname} {newname}...]
         {*      } {*       }

[/ERROR={WITHIN            } ]
        {RESIDUAL          }
        {WITHIN + RESIDUAL}
        {n                 }

[/CONTRAST (factorname)={DEVIATION** [(refcat)]      }] †
                        {POLYNOMIAL**[({1,2,3...})]]}
                        {            {metric  }  }
                        {SIMPLE [(refcat)]         }
                        {DIFFERENCE                }
                        {HELMERT                   }
                        {REPEATED                  }
                        {SPECIAL (matrix)          }

[/PARTITION (factorname)[=({1,1...  })]]]
                          {n1,n2...}

[/METHOD=[{UNIQUE**   }] [{CONSTANT**}] [{QR**     }]]
         {SEQUENTIAL} {NOCONSTANT} {CHOLESKY}

[/{PRINT  }= [CELLINFO [(([MEANS] [SSCP] [COV] [COR] [ALL])]]
  {NOPRINT} [HOMOGENEITY [(([ALL] [BARTLETT] [COCHRAN] [BOXM])]]
            [DESIGN [(([OVERALL] [ONEWAY] [DECOMP] [BIAS] [SOLUTION]
                      [REDUNDANCY] [COLLINEARITY] [ALL])]]
            [PARAMETERS [(([ESTIM] [ORTHO][COR][NEGSUM][EFSIZE][OPTIMAL][ALL])]]
            [SIGNIF [[(SINGLEDF)]
                    [(MULTIV**)] [(EIGEN)] [(DIMENR)]
                    [(UNIV**)] [(HYPOTH)][(STEPDOWN)] [(BRIEF)]
                    [((AVERF**)}] [(HF)] [(GG)] [(EFSIZE)]]
                    {(AVONLY) }
            [ERROR[(STDDEV)][(COR)][(COV)][(SSCP)]]

[/OMEANS =[VARIABLES(varlist)] [TABLES (({factor name      }] ]
                                        {factor BY factor}
                                        {CONSTANT         }

[/PMEANS =[VARIABLES(varlist)] [TABLES (({factor name      })] [PLOT]] ]
                                        {factor BY factor}
                                        {CONSTANT         }
```

```
[/RESIDUALS=[CASEWISE] [PLOT] ]

[/POWER=[T({.05**})] [F({.05**})] [{APPROXIMATE}]]
            {a     }     {a     }   {EXACT      }

[/CINTERVAL=[{INDIVIDUAL}][({.95}) ]
            {JOINT     }  {a   }
            [UNIVARIATE ({SCHEFFE})]
                         {BONFER }
              [MULTIVARIATE ({ROY      })] ]
                            {PILLAI   }
                            {BONFER   }
                            {HOTELLING}
                            {WILKS    }
[/PCOMPS [COR] [COV] [ROTATE(rottype)]
         [NCOMP(n)] [MINEIGEN(eigencut)] [ALL] ]

[/PLOT=[BOXPLOTS] [CELLPLOTS] [NORMAL]  [ALL] ]

[/DISCRIM [RAW] [STAN] [ESTIM] [COR] [ALL]
          [ROTATE(rottype)] [ALPHA({.25**})]]
                                   {a      }

[/MISSING=[LISTWISE**]  [{EXCLUDE**}] ]
                         {INCLUDE  }

[/MATRIX=[IN({file})]   [OUT({file})]]
            {[*] }         {[*] }

[/ANALYSIS [({UNCONDITIONAL**})]=[()]dependent varlist
            {CONDITIONAL    }      [WITH covariate varlist]
                                      [/dependent varlist...][)][WITH varlist] ]

[/DESIGN={factor [(n)]  }[BY factor[(n)]] [WITHIN factor[(n)]][WITHIN...]
         {[POOL(varlist)}

         [+ {factor [(n)] }...]
            {POOL(varlist)}

         [[= n] {AGAINST} {WITHIN  }
                {VS     } {RESIDUAL}
                          {WR      }
                          {n       }

         [{factor [(n)] } ... ]
          {POOL(varlist)}

         [MWITHIN factor(n)]
         [MUPLUS]
         [CONSTANT [=n] ]
```

* WSDESIGN uses the same specification as DESIGN, with only within-subjects factors.

† DEVIATION is the default for between-subjects factors, while POLYNOMIAL is the default for within-subjects factors.

** Default if subcommand or keyword is omitted.

Example 1

```
* Analysis of Variance

MANOVA RESULT BY TREATMNT(1,4) GROUP(1,2).
```

Example 2

```
* Analysis of Covariance

MANOVA RESULT BY TREATMNT(1,4) GROUP(1,2) WITH RAINFALL.
```

Example 3

```
* Repeated Measures Analysis

MANOVA SCORE1 TO SCORE4 BY CLASS(1,2)
  /WSFACTORS=MONTH(4).
```

Example 4

```
* Parallelism Test with Crossed Factors

MANOVA YIELD BY PLOT(1,4) TYPEFERT(1,3) WITH FERT
  /ANALYSIS YIELD
  /DESIGN FERT, PLOT, TYPEFERT, PLOT BY TYPEFERT,
  FERT BY PLOT + FERT BY TYPEFERT
  + FERT BY PLOT BY TYPEFERT.
```

Overview

MANOVA (multivariate analysis of variance) is a generalized procedure for analysis of variance and covariance. MANOVA is a powerful analysis-of-variance procedure and can be used for both univariate and multivariate designs. MANOVA allows you to perform the following tasks:

- Specify nesting of effects.
- Specify individual error terms for effects in mixed-model analyses.
- Estimate covariate-by-factor interactions to test the assumption of homogeneity of regressions.
- Obtain parameter estimates for a variety of contrast types, including irregularly spaced polynomial contrasts with multiple factors.
- Test user-specified special contrasts with multiple factors.
- Partition effects in models.
- Pool effects in models.

MANOVA and General Linear Model (GLM)

MANOVA is available only in syntax. GLM (general linear model), the other generalized procedure for analysis of variance and covariance in SPSS, is available both in syntax and via the dialog boxes. The major distinction between GLM and MANOVA in terms of statistical design and functionality is that GLM uses a non-full-rank, or overparameterized, indicator variable approach to parameterization of linear models instead of the full-rank reparameterization approach used in MANOVA. The generalized inverse approach and the aliasing of redundant parameters to zero used by GLM allow greater flexibility in handling a variety of data situations, particularly those involving empty cells. For features provided by GLM but unavailable in MANOVA, refer to "General Linear Model (GLM) and MANOVA" on p. 463.

To simplify the presentation, reference material on MANOVA is divided into three sections: *univariate* designs with one dependent variable; *multivariate* designs with several interrelated dependent variables; and *repeated measures* designs in which the dependent variables represent the same types of measurements taken at more than one time.

The full syntax diagram for MANOVA is presented here. The MANOVA sections that follow include partial syntax diagrams showing the subcommands and specifications discussed in that section. Individually, those diagrams are incomplete. Subcommands listed for univariate designs are available for any analysis, and subcommands listed for multivariate designs can be used in any multivariate analysis, including repeated measures.

MANOVA was designed and programmed by Philip Burns of Northwestern University.

MANOVA: Univariate

MANOVA is available in the Advanced Models option.

```
MANOVA dependent var [BY factor list (min,max)][factor list...]
                    [WITH covariate list]
 [/ERROR={WITHIN            } ]
         {RESIDUAL          }
         {WITHIN + RESIDUAL}
         {n                 }
 [/CONTRAST (factor name)={DEVIATION** [(refcat)]    }]
                          {POLYNOMIAL  [({1,2,3...})]}
                          {                {metric }  }
                          {SIMPLE [(refcat)]         }
                          {DIFFERENCE                }
                          {HELMERT                   }
                          {REPEATED                  }
                          {SPECIAL (matrix)          }
 [/PARTITION (factor name)[=({1,1... })]]
                            {n1,n2...}
 [/METHOD=[{UNIQUE**  }] [{CONSTANT**}] [{QR**    }]]
           {SEQUENTIAL}   {NOCONSTANT}   {CHOLESKY}
 [/{PRINT  }= [CELLINFO [([MEANS] [SSCP] [COV] [COR] [ALL])]]
   {NOPRINT}  [HOMOGENEITY [([ALL] [BARTLETT] [COCHRAN])]]
             [DESIGN [([OVERALL] [ONEWAY] [DECOMP] [BIAS] [SOLUTION]
                      [REDUNDANCY] [COLLINEARITY])]]
             [PARAMETERS [([ESTIM][ORTHO][COR][NEGSUM][EFSIZE][OPTIMAL][ALL])]]
             [SIGNIF[(SINGLEDF)]]
             [ERROR[(STDDEV)]]                                              ]
 [/OMEANS =[VARIABLES(varlist)] [TABLES ({factor name      }] ]
                                         {factor BY factor}
                                         {CONSTANT         }
 [/PMEANS =[TABLES ({factor name   })] [PLOT]] ]
                    {factor BY factor}
                    {CONSTANT        }
 [/RESIDUALS=[CASEWISE] [PLOT] ]
 [/POWER=[T({.05**})] [F({.05**})] [{APPROXIMATE}]]
           {a    }      {a    }     {EXACT      }
 [/CINTERVAL=[{INDIVIDUAL}][({.95}) ]] [UNIVARIATE ({SCHEFFE})]
             {JOINT     } {  a}                    {BONFER }
 [/PLOT=[BOXPLOTS] [CELLPLOTS] [NORMAL]   [ALL] ]
 [/MISSING=[LISTWISE**] [{EXCLUDE**}] ]
                        {INCLUDE  }
 [/MATRIX=[IN({file})]  [OUT({file})]]
          {[*] }        {[*] }
 [/ANALYSIS=dependent var [WITH covariate list]]
 [/DESIGN={factor [(n)]  }[BY factor[(n)]] [WITHIN factor[(n)]][WITHIN...]
          {[POOL(varlist)}
          [+ {factor [(n)] }...]
             {POOL(varlist)}
          [[= n] {AGAINST} {WITHIN  }
                 {VS     } {RESIDUAL}
                           {WR      }
                           {n       }
          [{factor [(n)] } ... ]
           {POOL(varlist)}
          [MUPLUS]
          [MWITHIN factor(n)]
          [CONSTANT [=n] ]
```

** Default if subcommand or keyword is omitted.

Example

```
MANOVA YIELD BY SEED(1,4) FERT(1,3)
  /DESIGN.
```

Overview

This section describes the use of MANOVA for univariate analyses. However, the subcommands described here can be used in any type of analysis with MANOVA. For additional subcommands used in those types of analysis, see MANOVA: Multivariate and MANOVA: Repeated Measures. For basic specification, syntax rules, and limitations of the MANOVA procedures, see MANOVA: Overview.

Options

Design Specification. You can specify which terms to include in the design on the DESIGN subcommand. This allows you to estimate a model other than the default full factorial model, incorporate factor-by-covariate interactions, indicate nesting of effects, and indicate specific error terms for each effect in mixed models. You can specify a different continuous variable as a dependent variable or work with a subset of the continuous variables with the ANALYSIS subcommand.

Contrast Types. You can specify contrasts other than the default deviation contrasts on the CONTRAST subcommand. You can also subdivide the degrees of freedom associated with a factor using the PARTITION subcommand and test the significance of a specific contrast or group of contrasts.

Optional Output. You can choose from a wide variety of optional output on the PRINT subcommand or suppress output using the NOPRINT subcommand. Output appropriate to univariate designs includes cell means, design or other matrices, parameter estimates, and tests for homogeneity of variance across cells. Using the OMEANS, PMEANS, RESIDUAL, and PLOT subcommands, you can also request tables of observed and/or predicted means, casewise values and residuals for your model, and various plots useful in checking assumptions. In addition, you can request observed power values based on fixed-effect assumptions using the POWER subcommand and request simultaneous confidence intervals for each parameter estimate and regression coefficient using the CINTERVAL subcommand.

Matrix Materials. You can write matrices of intermediate results to a matrix data file, and you can read such matrices in performing further analyses using the MATRIX subcommand.

Basic Specification

- The basic specification is a variable list identifying the dependent variable, the factors (if any), and the covariates (if any).
- By default, MANOVA uses a full factorial model, which includes all main effects and all possible interactions among factors. Estimation is performed using the cell-means model and UNIQUE (regression-type) sums of squares, adjusting each effect for all other effects

in the model. Parameters are estimated using DEVIATION contrasts to determine if their categories differ significantly from the mean.

Subcommand Order

- The variable list must be specified first.
- Subcommands applicable to a specific design must be specified before that DESIGN subcommand. Otherwise, subcommands can be used in any order.

Syntax Rules

- For many analyses, the MANOVA variable list and the DESIGN subcommand are the only specifications needed. If a full factorial design is desired, DESIGN can be omitted.
- All other subcommands apply only to designs that follow. If you do not enter a DESIGN subcommand or if the last subcommand is not DESIGN, MANOVA will use a full factorial model.
- Unless replaced, MANOVA subcommands other than DESIGN remain in effect for all subsequent models.
- MISSING can be specified only once.
- The following words are reserved as keywords or internal commands in the MANOVA procedure: AGAINST, CONSPLUS, CONSTANT, CONTIN, MUPLUS, MWITHIN, POOL, R, RESIDUAL, RW, VERSUS, VS, W, WITHIN, and WR. Variable names that duplicate these words should be changed before you invoke MANOVA.
- If you enter one of the multivariate specifications in a univariate analysis, MANOVA will ignore it.

Limitations

- Maximum 20 factors.
- Maximum 200 dependent variables.
- Memory requirements depend primarily on the number of cells in the design. For the default full factorial model, this equals the product of the number of levels or categories in each factor.

Example

```
MANOVA YIELD BY SEED(1,4) FERT(1,3) WITH RAINFALL
   /PRINT=CELLINFO(MEANS) PARAMETERS(ESTIM)
   /DESIGN.
```

- *YIELD* is the dependent variable; *SEED* (with values 1, 2, 3, and 4) and *FERT* (with values 1, 2, and 3) are factors; *RAINFALL* is a covariate.
- The PRINT subcommand requests the means of the dependent variable for each cell and the default deviation parameter estimates.

- The DESIGN subcommand requests the default design, a full factorial model. This subcommand could have been omitted or could have been specified in full as:

```
/DESIGN = SEED, FERT, SEED BY FERT.
```

MANOVA Variable List

The variable list specifies all variables that will be used in any subsequent analyses.

- The dependent variable must be the first specification on MANOVA.
- By default, MANOVA treats a list of dependent variables as jointly dependent, implying a multivariate design. However, you can change the role of a variable or its inclusion status in the analysis on the ANALYSIS subcommand.
- The names of the factors follow the dependent variable. Use the keyword BY to separate the factors from the dependent variable.
- Factors must have adjacent integer values, and you must supply the minimum and maximum values in parentheses after the factor name(s).
- If several factors have the same value range, you can specify a list of factors followed by a single value range in parentheses.
- Certain one-cell designs, such as univariate and multivariate regression analysis, canonical correlation, and one-sample Hotelling's T^2, do not require a factor specification. To perform these analyses, omit the keyword BY and the factor list.
- Enter the covariates, if any, following the factors and their ranges. Use the keyword WITH to separate covariates from factors (if any) and the dependent variable.

Example

```
MANOVA DEPENDNT BY FACTOR1 (1,3) FACTOR2, FACTOR3 (1,2).
```

- In this example, three factors are specified.
- *FACTOR1* has values 1, 2, and 3, while *FACTOR2* and *FACTOR3* have values 1 and 2.
- A default full factorial model is used for the analysis.

Example

```
MANOVA Y BY A(1,3) WITH X
   /DESIGN.
```

- In this example, the *A* effect is tested after adjusting for the effect of the covariate *X*. It is a test of equality of adjusted *A* means.
- The test of the covariate *X* is adjusted for *A*. It is a test of the pooled within-groups regression of *Y* on *X*.

ERROR Subcommand

ERROR allows you to specify or change the error term used to test all effects for which you do not explicitly specify an error term on the DESIGN subcommand. ERROR affects all terms in all subsequent designs, except terms for which you explicitly provide an error term.

WITHIN	*Terms in the model are tested against the within-cell sum of squares.* This specification can be abbreviated to W. This is the default unless there is no variance within cells or unless a continuous variable is named on the DESIGN subcommand.
RESIDUAL	*Terms in the model are tested against the residual sum of squares.* This specification can be abbreviated to R. This includes all terms not named on the DESIGN subcommand.
WITHIN+RESIDUAL	*Terms are tested against the pooled within-cells and residual sum of squares.* This specification can be abbreviated to WR or RW. This is the default for designs in which a continuous variable appears on the DESIGN subcommand.
error number	*Terms are tested against a numbered error term.* The error term must be defined on each DESIGN subcommand (for a discussion of error terms, see the DESIGN subcommand on p. 669).

- If you specify ERROR=WITHIN+RESIDUAL and one of the components does not exist, MANOVA uses the other component alone.
- If you specify your own error term by number and a design does not have an error term with the specified number, MANOVA does not carry out significance tests. It will, however, display hypothesis sums of squares and, if requested, parameter estimates.

Example

```
MANOVA DEP BY A(1,2) B(1,4)
   /ERROR = 1
   /DESIGN = A, B, A BY B = 1 VS WITHIN
   /DESIGN = A, B.
```

- ERROR defines error term 1 as the default error term.
- In the first design, *A* by *B* is defined as error term 1 and is therefore used to test the *A* and *B* effects. The *A* by *B* effect itself is explicitly tested against the within-cells error.
- In the second design, no term is defined as error term 1, so no significance tests are carried out. Hypothesis sums of squares are displayed for *A* and *B*.

CONTRAST Subcommand

CONTRAST specifies the type of contrast desired among the levels of a factor. For a factor with k levels or values, the contrast type determines the meaning of its $k - 1$ degrees of freedom. If the subcommand is omitted or is specified with no keyword, the default is DEVIATION for between-subjects factors.

- Specify the factor name in parentheses following the subcommand CONTRAST.
- You can specify only one factor per CONTRAST subcommand, but you can enter multiple CONTRAST subcommands.
- After closing the parentheses, enter an equals sign followed by one of the contrast keywords.

- To obtain *F* tests for individual degrees of freedom for the specified contrast, enter the factor name followed by a number in parentheses on the DESIGN subcommand. The number refers to a partition of the factor's degrees of freedom. If you do not use the PARTITION subcommand, each degree of freedom is a distinct partition.

The following contrast types are available:

DEVIATION *Deviations from the grand mean.* This is the default for between-subjects factors. Each level of the factor except one is compared to the grand mean. One category (by default the last) must be omitted so that the effects will be independent of one another. To omit a category other than the last, specify the number of the omitted category (which is not necessarily the same as its value) in parentheses after the keyword DEVIATION. For example,

```
MANOVA A BY B(2,4)
    /CONTRAST(B)=DEVIATION(1).
```

The specified contrast omits the first category, in which *B* has the value 2. Deviation contrasts are not orthogonal.

POLYNOMIAL *Polynomial contrasts.* This is the default for within-subjects factors. The first degree of freedom contains the linear effect across the levels of the factor, the second contains the quadratic effect, and so on. In a balanced design, polynomial contrasts are orthogonal. By default, the levels are assumed to be equally spaced; you can specify unequal spacing by entering a metric consisting of one integer for each level of the factor in parentheses after the keyword POLYNOMIAL. For example,

```
MANOVA RESPONSE BY STIMULUS (4,6)
    /CONTRAST(STIMULUS) = POLYNOMIAL(1,2,4).
```

The specified contrast indicates that the three levels of *STIMULUS* are actually in the proportion 1:2:4. The default metric is always $(1,2,...,k)$, where k levels are involved. Only the relative differences between the terms of the metric matter (1,2,4) is the same metric as (2,3,5) or (20,30,50) because, in each instance, the difference between the second and third numbers is twice the difference between the first and second.

DIFFERENCE *Difference or reverse Helmert contrasts.* Each level of the factor except the first is compared to the mean of the previous levels. In a balanced design, difference contrasts are orthogonal.

HELMERT *Helmert contrasts.* Each level of the factor except the last is compared to the mean of subsequent levels. In a balanced design, Helmert contrasts are orthogonal.

SIMPLE *Each level of the factor except the last is compared to the last level.* To use a category other than the last as the omitted reference category, specify its number (which is not necessarily the same as its value) in parentheses following the keyword SIMPLE. For example,

```
MANOVA A BY B(2,4)
    /CONTRAST(B)=SIMPLE(1).
```

The specified contrast compares the other levels to the first level of *B*, in which *B* has the value 2. Simple contrasts are not orthogonal.

REPEATED   *Comparison of adjacent levels.* Each level of the factor except the first is compared to the previous level. Repeated contrasts are not orthogonal.

SPECIAL   *A user-defined contrast.* After this keyword, enter a square matrix in parentheses with as many rows and columns as there are levels in the factor. The first row represents the mean effect of the factor and is generally a vector of 1's. It represents a set of weights indicating how to collapse over the categories of this factor in estimating parameters for other factors. The other rows of the contrast matrix contain the special contrasts indicating the desired comparisons between levels of the factor. If the special contrasts are linear combinations of each other, MANOVA reports the linear dependency and stops processing.

Orthogonal contrasts are particularly useful. In a balanced design, contrasts are orthogonal if the sum of the coefficients in each contrast row is 0 and if, for any pair of contrast rows, the products of corresponding coefficients sum to 0. DIFFERENCE, HELMERT, and POLYNOMIAL contrasts always meet these criteria in balanced designs. For illustration of contrast types, see the appendix.

Example

```
MANOVA DEP BY FAC(1,5)
  /CONTRAST(FAC)=DIFFERENCE
  /DESIGN=FAC(1) FAC(2) FAC(3) FAC(4).
```

- The factor *FAC* has five categories and therefore four degrees of freedom.
- CONTRAST requests DIFFERENCE contrasts, which compare each level (except the first) with the mean of the previous levels.
- Each of the four degrees of freedom is tested individually on the DESIGN subcommand.

PARTITION Subcommand

PARTITION subdivides the degrees of freedom associated with a factor. This permits you to test the significance of the effect of a specific contrast or group of contrasts of the factor instead of the overall effect of all contrasts of the factor. The default is a single degree of freedom for each partition.

- Specify the factor name in parentheses following the PARTITION subcommand.
- Specify an integer list in parentheses after the optional equals sign to indicate the degrees of freedom for each partition.
- Each value in the partition list must be a positive integer, and the sum of the values cannot exceed the degrees of freedom for the factor.
- The degrees of freedom available for a factor are one less than the number of levels of the factor.
- The meaning of each degree of freedom depends upon the contrast type for the factor. For example, with deviation contrasts (the default for between-subjects factors), each degree

of freedom represents the deviation of the dependent variable in one level of the factor from its grand mean over all levels. With polynomial contrasts, the degrees of freedom represent the linear effect, the quadratic effect, and so on.

- If your list does not account for all the degrees of freedom, MANOVA adds one final partition containing the remaining degrees of freedom.
- You can use a repetition factor of the form $n*$ to specify a series of partitions with the same number of degrees of freedom.
- To specify a model that tests only the effect of a specific partition of a factor in your design, include the number of the partition in parentheses on the DESIGN subcommand (see the example below).
- If you want the default single degree-of-freedom partition, you can omit the PARTITION subcommand and simply enter the appropriate term on the DESIGN subcommand.

Example

```
MANOVA OUTCOME BY TREATMNT(1,12)
  /PARTITION(TREATMNT) = (3*2,4)
  /DESIGN TREATMNT(2).
```

- The factor *TREATMNT* has 12 categories, hence 11 degrees of freedom.
- PARTITION divides the effect of *TREATMNT* into four partitions, containing, respectively, 2, 2, 2, and 4 degrees of freedom. A fifth partition is formed to contain the remaining 1 degree of freedom.
- DESIGN specifies a model in which only the second partition of *TREATMNT* is tested. This partition contains the third and fourth degrees of freedom.
- Since the default contrast type for between-subjects factors is DEVIATION, this second partition represents the deviation of the third and fourth levels of *TREATMNT* from the grand mean.

METHOD Subcommand

METHOD controls the computational aspects of the MANOVA analysis. You can specify one of two different methods for partitioning the sums of squares. The default is UNIQUE.

UNIQUE *Regression approach.* Each term is corrected for every other term in the model. With this approach, sums of squares for various components of the model do not add up to the total sum of squares unless the design is balanced. This is the default if the METHOD subcommand is omitted or if neither of the two keywords is specified.

SEQUENTIAL *Hierarchical decomposition of the sums of squares.* Each term is adjusted only for the terms that precede it on the DESIGN subcommand. This is an orthogonal decomposition, and the sums of squares in the model add up to the total sum of squares.

You can control how parameters are to be estimated by specifying one of the following two keywords available on MANOVA. The default is QR.

QR   *Use modified Givens rotations.* QR bypasses the normal equations and the inaccuracies that can result from creating the cross-products matrix, and it generally results in extremely accurate parameter estimates. This is the default if the METHOD subcommand is omitted or if neither of the two keywords is specified.

CHOLESKY   *Use Cholesky decomposition of the cross-products matrix.* Useful for large data sets with covariates entered on the DESIGN subcommand.

You can also control whether a constant term is included in all models. Two keywords are available on METHOD. The default is CONSTANT.

CONSTANT   *All models include a constant (grand mean) term, even if none is explicitly specified on the DESIGN subcommand.* This is the default if neither of the two keywords is specified.

NOCONSTANT   *Exclude constant terms from models that do not include the keyword CONSTANT on the DESIGN subcommand.*

Example

```
MANOVA DEP BY A B C (1,4)
  /METHOD=NOCONSTANT
  /DESIGN=A, B, C
  /METHOD=CONSTANT SEQUENTIAL
  /DESIGN.
```

- For the first design, a main-effects model, the METHOD subcommand requests the model to be fitted with no constant.
- The second design requests a full factorial model to be fitted with a constant and with a sequential decomposition of sums of squares.

PRINT and NOPRINT Subcommands

PRINT and NOPRINT control the display of optional output.

- Specifications on PRINT remain in effect for all subsequent designs.
- Some PRINT output, such as CELLINFO, applies to the entire MANOVA procedure and is displayed only once.
- You can turn off optional output that you have requested on PRINT by entering a NOPRINT subcommand with the specifications originally used on the PRINT subcommand.
- Additional output can be obtained on the PCOMPS, DISCRIM, OMEANS, PMEANS, PLOT, and RESIDUALS subcommands.
- Some optional output greatly increases the processing time. Request only the output you want to see.

The following specifications are appropriate for univariate MANOVA analyses. For information on PRINT specifications appropriate for other MANOVA models, see MANOVA: Multivariate and MANOVA: Repeated Measures.

CELLINFO   *Basic information about each cell in the design.*

PARAMETERS *Parameter estimates.*

HOMOGENEITY *Tests of homogeneity of variance.*

DESIGN *Design information.*

ERROR *Error standard deviations.*

CELLINFO Keyword

You can request any of the following cell information by specifying the appropriate keyword(s) in parentheses after CELLINFO. The default is MEANS.

MEANS *Cell means, standard deviations, and counts for the dependent variable and covariates.* Confidence intervals for the cell means are displayed if you have set a wide width. This is the default when CELLINFO is requested with no further specification.

SSCP *Within-cell sum-of-squares and cross-products matrices for the dependent variable and covariates.*

COV *Within-cell variance-covariance matrices for the dependent variable and covariates.*

COR *Within-cell correlation matrices, with standard deviations on the diagonal, for the dependent variable and covariates.*

ALL *MEANS, SSCP, COV, and COR.*

- Output from CELLINFO is displayed once before the analysis of any particular design. Specify CELLINFO only once.
- When you specify SSCP, COV, or COR, the cells are numbered for identification, beginning with cell 1.
- The levels vary most rapidly for the factor named last on the MANOVA variables specification.
- Empty cells are neither displayed nor numbered.
- A table showing the levels of each factor corresponding to each cell number is displayed at the beginning of MANOVA output.

Example

```
MANOVA DEP BY A(1,4) B(1,2) WITH COV
  /PRINT=CELLINFO(MEANS COV)
  /DESIGN.
```

- For each combination of levels of *A* and *B*, MANOVA displays separately the means and standard deviations of *DEP* and *COV*. Beginning with cell 1, it will then display the variance-covariance matrix of *DEP* and *COV* within each non-empty cell.
- A table of cell numbers will be displayed to show the factor levels corresponding to each cell.
- The keyword COV, as a parameter of CELLINFO, is not confused with the variable *COV*.

PARAMETERS Keyword

The keyword PARAMETERS displays information relating to the estimated size of the effects in the model. You can specify any of the following keywords in parentheses on PARAME-TERS. The default is ESTIM.

ESTIM   *The estimated parameters themselves, along with their standard errors, t tests, and confidence intervals.* Only nonredundant parameters are displayed. This is the default if PARAMETERS is requested without further specification.

NEGSUM   *The negative of the sum of parameters for each effect.* For DEVIATION main effects, this equals the parameter for the omitted (redundant) contrast. NEGSUM is displayed along with the parameter estimates.

ORTHO   *The orthogonal estimates of parameters used to produce the sums of squares.*

COR   *Covariance factors and correlations among the parameter estimates.*

EFSIZE   *The effect size values.*

OPTIMAL   *Optimal Scheffé contrast coefficients.*

ALL   *ESTIM, NEGSUM, ORTHO, COR, EFSIZE, and OPTIMAL.*

SIGNIF Keyword

SIGNIF requests special significance tests, most of which apply to multivariate designs (see MANOVA: Multivariate). The following specification is useful in univariate applications of MANOVA:

SINGLEDF   *Significance tests for each single degree of freedom making up each effect for analysis-of-variance tables.*

- When non-orthogonal contrasts are requested or when the design is unbalanced, the SINGLEDF effects will differ from single degree-of-freedom partitions. SINGLEDEF effects are orthogonal within an effect; single degree-of-freedom partitions are not.

Example

```
MANOVA DEP BY FAC(1,5)
  /CONTRAST(FAC)=POLY
  /PRINT=SIGNIF(SINGLEDF)
  /DESIGN.
```

- POLYNOMIAL contrasts are applied to *FAC*, testing the linear, quadratic, cubic, and quartic components of its five levels. POLYNOMIAL contrasts are orthogonal in balanced designs.
- The SINGLEDF specification on SIGNIF requests significance tests for each of these four components.

HOMOGENEITY Keyword

HOMOGENEITY requests tests for the homogeneity of variance of the dependent variable across the cells of the design. You can specify one or more of the following specifications in parentheses. If HOMOGENEITY is requested without further specification, the default is ALL.

BARTLETT	*Bartlett-Box* F *test.*
COCHRAN	*Cochran's* C.
ALL	*Both BARTLETT and COCHRAN.* This is the default.

DESIGN Keyword

You can request the following by entering one or more of the specifications in parentheses following the keyword DESIGN. If DESIGN is requested without further specification, the default is OVERALL.

The DECOMP and BIAS matrices can provide valuable information on the confounding of the effects and the estimability of the chosen contrasts. If two effects are confounded, the entry corresponding to them in the BIAS matrix will be nonzero; if they are orthogonal, the entry will be zero. This is particularly useful in designs with unpatterned empty cells. For further discussion of the matrices, see Bock (1985).

OVERALL	*The overall reduced-model design matrix (not the contrast matrix).* This is the default.
ONEWAY	*The one-way basis matrix (not the contrast matrix) for each factor.*
DECOMP	*The upper triangular QR/CHOLESKY decomposition of the design.*
BIAS	*Contamination coefficients displaying the bias present in the design.*
SOLUTION	*Coefficients of the linear combinations of the cell means used in significance testing.*
REDUNDANCY	*Exact linear combinations of parameters that form a redundancy.* This keyword displays a table only if QR (the default) is the estimation method.
COLLINEARITY	*Collinearity diagnostics for design matrices.* These diagnostics include the singular values of the normalized design matrix (which are the same as those of the normalized decomposition matrix), condition indexes corresponding to each singular value, and the proportion of variance of the corresponding parameter accounted for by each principal component. For greatest accuracy, use the QR method of estimation whenever you request collinearity diagnostics.
ALL	*All available options.*

ERROR Keyword

Generally, the keyword ERROR on PRINT produces error matrices. In univariate analyses, the only valid specification for ERROR is STDDEV, which is the default if ERROR is specified by itself.

STDDEV *The error standard deviation.* Normally, this is the within-cells standard deviation of the dependent variable. If you specify multiple error terms on DESIGN, this specification will display the standard deviation for each.

OMEANS Subcommand

OMEANS (observed means) displays tables of the means of continuous variables for levels or combinations of levels of the factors.

- Use the keywords VARIABLES and TABLES to indicate which observed means you want to display.
- With no specifications, the OMEANS subcommand is equivalent to requesting CELLINFO (MEANS) on PRINT.
- OMEANS displays confidence intervals for the cell means if you have set the width to 132.
- Output from OMEANS is displayed once before the analysis of any particular design. This subcommand should be specified only once.

VARIABLES   *Continuous variables for which you want means.* Specify the variables in parentheses after the keyword VARIABLES. You can request means for the dependent variable or any covariates. If you omit the VARIABLES keyword, observed means are displayed for the dependent variable and all covariates. If you enter the keyword VARIABLES, you must also enter the keyword TABLES, discussed below.

TABLES   *Factors for which you want the observed means displayed.* List in parentheses the factors, or combinations of factors, separated with BY. Observed means are displayed for each level, or combination of levels, of the factors named (see the example below). Both weighted means and unweighted means (where all cells are weighted equally, regardless of the number of cases they contain) are displayed. If you enter the keyword CONSTANT, the grand mean is displayed.

Example

```
MANOVA DEP BY A(1,3) B(1,2)
  /OMEANS=TABLES(A,B)
  /DESIGN.
```

- Because there is no VARIABLES specification on the OMEANS subcommand, observed means are displayed for all continuous variables. *DEP* is the only dependent variable here, and there are no covariates.
- The TABLES specification on the OMEANS subcommand requests tables of observed means for each of the three categories of *A* (collapsing over *B*) and for both categories of *B* (collapsing over *A*).
- MANOVA displays both weighted means, in which all cases count equally, and unweighted means, in which all cells count equally.

PMEANS Subcommand

PMEANS (predicted means) displays a table of the predicted cell means of the dependent variable, both adjusted for the effect of covariates in the cell and unadjusted for covariates. For comparison, it also displays the observed cell means.

- Output from PMEANS can be computationally expensive.

- PMEANS without any additional specifications displays a table showing for each cell the observed mean of the dependent variable, the predicted mean adjusted for the effect of covariates in that cell (*ADJ. MEAN*), the predicted mean unadjusted for covariates (*EST. MEAN*), and the raw and standardized residuals from the estimated means.

- Cells are numbered in output from PMEANS so that the levels vary most rapidly on the factor named last in the MANOVA variables specification. A table showing the levels of each factor corresponding to each cell number is displayed at the beginning of the MANOVA output.

- Predicted means are suppressed for any design in which the MUPLUS keyword appears.

- Covariates are not predicted.

- In designs with covariates and multiple error terms, use the ERROR subcommand to designate which error term's regression coefficients are to be used in calculating the standardized residuals.

For univariate analysis, the following keywords are available on the PMEANS subcommand:

TABLES   *Additional tables showing adjusted predicted means for specified factors or combinations of factors.* Enter the names of factors or combinations of factors in parentheses after this keyword. For each factor or combination, MANOVA displays the predicted means (adjusted for covariates) collapsed over all other factors.

PLOT   *A plot of the predicted means for each cell.*

Example

```
MANOVA DEP BY A(1,4) B(1,3)
  /PMEANS TABLES(A, B, A BY B)
  /DESIGN = A, B.
```

- PMEANS displays the default table of observed and predicted means for *DEP* and raw and standardized residuals in each of the 12 cells in the model.

- The TABLES specification on PMEANS displays tables of predicted means for *A* (collapsing over *B*), for *B* (collapsing over *A*), and all combinations of *A* and *B*.

- Because *A* and *B* are the only factors in the model, the means for *A* by *B* in the TABLES specification come from every cell in the model. They are identical to the adjusted predicted means in the default PMEANS table, which always includes all non-empty cells.

- Predicted means for *A* by *B* can be requested in the TABLES specification, even though the *A* by *B* effect is not in the design.

RESIDUALS Subcommand

Use RESIDUALS to display and plot casewise values and residuals for your models.

- Use the ERROR subcommand to specify an error term other than the default to be used to standardize the residuals.

- If a designated error term does not exist for a given design, no predicted values or residuals are calculated.

- If you specify RESIDUALS without any keyword, CASEWISE output is displayed.

The following keywords are available:

CASEWISE   *A case-by-case listing of the observed, predicted, residual, and standardized residual values for each dependent variable.*

PLOT   *A plot of observed values, predicted values, and case numbers versus the standardized residuals, plus normal and detrended normal probability plots for the standardized residuals (five plots in all).*

POWER Subcommand

POWER requests observed power values based on fixed-effect assumptions for all univariate and multivariate F tests and t tests. Both approximate and exact power values can be computed, although exact multivariate power is displayed only when there is one hypothesis degree of freedom. If POWER is specified by itself, with no keywords, MANOVA calculates the approximate observed power values of all F tests at 0.05 significance level.

The following keywords are available on the POWER subcommand:

APPROXIMATE   *Approximate power values.* This is the default if POWER is specified without any keyword. Approximate power values for univariate tests are derived from an Edgeworth-type normal approximation to the noncentral beta distribution. Approximate values are normally accurate to three decimal places and are much cheaper to compute than exact values.

EXACT   *Exact power values.* Exact power values for univariate tests are computed from the noncentral incomplete beta distribution.

F(a)   *Alpha level at which the power is to be calculated for* F *tests.* The default is 0.05. To change the default, specify a decimal number between 0 and 1 in parentheses after F. The numbers 0 and 1 themselves are not allowed. F test at 0.05 significance level is the default when POWER is omitted or specified without any keyword.

T(a)   *Alpha level at which the power is to be calculated for* t *tests.* The default is 0.05. To change the default, specify a decimal number between 0 and 1 in parentheses after t. The numbers 0 and 1 themselves are not allowed.

- For univariate F tests and t tests, MANOVA computes a measure of the effect size based on partial η^2:

$$\text{partial } \eta^2 = (ssh)/(ssh + sse)$$

where *ssh* is the hypothesis sum of squares and *sse* is the error sum of squares. The measure is an overestimate of the actual effect size. However, it is consistent and is applicable to all F tests and t tests. For a discussion of effect size measures, see Cohen (1977) or Hays (1981).

CINTERVAL Subcommand

CINTERVAL requests simultaneous confidence intervals for each parameter estimate and regression coefficient. MANOVA provides either individual or joint confidence intervals at any desired confidence level. You can compute joint confidence intervals using either Scheffé or Bonferroni intervals. Scheffé intervals are based on all possible contrasts, while Bonferroni intervals are based on the number of contrasts actually made. For a large number of contrasts, Bonferroni intervals will be larger than Scheffé intervals. Timm (1975) provides a good discussion of which intervals are best for certain situations. Both Scheffé and Bonferroni intervals are computed separately for each term in the design. You can request only one type of confidence interval per design.

The following keywords are available on the CINTERVAL subcommand. If the subcommand is specified without any keyword, CINTERVAL automatically displays individual univariate confidence intervals at the 0.95 level.

INDIVIDUAL(a)   *Individual confidence intervals.* Specify the desired confidence level in parentheses following the keyword. The desired confidence level can be any decimal number between 0 and 1. When individual intervals are requested, BONFER and SCHEFFE have no effect.

JOINT(a)   *Joint confidence intervals.* Specify the desired confidence level in parentheses after the keyword. The default is 0.95. The desired confidence level can be any decimal number between 0 and 1.

UNIVARIATE(type)   *Univariate confidence interval.* Specify either SCHEFFE for Scheffé intervals or BONFER for Bonferroni intervals in parentheses after the keyword. The default specification is SCHEFFE.

PLOT Subcommand

MANOVA can display a variety of plots useful in checking the assumptions needed in the analysis. Plots are produced only once in the MANOVA procedure, regardless of how many DESIGN subcommands you enter. Use the following keywords on the PLOT subcommand to request plots. If the PLOT subcommand is specified by itself, the default is BOXPLOT.

BOXPLOTS   *Boxplots.* Plots are displayed for each continuous variable (dependent or covariate) named on the MANOVA variable list. Boxplots provide a simple graphical means of comparing the cells in terms of mean location and spread. The data must be stored in memory for these plots; if there is not enough memory, boxplots are not produced and a warning message is issued. This is the default if the PLOT subcommand is specified without a keyword.

CELLPLOTS   *Cell statistics, including a plot of cell means versus cell variances, a plot of cell means versus cell standard deviations, and a histogram of cell means.* Plots are produced for each continuous variable (dependent or covariate) named on the MANOVA variable list. The first two plots aid in detecting heteroscedasticity (nonhomogeneous variances) and in determining an appropriate data transformation if one is needed. The third plot gives distributional information for the cell means.

NORMAL   *Normal and detrended normal plots.* Plots are produced for each continuous variable (dependent or covariate) named on the MANOVA variable list. MANOVA ranks the scores and then plots the ranks against the expected normal deviate, or detrended expected normal deviate, for that rank. These plots aid in detecting non-normality and outlying observations. All data must be held in memory to compute ranks. If not enough memory is available, MANOVA displays a warning and skips the plots.

- ZCORR, an additional plot available on the PLOT subcommand, is described in MANOVA: Multivariate.

- You can request other plots on PMEANS and RESIDUALS (see respective subcommands).

MISSING Subcommand

By default, cases with missing values for any of the variables on the MANOVA variable list are excluded from the analysis. The MISSING subcommand allows you to include cases with user-missing values. If MISSING is not specified, the defaults are LISTWISE and EXCLUDE.

- The same missing-value treatment is used to process all designs in a single execution of MANOVA.

- If you enter more than one MISSING subcommand, the last one entered will be in effect for the entire procedure, including designs specified before the last MISSING subcommand.

- Pairwise deletion of missing data is not available in MANOVA.

- Keywords INCLUDE and EXCLUDE are mutually exclusive; either can be specified with LISTWISE.

LISTWISE   *Cases with missing values for any variable named on the MANOVA variable list are excluded from the analysis.* This is always true in the MANOVA procedure.

EXCLUDE   *Exclude both user-missing and system-missing values.* This is the default when MISSING is not specified.

INCLUDE   *User-missing values are treated as valid.* For factors, you must include the missing-value codes within the range specified on the MANOVA variable list. It may be necessary to recode these values so that they will be adjacent to the other factor values. System-missing values cannot be included in the analysis.

MATRIX Subcommand

MATRIX reads and writes SPSS matrix data files. It writes correlation matrices that can be read by subsequent MANOVA procedures.

- Either IN or OUT is required to specify the matrix file in parentheses. When both IN and OUT are used on the same MANOVA procedure, they can be specified on separate MATRIX subcommands or on the same subcommand.

- The matrix materials include the *N*, mean, and standard deviation. Documents from the file that form the matrix are not included in the matrix data file.

- MATRIX=IN cannot be used in place of GET or DATA LIST to begin a new SPSS command file. MATRIX is a subcommand on MANOVA, and MANOVA cannot run before a working data file is defined. To begin a new command file and immediately read a matrix, first GET the matrix file, and then specify IN(*) on MATRIX.

- Records in the matrix data file read by MANOVA can be in any order, with the following exceptions: the order of split-file groups cannot be violated, and all *CORR* vectors must appear contiguously within each split-file group.

- When MANOVA reads matrix materials, it ignores the record containing the total number of cases. In addition, it skips unrecognized records. MANOVA does not issue a warning when it skips records.

The following two keywords are available on the MATRIX subcommand:

OUT   *Write an SPSS matrix data file.* Specify either a file or an asterisk, and enclose the specification in parentheses. If you specify a file, the file is stored on disk and can be retrieved at any time. If you specify an asterisk (*) or leave the parentheses empty, the matrix file replaces the working data file but is not stored on disk unless you use SAVE or XSAVE.

IN   *Read an SPSS matrix data file.* If the matrix file *is not* the current working data file, specify a file in parentheses. If the matrix file *is* the current working data file, specify an asterisk (*) or leave the parentheses empty.

Format of the SPSS Matrix Data File

The SPSS matrix data file includes two special variables created by SPSS: *ROWTYPE_* and *VARNAME_*.

- Variable *ROWTYPE_* is a short string variable having values *N*, *MEAN*, *CORR* (for Pearson correlation coefficients), and *STDDEV*.

- Variable *VARNAME_* is a short string variable whose values are the names of the variables and covariates used to form the correlation matrix. When *ROWTYPE_* is *CORR*, *VARNAME_* gives the variable associated with that row of the correlation matrix.

- Between *ROWTYPE_* and *VARNAME_* are the factor variables (if any) defined in the BY portion of the MANOVA variable list. (Factor variables receive the system-missing value on vectors that represent pooled values.)

- Remaining variables are the variables used to form the correlation matrix.

Split Files and Variable Order

- When split-file processing is in effect, the first variables in the matrix system file will be the split variables, followed by *ROWTYPE_*, the factor variable(s), *VARNAME_*, and then the variables used to form the correlation matrix.

- A full set of matrix materials is written for each subgroup defined by the split variable(s).

- A split variable cannot have the same variable name as any other variable written to the matrix data file.

- If a split file is in effect when a matrix is written, the same split file must be in effect when that matrix is read into another procedure.

Additional Statistics

In addition to the *CORR* values, MANOVA always includes the following with the matrix materials:

- The total weighted number of cases used to compute each correlation coefficient.
- A vector of *N*'s for each cell in the data.
- A vector of *MEAN*'s for each cell in the data.
- A vector of pooled standard deviations, *STDDEV*. This is the square root of the within-cells mean square error for each variable.

Example

```
GET FILE IRIS.
MANOVA SEPALLEN SEPALWID PETALLEN PETALWID BY TYPE(1,3)
    /MATRIX=OUT(MANMTX).
```

- MANOVA reads data from the SPSS data file *IRIS* and writes one set of matrix materials to the file *MANMTX*.
- The working data file is still *IRIS*. Subsequent commands are executed on the file *IRIS*.

Example

```
GET FILE IRIS.
MANOVA SEPALLEN SEPALWID PETALLEN PETALWID BY TYPE(1,3)
    /MATRIX=OUT(*).
LIST.
```

- MANOVA writes the same matrix as in the example above. However, the matrix file replaces the working data file. The LIST command is executed on the matrix file, not on the file *IRIS*.

Example

```
GET FILE=PRSNNL.
FREQUENCIES VARIABLE=AGE.

MANOVA SEPALLEN SEPALWID PETALLEN PETALWID BY TYPE(1,3)
    /MATRIX=IN(MANMTX).
```

- This example assumes that you want to perform a frequencies analysis on the file *PRSNNL* and then use MANOVA to read a different file. The file you want to read is an existing SPSS matrix data file. The external matrix file *MANMTX* is specified in parentheses after IN on the MATRIX subcommand.
- *MANMTX* does not replace *PRSNNL* as the working file.

Example

```
GET FILE=MANMTX.
MANOVA SEPALLEN SEPALWID PETALLEN PETALWID BY TYPE(1,3)
    /MATRIX=IN(*).
```

- This example assumes that you are starting a new session and want to read an existing SPSS matrix data file. GET retrieves the matrix file *MANMTX*.
- An asterisk is specified in parentheses after IN on the MATRIX subcommand to read the working data file. You can also leave the parentheses empty to indicate the default.

- If the GET command is omitted, SPSS issues an error message.
- If you specify *MANMTX* in parentheses after IN, SPSS issues an error message.

ANALYSIS Subcommand

ANALYSIS allows you to work with a subset of the continuous variables (dependent variable and covariates) you have named on the MANOVA variable list. In univariate analysis of variance, you can use ANALYSIS to allow factor-by-covariate interaction terms in your model (see the DESIGN subcommand below). You can also use it to switch the roles of the dependent variable and a covariate.

- In general, ANALYSIS gives you complete control over which continuous variables are to be dependent variables, which are to be covariates, and which are to be neither.
- ANALYSIS specifications are like the MANOVA variables specification, except that factors are not named. Enter the dependent variable and, if there are covariates, the keyword WITH and the covariates.
- Only variables listed as dependent variables or covariates on the MANOVA variable list can be entered on the ANALYSIS subcommand.
- In a univariate analysis of variance, the most important use of ANALYSIS is to omit covariates altogether from the analysis list, thereby making them available for inclusion on DESIGN (see the example below and the DESIGN subcommand examples).
- For more information on ANALYSIS, refer to MANOVA: Multivariate.

Example

```
MANOVA DEP BY FACTOR(1,3) WITH COV
  /ANALYSIS DEP
  /DESIGN FACTOR, COV, FACTOR BY COV.
```

- *COV*, a continuous variable, is included on the MANOVA variable list as a covariate.
- *COV* is not mentioned on ANALYSIS, so it will not be included in the model as a dependent variable or covariate. It can, therefore, be explicitly included on the DESIGN subcommand.
- DESIGN includes the main effects of *FACTOR* and *COV* and the *FACTOR* by *COV* interaction.

DESIGN Subcommand

DESIGN specifies the effects included in a specific model. It must be the last subcommand entered for any model.

The cells in a design are defined by all of the possible combinations of levels of the factors in that design. The number of cells equals the product of the number of levels of all the factors. A design is *balanced* if each cell contains the same number of cases. MANOVA can analyze both balanced and unbalanced designs.

- Specify a list of terms to be included in the model, separated by spaces or commas.
- The default design, if the DESIGN subcommand is omitted or is specified by itself, is a full factorial model containing all main effects and all orders of factor-by-factor interaction.
- If the last subcommand specified is not DESIGN, a default full factorial design is estimated.

- To include a term for the main effect of a factor, enter the name of the factor on the DESIGN subcommand.
- To include a term for an interaction between factors, use the keyword BY to join the factors involved in the interaction.
- Terms are entered into the model in the order in which you list them on DESIGN. If you have specified SEQUENTIAL on the METHOD subcommand to partition the sums of squares in a hierarchical fashion, this order may affect the significance tests.
- You can specify other types of terms in the model, as described in the following sections.
- Multiple DESIGN subcommands are accepted. An analysis of one model is produced for each DESIGN subcommand.

Example

```
MANOVA Y BY A(1,2) B(1,2) C(1,3)
  /DESIGN
  /DESIGN A, B, C
  /DESIGN A, B, C, A BY B, A BY C.
```

- The first DESIGN produces the default full factorial design, with all main effects and interactions for factors A, B, and C.
- The second DESIGN produces an analysis with main effects only for A, B, and C.
- The third DESIGN produces an analysis with main effects and the interactions between A and the other two factors. The interaction between B and C is not in the design, nor is the interaction between all three factors.

Partitioned Effects: Number in Parentheses

You can specify a number in parentheses following a factor name on the DESIGN subcommand to identify individual degrees of freedom or partitions of the degrees of freedom associated with an effect.

- If you specify PARTITION, the number refers to a partition. Partitions can include more than one degree of freedom (see the PARTITION subcommand on p. 656). For example, if the first partition of SEED includes two degrees of freedom, the term SEED(1) on a DESIGN subcommand tests the two degrees of freedom.
- If you do not use PARTITION, the number refers to a single degree of freedom associated with the effect.
- The number refers to an individual level for a factor if that factor follows the keyword WITHIN or MWITHIN (see the sections on nested effects and pooled effects below).
- A factor has one less degree of freedom than it has levels or values.

Example

```
MANOVA YIELD BY SEED(1,4) WITH RAINFALL
  /PARTITION(SEED)=(2,1)
  /DESIGN=SEED(1) SEED(2).
```

- Factor SEED is subdivided into two partitions, one containing the first two degrees of freedom and the other the last degree of freedom.

- The two partitions of *SEED* are treated as independent effects.

Nested Effects: WITHIN Keyword

Use the WITHIN keyword (alias W) to nest the effects of one factor within those of another factor or an interaction term.

Example

```
MANOVA YIELD BY SEED(1,4) FERT(1,3) PLOT (1,4)
  /DESIGN = FERT WITHIN SEED BY PLOT.
```

- The three factors in this example are type of seed (*SEED*), type of fertilizer (*FERT*), and location of plots (*PLOT*).
- The DESIGN subcommand nests the effects of *FERT* within the interaction term of *SEED* by *PLOT*. The levels of *FERT* are considered distinct for each combination of levels of *SEED* and *PLOT*.

Simple Effects: WITHIN and MWITHIN Keywords

A factor can be nested within one specific level of another factor by indicating the level in parentheses. This allows you to estimate simple effects or the effect of one factor within only one level of another. Simple effects can be obtained for higher-order interactions as well.

Use WITHIN to request simple effects of between-subjects factors.

Example

```
MANOVA YIELD BY SEED(2,4) FERT(1,3) PLOT (1,4)
  /DESIGN = FERT WITHIN SEED (1).
```

- This example requests the simple effect of *FERT* within the first level of *SEED*.
- The number (*n*) specified after a WITHIN factor refers to the level of that factor. It is the ordinal position, which is not necessarily the value of that level. In this example, the first level is associated with value 2.
- The number does *not* refer to the number of partitioned effects (see "Partitioned Effects: Number in Parentheses" on p. 670).

Example

```
MANOVA YIELD BY SEED(2,4) FERT(1,3) PLOT (3,5)
  /DESIGN = FERT WITHIN PLOT(1) WITHIN SEED(2)
```

- This example requests the effect of *FERT* within the second *SEED* level of the first *PLOT* level.
- The second *SEED* level is associated with value 3 and the first *PLOT* level is associated with value 3.

Use MWITHIN to request simple effects of within-subjects factors in repeated measures analysis (see MANOVA: Repeated Measures).

Pooled Effects: Plus Sign

To pool different effects for the purpose of significance testing, join the effects with a plus sign (+). A single test is made for the combined effect of the pooled terms.

- The keyword BY is evaluated before effects are pooled together.
- Parentheses are not allowed to change the order of evaluation. For example, it is illegal to specify `(A + B) BY C`. You must specify `/DESIGN=A BY C + B BY C`.

Example

```
MANOVA Y BY A(1,3) B(1,4) WITH X
 /ANALYSIS=Y
 /DESIGN=A, B, A BY B, A BY X + B BY X + A BY B BY X.
```

- This example shows how to test homogeneity of regressions in a two-way analysis of variance.
- The + signs are used to produce a pooled test of all interactions involving the covariate *X*. If this test is significant, the assumption of homogeneity of variance is questionable.

MUPLUS Keyword

MUPLUS combines the constant term (μ) in the model with the term specified after it. The normal use of this specification is to obtain parameter estimates that represent weighted means for the levels of some factor. For example, `MUPLUS SEED` represents the constant, or overall, mean plus the effect for each level of *SEED*. The significance of such effects is usually uninteresting, but the parameter estimates represent the weighted means for each level of *SEED*, adjusted for any covariates in the model.

- MUPLUS cannot appear more than once on a given DESIGN subcommand.
- MUPLUS is the only way to get standard errors for the predicted mean for each level of the factor specified.
- Parameter estimates are not displayed by default; you must explicitly request them on the PRINT subcommand or via a CONTRAST subcommand.
- You can obtain the unweighted mean by specifying the full factorial model, excluding those terms contained by an effect, and prefixing the effect whose mean is to be found by MUPLUS.

Effects of Continuous Variables

Usually you name factors but not covariates on the DESIGN subcommand. The linear effects of covariates are removed from the dependent variable before the design is tested. However, the design can include variables measured at the interval level and originally named as covariates or as additional dependent variables.

- Continuous variables on a DESIGN subcommand must be named as dependents or covariates on the MANOVA variable list.

- Before you can name a continuous variable on a DESIGN subcommand, you must supply an ANALYSIS subcommand that does *not* name the variable. This excludes it from the analysis as a dependent variable or covariate and makes it eligible for inclusion on DESIGN.

- More than one continuous variable can be pooled into a single effect (provided that they are all excluded on an ANALYSIS subcommand) with the keyword POOL(varlist). For a single continuous variable, `POOL(VAR)` is equivalent to `VAR`.

- The TO convention in the variable list for POOL refers to the order of continuous variables (dependent variables and covariates) on the original MANOVA variable list, which is not necessarily their order on the working data file. This is the only allowable use of the keyword TO on a DESIGN subcommand.

- You can specify interaction terms between factors and continuous variables. If *FAC* is a factor and *COV* is a covariate that has been omitted from an ANALYSIS subcommand, `FAC BY COV` is a valid specification on a DESIGN statement.

- You cannot specify an interaction between two continuous variables. Use the COMPUTE command to create a variable representing the interaction prior to MANOVA.

Example

```
*  This example tests whether the regression of the dependent
   variable Y on the two variables X1 and X2 is the same across
   all the categories of the factors AGE and TREATMNT.
MANOVA Y BY AGE(1,5) TREATMNT(1,3) WITH X1, X2
  /ANALYSIS = Y
  /DESIGN = POOL(X1,X2),
            AGE, TREATMNT, AGE BY TREATMNT,
            POOL(X1,X2) BY AGE + POOL(X1,X2) BY TREATMNT
              + POOL(X1,X2) BY AGE BY TREATMNT.
```

- ANALYSIS excludes *X1* and *X2* from the standard treatment of covariates, so that they can be used in the design.

- DESIGN includes five terms. `POOL(X1,X2)`, the overall regression of the dependent variable on *X1* and *X2*, is entered first, followed by the two factors and their interaction.

- The last term is the test for equal regressions. It consists of three factor-by-continuous-variable interactions pooled together. `POOL(X1,X2) BY AGE` is the interaction between *AGE* and the combined effect of the continuous variables *X1* and *X2*. It is combined with similar interactions between *TREATMNT* and the continuous variables and between the *AGE* by *TREATMNT* interaction and the continuous variables.

- If the last term is not statistically significant, there is no evidence that the regression of *Y* on *X1* and *X2* is different across any combination of the categories of *AGE* and *TREATMNT*.

Error Terms for Individual Effects

The "error" sum of squares against which terms in the design are tested is specified on the ERROR subcommand. For any particular term on a DESIGN subcommand, you can specify a different error term to be used in the analysis of variance. To do so, name the term followed by the keyword VS (or AGAINST) and the error term keyword.

- To test a term against only the within-cells sum of squares, specify the term followed by VS WITHIN on the DESIGN subcommand. For example, `GROUP VS WITHIN` tests the effect of the factor *GROUP* against only the within-cells sum of squares. For most analyses, this is the default error term.

- To test a term against only the residual sum of squares (the sum of squares for all terms not included in your DESIGN), specify the term followed by VS RESIDUAL.

- To test against the combined within-cells and residual sums of squares, specify the term followed by VS WITHIN+RESIDUAL.

- To test against any other sum of squares in the analysis of variance, include a term corresponding to the desired sum of squares in the design and assign it to an integer between 1 and 10. You can then test against the number of the error term. It is often convenient to test against the term before you define it. This is perfectly acceptable as long as you define the error term on the same DESIGN subcommand.

Example

```
MANOVA DEP BY A, B, C (1,3)
    /DESIGN=A VS 1,
            B WITHIN A = 1 VS 2,
            C WITHIN B WITHIN A = 2 VS WITHIN.
```

- In this example, the factors *A*, *B*, and *C* are completely nested; levels of *C* occur within levels of *B*, which occur within levels of *A*. Each factor is tested against everything within it.

- *A*, the outermost factor, is tested against the *B* within *A* sum of squares, to see if it contributes anything beyond the effects of *B* within each of its levels. The *B* within *A* sum of squares is defined as error term number 1.

- *B* nested within *A*, in turn, is tested against error term number 2, which is defined as the *C* within *B* within *A* sum of squares.

- Finally, *C* nested within *B* nested within *A* is tested against the within-cells sum of squares.

User-defined error terms are specified by simply inserting = n after a term, where *n* is an integer from 1 to 10. The equals sign is required. Keywords used in building a design term, such as BY or WITHIN, are evaluated first. For example, error term number 2 in the above example consists of the entire term `C WITHIN B WITHIN A`. An error-term *number,* but not an error-term *definition,* can follow the keyword VS.

CONSTANT Keyword

By default, the constant (grand mean) term is included as the first term in the model.

- If you have specified NOCONSTANT on the METHOD subcommand, a constant term will not be included in any design unless you request it with the CONSTANT keyword on DESIGN.

- You can specify an error term for the constant.

- A factor named CONSTANT will not be recognized on the DESIGN subcommand.

MANOVA: Multivariate

MANOVA is available in the Advanced Models option.

```
MANOVA dependent varlist [BY factor list (min,max) [factor list...]]
                        [WITH covariate list]

[/TRANSFORM [(dependent varlist [/dependent varlist])]=
                        [ORTHONORM] [{CONTRAST}] {DEVIATIONS (refcat)     }]
                                    {BASIS   }  {DIFFERENCE              }
                                                {HELMERT                 }
                                                {SIMPLE (refcat)         }
                                                {REPEATED                }
                                                {POLYNOMIAL[({1,2,3...})]}]
                                                            {metric }
                                                {SPECIAL (matrix)        }

[/RENAME={newname} {newname}...]
         {*       } {*       }

[/{PRINT  }=[HOMOGENEITY [(BOXM)]]
  {NOPRINT} [ERROR [([COV] [COR] [SSCP] [STDDEV])]]
            [SIGNIF [([MULTIV**] [EIGEN] [DIMENR]
                     [UNIV**] [HYPOTH][STEPDOWN] [BRIEF])]]
            [TRANSFORM]                                    ]

[/PCOMPS=[COR] [COV] [ROTATE(rottype)]
         [NCOMP(n)] [MINEIGEN(eigencut)] [ALL]]

[/PLOT=[ZCORR]]

[/DISCRIM [RAW] [STAN] [ESTIM] [COR] [ALL]
          [ROTATE(rottype)] [ALPHA({.25**})]]
                                   {a   }

[/POWER=[T({.05**})] [F({.05**})] [{APPROXIMATE}]]
           {a    }      {a    }   {EXACT      }

[/CINTERVAL=[MULTIVARIATE  ({ROY     })]]
                           {PILLAI  }
                           {BONFER  }
                           {HOTELLING}
                           {WILKS   }

[/ANALYSIS [({UNCONDITIONAL**})]=[()]dependent varlist
            {CONDITIONAL    }      [WITH covariate varlist]
                                   [/dependent varlist...][()][WITH varlist]]

[/DESIGN...]*
```

* The **DESIGN** subcommand has the same syntax as is described in MANOVA: Univariate.

**Default if subcommand or keyword is omitted.

Example
```
MANOVA SCORE1 TO SCORE4 BY METHOD(1,3).
```

Overview

This section discusses the subcommands that are used in multivariate analysis of variance and covariance designs with several interrelated dependent variables. The discussion focuses on subcommands and keywords that do not apply, or apply in different manners, to univariate analyses. It does not contain information on all of the subcommands you will need to specify the design. For subcommands not covered here, see MANOVA: Univariate.

Options

Dependent Variables and Covariates. You can specify subsets and reorder the dependent variables and covariates using the ANALYSIS subcommand. You can specify linear transformations of the dependent variables and covariates using the TRANSFORM subcommand. When transformations are performed, you can rename the variables using the RENAME subcommand and request the display of a transposed transformation matrix currently in effect using the PRINT subcommand.

Optional Output. You can request or suppress output on the PRINT and NOPRINT subcommands. Additional output appropriate to multivariate analysis includes error term matrices, Box's M statistic, multivariate and univariate F tests, and other significance analyses. You can also request predicted cell means for specific dependent variables on the PMEANS subcommand, produce a canonical discriminant analysis for each effect in your model with the DISCRIM subcommand, specify a principal components analysis of each error sum-of-squares and cross-product matrix in a multivariate analysis on the PCOMPS subcommand, display multivariate confidence intervals using the CINTERVAL subcommand, and generate a half-normal plot of the within-cells correlations among the dependent variables with the PLOT subcommand.

Basic Specification

- The basic specification is a variable list identifying the dependent variables, with the factors (if any) named after BY and the covariates (if any) named after WITH.
- By default, MANOVA produces multivariate and univariate F tests.

Subcommand Order

- The variable list must be specified first.
- Subcommands applicable to a specific design must be specified before that DESIGN subcommand. Otherwise, subcommands can be used in any order.

Syntax Rules

- All syntax rules applicable to univariate analysis apply to multivariate analysis. See "Syntax Rules" on p. 652 in MANOVA: Univariate.

- If you enter one of the multivariate specifications in a univariate analysis, MANOVA ignores it.

Limitations

- Maximum 20 factors.
- Memory requirements depend primarily on the number of cells in the design. For the default full factorial model, this equals the product of the number of levels or categories in each factor.

MANOVA Variable List

- Multivariate MANOVA calculates statistical tests that are valid for analyses of dependent variables that are correlated with one another. The dependent variables must be specified first.
- The factor and covariate lists follow the same rules as in univariate analyses.
- If the dependent variables are uncorrelated, the univariate significance tests have greater statistical power.

TRANSFORM Subcommand

TRANSFORM performs linear transformations of some or all of the continuous variables (dependent variables and covariates). Specifications on TRANSFORM include an optional list of variables to be transformed, optional keywords to describe how to generate a transformation matrix from the specified contrasts, and a required keyword specifying the transformation contrasts.

- Transformations apply to all subsequent designs unless replaced by another TRANSFORM subcommand.
- TRANSFORM subcommands are not cumulative. Only the transformation specified most recently is in effect at any time. You can restore the original variables in later designs by specifying SPECIAL with an identity matrix.
- You should not use TRANSFORM when you use the WSFACTORS subcommand to request repeated measures analysis; a transformation is automatically performed in repeated measures analysis (see MANOVA: Repeated Measures).
- Transformations are in effect for the duration of the MANOVA procedure only. After the procedure is complete, the original variables remain in the working data file.
- By default, the transformation matrix is not displayed. Specify the keyword TRANSFORM on the PRINT subcommand to see the matrix generated by the TRANSFORM subcommand.
- If you do not use the RENAME subcommand with TRANSFORM, the variables specified on TRANSFORM are renamed temporarily (for the duration of the procedure) as *T1*, *T2*, etc. Explicit use of RENAME is recommended.
- Subsequent references to transformed variables should use the new names. The only exception is when you supply a VARIABLES specification on the OMEANS subcommand af-

ter using TRANSFORM. In this case, specify the original names. OMEANS displays observed means of original variables (see the OMEANS subcommand on p. 662 in MANOVA: Univariate).

Variable Lists

- By default, MANOVA applies the transformation you request to all continuous variables (dependent variables and covariates).

- You can enter a variable list in parentheses following the TRANSFORM subcommand. If you do, only the listed variables are transformed.

- You can enter multiple variable lists, separated by slashes, within a single set of parentheses. Each list must have the same number of variables, and the lists must not overlap. The transformation is applied separately to the variables on each list.

- In designs with covariates, transform only the dependent variables, or, in some designs, apply the same transformation separately to the dependent variables and the covariates.

CONTRAST, BASIS, and ORTHONORM Keywords

You can control how the transformation matrix is to be generated from the specified contrasts. If none of these three keywords is specified on TRANSFORM, the default is CONTRAST.

CONTRAST   *Generate the transformation matrix directly from the contrast matrix speci-fied* (see the CONTRAST subcommand on p. 654 in MANOVA: Univariate). This is the default.

BASIS   *Generate the transformation matrix from the one-way basis matrix corre-sponding to the specified contrast matrix.* BASIS makes a difference only if the transformation contrasts are not orthogonal.

ORTHONORM   *Orthonormalize the transformation matrix by rows before use.* MANOVA eliminates redundant rows. By default, orthonormalization is not done.

- CONTRAST and BASIS are alternatives and are mutually exclusive.

- ORTHONORM is independent of the CONTRAST/BASIS choice; you can enter it before or after either of those keywords.

Transformation Methods

To specify a transformation method, use one of the following keywords available on the TRANSFORM subcommand. Note that these are identical to the keywords available for the CONTRAST subcommand (see the CONTRAST subcommand on p. 654 in MANOVA: Univariate). However, in univariate designs, they are applied to the different levels of a factor. Here they are applied to the continuous variables in the analysis. This reflects the fact that the different dependent variables in a multivariate MANOVA setup can often be thought of as corresponding to different levels of some factor.

- The transformation keyword (and its specifications, if any) must follow all other specifi-cations on the TRANSFORM subcommand.

DEVIATION   *Deviations from the mean of the variables being transformed.* The first transformed variable is the mean of all variables in the transformation. Other transformed variables represent deviations of individual variables from the mean. One of the original variables (by default the last) is omitted as redundant. To omit a variable other than the last, specify the number of the variable to be omitted in parentheses after the DEVIATION keyword. For example,

```
/TRANSFORM (A B C) = DEVIATION(1)
```

omits *A* and creates variables representing the mean, the deviation of *B* from the mean, and the deviation of *C* from the mean. A DEVIATION transformation is not orthogonal.

DIFFERENCE   *Difference or reverse Helmert transformation.* The first transformed variable is the mean of the original variables. Each of the original variables except the first is then transformed by subtracting the mean of those (original) variables that precede it. A DIFFERENCE transformation is orthogonal.

HELMERT   *Helmert transformation.* The first transformed variable is the mean of the original variables. Each of the original variables except the last is then transformed by subtracting the mean of those (original) variables that follow it. A HELMERT transformation is orthogonal.

SIMPLE   *Each original variable, except the last, is compared to the last of the original variables.* To use a variable other than the last as the omitted reference variable, specify its number in parentheses following the keyword SIMPLE. For example,

```
/TRANSFORM(A B C) = SIMPLE(2)
```

specifies the second variable, *B*, as the reference variable. The three transformed variables represent the mean of *A*, *B*, and *C*, the difference between *A* and *B*, and the difference between *C* and *B*. A SIMPLE transformation is not orthogonal.

POLYNOMIAL   *Orthogonal polynomial transformation.* The first transformed variable represents the mean of the original variables. Other transformed variables represent the linear, quadratic, and higher-degree components. By default, values of the original variables are assumed to represent equally spaced points. You can specify unequal spacing by entering a metric consisting of one integer for each variable in parentheses after the keyword POLYNOMIAL. For example,

```
/TRANSFORM(RESP1 RESP2 RESP3) = POLYNOMIAL(1,2,4)
```

might indicate that three response variables correspond to levels of some stimulus that are in the proportion 1:2:4. The default metric is always $(1,2,...,k)$, where k variables are involved. Only the relative differences between the terms of the metric matter: (1,2,4) is the same metric as (2,3,5) or (20,30,50) because in each instance the difference between the second and third numbers is twice the difference between the first and second.

REPEATED   *Comparison of adjacent variables.* The first transformed variable is the mean of the original variables. Each additional transformed variable is the difference between one of the original variables and the original variable that followed it. Such transformed variables are often called *difference scores*. A REPEATED transformation is not orthogonal.

SPECIAL   *A user-defined transformation.* After the keyword SPECIAL, enter a square matrix in parentheses with as many rows and columns as there are variables to transform. MANOVA multiplies this matrix by the vector of original variables to obtain the transformed variables (see the examples below).

Example

```
MANOVA X1 TO X3 BY A(1,4)
  /TRANSFORM(X1 X2 X3) = SPECIAL( 1  1  1,
                                  1  0 -1,
                                  2 -1 -1)
  /DESIGN.
```

- The given matrix will be post-multiplied by the three continuous variables (considered as a column vector) to yield the transformed variables. The first transformed variable will therefore equal $X1 + X2 + X3$, the second will equal $X1 - X3$, and the third will equal $2X1 - X2 - X3$.

- The variable list is optional in this example since all three interval-level variables are transformed.

- You do not need to enter the matrix one row at a time, as shown above. For example,

```
  /TRANSFORM = SPECIAL(1 1 1 1 0 -1 2 -1 -1)
```

is equivalent to the TRANSFORM specification in the above example.

- You can specify a repetition factor followed by an asterisk to indicate multiple consecutive elements of a SPECIAL transformation matrix. For example,

```
  /TRANSFORM = SPECIAL (4*1 0 -1 2 2*-1)
```

is again equivalent to the TRANSFORM specification above.

Example

```
MANOVA X1 TO X3, Y1 TO Y3 BY A(1,4)
  /TRANSFORM (X1 X2 X3/Y1 Y2 Y3) = SPECIAL( 1  1  1,
                                            1  0 -1,
                                            2 -1 -1)
  /DESIGN.
```

- Here the same transformation shown in the previous example is applied to *X1*, *X2*, *X3* and to *Y1*, *Y2*, *Y3*.

RENAME Subcommand

Use RENAME to assign new names to transformed variables. Renaming variables after a transformation is strongly recommended. If you transform but do not rename the variables, the names *T1*, *T2*,...,*Tn* are used as names for the transformed variables.

- Follow RENAME with a list of new variable names.

- You must enter a new name for each dependent variable and covariate on the MANOVA variable list.

- Enter the new names in the order in which the original variables appeared on the MANOVA variable list.

- To retain the original name for one or more of the interval variables, you can either enter an asterisk or reenter the old name as the new name.

- References to dependent variables and covariates on subcommands following RENAME must use the new names. The original names will not be recognized within the MANOVA procedure. The only exception is the OMEANS subcommand, which displays observed means of the original (untransformed) variables. Use the original names on OMEANS.

- The new names exist only during the MANOVA procedure that created them. They do not remain in the working data file after the procedure is complete.

Example

```
MANOVA A, B, C, V4, V5 BY TREATMNT(1,3)
   /TRANSFORM(A, B, C) = REPEATED
   /RENAME = MEANABC, AMINUSB, BMINUSC, *, *
   /DESIGN.
```

- The REPEATED transformation produces three transformed variables, which are then assigned mnemonic names *MEANABC*, *AMINUSB*, and *BMINUSC*.

- *V4* and *V5* retain their original names.

Example

```
MANOVA WT1, WT2, WT3, WT4 BY TREATMNT(1,3) WITH COV
   /TRANSFORM (WT1 TO WT4) = POLYNOMIAL
   /RENAME = MEAN, LINEAR, QUAD, CUBIC, *
   /ANALYSIS = MEAN, LINEAR, QUAD WITH COV
   /DESIGN.
```

- After the polynomial transformation of the four *WT* variables, RENAME assigns appropriate names to the various trends.

- Even though only four variables were transformed, RENAME applies to all five continuous variables. An asterisk is required to retain the original name for *COV*.

- The ANALYSIS subcommand following RENAME refers to the interval variables by their new names.

PRINT and NOPRINT Subcommands

All of the PRINT specifications described in MANOVA: Univariate are available in multivariate analyses. The following additional output can be requested. To suppress any optional output, specify the appropriate keyword on NOPRINT.

ERROR   *Error matrices.* Three types of matrices are available.

SIGNIF   *Significance tests.*

TRANSFORM   *Transformation matrix.* It is available if you have transformed the dependent variables with the TRANSFORM subcommand.

HOMOGENEITY   *Test for homogeneity of variance.* BOXM is available for multivariate analyses.

ERROR Keyword

In multivariate analysis, error terms consist of entire matrices, not single values. You can display any of the following error matrices on a PRINT subcommand by requesting them in parentheses following the keyword ERROR. If you specify ERROR by itself, without further specifications, the default is to display COV and COR.

SSCP   *Error sums-of-squares and cross-products matrix.*

COV   *Error variance-covariance matrix.*

COR   *Error correlation matrix with standard deviations on the diagonal.* This also displays the determinant of the matrix and Bartlett's test of sphericity, a test of whether the error correlation matrix is significantly different from an identity matrix.

SIGNIF Keyword

You can request any of the optional output listed below by entering the appropriate specification in parentheses after the keyword SIGNIF on the PRINT subcommand. Further specifications for SIGNIF are described in MANOVA: Repeated Measures.

MULTIV   *Multivariate* F *tests for group differences.* MULTIV is always printed unless explicitly suppressed with the NOPRINT subcommand.

EIGEN   *Eigenvalues of the $S_h S_e^{-1}$ matrix.* This matrix is the product of the hypothesis sums-of-squares and cross-products (SSCP) matrix and the inverse of the error SSCP matrix. To print EIGEN, request it on the PRINT subcommand.

DIMENR   *A dimension-reduction analysis.* To print DIMENR, request it on the PRINT subcommand.

UNIV   *Univariate* F *tests.* UNIV is always printed except in repeated measures analysis. If the dependent variables are uncorrelated, univariate tests have greater statistical power. To suppress UNIV, use the NOPRINT subcommand.

HYPOTH   *The hypothesis SSCP matrix.* To print HYPOTH, request it on the PRINT subcommand.

STEPDOWN   *Roy-Bargmann stepdown* F *tests.* To print STEPDOWN, request it on the PRINT subcommand.

BRIEF   *Abbreviated multivariate output.* This is similar to a univariate analysis of variance table but with Wilks' multivariate *F* approximation (lambda) replacing the univariate *F*. BRIEF overrides any of the SIGNIF specifications listed above.

SINGLEDF   *Significance tests for the single degree of freedom making up each effect for ANOVA tables.* Results are displayed separately corresponding to each hypothesis degree of freedom. See MANOVA: Univariate.

- If neither PRINT nor NOPRINT is specified, MANOVA displays the results corresponding to MULTIV and UNIV for a multivariate analysis not involving repeated measures.
- If you enter any specification except BRIEF or SINGLEDF for SIGNIF on the PRINT subcommand, the requested output is displayed in addition to the default.
- To suppress the default, specify the keyword(s) on the NOPRINT subcommand.

TRANSFORM Keyword

The keyword TRANSFORM specified on PRINT displays the transposed transformation matrix in use for each subsequent design. This matrix is helpful in interpreting a multivariate analysis in which the interval-level variables have been transformed with either TRANSFORM or WSFACTORS.

- The matrix displayed by this option is the transpose of the transformation matrix.
- Original variables correspond to the rows of the matrix, and transformed variables correspond to the columns.
- A **transformed variable** is a linear combination of the original variables using the coefficients displayed in the column corresponding to that transformed variable.

HOMOGENEITY Keyword

In addition to the BARTLETT and COCHRAN specifications described in MANOVA: Univariate, the following test for homogeneity is available for multivariate analyses:

BOXM   *Box's M statistic.* BOXM requires at least two dependent variables. If there is only one dependent variable when BOXM is requested, MANOVA prints Bartlett-Box *F* test statistic and issues a note.

PLOT Subcommand

In addition to the plots described in MANOVA: Univariate, the following is available for multivariate analyses:

ZCORR   *A half-normal plot of the within-cells correlations among the dependent variables.* MANOVA first transforms the correlations using Fisher's Z transformation. If errors for the dependent variables are uncorrelated, the plotted points should lie close to a straight line.

PCOMPS Subcommand

PCOMPS requests a principal components analysis of each error matrix in a multivariate analysis. You can display the principal components of the error correlation matrix, the error variance-covariance matrix, or both. These principal components are corrected for differences due to the factors and covariates in the MANOVA analysis. They tend to be more useful than principal components extracted from the raw correlation or covariance matrix when there are significant group differences between the levels of the factors or when a significant amount of error variance is accounted for by the covariates. You can specify any of the keywords listed below on PCOMPS.

COR   *Principal components analysis of the error correlation matrix.*

COV   *Principal components analysis of the error variance-covariance matrix.*

ROTATE   *Rotate the principal components solution.* By default, no rotation is performed. Specify a rotation type (either VARIMAX, EQUAMAX, or QUARTIMAX) in parentheses after the keyword ROTATE. To cancel a rotation specified for a previous design, enter NOROTATE in the parentheses after ROTATE.

NCOMP(n)   *The number of principal components to rotate.* Specify a number in parentheses. The default is the number of dependent variables.

MINEIGEN(n) *The minimum eigenvalue for principal component extraction.* Specify a cutoff value in parentheses. Components with eigenvalues below the cutoff will not be retained in the solution. The default is 0; all components (or the number specified on NCOMP) are extracted.

ALL   *COR, COV, and ROTATE.*

- You must specify either COR or COV (or both). Otherwise, MANOVA will not produce any principal components.

- Both NCOMP and MINEIGEN limit the number of components that are rotated.

- If the number specified on NCOMP is less than two, two components are rotated provided that at least two components have eigenvalues greater than any value specified on MINEIGEN.

- Principal components analysis is computationally expensive if the number of dependent variables is large.

DISCRIM Subcommand

DISCRIM produces a canonical discriminant analysis for each effect in a design. (For covariates, DISCRIM produces a canonical correlation analysis.) These analyses aid in the interpretation of multivariate effects. You can request the following statistics by entering the appropriate keywords after the subcommand DISCRIM:

RAW   *Raw discriminant function coefficients.*

STAN   *Standardized discriminant function coefficients.*

ESTIM   *Effect estimates in discriminant function space.*

COR   *Correlations between the dependent variables and the canonical variables defined by the discriminant functions.*

ROTATE *Rotation of the matrix of correlations between dependent and canonical variables.* Specify rotation type VARIMAX, EQUAMAX, or QUARTIMAX in parentheses after this keyword.

ALL *RAW, STAN, ESTIM, COR, and ROTATE.*

By default, the significance level required for the extraction of a canonical variable is 0.25. You can change this value by specifying the keyword ALPHA and a value between 0 and 1 in parentheses:

ALPHA *The significance level required before a canonical variable is extracted.* The default is 0.25. To change the default, specify a decimal number between 0 and 1 in parentheses after ALPHA.

- The correlations between dependent variables and canonical functions are not rotated unless at least two functions are significant at the level defined by ALPHA.
- If you set ALPHA to 1.0, all discriminant functions are reported (and rotated, if you so request).
- If you set ALPHA to 0, no discriminant functions are reported.

POWER Subcommand

The following specifications are available for POWER in multivariate analysis. For applications of POWER in univariate analysis, see MANOVA: Univariate.

APPROXIMATE *Approximate power values.* This is the default. Approximate power values for multivariate tests are derived from procedures presented by Muller and Peterson (1984). Approximate values are normally accurate to three decimal places and are much cheaper to compute than exact values.

EXACT *Exact power values.* Exact power values for multivariate tests are computed from the noncentral F distribution. Exact multivariate power values will be displayed only if there is one hypothesis degree of freedom, where all the multivariate criteria have identical power.

- For information on the multivariate generalizations of power and effect size, see Muller and Peterson (1984), Green (1978), and Huberty (1972).

CINTERVAL Subcommand

In addition to the specifications described in MANOVA: Univariate, the keyword MULTIVARIATE is available for multivariate analysis. You can specify a type in parentheses after the MULTIVARIATE keyword. The following type keywords are available on MULTIVARIATE:

ROY *Roy's largest root.* An approximation given by Pillai (1967) is used. This approximation is accurate for upper percentage points (0.95 to 1), but it is not as good for lower percentage points. Thus, for Roy intervals, the user is restricted to the range 0.95 to 1.

PILLAI *Pillai's trace.* The intervals are computed by approximating the percentage points with percentage points of the F distribution.

WILKS   *Wilks' lambda.* The intervals are computed by approximating the percentage points with percentage points of the *F* distribution.

HOTELLING   *Hotelling's trace.* The intervals are computed by approximating the percentage points with percentage points of the *F* distribution.

BONFER   *Bonferroni intervals.* This approximation is based on Student's *t* distribution.

- The Wilks', Pillai's, and Hotelling's approximate confidence intervals are thought to match exact intervals across a wide range of alpha levels, especially for large sample sizes (Burns, 1984). Use of these intervals, however, has not been widely investigated.

- To obtain multivariate intervals separately for each parameter, choose individual multivariate intervals. For individual multivariate confidence intervals, the hypothesis degree of freedom is set to 1, in which case Hotelling's, Pillai's, Wilks', and Roy's intervals will be identical and equivalent to those computed from percentage points of Hotelling's T^2 distribution. Individual Bonferroni intervals will differ and, for a small number of dependent variables, will generally be shorter.

- If you specify MULTIVARIATE on CINTERVAL, you must specify a type keyword. If you specify CINTERVAL without any keyword, the default is the same as with univariate analysis—CINTERVAL displays individual-univariate confidence intervals at the 0.95 level.

ANALYSIS Subcommand

ANALYSIS is discussed in MANOVA: Univariate as a means of obtaining factor-by-covariate interaction terms. In multivariate analyses, it is considerably more useful.

- ANALYSIS specifies a subset of the continuous variables (dependent variables and covariates) listed on the MANOVA variable list and completely redefines which variables are dependent and which are covariates.

- All variables named on an ANALYSIS subcommand must have been named on the MANOVA variable list. It does not matter whether they were named as dependent variables or as covariates.

- Factors cannot be named on an ANALYSIS subcommand.

- After the keyword ANALYSIS, specify the names of one or more dependent variables and, optionally, the keyword WITH followed by one or more covariates.

- An ANALYSIS specification remains in effect for all designs until you enter another ANALYSIS subcommand.

- Continuous variables named on the MANOVA variable list but omitted from the ANALYSIS subcommand currently in effect can be specified on the DESIGN subcommand. See the DESIGN subcommand on p. 669 in MANOVA: Univariate.

- You can use an ANALYSIS subcommand to request analyses of several groups of variables provided that the groups do not overlap. Separate the groups of variables with slashes and enclose the entire ANALYSIS specification in parentheses.

CONDITIONAL and UNCONDITIONAL Keywords

When several analysis groups are specified on a single ANALYSIS subcommand, you can control how each list is to be processed by specifying CONDITIONAL or UNCONDITIONAL in the parentheses immediately following the ANALYSIS subcommand. The default is UNCONDITIONAL.

UNCONDITIONAL   *Process each analysis group separately, without regard to other lists. This is the default.*

CONDITIONAL   *Use variables specified in one analysis group as covariates in subsequent analysis groups.*

- CONDITIONAL analysis is not carried over from one ANALYSIS subcommand to another.
- You can specify a final covariate list outside the parentheses. These covariates apply to every list within the parentheses, regardless of whether you specify CONDITIONAL or UNCONDITIONAL. The variables on this global covariate list must not be specified in any individual lists.

Example

```
MANOVA A B C BY FAC(1,4) WITH D, E
  /ANALYSIS = (A, B / C / D WITH E)
  /DESIGN.
```

- The first analysis uses *A* and *B* as dependent variables and uses no covariates.
- The second analysis uses *C* as a dependent variable and uses no covariates.
- The third analysis uses *D* as the dependent variable and uses *E* as a covariate.

Example

```
MANOVA A, B, C, D, E BY FAC(1,4) WITH F G
  /ANALYSIS = (A, B / C / D WITH E) WITH F G
  /DESIGN.
```

- A final covariate list WITH F G is specified outside the parentheses. The covariates apply to every list within the parentheses.
- The first analysis uses *A* and *B*, with *F* and *G* as covariates.
- The second analysis uses *C*, with *F* and *G* as covariates.
- The third analysis uses *D*, with *E*, *F*, and *G* as covariates.
- Factoring out *F* and *G* is the only way to use them as covariates in all three analyses, since no variable can be named more than once on an ANALYSIS subcommand.

Example

```
MANOVA A B C BY FAC(1,3)
  /ANALYSIS(CONDITIONAL) = (A WITH B / C)
  /DESIGN.
```

- In the first analysis, *A* is the dependent variable, *B* is a covariate, and *C* is not used.
- In the second analysis, *C* is the dependent variable, and both *A* and *B* are covariates.

MANOVA: Repeated Measures

MANOVA is available in the Advanced Models option.

```
MANOVA dependent varlist [BY factor list (min,max)[factor list...]
        [WITH [varying covariate list] [(constant covariate list)]]

  /WSFACTORS = varname (levels) [varname...]

[/WSDESIGN = [effect effect...]

[/MEASURE = newname newname...]

[/RENAME = newname newname...]

[/{PRINT  }=[SIGNIF({AVERF**}) (HF) (GG) (EFSIZE)]]
  {NOPRINT}         {AVONLY }

[/DESIGN]*
```

* The DESIGN subcommand has the same syntax as is described in MANOVA: Univariate.

** Default if subcommand or keyword is omitted.

Example
```
MANOVA Y1 TO Y4 BY GROUP(1,2)
  /WSFACTORS=YEAR(4).
```

Overview

This section discusses the subcommands that are used in repeated measures designs, in which the dependent variables represent measurements of the same variable (or variables) at different times. This section does not contain information on all subcommands you will need to specify the design. For some subcommands or keywords not covered here, such as DESIGN, see MANOVA: Univariate. For information on optional output and the multivariate significance tests available, see MANOVA: Multivariate.

- In a simple repeated measures analysis, all dependent variables represent different measurements of the same variable for different values (or levels) of a within-subjects factor. Between-subjects factors and covariates can also be included in the model, just as in analyses not involving repeated measures.

- A **within-subjects factor** is simply a factor that distinguishes measurements made on the same subject or case, rather than distinguishing different subjects or cases.

- MANOVA permits more complex analyses, in which the dependent variables represent levels of two or more within-subjects factors.

- MANOVA also permits analyses in which the dependent variables represent measurements of several variables for the different levels of the within-subjects factors. These are known as **doubly multivariate designs**.

- A repeated measures analysis includes a within-subjects design describing the model to be tested with the within-subjects factors, as well as the usual between-subjects design

688

- describing the effects to be tested with between-subjects factors. The default for both types of design is a full factorial model.
- MANOVA always performs an orthonormal transformation of the dependent variables in a repeated measures analysis. By default, MANOVA renames them as *T1*, *T2*, and so forth.

Basic Specification

- The basic specification is a variable list followed by the WSFACTORS subcommand.
- By default, MANOVA performs special repeated measures processing. Default output includes SIGNIF(AVERF) but not SIGNIF(UNIV). In addition, for any within-subjects effect involving more than one transformed variable, the Mauchly test of sphericity is displayed to test the assumption that the covariance matrix of the transformed variables is constant on the diagonal and zero off the diagonal. The Greenhouse-Geiser epsilon and the Huynh-Feldt epsilon are also displayed for use in correcting the significance tests in the event that the assumption of sphericity is violated.

Subcommand Order

- The list of dependent variables, factors, and covariates must be first.
- WSFACTORS must be the first subcommand used after the variable list.

Syntax Rules

- The WSFACTORS (within-subjects factors), WSDESIGN (within-subjects design), and MEASURE subcommands are used only in repeated measures analysis.
- WSFACTORS is required for any repeated measures analysis.
- If WSDESIGN is not specified, a full factorial within-subjects design consisting of all main effects and interactions among within-subjects factors is used by default.
- The MEASURE subcommand is used for doubly multivariate designs, in which the dependent variables represent repeated measurements of more than one variable.
- Do not use the TRANSFORM subcommand with the WSFACTORS subcommand because WSFACTORS automatically causes an orthonormal transformation of the dependent variables.

Limitations

- Maximum 20 between-subjects factors. There is no limit on the number of measures for doubly multivariate designs.
- Memory requirements depend primarily on the number of cells in the design. For the default full factorial model, this equals the product of the number of levels or categories in each factor.

Example

```
MANOVA Y1 TO Y4 BY GROUP(1,2)
  /WSFACTORS=YEAR(4)
  /CONTRAST(YEAR)=POLYNOMIAL
  /RENAME=CONST, LINEAR, QUAD, CUBIC
  /PRINT=TRANSFORM PARAM(ESTIM)
  /WSDESIGN=YEAR
  /DESIGN=GROUP.
```

- WSFACTORS immediately follows the MANOVA variable list and specifies a repeated measures analysis in which the four dependent variables represent a single variable measured at four levels of the within-subjects factor. The within-subjects factor is called *YEAR* for the duration of the MANOVA procedure.

- CONTRAST requests polynomial contrasts for the levels of *YEAR*. Because the four variables, *Y1*, *Y2*, *Y3*, and *Y4*, in the working data file represent the four levels of *YEAR*, the effect is to perform an orthonormal polynomial transformation of these variables.

- RENAME assigns names to the dependent variables to reflect the transformation.

- PRINT requests that the transformation matrix and the parameter estimates be displayed.

- WSDESIGN specifies a within-subjects design that includes only the effect of the *YEAR* within-subjects factor. Because *YEAR* is the only within-subjects factor specified, this is the default design, and WSDESIGN could have been omitted.

- DESIGN specifies a between-subjects design that includes only the effect of the *GROUP* between-subjects factor. This subcommand could have been omitted.

MANOVA Variable List

The list of dependent variables, factors, and covariates must be specified first.

- WSFACTORS determines how the dependent variables on the MANOVA variable list will be interpreted.

- The number of dependent variables on the MANOVA variable list must be a multiple of the number of cells in the within-subjects design. If there are six cells in the within-subjects design, each group of six dependent variables represents a single within-subjects variable that has been measured in each of the six cells.

- Normally, the number of dependent variables should equal the number of cells in the within-subjects design multiplied by the number of variables named on the MEASURE subcommand (if one is used). If you have more groups of dependent variables than are accounted for by the MEASURE subcommand, MANOVA will choose variable names to label the output, which may be difficult to interpret.

- Covariates are specified after the keyword WITH. You can specify either varying covariates or constant covariates, or both. **Varying covariates**, similar to dependent variables in a repeated measures analysis, represent measurements of the same variable (or variables) at different times while **constant covariates** represent variables whose values remain the same at each within-subjects measurement.

- If you use varying covariates, the number of covariates specified must be an integer multiple of the number of dependent variables.

- If you use constant covariates, you must specify them in parentheses. If you use both constant and varying covariates, constant variates must be specified after all varying covariates.

Example

```
MANOVA MATH1 TO MATH4 BY METHOD(1,2) WITH PHYS1 TO PHYS4 (SES)
   /WSFACTORS=SEMESTER(4).
```

- The four dependent variables represent a score measured four times (corresponding to the four levels of *SEMESTER*).
- The four varying covariates *PHYS1* to *PHYS4* represents four measurements of another score.
- *SES* is a constant covariate. Its value does not change over the time covered by the four levels of *SEMESTER*.
- Default contrast (POLYNOMIAL) is used.

WSFACTORS Subcommand

WSFACTORS names the within-subjects factors and specifies the number of levels for each.

- For repeated measures designs, WSFACTORS must be the first subcommand after the MANOVA variable list.
- Only one WSFACTORS subcommand is permitted per execution of MANOVA.
- Names for the within-subjects factors are specified on the WSFACTORS subcommand. Factor names must not duplicate any of the dependent variables, factors, or covariates named on the MANOVA variable list.
- If there are more than one within-subjects factors, they must be named in the order corresponding to the order of the dependent variables on the MANOVA variable list. MANOVA varies the levels of the last-named within-subjects factor most rapidly when assigning dependent variables to within-subjects cells (see the example below).
- Levels of the factors must be represented in the data by the dependent variables named on the MANOVA variable list.
- Enter a number in parentheses after each factor to indicate how many levels the factor has. If two or more adjacent factors have the same number of levels, you can enter the number of levels in parentheses after all of them.
- Enter only the number of levels for within-subjects factors, not a range of values.
- The number of cells in the within-subjects design is the product of the number of levels for all within-subjects factors.

Example

```
MANOVA X1Y1 X1Y2 X2Y1 X2Y2 X3Y1 X3Y2 BY TREATMNT(1,5) GROUP(1,2)
   /WSFACTORS=X(3) Y(2)
   /DESIGN.
```

- The MANOVA variable list names six dependent variables and two between-subjects factors, *TREATMNT* and *GROUP*.

- WSFACTORS identifies two within-subjects factors whose levels distinguish the six dependent variables. *X* has three levels and *Y* has two. Thus, there are $3 \times 2 = 6$ cells in the within-subjects design, corresponding to the six dependent variables.
- Variable *X1Y1* corresponds to levels 1,1 of the two within-subjects factors; variable *X1Y2* corresponds to levels 1,2; *X2Y1* to levels 2,1; and so on up to *X3Y2*, which corresponds to levels 3,2. The first within-subjects factor named, *X*, varies most slowly, and the last within-subjects factor named, *Y*, varies most rapidly on the list of dependent variables.
- Because there is no WSDESIGN subcommand, the within-subjects design will include all main effects and interactions: *X*, *Y*, and *X* by *Y*.
- Likewise, the between-subjects design includes all main effects and interactions: *TREATMNT*, *GROUP*, and *TREATMNT* by *GROUP*.
- In addition, a repeated measures analysis always includes interactions between the within-subjects factors and the between-subjects factors. There are three such interactions for each of the three within-subjects effects.

CONTRAST for WSFACTORS

The levels of a within-subjects factor are represented by different dependent variables. Therefore, contrasts between levels of such a factor compare these dependent variables. Specifying the type of contrast amounts to specifying a transformation to be performed on the dependent variables.

- An orthonormal transformation is automatically performed on the dependent variables in a repeated measures analysis.
- To specify the type of orthonormal transformation, use the CONTRAST subcommand for the within-subjects factors.
- Regardless of the contrast type you specify, the transformation matrix is orthonormalized before use.
- If you do not specify a contrast type for within-subjects factors, the default contrast type is orthogonal POLYNOMIAL. Intrinsically orthogonal contrast types are recommended for within-subjects factors if you wish to examine each degree-of-freedom test. Other orthogonal contrast types are DIFFERENCE and HELMERT. MULTIV and AVERF tests are identical, no matter what contrast was specified.
- To perform non-orthogonal contrasts, you must use the TRANSFORM subcommand instead of CONTRAST. The TRANSFORM subcommand is discussed in MANOVA: Multivariate.
- When you implicitly request a transformation of the dependent variables with CONTRAST for within-subjects factors, the same transformation is applied to any covariates in the analysis. The number of covariates must be an integer multiple of the number of dependent variables.
- You can display the transpose of the transformation matrix generated by your within-subjects contrast using the keyword TRANSFORM on the PRINT subcommand.

Example

```
MANOVA SCORE1 SCORE2 SCORE3 BY GROUP(1,4)
  /WSFACTORS=ROUND(3)
  /CONTRAST(ROUND)=DIFFERENCE
  /CONTRAST(GROUP)=DEVIATION
  /PRINT=TRANSFORM PARAM(ESTIM).
```

- This analysis has one between-subjects factor, *GROUP*, with levels 1, 2, 3, and 4, and one within-subjects factor, *ROUND*, with three levels that are represented by the three dependent variables.

- The first CONTRAST subcommand specifies difference contrasts for *ROUND*, the within-subjects factor.

- There is no WSDESIGN subcommand, so a default full factorial within-subjects design is assumed. This could also have been specified as WSDESIGN=ROUND, or simply WSDESIGN.

- The second CONTRAST subcommand specifies deviation contrasts for *GROUP*, the between-subjects factor. This subcommand could have been omitted because deviation contrasts are the default.

- PRINT requests the display of the transformation matrix generated by the within-subjects contrast and the parameter estimates for the model.

- There is no DESIGN subcommand, so a default full factorial between-subjects design is assumed. This could also have been specified as DESIGN=GROUP, or simply DESIGN.

PARTITION for WSFACTORS

The PARTITION subcommand also applies to factors named on WSFACTORS. (See the PARTITION subcommand on p. 656 in MANOVA: Univariate.)

WSDESIGN Subcommand

WSDESIGN specifies the design for within-subjects factors. Its specifications are like those of the DESIGN subcommand, but it uses the within-subjects factors rather than the between-subjects factors.

- The default WSDESIGN is a full factorial design, which includes all main effects and all interactions for within-subjects factors. The default is in effect whenever a design is processed without a preceding WSDESIGN or when the preceding WSDESIGN subcommand has no specifications.

- A WSDESIGN specification can include main effects, factor-by-factor interactions, nested terms (term within term), terms using the keyword MWITHIN, and pooled effects using the plus sign. The specification is the same as on the DESIGN subcommand but involves only within-subjects factors.

- A WSDESIGN specification cannot include between-subjects factors or terms based on them, nor does it accept interval-level variables, the keywords MUPLUS or CONSTANT, or error-term definitions or references.

- The WSDESIGN specification applies to all subsequent within-subjects designs until another WSDESIGN subcommand is encountered.

Example

```
MANOVA JANLO,JANHI,FEBLO,FEBHI,MARLO,MARHI BY SEX(1,2)
  /WSFACTORS MONTH(3) STIMULUS(2)
  /WSDESIGN MONTH, STIMULUS
  /WSDESIGN
  /DESIGN SEX.
```

- There are six dependent variables, corresponding to three months and two different levels of stimulus.

- The dependent variables are named on the MANOVA variable list in such an order that the level of stimulus varies more rapidly than the month. Thus, *STIMULUS* is named last on the WSFACTORS subcommand.

- The first WSDESIGN subcommand specifies only the main effects for within-subjects factors. There is no *MONTH* by *STIMULUS* interaction term.

- The second WSDESIGN subcommand has no specifications and, therefore, invokes the default within-subjects design, which includes the main effects and their interaction.

MWITHIN Keyword for Simple Effects

You can use MWITHIN on either the WSDESIGN or the DESIGN subcommand in a model with both between- and within-subjects factors to estimate simple effects for factors nested within factors of the opposite type.

Example

```
MANOVA WEIGHT1 WEIGHT2 BY TREAT(1,2)
 /WSFACTORS=WEIGHT(2)
 /DESIGN=MWITHIN TREAT(1) MWITHIN TREAT(2)
MANOVA WEIGHT1 WEIGHT2 BY TREAT(1,2)
 /WSFACTORS=WEIGHT(2)
 /WSDESIGN=MWITHIN WEIGHT(1) MWITHIN WEIGHT(2)
 /DESIGN.
```

- The first DESIGN tests the simple effects of *WEIGHT* within each level of *TREAT*.

- The second DESIGN tests the simple effects of *TREAT* within each level of *WEIGHT*.

MEASURE Subcommand

In a doubly multivariate analysis, the dependent variables represent multiple variables measured under the different levels of the within-subjects factors. Use MEASURE to assign names to the variables that you have measured for the different levels of within-subjects factors.

- Specify a list of one or more variable names to be used in labeling the averaged results. If no within-subjects factor has more than two levels, MEASURE has no effect.

- The number of dependent variables on the DESIGN subcommand should equal the product of the number of cells in the within-subjects design and the number of names on MEASURE.

- If you do not enter a MEASURE subcommand and there are more dependent variables than cells in the within-subjects design, MANOVA assigns names (normally *MEAS.1*, *MEAS.2*, etc.) to the different measures.

- All of the dependent variables corresponding to each measure should be listed together and ordered so that the within-subjects factor named last on the WSFACTORS subcommand varies most rapidly.

Example

```
MANOVA TEMP1 TO TEMP6, WEIGHT1 TO WEIGHT6 BY GROUP(1,2)
  /WSFACTORS=DAY(3) AMPM(2)
  /MEASURE=TEMP WEIGHT
  /WSDESIGN=DAY, AMPM, DAY BY AMPM
  /PRINT=SIGNIF(HYPOTH AVERF)
  /DESIGN.
```

- There are 12 dependent variables: 6 temperatures and 6 weights, corresponding to morning and afternoon measurements on three days.

- WSFACTORS identifies the two factors (*DAY* and *AMPM*) that distinguish the temperature and weight measurements for each subject. These factors define six within-subjects cells.

- MEASURE indicates that the first group of six dependent variables correspond to *TEMP* and the second group of six dependent variables correspond to *WEIGHT*.

- These labels, *TEMP* and *WEIGHT*, are used on the output requested by PRINT.

- WSDESIGN requests a full factorial within-subjects model. Because this is the default, WSDESIGN could have been omitted.

RENAME Subcommand

Because any repeated measures analysis involves a transformation of the dependent variables, it is always a good idea to rename the dependent variables. Choose appropriate names depending on the type of contrast specified for within-subjects factors. This is easier to do if you are using one of the orthogonal contrasts. The most reliable way to assign new names is to inspect the transformation matrix.

Example

```
MANOVA LOW1 LOW2 LOW3 HI1 HI2 HI3
  /WSFACTORS=LEVEL(2) TRIAL(3)
  /CONTRAST(TRIAL)=DIFFERENCE
  /RENAME=CONST LEVELDIF TRIAL21 TRIAL312 INTER1 INTER2
  /PRINT=TRANSFORM
  /DESIGN.
```

- This analysis has two within-subjects factors and no between-subjects factors.

- Difference contrasts are requested for *TRIAL*, which has three levels.

- Because all orthonormal contrasts produce the same F test for a factor with two levels, there is no point in specifying a contrast type for *LEVEL*.

- New names are assigned to the transformed variables based on the transformation matrix. These names correspond to the meaning of the transformed variables: the mean or constant, the average difference between levels, the average effect of trial 2 compared to 1, the average effect of trial 3 compared to 1 and 2; and the two interactions between *LEVEL* and *TRIAL*.

- The transformation matrix requested by the PRINT subcommand looks like Figure 1.

Figure 1   Transformation matrix

	CONST	LEVELDIF	TRIAL1	TRIAL2	INTER1	INTER2
LOW1	0.408	0.408	-0.500	-0.289	-0.500	-0.289
LOW2	0.408	0.408	0.500	-0.289	0.500	-0.289
LOW3	0.408	0.408	0.000	0.577	0.000	0.577
HI1	0.408	-0.408	-0.500	-0.289	0.500	0.289
HI2	0.408	-0.408	0.500	-0.289	-0.500	0.289
HI3	0.408	-0.408	0.000	0.577	0.000	-0.577

PRINT Subcommand

The following additional specifications on PRINT are useful in repeated measures analysis:

SIGNIF(AVERF)   *Averaged* F *tests for use with repeated measures.* This is the default display in repeated measures analysis. The averaged *F* tests in the multivariate setup for repeated measures are equivalent to the univariate (or split-plot or mixed-model) approach to repeated measures.

SIGNIF(AVONLY)   *Only the averaged* F *test for repeated measures.* AVONLY produces the same output as AVERF and suppresses all other SIGNIF output.

SIGNIF(HF)   *The Huynh-Feldt corrected significance values for averaged univariate* F *tests.*

SIGNIF(GG)   *The Greenhouse-Geisser corrected significance values for averaged univariate* F *tests.*

SIGNIF(EFSIZE)   *The effect size for the univariate* F *and* t *tests.*

- The keywords AVERF and AVONLY are mutually exclusive.
- When you request repeated measures analysis with the WSFACTORS subcommand, the default display includes SIGNIF(AVERF) but does not include the usual SIGNIF(UNIV).
- The averaged *F* tests are appropriate in repeated measures because the dependent variables that are averaged actually represent contrasts of the WSFACTOR variables. When the analysis is not doubly multivariate, as discussed above, you can specify PRINT=SIGNIF(UNIV) to obtain significance tests for each degree of freedom, just as in univariate MANOVA.

MATCH FILES

```
MATCH FILES FILE={file}  [TABLE={file}]
               {*   }           {*   }

[/RENAME=(old varnames=new varnames)...]

[/IN=varname]

/FILE==...  [TABLE= ...]

[/BY varlist]

[/MAP]

[/KEEP={ALL**  }] [/DROP=varlist]
        {varlist}

[/FIRST=varname]  [/LAST=varname]
```

**Default if the subcommand is omitted.

Example

```
MATCH FILES FILE=PART1 /FILE=PART2 /FILE=*.
```

Overview

MATCH FILES combines variables from 2 up to 50 SPSS-format data files. MATCH FILES can make parallel or nonparallel matches between different files or perform table lookups. **Parallel matches** combine files sequentially by case (they are sometimes referred to as **sequential matches**). **Nonparallel matches** combine files according to the values of one or more key variables. In a table lookup, MATCH FILES looks up variables in one file and transfers those variables to a case file.

The files specified on MATCH FILES can be SPSS-format data files created with SAVE or XSAVE or the working data file. The combined file becomes the new working data file. Statistical procedures following MATCH FILES use this combined file unless you replace it by building another working file. You must use the SAVE or XSAVE commands if you want to save the combined file as an SPSS-format data file.

In general, MATCH FILES is used to combine files containing the same cases but different variables. To combine files containing the same variables but different cases, use ADD FILES. To update existing SPSS-format data files, use UPDATE.

MATCH FILES is often used with the AGGREGATE command to add variables with summary measures (sum, mean, and so forth) to the data. For an example, see p. 94.

Options

Variable Selection. You can specify which variables from each input file are included in the new working file using the DROP and KEEP subcommands.

Variable Names. You can rename variables in each input file before combining the files using the RENAME subcommand. This permits you to combine variables that are the same but whose names differ in different input files, or to separate variables that are different but have the same name.

Variable Flag. You can create a variable that indicates whether a case came from a particular input file using IN. You can use the FIRST or LAST subcommands to create a variable that flags the first or last case of a group of cases with the same value for the key variable.

Variable Map. You can request a map showing all variables in the new working file, their order, and the input files from which they came using the MAP subcommand.

Basic Specification

The basic specification is two or more FILE subcommands, each of which specifies a file to be matched. In addition, BY is required to specify the key variables for nonparallel matches. Both BY and TABLE are required to match table-lookup files.

- All variables from all input files are included in the new working file unless DROP or KEEP is specified.

Subcommand Order

- RENAME and IN must immediately follow the FILE subcommand to which they apply.
- BY must follow the FILE and TABLE subcommands and any associated RENAME and IN subcommands.
- FIRST and LAST must follow all TABLE and FILE subcommands and any associated RENAME and IN subcommands.
- MAP, DROP, and KEEP must follow all FILE, TABLE, and RENAME subcommands.

Syntax Rules

- RENAME can be repeated after each FILE or TABLE subcommand and applies only to variables in the file named on the immediately preceding FILE or TABLE.
- IN can be used only for a nonparallel match or for a table lookup. (Thus, IN can be used only if BY is specified.)
- BY can be specified only once. However, multiple variables can be specified on BY. When BY is used, all files must be sorted in ascending order of the key variables named on BY.
- MAP can be repeated as often as desired.

Operations

- MATCH FILES reads all files named on FILE or TABLE and builds a new working data file that replaces any working file created earlier in the session.

- The new working data file contains complete dictionary information from the input files, including variable names, labels, print and write formats, and missing-value indicators. The new file also contains the documents from each of the input files. See DROP DOCUMENTS for information on deleting documents.

- Variables are copied in order from the first file specified, then from the second file specified, and so on.

- If the same variable name is used in more than one input file, data are taken from the file specified first. Dictionary information is taken from the first file containing value labels, missing values, or a variable label for the common variable. If the first file has no such information, MATCH FILES checks the second file, and so on, seeking dictionary information.

- All cases from all input files are included in the combined file. Cases that are absent from one of the input files will be assigned system-missing values for variables unique to that file.

- BY specifies that cases should be combined according to a common value on one or more key variables. All input files must be sorted in ascending order of the key variables.

- If BY is not used, the program performs a parallel (sequential) match, combining the first case from each file, then the second case from each file, and so on, without regard to any identifying values that may be present.

- If the working file is named as an input file, any N and SAMPLE commands that have been specified are applied to that file before files are matched.

Limitations

- Maximum 50 files can be combined on one MATCH FILES command.
- Maximum one BY subcommand. However, BY can specify multiple variables.
- The TEMPORARY command cannot be in effect if the working data file is used as an input file.

Example

```
MATCH FILES FILE=PART1 /FILE=PART2 /FILE=*.
```

- MATCH FILES combines three files (the working data file and two SPSS-format data files) in a parallel match. Cases are combined according to their order in each file.

- The new working data file contains as many cases as are contained in the largest of the three input files.

FILE Subcommand

FILE identifies the files to be combined (except table files). At least one FILE subcommand is required on MATCH FILES. A separate FILE subcommand must be used for each input file.

- An asterisk can be specified on FILE to refer to the working data file.

- The order in which files are specified determines the order of variables in the new working file. In addition, if the same variable name occurs in more than one input file, the variable is taken from the file specified first.

- If the files have unequal numbers of cases, cases are generated from the longest file. Cases that do not exist in the shorter files have system-missing values for variables that are unique to those files.

Raw Data Files

To add variables from a raw data file, you must first define the raw data as the working data file using the DATA LIST command. MATCH FILES can then combine the working data file with an SPSS-format data file.

Example

```
DATA LIST FILE=GASDATA/1 OZONE 10-12 CO 20-22 SULFUR 30-32.

VARIABLE LABELS OZONE 'LEVEL OF OZONE'
   CO 'LEVEL OF CARBON MONOXIDE'
   SULFUR 'LEVEL OF SULFUR DIOXIDE'.

MATCH FILES  FILE=PARTICLE /FILE=*.

SAVE  OUTFILE=POLLUTE.
```

- The *PARTICLE* file is a previously saved SPSS-format data file.
- The *GASDATA* file is a raw data file and is defined on the DATA LIST command. Variable labels are assigned on the VARIABLE LABELS command.
- MATCH FILES adds the working data file (*), which now contains the gas data, to SPSS-format data file *PARTICLE*.
- SAVE saves the new working file as an SPSS-format data file with the filename *POLLUTE*.

BY Subcommand

BY specifies one or more identification, or key, variables that determine which cases are to be combined. When BY is specified, cases from one file are matched only with cases from other files that have the same values for the key variables. BY is required unless all input files are to be matched sequentially according to the order of cases.

- BY must follow the FILE and TABLE subcommands and any associated RENAME and IN subcommands.
- BY specifies the names of one or more key variables. The key variables must exist in all input files. The key variables can be numeric or long or short strings.
- All input files must be sorted in ascending order of the key variables. If necessary, use SORT CASES before MATCH FILES.
- Missing values for key variables are handled like any other values.
- Unmatched cases are assigned system-missing values (for numeric variables) or blanks (for string variables) for variables from files that do not contain a match.

Duplicate Cases

Duplicate cases are those with the same values for the key variables named on the BY subcommand.

- Duplicate cases are permitted in any input files except table files.
- When there is no table file, the first duplicate case in each file is matched with the first matching case (if any) from the other files; the second duplicate case is matched with a second matching duplicate, if any; and so on. (In effect, a parallel match is performed within groups of duplicate cases.) Unmatched cases are assigned system-missing values (for numeric variables) or blanks (for string variables) for variables from files that do not contain a match.
- The program displays a warning if it encounters duplicate keys in one or more of the files being matched.

TABLE Subcommand

TABLE specifies a table lookup (or keyed table) file. A lookup file contributes variables but not cases to the new working file. Variables from the table file are added to all cases from other files that have matching values for the key variables. FILE specifies the files that supply the cases.

- A separate TABLE subcommand must be used to specify each lookup file, and a separate FILE subcommand must be used to specify each case file.
- The BY subcommand is required when TABLE is used.
- All specified files must be sorted in ascending order of the key variables. If necessary, use SORT CASES before MATCH FILES.
- A lookup file cannot contain duplicate cases (cases for which the key variable(s) named on BY have identical values).
- An asterisk on TABLE refers to the working data file.
- Cases in a case file that do not have matches in a table file are assigned system-missing values (for numeric variables) or blanks (for string variables) for variables from that table file.
- Cases in a table file that do not match any cases in a case file are ignored.

Example

```
MATCH FILES FILE=* /TABLE=MASTER /BY EMP_ID.
```

- MATCH FILES combines variables from the SPSS-format data file *MASTER* with the working data file, matching cases by the variable *EMP_ID*.
- No new cases are added to the working file as a result of the table lookup.
- Cases whose value for *EMP_ID* is not included in the *MASTER* file are assigned system-missing values for variables taken from the table.

RENAME Subcommand

RENAME renames variables on the input files *before* they are processed by MATCH FILES. RENAME must follow the FILE or TABLE subcommand that contains the variables to be renamed.

- RENAME applies only to the immediately preceding FILE or TABLE subcommand. To rename variables from more than one input file, specify a RENAME subcommand after each FILE or TABLE subcommand.
- Specifications for RENAME consist of a left parenthesis, a list of old variable names, an equals sign, a list of new variable names, and a right parenthesis. The two variable lists must name or imply the same number of variables. If only one variable is renamed, the parentheses are optional.
- More than one rename specification can be specified on a single RENAME subcommand, each enclosed in parentheses.
- The TO keyword can be used to refer to consecutive variables in the file and to generate new variable names. (See the TO keyword on p. 29.)
- RENAME takes effect immediately. Any KEEP and DROP subcommands entered prior to a RENAME must use the old names, while KEEP and DROP subcommands entered after a RENAME must use the new names.
- All specifications within a single set of parentheses take effect simultaneously. For example, the specification RENAME (A,B = B,A) swaps the names of the two variables.
- Variables cannot be renamed to scratch variables.
- Input SPSS-format data files are not changed on disk; only the copy of the file being combined is affected.

Example

```
MATCH FILES FILE=UPDATE /RENAME=(NEWID = ID)
 /FILE=MASTER /BY ID.
```

- MATCH FILES matches a master SPSS-format data file (*MASTER*) with an update data file (*UPDATE*).
- Variable *NEWID* in the *UPDATE* file is renamed *ID* so that it will have the same name as the identification variable in the master file and can be used on the BY subcommand.

DROP and KEEP Subcommands

DROP and KEEP are used to include a subset of variables in the new working data file. DROP specifies a set of variables to exclude and KEEP specifies a set of variables to retain.

- DROP and KEEP do not affect the input files on disk.
- DROP and KEEP must follow all FILE, TABLE, and RENAME subcommands.
- DROP and KEEP must specify one or more variables. If RENAME is used to rename variables, specify the new names on DROP and KEEP.
- The keyword ALL can be specified on KEEP. ALL must be the last specification on KEEP, and it refers to all variables not previously named on KEEP.

- DROP cannot be used with variables created by the IN, FIRST, or LAST subcommands.
- KEEP can be used to change the order of variables in the resulting file. By default, MATCH FILES first copies the variables in order from the first file, then copies the variables in order from the second file, and so on. With KEEP, variables are kept in the order in which they are listed on the subcommand. If a variable is named more than once on KEEP, only the first mention of the variable is in effect; all subsequent references to that variable name are ignored.

Example

```
MATCH FILES FILE=PARTICLE /RENAME=(PARTIC=POLLUTE1)
   /FILE=GAS /RENAME=(OZONE TO SULFUR=POLLUTE2 TO POLLUTE4)
   /DROP=POLLUTE4.
```

- The renamed variable *POLLUTE4* is dropped from the resulting file. DROP is specified after all of the FILE and RENAME subcommands, and it refers to the dropped variable by its new name.

IN Subcommand

IN creates a new variable in the resulting file that indicates whether a case came from the input file named on the preceding FILE subcommand. IN applies only to the file specified on the immediately preceding FILE subcommand.

- IN can be used only for a nonparallel match or table lookup.
- IN has only one specification—the name of the flag variable.
- The variable created by IN has the value 1 for every case that came from the associated input file and the value 0 if the case came from a different input file.
- Variables created by IN are automatically attached to the end of the resulting file and cannot be dropped. If FIRST or LAST is used, the variable created by IN precedes the variables created by FIRST or LAST.

Example

```
MATCH FILES  FILE=WEEK10 /FILE=WEEK11 /IN=INWEEK11 /BY=EMPID.
```

- IN creates the variable *INWEEK11*, which has the value 1 for all cases in the resulting file that had values in the input file *WEEK11* and the value 0 for those cases that were not in file *WEEK11*.

FIRST and LAST Subcommands

FIRST and LAST create logical variables that flag the first or last case of a group of cases with the same value for the BY variables.

- FIRST and LAST must follow all TABLE and FILE subcommands and any associated RENAME and IN subcommands.
- FIRST and LAST have only one specification—the name of the flag variable.

- FIRST creates a variable with the value 1 for the first case of each group and the value 0 for all other cases.

- LAST creates a variable with the value 1 for the last case of each group and the value 0 for all other cases.

- Variables created by FIRST and LAST are automatically attached to the end of the resulting file and cannot be dropped.

- If one file has several cases with the same values for the key variables, FIRST or LAST can be used to create a variable that flags the first or last case of the group.

Example

```
MATCH FILES  TABLE=HOUSE /FILE=PERSONS
 /BY=HOUSEID /FIRST=HEAD.
```

- The variable *HEAD* contains the value 1 for the first person in each household and the value 0 for all other persons. Assuming that the *PERSONS* file is sorted with the head of household as the first case for each household, the variable *HEAD* identifies the case for the head of household.

Example

```
* Using match files with only one file.

* This example flags the first of several cases with
  the same value for a key variable.

MATCH FILES  FILE=PERSONS /BY HOUSEID /FIRST=HEAD.
SELECT IF  (HEAD EQ 1).
CROSSTABS  JOBCAT BY SEX.
```

- MATCH FILES is used instead of GET to read the SPSS-format data file *PERSONS*. The BY subcommand identifies the key variable (*HOUSEID*), and FIRST creates the variable *HEAD* with the value 1 for the first case in each household and the value 0 for all other cases.

- SELECT IF selects only the cases with the value 1 for *HEAD*, and the CROSSTABS procedure is run on these cases.

MAP Subcommand

MAP produces a list of the variables that are in the new working file and the file or files from which they came. Variables are listed in the order in which they appear in the resulting file. MAP has no specifications and must be placed after all FILE, TABLE, and RENAME subcommands.

- Multiple MAP subcommands can be used. Each MAP shows the current status of the working data file and reflects only the subcommands that precede the MAP subcommand.

- To obtain a map of the resulting file in its final state, specify MAP last.

- If a variable is renamed, its original and new names are listed. Variables created by IN, FIRST, and LAST are not included in the map, since they are automatically attached to the end of the file and cannot be dropped.

MATRIX—END MATRIX

This command is not available on all operating systems.

```
MATRIX

matrix statements

END MATRIX
```

The following matrix language statements can be used in a matrix program:

BREAK	DO IF	END LOOP	MSAVE	SAVE
CALL	ELSE	GET	PRINT	WRITE
COMPUTE	ELSE IF	LOOP	READ	
DISPLAY	END IF	MGET	RELEASE	

The following functions can be used in matrix language statements:

ABS	Absolute values of matrix elements
ALL	Test if all elements are positive
ANY	Test if any element is positive
ARSIN	Arcsines of matrix elements
ARTAN	Arctangents of matrix elements
BLOCK	Create block diagonal matrix
CDFNORM	Cumulative normal distribution function
CHICDF	Cumulative chi-squared distribution function
CHOL	Cholesky decomposition
CMAX	Column maxima
CMIN	Column minima
COS	Cosines of matrix elements
CSSQ	Column sums of squares
CSUM	Column sums
DESIGN	Create design matrix
DET	Determinant
DIAG	Diagonal of matrix
EOF	Check end of file
EVAL	Eigenvalues of symmetric matrix
EXP	Exponentials of matrix elements
FCDF	Cumulative F distribution function
GINV	Generalized inverse
GRADE	Rank elements in matrix, using sequential integers for ties
GSCH	Gram-Schmidt orthonormal basis
IDENT	Create identity matrix

INV	Inverse
KRONECKER	Kronecker product of two matrices
LG10	Logarithms to base 10 of matrix elements
LN	Logarithms to base e of matrix elements
MAGIC	Create magic square
MAKE	Create a matrix with all elements equal
MDIAG	Create a matrix with the given diagonal
MMAX	Maximum element in matrix
MMIN	Minimum element in matrix
MOD	Remainders after division
MSSQ	Matrix sum of squares
MSUM	Matrix sum
NCOL	Number of columns
NROW	Number of rows
RANK	Matrix rank
RESHAPE	Change shape of matrix
RMAX	Row maxima
RMIN	Row minima
RND	Round off matrix elements to nearest integer
RNKORDER	Rank elements in matrix, averaging ties
RSSQ	Row sums of squares
RSUM	Row sums
SIN	Sines of matrix elements
SOLVE	Solve systems of linear equations
SQRT	Square roots of matrix elements
SSCP	Sums of squares and cross-products
SVAL	Singular values
SWEEP	Perform sweep transformation
T	(Synonym for TRANSPOS)
TCDF	Cumulative normal t distribution function
TRACE	Calculate trace (sum of diagonal elements)
TRANSPOS	Transposition of matrix
TRUNC	Truncation of matrix elements to integer
UNIFORM	Create matrix of uniform random numbers

Example

```
MATRIX.
READ A /FILE=MATRDATA /SIZE={6,6} /FIELD=1 TO 60.
CALL EIGEN(A,EIGENVEC,EIGENVAL).
LOOP J=1 TO NROW(EIGENVAL).
+ DO IF (EIGENVAL(J) > 1.0).
+   PRINT EIGENVAL(J) / TITLE="Eigenvalue:" /SPACE=3.
+   PRINT T(EIGENVEC(:,J)) / TITLE="Eigenvector:" /SPACE=1.
+ END IF.
END LOOP.
END MATRIX.
```

Overview

The MATRIX and END MATRIX commands enclose statements that are executed by the SPSS matrix processor. Using matrix programs, you can write your own statistical routines in the compact language of matrix algebra. Matrix programs can include mathematical calculations, control structures, display of results, and reading and writing matrices as character files or SPSS data files.

As discussed below, a matrix program is for the most part independent of the rest of the SPSS session, although it can read and write SPSS data files, including the working data file.

This section does not attempt to explain the rules of matrix algebra. Many textbooks, such as Hadley (1961) and O'Nan (1971), teach the application of matrix methods to statistics.

The SPSS MATRIX procedure was originally developed at the Madison Academic Computing Center, University of Wisconsin.

Terminology

A variable within a matrix program represents a **matrix**, which is simply a set of values arranged in a rectangular array of rows and columns.

- An $n \times m$ (read "n by m") matrix is one that has n rows and m columns. The integers n and m are the dimensions of the matrix. An $n \times m$ matrix contains $n \times m$ elements, or data values.

- An $n \times 1$ matrix is sometimes called a **column vector**, and a $1 \times n$ matrix is sometimes called a **row vector**. A vector is a special case of a matrix.

- A 1×1 matrix, containing a single data value, is often called a **scalar**. A scalar is also a special case of a matrix.

- An **index** to a matrix or vector is an integer that identifies a specific row or column. Indexes normally appear in printed works as subscripts, as in A_{31}, but are specified in the matrix language within parentheses, as in $A(3,1)$. The row index for a matrix precedes the column index.

- The **main diagonal** of a matrix consists of the elements whose row index equals their column index. It begins at the top left corner of the matrix; in a square matrix, it runs to the bottom right corner.

- The **transpose** of a matrix is the matrix with rows and columns interchanged. The transpose of an $n \times m$ matrix is an $m \times n$ matrix.

- A **symmetric matrix** is a square matrix that is unchanged if you flip it about the main diagonal. That is, the element in row *i*, column *j* equals the element in row *j*, column *i*. A symmetric matrix equals its transpose.
- Matrices are always rectangular, although it is possible to read or write symmetric matrices in triangular form. Vectors and scalars are considered degenerate rectangles.
- It is an error to try to create a matrix whose rows have different numbers of elements.

A matrix program does not process individual cases unless you so specify, using the control structures of the matrix language. Unlike ordinary SPSS variables, matrix variables do not have distinct values for different cases. A matrix is a single entity.

Vectors in matrix processing should not be confused with the vectors temporarily created by the VECTOR command in SPSS. The latter are shorthand for a list of SPSS variables and, like all ordinary SPSS variables, are unavailable during matrix processing.

Matrix Variables

A matrix variable is created by a matrix statement that assigns a value to a variable name.

- A matrix variable name follows the same rules as those applicable to an ordinary SPSS variable name.
- The names of matrix functions and procedures cannot be used as variable names within a matrix program. (In particular, the letter *T* cannot be used as a variable name because T is an alias for the TRANSPOS function.)
- The COMPUTE, READ, GET, MGET, and CALL statements create matrices. An index variable named on a LOOP statement creates a scalar with a value assigned to it.
- A variable name can be redefined within a matrix program without regard to the dimensions of the matrix it represents. The same name can represent scalars, vectors, and full matrices at different points in the matrix program.
- MATRIX—END MATRIX does not include any special processing for missing data. When reading a data matrix from an SPSS data file, you must therefore specify whether missing data are to be accepted as valid or excluded from the matrix.

String Variables in Matrix Programs

Matrix variables can contain short string data. Support for string variables is limited, however.

- MATRIX will attempt to carry out calculations with string variables if you so request. The results will not be meaningful.
- You must specify a format (such as A8) when you display a matrix that contains string data.

Syntax of Matrix Language

A matrix program consists of statements. Matrix statements must appear in a matrix program, between the MATRIX and END MATRIX commands. They are analogous to SPSS commands and follow the rules of the SPSS command language regarding the abbreviation of keywords; the equivalence of upper and lower case; the use of spaces, commas, and equals signs; and the splitting of statements across multiple lines. However, commas are required to separate arguments to matrix functions and procedures and to separate variable names on the RELEASE statement.

Matrix statements are composed of the following elements:

- Keywords, such as the names of matrix statements.
- Variable names.
- Explicitly written matrices, which are enclosed within braces ({ }).
- Arithmetic and logical operators.
- Matrix functions.
- The SPSS command terminator, which serves as a statement terminator within a matrix program.

Comments in Matrix Programs

Within a matrix program, you can enter comments in any of the forms recognized by SPSS: on lines beginning with the COMMENT command, on lines beginning with an asterisk, or between the characters /* and */ on a command line.

Matrix Notation in SPSS

To write a matrix explicitly:

- Enclose the matrix within braces ({ }).
- Separate the elements of each row by commas.
- Separate the rows by semicolons.
- String elements must be enclosed in either apostrophes or quotation marks, as is generally true in the SPSS command language.

Example

{1,2,3;4,5,6}

- The example represents the following matrix:

$$\begin{bmatrix} 1 & 2 & 3 \\ 4 & 5 & 6 \end{bmatrix}$$

Example

{1,2,3}

- This example represents a row vector:

$$\begin{bmatrix} 1 & 2 & 3 \end{bmatrix}$$

Example

`{11;12;13}`

- This example represents a column vector:

$$\begin{bmatrix} 11 \\ 12 \\ 13 \end{bmatrix}$$

Example

`{3}`

- This example represents a scalar. The braces are optional. You can specify the same scalar as `3`.

Matrix Notation Shorthand

You can simplify the construction of matrices using notation shorthand.

Consecutive Integers. Use a colon to indicate a range of consecutive integers. For example, the vector `{1,2,3,4,5,6}` can be written as `{1:6}`.

Incremented Ranges of Integers. Use a second colon followed by an integer to indicate the increment. The matrix `{1,3,5,7;2,5,8,11}` can be written as `{1:7:2;2:11:3}`, where `1:7:2` indicates the integers from 1 to 7 incrementing by 2, and `2:11:3` indicates the integers from 2 to 11 incrementing by 3.

- You must use integers when specifying a range in either of these ways. Numbers with fractional parts are truncated to integers.
- If an arithmetic expression is used, it should be enclosed in parentheses.

Extraction of an Element, a Vector, or a Submatrix

You can use indexes in parentheses to extract an element from a vector or matrix, a vector from a matrix, or a submatrix from a matrix. In the following discussion, an **integer index** refers to an integer expression used as an index, which can be a scalar matrix with an integer value or an integer element extracted from a vector or matrix. Similarly, a **vector index** refers to a vector expression used as an index, which can be a vector matrix or a vector extracted from a matrix.

For example, if S is a scalar matrix, $S = \begin{bmatrix} 2 \end{bmatrix}$, R is a row vector, $R = \begin{bmatrix} 1 & 3 & 5 \end{bmatrix}$, C is a

column vector, $C = \begin{bmatrix} 2 \\ 3 \\ 4 \end{bmatrix}$, and A is a 5×5 matrix, $A = \begin{bmatrix} 11 & 12 & 13 & 14 & 15 \\ 21 & 22 & 23 & 24 & 25 \\ 31 & 32 & 33 & 34 & 35 \\ 41 & 42 & 43 & 44 & 45 \\ 51 & 52 & 53 & 54 & 55 \end{bmatrix}$, then:

$R(S) = R(2) = \{3\}$
$C(S) = C(2) = \{3\}$

- An integer index extracts an element from a vector matrix.
- The distinction between a row and a column vector does not matter when an integer index is used to extract an element from it.

$A(2,3) = A(S,3) = \{23\}$

- Two integer indexes separated by a comma extract an element from a rectangular matrix.

$A(R,2)=A(1:5:2,2)=\{12; 32; 52\}$
$A(2,R)=A(2,1:5:2)=\{21, 23, 25\}$
$A(C,2)=A(2:4,2)= \{22;32;42\}$
$A(2,C)=A(2,2:4)= \{22,23,24\}$

- An integer and a vector index separated by a comma extract a vector from a matrix.
- The distinction between a row and a column vector does not matter when used as indexes in this way.

$A(2,:)=A(S,:) = \{21, 22, 23, 24, 25\}$
$A(:,2) =A(:,S)= \{12; 22; 32; 42; 52\}$

- A colon by itself used as an index extracts an entire row or column vector from a matrix.

$A(R,C)=A(R,2:4)=A(1:5:2,C)=A(1:5:2,2:4)=\{12,13,14;32,33,34;52,53,54\}$
$A(C,R)=A(C,1:5:2)=A(2:4,R)=A(2:4,1:5:2)=\{21,23,25;31,33,35;41,43,45\}$

- Two vector indexes separated by a comma extract a submatrix from a matrix.
- The distinction between a row and a column vector does not matter when used as indexes in this way.

Construction of a Matrix from Other Matrices

You can use vector or rectangular matrices to construct a new matrix, separating row expressions by semicolons and components of row expressions by commas. If a column vector V_c has n elements and matrix M has the dimensions $n \times m$, then $\{M, V_c\}$ is an $n \times (m + 1)$ matrix. Similarly, if the row vector V_r has m elements and M is the same, then $\{M;V_r\}$ is an $(n + 1) \times m$ matrix. In fact, you can paste together any number of matrices and vectors this way.

- All of the components of each column expression must have the same number of actual rows, and all of the row expressions must have the same number of actual columns.
- The distinction between row vectors and column vectors must be observed carefully when constructing matrices in this way, so that the components will fit together properly.
- Several of the matrix functions are also useful in constructing matrices; see in particular the MAKE, UNIFORM, and IDENT functions in "Matrix Functions" on p. 719.

Example

```
COMPUTE M={CORNER, COL3; ROW3}.
```

- This example constructs the matrix *M* from the matrix *CORNER*, the column vector *COL3*, and the row vector *ROW3*.
- *COL3* supplies new row components and is separated from *CORNER* by a comma.
- *ROW3* supplies column elements and is separated from previous expressions by a semicolon.
- *COL3* must have the same number of rows as *CORNER*.
- *ROW3* must have the same number of columns as the matrix resulting from the previous expressions.
- For example, if $CORNER = \begin{bmatrix} 11 & 12 \\ 21 & 22 \end{bmatrix}$, $COL3 = \begin{bmatrix} 13 \\ 23 \end{bmatrix}$, and $ROW3 = \begin{bmatrix} 31 & 32 & 33 \end{bmatrix}$,

  then: $M = \begin{bmatrix} 11 & 12 & 13 \\ 21 & 22 & 23 \\ 31 & 32 & 33 \end{bmatrix}$

Matrix Operations

You can perform matrix calculations according to the rules of matrix algebra and compare matrices using relational or logical operators.

Conformable Matrices

Many operations with matrices make sense only if the matrices involved have "suitable" dimensions. Most often, this means that they should be the same size, with the same number of rows and the same number of columns. Matrices that are the right size for an operation are said to be **conformable matrices**. If you attempt to do something in a matrix program with a matrix that is not conformable for that operation—a matrix that has the wrong dimensions—you will receive an error message, and the operation will not be performed. An important exception, where one of the matrices is a scalar, is discussed below.

Requirements for carrying out matrix operations include:

- Matrix addition and subtraction require that the two matrices be the same size.

- The relational and logical operations described below require that the two matrices be the same size.
- Matrix multiplication requires that the number of columns of the first matrix equal the number of rows of the second matrix.
- Raising a matrix to a power can be done only if the matrix is square. This includes the important operation of *inverting* a matrix, where the power is -1.
- Conformability requirements for matrix functions are noted in "Matrix Functions" on p. 719 and in "COMPUTE Statement" on p. 718.

Scalar Expansion

When one of the matrices involved in an operation is a scalar, the scalar is treated as a matrix of the correct size in order to carry out the operation. This internal scalar expansion is performed for the following operations:

- Addition and subtraction.
- Elementwise multiplication, division, and exponentiation. Note that multiplying a matrix elementwise by an expanded scalar is equivalent to ordinary scalar multiplication—each element of the matrix is multiplied by the scalar.
- All relational and logical operators.

Arithmetic Operators

You can add, subtract, multiply, or exponentiate matrices according to the rules of matrix algebra, or you can perform elementwise arithmetic, in which you multiply, divide, or exponentiate each element of a matrix separately. The arithmetic operators are listed below.

Unary – *Sign reversal.* A minus sign placed in front of a matrix reverses the sign of each element. (The unary + is also accepted but has no effect.)

+ *Matrix addition.* Corresponding elements of the two matrices are added. The matrices must have the same dimensions, or one must be a scalar.

– *Matrix subtraction.* Corresponding elements of the two matrices are subtracted. The matrices must have the same dimensions, or one must be a scalar.

* *Multiplication.* There are two cases. First, *scalar multiplication*: if either of the matrices is a scalar, each element of the other matrix is multiplied by that scalar. Second, *matrix multiplication*: if A is an $m \times n$ matrix and B is an $n \times p$ matrix, $A*B$ is an $m \times p$ matrix in which the element in row i, column k, is equal to $\Sigma_{j=1}^{n} A(i,j) \times B(j,k)$.

/ *Division.* The division operator performs elementwise division (described below). True matrix division, the inverse operation of matrix multiplication, is accomplished by taking the INV function (square matrices) or the GINV function (rectangular matrices) of the denominator and multiplying.

** *Matrix exponentiation.* A matrix can be raised only to an integer power. The matrix, which must be square, is multiplied by itself as many times as the absolute value of the exponent. If the exponent is negative, the result is then inverted.

&* *Elementwise multiplication.* Each element of the matrix is multiplied by the corresponding element of the second matrix. The matrices must have the same dimensions, or one must be a scalar.

&/ *Elementwise division.* Each element of the matrix is divided by the corresponding element of the second matrix. The matrices must have the same dimensions, or one must be a scalar.

&** *Elementwise exponentiation.* Each element of the first matrix is raised to the power of the corresponding element of the second matrix. The matrices must have the same dimensions, or one must be a scalar.

: *Sequential integers.* This operator creates a vector of consecutive integers from the value preceding the operator to the value following it. You can specify an optional increment following a second colon. See "Matrix Notation Shorthand" on p. 710 for the principal use of this operator.

- Use these operators only with numeric matrices. The results are undefined when they are used with string matrices.

Relational Operators

The relational operators are used to compare two matrices, element by element. The result is a matrix of the same size as the (expanded) operands and containing either 1 or 0. The value of each element, 1 or 0, is determined by whether the comparison between the corresponding element of the first matrix with the corresponding element of the second matrix is true or false, 1 for true and 0 for false. The matrices being compared must be of the same dimensions unless one of them is a scalar. The relational operators are listed in Table 1.

Table 1 Relational operators in matrix programs

>	GT	Greater than
<	LT	Less than
<> or ~= (¬=)	NE	Not equal to
<=	LE	Less than or equal to
>=	GE	Greater than or equal to
=	EQ	Equal to

- The symbolic and alphabetic forms of these operators are equivalent.
- The symbols representing NE (~= or ¬=) are system dependent. In general, the tilde (~) is valid for ASCII systems, while the logical-not sign (¬), or whatever symbol is over the number 6 on the keyboard, is valid for IBM EBCDIC systems.
- Use these operators only with numeric matrices. The results are undefined when they are used with string matrices.

Logical Operators

Logical operators combine two matrices, normally containing values of 1 (true) or 0 (false). When used with other numerical matrices, they treat all positive values as true and all negative and 0 values as false. The logical operators are:

NOT *Reverses the truth of the matrix that follows it.* Positive elements yield 0, and negative or 0 elements yield 1.

AND *Both must be true.* The matrix *A* AND *B* is 1 where the corresponding elements of *A* and *B* are both positive, and 0 elsewhere.

OR *Either must be true.* The matrix *A* OR *B* is 1 where the corresponding element of either *A* or *B* is positive, and 0 where both elements are negative or 0.

XOR *Either must be true, but not both.* The matrix *A* XOR *B* is 1 where one, but not both, of the corresponding elements of *A* and *B* is positive, and 0 where both are positive or neither is positive.

Precedence of Operators

Parentheses can be used to control the order in which complex expressions are evaluated. When the order of evaluation is not specified by parentheses, operations are carried out in the order listed below. The operations higher on the list take precedence over the operations lower on the list.

```
+ -  (Unary)
:
** &**
* &* &/
+ -  (Addition and Subtraction)
> >= < <= <>=
NOT
AND
OR XOR
```

Operations of equal precedence are performed left to right of the expressions.

Examples

```
COMPUTE A = {1,2,3;4,5,6}.
COMPUTE B = A + 4.
COMPUTE C = A &** 2.
COMPUTE D = 2 &** A.
COMPUTE E = A < 5.
COMPUTE F = (C &/ 2) < B.
```

- The results of these COMPUTE statements are:

$$A = \begin{bmatrix} 1 & 2 & 3 \\ 4 & 5 & 6 \end{bmatrix} \qquad B = \begin{bmatrix} 5 & 6 & 7 \\ 8 & 9 & 10 \end{bmatrix} \qquad C = \begin{bmatrix} 1 & 4 & 9 \\ 16 & 25 & 36 \end{bmatrix}$$

$$D = \begin{bmatrix} 2 & 4 & 8 \\ 16 & 32 & 64 \end{bmatrix} \qquad E = \begin{bmatrix} 1 & 1 & 1 \\ 1 & 0 & 0 \end{bmatrix} \qquad F = \begin{bmatrix} 1 & 1 & 1 \\ 0 & 0 & 0 \end{bmatrix}$$

MATRIX and Other SPSS Commands

A matrix program is a single procedure within an SPSS session.

- No working data file is needed to run a matrix program. If one exists, it is ignored during matrix processing unless you specifically reference it (with an asterisk) on the GET, SAVE, MGET, or MSAVE statements.
- Variables defined in the SPSS working data file are unavailable during matrix processing, except with the GET or MGET statements.
- Matrix variables are unavailable after the END MATRIX command, unless you use SAVE or MSAVE to write them to the working data file.
- You cannot run a matrix program from a syntax window if split-file processing is in effect. If you save the matrix program into a syntax file, however, you can use the INCLUDE command to run the program even if split-file processing is in effect.

Matrix Statements

Table 2 lists all of the statements that are accepted within a matrix program. Most of them have the same name as an analogous SPSS command and perform an exactly analogous function. Use only these statements between the MATRIX and END MATRIX commands. Any command not recognized as a valid matrix statement will be rejected by the matrix processor.

Table 2   Valid matrix statements

BREAK	ELSE IF	MSAVE
CALL	END IF	PRINT
COMPUTE	END LOOP	READ
DISPLAY	GET	RELEASE
DO IF	LOOP	SAVE
ELSE	MGET	WRITE

Exchanging Data with SPSS Data Files

Matrix programs can read and write SPSS data files.

- The GET and SAVE statements read and write ordinary (case-oriented) SPSS data files, treating each case as a row of a matrix and each ordinary variable as a column.

- The MGET and MSAVE statements read and write matrix-format SPSS data files, respecting the structure defined by SPSS when it creates the file. These statements are discussed below.
- Case weighting in an SPSS data file is ignored when the file is read into a matrix program.

Using a Working Data File

You can use the GET statement to read a case-oriented working data file into a matrix variable. The result is a rectangular data matrix in which cases have become rows and variables have become columns. Special circumstances can affect the processing of this data matrix.

Split-File Processing. After a SPLIT FILE command in SPSS, a matrix program executed with the INCLUDE command will read one split-file group with each execution of a GET statement. This enables you to process the subgroups separately within the matrix program.

Case Selection. When a subset of cases is selected for processing, as the result of a SELECT IF, SAMPLE, or N OF CASES command, only the selected cases will be read by the GET statement in a matrix program.

Temporary Transformations. The entire matrix program is treated as a single procedure by the SPSS system. Temporary transformations—those preceded by the TEMPORARY command—entered immediately before a matrix program are in effect throughout that program (even if you GET the working data file repeatedly) and are no longer in effect at the end of the matrix program.

Case Weighting. Case weighting in a working data file is ignored when the file is read into a matrix program.

MATRIX and END MATRIX Commands

The MATRIX command, when encountered in an SPSS session, invokes the matrix processor, which reads matrix statements until the END MATRIX or FINISH command is encountered.

- MATRIX is a procedure and cannot be entered inside a transformation structure such as DO IF or LOOP.
- The MATRIX procedure does not require a working data file.
- Comments are removed before subsequent lines are passed to the matrix processor.
- Macros are expanded before subsequent lines are passed to the matrix processor.

The END MATRIX command terminates matrix processing and returns control to the SPSS command processor.

- The contents of matrix variables are lost after an END MATRIX command.
- The working data file, if present, becomes available again after an END MATRIX command.

COMPUTE Statement

The COMPUTE statement carries out most of the calculations in the matrix program. It closely resembles the COMPUTE command in the SPSS transformation language.

- The basic specification is the target variable, an equals sign, and the assignment expression. Values of the target variable are calculated according to the specification on the assignment expression.

- The target variable must be named first, and the equals sign is required. Only one target variable is allowed per COMPUTE statement.

- Expressions that extract portions of a matrix, such as $M(1,:)$ or $M(1:3,4)$, are allowed to assign values. (See "Matrix Notation Shorthand" on p. 710.) The target variable must be specified as a variable.

- Matrix functions must specify at least one argument enclosed in parentheses. If an expression has two or more arguments, each argument must be separated by a comma. For a complete discussion of the functions and their arguments, see "Matrix Functions" on p. 719.

String Values on COMPUTE Statements

Matrix variables, unlike those in the SPSS transformation language, are not checked for data type (numeric or string) when you use them in a COMPUTE statement.

- Numerical calculations with matrices containing string values will produce meaningless results.

- One or more elements of a matrix can be set equal to string constants by enclosing the string constants in apostrophes or quotation marks on a COMPUTE statement.

- String values can be copied from one matrix to another with the COMPUTE statement.

- There is no way to display a matrix that contains both numeric and string values, if you compute one for some reason.

Example

```
COMPUTE LABELS={"Observe", "Predict", "Error"}.
PRINT LABELS /FORMAT=A7.
```

- *LABELS* is a row vector containing three string values.

Arithmetic Operations and Comparisons

The expression on a COMPUTE statement can be formed from matrix constants and variables, combined with the arithmetic, relational, and logical operators discussed above. Matrix constructions and matrix functions are also allowed.

Examples

```
COMPUTE PI = 3.14159265.
COMPUTE RSQ = R * R.
COMPUTE FLAGS = EIGENVAL >= 1.
COMPUTE ESTIM = {OBS, PRED, ERR}.
```

- The first statement computes a scalar. Note that the braces are optional on a scalar constant.
- The second statement computes the square of the matrix *R*. *R* can be any square matrix, including a scalar.
- The third statement computes a vector named *FLAGS*, which has the same dimension as the existing vector *EIGENVAL*. Each element of *FLAGS* equals 1 if the corresponding element of *EIGENVAL* is greater than or equal to 1, and 0 if the corresponding element is less than 1.
- The fourth statement constructs a matrix *ESTIM* by concatenating the three vectors or matrices *OBS*, *PRED*, and *ERR*. The component matrices must have the same number of rows.

Matrix Functions

The following functions are available in the matrix program. Except where noted, each takes one or more numeric matrices as arguments and returns a matrix value as its result. The arguments must be enclosed in parentheses, and multiple arguments must be separated by commas.

On the following list, matrix arguments are represented by names beginning with *M*. Unless otherwise noted, these arguments can be vectors or scalars. Arguments that must be vectors are represented by names beginning with *V*, and arguments that must be scalars are represented by names beginning with *S*.

ABS(M)   *Absolute value.* Takes a single argument. Returns a matrix having the same dimensions as the argument, containing the absolute values of its elements.

ALL(M)   *Test for all elements nonzero.* Takes a single argument. Returns a scalar: 1 if all elements of the argument are nonzero and 0 if any element is zero.

ANY(M)   *Test for any element nonzero.* Takes a single argument. Returns a scalar: 1 if any element of the argument is nonzero and 0 if all elements are zero.

ARSIN(M)   *Inverse sine.* Takes a single argument, whose elements must be between -1 and 1. Returns a matrix having the same dimensions as the argument, containing the inverse sines (arcsines) of its elements. The results are in radians and are in the range from $-\pi/2$ to $\pi/2$.

ARTAN(M)   *Inverse tangent.* Takes a single argument. Returns a matrix having the same dimensions as the argument, containing the inverse tangents (arctangents) of its elements, in radians. To convert radians to degrees, multiply by $180/\pi$, which you can compute as `45/ARTAN(1)`. For example, the statement `COMPUTE DEGREES=ARTAN(M)*45/ARTAN(1)` returns a matrix containing inverse tangents in degrees.

BLOCK(M1,M2,...)   *Create a block diagonal matrix.* Takes any number of arguments. Returns a matrix with as many rows as the sum of the rows in all the arguments, and as many columns as the sum of the columns in all the arguments, with the argument matrices down the diagonal and zeros elsewhere. For example, if:

$$A = \begin{bmatrix} 1 & 1 & 1 \\ 1 & 1 & 1 \end{bmatrix}, \quad B = \begin{bmatrix} 2 & 2 \\ 2 & 2 \end{bmatrix}, \quad C = \begin{bmatrix} 3 & 3 & 3 \\ 3 & 3 & 3 \\ 3 & 3 & 3 \\ 3 & 3 & 3 \end{bmatrix}, \text{ and } D = \begin{bmatrix} 4 & 4 & 4 \end{bmatrix},$$

then: $\text{BLOCK}(A, B, C, D) = \begin{bmatrix} 1 & 1 & 1 & 0 & 0 & 0 & 0 & 0 & 0 & 0 \\ 1 & 1 & 1 & 0 & 0 & 0 & 0 & 0 & 0 & 0 \\ 0 & 0 & 0 & 2 & 2 & 0 & 0 & 0 & 0 & 0 \\ 0 & 0 & 0 & 2 & 2 & 0 & 0 & 0 & 0 & 0 \\ 0 & 0 & 0 & 0 & 0 & 3 & 3 & 3 & 0 & 0 \\ 0 & 0 & 0 & 0 & 0 & 3 & 3 & 3 & 0 & 0 \\ 0 & 0 & 0 & 0 & 0 & 3 & 3 & 3 & 0 & 0 \\ 0 & 0 & 0 & 0 & 0 & 3 & 3 & 3 & 0 & 0 \\ 0 & 0 & 0 & 0 & 0 & 0 & 0 & 0 & 4 & 4 & 4 \end{bmatrix}$

CDFNORM(M) *Standard normal cumulative distribution function of elements.* Takes a single argument. Returns a matrix having the same dimensions as the argument, containing the values of the cumulative normal distribution function for each of its elements. If an element of the argument is x, the corresponding element of the result is a number between 0 and 1, giving the proportion of a normal distribution that is less than x. For example, CDFNORM({-1.96,0,1.96}) results in, approximately, {.025,.5,.975}.

CHICDF(M,S) *Chi-square cumulative distribution function of elements.* Takes two arguments, a matrix of chi-square values and a scalar giving the degrees of freedom (which must be positive). Returns a matrix having the same dimensions as the first argument, containing the values of the cumulative chi-square distribution function for each of its elements. If an element of the first argument is x and the second argument is S, the corresponding element of the result is a number between 0 and 1, giving the proportion of a chi-square distribution with S degrees of freedom that is less than x. If x is not positive, the result is 0.

CHOL(M) *Cholesky decomposition.* Takes a single argument, which must be a symmetric positive-definite matrix (a square matrix, symmetric about the main diagonal, with positive eigenvalues). Returns a matrix having the same dimensions as the argument. If M is a symmetric positive-definite matrix and B=CHOL(M), then T(B)*B=M, where T is the transpose function defined below.

CMAX(M)

Column maxima. Takes a single argument. Returns a row vector with the same number of columns as the argument. Each column of the result contains the maximum value of the corresponding column of the argument.

CMIN(M)

Column minima. Takes a single argument. Returns a row vector with the same number of columns as the argument. Each column of the result contains the minimum value of the corresponding column of the argument.

COS(M)

Cosines. Takes a single argument. Returns a matrix having the same dimensions as the argument, containing the cosines of the elements of the argument. Elements of the argument matrix are assumed to be measured in radians. To convert degrees to radians, multiply by $\pi/180$, which you can compute as ARTAN(1)/45. For example, the statement COMPUTE COSINES=COS(DEGREES*ARTAN(1)/45) returns cosines from a matrix containing elements measured in degrees.

CSSQ(M)

Column sums of squares. Takes a single argument. Returns a row vector with the same number of columns as the argument. Each column of the result contains the sum of the squared values of the elements in the corresponding column of the argument.

CSUM(M)

Column sums. Takes a single argument. Returns a row vector with the same number of columns as the argument. Each column of the result contains the sum of the elements in the corresponding column of the argument.

DESIGN(M)

Main-effects design matrix from the columns of a matrix. Takes a single argument. Returns a matrix having the same number of rows as the argument, and as many columns as the sum of the numbers of unique values in each column of the argument. Constant columns in the argument are skipped with a warning message. The result contains 1 in the row(s) where the value in question occurs in the argument and 0 otherwise. For example, if:

$$A = \begin{bmatrix} 1 & 2 & 8 \\ 1 & 3 & 8 \\ 2 & 6 & 5 \\ 3 & 3 & 8 \\ 3 & 6 & 5 \end{bmatrix}, \text{ then: } \text{DESIGN}(A) = \begin{bmatrix} 1 & 0 & 0 & 1 & 0 & 0 & 1 & 0 \\ 1 & 0 & 0 & 0 & 1 & 0 & 1 & 0 \\ 0 & 1 & 0 & 0 & 0 & 1 & 0 & 1 \\ 0 & 0 & 1 & 0 & 1 & 0 & 1 & 0 \\ 0 & 0 & 1 & 0 & 0 & 1 & 0 & 1 \end{bmatrix}$$

The first three columns of the result correspond to the three distinct values 1, 2, and 3 in the first column of A; the fourth through sixth columns of the result correspond to the three distinct values 2, 3, and 6 in the second column of A; and the last two columns of the result correspond to the two distinct values 8 and 5 in the third column of A.

DET(M)

Determinant. Takes a single argument, which must be a square matrix. Returns a scalar, which is the determinant of the argument.

DIAG(M)

Diagonal of a matrix. Takes a single argument. Returns a column vector with as many rows as the minimum of the number of rows and the number of columns in the argument. The *i*th element of the result is the value in row *i*, column *i*, of the argument.

EOF(file)

End of file indicator. Normally used after a READ statement. Takes a single argument, which must be either a filename in apostrophes or quotation marks, or a file handle defined on a FILE HANDLE command that precedes the matrix program. Returns a scalar equal to 1 if the last attempt to read that file encountered the last record in the file, and equal to 0 if the last attempt did not encounter the last record in the file. Calling the EOF function causes a REREAD specification on the READ statement to be ignored on the next attempt to read the file.

EVAL(M)

Eigenvalues of a symmetric matrix. Takes a single argument, which must be a symmetric matrix. Returns a column vector with the same number of rows as the argument, containing the eigenvalues of the argument in decreasing numerical order.

EXP(M)

Exponentials of matrix elements. Takes a single argument. Returns a matrix having the same dimensions as the argument, in which each element equals e raised to the power of the corresponding element in the argument matrix.

FCDF(M,S1,S2)

Cumulative F distribution function of elements. Takes three arguments, a matrix of F values and two scalars giving the degrees of freedom (which must be positive). Returns a matrix having the same dimensions as the first argument M, containing the values of the cumulative F distribution function for each of its elements. If an element of the first argument is x and the second and third arguments are $S1$ and $S2$, the corresponding element of the result is a number between 0 and 1, giving the proportion of an F distribution with $S1$ and $S2$ degrees of freedom that is less than x. If x is not positive, the result is 0.

GINV(M)

Moore-Penrose generalized inverse of a matrix. Takes a single argument. Returns a matrix with the same dimensions as the transpose of the argument. If A is the generalized inverse of a matrix M, then $M*A*M=M$ and $A*M*A=A$. Both $A*M$ and $M*A$ are symmetric.

GRADE(M)

Ranks elements in a matrix. Takes a single argument. Uses sequential integers for ties.

GSCH(M)

Gram-Schmidt orthonormal basis for the space spanned by the column vectors of a matrix. Takes a single argument, in which there must be as many linearly independent columns as there are rows. (That is, the rank of the argument must equal the number of rows.) Returns a square matrix with as many rows as the argument. The columns of the result form a basis for the space spanned by the columns of the argument.

IDENT(S1 [,S2])	*Create an identity matrix.* Takes either one or two arguments, which must be scalars. Returns a matrix with as many rows as the first argument and as many columns as the second argument, if any. If the second argument is omitted, the result is a square matrix. Elements on the main diagonal of the result equal 1, and all other elements equal 0.
INV(M)	*Inverse of a matrix.* Takes a single argument, which must be square and nonsingular (that is, its determinant must not be 0). Returns a square matrix having the same dimensions as the argument. If A is the inverse of M, then $M*A=A*M=I$, where I is the identity matrix.
KRONEKER(M1,M2)	*Kronecker product of two matrices.* Takes two arguments. Returns a matrix whose row dimension is the product of the row dimensions of the arguments and whose column dimension is the product of the column dimensions of the arguments. The Kronecker product of two matrices A and B takes the form of an array of scalar products:

$$A(1,1)*B \quad A(1,2)*B \quad ...A(1,N)*B$$
$$A(2,1)*B \quad A(2,2)*B \quad ...A(2,N)*B$$
$$...$$
$$A(M,1)*B \quad A(M,2)*B \quad ...A(M,N)*B$$

LG10(M)	*Base 10 logarithms of the elements.* Takes a single argument, all of whose elements must be positive. Returns a matrix having the same dimensions as the argument, in which each element is the logarithm to base 10 of the corresponding element of the argument.
LN(M)	*Natural logarithms of the elements.* Takes a single argument, all of whose elements must be positive. Returns a matrix having the same dimensions as the argument, in which each element is the logarithm to base e of the corresponding element of the argument.
MAGIC(S)	*Magic square.* Takes a single scalar, which must be 3 or larger, as an argument. Returns a square matrix with S rows and S columns containing the integers from 1 through S^2. All the row sums and all the column sums are equal in the result matrix. (The result matrix is only one of several possible magic squares.)
MAKE(S1,S2,S3)	*Create a matrix, all of whose elements equal a specified value.* Takes three scalars as arguments. Returns an $S1 \times S2$ matrix, all of whose elements equal $S3$.
MDIAG(V)	*Create a square matrix with a specified main diagonal.* Takes a single vector as an argument. Returns a square matrix with as many rows and columns as the dimension of the vector. The elements of the vector appear on the main diagonal of the matrix, and the other matrix elements are all 0.
MMAX(M)	*Maximum element in a matrix.* Takes a single argument. Returns a scalar equal to the numerically largest element in the argument M.
MMIN(M)	*Minimum element in a matrix.* Takes a single argument. Returns a scalar equal to the numerically smallest element in the argument M.

MOD(M,S)   *Remainders after division by a scalar.* Takes two arguments, a matrix and a scalar (which must not be 0). Returns a matrix having the same dimensions as M, each of whose elements is the remainder after the corresponding element of M is divided by S. The sign of each element of the result is the same as the sign of the corresponding element of the matrix argument M.

MSSQ(M)   *Matrix sum of squares.* Takes a single argument. Returns a scalar that equals the sum of the squared values of all the elements in the argument.

MSUM(M)   *Matrix sum.* Takes a single argument. Returns a scalar that equals the sum of all of the elements in the argument.

NCOL(M)   *Number of columns in a matrix.* Takes a single argument. Returns a scalar that equals the number of columns in the argument.

NROW(M)   *Number of rows in a matrix.* Takes a single argument. Returns a scalar that equals the number of rows in the argument.

RANK(M)   *Rank of a matrix.* Takes a single argument. Returns a scalar that equals the number of linearly independent rows or columns in the argument.

RESHAPE(M,S1,S2)   *Matrix of different dimensions.* Takes three arguments, a matrix and two scalars, whose product must equal the number of elements in the matrix. Returns a matrix whose dimensions are given by the scalar arguments. For example, if M is any matrix with exactly 50 elements, then RESHAPE(M, 5, 10) is a matrix with 5 rows and 10 columns. Elements are assigned to the reshaped matrix in order by row.

RMAX(M)   *Row maxima.* Takes a single argument. Returns a column vector with the same number of rows as the argument. Each row of the result contains the maximum value of the corresponding row of the argument.

RMIN(M)   *Row minima.* Takes a single argument. Returns a column vector with the same number of rows as the argument. Each row of the result contains the minimum value of the corresponding row of the argument.

RND(M)   *Elements rounded to the nearest integers.* Takes a single argument. Returns a matrix having the same dimensions as the argument. Each element of the result equals the corresponding element of the argument rounded to an integer.

RNKORDER(M)   *Ranking of matrix elements in ascending order.* Takes a single argument. Returns a matrix having the same dimensions as the argument M. The smallest element of the argument corresponds to a result element of 1, and the largest element of the argument to a result element equal to the number of elements, except that ties (equal elements in M) are resolved by assigning a rank equal to the arithmetic mean of the applicable ranks. For example, if:

$$M = \begin{bmatrix} -1 & -21.7 & 8 \\ 0 & 3.91 & -21.7 \\ 8 & 9 & 10 \end{bmatrix}, \text{ then: } \text{RNKORDER}(M) = \begin{bmatrix} 3 & 1.5 & 6.5 \\ 4 & 5 & 1.5 \\ 6.5 & 8 & 9 \end{bmatrix}$$

RSSQ(M)	*Row sums of squares.* Takes a single argument. Returns a column vector having the same number of rows as the argument. Each row of the result contains the sum of the squared values of the elements in the corresponding row of the argument.
RSUM(M)	*Row sums.* Takes a single argument. Returns a column vector having the same number of rows as the argument. Each row of the result contains the sum of the elements in the corresponding row of the argument.
SIN(M)	*Sines.* Takes a single argument. Returns a matrix having the same dimensions as the argument, containing the sines of the elements of the argument. Elements of the argument matrix are assumed to be measured in radians. To convert degrees to radians, multiply by $\pi/180$, which you can compute as ARTAN(1)/45. For example, the statement COMPUTE SINES=SIN(DEGREES*ARTAN(1)/45) computes sines from a matrix containing elements measured in degrees.
SOLVE(M1,M2)	*Solution of systems of linear equations.* Takes two arguments, the first of which must be square and nonsingular (its determinant must be nonzero), and the second of which must have the same number of rows as the first. Returns a matrix with the same dimensions as the second argument. If *M1*X=M2*, then *X*=SOLVE(*M1, M2*). In effect, this function sets its result *X* equal to INV(*M1*)*M2.
SQRT(M)	*Square roots of elements.* Takes a single argument, whose elements must not be negative. Returns a matrix having the same dimensions as the arguments, whose elements are the positive square roots of the corresponding elements of the argument.
SSCP(M)	*Sums of squares and cross-products.* Takes a single argument. Returns a square matrix having as many rows (and columns) as the argument has columns. SSCP *(M)* equals T*(M)*M*, where T is the transpose function defined below.
SVAL(M)	*Singular values of a matrix.* Takes a single argument. Returns a column vector containing as many rows as the minimum of the numbers of rows and columns in the argument, containing the singular values of the argument in decreasing numerical order. The singular values of a matrix *M* are the square roots of the eigenvalues of T*(M)*M*, where T is the transpose function discussed below.
SWEEP(M,S)	*Sweep transformation of a matrix.* Takes two arguments, a matrix and a scalar, which must be less than or equal to both the number of rows and the number of columns of the matrix. In other words, the pivot

element of the matrix, which is $M(S,S)$, must exist. Returns a matrix of the same dimensions as M. Suppose that $S=\{k\}$ and $A=\text{SWEEP}(M,S)$. If $M(k,k)$ is not 0, then

$A(k, k) \ = \ 1/M(k, k)$

$A(i, k) \ = \ -M(i, k)/M(k, k)$ for i not equal to k

$A(k, j) \ = \ M(k, j)/(M(k, k))$ for j not equal to k

$A(i, j) \ = \ (M(k, k)*M(i, j) - M(i, k)*M(k, j))/M(k, k)$

$$\text{for } i,j \text{ not equal to } k$$

and if $M(k,k)$ equals 0, then

$A(i, k) \ = \ A(k, i) \ = \ 0$ for all i

$A(i, j) \ = \ M(i, j)$ for i,j not equal to k

TCDF(M,S)   *Cumulative* t *distribution function of elements.* Takes two arguments, a matrix of t values and a scalar giving the degrees of freedom (which must be positive). Returns a matrix having the same dimensions as M, containing the values of the cumulative t distribution function for each of its elements. If an element of the first argument is x and the second argument is S, then the corresponding element of the result is a number between 0 and 1, giving the proportion of a t distribution with S degrees of freedom that is less than x.

TRACE(M)   *Sum of the main diagonal elements.* Takes a single argument. Returns a scalar, which equals the sum of the elements on the main diagonal of the argument.

TRANSPOS(M)   *Transpose of the matrix.* Takes a single argument. Returns the transpose of the argument. TRANSPOS can be shortened to T.

TRUNC(M)   *Truncation of elements to integers.* Takes a single argument. Returns a matrix having the same dimensions as the argument, whose elements equal the corresponding elements of the argument truncated to integers.

UNIFORM(S1,S2)   *Uniformly distributed pseudo-random numbers between 0 and 1.* Takes two scalars as arguments. Returns a matrix with the number of rows specified by the first argument and the number of columns specified by the second argument, containing pseudo-random numbers uniformly distributed between 0 and 1.

CALL Statement

Closely related to the matrix functions are the matrix procedures, which are invoked with the CALL statement. Procedures, similarly to functions, accept arguments enclosed in parentheses and separated by commas. They return their result in one or more of the arguments as noted in the individual descriptions below. They are implemented as procedures rather than as functions so that they can return more than one value or (in the case of SETDIAG) modify a matrix without making a copy of it.

EIGEN(M,var1,var2)   *Eigenvectors and eigenvalues of a symmetric matrix.* Takes three arguments: a symmetric matrix and two valid variable names to which the results are assigned. If M is a symmetric matrix, the statement

CALL EIGEN(M, A, B) will assign to *A* a matrix having the same dimensions as *M*, containing the eigenvectors of *M* as its columns, and will assign to *B* a column vector having as many rows as *M*, containing the eigenvalues of *M* in descending numerical order. The eigenvectors in *A* are ordered to correspond with the eigenvalues in *B*; thus, the first column corresponds to the largest eigenvalue, the second to the second largest, and so on.

SETDIAG(M,V)   *Set the main diagonal of a matrix.* Takes two arguments, a matrix and a vector. Elements on the main diagonal of *M* are set equal to the corresponding elements of *V*. If *V* is a scalar, all the diagonal elements are set equal to that scalar. Otherwise, if *V* has fewer elements than the main diagonal of *M*, remaining elements on the main diagonal are unchanged. If *V* has more elements than are needed, the extra elements are not used. See also MDIAG on p. 723.

SVD(M,var1,var2,var3)   *Singular value decomposition of a matrix.* Takes four arguments: a matrix and three valid variable names to which the results are assigned. If *M* is a matrix, the statement CALL SVD(M,U,Q,V) will assign to *Q* a diagonal matrix of the same dimensions as *M*, and to *U* and *V* unitary matrices (matrices whose inverses equal their transposes) of appropriate dimensions, such that $M=U*Q*T(V)$, where T is the transpose function defined above. The singular values of *M* are in the main diagonal of *Q*.

PRINT Statement

The PRINT statement displays matrices or matrix expressions. Its syntax is as follows:

```
PRINT [matrix expression]
      [/FORMAT="format descriptor"]
      [/TITLE="title"]
      [/SPACE={NEWPAGE}]
             {n      }
      [{/RLABELS=list of quoted names}]
       {/RNAMES=vector of names      }

      [{/CLABELS=list of quoted names}]
       {/CNAMES=vector of names       }
```

Matrix Expression

Matrix expression is a single matrix variable name or an expression that evaluates to a matrix. PRINT displays the specified matrix.

- The matrix specification must precede any other specifications on the PRINT statement. If no matrix is specified, no data will be displayed, but the TITLE and SPACE specifications will be honored.

- You can specify a matrix name, a matrix raised to a power, or a matrix function (with its arguments in parentheses) by itself, but you must enclose other matrix expressions in parentheses. For example, PRINT A, PRINT INV(A), and PRINT B**DET(T(C)*D) are all legal, but PRINT A+B is not. You must specify PRINT (A+B).

- Constant expressions are allowed.
- A matrix program can consist entirely of PRINT statements, without defining any matrix variables.

FORMAT Keyword

FORMAT specifies a single format descriptor for display of the matrix data.

- All matrix elements are displayed with the same format.
- You can use any printable numeric format (for numeric matrices) or string format (for string matrices) as defined in FORMATS.
- The matrix processor will choose a suitable numeric format if you omit the FORMAT specification, but a string format such as A8 is essential when displaying a matrix containing string data.
- String values exceeding the width of a string format are truncated.
- See "Scaling Factor in Displays" on p. 729 for default formatting of matrices containing large or small values.

TITLE Keyword

TITLE specifies a title for the matrix displayed. The title must be enclosed in quotation marks or apostrophes. If it exceeds the maximum display width, it is truncated. The slash preceding TITLE is required, even if it is the only specification on the PRINT statement. If you omit the TITLE specification, the matrix name or expression from the PRINT statement is used as a default title.

SPACE Keyword

SPACE controls output spacing before printing the title and the matrix. You can specify either a positive number or the keyword NEWPAGE. The slash preceding SPACE is required, even if it is the only specification on the PRINT statement.

NEWPAGE   *Start a new page before printing the title.*

n   *Skip* n *lines before displaying the title.*

RLABELS Keyword

RLABELS allows you to supply row labels for the matrix.

- The labels must be separated by commas.
- Enclose individual labels in quotation marks or apostrophes if they contain imbedded commas or if you want to preserve lowercase letters. Otherwise, quotation marks or apostrophes are optional.
- If too many names are supplied, the extras are ignored. If not enough names are supplied, the last rows remain unlabeled.

RNAMES Keyword

RNAMES allows you to supply the name of a vector or a vector expression containing row labels for the matrix.

- Either a row vector or a column vector can be used, but the vector must contain string data.
- If too many names are supplied, the extras are ignored. If not enough names are supplied, the last rows remain unlabeled.

CLABELS Keyword

CLABELS allows you to supply column labels for the matrix.

- The labels must be separated by commas.
- Enclose individual labels in quotation marks or apostrophes if they contain imbedded commas or if you want to preserve lowercase letters. Otherwise, quotation marks or apostrophes are optional.
- If too many names are supplied, the extras are ignored. If not enough names are supplied, the last columns remain unlabeled.

CNAMES Keyword

CNAMES allows you to supply the name of a vector or a vector expression containing column labels for the matrix.

- Either a row vector or a column vector can be used, but the vector must contain string data.
- If too many names are supplied, the extras are ignored. If not enough names are supplied, the last columns remain unlabeled.

Scaling Factor in Displays

When a matrix contains very large or very small numbers, it may be necessary to use scientific notation to display the data. If you do not specify a display format, the matrix processor chooses a power-of-10 multiplier that will allow the largest value to be displayed, and it displays this multiplier on a heading line before the data. The multiplier is not displayed for each element in the matrix. The displayed values, multiplied by the power of 10 that is indicated in the heading, equal the actual values (possibly rounded).

- Values that are very small, relative to the multiplier, are displayed as 0.
- If you explicitly specify a scientific-notation format (Ew.d), each matrix element is displayed using that format. This permits you to display very large and very small numbers in the same matrix without losing precision.

Example

```
COMPUTE M = {.0000000001357, 2.468, 3690000000}.
PRINT M /TITLE "Default format".
PRINT M /FORMAT "E13" /TITLE "Explicit exponential format".
```

- The first PRINT subcommand uses the default format with 10^9 as the multiplier for each element of the matrix. This results in the following output:

```
Default format
   10 ** 9   X
     .000000000    .000000002   3.690000000
```

Note that the first element is displayed as 0 and the second is rounded to one significant digit.

- An explicitly specified exponential format on the second PRINT subcommand allows each element to be displayed with full precision, as the following output shows:

```
Explicit exponential format
 1.3570000E-10 2.4680000E+00 3.6900000E+09
```

Matrix Control Structures

The matrix language includes two structures that allow you to alter the flow of control within a matrix program.

- The DO IF statement tests a logical expression to determine whether one or more subsequent matrix statements should be executed.
- The LOOP statement defines the beginning of a block of matrix statements that should be executed repeatedly until a termination criterion is satisfied or a BREAK statement is executed.

These statements closely resemble the DO IF and LOOP commands in the SPSS transformation language. In particular, these structures can be nested within one another as deeply as the available memory allows.

DO IF Structures

A DO IF structure in a matrix program affects the flow of control exactly as the analogous commands affect an SPSS transformation program, except that missing-value considerations do not arise in a matrix program. The syntax of the DO IF structure is as follows:

```
DO IF [(]logical expression[)]

  matrix statements

[ELSE IF [(]logical expression[)]]

  matrix statements

[ELSE IF...]

   .
   .
   .

[ELSE]

 matrix statements

END IF.
```

- The DO IF statement marks the beginning of the structure, and the END IF statement marks its end.

- The ELSE IF statement is optional and can be repeated as many times as desired within the structure.
- The ELSE statement is optional. It can be used only once and must follow any ELSE IF statements.
- The END IF statement must follow any ELSE IF and ELSE statements.
- The DO IF and ELSE IF statements must contain a logical expression, normally one involving the relational operators EQ, GT, and so on. However, the matrix language allows any expression that evaluates to a scalar to be used as the logical expression. Scalars greater than 0 are considered true, and scalars less than or equal to 0 are considered false.

A DO IF structure affects the flow of control within a matrix program as follows:

- If the logical expression on the DO IF statement is true, the statements immediately following the DO IF are executed up to the next ELSE IF or ELSE in the structure. Control then passes to the first statement following the END IF for that structure.
- If the expression on the DO IF statement is false, control passes to the first ELSE IF, where the logical expression is evaluated. If this expression is true, statements following the ELSE IF are executed up to the next ELSE IF or ELSE statement, and control passes to the first statement following the END IF for that structure.
- If the expressions on the DO IF and the first ELSE IF statements are both false, control passes to the next ELSE IF, where that logical expression is evaluated. If none of the expressions is true on any of the ELSE IF statements, statements following the ELSE statement are executed up to the END IF statement, and control falls out of the structure.
- If none of the expressions on the DO IF statement or the ELSE IF statements is true and there is no ELSE statement, control passes to the first statement following the END IF for that structure.

LOOP Structures

A LOOP structure in a matrix program affects the flow of control exactly as the analogous commands affect an SPSS transformation program, except that missing-value considerations do not arise in a matrix program. Its syntax is as follows:

```
LOOP [varname=n TO m [BY k]] [IF [(]logical expression[)]]

matrix statements

[BREAK]

matrix statements

END LOOP [IF [(]logical expression[)]]
```

The matrix statements specified between LOOP and END LOOP are executed repeatedly until one of the following four conditions is met:

- A logical expression on the IF clause of the LOOP statement is evaluated as false.
- An index variable used on the LOOP statement passes beyond its terminal value.
- A logical expression on the IF clause of the END LOOP statement is evaluated as true.
- A BREAK statement is executed within the loop structure (but outside of any nested loop structures).

Index Clause on the LOOP Statement

An index clause on a LOOP statement creates an index variable whose name is specified immediately after the keyword LOOP. The variable is assigned an initial value of n. Each time through the loop, the variable is tested against the terminal value m and incremented by the increment value k if k is specified, or by 1 if k is not specified. When the index variable is greater than m for positive increments or less than m for negative increments, control passes to the statement after the END LOOP statement.

- Both the index clause and the IF clause are optional. If both are present, the index clause must appear first.
- The index variable must be scalar with a valid matrix variable name.
- The initial value, n, the terminal value, m, and the increment, k (if present), must be scalars or matrix expressions evaluating to scalars. Non-integer values are truncated to integers before use.
- If the keyword BY and the increment k are absent, an increment of 1 is used.

IF Clause on the LOOP Statement

The logical expression is evaluated before each iteration of the loop structure. If it is false, the loop terminates and control passes to the statement after END LOOP.

- The IF clause is optional. If both the index clause and the IF clause are present, the index clause must appear first.
- As in the DO IF structure, the logical expression of the IF clause is evaluated as scalar, with positive values being treated as true and 0 or negative values, as false.

IF Clause on the END LOOP Statement

When an IF clause is present on an END LOOP statement, the logical expression is evaluated after each iteration of the loop structure. If it is true, the loop terminates and control passes to the statement following the END LOOP statement.

- The IF clause is optional.
- As in the LOOP statement, the logical expression of the IF clause is evaluated as scalar, with positive values being treated as true and 0 or negative values, as false.

BREAK Statement

The BREAK statement within a loop structure transfers control immediately to the statement following the (next) END LOOP statement. It is normally placed within a DO IF structure inside the LOOP structure to exit the loop when specified conditions are met.

Example

```
LOOP LOCATION = 1, NROW(VEC).
+  DO IF (VEC(LOCATION) = TARGET).
+     BREAK.

+  END IF.
END LOOP.
```

- This loop searches for the (first) location of a specific value, *TARGET*, in a vector, *VEC*.

- The DO IF statement checks whether the vector element indexed by *LOCATION* equals the target.

- If so, the BREAK statement transfers control out of the loop, leaving *LOCATION* as the index of *TARGET* in *VEC*.

READ Statement: Reading Character Data

The READ statement reads data into a matrix or submatrix from a character-format file—that is, a file containing ordinary numbers or words in readable form. The syntax for the READ statement is:

```
READ  variable reference
  [/FILE = file reference]
   /FIELD = c1 TO c2 [BY w]
  [/SIZE = size expression]
  [/MODE = {RECTANGULAR}]
           {SYMMETRIC  }
  [/REREAD]
  [/FORMAT = format descriptor]
```

- The file can contain values in freefield or fixed-column format. The data can appear in any of the field formats supported by DATA LIST.

- More than one matrix can be read from a single input record by rereading the record.

- If the end of the file is encountered during a READ operation (that is, fewer values are available than the number of elements required by the specified matrix size), a warning message is displayed and the contents of the unread elements of the matrix are unpredictable.

Variable Specification

The variable reference on the READ statement is a matrix variable name, with or without indexes.

For a name without indexes:

- READ creates the specified matrix variable.

- The matrix need not exist when READ is executed.

- If the matrix already exists, it is replaced by the matrix read from the file.

- You must specify the size of the matrix using the SIZE specification.

For an indexed name:

- READ creates a submatrix from an existing matrix.

- The matrix variable named must already exist.
- You can define any submatrix with indexes; for example, M(:,I). To define an entire existing matrix, specify M(:,:).
- The SIZE specification can be omitted. If specified, its value must match the size of the specified submatrix.

FILE Specification

FILE designates the character file containing the data. It can be an actual filename in apostrophes or quotation marks, or a file handle defined on a FILE HANDLE command that precedes the matrix program.

- The filename or handle must specify an existing file containing character data, not an SPSS data file or a specially formatted file of another kind, such as a spreadsheet file.
- The FILE specification is required on the first READ statement in a matrix program (first in order of appearance, not necessarily in order of execution). If you omit the FILE specification from a later READ statement, the statement uses the most recently named file (in order of appearance) on a READ statement in the same matrix program.

FIELD Specification

FIELD specifies the column positions of a fixed-format record where the data for matrix elements are located.

- The FIELD specification is required.
- Startcol is the number of the leftmost column of the input area.
- Endcol is the number of the rightmost column of the input area.
- Both startcol and endcol are required and both must be constants. For example, FIELD = 9 TO 72 specifies that values to be read appear between columns 9 and 72 (inclusive) of each input record.
- The BY clause, if present, indicates that each value appears within a fixed set of columns on the input record; that is, one value is separated from the next by its column position rather than by a space or comma. Width is the width of the area designated for each value. For example, FIELD = 1 TO 80 BY 10 indicates that there are eight possible values per record and that one will appear between columns 1 and 10 (inclusive), another between columns 11 and 20, and so on, up to columns 71 and 80. The BY value must evenly divide the length of the field. That is, endcol − startcol + 1 must be a multiple of the width.
- You can use the FORMAT specification (see p. 736) to supply the same information as the BY clause of the FIELD specification. If you omit the BY clause and do not specify a format on the FORMAT specification, READ assumes that values are separated by blanks or commas within the designated field.

SIZE Specification

The SIZE specification is a matrix expression that, when evaluated, specifies the size of the matrix to be read.

- The expression should evaluate to a two-element row or column vector. The first element designates the number of rows in the matrix to be read; the second element gives the number of columns.
- Values of the SIZE specification are truncated to integers if necessary.
- The size expression may be a constant, such as {5;5}, or a matrix variable name, such as MSIZE, or any valid expression, such as INFO(1,:).
- If you use a scalar as the size expression, a column vector containing that number of rows is read. Thus, SIZE=1 reads a scalar, and SIZE=3 reads a 3 × 1 column vector.

You must include a SIZE specification whenever you name an entire matrix (rather than a submatrix) on the READ statement. If you specify a submatrix, the SIZE specification is optional but, if included, must agree with the size of the specified submatrix.

MODE Specification

MODE specifies the format of the matrix to be read in. It can be either rectangular or symmetric. If the MODE specification is omitted, the default is RECTANGULAR.

RECTANGULAR   *Matrix is completely represented in file.* Each row begins on a new record, and all entries in that row are present on that and (possibly) succeeding records. This is the default if the MODE specification is omitted.

SYMMETRIC   *Elements of the matrix below the main diagonal are the same as those above it.* Only matrix elements on and below the main diagonal are read; elements above the diagonal are set equal to the corresponding symmetric elements below the diagonal. Each row is read beginning on a new record, although it may span more than one record. Only a single value is read from the first record, two values are read from the second, and so on.

- If SYMMETRIC is specified, the matrix processor first checks that the number of rows and the number of columns are the same. If the numbers, specified either on SIZE or on the variable reference, are not the same, an error message is displayed and the command is not executed.

REREAD Specification

The REREAD specification indicates that the current READ statement should begin with the last record read by a previous READ statement.

- REREAD has no further specifications.
- REREAD cannot be used on the first READ statement to read from a file.
- If you omit REREAD, the READ statement begins with the first record following the last one read by the previous READ statement.
- The REREAD specification is ignored on the first READ statement following a call to the EOF function for the same file.

FORMAT Specification

FORMAT specifies how the matrix processor should interpret the input data. The format descriptor can be any valid SPSS data format, such as `F6`, `E12.2`, or `A6`, or it can be a type code; for example, `F`, `E`, or `A`.

- If you omit the FORMAT specification, the default is `F`.

- You can specify the width of fixed-size data fields with either a FORMAT specification or a BY clause on a FIELD specification. You can include it in both places only if you specify the same value.

- If you do not include either a FORMAT or a BY clause on FIELD, READ expects values separated by blanks or commas.

- An additional way of specifying the width is to supply a repetition factor without a width (for example, `10F`, `5COMMA`, or `3E`). The field width is then calculated by dividing the width of the whole input area on the FIELD specification by the repetition factor. A format with a digit for the repetition factor must be enclosed in quotes.

- Only one format can be specified. A specification such as `FORMAT='5F2.0  3F3.0 F2.0'` is invalid.

WRITE Statement: Writing Character Data

WRITE writes the value of a matrix expression to an external file. The syntax of the WRITE statement is:

```
WRITE  matrix expression
   [/OUTFILE = file reference]
    /FIELD = startcol TO endcol [BY width]
   [/MODE = {RECTANGULAR}]
           {TRIANGULAR }
   [/HOLD]
   [/FORMAT = format descriptor]
```

Matrix Expression Specification

Specify any matrix expression that evaluates to the value(s) to be written.

- The matrix specification must precede any other specifications on the WRITE statement.

- You can specify a matrix name, a matrix raised to a power, or a matrix function (with its arguments in parentheses) by itself, but you must enclose other matrix expressions in parentheses. For example, `WRITE A`, `WRITE INV(A)`, or `WRITE B**DET(T(C)*D)` is legal, but `WRITE A+B` is not. You must specify `WRITE (A+B)`.

- Constant expressions are allowed.

OUTFILE Specification

OUTFILE designates the character file to which the matrix expression is to be written. The file reference can be an actual filename in apostrophes or quotation marks, or a file handle defined on a FILE HANDLE command that precedes the matrix program. The filename or file handle must be a valid file specification.

- The OUTFILE specification is required on the first WRITE statement in a matrix program (first in order of appearance, not necessarily in order of execution).

- If you omit the OUTFILE specification from a later WRITE statement, the statement uses the most recently named file (in order of appearance) on a WRITE statement in the same matrix program.

FIELD Specification

FIELD specifies the column positions of a fixed-format record to which the data should be written.

- The FIELD specification is required.

- The start column, $c1$, is the number of the leftmost column of the output area.

- The end column, $c2$, is the number of the rightmost column of the output area.

- Both $c1$ and $c2$ are required, and both must be constants. For example, FIELD = 9 TO 72 specifies that values should be written between columns 9 and 72 (inclusive) of each output record.

- The BY clause, if present, indicates how many characters should be allocated to the output value of a single matrix element. The value w is the width of the area designated for each value. For example, FIELD = 1 TO 80 BY 10 indicates that up to eight values should be written per record, and that one should go between columns 1 and 10 (inclusive), another between columns 11 and 20, and so on up to columns 71 and 80. The value on the BY clause must evenly divide the length of the field. That is, $c2 - c1 + 1$ must be a multiple of w.

- You can use the FORMAT specification (see below) to supply the same information as the BY clause. If you omit the BY clause from the FIELD specification and do not specify a format on the FORMAT specification, WRITE uses freefield format, separating matrix elements by single blank spaces.

MODE Specification

MODE specifies the format of the matrix to be written. If MODE is not specified, the default is RECTANGULAR.

RECTANGULAR   *Write the entire matrix.* Each row starts a new record, and all of the values in that row are present in that and (possibly) subsequent records. This is the default if the MODE specification is omitted.

TRIANGULAR   *Write only the lower triangular entries and the main diagonal.* Each row begins a new record and may span more than one record. This mode may save file space.

- A matrix written with MODE = TRIANGULAR must be square, but it need not be symmetric. If it is not, values in the upper triangle are not written.

- A matrix written with MODE = TRIANGULAR may be read with MODE = SYMMETRIC.

HOLD Specification

HOLD causes the last line written by the current WRITE statement to be held so that the next WRITE to that file will write on the same line. Use HOLD to write more than one matrix on a line.

FORMAT Specification

FORMAT indicates how the internal (binary) values of matrix elements should be converted to character format for output.

- The format descriptor is any valid SPSS data format, such as F6, E12.2, or A6, or it can be a format type code, such as F, E, or A. It specifies how the written data are encoded and, if a width is specified, how wide the fields containing the data are. (See FORMATS for valid formats.)
- If you omit the FORMAT specification, the default is F.
- The data field widths may be specified either here or after BY on the FIELD specification. You may specify the width in both places only if you give the same value.
- An additional way of specifying the width is to supply a repetition factor without a width (for example, 10F or 5COMMA). The field width is then calculated by dividing the width of the whole output area on the FIELD specification by the repetition factor. A format with a digit for the repetition factor must be enclosed in quotes.
- If the field width is not specified in any of these ways, then the freefield format is used— matrix values are written separated by one blank, and each value occupies as many positions as necessary to avoid the loss of precision. Each row of the matrix is written starting with a new output record.
- Only one format descriptor can be specified. Do *not* try to specify more than one format; for example, '5F2.0 3F3.0 F2.0' is invalid as a FORMAT specification on WRITE.

GET Statement: Reading SPSS Data Files

GET reads matrices from an external SPSS data file or from the working data file. The syntax of GET is as follows:

```
GET variable reference
  [/FILE={file reference}]
        {*            }
  [/VARIABLES = variable list]
  [/NAMES = names vector]
  [/MISSING = {ACCEPT}]
             {OMIT  }
             {value }
  [/SYSMIS = {OMIT }]
            {value}
```

Variable Specification

The variable reference on the GET statement is a matrix variable name with or without indexes.

For a name without indexes:

- GET creates the specified matrix variable.
- The size of the matrix is determined by the amount of data read from the SPSS data file or the working file.
- If the matrix already exists, it is replaced by the matrix read from the file.

For an indexed name:

- GET creates a submatrix from an existing matrix.
- The matrix variable named must already exist.
- You can define any submatrix with indexes; for example, $M(:,I)$. To define an entire existing matrix, specify $M(:,:)$.
- The indexes, along with the size of the existing matrix, specify completely the size of the submatrix, which must agree with the dimensions of the data read from the SPSS data file.
- The specified submatrix is replaced by the matrix elements read from the SPSS data file.

FILE Specification

FILE designates the SPSS data file to be read. Use an asterisk, or simply omit the FILE specification, to designate the current working data file.

- The file reference can be either a filename enclosed in apostrophes or quotation marks, or a file handle defined on a FILE HANDLE command that precedes the matrix program.
- If you omit the FILE specification, the working data file is used.
- In a matrix program executed with the INCLUDE command, if a SPLIT FILE command is in effect, a GET statement that references the working data file will read a single split-file group of cases. (A matrix program cannot be executed from a syntax window if a SPLIT FILE command is in effect.)

VARIABLES Specification

VARIABLES specifies a list of variables to be read from the SPSS data file.

- The variable list is entered much the same as in other SPSS procedures except that the variable names *must* be separated by commas.
- The keyword TO can be used to reference consecutive variables on the SPSS data file.
- The variable list can consist of the keyword ALL to get all the variables in the SPSS data file. ALL is the default if the VARIABLES specification is omitted.
- All variables read from the SPSS data file should be numeric. If a string variable is specified, a warning message is issued and the string variable is skipped.

Example

```
GET M /VARIABLES = AGE, RESIDE, INCOME TO HEALTH.
```

- The variables *AGE*, *RESIDE*, and *INCOME* to *HEALTH* from the working data file will form the columns of the matrix *M*.

NAMES Specification

NAMES specifies a vector to store the variable names from the SPSS data file.

- If you omit the NAMES specification, the variable names are not available to the MATRIX procedure.
- In place of a vector name, you can use a matrix expression that evaluates to a vector, such as A(N+1,:).

MISSING Specification

MISSING specifies how missing values declared for the SPSS data file should be handled.

- The MISSING specification is required if the SPSS data file contains missing values for any variable being read.
- If you omit the MISSING specification and a missing value is encountered for a variable being read, an error message is displayed and the GET statement is not executed.

The following keywords are available on the MISSING specification. There is no default.

ACCEPT *Accept user-missing values for entry.* If the system-missing value exists for a variable to be read, you must specify SYSMIS to indicate how the system-missing value should be handled (see "SYSMIS Specification" below).

OMIT *Skip an entire observation when a variable with a missing value is encountered.*

value *Recode all missing values encountered (including the system-missing value) to the specified value for entry.* The replacement value can be any numeric constant.

SYSMIS Specification

SYSMIS specifies how system-missing values should be handled when you have specified ACCEPT on MISSING.

- The SYSMIS specification is ignored unless ACCEPT is specified on MISSING.
- If you specify ACCEPT on MISSING but omit the SYSMIS specification, and a system-missing value is encountered for a variable being read, an error message is displayed and the GET statement is not executed.

The following keywords are available on the SYSMIS specification. There is no default.

OMIT *Skip an entire observation when a variable with a system-missing value is encountered.*

value *Recode all system-missing values encountered to the specified value for entry.* The replacement value can be any numeric constant.

Example

```
GET SCORES
  /VARIABLES = TEST1,TEST2,TEST3
  /NAMES = VARNAMES
  /MISSING = ACCEPT
  /SYSMIS = -1.0.
```

- A matrix named *SCORES* is read from the working data file.
- The variables *TEST1*, *TEST2*, and *TEST3* form the columns of the matrix, while the cases in the working file form the rows.
- A vector named *VARNAMES*, whose three elements contain the variable names *TEST1*, *TEST2*, and *TEST3*, is created.
- User-missing values defined in the working data file are accepted into the matrix *SCORES*.
- System-missing values in the working data file are converted to the value −1 in the matrix *SCORES*.

SAVE Statement: Writing SPSS Data Files

SAVE writes matrices to an SPSS data file or to the current working data file. The rows of the matrix expression become cases, and the columns become variables. The syntax of the SAVE statement is as follows:

```
SAVE matrix expression
  [/OUTFILE = {file reference}]
              {*             }
  [/VARIABLES = variable list]
  [/NAMES = names vector]
  [/STRINGS = variable list]
```

Matrix Expression Specification

The matrix expression following the keyword SAVE is any matrix language expression that evaluates to the value(s) to be written to an SPSS data file.

- The matrix specification must precede any other specifications on the SAVE statement.
- You can specify a matrix name, a matrix raised to a power, or a matrix function (with its arguments in parentheses) by itself, but you must enclose other matrix expressions in parentheses. For example, SAVE A, SAVE INV(A), or SAVE B**DET(T(C)*D) is legal, but SAVE A+B is not. You must specify SAVE (A+B).
- Constant expressions are allowed.

OUTFILE Specification

OUTFILE designates the file to which the matrix expression is to be written. It can be an actual filename in apostrophes or quotation marks, or a file handle defined on a FILE HANDLE command that precedes the matrix program. The filename or handle must be a valid file specification.

- To save a matrix expression as the working data file, specify an asterisk (*). If there is no working data file, one will be created; if there is one, it is replaced by the saved matrices.
- The OUTFILE specification is required on the first SAVE statement in a matrix program (first in order of appearance, not necessarily in order of execution). If you omit the OUTFILE specification from a later SAVE statement, the statement uses the most recently named file (in order of appearance) on a SAVE statement in the same matrix program.

- If more than one SAVE statement writes to the working data file in a single matrix program, the dictionary of the new working data file is written on the basis of the information given by the first such SAVE. All the subsequently saved matrices are appended to the new working data file as additional cases. If the number of columns differs, an error occurs.

- When you execute a matrix program with the INCLUDE command, the SAVE statement creates a new SPSS data file at the end of the matrix program's execution, so any attempt to GET the data file obtains the original data file, if any.

- When you execute a matrix program from a syntax window, SAVE creates a new SPSS data file immediately, but the file remains open, so you cannot GET it until after the END MATRIX statement.

VARIABLES Specification

You can provide variable names for the SPSS data file with the VARIABLES specification. The variable list is a list of valid SPSS variable names separated by commas.

- You can use the TO convention, as shown in the example below.

- You can also use the NAMES specification, discussed below, to provide variable names.

Example

```
SAVE {A,B,X,Y} /OUTFILE=*
    /VARIABLES = A,B,X1 TO X50,Y1,Y2.
```

- The matrix expression on the SAVE statement constructs a matrix from two column vectors A and B and two matrices X and Y. All four matrix variables must have the same number of rows so that this matrix construction will be valid.

- The VARIABLES specification provides descriptive names so that the SPSS variable names in the new working data file will resemble the names used in the matrix program.

NAMES Specification

As an alternative to the explicit list on the VARIABLES specification, you can specify a name list with a matrix expression that evaluates to a vector containing string values. The elements of this vector are used as names for the variables.

- The NAMES specification on SAVE is designed to complement the NAMES specification on the GET statement. Names extracted from an SPSS data file can be used in a new data file by specifying the same vector name on both NAMES specifications.

- If you specify both VARIABLES and NAMES, a warning message is displayed and the VARIABLES specification is used.

- If you omit both the VARIABLES and NAMES specifications, or if you do not specify names for all columns of the matrix, the MATRIX procedure creates default names. The names have the form *COLn*, where n is the column number.

STRINGS Specification

The STRINGS specification provides the names of variables that contain short string data rather than numeric data.

- By default, all variables are assumed to be numeric.
- The variable list specification following STRINGS consists of a list of SPSS variable names separated by commas. The names must be among those used by SAVE.

MGET Statement: Reading SPSS Matrix Data Files

MGET reads an SPSS matrix-format data file. MGET puts the data it reads into separate matrix variables. It also names these new variables automatically. The syntax of MGET is as follows:

```
MGET [ [/] FILE = file reference]
  [/TYPE = {COV   }]
          {CORR  }
          {MEAN  }
          {STDDEV}
          {N     }
          {COUNT }
```

- Since MGET assigns names to the matrices it reads, do not specify matrix names on the MGET statement.

FILE Specification

FILE designates an SPSS matrix-format data file. (See MATRIX DATA for a discussion of matrix-format data files.) To designate the working data file (if it is a matrix-format data file), use an asterisk, or simply omit the FILE specification.

- The file reference can be either a filename enclosed in apostrophes or quotation marks, or a file handle defined on a FILE HANDLE command that precedes the matrix program.
- The same matrix-format SPSS data file can be read more than once.
- If you omit the FILE specification, the current working data file is used.
- MGET ignores the SPLIT FILE command in SPSS when reading the working data file. It does honor the split-file groups that were in effect when the matrix-format data file was created.
- The maximum number of split-file groups that can be read is 99.
- The maximum number of cells that can be read is 99.

TYPE Specification

TYPE specifies the rowtype(s) to read from the matrix-format data file.

- By default, records of all rowtypes are read.
- If the matrix-format data file does not contain rows of the requested type, an error occurs.

Valid keywords on the TYPE specification are:

COV   *A matrix of covariances.*

CORR   *A matrix of correlation coefficients.*

MEAN   *A vector of means.*

STDDEV *A vector of standard deviations.*

N   *A vector of numbers of cases.*

COUNT *A vector of counts.*

Names of Matrix Variables from MGET

- The MGET statement automatically creates matrix variable names for the matrices it reads.
- All new variables created by MGET are reported to the user.
- If a matrix variable already exists with the same name that MGET chose for a new variable, the new variable is not created and a warning is issued. The RELEASE statement can be used to get rid of a variable. A COMPUTE statement followed by RELEASE can be used to change the name of an existing matrix variable.

MGET constructs variable names in the following manner:

- The first two characters of the name identify the row type. If there are no cells and no split file groups, these two characters constitute the name:

  CV   A covariance matrix (rowtype COV)

  CR   A correlation matrix (rowtype CORR)

  MN   A vector of means (rowtype MEAN)

  SD   A vector of standard deviations (rowtype STDDEV)

  NC   A vector of numbers of cases (rowtype N)

  CN   A vector of counts (rowtype COUNT)

- Characters 3–5 of the variable name identify the cell number or the split-group number. Cell identifiers consist of the letter *F* and a two-digit cell number. Split-group identifiers consist of the letter *S* and a two-digit split-group number; for example, *MNF12* or *SDS22*.
- If there are both cells and split groups, characters 3–5 identify the cell and characters 6–8 identify the split group. The same convention for cell or split-file numbers is used—for example, *CRF12S21*.
- After the name is constructed as described above, any leading zeros are removed from the cell number and the split-group number—for example, *CNF2S99* or *CVF2S1*.

MSAVE Statement: Writing SPSS Matrix Data Files

The MSAVE statement writes matrix expressions to an SPSS matrix-format data file that can be used as matrix input to other SPSS procedures. (See MATRIX DATA for a discussion of matrix-format data files.) The syntax of MSAVE is as follows:

```
MSAVE matrix expression
   /TYPE = {COV   }
           {CORR  }
           {MEAN  }
           {STDDEV}
           {N     }
           {COUNT }
  [/OUTFILE = {file reference}]
             {*             }
  [/VARIABLES = variable list]
  [/SNAMES = variable list]
  [/SPLIT = split vector]
  [/FNAMES = variable list]
  [/FACTOR = factor vector]
```

- Only one matrix-format data file can be saved in a single matrix program.

- Each MSAVE statement writes records of a single rowtype. Therefore, several MSAVE statements will normally be required to write a complete matrix-format data file.

- Most specifications are retained from one MSAVE statement to the next so that it is not necessary to repeat the same specifications on a series of MSAVE statements. The exception is the FACTOR specification, as noted below.

Example

```
MSAVE M /TYPE=MEAN /OUTFILE=CORRMAT /VARIABLES=V1 TO V8.
MSAVE S /TYPE STDDEV.
MSAVE MAKE(1,8,24) /TYPE N.
MSAVE C /TYPE CORR.
```

- The series of MSAVE statements save the matrix variables *M*, *S*, and *C*, which contain, respectively, vectors of means and standard deviations and a matrix of correlation coefficients. The SPSS matrix-format data file thus created is suitable for use in a procedure such as FACTOR.

- The first MSAVE statement saves *M* as a vector of means. This statement specifies OUTFILE, a previously defined file handle, and VARIABLES, a list of variable names to be used in the SPSS data file.

- The second MSAVE statement saves *S* as a vector of standard deviations. Note that the OUTFILE and VARIABLES specifications do not have to be repeated.

- The third MSAVE statement saves a vector of case counts. The matrix function MAKE constructs an eight-element vector with values equal to the case count (24 in this example).

- The last MSAVE statement saves *C*, an 8×8 matrix, as the correlation matrix.

Matrix Expression Specification

- The matrix expression must be specified first on the MSAVE statement.

- The matrix expression specification can be any matrix language expression that evaluates to the value(s) to be written to the matrix-format file.
- You can specify a matrix name, a matrix raised to a power, or a matrix function (with its arguments in parentheses) by itself, but you must enclose other matrix expressions in parentheses. For example, MSAVE A, SAVE INV(A), or MSAVE B**DET(T(C)*D) is legal, but MSAVE N * WT is not. You must specify MSAVE (N * WT).
- Constant expressions are allowed.

TYPE Specification

TYPE specifies the rowtype to write to the matrix-format data file. Only a single rowtype can be written by any one MSAVE statement. Valid keywords on the TYPE specification are:

COV   *A matrix of covariances.*

CORR   *A matrix of correlation coefficients.*

MEAN   *A vector of means.*

STDDEV *A vector of standard deviations.*

N   *A vector of numbers of cases.*

COUNT   *A vector of counts.*

OUTFILE Specification

OUTFILE designates the SPSS matrix-format data file to which the matrices are to be written. It can be an asterisk, an actual filename in apostrophes or quotation marks, or a file handle defined on a FILE HANDLE command that precedes the matrix program. The filename or handle must be a valid file specification.

- The OUTFILE specification is required on the first MSAVE statement in a matrix program.
- To save a matrix expression as the working data file (replacing any working data file created before the matrix program), specify an asterisk (*).
- Since only one matrix-format data file can be written in a single matrix program, any OUTFILE specification on the second and later MSAVE statements in one matrix program must be the same as that on the first MSAVE statement.

VARIABLES Specification

You can provide variable names for the matrix-format data file with the VARIABLES specification. The variable list is a list of valid SPSS variable names separated by commas. You can use the TO convention.

- The VARIABLES specification names only the data variables in the matrix. Split-file variables and grouping or factor variables are named on the SNAMES and FNAMES specifications.
- The names in the VARIABLES specification become the values of the special variable *VARNAME_* in the matrix-format data file for rowtypes of CORR and COV.

- You cannot specify the reserved names *ROWTYPE_* and *VARNAME_* on the VARIABLES specification.

- If you omit the VARIABLES specification, the default names *COL1, COL2,...*, etc., are used.

FACTOR Specification

To write an SPSS matrix-format data file with factor or group codes, you must use the FACTOR specification to provide a row matrix containing the values of each of the factors or group variables for the matrix expression being written by the current MSAVE statement.

- The factor vector must have the same number of columns as there are factors in the matrix data file being written. You can use a scalar when the groups are defined by a single variable. For example, FACTOR=1 indicates that the matrix data being written are for the value 1 of the factor variable.

- The values of the factor vector are written to the matrix-format data file as values of the factors in the file.

- To create a complete matrix-format data file with factors, you must execute an MSAVE statement for every combination of values of the factors or grouping variables (in other words, for every group). If split-file variables are also present, you must execute an MSAVE statement for every combination of factor codes within every combination of values of the split-file variables.

Example

```
MSAVE M11 /TYPE=MEAN /OUTFILE=CORRMAT /VARIABLES=V1 TO V8
   /FNAMES=SEX, GROUP /FACTOR={1,1}.
MSAVE S11 /TYPE STDDEV.
MSAVE MAKE(1,8,N(1,1)) /TYPE N.
MSAVE C11 /TYPE CORR.

MSAVE M12 /TYPE=MEAN /FACTOR={1,2}.
MSAVE S12 /TYPE STDDEV.
MSAVE MAKE(1,8,N(1,2)) /TYPE N.
MSAVE C12 /TYPE CORR.

MSAVE M21 /TYPE=MEAN /FACTOR={2,1}.
MSAVE S21 /TYPE STDDEV.
MSAVE MAKE(1,8,N(2,1)) /TYPE N.
MSAVE C21 /TYPE CORR.

MSAVE M22 /TYPE=MEAN /FACTOR={2,2}.
MSAVE S22 /TYPE STDDEV.
MSAVE MAKE(1,8,N(2,2)) /TYPE N.
MSAVE C22 /TYPE CORR.
```

- The first four MSAVE statements provide data for a group defined by the variables *SEX* and *GROUP*, with both factors having the value 1.

- The second, third, and fourth groups of four MSAVE statements provide the corresponding data for the other groups, in which *SEX* and *GROUP*, respectively, equal 1 and 2, 2 and 1, and 2 and 2.

- Within each group of MSAVE statements, a suitable number-of-cases vector is created with the matrix function MAKE.

FNAMES Specification

To write an SPSS matrix-format data file with factor or group codes, you can use the FNAMES specification to provide variable names for the grouping or factor variables.

- The variable list following the keyword FNAMES is a list of valid SPSS variable names, separated by commas.
- If you omit the FNAMES specification, the default names *FAC1, FAC2*,..., etc., are used.

SPLIT Specification

To write an SPSS matrix-format data file with split-file groups, you must use the SPLIT specification to provide a row matrix containing the values of each of the split-file variables for the matrix expression being written by the current MSAVE statement.

- The split vector must have the same number of columns as there are split-file variables in the matrix data file being written. You can use a scalar when there is only one split-file variable. For example, `SPLIT=3` indicates that the matrix data being written are for the value 3 of the split-file variable.
- The values of the split vector are written to the matrix-format data file as values of the split-file variable(s).
- To create a complete matrix-format data file with split-file variables, you must execute MSAVE statements for every combination of values of the split-file variables. (If factor variables are present, you must execute MSAVE statements for every combination of factor codes within every combination of values of the split-file variables.)

SNAMES Specification

To write an SPSS matrix-format data file with split-file groups, you can use the SNAMES specification to provide variable names for the split-file variables.

- The variable list following the keyword SNAMES is a list of valid SPSS variable names separated by commas.
- If you omit the SNAMES specification, the default names *SPL1, SPL2*,..., etc., are used.

DISPLAY Statement

DISPLAY provides information on the matrix variables currently defined in a matrix program and on usage of internal memory by the matrix processor. Two keywords are available on DISPLAY:

DICTIONARY   *Display variable name and row and column dimensions for each matrix variable currently defined.*

STATUS   *Display the status and size of internal tables.* This display is intended as a debugging aid when writing large matrix programs that approach the memory limitations of your system.

If you enter the DISPLAY statement with no specifications, both DICTIONARY and STATUS information is displayed.

RELEASE Statement

Use the RELEASE statement to release the work areas in memory assigned to matrix variables that are no longer needed.

- Specify a list of currently defined matrix variables. Variable names on the list must be separated by commas.

- RELEASE discards the contents of the named matrix variables. Releasing a large matrix when it is no longer needed makes memory available for additional matrix variables.

- All matrix variables are released when the END MATRIX statement is encountered.

Macros Using the Matrix Language

Macro expansion (see DEFINE—END DEFINE) occurs before command lines are passed to the matrix processor. Therefore, previously defined macro names can be used within a matrix program. If the macro name expands to one or more valid matrix statements, the matrix processor will execute those statements. Similarly, you can define an entire matrix program, including the MATRIX and END MATRIX commands, as a macro, but you cannot define a macro within a matrix program, since DEFINE and END DEFINE are not valid matrix statements.

MATRIX DATA

```
MATRIX DATA VARIABLES=varlist    [/FILE={INLINE**}]
                                       {file     }

[/FORMAT=[{LIST**}]   [{LOWER**}]   [{DIAGONAL**}]]
         {FREE  }     {UPPER  }     {NODIAGONAL}
                      {FULL   }

[/SPLIT=varlist]     [/FACTORS=varlist]

[/CELLS=number of cells]     [/N=sample size]

[/CONTENTS= [CORR**]   [COV]   [MAT]   [MSE]   [DFE]   [MEAN]   [PROX]

            [{STDDEV}]   [N_SCALAR]   [{N_VECTOR}]   [N_MATRIX]   [COUNT]]
            {SD    }                  {N       }
```

**Default if the subcommand is omitted.

Example

```
MATRIX DATA VARIABLES=ROWTYPE_ SAVINGS POP15 POP75 INCOME GROWTH.
BEGIN DATA
MEAN 9.6710 35.0896 2.2930 1106.7784 3.7576
STDDEV 4.4804 9.1517 1.2907 990.8511 2.8699
N 50 50 50 50 50
CORR 1
CORR -.4555 1
CORR .3165 -.9085 1
CORR .2203 -.7562 .7870 1
CORR .3048 -.0478 .0253 -.1295  1
END DATA.
```

Overview

MATRIX DATA reads raw matrix materials and converts them to a matrix data file that can be read by procedures that handle matrix materials. The data can include vector statistics such as means and standard deviations as well as matrices.

MATRIX DATA is similar to a DATA LIST command: it defines variable names and their order in a raw data file. However, MATRIX DATA can read only data that conform to the general format of SPSS-format matrices.

Matrix Files

Like the matrix data files created by procedures, the file that MATRIX DATA creates contains the following variables in the indicated order. If the variables are in a different order in the raw data file, MATRIX DATA rearranges them in the working data file.

- *Split-file variables.* These optional variables define split files. There can be up to eight split variables, and they must have numeric values. Split-file variables will appear in the order in which they are specified on the SPLIT subcommand.

- *ROWTYPE_.* This is a string variable with A8 format. Its values define the data type for each record. For example, it might identify a row of values as means, standard deviations, or correlation coefficients. Every SPSS-format matrix data file has a *ROWTYPE_* variable.

- *Factor variables.* There can be any number of factors. They occur only if the data include within-cells information, such as the within-cells means. Factors have the system-missing value on records that define pooled information. Factor variables appear in the order in which they are specified on the FACTORS subcommand.

- *VARNAME_.* This is a string variable with A8 format. MATRIX DATA automatically generates *VARNAME_* and its values based on the variables named on VARIABLES. You never enter values for *VARNAME_.* Values for *VARNAME_* are blank for records that define vector information. Every matrix in the program has a *VARNAME_* variable.

- *Continuous variables.* These are the variables that were used to generate the correlation coefficients or other aggregated data. There can be any number of them. Continuous variables appear in the order in which they are specified on VARIABLES.

Options

Data Files. You can define both inline data and data in an external file.

Data Format. By default, data are assumed to be entered in freefield format with each vector or row beginning on a new record (the keyword LIST on the FORMAT subcommand). If each vector or row does not begin on a new record, use the keyword FREE. You can also use FORMAT to indicate whether matrices are entered in upper or lower triangular or full square or rectangular format, and whether or not they include diagonal values.

Variable Types. You can specify split-file and factor variables using the SPLIT and FACTORS subcommands. You can identify record types by specifying ROWTYPE_ on the VARIABLES subcommand if *ROWTYPE_* values are included in the data, or by implying *ROWTYPE_* values on CONTENTS.

Basic Specification

The basic specification is VARIABLES and a list of variables. Additional specifications are required as follows:

- FILE is required to specify the data file if the data are not inline.

- If data are in any format other than lower-triangular with diagonal values included, FORMAT is required.

- If the data contain values in addition to matrix coefficients, such as the mean and standard deviation, either variable *ROWTYPE_* must be specified on VARIABLES and *ROWTYPE_* values must be included in the data, or CONTENTS must be used to describe the data.

- If the data include split-file variables, SPLIT is required. If there are factors, FACTORS is required.

Specifications on most MATRIX DATA subcommands depend on whether *ROWTYPE_* is included in the data and specified on VARIABLES, or whether it is implied using CONTENTS.

Table 1 summarizes the status of each MATRIX DATA subcommand in relation to the *ROWTYPE_* specification.

Table 1   Subcommand requirements in relation to ROWTYPE_

Subcommand	Implicit ROWTYPE_ using CONTENTS	Explicit ROWTYPE_ on VARIABLES
FILE	Defaults to INLINE	Defaults to INLINE
VARIABLES	Required	Required
FORMAT	Defaults to LOWER DIAG	Defaults to LOWER DIAG
SPLIT	Required if split files*	Required if split files
FACTORS	Required if factors	Required if factors
CELLS	Required if factors	Inapplicable
CONTENTS	Defaults to CORR	Optional
N	Optional	Optional

* If the data do not contain values for the split-file variables, this subcommand can specify a single variable, which is not specified on the VARIABLES subcommand.

Subcommand Order

- SPLIT and FACTORS, when used, must follow VARIABLES.
- The remaining subcommands can be specified in any order.

Syntax Rules

- No commands can be specified between MATRIX DATA and BEGIN DATA, not even a VARIABLE LABELS or FORMAT command. Data transformations cannot be used until after MATRIX DATA is executed.

Operations

- MATRIX DATA defines and writes data in one step.
- MATRIX DATA clears the working data file and defines a new working file.
- If CONTENTS is not specified and *ROWTYPE_* is not specified on VARIABLES, MATRIX DATA assumes that the data contain only CORR values and issues warning messages to alert you to its assumptions.
- With the default format, data values, including diagonal values, must be in the lower triangle of the matrix. If MATRIX DATA encounters values in the upper triangle, it ignores those values and issues a series of warnings.
- With the default format, if any matrix rows span records in the data file, MATRIX DATA cannot form the matrix properly.
- MATRIX DATA does not allow format specifications for matrix materials. The procedure assigns the formats shown in Table 2. To change data formats, execute MATRIX DATA

and then assign new formats with the FORMATS, PRINT FORMATS, or WRITE FORMATS commands.

Table 2   Print and write formats for matrix variables

Variable type	Format
*ROWTYPE_, VARNAME_*	A8
Split-file variables	F4.0
Factors	F4.0
Continuous variables	F10.4

Format of the Raw Matrix Data File

- If LIST is in effect on the FORMAT subcommand, the data are entered in freefield format, with blanks and commas used as separators and each scalar, vector, or row of the matrix beginning on a new record. Unlike LIST format with DATA LIST, a vector or row of the matrix can be contained on multiple records. The continuation records do not have a value for *ROWTYPE_*.

- *ROWTYPE_* values can be enclosed in apostrophes or quotes.

- The order of variables in the raw data file must match the order in which they are specified on VARIABLES. However, this order does not have to correspond to the order of variables in the resulting SPSS-format matrix data file.

- The way records are entered for pooled vectors or matrices when factors are present depends upon whether *ROWTYPE_* is specified on the VARIABLES subcommand (see the FACTORS subcommand on p. 762).

- MATRIX DATA recognizes plus and minus signs as field separators when they are not preceded by the letter *D* or *E*. This allows MATRIX DATA to read scientific notation as well as correlation matrices written by FORTRAN in F10.8 format. A plus sign preceded by a *D* or *E* is read as part of the number in scientific notation.

Example

```
MATRIX DATA
    VARIABLES=ROWTYPE_ SAVINGS POP15 POP75 INCOME GROWTH.
BEGIN DATA
MEAN 9.6710 35.0896 2.2930 1106.7784 3.7576
STDDEV 4.4804 9.1517 1.2907 990.8511 2.8699
N 50 50 50 50 50
CORR 1
CORR -.4555 1
CORR .3165 -.9085 1
CORR .2203 -.7562 .7870 1
CORR .3048 -.0478 .0253 -.1295  1
END DATA.
```

- The variable *ROWTYPE_* is specified on VARIABLES. *ROWTYPE_* values are included in the data.

- No other specifications are required.

Example

```
* Matrix data with procedure DISCRIMINANT'.

MATRIX DATA VARIABLES=WORLD ROWTYPE_ FOOD APPL SERVICE RENT
  /FACTORS=WORLD.
BEGIN DATA
1 N       25 25 25 25
1 MEAN    76.64 77.32 81.52 101.40
2 N       7 7 7 7
2 MEAN    76.1428571 85.2857143 60.8571429 249.571429
3 N       13 13 13 13
3 MEAN    55.5384615 76 63.4615385 86.3076923
. SD      16.4634139 22.5509310 16.8086768 77.1085326
. CORR    1
. CORR    .1425366 1
. CORR    .5644693 .2762615 1
. CORR    .2133413 -.0499003 .0417468 1
END DATA.

DISCRIMINANT GROUPS=WORLD(1,3)
  /VARIABLES=FOOD APPL SERVICE RENT /METHOD=WILKS /MATRIX=IN(*).
```

- **MATRIX DATA** is used to generate a working data file that **DISCRIMINANT** can read. **DISCRIMINANT** reads the mean, count (unweighted N), and N (weighted N) for each cell in the data, as well as pooled values for the standard deviation and correlation coefficients. If count equals N, only N needs to be supplied.

- *ROWTYPE_* is specified on VARIABLES to identify record types in the data. Though CONTENTS and CELLS can be used to identify record types and distinguish between within-cells data and pooled values, it is usually easier to specify *ROWTYPE_* on VARIABLES and enter the *ROWTYPE_* values in the data.

- Because factors are present in the data, the continuous variables (*FOOD, APPL, SERVICE,* and *RENT*) must be specified last on VARIABLES and must be last in the data.

- The FACTORS subcommand identifies *WORLD* as the factor variable.

- BEGIN DATA immediately follows MATRIX DATA.

- N and *MEAN* values for each cell are entered in the data.

- *ROWTYPE_* values for the pooled records are *SD* and *COR*. MATRIX DATA assigns the values *STDDEV* and *CORR* to the corresponding vectors in the matrix. Records with pooled information have the system-missing value (.) for the factors.

- The DISCRIMINANT procedure reads the data matrix. An asterisk (*) is specified as the input file on the MATRIX subcommand because the data are in the working file.

Example

```
* Matrix data with procedure REGRESSION.

MATRIX DATA VARIABLES=SAVINGS POP15 POP75 INCOME GROWTH
   /CONTENTS=MEAN SD N CORR /FORMAT=UPPER NODIAGONAL.

BEGIN DATA
9.6710 35.0896 2.2930 1106.7784 3.7576
4.4804 9.1517 1.2908 990.8511 2.8699
50 50 50 50 50
-.4555 .3165 .2203 .3048
-.9085 -.7562 -.0478
 .7870 .0253
-.1295
END DATA.

REGRESSION MATRIX=IN(*) /VARIABLES=SAVINGS TO GROWTH
   /DEP=SAVINGS /ENTER.
```

- **MATRIX DATA** is used to generate a matrix that REGRESSION can read. REGRESSION reads and writes matrices that always contain the mean, standard deviation, *N*, and Pearson correlation coefficients. Data in this example do not have *ROWTYPE_* values, and the correlation values are from the upper triangle of the matrix without the diagonal values.

- *ROWTYPE_* is not specified on VARIABLES because its values are not included in the data.

- Because there are no *ROWTYPE_* values, CONTENTS is required to define the record types and the order of the records in the file.

- By default, MATRIX DATA reads values from the lower triangle of the matrix, including the diagonal values. FORMAT is required in this example to indicate that the data are in the upper triangle and do not include diagonal values.

- BEGIN DATA immediately follows the MATRIX DATA command.

- The REGRESSION procedure reads the data matrix. An asterisk (*) is specified as the input file on the MATRIX subcommand because the data are in the working file. Since there is a single vector of *N*'s in the data, missing values are handled listwise (the default for REGRESSION).

Example

```
* Matrix data with procedure ONEWAY.
MATRIX DATA VARIABLES=EDUC ROWTYPE_ WELL /FACTORS=EDUC.
BEGIN DATA
1 N 65
2 N 95
3 N 181
4 N 82
5 N 40
6 N 37
1 MEAN 2.6462
2 MEAN 2.7737
3 MEAN 4.1796
4 MEAN 4.5610
5 MEAN 4.6625
6 MEAN 5.2297
. MSE 6.2699
. DFE 494
END DATA.

ONEWAY WELL BY EDUC(1,6) /MATRIX=IN(*)
```

- One of the two types of matrices that the ONEWAY procedure reads includes a vector of frequencies for each factor level, a vector of means for each factor level, a record containing the pooled variance (within-group mean square error), and the degrees of freedom for the mean square error. MATRIX DATA is used to generate a working data file containing this type of matrix data for the ONEWAY procedure.
- *ROWTYPE_* is explicit on VARIABLES and identifies record types.
- Because factors are present in the data, the continuous variables (*WELL*) must be specified last on VARIABLES and must be last in the data.
- The FACTORS subcommand identifies *EDUC* as the factor variable.
- *MSE* is entered in the data as the *ROWTYPE_* value for the vector of square pooled standard deviations.
- *DFE* is entered in the data as the *ROWTYPE_* value for the vector of degrees of freedom.
- Records with pooled information have the system-missing value (.) for the factors.

VARIABLES Subcommand

VARIABLES specifies the names of the variables in the raw data and the order in which they occur.

- VARIABLES is required.
- There is no limit to the number of variables that can be specified.
- If *ROWTYPE_* is specified on VARIABLES, the continuous variables must be the last variables specified on the subcommand and must be last in the data.
- If split-file variables are present, they must also be specified on SPLIT.
- If factor variables are present, they must also be specified on FACTORS.

When either of the following is true, the only variables that must be specified on VARIABLES are the continuous variables:

1. The data contain only correlation coefficients. There can be no additional information, such as the mean and standard deviation, and no factor information or split-file variables. MATRIX DATA assigns the record type *CORR* to all records.

2. CONTENTS is used to define all record types. The data can then contain information such as the mean and standard deviation, but no factor, split-file, or *ROWTYPE_* variables. MATRIX DATA assigns the record types defined on the CONTENTS subcommand.

Variable VARNAME_

*VARNAME_* cannot be specified on the VARIABLES subcommand or anywhere on MATRIX DATA, and its values cannot be included in the data. The MATRIX DATA command generates the variable *VARNAME_* automatically.

Variable ROWTYPE_

- *ROWTYPE_* is a string variable with A8 format. Its values define the data types. All SPSS-format matrix data files contain a *ROWTYPE_* variable.

- If *ROWTYPE_* is specified on VARIABLES and its values are entered in the data, MATRIX DATA is primarily used to define the names and order of the variables in the raw data file.

- *ROWTYPE_* must precede the continuous variables.

- Valid values for *ROWTYPE_* are *CORR, COV, MAT, MSE, DFE, MEAN, STDDEV* (or *SD*), *N_VECTOR* (or *N*), *N_SCALAR, N_MATRIX, COUNT*, or *PROX*. For definitions of these values, see the CONTENTS subcommand on p. 764. Three-character abbreviations for these values are permitted. These values can also be enclosed in quotes or apostrophes.

- If *ROWTYPE_* is not specified on VARIABLES, CONTENTS must be used to define the order in which the records occur within the file. MATRIX DATA follows these specifications strictly and generates a *ROWTYPE_* variable according to the CONTENTS specifications. A data-entry error, especially skipping a record, can cause the procedure to assign the wrong values to the wrong records.

Example

```
* ROWTYPE_ is specified on VARIABLES.

MATRIX DATA
     VARIABLES=ROWTYPE_ SAVINGS POP15 POP75 INCOME GROWTH.
BEGIN DATA
MEAN 9.6710 35.0896 2.2930 1106.7784 3.7576
STDDEV 4.4804 9.1517 1.2907 990.8511 2.8699
N 50 50 50 50 50
CORR 1
CORR -.4555 1
CORR .3165 -.9085 1
CORR .2203 -.7562 .7870 1
CORR .3048 -.0478 .0253 -.1295  1
END DATA.
```

- *ROWTYPE_* is specified on VARIABLES. *ROWTYPE_* values in the data identify each record type.
- Note that *VARNAME_* is not specified on VARIABLES, and its values are not entered in the data.

Example

```
* ROWTYPE_ is specified on VARIABLES.

MATRIX DATA
    VARIABLES=ROWTYPE_ SAVINGS POP15 POP75 INCOME GROWTH.
BEGIN DATA
'MEAN     ' 9.6710 35.0896 2.2930 1106.7784 3.7576
'SD       ' 4.4804 9.1517 1.2907 990.8511 2.8699
'N        ' 50 50 50 50 50
"CORR     " 1
"CORR     " -.4555 1
"CORR     " .3165 -.9085 1
"CORR     " .2203 -.7562 .7870 1
"CORR     " .3048 -.0478 .0253 -.1295  1
END DATA.
```

- *ROWTYPE_* values for the mean, standard deviation, *N*, and Pearson correlation coefficients are abbreviated and enclosed in apostrophes or quotations.

Example

```
* ROWTYPE_ is not specified on VARIABLES.

MATRIX DATA VARIABLES=SAVINGS POP15 POP75 INCOME GROWTH
  /CONTENTS=MEAN SD N CORR.
BEGIN DATA
9.6710 35.0896 2.2930 1106.7784 3.7576
4.4804 9.1517 1.2907 990.8511 2.8699
50 50 50 50 50
 1
-.4555 1
 .3165 -.9085 1
 .2203 -.7562 .7870 1
 .3048 -.0478 .0253 -.1295 1
END DATA.
```

- *ROWTYPE_* is not specified on VARIABLES, and its values are not included in the data.
- CONTENTS is required to define the record types and the order of the records in the file.

FILE Subcommand

FILE specifies the matrix file containing the data. The default specification is INLINE, which indicates that the data are included within the command sequence between the BEGIN DATA and END DATA commands.

- If the data are in an external file, FILE must specify the file.
- If the FILE subcommand is omitted, the data must be inline.

Example

```
MATRIX DATA FILE=RAWMTX /VARIABLES=varlist.
```

- FILE indicates that the data are in the file *RAWMTX*.

FORMAT Subcommand

FORMAT indicates how the matrix data are formatted. It applies only to matrix values in the data, not to vector values, such as the mean and standard deviation.

- FORMAT can specify up to three keywords: one to specify the data-entry format, one to specify matrix shape, and one to specify whether the data include diagonal values.
- The minimum specification is a single keyword.
- Default settings remain in effect unless explicitly overridden.

Data-Entry Format

FORMAT has two keywords that specify the data-entry format:

LIST   *Each scalar, vector, and matrix row must begin on a new record.* A vector or row of the matrix may be continued on multiple records. This is the default.

FREE   *Matrix rows do not need to begin on a new record.* Any item can begin in the middle of a record.

Matrix Shape

FORMAT has three keywords that specify the matrix shape. With either triangular shape, no values—not even missing indicators—are entered for the implied values in the matrix.

LOWER   *Read data values from the lower triangle.* This is the default.

UPPER   *Read data values from the upper triangle.*

FULL   *Read the full square matrix of data values.* FULL cannot be specified with NODIAGONAL.

Diagonal Values

FORMAT has two keywords that refer to the diagonal values:

DIAGONAL   *Data include the diagonal values.* This is the default.

NODIAGONAL   *Data do not include diagonal values.* The diagonal value is set to the system-missing value for all matrices except the correlation matrices. For correlation matrices, the diagonal value is set to 1. NODIAGONAL cannot be specified with FULL.

Table 3 shows how data might be entered for each combination of FORMAT settings that govern matrix shape and diagonal values. With UPPER NODIAGONAL and LOWER NODIAGONAL, you do not enter the matrix row that has blank values for the continuous variables. If you enter that row, MATRIX DATA cannot properly form the matrix.

Table 3   Various FORMAT settings

FULL	UPPER DIAGONAL	UPPER NODIAGONAL	LOWER DIAGONAL	LOWER NODIAGONAL
MEAN 5 4 3	MEAN 5 4 3	MEAN 5 4 3	MEAN 5 4 3	MEAN 5 4 3
SD 3 2 1	SD 3 2 1	SD 3 2 1	SD 3 2 1	SD 3 2 1
N 9 9 9	N 9 9 9	N 9 9 9	N 9 9 9	N 9 9 9
CORR 1 .6 .7	CORR 1 .6 .7	CORR .6 .7	CORR 1	CORR .6
CORR .6 1 .8	CORR 1 .8	CORR .8	CORR .6 1	CORR .7 .8
CORR .7 .8 1	CORR 1		CORR .7 .8 1	

Example

```
MATRIX DATA VARIABLES=ROWTYPE_ V1 TO V3
   /FORMAT=UPPER NODIAGONAL.
BEGIN DATA
MEAN    5    4    3
SD      3    2    1
N       9    9    9
CORR         .6  .7
CORR              .8
END DATA.
LIST.
```

- FORMAT specifies the upper-triangle format with no diagonal values. The default LIST is in effect for the data-entry format.

Example

```
MATRIX DATA VARIABLES=ROWTYPE_ V1 TO V3
   /FORMAT=UPPER NODIAGONAL.
BEGIN DATA
MEAN 5 4 3
SD 3 2 1
N 9 9 9
CORR .6 .7
CORR .8
END DATA.
LIST.
```

- This example is identical to the previous example. It shows that data do not have to be aligned in columns. Data throughout this section are aligned in columns to emphasize the matrix format.

SPLIT Subcommand

SPLIT specifies the variables whose values define the split files. SPLIT must follow the VARIABLES subcommand.

- SPLIT can specify a subset of up to eight of the variables named on VARIABLES. All split variables must be numeric. The keyword TO can be used to imply variables in the order in which they are named on VARIABLES.
- A separate matrix must be included in the data for each value of each split variable. MATRIX DATA generates a complete set of matrix materials for each.
- If the data contain neither *ROWTYPE_* nor split-file variables, a single split-file variable can be specified on SPLIT. This variable is *not* specified on the VARIABLES subcommand. MATRIX DATA generates a complete set of matrix materials for each set of matrix materials in the data and assigns values 1, 2, 3, etc., to the split variable until the end of the data is encountered.

Example

```
MATRIX DATA  VARIABLES=S1 ROWTYPE_ V1 TO V3 /SPLIT=S1.
BEGIN DATA
0 MEAN    5   4   3
0 SD      1   2   3
0 N       9   9   9
0 CORR    1
0 CORR   .6   1
0 CORR   .7  .8   1
1 MEAN    9   8   7
1 SD      5   6   7
1 N       9   9   9
1 CORR    1
1 CORR   .4   1
1 CORR   .3  .2   1
END DATA.
LIST.
```

- The split variable *S1* has two values: 0 and 1. Two separate matrices are entered in the data, one for each value *S1*.
- *S1* must be specified on both VARIABLES and SPLIT.

Example

```
MATRIX DATA VARIABLES=V1 TO V3 /CONTENTS=MEAN SD N CORR
   /SPLIT=SPL.
BEGIN DATA
   5   4   3
   1   2   3
   9   9   9
   1
  .6   1
  .7  .8   1
   9   8   7
   5   6   7
   9   9   9
   1
  .4   1
  .3  .2   1
END DATA.
LIST.
```

- The split variable *SPL* is not specified on VARIABLES, and values for *SPL* are not included in the data.

- Two sets of matrix materials are included in the data. MATRIX DATA therefore assigns values 1 and 2 to variable *SPL* and generates two matrices in the matrix data file.

FACTORS Subcommand

FACTORS specifies the variables whose values define the cells represented by the within-cells data. FACTORS must follow the VARIABLES subcommand.

- FACTORS specifies a subset of the variables named on the VARIABLES subcommand. The keyword TO can be used to imply variables in the order in which they are named on VARIABLES.
- If *ROWTYPE_* is explicit on VARIABLES and its values are included in the data, records that represent pooled information have the system-missing value (indicated by a period) for the factors, since the values of *ROWTYPE_* are ambiguous.
- If *ROWTYPE_* is not specified on VARIABLES and its values are not in the data, enter data values for the factors only for records that represent within-cells information. Enter nothing for the factors for records that represent pooled information. CELLS must be specified to indicate the number of within-cells records, and CONTENTS must be specified to indicate which record types have within-cells data.

Example

```
* Rowtype is explicit.

MATRIX DATA VARIABLES=ROWTYPE_ F1 F2   VAR1 TO VAR3
  /FACTORS=F1 F2.
BEGIN DATA.
MEAN 1 1  1   2   3
SD   1 1  5   4   3
N    1 1  9   9   9
MEAN 1 2  4   5   6
SD   1 2  6   5   4
N    1 2  9   9   9
MEAN 2 1  7   8   9
SD   2 1  7   6   5
N    2 1  9   9   9
MEAN 2 2  9   8   7
SD   2 2  8   7   6
N    2 2  9   9   9
CORR  . . .1
CORR  . . .6  1
CORR  . . .7 .8   1
END DATA.
```

- *ROWTYPE_* is specified on VARIABLES.
- Factor variables must be specified on both VARIABLES and FACTORS.
- Periods in the data represent missing values for the *CORR* factor values.

Example

```
* Rowtype is implicit.

MATRIX DATA VARIABLES=F1 F2  VAR1 TO VAR3
  /FACTORS=F1 F2 /CONTENTS=(MEAN SD N) CORR /CELLS=4.
BEGIN DATA
1 1  1   2   3
1 1  5   4   3
1 1  9   9   9
1 2  4   5   6
1 2  6   5   4
1 2  9   9   9
2 1  7   8   9
2 1  7   6   5
2 1  9   9   9
2 2  9   8   7
2 2  8   7   6
2 2  9   9   9
     1
    .6  1
    .7 .8 1
END DATA.
```

- *ROWTYPE_* is not specified on VARIABLES.
- Nothing is entered for the *CORR* factor values because the records contain pooled information.
- CELLS is required because there are factors in the data and *ROWTYPE_* is implicit.
- CONTENTS is required to define the record types and to differentiate between the within-cells and pooled types.

CELLS Subcommand

CELLS specifies the number of within-cells records in the data. The only valid specification for CELLS is a single integer, which indicates the number of sets of within-cells information that MATRIX DATA must read.

- CELLS is required when there are factors in the data and *ROWTYPE_* is implicit.
- If CELLS is used when *ROWTYPE_* is specified on VARIABLES, MATRIX DATA issues a warning and ignores the CELLS subcommand.

Example

```
MATRIX DATA VARIABLES=F1 VAR1 TO VAR3 /FACTORS=F1 /CELLS=2
  /CONTENTS=(MEAN SD N) CORR.
BEGIN DATA
1  5   4   3
1  3   2   1
1  9   9   9
2  8   7   6
2  6   7   8
2  9   9   9
   1
  .6  1
  .7 .8  1
END DATA.
```

- The specification for CELLS is 2 because the factor variable *F1* has two values (1 and 2) and there are therefore two sets of within-cells information.
- If there were two factor variables, *F1* and *F2*, and each had two values, 1 and 2, CELLS would equal 4 to account for all four possible factor combinations (assuming all 4 combinations are present in the data).

CONTENTS Subcommand

CONTENTS defines the record types when *ROWTYPE_* is not included in the data. The minimum specification is a single keyword indicating a type of record. The default is CORR.

- CONTENTS is required to define record types and record order whenever *ROWTYPE_* is not specified on VARIABLES and its values are not in the data. The only exception to this rule is the rare situation in which all data values represent pooled correlation records and there are no factors. In that case, MATRIX DATA reads the data values and assigns the default *ROWTYPE_* of *CORR* to all records.
- The order in which keywords are specified on CONTENTS must correspond to the order in which records appear in the data. If the keywords on CONTENTS are in the wrong order, MATRIX DATA will incorrectly assign values.

CORR
: *Matrix of correlation coefficients.* This is the default. If *ROWTYPE_* is not specified on the VARIABLES subcommand and you omit the CONTENTS subcommand, MATRIX DATA assigns the *ROWTYPE_* value *CORR* to all matrix rows.

COV
: *Matrix of covariance coefficients.*

MAT
: *Generic square matrix.*

MSE
: *Vector of mean squared errors.*

DFE
: *Vector of degrees of freedom.*

MEAN
: *Vector of means.*

STDDEV
: *Vector of standard deviations.* SD is a synonym for STDDEV. MATRIX DATA assigns the *ROWTYPE_* value STDDEV to the record if either STDDEV or SD is specified.

N_VECTOR
: *Vector of counts.* N is a synonym for N_VECTOR. MATRIX DATA assigns the *ROWTYPE_* value *N* to the record.

N_SCALAR
: *Count.* Scalars are a shorthand mechanism for representing vectors in which all elements have the same value, such as when a vector of *N*'s is calculated using listwise deletion of missing values. Enter N_SCALAR as the *ROWTYPE_* value in the data and then the N_SCALAR value for the first continuous variable only. MATRIX DATA assigns the *ROWTYPE_* value *N* to the record and copies the specified N_SCALAR value across all the continuous variables.

N_MATRIX
: *Square matrix of counts.* Enter N_MATRIX as the *ROWTYPE_* value for each row of counts in the data. MATRIX DATA assigns the *ROWTYPE_* value *N* to each of those rows.

COUNT   *Count vector accepted by procedure DISCRIMINANT.* This contains unweighted *N*'s.

Example

```
MATRIX DATA VARIABLES=V1 TO V3 /CONTENTS=MEAN SD N_SCALAR CORR.
BEGIN DATA
  5  4  3
  3  2  1
  9
  1
 .6  1
 .7 .8  1
END DATA.
LIST.
```

- *ROWTYPE_* is not specified on VARIABLES, and *ROWTYPE_* values are not in the data. CONTENTS is therefore required to identify record types.
- CONTENTS indicates that the matrix records are in the following order: mean, standard deviation, *N*, and correlation coefficients.
- The *N_SCALAR* value is entered for the first continuous variable only.

Within-Cells Record Definition

When the data include factors and *ROWTYPE_* is not specified, CONTENTS distinguishes between within-cells and pooled records by enclosing the keywords for within-cells records in parentheses.

- If the records associated with the within-cells keywords appear together for each set of factor values, enclose the keywords together within a single set of parentheses.
- If the records associated with each within-cells keyword are grouped together across factor values, enclose the keyword within its own parentheses

Example

```
MATRIX DATA VARIABLES=F1 VAR1 TO VAR3 /FACTORS=F1 /CELLS=2
  /CONTENTS=(MEAN SD N) CORR.
```

- MEAN, SD, and N contain within-cells information and are therefore specified within parentheses. CORR is outside the parentheses because it identifies pooled records.
- CELLS is required because there is a factor specified and *ROWTYPE_* is implicit.

Example

```
MATRIX DATA VARIABLES=F1 VAR1 TO VAR3 /FACTORS=F1 /CELLS=2
  /CONTENTS=(MEAN SD N) CORR.
BEGIN DATA
1  5  4  3
1  3  2  1
1  9  9  9
2  4  5  6
2  6  5  4
2  9  9  9
   1
  .6  1
  .7 .8  1
END DATA.
```

- The parentheses around the CONTENTS keywords indicate that the mean, standard deviation, and *N* for value 1 of factor *F1* are together, followed by the mean, standard deviation, and *N* for value 2 of factor *F1*.

Example

```
MATRIX DATA VARIABLES=F1 VAR1 TO VAR3 /FACTORS=F1 /CELLS=2
  /CONTENTS=(MEAN) (SD) (N) CORR.
BEGIN DATA
1  5  4  3
2  4  5  6
1  3  2  1
2  6  5  4
1  9  9  9
2  9  9  9
   1
  .6  1
  .7 .8  1
END DATA.
```

- The parentheses around each CONTENTS keyword indicate that the data include the means for all cells, followed by the standard deviations for all cells, followed by the *N* values for all the cells.

Example

```
MATRIX DATA VARIABLES=F1 VAR1 TO VAR3 /FACTORS=F1 /CELLS=2
  /CONTENTS=(MEAN SD) (N) CORR.
BEGIN DATA
1  5  4  3
1  3  2  1
2  4  5  6
2  6  5  4
1  9  9  9
2  9  9  9
   1
  .6  1
  .7 .8  1
END DATA.
```

- The parentheses around the CONTENTS keywords indicate that the data include the mean and standard deviation for value 1 of *F1*, followed by the mean and standard deviation for value 2 of *F1*, followed by the *N* values for all cells.

Optional Specification When ROWTYPE_ Is Explicit

When *ROWTYPE_* is explicitly named on VARIABLES, MATRIX DATA uses *ROWTYPE_* values to determine record types.

- When *ROWTYPE_* is explicitly named on VARIABLES, CONTENTS can be used for informational purposes. However, *ROWTYPE_* values in the data determine record types.
- If MATRIX DATA reads values for *ROWTYPE_* that are not specified on CONTENTS, it issues a warning.
- Missing values for factors are entered as periods, even though CONTENTS is specified (see the FACTORS subcommand on p. 762).

Example

```
MATRIX DATA VARIABLES=ROWTYPE_ F1 F2 VAR1 TO VAR3
  /FACTORS=F1 F2 /CONTENTS=(MEAN SD N) CORR.
BEGIN DATA
MEAN 1 1   1   2   3
SD   1 1   5   4   3
N    1 1   9   9   9
MEAN 1 2   4   5   6
SD   1 2   6   5   4
N    1 2   9   9   9
CORR . .   1
CORR . .  .6  1
CORR . .  .7 .8  1
END DATA.
```

- *ROWTYPE_* is specified on VARIABLES. MATRIX DATA therefore uses *ROWTYPE_* values in the data to identify record types.
- Because *ROWTYPE_* is specified on VARIABLES, CONTENTS is optional. However, CONTENTS is specified for informational purposes. This is most useful when data are in an external file and the *ROWTYPE_* values cannot be seen in the data.
- Missing values for factors are entered as periods, even though CONTENTS is specified.

N Subcommand

N specifies the population *N* when the data do not include it. The only valid specification is an integer, which indicates the population *N*.

- MATRIX DATA generates one record with a *ROWTYPE_* of N for each split file, and it uses the specified *N* value for each continuous variable.

Example

```
MATRIX DATA VARIABLES=V1 TO V3 /CONTENTS=MEAN SD CORR
   /N=99.
BEGIN DATA
   5   4   3
   3   4   5
   1
  .6   1
  .7  .8   1
END DATA.
```

- MATRIX DATA uses 99 as the *N* value for all continuous variables.

MCONVERT

```
MCONVERT [[/MATRIX=] [IN({*    })] [OUT({*    })]]
                         {file}        {file}
         [{/REPLACE}]
          {/APPEND }
```

Example

```
MCONVERT MATRIX=OUT(CORMTX) /APPEND.
```

Overview

MCONVERT converts covariance matrix materials to correlation matrix materials, or vice versa. For MCONVERT to convert a correlation matrix, the matrix data must contain *CORR* values (Pearson correlation coefficients) and a vector of standard deviations (*STDDEV*). For MCONVERT to convert a covariance matrix, only *COV* values are required in the data.

Options

Matrix Files. MCONVERT can read matrix materials from an external matrix data file, and it can write converted matrix materials to an external file.

Matrix Materials. MCONVERT can write the converted matrix only or both the converted matrix and the original matrix to the resulting matrix data file.

Basic Specification

The minimum specification is the command itself. By default, MCONVERT reads the original matrix from the working data file and then replaces it with the converted matrix.

Syntax Rules

- The keywords IN and OUT cannot specify the same external file.
- The APPEND and REPLACE subcommands cannot be specified on the same MCONVERT command.

Operations

- If the data are covariance matrix materials, MCONVERT converts them to a correlation matrix plus a vector of standard deviations.
- If the data are a correlation matrix and vector of standard deviations, MCONVERT converts them to a covariance matrix.

- If there are multiple *CORR* or *COV* matrices (for example, one for each grouping (factor) or one for each split variable), each will be converted to a separate matrix, preserving the values of any factor or split variables.
- All cases with *ROWTYPE_* values other than *CORR* or *COV*, such as *MEAN*, *N*, and *STDDEV*, are always copied into the new matrix data file.
- MCONVERT cannot read raw matrix values. If your data are raw values, use the MATRIX DATA command.
- Split variables (if any) must occur first in the file that MCONVERT reads, followed by the variable *ROWTYPE_*, the grouping variables (if any), and the variable *VARNAME_*. All variables following *VARNAME_* are the variables for which a matrix will be read and created.

Limitations

- The total number of split variables plus grouping variables cannot exceed eight.

Example

```
MATRIX DATA VARIABLES=ROWTYPE_ SAVINGS POP15 POP75 INCOME GROWTH
  /FORMAT=FULL.
BEGIN DATA
COV     20.0740459  -18.678638    1.8304990  978.181242 3.9190106
COV    -18.678638    83.7541100 -10.731666 -6856.9888   -1.2561071
COV      1.8304990  -10.731666    1.6660908 1006.52742    .0937992
COV    978.181242  -6856.9888    1006.52742 981785.907 -368.18652
COV      3.9190106   -1.2561071    .0937992 -368.18652  8.2361574
END DATA.
MCONVERT.
```

- MATRIX DATA defines the variables in the file and creates a working data file of matrix materials. The values for the variable *ROWTYPE_* are *COV*, indicating that the matrix contains covariance coefficients. The FORMAT subcommand indicates that data are in full square format.
- MCONVERT converts the covariance matrix to a correlation matrix plus a vector of standard deviations. By default, the converted matrix is written to the working data file.

MATRIX Subcommand

The MATRIX subcommand specifies the file for the matrix materials. By default, MATRIX reads the original matrix from the working data file and replaces the working data file with the converted matrix.

- MATRIX has two keywords, IN and OUT. The specification on both IN and OUT is the name of an external file in parentheses or an asterisk (*) to refer to the working data file (the default).
- The actual keyword MATRIX is optional.
- IN and OUT cannot specify the same external file.

- MATRIX=IN cannot be specified unless a working data file has already been defined. To convert an existing matrix at the beginning of a session, use GET to retrieve the matrix file and then specify IN(*) on MATRIX.

IN   *The matrix file to read.*

OUT   *The matrix file to write.*

Example

```
GET FILE=COVMTX.
MCONVERT MATRIX=OUT(CORMTX).
```

- GET retrieves the SPSS-format matrix data file *COVMTX*. *COVMTX* becomes the working data file.
- By default, MCONVERT reads the original matrix from the working data file. IN(*) can be specified to make the default explicit.
- The keyword OUT on MATRIX writes the converted matrix to file *CORMTX*.

REPLACE and APPEND Subcommands

By default, MCONVERT writes only the converted matrix to the resulting matrix file. Use APPEND to copy both the original matrix and the converted matrix.

- The only specification is the keyword REPLACE or APPEND.
- REPLACE and APPEND are alternatives.
- REPLACE and APPEND affect the resulting matrix file only. The original matrix materials, whether in the working file or in an external file, remain intact.

APPEND   *Write the original matrix followed by the converted matrix to the matrix file. If there are multiple sets of matrix materials, APPEND appends each converted matrix to the end of a copy of its original matrix.*

REPLACE   *Write the original matrix followed by the covariance matrix to the matrix file.*

Example

```
MCONVERT MATRIX=OUT(COVMTX) /APPEND.
```

- MCONVERT reads matrix materials from the working file.
- The APPEND subcommand copies original matrix materials, appends each converted matrix to the end of the copy of its original matrix, and writes both sets to the file *COVMTX*.

MEANS

```
MEANS [TABLES=]{varlist} BY varlist [BY...] [/varlist...]
                {ALL    }

[/MISSING={TABLE    }]
          {INCLUDE  }
          {DEPENDENT}

[/CELLS= [MEAN**   ] [COUNT**   ] [STDDEV**]
         [MEDIAN] [GMEDIAN] [SEMEAN]  [SUM ]
         [MIN] [MAX] [RANGE] [VARIANCE]
         [KURT] [SEKURT] [SKEW] [SESKEW]
         [FIRST] [LAST]
         [NPCT] [SPCT] [NPCT(var)]  [SPCT(var)]
         [HARMONIC] [GEOMETRIC]
         [DEFAULT]
         [ALL] [NONE]   ]

[/STATISTICS=[ANOVA] [{LINEARITY}]  [NONE**]]
                     {ALL       }
```

**Default if the subcommand is omitted.

Example

```
MEANS TABLES=V1 TO V5 BY GROUP
  /STATISTICS=ANOVA.
```

Overview

By default, MEANS (alias BREAKDOWN) displays means, standard deviations, and group counts for a numeric dependent variable and group counts for a string variable within groups defined by one or more control (independent) variables. Other procedures that display univariate statistics are SUMMARIZE, FREQUENCIES, and DESCRIPTIVES.

Options

Cell Contents. By default, MEANS displays means, standard deviations, and cell counts for a dependent variable across groups defined by one or more control variables. You can also display sums and variances using the CELLS subcommand.

Statistics. In addition to the statistics displayed for each cell of the table, you can obtain a one-way analysis of variance and test of linearity using the STATISTICS subcommand.

Basic Specification

The basic specification is TABLES with a table list. The actual keyword TABLES can be omitted.

- The minimum table list specifies a dependent variable, the keyword BY, and a control variable.

- By default, MEANS displays means, standard deviations, and number of cases.

Subcommand Order

The table list must be first if the keyword TABLES is omitted. If the keyword TABLES is explicitly used, subcommands can be specified in any order.

Operations

- MEANS displays the number and percentage of the processed and missing cases in the Case Process Summary table.
- MEANS displays univariate statistics for the population as a whole and for each value of each successive control variable defined by the BY keyword on the TABLE subcommand in the Group Statistics table.
- ANOVA and linearity statistics, if requested, are displayed in the ANOVA and Measures of Association tables.
- If a control variable is a long string, only the short-string portion is used to identify groups in the analysis.
- If a string variable is specified as a dependent variable on any table lists, the MEANS procedure produces limited statistics (COUNT, FIRST, and LAST).

Limitations

- Maximum 200 variables total per MEANS command.
- Maximum 250 tables.

Example

```
MEANS TABLES=V1 TO V5 BY GROUP
    /STATISTICS=ANOVA.
```

- TABLES specifies that *V1* through *V5* are the dependent variables. *GROUP* is the control variable.
- Assuming that variables *V2, V3,* and *V4* lie between *V1* and *V5* in the working data file, five tables are produced: *V1* by *GROUP*, *V2* by *GROUP*, *V3* by *GROUP*, and so on.
- STATISTICS requests one-way analysis-of-variance tables of *V1* through *V5* by *GROUP*.

Example

```
MEANS VARA BY VARB BY VARC/V1 V2 BY V3 V4 BY V5.
```

- This command contains two TABLES subcommands that omit the optional TABLES keyword.

- The first table list produces a Group Statistics table for *VARA* within groups defined by each combination of values as well as the totals of *VARB* and *VARC*.
- The second table list produces a Group Statistics table displaying statistics for *V1* by *V3* by *V5*, *V1* by *V4* by *V5*, *V2* by *V3* by *V5*, and *V2* by *V4* by *V5*.

TABLES Subcommand

TABLES specifies the table list.

- You can specify multiple TABLES subcommands on a single MEANS command. The slash between the subcommands is required. You can also name multiple table lists separated by slashes on one TABLES subcommand.
- The dependent variable is specified first. If the dependent variable is a string variable, MEANS produces only limited statistics (COUNT, FIRST, and LAST). The control (independent) variables follow the BY keyword and can be numeric (integer or non-integer) or string.
- Each use of the keyword BY in a table list adds a dimension to the table requested. Statistics are displayed for each dependent variable by each combination of values and the totals of the control variables across dimensions.
- The order in which control variables are displayed is the same as the order in which they are specified on TABLES. The values of the first control variable defined for the table appear in the leftmost column of the table and change the most slowly in the definition of groups.
- More than one dependent variable can be specified in a table list, and more than one control variable can be specified in each dimension of a table list.

CELLS Subcommand

By default, SUMMARIZE displays the means, standard deviations, and cell counts in each cell. Use CELLS to modify cell information.

- If CELLS is specified without keywords, SUMMARIZE displays the default statistics.
- If any keywords are specified on CELLS, only the requested information is displayed.
- MEDIAN and GMEDIAN are expensive in terms of computer resources and time. Requesting these statistics (via these keywords or ALL) may slow down performance.

DEFAULT	*Means, standard deviations, and cell counts.* This is the default if CELLS is omitted.
MEAN	*Cell means.*
STDDEV	*Cell standard deviations.*
COUNT	*Cell counts.*
MEDIAN	*Cell median.*
GMEDIAN	*Grouped median.*

SEMEAN	*Standard error of cell mean.*
SUM	*Cell sums.*
MIN	*Cell minimum.*
MAX	*Cell maximum.*
RANGE	*Cell range.*
VARIANCE	*Variances.*
KURT	*Cell kurtosis.*
SEKURT	*Standard error of cell kurtosis.*
SKEW	*Cell skewness.*
SESKEW	*Standard error of cell skewness.*
FIRST	*First value.*
LAST	*Last value.*
NPCT	*Percentage of the total number of cases.*
SPCT	*Percentage of the total sum.*
NPCT(var)	*Percentage of the total number of cases within the specified variable.* The specified variable must be one of the control variables.
SPCT(var)	*Percentage of the total sum within the specified variable.* The specified variable must be one of the control variables.
HARMONIC	*Harmonic mean.*
GEOMETRIC	*Geometric mean.*
ALL	*All cell information.*

STATISTICS Subcommand

Use STATISTICS to request a one-way analysis of variance and a test of linearity for each TABLE list.

- Statistics requested on STATISTICS are computed in addition to the statistics displayed in the Group Statistics table.
- If STATISTICS is specified without keywords, MEANS computes ANOVA.
- If two or more dimensions are specified, the second and subsequent dimensions are ignored in the analysis-of-variance table. To obtain a two-way and higher analysis of variance, use the ANOVA or MANOVA procedure. The ONEWAY procedure calculates a one-way analysis of variance with multiple comparison tests.

ANOVA	*Analysis of variance.* ANOVA displays a standard analysis-of-variance table and calculates eta and eta squared (displayed in the Measures of Association table). This is the default if STATISTICS is specified without keywords.

LINEARITY	*Test of linearity.* LINEARITY (alias ALL) displays additional statistics to the tables created by the ANOVA keyword: the sums of squares, degrees of freedom, and mean square associated with linear and nonlinear components, the F ratio, and significance level for the ANOVA table and Pearson's r and r^2 for the Measures of Association table. LINEARITY is ignored if the control variable is a string.
NONE	*No additional statistics.* This is the default if STATISTICS is omitted.

Example

```
MEANS TABLES=INCOME BY SEX BY RACE
  /STATISTICS=ANOVA.
```

- MEANS produces a Group Statistics table of *INCOME* by *RACE* within *SEX* and computes an analysis of variance only for *INCOME* by *SEX*.

MISSING Subcommand

MISSING controls the treatment of missing values. If no MISSING subcommand is specified each combination of a dependent variable and control variables is handled separately.

TABLE	*Delete cases with missing values on a tablewise basis.* A case with a missing value for any variable specified for a table is not used. Thus, every case contained in a table has a complete set of nonmissing values for all variables in that table. When you separate table requests with a slash, missing values are handled separately for each list. Any MISSING specification will result in tablewise treatment of missing values.
INCLUDE	*Include user-missing values.* This option treats user-missing values as valid values.
DEPENDENT	*Exclude user-missing values for dependent variables only.* DEPENDENT treats user-missing values for all control variables as valid.

References

Hays, W. L. 1981. *Statistics for the social sciences*, 3rd ed. New York: Holt, Rinehart, and Wilson.

MISSING VALUES

```
MISSING VALUES {varlist}(value list) [[/]{varlist} ...]
               {ALL    }                {ALL    }
```

Keywords for numeric value lists:

LO, LOWEST, HI, HIGHEST, THRU

Example

```
MISSING VALUES V1 (8,9) V2 V3 (0) V4 ('X') V5 TO V9 ('    ').
```

Overview

MISSING VALUES declares values for numeric and short string variables as user-missing. These values can then receive special treatment in data transformations, statistical calculations, and case selection. By default, user-missing values are treated the same as the system-missing values. System-missing values are automatically assigned by the program when no legal value can be produced, such as when an alphabetical character is encountered in the data for a numeric variable, or when an illegal calculation, such as division by 0, is requested in a data transformation.

Basic Specification

The basic specification is a single variable followed by the user-missing value or values in parentheses. Each specified value for the variable is treated as user-missing for any analysis.

Syntax Rules

- Each variable can have a maximum of three individual user-missing values. A space or comma must separate each value. For numeric variables, you can also specify a range of missing values. See "Specifying Ranges of Missing Values" on p. 779.
- The missing-value specification must correspond to the variable type (numeric or string).
- The same values can be declared missing for more than one variable by specifying a variable list followed by the values in parentheses. Variable lists must have either all numeric or all string variables.
- Different values can be declared missing for different variables by specifying separate values for each variable. An optional slash can be used to separate specifications.
- Missing values cannot be assigned to long string variables or to scratch variables.

777

- Missing values for short string variables must be enclosed in apostrophes or quotation marks. The value specifications must include any leading or trailing blanks. (See "String Values in Command Specifications" on p. 15.)

- A variable list followed by an empty set of parentheses ( ) deletes any user-missing specifications for those variables.

- The keyword ALL can be used to refer to all user-defined variables in the working file, provided the variables are either all numeric or all string. ALL can refer to both numeric and string variables if it is followed by an empty set of parentheses. This will delete all user-missing specifications in the working data file.

- More than one MISSING VALUES command can be specified per session.

Operations

- Unlike most transformations, MISSING VALUES takes effect as soon as it is encountered. Special attention should be paid to its position among commands. See "Command Order" on p. 16 for more information.

- Missing-value specifications can be changed between procedures. New specifications replace previous ones. If a variable is mentioned more than once on one or more MISSING VALUES commands before a procedure, only the last specification is used.

- Missing-value specifications are saved in SPSS-format data files (see SAVE) and portable files (see EXPORT).

Example

```
MISSING VALUES V1 (8,9) V2 V3 (0) V4 ('X') V5 TO V9 ('    ').
```

- The values 8 and 9 are declared missing for the numeric variable *V1*.
- The value 0 is declared missing for the numeric variables *V2* and *V3*.
- The value X is declared missing for the string variable *V4*.
- Blanks are declared missing for the string variables between and including *V5* and *V9*. All of these variables must have a width of four columns.

Example

```
MISSING VALUES V1 ().
```

- Any previously declared missing values for *V1* are deleted.

Example

```
MISSING VALUES ALL (9).
```

- The value 9 is declared missing for all variables in the working data file; the variables must all be numeric. All previous user-missing specifications are overridden.

Example

```
MISSING VALUES ALL ().
```

- All previously declared user-missing values for all variables in the working data file are deleted. The variables in the working data file can be both numeric and string.

Specifying Ranges of Missing Values

A range of values can be specified as missing for numeric variables but *not* for string variables.

- The keyword THRU indicates an inclusive list of values. Values must be separated from THRU by at least one blank space.
- The keywords HIGHEST and LOWEST with THRU indicate the highest and lowest values of a variable. HIGHEST and LOWEST can be abbreviated to HI and LO.
- Only one THRU specification can be used for each variable or variable list. Each THRU specification can be combined with one additional missing value.

Example

```
MISSING VALUES  V1 (LOWEST THRU 0).
```

- All negative values and 0 are declared missing for the variable *V1*.

Example

```
MISSING VALUES  V1 (0 THRU 1.5).
```

- Values from 0 through and including 1.5 are declared missing.

Example

```
MISSING VALUES V1 (LO THRU 0, 999).
```

- All negative values, 0, and 999 are declared missing for the variable *V1*.

MULT RESPONSE

```
MULT RESPONSE†

{/GROUPS=groupname['label'](varlist ({value1,value2})))}
                                     {value           }
      ...[groupname...]

{/VARIABLES=varlist(min,max)  [varlist...]              }


{/FREQUENCIES=varlist                                   }

{/TABLES=varlist BY varlist... [BY varlist] [(PAIRED)]}
      [/varlist BY...]


[/MISSING=[{TABLE**}]  [INCLUDE]]
          {MDGROUP}
          {MRGROUP}

[/FORMAT={LABELS**}   {TABLE**  }   [DOUBLE]]
         {NOLABELS}   {CONDENSE}
                      {ONEPAGE }

[/BASE={CASES**   }]
       {RESPONSES}

[/CELLS=[COUNT**]  [ROW]  [COLUMN]  [TOTAL]  [ALL]]
```

†A minimum of two subcommands must be used: at least one from the pair GROUPS or VARIABLES and one from the pair FREQUENCIES or TABLES.
**Default if the subcommand is omitted.

Example

```
MULT RESPONSE  GROUPS=MAGS (TIME TO STONE (2))
   /FREQUENCIES=MAGS .
```

Overview

MULT RESPONSE displays frequencies and optional percentages for multiple-response items in univariate tables and multivariate crosstabulations. Another procedure that analyzes multiple-response items is TABLES, which has most, but not all, of the capabilities of MULT RESPONSE. TABLES has special formatting capabilities that make it useful for presentations.

   Multiple-response items are questions that can have more than one value for each case. For example, the respondent may have been asked to circle all magazines read within the last month in a list of magazines. You can organize multiple-response data in one of two ways for use in the program. For each possible response, you can create a variable that can have one of two values, such as 1 for *no* and 2 for *yes*; this is the multiple-dichotomy method. Alternatively, you can estimate the maximum number of possible answers from a respondent and create that number of variables, each of which can have a value representing one of the possible answers, such as 1 for *Time*, 2 for *Newsweek*, and 3 for *PC Week*. If an individual did not give the maximum number of answers, the extra variables receive a missing-value code. This is the multiple-response or multiple-category method of coding answers.

To analyze the data entered by either method, you combine variables into groups. The technique depends on whether you have defined multiple-dichotomy or multiple-response variables. When you create a multiple-dichotomy group, each component variable with at least one *yes* value across cases becomes a category of the group variable. When you create a multiple-response group, each value becomes a category and the program calculates the frequency for a particular value by adding the frequencies of all component variables with that value. Both multiple-dichotomy and multiple-response groups can be crosstabulated with other variables in MULT RESPONSE.

Options

Cell Counts and Percentages. By default, crosstabulations include only counts and no percentages. You can request row, column, and total table percentages using the CELLS subcommand. You can also base percentages on responses instead of respondents using BASE.

Format. You can suppress the display of value labels and request condensed format for frequency tables using the FORMAT subcommand.

Basic Specification

The subcommands required for the basic specification fall into two groups: GROUPS and VARIABLES name the elements to be included in the analysis; FREQUENCIES and TABLES specify the type of table display to be used for tabulation. The basic specification requires at least one subcommand from each group:

- GROUPS defines groups of multiple-response items to be analyzed and specifies how the component variables will be combined.
- VARIABLES identifies all individual variables to be analyzed.
- FREQUENCIES requests frequency tables for the groups and/or individual variables specified on GROUPS and VARIABLES.
- TABLES requests crosstabulations of groups and/or individual variables specified on GROUPS and VARIABLES.

Subcommand Order

- The basic subcommands must be used in the following order: GROUPS, VARIABLES, FREQUENCIES, and TABLES. Only one set of basic subcommands can be specified.
- All basic subcommands must precede all optional subcommands. Optional subcommands can be used in any order.

Operations

- Empty categories are not displayed in either frequency tables or crosstabulations.
- If you define a multiple-response group with a very wide range, the tables require substantial amounts of workspace. If the component variables are sparsely distributed, you should recode them to minimize the workspace required.
- MULT RESPONSE stores category labels in the workspace. If there is insufficient space to store the labels after the tables are built, the labels are not displayed.

Limitations

- The component variables must have integer values. Non-integer values are truncated.
- Maximum 100 existing variables named or implied by GROUPS and VARIABLES together.
- Maximum 20 groups defined on GROUPS.
- Maximum 32,767 categories for a multiple-response group or an individual variable.
- Maximum 10 table lists on TABLES.
- Maximum 5 dimensions per table.
- Maximum 100 groups and variables named or implied on FREQUENCIES and TABLES together.
- Maximum 200 non-empty rows and 200 non-empty columns in a single table.

GROUPS Subcommand

GROUPS defines both multiple-dichotomy and multiple-response groups.

- Specify a name for the group and an optional label, followed by a list of the component variables and the value or values to be used in the tabulation.
- Enclose the variable list in parentheses and enclose the values in an inner set of parentheses following the last variable in the list.
- The label for the group is optional and can be up to 40 characters in length, including imbedded blanks. Apostrophes or quotes around the label are not required.
- To define a multiple-dichotomy group, specify only one tabulating value (the value that represents *yes*) following the variable list. Each component variable becomes a value of the group variable, and the number of cases that have the tabulating value becomes the frequency. If there are no cases with the tabulating value for a given component variable, that variable does not appear in the tabulation.
- To define a multiple-response group, specify two values following the variable list. These are the minimum and maximum values of the component variables. The group variable will have the same range of values. The frequency for each value is tabulated across all component variables in the list.
- You can use any valid variable name for the group except the name of an existing variable specified on the same MULT RESPONSE command. However, you can reuse a group name on another MULT RESPONSE command.

- The group names and labels exist only during MULT RESPONSE and disappear once MULT RESPONSE has been executed. If group names are referred to in other procedures, an error results.

- For a multiple-dichotomy group, the category labels come from the variable labels defined for the component variables.

- For a multiple-response group, the category labels come from the value labels for the first component variable in the group. If categories are missing for the first variable but are present for other variables in the group, you must define value labels for the missing categories. (You can use the ADD VALUE LABELS command to define extra value labels.)

Example

```
MULT RESPONSE  GROUPS=MAGS 'MAGAZINES READ' (TIME TO STONE (2))
   /FREQUENCIES=MAGS.
```

- The GROUPS subcommand creates a multiple-dichotomy group named *MAGS*. The variables between and including *TIME* and *STONE* become categories of *MAGS*, and the frequencies are cases with the value 2 (indicating *yes, read the magazine*) for the component variables.

- The group label is *MAGAZINES READ*.

Example

```
MULT RESPONSE  GROUPS=PROBS 'PERCEIVED NATIONAL PROBLEMS'
   (PROB1 TO PROB3 (1,9))
   /FREQUENCIES=PROBS.
```

- The GROUPS subcommand creates the multiple-response group *PROBS*. The component variables are the existing variables between and including *PROB1* and *PROB3*, and the frequencies are tabulated for the values 1 through 9.

- The frequency for a given value is the number of cases that have that value in any of the variables *PROB1* to *PROB3*.

VARIABLES Subcommand

VARIABLES specifies existing variables to be used in frequency tables and crosstabulations. Each variable is followed by parentheses enclosing a minimum and a maximum value, which are used to allocate cells for the tables for that variable.

- You can specify any numeric variable on VARIABLES, but non-integer values are truncated.

- If GROUPS is also specified, VARIABLES follows GROUPS.

- To provide the same minimum and maximum for each of a set of variables, specify a variable list followed by a range specification.

- The component variables specified on GROUPS can be used in frequency tables and crosstabulations, but you must specify them again on VARIABLES, along with a range for the values. You do not have to respecify the component variables if they will not be used as individual variables in any tables.

Example

```
MULT RESPONSE  GROUPS=MAGS 'MAGAZINES READ' (TIME TO STONE (2))
   /VARIABLES SEX(1,2) EDUC(1,3)
   /FREQUENCIES=MAGS SEX EDUC.
```

- The VARIABLES subcommand names the variables *SEX* and *EDUC* so that they can be used in a frequencies table.

Example

```
MULT RESPONSE  GROUPS=MAGS 'MAGAZINES READ' (TIME TO STONE (2))
   /VARIABLES=EDUC (1,3) TIME (1,2).
   /TABLES=MAGS BY EDUC TIME.
```

- The variable *TIME* is used in a group and also in a table.

FREQUENCIES Subcommand

FREQUENCIES requests frequency tables for groups and individual variables. By default, a frequency table contains the count for each value, the percentage of responses, and the percentage of cases. For another method of producing frequency tables for individual variables, see the FREQUENCIES procedure.

- All groups must be created by GROUPS, and all individual variables to be tabulated must be named on VARIABLES.
- You can use the keyword TO to imply a set of group or individual variables. TO refers to the order in which variables are specified on the GROUPS or VARIABLES subcommand.

Example

```
MULT RESPONSE  GROUPS=MAGS 'MAGAZINES READ' (TIME TO STONE (2))
   /FREQUENCIES=MAGS.
```

- The FREQUENCIES subcommand requests a frequency table for the multiple-dichotomy group *MAGS*, tabulating the frequency of the value 2 for each of the component variables *TIME* to *STONE*.

Example

```
MULT RESPONSE
 GROUPS=MAGS 'MAGAZINES READ' (TIME TO STONE (2))
     PROBS 'PERCEIVED NATIONAL PROBLEMS' (PROB1 TO PROB3 (1,9))
     MEMS 'SOCIAL ORGANIZATION MEMBERSHIPS' (VFW AMLEG ELKS (1))
 /VARIABLES SEX(1,2) EDUC(1,3)
 /FREQUENCIES=MAGS TO MEMS SEX EDUC.
```

- The FREQUENCIES subcommand requests frequency tables for *MAGS*, *PROBS*, *MEMS*, *SEX*, and *EDUC*.
- You cannot specify MAGS TO EDUC because *SEX* and *EDUC* are individual variables, and *MAGS*, *PROBS*, and *MEMS* are group variables.

TABLES Subcommand

TABLES specifies the crosstabulations to be produced by MULT RESPONSE. Both individual variables and group variables can be tabulated together.

- The first list defines the rows of the tables; the next list (following BY) defines the columns. Subsequent lists following BY keywords define control variables, which produce subtables. Use the keyword BY to separate the dimensions. You can specify up to five dimensions (four BY keywords) for a table.

- To produce more than one table, name one or more variables for each dimension of the tables. You can also specify multiple table lists separated by a slash. If you use the keyword TO to imply a set of group or individual variables, TO refers to the order in which groups or variables are specified on the GROUPS or VARIABLES subcommand.

- If FREQUENCIES is also specified, TABLES follows FREQUENCIES.

- The value labels for columns are displayed on three lines with eight characters per line. To avoid splitting words, reverse the row and column variables, or redefine the variable or value labels (depending on whether the variables are multiple-dichotomy or multiple-response variables).

Example

```
MULT RESPONSE  GROUPS=MAGS 'MAGAZINES READ' (TIME TO STONE (2))
   /VARIABLES=EDUC (1,3)/TABLES=EDUC BY MAGS.
```

- The TABLES subcommand requests a crosstabulation of variable *EDUC* by the multiple-dichotomy group *MAGS*.

Example

```
MULT RESPONSE  GROUPS=MAGS 'MAGAZINES READ' (TIME TO STONE (2))
   MEMS 'SOCIAL ORGANIZATION MEMBERSHIPS' (VFW AMLEG ELKS (1))
   /VARIABLES EDUC (1,3)/TABLES=MEMS MAGS BY EDUC.
```

- The TABLES subcommand specifies two crosstabulations—*MEMS* by *EDUC*, and *MAGS* by *EDUC*.

Example

```
MULT RESPONSE  GROUPS=MAGS 'MAGAZINES READ' (TIME TO STONE (2))
   /VARIABLES SEX (1,2) EDUC (1,3)
   /TABLES=MAGS BY EDUC SEX/EDUC BY SEX/MAGS BY EDUC BY SEX.
```

- The TABLES subcommand uses slashes to separate three table lists. It produces two tables from the first table list (*MAGS* by *EDUC* and *MAGS* by *SEX*) and one table from the second table list (*EDUC* by *SEX*). The third table list produces separate tables for each sex (*MAGS* by *EDUC* for male and for female).

Example

```
MULT RESPONSE  GROUPS=MAGS 'MAGAZINES READ' (TIME TO STONE (2))
   PROBS 'NATIONAL PROBLEMS MENTIONED' (PROB1 TO PROB3 (1,9))
   /TABLES=MAGS BY PROBS.
```

- The TABLES subcommand requests a crosstabulation of the multiple-dichotomy group *MAGS* with the multiple-response group *PROBS*.

PAIRED Keyword

When MULT RESPONSE crosstabulates two multiple-response groups, by default it tabulates each variable in the first group with each variable in the second group and sums the counts for each cell. Thus, some responses can appear more than once in the table. Use PAIRED to pair the first variable in the first group with the first variable in the second group, the second variable in the first group with the second variable in the second group, and so on.

- The keyword PAIRED is specified in parentheses on the TABLES subcommand following the last variable named for a specific table list.
- When you request paired crosstabulations, the order of the component variables on the GROUPS subcommand determines the construction of the table.
- Although the tables can contain individual variables and multiple-dichotomy groups in a paired table request, only variables within multiple-response groups are paired.
- PAIRED also applies to a multiple-response group used as a control variable in a three-way or higher-order table.
- Paired tables are identified in the output by the label *PAIRED GROUP*.
- Percentages in paired tables are always based on responses rather than cases.

Example

```
MULT RESPONSE GROUPS=PSEX 'SEX OF CHILD'(P1SEX P2SEX P3SEX (1,2))
    /PAGE 'AGE OF ONSET OF PREGNANCY' (P1AGE P2AGE P3AGE (1,4))
    /TABLES=PSEX BY PAGE (PAIRED).
```

- The PAIRED keyword produces a paired crosstabulation of *PSEX* by *PAGE*, which is a combination of the tables *P1SEX* by *P1AGE*, *P2SEX* by *P2AGE*, and *P3SEX* by *P3AGE*.

Example

```
MULT RESPONSE GROUPS=PSEX 'SEX OF CHILD'(P1SEX P2SEX P3SEX (1,2))
    PAGE 'AGE OF ONSET OF PREGNANCY' (P1AGE P2AGE P3AGE (1,4))
    /VARIABLES=EDUC (1,3)
    /TABLES=PSEX BY PAGE BY EDUC (PAIRED).
```

- The TABLES subcommand pairs only *PSEX* with *PAGE*. *EDUC* is not paired because it is an individual variable, not a multiple-response group.

CELLS Subcommand

By default, MULT RESPONSE displays cell counts but not percentages in crosstabulations. CELLS requests percentages for crosstabulations.

- If you specify one or more keywords on CELLS, MULT RESPONSE displays cell counts plus the percentages you request. The count cannot be eliminated from the table cells.

COUNT   *Cell counts. This is the default if you omit the CELLS subcommand.*

ROW   *Row percentages.*

COLUMN   *Column percentages.*

TOTAL   *Two-way table total percentages.*

ALL   *Cell counts, row percentages, column percentages, and two-way table total percentages.* This is the default if you specify the CELLS subcommand without keywords.

Example

```
MULT RESPONSE  GROUPS=MAGS 'MAGAZINES READ' (TIME TO STONE (2))
  /VARIABLES=SEX (1,2) (EDUC (1,3)
  /TABLES=MAGS BY EDUC SEX
  /CELLS=ROW COLUMN.
```

- The CELLS subcommand requests row and column percentages in addition to counts.

BASE Subcommand

BASE lets you obtain cell percentages and marginal frequencies based on responses rather than respondents. Specify one of two keywords:

CASES   *Base cell percentages on cases.* This is the default if you omit the BASE subcommand and do not request paired tables. You cannot use this specification if you specify PAIRED on TABLE.

RESPONSES *Base cell percentages on responses.* This is the default if you request paired tables.

Example

```
MULT RESPONSE  GROUPS=PROBS 'NATIONAL PROBLEMS MENTIONED'
  (PROB1 TO PROB3 (1,9))/VARIABLES=EDUC (1,3)
  /TABLES=EDUC BY PROBS
  /CELLS=ROW COLUMN
  /BASE=RESPONSES.
```

- The BASE subcommand requests marginal frequencies and cell percentages based on responses.

MISSING Subcommand

MISSING controls missing values. Its minimum specification is a single keyword.

- By default, MULT RESPONSE deletes cases with missing values on a table-by-table basis for both individual variables and groups. In addition, values falling outside the specified range are not tabulated and are included in the missing category. Thus, specifying a range that excludes missing values is equivalent to the default missing-value treatment.
- For a multiple-dichotomy group, a case is considered missing by default if none of the component variables contains the tabulating value for that case. Keyword MDGROUP overrides the default and specifies listwise deletion for multiple-dichotomy groups.
- For a multiple-response group, a case is considered missing by default if none of the components has valid values falling within the tabulating range for that case. Thus, cases with missing or excluded values on some (but not all) of the components of a group are

included in tabulations of the group variable. The keyword MRGROUP overrides the default and specifies listwise deletion for multiple-response groups.

- You can use INCLUDE with MDGROUP, MRGROUP, or TABLE. The user-missing value is tabulated if it is included in the range specification.

TABLE   *Exclude missing values on a table-by-table basis.* Missing values are excluded on a table-by-table basis for both component variables and groups. This is the default if you omit the MISSING subcommand.

MDGROUP   *Exclude missing values listwise for multiple-dichotomy groups.* Cases with missing values for any component dichotomy variable are excluded from the tabulation of the multiple-dichotomy group.

MRGROUP   *Exclude missing values listwise for multiple-response groups.* Cases with missing values for any component variable are excluded from the tabulation of the multiple-response group.

INCLUDE   *Include user-missing values.* User-missing values are treated as valid values if they are included in the range specification on the GROUPS or VARIABLES subcommands.

Example

```
MULT RESPONSE  GROUPS=FINANCL 'FINANCIAL PROBLEMS MENTIONED'
  (FINPROB1 TO FINPROB3 (1,3))
  SOCIAL 'SOCIAL PROBLEMS MENTIONED'(SOCPROB1 TO SOCPROB4 (4,9))
  /VARIABLES=EDUC (1,3)
  /TABLES=EDUC BY FINANCL SOCIAL
  /MISSING=MRGROUP.
```

- The MISSING subcommand indicates that a case will be excluded from counts in the first table if any of the variables in the group *FINPROB1* to *FINPROB3* has a missing value or a value outside the range 1 to 3. A case is excluded from the second table if any of the variables in the group *SOCPROB1* to *SOCPROB4* has a missing value or value outside the range 4 to 9.

FORMAT Subcommand

FORMAT controls table formats. The minimum specification on FORMAT is a single keyword.

Labels are controlled by two keywords:

LABELS   *Display value labels in frequency tables and crosstabulations.* This is the default.

NOLABELS   *Suppress value labels in frequency tables and crosstabulations for multiple-response variables and individual variables.* You cannot suppress the display of variable labels used as value labels for multiple-dichotomy groups.

The following keywords apply to the format of frequency tables:

DOUBLE   *Double spacing for frequency tables.* By default, MULT RESPONSE uses single spacing.

TABLE *One-column format for frequency tables.* This is the default if you omit the FORMAT subcommand.

CONDENSE *Condensed format for frequency tables.* This option uses a three-column condensed format for frequency tables for all multiple-response groups and individual variables. Labels are suppressed. This option does not apply to multiple-dichotomy groups.

ONEPAGE *Conditional condensed format for frequency tables.* Three-column condensed format is used if the resulting table would not fit on a page. This option does not apply to multiple-dichotomy groups.

Example

```
MULT RESPONSE  GROUPS=PROBS 'NATIONAL PROBLEMS MENTIONED'
   (PROB1 TO PROB3 (1,9))/VARIABLES=EDUC (1,3)
   /FREQUENCIES=EDUC PROBS
   /FORMAT=CONDENSE.
```

- The FORMAT subcommand specifies condensed format, which eliminates category labels and displays the categories in three parallel sets of columns, each set containing one or more rows of categories (rather than displaying one set of columns aligned vertically down the page).

NEW FILE

```
NEW FILE
```

Overview

The NEW FILE command clears the working data file. It is used when you want to build a new working data file by generating data within an input program (see INPUT PROGRAM— END INPUT PROGRAM).

Basic Specification

NEW FILE is always specified by itself. No other keyword is required or allowed.

Operations

- NEW FILE clears the working data file. The command takes effect as soon as it is encountered. You *must* build a new working data file after this command to continue your session. Transformations or procedures cannot be used before a working data file is created.
- When you build a working data file with GET, DATA LIST, or other file definition commands (such as ADD FILES or MATCH FILES), the working data file is automatically replaced. It is not necessary to specify NEW FILE.

NLR

NLR and CNLR are available in the Regression Models option.

```
MODEL PROGRAM parameter=value [parameter=value ...]
transformation commands

[DERIVATIVES
transformation commands]

[CLEAR MODEL PROGRAMS]
```

Procedure CNLR (Constrained Nonlinear Regression):

```
[CONSTRAINED FUNCTIONS
transformation commands]

CNLR dependent var

  [/FILE=file]    [/OUTFILE=file]

  [/PRED=varname]

  [/SAVE [PRED] [RESID[(varname)]] [DERIVATIVES] [LOSS]]

  [/CRITERIA=[ITER n] [MITER n] [CKDER {0.5**}]
                                      {n     }
             [ISTEP {1E+20**}] [FPR n] [LFTOL n]
                    {n       }
             [LSTOL n] [STEPLIMIT {2**}] [NFTOL n]
                                  {n  }
             [FTOL n] [OPTOL n] [CRSHTOL {.01**}]]
                                         {n    }

  [/BOUNDS=expression, expression, ...]

  [/LOSS=varname]

  [/BOOTSTRAP [=n]]
```

Procedure NLR (Nonlinear Regression):

```
NLR dependent var

  [/FILE=file]    [/OUTFILE=file]

  [/PRED=varname]

  [/SAVE [PRED] [RESID [(varname)] [DERIVATIVES]]]

  [/CRITERIA=[ITER {100**}] [CKDER {0.5**}]
                   {n     }        {n     }
             [SSCON {1E-8**}]  [PCON {1E-8**}]   [RCON {1E-8**}]]
                    {n       }       {n       }        {n       }
```

**Default if the subcommand or keyword is omitted.

Example

```
MODEL PROGRAM A=.6.
COMPUTE PRED=EXP(A*X).

NLR Y.
```

Overview

Nonlinear regression is used to estimate parameter values and regression statistics for models that are not linear in their parameters. SPSS has two procedures for estimating nonlinear equations. CNLR (constrained nonlinear regression), which uses a sequential quadratic programming algorithm, is applicable for both constrained and unconstrained problems. NLR (nonlinear regression), which uses a Levenberg-Marquardt algorithm, is applicable only for unconstrained problems.

CNLR is more general. It allows linear and nonlinear constraints on any combination of parameters. It will estimate parameters by minimizing any smooth loss function (objective function), and can optionally compute bootstrap estimates of parameter standard errors and correlations. The individual bootstrap parameter estimates can optionally be saved in a separate SPSS data file.

Both programs estimate the values of the parameters for the model and, optionally, compute and save predicted values, residuals, and derivatives. Final parameter estimates can be saved in an SPSS data file and used in subsequent analyses.

CNLR and NLR use much of the same syntax. Some of the following sections discuss features common to both procedures. In these sections, the notation [C]NLR means that either the CNLR or NLR procedure can be specified. Sections that apply only to CNLR or only to NLR are clearly identified.

Options

The Model. You can use any number of transformation commands under MODEL PROGRAM to define complex models.

Derivatives. You can use any number of transformation commands under DERIVATIVES to supply derivatives.

Adding Variables to Working Data File. You can add predicted values, residuals, and derivatives to the working data file with the SAVE subcommand.

Writing Parameter Estimates to a New Data File. You can save final parameter estimates as an external SPSS data file using the OUTFILE subcommand; you can retrieve them in subsequent analyses using the FILE subcommand.

Controlling Model-Building Criteria. You can control the iteration process used in the regression with the CRITERIA subcommand.

Additional CNLR Controls. For CNLR, you can impose linear and nonlinear constraints on the parameters with the BOUNDS subcommand. Using the LOSS subcommand, you can specify a loss function for CNLR to minimize and, using the BOOTSTRAP subcommand, you can provide bootstrap estimates of the parameter standard errors, confidence intervals, and correlations.

Basic Specification

The basic specification requires three commands: MODEL PROGRAM, COMPUTE (or any other computational transformation command), and [C]NLR.

- The MODEL PROGRAM command assigns initial values to the parameters and signifies the beginning of the model program.
- The computational transformation command generates a new variable to define the model. The variable can take any legitimate name, but if the name is not *PRED*, the PRED subcommand will be required.
- The [C]NLR command provides the regression specifications. The minimum specification is the dependent variable.
- By default, the residual sum of squares and estimated values of the model parameters are displayed for each iteration. Statistics generated include regression and residual sums of squares and mean squares, corrected and uncorrected total sums of squares, R^2, parameter estimates with their asymptotic standard errors and 95% confidence intervals, and an asymptotic correlation matrix of the parameter estimates.

Command Order

- The model program, beginning with the MODEL PROGRAM command, must precede the [C]NLR command.
- The derivatives program (when used), beginning with the DERIVATIVES command, must follow the model program but precede the [C]NLR command.
- The constrained functions program (when used), beginning with the CONSTRAINED FUNCTIONS command, must immediately precede the CNLR command. The constrained functions program cannot be used with the NLR command.
- The CNLR command must follow the block of transformations for the model program and the derivatives program when specified; the CNLR command must also follow the constrained functions program when specified.
- Subcommands on [C]NLR can be named in any order.

Syntax Rules

- The FILE, OUTFILE, PRED, and SAVE subcommands work the same way for both CNLR and NLR.
- The CRITERIA subcommand is used by both CNLR and NLR, but iteration criteria are different. Therefore, the CRITERIA subcommand is documented separately for CNLR and NLR.
- The BOUNDS, LOSS, and BOOTSTRAP subcommands can be used only with CNLR. They cannot be used with NLR.

Operations

- By default, the predicted values, residuals, and derivatives are created as temporary variables. To save these variables, use the SAVE subcommand.

Weighting Cases

- If case weighting is in effect, [C]NLR uses case weights when calculating the residual sum of squares and derivatives. However, the degrees of freedom in the ANOVA table are always based on unweighted cases.
- When the model program is first invoked for each case, the weight variable's value is set equal to its value in the working data file. The model program may recalculate that value. For example, to effect a robust estimation, the model program may recalculate the weight variable's value as an inverse function of the residual magnitude. [C]NLR uses the weight variable's value after the model program is executed.

Missing Values

Cases with missing values for any of the dependent or independent variables named on the [C]NLR command are excluded.

- Predicted values, but not residuals, can be calculated for cases with missing values on the dependent variable.
- [C]NLR ignores cases that have missing, negative, or zero weights. The procedure displays a warning message if it encounters any negative or zero weights at any time during its execution.
- If a variable used in the model program or the derivatives program is omitted from the independent variable list on the [C]NLR command, the predicted value and some or all of the derivatives may be missing for every case. If this happens, SPSS generates an error message.

Example

```
MODEL PROGRAM A=.5 B=1.6.
COMPUTE PRED=A*SPEED**B.

DERIVATIVES.
COMPUTE D.A=SPEED**B.
COMPUTE D.B=A*LN(SPEED)*SPEED**B.

NLR STOP.
```

- MODEL PROGRAM assigns values to the model parameters *A* and *B*.
- COMPUTE generates the variable *PRED* to define the nonlinear model using parameters *A* and *B* and the variable *SPEED* from the working data file. Because this variable is named *PRED*, the PRED subcommand is not required on NLR.
- DERIVATIVES indicates that calculations for derivatives are being supplied.

- The two COMPUTE statements on the DERIVATIVES transformations list calculate the derivatives for the parameters *A* and *B*. If either one had been omitted, NLR would have calculated it numerically.

- NLR specifies *STOP* as the dependent variable. It is not necessary to specify *SPEED* as the independent variable since it has been used in the model and derivatives programs.

MODEL PROGRAM Command

The MODEL PROGRAM command assigns initial values to the parameters and signifies the beginning of the model program. The model program specifies the nonlinear equation chosen to model the data. There is no default model.

- The model program is required and must precede the [C]NLR command.

- The MODEL PROGRAM command must specify all parameters in the model program. Each parameter must be individually named. Keyword TO is not allowed.

- Parameters can be assigned any acceptable SPSS variable name. However, if you intend to write the final parameter estimates to a file with the OUTFILE subcommand, do not use the name *SSE* or *NCASES* (see the OUTFILE subcommand on p. 798).

- Each parameter in the model program must have an assigned value. The value can be specified on MODEL PROGRAM or read from an existing parameter data file named on the FILE subcommand.

- Zero should be avoided as an initial value because it provides no information on the scale of the parameters. This is especially true for CNLR.

- The model program must include at least one command that uses the parameters and the independent variables (or preceding transformations of these) to calculate the predicted value of the dependent variable. This predicted value defines the nonlinear model. There is no default model.

- By default, the program assumes that *PRED* is the name assigned to the variable for the predicted values. If you use a different variable name in the model program, you must supply the name on the PRED subcommand (see the PRED subcommand on p. 799).

- In the model program, you can assign a label to the variable holding predicted values and also change its print and write formats, but you should not specify missing values for this variable.

- You can use any computational commands (such as COMPUTE, IF, DO IF, LOOP, END LOOP, END IF, RECODE, or COUNT) or output commands (WRITE, PRINT, or XSAVE) in the model program, but you cannot use input commands (such as DATA LIST, GET, MATCH FILES, or ADD FILES).

- Transformations in the model program are used only by [C]NLR, and they do not affect the working data file. The parameters created by the model program do not become a part of the working data file. Permanent transformations should be specified before the model program.

Caution

The selection of good initial values for the parameters in the model program is very important to the operation of [C]NLR. The selection of poor initial values can result in no solution, a local rather than a general solution, or a physically impossible solution.

Example

```
MODEL PROGRAM A=10 B=1 C=5 D=1.
COMPUTE PRED= A*exp(B*X) + C*exp(D*X).
```

- The MODEL PROGRAM command assigns starting values to the four parameters *A, B, C,* and *D.*

- COMPUTE defines the model to be fit as the sum of two exponentials.

DERIVATIVES Command

The optional DERIVATIVES command signifies the beginning of the derivatives program. The derivatives program contains transformation statements for computing some or all of the derivatives of the model. The derivatives program must follow the model program but precede the [C]NLR command.

If the derivatives program is not used, [C]NLR numerically estimates derivatives for all the parameters. Providing derivatives reduces computation time and, in some situations, may result in a better solution.

- The DERIVATIVES command has no further specifications but must be followed by the set of transformation statements that calculate the derivatives.

- You can use any computational commands (such as COMPUTE, IF, DO IF, LOOP, END LOOP, END IF, RECODE, or COUNT) or output commands (WRITE, PRINT, or XSAVE) in the derivatives program, but you cannot use input commands (such as DATA LIST, GET, MATCH FILES, or ADD FILES).

- To name the derivatives, specify the prefix *D.* before each parameter name. For example, the derivative name for the parameter *PARM1* must be *D.PARM1.*

- Once a derivative has been calculated by a transformation, the variable for that derivative can be used in subsequent transformations.

- You do not need to supply all of the derivatives. Those that are not supplied will be estimated by the program. During the first iteration of the nonlinear estimation procedure, derivatives calculated in the derivatives program are compared with numerically calculated derivatives. This serves as a check on the supplied values (see the CRITERIA subcommand on p. 801).

- Transformations in the derivatives program are used by [C]NLR only and do not affect the working data file.

- For NLR, the derivative of each parameter must be computed with respect to the predicted function. (For computation of derivatives in CNLR, see the LOSS subcommand on p. 805.)

Example

```
MODEL PROGRAM A=1, B=0, C=1, D=0
COMPUTE PRED = Ae^Bx + Ce^Dx
DERIVATIVES.
COMPUTE D.A = exp (B * X).
COMPUTE D.B = A * exp (B * X) * X.
COMPUTE D.C = exp (D * X).
COMPUTE D.D = C * exp (D * X) * X.
```

- The derivatives program specifies derivatives of the PRED function for the sum of the two exponentials in the model described by the following equation:

$$Y = Ae^{Bx} + Ce^{Dx}$$

Example

```
DERIVATIVES.
COMPUTE D.A = exp (B * X).
COMPUTE D.B = A * X * D.A.
COMPUTE D.C = exp (D * X).
COMPUTE D.D = C * X * D.C.
```

- This is an alternative way to express the same derivatives program specified in the previous example.

CONSTRAINED FUNCTIONS Command

The optional CONSTRAINED FUNCTIONS command signifies the beginning of the constrained functions program, which specifies nonlinear constraints. The constrained functions program is specified after the model program and the derivatives program (when used). It can only be used with, and must precede, the CNLR command. For more information, see the BOUNDS subcommand on p. 804.

Example

```
MODEL PROGRAM A=.5 B=1.6.
COMPUTE PRED=A*SPEED**B.

CONSTRAINED FUNCTIONS.
COMPUTE CF=A-EXP(B).

CNLR STOP
  /BOUNDS CF LE 0.
```

CLEAR MODEL PROGRAMS Command

CLEAR MODEL PROGRAMS deletes all transformations associated with the model program, the derivative program, and/or the constrained functions program previously submitted. It is primarily used in interactive mode to remove temporary variables created by these programs without affecting the working data file or variables created by other transformation programs or temporary programs. It allows you to specify new models, derivatives, or constrained functions without having to run [C]NLR.

It is not necessary to use this command if you have already executed the [C]NLR procedure. Temporary variables associated with the procedure are automatically deleted.

CNLR/NLR Command

Either the CNLR or the NLR command is required to specify the dependent and independent variables for the nonlinear regression.

- For either CNLR or NLR, the minimum specification is a dependent variable.
- Only one dependent variable can be specified. It must be a numeric variable in the working data file and cannot be a variable generated by the model or the derivatives program.

OUTFILE Subcommand

OUTFILE stores final parameter estimates for use on a subsequent [C]NLR command. The only specification on OUTFILE is the target file. Some or all of the values from this file can be read into a subsequent [C]NLR procedure with the FILE subcommand. The parameter data file created by OUTFILE stores the following variables:

- All of the split-file variables. OUTFILE writes one case of values for each split-file group in the working data file.
- All of the parameters named on the MODEL PROGRAM command.
- The labels, formats, and missing values of the split-file variables and parameters defined for them previous to their use in the [C]NLR procedure.
- The sum of squared residuals (named *SSE*). *SSE* has no labels or missing values. The print and write format for *SSE* is F10.8.
- The number of cases on which the analysis was based (named *NCASES*). *NCASES* has no labels or missing values. The print and write format for *NCASES* is F8.0.

When OUTFILE is used, the model program cannot create variables named *SSE* or *NCASES*.

Example

```
MODEL PROGRAM A=.5 B=1.6.
COMPUTE PRED=A*SPEED**B.
NLR STOP /OUTFILE=PARAM.
```

- OUTFILE generates a parameter data file containing one case for four variables: *A*, *B*, *SSE*, and *NCASES*.

FILE Subcommand

FILE reads starting values for the parameters from a parameter data file created by an OUTFILE subcommand from a previous [C]NLR procedure. When starting values are read from a file, they do not have to be specified on the MODEL PROGRAM command. Rather, the MODEL PROGRAM command simply names the parameters that correspond to the parameters in the data file.

- The only specification on FILE is the file that contains the starting values.

- Some new parameters may be specified for the model on the MODEL PROGRAM command while others are read from the file specified on the FILE subcommand.
- You do not have to name the parameters on MODEL PROGRAM in the order in which they occur in the parameter data file. In addition, you can name a partial list of the variables contained in the file.
- If the starting value for a parameter is specified on MODEL PROGRAM, the specification overrides the value read from the parameter data file.
- If split-file processing is in effect, the starting values for the first subfile are taken from the first case of the parameter data file. Subfiles are matched with cases in order until the starting value file runs out of cases. All subsequent subfiles use the starting values for the last case.
- To read starting values from a parameter data file and then replace those values with the final results from [C]NLR, specify the same file on the FILE and OUTFILE subcommands. The input file is read completely before anything is written in the output file.

Example

```
MODEL PROGRAM A B C=1 D=3.
COMPUTE PRED=A*SPEED**B + C*SPEED**D.
NLR STOP /FILE=PARAM /OUTFILE=PARAM.
```

- MODEL PROGRAM names four of the parameters used to calculate *PRED*, but assigns values to only *C* and *D*. The values of *A* and *B* are read from the existing data file *PARAM*.
- After NLR computes the final estimates of the four parameters, OUTFILE writes over the old input file. If, in addition to these new final estimates, the former starting values of *A* and *B* are still desired, specify a different file on the OUTFILE subcommand.

PRED Subcommand

PRED identifies the variable holding the predicted values.

- The only specification is a variable name, which must be identical to the variable name used to calculate predicted values in the model program.
- If the model program names the variable *PRED*, the PRED subcommand can be omitted. Otherwise, the PRED subcommand is required.
- The variable for predicted values is not saved in the working data file unless the SAVE subcommand is used.

Example

```
MODEL PROGRAM A=.5 B=1.6.
COMPUTE PSTOP=A*SPEED**B.
NLR STOP /PRED=PSTOP.
```

- COMPUTE in the model program creates a variable named *PSTOP* to temporarily store the predicted values for the dependent variable *STOP*.
- PRED identifies *PSTOP* as the variable used to define the model for the NLR procedure.

SAVE Subcommand

SAVE is used to save the temporary variables for the predicted values, residuals, and derivatives created by the model and the derivatives programs.

- The minimum specification is a single keyword.
- The variables to be saved must have unique names on the working data file. If a naming conflict exists, the variables are not saved.
- Temporary variables, for example, variables created after a TEMPORARY command and parameters specified by the model program, are not saved in the working data file. They will not cause naming conflicts.

The following keywords are available and can be used in any combination and in any order. The new variables are always appended to the working data file in the order in which these keywords are presented here:

PRED
Save the predicted values. The variable's name, label, and formats are those specified for it (or assigned by default) in the model program.

RESID [(varname)]
Save the residuals variable. You can specify a variable name in parentheses following the keyword. If no variable name is specified, the name of this variable is the same as the specification you use for this keyword. For example, if you use the three-character abbreviation RES, the default variable name will be RES. The variable has the same print and write format as the predicted values variable created by the model program. It has no variable label and no user-defined missing values. It is system-missing for any case in which either the dependent variable is missing or the predicted value cannot be computed.

DERIVATIVES
Save the derivative variables. The derivative variables are named with the prefix D. to the first six characters of the parameter names. Derivative variables use the print and write formats of the predicted values variable and have no value labels or user-missing values. Derivative variables are saved in the same order as the parameters named on MODEL PROGRAM. Derivatives are saved for all parameters, whether or not the derivative was supplied in the derivatives program.

LOSS
Save the user-specified loss function variable. This specification is available only with CNLR and only if the LOSS subcommand has been specified.

Asymptotic standard errors of predicted values and residuals, and special residuals used for outlier detection and influential case analysis are not provided by the [C]NLR procedure. However, for a squared loss function, the asymptotically correct values for all these statistics can be calculated using the SAVE subcommand with [C]NLR and then using the REGRESSION procedure. In REGRESSION, the dependent variable is still the same, and derivatives of the model parameters are used as independent variables. Casewise plots, standard errors of prediction, partial regression plots, and other diagnostics of the regression are valid for the nonlinear model.

Example

```
MODEL PROGRAM A=.5 B=1.6.
COMPUTE PSTOP=A*SPEED**B.
NLR STOP /PRED=PSTOP
  /SAVE=RESID(RSTOP) DERIVATIVES PRED.
REGRESSION VARIABLES=STOP D.A D.B /ORIGIN
  /DEPENDENT=STOP /ENTER D.A D.B /RESIDUALS.
```

- The SAVE subcommand creates the residuals variable *RSTOP* and the derivative variables *D.A* and *D.B*.

- Because the PRED subcommand identifies *PSTOP* as the variable for predicted values in the nonlinear model, keyword PRED on SAVE adds the variable *PSTOP* to the working data file.

- The new variables are added to the working data file in the following order: *PSTOP*, *RSTOP*, *D.A*, and *D.B*.

- The subcommand RESIDUALS for REGRESSION produces the default analysis of residuals.

CRITERIA Subcommand

CRITERIA controls the values of the cutoff points used to stop the iterative calculations in [C]NLR.

- The minimum specification is any of the criteria keywords and an appropriate value. The value can be specified in parentheses after an equals sign, a space, or a comma. Multiple keywords can be specified in any order. Defaults are in effect for keywords not specified.

- Keywords available for CRITERIA differ between CNLR and NLR and are discussed separately. However, with both CNLR and NLR, you can specify the critical value for derivative checking.

Checking Derivatives for CNLR and NLR

Upon entering the first iteration, [C]NLR always checks any derivatives calculated on the derivatives program by comparing them with numerically calculated derivatives. For each comparison, it computes an agreement score. A score of 1 indicates agreement to machine precision; a score of 0 indicates definite disagreement. If a score is less than 1, either an incorrect derivative was supplied or there were numerical problems in estimating the derivative. The lower the score, the more likely it is that the supplied derivatives are incorrect. Highly correlated parameters may cause disagreement even when a correct derivative is supplied. Be sure to check the derivatives if the agreement score is not 1.

During the first iteration, [C]NLR checks each derivative score. If any score is below 1, it begins displaying a table to show the worst (lowest) score for each derivative. If any score is below the critical value, the program stops.

To specify the critical value, use the following keyword on CRITERIA:

CKDER n   *Critical value for derivative checking.* Specify a number between 0 and 1 for *n*. The default is 0.5. Specify 0 to disable this criterion.

Iteration Criteria for CNLR

The CNLR procedure uses NPSOL (Version 4.0) Fortran Package for Nonlinear Programming (Gill et al., 1986). The CRITERIA subcommand of CNLR gives the control features of NPSOL. The following section summarizes the NPSOL documentation.

CNLR uses a sequential quadratic programming algorithm, with a quadratic programming subproblem to determine the search direction. If constraints or bounds are specified, the first step is to find a point that is feasible with respect to those constraints. Each major iteration sets up a quadratic program to find the search direction, p. Minor iterations are used to solve this subproblem. Then, the major iteration determines a steplength α by a line search, and the function is evaluated at the new point. An optimal solution is found when the optimality tolerance criterion is met.

The CRITERIA subcommand has the following keywords when used with CNLR:

ITER n *Maximum number of major iterations.* Specify any positive integer for n. The default is $\max(50, 3(p + m_L) + 10m_N)$, where p is the number of parameters, m_L is the number of linear constraints, and m_N is the number of nonlinear constraints. If the search for a solution stops because this limit is exceeded, CNLR issues a warning message.

MINORITERATION n *Maximum number of minor iterations.* Specify any positive integer. This is the number of minor iterations allowed within each major iteration. The default is $\max(50, 3(n + m_L + m_N))$.

CRSHTOL n *Crash tolerance.* CRSHTOL is used to determine if initial values are within their specified bounds. Specify any value between 0 and 1. The default value is 0.01. A constraint of the form $a'X \geq l$ is considered a valid part of the working set if $|a'X - l| < \text{CRSHTOL}(1 + |l|)$.

STEPLIMIT n *Step limit.* The CNLR algorithm does not allow changes in the length of the parameter vector to exceed a factor of n. The limit prevents very early steps from going too far from good initial estimates. Specify any positive value. The default value is 2.

FTOLERANCE n *Feasibility tolerance.* This is the maximum absolute difference allowed for both linear and nonlinear constraints for a solution to be considered feasible. Specify any value greater than 0. The default value is the square root of your machine's epsilon.

LFTOLERANCE n *Linear feasibility tolerance.* If specified, this overrides FTOLERANCE for linear constraints and bounds. Specify any value greater than 0. The default value is the square root of your machine's epsilon.

NFTOLERANCE n *Nonlinear feasibility tolerance.* If specified, this overrides FTOLERANCE for nonlinear constraints. Specify any value greater than 0. The default value is the square root of your machine's epsilon.

LSTOLERANCE n *Line search tolerance.* This value must be between 0 and 1 (but not including 1). It controls the accuracy required of the line search that forms the innermost search loop. The default value, 0.9, specifies an inaccurate search. This is appropriate for many problems, particularly if nonlinear constraints are involved. A smaller positive value, corresponding to a more accurate line search, may give better performance if there are no nonlinear constraints, all (or most) derivatives are supplied in the derivatives program, and the data fit in memory.

OPTOLERANCE n   *Optimality tolerance.* If an iteration point is a feasible point and the next step will not produce a relative change in either the parameter vector or the objective function of more than the square root of OPTOLERANCE, an optimal solution has been found. OPTOLERANCE can also be thought of as the number of significant digits in the objective function at the solution. For example, if OPTOLERANCE=10^{-6}, the objective function should have approximately six significant digits of accuracy. Specify any number between the FPRECISION value and 1. The default value for OPTOLERANCE is epsilon**0.8.

FPRECISION n   *Function precision.* This is a measure of the accuracy with which the objective function can be checked. It acts as a relative precision when the function is large, and an absolute precision when the function is small. For example, if the objective function is larger than 1, and six significant digits are desired, FPRECISION should be $1E-6$. If, however, the objective function is of the order 0.001, FPRECISION should be $1E-9$ to get six digits of accuracy. Specify any number between 0 and 1. The choice of FPRECISION can be very complicated for a badly scaled problem. Chapter 8 of Gill et al. (1981) gives some scaling suggestions. The default value is epsilon**0.9.

ISTEP n   *Infinite step size.* This value is the magnitude of the change in parameters that is defined as infinite. That is, if the change in the parameters at a step is greater than ISTEP, the problem is considered unbounded, and estimation stops. Specify any positive number. The default value is $1E+20$.

Iteration Criteria for NLR

The NLR procedure uses an adaptation of subroutine LMSTR from the MINPACK package by Garbow et al. Because the NLR algorithm differs substantially from CNLR, the CRITERIA subcommand for NLR has a different set of keywords.

NLR computes parameter estimates using the Levenberg-Marquardt method. At each iteration, NLR evaluates the estimates against a set of control criteria. The iterative calculations continue until one of five cutoff points is met, at which point the iterations stop and the reason for stopping is displayed.

The CRITERIA subcommand has the following keywords when used with NLR:

ITER n   *Maximum number of major and minor iterations allowed.* Specify any positive integer for *n*. The default is 100 iterations per parameter. If the search for a solution stops because this limit is exceeded, NLR issues a warning message.

SSCON n   *Convergence criterion for the sum of squares.* Specify any non-negative number for *n*. The default is $1E-8$. If successive iterations fail to reduce the sum of squares by this proportion, the procedure stops. Specify 0 to disable this criterion.

PCON n | *Convergence criterion for the parameter values.* Specify any non-negative number for *n*. The default is $1E-8$. If successive iterations fail to change any of the parameter values by this proportion, the procedure stops. Specify 0 to disable this criterion.

RCON n | *Convergence criterion for the correlation between the residuals and the derivatives.* Specify any non-negative number for *n*. The default is $1E-8$. If the largest value for the correlation between the residuals and the derivatives equals this value, the procedure stops because it lacks the information it needs to estimate a direction for its next move. This criterion is often referred to as a gradient convergence criterion. Specify 0 to disable this criterion.

Example

```
MODEL PROGRAM A=.5 B=1.6.
COMPUTE PRED=A*SPEED**B.
NLR STOP /CRITERIA=ITER(80) SSCON=.000001.
```

• CRITERIA changes two of the five cutoff values affecting iteration, ITER and SSCON, and leaves the remaining three, PCON, RCON, and CKDER, at their default values.

BOUNDS Subcommand

The BOUNDS subcommand can be used to specify both linear and nonlinear constraints. It can be used only with CNLR; it cannot be used with NLR.

Simple Bounds and Linear Constraints

BOUNDS can be used to impose bounds on parameter values. These bounds can involve either single parameters or a linear combination of parameters and can be either equalities or inequalities.

• All bounds are specified on the same BOUNDS subcommand and separated by semicolons.

• The only variables allowed on BOUNDS are parameter variables (those named on MODEL PROGRAM).

• Only * (multiplication), + (addition), − (subtraction), = or EQ, >= or GE, and <= or LE can be used. When two relational operators are used (as in the third bound in the example below), they must both be in the same direction.

Example

```
/BOUNDS 5 >= A;
        B >= 9;
        .01 <= 2*A + C <= 1;
        D + 2*E = 10
```

• BOUNDS imposes bounds on the parameters *A, B, C,* and *D*. Specifications for each parameter are separated by a semicolon.

Nonlinear Constraints

Nonlinear constraints on the parameters can also be specified with the BOUNDS subcommand. The constrained function must be calculated and stored in a variable by a constrained functions program directly preceding the CNLR command. The constraint is then specified on the BOUNDS subcommand.

In general, nonlinear bounds will not be obeyed until an optimal solution has been found. This is different from simple and linear bounds, which are satisfied at each iteration. The constrained functions must be smooth near the solution.

Example

```
MODEL PROGRAM A=.5 B=1.6.
COMPUTE PRED=A*SPEED**B.

CONSTRAINED FUNCTIONS.
COMPUTE DIFF=A-10**B.

CNLR STOP /BOUNDS DIFF LE 0.
```

- The constrained function is calculated by a constrained functions program and stored in variable *DIFF*. The constrained functions program immediately precedes CNLR.
- BOUNDS imposes bounds on the function (less than or equal to 0).
- CONSTRAINED FUNCTIONS variables and parameters named on MODEL PROGRAM cannot be combined in the same BOUNDS expression. For example, you *cannot* specify $(DIFF + A) > = 0$ on the BOUNDS subcommand.

LOSS Subcommand

LOSS specifies a loss function for CNLR to minimize. By default, CNLR minimizes the sum of squared residuals. LOSS can be used only with CNLR; it cannot be used with NLR.

- The loss function must first be computed in the model program. LOSS is then used to specify the name of the computed variable.
- The minimizing algorithm may fail if it is given a loss function that is not smooth, such as the absolute value of residuals.
- If derivatives are supplied, the derivative of each parameter must be computed with respect to the loss function, rather than the predicted value. The easiest way to do this is in two steps: first compute derivatives of the model, and then compute derivatives of the loss function with respect to the model and multiply by the model derivatives.
- When LOSS is used, the usual summary statistics are not computed. Standard errors, confidence intervals, and correlations of the parameters are available only if the BOOTSTRAP subcommand is specified.

Example

```
MODEL PROGRAM  A=1 B=1.
COMPUTE PRED=EXP(A+B*T)/(1+EXP(A+B*T)).
COMPUTE LOSS=-W*(Y*LN(PRED)+(1-Y)*LN(1-PRED)).

DERIVATIVES.
COMPUTE D.A=PRED/(1+EXP(A+B*T)).
COMPUTE D.B=T*PRED/(1+EXP(A+B*T)).
COMPUTE D.A=(-W*(Y/PRED - (1-Y)/(1-PRED)) * D.A).
COMPUTE D.B=(-W*(Y/PRED - (1-Y)/(1-PRED)) * D.B).

CNLR Y /LOSS=LOSS.
```

- The second COMPUTE command in the model program computes the loss functions and stores its values in the variable *LOSS*, which is then specified on the LOSS subcommand.

- Because derivatives are supplied in the derivatives program, the derivatives of all parameters are computed with respect to the loss function, rather than the predicted value.

BOOTSTRAP Subcommand

BOOTSTRAP provides bootstrap estimates of the parameter standard errors, confidence intervals, and correlations. BOOTSTRAP can be used only with CNLR; it cannot be used with NLR.

Bootstrapping is a way of estimating the standard error of a statistic, using repeated samples from the original data set. This is done by sampling with replacement to get samples of the same size as the original data set.

- The minimum specification is the subcommand keyword. Optionally, specify the number of samples to use for generating bootstrap results.

- By default, BOOTSTRAP generates bootstrap results based on $10*p*(p+1)/2$ samples, where p is the number of parameters. That is, 10 samples are drawn for each statistic (standard error or correlation) to be calculated.

- When BOOTSTRAP is used, the nonlinear equation is estimated for each sample. The standard error of each parameter estimate is then calculated as the standard deviation of the bootstrapped estimates. Parameter values from the original data are used as starting values for each bootstrap sample. Even so, bootstrapping is computationally expensive.

- If the OUTFILE subcommand is specified, a case is written to the output file for each bootstrap sample. The first case in the file will be the actual parameter estimates, followed by the bootstrap samples. After the first case is eliminated (using SELECT IF), other SPSS procedures (such as FREQUENCIES) can be used to examine the bootstrap distribution.

Example

```
MODEL PROGRAM A=.5 B=1.6.
COMPUTE PSTOP=A*SPEED**B.
CNLR STOP /BOOTSTRAP /OUTFILE=PARAM.
GET FILE=PARAM.
LIST.
COMPUTE ID=$CASENUM.
SELECT IF (ID > 1).
FREQUENCIES A B /FORMAT=NOTABLE /HISTOGRAM.
```

- CNLR generates the bootstrap standard errors, confidence intervals, and parameter correlation matrix. OUTFILE saves the bootstrap estimates in the file *PARAM*.
- GET retrieves the system file *PARAM*.
- LIST lists the different sample estimates along with the original estimate. *NCASES* in the listing (see the OUTFILE subcommand on p. 798) refers to the number of distinct cases in the sample because cases are duplicated in each bootstrap sample.
- FREQUENCIES generates histograms of the bootstrapped parameter estimates.

N OF CASES

```
N OF CASES n
```

Example

```
N OF CASES 100.
```

Overview

N OF CASES (alias N) limits the number of cases in the working data file to the first n cases.

Basic Specification

The basic specification is N OF CASES followed by at least one space and a positive integer. Cases in the working data file are limited to the specified number.

Syntax Rules

- To limit the number of cases for the next procedure only, use the TEMPORARY command before N OF CASES (see TEMPORARY).
- In some versions of the program, N OF CASES can be specified only after a working data file is defined.

Operations

- Unlike most transformations, N OF CASES takes effect as soon as it is encountered in the command sequence. Thus, special attention should be paid to its position among commands. See "Command Order" on p. 16 for more information.
- N OF CASES limits the number of cases analyzed by all subsequent procedures in the session. The working data file will have no more than n cases after the first data pass following the N OF CASES command. Any subsequent N OF CASES command specifying a greater number of cases will be ignored.
- If N OF CASES specifies more cases than can actually be built, the program builds as many cases as possible.
- If N OF CASES is used with SAMPLE or SELECT IF, the program reads as many records as required to build the specified n cases. It makes no difference whether the N OF CASES precedes or follows the SAMPLE or SELECT IF command.

Example

```
GET FILE=CITY.
N 100.
```

- N OF CASES limits the number of cases on the working data file to the first 100 cases. Cases are limited for all subsequent analyses.

Example

```
DATA LIST FILE=PRSNNL / NAME 1-20 (A) AGE 22-23 SALARY 25-30.
N 25.
SELECT IF (SALARY GT 20000).
LIST.
```

- DATA LIST defines variables from file *PRSNNL*.
- N OF CASES limits the working data file to 25 cases after cases have been selected by SELECT IF.
- SELECT IF selects only cases in which *SALARY* is greater than $20,000.
- LIST produces a listing of the cases in the working data file. If the original working data file has fewer than 25 cases in which salary is greater than 20,000, fewer than 25 cases will be listed.

Example

```
DATA LIST FILE=PRSNNL / NAME 1-20(A) AGE 22-23
                       SALARY 25-30 DEPT 32.
LIST.
TEMPORARY.
N 25.
FREQUENCIES VAR=SALARY.
N 50.
FREQUENCIES VAR=AGE.
REPORT FORMAT=AUTO /VARS=NAME AGE SALARY /BREAK=DEPT
  /SUMMARY=MEAN.
```

- The first N OF CASES command is temporary. Only 25 cases are used in the first FREQUENCIES procedure.
- The second N OF CASES command is permanent. The second frequency table and the report are based on 50 cases from file *PRSNNL*. The working data file now contains 50 cases (assuming the original working file had at least that many).

NOMREG

NOMREG is available in the Regression Models option.

```
NOMREG dependent varname [BY factor list] [WITH covariate list]

[/CRITERIA = [CIN({95**})] [DELTA({0**})] [MXITER({100**})] [MXSTEP({5**})]
                  {n  }         {n  }           {n   }            {n  }
              [LCONVERGE({0**})] [PCONVERGE({1.0E-6**})] [SINGULAR({1E-8**})]
                        {n  }              {n      }                {n    }
              [BIAS({0**})] ]
                   {n  }

[/FULLFACTORIAL]

[/INTERCEPT = {EXCLUDE   }]
             {INCLUDE**}

[/MISSING = {EXCLUDE**}]
           {INCLUDE  }

[/MODEL = {[effect effect ...]}]

[/OUTFILE = [MODEL(filename)]]

[/PRINT = [CELLPROB] [CLASSTABLE] [CORB] [HISTORY({1**})] ]
                                                 {n  }
          [SUMMARY ] [PARAMETER ] [COVB] [FIT] [LRT] [KERNEL]

[/SCALE = {1**      }]
          {n       }
          {DEVIANCE}
          {PEARSON }

[/SUBPOP = varlist]

[/TEST[(valuelist)] = {['label'] effect valuelist effect valuelist...;}]
                      {['label'] ALL list;                            }
                      {['label'] ALL list                             }
```

**The default value.

Overview

NOMREG is a procedure for fitting a multinomial logit model to a polytomous nominal
dependent variable.

Options

Tuning the algorithm. You can control the values of algorithm-tuning parameters with the
CRITERIA subcommand.

Optional output. You can request additional output through the PRINT subcommand.

Basic Specification

The basic specification is one dependent variable.

Syntax Rules

- Minimum syntax—at least one dependent variable must be specified.
- The variable specification must come first.
- Subcommands can be specified in any order.
- Empty subcommands except the MODEL subcommand are ignored.
- The MODEL and the FULLFACTORIAL subcommands are mutually exclusive. Only one of them can be specified at any time.
- When repeated subcommands except the TEST subcommand are specified, all specifications except the last valid one are discarded.
- The following words are reserved as keywords or internal commands in the NOMREG procedure: BY, WITH, WITHIN.

Variable List

The variable list specifies the dependent variable and the factors in the model.

- The dependent variable must be the first specification on NOMREG. It can be of any type (numeric or string). Values of the dependent variable are sorted in ascending order. The lowest value defines the first category, and the highest value defines the last category.
- Factor variables can be of any type (numeric or string). The factors follow the dependent variable separated by the keyword BY.
- Covariate variables must be numeric. The covariates follow the factors, separated by the keyword WITH.
- If the WEIGHT command is specified, then the weight values are used as frequency counts for the respective category combination. Also, positive fractional weight values are rounded to the nearest integral value.

CRITERIA Subcommand

The CRITERIA subcommand offers controls on the iterative algorithm used for estimation and specifies numerical tolerance for checking singularity.

BIAS(n)   *Bias value added to observed cell frequency.* Specify a nonnegative value less than 1. The default value is 0.

CIN(n)   *Confidence interval level.* Specify a value greater than or equal to 0 and less than 100. The default value is 95.

DELTA(n)   *Delta value added to zero cell frequency.* Specify a nonnegative value less than 1. The default value is 0.

LCONVERGE(n)	*Log-likelihood function convergence criterion.* Convergence is assumed if the absolute change or relative change in the log-likelihood function is less than this value. The criterion is not used if the value is 0. Specify a nonnegative value. The default value is 0.
MXITER(n)	*Maximum number of iterations.* Specify a positive integer. The default value is 100.
MXSTEP(n)	*Maximum step-halving allowed.* Specify a positive integer. The default value is 5.
PCONVERGE(a)	*Parameter estimates convergence criterion.* Convergence is assumed if the absolute change or relative change in the parameter estimates is less than this value. The criterion is not used if the value is 0. Specify a nonnegative value. The default value is 10^{-6}.
SINGULAR(a)	*Value used as tolerance in checking singularity.* Specify a positive value. The default value is 10^{-8}.

FULLFACTORIAL Subcommand

The FULLFACTORIAL subcommand generates a specific model: first, the intercept (if included); second, all of the covariates (if specified), in the order in which they are specified; next, all of the main factorial effects; next, all the two-way factorial interaction effects, all of the three-way factorial interaction effects, and so on, up to the highest possible interaction effect.

- The FULLFACTORIAL and the MODEL subcommands are mutually exclusive. Only one of them can be specified at any time.
- The FULLFACTORIAL subcommand does not take any keywords.

INTERCEPT Subcommand

The INTERCEPT subcommand controls whether intercept terms are included in the model. The number of intercept terms is the number of response categories less one.

INCLUDE	*Includes the intercept term.* This is the default.
EXCLUDE	*Excludes the intercept terms.*

MISSING Subcommand

By default, cases with missing values for any of the variables on the NOMREG variable list are excluded from the analysis. The MISSING subcommand allows you to include cases with user-missing values.

- Note that missing values are deleted at the subpopulation level.

EXCLUDE	*Excludes both user-missing and system-missing values.* This is the default.

INCLUDE   *User-missing values are treated as valid.* System-missing values cannot be included in the analysis.

MODEL Subcommand

The MODEL subcommand specifies the effects in the model.

- The MODEL and the FULLFACTORIAL subcommands are mutually exclusive. Only one of them can be specified at any time.
- If more than one MODEL subcommand is specified, only the last one is in effect.
- Specify a list of terms to be included in the model, separated by commas or spaces. If the MODEL subcommand is omitted or empty, the default model is generated. The default model contains: first, the intercept (if included); second, all of the covariates (if specified), in the order in which they are specified; and next, all of the main factorial effects, in the order in which they are specified.
- To include a main-effect term, enter the name of the factor on the MODEL subcommand.
- To include an interaction-effect term among factors, use the keyword BY or the asterisk (*) to join factors involved in the interaction. For example, A*B*C means a three-way interaction effect of A, B, and C, where A, B, and C are factors. The expression A BY B BY C is equivalent to A*B*C. Factors inside an interaction effect must be distinct. Expressions like A*C*A and A*A are invalid.
- To include a nested effect term, use the keyword WITHIN or a pair of parentheses on the MODEL subcommand. For example, A(B) means that A is nested within B, where A and B are factors. The expression A WITHIN B is equivalent to A(B). Factors inside a nested effect must be distinct. Expressions like A(A) and A(B*A) are invalid.
- Multiple level nesting is supported. For example, A(B(C)) means that B is nested within C, and A is nested within B(C). When more than one pair of parentheses is present, each pair of parentheses must be enclosed or nested within another pair of parentheses. Thus, A(B)(C) is not valid.
- Nesting within an interaction effect is valid. For example, A(B*C) means that A is nested within B*C.
- Interactions among nested effects are allowed. The correct syntax is the interaction followed by the common nested effect inside the parentheses. For example, interaction between A and B within levels of C should be specified as A*B(C) instead of A(C)*B(C).
- To include a covariate term in the model, enter the name of the covariate on the MODEL subcommand.
- Covariates can be connected, but not nested, using the keyword BY or the asterisk (*) operator. For example, X*X is the product of X and itself. This is equivalent to a covariate whose values are the square of those of X. However, X(Y) is invalid.
- Factor and covariate effects can be connected in many ways. No effects can be nested within a covariate effect. Suppose A and B are factors, and X and Y are covariates. Examples of valid combination of factor and covariate effects are A*X, A*B*X, X(A), X(A*B), X*A(B), X*Y(A*B), and A*B*X*Y.

OUTFILE Subcommand

The OUTFILE subcommand allows you to specify files to which output is written.

- Only one OUTFILE subcommand is allowed. If you specify more than one, only the last one is executed.

- You must specify at least one keyword and a valid filename in parentheses. There is no default.

- MODEL cannot be used if split file processing is on (SPLIT FILE command) or if more than one dependent (DEPENDENT subcommand)variable is specified.

MODEL	*Write model information to an XML file.* Specify the filename in full. NOMREG does not supply an extension. *SmartScore* and future releases of *WhatIf?* will be able to use this file.

PRINT Subcommand

The PRINT subcommand displays optional output. If no PRINT subcommand is specified, default output includes a factor information table.

CELLPROB	*Observed proportion, expected probability, and the residual for each covariate pattern and each response category.*
CLASSTABLE	*Classification table.* The square table of frequencies of observed response categories versus the predicted response categories. Each case is classified into the category with the highest predicted probability.
CORB	*Asymptotic correlation matrix of the parameter estimates.*
COVB	*Asymptotic covariance matrix of the parameter estimates.*
FIT	*Goodness-of-fit statistics.* The change in chi-square statistics with respect to a model with intercept terms only (or to a null model when INTERCEPT=EXCLUDE). The table contains the Pearson chi-square and the likelihood-ratio chi-square statistics. The statistics are computed based on the subpopulation classification specified on the SUBPOP subcommand or the default classification.
HISTORY(n)	*Iteration history.* The table contains log-likelihood function value and parameter estimates at every nth iteration beginning with the 0th iteration (the initial estimates). The default is to print every iteration ($n = 1$). The last iteration is always printed if HISTORY is specified, regardless of the value of n.
KERNEL	*Kernel of the log-likelihood.* Displays the value of the kernel of the -2 log-likelihood. The default is to display the full -2 log-likelihood.
LRT	*Likelihood-ratio tests.* The table contains the likelihood-ratio test statistics for the model and model partial effects. If LRT is not specified, just the model test statistic is printed.

PARAMETER	*Parameter estimates.*
SUMMARY	*Model summary.* Cox and Snell's, Nagelkerke's, and McFadden's R^2 statistics.

SCALE Subcommand

The SCALE subcommand specifies the dispersion scaling value. Model estimation is not affected by this scaling value. Only the asymptotic covariance matrix of the parameter estimates is affected.

N	*A positive number corresponding to the amount of overdispersion or underdispersion.* The default scaling value is 1, which corresponds to no overdispersion or underdispersion.
DEVIANCE	*Estimates the scaling value by using the deviance function statistic.*
PEARSON	*Estimates the scaling value by using the Pearson chi-square statistic.*

SUBPOP Subcommand

The SUBPOP subcommand allows you to define the subpopulation classification used in computing the goodness-of-fit statistics.

- A variable list is expected if the SUBPOP subcommand is specified. The variables in the list must be a subset of the combined list of factors and covariates specified on the command line.
- Variables specified or implied on the MODEL subcommand must be a subset of the variables specified or implied on the SUBPOP subcommand.
- If the SUBPOP subcommand is omitted, the default classification is based on all of the factors and the covariates specified.
- Missing values are deleted listwise on the subpopulation level.

TEST Subcommand

The TEST subcommand allows you to customize your hypothesis tests by directly specifying null hypotheses as linear combinations of parameters.

- TEST is offered only through syntax.
- Multiple TEST subcommands are allowed. Each is handled independently.
- The basic format for the TEST subcommand is an optional list of values enclosed in parentheses, an optional label in quotes, an effect name or the keyword ALL, and a list of values.
- The value list preceding the first effect or the keyword ALL are the constants to which the linear combinations are equated under the null hypotheses. If this value list is omitted, the constants are assumed to be all zeros.

- The label is a string with a maximum length of 255 characters (or 127 double-byte characters). Only one label per linear combination can be specified.
- When ALL is specified, only a list of values can follow. The number of values must equal the number of parameters (including the redundant ones) in the model.
- When effects are specified, only valid effects appearing or implied on the MODEL subcommand can be named. The number of values following an effect name must equal the number of parameters (including the redundant ones) corresponding to that effect. For example, if the effect A*B takes up six parameters, then exactly six values must follow A*B. To specify the coefficient for the intercept, use the keyword INTERCEPT. Only one value is expected to follow INTERCEPT.
- When multiple linear combinations are specified within the same TEST subcommand, use semicolons to separate each hypothesis.
- The linear combinations are first separately tested for each logit, and then simultaneously tested for all of the logits.
- A number can be specified as a fraction with a positive denominator. For example, 1/3 or −1/3 are valid, but 1/−3 is invalid.
- Effects appearing or implied on the MODEL subcommand but not specified on the TEST are assumed to take the value 0 for all of their parameters.

NONPAR CORR

```
NONPAR CORR [VARIABLES=] varlist [WITH varlist] [/varlist...]

[/PRINT={TWOTAIL**}  {SIG**}  {SPEARMAN**}]
        {ONETAIL }  {NOSIG}  {KENDALL  }
                             {BOTH     }

[/SAMPLE]

[/MISSING=[{PAIRWISE**} [INCLUDE]]]
          {LISTWISE  }

[/MATRIX=OUT({*   })]
            {file}
```

**Default if the subcommand is omitted.

Example

```
NONPAR CORR VARIABLES=PRESTIGE SPPRES PAPRES16 DEGREE PADEG MADEG.
```

Overview

NONPAR CORR computes two rank-order correlation coefficients, Spearman's rho and Kendall's tau-*b*, with their significance levels. You can obtain either or both coefficients. NONPAR CORR automatically computes the ranks and stores the cases in memory. Therefore, memory requirements are directly proportional to the number of cases being analyzed.

Options

Coefficients and Significance Levels. By default, NONPAR CORR computes Spearman coefficients and displays the two-tailed significance level. You can request a one-tailed test, and you can display the significance level for each coefficient as an annotation using the PRINT subcommand.

Random Sampling. You can request a random sample of cases using the SAMPLE subcommand when there is not enough space to store all the cases.

Matrix Output. You can write matrix materials to an SPSS-format data file using the MATRIX subcommand. The matrix materials include the number of cases used to compute each coefficient and the Spearman or Kendall coefficients for each variable. These materials can be read by other procedures.

Basic Specification

The basic specification is VARIABLES and a list of numeric variables. The actual keyword VARIABLES can be omitted. By default, Spearman correlation coefficients are calculated.

Subcommand Order

- VARIABLES must be specified first.
- The remaining subcommands can be used in any order.

Operations

- NONPAR CORR produces one or more matrices of correlation coefficients. For each coefficient, NONPAR CORR displays the number of cases used and the significance level.
- The number of valid cases is always displayed. Depending on the specification on the MISSING subcommand, it can be displayed for each pair or in a single annotation.
- If all cases have a missing value for a given pair of variables, or if they all have the same value for a variable, the coefficient cannot be computed. If a correlation cannot be computed, NONPAR CORR displays a decimal point.
- If both Spearman and Kendall coefficients are requested and MATRIX is used to write matrix materials to an SPSS-format matrix data file, only Spearman's coefficient will be written with the matrix materials.

Limitations

- Maximum 25 variable lists.
- Maximum 100 variables total per NONPAR CORR command.

Example

```
NONPAR CORR VARIABLES=PRESTIGE SPPRES PAPRES16 DEGREE PADEG MADEG.
```

- By default, Spearman correlation coefficients are calculated. The number of cases upon which the correlations are based and the two-tailed significance level are displayed for each correlation.

VARIABLES Subcommand

VARIABLES specifies the variable list. The keyword VARIABLES is optional.
- All variables must be numeric.
- If keyword WITH is not used, NONPAR CORR displays the correlations of each variable with every other variable in the list.
- To obtain a rectangular matrix, specify two variable lists separated by keyword WITH. NONPAR CORR writes a rectangular matrix of variables in the first list correlated with variables in the second list.
- Keyword WITH cannot be used when the MATRIX subcommand is used.
- You can request more than one analysis. Use a slash to separate the specifications for each analysis.

Example

```
NONPAR CORR VARS=PRESTIGE SPPRES PAPRES16 WITH DEGREE PADEG MADEG.
```

- The three variables listed before WITH define the rows; the three variables listed after WITH define the columns of the correlation matrix.
- Spearman's rho is displayed by default.

Example

```
NONPAR CORR VARIABLES=SPPRES PAPRES16 PRESTIGE
                     /SATCITY WITH SATHOBBY SATFAM.
```

- NONPAR CORR produces two Correlations tables.
- By default, Spearman's rho is displayed.

PRINT Subcommand

By default, NONPAR CORR displays Spearman correlation coefficients. The significance level(s) are displayed below the coefficients. The significance level is based on a two-tailed test. Use PRINT to change these defaults.

- The Spearman and Kendall coefficients are both based on ranks.

SPEARMAN   *Spearman's rho.* Only Spearman coefficients are displayed. This is the default.

KENDALL   *Kendall's tau-b.* Only Kendall coefficients are displayed.

BOTH   *Kendall and Spearman coefficients.* Both coefficients are displayed. If MATRIX is used to write the correlation matrix to a matrix data file, only Spearman coefficients are written with the matrix materials.

SIG   *Display the significance level.* This is the default.

NOSIG   *Display the significance level in an annotation.*

TWOTAIL   *Two-tailed test of significance.* This test is appropriate when the direction of the relationship cannot be determined in advance, as is often the case in exploratory data analysis. This is the default.

ONETAIL   *One-tailed test of significance.* This test is appropriate when the direction of the relationship between a pair of variables can be specified in advance of the analysis.

SAMPLE Subcommand

NONPAR CORR must store cases in memory to build matrices. SAMPLE selects a random sample of cases when computer resources are insufficient to store all the cases. To request a random sample, simply specify the subcommand. SAMPLE has no additional specifications.

MISSING Subcommand

MISSING controls missing-value treatments.

- PAIRWISE and LISTWISE are alternatives. You can specify INCLUDE with either PAIRWISE or LISTWISE.

PAIRWISE   *Exclude missing values pairwise.* Cases with a missing value for one or both of a pair of variables for a specific correlation coefficient are excluded from the computation of that coefficient. This allows the maximum information available to be used in every calculation. This also results in a set of coefficients based on a varying number of cases. The number is displayed for each pair. This is the default.

LISTWISE   *Exclude missing values listwise.* Cases with a missing value for any variable named in a list are excluded from the computation of all coefficients in the Correlations table. The number of cases used is displayed in a single annotation. Each variable list on a command is evaluated separately. Thus, a case missing for one matrix might be used in another matrix. This option decreases the amount of memory required and significantly decreases computational time.

INCLUDE   *Include user-missing values.* User-missing values are treated as valid values.

MATRIX Subcommand

MATRIX writes matrix materials to a matrix data file. The matrix materials always include the number of cases used to compute each coefficient, and either the Spearman or the Kendall correlation coefficient for each variable, whichever is requested. See "Format of the Matrix Data File" on page 821 for a description of the file.

- You cannot write both Spearman's and Kendall's coefficients to the same matrix data file. To obtain both Spearman's and Kendall's coefficients in matrix format, specify separate NONPAR CORR commands for each coefficient and define different matrix data files for each command.

- If PRINT=BOTH is in effect, NONPAR CORR displays a matrix in the listing file for both coefficients but writes only the Spearman coefficients to the matrix data file.

- NONPAR CORR cannot write matrix materials for rectangular matrices (variable lists containing keyword WITH). If more than one variable list is specified, only the last variable list that does not use keyword WITH is written to the matrix data file.

- The specification on MATRIX is keyword OUT and the name of the matrix file in parentheses.

- If you want to use a correlation matrix written by NONPAR CORR in another procedure, change the *ROWTYPE_* value RHO or TAUB to CORR using the RECODE command.

- Any documents contained in the working data file are not transferred to the matrix file.

OUT (filename)   *Write a matrix data file.* Specify either a file or an asterisk, enclosed in parentheses. If you specify a file, the file is stored on disk and can be retrieved at any time. If you specify an asterisk (*), the matrix data file replaces the working file but is not stored on disk unless you use SAVE or XSAVE.

Format of the Matrix Data File

- The matrix data file has two special variables created by the program: *ROWTYPE_* and *VARNAME_*.
- Variable *ROWTYPE_* is a short string variable with values N and RHO for Spearman's correlation coefficient. If you specify Kendall's coefficient, the values are N and TAUB.
- *VARNAME_* is a short string variable whose values are the names of the variables used to form the correlation matrix. When *ROWTYPE_* is RHO (or TAUB), VARNAME_ gives the variable associated with that row of the correlation matrix.
- The remaining variables in the file are the variables used to form the correlation matrix.

Split Files

- When split-file processing is in effect, the first variables in the matrix data file are the split variables, followed by *ROWTYPE_*, *VARNAME_*, and the variables used to form the correlation matrix.
- A full set of matrix materials is written for each split-file group defined by the split variables.
- A split variable cannot have the same name as any other variable written to the matrix data file.
- If split-file processing is in effect when a matrix is written, the same split file must be in effect when that matrix is read by a procedure.

Missing Values

- With PAIRWISE treatment of missing values (the default), the matrix of N's used to compute each coefficient is included with the matrix materials.
- With LISTWISE or INCLUDE treatments, a single N used to calculate all coefficients is included with the matrix materials.

Example

```
GET FILE GSS80 /KEEP PRESTIGE SPPRES PAPRES16 DEGREE PADEG MADEG.
NONPAR CORR VARIABLES=PRESTIGE TO MADEG
  /MATRIX OUT(NPMAT).
```

- NONPAR CORR reads data from file *GSS80* and writes one set of correlation matrix materials to the file *NPMAT*.
- The working data file is still *GSS80*. Subsequent commands are executed on file *GSS80*.

Example

```
GET FILE GSS80 /KEEP PRESTIGE SPPRES PAPRES16 DEGREE PADEG MADEG.
NONPAR CORR VARIABLES=PRESTIGE TO MADEG
  /MATRIX OUT(*).
LIST.
DISPLAY DICTIONARY.
```

- **NONPAR CORR** writes the same matrix as in the example above. However, the matrix data file replaces the working file. The LIST and DISPLAY commands are executed on the matrix file, not on the original working file *GSS80*.

Example

```
NONPAR CORR VARIABLES=PRESTIGE SPPRES PAPRES16 DEGREE PADEG MADEG
    /PRESTIGE TO DEGREE /PRESTIGE WITH DEGREE
  /MATRIX OUT(NPMAT).
```

- Only the matrix for *PRESTIGE* to *DEGREE* is written to the matrix data file because it is the last variable list that does not use keyword WITH.

NPAR TESTS

```
NPAR TESTS [CHISQUARE=varlist[(lo,hi)]/] [/EXPECTED={EQUAL       }]
                                                     {f1,f2,...fn}

[/K-S({UNIFORM [min,max]   })=varlist]
      {NORMAL [mean,stddev]}
      {POISSON [mean]      }
      {EXPONENTIAL [mean]  }

[/RUNS({MEAN  })=varlist]
       {MEDIAN}
       {MODE  }
       {value }

[/BINOMIAL[({.5})]=varlist[(({value1,value2})]]
           { p}             {value        }

[/MCNEMAR=varlist [WITH varlist [(PAIRED)]]]

[/SIGN=varlist [WITH varlist [(PAIRED)]]]

[/WILCOXON=varlist [WITH varlist [(PAIRED)]]]

|/MH=varlist [WITH varlist [(PAIRED)]]]††

[/COCHRAN=varlist]

[/FRIEDMAN=varlist]

[/KENDALL=varlist]

[/M-W=varlist BY var (value1,value2)]

[/K-S=varlist BY var (value1,value2)]

[/W-W=varlist BY var (value1,value2)]

[/MOSES[(n)]=varlist BY var (value1,value2)]

[/K-W=varlist BY var (value1,value2)]

[/J-T=varlist BY var (value1, value2)]††

[/MEDIAN[(value)]=varlist BY var (value1,value2)]

[/MISSING=[{ANALYSIS**}]  [INCLUDE]]
          {LISTWISE  }

[/SAMPLE]

[/STATISTICS=[DESCRIPTIVES]  [QUARTILES] [ALL]]

[/METHOD={MC [CIN({99.0 })] [SAMPLES({10000})] }]††
                 {value}            {value}
         {EXACT [TIMER({5   })]                  }
                      {value}
```

**Default if the subcommand is omitted.
††Available only if the Exact Tests option is installed.

Example

```
NPAR TESTS K-S(UNIFORM)=V1 /K-S(NORMAL,0,1)=V2.
```

Overview

NPAR TESTS is a collection of nonparametric tests. These tests make minimal assumptions about the underlying distribution of the data and are described in Siegel (1956). In addition to the nonparametric tests available in NPAR TESTS, the k-sample chi-square and Fisher's exact test are available in procedure CROSSTABS.

The tests available in NPAR TESTS can be grouped into three broad categories based on how the data are organized: one-sample tests, related-samples tests, and independent-samples tests. A one-sample test analyzes one variable. A test for related samples compares two or more variables for the same set of cases. An independent-samples test analyzes one variable grouped by categories of another variable.

The one-sample tests available in procedure NPAR TESTS are:

- BINOMIAL
- CHISQUARE
- K-S (Kolmogorov-Smirnov)
- RUNS

Tests for two related samples are:

- MCNEMAR
- SIGN
- WILCOXON

Tests for k related samples are:

- COCHRAN
- FRIEDMAN
- KENDALL

Tests for two independent samples are:

- M-W (Mann-Whitney)
- K-S (Kolmogorov-Smirnov)
- W-W (Wald-Wolfowitz)
- MOSES

Tests for k independent samples are:

- K-W (Kruskal-Wallis)
- MEDIAN

Tests are described below in alphabetical order.

Options

Statistical Display. In addition to the tests, you can request univariate statistics, quartiles, and counts for all variables specified on the command. You can also control the pairing of variables in tests for two related samples.

Random Sampling. NPAR TESTS must store cases in memory when computing tests that use ranks. You can use random sampling when there is not enough space to store all cases.

Basic Specification

The basic specification is a single test subcommand and a list of variables to be tested. Some tests require additional specifications. CHISQUARE has an optional subcommand.

Subcommand Order

Subcommands can be used in any order.

Syntax Rules

- The STATISTICS, SAMPLE, and MISSING subcommands are optional. Each can be specified only once per NPAR TESTS command.
- You can request any or all tests, and you can specify a test subcommand more than once on a single NPAR TESTS command.
- If you specify a variable more than once on a test subcommand, only the first is used.
- Keyword ALL in any variable list refers to all user-defined variables in the working data file.
- Keyword WITH controls pairing of variables in two-related-samples tests.
- Keyword BY introduces the grouping variable in two- and k-independent-samples tests.
- Keyword PAIRED can be used with keyword WITH on the MCNEMAR, SIGN, and WILCOXON subcommands to obtain sequential pairing of variables for two related samples.

Operations

- If a string variable is specified on any subcommand, NPAR TESTS will stop executing.
- When ALL is used, requests for tests of variables with themselves are ignored and a warning is displayed.

Limitations

- Maximum 100 subcommands.
- Maximum 500 variables total per NPAR TESTS command.
- Maximum 200 values for subcommand CHISQUARE.

BINOMIAL Subcommand

```
NPAR TESTS BINOMIAL [({.5})]=varlist[({value,value})]
                      {p }               {value       }
```

BINOMIAL tests whether the observed distribution of a dichotomous variable is the same as that expected from a specified binomial distribution. By default, each variable named is assumed to have only two values, and the distribution of each variable named is compared to a binomial distribution with p (the proportion of cases expected in the first category) equal to 0.5. The default output includes the number of valid cases in each group, the test proportion, and the two-tailed probability of the observed proportion.

Syntax

- The minimum specification is a list of variables to be tested.
- To change the default 0.5 test proportion, specify a value in parentheses immediately after keyword BINOMIAL.
- A single value in parentheses following the variable list is used as a cutting point. Cases with values equal to or less than the cutting point form the first category; the remaining cases form the second.
- If two values appear in parentheses after the variable list, cases with values equal to the first value form the first category, and cases with values equal to the second value form the second category.
- If no values are specified, the variables must be dichotomous.

Operations

- The proportion observed in the first category is compared to the test proportion. The probability of the observed proportion occurring given the test proportion and a binomial distribution is then computed. A test statistic is calculated for each variable specified.
- If the test proportion is the default (0.5), a two-tailed probability is displayed. For any other test proportion, a one-tailed probability is displayed. The direction of the one-tailed test depends on the observed proportion in the first category. If the observed proportion is more than the test proportion, the significance of observing that many or more in the first category is reported. If the observed proportion is less than or equal to the test proportion, the significance of observing that many or fewer in the first category is reported. In other words, the test is always done in the observed direction.

Example

```
NPAR TESTS BINOMIAL(.667)=V1(0,1).
```

- NPAR TESTS displays the Binomial Test table showing the number of cases, observed proportion, test proportion (0.667), and the one-tailed significance for each category.

- If more than 0.667 of the cases have value 0 for *V1*, BINOMIAL gives the probability of observing that many or more values of 0 in a binomial distribution with probability 0.667. If fewer than 0.667 of the cases are 0, the test will be of observing that many or fewer.

CHISQUARE Subcommand

```
NPAR TESTS CHISQUARE=varlist [(lo,hi)] [/EXPECTED={EQUAL**    }]
                                                  {f1,f2,... fn}
```

The CHISQUARE (alias CHI-SQUARE) one-sample test computes a chi-square statistic based on the differences between the observed and expected frequencies of categories of a variable. By default, equal frequencies are expected in each category. The output includes the frequency distribution, expected frequencies, residuals, chi-square, degrees of freedom, and probability.

Syntax

- The minimum specification is a list of variables to be tested. Optionally, you can specify a value range in parentheses following the variable list. You can also specify expected proportions with the EXPECTED subcommand.
- If you use the EXPECTED subcommand to specify unequal expected frequencies, you must specify a value greater than 0 for each observed category of the variable. The expected frequencies are specified in ascending order of category value. You can use the notation *n*f* to indicate that frequency *f* is expected for *n* consecutive categories.
- Specifying keyword EQUAL on the EXPECTED subcommand has the same effect as omitting the EXPECTED subcommand.
- EXPECTED applies to all variables specified on the CHISQUARE subcommand. Use multiple CHISQUARE and EXPECTED subcommands to specify different expected proportions for variables.

Operations

- If no range is specified for the variables to be tested, a separate Chi-Square Frequency table is produced for each variable. Each distinct value defines a category.
- If a range is specified, integer-valued categories are established for each value within the range. Noninteger values are truncated before classification. Cases with values outside the specified range are excluded. One combined Chi-Square Frequency table is produced for all specified variables.
- Expected values are interpreted as proportions, not absolute values. Values are summed, and each value is divided by the total to calculate the proportion of cases expected in the corresponding category.
- A test statistic is calculated for each variable specified.

Example

```
NPAR TESTS CHISQUARE=V1 (1,5) /EXPECTED= 12, 3*16, 18.
```

- This example requests the chi-square test for values 1 through 5 of variable *V1*.
- The observed frequencies for variable *V1* are compared with the hypothetical distribution of 12/78 occurrences of value 1; 16/78 occurrences each of values 2, 3, and 4; and 18/78 occurrences of value 5.

COCHRAN Subcommand

```
NPAR TESTS COCHRAN=varlist
```

COCHRAN calculates Cochran's Q, which tests whether the distribution of values is the same for k related dichotomous variables. The output shows the frequency distribution for each variable in the Cochran Frequencies table and the number of cases, Cochran's Q, degrees of freedom, and probability in the Test Statistics table.

Syntax

- The minimum specification is a list of two variables.
- The variables must be dichotomous and must be coded with the same two values.

Operations

- A $k \times 2$ contingency table (variables by categories) is constructed for dichotomous variables and the proportions for each variable are computed. A single test comparing all variables is calculated.
- Cochran's Q statistic has approximately a chi-square distribution.

Example

```
NPAR TESTS COCHRAN=RV1 TO RV3.
```

- This example tests whether the distribution of values 0 and 1 for *RV1*, *RV2*, and *RV3* is the same.

FRIEDMAN Subcommand

```
NPAR TESTS FRIEDMAN=varlist
```

FRIEDMAN tests whether k related samples have been drawn from the same population. The output shows the mean rank for each variable in the Friedman Ranks table and the number of valid cases, chi-square, degrees of freedom, and probability in the Test Statistics table.

Syntax

- The minimum specification is a list of two variables.
- Variables should be at least at the ordinal level of measurement.

Operations

- The values of k variables are ranked from 1 to k for each case, and the mean rank is calculated for each variable over all cases.
- The test statistic has approximately a chi-square distribution. A single test statistic comparing all variables is calculated.

Example

```
NPAR TESTS FRIEDMAN=V1 V2 V3
  /STATISTICS=DESCRIPTIVES.
```

- This example tests variables *V1, V2*, and *V3*, and requests univariate statistics for all three.

J-T Subcommand

```
NPAR TESTS /J-T=varlist BY variable(value1,value2)
```

J-T (alias JONCKHEERE-TERPSTRA) performs the Jonckheere-Terpstra test, which tests whether k independent samples defined by a grouping variable are from the same population. This test is particularly powerful when the k populations have a natural ordering. The output shows the number of levels in the grouping variable, the total number of cases, observed, standardized, mean, and standard deviation of the test statistic, the two-tailed asymptotic significance, and, if a /METHOD subcommand is specified, one-tailed and two-tailed exact or Monte Carlo probabilities. This subcommand is available only if the SPSS Exact Tests option is installed.

Syntax

- The minimum specification is a test variable, the keyword BY, a grouping variable, and a pair of values in parentheses.
- Every value in the range defined by the pair of values for the grouping variable forms a group.
- If the /METHOD subcommand is specified, and the number of populations, k, is greater than 5, the p value is estimated using the Monte Carlo sampling method. The exact p value is not available when k exceeds 5.

Operations

- Cases from the k groups are ranked in a single series, and the rank sum for each group is computed. A test statistic is calculated for each variable specified before BY.
- The Jonckheere-Terpstra statistic has approximately a normal distribution.
- Cases with values other than those in the range specified for the grouping variable are excluded.
- The direction of a one-tailed inference is indicated by the sign of the standardized test statistic.

Example

```
NPAR TESTS /J-T=V1 BY V2(0,4)
  /METHOD=EXACT.
```

- This example performs the Jonckheere-Terpstra test for groups defined by values 0 through 4 of *V2*. The exact *p* values are calculated.

K-S Subcommand (One-Sample)

```
NPAR TESTS K-S({NORMAL [mean,stddev]})=varlist
              {POISSON [mean]      }
              {UNIFORM [min,max]   }
              {EXPONENTIAL [mean]  }
```

The K-S (alias KOLMOGOROV-SMIRNOV) one-sample test compares the cumulative distribution function for a variable with a uniform, normal, Poisson, or exponential distribution, and it tests whether the distributions are homogeneous. The parameters of the test distribution can be specified; the defaults are the observed parameters. The output shows the number of valid cases, parameters of the test distribution, most-extreme absolute, positive, and negative differences, Kolmogorov-Smirnov Z, and two-tailed probability for each variable.

Syntax

The minimum specification is a distribution keyword and a list of variables. The distribution keywords are NORMAL, POISSON, EXPONENTIAL, and UNIFORM.

- The distribution keyword and its optional parameters must be enclosed within parentheses.
- The distribution keyword must be separated from its parameters by blanks or commas.

NORMAL [mean, stdev] *Normal distribution.* The default parameters are the observed mean and standard deviation.

POISSON [mean] *Poisson distribution.* The default parameter is the observed mean.

UNIFORM [min,max] *Uniform distribution.* The default parameters are the observed minimum and maximum values.

EXPONENTIAL [mean] *Exponential distribution.* The default parameter is the observed mean.

Operations

- The Kolmogorov-Smirnov Z is computed from the largest difference in absolute value between the observed and test distribution functions.
- The K-S probability levels assume that the test distribution is specified entirely in advance. The distribution of the test statistic and resulting probabilities are different when the parameters of the test distribution are estimated from the sample. No correction is made.
- For a mean of 100,000 or larger, a normal approximation to the Poisson distribution is used.
- A test statistic is calculated for each variable specified.

Example

```
NPAR TESTS K-S(UNIFORM)=V1 /K-S(NORMAL,0,1)=V2.
```

- The first K-S subcommand compares the distribution of *V1* with a uniform distribution that has the same range as *V1*.
- The second K-S subcommand compares the distribution of *V2* with a normal distribution that has a mean of 0 and a standard deviation of 1.

K-S Subcommand (Two-Sample)

```
NPAR TESTS K-S=varlist BY variable(value1,value2)
```

K-S (alias KOLMOGOROV-SMIRNOV) tests whether the distribution of a variable is the same in two independent samples defined by a grouping variable. The test is sensitive to any difference in median, dispersion, skewness, and so forth, between the two distributions. The output shows the valid number of cases in each group in the Frequency table and the largest absolute, positive, and negative differences between the two groups, the Kolmogorov-Smirnov Z, and the two-tailed probability for each variable in the Test Statistics table.

Syntax

- The minimum specification is a test variable, the keyword BY, a grouping variable, and a pair of values in parentheses.
- The test variable should be at least at the ordinal level of measurement.
- Cases with the first value form one group and cases with the second value form the other. The order in which values are specified determines which difference is the largest positive and which is the largest negative.

Operations

- The observed cumulative distributions for both groups are computed, as are the maximum positive, negative, and absolute differences. A test statistic is calculated for each variable named before BY.
- Cases with values other than those specified for the grouping variable are excluded.

Example

```
NPAR TESTS K-S=V1 V2 BY V3(0,1).
```

- This example specifies two tests. The first compares the distribution of *V1* for cases with value 0 for *V3* with the distribution of *V1* for cases with value 1 for *V3*.
- A parallel test is calculated for *V2*.

K-W Subcommand

```
NPAR TESTS K-W=varlist BY variable(value1,value2)
```

K-W (alias KRUSKAL-WALLIS) tests whether k independent samples defined by a grouping variable are from the same population. The output shows the number of valid cases and the mean rank of the variable in each group in the Ranks table and the chi-square, degrees of freedom, and probability in the Test Statistics table.

Syntax

- The minimum specification is a test variable, the keyword BY, a grouping variable, and a pair of values in parentheses.
- Every value in the range defined by the pair of values for the grouping variable forms a group.

Operations

- Cases from the k groups are ranked in a single series, and the rank sum for each group is computed. A test statistic is calculated for each variable specified before BY.
- Kruskal-Wallis H has approximately a chi-square distribution.
- Cases with values other than those in the range specified for the grouping variable are excluded.

Example

```
NPAR TESTS K-W=V1 BY V2(0,4).
```

- This example tests *V1* for groups defined by values 0 through 4 of *V2*.

KENDALL Subcommand

```
NPAR TESTS KENDALL=varlist
```

KENDALL tests whether k related samples are from the same population. W is a measure of agreement among judges or raters where each case is one judge's rating of several items (variables). The output includes the mean rank for each variable in the Ranks table and the valid number of cases, Kendall's W, chi-square, degrees of freedom, and probability in the Test Statistics table.

Syntax

The minimum specification is a list of two variables.

Operations

- The values of the k variables are ranked from 1 to k for each case, and the mean rank is calculated for each variable over all cases. Kendall's W and a corresponding chi-square statistic are calculated, correcting for ties. In addition, a single test statistic is calculated for all variables.
- W ranges between 0 (no agreement) and 1 (complete agreement).

Example

```
DATA LIST /V1 TO V5 1-10.
BEGIN DATA
2 5 4 5 1
3 3 4 5 3
3 4 4 6 2
2 4 3 6 2
END DATA.
NPAR TESTS KENDALL=ALL.
```

- This example tests four judges (cases) on five items (variables *V1* through *V5*).

M-W Subcommand

```
NPAR TESTS M-W=varlist BY variable(value1,value2)
```

M-W (alias MANN-WHITNEY) tests whether two independent samples defined by a grouping variable are from the same population. The test statistic uses the rank of each case to test whether the groups are drawn from the same population. The output shows the number of valid cases of each group, the mean rank of the variable within each group and the sum of ranks in the Ranks table and the Mann-Whitney U, Wilcoxon W (the rank sum of the smaller group), Z statistic, and probability in the Test Statistics table.

Syntax

- The minimum specification is a test variable, the keyword BY, a grouping variable, and a pair of values in parentheses.
- Cases with the first value form one group and cases with the second value form the other. The order in which the values are specified is unimportant.

Operations

- Cases are ranked in order of increasing size, and test statistic U (the number of times a score from group 1 precedes a score from group 2) is computed.
- An exact significance level is computed if there are 40 or fewer cases. For more than 40 cases, U transformed into a normally distributed Z statistic, and a normal approximation p value is computed.
- A test statistic is calculated for each variable named before BY.

- Cases with values other than those specified for the grouping variable are excluded.

Example

```
NPAR TESTS M-W=V1 BY V2(1,2).
```

- This example tests *V1* based on the two groups defined by values 1 and 2 of *V2*.

MCNEMAR Subcommand

```
NPAR TESTS MCNEMAR=varlist [WITH varlist [(PAIRED)]]
```

MCNEMAR tests whether combinations of values between two dichotomous variables are equally likely. The output includes a Crosstabulation table for each pair and a Test Statistics table for all pairs showing the number of valid cases, chi-square, and probability for each pair.

Syntax

- The minimum specification is a list of two variables. Variables must be dichotomous and must have the same two values.
- If keyword WITH is not specified, each variable is paired with every other variable in the list.
- If WITH is specified, each variable before WITH is paired with each variable after WITH. If PAIRED is also specified, the first variable before WITH is paired with the first variable after WITH, the second variable before WITH with the second variable after WITH, and so on. PAIRED cannot be specified without WITH.
- With PAIRED, the number of variables specified before and after WITH must be the same. PAIRED must be specified in parentheses after the second variable list.

Operations

- In computing the test statistics, only combinations for which the values for the two variables are different are considered.
- If fewer than 25 cases change values from the first variable to the second variable, the binomial distribution is used to compute the probability.

Example

```
NPAR TESTS MCNEMAR=V1 V2 V3.
```

- This example performs the MCNEMAR test on variable pairs *V1* and *V2*, *V1* and *V3*, and *V2* and *V3*.

MEDIAN Subcommand

```
NPAR TESTS MEDIAN [(value)]=varlist BY variable(value1,value2)
```

MEDIAN determines if k independent samples are drawn from populations with the same median. The independent samples are defined by a grouping variable. For each variable, the output shows a table of the number of cases greater than and less than or equal to the median in each category in the Frequency table and the number of valid cases, the median, chi-square, degrees of freedom, and probability in the Test Statistics table.

Syntax

- The minimum specification is a single test variable, the keyword BY, a grouping variable, and two values in parentheses.
- If the first grouping value is less than the second, every value in the range defined by the pair of values forms a group and a k-sample test is performed.
- If the first value is greater than the second, two groups are formed using the two values and a two-sample test is performed.
- By default, the median is calculated from all cases included in the test. To override the default, specify a median value in parentheses following the MEDIAN subcommand keyword.

Operations

- A $2 \times k$ contingency table is constructed with counts of the number of cases greater than the median and less than or equal to the median for the k groups.
- Test statistics are calculated for each variable specified before BY.
- For more than 30 cases, a chi-square statistic is computed. For 30 or fewer cases, Fisher's exact procedure (two-tailed) is used instead of chi-square.
- For a two-sample test, cases with values other than the two specified are excluded.

Example

```
NPAR TESTS MEDIAN(8.4)=V1 BY V2(1,2) /MEDIAN=V1 BY V2(1,2)
   /MEDIAN=V1 BY V3(1,4) /MEDIAN=V1 BY V3(4,1).
```

- The first two MEDIAN subcommands test variable *V1* grouped by values 1 and 2 of variable *V2*. The first test specifies a median of 8.4 and the second uses the observed median.
- The third MEDIAN subcommand requests a four-samples test, dividing the sample into four groups based on values 1, 2, 3, and 4 of variable *V3*.
- The last MEDIAN subcommand requests a two-samples test, grouping cases based on values 1 and 4 of *V3* and ignoring all other cases.

MH Subcommand

```
NPAR TESTS /MH=varlist [WITH varlist [(PAIRED)]]
```

MH performs the marginal homogeneity test, which tests whether combinations of values between two paired ordinal variables are equally likely. The marginal homogeneity test is typically used in repeated measures situations. This test is an extension of the McNemar test from binary response to multinomial response. The output shows the number of distinct values for all test variables, the number of valid off-diagonal cell counts, mean, standard deviation, observed and standardized values of the test statistics, the asymptotic two-tailed probability for each pair of variables, and, if a /METHOD subcommand is specified, one-tailed and two-tailed exact or Monte Carlo probabilities. This subcommand is available only if the SPSS Exact Tests option has been installed.

Syntax

- The minimum specification is a list of two variables. Variables must be polychotomous and must have more than two values. If the variables contain only two values, the McNemar test is performed.

- If keyword WITH is not specified, each variable is paired with every other variable in the list.

- If WITH is specified, each variable before WITH is paired with each variable after WITH. If PAIRED is also specified, the first variable before WITH is paired with the first variable after WITH, the second variable before WITH with the second variable after WITH, and so on. PAIRED cannot be specified without WITH.

- With PAIRED, the number of variables specified before and after WITH must be the same. PAIRED must be specified in parentheses after the second variable list.

Operations

- The data consist of paired, dependent responses from two populations. The marginal homogeneity test tests the equality of two multinomial $c \times 1$ tables, and the data can be arranged in the form of a square $c \times c$ contingency table. A $2 \times c$ table is constructed for each off-diagonal cell count. The marginal homogeneity test statistic is computed for cases with different values for the two variables. Only combinations for which the values for the two variables are different are considered. The first row of each $2 \times c$ table specifies the category chosen by population 1, and the second row specifies the category chosen by population 2. The test statistic is calculated by summing the first row scores across all $2 \times c$ tables.

Example

```
NPAR TESTS /MH=V1 V2 V3
   /METHOD=MC .
```

- This example performs the marginal homogeneity test on variable pairs *V1* and *V2*, *V1* and *V3*, and *V2* and *V3*. The exact *p* values are estimated using the Monte Carlo sampling method.

MOSES Subcommand

```
NPAR TESTS MOSES[(n)]=varlist BY variable(value1,value2)
```

The MOSES test of extreme reactions tests whether the range of an ordinal variable is the same in a control group and a comparison group. The control and comparison groups are defined by a grouping variable. The output includes a Frequency table showing for each variable before *BY* the total number of cases and the number of cases in each group and a Test Statistics table showing the number of outliers removed, span of the control group before and after outliers are removed, and one-tailed probability of the span with and without outliers.

Syntax

- The minimum specification is a test variable, the keyword BY, a grouping variable, and two values in parentheses.
- The test variable must be at least at the ordinal level of measurement.
- The first value of the grouping variable defines the control group and the second value defines the comparison group.
- By default, 5% of the cases are trimmed from each end of the range of the control group to remove outliers. You can override the default by specifying a value in parentheses following the MOSES subcommand keyword. This value represents an actual number of cases, not a percentage.

Operations

- Values from the groups are arranged in a single ascending sequence. The span of the control group is computed as the number of cases in the sequence containing the lowest and highest control values.
- No adjustments are made for tied cases.
- Cases with values other than those specified for the grouping variable are excluded.
- Test statistics are calculated for each variable named before BY.

Example

```
NPAR TESTS MOSES=V1 BY V3(0,1) /MOSES=V1 BY V3(1,0).
```

- The first MOSES subcommand tests *V1* using value 0 of *V3* to define the control group and value 1 for the comparison group. The second MOSES subcommand reverses the comparison and control groups.

RUNS Subcommand

```
NPAR TESTS RUNS({MEAN  })=varlist
              {MEDIAN}
              {MODE  }
              {value }
```

RUNS tests whether the sequence of values of a dichotomized variable is random. The output includes a Run Test table showing the test value (cut point used to dichotomize the variable tested), number of runs, number of cases below the cut point, number of cases greater than or equal to the cut point, and test statistic Z with its two-tailed probability for each variable.

Syntax

- The minimum specification is a cut point in parentheses followed by a test variable.
- The cut point can be specified by an exact value or one of the keywords MEAN, MEDIAN, or MODE.

Operations

- All variables tested are treated as dichotomous: cases with values less than the cut point form one category, and cases with values greater than or equal to the cut point form the other category.
- Test statistics are calculated for each variable specified.

Example

```
NPAR TESTS RUNS(MEDIAN)=V2 /RUNS(24.5)=V2 /RUNS(1)=V3.
```

- This example performs three runs tests. The first tests variable *V2* using the median as the cut point. The second also tests *V2*, this time using 24.5 as the cut point. The third tests variable *V3* with value 1 specified as the cut point.

SIGN Subcommand

```
NPAR TESTS SIGN=varlist [WITH varlist [(PAIRED)] ]
```

SIGN tests whether the distribution of two paired variables in a two-related-samples test is the same. The output includes a Frequency table showing for each pair the number of positive differences, number of negative differences, number of ties, and the total number and a Test Statistics table showing the Z statistic and two-tailed probability.

Syntax

- The minimum specification is a list of two variables.
- Variables should be at least at the ordinal level of measurement.

- If keyword WITH is not specified, each variable in the list is paired with every other variable in the list.

- If keyword WITH is specified, each variable before WITH is paired with each variable after WITH. If PAIRED is also specified, the first variable before WITH is paired with the first variable after WITH, the second variable before WITH with the second variable after WITH, and so on. PAIRED cannot be specified without WITH.

- With PAIRED, the number of variables specified before and after WITH must be the same. PAIRED must be specified in parentheses after the second variable list.

Operations

- The positive and negative differences between the pair of variables are counted. Ties are ignored.

- The probability is taken from the binomial distribution if 25 or fewer differences are observed. Otherwise, the probability comes from the Z distribution.

- Under the null hypothesis for large sample sizes, Z is approximately normally distributed with a mean of 0 and a variance of 1.

Example

```
NPAR TESTS SIGN=N1,M1 WITH N2,M2 (PAIRED).
```

- *N1* is tested with *N2*, and *M1* is tested with *M2*.

W-W Subcommand

```
NPAR TESTS W-W=varlist BY variable(value1,value2)
```

W-W (alias WALD-WOLFOWITZ) tests whether the distribution of a variable is the same in two independent samples. A runs test is performed with group membership as the criterion. The output includes a Frequency table showing the total number of valid cases for each variable specified before BY and the number of valid cases in each group, and a Test Statistics table showing the number of runs, Z, and one-tailed probability of Z. If ties are present, the minimum and maximum number of runs possible, their Z statistics, and one-tailed probabilities are displayed.

Syntax

- The minimum specification is a single test variable, the keyword BY, a grouping variable, and two values in parentheses.

- Cases with the first value form one group and cases with the second value form the other. The order in which values are specified is unimportant.

Operations

- Cases are combined from both groups and ranked from lowest to highest, and a runs test is performed using group membership as the criterion. For ties involving cases from both groups, both the minimum and maximum number of runs possible are calculated. Test statistics are calculated for each variable specified before BY.
- For a sample size of 30 or less, the exact one-tailed probability is calculated. For a sample size greater than 30, the normal approximation is used.
- Cases with values other than those specified for the grouping variable are excluded.

Example

```
NPAR TESTS W-W=V1 BY V3(0,1).
```

- This example ranks cases from lowest to highest based on their values for *V1* and a runs test is performed. Cases with value 0 for *V3* form one group and cases with value 1 form the other.

WILCOXON Subcommand

```
NPAR TESTS WILCOXON=varlist [WITH varlist [(PAIRED)] ]
```

WILCOXON tests whether the distribution of two paired variables in two related samples is the same. This test takes into account the magnitude of the differences between two paired variables. The output includes a Ranks table showing for each pair the number of valid cases, positive and negative differences, their respective mean and sum of ranks, and the number of ties and a Test Statistics table showing Z and probability of Z.

Syntax

- The minimum specification is a list of two variables.
- If keyword WITH is not specified, each variable is paired with every other variable in the list.
- If keyword WITH is specified, each variable before WITH is paired with each variable after WITH. If PAIRED is also specified, the first variable before WITH is paired with the first variable after WITH, the second variable before WITH with the second variable after WITH, and so on. PAIRED cannot be specified without WITH.
- With PAIRED, the number of variables specified before and after WITH must be the same. PAIRED must be specified in parentheses after the second variable list.

Operations

- The differences between the pair of variables are counted, the absolute differences ranked, the positive and negative ranks summed, and the test statistic Z computed from the positive and negative rank sums.

- Under the null hypothesis for large sample sizes, Z is approximately normally distributed with a mean of 0 and a variance of 1.

Example

```
NPAR TESTS WILCOXON=A B WITH C D (PAIRED).
```

- This example pairs *A* with *C* and *B* with *D*. If PAIRED were not specified, it would also pair *A* with *D* and *B* with *C*.

STATISTICS Subcommand

STATISTICS requests summary statistics for variables named on the NPAR TESTS command. Summary statistics are displayed in the Descriptive Statistics table before all test output.

- If STATISTICS is specified without keywords, univariate statistics (keyword DESCRIPTIVES) are displayed.

DESCRIPTIVES   *Univariate statistics.* The displayed statistics include the mean, maximum, minimum, standard deviation, and number of valid cases for each variable named on the command.

QUARTILES   *Quartiles and number of cases.* The 25th, 50th, and 75th percentiles are displayed for each variable named on the command.

ALL   *All statistics available on* NPAR TESTS.

MISSING Subcommand

MISSING controls the treatment of cases with missing values.

- ANALYSIS and LISTWISE are alternatives. However, each can be specified with INCLUDE.

ANALYSIS   *Exclude cases with missing values on a test-by-test basis.* Cases with missing values for a variable used for a specific test are omitted from that test. On subcommands that specify several tests, each test is evaluated separately. This is the default.

LISTWISE   *Exclude cases with missing values listwise.* Cases with missing values for any variable named on any subcommand are excluded from all analyses.

INCLUDE   *Include user-missing values.* User-missing values are treated as valid values.

SAMPLE Subcommand

NPAR TESTS must store cases in memory. SAMPLE allows you to select a random sample of cases when there is not enough space on your computer to store all the cases. SAMPLE has no additional specifications.

- Because sampling would invalidate a runs test, this option is ignored when the RUNS sub-command is used.

METHOD Subcommand

METHOD displays additional results for each statistic requested. If no METHOD subcommand is specified, the standard asymptotic results are displayed. If fractional weights have been specified, results for all methods will be calculated on the weight rounded to the nearest integer. This subcommand is available only if the SPSS Exact Tests option has been installed.

MC   Displays an unbiased point estimate and confidence interval based on the Monte Carlo sampling method, for all statistics. Asymptotic results are also displayed. When exact results can be calculated, they will be provided instead of the Monte Carlo results. See *SPSS Exact Tests* for details of the situations under which exact results are provided instead of Monte Carlo results.

CIN(n)   Controls the confidence level for the Monte Carlo estimate. CIN is available only when /METHOD=MC is specified. CIN has a default value of 99.0. You can specify a confidence interval between 0.01 and 99.9, inclusive.

SAMPLES   Specifies the number of tables sampled from the reference set when calculating the Monte Carlo estimate of the exact *p* value. Larger sample sizes lead to narrower confidence limits but also take longer to calculate. You can specify any integer between 1 and 1,000,000,000 as the sample size. SAMPLES has a default value of 10,000.

EXACT   Computes the exact significance level for all statistics, in addition to the asymptotic results. If both the EXACT and MC keywords are specified, only exact results are provided. Calculating the exact *p* value can be memory-intensive. If you have specified /METHOD=EXACT and find that you have insufficient memory to calculate results, you should first close any other applications that are currently running in order to make more memory available. You can also enlarge the size of your swap file (see your Windows manual for more information). If you still cannot obtain exact results, specify /METHOD=MC to obtain the Monte Carlo estimate of the exact *p* value. An optional TIMER keyword is available if you choose /METHOD=EXACT.

TIMER(n)   Specifies the maximum number of minutes allowed to run the exact analysis for each statistic. If the time limit is reached, the test is terminated, no exact results are provided, and the program begins to calculate the next test in the analysis. TIMER is available only when /METHOD=EXACT is specified. You can specify any integer value for TIMER. Specifying a value of 0 for TIMER turns the timer off completely. TIMER has a default value of 5 minutes. If a test exceeds a time limit of 30 minutes, it is recommended that you use the Monte Carlo, rather than the exact, method.

References

Siegel, S. 1956. *Nonparametric statistics for the behavioral sciences.* New York: McGraw-Hill.

NUMBERED and UNNUMBERED

This command is not available on all operating systems.

```
{NUMBERED  }
{UNNUMBERED}
```

Overview

NUMBERED and UNNUMBERED are IBM-specific commands. Usually IBM systems reserve columns 73–80 of each input line for line numbers. NUMBERED reserves columns 73–80 for those line numbers; UNNUMBERED indicates that the columns are not reserved for numbers. The default may vary by installation. Use the SHOW command to see the default for your installation.

Basic Specification

The only specification is either NUMBERED or UNNUMBERED. NUMBERED instructs the program to check only the first 72 columns for data. UNNUMBERED instructs the program to check all 80 columns for data.

Operations

- If NUMBERED is in effect and data extend beyond column 72, the program issues a warning message.
- NUMBERED and UNNUMBERED column settings apply only to inline data; they do not apply to data in an external file.

Example

```
UNNUMBERED.
```

- The program checks up to 80 columns of each input line for data.

NUMERIC

```
NUMERIC varlist[(format)] [/varlist...]
```

Example

```
NUMERIC V1 V2 (F4.0) / V3 (F1.0).
```

Overview

NUMERIC declares new numeric variables that can be referred to in the transformation language before they are assigned values. Commands such as COMPUTE, IF, RECODE, and COUNT can be used to assign values to the new numeric variables.

Basic Specification

The basic specification is the name of the new variables. By default, variables are assigned a format of F8.2 (or the format specified on the SET command).

Syntax Rules

- A FORTRAN-like format can be specified in parentheses following a variable or variable list. Each format specified applies to all variables in the list. To specify different formats for different groups of variables, separate each format group with a slash.
- Keyword TO can be used to declare multiple numeric variables. The specified format applies to each variable named and implied by the TO construction.
- NUMERIC can be used within an input program to predetermine the order of numeric variables in the dictionary of the working data file. When used for this purpose, NUMERIC must precede DATA LIST in the input program.

Operations

- Unlike most transformations, NUMERIC takes effect as soon as it is encountered in the command sequence. Special attention should be paid to its position among commands. For more information, see "Command Order" on p. 16.
- The specified formats (or the defaults) are used as both print and write formats.
- Permanent or temporary variables are initialized to the system-missing value. Scratch variables are initialized to 0.
- Variables named on NUMERIC are added to the working file in the order in which they are specified. The order in which they are used in transformations does not affect their order in the working data file.

Example

```
NUMERIC V1 V2 (F4.0) / V3 (F1.0).
```

- NUMERIC declares variables *V1* and *V2* with format F4.0, and variable *V3* with format F1.0.

Example

```
NUMERIC V1 TO V6 (F3.1) / V7 V10 (F6.2).
```

- NUMERIC declares variables *V1*, *V2*, *V3*, *V4*, *V5*, and *V6* each with format F3.1, and variables *V7* and *V10*, each with format F6.2.

Example

```
NUMERIC SCALE85 IMPACT85 SCALE86 IMPACT86 SCALE87 IMPACT87
        SCALE88 IMPACT88.
```

- Variables *SCALE85* to *IMPACT88* are added to the working data file in the order specified on NUMERIC. The order in which they are used in transformations does not affect their order in the working data file.

Example

```
* Predetermine variable order.

INPUT PROGRAM.
STRING CITY (A24).
NUMERIC POP81 TO POP83 (F9)/ REV81 TO REV83(F10).
DATA LIST FILE=POPDATA RECORDS=3
  /1 POP81 22-30 REV81 31-40
  /2 POP82 22-30 REV82 31-40
  /3 POP83 22-30 REV83 31-40
  /4 CITY 1-24(A).
END INPUT PROGRAM.
```

- STRING and NUMERIC are specified within an input program to predetermine variable order in the working data file. Though data in the file are in a different order, the working file dictionary uses the order specified on STRING and NUMERIC. Thus, *CITY* is the first variable in the dictionary, followed by *POP81*, *POP82*, *POP83*, *REV81*, *REV82*, and *REV83*.
- Formats are specified for the variables on NUMERIC. Otherwise, the program uses the default numeric format (F8.2) from the NUMERIC command for the dictionary format, even though it uses the format on DATA LIST to read the data. In other words, the dictionary uses the first formats specified, even though DATA LIST may use different formats to read cases.

OLAP CUBE

```
OLAP CUBE {varlist} BY varlist [BY...]

[/CELLS= [MEAN**] [COUNT**] [STDDEV**]
         [NPCT**] [SPCT**] [SUM** ]
         [MEDIAN] [GMEDIAN] [SEMEAN]
         [MIN] [MAX] [RANGE]
         [VARIANCE] [KURT] [SEKURT]
         [SKEW] [SESKEW] [FIRST] [LAST]
         [NPCT(var)][SPCT(var)]
         [HARMONIC] [GEOMETRIC]
         [DEFAULT]
         [ALL] [NONE] ]

[/TITLE ='string'][FOOTNOTE= 'string']
```

**Default if the subcommand is omitted.

Example

```
OLAP CUBE sales BY region by industry
  /CELLS=MEAN MEDIAN SUM SPCT(region).
```

Overview

OLAP CUBE produces summary statistics for continuous, quantitative variables within categories defined by one or more categorical grouping variables.

Options

Cell Contents. By default, OLAP CUBE displays means, standard deviations, cell counts, sums, percentage of total N, and percentage of total sum. Optionally, you can request any combination of available statistics.

Format. You can specify a title and a caption for the report using the TITLE and FOOTNOTE subcommands.

Basic Specification

The basic specification is the command name, OLAP CUBE, with a summary variable, the keyword BY, and one or more grouping variables.

- The minimum specification is a summary variable, the keyword BY, and a grouping variable.
- By default, OLAP CUBE displays a Case Processing Summary table showing the number and percentage of cases included, excluded, and their total, and a Layered Report showing means, standard deviations, sums, number of cases for each category, percentage of total N, and percentage of total sum.

Syntax Rules

- Both numeric and string variables can be specified. String variables can be short or long. Summary variables must be numeric.
- String specifications for TITLE and FOOTNOTE cannot exceed 255 characters. Quotation marks or apostrophes are required. When the specification breaks on multiple lines, enclose each line in apostrophes or quotes and separate the specifications for each line by at least one blank. To specify line breaks in titles and footnotes, use the /n specification.
- Each subcommand can be specified only once. Multiple use results in a warning, and the last specification is used.
- When a variable is specified more than once, only the first occurrence is honored. The same variables specified after different BY keywords will result in an error.

Limitations

- Only 5 BY keywords can be specified.

Operations

- The data are processed sequentially. It is not necessary to sort the cases before processing. If a BY keyword is used, the output is always sorted.
- A Case Processing Summary table is always generated, showing the number and percentage of the cases included, excluded, and the total.
- For each combination of grouping variables specified after different BY keywords, OLAP CUBE produces a group in the report.

Example

```
OLAP CUBE SALES BY REGION BY INDUSTRY
  /CELLS=MEAN MEDIAN SUM.
```

- A Case Processing Summary table lists the number and percentage of cases included, excluded, and the total.
- A Layered Report displays the requested statistics for sales for each group defined by each combination of *REGION* and *INDUSTRY*.

TITLE and FOOTNOTE Subcommands

TITLE and FOOTNOTE provide a title and a caption for the Layered Report.

- TITLE and FOOTNOTE are optional and can be placed anywhere.
- The specification on TITLE or FOOTNOTE is a string within apostrophes or quotation marks. To specify a multiple-line title or footnote, enclose each line in apostrophes or quotation marks and separate the specifications for each line by at least one blank.

- To insert line breaks in the displayed title or footnote, use the /n specification.
- The string you specify cannot exceed 255 characters.

CELLS Subcommand

By default, OLAP CUBE displays the means, standard deviations, number of cases, sum, percentage of total cases, and percentage of total sum.

- If CELLS is specified without keywords, OLAP CUBE displays the default statistics.
- If any keywords are specified on CELLS, only the requested information is displayed.

DEFAULT   *Means, standard deviations, cell counts, sum, percentage of total N, and percentage of total sum.* This is the default if CELLS is omitted.

MEAN   *Cell means.*

STDDEV   *Cell standard deviations.*

COUNT   *Cell counts.*

MEDIAN   *Cell median.*

GMEDIAN   *Grouped median.*

SEMEAN   *Standard error of cell mean.*

SUM   *Cell sums.*

MIN   *Cell minimum.*

MAX   *Cell maximum.*

RANGE   *Cell range.*

VARIANCE   *Variances.*

KURT   *Cell kurtosis.*

SEKURT   *Standard error of cell kurtosis.*

SKEW   *Cell skewness.*

SESKEW   *Standard error of cell skewness.*

FIRST   *First value.*

LAST   *Last value.*

SPCT   *Percentage of total sum.*

NPCT   *Percentage of total number of cases.*

SPCT(var)   *Percentage of total sum within specified variable.* The specified variable must be one of the grouping variables.

NPCT(var)   *Percentage of total number of cases within specified variable.* The specified variable must be one of the grouping variables.

HARMONIC   *Harmonic mean.*

GEOMETRIC   *Geometric mean.*

ALL   *All cell information.*

ONEWAY

```
ONEWAY  varlist BY varname

[/POLYNOMIAL=n]  [/CONTRAST=coefficient list]  [/CONTRAST=... ]

[/POSTHOC=([SNK] [TUKEY] [BTUKEY] [DUNCAN] [SCHEFFE] [DUNNETT[refcat]]
          [DUNNETTL(refcat)] [DUNNETTR(refcat)] [BONFERRONI] [;SD]
          [SIDAK] [GT2] [GABRIEL] [FREGW] [QREGW] [T2] [T3] [GH] [C]
          [WALLER({100** })]) [ALPHA({0.05**})]
                  {Kratio}          {α       }

[/RANGES={LSD       }([[{0.05**}])] [/RANGES=...]
         {DUNCAN    } {α       }
         {SNK       }
         {TUKEYB    }
         {TUKEY     }
         {MODLSD    }
         {SCHEFFE   }

[/STATISTICS=[NONE**] [DESCRIPTIVES] [EFFECTS] [HOMOGENEITY] [ALL]

[/PLOT MEANS

[/MISSING=[{ANALYSIS**}]  [{EXCLUDE**}]]
          {LISTWISE  }    {INCLUDE  }

[/MATRIX =[IN({*   })] [OUT({*   })]  [NONE]]
             {file}       {file}
```

**Default if the subcommand is omitted.

Example

```
ONEWAY V1 BY V2(1,4).
```

Overview

ONEWAY produces a one-way analysis of variance for an interval-level dependent variable by one numeric independent variable that defines the groups for the analysis. Other procedures that perform an analysis of variance are SUMMARIZE, UNIANOVA, and GLM (GLM is available in the SPSS Advanced Models option). Some tests not included in the other procedures are available as options in ONEWAY.

Options

Trend and Contrasts. You can partition the between-groups sums of squares into linear, quadratic, cubic, and higher-order trend components using the POLYNOMIAL subcommand. You can specify up to 10 contrasts to be tested with the *t* statistic on the CONTRAST subcommand.

Post Hoc Tests. You can specify 20 different post hoc tests for comparisons of all possible pairs of group means or multiple comparisons using the POSTHOC subcommand.

Statistical Display. In addition to the default display, you can obtain means, standard deviations, and other descriptive statistics for each group using the STATISTICS subcommand. Fixed- and random-effects statistics as well as Leven's test for homogeneity of variance are also available.

Matrix Input and Output. You can write means, standard deviations, and category frequencies to a matrix data file that can be used in subsequent ONEWAY procedures using the MATRIX subcommand. You can also read matrix materials consisting of means, category frequencies, pooled variance, and degrees of freedom for the pooled variance.

Basic Specification

The basic specification is a dependent variable, keyword BY, and an independent variable. ONEWAY produces an ANOVA table displaying the between- and within-groups sums of squares, mean squares, degrees of freedom, the F ratio, and the probability of F for each dependent variable by the independent variable.

Subcommand Order

- The variable list must be specified first.
- The remaining subcommands can be specified in any order.

Operations

- All values of the independent variable are used. Each different value creates one category.
- If a string variable is specified as an independent or dependent variable, ONEWAY is not executed.

Limitations

- Maximum 100 dependent variables and 1 independent variable.
- An unlimited number of categories for the independent variable. However, post hoc tests are not performed if the number of nonempty categories exceeds 50. Contrast tests are not performed if the total of empty and nonempty categories exceeds 50.
- Maximum 1 POLYNOMIAL subcommand.
- Maximum 1 POSTHOC subcommand.
- Maximum 10 CONTRAST subcommands.

Example

```
ONEWAY V1 BY V2.
```

- ONEWAY names *V1* as the dependent variable and *V2* as the independent variable.

Analysis List

The analysis list consists of a list of dependent variables, keyword BY, and an independent (grouping) variable.

- Only one analysis list is allowed, and it must be specified before any of the optional sub-commands.
- All variables named must be numeric.

POLYNOMIAL Subcommand

POLYNOMIAL partitions the between-groups sums of squares into linear, quadratic, cubic, or higher-order trend components. The display is an expanded analysis-of-variance table that provides the degrees of freedom, sums of squares, mean square, F, and probability of F for each partition.

- The value specified on POLYNOMIAL indicates the highest-degree polynomial to be used.
- The polynomial value must be a positive integer less than or equal to 5 and less than the number of groups. If the polynomial specified is greater than the number of groups, the highest-degree polynomial possible is assumed.
- Only one POLYNOMIAL subcommand can be specified per ONEWAY command. If more than one is used, only the last one specified is in effect.
- ONEWAY computes the sums of squares for each order polynomial from weighted poly-nomial contrasts, using the category of the independent variable as the metric. These contrasts are orthogonal.
- With unbalanced designs and equal spacing between groups, ONEWAY also computes sums of squares using the unweighted polynomial contrasts. These contrasts are not orthogonal.
- The deviation sums of squares are always calculated from the weighted sums of squares (Speed, 1976).

Example

```
ONEWAY WELL BY EDUC6
  /POLYNOMIAL=2.
```

- ONEWAY requests an analysis of variance of *WELL* by *EDUC6* with second-order (quadratic) polynomial contrasts.
- The ANOVA table is expanded to include both linear and quadratic terms.

CONTRAST Subcommand

CONTRAST specifies a priori contrasts to be tested by the t statistic. The specification on CONTRAST is a vector of coefficients, where each coefficient corresponds to a category of the independent variable. The Contrast Coefficients table displays the specified contrasts for each group and the Contrast Tests table displays the value of the contrast and its standard error, the t statistic, and the degrees of freedom and two-tailed probability of t for each variable. Both pooled- and separate-variance estimates are displayed.

- A contrast coefficient must be specified or implied for every group defined for the independent variable. If the number of contrast values is not equal to the number of groups, the contrast test is not performed.
- The contrast coefficients for a set should sum to 0. If they do not, a warning is issued. ONEWAY will still give an estimate of this contrast.
- Coefficients are assigned to groups defined by ascending values of the independent variable.
- The notation $n*c$ can be used to indicate that coefficient c is repeated n times.

Example

```
ONEWAY V1 BY V2
  /CONTRAST = -1 -1 1 1
  /CONTRAST = -1 0 0 1
  /CONTRAST = -1 0 .5 .5.
```

- *V2* has four levels.
- The first CONTRAST subcommand contrasts the combination of the first two groups with the combination of the last two groups.
- The second CONTRAST subcommand contrasts the first group with the last group.
- The third CONTRAST subcommand contrasts the first group with the combination of the third and fourth groups.

Example

```
ONEWAY V1 BY V2
  /CONTRAST = -1 1 2*0
  /CONTRAST = -1 1 0 0
  /CONTRAST = -1 1.
```

- The first two CONTRAST subcommands specify the same contrast coefficients for a four-group analysis. The first group is contrasted with the second group in both cases.
- The first CONTRAST uses the $n*c$ notation.
- The last CONTRAST does not work because only two coefficients are specified for four groups.

POSTHOC Subcommand

POSTHOC produces post hoc tests for comparisons of all possible pairs of group means or multiple comparisons. In contrast to a priori analyses specified on the CONTRAST subcommand, post hoc analyses are usually not planned at the beginning of the study but are suggested by the data in the course of the study.

- Twenty post hoc tests are available. Some detect homogeneity subsets among the groups of means, some produce pairwise comparisons, and others perform both. POSTHOC produces a Multiple Comparison table showing up to 10 test categories. Nonempty group means are sorted in ascending order, with asterisks indicating significantly different groups. In addition, homogeneous subsets are calculated and displayed in the Homogeneous Subsets table if the test is designed to detect homogeneity subsets.

- When the number of valid cases in the groups varies, the harmonic mean of the group sizes is used as the sample size in the calculation for homogeneity subsets except for QREGW and FREGW. For QREGW and FREGW and tests for pairwise comparison, the sample sizes of individual groups are always used.

- You can specify only one POSTHOC subcommand per ONEWAY command. If more than one is specified, the last specification takes effect.

- You can specify one alpha value used in all POSTHOC tests using keyword ALPHA. The default is 0.05.

SNK	*Student-Newman-Keuls procedure based on the Studentized range test.* Used for detecting homogeneity subsets.
TUKEY	*Tukey's honestly significant difference.* This test uses the Studentized range statistic to make all pairwise comparisons between groups. Used for pairwise comparison and for detecting homogeneity subsets.
BTUKEY	*Tukey's* b. Multiple comparison procedure based on the average of Studentized range tests. Used for detecting homogeneity subsets.
DUNCAN	*Duncan's multiple comparison procedure based on the Studentized range test.* Used for detecting homogeneity subsets.
SCHEFFE	*Scheffé's multiple comparison* t *test.* Used for pairwise comparison and for detecting homogeneity subsets.
DUNNETT(refcat)	*Dunnett's two-tailed* t *test.* Used for pairwise comparison. Each group is compared to a reference category. You can specify a reference category in parentheses. The default is the last category. This keyword must be spelled out in full.
DUNNETTL(refcat)	*Dunnett's one-tailed* t *test.* Used for pairwise comparison. This test indicates whether the mean of each group (except the reference category) is *smaller* than that of the reference category. You can specify a reference category in parentheses. The default is the last category. This keyword must be spelled out in full.
DUNNETTR(refcat)	*Dunnett's one-tailed* t *test.* Used for pairwise comparison. This test indicates whether the mean of each group (except the reference category) is *larger* than that of the reference category. You can specify a reference category in parentheses. The default is the last category. This keyword must be spelled out in full.
BONFERRONI	*Bonferroni* t *test.* This test is based on Student's *t* statistic and adjusts the observed significance level for the fact that multiple comparisons are made. Used for pairwise comparison.
LSD	*Least significant difference* t *test.* Equivalent to multiple *t* tests between all pairs of groups. Used for pairwise comparison. This test does not control the overall probability of rejecting the hypotheses that some pairs of means are different, while in fact they are equal.

SIDAK	*Sidak* t *test.* Used for pairwise comparison. This test provides tighter bounds than the Bonferroni test.
GT2	*Hochberg's GT2.* Used for pairwise comparison and for detecting homogeneity subsets. This test is based on the Studentized maximum modulus test. Unless the cell sizes are extremely unbalanced, this test is fairly robust even for unequal variances.
GABRIEL	*Gabriel's pairwise comparisons test based on the Studentized maximum modulus test.* Used for pairwise comparison and for detecting homogeneity subsets.
FREGW	*Ryan-Einot-Gabriel-Welsch's multiple stepdown procedure based on an* F *test.* Used for detecting homogeneity subsets.
QREGW	*Ryan-Einot-Gabriel-Welsch's multiple stepdown procedure based on the Studentized range test.* Used for detecting homogeneity subsets.
T2	*Tamhane's T2.* Used for pairwise comparison. This test is based on a *t* test and can be applied in situations where the variances are unequal.
T3	*Tamhane's T3.* Used for pairwise comparison. This test is based on the Studentized maximum modulus test and can be applied in situations where the variances are unequal.
GH	*Games and Howell's pairwise comparisons test based on the Studentized range test.* Used for pairwise comparison. This test can be applied in situations where the variances are unequal.
C	*Dunnett's C.* Used for pairwise comparison. This test is based on the weighted average of Studentized ranges and can be applied in situations where the variances are unequal.
WALLER(kratio)	*Waller-Duncan* t *test.* Used for detecting homogeneity subsets. This test uses a Bayesian approach. The k-ratio is the Type 1/Type 2 error seriousness ratio. The default value is 100. You can specify an integer greater than 1 within parentheses.

Example

```
ONEWAY WELL BY EDUC6
  /POSTHOC=SNK SCHEFFE ALPHA=.01.
```

- ONEWAY requests two different post hoc tests. The first uses the Student-Newman-Keuls test and the second uses Scheffé's test. Both tests use an alpha of 0.01.

RANGES Subcommand

RANGES produces results for some post hoc tests. It is available only through syntax. You can always produce the same results using the POSTHOC subcommand.

- Up to 10 RANGE subcommands are allowed. The effect is cumulative. If you specify more than one alpha value for different range tests, the last specified value takes effect for all tests. The default is 0.05.

- Keyword MODLSD on the RANGE subcommand is equivalent to keyword BONFERRONI on the POSTHOC subcommand. Keyword LSDMOD is an alias for MODLSD.

PLOT MEANS Subcommand

PLOT MEANS produces a chart that plots the subgroup means (the means for each group defined by values of the factor variable).

STATISTICS Subcommand

By default, ONEWAY displays the ANOVA table showing between- and within-groups sums of squares, mean squares, degrees of freedom, F ratio, and probability of F. Use STATISTICS to obtain additional statistics.

DESCRIPTIVES   *Group descriptive statistics.* The statistics include the number of cases, mean, standard deviation, standard error, minimum, maximum, and 95% confidence interval for each dependent variable for each group.

EFFECTS   *Fixed- and random-effects statistics.* The statistics include the standard deviation, standard error, and 95% confidence interval for the fixed-effects model, and the standard error, 95% confidence interval, and estimate of between-components variance for the random-effects model.

HOMOGENEITY   *Homogeneity-of-variance tests.* The statistics include Levene statistic, degrees of freedom, and the significance level displayed in the Test of Homogeneity of Variances table.

NONE   *No optional statistics.* This is the default.

ALL   *All statistics available for* ONEWAY.

MISSING Subcommand

MISSING controls the treatment of missing values.

- Keywords ANALYSIS and LISTWISE are alternatives. Each can be used with INCLUDE or EXCLUDE. The default is ANALYSIS and EXCLUDE.
- A case outside the range specified for the grouping variable is not used.

ANALYSIS   *Exclude cases with missing values on a pair-by-pair basis.* A case with a missing value for the dependent or grouping variable for a given analysis is not used for that analysis. This is the default.

LISTWISE   *Exclude cases with missing values listwise.* Cases with missing values for any variable named are excluded from all analyses.

EXCLUDE   *Exclude cases with user-missing values.* User-missing values are treated as missing. This is the default.

INCLUDE   *Include user-missing values.* User-missing values are treated as valid values.

MATRIX Subcommand

MATRIX reads and writes matrix data files.

- Either IN or OUT and a matrix file in parentheses are required.
- You cannot specify both IN and OUT on the same ONEWAY procedure.
- Use MATRIX=NONE to explicitly indicate that a matrix data file is not being written or read.

OUT (filename)   *Write a matrix data file.* Specify either a filename or an asterisk, enclosed in parentheses. If you specify a filename, the file is stored on disk and can be retrieved at any time. If you specify an asterisk (*), the matrix data file replaces the working file but is not stored on disk unless you use SAVE or XSAVE.

IN (filename)   *Read a matrix data file.* If the matrix data file is the working data file, specify an asterisk (*) in parentheses. If the matrix data file is another file, specify the filename in parentheses. A matrix file read from an external file does not replace the working data file.

NONE   *Do not read or write matrix data materials.* This is the default.

Matrix Output

- ONEWAY writes means, standard deviations, and frequencies to a matrix data file that can be used by subsequent ONEWAY procedures. See "Format of the Matrix Data File" below for a description of the file.

Matrix Input

- ONEWAY can read the matrices it writes, and it can also read matrix materials that include the means, category frequencies, pooled variance, and degrees of freedom for the pooled variance. The pooled variance has a *ROWTYPE_* value MSE, and the vector of degrees of freedom for the pooled variance has the *ROWTYPE_* value DFE.
- The dependent variables named on ONEWAY can be a subset of the dependent variables in the matrix data file.
- MATRIX=IN cannot be specified unless a working data file has already been defined. To read an existing matrix data file at the beginning of a session, use GET to retrieve the matrix file and then specify IN(*) on MATRIX.

Format of the Matrix Data File

- The matrix data file includes two special variables created by the program: *ROWTYPE_* and *VARNAME_*.
- *ROWTYPE_* is a short string variable with values MEAN, STDDEV, and N.

- *VARNAME_* is a short string variable that never has values for procedure ONEWAY. *VARNAME_* is included with the matrix materials so that matrices written by ONEWAY can be read by procedures that expect to read a *VARNAME_* variable.
- The independent variable is between variables *ROWTYPE_* and *VARNAME_*.
- The remaining variables in the matrix file are the dependent variables.

Split Files

- When split-file processing is in effect, the first variables in the matrix data file are the split variables, followed by *ROWTYPE_*, the independent variable, *VARNAME_*, and the dependent variables.
- A full set of matrix materials is written for each split-file group defined by the split variable(s).
- A split variable cannot have the same variable name as any other variable written to the matrix data file.
- If split-file processing is in effect when a matrix is written, the same split file must be in effect when that matrix is read by any procedure.
- Generally, matrix rows, independent variables, and dependent variables can be in any order in the matrix data file read by keyword IN. However, all split-file variables must precede variable *ROWTYPE_*, and all split-group rows must be consecutive. ONEWAY ignores unrecognized *ROWTYPE_* values.

Missing Values

Missing-value treatment affects the values written to an matrix data file. When reading a matrix data file, be sure to specify a missing-value treatment on ONEWAY that is compatible with the treatment that was in effect when the matrix materials were generated.

Example

```
GET FILE=GSS80.
ONEWAY   WELL BY EDUC6
  /MATRIX=OUT(ONEMTX).
```

- ONEWAY reads data from file *GSS80* and writes one set of matrix materials to the file *ONEMTX*.
- The working data file is still *GSS80*. Subsequent commands are executed on *GSS80*.

Example

```
GET FILE=GSS80.
ONEWAY   WELL BY EDUC6
  /MATRIX=OUT(*).
LIST.
```

- ONEWAY writes the same matrix as in the example above. However, the matrix data file replaces the working data file. The LIST command is executed on the matrix file, not on the *GSS80* file.

Example

```
GET FILE=PRSNNL.
FREQUENCIES VARIABLE=AGE.
ONEWAY  WELL BY EDUC6
 /MATRIX=IN(ONEMTX).
```

- This example performs a frequencies analysis on *PRSNNL* and then uses a different file for ONEWAY. The file is an existing matrix data file.
- MATRIX=IN specifies the matrix data file.
- *ONEMTX* does not replace *PRSNNL* as the working data file.

Example

```
GET FILE=ONEMTX.
ONEWAY  WELL BY EDUC6
 /MATRIX=IN(*).
```

- The GET command retrieves the matrix data file *ONEMTX*.
- MATRIX=IN specifies an asterisk because the working data file is the matrix data file *ONEMTX*. If MATRIX=IN(ONEMTX) is specified, the program issues an error message, since *ONEMTX* is already open.
- If the GET command is omitted, the program issues an error message.

References

Speed, M. F. 1976. Response curves in the one way classification with unequal numbers of observations per cell. *Proceedings of the Statistical Computing Section.* American Statistical Association.

PACF

```
PACF [VARIABLES=] series names

[/DIFF={1}]
       {n}

[/SDIFF={1}]
        {n}

[/PERIOD=n]

[/{NOLOG**}]
  {LN    }

[/SEASONAL]

[/MXAUTO={16**}]
         {n   }

[/APPLY [='model name']]
```

**Default if the subcommand is omitted and there is no corresponding specification on the TSET command.

Example
```
PACF TICKETS
  /LN
  /DIFF=1
  /SDIFF=1
  /PERIOD=12
  /MXAUTO=25.
```

Overview

PACF displays and plots the sample partial autocorrelation function of one or more time series. You can also display and plot the partial autocorrelations of transformed series by requesting natural log and differencing transformations from within the procedure.

Options

Modifying the Series. You can request a natural log transformation of the series using the LN subcommand and seasonal and nonseasonal differencing to any degree using the SDIFF and DIFF subcommands. With seasonal differencing, you can specify the periodicity on the PERIOD subcommand.

Statistical Output. With the MXAUTO subcommand, you can specify the number of lags for which you want values displayed and plotted, overriding the maximum specified on TSET. You can also display and plot values only at periodic lags using the SEASONAL subcommand.

Basic Specification

The basic specification is one or more series names. For each series specified, PACF automatically displays the partial autocorrelation value and standard error value for each lag. It also plots the partial autocorrelations and marks the bounds of two standard errors on the plot. By default, PACF displays and plots partial autocorrelations for up to 16 lags or the number of lags specified on TSET.

Subcommand Order

- Subcommands can be specified in any order.

Syntax Rules

- VARIABLES can be specified only once.
- Other subcommands can be specified more than once, but only the last specification of each one is executed.

Operations

- Subcommand specifications apply to all series named on the PACF command.
- If the LN subcommand is specified, any differencing requested on that PACF command is done on log-transformed series.
- Confidence limits are displayed in the plot, marking the bounds of two standard errors at each lag.

Limitations

- Maximum 1 VARIABLES subcommand. There is no limit on the number of series named on the list.

Example

```
PACF TICKETS
  /LN
  /DIFF=1
  /SDIFF=1
  /PERIOD=12
  /MXAUTO=25.
```

- This example produces a plot of the partial autocorrelation function for the series *TICKETS* after a natural log transformation, differencing, and seasonal differencing have been applied to the series. Along with the plot, the partial autocorrelation value and standard error are displayed for each lag.

- LN transforms the data using the natural logarithm (base e) of the series.
- DIFF differences the series once.
- SDIFF and PERIOD apply one degree of seasonal differencing with a period of 12.
- MXAUTO specifies that the maximum number of lags for which output is to be produced is 25.

VARIABLES Subcommand

VARIABLES specifies the series names and is the only required subcommand. The actual keyword VARIABLES can be omitted.

DIFF Subcommand

DIFF specifies the degree of differencing used to convert a nonstationary series to a stationary one with a constant mean and variance before the partial autocorrelations are computed.
- You can specify any positive integer on DIFF.
- If DIFF is specified without a value, the default is 1.
- The number of values used in the calculations decreases by 1 for each degree of differencing.

Example

```
PACF SALES
  /DIFF=1.
```

- In this example, the series *SALES* will be differenced once before the partial autocorrelations are computed and plotted.

SDIFF Subcommand

If the series exhibits a seasonal or periodic pattern, you can use the SDIFF subcommand to seasonally difference the series before obtaining partial autocorrelations.
- The specification on SDIFF indicates the degree of seasonal differencing and can be any positive integer.
- If SDIFF is specified without a value, the degree of seasonal differencing defaults to 1.
- The number of seasons used in the calculations decreases by 1 for each degree of seasonal differencing.
- The length of the period used by SDIFF is specified on the PERIOD subcommand. If the PERIOD subcommand is not specified, the periodicity established on the TSET or DATE command is used (see the PERIOD subcommand).

PERIOD Subcommand

PERIOD indicates the length of the period to be used by the SDIFF or SEASONAL subcommand.

- The specification on PERIOD indicates how many observations are in one period or season and can be any positive integer.
- PERIOD is ignored if it is used without the SDIFF or SEASONAL subcommand.
- If PERIOD is not specified, the periodicity established on TSET PERIOD is in effect. If TSET PERIOD is not specified, the periodicity established on the DATE command is used. If periodicity was not established anywhere, the SDIFF and SEASONAL subcommands will not be executed.

Example

```
PACF SALES
  /SDIFF=1
  /PERIOD=12.
```

- This PACF command applies one degree of seasonal differencing with a periodicity of 12 to the series *SALES* before partial autocorrelations are computed and plotted.

LN and NOLOG Subcommands

LN transforms the data using the natural logarithm (base *e*) of the series and is used to remove varying amplitude over time. NOLOG indicates that the data should not be log transformed. NOLOG is the default.

- If you specify LN on a PACF command, any differencing requested on that command will be done on the log-transformed series.
- There are no additional specifications on LN or NOLOG.
- Only the last LN or NOLOG subcommand on a PACF command is executed.
- If a natural log transformation is requested when there are values in the series that are less than or equal to 0, the PACF will not be produced for that series because nonpositive values cannot be log transformed.
- NOLOG is generally used with an APPLY subcommand to turn off a previous LN specification.

Example

```
PACF SALES
  /LN.
```

- This command transforms the series *SALES* using the natural log transformation and then computes and plots partial autocorrelations.

SEASONAL Subcommand

Use SEASONAL to focus attention on the seasonal component by displaying and plotting autocorrelations only at periodic lags.

- There are no additional specifications on SEASONAL.

- If SEASONAL is specified, values are displayed and plotted at the periodic lags indicated on the PERIOD subcommand. If PERIOD is not specified, the periodicity established on the TSET or DATE command is used (see the PERIOD subcommand on p. 863).
- If SEASONAL is not specified, partial autocorrelations for all lags up to the maximum are displayed and plotted.

Example

```
PACF SALES
 /SEASONAL
 /PERIOD=12.
```

- In this example, partial autocorrelations are displayed and plotted at every 12th lag.

MXAUTO Subcommand

MXAUTO specifies the maximum number of lags for a series.
- The specification on MXAUTO must be a positive integer.
- If MXAUTO is not specified, the default number of lags is the value set on TSET MXAUTO. If TSET MXAUTO is not specified, the default is 16.
- The value on MXAUTO overrides the value set on TSET MXAUTO.

Example

```
PACF SALES
 /MXAUTO=14.
```

- This command specifies 14 for the maximum number of partial autocorrelations that can be displayed and plotted for series *SALES*.

APPLY Subcommand

APPLY allows you to use a previously defined PACF model without having to repeat the specifications.
- The only specification on APPLY is the name of a previous model enclosed in apostrophes. If a model name is not specified, the model specified on the previous PACF command is used.
- To change one or more model specifications, specify the subcommands of only those portions you want to change after the APPLY subcommand.
- If no series are specified on the PACF command, the series that were originally specified with the model being reapplied are used.
- To change the series used with the model, enter new series names before or after the APPLY subcommand.

Example

```
PACF TICKETS
  /LN
  /DIFF=1
  /SDIFF=1
  /PER=12
  /MXAUTO=25.
PACF ROUNDTRP
  /APPLY.
```

- The first command specifies a maximum of 25 partial autocorrelations for the series *TICKETS* after it has been log transformed, differenced once, and had one degree of seasonal differencing with a periodicity of 12 applied to it. This model is assigned the default name *MOD_1*.

- The second command displays and plots partial autocorrelations for series *ROUNDTRP* using the same model that was specified for series *TICKETS*.

References

Box, G. E. P., and G. M. Jenkins. 1976. *Time series analysis: Forecasting and control.* San Francisco: Holden-Day.

PARTIAL CORR

```
PARTIAL CORR [VARIABLES=] varlist [WITH varlist]
    BY varlist [(levels)] [/varlist...]

[/SIGNIFICANCE={TWOTAIL**}]
              {ONETAIL  }

[/STATISTICS=[NONE**] [CORR] [DESCRIPTIVES] [BADCORR] [ALL]]

[/FORMAT={MATRIX** }]
         {SERIAL   }
         {CONDENSED}

[/MISSING=[{LISTWISE**}]  [{EXCLUDE**}]]
          {ANALYSIS  }    {INCLUDE  }

[/MATRIX= [IN({*    })] [OUT({*    })]]
             {file}         {file}
```

**Default if the subcommand is omitted.

Example

```
PARTIAL CORR VARIABLES=PUBTRANS MECHANIC BUSDRVER BY NETPURSE(1).
```

Overview

PARTIAL CORR produces partial correlation coefficients that describe the relationship between two variables while adjusting for the effects of one or more additional variables. PARTIAL CORR calculates a matrix of Pearson product-moment correlations. It can also read the zero-order correlation matrix as input. Other procedures producing zero-order correlation matrices that can be read by PARTIAL CORR include CORRELATIONS, REGRESSION, DISCRIMINANT, and FACTOR.

Options

Significance Levels. By default, the significance level for each partial correlation coefficient is based on a two-tailed test. Optionally, you can request a one-tailed test using the SIGNIFICANCE subcommand.

Statistics. In addition to the partial correlation coefficient, degrees of freedom, and significance level, you can obtain the mean, standard deviation, and number of nonmissing cases for each variable, and zero-order correlation coefficients for each pair of variables using the STATISTICS subcommand.

Format. You can specify condensed format, which suppresses the degrees of freedom and significance level for each coefficient, and you can print only nonredundant coefficients in serial string format using the FORMAT subcommand.

Matrix Input and Output. You can read and write zero-order correlation matrices using the MATRIX subcommand.

Basic Specification

The basic specification is the VARIABLES subcommand, which specifies a list of variables to be correlated and one or more control variables following keyword BY. PARTIAL CORR calculates the partial correlation of each variable with every other variable specified on the correlation variable list.

Subcommand Order

Subcommands can be specified in any order.

- If VARIABLES is the first subcommand used on PARTIAL CORR, keyword VARIABLES can be omitted.
- If VARIABLES is not the first subcommand specified on PARTIAL CORR, both the subcommand keyword VARIABLES and the equals sign are required.

Operations

PARTIAL CORR produces one matrix of partial correlation coefficients for each of up to five order values. For each coefficient, PARTIAL CORR prints the degrees of freedom and the significance level.

Limitations

- Maximum 25 variable lists on a single PARTIAL CORR command. Each variable list contains a correlation list, a control list, and order values.
- Maximum 400 variables total can be named or implied per PARTIAL CORR command.
- Maximum 100 control variables.
- Maximum 5 different order values per single list. The largest order value that can be specified is 100.

Example

```
PARTIAL CORR VARIABLES=PUBTRANS MECHANIC BUSDRVER BY NETPURSE(1).
```

- PARTIAL CORR produces a square matrix containing three unique first-order partial correlations: *PUBTRANS* with *MECHANIC* controlling for *NETPURSE*; *PUBTRANS* with *BUSDRVER* controlling for *NETPURSE*; and *MECHANIC* with *BUSDRVER* controlling for *NETPURSE*.

VARIABLES Subcommand

VARIABLES requires a *correlation list* of one or more pairs of variables for which partial correlations are desired and a *control list* of one or more variables that will be used as controls for the variables in the correlation list, followed by optional order values in parentheses.

- The correlation list specifies pairs of variables to be correlated while controlling for the variables in the control list.

- To request a square or lower-triangular matrix, do not use keyword WITH in the correlation list. This obtains the partial correlation of every variable with every other variable in the list.

- To request a rectangular matrix, specify a list of correlation variables followed by keyword WITH and a second list of variables. This obtains the partial correlation of specific variable pairs. The first variable list defines the rows of the matrix and the second list defines the columns.

- The control list is specified after keyword BY.

- The correlation between a pair of variables is referred to as a zero-order correlation. Controlling for one variable produces a first-order partial correlation, controlling for two variables produces a second-order partial, and so on.

- You can specify order values in parentheses following the control list to indicate the exact partials to be computed. These values also determine the partial correlation matrix or matrices to be printed. Up to five order values can be specified. Separate each value with at least one space or comma. The default order value is the number of control variables.

- One partial is produced for every unique combination of control variables for each order value.

- To specify multiple analyses, use multiple VARIABLES subcommands or a slash to separate each set of specifications on one VARIABLES subcommand. PARTIAL CORR computes the zero-order correlation matrix for each analysis list separately.

Example

```
PARTIAL CORR RENT FOOD PUBTRANS WITH TEACHER MANAGER BY NETSALRY(1).
```

- PARTIAL CORR produces a rectangular matrix. Variables *RENT*, *FOOD*, and *PUBTRANS* form the matrix rows, and variables *TEACHER* and *MANAGER* form the columns.

- Keyword VARIABLES is omitted. This is allowed because the variable list is the first specification on PARTIAL CORR.

Example

```
PARTIAL CORR   RENT WITH TEACHER BY NETSALRY, NETPRICE (1).
PARTIAL CORR   RENT WITH TEACHER BY NETSALRY, NETPRICE (2).
PARTIAL CORR   RENT WITH TEACHER BY NETSALRY, NETPRICE (1,2).
PARTIAL CORR   RENT FOOD PUBTRANS BY NETSALRY NETPURSE NETPRICE
(1,3).
```

- The first PARTIAL CORR produces two first-order partials: *RENT* with *TEACHER* controlling for *NETSALRY*, and *RENT* with *TEACHER* controlling for *NETPRICE*.

- The second PARTIAL CORR produces one second-order partial of *RENT* with *TEACHER* controlling simultaneously for *NETSALRY* and *NETPRICE*.
- The third PARTIAL CORR specifies both sets of partials specified by the previous two commands.
- The fourth PARTIAL CORR produces three first-order partials (controlling for *NETSALRY*, *NETPURSE*, and *NETPRICE* individually) and one third-order partial (controlling for all three control variables simultaneously).

Example

```
PARTIAL CORR RENT FOOD WITH TEACHER BY NETSALRY NETPRICE (1,2)
    /WCLOTHES MCLOTHES BY NETPRICE (1).
```

- PARTIAL CORR produces three matrices for the first correlation list, control list, and order values.
- The second correlation list, control list, and order value produce one matrix.

SIGNIFICANCE Subcommand

SIGNIFICANCE determines whether the significance level is based on a one-tailed or two-tailed test.

- By default, the significance level is based on a two-tailed test. This is appropriate when the direction of the relationship between a pair of variables cannot be specified in advance of the analysis.
- When the direction of the relationship can be determined in advance, a one-tailed test is appropriate.

TWOTAIL *Two-tailed test of significance.* This is the default.

ONETAIL *One-tailed test of significance.*

STATISTICS Subcommand

By default, the partial correlation coefficient, degrees of freedom, and significance level are displayed. Use STATISTICS to obtain additional statistics.

- If both CORR and BADCORR are requested, CORR takes precedence over BADCORR and the zero-order correlations are displayed.

CORR *Zero-order correlations with degrees of freedom and significance level.*

DESCRIPTIVES *Mean, standard deviation, and number of nonmissing cases.* Descriptive statistics are not available with matrix input.

BADCORR *Zero-order correlation coefficients only if any of the zero-order correlations cannot be computed.* Noncomputable coefficients are displayed as a period.

NONE *No additional statistics.* This is the default.

ALL *All additional statistics available with* PARTIAL CORR.

FORMAT Subcommand

FORMAT determines page format.

- If both CONDENSED and SERIAL are specified, only SERIAL is in effect.

MATRIX   *Display degrees of freedom and significance level in matrix format.* This format requires four lines per matrix row and displays the degrees of freedom and the significance level. The output includes redundant coefficients. This is the default.

CONDENSED   *Suppress the degrees of freedom and significance level.* This format requires only one line per matrix row and suppresses the degrees of freedom and significance. A single asterisk (*) following a coefficient indicates a significance level of 0.05 or less. Two asterisks (**) following a coefficient indicate a significance level of 0.01 or less.

SERIAL   *Display only the nonredundant coefficients in serial string format.* The coefficients, degrees of freedom, and significance levels from the first row of the matrix are displayed first, followed by all the unique coefficients from the second row and so on for all the rows of the matrix.

MISSING Subcommand

MISSING controls the treatment of cases with missing values.

- When multiple analysis lists are specified, missing values are handled separately for each analysis list. Thus, different sets of cases can be used for different lists.
- When pairwise deletion is in effect (keyword ANALYSIS), the degrees of freedom for a particular partial coefficient are based on the smallest number of cases used in the calculation of any of the simple correlations.
- LISTWISE and ANALYSIS are alternatives. However, each can be used with either INCLUDE or EXCLUDE. The default is LISTWISE and EXCLUDE.

LISTWISE   *Exclude cases with missing values listwise.* Cases with missing values for any of the variables listed for an analysis, including control variables, are not used in the calculation of the zero-order correlation coefficient. This is the default.

ANALYSIS   *Exclude cases with missing values on a pair-by-pair basis.* Cases with missing for one or both of a pair of variables are not used in the calculation of zero-order correlation coefficients.

EXCLUDE   *Exclude user-missing values.* User-missing values are treated as missing. This is the default.

INCLUDE   *Include user-missing values.* User-missing values are treated as valid values.

MATRIX Subcommand

MATRIX reads and writes matrix data files.

- Either IN or OUT and a matrix file in parentheses is required. When both IN and OUT are used on the same PARTIAL CORR procedure, they can be specified on separate MATRIX subcommands or both on the same subcommand.

OUT (filename)   *Write the (zero-order) correlation matrix to a file.* Specify either a filename or an asterisk, enclosed in parentheses. If you specify a filename, the file is stored on disk and can be retrieved at any time. If you specify an asterisk (*), the matrix data file replaces the working data file but is not stored on disk unless you use SAVE or XSAVE.

IN (filename)   *Read a matrix data file.* If the matrix data file is the working data file, specify an asterisk (*) in parentheses. If the matrix data file is another file, specify a filename in parentheses. Both the working data file and the matrix data file must contain all the variables specified on the VARIABLES subcommands on PARTIAL CORR. A matrix file read from an external file does not replace the working data file.

Matrix Output

- The matrix materials that PARTIAL CORR writes can be used by subsequent PARTIAL CORR procedures or by other procedures that read correlation-type matrices.

- In addition to the Pearson correlation coefficients, the matrix materials PARTIAL CORR writes include the mean, standard deviation, and number of cases used to compute each coefficient (see "Format of the Matrix Data File" on p. 872 for a description of the file). If PARTIAL CORR reads matrix data and then writes matrix materials based on those data, the matrix data file that it writes will not include means and standard deviations.

- PARTIAL CORR writes a full square matrix for the analysis specified on the first VARIABLES subcommand (or the first analysis list if keyword VARIABLES is omitted). No matrix is written for subsequent variable lists.

- Any documents contained in the working data file are not transferred to the matrix file.

Matrix Input

- When matrix materials are read from a file other than the working data file, both the working data file and the matrix data file specified on IN must contain all the variables specified on the VARIABLES subcommands.

- MATRIX=IN cannot be specified unless a working data file has already been defined. To read an existing matrix data file at the beginning of a session, use GET to retrieve the matrix file and then specify IN(*) on MATRIX.

- PARTIAL CORR can read correlation-type matrices written by other procedures.

- The program reads variable names, variable and value labels, and print and write formats from the dictionary of the matrix data file.

Format of the Matrix Data File

- The matrix data file includes two special variables created by the program: *ROWTYPE_* and *VARNAME_*.
- *ROWTYPE_* is a short string variable with values N, MEAN, STDDEV, and CORR (for Pearson's correlation coefficient).
- *VARNAME_* is a short string variable whose values are the names of the variables used to form the correlation matrix. When *ROWTYPE_* is CORR, *VARNAME_* gives the variable associated with that row of the correlation matrix.
- The remaining variables in the file are the variables used to form the correlation matrix.

Split Files

- When split-file processing is in effect, the first variables in the matrix data file are the split variables, followed by *ROWTYPE_*, *VARNAME_*, and the variables used to form the correlation matrix.
- A full set of matrix materials is written for each split-file group defined by the split variables.
- A split variable cannot have the same variable name as any other variable written to the matrix data file.
- If split-file processing is in effect when a matrix is written, the same split file must be in effect when that matrix is read by any procedure.

Missing Values

- With pairwise treatment of missing values (MISSING=ANALYSIS is specified), the matrix of N's used to compute each coefficient is included with the matrix materials.
- With LISTWISE treatment, a single N used to calculate all coefficients is included with the matrix materials.
- When reading a matrix data file, be sure to specify a missing-value treatment on PARTIAL CORR that is compatible with the missing-value treatment that was in effect when the matrix materials were produced.

Example

```
GET FILE=CITY.
PARTIAL CORR VARIABLES=BUSDRVER MECHANIC ENGINEER TEACHER COOK
                        BY  NETSALRY(1)
  /MATRIX=OUT(PTMTX).
```

- PARTIAL CORR reads data from file *CITY* and writes one set of matrix materials to file *PTMTX*.
- The working data file is still *CITY*. Subsequent commands are executed on *CITY*.

Example

```
GET FILE=CITY.
PARTIAL CORR VARIABLES=BUSDRVER MECHANIC ENGINEER TEACHER COOK
  BY  NETSALRY(1)   /MATRIX=OUT(*).
LIST.
```

- PARTIAL CORR writes the same matrix as in the example above. However, the matrix data file replaces the working data file. The LIST command is executed on the matrix file, not on the *CITY* file.

Example

```
GET FILE=PRSNNL.
FREQUENCIES VARIABLE=AGE.
PARTIAL CORR VARIABLES=BUSDRVER MECHANIC ENGINEER TEACHER COOK
   BY  NETSALRY(1)   /MATRIX=IN(CORMTX).
```

- This example performs a frequencies analysis on file *PRSNNL* and then uses a different file for PARTIAL CORR. The file is an existing matrix data file.
- MATRIX=IN specifies the matrix data file. Both the working data file and the *CORMTX* file must contain all variables specified on the VARIABLES subcommand on PARTIAL CORR.
- *CORMTX* does not replace *PRSNNL* as the working data file.

Example

```
GET FILE=CORMTX.
PARTIAL CORR VARIABLES=BUSDRVER MECHANIC ENGINEER TEACHER COOK
                      BY NETSALRY(1)
  /MATRIX=IN(*).
```

- The GET command retrieves the matrix data file *CORMTX*.
- MATRIX=IN specifies an asterisk because the working data file is the matrix file *CORMTX*. If MATRIX=IN(CORMTX) is specified, the program issues an error message.
- If the GET command is omitted, the program issues an error message.

Example

```
GET FILE=CITY.
REGRESSION MATRIX=OUT(*)
  /VARIABLES=NETPURSE PUBTRANS MECHANIC BUSDRVER
  /DEPENDENT=NETPURSE /ENTER.
PARTIAL CORR  PUBTRANS MECHANIC BUSDRVER BY NETPURSE(1) /MATRIX=IN(*).
```

- GET retrieves the SPSS-format data file *CITY*.

- REGRESSION computes correlations among the specified variables. MATRIX=OUT(*) writes a matrix data file that replaces the working data file.
- The MATRIX=IN(*) specification on PARTIAL CORR reads the matrix materials in the working data file.

PLOT

```
PLOT
 [/MISSING=[{PLOTWISE**}] [INCLUDE] [DEFAULT**]]
            {LISTWISE  }

 [/FORMAT={DEFAULT**        }]
          {OVERLAY          }
          {CONTOUR††[({10})]}
          {          {n }  }
          {REGRESSION       }

 [/TITLE='title']

 [/HORIZONTAL=['label'] [STANDARDIZE] [REFERENCE(value list)]
              [MIN(n)] [MAX(n)] [UNIFORM]]

 [/VERTICAL=['label'] [STANDARDIZE] [REFERENCE(value list)]
            [MIN(n)] [MAX(n)] [UNIFORM]]

 /PLOT={varlist} WITH varlist [(PAIR)] [BY varname] [;varlist...]
       {ALL     }

 [/PLOT=...]
```

**Default if the subcommand is omitted.

Example

```
PLOT FORMAT=OVERLAY
  /TITLE='Marriage and Divorce Rates'
  /VERTICAL='Rates per 1000 population'
  /HORIZONTAL='Year' REFERENCE (1918, 1945) MIN (1880) MAX (2000)
  /PLOT=MARRATE DIVRATE WITH YEAR.
```

Overview

PLOT produces two-dimensional plots, including simple bivariate scatterplots, scatterplots with a control variable, contour plots, and overlay plots. You can also request bivariate regression statistics. You can choose from a variety of options for plot symbols, and you can add reference lines. You have control over size, labeling, and scaling of each axis, and you can constrain the axes to be uniform for a series of plots. Many of these plots can also be produced with the GRAPH command.

Options

Types of Plots. You can introduce a control variable for bivariate scatterplots and request regression plots with or without a control variable, contour plots, and overlay plots using the FORMAT subcommand.

Basic Specification

The basic specification is a PLOT subcommand that names the variables for the vertical (*y*) axis, keyword WITH, and the variables for the horizontal (*x*) axis. By default, PLOT produces separate bivariate scatterplots for all combinations formed by each variable on the left side of WITH with each variable on the right.

Subcommand Order

- No subcommand can be specified after the last PLOT subcommand specified. Other than this, subcommands can be specified in any order.

Syntax Rules

- The PLOT subcommand can be specified more than once.
- Subcommands HORIZONTAL, VERTICAL, FORMAT, and TITLE can be specified more than once and apply only to the following PLOT subcommand.

Limitations

There are no limitations on the number of plots requested or on the number of variables specified on a PLOT command. The following limitations apply to the optional subcommands:

- Maximum 60 characters for a title specified on TITLE.
- Maximum 10 reference points on each HORIZONTAL or VERTICAL subcommand.
- Maximum 40 characters per label on each HORIZONTAL or VERTICAL subcommand.

Example

```
PLOT FORMAT=OVERLAY
  /TITLE='Marriage and Divorce Rates'
  /VERTICAL='Rates per 1000 population'
  /HORIZONTAL='Year' REFERENCE (1918, 1945) MIN (1900) MAX (1983)
  /PLOT=MARRATE DIVRATE WITH YEAR.
```

- This example produces an overlay plot of marriage and divorce rates by year.
- TITLE specifies a plot title.
- VERTICAL provides a title for the vertical axis.
- HORIZONTAL provides a title for the horizontal axis. The REFERENCE keyword provides reference lines at values 1918 and 1945. MIN and MAX specify minimum and maximum scale values for the horizontal axis.

PLOT Subcommand

The PLOT subcommand names the variables to be plotted on each axis. PLOT can also name a control or contour variable.

- PLOT is the only required subcommand.
- Multiple PLOT subcommands are allowed.
- No other subcommands can follow the last PLOT subcommand.
- The basic specification on PLOT is a list of variables to be plotted on the vertical axis, keyword WITH, and a list of variables to be plotted on the horizontal axis.
- By default, PLOT creates a separate plot for each variable specified before WITH with each variable specified after WITH.
- To request special pairing of variables, specify keyword PAIR in parentheses following the second variable list. The first variable before WITH is plotted against the first variable after WITH, the second against the second, and so on.
- Use semicolons to separate multiple plot lists on a single PLOT subcommand.
- Keyword ALL can be used to refer to all user-defined variables.
- An optional control variable can be specified following keyword BY. Only one control variable can be specified on any plot list.
- If a control variable is specified for a bivariate scatterplot (the default), PLOT uses the first character of the control variable's value label as the plot symbol. If value labels have not been specified, the first character of the value is used. The symbol $ indicates that more than one control value occurs at that position.

Example

```
PLOT PLOT=MARRATE WITH YEAR AGE;
         BIRTHS DEATHS WITH INCOME1 INCOME2 (PAIR);
         DIVRATE WITH AGE BY YEAR.
```

- The PLOT subcommand contains three plot lists. The first requests a plot of *MARRATE* with *YEAR* and of *MARRATE* with *AGE*.
- The second uses the keyword PAIR to request two plots: *BIRTHS* with *INCOME1* and *DEATHS* with *INCOME2*.
- The third requests a plot of *DIVRATE* with *AGE* using *YEAR* as a control variable. The first character of the value labels for *YEAR* is used as the plot symbol.

FORMAT Subcommand

FORMAT controls the type of plot produced.

- FORMAT can be specified once before each PLOT subcommand and applies only to plots requested on that PLOT subcommand.
- If FORMAT is not used or keyword DEFAULT is specified, bivariate scatterplots are displayed.
- Only one keyword can be specified on each FORMAT subcommand.

DEFAULT	*Bivariate scatterplot.* When there is no control variable, each symbol represents the case count at that position. When a control variable is specified, each symbol represents the first character of the control variable's value label, or the first character of the value if no labels have been defined.
OVERLAY	*Overlay plots.* All bivariate plots on the next PLOT subcommand appear in one plot frame. PLOT selects a unique symbol for each plot to be overlaid, plus a symbol to represent multiple plot points at one position.
REGRESSION	*Regression of the* y *axis variable on the* x *axis variable.* The regression-line intercepts are marked with the letter *R*. When there is no control variable, each symbol represents the frequency of cases at that position. If a control variable is specified, regression statistics are pooled over all categories and each symbol represents the first character of the control variable's value label, or the first character of the value if no labels have been defined.

VERTICAL and HORIZONTAL Subcommands

VERTICAL and HORIZONTAL control labeling and scaling for the vertical and horizontal axes.

- VERTICAL and HORIZONTAL can each be specified once before each PLOT subcommand and apply only to plots requested by that subcommand.
- If VERTICAL and HORIZONTAL are omitted, all defaults are in effect. If VERTICAL and HORIZONTAL are included, only those defaults explicitly altered are changed.

The following keywords are available for both VERTICAL and HORIZONTAL:

'label'	*Label for axis.* The label can contain up to 40 characters. A label that cannot fit in the frame is truncated. The default is the variable label for the variable plotted on that axis, or the variable name if no variable label has been specified.
MIN (n)	*Minimum axis value.* If you specify a minimum value greater than the observed minimum value, some points will not be included in the plot. The default is the minimum observed value.
MAX (n)	*Maximum axis value.* If you specify a maximum value less than the observed maximum value, some points will not be included in the plot. The default is the maximum observed value.
UNIFORM	*Uniform values on axis.* All plots specified on that PLOT subcommand will have the same scale on that axis. A uniform scale is implied when both MIN and MAX are specified. If UNIFORM is specified, PLOT determines the minimum and maximum observed values across all variables on the PLOT subcommand.
REFERENCE(values)	*Reference lines.* The values at which reference lines should be drawn are separated by blanks or commas. The default is no reference lines.
STANDARDIZE	*Plot standardized variables.* Standardized variables are useful for overlay plots of variables with different scales. The default is to plot observed values.

TITLE Subcommand

TITLE provides titles for plots.

- TITLE can be specified once before each PLOT subcommand and applies to all plots named on that PLOT subcommand.
- The default title for a bivariate scatterplot or regression plot is the names of the variables in the plot. For other plots, the default is the plot type requested on FORMAT.
- The title can be up to 60 characters long and follows the usual rules for specifying strings (see "String Values in Command Specifications" on p. 15).
- The title is truncated if it exceeds the width specified on the HSIZE subcommand.

MISSING Subcommand

MISSING controls the treatment of cases with missing values.

- MISSING can be specified only once per PLOT command and applies to all plots requested.
- Keywords LISTWISE and PLOTWISE are alternatives. Either one can be specified with INCLUDE. The default is PLOTWISE.

DEFAULT *Exclude cases with system-missing or user-missing values for any variables in a plot from that plot.*

PLOTWISE *Delete cases with missing values plotwise.* Cases with missing values for any variable in a plot are not included in that plot. In overlay plots, PLOTWISE applies separately to each overlaid plot in the frame, not to the full list specified on the PLOT subcommand.

LISTWISE *Delete cases with missing values listwise.* Cases with missing values for any variable named on the PLOT subcommand are deleted from all plots specified on that PLOT subcommand.

INCLUDE *Treat user-missing values as valid values.* Only cases with system-missing values are excluded according to the missing-value treatment specified.

PLUM

PLUM is available in the Advanced Models option.

```
PLUM dependent variable [BY factor varlist] [WITH covariate varlist]

[/CRITERIA = [CIN({95** })]] [DELTA({0**   })] [MXITER({100**})]] [MXSTEP({5**})]]
                  {value}        {value }         {n    }          {n  }
              [LCONVERGE({0**  })]] [PCONVERGE({1.0E-6**})]] [SINGULAR({1.0E-8**})]]
                        {value}              {value   }              {value   }
              [BIAS] ]

[/LINK = {CAUCHIT}]
         {CLOGLOG}
         {LOGIT**}
         {NLOGLOG}
         {PROBIT }

[/LOCATION = [effect effect ...] ]

[/MISSING = {EXCLUDE**}]
            {INCLUDE  }

[/PRINT = [CELLINFO] [CORB] [COVB] [FIT] [HISTORY({1})] [KERNEL]
                                                 {n}
          [TPARALLEL] [PARAMETER] [SUMMARY]]

[/SAVE = [ESTPROB [(rootname [:{25**}])]] [PREDCAT [(newname)]] [PCPROB [(newname)]]
                              {n  }        [ACPROB [(newname)] ]

[/SCALE = [effect effect ...] ]

[/TEST [(valuelist)] = ['label'] effect valuelist [effect valuelist] ...;
       [effect valuelist [effect valuelist] ...;] ... ]

[/TEST [(valuelist)] = ['label'] ALL list; [ALL list;] ... ].
```

Note: Default parameters are shown in **bold**. Passive default parameters (i.e., those in effect when a subcommand and a keyword are specified without the parameter value) are not further marked. Active defaults (i.e., those in effect even if a subcommand or/and a keyword is omitted) are marked with **.

Overview

This procedure makes use of a general class of models to allow you to analyze the relationship between a polytomous ordinal dependent variable and a set of predictors. These models utilize the ordinal nature of the dependent variable and eliminate the need for rescaling.

Options

Link Functions. Five link functions are available for specifying the model with the LINK subcommand.

Tuning the Algorithm. You can control the values of algorithm-tuning parameters with the CRITERIA subcommand.

Optional Output. You can request additional output through the PRINT subcommand.

880

Basic Specification

The basic specification is one dependent variable.

Syntax Rules

- Minimum syntax—one dependent variable must be specified.
- The variable specification must come first and can be specified only once.
- Subcommands can be specified in any order.
- When subcommands (except the TEST subcommand) are repeated, previous specifications are discarded and the last subcommand is in effect.
- Empty subcommands except the LOCATION and the SCALE subcommands are ignored. An empty LOCATION or SCALE subcommand indicates a simple additive model.
- The words BY, WITH, and WITHIN are reserved keywords in this procedure.

Variable List

The variable list specifies the dependent variable, factors, and covariates in the model.

- The dependent variable must be the first specification on the command line.
- The dependent variable is assumed to be an ordinal variable and can be of any type (numeric versus string). The order is determined by sorting the level of the dependent variable in ascending order. The lowest value defines the first category.
- Factor variables can be of any type (numeric versus string). Factor levels are sorted in ascending order. The lowest value defines the first category.
- Covariate variables must be numeric.
- Names of the factors follow the dependent variable separated by the keyword BY.
- Enter the covariates, if any, following the factors. Use the keyword WITH to separate covariates from factors (if any) and the dependent variable.

Weight Variable

- If an SPSS WEIGHT variable is specified, this procedure will take the non-missing weight values, rounded to the nearest integer, as frequencies.
- Cases with negative frequencies are always excluded.

CRITERIA Subcommand

The CRITERIA subcommand offers controls on the iterative algorithm used for estimation, specifies numerical tolerance for checking singularity, and offers options to customize your output.

BIAS	*Bias Value Added to All Observed Cell Frequencies.* Specify a non-negative value less than 1. The default value is 0.0.
CIN	*Confidence Interval Level.* Specify a value greater than or equal to 0 and less than 100. The default value is 95.
DELTA	*Delta Value Added to Observed Zero Frequency.* Specify a non-negative value less than 1. The default value is 0.0.
LCONVERGE	*Log-Likelihood Function Convergence Criterion.* Convergence is assumed if the absolute change or relative change in the log-likelihood function is less than this value. The criterion is not used if the value is 0. Specify a non-negative value. The default value is 0.
MXITER	*Maximum Number of Iterations.* Specify a non-negative integer. The default value is 100. Specifying 0 gives the initial estimates.
MXSTEP	*Maximum Step-Halving Allowed.* Specify a positive integer. The default value is 5.
PCONVERGE	*Parameter Estimates Convergence Criterion.* Convergence is assumed if the maximum absolute change in each of the parameter estimates is less than this value. The criterion is not used if the value is 0. Specify a non-negative value. The default value is 10^{-6}.
SINGULAR	*Value Used as Tolerance in Checking Singularity.* Specify a positive value. The default value is 10^{-8}.

LINK Subcommand

The LINK subcommand offers five link functions to specify the model.

- If LINK is not specified, LOGIT is the default.
- The five keywords are mutually exclusive. Only one of them can be specified and only once.

CAUCHIT	*Cauchit Function.* $f(x) = \tan(\pi(x - 0.5))$.
CLOGLOG	*Complementary Log-log Function.* $f(x) = \log(-\log(1 - x))$.
LOGIT	*Logit Function.* $f(x) = \log(x / (1 - x))$. This is the default link function.
NLOGLOG	*Negative Log-log Function.* $f(x) = -\log(-\log(x))$.
PROBIT	*Probit Function.* $f(x) = \Phi^{-1}(x)$, where Φ^{-1} is the inverse standard normal cumulative distribution function.

LOCATION Subcommand

The LOCATION subcommand specifies the location model.

- Specify a list of terms to be included in the location model, separated by commas or spaces.
- The default location model is generated if the subcommand is not specified or empty. The default model contains: 1) the intercept, 2) all the covariates (if specified) in the order they are specified, and 3) all the main factorial effects in the order they are specified in the variable list.
- To include the intercept term explicitly, enter the keyword INTERCEPT on the subcommand.
- To include a main effect term, enter the name of the factor on the subcommand.
- To include an interaction effect term among factors, use the keyword BY or the asterisk (*) to join factors involved in the interaction. For example, A*B*C means a three-way interaction effect of A, B, and C, where A, B, and C are factors. The expression A BY B BY C is equivalent to A*B*C. Factors inside an interaction effect must be distinct. Expressions such as A*C*A and A*A are invalid. The keyword INTERCEPT cannot be used to construct an interaction term.
- To include a nested effect term, use the keyword WITHIN or a pair of parentheses on the subcommand. For example, A(B) means that A is nested within B, where A and B are factors. The expression A WITHIN B is equivalent to A(B). Factors inside a nested effect must be distinct. Expressions such as A(A) and A(B*A) are invalid.
- Multiple level nesting is supported. For example, A(B(C)) means that B is nested within C, and A is nested within B(C). When more than one pair of parentheses is present, each pair of parentheses must be enclosed or nested within another pair of parentheses. Thus, A(B)(C) is not valid.
- Nesting within an interaction effect is valid. For example, A(B*C) means A is nested within B*C.
- Interactions among nested effects are allowed. The correct syntax is the interaction followed by the common nested effect inside the parentheses. For example, interaction between A and B within levels of C should be specified as A*B(C) instead of A(C)*B(C).
- To include a covariate term in the model, enter the name of the covariate on the subcommand.
- Covariates can be connected, but not nested, using the keyword BY or the asterisk (*) operator. For example, X*X is the product of X and itself. This is equivalent to a covariate whose values are the square of those of X. On the contrary, X(Y) is invalid.
- Factor and covariate effects can be connected in many ways. No effects can be nested within a covariate effect. Suppose A and B are factors and X and Y are covariates. Examples of valid combination of factor and covariate effects are A*X, A*B*X, X(A), X(A*B), X*A(B), X*Y(A*B), and A*B*X*Y.

MISSING Subcommand

By default, cases with missing values for any of the variables on the variable list are excluded from the analysis. The MISSING subcommand allows you to include cases with user-missing values.

- If MISSING is not specified, the default is EXCLUDE.
- Listwise deletion is always used in this procedure.
- Keywords EXCLUDE and INCLUDE are mutually exclusive. Only one of them can be specified and only once.

EXCLUDE   *Exclude Both User-Missing and System-Missing Values.* This is the default.

INCLUDE   *User-Missing Values are Treated as Valid.* System-missing values cannot be included in the analysis.

PRINT Subcommand

The PRINT subcommand controls the display of optional output. If no PRINT subcommand is specified, default output includes a case-processing summary table.

CELLINFO   *Cell Information.* Observed and expected frequencies by category and cumulative, Pearson residual for cumulative and category frequencies, and observed and expected probabilities of each response category separately and cumulatively by covariate pattern combination.

CORB   *Asymptotic Correlation Matrix of the Parameter Estimates.*

COVB   *Asymptotic Covariance Matrix of the Parameter Estimates.*

FIT   *Goodness-of-Fit Statistics.* The Pearson's Chi-square and the Likelihood Ratio Chi-square statistics. The statistics are computed based on the classification specified on the variable list.

HISTORY   *Iteration History.* The table contains log-likelihood function value and parameter estimates every *n* iterations. The default value is $n = 1$. The first and the last iterations are always printed if HISTORY is specified and regardless of the value of *n*.

KERNEL   *Use the kernel of the log-likelihood function for display instead of the complete log-likelihood function.*

TPARALLEL   *Test of Parallel Lines Assumption.* Produce a chi-squared score test of the parallel lines assumption.

PARAMETER   *Parameter Statistics.* The parameter estimates, the standard errors, the significances, and the confidence interval.

SUMMARY   *Model Summary.* The Cox & Snell's R^2, the Nagelkerke's R^2, and the McFadden's R^2 statistics.

SAVE Subcommand

The SAVE subcommand puts casewise post-estimation statistics back into the active file.

- The new variables must have valid SPSS variable names that are not in use in the working file.
- The rootname must be a valid SPSS variable name.
- The new variables are saved to the working file in the order the keywords are specified on the subcommand.

ESTPROB   *Estimated probabilities of classifying a factor/covariate pattern into the response categories.* The predicted probabilities of the first n categories are saved. The default number of categories is 25. To specify a number of categories without a rootname, put a colon before the number.

PREDCAT   *The response category that has the maximum expected probability for a factor/covariate pattern.*

PCPROB   *Estimated probability of classifying a factor/covariate pattern into the predicted category.* This probability is the maximum of the estimated probabilities of the factor/covariate pattern.

ACPROB   *Estimated probability of classifying a factor/covariate pattern into the actual category.*

SCALE Subcommand

The SCALE subcommand specifies the scale component in the model.

- Specify a list of terms to be included in the model, separated by commas or spaces.
- The model will have no scale component if the subcommand is omitted.
- No scale component is generated if the subcommand is not specified or empty.
- To include a main effect term, enter the name of the factor on the subcommand.
- The keyword INTERCEPT is not allowed on the subcommand.
- To include an interaction effect term among factors, use the keyword BY or the asterisk (*) to join factors involved in the interaction. For example, A*B*C means a three-way interaction effect of A, B, and C, where A, B, and C are factors. The expression A BY B BY C is equivalent to A*B*C. Factors inside an interaction effect must be distinct. Expressions such as A*C*A and A*A are invalid.
- To include a nested effect term, use the keyword WITHIN or a pair of parentheses on the subcommand. For example, A(B) means that A is nested within B, where A and B are factors. The expression A WITHIN B is equivalent to A(B). Factors inside a nested effect must be distinct. Expressions such as A(A) and A(B*A) are invalid.
- Multiple level nesting is supported. For example, A(B(C)) means that B is nested within C, and A is nested within B(C). When more than one pair of parentheses is present, each pair of parentheses must be enclosed or nested within another pair of parentheses. Thus, A(B)(C) is not valid.

- Nesting within an interaction effect is valid. For example, A(B*C) means that A is nested within B*C.

- Interactions among nested effects are allowed. The correct syntax is the interaction followed by the common nested effect inside the parentheses. For example, interaction between A and B within levels of C should be specified as A*B(C) instead of A(C)*B(C).

- To include a covariate term in the model, enter the name of the covariate on the subcommand.

- Covariates can be connected, but not nested, using the keyword BY or the asterisk (*) operator. For example, X*X is the product of X and itself. This is equivalent to a covariate whose values are the square of those of X. On the contrary, X(Y) is invalid.

- Factor and covariate effects can be connected in many ways. No effects can be nested within a covariate effect. Suppose A and B are factors, and X and Y are covariates. Examples of valid combination of factor and covariate effects are A*X, A*B*X, X(A), X(A*B), X*A(B), X*Y(A*B), and A*B*X*Y.

TEST Subcommand

The TEST subcommand allows you to customize your hypothesis tests by directly specifying null hypotheses as linear combinations of parameters.

- TEST is offered only through syntax.

- Multiple TEST subcommands are allowed. Each is handled independently.

- The basic format of the TEST subcommand is an optional list of values enclosed in a pair of parentheses, an optional label in quotes, an effect name or the keyword ALL, and a list of values.

- To specify the coefficient for the intercept, use the keyword INTERCEPT. The number of values after INTERCEPT must be equal to the number of response categories minus 1.

- When multiple linear combinations are specified within the same TEST subcommand, a semicolon terminates each linear combination, except the last one.

- The linear combinations are separately tested for each category of the dependent variable and then simultaneously tested for all the categories.

- If specified, the value list that immediately follows the subcommand name is the constant that the linear combinations are equated to under the null hypotheses. If this value list is omitted, the constants are assumed to be all zeros.

- The optional label is a string with a maximum length of 255 characters (or 127 double-byte characters). Only one label per TEST subcommand can be specified.

- Only valid effects appearing or implied on the LOCATION or the SCALE subcommands can be specified in a linear combination. If an effect appears in both subcommands, then enter the effect only once on the TEST subcommand.

- To specify coefficient for the intercept, use the keyword INTERCEPT. Only one value is expected to follow INTERCEPT.

- The number of values following an effect name must equal the number of parameters (including the redundant ones) corresponding to that effect. For example, if the effect A*B takes up six parameters, then exactly six values must follow A*B.

- A number can be specified as a fraction with a positive denominator. For example, 1/3 or -1/3 are valid, but 1/-3 is invalid.

- When ALL is specified, only a list of values can follow. The number of values must equal the combined number of LOCATION and SCALE parameters (including the redundant ones).

- Effects appearing or implied on the LOCATION or the SCALE subcommands but not specified on the TEST are assumed to take the value 0 for all their parameters.

- Effect names and the ALL keywords are mutually exclusive within a single TEST subcommand.

- If ALL is specified for the first row in a TEST matrix, then all subsequent rows should begin with the ALL keyword.

- If effects are specified for the first row in a TEST matrix, then all subsequent rows should use effect name (thus ALL is not allowed).

POINT

```
POINT KEY=varname [FILE=file]
```

Example

```
FILE HANDLE DRIVERS/ file specifications.
POINT FILE=DRIVERS /KEY=#FRSTAGE.
```

Overview

POINT establishes the location at which sequential access begins (or resumes) in a keyed file. A keyed file is a file that provides access to information by a record key. An example of a keyed file is a file containing a social security number and other information about a firm's employees. The social security number can be used to identify the records in the file. For additional information on keyed files, see KEYED DATA LIST.

POINT prepares for reading the key-sequenced data set sequentially from a point that the key value controls. Data selection commands can then be used to limit the file to the portion you want to analyze. A DATA LIST command is used to read the data. To read keyed files (and also direct access files), see the KEYED DATA LIST command.

Basic Specification

The basic specification is the KEY subcommand and a string variable. The value of the string variable is used as the file key for determining where sequential retrieval (via DATA LIST) begins or resumes.

Subcommand Order

- Subcommands can be named in any order.
- Each POINT command must precede its corresponding DATA LIST command.

Syntax Rules

- POINT can be used more than once to change the order of retrieval during processing.
- POINT must be specified in an input program and therefore cannot be used to add cases to an existing file.

Operations

- The next DATA LIST command executed after the POINT command (for the same file) will read a record whose key value is at least as large as that of the specified key. To prevent an infinite loop in which the same record is read again and again, either the value of the variable specified on KEY must change from case to case or the POINT command must be set up to execute only once.

- If the file contains a record whose key exactly matches the value of the KEY variable, the next execution of DATA LIST will read that record, the second execution of DATA LIST will read the next record, and so on.

- If an exact match is not found, the results depend on the operating system. On IBM implementations, reading will begin or resume at the record that has the next higher key. If the value of the key is shorter than the file key, the value of the key variable is logically extended with the lowest character in the collating sequence. For example, if the value of the key variable is the single letter M, retrieval would begin or resume at the first record that had a key (regardless of length) beginning with the letter M or a character higher in the collating sequence.

- POINT does not report on whether the file contains a record that exactly matches the specified key. The only way to check for missing records is to display the data read by the subsequent DATA LIST command using LIST.

Example

```
* Select a subset of records from a keyed file.

FILE HANDLE      DRIVERS/ file specifications.
INPUT PROGRAM.
STRING           #FRSTAGE(A2).
DO IF            #FRSTAGE = ' '.     /* First case check
+  COMPUTE       #FRSTAGE = '26'.    /* Initial key
+  POINT         FILE=DRIVERS /KEY=#FRSTAGE.
END IF.
DATA LIST        FILE=DRIVERS NOTABLE/
                 AGE 19-20(A) SEX 21(A) TICKETS 12-13.
DO IF            AGE > '30'.
+  END FILE.
END IF.
END INPUT PROGRAM.
LIST.
```

- This example illustrates how to execute POINT for only the first case. The file contains information about traffic violations, and it uses the individual's age as the key. Ages between 26 and 30 are selected.

- FILE HANDLE specifies the file handle DRIVERS.

- The INPUT PROGRAM and END INPUT PROGRAM commands begin and end the block of commands that build cases. POINT must appear in an input program.

- STRING declares the string variable *#FRSTAGE*, whose value will be used as the key on the POINT command. Since *#FRSTAGE* is a string variable, it is initialized as blanks.

- The first DO IF—END IF structure is executed only if no records have been read; that is, when *#FRSTAGE* is blank. When *#FRSTAGE* is blank, COMPUTE resets *#FRSTAGE* to 26, which is the initial value. POINT is executed, and it causes the first execution of DATA LIST to read a record whose key is at least 26. Since the value of *#FRSTAGE* is now 26, the DO IF—END IF structure is not executed again.

- DATA LIST reads the variables *AGE*, *SEX*, and *TICKETS* from the file *DRIVERS*.
- The second DO IF—END IF structure executes an END FILE command as soon as a record is read that contains a driver's age greater than 30. The program does not add this last case to the working file when it ends the file (see END FILE).

Example

```
FILE HANDLE DRIVERS/ file specifications.
POINT FILE=DRIVERS /KEY=#FRSTAGE.
```

- FILE HANDLE defines the handle for the data file to be read by POINT. The handle is specified on the FILE subcommand on POINT.
- KEY on POINT specifies the key variable. The key variable must be a string, and it must already exist as the result of a prior DATA LIST, KEYED DATA LIST, or transformation command.

FILE Subcommand

FILE specifies a file handle for the keyed data file. The file handle must have been previously defined on a FILE HANDLE command.

- FILE is optional.
- If FILE is omitted, POINT reads from the last file specified on an input command, such as DATA LIST.

Example

```
FILE HANDLE DRIVERS/ file specifications.
POINT FILE=DRIVERS /KEY=#NXTCASE.
```

- FILE HANDLE specifies *DRIVERS* as the file handle for the data. The FILE subcommand on POINT specifies file handle *DRIVERS*.

KEY Subcommand

KEY specifies the variable whose value will be used as the file key for determining where sequential retrieval by DATA LIST will begin or resume. This variable must be a string variable, and it must already exist as the result of a prior DATA LIST, KEYED DATA LIST, or transformation command.

- KEY is required. Its only specification is a single variable. The variable can be a permanent variable or a scratch variable.
- Where the keys on a file are inherently numbers, such as social security numbers, the STRING function can be used to convert the numeric variable to a string (see "Conversion Functions" on p. 53).

Example

```
FILE HANDLE DRIVERS/ file specifications.
POINT FILE=DRIVERS /KEY=#NXTCASE.
```

- KEY indicates that the value of the existing scratch variable *#FRSTAGE* will be used as the key to reading each record.
- Variable *#FRSTAGE* must be an existing string variable.

PPLOT

```
PPLOT [VARIABLES=] varlist

[/DISTRIBUTION={NORMAL(a,b)** }   ]
               {EXPONENTIAL(a) }
               {WEIBUL(a,b)    }
               {PARETO(a,b)    }
               {LNORMAL(a,b)   }
               {BETA(a,b)      }
               {GAMMA(a,b)     }
               {LOGISTIC(a,b)  }
               {LAPLACE(a,b)   }
               {UNIFORM(a,b)   }
               {HNORMAL(a)     }
               {CHI(df)        }
               {STUDENT(df)    }

[/FRACTION={BLOM**}]
           {RANKIT}
           {TUKEY }
           {VW    }

[/TIES={MEAN**  }]
       {LOW     }
       {HIGH    }
       {CONDENSE}

[/{NOSTANDARDIZE**}]
  {STANDARDIZE     }

[/TYPE={Q-Q**}]
       {P-P  }

[/PLOT={BOTH**   }]
       {NORMAL   }
       {DETRENDED}

[/DIFF={1}]
       {n}

[/SDIFF={1}]
        {n}

[/PERIOD=n]

[/{NOLOG**}]
  {LN     }

[/APPLY [='model name']]
```

**Default if the subcommand is omitted.

Example

```
PPLOT VARX
  /FRACTION=TUKEY
  /DIFF=2.
```

Overview

PPLOT (alias NPPLOT) produces probability plots of one or more sequence or time series variables. The variables can be standardized, differenced, and/or transformed before plotting. Expected normal values or deviations from expected normal values can be plotted.

Options

Modifying the Variables. You can request a natural log transformation of the sequence or time series variables using the LN subcommand and seasonal and nonseasonal differencing to any degree using the SDIFF and DIFF subcommands. With seasonal differencing, you can specify the periodicity on the PERIOD subcommand. You can also plot standardized series using the STANDARDIZE subcommand.

Plot Type. You can request p-p (proportion-proportion) or q-q (quantile-quantile) plots on the TYPE subcommand. With the PLOT subcommand you can display normal plots, detrended plots, or both.

Distribution Type. You can specify the distribution type on the DISTRIBUTION subcommand. The cumulative distribution function (CDF) and the inverse distribution function (IDF) for the specified distribution type are used to compute the expected values in the p-p and q-q plots, respectively.

Score Calculations. On the FRACTION subcommand, you can specify one of several fractional rank formulas to use for estimating the empirical distribution in p-p plots and computing expected quantiles in q-q plots. You can specify the treatment of tied values on the TIE subcommand.

Basic Specification

The basic specification is one or more variable names.
- For each variable specified, PPLOT produces two q-q plots of the observed values, one versus expected normal values and the other versus deviations from normal values. By default, expected normal values are calculated using Blom's transformation.
- Observed values define the horizontal axis, and expected normal values or deviations define the vertical axis.

Subcommand Order

- Subcommands can be specified in any order.

Syntax Rules

- VARIABLES can be specified only once.
- Other subcommands can be specified more than once, but only the last specification of each one is executed.

Operations

- Subcommand specifications apply to all plots produced by PPLOT.
- If the LN subcommand is specified, any differencing or standardization requested on that PPLOT is done on the log-transformed series.
- If differencing (DIFF or SDIFF) is specified, any standardization is done on the differenced series.

Limitations

- Maximum 1 VARIABLES subcommand. There is no limit on the number of variables named on the list.

Example

```
PPLOT VARX
  /FRACTION=TUKEY
  /DIFF=2.
```

- This command produces two normal q-q plots of *VARX*, one not detrended and the other detrended.
- The expected quantile values are calculated using Tukey's transformation.
- The variable is differenced twice before plotting.

VARIABLES Subcommand

VARIABLES specifies the sequence or time series variables to be plotted and is the only required subcommand. The actual keyword VARIABLES can be omitted.

DISTRIBUTION Subcommand

DISTRIBUTION specifies the distribution type of your data. The default is NORMAL if the subcommand is not specified or is specified without a keyword. If the parameters of the distribution type are not specified, DISTRIBUTION estimates them from the sample data and displays them with the plots.

NORMAL(a,b)   *Normal distribution.* The location parameter a can be any numeric value, while the scale parameter b must be positive. If they are not specified, DISTRIBUTION estimates them from the sample mean and sample standard deviation.

EXPONENTIAL(a)   *Exponential distribution.* The scale parameter a must be positive. If the parameter is not specified, DISTRIBUTION estimates it from the sample mean. Negative observations are not allowed.

WEIBULL(a,b)	*Weibull distribution.* The scale and shape parameters *a* and *b* must be positive. If they are not specified, DISTRIBUTION estimates them using the least square method. Negative observations are not allowed.
PARETO(a,b)	*Pareto distribution.* The threshold and shape parameters *a* and *b* must be positive. If they are not specified, DISTRIBUTION assumes *a* equals the minimum observation and estimates *b* by the maximum likelihood method. Negative observations are not allowed.
LNORMAL(a,b)	*Lognormal distribution.* The scale and shape parameters *a* and *b* must be positive. If they are not specified, DISTRIBUTION estimates them from the mean and standard deviation of the natural logarithm of the sample data. Negative observations are not allowed.
BETA(a,b)	*Beta distribution.* The shape1 and shape2 parameters *a* and *b* must be positive. If they are not specified, DISTRIBUTION estimates them from the sample mean and sample standard deviation. All observations must be between 0 and 1, inclusive.
GAMMA(a,b)	*Gamma distribution.* The shape and scale parameters *a* and *b* must be positive. If they are not specified, DISTRIBUTION estimates them from the sample mean and sample standard deviation if they are not specified. Negative observations are not allowed.
LOGISTIC(a,b)	*Logistic distribution.* LOGISTIC takes a location and a scale parameter (*a* and *b*). The scale parameter (*b*) must be positive. If the parameters are not specified, DISTRIBUTION estimates them from the sample mean and sample standard deviation.
LAPLACE(a,b)	*Laplace or double exponential distribution.* LAPLACE takes a location and a scale parameter (*a* and *b*). The scale parameter (*b*) must be positive. If the parameters are not specified, DISTRIBUTION estimates them from the sample mean and sample standard deviation.
UNIFORM(a,b)	*Uniform distribution.* UNIFORM takes a minimum and a maximum parameter (*a* and *b*). *a* must be equal to or greater than *b*. If the parameters are not specified, DISTRIBUTION assumes them from the sample data.
HNORMAL(a)	*Half-normal distribution.* Data are assumed to be location free or centralized. (Location parameter=0.) You can specify the scale parameter *a* or let DISTRIBUTION estimate it using the maximum likelihood method.
CHI (df)	*Chi-square distribution.* You must specify the degrees of freedom *df*. Negative observations are not allowed.
STUDENT(df)	*Student's t distribution.* You must specify the degrees of freedom *df*.

FRACTION Subcommand

FRACTION specifies the formula to be used in estimating the empirical distribution in p-p plots and calculating the expected quantile values in q-q plots.

- Only one formula can be specified. If more than one is specified, only the first is used.
- If the FRACTION subcommand is not specified, BLOM is used by default.
- These formulas will produce noticeable differences only for short series.

Four formulas are available:

BLOM   Blom's transformation, defined by the formula $(r - (3/8)) / (n + (1/4))$, where n is the number of observations and r is the rank, ranging from 1 to n (Blom, 1958).

RANKIT   Uses the formula $(r - (1/2)) / n$, where n is the number of observations and r is the rank, ranging from 1 to n (Chambers et al., 1983).

TUKEY   Tukey's transformation, defined by the formula $(r - (1/3)) / (n + (1/3))$, where n is the number of observations and r is the rank, ranging from 1 to n (Tukey, 1962).

VW   Van der Waerden's transformation, defined by the formula $r / (n + 1)$, where n is the number of observations and r is the rank, ranging from 1 to n (Lehmann, 1975).

Example

```
PPLOT VARX
  /FRACTION=VW.
```

- This PPLOT command uses van der Waerden's transformation to approximate the proportion estimate p, which is used in the inverse distribution function.
- By default, two q-q plots are produced.

TIES Subcommand

TIES determines the way tied values are handled. The default method is MEAN.

MEAN   *Mean rank of tied values is used for ties.* This is the default.

LOW   *Lowest rank of tied values is used for ties.*

HIGH   *Highest rank of tied values is used for ties.*

CONDENSE   *Consecutive ranks with ties sharing the same value.* Each distinct value of the ranked variable is assigned a consecutive rank. Ties share the same rank.

TYPE Subcommand

TYPE specifies the type of plot to produce. The default is Q-Q. Figure 1 shows a quantile-quantile plot and Figure 2 shows a proportion-proportion plot using the same data (with a normal distribution).

Q-Q   *Quantile-quantile plots.* The quantiles of the observed values are plotted against the quantiles of the specified distribution.

P-P   *Proportion-proportion plots.* The observed cumulative proportion is plotted against the expected cumulative proportion if the data were a sample from a specified distribution.

Figure 1   Normal q-q plot of current salary

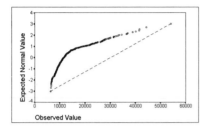

Figure 2   Normal p-p plot of current salary

PLOT Subcommand

PLOT specifies whether to produce a plot of observed values versus expected values, a plot of observed values versus deviations from expected values, or both. Figure 1 and Figure 2 are nondetrended plots. Figure 3 shows a detrended q-q plot.

BOTH   *Display both detrended and nondetrended normal plots.* This is the default.

NORMAL   *Display nondetrended normal plots.* The observed values are plotted against the expected values.

DETRENDED   *Display detrended plots.* The observed values are plotted against the deviations from the expected values.

- If you specify PLOT more than once, only the last specification is executed.
- Deviations are calculated by subtracting the expected value from the observed value.

- In low resolution, a dash is used in a detrended plot to indicate where the deviation from the expected is 0.

Figure 3   Detrended normal q-q plot of current salary

STANDARDIZE and NOSTANDARDIZE Subcommands

STANDARDIZE transforms the sequence or time series variables into a sample with a mean of 0 and a standard deviation of 1. NOSTANDARDIZE indicates that the series should not be standardized and is the default.

- There are no additional specifications on the STANDARDIZE or NOSTANDARDIZE subcommands.
- Only the last STANDARDIZE or NOSTANDARDIZE subcommand on the PPLOT command is executed.
- The STANDARDIZE and NOSTANDARDIZE subcommands have no effect on expected values, which are always standardized.
- NOSTANDARDIZE is generally used with an APPLY subcommand to turn off a previous STANDARDIZE specification.

Example

```
PPLOT VARX
  /STANDARDIZE.
```

- This example produces two q-q normal probability plots of *VARX* with standardized observed values.

DIFF Subcommand

DIFF specifies the degree of differencing used before plotting to convert a nonstationary variable to a stationary one with a constant mean and variance.

- You can specify any positive integer on DIFF.
- If DIFF is specified without a value, the default is 1.
- The number of values plotted decreases by 1 for each degree of differencing.

Example

```
PPLOT TICKETS
  /DIFF=2.
```

- In this example, *TICKETS* is differenced twice before the expected and observed values are plotted.

SDIFF Subcommand

If the variable exhibits a seasonal or periodic pattern, you can use the SDIFF subcommand to seasonally difference the variable before plotting.

- The specification on SDIFF indicates the degree of seasonal differencing and can be any positive integer.
- If SDIFF is specified without a value, the degree of seasonal differencing defaults to 1.
- The number of seasons plotted decreases by 1 for each degree of seasonal differencing.
- The length of the period used by SDIFF is specified on the PERIOD subcommand. If the PERIOD subcommand is not specified, the periodicity established on the TSET or DATE command is used (see the PERIOD subcommand below).

PERIOD Subcommand

PERIOD indicates the length of the period to be used by the SDIFF subcommand.

- The specification on PERIOD indicates how many observations are in one period or season. You can specify any positive integer on PERIOD.
- The PERIOD subcommand is ignored if it is used without the SDIFF subcommand.
- If PERIOD is not specified, the periodicity established on TSET PERIOD is in effect. If TSET PERIOD is not specified either, the periodicity established on the DATE command is used. If periodicity was not established anywhere, the SDIFF subcommand will not be executed.

Example

```
PPLOT TICKETS
  /SDIFF=1
  /PERIOD=12.
```

- This command applies 1 degree of seasonal differencing with 12 observations per season to the variable *TICKETS*.

LN and NOLOG Subcommands

LN transforms the data using the natural logarithm (base e) to remove varying amplitude. NOLOG indicates that the data should not be log transformed. NOLOG is the default.

- There are no additional specifications on LN or NOLOG.
- Only the last LN or NOLOG subcommand on a PPLOT command is executed.

- If a natural log transformation is requested, cases with values that are less than or equal to 0 will be set to system-missing, since nonpositive values cannot be log-transformed.
- NOLOG is generally used with an APPLY subcommand to turn off a previous LN specification.

Example

```
PPLOT TICKETS
  /FRACTION=TUKEY
  /DIFF=1
  /LN.
PPLOT EARNINGS
  /APPLY
  /NOLOG.
```

- The first command requests a natural log transformation of variable *TICKETS* before plotting.
- The second command applies the previous PPLOT specifications to variable *EARNINGS*. However, *EARNINGS* is not log-transformed before plotting.

APPLY Subcommand

APPLY allows you to produce a plot using previously defined specifications without having to repeat the PPLOT subcommands.

- The only specification on APPLY is the name of a previous model in quotes. If a model name is not specified, the model specified on the previous PPLOT command is used.
- To change any plot specifications, specify the subcommands of only those portions you want to change after the APPLY subcommand.
- If no variables are specified, the variables that were specified for the original plot are used.
- To change the variables used with the model, enter new variable names before or after the APPLY subcommand.
- The distribution type is applied but the parameters are not.

Example

```
PPLOT X1
  /FRACTION=TUKEY.
PPLOT Z1
  /APPLY.
```

- The first command produces two q-q normal probability plots of *X1* using Tukey's transformation to compute the expected values.
- The second command requests the same plots for variable *Z1*.

Example

```
PPLOT X1 Y1 Z1
  /FRACTION=VW.
PPLOT APPLY
  /FRACTION=BLOM.
```

- The first command uses van der Waerden's transformation to calculate expected normal values of *X1*, *Y1*, and *Z1*.
- The second command uses Blom's transformation for the same three series.

Example

```
PPLOT VARX
  /FRACTION=RANKIT
  /DIFF
  /STANDARDIZE.
PPLOT VARY
  /APPLY
  /NOSTANDARDIZE.
```

- The first command differences and standardizes series *VARX* and then produces a normal probability plot using the RANKIT transformation.
- The second command applies the previous plot specifications to *VARY* but does not standardize the series.

References

Blom, G. 1958. *Statistical estimates and transformed beta variables.* New York: John Wiley and Sons.

Chambers, J. M., W. S. Cleveland, B. Kleiner, and P. A. Tukey. 1983. *Graphical methods for data analysis.* Belmont, Calif.: Wadsworth International Group; Boston: Duxbury Press.

Lehmann, E. L. 1975. *Nonparametrics: Statistical methods based on ranks.* San Francisco: Holden-Day.

Tukey, J. W. 1962. The future of data analysis. *Annals of Mathematical Statistics,* 33:22.

PREDICT

```
PREDICT  [{start date      }] [THRU [{end date       }]]
         {start case number}           {end case number}
                                       {END            }
```

Example

```
PREDICT Y 61 THRU Y 65.
```

Overview

PREDICT specifies the observations that mark the beginning and end of the forecast period. If the forecast period extends beyond the length of the series, PREDICT extends the series in the working data file to allow room for the forecast observations.

Basic Specification

The minimum specification on PREDICT is either the start or the end of the range, or keyword THRU. PREDICT sets up a forecast period beginning and ending with the dates or case numbers specified. The default starting point is the observation immediately after the end of the series or, if USE is specified, the observation immediately after the end of the use range (the historical period). The default end is the last observation in the series.

Syntax Rules

- You can specify a start, an end, or both.
- The start and end are specified as either date specifications or case (observation) numbers.
- Date specifications and case numbers cannot be mixed on one PREDICT command.
- Keyword THRU is required if the end of the range is specified.
- Keyword THRU by itself defines a PREDICT range starting with the first observation after the use range and ending with the end of the series. If USE has not been specified, PREDICT THRU is meaningless.

Date Specifications

- A date specification consists of DATE keyword(s) and value(s) (see DATE). These specifications must correspond to existing date variables.
- If more than one date variable exists, the highest-order one must be included in the date specification.

- Values on keyword YEAR must have the same format (2 or 4 digits) as the YEAR specifications on the DATE command.

Case Specifications

The case number specification is the sequence number of the case (observation) as it is read by the program.

Valid Range

- The start date must precede the end date.
- The start case number must be less than the end case number.
- The start can be any observation ranging from the second observation in the historical period specified on USE to the observation immediately following the end of the historical period. If USE is not specified, the start can be any observation ranging from the second observation in the series to the observation immediately following the end of the series.
- For most models, the start of the predict period should not be too close to the start of the use period.
- The predict and use periods should not be exactly the same.
- The start of the predict period should not precede the start of the use period.

Operations

- PREDICT is executed when the data are read for the next forecasting procedure (ARIMA in SPSS Trends, CURVEFIT in SPSS Base system, and 2SLS in SPSS Regression Models).
- PREDICT is ignored by non-forecasting procedures.
- Case number specifications refer to the sequential numbers assigned to cases as they are read.
- If the forecast period extends beyond the length of the series, PREDICT extends the series in the working data file to allow room for the forecast observations.
- New observations added to the end of existing series will contain non-missing date variables, forecast values (variable *FIT#n*), confidence interval limits (variables *LCL#n* and *UCL#n*), and, for ARIMA models, standard error of the predicted value (*SEP#n*). For all other variables, including the original series, the new cases will be system-missing.
- PREDICT cannot forecast beyond the end of the series for ARIMA with regressors and 2SLS. However, it *can* forecast values for the dependent variable if the independent variables have valid values in the predict period.
- If the use and predict periods overlap, the model is still estimated using all observations in the use period.
- USE and PREDICT can be used together to perform forecasting validation. To do this, specify a use period that ends before the existing end of the series, and specify a predict period starting with the next observation.

- If there is a gap between the end of the use period and the start of the specified predict period, the program will use the first observation after the end of the use period as the start of the predict period. (This is the default.)
- The DATE command turns off all existing USE and PREDICT specifications.
- PREDICT remains in effect in a session until it is changed by another PREDICT command or until a new DATE command is issued.
- If more than one forecasting procedure is specified after PREDICT, the USE command should be specified between procedures so that the original series without any new, system-missing cases will be used each time. Alternatively, you can specify

```
TSET NEWVAR = NONE
```

before the first forecasting procedure so that you can evaluate model statistics without creating new variables or adding new cases with missing values to the original series.

Limitations

Maximum 1 range (one start and/or one end) can be specified per PREDICT command.

Example

```
PREDICT Y 61 THRU Y 65.
```

- This command specifies a forecast period from 1961 to 1965.
- The working data file must include variable *YEAR_*, which in this example contains only the last 2 digits of each year.
- If variable *MONTH_* also exists, the above command is equivalent to

```
PREDICT Y 61 M 1 THRU Y 65 M 12.
```

Example

```
PREDICT 61 THRU 65.
```

- This command specifies a forecast period from the 61st case (observation) to the 65th case.

Example

```
PREDICT W 28 THRU W 56.
```

- This command specifies a forecast period from the 28th week to the 56th week.
- The working data file must include variable *WEEK_*.

- If variable *DAY_* also exists, the above command is equivalent to

  ```
  PREDICT W 28 D 1 THRU W 56 D 7.
  ```

Example

```
PREDICT THRU Y 65.
```

- This command uses the default start date, which is the observation immediately following the end of the use period. If USE is not specified, the default start is the observation immediately following the end of the series.
- The forecast period extends from the start date through year '65.
- The working data file must include variable *YEAR_*.
- Keyword THRU is required.

Example

```
PREDICT THRU CYCLE 4 OBS 17.
```

- This example uses the date variables *OBS_* and *CYCLE_*, which must exist in the working data file.
- *CYCLE*, the highest order, must be included on PREDICT.
- Keyword THRU is required.
- The forecast period extends from the default start up to the 17th observation of cycle 4.

PRESERVE

```
PRESERVE
```

Overview

PRESERVE stores current SET specifications that can later be restored by the RESTORE command. PRESERVE and RESTORE are especially useful with the macro facility. PRE-SERVE—RESTORE sequences can be nested up to five levels.

Basic Specification

The only specification is the command keyword. PRESERVE has no additional specifications.

Example

```
GET FILE=PRSNNL.
FREQUENCIES VAR=DIVISION /STATISTICS=ALL.
PRESERVE.
SET XSORT=NO WIDTH=90 UNDEFINED=NOWARN BLANKS=000 CASE=UPLOW.
SORT CASES BY DIVISION.
REPORT FORMAT=AUTO LIST /VARS=LNAME FNAME DEPT SOCSEC SALARY
  /BREAK=DIVISION /SUMMARY=MEAN.
RESTORE.
```

- GET reads SPSS-format data file *PRSNNL.*
- FREQUENCIES requests a Frequency table and all statistics for variable *DIVISION.*
- PRESERVE stores all current SET specifications.
- SET changes several subcommand settings.
- SORT sorts cases in preparation for a report. Because SET XSORT=NO, the sort program is not used to sort cases; another sort program must be available.
- REPORT requests a report organized by variable *DIVISION.*
- RESTORE reestablishes the SET specifications that were in effect when PRESERVE was specified.

PRINT

```
PRINT [OUTFILE=file] [RECORDS={1}] [{NOTABLE}]
                               {n}   {TABLE  }

 /{1     } varlist [{col location [(format)]}] [varlist...]
  {rec #}           {(format list)          }
                    {*                       }

 [/{2     }...]
   {rec #}
```

Example

```
PRINT / MOHIRED YRHIRED DEPT SALARY NAME.
EXECUTE.
```

Overview

PRINT displays the values of variables for each case in the data. PRINT is designed to be simple enough for a quick check on data definitions and transformations and yet flexible enough for formatting simple reports.

Options

Formats. You can specify formats for the variables (see "Formats" on p. 909).

Strings. You can specify string values within the variable specifications. The strings can be used to label values or to create extra space between values. Strings can also be used as column headings. (See "Strings" on p. 910.)

Output File. You can direct the output to a specified file using the OUTFILE subcommand.

Summary Table. You can display a table that summarizes variable formats with the TABLE subcommand.

Basic Specification

The basic specification is a slash followed by a variable list. The values for all variables named on the list are displayed in the output.

Subcommand Order

Subcommands can be specified in any order. However, all subcommands must be specified before the slash that precedes the start of the variable specifications.

Syntax Rules

- A slash must precede the variable specifications. The first slash begins the definition of the first (and possibly only) line per case of the PRINT display.
- Specified variables must already exist, but they can be numeric, string, scratch, temporary, or system variables. Subscripted variable names, such as *X(1)* for the first element in vector *X,* cannot be used.
- Keyword ALL can be used to display the values of all user-defined variables in the working data file.

Operations

- PRINT is executed once for each case constructed from the data file.
- PRINT is a transformation and will not be executed unless it is followed by a procedure or the EXECUTE command.
- Because PRINT is a transformation command, the output might be mixed with casewise procedure output. Procedures that produce individual case listings (such as LIST) should not be used immediately after PRINT. An intervening EXECUTE or procedure command should be specified.
- Values are displayed with a blank space between them. However, if a format is specified for a variable, the blank space for that variable's values is suppressed.
- Values are displayed in the output as the data are read. The PRINT output appears before the output from the first procedure.
- If more variables are specified than can be displayed in 132 columns or within the width specified on SET WIDTH, the program displays an error message. You must reduce the number of variables or split the output into several records.
- User-missing values are displayed just like valid values. System-missing values are represented by a period.

Example

```
PRINT   / MOHIRED YRHIRED DEPT SALARY NAME.
FREQUENCIES VARIABLES=DEPT.
```

- PRINT displays values for each variable on the variable list. The FREQUENCIES procedure reads the data and causes PRINT to be executed.
- All variables are displayed using their dictionary formats. One blank space separates the values of each variable.

Example

```
PRINT /ALL.
EXECUTE.
```

- PRINT displays values for all user-defined variables in the working data file. The EXECUTE command executes PRINT.

Formats

By default, PRINT uses the dictionary print formats. You can specify formats for some or all variables specified on PRINT. For a string variable, the specified format must have a width at least as large as that of the dictionary format. String values are truncated if the specified width is smaller than that of the dictionary format.

- Format specifications can be either column-style or FORTRAN-like (see DATA LIST). The column location specified with column-style formats or implied with FORTRAN-like formats refers to the column in which the variable will be displayed.

- A format specification following a list of variables applies to all of the variables in the list. Use an asterisk to prevent the specified format from applying to variables preceding the asterisk. The specification of columns locations implies a default print format, and that format will apply to all previous variables if no asterisk is used.

- Printable numeric formats are F, COMMA, DOLLAR, CC, DOT, N, E, PCT, PIBHEX, RBHEX, Z, and the date and time formats. Printable string formats are A and AHEX. Note that hex and binary formats use different widths. For example, the AHEX format must have a width twice that of the corresponding A format. For more information on specifying formats and on the formats available, see DATA LIST and "Variable Formats" on p. 31.

- Format specifications are in effect only for the PRINT command. They do not change the dictionary print formats.

- When a format is specified for a variable, the automatic blank following the variable in the output is suppressed. To preserve the blank between variables, use a string (see "Strings" on p. 910), specify blank columns in the format, or use an X or T format element (see DATA LIST for information on X and T).

Example

```
PRINT / TENURE (F2.0) ' ' MOHIRED YRHIRED DEPT *
        SALARY85 TO SALARY88 (4(DOLLAR8,1X)) NAME.
EXECUTE.
```

- Format F2.0 is specified for *TENURE*. A blank string is specified after *TENURE* because the automatic blank following the variable is suppressed by the format specification.

- *MOHIRED, YRHIRED,* and *DEPT* are displayed with default formats because the asterisk prevents them from receiving the DOLLAR8 format specified for *SALARY85* to *SALARY88*. The automatic blank is preserved for *MOHIRED, YRHIRED,* and *DEPT,* but the blank is suppressed for *SALARY85* to *SALARY88* by the format specification. The 1X format element is therefore specified with DOLLAR8 to add one blank after each value of *SALARY85* to *SALARY88*.

- NAME uses the default dictionary format.

Strings

You can specify string values within the variable list. Strings must be enclosed in apostrophes or quotation marks.

- If a format is specified for a variable list, the application of the format is interrupted by a specified string. Thus, the string has the same effect within a variable list as an asterisk.
- Strings can be used to create column headings for the displayed variables. The PRINT command that specifies the column headings must be used within a DO IF—END IF structure. If you want the column headings to begin a new page in the output, use a PRINT EJECT command rather than PRINT to specify the headings (see PRINT EJECT).

Example

```
PRINT / NAME 'HIRED=' MOHIRED(F2) '/' YRHIRED
             ' SALARY=' SALARY (DOLLAR8).
EXECUTE.
```

- Three strings are specified. The strings HIRED= and SALARY= label the values being displayed. The slash specified between month hired (*MOHIRED*) and year hired (*YRHIRED*) creates a composite hiring date. The F2 format is supplied for variable *MOHIRED* in order to suppress the blank that would follow it if the dictionary format were used.
- *NAME* and *YRHIRED* are displayed with default formats. The 'HIRED=' specification prevents the F2 format from applying to *NAME*, and the 'SALARY=' specification prevents the DOLLAR8 format from applying to *YRHIRED*.

Example

```
DO IF $CASENUM EQ 1.
PRINT /'    NAME ' 1 'DEPT' 25 'HIRED' 30 '   SALARY' 35.
END IF.
PRINT / NAME DEPT *
        MOHIRED 30-31 '/' YRHIRED *
        SALARY 35-42(DOLLAR).
EXECUTE.
```

- The first PRINT command specifies strings only. The integer after each string specifies the beginning column number of the string. The strings will be used as column headings for the variables. DO IF $CASENUM EQ 1 causes the first PRINT command to be executed only once, as the first case is processed. END IF closes the structure.
- The second PRINT command specifies the variables to be displayed. It is executed once for each case in the data. Column locations are specified to align the values with the column headings. In this example, the T format element could also have been used to align the variables and the column headings. For example, MOHIRED (T30,F2) begins the display of values for variable *MOHIRED* in column 30.
- The asterisk after *DEPT* prevents the format specified for *MOHIRED* from applying to *NAME* and *DEPT*. The asterisk after *YRHIRED* prevents the format specified for *SALARY* from applying to *YRHIRED*.

RECORDS Subcommand

RECORDS indicates the total number of lines displayed per case. The number specified on RECORDS is informational only. The actual specification that causes variables to display on a new line is a slash within the variable specifications. Each new line is requested by another slash.

- RECORDS must be specified before the slash that precedes the start of the variable specifications.
- The only specification on RECORDS is an integer to indicate the number of records for the output. If the number does not agree with the actual number of records indicated by slashes, the program issues a warning and ignores the specification on RECORDS.
- Specifications for each line of output must begin with a slash. An integer can follow the slash, indicating the line on which values are to be displayed. The integer is informational only. It cannot be used to rearrange the order of records in the output. If the integer does not agree with the actual record number indicated by the number of slashes in the variable specifications, the integer is ignored.
- A slash that is not followed by a variable list generates a blank line in the output.

Example

```
PRINT RECORDS=3 /EMPLOYID NAME DEPT
                /EMPLOYID TENURE SALARY
                /.
EXECUTE.
```

- PRINT displays the values of an individual's name and department on one line, tenure and salary on the next line, and the employee identification number on both lines, followed by a blank third line. Two lines are displayed for each case, and cases in the output are separated by a blank line.

Example

```
PRINT RECORDS=3 /1 EMPLOYID NAME DEPT
                /2 EMPLOYID TENURE SALARY
                /3.
```

- This PRINT command is equivalent to that in the preceding example.

Example

```
PRINT / EMPLOYID NAME DEPT / EMPLOYID TENURE SALARY /.
```

- This PRINT command is equivalent to those in the two preceding examples.

OUTFILE Subcommand

OUTFILE specifies a file for the output from the PRINT command. By default, PRINT output is included with the rest of the output from the session.

- OUTFILE must be specified before the slash preceding the start of the variable specifications.
- The output from PRINT cannot exceed 132 characters, even if the external file is defined with a longer record length.

Example

```
PRINT OUTFILE=PRINTOUT
  /1 EMPLOYID DEPT SALARY /2 NAME.
EXECUTE.
```

- OUTFILE specifies *PRINTOUT* as the file that receives the PRINT output.

TABLE Subcommand

TABLE requests a table showing how the variable information is formatted. NOTABLE, which suppresses the format table, is the default.

- TABLE must be specified before the slash that precedes the start of the variable specifications.

Example

```
PRINT TABLE /1 EMPLOYID DEPT SALARY /2  NAME.
EXECUTE.
```

- TABLE requests a summary table describing the PRINT specifications. The table is included with the PRINT output.

PRINT EJECT

```
PRINT EJECT [OUTFILE=file] [RECORDS={1}] [{NOTABLE}]
                                     {n}  {TABLE  }

  /{1   } varlist [{col location [(format)]}] [varlist...]
  {rec #}          {(format list)           }
                   {*                       }

 [/{2    }...]
   {rec #}
```

Example

```
DO IF $CASENUM EQ 1.
PRINT EJECT /'   NAME ' 1 'DEPT' 25 'HIRED' 30 '  SALARY' 35.
END IF.
PRINT / NAME DEPT *
        MOHIRED(T30,F2) '/' YRHIRED *
        SALARY (T35,DOLLAR8).
EXECUTE.
```

Overview

PRINT EJECT displays specified information at the top of a new page of the output. PRINT EJECT causes a page ejection each time it is executed. If PRINT EJECT is not used in a DO IF—END IF structure, it is executed for each case in the data, and each case is displayed on a separate page.

PRINT EJECT is designed to be used with the PRINT command to insert titles and column headings above the values displayed by PRINT. PRINT can also generate titles and headings, but PRINT cannot be used to control page ejections.

PRINT EJECT and PRINT can be used for writing simple reports.

Options

The options available for PRINT EJECT are identical to those available for PRINT:

- You can specify formats for the variables.
- You can specify string values within the variable specifications. With PRINT EJECT, the strings are usually used as titles or column headings and often include a specification for column location.
- You can display each case on more than one line using the RECORDS subcommand.
- You can direct the output to a specified file using the OUTFILE subcommand.
- You can display a table that summarizes variable formats with the TABLE subcommand.

All of these features are documented in detail for the PRINT command and work identically for PRINT EJECT. Refer to PRINT for additional information.

Basic Specification

The basic specification is a slash followed by a variable list and/or a list of string values that will be used as column headings or titles. The values for each variable or string are displayed on the top line of a new page in the output. PRINT EJECT is usually used within a DO IF—END IF structure to control the page ejections.

Operations

- PRINT EJECT is a transformation and will not be executed unless it is followed by a procedure or the EXECUTE command.
- If PRINT EJECT is not used within a DO IF—END IF structure, it is executed for each case in the data and displays the values for each case on a separate page.
- Values are displayed with a blank space between them. However, if a format is specified for a variable, the blank space for that variable's values is suppressed.
- Values are displayed in the output as the data are read. The PRINT output appears before the output from the first procedure.
- If more variables are specified than can be displayed in 132 columns or within the width specified on SET WIDTH, the program displays an error message. You must reduce the number of variables or split the output into several records.
- User-missing values are displayed just like valid values. System-missing values are represented by a period.

Example

```
DO IF $CASENUM EQ 1.
PRINT EJECT /'   NAME ' 1 'DEPT' 25 'HIRED' 30 '   SALARY' 35.
END IF.
PRINT / NAME DEPT *
        MOHIRED(T30,F2) '/' YRHIRED *
        SALARY (T35,DOLLAR8).
EXECUTE.
```

- PRINT EJECT specifies strings to be used as column headings and causes a page ejection. DO IF—END IF causes the PRINT EJECT command to be executed only once, when the system variable $CASENUM equals 1 (the value assigned to the first case in the file). Thus, column headings are displayed on the first page of the output only. The next example shows how to display column headings at the top of every page of the output.
- If a PRINT command were used in place of PRINT EJECT, the column headings would begin immediately after the command printback.

Example

```
DO IF MOD($CASENUM,50) = 1.
PRINT   EJECT
FILE=OUT /'    NAME ' 1 'DEPT' 25 'HIRED' 30 '   SALARY' 35.
END IF.
PRINT FILE=OUT / NAME DEPT *
        MOHIRED 30-31 '/' YRHIRED *
        SALARY 35-42(DOLLAR).
EXECUTE.
```

- In this example, DO IF specifies that PRINT EJECT is executed if MOD (the remainder) of *$CASENUM* divided by 50 equals 1 (see p. 44 for a description of MOD). Thus, column headings are displayed on a new page after every 50th case.

- If PRINT were used instead of PRINT EJECT, column headings would display after every 50th case but would not appear at the top of a new page.

- Both PRINT EJECT and PRINT specify the same file for the output. If the FILE subcommands on PRINT EJECT and PRINT do not specify the same file, the column headings and the displayed values end up in different files.

PRINT FORMATS

```
PRINT FORMATS varlist(format) [varlist...]
```

Example

```
PRINT FORMATS SALARY (DOLLAR8) / HOURLY (DOLLAR7.2)
               / RAISE BONUS (PCT2).
```

Overview

PRINT FORMATS changes variable print formats. Print formats are output formats and control the form in which values are displayed by a procedure or by the PRINT command.

PRINT FORMATS changes only print formats. To change write formats, use the WRITE FORMATS command. To change both the print and write formats with a single specification, use the FORMATS command. For information on assigning input formats during data definition, see DATA LIST. For a more detailed discussion of input and output formats, see "Variable Formats" on p. 31.

Basic Specification

The basic specification is a variable list followed by the new format specification in parentheses. All specified variables receive the new format.

Syntax Rules

- You can specify more than one variable or variable list, followed by a format in parentheses. Only one format can be specified after each variable list. For clarity, each set of specifications can be separated by a slash.
- You can use keyword TO to refer to consecutive variables in the working data file.
- The specified width of a format must include enough positions to accommodate any punctuation characters such as decimal points, commas, dollar signs, or date and time delimiters. (This differs from assigning an *input* format on DATA LIST, where the program automatically expands the input format to accommodate punctuation characters in output.)
- Custom currency formats (CCw, CCw.d) must first be defined on the SET command before they can be used on PRINT FORMATS.
- PRINT FORMATS cannot be used with string variables. To change the length of a string variable, declare a new variable of the desired length with the STRING command and then use COMPUTE to copy values from the existing string into the new string.

Operations

- Unlike most transformations, PRINT FORMATS takes effect as soon as it is encountered in the command sequence. Special attention should be paid to its position among commands.

- Variables not specified on PRINT FORMATS retain their current print formats in the working data file. To see the current formats, use the DISPLAY command.

- The new print formats are changed only in the working file and are in effect for the duration of the session or until changed again with a PRINT FORMATS or FORMATS command. Print formats in the original data file (if one exists) are not changed, unless the file is re-saved with the SAVE or XSAVE command.

- New numeric variables created with transformation commands are assigned default print formats of F8.2 (or the format specified on the FORMAT subcommand of SET). The FORMATS command can be used to change the new variable's print formats.

- New string variables created with transformation commands are assigned the format specified on the STRING command that declares the variable. PRINT FORMATS cannot be used to change the format of a new string variable.

- If a numeric data value exceeds its width specification, the program attempts to display some value nevertheless. First the program rounds decimal values, then removes punctuation characters, then tries scientific notation, and finally, if there is still not enough space, produces asterisks indicating that a value is present but cannot be displayed in the assigned width.

Example

```
PRINT FORMATS SALARY (DOLLAR8) / HOURLY (DOLLAR7.2)
          / RAISE BONUS (PCT2).
```

- The print format for *SALARY* is changed to DOLLAR with eight positions, including the dollar sign and comma when appropriate. The value 11550 is displayed as $11,550. An eight-digit number would require a DOLLAR11 format specification: eight characters for digits, two characters for commas, and one character for the dollar sign.

- The print format for *HOURLY* is changed to DOLLAR with seven positions, including the dollar sign, decimal point, and two decimal places. The number 115 is displayed as $115.00. If DOLLAR6.2 had been specified, the value 115 would be displayed as $115.0. the program would truncate the last 0 because a width of 6 is not enough to display the full value.

- The print format for both *RAISE* and *BONUS* is changed to PCT with two positions: one position for the percentage and one position for the percent sign. The value 9 displays as 9%. Because the width allows for only two positions, the value 10 displays as 10, since the percent sign is truncated.

Example

```
COMPUTE V3=V1 + V2.
PRINT FORMATS V3 (F3.1).
```

- COMPUTE creates the new numeric variable *V3*. By default, *V3* is assigned an F8.2 format (or the default format specified on SET).
- PRINT FORMATS changes the print format for *V3* to F3.1.

Example

```
SET CCA='-/-.Dfl ..-'.
PRINT FORMATS COST (CCA14.2).
```

- SET defines a European currency format for the custom currency format type CCA.
- PRINT FORMATS assigns the print format CCA to variable *COST*. With the format defined for CCA on SET, the value 37419 is displayed as Dfl'37.419,00. See the SET command for more information on custom currency formats.

PRINT SPACE

```
PRINT SPACE [OUTFILE=file] [numeric expression]
```

Example

```
PRINT / NAME DEPT82 *
       MOHIRED(T30,F2) '/' YRHIRED *
       SALARY82 (T35,DOLLAR8).
PRINT SPACE.
EXECUTE.
```

Overview

PRINT SPACE displays blank lines in the output and is generally used with a PRINT or WRITE command. Because PRINT SPACE displays a blank line each time it is executed, it is often used in a DO IF—END IF structure.

Basic Specification

The basic specification is simply the command PRINT SPACE.

Syntax Rules

- To display more than one blank line, specify a numeric expression after PRINT SPACE. The expression can be an integer or a complex expression.
- OUTFILE directs the output to a specified file. OUTFILE should be specified if an OUTFILE subcommand is specified on the PRINT or WRITE command that is used with PRINT SPACE. The OUTFILE subcommand on PRINT SPACE and PRINT or WRITE should specify the same file.

Operations

- If PRINT SPACE is not used in a DO IF—END IF structure, it is executed for each case in the data and displays a blank line for every case.

Example

```
PRINT / NAME DEPT82 *
       MOHIRED(T30,F2) '/' YRHIRED *
       SALARY82 (T35,DOLLAR8).
PRINT SPACE.
EXECUTE.
```

- PRINT SPACE displays one blank line each time it is executed. Because PRINT SPACE is not used in a DO IF—END IF structure, it is executed once for each case. In effect, the output is double-spaced.

Example

```
NUMERIC #LINE.
DO IF MOD(#LINE,5) = 0.
PRINT SPACE 2.
END IF.
COMPUTE #LINE=#LINE + 1.
PRINT / NAME DEPT *
       MOHIRED 30-31 '/' YRHIRED *
       SALARY 35-42(DOLLAR).
EXECUTE.
```

- DO IF specifies that PRINT SPACE will be executed if MOD (the remainder) of *#LINE* divided by 5 equals 1. Since *#LINE* is incremented by 1 for each case, PRINT SPACE is executed once for every five cases. (See p. 44 for information on the MOD function.)
- PRINT SPACE specifies two blank lines. Cases are displayed in groups of five with two blank lines between each group.

Example

```
* Printing addresses on labels.

COMPUTE #LINES=0.                  /*Initiate #LINES to 0
DATA LIST FILE=ADDRESS/RECORD 1-40 (A).  /*Read a record
COMPUTE #LINES=#LINES+1.           /*Bump counter and print
WRITE OUTFILE=LABELS /RECORD.

DO IF RECORD EQ ' '.               /*Blank between addresses
+  PRINT SPACE OUTFILE=LABELS 8 - #LINES.  /*Add extra blank #LINES
+  COMPUTE #LINES=0.
END IF.
EXECUTE.
```

- PRINT SPACE uses a complex expression for specifying the number of blank lines to display. The data contain a variable number of input records for each name and address, which must be printed in a fixed number of lines for mailing labels. The goal is to know when the last line for each address has been printed, how many lines have printed, and therefore how many blank records must be printed in order for the next address to fit on the next label. The example assumes that there is already one blank line between each address on input and that you want to print eight lines per label.
- The DATA LIST command defines the data. Each line of the address is contained in columns 1–40 of the data file and is assigned the variable name *RECORD*. For the blank line between each address, *RECORD* is blank.
- Variable *#LINES* is the key to this example. *#LINES* is initialized to 0 as a scratch variable. It is incremented for each record written. When the program encounters a blank line

(RECORD EQ ' '), PRINT SPACE prints a number of blank lines equal to 8 minus the number already printed, and *#LINES* is then reset to 0.

- OUTFILE on PRINT SPACE specifies the same file specified by OUTFILE on WRITE.

PROBIT

PROBIT is available in the Regression Models option.

```
PROBIT response-count varname OF observation-count varname
       WITH varlist [BY varname(min,max)]

[/MODEL={PROBIT**}]
       {LOGIT   }
       {BOTH    }

[/LOG=[{10**  }]
       {2.718}
       {value}
       {NONE }

[/CRITERIA=[{OPTOL   }({epsilon**0.8})][P({0.15**})][STEPLIMIT({0.1**})]
            {CONVERGE} {n           }   {p      }              {n     }

           [ITERATE({max(50,3(p+1)**})]]
                    {n              }

[/NATRES[=value]]

[/PRINT={[CI**] [FREQ**] [RMP**]} [PARALL] [NONE] [ALL]]
        {DEFAULT**              }

[/MISSING=[{EXCLUDE**}]   ]
           {INCLUDE  }
```

**Default if the subcommand or keyword is omitted.

Example

```
PROBIT  R OF N BY ROOT(1,2) WITH X
  /MODEL = BOTH.
```

Overview

PROBIT can be used to estimate the effects of one or more independent variables on a dichotomous dependent variable (such as dead or alive, employed or unemployed, product purchased or not). The program is designed for dose-response analyses and related models, but PROBIT can also estimate logistic regression models.

Options

The Model. You can request a probit or logit response model, or both, for the observed response proportions with the MODEL subcommand.

Transform Predictors. You can control the base of the log transformation applied to the predictors or request no log transformation with the LOG subcommand.

Natural Response Rates. You can instruct PROBIT to estimate the natural response rate (threshold) of the model or supply a known natural response rate to be used in the solution with the NATRES subcommand.

Algorithm Control Parameters. You can specify values of algorithm control parameters, such as the limit on iterations, using the CRITERIA subcommand.

Statistics. By default, PROBIT calculates frequencies, fiducial confidence intervals, and the relative median potency. It also produces a plot of the observed probits or logits against the values of a single independent variable. Optionally, you can use the PRINT subcommand to request a test of the parallelism of regression lines for different levels of the grouping variable or to suppress any or all of these statistics.

Basic Specification

- The basic specification is the response-count variable, keyword OF, the observation-count variable, keyword WITH, and at least one independent variable.
- PROBIT calculates maximum-likelihood estimates for the parameters of the default probit response model and automatically displays estimates of the regression coefficient and intercept terms, their standard errors, a covariance matrix of parameter estimates, and a Pearson chi-square goodness-of-fit test of the model.

Subcommand Order

- The variable specification must be first.
- Subcommands can be named in any order.

Syntax Rules

- The variables must include a response count, an observation count, and at least one predictor. A categorical grouping variable is optional.
- All subcommands are optional and each can appear only once.
- Generally, data should not be entered for individual observations. PROBIT expects predictor values, response counts, and the total number of observations as the input case.
- If the data are available only in a case-by-case form, use AGGREGATE first to compute the required response and observation counts.

Operations

- The transformed response variable is predicted as a linear function of other variables using the nonlinear-optimization method. Note that the previous releases used the iteratively weighted least-squares method, which has a different way of transforming the response variables. See the MODEL subcommand on p. 926.

- If individual cases are entered in the data, PROBIT skips the plot of transformed response proportions and predictor values.
- If individual cases are entered, the chi-square goodness-of-fit statistic and associated degrees of freedom are based on the individual cases. The case-based chi-square goodness-of-fit statistic generally differs from that calculated for the same data in aggregated form.

Limitations

- Only one prediction model can be tested on a single PROBIT command, although both probit and logit response models can be requested for that prediction.
- Confidence limits, the plot of transformed response proportions and predictor values, and computation of relative median potency are necessarily limited to single-predictor models.

Example

```
PROBIT  R OF N BY ROOT(1,2) WITH X
/MODEL = BOTH.
```

- This example specifies that both the probit and logit response models be applied to the response frequency R, given N total observations and the predictor X.
- By default, the predictor is log transformed.

Example

```
* Using data in a case-by-case form

DATA LIST FREE / PREPARTN DOSE RESPONSE.
BEGIN DATA
1 1.5 0
 ...
4 20.0 1
END DATA.
COMPUTE SUBJECT = 1.
PROBIT RESPONSE OF SUBJECT BY PREPARTN(1,4) WITH DOSE.
```

- This dose-response model (Finney, 1971) illustrates a case-by-case analysis. A researcher tests four different preparations at varying doses and observes whether each subject responds. The data are individually recorded for each subject, with 1 indicating a response and 0 indicating no response. The number of observations is always 1 and is stored in variable SUBJECT.
- PROBIT warns that the data are in a case-by-case form and that the plot is therefore skipped.
- The goodness-of-fit test and associated degrees of freedom are based on individual cases, not dosage groups.
- PROBIT displays predicted and observed frequencies for all individual input cases.

Example

```
* Aggregating case-by-case data

DATA LIST FREE/PREPARTN DOSE RESPONSE.
BEGIN DATA
      1.00      1.50        .00
      ...
      4.00     20.00       1.00
END DATA.
AGGREGATE OUTFILE=*
  /BREAK=PREPARTN DOSE
  /SUBJECTS=N(RESPONSE)
  /NRESP=SUM(RESPONSE).
PROBIT NRESP OF SUBJECTS BY PREPARTN(1,4) WITH DOSE.
```

- This example analyzes the same dose-response model as the previous example, but the data are first aggregated.
- AGGREGATE summarizes the data by cases representing all subjects who received the same preparation (*PREPARTN*) at the same dose (*DOSE*).
- The number of cases having a nonmissing response is recorded in the aggregated variable *SUBJECTS*.
- Because *RESPONSE* is coded 0 for no response and 1 for a response, the sum of the values gives the number of observations with a response.
- PROBIT requests a default analysis.
- The parameter estimates for this analysis are the same as those calculated for individual cases in the example above. The chi-square test, however, is based on the number of dosages.

Variable Specification

The variable specification on PROBIT identifies the variables for response count, observation count, groups, and predictors. The variable specification is required.

- The variables must be specified first. The specification must include the response-count variable, followed by the keyword OF and then the observation-count variable.
- If the value of the response-count variable exceeds that of the observation-count variable, a procedure error occurs and PROBIT is not executed.
- At least one predictor (covariate) must be specified following the keyword WITH. The number of predictors is limited only by available workspace. All predictors must be continuous variables.
- You can specify a grouping variable (factor) after the keyword BY. Only one variable can be specified. It must be numeric and can contain only integer values. You must specify, in parentheses, a range indicating the minimum and maximum values for the grouping variable. Each integer value in the specified range defines a group.
- Cases with values for the grouping variable that are outside the specified range are excluded from the analysis.

- Keywords BY and WITH can appear in either order. However, both must follow the response- and observation-count variables.

Example

```
PROBIT R OF N WITH X.
```

- The number of observations having the measured response appears in variable *R*, and the total number of observations is in *N*. The predictor is *X*.

Example

```
PROBIT  R OF N BY ROOT(1,2) WITH X.

PROBIT  R OF N WITH X BY ROOT(1,2).
```

- Because keywords BY and WITH can be used in either order, these two commands are equivalent. Each command specifies *X* as a continuous predictor and *ROOT* as a categorical grouping variable.
- Groups are identified by the levels of variable *ROOT*, which may be 1 or 2.
- For each combination of predictor and grouping variables, the variable *R* contains the number of observations with the response of interest, and *N* contains the total number of observations.

MODEL Subcommand

MODEL specifies the form of the dichotomous-response model. Response models can be thought of as transformations (T) of response rates, which are proportions or probabilities (p). Note the difference in the transformations between the current version and the previous versions.

- A **probit** is the inverse of the cumulative standard normal distribution function. Thus, for any proportion, the probit transformation returns the value below which that proportion of standard normal deviates is found. For the probit response model, the program uses $T(p) = \text{PROBIT}(p)$. Hence:

$T(0.025) = \text{PROBIT}(0.025) = -1.96$

$T(0.400) = \text{PROBIT}(0.400) = -0.25$

$T(0.500) = \text{PROBIT}(0.500) = 0.00$

$T(0.950) = \text{PROBIT}(0.950) = 1.64$

- A **logit** is simply the natural log of the odds ratio, $p/(1-p)$. In the Probit procedure, the response function is given as $T(p) = \log_e(p/(1-p))$. Hence:

$T(0.025) = \text{LOGIT}(0.025) = -3.66$

$T(0.400) = \text{LOGIT}(0.400) = -0.40$

$T(0.500) = \text{LOGIT}(0.500) = 0.00$

$T(0.950) = \text{LOGIT}(0.950) = 2.94$

You can request one or both of the models on the MODEL subcommand. The default is PROBIT if the subcommand is not specified or is specified with no keyword.

PROBIT   *Probit response model.* This is the default.

LOGIT   *Logit response model.*

BOTH   *Both probit and logit response models.* PROBIT displays all the output for the logit model followed by the output for the probit model.

- If subgroups and multiple-predictor variables are defined, PROBIT estimates a separate intercept, a_j, for each subgroup and a regression coefficient, b_i, for each predictor.

LOG Subcommand

LOG specifies the base of the logarithmic transformation of the predictor variables or suppresses the default log transformation.

- LOG applies to all predictors.
- To transform only selected predictors, use COMPUTE commands before the Probit procedure. Then specify NONE on the LOG subcommand.
- If LOG is omitted, a logarithm base of 10 is used.
- If LOG is used without a specification, the natural logarithm base e (2.718) is used.
- If you have a control group in your data and specify NONE on the LOG subcommand, the control group is included in the analysis. See the NATRES subcommand on p. 928.

You can specify one of the following on LOG:

value   *Logarithm base to be applied to all predictors.*

NONE   *No transformation of the predictors.*

Example
```
PROBIT R OF N BY ROOT (1,2) WITH X
  /LOG = 2.
```
- LOG specifies a base-2 logarithmic transformation.

CRITERIA Subcommand

Use CRITERIA to specify the values of control parameters for the PROBIT algorithm. You can specify any or all of the keywords below. Defaults remain in effect for parameters that are not changed.

OPTOL(n)   *Optimality tolerance.* Alias CONVERGE. If an iteration point is a feasible point and the next step will not produce a relative change in either the parameter vector or the log-likelihood function of more than the square root of n, an optimal solution has been found. OPTOL can also be thought of as the number of significant digits in the log-likelihood function at the solution. For example, if OPTOL=10^{-6}, the log-likelihood function should have approximately six significant digits of accuracy. The default value is machine epsilon**0.8.

ITERATE(n)   *Iteration limit.* Specify the maximum number of iterations. The default is $\max(50, 3(p + 1))$, where p is the number of parameters in the model.

P(p)   *Heterogeneity criterion probability.* Specify a cutoff value between 0 and 1 for the significance of the goodness-of-fit test. The cutoff value determines whether a heterogeneity factor is included in calculations of confidence levels for effective levels of a predictor. If the significance of chi-square is greater than the cutoff, the heterogeneity factor is not included. If you specify 0, this criterion is disabled; if you specify 1, a heterogeneity factor is automatically included. The default is 0.15.

STEPLIMIT(n)   *Step limit.* The PROBIT algorithm does not allow changes in the length of the parameter vector to exceed a factor of n. This limit prevents very early steps from going too far from good initial estimates. Specify any positive value. The default value is 0.1.

CONVERGE(n)   *Alias of OPTOL.*

NATRES Subcommand

You can use NATRES either to supply a known natural response rate to be used in the solution or to instruct PROBIT to estimate the natural (or threshold) response rate of the model.

- To supply a known natural response rate as a constraint on the model solution, specify a value less than 1 on NATRES.

- To instruct PROBIT to estimate the natural response rate of the model, you can indicate a control group by giving a 0 value to any of the predictor variables. PROBIT displays the estimate of the natural response rate and the standard error and includes the estimate in the covariance/correlation matrix as NAT RESP.

- If no control group is indicated and NATRES is specified without a given value, PROBIT estimates the natural response rate from the entire data and informs you that no control group has been provided. The estimate of the natural response rate and the standard error are displayed and NAT RESP is included in the covariance/correlation matrix.

- If you have a control group in your data and specify NONE on the LOG subcommand, the control group is included in the analysis.

Example

```
DATA LIST FREE / SOLUTION DOSE NOBSN NRESP.
BEGIN DATA
1   5 100 20
1  10   80 30
1   0 100 10
...
END DATA.

PROBIT NRESP OF NOBSN BY SOLUTION(1,4) WITH DOSE
  /NATRES.
```

- This example reads four variables and requests a default analysis with an estimate of the natural response rate.
- The predictor variable, *DOSE*, has a value of 0 for the third case.
- The response count (10) and the observation count (100) for this case establish the initial estimate of the natural response rate.
- Because the default log transformation is performed, the control group is not included in the analysis.

Example

```
DATA LIST FREE / SOLUTION DOSE NOBSN NRESP.
BEGIN DATA
1   5 100 20
1 10   80 30
1   0 100 10
  . . .
END DATA.

PROBIT NRESP OF NOBSN BY SOLUTION(1,4) WITH DOSE
  /NATRES = 0.10.
```

- This example reads four variables and requests an analysis in which the natural response rate is set to 0.10. The values of the control group are ignored.
- The control group is excluded from the analysis because the default log transformation is performed.

PRINT Subcommand

Use PRINT to control the statistics calculated by PROBIT.

- PROBIT always displays the plot (for a single-predictor model) and the parameter estimates and covariances for the probit model.
- If PRINT is used, the requested statistics are calculated and displayed in addition to the parameter estimates and plot.
- If PRINT is not specified or is specified without any keyword, FREQ, CI, and RMP are calculated and displayed in addition to the parameter estimates and plot.

DEFAULT   *FREQ, CI, and RMP.* This is the default if PRINT is not specified or is specified by itself.

FREQ   *Frequencies.* Display a table of observed and predicted frequencies with their residual values. If observations are entered on a case-by-case basis, this listing can be quite lengthy.

CI   *Fiducial confidence intervals.* Print Finney's (1971) fiducial confidence intervals for the levels of the predictor needed to produce each proportion of responses. PROBIT displays this default output for single-predictor models only. If a categorical grouping variable is specified, PROBIT produces a table of confidence intervals for each group. If the Pearson chi-square goodness-of-fit test is significant ($p < 0.15$ by default), PROBIT uses a heterogeneity factor to calculate the limits.

RMP   *Relative median potency.* Display the relative median potency (RMP) of each pair of groups defined by the grouping variable. PROBIT displays this default output for single-predictor models only. For any pair of groups, the RMP is the ratio of the stimulus tolerances in those groups. **Stimulus tolerance** is the value of the predictor necessary to produce a 50% response rate. If the derived model for one predictor and two groups estimates that a predictor value of 21 produces a 50% response rate in the first group, and that a predictor value of 15 produces a 50% response rate in the second group, the relative median potency would be 21/15 = 1.40. In biological assay analyses, RMP measures the comparative strength of preparations.

PARALL   *Parallelism test.* Produce a test of the parallelism of regression lines for different levels of the grouping variable. This test displays a chi-square value and its associated probability. It requires an additional pass through the data and, thus, additional processing time.

NONE   *Display only the unconditional output.* This option can be used to override any other specification on the PRINT subcommand for PROBIT.

ALL   *All available output.* This is the same as requesting FREQ, CI, RMP, and PARALL.

MISSING Subcommand

PROBIT always deletes cases having a missing value for any variable. In the output, PROBIT indicates how many cases it rejected because of missing data. This information is displayed with the DATA Information that prints at the beginning of the output. You can use the MISSING subcommand to control the treatment of user-missing values.

EXCLUDE   *Delete cases with user-missing values.* This is the default. You can also make it explicit by using the keyword DEFAULT.

INCLUDE   *Include user-missing values.* PROBIT treats user-missing values as valid. Only cases with system-missing values are rejected.

PROCEDURE OUTPUT

```
PROCEDURE OUTPUT OUTFILE=file
```

Example

```
PROCEDURE OUTPUT OUTFILE=CELLDATA.
CROSSTABS VARIABLES=FEAR SEX (1,2)
  /TABLES=FEAR BY SEX
  /WRITE=ALL.
```

Overview

PROCEDURE OUTPUT specifies the files to which CROSSTABS, FREQUENCIES, and SURVIVAL (included in the SPSS Advanced Models option) can write procedure output. PROCEDURE OUTPUT has no other applications.

Basic Specification

The only specification is OUTFILE and the file specification. PROCEDURE OUTPUT must precede the command to which it applies.

Operations

Commands with the WRITE subcommand or keyword write to the output file specified on the most recent PROCEDURE OUTPUT command. If only one output file has been specified, the output from the last such procedure overwrites all previous ones.

Example

```
PROCEDURE OUTPUT OUTFILE=CELLDATA.
CROSSTABS VARIABLES=FEAR SEX (1,2)
  /TABLES=FEAR BY SEX
  /WRITE=ALL.
```

- PROCEDURE OUTPUT precedes CROSSTABS and specifies *CELLDATA* as the file to receive the cell frequencies.
- The WRITE subcommand on CROSSTABS is required for writing cell frequencies to a procedure output file.

Example

```
PROCEDURE OUTPUT OUTFILE=CODEBOOK.
FREQUENCIES VARIABLES=ALL
  /FORMAT=ONEPAGE WRITE.
PROCEDURE OUTPUT OUTFILE=CELLDATA.
CROSSTABS VARIABLES=FEAR SEX (1 2)
  /TABLES=FEAR BY SEX
  /WRITE=ALL.
```

- The first PROCEDURE OUTPUT command precedes FREQUENCIES and specifies *CODEBOOK* as the file to receive frequency tables.

- The WRITE keyword on the FORMAT subcommand on FREQUENCIES is required for writing the display to a procedure output file.

- The second PROCEDURE OUTPUT command is required to specify *CELLDATA* as the file to receive the cell frequencies of the crosstabulation. Without this command, the cell frequencies would overwrite the FREQUENCIES output.

Example

```
PROCEDURE OUTPUT OUTFILE=SURVTBL.
SURVIVAL   TABLES=ONSSURV,RECSURV BY TREATMNT(1,3)
  /STATUS = RECURSIT(1,9) FOR RECSURV
  /STATUS = STATUS(3,4) FOR ONSSURV
  /INTERVAL=THRU 50 BY 5 THRU 100 BY 10/PLOTS/COMPARE
  /CALCULATE=CONDITIONAL PAIRWISE
  /WRITE=TABLES.
```

- PROCEDURE OUTPUT precedes SURVIVAL and specifies *SURVTBL* as the file to receive the survival tables.

- The WRITE subcommand on SURVIVAL is required for writing survival tables to a procedure output file.

PROXIMITIES

```
PROXIMITIES  varlist  [/VIEW={CASE**  }]
                            {VARIABLE}

  [/STANDARDIZE=[{VARIABLE}]  [{NONE** }]]
                {CASE    }   {Z      }
                             {SD     }
                             {RANGE  }
                             {MAX    }
                             {MEAN   }
                             {RESCALE}

  [/MEASURE=[{EUCLID**          }]  [ABSOLUTE] [REVERSE] [RESCALE]
             {SEUCLID           }
             {COSINE            }
             {CORRELATION       }
             {BLOCK             }
             {CHEBYCHEV         }
             {POWER(p,r)        }
             {MINKOWSKI(p)      }
             {CHISQ             }
             {PH2               }
             {RR[(p[,np])]      }
             {SM[(p[,np])]      }
             {JACCARD[(p[,np])] }
             {DICE[(p[,np])]    }
             {SS1[(p[,np])]     }
             {RT[(p[,np])]      }
             {SS2[(p[,np])]     }
             {K1[(p[,np])]      }
             {SS3[(p[,np])]     }
             {K2[(p[,np])]      }
             {SS4[(p[,np])]     }
             {HAMANN[(p[,np])]  }
             {OCHIAI[(p[,np])]  }
             {SS5[(p[,np])]     }
             {PHI[(p[,np])]     }
             {LAMBDA[(p[,np])]  }
             {D[(p[,np])]       }
             {Y[(p[,np])]       }
             {Q[(p[,np])]       }
             {BEUCLID[(p[,np])] }
             {SIZE[(p[,np])]    }
             {PATTERN[(p[,np])] }
             {BSEUCLID[(p[,np])]}
             {BSHAPE[(p[,np])]  }
             {DISPER[(p[,np])]  }
             {VARIANCE[(p[,np])]}
             {BLWMN[(p[,np])]   }
             {NONE              }

  [/PRINT=[{PROXIMITIES**}]]  [/ID=varname]
           {NONE          }

  [/MISSING=[LISTWISE**]  [INCLUDE]

  [/MATRIX=[IN({file})]  [OUT({file})]]]
               {*   }        {*   }
```

**Default if subcommand or keyword is omitted.

Example

```
PROXIMITIES A B C.
```

Overview

PROXIMITIES computes a variety of measures of similarity, dissimilarity, or distance between pairs of cases or pairs of variables for moderate-sized data sets (see "Limitations" below). PROXIMITIES matrix output can be used as input to procedures ALSCAL, CLUSTER, and FACTOR. To learn more about proximities matrices and their uses, consult Anderberg (1973) and Romesburg (1984).

Options

Standardizing Data. With the STANDARDIZE subcommand you can standardize the values for each variable or for each case by any of several different methods.

Proximity Measures. You can compute a variety of similarity, dissimilarity, and distance measures using the MEASURE subcommand. (Similarity measures increase with greater similarity; dissimilarity and distance measures decrease.) MEASURE can compute measures for interval data, frequency count data, and binary data. Only one measure can be requested in any one PROXIMITIES procedure. With the VIEW subcommand, you can control whether proximities are computed between variables or between cases.

Output. You can display a computed matrix using the PRINT subcommand.

Matrix Input and Output. You can write a computed proximities matrix to an SPSS-format data file using the MATRIX subcommand. This matrix can be used as input to procedures CLUSTER, ALSCAL, and FACTOR. You can also use MATRIX to read a similarity, dissimilarity, or distance matrix. This option lets you rescale or transform existing proximity matrices.

Basic Specification

The basic specification is a variable list, which obtains Euclidean distances between cases based on the values of each specified variable.

Subcommand Order

- The variable list must be first.
- Subcommands can be named in any order.

Operations

- PROXIMITIES ignores case weights when computing coefficients.

Limitations

- PROXIMITIES keeps the raw data for the current split-file group in memory. Storage requirements increase rapidly with the number of cases and the number of items (cases or variables) for which PROXIMITIES computes coefficients.

Example

```
PROXIMITIES A B C.
```

- PROXIMITIES computes Euclidean distances between cases based on the values of variables *A*, *B*, and *C*.

Variable Specification

- The variable list must be specified first.
- The variable list can be omitted when an input matrix data file is specified. A slash must then be specified before the first subcommand to indicate that the variable list is omitted.

STANDARDIZE Subcommand

Use STANDARDIZE to standardize data values for either cases or variables before computing proximities. One of two options can be specified to control the direction of standardization:

VARIABLE   *Standardize the values for each variable.* This is the default.

CASE   *Standardize the values within each case.*

Several standardization methods are available. These allow you to equalize selected properties of the values. All methods can be used with either VARIABLE or CASE. Only one standardization method can be specified.

- If STANDARDIZE is omitted, proximities are computed using the original values (keyword NONE).
- If STANDARDIZE is used without specifications, proximities are computed using Z scores (keyword Z).
- STANDARDIZE cannot be used with binary measures.

NONE   *Do not standardize.* Proximities are computed using the original values. This is the default if STANDARDIZE is omitted.

Z   *Standardize values to Z scores, with a mean of 0 and a standard deviation of 1.* PROXIMITIES subtracts the mean value for the variable or case from each value being standardized and then divides by the standard deviation. If the standard deviation is 0, PROXIMITIES sets all values for the case or variable to 0. This is the default if STANDARDIZE is used without specifications.

RANGE   *Standardize values to have a range of 1.* PROXIMITIES divides each value being standardized by the range of values for the variable or case. If the range is 0, PROXIMITIES leaves all values unchanged.

RESCALE   *Standardize values to have a range from 0 to 1.* From each value being standardized, PROXIMITIES subtracts the minimum value and then divides by the range for the variable or case. If a range is 0, PROXIMITIES sets all values for the case or variable to 0.50.

MAX   *Standardize values to a maximum magnitude of 1.* PROXIMITIES divides each value being standardized by the maximum value for the variable or case. If the maximum of the values is 0, PROXIMITIES divides each value by the absolute magnitude of the smallest value and adds 1.

MEAN   *Standardize values to a mean of 1.* PROXIMITIES divides each value being standardized by the mean of the values for the variable or case. If the mean is 0, PROXIMITIES adds 1 to all values for the case or variable to produce a mean of 1.

SD   *Standardize values to unit standard deviation.* PROXIMITIES divides each value being standardized by the standard deviation of the values for the variable or case. PROXIMITIES does not change the values if their standard deviation is 0.

Example

```
PROXIMITIES A B C
  /STANDARDIZE=CASE RANGE.
```

- Within each case, values are standardized to have ranges of 1.

VIEW Subcommand

VIEW indicates whether proximities are computed between cases or between variables.

CASE   *Compute proximity values between cases.* This is the default.

VARIABLE   *Compute proximity values between variables.*

MEASURE Subcommand

MEASURE specifies the similarity, dissimilarity, or distance measure that PROXIMITIES computes. Three transformations are available with any of these measures:

ABSOLUTE   *Take the absolute values of the proximities.* Use ABSOLUTE when the sign of the values indicates the direction of the relationship (as with correlation coefficients) but only the magnitude of the relationship is of interest.

REVERSE   *Transform similarity values into dissimilarities, or vice versa.* Use this specification to reverse the ordering of the proximities by negating the values.

RESCALE   *Rescale the proximity values to a range of 0 to 1.* RESCALE standardizes the proximities by first subtracting the value of the smallest and then dividing by the range. You would not usually use RESCALE with measures that are already standardized on meaningful scales, as are correlations, cosines, and many binary coefficients.

PROXIMITIES can compute any one of a number of measures between items. You can choose among measures for interval data, frequency count data, or binary data. Available keywords for each of these types of measures are defined in the following sections.

- Only one measure can be specified. However, each measure can be specified with any of the transformations ABSOLUTE, REVERSE, or RESCALE. To apply a transformation to an existing matrix of proximity values without computing any measures, use keyword NONE (see p. 945).

- If more than one transformation is specified, PROXIMITIES does them in the order listed above: first ABSOLUTE, then REVERSE, and then RESCALE regardless of the order they are specified.

- Each entry in the resulting proximity matrix represents a pair of items. The items can be either cases or variables, whichever is specified on the VIEW subcommand.

- When the items are cases, the computation for each pair of cases involves pairs of values for the specified variables.

- When the items are variables, the computation for each pair of variables involves pairs of values for the variables across all cases.

Example

```
PROXIMITIES A B C
  /MEASURE=EUCLID REVERSE.
```

- MEASURE specifies a EUCLID measure and a REVERSE transformation.

Measures for Interval Data

To obtain proximities for interval data, use any one of the following keywords on MEASURE:

EUCLID   *Euclidean distance.* The distance between two items, x and y, is the square root of the sum of the squared differences between the values for the items. This is the default.

$$\text{EUCLID}(x, y) = \sqrt{\Sigma_i (x_i - y_i)^2}$$

SEUCLID   *Squared Euclidean distance.* The distance between two items is the sum of the squared differences between the values for the items.

$$\text{SEUCLID}(x, y) = \Sigma_i (x_i - y_i)^2$$

CORRELATION   *Correlation between vectors of values.* This is a pattern similarity measure.

$$\text{CORRELATION}(x, y) = \frac{\Sigma_i(Z_{xi}Z_{yi})}{N-1}$$

where Z_{xi} is the Z-score (standardized) value of x for the ith case or variable, and N is the number of cases or variables.

COSINE   *Cosine of vectors of values.* This is a pattern similarity measure.

$$\text{COSINE}(x, y) = \frac{\Sigma_i(x_i y_i)}{\sqrt{(\Sigma_i x_i^2)(\Sigma_i y_i^2)}}$$

CHEBYCHEV   *Chebychev distance metric.* The distance between two items is the maximum absolute difference between the values for the items.

$$\text{CHEBYCHEV}(x, y) = \max_i |x_i - y_i|$$

BLOCK   *City-block or Manhattan distance.* The distance between two items is the sum of the absolute differences between the values for the items.

$$\text{BLOCK}(x, y) = \Sigma_i |x_i - y_i|$$

MINKOWSKI(p)   *Distance in an absolute Minkowski power metric.* The distance between two items is the pth root of the sum of the absolute differences to the pth power between the values for the items. Appropriate selection of the integer parameter p yields Euclidean and many other distance metrics.

$$\text{MINKOWSKI}(x, y) = (\Sigma_i |x_i - y_i|^p)^{1/p}$$

POWER(p,r)   *Distance in an absolute power metric.* The distance between two items is the rth root of the sum of the absolute differences to the pth power between the values for the items. Appropriate selection of the integer parameters p and r yields Euclidean, squared Euclidean, Minkowski, city-block, and many other distance metrics.

$$\text{POWER}(x, y) = (\Sigma_i |x_i - y_i|^p)^{1/r}$$

Measures for Frequency Count Data

To obtain proximities for frequency count data, use either of the following keywords on MEASURE:

CHISQ   *Based on the chi-square test of equality for two sets of frequencies.* The magnitude of this dissimilarity measure depends on the total frequencies of the two cases or variables whose dissimilarity is computed. Expected values are from the model of independence of cases or variables x and y.

$$\text{CHISQ}(x, y) = \sqrt{\frac{\Sigma_i(x_i - E(x_i))^2}{E(x_i)} + \frac{\Sigma_i(y_i - E(y_i))^2}{E(y_i)}}$$

PH2   *Phi-square between sets of frequencies.* This is the CHISQ measure normalized by the square root of the combined frequency. Therefore, its value does not depend on the total frequencies of the two cases or variables whose dissimilarity is computed.

$$\text{PH2}(x, y) = \sqrt{\frac{\dfrac{\Sigma_i(x_i - E(x_i))^2}{E(x_i)} + \dfrac{\Sigma_i(y_i - E(y_i))^2}{E(y_i)}}{N}}$$

Measures for Binary Data

Different binary measures emphasize different aspects of the relationship between sets of binary values. However, all the measures are specified in the same way. Each measure has two optional integer-valued parameters, p (present) and np (not present).

- If both parameters are specified, PROXIMITIES uses the value of the first as an indicator that a characteristic is present and the value of the second as an indicator that a characteristic is absent. PROXIMITIES skips all other values.

- If only the first parameter is specified, PROXIMITIES uses that value to indicate presence and all other values to indicate absence.

- If no parameters are specified, PROXIMITIES assumes that 1 indicates presence and 0 indicates absence.

Using the indicators for presence and absence within each item (case or variable), PROXIMITIES constructs a 2×2 contingency table for each pair of items in turn. It uses this table to compute a proximity measure for the pair.

	Item 2 characteristics	
	Present	**Absent**
Item 1 characteristics		
Present	a	b
Absent	c	d

PROXIMITIES computes all binary measures from the values of a, b, c, and d. These values are tallied across variables (when the items are cases) or cases (when the items are variables). For example, if variables *V, W, X, Y, Z* have values 0, 1, 1, 0, 1 for case 1 and values 0, 1, 1, 0,

0 for case 2 (where 1 indicates presence and 0 indicates absence), the contingency table is as follows:

Case 2 characteristics

	Present	**Absent**
Case 1 characteristics		
Present	2	1
Absent	0	2

The contingency table indicates that both cases are present for two variables (*W* and *X*), both cases are absent for two variables (*V* and *Y*), and case 1 is present and case 2 is absent for one variable (*Z*). There are no variables for which case 1 is absent and case 2 is present.

The available binary measures include matching coefficients, conditional probabilities, predictability measures, and others.

Matching Coefficients. Table 1 shows a classification scheme for PROXIMITIES matching coefficients. In this scheme, *matches* are joint presences (value *a* in the contingency table) or joint absences (value *d*). *Nonmatches* are equal in number to value *b* plus value *c*. Matches and nonmatches may be weighted equally or not. The three coefficients JACCARD, DICE, and SS2 are related monotonically, as are SM, SS1, and RT. All coefficients in Table 1 are similarity measures, and all except two (K1 and SS3) range from 0 to 1. K1 and SS3 have a minimum value of 0 and no upper limit.

Table 1   Binary matching coefficients in PROXIMITIES

	Joint absences excluded from numerator	Joint absences included in numerator
All matches included in denominator		
Equal weight for matches and nonmatches	RR	SM
Double weight for matches		SS1
Double weight for nonmatches		RT
Joint absences excluded from denominator		
Equal weight for matches and nonmatches	JACCARD	
Double weight for matches	DICE	

Table 1   Binary matching coefficients in PROXIMITIES (Continued)

	Joint absences excluded from numerator	Joint absences included in numerator
Double weight for nonmatches	SS2	
All matches excluded from denominator		
Equal weight for matches and nonmatches	K1	SS3

RR[(p[,np])]

Russell and Rao similarity measure. This is the binary dot product.

$$RR(x, y) = \frac{a}{a + b + c + d}$$

SM[(p[,np])]

Simple matching similarity measure. This is the ratio of the number of matches to the total number of characteristics.

$$SM(x, y) = \frac{a + d}{a + b + c + d}$$

JACCARD[(p[,np])]

Jaccard similarity measure. This is also known as the *similarity ratio.*

$$JACCARD(x, y) = \frac{a}{a + b + c}$$

DICE[(p[,np])]

Dice (or Czekanowski or Sorenson) similarity measure.

$$DICE(x, y) = \frac{2a}{2a + b + c}$$

SS1[(p[,np])]

Sokal and Sneath similarity measure 1.

$$SS1(x, y) = \frac{2(a + d)}{2(a + d) + b + c}$$

RT[(p[,np])]

Rogers and Tanimoto similarity measure.

$$RT(x, y) = \frac{a + d}{a + d + 2(b + c)}$$

SS2[(p[,np])]

Sokal and Sneath similarity measure 2.

$$SS2(x, y) = \frac{a}{a + 2(b + c)}$$

K1[(p[,np])]

Kulczynski similarity measure 1. This measure has a minimum value of 0 and no upper limit. It is undefined when there are no nonmatches (*b*=0 and *c*=0). PROXIMITIES assigns an artificial upper limit of 10,000 to K1 when it is undefined or exceeds this value.

$$K1(x, y) = \frac{a}{b + c}$$

SS3[(p[,np])]

Sokal and Sneath similarity measure 3. This measure has a minimum value of 0 and no upper limit. It is undefined when there are no non-matches (*b*=0 and *c*=0). PROXIMITIES assigns an artificial upper limit of 10,000 to SS3 when it is undefined or exceeds this value.

$$SS3(x, y) = \frac{a + d}{b + c}$$

Conditional Probabilities. The following binary measures yield values that can be interpreted in terms of conditional probability. All three are similarity measures.

K2[(p[,np])]

Kulczynski similarity measure 2. This yields the average conditional probability that a characteristic is present in one item given that the characteristic is present in the other item. The measure is an average over both items acting as predictors. It has a range of 0 to 1.

$$K2(x, y) = \frac{a/(a + b) + a/(a + c)}{2}$$

SS4[(p[,np])]

Sokal and Sneath similarity measure 4. This yields the conditional probability that a characteristic of one item is in the same state (presence or absence) as the characteristic of the other item. The measure is an average over both items acting as predictors. It has a range of 0 to 1.

$$SS4(x, y) = \frac{a/(a + b) + a/(a + c) + d/(b + d) + d/(c + d)}{4}$$

HAMANN[(p[,np])]

Hamann similarity measure. This measure gives the probability that a characteristic has the same state in both items (present in both or absent from both) minus the probability that a characteristic has different states in the two items (present in one and absent from the other). HAMANN has a range of −1 to +1 and is monotonically related to SM, SS1, and RT.

$$HAMANN(x, y) = \frac{(a + d) - (b + c)}{a + b + c + d}$$

Predictability Measures. The following four binary measures assess the association between items as the predictability of one given the other. All four measures yield similarities.

LAMBDA[(p[,np])]

Goodman and Kruskal's lambda (similarity). This coefficient assesses the predictability of the state of a characteristic on one item (present or absent) given the state on the other item. Specifically, LAMBDA measures the proportional reduction in error using one item to predict the other when the directions of prediction are of equal importance. LAMBDA has a range of 0 to 1.

$$\text{LAMBDA}(x, y) = \frac{t_1 - t_2}{2(a + b + c + d) - t_2}$$

where
$t_1 = \max(a,b) + \max(c,d) + \max(a,c) + \max(b,d)$
$t_2 = \max(a + c, b + d) + \max(a + d, c + d).$

D[(p[,np])] *Anderberg's D (similarity).* This coefficient assesses the predictability of the state of a characteristic on one item (present or absent) given the state on the other. D measures the actual reduction in the error probability when one item is used to predict the other. The range of D is 0 to 1.

$$D(x, y) = \frac{t_1 - t_2}{2(a + b + c + d)}$$

where
$t_1 = \max(a,b) + \max(c,d) + \max(a,c) + \max(b,d)$
$t_2 = \max(a + c, b + d) + \max(a + d, c + d)$

Y[(p[,np])] *Yule's Y coefficient of colligation (similarity).* This is a function of the cross ratio for a 2×2 table. It has a range of -1 to $+1$.

$$Y(x, y) = \frac{\sqrt{ad} - \sqrt{bc}}{\sqrt{ad} + \sqrt{bc}}$$

Q[(p[,np])] *Yule's Q (similarity).* This is the 2×2 version of Goodman and Kruskal's ordinal measure *gamma*. Like Yule's Y, Q is a function of the cross ratio for a 2×2 table and has a range of -1 to $+1$.

$$Q(x, y) = \frac{ad - bc}{ad + bc}$$

Other Binary Measures. The remaining binary measures available in PROXIMITIES are either binary equivalents of association measures for continuous variables or measures of special properties of the relationship between items.

OCHIAI[(p[,np])] *Ochiai similarity measure.* This is the binary form of the cosine. It has a range of 0 to 1.

$$OCHIAI(x, y) = \sqrt{\frac{a}{a + b} \cdot \frac{a}{a + c}}$$

SS5[(p[,np])]

Sokal and Sneath similarity measure 5. The range is 0 to 1.

$$SS5(x, y) = \frac{ad}{\sqrt{(a + b)(a + c)(b + d)(c + d)}}$$

PHI[(p[,np])]

Fourfold point correlation (similarity). This is the binary form of the Pearson product-moment correlation coefficient.

$$PHI(x, y) = \frac{ad - bc}{\sqrt{(a + b)(a + c)(b + d)(c + d)}}$$

BEUCLID[(p[,np])]

Binary Euclidean distance. This is a distance measure. Its minimum value is 0, and it has no upper limit.

$$BEUCLID(x, y) = \sqrt{b + c}$$

BSEUCLID[(p[,np])]

Binary squared Euclidean distance. This is a distance measure. Its minimum value is 0, and it has no upper limit.

$$BSEUCLID(x, y) = b + c$$

SIZE[(p[,np])]

Size difference. This is a dissimilarity measure with a minimum value of 0 and no upper limit.

$$SIZE(x, y) = \frac{(b - c)^2}{(a + b + c + d)^2}$$

PATTERN[(p[,np])]

Pattern difference. This is a dissimilarity measure. The range is 0 to 1.

$$PATTERN(x, y) = \frac{bc}{(a + b + c + d)^2}$$

BSHAPE[(p[,np])]

Binary shape difference. This dissimilarity measure has no upper or lower limit.

$$BSHAPE(x, y) = \frac{(a + b + c + d)(b + c) - (b - c)^2}{(a + b + c + d)^2}$$

DISPER[(p[,np])]

Dispersion similarity measure. The range is −1 to +1.

$$DISPER(x, y) = \frac{ad - bc}{(a + b + c + d)^2}$$

VARIANCE[(p[,np])]

Variance dissimilarity measure. This measure has a minimum value of 0 and no upper limit.

$$\text{VARIANCE}(x, y) = \frac{b + c}{4(a + b + c + d)}$$

BLWMN[(p[,np])]   *Binary Lance-and-Williams nonmetric dissimilarity measure.* This measure is also known as the Bray-Curtis nonmetric coefficient. The range is 0 to 1.

$$\text{BLWMN}(x, y) = \frac{b + c}{2a + b + c}$$

Example

```
PROXIMITIES A B C
  /MEASURE=RR(1,2).
```

- MEASURE computes Russell and Rao coefficients from data in which 1 indicates the presence of a characteristic and 2 indicates the absence. Other values are ignored.

Example

```
PROXIMITIES A B C
  /MEASURE=SM(2).
```

- MEASURE computes simple matching coefficients from data in which 2 indicates presence and all other values indicate absence.

Transforming Measures in Proximity Matrix

Use keyword NONE to apply the ABSOLUTE, REVERSE, and/or RESCALE transformations to an existing matrix of proximity values without computing any proximity measures.

NONE   *Do not compute proximity measures.* Use NONE only if you have specified an existing proximity matrix on keyword IN on the MATRIX subcommand.

PRINT Subcommand

PROXIMITIES always prints the name of the measure it computes and the number of cases. Use PRINT to control printing of the proximity matrix.

PROXIMITIES   *Print the matrix of the proximities between items.* This is the default. The matrix may have been either read or computed. When the number of cases or variables is large, this specification produces a large volume of output and uses significant CPU time.

NONE   *Do not print the matrix of proximities.*

ID Subcommand

By default, PROXIMITIES identifies cases by case number alone. Use ID to specify an identifying string variable for cases.

- Any string variable in the working data file can be named as the identifier. PROXIMITIES uses the first eight characters of this variable to identify cases in the output.

MISSING Subcommand

MISSING controls the treatment of cases with missing values.

- By default, PROXIMITIES deletes cases with missing values listwise and excludes user-missing values from the analysis.

LISTWISE *Delete cases with missing values listwise.* This is the default.

INCLUDE *Include cases with user-missing values.* Only cases with system-missing values are deleted.

MATRIX Subcommand

MATRIX reads and writes matrix data files.

- Either IN or OUT and the matrix file in parentheses are required. When both IN and OUT are used on the same PROXIMITIES command, they can be specified on separate MATRIX subcommands or on the same subcommand.

OUT (filename) *Write a matrix data file.* Specify either a filename or an asterisk (*), enclosed in parentheses. If you specify a filename, the file is stored on disk and can be retrieved at any time. If you specify an asterisk, the matrix data file replaces the working data file but is not stored on disk unless you use SAVE or XSAVE.

IN (filename) *Read a matrix data file.* If the matrix data file is the working data file, specify an asterisk in parentheses. If the matrix data file is another file, specify the filename in parentheses. A matrix file read from an external file does not replace the working data file.

Matrix Output

- PROXIMITIES writes a variety of proximity matrices, each with *ROWTYPE_* values of PROX. PROXIMITIES neither reads nor writes additional statistics with its matrix materials. See "Format of the Matrix Data File" on p. 947 for a description of the file.
- The matrices PROXIMITIES writes can be used by PROXIMITIES or other procedures. Procedures CLUSTER and ALSCAL can read a proximity matrix directly. Procedure FACTOR can read a correlation matrix written by PROXIMITIES, but RECODE must first be used to change the *ROWTYPE_* value PROX to *ROWTYPE_* value CORR. Also, the ID subcommand cannot be used on PROXIMITIES if the matrix will be used in FACTOR. For more information, see "Universals" on p. 11.
- If VIEW=VARIABLE, the variables in the matrix file will have the names and labels of the original variables.
- If VIEW=CASE (the default), the variables in the matrix file will be named *VAR1, VAR2, ...VARn*, where *n* is the sequential number of the variable in the new file. The numeric suf-

fix *n* is consecutive and does not necessarily match the number of the actual case. If there are no split files, the case number appears in the variable label in the form *CASE m*. The numeric suffix *m* is the actual case number and may not be consecutive (for example, if cases were selected before PROXIMITIES was executed).

- The new file preserves the names and values of any split-file variables in effect. When split-file processing is in effect, no labels are generated for variables in the new file. The actual case number is retained by the variable *ID*.

- Any documents contained in the working data file are not transferred to the matrix file.

Matrix Input

- PROXIMITIES can read a matrix file written by a previous PROXIMITIES procedure.

- The order among rows and variables in the input matrix file is unimportant as long as values for split-file variables precede values for *ROWTYPE_*.

- PROXIMITIES ignores unrecognized *ROWTYPE_* values. In addition, it ignores variables present in the matrix file that are not specified (or used by default) on the PROXIMITIES variable list.

- The program reads variable names, variable and value labels, and print and write formats from the dictionary of the matrix data file.

- MATRIX=IN cannot be used unless a working data file has already been defined. To read an existing matrix data file at the beginning of a session, first use GET to retrieve the matrix file and then specify IN(*) on MATRIX.

- When you read a matrix created with MATRIX DATA, you should supply a value label for PROX of either *SIMILARITY* or *DISSIMILARITY* so the matrix is correctly identified. If you do not supply a label, PROXIMITIES assumes *DISSIMILARITY*. (See "Format of the Matrix Data File" below.)

- The variable list on PROXIMITIES can be omitted when a matrix file is used as input. When the variable list is omitted, all variables in the matrix data file are used in the analysis. If a variable list is specified, the specified variables can be a subset of the variables in the matrix file.

- With a large number of variables, the matrix data file will wrap when it is displayed (as with LIST) and will be difficult to read. Nonetheless, the matrix values are accurate and can be used as matrix input.

Format of the Matrix Data File

- The matrix data file includes two special variables created by the program: *ROWTYPE_* and *VARNAME_*. Variable *ROWTYPE_* is a short string variable with value PROX (for proximity measure). PROX is assigned value labels containing the distance measure used to create the matrix and either *SIMILARITY* or *DISSIMILARITY* as an identifier. Variable *VARNAME_* is a short string variable whose values are the names of the new variables.

- The matrix file includes the string variable named on the ID subcommand. This variable is used to identify cases. Up to 20 characters can be displayed for the identifier variable;

longer values are truncated. The identifier variable is present only when VIEW=CASE (the default) and when the ID subcommand is used.

- The remaining variables in the matrix file are the variables used to form the matrix.

Split Files

- When split-file processing is in effect, the first variables in the matrix system file are the split variables, followed by *ROWTYPE_*, the case-identifier variable (if VIEW=CASE and ID are used), *VARNAME_*, and the variables that make up the matrix.
- A full set of matrix materials is written for each split-file group defined by the split variables.
- A split variable cannot have the same name as any other variable written to the matrix data file.
- If split-file processing is in effect when a matrix is written, the same split file must be in effect when that matrix is read by any procedure.

Example

```
PROXIMITIES  V1 TO V20
  /MATRIX=OUT(DISTOUT).
```

- PROXIMITIES produces a default Euclidean distance matrix for cases using variables *V1* through *V20* and saves the matrix in the SPSS-format file *DISTOUT*.
- The names of the variables on the matrix file will be *VAR1, VAR2, ...VARn*.

Example

```
GET FILE=CRIME.
PROXIMITIES MURDER TO MOTOR
  /ID=CITY
  /MEASURE=EUCLID
  /MATRIX=OUT(PROXMTX).
```

- PROXIMITIES reads data from the SPSS-format data file *CRIME* and writes one set of matrix materials to file *PROXMTX*.
- The working data file is still *CRIME*. Subsequent commands are executed on this file.

Example

```
GET FILE=CRIME.
PROXIMITIES MURDER TO MOTOR
  /ID=CITY
  /MEASURE=EUCLID
  /MATRIX=OUT(*).
LIST.
```

- PROXIMITIES writes the same matrix as in the example above. However, the matrix data file replaces the working data file. The LIST command is executed on the matrix file, not on the *CRIME* file.

Example

```
GET FILE PRSNNL.
FREQUENCIES VARIABLE=AGE.

PROXIMITIES CASE1 TO CASE8
  /ID=CITY
  /MATRIX=IN(PROXMTX).
```

- This example performs a frequencies analysis on file *PRSNNL* and then uses a different file containing matrix data for PROXIMITIES.

- MATRIX=IN specifies the matrix data file *PROXMTX*. *PROXMTX* does not replace *PRSNNL* as the working data file.

Example

```
GET FILE PROXMTX.
PROXIMITIES CASE1 TO CASE8
  /ID=CITY
  /MATRIX=IN(*).
```

- This example assumes that you are starting a new session and want to read an existing matrix data file. GET retrieves the matrix file *PROXMTX*.

- MATRIX=IN specifies an asterisk because the matrix data file is the working data file. If MATRIX=IN(PROXMTX) is specified, the program issues an error message.

- If the GET command is omitted, the program issues an error message.

Example

```
GET FILE=CRIME.
PROXIMITIES MURDER TO MOTOR
  /ID=CITY
  /MATRIX=OUT(*).
PROXIMITIES
  /MATRIX=IN(*)
  /STANDARDIZE.
```

- GET retrieves the SPSS-format data file *CRIME.*

- The first PROXIMITIES command specifies variables for the analysis and reads data from file *CRIME.* ID specifies *CITY* as the case identifier. MATRIX writes the resulting matrix to the working data file.

- The second PROXIMITIES command uses the matrix file written by the first PROXIMITIES command as input. The asterisk indicates that the matrix file is the working data file. The variable list is omitted, indicating that all variables in the matrix are to be used.

- The slash preceding the MATRIX subcommand on the second PROXIMITIES is required. Without the slash, PROXIMITIES would attempt to interpret MATRIX as a variable name rather than as a subcommand.

Example

In this example, PROXIMITIES and FACTOR are used for a *Q*-factor analysis, in which factors account for variance shared among observations rather than among variables. Procedure

FACTOR does not perform *Q*-factor analysis without some preliminary transformation such as that provided by PROXIMITIES. Because the number of cases exceeds the number of variables, the model is not of full rank and FACTOR will print a warning. This is a common occurrence when case-by-case matrices from PROXIMITIES are used as input to FACTOR.

```
* Recoding a PROXIMITIES matrix for procedure FACTOR.

GET FILE=CRIME.
PROXIMITIES    MURDER TO MOTOR
  /MEASURE=CORR
  /MATRIX=OUT(TEMPFILE).
GET FILE=TEMPFILE/DROP=ID.
RECODE ROWTYPE_ ('PROX' = 'CORR').
FACTOR MATRIX IN(COR=*).
```

- The MATRIX subcommand on PROXIMITIES writes the correlation matrix to the working data file. Because the matrix materials will be used in procedure FACTOR, the ID subcommand is not specified.

- RECODE recodes *ROWTYPE_* values PROX to CORR so procedure FACTOR can read the matrix.

- When FACTOR reads matrix materials, it reads all the variables in the file. The MATRIX subcommand on FACTOR indicates that the matrix is a correlation matrix and data are in the working data file.

QUICK CLUSTER

```
QUICK CLUSTER {varlist}
              {ALL     }

[/MISSING=[{LISTWISE**}] [INCLUDE]]
           {PAIRWISE  }
           {DEFAULT   }

[/FILE=file]

[/INITIAL=(value list)]

[/CRITERIA=[CLUSTER({2**})][NOINITIAL][MXITER({10**})] [CONVERGE({0**})]]]
                    {n  }                        {n  }            {n  }

[/METHOD=[{KMEANS[(NOUPDATE)]**}]
          {KMEANS(UPDATE)}      }
          {CLASSIFY             }

[/PRINT=[INITIAL**] [CLUSTER] [ID(varname)] [DISTANCE] [ANOVA] [NONE]]

[/OUTFILE=file]

[/SAVE=[CLUSTER[(varname)]] [DISTANCE[(varname)]]]
```

**Default if subcommand or keyword is omitted.

Example

```
QUICK CLUSTER V1 TO V4
  /CRITERIA=CLUSTER(4)
  /SAVE=CLUSTER(GROUP).
```

Overview

When the desired number of clusters is known, QUICK CLUSTER groups cases efficiently into clusters. It is not as flexible as CLUSTER, but it uses considerably less processing time and memory, especially when the number of cases is large.

Options

Algorithm Specifications. You can specify the number of clusters to form with the CRITERIA subcommand. You can also use CRITERIA to control initial cluster selection and the criteria for iterating the clustering algorithm. With the METHOD subcommand, you can specify how to update cluster centers, and you can request classification only when working with very large data files (see "Operations" on p. 952).

Initial Cluster Centers. By default, QUICK CLUSTER chooses the initial cluster centers. Alternatively, you can provide initial centers on the INITIAL subcommand. You can also read initial cluster centers from an SPSS-format data file using the FILE subcommand.

Optional Output. With the PRINT subcommand you can display the cluster membership of each case and the distance of each case from its cluster center. You can also display the distances between the final cluster centers and a univariate analysis of variance between clusters for each clustering variable.

Saving Results. You can write the final cluster centers to an SPSS-format data file using the OUTFILE subcommand. In addition, you can save the cluster membership of each case and the distance from each case to its classification cluster center as new variables in the working data file using the SAVE subcommand.

Basic Specification

The basic specification is a list of variables. By default, QUICK CLUSTER produces two clusters. The two cases that are farthest apart based on the values of the clustering variables are selected as initial cluster centers and the rest of the cases are assigned to the nearer center. The new cluster centers are calculated as the means of all cases in each cluster, and if neither the minimum change nor the maximum iteration criterion is met, all cases are assigned to the new cluster centers again. When one of the criteria is met, iteration stops, the final cluster centers are updated, and the distance of each case is computed.

Subcommand Order

- The variable list must be specified first.
- Subcommands can be named in any order.

Operations

The procedure generally involves four steps:

- First, initial cluster centers are selected, either by choosing one case for each cluster requested or by using the specified values.
- Second, each case is assigned to the nearest cluster center, and the mean of each cluster is calculated to obtain the new cluster centers.
- Third, the maximum change between the new cluster centers and the initial cluster centers is computed. If the maximum change is not less than the minimum change value and the maximum iteration number is not reached, the second step is repeated and the cluster centers are updated. The process stops when either the minimum change or maximum iteration criterion is met. The resulting clustering centers are used as classification centers in the last step.
- In the last step, all cases are assigned to the nearest classification center. The final cluster centers are updated and the distance for each case is computed.

When the number of cases is large, directly clustering all cases may be impractical. As an alternative, you can cluster a sample of cases and then use the cluster solution for the sample to classify the entire group. This can be done in two phases:

- The first phase obtains a cluster solution for the sample. This involves all four steps of the QUICK CLUSTER algorithm. OUTFILE then saves the final cluster centers to an SPSS-format data file.

- The second phase requires only one pass through the data. First, the FILE subcommand specifies the file containing the final cluster centers from the first analysis. These final cluster centers are used as the initial cluster centers for the second analysis. CLASSIFY is specified on the METHOD subcommand to skip the second and third steps of the clustering algorithm, and cases are classified using the initial cluster centers. When all cases are assigned, the cluster centers are updated and the distance of each case is computed. This phase can be repeated until final cluster centers are stable.

Example

```
QUICK CLUSTER V1 TO V4
  /CRITERIA=CLUSTERS(4)
  /SAVE=CLUSTER(GROUP).
```

- This example clusters cases based on their values for all variables between and including *V1* and *V4* in the working data file.
- Four clusters, rather than the default two, will be formed.
- Initial cluster centers are chosen by finding four widely spaced cases. This is the default.
- The cluster membership of each case is saved in variable *GROUP* in the working data file. *GROUP* has integer values from 1 to 4, indicating the cluster to which each case belongs.

Variable List

The variable list identifies the clustering variables.
- The variable list is required and must be the first specification on QUICK CLUSTER.
- You can use keyword ALL to refer to all user-defined variables in the working data file.
- QUICK CLUSTER uses squared Euclidean distances, which equally weight all clustering variables. If the variables are measured in units that are not comparable, the procedure will give more weight to variables with large variances. Therefore, you should standardize variables measured on different scales using procedure DESCRIPTIVES before performing QUICK CLUSTER.

CRITERIA Subcommand

CRITERIA specifies the number of clusters to form and controls options for the clustering algorithm. You can use any or all of the keywords below.
- The NOINITIAL option followed by the remaining steps of the default QUICK CLUSTER algorithm makes QUICK CLUSTER equivalent to MacQueen's *n*-means clustering method.

CLUSTER(n)   *Number of clusters.* QUICK CLUSTER assigns cases to *n* clusters. The default is 2.

NOINITIAL   *No initial cluster center selection.* By default, initial cluster centers are formed by choosing one case (with valid data for the clustering variables) for each cluster requested. The initial selection requires a pass through the data to ensure that the centers are well separated from one another. If NOINITIAL is specified, QUICK CLUSTER selects the first *n* cases without missing values as initial cluster centers.

MXITER(n) *Maximum number of iterations for updating cluster centers.* The default is 10. Iteration stops when the maximum number of iterations has been reached. MXITER is ignored when METHOD=CLASSIFY.

CONVERGE(n) *Convergence criterion controlling minimum change in cluster centers.* The default value for *n* is 0. The minimum change value equals the convergence value (*n*) times the minimum distance between initial centers. Iteration stops when the largest change of any cluster center is less than or equal to the minimum change value. CONVERGE is ignored when METHOD=CLASSIFY.

METHOD Subcommand

By default, QUICK CLUSTER recalculates cluster centers after assigning all the cases and repeats the process until one of the criteria is met. You can use the METHOD subcommand to recalculate cluster centers after each case is assigned or to suppress recalculation until after classification is complete. When METHOD=KMEANS is specified, QUICK CLUSTER displays the iteration history table.

KMEANS(NOUPDATE) *Recalculate cluster centers after all cases are assigned for each iteration.* This is the default.

KMEANS(UPDATE) *Recalculate a cluster center each time a case is assigned.* QUICK CLUSTER calculates the mean of cases currently in the cluster and uses this new cluster center in subsequent case assignment.

CLASSIFY *Do not recalculate cluster centers.* QUICK CLUSTER uses the initial cluster centers for classification and computes the final cluster centers as the means of all the cases assigned to the same cluster. When CLASSIFY is specified, the CONVERGE or MXITER specifications on CRITERIA are ignored.

INITIAL Subcommand

INITIAL specifies the initial cluster centers. Initial cluster centers can also be read from an SPSS-format data file (see the FILE subcommand on p. 955).

- One value for each clustering variable must be included for each cluster requested. Values are specified in parentheses cluster by cluster.

Example

```
QUICK CLUSTER  A  B  C  D
  /CRITERIA = CLUSTER(3)
  /INITIAL = (13 24  1  8
               7 12  5  9
              10 18 17 16).
```

- This example specifies four clustering variables and requests three clusters. Thus, twelve values are supplied on INITIAL.
- The initial center of the first cluster has a value of 13 for variable *A*, 24 for variable *B*, 1 for *C*, and 8 for *D*.

FILE Subcommand

Use FILE to obtain initial cluster centers from an SPSS-format data file.

- The only specification is the name of the file.

Example

```
QUICK CLUSTER  A  B  C  D
  /FILE=INIT
  /CRITERIA = CLUSTER(3).
```

- In this example, the initial cluster centers are read from file *INIT*. The file must contain cluster centers for the same four clustering variables specified (*A*, *B*, *C*, and *D*).

PRINT Subcommand

QUICK CLUSTER always displays in a Final Cluster Centers table listing the centers used to classify cases and the mean values of the cases in each cluster and a Number of Cases in Each Cluster table listing the number of weighted (if weighting is on) and unweighted cases in each cluster. Use PRINT to request other types of output.

- If PRINT is not specified or is specified without keywords, the default is INITIAL.

INITIAL
Initial cluster centers. When SPLIT FILES is in effect, the initial cluster center for each split file is displayed. This is the default.

CLUSTER
Cluster membership. Each case displays an identifying number or value, the number of the cluster to which it was assigned, and its distance from the center of that cluster. This output is extensive when the number of cases is large.

ID(varname)
Case identification. The value of the specified variable is used in addition to the case numbers to identify cases in output. Case numbers may not be sequential if cases have been selected.

DISTANCE
Pairwise distances between all final cluster centers. This output can consume a great deal of processing time when the number of clusters requested is large.

ANOVA
Descriptive univariate F *tests for the clustering variables.* Since cases are systematically assigned to clusters to maximize differences on the clustering variables, these tests are descriptive only and should not be used to test the null hypothesis that there are no differences between clusters. Statistics after clustering are also available through procedure DISCRIMINANT or GLM (GLM is available in the SPSS Advanced Models option).

NONE   *No additional output.* Only the default output is displayed. NONE overrides any other specifications on PRINT.

Example

```
QUICK CLUSTER A B C D E
  /CRITERIA=CLUSTERS(6)
  /PRINT=CLUSTER ID(CASEID) DISTANCE.
```

- Six clusters are formed on the basis of the five variables *A*, *B*, *C*, *D*, and *E*.
- For each case in the file, cluster membership and distance from cluster center are displayed. Cases are identified by the values of the variable *CASEID*.
- Distances between all cluster centers are printed.

OUTFILE Subcommand

OUTFILE saves the final cluster centers in an SPSS-format data file. You can later use these final cluster centers as initial cluster centers for a different sample of cases that use the same variables. You can also cluster the final cluster centers themselves to obtain clusters of clusters.

- The only specification is a filename for the file.
- The program displays the name of the saved file in the procedure information notes.

Example

```
QUICK CLUSTER A B C D
  /CRITERIA = CLUSTER(3)
  /OUTFILE = QC1.
```

- QUICK CLUSTER writes the final cluster centers to the file *QC1*.

SAVE Subcommand

Use SAVE to save results of cluster analysis as new variables in the working data file.

- You can specify a variable name in parentheses following either keyword. If no variable name is specified, QUICK CLUSTER forms unique variable names by appending an underscore and a sequential number to the rootname *QCL*. The number increments with each new variable saved.
- The program displays the new variables and a short description of each in the procedure information notes.

CLUSTER[(varname)]   *The cluster number of each case.* The value of the new variable is set to an integer from 1 to the number of clusters.

DISTANCE[(varname)]   *The distance of each case from its classification cluster center.*

Example

```
QUICK CLUSTER A B C D
  /CRITERIA=CLUSTERS(6)
  /SAVE=CLUSTER DISTANCE.
```

- Six clusters of cases are formed on the basis of the variables *A*, *B*, *C*, and *D*.
- A new variable *QCL_1* is created and set to an integer between 1 and 6 to indicate cluster membership for each case.
- Another new variable *QCL_2* is created and set to the Euclidean distance between a case and the center of the cluster to which it is assigned.

MISSING Subcommand

MISSING controls the treatment of cases with missing values.

- LISTWISE, PAIRWISE, and DEFAULT are alternatives. However, each can be used with INCLUDE.

LISTWISE   *Delete cases with missing values listwise.* A case with a missing value for any of the clustering variables is deleted from the analysis and will not be assigned to a cluster. This is the default.

PAIRWISE   *Assign each case to the nearest cluster on the basis of the clustering variables for which the case has nonmissing values.* Only cases with missing values for *all* clustering variables are deleted.

INCLUDE   *Treat user-missing values as valid.*

DEFAULT   *Same as LISTWISE.*

RANK

```
RANK [VARIABLES=] varlist [({A**})] [BY varlist]
                          {D  }

  [/TIES={MEAN**  }]
         {LOW     }
         {HIGH    }
         {CONDENSE}

  [/FRACTION={BLOM**}]
             {TUKEY }
             {VW    }
             {RANKIT}

  [/PRINT={YES**}]
          {NO   }

  [/MISSING={EXCLUDE**}]
            {INCLUDE  }
```

The following function subcommands can each be specified once:

```
  [/RANK**] [/NTILES(k)] [/NORMAL] [/PERCENT]

  [/RFRACTION] [/PROPORTION] [/N] [/SAVAGE]
```

The following keyword can be used with any function subcommand:

```
  [INTO varname]
```

**Default if the subcommand is omitted.

Example

```
RANK VARIABLES=SALARY JOBTIME.
```

Overview

RANK produces new variables containing ranks, normal scores, and Savage and related scores for numeric variables.

Options

Methods. You can rank variables in ascending or descending order by specifying A or D on the VARIABLES subcommand. You can compute different rank functions and also name the new variables using the function subcommands. You can specify the method for handling ties on the TIES subcommand, and you can specify how the proportion estimate is computed for the NORMAL and PROPORTIONAL functions on the FRACTION subcommand.

Format. You can suppress the display of the summary table that lists the ranked variables and their associated new variables in the working data file using the PRINT subcommand.

Basic Specification

The basic specification is VARIABLES and at least one variable from the working data file. By default, the ranking function is RANK. Direction is ascending, and ties are handled by assigning the mean rank to tied values. A summary table that lists the ranked variables and the new variables into which computed ranks have been stored is displayed.

Subcommand Order

- VARIABLES must be specified first.
- The remaining subcommands can be specified in any order.

Operations

- RANK does not change the way the working data file is sorted.
- If new variable names are not specified with the INTO keyword on the function subcommand, RANK creates default names. (See the INTO keyword on p. 961.)
- RANK automatically assigns variable labels to the new variables. The labels identify the source variables. For example, the label for a new variable with the default name *RSALARY* is *RANK of SALARY*.

Example

```
RANK VARIABLES=SALARY JOBTIME.
```

- RANK ranks *SALARY* and *JOBTIME* and creates two new variables in the working file, *RSALARY* and *RJOBTIME*, which contain the ranks.

VARIABLES Subcommand

VARIABLES specifies the variables to be ranked. Keyword VARIABLES can be omitted.

- VARIABLES is required and must be the first specification on RANK. The minimum specification is a single numeric variable. To rank more than one variable, specify a variable list.
- After the variable list you can specify the direction for ranking in parentheses. Specify A for ascending (smallest value gets smallest rank) or D for descending (largest value gets smallest rank). A is the default.
- To rank some variables in ascending order and others in descending order, use both A and D in the same variable list. A or D applies to all preceding variables in the list up to the previous A or D specification.
- To organize ranks into subgroups, specify keyword BY followed by the variable whose values determine the subgroups. The working data file does not have to be sorted by this variable.

- String variables cannot be specified. Use AUTORECODE to recode string variables for ranking.

Example

```
RANK VARIABLES=MURDERS ROBBERY (D).
```

- RANK ranks *MURDERS* and *ROBBERY* and creates two new variables in the working data file: *RMURDERS* and *RROBBERY*.
- D specifies descending order of rank. D applies to both *MURDERS* and *ROBBERY*.

Example

```
RANK VARIABLES=MURDERS (D) ROBBERY (A) BY ETHNIC.
```

- Ranks are computed within each group defined by *ETHNIC*. *MURDERS* is ranked in descending order and *ROBBERY* in ascending order within each group of *ETHNIC*. The working data file does not have to be sorted by *ETHNIC*.

Function Subcommands

The optional function subcommands specify different rank functions. RANK is the default function.

- Any combination of function subcommands can be specified for a RANK procedure, but each function can be specified only once.
- Each function subcommand must be preceded by a slash.
- The functions assign default names to the new variables unless keyword INTO is specified (see the INTO keyword on p. 961).

RANK *Simple ranks.* The values for the new variable are the ranks. Rank can either be ascending or descending, as indicated on the VARIABLES subcommand. Rank values can be affected by the specification on the TIES subcommand.

RFRACTION *Fractional ranks.* The values for the new variable equal the ranks divided by the sum of the weights of the nonmissing cases. If HIGH is specified on TIES, fractional rank values are an empirical cumulative distribution.

NORMAL *Normal scores* (Lehmann, 1975). The new variable contains the inverse of the standard normal cumulative distribution of the proportion estimate defined by the FRACTION subcommand. The default for FRACTION is BLOM.

PERCENT *Fractional ranks as a percentage.* The new variable contains fractional ranks multiplied by 100.

PROPORTION *Proportion estimates.* The estimation method is specified by the FRACTION subcommand. The default for FRACTION is BLOM.

N *Sum of case weights.* The new variable is a constant.

SAVAGE *Savage scores* (Lehmann, 1975). The new variable contains Savage (exponential) scores.

NTILES(k)   *Percentile groups.* The new variable contains values from 1 to k, where k is the number of groups to be generated. Each case is assigned a group value, which is the integer part of $1+rk/(w+1)$, where r is the rank of the case, k is the number of groups specified on NTILES, and w is the sum of the case weights. Group values can be affected by the specification on TIES. There is no default for k.

INTO Keyword

INTO specifies variable names for the new variable(s) added to the working data file. INTO can be used with any of the function subcommands.

- INTO must follow a function subcommand. You must specify the INTO subcommand to assign names to the new variables created by the function.
- You can specify multiple variable names on INTO. The names are assigned to the new variables in the order they are created (the order the variables are specified on the VARIABLES subcommand).
- If you specify fewer names than the new variables, default names are used for the remaining new variables. If you specify more names, the program issues a message and the command is not executed.

If INTO is not specified on a function, RANK creates default names for the new variables according to the following rules:

- The first letter of the ranking function is added to the first seven characters of the original variable name.
- New variable names cannot duplicate variable names in the working data file or names specified after INTO or generated by default.
- If a new default name is a duplicate, the scheme *XXXnnn* is used, where *XXX* represents the first three characters of the function and *nnn* is a three-digit number starting with 001 and increased by 1 for each variable. (If the ranking function is N, *XXX* is simply *N*.) If this naming scheme generates duplicate names, the duplicates are named *RNKXXnn*, where *XX* is the first two characters of the function and *nn* is a two-digit number starting with 01 and increased by 1 for each variable.
- If it is not possible to generate unique names, an error results.

Example

```
RANK VARIABLES=SALARY
 /NORMAL INTO SALNORM
 /SAVAGE INTO SALSAV
 /NTILES(4) INTO SALQUART.
```

- RANK generates three new variables from variable *SALARY*.
- NORMAL produces the new variable *SALNORM*. *SALNORM* contains normal scores for *SALARY* computed with the default formula BLOM.
- SAVAGE produces the new variable *SALSAV*. *SALSAV* contains Savage scores for *SALARY*.
- NTILES(4) produces the new variable *SALQUART*. *SALQUART* contains the value 1, 2, 3, or 4 to represent one of the four percentile groups of *SALARY*.

TIES Subcommand

TIES determines the way tied values are handled. The default method is MEAN.

MEAN   *Mean rank of tied values is used for ties.* This is the default.

LOW   *Lowest rank of tied values is used for ties.*

HIGH   *Highest rank of tied values is used for ties.*

CONDENSE *Consecutive ranks with ties sharing the same value.* Each distinct value of the ranked variable is assigned a consecutive rank. Ties share the same rank.

Example

```
RANK VARIABLES=BURGLARY /RANK INTO RMEAN /TIES=MEAN.
RANK VARIABLES=BURGLARY /RANK INTO RCONDS /TIES=CONDENSE.
RANK VARIABLES=BURGLARY /RANK INTO RHIGH /TIES=HIGH.
RANK VARIABLES=BURGLARY /RANK INTO RLOW /TIES=LOW.
```

- The values of *BURGLARY* and the four new ranking variables are shown below:

BURGLARY	RMEAN	RCONDS	RHIGH	RLOW
0	3	1	5	1
0	3	1	5	1
0	3	1	5	1
0	3	1	5	1
0	3	1	5	1
1	6.5	2	7	6
1	6.5	2	7	6
3	8	3	8	8

FRACTION Subcommand

FRACTION specifies the way to compute a proportion estimate P for the NORMAL and PROPORTION rank functions.

- FRACTION can be used only with function subcommands NORMAL or PROPORTION. If it is used with other function subcommands, FRACTION is ignored and a warning message is displayed.

- Only one formula can be specified for each RANK procedure. If more than one is specified, an error results.

In the following formulas, r is the rank and w is the sum of case weights.

BLOM   *Blom's transformation, defined by the formula $(r - 3/8)/(w + 1/4)$.* (Blom, 1958.) This is the default.

RANKIT *The formula is $(r - 1/2)/w$.* (Chambers et al., 1983.)

TUKEY   *Tukey's transformation, defined by the formula $(r - 1/3)/(w + 1/3)$.* (Tukey, 1962.)

VW   *Van der Waerden's transformation, defined by the formula $r/(w + 1)$.* (Lehmann, 1975.)

Example

```
RANK VARIABLES=MORTGAGE VALUE /FRACTION=BLOM
   /NORMAL INTO MORTNORM VALNORM.
```

- RANK generates new variables *MORTNORM* and *VALNORM*. *MORTNORM* contains normal scores for *MORTGAGE*, and *VALNORM* contains normal scores for *VALUE*.

PRINT Subcommand

PRINT determines whether the summary tables are displayed. The summary table lists the ranked variables and their associated new variables in the working data file.

YES   *Display the summary tables.* This is the default.

NO   *Suppress the summary tables.*

MISSING Subcommand

MISSING controls the treatment of user-missing values.

INCLUDE   *Include user-missing values.* User-missing values are treated as valid values.

EXCLUDE   *Exclude all missing values.* User-missing values are treated as missing. This is the default.

Example

```
MISSING VALUE SALARY (0).
RANK VARIABLES=SALARY /RANK INTO SALRANK /MISSING=INCLUDE.
```

- RANK generates the new variable *SALRANK*.
- INCLUDE causes the user-missing value 0 to be included in the ranking process.

References

Blom, G. 1958. *Statistical estimates and transformed beta variables.* New York: John Wiley and Sons.

Chambers, J. M., W. S. Cleveland, B. Kleiner, and P. A. Tukey. 1983. *Graphical methods for data analysis.* Belmont, California: Wadsworth International Group; Boston: Duxbury Press.

Fisher, R. A. 1973. *Statistical methods for research workers.* 14th ed. New York: Hafner Publishing Company.

Frigge, M., D. C. Hoaglin, and B. Iglewicz. 1987. Some implementations of the boxplot. In: *Computer Science and Statistics Proceedings of the 19th Symposium on the Interface*, R. M. Heiberger and M. Martin, eds. Alexandria, Virginia: American Statistical Association.

Lehmann, E. L. 1975. *Nonparametrics: Statistical methods based on ranks.* San Francisco: Holden-Day.

Tukey, J. W. 1962. The future of data analysis. *Annals of Mathematical Statistics*, 33:22.

RECODE

For numeric variables:

```
RECODE varlist (value list=value)...(value list=value) [INTO varlist]
       [/varlist...]
```

Input keywords:

LO, LOWEST, HI, HIGHEST, THRU, MISSING, SYSMIS, ELSE

Output keywords:

COPY, SYSMIS

For string variables:

```
RECODE varlist [('string',['string'...]='string')][INTO varlist]
       [/varlist...]
```

Input keywords:

CONVERT, ELSE

Output keyword:

COPY

Examples

```
RECODE V1 TO V3 (0=1) (1=0) (2,3=-1) (9=9) (ELSE=SYSMIS).

RECODE STRNGVAR ('A','B','C'='A')('D','E','F'='B')(ELSE=' ').
```

Overview

RECODE changes, rearranges, or consolidates the values of an existing variable. RECODE can be executed on a value-by-value basis or for a range of values. Where it can be used, RECODE is much more efficient than the series of IF commands that produce the same transformation.

With RECODE, you must specify the new values. Use AUTORECODE to automatically recode the values of string or numeric variables to consecutive integers.

Options

You can generate a new variable as the recoded version of an existing variable using keyword INTO. You can also use INTO to recode a string variable into a new numeric variable for more efficient processing, or to recode a numeric variable into a new string variable to provide more descriptive values.

Basic Specification

The basic specification is a variable name and, within parentheses, the original values followed by a required equals sign and a new value. RECODE changes the values on the left of the equals sign into the single value on the right of the equals sign.

Syntax Rules

- The variables to be recoded must already exist and must be specified before the value specifications.
- Value specifications are enclosed in parentheses. The original value or values must be specified to the left of an equals sign. A single new value is specified to the right of the equals sign.
- Multiple values can be consolidated into a single recoded value by specifying, to the left of the equals sign, a list of values separated by blanks or commas. Only one recoded value per set is allowed to the right of the equals sign.
- Multiple sets of value specifications are permitted. Each set must be enclosed in parentheses and can result in only one new value.
- To recode multiple variables using the same set of value specifications, specify a variable list before the value specifications. Each variable in the list is recoded identically.
- To recode variables using different value specifications, separate each variable (or variable list) and its specifications from the others by a slash.
- Original values that are not mentioned remain unchanged unless keyword ELSE is used. ELSE refers to all original values not previously mentioned, including the system-missing value. ELSE should be the last specification for the variable.
- COPY replicates original values without recoding them.
- INTO is required to recode a string variable into a numeric variable or a numeric variable into a string variable (see the INTO keyword on p. 967).

Numeric Variables

- Keywords that can be used in the list of original values are LO (or LOWEST), HI (or HIGHEST), THRU, MISSING, SYSMIS, and ELSE. Keywords that can be used in place of a new value are COPY and SYSMIS.
- THRU specifies a value range and includes the specified end values.
- LOWEST and HIGHEST (LO and HI) specify the lowest and highest values encountered in the data. LOWEST and HIGHEST include user-missing values but not the system-missing value.
- MISSING specifies user-missing and system-missing values for recoding. MISSING can be used in the list of original values only.
- SYSMIS specifies the system-missing value and can be used as both an original value and a new value.
- See "Syntax Rules" above for a description of ELSE and COPY.

String Variables

- Keywords that can be used in the list of original values are CONVERT and ELSE. The only keyword that can be used in place of a new value is COPY. See p. 968 for a description of CONVERT, and "Syntax Rules" on p. 965 for a description of ELSE and COPY.
- Both short and long string variables can be recoded.
- Values must be enclosed in apostrophes or quotation marks.
- Blanks are significant characters.

Operations

- Value specifications are scanned left to right.
- A value is recoded only once per RECODE command.
- Invalid specifications on a RECODE command that result in errors stop all processing of that RECODE command. No variables are recoded.

Numeric Variables

- Blank fields for numeric variables are handled according to the SET BLANKS specification prior to recoding.
- When you recode a value that was previously defined as user-missing on the MISSING VALUE command, the new value is not missing.

String Variables

- If the original or new value specified is shorter than the format width defined for the variable, the string is right-padded with blanks.
- If the original or recoded value specified is longer than the format width defined for that variable, the program issues an error message and RECODE is not executed.

Limitations

- You can recode (and count using the COUNT command) approximately 400 values.

Example

```
RECODE V1 TO V3 (0=1) (1=0) (2,3=-1) (9=9) (ELSE=SYSMIS)
   /QVAR(1 THRU 5=1)(6 THRU 10=2)(11 THRU HI=3)(ELSE=0).
```

- The numeric variables between and including *V1* and *V3* are recoded: original values 0 and 1 are switched respectively to 1 and 0; 2 and 3 are changed to −1; 9 remains 9; and any other value is changed to the system-missing value.

- Variable *QVAR* is also recoded: original values 1 through 5 are changed to 1; 6 through 10 are changed to 2; 11 through the highest value in the data are changed to 3; and any other value, including system-missing, is changed to 0.

Example

```
RECODE STRNGVAR ('A','B','C'='A')('D','E','F'='B')(ELSE=' ').
RECODE PET ('IGUANA', 'SNAKE ' = 'WILD  ').
```

- Values A, B, and C are changed to value A. Values D, E, and F are changed to value B. All other values are changed to a blank.

- Values IGUANA and SNAKE are changed to value WILD. The defined width of variable *PET* is 6. Thus, values SNAKE and WILD include trailing blanks for a total of six characters. If blanks are not specified, the values are right-padded. In this example, the results will be the same.

- Each string value is enclosed within apostrophes.

INTO Keyword

INTO specifies a **target** variable to receive recoded values from the original, or **source**, variable. Source variables remain unchanged after the recode.

- INTO must follow the value specifications for the source variables that are being recoded into the target variables.

- The number of target variables must equal the number of source variables.

Numeric Variables

- Target variables can be existing or new variables. For existing variables, cases with values not mentioned in the value specifications are not changed. For new variables, cases with values not mentioned are assigned the system-missing value.

- New numeric variables have default print and write formats of F8.2 (or the format specified on SET FORMAT).

Example

```
RECODE AGE (MISSING=9) (18 THRU HI=1) (0 THRU 18=0) INTO VOTER.
```

- The recoded *AGE* values are stored in target variable *VOTER*, leaving *AGE* unchanged.

- Value 18 and higher values are changed to value 1. Values between 0 and 18, but not including 18, are recoded to 0. If the specification 0 THRU 18 preceded the specification 18 THRU HI, value 18 would be recoded to 0.

Example

```
RECODE V1 TO V3 (0=1) (1=0) (2=-1) INTO DEFENSE WELFARE HEALTH.
```

- Values for *V1* through *V3* are recoded and stored in *DEFENSE*, *WELFARE*, and *HEALTH*. *V1*, *V2*, and *V3* are not changed.

String Variables

- Target variables must already exist. To create a new string variable, declare the variable with the STRING command before specifying it on RECODE.
- The new string values cannot be longer than the defined width of the target variable.
- If the new values are shorter than the defined width of the target variable, the values are right-padded with blanks.
- Multiple target variables are allowed. The target variables must all be the same defined width; the source variables can have different widths.
- If the source and target variables have different widths, the criterion for the width of the original values is the width defined for the source variable; the criterion for the width of the recoded values is the width defined for the target variable.

Example

```
STRING STATE1 (A2).
RECODE STATE ('IO'='IA') (ELSE=COPY) INTO STATE1.
```

- STRING declares variable *STATE1* so that it can be used as a target variable on RECODE.
- RECODE specifies *STATE* as the source variable and *STATE1* as the target variable. The original value IO is recoded to IA. Keywords ELSE and COPY copy all other state codes over unchanged. Thus, *STATE* and *STATE1* are identical except for cases with the original value IO.

Example

```
RECODE SEX ('M'=1) ('F'=2) INTO NSEX.
```

- RECODE recodes string variable *SEX* into numeric variable *NSEX*. Any value other than M or F becomes system-missing.
- The program can process a large number of cases more efficiently with the numeric variable *NSEX* than it can with the string variable *SEX*.

CONVERT Keyword

CONVERT recodes the string representation of numbers to their numeric representation.

- If keyword CONVERT precedes the value specifications, cases with numbers are recoded immediately and blanks are recoded to the system-missing value, even if you specifically recode blanks into a value.
- To recode blanks to a value other than system-missing or to recode a string value to a non-corresponding numeric value (for example '0' to 10), you must specify a recode specification *before* the keyword CONVERT.
- RECODE converts numbers as if the variable were being reread using the F format.
- If RECODE encounters a value that cannot be converted, it scans the remaining value specifications. If there is no specific recode specification for that value, the target variable will be system-missing for that case.

Example

```
RECODE #JOB (CONVERT) ('-'=11) ('&'=12) INTO JOB.
```

- RECODE first recodes all numbers in string variable #JOB to numbers. The target variable is JOB.
- RECODE then specifically recodes the minus sign (the "eleven" punch) to 11 and the ampersand (or "twelve" punch in EBCDIC) to 12. Keyword CONVERT is specified first as an efficiency measure to recode cases with numbers immediately. Blanks are recoded to the system-missing value.

Example

```
RECODE #JOB (' '=-99) (CONVERT) ('-'=11) ('&'=12) INTO JOB.
```

- The result is the same as in the above example, except that blanks are changed to −99.

RECORD TYPE

For mixed file types:

```
RECORD TYPE {value list} [SKIP]
            {OTHER     }
```

For grouped file types:

```
RECORD TYPE {value list} [SKIP] [CASE=col loc]
            {OTHER     }

 [DUPLICATE={WARN  }] [MISSING={WARN  }]
           {NOWARN}            {NOWARN}
```

For nested file types:

```
RECORD TYPE {value list} [SKIP] [CASE=col loc]
            {OTHER     }

 [SPREAD={YES}] [MISSING={WARN  }]
         {NO }           {NOWARN}
```

Example
```
FILE TYPE   MIXED RECORD=RECID 1-2.
RECORD TYPE 23.
DATA LIST    /SEX 5 AGE 6-7 DOSAGE 8-10 RESULT 12.
END FILE TYPE.

BEGIN DATA
21    145010 1
22    257200 2
25    235   250  2
35    167          300      3
24    125150 1
23    272075 1
21    149050 2
25    134   035  3
30    138          300      3
32    229          500      3
END DATA.
```

Overview

RECORD TYPE is used with DATA LIST within a FILE TYPE—END FILE TYPE structure to define any one of the three types of complex raw data files: **mixed files**, which contain several types of records that define different types of cases; **hierarchical** or **nested files**, which contain several types of records with a defined relationship among the record types; or **grouped files**, which contain several records for each case with some records missing or duplicated (see FILE TYPE for more complete information). A fourth type of complex file, files with **repeating groups** of information, can be read with the REPEATING DATA command. REPEATING DATA can also be used to read mixed files and the lowest level of nested files.

Each type of complex file has varying types of records. One set of RECORD TYPE and DATA LIST commands is used to define each type of record in the data. The specifications available for RECORD TYPE vary according to whether MIXED, GROUPED, or NESTED is specified on FILE TYPE.

Basic Specification

For each record type being defined, the basic specification is the value of the record type variable defined on the RECORD subcommand on FILE TYPE.

- RECORD TYPE must be followed by a DATA LIST command defining the variables for the specified records, unless SKIP is used.
- One pair of RECORD TYPE and DATA LIST commands must be used for each defined record type.

Syntax Rules

- A list of values can be specified if a set of different record types has the same variable definitions. Each value must be separated by a space or comma.
- String values must be enclosed in apostrophes or quotation marks.
- For mixed files, each DATA LIST can specify variables with the same variable name, since each record type defines a separate case. For grouped and nested files, the variable names on each DATA LIST must be unique, since a case is built by combining all record types together onto a single record.
- For mixed files, if the same variable is defined for more than one record type, the format type and width of the variable should be the same on all DATA LIST commands. The program refers to the first DATA LIST command that defines a variable for the print and write formats to include in the dictionary of the working data file.
- For nested files, the order of the RECORD TYPE commands defines the hierarchical structure of the file. The first RECORD TYPE defines the highest-level record type, the next RECORD TYPE defines the next highest-level record, and so forth. The last RECORD TYPE command defines a case in the working data file.

Operations

- If a record type is specified on more than one RECORD TYPE command, the program uses the DATA LIST command associated with the first specification and ignores all others.
- For NESTED files, the first record in the file should be the type specified on the first RECORD TYPE command—the highest-level record of the hierarchy. If the first record in the file is not the highest-level type, the program skips all records until it encounters a record of the highest-level type. If the MISSING or DUPLICATE subcommands have been specified on the FILE TYPE command, these records may produce warning messages but will not be used to build a case in the working data file.

Example

```
* Reading only one record type from a mixed file.

FILE TYPE  MIXED RECORD=RECID 1-2.
RECORD TYPE 23.
DATA LIST   /SEX 5 AGE 6-7 DOSAGE 8-10 RESULT 12.
END FILE TYPE.

BEGIN DATA
21   145010 1
22   257200 2
25   235   250   2
35   167             300       3
24   125150 1
23   272075 1
21   149050 2
25   134   035   3
30   138             300       3
32   229             500       3
END DATA.
```

- FILE TYPE begins the file definition, and END FILE TYPE indicates the end of file definition. FILE TYPE specifies a mixed file type. Since the data are included between BEGIN DATA—END DATA, the FILE subcommand is omitted. The record identification variable *RECID* is located in columns 1 and 2.

- RECORD TYPE indicates that records with value 23 for variable *RECID* will be copied into the working data file. All other records are skipped. The program does not issue a warning when it skips records in mixed files.

- DATA LIST defines variables on records with the value 23 for variable *RECID*.

Example

```
* Reading multiple record types from a mixed file.

FILE TYPE  MIXED FILE=TREATMNT RECORD=RECID 1-2.
+ RECORD TYPE 21,22,23,24.
+ DATA LIST   /SEX 5 AGE 6-7 DOSAGE 8-10 RESULT 12.
+ RECORD TYPE 25.
+ DATA LIST   /SEX 5 AGE 6-7 DOSAGE 10-12 RESULT 15.
END FILE TYPE.
```

- Variable *DOSAGE* is read from columns 8–10 for record types 21, 22, 23, and 24 and from columns 10–12 for record type 25. *RESULT* is read from column 12 for record types 21, 22, 23, and 24 and from column 15 for record type 25.

- The working data file contains values for all variables defined on the DATA LIST commands for record types 21 through 25. All other record types are skipped.

Example

```
* A nested file of accident records.

FILE TYPE NESTED RECORD=6 CASE=ACCID 1-4.
RECORD TYPE 1.
DATA LIST /ACC_ID 9-11 WEATHER 12-13 STATE 15-16 (A) DATE 18-24 (A).
RECORD TYPE 2.
DATA LIST /STYLE 11 MAKE 13 OLD 14 LICENSE 15-16(A) INSURNCE 18-21 (A).
RECORD TYPE 3.
DATA LIST /PSNGR_NO 11 AGE 13-14 SEX 16 (A) INJURY 18 SEAT 20-21 (A)
          COST 23-24.
END FILE TYPE.

BEGIN DATA
0001 1   322 1 IL 3/13/88   /* Type 1:  accident record
0001 2     1 44MI 134M      /* Type 2:    vehicle record
0001 3     1 34 M 1 FR   3  /* Type 3:      person record
0001 2     2 16IL 322F      /*              vehicle record
0001 3     1 22 F 1 FR 11   /*              person record
0001 3     2 35 M 1 FR   5  /*              person record
0001 3     3 59 M 1 BK   7  /*              person record
0001 2     3 21IN 146M      /*              vehicle record
0001 3     1 46 M 0 FR   0  /*              person record
END DATA.
```

- FILE TYPE specifies a nested file type. The record identifier, located in column 6, is not assigned a variable name, so the default scratch variable name *####RECD* is used. The case identification variable *ACCID* is located in columns 1–4.

- Because there are three record types, there are three RECORD TYPE commands. For each RECORD TYPE there is a DATA LIST command to define variables on that record type. The order of the RECORD TYPE commands defines the hierarchical structure of the file.

- END FILE TYPE signals the end of file definition.

- The program builds a case for each lowest-level (type 3) record, representing each person in the file. There can be only one type 1 record for each type 2 record, and one type 2 record for each type 3 record. Each vehicle can be in only one accident, and each person can be in only one vehicle. The variables from the type 1 and type 2 records are spread to their corresponding type 3 records.

OTHER Keyword

OTHER specifies all record types that have not been mentioned on previous RECORD TYPE commands.

- OTHER can be specified only on the last RECORD TYPE command in the file definition.

- OTHER can be used with SKIP to skip all undefined record types.

- For nested files, OTHER can be used only with SKIP. Neither can be used separately.

- If WILD=WARN is in effect for the FILE TYPE command, OTHER cannot be specified on the RECORD TYPE command.

Example

```
* A mixed file.

FILE TYPE  MIXED FILE=TREATMNT RECORD=RECID 1-2.
RECORD TYPE 21,22,23,24.
DATA LIST    /SEX 5 AGE 6-7 DOSAGE 8-10 RESULT 12.
RECORD TYPE 25.
DATA LIST    /SEX 5 AGE 6-7 DOSAGE 10-12 RESULT 15.
RECORD TYPE OTHER.
DATA LIST    /SEX 5 AGE 6-7 DOSAGE 18-20 RESULT 25.
END FILE TYPE.
```

- The first two RECORD TYPE commands specify record types 21–25. All other record types are specified by the third RECORD TYPE.

Example

```
* A nested file.

FILE TYPE NESTED FILE=ACCIDENT RECORD=#RECID 6 CASE=ACCID 1-4.
RECORD TYPE 1.          /* Accident record
DATA LIST    /WEATHER 12-13.
RECORD TYPE 2.          /* Vehicle record
DATA LIST /STYLE 16.
RECORD TYPE OTHER SKIP.
END FILE TYPE.
```

- The third RECORD TYPE specifies OTHER SKIP. Type 2 records are therefore the lowest-level records included in the working data file. These commands build one case for each vehicle record. The person records are skipped.
- Because the data are in a nested file, OTHER can be specified only with SKIP.

SKIP Subcommand

SKIP specifies record types to skip.

- To skip selected record types, specify the values for the types you want to skip and then specify SKIP. To skip all record types other than those specified on previous RECORD TYPE commands, specify OTHER and then SKIP.
- For nested files, SKIP can be used only with OTHER. Neither can be used separately.
- For grouped files, OTHER cannot be specified on SKIP if WILD=WARN (the default) is in effect for FILE TYPE.
- For mixed files, all record types that are not specified on a RECORD TYPE command are skipped by default. No warning is issued (WILD=NOWARN on FILE TYPE is the default for mixed files).
- For grouped files, a warning message is issued by default for all record types not specified on a RECORD TYPE command (WILD=WARN on FILE TYPE is the default for grouped files). If the record types are explicitly specified on SKIP, no warning is issued.

Example

```
FILE TYPE GROUPED FILE=HUBDATA RECORD=#RECID 80 CASE=ID 1-5
                                WILD=NOWARN.
RECORD TYPE 1.
DATA LIST    /MOHIRED YRHIRED 12-15 DEPT79 TO DEPT82 SEX 16-20.
RECORD TYPE OTHER SKIP.
END FILE TYPE.
```

- The program reads variables from type 1 records and skips all other types.

- WILD=NOWARN on the FILE TYPE command suppresses the warning messages that is issued by default for undefined record types for grouped files. Keyword OTHER cannot be used when the default WILD=WARN specification is in effect.

Example

```
FILE TYPE GROUPED FILE=HUBDATA RECORD=#RECID 80 CASE=ID 1-5.
RECORD TYPE 1.
DATA LIST    /MOHIRED YRHIRED 12-15 DEPT79 TO DEPT82 SEX 16-20.
RECORD TYPE 2,3 SKIP.
END FILE TYPE.
```

- Record type 1 is defined for each case, and record types 2 and 3 are skipped.

- WILD=WARN (the default) on FILE TYPE GROUPED is in effect. The program therefore issues a warning message for any record types it encounters other than types 1, 2, and 3. No warning is issued for record types 2 and 3 because they are explicitly specified on a RECORD TYPE command.

CASE Subcommand

CASE specifies the column locations of the case identification variable when that variable is not in the location defined by the CASE subcommand on FILE TYPE.

- CASE on RECORD TYPE applies only to those records specified by that RECORD TYPE command. The identifier for record types without CASE on RECORD TYPE must be in the location specified by CASE on FILE TYPE.

- CASE can be used for nested and grouped files only. CASE cannot be used for mixed files.

- CASE can be used on RECORD TYPE only if a CASE subcommand is specified on FILE TYPE.

- The format type of the case identification variable must be the same on all records, and the same format must be assigned on the RECORD TYPE and FILE TYPE commands. For example, if the case identification variable is defined as a string on FILE TYPE, it cannot be defined as a numeric variable on RECORD TYPE.

Example

```
* Specifying case on the record type command for a grouped file.

FILE TYPE GROUPED FILE=HUBDATA RECORD=#RECID 80 CASE=ID 1-5.
RECORD TYPE 1.
DATA LIST    /MOHIRED YRHIRED 12-15 DEPT79 TO DEPT82 SEX 16-20.
RECORD TYPE 2.
DATA LIST    /SALARY79 TO SALARY82 6-25
               HOURLY81 HOURLY82 40-53 (2)
                PROMO81 72   AGE 54-55 RAISE82 66-70.
RECORD TYPE 3   CASE=75-79.
DATA LIST    /JOBCAT 6 NAME 25-48 (A).
END FILE TYPE.
```

- CASE on FILE TYPE indicates that the case identification variable is located in columns 1–5. On the third RECORD TYPE command, the CASE subcommand overrides the identifier location for type 3 records. For type 3 records, the case identification variable is located in columns 75–79.

MISSING Subcommand

MISSING controls whether the program issues a warning when it encounters a missing record type for a case. Regardless of whether the program issues the warning, it builds the case in the working data file with system-missing values for the variables defined on the missing record.

- The only specification is a single keyword. NOWARN is the default for nested files. WARN is the default for grouped files. MISSING cannot be used with MIXED files.

- MISSING on RECORD TYPE applies only to those records specified by that RECORD TYPE command. The treatment of missing records for record types without the MISSING specification on RECORD TYPE is determined by the MISSING subcommand on FILE TYPE.

- For grouped files, the program checks whether there is a record for each case identification number. For nested files, the program verifies that each defined case includes one record of each type.

WARN   *Issue a warning message when a record type is missing for a case.* This is the default for grouped files.

NOWARN   *Suppress the warning message when a record type is missing for a case.* This is the default for nested files.

Example

```
FILE TYPE GROUPED FILE=HUBDATA RECORD=#RECID 80 CASE=ID 1-5.
RECORD TYPE 1.
DATA LIST    /MOHIRED YRHIRED 12-15 DEPT79 TO DEPT82 SEX 16-20.
RECORD TYPE 2  MISSING=NOWARN.
DATA LIST    /SALARY79 TO SALARY82 6-25
   HOURLY81 HOURLY82 40-53 (2) PROMO81 72 AGE 54-55 RAISE82 66-70.
RECORD TYPE 3.
DATA LIST    /JOBCAT 6 NAME 25-48 (A).
END FILE TYPE.
```

- MISSING is not specified on FILE TYPE. Therefore the default MISSING=WARN is in effect for all record types.
- MISSING=NOWARN is specified on the second RECORD TYPE, overriding the default setting for type 2 records. WARN is still in effect for type 1 and type 3 records.

DUPLICATE Subcommand

DUPLICATE controls whether the program issues a warning when it encounters more than one record of each type for a single case.

- DUPLICATE on RECORD TYPE can be used for grouped files only. DUPLICATE cannot be used for mixed or nested files.
- The only specification is a single keyword. WARN is the default.
- DUPLICATE on RECORD TYPE applies only to those records specified by that RECORD TYPE command. The treatment of duplicate records for record types without DUPLICATE specification is determined by the DUPLICATE subcommand on FILE TYPE.
- Regardless of the specification on DUPLICATE, only the last record from a set of duplicates is included in the working data file.

WARN   *Issue a warning message.* The program issues a message and the first 80 characters of the last record of the duplicate set of record types. This is the default.

NOWARN   *Suppress the warning message.*

Example

```
* Specifying DUPLICATE on RECORD TYPE for a grouped file.

FILE TYPE GROUPED FILE=HUBDATA RECORD=#RECID 80 CASE=ID 1-5.
RECORD TYPE 1.
DATA LIST    /MOHIRED YRHIRED 12-15 DEPT79 TO DEPT82 SEX 16-20.
RECORD TYPE 2   DUPLICATE=NOWARN.
DATA LIST    /SALARY79 TO SALARY82 6-25
  HOURLY81 HOURLY82 40-53 (2) PROMO81 72  AGE 54-55 RAISE82 66-70.
RECORD TYPE 3.
DATA LIST    /JOBCAT 6 NAME 25-48 (A).
END FILE TYPE.
```

- DUPLICATE is not specified on FILE TYPE. Therefore the default DUPLICATE=WARN is in effect for all record types.
- DUPLICATE=NOWARN is specified on the second RECORD TYPE, overriding the FILE TYPE setting for type 2 records. WARN is still in effect for type 1 and type 3 records.

SPREAD Subcommand

SPREAD controls whether the values for variables defined for a record type are spread to all related cases.

- SPREAD can be used for nested files only. SPREAD cannot be used for mixed or grouped files.
- The only specification is a single keyword. YES is the default.
- SPREAD=NO applies only to the record type specified on that RECORD TYPE command. The default YES is in effect for all other defined record types.

YES   *Spread the values from the specified record type to all related cases.* This is the default.

NO   *Spread the values from the specified type only to the first related case.* All other cases built from the same record are assigned the system-missing value for the variables defined on the record type.

Example

```
* A nested file.

FILE TYPE NESTED RECORD=#RECID 6 CASE=ACCID 1-4.
RECORD TYPE 1.
DATA LIST    /ACC_NO 9-11 WEATHER 12-13
                STATE 15-16 (A) DATE 18-24 (A).
RECORD TYPE 2  SPREAD=NO.
DATA LIST /STYLE 11 MAKE 13 OLD 14
            LICENSE 15-16 (A) INSURNCE 18-21 (A).
RECORD TYPE 3.
DATA LIST /PSNGR_NO 11 AGE 13-14 SEX 16 (A)
        INJURY 18 SEAT 20-21 (A) COST 23-24.
END FILE TYPE.

BEGIN DATA
0001 1   322 1 IL 3/13/88    /* Type 1:   accident record
0001 2     1 44MI 134M       /* Type 2:    vehicle record
0001 3     1 34 M 1 FR   3   /* Type 3:    person record
0001 2     2 16IL 322F       /*            vehicle record
0001 3     1 22 F 1 FR 11    /*            person record
0001 3     2 35 M 1 FR   5   /*            person record
0001 3     3 59 M 1 BK   7   /*            person record
0001 2     3 21IN 146M       /*            vehicle record
0001 3     1 46 M 0 FR   0   /*            person record
END DATA.
```

- The accident record (type 1) is spread to all related cases (in this example, all cases).
- The first vehicle record has one related person record. The values for *STYLE, MAKE, OLD, LICENSE*, and *INSURNCE* are spread to the case built for the person record.
- The second vehicle record has three related person records. The values for *STYLE, MAKE, OLD, LICENSE*, and *INSURNCE* are spread only to the case built from the first person record. The other two cases have the system-missing values for *STYLE, MAKE, OLD, LICENSE*, and *INSURNCE*.
- The third vehicle record has one related person record, and the values for type 2 records are spread to that case.

REFORMAT

```
REFORMAT   {ALPHA  } = varlist [/...]
           {NUMERIC}
```

Example

```
REFORMAT ALPHA=STATE /NUMERIC=HOUR1 TO HOUR6.
```

Overview

REFORMAT converts variables from BMDP files to variables for SPSS-format data files. It also converts very old versions of SPSS-format data files to current SPSS-format data files. REFORMAT can change the print formats, write formats, and missing-value specifications for variables from alphanumeric to numeric, or from numeric to alphanumeric.

Basic Specification

The basic specification is ALPHA and a list of variables or NUMERIC and a list of variables.

- The ALPHA subcommand declares variables as string variables. The NUMERIC subcommand declares variables as numeric variables.

- If both ALPHA and NUMERIC are specified, they must be separated by a slash.

Operations

- REFORMAT always assigns the print and write format F8.2 (or the format specified on the SET command) to variables specified after NUMERIC and format A4 to variables specified after ALPHA.

- Formats cannot be specified on REFORMAT. To define different formats for numeric variables, use the PRINT FORMATS, WRITE FORMATS, or FORMATS commands. To declare new format widths for string variables, use the STRING and COMPUTE commands to perform data transformations.

- Missing-value specifications for variables named with both ALPHA and NUMERIC are also changed to conform to the new formats.

- The SAVE or XSAVE commands can be used to save the reformatted variables in an SPSS-format data file. This avoids having to reformat the variables each time the SPSS-format or BMDP data set is used.

Example

```
* Convert an old SPSS-format file to a new SPSS-format data file.

GET FILE R9FILE.
REFORMAT ALPHA=STATE /NUMERIC=HOUR1 TO HOUR6.
STRING XSTATE (A2) /NAME1 TO NAME6 (A15).
COMPUTE XSTATE=STATE.
FORMATS HOUR1 TO HOUR6 (F2.0).
SAVE OUTFILE=NEWFILE /DROP=STATE
    /RENAME=(XSTATE=STATE).
```

- GET accesses the old SPSS-format data file.

- REFORMAT converts variable STATE to a string variable with an A4 format and variables *HOUR1* to *HOUR6* to numeric variables with F8.2 formats.

- STRING declares *XSTATE* as a string variable with two positions.

- COMPUTE transfers the information from the variable *STATE* to the new string variable *XSTATE*.

- FORMATS changes the F8.2 formats for *HOUR1* to *HOUR6* to F2.0 formats.

- SAVE saves a new SPSS-format data file. The DROP subcommand drops the old variable *STATE*. RENAME renames the new string variable *XSTATE* to the original variable name *STATE*.

REGRESSION

```
REGRESSION [MATRIX=[IN({file})]   [OUT({file})]]
                     {*    }          {*   }

[/VARIABLES={varlist    }]
           {(COLLECT)**}
           {ALL        }

[/DESCRIPTIVES=[DEFAULTS] [MEAN] [STDDEV] [CORR] [COV]
               [VARIANCE] [XPROD] [SIG] [N] [BADCORR]
               [ALL] [NONE**]]

[/SELECT={varname relation value}

[/MISSING=[{LISTWISE**        }] [INCLUDE]]
          {PAIRWISE          }
          {MEANSUBSTITUTION}

[/REGWGT=varname]

[/STATISTICS=[DEFAULTS**] [R**] [COEFF**] [ANOVA**] [OUTS**]
             [ZPP] [LABEL] [CHA] [CI] [F] [BCOV] [SES]
             [XTX] [COLLIN] [TOL] [SELECTION] [ALL]]

[/CRITERIA=[DEFAULTS**]  [TOLERANCE({0.0001**})] [MAXSTEPS(n)]
                                   {value    }

           [PIN[({0.05**})]]  [POUT[({0.10**})]]
                {value }            {value }

           [FIN[({3.84 })]]  [FOUT[({2.71 })]]
                {value}            {value}

           [CIN[({ 95**})]]]]
                {value}

[/{NOORIGIN**}]
  {ORIGIN    }

/DEPENDENT=varlist

[/METHOD=]{STEPWISE [varlist]  } [...] [/...]
          {FORWARD  [varlist]  }
          {BACKWARD [varlist]  }
          {ENTER    [varlist]  }
          {REMOVE   varlist    }
          {TEST(varlist)(varlist)...}

[/OUTFILE={COVB (filename)}]  [MODEL (filename)]
          {CORB (filename)}
```

**Default if the subcommand is omitted.

Example

```
REGRESSION VARIABLES=POP15,POP75,INCOME,GROWTH,SAVINGS
 /DEPENDENT=SAVINGS
 /METHOD=ENTER POP15,POP75,INCOME
 /METHOD=ENTER GROWTH.
```

Overview

REGRESSION calculates multiple regression equations and associated statistics and plots. REGRESSION also calculates collinearity diagnostics, predicted values, residuals, measures of fit and influence, and several statistics based on these measures (see the section on residuals beginning on p. 997).

Options

Input and Output Control Subcommands. DESCRIPTIVES requests descriptive statistics on the variables in the analysis. SELECT estimates the model based on a subset of cases. REGWGT specifies a weight variable for estimating weighted least-squares models. MISSING specifies the treatment of cases with missing values. MATRIX reads and writes matrix data files.

Equation-Control Subcommands. These optional subcommands control the calculation and display of statistics for each equation. STATISTICS controls the statistics displayed for the equation(s) and the independent variable(s), CRITERIA specifies the criteria used by the variable selection method, and ORIGIN specifies whether regression is through the origin.

Analysis of Residuals, Fit, and Influence. The optional subcommands that analyze and plot residuals and add new variables to the working data file containing predicted values, residuals, measures of fit and influence, or related information, are described starting on p. 997. These subcommands apply to the final equation.

Basic Specification

The basic specification is DEPENDENT, which initiates the equation(s) and defines at least one dependent variable, followed by METHOD, which specifies the method for selecting independent variables.

- By default, all variables named on DEPENDENT and METHOD are used in the analysis.
- The default display for each equation includes a Model Summary table showing R^2, an ANOVA table, a Coefficients table displaying related statistics for variables in the equation, and an Excluded Variables table displaying related statistics for variables not yet in the equation.
- By default, all cases in the working data file with valid values for all selected variables are used to compute the correlation matrix on which the regression equations are based. The default equations include a constant (intercept).

Subcommand Order

The standard subcommand order for REGRESSION is

```
REGRESSION MATRIX=...
    /VARIABLES=...
    /DESCRIPTIVES=...
    /SELECT=...
    /MISSING=...
    /REGWGT=...
```

Equation Block

```
/STATISTICS=...
/CRITERIA=...
/ORIGIN
/DEPENDENT=...
```

Method Block(s)

```
/METHOD=...
[/METHOD...]...
```

```
/RESIDUALS=...
/SAVE=...
/CASEWISE=...
/SCATTERPLOT=...
/PARTIALPLOT=...
/OUTFILE = ...
```

- Only one equation block is allowed per REGRESSION command.

- Subcommands listed outside the equation block must be specified before any subcommands within the block.

- When used, MATRIX must be specified first.

- An equation block can contain multiple METHOD subcommands. These methods are applied, one after the other, to the estimation of the equation for that block.

- The STATISTICS, CRITERIA, and ORIGIN/NOORIGIN subcommands must precede the DEPENDENT subcommand.

- The RESIDUALS, CASEWISE, SCATTERPLOT, SAVE, PARTIALPLOT and OUTFILE subcommands must follow the last METHOD subcommand in an equation block and apply only to the final equation after all METHOD subcommands have been processed. These subcommands are discussed in the section on residuals beginning on p. 997.

Syntax Rules

- VARIABLES can be specified only once. If omitted, VARIABLES defaults to COLLECT.

- The DEPENDENT subcommand can be specified only once and must be followed immediately by one or more METHOD subcommands.
- CRITERIA, STATISTICS, and ORIGIN must be specified before DEPENDENT and METHOD. If any of these subcommands are specified more than once, only the last specified is in effect for all subsequent equations.
- More than one variable can be specified on the DEPENDENT subcommand. An equation is estimated for each.
- If no variables are specified on METHOD, all variables named on VARIABLES but not on DEPENDENT are considered for selection.

Operations

- REGRESSION calculates a correlation matrix that includes all variables named on VARIABLES. All equations requested on the REGRESSION command are calculated from the same correlation matrix.
- The MISSING, DESCRIPTIVES, and SELECT subcommands control the calculation of the correlation matrix and associated displays.
- If multiple METHOD subcommands are specified, they operate in sequence on the equations defined by the preceding DEPENDENT subcommand.
- Only independent variables that pass the tolerance criterion are candidates for entry into the equation (see the CRITERIA subcommand on p. 989).

Example

```
REGRESSION VARIABLES=POP15,POP75,INCOME,GROWTH,SAVINGS
 /DEPENDENT=SAVINGS
 /METHOD=ENTER POP15,POP75,INCOME
 /METHOD=ENTER GROWTH.
```

- VARIABLES calculates a correlation matrix of five variables for use by REGRESSION.
- DEPENDENT defines a single equation, with *SAVINGS* as the dependent variable.
- The first METHOD subcommand enters *POP15*, *POP75*, and *INCOME* into the equation.
- The second METHOD subcommand adds *GROWTH* to the equation containing *POP15* to *INCOME*.

VARIABLES Subcommand

VARIABLES names all the variables to be used in the analysis.
- The minimum specification is a list of two variables or the keyword ALL or COLLECT. COLLECT, which must be specified in parentheses, is the default.
- Only one VARIABLES subcommand is allowed and it must precede any DEPENDENT or METHOD subcommands.
- You can use keyword TO to refer to consecutive variables in the working data file.

- The order of variables in the correlation matrix constructed by REGRESSION is the same as their order on VARIABLES. If (COLLECT) is used, the order of variables in the correlation matrix is the order in which they are first listed on the DEPENDENT and METHOD subcommands.

ALL   *Include all user-defined variables in the working data file.*

(COLLECT)   *Include all variables named on the DEPENDENT and METHOD subcommands.* COLLECT is the default if the VARIABLES subcommand is omitted. COLLECT must be specified in parentheses. If COLLECT is used, the METHOD subcommands must specify variable lists.

Example

```
REGRESSION VARIABLES=(COLLECT)
 /DEPENDENT=SAVINGS
 /METHOD=STEP POP15 POP75 INCOME
 /METHOD=ENTER GROWTH.
```

- COLLECT requests that the correlation matrix include *SAVINGS, POP15, POP75, INCOME*, and *GROWTH*. Since COLLECT is the default, the VARIABLES subcommand could have been omitted.
- The DEPENDENT subcommand defines a single equation in which *SAVINGS* is the dependent variable.
- The first METHOD subcommand requests that the block of variables *POP15, POP75,* and *INCOME* be considered for inclusion using a stepwise procedure.
- The second METHOD subcommand adds variable *GROWTH* to the equation.

DEPENDENT Subcommand

DEPENDENT specifies a list of variables and requests that an equation be built for each. DEPENDENT is required.

- The minimum specification is a single variable. There is no default variable list.
- Only one DEPENDENT subcommand can be specified. It must be followed by at least one METHOD subcommand.
- Keyword TO on a DEPENDENT subcommand refers to the order in which variables are specified on the VARIABLES subcommand. If VARIABLES=(COLLECT), TO refers to the order of variables in the working data file.
- If DEPENDENT names more than one variable, an equation is built for each using the same independent variables and methods.

METHOD Subcommand

METHOD specifies a variable selection method and names a block of variables to be evaluated using that method. METHOD is required.

- The minimum specification is a method keyword and, for some methods, a list of variables. The actual keyword METHOD can be omitted.

- When more than one METHOD subcommand is specified, each METHOD subcommand is applied to the equation that resulted from the previous METHOD subcommands.
- The default variable list for methods FORWARD, BACKWARD, STEPWISE, and ENTER consists of all variables named on VARIABLES that are not named on the DEPENDENT subcommand. If VARIABLES=(COLLECT), the variables must be specified for these methods.
- There is no default variable list for the REMOVE and TEST methods.
- Keyword TO in a variable list on METHOD refers to the order in which variables are specified on the VARIABLES subcommand. If VARIABLES=(COLLECT), TO refers to the order of variables in the working data file.

The available stepwise methods are as follows:

BACKWARD [varlist]   *Backward elimination.* Variables in the block are considered for removal. At each step, the variable with the largest probability-of-F value is removed, provided that the value is larger than POUT (see the CRITERIA subcommand on p. 989). If no variables are in the equation when BACKWARD is specified, all independent variables in the block are first entered.

FORWARD [varlist]   *Forward entry.* Variables in the block are added to the equation one at a time. At each step, the variable not in the equation with the smallest probability of F is entered if the value is smaller than PIN (see the CRITERIA subcommand on p. 989).

STEPWISE [varlist]   *Stepwise selection.* If there are independent variables already in the equation, the variable with the largest probability of F is removed if the value is larger than POUT. The equation is recomputed without the variable and the process is repeated until no more independent variables can be removed. Then, the independent variable not in the equation with the smallest probability of F is entered if the value is smaller than PIN. All variables in the equation are again examined for removal. This process continues until no variables in the equation can be removed and no variables not in the equation are eligible for entry, or until the maximum number of steps has been reached (see the CRITERIA subcommand on p. 989).

The methods that enter or remove the entire variable block in a single step are as follows:

ENTER [varlist]   *Forced entry.* All variables specified are entered in a single step in order of decreasing tolerance. You can control the order in which variables are entered by specifying the variables on multiple METHOD=ENTER subcommands.

REMOVE varlist   *Forced removal.* All variables specified are removed in a single step. REMOVE requires a variable list.

TEST (varlist) (varlist) R^2 *change and its significance for sets of independent variables.* This method first adds all variables specified on TEST to the current equation. It then removes in turn each subset from the equation and displays requested statistics. Specify test subsets in parentheses. A variable can be used in more than one subset, and each subset can include any number of variables. Variables named on TEST remain in the equation when the method is completed.

Example

```
REGRESSION VARIABLES=POP15 TO GROWTH, SAVINGS
 /DEPENDENT=SAVINGS
 /METHOD=STEPWISE
 /METHOD=ENTER.
```

- STEPWISE applies the stepwise procedure to variables *POP15* to *GROWTH*.
- All variables not in the equation when the STEPWISE method is completed will be forced into the equation with ENTER.

Example

```
REGRESSION VARIABLES=(COLLECT)
 /DEPENDENT=SAVINGS
 /METHOD=TEST(MEASURE3 TO MEASURE9)(MEASURE3,INCOME)
 /METHOD=ENTER GROWTH.
```

- The VARIABLES=(COLLECT) specification assembles a correlation matrix that includes all variables named on the DEPENDENT and METHOD subcommands.
- REGRESSION first builds the full equation of all the variables named on the first METHOD subcommand: *SAVINGS* regressed on *MEASURE3* to *MEASURE9* and *INCOME*. For each set of test variables (MEASURE3 to MEASURE9, and MEASURE3 and INCOME), the R^2 change, F, probability, sums of squares, and degrees of freedom are displayed.
- *GROWTH* is added to the equation by the second METHOD subcommand. Variables *MEASURE3* to *MEASURE9* and *INCOME* are still in the equation when this subcommand is executed.

STATISTICS Subcommand

STATISTICS controls the display of statistics for the equation and for the independent variables.

- If STATISTICS is omitted or if it is specified without keywords, R, ANOVA, COEFF, and OUTS are displayed (see below).
- If any statistics are specified on STATISTICS, only those statistics specifically requested are displayed.
- STATISTICS must be specified before DEPENDENT and METHOD subcommands. The last specified STATISTICS affects all equations.

Global Statistics

DEFAULTS   *R, ANOVA, COEFF, and OUTS.* These are displayed if STATISTICS is omitted or if it is specified without keywords.

ALL   *All statistics except F.*

Equation Statistics

R
Multiple R. R includes R^2, adjusted R^2, and standard error of the estimate displayed in the Model Summary table.

ANOVA
Analysis of variance table. This option includes regression and residual sums of squares, mean square, F, and probability of F displayed in the ANOVA table.

CHA
Change in R^2. This option includes the change in R^2 between steps, along with the corresponding F and its probability, in the Model Summary table. For each equation, F and its probability are also displayed.

BCOV
Variance-covariance matrix for unstandardized regression coefficients. The statistics are displayed in the Coefficient Correlations table.

XTX
Swept correlation matrix.

COLLIN
Collinearity diagnostics (Belsley et al., 1980). COLLIN includes the variance-inflation factors (VIF) displayed in the Coefficients table, and the eigenvalues of the scaled and uncentered cross-products matrix, condition indexes, and variance-decomposition proportions displayed in the Collinearity Diagnostics table.

SELECTION
Selection statistics. This option includes Akaike information criterion (AIK), Ameniya's prediction criterion (PC), Mallows conditional mean squared error of prediction criterion (C_p), and Schwarz Bayesian criterion (SBC) (Judge et al., 1980). The statistics are displayed in the Model Summary table.

Statistics for the Independent Variables

COEFF
Regression coefficients. This option includes regression coefficients (B), standard errors of the coefficients, standardized regression coefficients (beta), t, and two-tailed probability of t. The statistics are displayed in the Coefficients table.

OUTS
Statistics for variables not yet in the equation that have been named on METHOD subcommands for the equation. OUTS displays the Excluded Variables table showing beta, t, two-tailed probability of t, and minimum tolerance of the variable if it were the only variable entered next.

ZPP
Zero-order, part, and partial correlation. The statistics are displayed in the Coefficients table.

CI
95% confidence interval for the unstandardized regression coefficients. The statistics are displayed in the Coefficients table.

SES
Approximate standard error of the standardized regression coefficients. (Meyer & Younger, 1976.) The statistics are displayed in the Coefficients table.

TOL
Tolerance. This option displays tolerance for variables in the equation in the Coefficients table. For variables not yet entered into the equation, TOL displays in the

Excluded Variables table the tolerance each variable would have if it were the only variable entered next.

F   *F value for B and its probability.* This is displayed instead of the *t* value in the Coefficients or Excluded Variables table.

CRITERIA Subcommand

CRITERIA controls the statistical criteria used to build the regression equations. The way in which these criteria are used depends on the method specified on METHOD. The default criteria are noted in the description of each CRITERIA keyword below.

- The minimum specification is a criterion keyword and its arguments, if any.
- If CRITERIA is omitted or included without specifications, the default criteria are in effect.
- The CRITERIA subcommand must be specified before DEPENDENT and METHOD subcommands. The last specified CRITERIA affects all equations.

Tolerance and Minimum Tolerance Tests

Variables must pass both tolerance and minimum tolerance tests in order to enter and remain in a regression equation. Tolerance is the proportion of the variance of a variable in the equation that is not accounted for by other independent variables in the equation. The minimum tolerance of a variable not in the equation is the smallest tolerance any variable already in the equation would have if the variable being considered were included in the analysis.

If a variable passes the tolerance criteria, it is eligible for inclusion based on the method in effect.

Criteria for Variable Selection

- The ENTER, REMOVE, and TEST methods use only the TOLERANCE criterion.
- BACKWARD removes variables according to the probability of *F*-to-remove (keyword POUT). Specify FOUT to use *F*-to-remove instead.
- FORWARD enters variables according to the probability of *F*-to-enter (keyword PIN). Specify FIN to use *F*-to-enter instead.
- STEPWISE uses both PIN and POUT (or FIN and FOUT) as criteria. If the criterion for entry (PIN or FIN) is less stringent than the criterion for removal (POUT or FOUT), the same variable can cycle in and out until the maximum number of steps is reached. Therefore, if PIN is larger than POUT or FIN is smaller than FOUT, REGRESSION adjusts POUT or FOUT and issues a warning.
- The values for these criteria are specified in parentheses. If a value is not specified, the default values are used.

DEFAULTS   *PIN(0.05), POUT(0.10), and TOLERANCE(0.0001).* These are the defaults if CRITERIA is omitted. If criteria have been changed, DEFAULTS restores these defaults.

PIN[(value)]	*Probability of* F-*to-enter.* The default value is 0.05. Either PIN or FIN can be specified. If more than one is used, the last one specified is in effect.
FIN[(value)]	F-*to-enter.* The default value is 3.84. Either PIN or FIN can be specified. If more than one is used, the last one specified is in effect.
POUT[(value)]	*Probability of* F-*to-remove.* The default value is 0.10. Either POUT or FOUT can be specified. If more than one is used, the last one specified is in effect.
FOUT[(value)]	F-*to-remove.* The default value is 2.71. Either POUT or FOUT can be specified. If more than one is used, the last one specified is in effect.
TOLERANCE[(value)]	*Tolerance.* The default value is 0.0001. If the specified tolerance is very low, REGRESSION issues a warning.
MAXSTEPS[(n)]	*Maximum number of steps.* The value of MAXSTEPS is the sum of the maximum number of steps for each method for the equation. The default values are, for the BACKWARD or FORWARD methods, the number of variables meeting PIN/POUT or FIN/FOUT criteria, and for the STEPWISE method, twice the number of independent variables.

Confidence Intervals

CIN[(value)]	*Reset the value of the percent for confidence intervals.* The default is 95%. The specified value sets the percentage interval used in the computation of temporary variable types MCIN and ICIN. (See the list of temporary variable types on p. 998.)

Example

```
REGRESSION VARIABLES=POP15 TO GROWTH, SAVINGS
 /CRITERIA=PIN(.1) POUT(.15)
 /DEPENDENT=SAVINGS
 /METHOD=FORWARD.
```

• The CRITERIA subcommand relaxes the default criteria for entry and removal for the FORWARD method. Note that the specified PIN is less than POUT.

ORIGIN and NOORIGIN Subcommands

ORIGIN and NOORIGIN control whether or not the constant is suppressed. By default, the constant is included in the model (NOORIGIN).

• The specification is either the ORIGIN or NOORIGIN subcommand.

• ORIGIN and NOORIGIN must be specified before the DEPENDENT and METHOD subcommands. The last specified remains in effect for all equations.

• ORIGIN requests regression through the origin. The constant term is suppressed.

• If you specify ORIGIN, statistics requested on the DESCRIPTIVES subcommand are computed as if the mean were 0.

- ORIGIN and NOORIGIN affect the way the correlation matrix is built. If matrix materials are used as input to REGRESSION, the keyword that was in effect when the matrix was written should be in effect when that matrix is read.

Example

```
REGRESSION VAR=(COL)
 /ORIGIN
 /DEP=HOMICIDE
 /METHOD=ENTER POVPCT.
```

- The REGRESSION command requests an equation that regresses *HOMICIDE* on *POVPCT* and suppresses the constant (ORIGIN).

REGWGT Subcommand

The only specification on REGWGT is the name of the variable containing the weights to be used in estimating a weighted least-squares model. With REGWGT the default display is the usual REGRESSION display.

- REGWGT is a global subcommand.
- If more than one REGWGT subcommand is specified on a REGRESSION procedure, only the last one is in effect.
- REGWGT can be used with MATRIX OUT but not with MATRIX IN.
- Residuals saved from equations using the REGWGT command are not weighted. To obtain weighted residuals, multiply the residuals created with SAVE by the square root of the weighting variable in a COMPUTE statement.
- REGWGT is in effect for all equations and affects the way the correlation matrix is built. Thus, if REGWGT is specified on a REGRESSION procedure that writes matrix materials to a matrix data file, subsequent REGRESSION procedures using that file will be automatically weighted.

Example

```
REGRESSION VARIABLES=GRADE GPA STARTLEV TREATMNT
 /DEPENDENT=GRADE
 /METHOD=ENTER
 /SAVE PRED(P).
COMPUTE WEIGHT=1/(P*(1-P)).
REGRESSION VAR=GRADE GPA STARTLEV TREATMNT
 /REGWGT=WEIGHT
 /DEP=GRADE
 /METHOD=ENTER.
```

- VARIABLES builds a correlation matrix that includes *GRADE*, *GPA*, *STARTLEV*, and *TREATMNT*.
- DEPENDENT identifies *GRADE* as the dependent variable.
- METHOD regresses *GRADE* on *GPA*, *STARTLEV*, and *TREATMNT*.
- SAVE saves the predicted values from the regression equation as variable *P* in the working data file (see the SAVE subcommand on p. 1004).

- COMPUTE creates the variable *WEIGHT* as a transformation of *P*.
- The second REGRESSION procedure performs a weighted regression analysis on the same set of variables using *WEIGHT* as the weighting variable.

Example

```
REGRESSION VAR=GRADE GPA STARTLEV TREATMNT
 /REGWGT=WEIGHT
 /DEP=GRADE
 /METHOD=ENTER
 /SAVE RESID(RGRADE).
COMPUTE WRGRADE=RGRADE * SQRT(WEIGHT).
```

- This example illustrates the use of COMPUTE with SAVE to weight residuals.
- REGRESSION performs a weighted regression analysis of *GRADE* on *GPA*, *STARTLEV*, and *TREATMNT*, using *WEIGHT* as the weighting variable.
- SAVE saves the residuals as *RGRADE* (see the SAVE subcommand on p. 1004). These residuals are not weighted.
- COMPUTE creates variable *WRGRADE*, which contains the weighted residuals.

DESCRIPTIVES Subcommand

DESCRIPTIVES requests the display of correlations and descriptive statistics. By default, descriptive statistics are not displayed.

- The minimum specification is simply the subcommand keyword DESCRIPTIVES, which obtains MEAN, STDDEV, and CORR.
- If DESCRIPTIVES is specified with keywords, only those statistics specifically requested are displayed.
- Descriptive statistics are displayed only once for all variables named or implied on VARIABLES.
- Descriptive statistics are based on all valid cases for each variable if PAIRWISE or MEANSUBSTITUTION has been specified on MISSING. Otherwise, only cases with valid values for all variables named or implied on the VARIABLES subcommand are included in the calculation of descriptive statistics.
- If regression through the origin has been requested (subcommand ORIGIN), statistics are computed as if the mean were 0.

NONE   *No descriptive statistics.* This is the default if the subcommand is omitted.

DEFAULTS   *MEAN, STDDEV, and CORR.* This is the same as specifying DESCRIPTIVES without specifications.

MEAN   *Display variable means in the Descriptive Statistics table.*

STDDEV   *Display variable standard deviations in the Descriptive Statistics table.*

VARIANCE   *Display variable variances in the Descriptive Statistics table.*

CORR   *Display Pearson correlation coefficients in the Correlations table.*

SIG	*Display one-tailed probabilities of the correlation coefficients in the Correlations table.*
BADCORR	*Display the correlation coefficients only if some coefficients cannot be computed.*
COV	*Display covariance in the Correlations table.*
XPROD	*Display sum of squares and cross-product deviations from the mean in the Correlations table.*
N	*Display numbers of cases used to compute correlation coefficients in the Correlations table.*
ALL	*All descriptive statistics.*

Example

```
REGRESSION DESCRIPTIVES=DEFAULTS SIG COV
 /VARIABLES=AGE,FEMALE,YRS_JOB,STARTPAY,SALARY
 /DEPENDENT=SALARY
 /METHOD=ENTER STARTPAY
 /METHOD=ENTER YRS_JOB.
```

- The variable means, standard deviations, and number of cases are displayed in the Descriptive Statistics table and the correlation coefficients, one-tailed probabilities of the correlation coefficients, and covariance are displayed in the Correlations table.
- Statistics are displayed for all variables named on VARIABLES, even though only variables *SALARY, STARTPAY,* and *YRS_JOB* are used to build the equations.
- *STARTPAY* is entered into the equation by the first METHOD subcommand. *YRS_JOB* is entered by the second METHOD subcommand.

SELECT Subcommand

By default, all cases in the working data file are considered for inclusion on REGRESSION. Use SELECT to include a subset of cases in the correlation matrix and resulting regression statistics.

- The required specification on SELECT is a logical expression.
- The syntax for the SELECT subcommand is as follows:

  ```
  /SELECT=varname relation value
  ```

- The variable named on SELECT should not be specified on the VARIABLES subcommand.
- The relation can be EQ, NE, LT, LE, GT, or GE.
- Only cases for which the logical expression on SELECT is true are included in the calculation of the correlation matrix and regression statistics.
- All other cases, including those with missing values for the variable named on SELECT, are not included in the computations.

- If SELECT is specified, residuals and predicted values are calculated and reported separately for both selected and unselected cases by default (see the RESIDUALS subcommand on p. 1000).

- Cases deleted from the working data file with SELECT IF, a temporary SELECT IF, or SAMPLE are not passed to REGRESSION and are not included among either the selected or unselected cases.

- You should not use a variable from a temporary transformation as a selection variable, since REGRESSION reads the data file more than once if any residuals subcommands are specified. A variable created from a temporary transformation (with IF and COMPUTE statements) will disappear when the data are read a second time, and a variable that is the result of a temporary RECODE will change.

Example

```
REGRESSION SELECT SEX EQ 'M'
 /VARIABLES=AGE,STARTPAY,YRS_JOB,SALARY
 /DEPENDENT=SALARY
 /METHOD=STEP
 /RESIDUALS=NORMPROB.
```

- Only cases with the value M for *SEX* are included in the correlation matrix calculated by REGRESSION.

- Separate normal P_P plots are displayed for cases with *SEX* equal to M and for other cases (see the RESIDUALS subcommand on p. 1000).

MATRIX Subcommand

MATRIX reads and writes matrix data files. It can read files written by previous REGRESSION procedures or files written by other procedures such as CORRELATIONS. The matrix materials REGRESSION writes also include the mean, standard deviation, and number of cases used to compute each coefficient. This information immediately precedes the correlation matrix in the matrix file (see "Format of the Matrix Data File" on p. 995).

- Either IN or OUT and a matrix file in parentheses are required on MATRIX.

- When used, MATRIX must be the first subcommand specified in a REGRESSION procedure.

- ORIGIN and NOORIGIN affect the way the correlation matrix is built. If matrix materials are used as input to REGRESSION, the keyword that was in effect when the matrix was written should be in effect when that matrix is read.

OUT (filename)   *Write a matrix data file.* Specify either a filename or an asterisk, enclosed in parentheses. If you specify a filename, the file is stored on disk and can be retrieved at any time. If you specify an asterisk (*), the matrix data file replaces the working file but is not stored on disk unless you use SAVE or XSAVE.

IN (filename)   *Read a matrix data file.* If the matrix data file is the working data file, specify an asterisk (*) in parentheses. If the matrix data file is another file, specify the filename in parentheses. A matrix file read from an external file does not replace the working data file.

Format of the Matrix Data File

- The file has two special variables created by the program: *ROWTYPE_* and *VARNAME_*.
- *ROWTYPE_* is a short string variable with values MEAN, STDDEV, N, and CORR (for Pearson correlation coefficient).
- *VARNAME_* is a short string variable whose values are the names of the variables used to form the correlation matrix. When *ROWTYPE_* is CORR, *VARNAME_* gives the variable associated with that row of the correlation matrix.
- The remaining variables in the file are the variables used to form the correlation matrix.
- To suppress the constant term when ORIGIN is used in the analysis, value OCORR (rather than value CORR) is written to the matrix system file. OCORR indicates that the regression passes through the origin.

Split Files

- When split-file processing is in effect, the first variables in the matrix data file are the split variables, followed by *ROWTYPE_*, the independent variable, *VARNAME_*, and the dependent variables.
- A full set of matrix materials is written for each subgroup defined by the split variable(s).
- A split variable cannot have the same variable name as any other variable written to the matrix data file.
- If a split file is in effect when a matrix is written, the same split file must be in effect when that matrix is read.

Missing Values

- With PAIRWISE treatment of missing values, the matrix of N's used to compute each coefficient is included with the matrix materials.
- With LISTWISE treatment (the default) or MEANSUBSTITUTION, a single N used to calculate all coefficients is included.

Example

```
REGRESSION MATRIX IN(PAY_DATA) OUT(*)
 /VARIABLES=AGE,STARTPAY,YRS_JOB,SALARY
 /DEPENDENT=SALARY
 /METHOD=STEP.
```

- MATRIX IN reads the matrix data file *PAY_DATA*.
- A stepwise regression analysis of *SALARY* is performed using *AGE*, *STARTPAY*, and *YRS_JOB*.
- MATRIX OUT replaces the working data file with the matrix data file that was previously stored in the *PAY_DATA* file.

MISSING Subcommand

MISSING controls the treatment of cases with missing values. By default, a case that has a user-missing or system-missing value for any variable named or implied on VARIABLES is omitted from the computation of the correlation matrix on which all analyses are based.

- The minimum specification is a keyword specifying a missing-value treatment.

LISTWISE
Delete cases with missing values listwise. Only cases with valid values for all variables named on the current VARIABLES subcommand are used. If INCLUDE is also specified, only cases with system-missing values are deleted listwise. LISTWISE is the default if the MISSING subcommand is omitted.

PAIRWISE
Delete cases with missing values pairwise. Each correlation coefficient is computed using cases with complete data for the pair of variables correlated. If INCLUDE is also specified, only cases with system-missing values are deleted pairwise.

MEANSUBSTITUTION
Replace missing values with the variable mean. All cases are included and the substitutions are treated as valid observations. If INCLUDE is also specified, user-missing values are treated as valid and are included in the computation of the means.

INCLUDE
Includes cases with user-missing values. All user-missing values are treated as valid values. This keyword can be specified along with the methods LISTWISE, PAIRWISE, or MEANSUBSTITUTION.

Example

```
REGRESSION  VARIABLES=POP15,POP75,INCOME,GROWTH,SAVINGS
 /DEPENDENT=SAVINGS
 /METHOD=STEP
 /MISSING=MEANSUBSTITUTION.
```

- System-missing and user-missing values are replaced with the means of the variables when the correlation matrix is calculated.

References

Belsley, D. A., E. Kuh, and R. E. Welsch. 1980. *Regression diagnostics: Identifying influential data and sources of collinearity.* New York: John Wiley and Sons.

Berk, K. N. 1977. Tolerance and condition in regression computation. *Journal of the American Statistical Association*, 72: 863–66.

Judge, G. G., W. E. Griffiths, R. C. Hill, H. Lutkepohl, and T. C. Lee. 1980. *The theory and practice of econometrics.* 2nd ed. New York: John Wiley and Sons.

Meyer, L. S., and M. S. Younger. 1976. Estimation of standardized coefficients. *Journal of the American Statistical Association*, 71: 154–57.

REGRESSION: Residuals

```
REGRESSION VARIABLES=varlist /DEPENDENT=varname /METHOD=method

 [/RESIDUALS=[DEFAULTS] [DURBIN] [OUTLIERS({ZRESID })] [ID (varname)]
                                          {tempvars}

        [NORMPROB({ZRESID })] [HISTOGRAM({ZRESID })]
                 {tempvars}             {tempvars}

        [SIZE({SEPARATE})]
              {POOLED  }

 [/CASEWISE=[DEFAULTS]  [{OUTLIERS({3     })}] [PLOT({ZRESID })]
                        {         {value} }         {tempvar}
                        {ALL            }

        [{DEPENDENT PRED RESID}]]
         {tempvars            }

 [/SCATTERPLOT [varname,varname]...[

 [/PARTIALPLOT=[{ALL    }]
               {varlist}

 [/OUTFILE={COVB (filename)}]  [MODEL (filename]
           {CORB (filename)}

 [/SAVE=tempvar[(newname)]  [tempvar[(newname)]...]  [FITS]]
```

Temporary residual variables are:

PRED, ADJPRED, SRESID, MAHAL, RESID, ZPRED, SDRESID, COOK, DRESID, ZRESID, SEPRED, LEVER, DFBETA, SDBETA, DFFIT, SDFFIT, COVRATIO, MCIN, ICIN

SAVE FITS saves:

DFFIT, SDFIT, DFBETA, SDBETA, COVRATIO

Example

```
REGRESSION VARIABLES=SAVINGS INCOME POP15 POP75
  /WIDTH=132
  /DEPENDENT=SAVINGS
  /METHOD=ENTER
  /RESIDUALS
  /CASEWISE
  /SCATTERPLOT (*ZRESID *ZPRED)
  /PARTIALPLOT
  /SAVE ZRESID(STDRES) ZPRED(STDPRED).
```

Overview

REGRESSION creates temporary variables containing predicted values, residuals, measures of fit and influence, and several statistics based on these measures. These temporary variables can be analyzed within REGRESSION in Casewise Diagnostics tables (CASEWISE subcommand), scatterplots (SCATTERPLOT subcommand), histograms and normal probability plots

(RESIDUALS subcommand), and partial regression plots (PARTIALPLOT subcommand). Any of the residuals subcommands can be specified to obtain descriptive statistics for the predicted values, residuals, and their standardized versions. Any of the temporary variables can be added to the working data file with the SAVE subcommand.

Basic Specification

All residuals analysis subcommands are optional. Most have defaults that can be requested by including the subcommand without any further specifications. These defaults are described in the discussion of each subcommand below.

Subcommand Order

- The residuals subcommands RESIDUALS, CASEWISE, SCATTERPLOT, and PARTIALPLOT follow the last METHOD subcommand of any equation for which residuals analysis is requested. Statistics are based on this final equation.
- Residuals subcommands can be specified in any order. All residuals subcommands must follow the DEPENDENT and METHOD subcommands.

Operations

- Residuals subcommands affect all equations.
- The temporary variables *PRED* (unstandardized predicted value), *ZPRED* (standardized predicted value), *RESID* (unstandardized residual), and *ZRESID* (standardized residual) are calculated and descriptive statistics are displayed whenever any residuals subcommand is specified. If any of the other temporary variables are referred to on the command, they are also calculated.
- Predicted values and statistics based on predicted values are calculated for every observation that has valid values for all variables in the equation. Residuals and statistics based on residuals are calculated for all observations that have a valid predicted value and a valid value for the dependent variable. The missing-values option therefore affects the calculation of residuals and predicted values.
- No residuals or predictors are generated for cases deleted from the working data file with SELECT IF, a temporary SELECT IF, or SAMPLE.
- All variables are standardized before plotting. If the unstandardized version of a variable is requested, the standardized version is plotted.
- Residuals processing is not available when the working data file is a matrix file or is replaced by a matrix file with MATRIX OUT(*) on REGRESSION. If RESIDUALS, CASEWISE, SCATTERPLOT, PARTIALPLOT, or SAVE are used when MATRIX IN(*) or MATRIX OUT(*) is specified, the REGRESSION command is not executed.

For each analysis, REGRESSION can calculate the following types of temporary variables:

PRED   *Unstandardized predicted values.*

RESID   *Unstandardized residuals.*

DRESID *Deleted residuals.*

ADJPRED *Adjusted predicted values.*

ZPRED *Standardized predicted values.*

ZRESID *Standardized residuals.*

SRESID *Studentized residuals.*

SDRESID *Studentized deleted residuals.* (See Hoaglin & Welsch, 1978.)

SEPRED *Standard errors of the predicted values.*

MAHAL *Mahalanobis distances.*

COOK *Cook's distances.* (See Cook, 1977.)

LEVER *Centered leverage values.* (See Velleman & Welsch, 1981.)

DFBETA *Change in the regression coefficient that results from the deletion of the ith case.* A DFBETA value is computed for each case for each regression coefficient generated by a model. (See Belsley et al., 1980.)

SDBETA *Standardized DFBETA.* An SDBETA value is computed for each case for each regression coefficient generated by a model. (See Belsley et al., 1980.)

DFFIT *Change in the predicted value when the ith case is deleted.* (See Belsley et al., 1980.)

SDFIT *Standardized DFFIT.* (See Belsley et al., 1980.)

COVRATIO *Ratio of the determinant of the covariance matrix with the ith case deleted to the determinant of the covariance matrix with all cases included.* (See Belsley et al., 1980.)

MCIN *Lower and upper bounds for the prediction interval of the mean predicted response.* A lowerbound *LMCIN* and an upperbound *UMCIN* are generated. The default confidence interval is 95%. The confidence interval can be reset with the CIN subcommand. (See Dillon & Goldstein, 1984.)

ICIN *Lower and upper bounds for the prediction interval for a single observation.* A lowerbound *LICIN* and an upperbound *UICIN* are generated. The default confidence interval is 95%. The confidence interval can be reset with the CIN subcommand. (See Dillon & Goldstein, 1984.)

Example

```
REGRESSION VARIABLES=SAVINGS INCOME POP15 POP75
  /DEPENDENT=SAVINGS
  /METHOD=ENTER
  /RESIDUALS
  /CASEWISE
  /SCATTERPLOT (*ZRESID *ZPRED)
  /PARTIALPLOT
  /SAVE ZRESID(STDRES) ZPRED(STDPRED).
```

- REGRESSION requests a single equation in which *SAVINGS* is the dependent variable and *INCOME*, *POP15*, and *POP75* are independent variables.
- RESIDUALS requests the default residuals output.
- Because residuals processing has been requested, statistics for predicted values, residuals, and standardized versions of predicted values and residuals are displayed in a Residuals Statistics table.
- CASEWISE requests a Casewise Diagnostics table for cases whose absolute value of *ZRESID* is greater than 3. Values of the dependent variable, predicted value, and residual are listed for each case.
- SCATTERPLOT requests a plot of the standardized predicted value and the standardized residual.
- PARTIALPLOT requests partial regression plots for all independent variables.
- SAVE adds the standardized residual and the standardized predicted value to the working data file as new variables named *STDRES* and *STDPRED*.

RESIDUALS Subcommand

RESIDUALS controls the display and labeling of summary information on outliers as well as the display of the Durbin-Watson statistic and histograms and normal probability plots for the temporary variables.

- If RESIDUALS is specified without keywords, it displays a histogram of residuals, a normal probability plot of residuals, the values of *$CASENUM* and *ZRESID* for the 10 cases with the largest absolute value of *ZRESID*, and the Durbin-Watson test statistic. The histogram and the normal plot are standardized.
- If any keywords are specified on RESIDUALS, only the requested information and plots are displayed.

DEFAULTS *DURBIN, NORMPROB(ZRESID), HISTOGRAM(ZRESID), OUTLIERS(ZRESID)*. These are the defaults if RESIDUALS is used without specifications.

HISTOGRAM(tempvars) *Histogram of the temporary variable or variables*. The default is *ZRESID*. You can request histograms for *PRED, RESID, ZPRED, DRESID, ADJPRED, SRESID, SDRESID, SEPRED, MAHAL, COOK*, and *LEVER*. The specification of any other temporary variable will result in an error.

NORMPROB(tempvars) *Normal probability (P-P) plot*. The default is *ZRESID*. The other temporary variables for which normal probability plots are available are *PRED, RESID, ZPRED, DRESID, SRESID*, and *SDRESID*. The specification of any other temporary variable will result in an error. Normal probability plots are always displayed in standardized form; therefore, when *PRED, RESID*, or *DRESID* is requested, the standardized equivalent *ZPRED, ZRESID* or *SDRESID* is displayed.

OUTLIERS(tempvars) *The 10 cases with the largest absolute values of the specified temporary variables*. The default is *ZRESID*. The output includes the values of *$CASENUM* and of the temporary variables for the 10 cases. The other temporary variables available for OUTLIERS are *RESID*, *SRESID*, *SDRESID*, *DRESID*, *MAHAL*, and *COOK*. The specification of any temporary variable other than these will result in an error.

DURBIN   *Display Durbin-Watson test statistic in the Model Summary table.*

ID(varname)   *ID variable providing case labels for use with point selection mode in the Chart Editor.* Applicable to scatterplots produced by SCATTERPLOT, PARTIALPLOT, and RESIDUALS. Any variable in the working data file can be named.

SEPARATE   *Separate reporting of residuals statistics and plots for selected and unselected cases.* This is the default.

POOLED   *Pooled plots and statistics using all cases in the working file when the SELECT subcommand is in effect.* (See the SELECT subcommand on p. 993.) This is an alternative to SEPARATE.

Example

```
/RESID=DEFAULT ID(SVAR)
```

- DEFAULT produces the default residuals statistics: Durbin-Watson statistic, a normal probability plot and histogram of *ZRESID*, and an outlier listing for *ZRESID*.
- Descriptive statistics for *ZRESID*, *RESID*, *PRED*, and *ZPRED* are automatically displayed.
- *SVAR* is specified as the case identifier on the outlier output.

CASEWISE Subcommand

CASEWISE requests a Casewise Diagnostics table of residuals. You can specify a temporary residual variable for casewise listing (via the PLOT keyword). You can also specify variables to be listed in the table for each case.

- If CASEWISE is used without any additional specifications, it displays a Casewise Diagnostics table of *ZRESID* for cases whose absolute value of *ZRESID* is at least 3. By default, the values of the case sequence number, *DEPENDENT*, *PRED*, and *RESID* are listed for each case.
- Defaults remain in effect unless specifically altered.

DEFAULTS   *OUTLIERS(3), PLOT(ZRESID), DEPENDENT, PRED, and RESID.* These are the defaults if the subcommand is used without specifications.

OUTLIERS(value) *List only cases for which the absolute standardized value of the listed variable is at least as large as the specified value.* The default value is 3. Keyword OUTLIERS is ignored if keyword ALL is also present.

ALL   *Include all cases in the Casewise Diagnostic table.* ALL is the alternative to keyword OUTLIERS.

PLOT(tempvar)   *List the values of the temporary variable in the Casewise Diagnostics table.* The default temporary variable is *ZRESID*. Other variables that can be listed

are *RESID*, *DRESID*, *SRESID*, and *SDRESID*. The specification of any temporary variable other than these will result in an error. When requested, *RESID*
is standardized and *DRESID* is Studentized in the output.

tempvars   *Display the values of these variables next to the casewise list entry for each*
case. The default variables are *DEPENDENT* (the dependent variable), *PRED*,
and *RESID*. Any of the other temporary variables can be specified. If an ID
variable is specified on RESIDUALS, the ID variable is also listed.

Example

```
/CASEWISE=DEFAULT ALL SRE MAH COOK SDR
```

- This example requests a Casewise Diagnostics table of the standardized residuals for all
cases.

- *ZRESID*, the dependent variable, and the temporary variables *PRED*, *RESID*, *SRESID*,
MAHAL, *COOK*, and *SDRESID* are for all cases.

SCATTERPLOT Subcommand

SCATTERPLOT names pairs of variables for scatterplots.

- The minimum specification for SCATTERPLOT is a pair of variables in parentheses. There
are no default specifications.

- You can specify as many pairs of variables in parentheses as you want.

- The first variable named in each set of parentheses is plotted along the vertical axis, and
the second variable is plotted along the horizontal axis.

- Plotting symbols are used to represent multiple points occurring at the same position.

- You can specify any variable named on the VARIABLES subcommand.

- You can specify *PRED*, *RESID*, *ZPRED*, *ZRESID*, *DRESID*, *ADJPRED*, *SRESID*, *SDRESID*,
SEPRED, *MAHAL*, *COOK*, and *LEVER*. The specification of any other temporary variables
will result in an error.

- Specify an asterisk before temporary variable names to distinguish them from user-
defined variables. For example, use **PRED* to specify *PRED*.

Example

```
/SCATTERPLOT (*RES,*PRE) (*RES,SAVINGS)
```

- This example specifies two scatterplots: residuals against predicted values and residuals
against the values of the variable *SAVINGS*.

PARTIALPLOT Subcommand

PARTIALPLOT requests partial regression plots. Partial regression plots are scatterplots of the
residuals of the dependent variable and an independent variable when both of these variables
are regressed on the rest of the independent variables.

- If PARTIALPLOT is included without any additional specifications, it produces a partial regression plot for every independent variable in the equation. The plots appear in the order the variables are specified or implied on the VARIABLES subcommand.

- If variables are specified on PARTIALPLOT, only the requested plots are displayed. The plots appear in the order the variables are listed on the PARTIALPLOT subcommand.

- At least two independent variables must be in the equation for partial regression plots to be produced.

ALL   *Plot all independent variables in the equation.* This is the default.

varlist   *Plot the specified variables.* Any variable entered into the equation can be specified.

Example

```
REGRESSION VARS=PLOT15 TO SAVINGS
  /DEP=SAVINGS
  /METH=ENTER
  /RESID=DEFAULTS
  /PARTIAL.
```

- A partial regression plot is produced for every independent variable in the equation.

OUTFILE Subcommand

OUTFILE saves in an SPSS-format data file the parameter covariance or correlation matrix with parameter estimates, standard errors, significance values, and residual degrees of freedom for each term in the final equation. It also saves model information in XML format.

- The OUTFILE subcommand must follow the last METHOD subcommand.

- Only one OUTFILE subcommand is allowed. If you specify more than one, only the last one is executed.

- You must specify at least one keyword and a valid filename in parentheses. There is no default.

- You cannot save the parameter statistics as the working data file.

- COVB and CORB are mutually exclusive.

- MODEL cannot be used if split file processing is on (SPLIT FILE command) or if more than one dependent (DEPENDENT subcommand)variable is specified.

COVB (filename)   *Write the parameter covariance matrix with other statistics.* Specify the filename in full. REGRESSION does not supply an extension.

CORB (filename)   *Write the parameter correlation matrix with other statistics.* Specify the filename in full. REGRESSION does not supply an extension.

MODEL (filename)   *Write model information to an XML file.* Specify the filename in full. REGRESSION does not supply an extension. *SmartScore* and future releases of *WhatIf?* will be able to use this file.

Example

```
REGRESSION DEPENDENT=Y
 /METHOD=ENTER X1 X2
 /OUTFILE CORB (covx1x2y.sav).
```

- The OUTFILE subcommand saves the parameter correlation matrix, and the parameter estimates, standard errors, significance values and residual degrees of freedom for the constant term, *X1* and *X2*.

SAVE Subcommand

Use SAVE to add one or more residual or fit variables to the working data file.

- The specification on SAVE is one or more of the temporary variable types listed on pp. 998–999, each followed by an optional name in parentheses for the new variable.
- New variable names must be unique.
- If new names are not specified, REGRESSION generates a rootname using a shortened form of the temporary variable name with a suffix to identify its creation sequence.
- If you specify DFBETA or SDBETA on the SAVE subcommand, the number of new variables saved is the total number of variables in the equation.

FITS   *Save all influence statistics.* FITS saves *DFFIT, SDFIT, DFBETA, SDBETA,* and *COVRATIO.* You cannot specify new variable names when using this keyword. Default names are generated.

Example

```
/SAVE=PRED(PREDVAL) RESID(RESIDUAL) COOK(CDISTANC)
```

- This subcommand adds three variables to the end of the working data file: *PREDVAL*, containing the unstandardized predicted value for each case; *RESIDUAL*, containing the unstandardized residual; and *CDISTANC*, containing Cook's distance.

Example

```
/SAVE=PRED RESID
```

- This subcommand adds two variables named *PRE_1* and *RES_1* to the end of the working data file.

Example

```
REGRESSION DEPENDENT=Y
 /METHOD=ENTER X1 X2
 /SAVE DFBETA(DFBVAR).
```

- The SAVE subcommand creates and saves three new variables with the names *DFBVAR0*, *DFBVAR1*, and *DFBVAR2*.

Example

```
REGRESSION VARIABLES=SAVINGS INCOME POP15 POP75 GROWTH
 /DEPENDENT=SAVINGS
 /METHOD=ENTER INCOME POP15 POP75
 /SAVE=PRED(PREDV) SDBETA(BETA) ICIN.
```

- The SAVE subcommand adds seven variables to the end of the file: *PREDV*, containing the unstandardized predicted value for the case; *BETA0*, the standardized *DFBETA* for the intercept; *BETA1*, *BETA2*, and *BETA3*, the standardized *DFBETA*'s for the three independent variables in the model; *LICL_1*, the lower bound for the prediction interval for an individual case; and *UICL_1*, the upper bound for the prediction interval for an individual case.

References

Belsley, D. A., E. Kuh, and R. E. Welsch. 1980. *Regression diagnostics: Identifying influential data and sources of collinearity.* New York: John Wiley and Sons.

Cook, R. D. 1977. Detection of influential observations in linear regression. *Technometrics*, 19: 15–18.

Dillon, W. R., and M. Goldstein. 1984. *Multivariate analysis: Methods and applications.* New York: John Wiley and Sons.

Hoaglin, D. C., and R. E. Welsch. 1978. The hat matrix in regression and ANOVA. *American Statistician*, 32: 17–22.

Velleman, P. F., and R. E. Welsch. 1981. Efficient computing of regression diagnostics. *American Statistician*, 35: 234–42.

RELIABILITY

```
RELIABILITY VARIABLES={varlist}
                     {ALL    }

[/SCALE(scalename)=varlist [/SCALE... ]]

[/MODEL={ALPHA         }] [/VARIABLES...]
        {SPLIT[(n)]    }
        {GUTTMAN       }
        {PARALLEL      }
        {STRICTPARALLEL}

[/STATISTICS=[DESCRIPTIVE]  [SCALE]      [{ANOVA          }]  [ALL]]
             [COVARIANCES]  [TUKEY]       {ANOVA FRIEDMAN}
             [CORRELATIONS] [HOTELLING]   {ANOVA COCHRAN }

[/SUMMARY=[MEANS] [VARIANCE] [COV] [CORR] [TOTAL] [ALL]]

[/ICC=[MODEL({MIXED**})][TYPE({CONSISTENCY**})][CIN={95**}]]
            {RANDOM}           {ABSOLUTE    }        {n   }
      [TESTVAL={0**}]
               {p  }


[/METHOD=COVARIANCE]

[/FORMAT={NOLABELS**}]
         {LABELS    }

[/MISSING={EXCLUDE**}]
          {INCLUDE  }

[/MATRIX =[IN({*    })] [OUT({*    })] [NOPRINT]]
             {file}        {file}
```

**Default if the subcommand or keyword is omitted.

Example

```
RELIABILITY  VARIABLES=SCORE1 TO SCORE10
  /SCALE (OVERALL) = ALL
  /MODEL = ALPHA
  /SUMMARY = MEANS TOTAL.
```

Overview

RELIABILITY estimates reliability statistics for the components of multiple-item additive scales. It uses any one of five models for reliability analysis and offers a variety of statistical displays. RELIABILITY can also be used to perform a repeated measures analysis of variance, a two-way factorial analysis of variance with one observation per cell, Tukey's test for additivity, Hotelling's *T*-square test for equality of means in repeated measures designs, and Friedman's two-way analysis of variance on ranks. For more complex repeated measures designs, use the GLM procedure (available in the SPSS Advanced Models option).

Options

Model Type. You can specify any one of five models on the MODEL subcommand.

Statistical Display. Statistics available on the STATISTICS subcommand include descriptive statistics, correlation and covariance matrices, a repeated measures analysis of variance table, Hotelling's *T*-square, Tukey's test for additivity, Friedman's chi-square for the analysis of ranked data, and Cochran's *Q*.

Computational Method. You can force RELIABILITY to use the covariance method, even when you are not requesting any output that requires it, by using the METHOD subcommand.

Matrix Input and Output. You can read data in the form of correlation matrices and you can write correlation-type matrix materials to a data file using the MATRIX subcommand.

Basic Specification

The basic specification is VARIABLES and a variable list. By default, RELIABILITY displays the number of cases, number of items, and Cronbach's alpha. Whenever possible, it uses an algorithm that does not require the calculation of the covariance matrix.

Subcommand Order

- VARIABLES must be specified first.
- The remaining subcommands can be named in any order.

Operations

- STATISTICS and SUMMARY are cumulative. If you enter them more than once, all requested statistics are produced for each scale.
- If you request output that is not available for your model or for your data, RELIABILITY ignores the request.
- RELIABILITY uses an economical algorithm whenever possible but calculates a covariance matrix when necessary (see the METHOD subcommand on p. 1011).

Limitations

- Maximum 10 VARIABLES subcommands.
- Maximum 50 SCALE subcommands.
- Maximum 500 variables on the combined VARIABLES subcommands. Each occurrence of a variable counts as 1 toward this limit.
- Maximum 500 variables on one SCALE subcommand.
- Maximum 1000 variables on all SCALE subcommands combined. Each mention of a variable counts one toward this limit.
- If the available workspace is insufficient to handle multiple VARIABLES subcommands, RELIABILITY deletes them in the reverse order of specification until the workspace is sufficient.

Example

```
RELIABILITY  VARIABLES=SCORE1 TO SCORE10
  /SCALE (OVERALL) = ALL
  /SCALE (ODD) = SCORE1 SCORE3 SCORE5 SCORE7 SCORE9
  /SUMMARY = MEANS TOTAL.
```

- This example analyzes two additive scales.
- One scale (labeled *OVERALL* in the output) includes all 10 items. Another (labeled *ODD*) includes every other item.
- Summary statistics are displayed for each scale, showing item means and the relationship of each item to the total scale.

Example

```
RELIABILITY  VARIABLES=SCORE1 TO SCORE10.
```

- This example analyzes one scale (labeled *ALL* in the display output) that includes all 10 items.
- Because there is no SUMMARY subcommand, no summary statistics are displayed.

VARIABLES Subcommand

VARIABLES specifies the variables to be used in the analysis. Only numeric variables can be used.

- VARIABLES is required and must be specified first.
- You can use keyword ALL to refer to all user-defined variables in the working data file.
- You can specify VARIABLES more than once on a single RELIABILITY command. A reliability analysis is performed on each set of variables.

SCALE Subcommand

SCALE defines a scale for analysis, providing a label for the scale and specifying its component variables. If SCALE is omitted, all variables named on VARIABLES are used, and the label for the scale is *ALL*.

- The label is specified in parentheses after SCALE. It can have a maximum of eight characters and can use only the letters A to Z and the numerals 0 to 9.
- RELIABILITY does not add any new variables to the working data file. The label is used only to identify the output. If the analysis is satisfactory, use COMPUTE to create a new variable containing the sum of the component items.
- Variables named on SCALE must have been named on the previous VARIABLES subcommand. Use the keyword ALL to refer to all variables named on the preceding VARIABLES subcommand.
- To analyze different groups of component variables, specify SCALE more than once following a VARIABLES subcommand.

Example

```
RELIABILITY VARIABLES = ITEM1 TO ITEM20
  /SCALE (A) = ITEM1 TO ITEM10
  /SCALE (B) = ITEM1 ITEM3 ITEM5 ITEM16 TO ITEM20
  /SCALE (C) = ALL.
```

- This command analyzes three different scales: scale A has 10 items, scale B has 8 items, and scale C has 20 items.

MODEL Subcommand

MODEL specifies the type of reliability analysis for the scale named on the preceding SCALE subcommand.

ALPHA
: *Cronbach's α.* Standardized item α is displayed. This is the default.

SPLIT [(n)]
: *Split-half coefficients.* You can specify a number in parentheses to indicate how many items should be in the second half. For example, MODEL SPLIT (6) uses the last six variables for the second half and all others for the first. By default, each half has an equal number of items, with the odd item, if any, going to the first half.

GUTTMAN
: *Guttman's lower bounds for true reliability.*

PARALLEL
: *Maximum-likelihood reliability estimate under parallel assumptions.* This model assumes that items have the same variance but not necessarily the same mean.

STRICTPARALLEL
: *Maximum-likelihood reliability estimate under strictly parallel assumptions.* This model assumes that items have the same means, the same true score variances over a set of objects being measured, and the same error variance over replications.

STATISTICS Subcommand

STATISTICS displays optional statistics. There are no default statistics.

- STATISTICS is cumulative. If you enter it more than once, all requested statistics are produced for each scale.

DESCRIPTIVES
: *Item means and standard deviations.*

COVARIANCES
: *Inter-item variance-covariance matrix.*

CORRELATIONS
: *Inter-item correlation matrix.*

SCALE
: *Scale means and scale variances.*

TUKEY
: *Tukey's test for additivity.* This helps determine whether a transformation of the items is needed to reduce nonadditivity. The test displays an estimate of the power to which the items should be raised in order to be additive.

HOTELLING	*Hotelling's* T-*square.* This is a test for equality of means among the items.
ANOVA	*Repeated measures analysis of variance table.*
FRIEDMAN	*Friedman's chi-square and Kendall's coefficient of concordance.* These apply to ranked data. You must request ANOVA in addition to FRIEDMAN; Friedman's chi-square appears in place of the usual *F* test.
COCHRAN	*Cochran's* Q. This applies when all items are dichotomies. You must request ANOVA in addition to COCHRAN; the *Q* statistic appears in place of the usual *F* test.
ALL	*All applicable statistics.*

ICC Subcommand

ICC displays intraclass correlation coefficients for single measure and average measure. Single measure applies to single measurements, for example, the rating of judges, individual item scores, or the body weights of individuals. Average measure, however, applies to average measurements, for example, the average rating of *k* judges, or the average score for a *k*-item test.

MODEL	*Model.* You can specify the model for the computation of ICC. There are three keywords for this option. ONEWAY is the one-way random effects model (people effects are random). RANDOM is the two-way random effect model (people effects and the item effects are random). MIXED is the two-way mixed (people effects are random and the item effects are fixed). MIXED is the default. Only one model can be specified.
TYPE	*Type of definition.* There are two keywords for this option. CONSISTENCY is the consistency definition and ABSOLUTE is the absolute agreement definition. For the consistency coefficient, the between measures variance is excluded from the denominator variance, and for absolute agreement, it is not.
CIN	*The value of the percent for confidence interval and significance level of the hypothesis testing.*
TESTVAL	*The value with which an estimate of ICC is compared.* The value should be between 0 and 1.

SUMMARY Subcommand

SUMMARY displays summary statistics for each individual item in the scale.

- SUMMARY is cumulative. If you enter it more than once, all requested statistics are produced for each scale.
- You can specify one or more of the following:

MEANS	*Statistics on item means.* The average, minimum, maximum, range, ratio of maximum to minimum, and variance of the item means.
VARIANCE	*Statistics on item variances.* This displays the same statistics as for MEANS.
COVARIANCES	*Statistics on item covariances.* This displays the same statistics as for MEANS.
CORRELATIONS	*Statistics on item correlations.* This displays the same statistics as for MEANS.
TOTAL	*Statistics comparing each individual item to the scale composed of the other items.* The output includes the scale mean, variance, and Cronbach's α without the item, and the correlation between the item and the scale without it.
ALL	*All applicable summary statistics.*

METHOD Subcommand

By default, RELIABILITY uses a computational method that does not require the calculation of a covariance matrix wherever possible. METHOD forces RELIABILITY to calculate the covariance matrix. Only a single specification applies to METHOD:

COVARIANCE *Calculate and use the covariance matrix, even if it is not needed.*

If METHOD is not specified, RELIABILITY computes the covariance matrix for all variables on each VARIABLES subcommand only if any of the following is true:

- You specify a model other than ALPHA or SPLIT.
- You request COV, CORR, FRIEDMAN, or HOTELLING on the STATISTICS subcommand.
- You request anything other than TOTAL on the SUMMARY subcommand.
- You write the matrix to a matrix data file, using the MATRIX subcommand.

FORMAT Subcommand

FORMAT controls the initial display of variable names and labels before the analysis.

NOLABELS *Do not display names and labels before the analysis.* This is the default.

LABELS *Display names and labels for all items before the analysis.*

MISSING Subcommand

MISSING controls the deletion of cases with user-missing data.

- RELIABILITY deletes cases from analysis if they have a missing value for any variable named on the current VARIABLES subcommand. By default, both system-missing and user-missing values are excluded.

EXCLUDE *Exclude user-missing and system-missing values.* This is the default.

INCLUDE *Treat user-missing values as valid.* Only system-missing values are excluded.

MATRIX Subcommand

MATRIX reads and writes SPSS matrix data files.

- Either IN or OUT and the matrix file in parentheses are required. When both IN and OUT are used on the same RELIABILITY procedure, they can be specified on separate MATRIX subcommands or on the same subcommand.

- If both IN and OUT are used on the same RELIABILITY command and there are grouping variables, these variables are treated as if they were split variables. Values of the grouping variables in the input matrix are passed on to the output matrix (see "Split Files" on p. 1013).

OUT (filename) *Write a matrix data file.* Specify either a filename or an asterisk (*), enclosed in parentheses. If you specify a filename, the file is stored on disk and can be retrieved at any time. If you specify an asterisk, the matrix file replaces the working data file but is not stored on disk unless you use SAVE or XSAVE.

IN (filename) *Read a matrix data file.* If the matrix data file is the working data file, specify an asterisk (*) in parentheses. If it is another file, specify the filename in parentheses. A matrix file read from an external file does not replace the working data file.

Matrix Output

- RELIABILITY writes correlation-type matrices that include the number of cases, means, and standard deviations with the matrix materials (see "Format of the Matrix Data File" below for a description of the file). These matrix materials can be used as input to RELIABILITY or other procedures.

- Any documents contained in the working data file are not transferred to the matrix file.

- RELIABILITY displays the scale analyses when it writes matrix materials. To suppress the display of scale analyses, specify keyword NOPRINT on MATRIX.

Matrix Input

- RELIABILITY can read a matrix data file created by a previous RELIABILITY command or by another SPSS procedure. The matrix input file must have records of type N, MEAN, STDDEV, and CORR for each split-file group. For more information, see the Universals section.

- SPSS reads variable names, variable and value labels, and print and write formats from the dictionary of the matrix data file.

- MATRIX=IN cannot be used unless a working data file has already been defined. To read an existing matrix data file at the beginning of a session, use GET to retrieve the matrix file and then specify IN(*) on MATRIX.

Format of the Matrix Data File

- The matrix data file includes two special variables created by SPSS: *ROWTYPE_* and *VARNAME_*. Variable *ROWTYPE_* is a short string variable having values N, MEAN, STDDEV, and CORR. Variable *VARNAME_* is a short string variable whose values are the names of the variables used to form the correlation matrix.

- When *ROWTYPE_* is CORR, *VARNAME_* gives the variable associated with that row of the correlation matrix.

- The remaining variables in the matrix file are the variables used to form the correlation matrix.

Split Files

- When split-file processing is in effect, the first variables in the matrix data file will be the split variables, followed by *ROWTYPE_*, *VARNAME_*, and the dependent variable(s).

- If grouping variables are in the matrix input file, their values are between *ROWTYPE_* and *VARNAME_*. The grouping variables are treated like split-file variables.

- A full set of matrix materials is written for each split-file group defined by the split variables.

- A split variable cannot have the same variable name as any other variable written to the matrix data file.

- If split-file processing is in effect when a matrix is written, the same split file must be in effect when that matrix is read by any procedure.

Missing Values

Missing-value treatment affects the values written to a matrix data file. When reading a matrix data file, be sure to specify a missing-value treatment on RELIABILITY that is compatible with the treatment that was in effect when the matrix materials were generated.

Example

```
DATA LIST / TIME1 TO TIME5 1-10.
BEGIN DATA
 0 0 0 0 0
 0 0 1 1 0
 0 0 1 1 1
 0 1 1 1 1
 0 0 0 0 1
 0 1 0 1 1
 0 0 1 1 1
 1 0 0 1 1
 1 1 1 1 1
 1 1 1 1 1
END DATA.
RELIABILITY  VARIABLES=TIME1 TO TIME5
  /MATRIX=OUT(RELMTX).
LIST.
```

- RELIABILITY reads data from the working data file and writes one set of matrix materials to file *RELMTX*.
- The working data file is still the file defined by DATA LIST. Subsequent commands are executed in this file.

Example

```
DATA LIST  / TIME1 TO TIME5 1-10.
BEGIN DATA
 0 0 0 0 0
 0 0 1 1 0
 0 0 1 1 1
 0 1 1 1 1
 0 0 0 0 1
 0 1 0 1 1
 0 0 1 1 1
 1 0 0 1 1
 1 1 1 1 1
 1 1 1 1 1
END DATA.
RELIABILITY  VARIABLES=TIME1 TO TIME5
  /MATRIX=OUT(*) NOPRINT.
LIST.
```

- RELIABILITY writes the same matrix as in the previous example. However, the matrix data file replaces the working data file. The LIST command is executed in the matrix file, not in the file defined by DATA LIST.
- Because NOPRINT is specified on MATRIX, scale analyses are not displayed.

Example

```
GET FILE=RELMTX.
RELIABILITY VARIABLES=ALL
  /MATRIX=IN(*).
```

- This example assumes that you are starting a new session and want to read an existing matrix data file. GET retrieves the matrix data file *RELMTX*.
- MATRIX=IN specifies an asterisk because the matrix data file is the working data file. If MATRIX=IN(RELMTX) is specified, SPSS issues an error message.
- If the GET command is omitted, SPSS issues an error message.

Example

```
GET FILE=PRSNNL.
FREQUENCIES VARIABLE=AGE.

RELIABILITY VARIABLES=ALL
  /MATRIX=IN(RELMTX).
```

- This example performs a frequencies analysis on file *PRSNNL* and then uses a different file containing matrix data for RELIABILITY. The file is an existing matrix data file. In order for this to work, the analysis variables named in *RELMTX* must also exist in *PRSNNL*.

- *RELMTX* must have records of type N, MEAN, STDDEV, and CORR for each split-file group.

- *RELMTX* does not replace *PRSNNL* as the working data file.

Example

```
GET FILE=PRSNNL.
CORRELATIONS VARIABLES=V1 TO V5
  /MATRIX=OUT(*).
RELIABILITY VARIABLES=V1 TO V5
  /MATRIX=IN(*).
```

- RELIABILITY uses matrix input from procedure CORRELATIONS. An asterisk is used to specify the working data file for both the matrix output from CORRELATIONS and the matrix input for RELIABILITY.

RENAME VARIABLES

```
RENAME VARIABLES {(varname=varname)  [(varname ...)]}
                 {(varnames=varnames)               }
```

Example

```
RENAME VARIABLES (JOBCAT=TITLE).
```

Overview

RENAME VARIABLES changes the names of variables in the working data file while preserving their original order, values, variable labels, value labels, missing values, and print and write formats.

Basic Specification

- The basic specification is an old variable name, an equals sign, and the new variable name. The equals sign is required.

Syntax Rules

- Multiple sets of variable specifications are allowed. Each set can be enclosed in parentheses.
- You can specify a list of old variable names followed by an equals sign and a list of new variable names. The same number of variables must be specified on both lists. A single set of parentheses enclosing the entire specification is required for this method.
- Keyword TO can be used on the left side of the equals sign to refer to variables in the working data file, and on the right side of the equals sign to generate new variable names (see the TO keyword on p. 29).
- Old variable names do not need to be specified according to their order in the working data file.
- Name changes take place in one operation. Therefore, variable names can be exchanged between two variables (see the example on p. 1016).
- Multiple RENAME VARIABLES commands are allowed.
- RENAME VARIABLES cannot follow either a TEMPORARY or a MODEL PROGRAM command.

Example

```
RENAME VARIABLES (MOHIRED=MOSTART) (YRHIRED=YRSTART).
```

- *MOHIRED* is renamed to *MOSTART* and *YRHIRED* to *YRSTART*. The parentheses are optional.

Example

```
RENAME VARIABLES (MOHIRED YRHIRED=MOSTART YRSTART).
```

- The same name changes are specified as in the previous example. The parentheses are required, since variable lists are used.

Example

```
RENAME VARIABLES (A=B) (B=A).
```

- Variable names are exchanged between two variables: *A* is renamed to *B*, and *B* is renamed to *A*.

REPEATING DATA

```
REPEATING DATA [FILE=file]

 /STARTS=beg col[-end col] /OCCURS={value  }
                                    {varname}

 [/LENGTH={value  }] [/CONTINUED[=beg col[-end col]]]
          {varname}

 [/ID={col loc}=varname] [/{TABLE  }]
      {format }             {NOTABLE}

 /DATA=variable specifications
```

Example

```
INPUT PROGRAM.
DATA LIST / SEQNUM 2-4 NUMPERS 6-7 NUMVEH 9-10.
REPEATING DATA STARTS=12 /OCCURS=NUMVEH
 /DATA=MAKE 1-8 (A) MODEL 9 (A) NUMCYL 10.
END INPUT PROGRAM.

BEGIN DATA
1001 02 02 FORD    T8PONTIAC C6
1002 04 01 CHEVY    C4
1003 02 03 CADILAC C8FORD    T6VW      C4
END DATA.
LIST.
```

Overview

REPEATING DATA reads input cases whose records contain repeating groups of data. For each repeating group, REPEATING DATA builds one output case in the working data file. All of the repeating groups in the data must contain the same type of information, although the number of groups for each input case may vary. Information common to the repeating groups for each input case can be recorded once for that case and then spread to each resulting output case. In this respect, a file with a repeating data structure is like a hierarchical file with both levels of information recorded on a single record rather than on separate record types. For information on reading hierarchical files, see FILE TYPE—END FILE TYPE.

REPEATING DATA must be used within an INPUT PROGRAM structure or within a FILE TYPE structure with mixed or nested data. In an INPUT PROGRAM structure, REPEATING DATA must be preceded by a DATA LIST command. In a FILE TYPE structure, DATA LIST is needed only if there are variables to be spread to each resulting output case.

Options

Length of Repeating Groups. If the length of the repeating groups varies across input cases, you can specify a variable that indicates the length on the LENGTH subcommand. You can also use LENGTH if you do not want to read all the data in each repeating group.

Continuation Records. You can use the CONTINUED subcommand to indicate that the repeating groups for each input case are contained on more than one record. You can check the value of an identification variable across records for the same input case using the ID subcommand.

Summary Tables. You can suppress the display of the table that summarizes the names, locations, and formats of the variables specified on the DATA subcommand using the NOTABLE subcommand.

Basic Specification

The basic specification requires three subcommands: STARTS, OCCURS, and DATA.

- STARTS specifies the beginning column of the repeating data segments. When there are continuation records, STARTS can specify the ending column of the last repeating group on the first record of each input case.
- OCCURS specifies the number of repeating groups on each input case. OCCURS can specify a number if the number of repeating groups is the same for all input cases. Otherwise, OCCURS should specify the name of a variable whose value for each input case indicates the number of repeating groups for that case.
- DATA specifies names, location within the repeating segment, and format for each variable to be read from the repeated groups.

Subcommand Order

- DATA must be the last subcommand specified on REPEATING DATA.
- The remaining subcommands can be named in any order.

Syntax Rules

- REPEATING DATA can be specified only within an INPUT PROGRAM structure, or within a FILE TYPE structure with mixed or nested data. DATA LIST, REPEATING DATA, and any transformation commands used to build the output cases must be placed within the INPUT PROGRAM or FILE TYPE structure. Transformations that apply to the output cases should be specified after the END INPUT PROGRAM or END FILE TYPE command.
- LENGTH must be used if the last variable specified on the DATA subcommand is not read from the last position of each repeating group or if the length of the repeating groups varies across input cases.
- CONTINUED must be used if repeating groups for each input case are continued on successive records.
- The DATA LIST command used with REPEATING DATA must define all fixed-format data for the records.

- Repeating groups are usually recorded at the end of the fixed-format records, but fixed-format data may follow the repeating data in data structures such as IBM SMF and RMF records. Use the following sequence in such cases.

```
DATA LIST .../* Read the fixed-format data before repeating data
REREAD  COLUMNS= .../* Skip repeating data
DATA LIST .../* Read the fixed-format data after repeating data
REPEATING DATA ... /*Read repeating data
```

Operations

- Fixed-location data specified on the DATA LIST are spread to each output case.
- If LENGTH is not specified, the program uses the default length for repeating data groups, which is determined from specifications on the DATA subcommand. For more information on the default length, see the LENGTH subcommand on p. 1027.

Cases Generated

- The number of output cases generated is the number specified on the OCCURS subcommand. Physical record length or whether fields are non-blank does not affect the number of cases generated.
- If the number specified for OCCURS is nonpositive or missing, no cases are generated.

Records Read

- If CONTINUED is not specified, all repeating groups are read from the first record of each input case.
- If CONTINUED is specified, the first continuation record is read when the first record for the input case is exhausted, that is, when the next repeating group would extend past the end of the record. The ending column for the first record is defined on STARTS. If the ending column is not specified on STARTS, the logical record length is used (see below).
- Subsequent continuation records are read when the current continuation record is exhausted. Exhaustion of the current continuation record is detected when the next repeating group would extend past the end of the record. The ending column for continuation records is defined on CONTINUED. If the ending column is not specified on CONTINUED, the logical record length is used (see below).
- For inline data, the record length is always 80. For data stored in a file, the record length is generally whatever was specified on the FILE HANDLE command or the default of 1024. Shorter records are extended with blanks when they are read. For IBM implementations, the physical record length is available and is used.

Reading Past End of Record

If one or more fields extend past the end of the actual record, or if CONTINUED is specified and the ending column specified on either STARTS or CONTINUED is beyond the end of the actual record, the program takes the following action:

- For string data with format A, the data record is considered to be extended logically with blanks. If the entire field lies past the end of the record, the resulting value will be all blanks.

- For numeric data, a warning is issued and the resulting value is system-missing.

Example

```
* Build a file with each case representing one vehicle and
  spread information about the household to each case.

INPUT PROGRAM.
DATA LIST / SEQNUM 2-4 NUMPERS 6-7 NUMVEH 9-10.
REPEATING DATA STARTS=12 /OCCURS=NUMVEH
 /DATA=MAKE 1-8 (A) MODEL 9 (A) NUMCYL 10.
END INPUT PROGRAM.

BEGIN DATA
1001 02 02 FORD    T8PONTIAC C6
1002 04 01 CHEVY   C4
1003 02 03 CADILAC C8FORD    T6VW      C4
END DATA.
LIST.
```

- Data are extracted from a file representing household records. Each input case is recorded on a single record; there are no continuation records.

- The total number of persons living in the house and number of vehicles owned by the household is recorded on each record. The first field of numbers (columns 1–4) for each record is an identification number unique to each record. The next two fields of numbers are number of persons in household and number of vehicles. The remainder of the record contains repeating groups of information about each vehicle: the make of vehicle, model, and number of cylinders.

- INPUT PROGRAM indicates the beginning of the input program and END INPUT PROGRAM indicates the end of the input program.

- DATA LIST reads the variables from the household portion of the record. All fixed-format variables are defined on DATA LIST.

- REPEATING DATA reads the information from the repeating groups and builds the output cases. Repeating groups start in column 12. The number of repeating groups for each input case is given by the value of variable *NUMVEH*. Three variables are defined for each repeating group: *MAKE*, *MODEL*, and *NUMCYL*.

- The first input record contains two repeating groups, producing two output cases in the working data file. One output case is built from the second input record which contains information on one vehicle, and three output cases are built from the third record. The values of the fixed-format variables defined on DATA LIST are spread to every new case built in the working data file. Six cases result, as shown in Figure 1.

Figure 1   Output cases built with REPEATING DATA

```
SEQNUM NUMPERS NUMVEH MAKE      MODEL NUMCYL

      1       2      2  FORD      T       8
      1       2      2  PONTIAC   C       6
      2       4      1  CHEVY     C       4
      3       2      3  CADILAC   C       8
      3       2      3  FORD      T       6
      3       2      3  VW        C       4


NUMBER OF CASES READ =         6    NUMBER OF CASES LISTED =          6
```

Example

```
* Use REPEATING DATA with FILE TYPE MIXED: read only type 3 records.

FILE TYPE  MIXED RECORD=#SEQNUM 2-4.
RECORD TYPE 003.
REPEATING DATA STARTS=12 /OCCURS=3
 /DATA=MAKE 1-8(A) MODEL 9(A) NUMCYL 10.
END FILE.
END FILE TYPE.

BEGIN DATA
1001 02 02 FORD     T8PONTIAC C6
1002 04 01 CHEVY    C4
1003 02 03 CADILAC C8FORD     T6VW      C4
END DATA.
LIST.
```

- The task in this example is to read only the repeating data for records with value 003 for variable *#SEQNUM*.

- REPEATING DATA is used within a FILE TYPE structure, which specifies a mixed file type. The record identification variable *#SEQNUM* is located in columns 2–4.

- RECORD TYPE specifies that only records with value 003 for *#SEQNUM* are copied into the working data file. All other records are skipped.

- REPEATING DATA indicates that the repeating groups start in column 12. The OCCURS subcommand indicates there are three repeating groups on each input case, and the DATA subcommand specifies names, locations, and formats for the variables in the repeating groups.

- The DATA LIST command is not required in this example, since none of the information on the input case is being spread to the output cases. However, if there were multiple input cases with value 003 for *#SEQNUM* and they did not all have three repeating groups, DATA LIST would be required to define a variable whose value for each input case indicated the number of repeating groups for that case. This variable would then be specified on the OCCURS subcommand.

Example

```
* Create a data set of child records.

INPUT PROGRAM.
DATA LIST / PARENTID 1 DATE 3-6 NCHILD 8.
REPEATING DATA STARTS=9 /OCCURS=NCHILD
 /DATA=BIRTHDAY 2-5 VACDATE 7-10.
END INPUT PROGRAM.

COMPUTE AGE=DATE - BIRTHDAY.
COMPUTE VACAGE=VACDATE - BIRTHDAY.

DO IF PARENTID NE LAG(PARENTID,1) OR $CASENUM EQ 1.
COMPUTE CHILD=1.
ELSE.
COMPUTE CHILD=LAG(CHILD,1)+1.
END IF.
FORMAT AGE VACAGE CHILD (F2).

BEGIN DATA
1 1987 2 1981 1983 1982 1984
2 1988 1 1979 1984
3 1988 3 1978 1981 1981 1986 1983 1986
4 1988 1 1984 1987
END DATA.
LIST.
```

- Data are from a file that contains information on parents within a school district. Each input case is recorded on a single record; there are no continuation records.

- Each record identifies the parents by a number and indicates how many children they have. The repeating groups give the year of birth and year of vaccination for each child.

- REPEATING DATA indicates that the repeating groups begin in column 9. The value of *NCHILD* indicates how many repeating groups there are for each record.

- The first two COMPUTE commands compute the age for each child and age at vaccination. These transformation commands are specified outside the input program.

- Because the repeating groups do not have descriptive values, the DO IF structure computes variable *CHILD* to distinguish between the first-born child, second-born child, etc. The value for *CHILD* will be 1 for the first-born, 2 for the second-born, and so forth. The LIST output is shown in Figure 2.

Figure 2   Output cases built with REPEATING DATA

```
PARENTID DATE NCHILD BIRTHDAY VACDATE AGE VACAGE CHILD

    1     1987    2     1981     1983    6     2      1
    1     1987    2     1982     1984    5     2      2
    2     1988    1     1979     1984    9     5      1
    3     1988    3     1978     1981   10     3      1
    3     1988    3     1981     1986    7     5      2
    3     1988    3     1983     1986    5     3      3
    4     1988    1     1984     1987    4     3      1

NUMBER OF CASES READ =      7    NUMBER OF CASES LISTED =      7
```

STARTS Subcommand

STARTS indicates the beginning location of the repeating data segment on the first record of each input case. STARTS is required and can specify either a number or a variable name.

- If the repeating groups on the first record of each input case begin in the same column, STARTS specifies a column number.

- If the repeating groups on the first record of each input case do not begin in the same column, STARTS specifies the name of a variable whose value for each input case indicates the beginning location of the repeating groups on the first record. The variable can be defined on DATA LIST or created by transformation commands that precede REPEATING DATA.

- When repeating groups are continued on multiple records for each input case, STARTS must also specify an ending location if there is room on the logical record length for more repeating groups than are contained on the first record of each input case. The ending column applies only to the first record of each input case. See the CONTINUED subcommand on p. 1028 for an example.

- The ending column can be specified as a number or a variable name. Specifications for the beginning column and the ending column are separated by a hyphen. The values of the variable used to define the ending column must be valid values and must be larger than the starting value.

- If the variable specified for the ending column is undefined or missing for an input case, the program displays a warning message and builds no output cases from that input case. If the variable specified for the ending column on STARTS has a value that is less than the value specified for the starting column, the program issues a warning and builds output cases only from the continuation records of that input case; it does not build cases from the first record of the case.

- If the ending location is required but not supplied, the program generates output cases with system-missing values for the variables specified on the DATA subcommand and may misread all data after the first or second record in the data file (see the CONTINUED subcommand on p. 1028).

Example

```
* Repeating groups in the same location.

INPUT PROGRAM.
DATA LIST FILE=VEHICLE / SEQNUM 2-4 NUMPERS 6-7 NUMVEH 9-10.
REPEATING DATA STARTS=12 /OCCURS=NUMVEH
 /DATA=MAKE 1-8 (A) MODEL 9 (A) NUMCYL 10.
END INPUT PROGRAM.
```

- STARTS specifies column number 12. The repeating groups must therefore start in column 12 of the first record of each input case.

Example

```
* Repeating groups in varying locations.

INPUT PROGRAM.
DATA LIST FILE=VEHICLE / SEQNUM 2-4 NUMPERS 6-7 NUMVEH 9-10.
+    DO IF   (SEQNUM LE 100).
+    COMPUTE FIRST=12.
+    ELSE.
+    COMPUTE FIRST=15.
+    END IF.
REPEATING DATA STARTS=FIRST /OCCURS=NUMVEH
 /DATA=MAKE 1-8 (A) MODEL 9 (A) NUMCYL 10.
END INPUT PROGRAM.
```

- This example assumes that each input case is recorded on a single record and that there are no continuation records. Repeating groups begin in column 12 for all records with sequence numbers 1 through 100 and in column 15 for all records with sequence numbers greater than 100.

- The sequence number for each record is defined as variable *SEQNUM* on the DATA LIST command. The DO IF—END IF structure creates the variable *FIRST* with value 12 for records with sequence numbers through 100 and value 15 for records with sequence numbers greater than 100.

- Variable *FIRST* is specified on the STARTS subcommand.

OCCURS Subcommand

OCCURS specifies the number of repeating groups for each input case. OCCURS is required and specifies a number if the number of groups is the same for all input cases or a variable if the number of groups varies across input cases. The variable must be defined on a DATA LIST command or created with transformation commands.

Example

```
INPUT PROGRAM.
DATA LIST / SEQNUM 2-4 NUMPERS 6-7 NUMVEH 9-10.
REPEATING DATA STARTS=12 /OCCURS=NUMVEH
 /DATA=MAKE 1-8 (A) MODEL 9 (A) NUMCYL 10.
END INPUT PROGRAM.

BEGIN DATA
1001 02 02 FORD    T8PONTIAC C6
1002 04 01 CHEVY   C4
1003 02 03 CADILAC C8FORD    T6VW       C4
END DATA.
LIST.
```

- Data for each input case are recorded on a single record; there are no continuation records.

- The value for variable *NUMVEH* in columns 9 and 10 indicates the number of repeating groups on each record. One output case is built in the working data file for each occurrence of a repeating group.

- In the data, *NUMVEH* has the value 2 for the first case, 1 for the second, and 3 for the third. Thus, six cases are built from these records. If the value of *NUMVEH* is 0, no cases are built from that record.

Example

```
* Read only the first repeating group from each record.

INPUT PROGRAM.
DATA LIST FILE=VEHICLE / SEQNUM 2-4 NUMPERS 6-7 NUMVEH 9-10.
REPEATING DATA STARTS=12 /OCCURS=1
 /DATA=MAKE 1-8 (A) MODEL 9 (A) NUMCYL 10.
END INPUT PROGRAM.
LIST.
```

- Since OCCURS specifies that there is only one repeating group for each input case, only one output case is built from each input case regardless of the actual number of repeating groups.

DATA Subcommand

DATA specifies a name, location within each repeating segment, and format for each variable to be read from the repeating groups. DATA is required and must be the last subcommand on REPEATING DATA.

- The specifications for DATA are the same as for the DATA LIST command.
- The specified location of the variables on DATA is their location within each repeating group—*not* their location within the record.
- Any input format available on the DATA LIST command can be specified on the DATA subcommand. Both FORTRAN-like and the column-style specifications can be used.

Example

```
INPUT PROGRAM.
DATA LIST FILE=VEHICLE / SEQNUM 2-4 NUMPERS 6-7 NUMVEH 9-10.
REPEATING DATA STARTS=12 /OCCURS=NUMVEH
 /DATA=MAKE 1-8 (A) MODEL 9 (A) NUMCYL 10.
END INPUT PROGRAM.
LIST.
```

- Variable *MAKE* is a string variable read from positions 1 through 8 of each repeating group; *MODEL* is a single-character string variable read from position 9; and *NUMCYL* is a one-digit numeric variable read from position 10.
- The DATA LIST command defines variables *SEQNUM, NUMPERS*, and *NUMVEH*. These variables are spread to each output case built from the repeating groups.

FILE Subcommand

REPEATING DATA always reads the file specified on its associated DATA LIST or FILE TYPE command. The FILE subcommand on REPEATING DATA explicitly specifies the name of the file.

- FILE must specify the same file as its associated DATA LIST or FILE TYPE command.

Example

```
INPUT PROGRAM.
DATA LIST FILE=VEHICLE / SEQNUM 2-4 NUMPERS 6-7 NUMVEH 9-10.
REPEATING DATA FILE=VEHICLE /STARTS=12 /OCCURS=NUMVEH
 /DATA=MAKE 1-8 (A) MODEL 9 (A) NUMCYL 10.
END INPUT PROGRAM.
LIST.
```

- FILE on REPEATING DATA specifically identifies the *VEHICLE* file, which is also specified on the DATA LIST command.

LENGTH Subcommand

LENGTH specifies the length of each repeating data group. The default length is the number of columns between the beginning column of the repeating data groups and the ending position of the last variable specified on DATA. (For the first record of each input case, STARTS specifies the beginning column of the repeating groups. For continuation records, repeating groups are read from column 1 by default or from the column specified on CONTINUED.)

- The specification on LENGTH can be a number or the name of a variable.

- LENGTH must be used if the last variable specified on the DATA subcommand is not read from the last position of each repeating group, or if the length of the repeating groups varies across input cases.

- If the length of the repeating groups varies across input cases, the specification must be a variable whose value for each input case is the length of the repeating groups for that case. The variable can be defined on DATA LIST or created with transformation commands.

- If the value of the variable specified on LENGTH is undefined or missing for an input case, the program displays a warning message and builds only one output case for that input case.

Example

```
* Read only the variable MAKE for each vehicle.

* The data contain two values that are not specified on the
  DATA subcommand.  The first is in position 9 of the repeating
  groups, and the second is in position 10.

INPUT PROGRAM.
DATA LIST FILE=VEHICLE / SEQNUM 2-4 NUMPERS 6-7 NUMVEH 9-10.
REPEATING DATA STARTS=12 /OCCURS=NUMVEH /LENGTH=10
 /DATA=MAKE 1-8 (A).
END INPUT PROGRAM.
```

- LENGTH indicates that each repeating group is 10 columns long. LENGTH is required because *MAKE* is not read from the last position of each repeating group. As illustrated in previous examples, each repeating group also includes variable *MODEL* (position 9) and *NUMCYL* (position 10).

- DATA specifies that *MAKE* is in positions 1 through 8 of each repeating group. Positions 9 and 10 of each repeating group are skipped.

CONTINUED Subcommand

CONTINUED indicates that the repeating groups are contained on more than one record for each input case.

- Each repeating group must be fully recorded on a single record: a repeating group cannot be split across records.
- The repeating groups must begin in the same column on all continuation records.
- If CONTINUED is specified without beginning and ending columns, the program assumes that the repeating groups begin in column 1 of continuation records and searches for repeating groups by scanning to the end of the record or to the value specified by OCCURS. See "Operations" on p. 1020 for additional information on how records are read.
- If the repeating groups on continuation records do not begin in column 1, CONTINUED must specify the column in which the repeating groups begin.
- If there is room on the logical record length for more repeating groups than are contained on the first record of each input case, the STARTS subcommand must indicate an ending column for the records. The ending column on STARTS applies only to the first record of each input case.
- If there is room on the logical record length for more repeating groups than are contained on the continuation records of each input case, the CONTINUED subcommand must indicate an ending column. The ending column on CONTINUED applies to all continuation records.

Example

```
* This example assumes the logical record length is 80.

INPUT PROGRAM.
DATA LIST / ORDERID 1-5 NITEMS 7-8.
REPEATING DATA STARTS=10 /OCCURS=NITEMS /CONTINUED=7
 /DATA=ITEM 1-9 (A) QUANTITY 11-13 PRICE (DOLLAR7.2,1X).
END INPUT PROGRAM.

BEGIN DATA
10020 07 01-923-89 001   25.99 02-899-56 100 101.99 03-574-54 064   61.29
10020 04-780-32 025   13.95 05-756-90 005   56.75 06-323-47 003   23.74
10020 07-350-95 014   11.46
20030 04 01-781-43 010   10.97 02-236-54 075 105.95 03-655-83 054   22.99
20030 04-569-38 015   75.00
END DATA.
LIST.
```

- Data are extracted from a mail-order file. Each input case represents one complete order. The data show two complete orders recorded on a total of five records.
- The order number is recorded in columns 1 through 5 of each record. The first three records contain information for order 10020; the next two records contain information for order 20030. The second field of numbers on the first record of each order indicates the total number of items ordered. The repeating groups begin in column 10 on the first record and in column 7 on continuation records. Each repeating data group represents one item ordered and contains three variables—the item inventory number, the quantity ordered, and the price.
- DATA LIST defines variables *ORDERID* and *NITEMS* on the first record of each input case.

- STARTS on REPEATING DATA indicates that the repeating groups on the first record of each input case begin in column 10.
- OCCURS indicates that the total number of repeating groups for each input case is the value of *NITEMS*.
- CONTINUED must be used because the repeating groups are continued on more than one record for each input case. CONTINUED specifies a beginning column because the repeating groups begin in column 7 rather than in column 1 on the continuation records.
- DATA defines variables *ITEM*, *QUANTITY*, and *PRICE* for each repeating data group. *ITEM* is in positions 1–9, *QUANTITY* is in positions 11–13, and *PRICE* is in positions 14–20 and is followed by one blank column. The length of the repeating groups is therefore 21 columns. The LIST output is shown in Figure 3.

Figure 3   Cases generated by REPEATING DATA

```
ORDERID NITEMS ITEM      QUANTITY      PRICE

 10020     7    01-923-89      1      $25.99
 10020     7    02-899-56    100     $101.99
 10020     7    03-574-54     64      $61.29
 10020     7    04-780-32     25      $13.95
 10020     7    05-756-90      5      $56.75
 10020     7    06-323-47      3      $23.74
 10020     7    07-350-95     14      $11.46
 20030     4    01-781-43     10      $10.97
 20030     4    02-236-54     75     $105.95
 20030     4    03-655-83     54      $22.99
 20030     4    04-569-38     15      $75.00


NUMBER OF CASES READ =      11   NUMBER OF CASES LISTED =       11
```

Example

```
* Specifying an ending column on the STARTS subcommand.
* This example assumes the logical record length is 80.

INPUT PROGRAM.
DATA LIST / ORDERID 1-5 NITEMS 7-8.
REPEATING DATA STARTS=10-55 /OCCURS=NITEMS /CONTINUED=7
 /DATA=ITEM 1-9 (A) QUANTITY 11-13 PRICE (DOLLAR7.2,1X).
END INPUT PROGRAM.

BEGIN DATA
10020 07 01-923-89 001  25.99 02-899-56 100 101.99
10020 03-574-54 064  61.29 04-780-32 025  13.95 05-756-90 005  56.75
10020 06-323-47 003  23.74 07-350-95 014  11.46
20030 04 01-781-43 010  10.97 02-236-54 075 105.95
20030 03-655-83 054  22.99 04-569-38 015  75.00
END DATA.
LIST.
```

- Data are the same as in the previous example; however, records are entered differently. The first record for each input case contains only two repeating groups.
- DATA LIST defines variables *ORDERID* and *NITEMS* in columns 1–8 on the first record of each input case. Column 9 is blank. DATA defines variables *ITEM*, *QUANTITY*, and *PRICE* in positions 1–20 of each repeating group, followed by a blank. Thus, each repeating

group is 21 columns wide. The length of the first record of each input case is therefore 51 columns: 21 columns for each of two repeating groups, plus the eight columns defined on DATA LIST, plus column 9, which is blank. The operating system's logical record length is 80, which allows room for one more repeating group on the first record of each input case. STARTS must therefore specify an ending column that does not provide enough columns for another repeating group; otherwise, the program creates an output case with missing values for the variables specified on DATA.

- STARTS specifies that the program is to scan only columns 10–55 of the first record of each input case looking for repeating data groups. It will scan continuation records beginning in column 7 until the value specified on the OCCURS subcommand is reached.

Example

```
* Specifying an ending column on the CONTINUED subcommand.
* This example assumes the logical record length is 80.

INPUT PROGRAM.
DATA LIST / ORDERID 1-5 NITEMS 7-8.
REPEATING DATA STARTS=10-55 /OCCURS=NITEMS /CONTINUED=7-55
 /DATA=ITEM 1-9 (A) QUANTITY 11-13 PRICE (DOLLAR7.2,1X).
END INPUT PROGRAM.

BEGIN DATA
10020 07 01-923-89 001  25.99 02-899-56 100 101.99
10020 03-574-54 064  61.29 04-780-32 025  13.95
10020 05-756-90 005  56.75 06-323-47 003  23.74
10020 07-350-95 014  11.46
20030 04 01-781-43 010  10.97 89-236-54 075 105.95
20030 03-655-83 054  22.99 04-569-38 015  75.00
END DATA.
LIST.
```

- The data are the same as in the previous two examples, but records are entered differently. The first record and the continuation records for each input case store only two repeating groups each.

- The operating system's logical record length is 80, which allows room for more repeating groups on all records.

- STARTS specifies that the program is to scan only columns 10-55 of the first record of each input case looking for repeating data groups.

- CONTINUED specifies that the program is to scan only columns 7–55 of all continuation records.

ID Subcommand

ID compares the value of an identification variable across records of the same input case. ID can be used only when CONTINUED is specified. The identification variable must be defined on a DATA LIST command and must be recorded on all records in the file.

- The ID subcommand has two specifications: the location of the variable on the continuation records and the name of the variable (as specified on the DATA LIST command). The specifications must be separated from each other by an equals sign.

- The format specified on the ID subcommand must be the same as the format specified for the variable on DATA LIST. However, the location can be different on the continuation records.
- If the values of the identification variable are not the same on all records for a single input case, the program displays an error message and stops reading data.

Example

```
INPUT PROGRAM.
DATA LIST / ORDERID 1-5 NITEMS 7-8.
REPEATING DATA STARTS=10-50 /OCCURS=NITEMS
 /CONTINUED=7 /ID=1-5=ORDERID
 /DATA=ITEM 1-9 (A) QUANTITY 11-13 PRICE 15-20 (2).
END INPUT PROGRAM.

BEGIN DATA
10020 04 45-923-89 001  25.9923-899-56 100 101.99
10020 63-780-32 025  13.9554-756-90 005  56.75
20030 03 45-781-43 010  10.9789-236-54 075 105.95
20030 32-569-38 015  75.00
END DATA.
LIST.
```

- The order number in the data is recorded in columns 1–5 of each record.
- *ORDERID* is defined on the DATA LIST command as a five-column integer variable. The first specification on the ID subcommand must therefore specify a five-column integer variable. The location of the variable can be different on continuation records.

TABLE and NOTABLE Subcommands

TABLE displays a table summarizing all variables defined on the DATA subcommand. The summary table lists the names, locations, and formats of the variables and is identical in format to the summary table displayed by the DATA LIST command. NOTABLE suppresses the table. TABLE is the default.

Example

```
INPUT PROGRAM.
DATA LIST FILE=VEHICLE /  SEQNUM 2-4 NUMPERS 6-7 NUMVEH 9-10.
REPEATING DATA STARTS=12 /OCCURS=NUMVEH /NOTABLE
 /DATA=MAKE 1-8 (A) MODEL 9 (A) NUMCYL 10.
END INPUT PROGRAM.
```

- NOTABLE suppresses the display of the summary table.

REPORT

```
REPORT [/FORMAT=[{MANUAL   }] [{NOLIST   }] [ALIGN({LEFT  })] [TSPACE({1})]
                 {AUTOMATIC}    {LIST[(n)]}        {CENTER}            {n}
                                                   {RIGHT }
         [CHDSPACE({1})] [FTSPACE({1})] [SUMSPACE({1})] [COLSPACE({4})]
                   {n}             {n}             {n}             {n}
         [BRKSPACE({ 1 })][LENGTH({1,length})] [MARGINS({1,width})]
                   { n }          {t,b     }           {l,r     }
                   {-1†}          {*,*     }           {*,*     }
         [CHALIGN({TOP    })] [UNDERSCORE({{OFF})] [PAGE1({{1})] [MISSING {'.'}]]
                  {BOTTOM†}                {ON†}          {n}            {'s'}
         [ONEBREAKCOLUMN {OFF**}] [INDENT {2**}] [CHWRAP {OFF**}] [PREVIEW {OFF**}]
                         {ON   }          {n  }          {ON   }           {ON   }
[/OUTFILE=file]
[/STRING=stringname (varname[(width)] [(BLANK)] ['literal'])
/VARIABLES=varname ({VALUE}) [+ varname({{VALUE})] ['col head'] [option list]
                    {LABEL}              {LABEL}
                    {DUMMY}              {DUMMY}
```

where option list can contain any of the following:

```
     (width)   (OFFSET({0     }))   ({LEFT  })
                       {n     }      {CENTER†}
                       {CENTER†}     {RIGHT }
[/MISSING={VAR                    }]
          {NONE                   }
          {LIST[([varlist][{1}])]}
                            {n}
[/TITLE=[{LEFT  }] 'line1' 'line2'...]   [/FOOTNOTE=[{LEFT  }] 'line1' 'line2'...]
         {CENTER}                                    {CENTER}
         {RIGHT }                                    {RIGHT }
         [)PAGE]   [)DATE]   [)var]
[/BREAK=varlist ['col head'] [option list]]
```

where option list can contain any of the following:

```
     (width)   ({VALUE })   ({NOTOTAL})   ({SKIP({1}    )))
               {LABEL†}     {TOTAL  }        {n}
                                          {PAGE[(RESET)]}
     (OFFSET({0     }))   (UNDERSCORE[(varlist)])   ({LEFT  })   ({NONAME})
             {n     }                                {CENTER†}    {NAME  }
             {CENTER†}                               {RIGHT  }
[/SUMMARY=function...['summary title'][(break col #)] [SKIP({0})]
                                                            {n}
     or
[/SUMMARY=PREVIOUS[({1})]]
                   {n}
```

where function is

```
aggregate [(varname[({PLAIN  })][(d)][varname...])]
                    {format††}
     or
composite(argument)[(report col[({PLAIN  })][(d)])]
                                 {format††}
```

**Default if the keyword is omitted.
†Default if FORMAT=AUTOMATIC.
††Any printable output format is valid. See FORMATS.

1032

Aggregate functions:

VALIDN	VARIANCE	PLT(n)
SUM	KURTOSIS	PIN(min,max)
MIN	SKEWNESS	FREQUENCY(min,max)
MAX	MEDIAN(min,max)	PERCENT(min,max)
MEAN	MODE(min,max)	
STDDEV	PGT(n)	

Composite functions:

DIVIDE(arg_1 arg_2 [factor])
MULTIPLY($arg_1...arg_n$)
PCT(arg_1 arg_2)
SUBTRACT(arg_1 arg_2)
ADD($arg_1...arg_n$)
GREAT($arg_1...arg_n$)
LEAST($arg_1...arg_n$)
AVERAGE($arg_1...arg_n$)

where arg is either one of the aggregate functions or a constant

Example

```
REPORT FORMAT=LIST
  /VARIABLES=PRODUCT (LABEL) ' ' 'Retail' 'Products'
          SALES 'Annual' 'Sales' '1981'
  /BREAK=DEPT 'Department' (LABEL)
  /SUMMARY=VALIDN (PRODUCT) MEAN (SALES).
```

Overview

REPORT produces case listings and summary statistics and gives you considerable control over the appearance of the output. REPORT calculates all the univariate statistics available in DESCRIPTIVES and the statistics and subpopulation means available in MEANS. In addition, REPORT calculates statistics not directly available in any other procedure, such as computations involving aggregated statistics.

REPORT provides complete report format defaults but also lets you customize a variety of table elements, including column widths, titles, footnotes, and spacing. Because REPORT is so flexible and the output has so many components, it is often efficient to preview report output using a small number of cases until you find the format that best suits your needs.

Defaults

Column Heads. REPORT uses variable labels as default column heads; if no variable labels have been specified, variable names are used. If ONEBREAKCOLUMN is ON, the default head for the first BREAK subcommand is used.

Column Widths. Default column widths are determined by REPORT, using the maximum of the following for each column:

- The widest print format in the column, whether it is a variable print format or a summary print format.

- The width of any temporary variable defined with the STRING subcommand on REPORT.

- If a column heading is assigned, the length of the longest title line in the heading when CHWRAP is off, and the longest word in the title when CHWRAP is on. Underscores, which are removed on printing, can be used to create longer words in the title.

- When no column heading is specified, the length of the longest word in the variable label, or the length of the variable name.

- If you specify LABEL on VARIABLES or BREAK, the length of the variable's longest value label. If FORMAT=MANUAL is in effect, 20 is the maximum value used for this criterion.

- The minimum column width is 8 when FORMAT=MANUAL; it can be less when FORMAT=AUTOMATIC.

Automatic Fit. When the above criteria for column width result in a report that is too wide for the report margins, FORMAT=AUTOMATIC shrinks the report. AUTOMATIC performs the following two steps sequentially, stopping as soon as the report fits within the margins:

1. AUTOMATIC reduces intercolumn spacing incrementally until it reaches a minimum intercolumn space of 1. It will never reduce it to 0.

2. AUTOMATIC shortens widths for strings specified on the STRING subcommand or for value label strings when the LABEL option is specified. It begins with the longest string if that string is at least 15 characters wide and shortens the column width as much as needed (up to 40% of its length), wrapping the string within the new width. If necessary, it repeats the step, using different defined strings. It will not shorten the column width of the same string twice.

REPORT does *not* implement the automatic fit unless AUTOMATIC is specified on the FORMAT subcommand.

AUTOMATIC versus MANUAL Defaults. Many default settings depend on whether you specify AUTOMATIC or MANUAL on FORMAT. Table 1 shows the defaults according to either of the specifications.

Table 1   Keyword default settings

Subcommand	Keyword	Default for AUTOMATIC	Default for MANUAL
FORMAT	ALIGN	left	left
	BRKSPACE		
	summary report	1	1
	listing report	−1	1
	CHALIGN	bottom	top
	CHDSPACE	1	1
	COLSPACE	4	4
	FTSPACE	1	1

Table 1   Keyword default settings (Continued)

Subcommand	Keyword	Default for AUTOMATIC	Default for MANUAL
	LENGTH	1,system length	1,system length
	LISTINOLIST	NOLIST	NOLIST
	MARGINS	1,system width	1,system width
	MISSING	.	.
	PAGE1	1	1
	SUMSPACE	1	1
	TSPACE	1	1
	UNDERSCORE	on	off
	ONEBREAKCOLUMN	off	off
	INDENT[1]	2	2
	CHWRAP	off	off
	PREVIEW	off	off
VARIABLES	LABELIVALUEIDUMMY	VALUE	VALUE
	LEFTICENTERIRIGHT	CENTER[2]	RIGHT for numbers LEFT for strings
	OFFSET	CENTER	0
BREAK	LABELIVALUE	LABEL	VALUE
	LEFTICENTERIRIGHT	CENTER[2]	RIGHT for numbers LEFT for strings
	NAMEINONAME	NONAME	NONAME
	OFFSET	CENTER[3]	0
	PAGE	off	off
	SKIP	1	1
	TOTALINOTOTAL	NOTOTAL	NOTOTAL
	UNDERSCORE	off	off
SUMMARY	PREVIOUS	1	1
	SKIP	0	0

[1] No effect when ONEBREAKCOLUMN is on.
[2] LEFT when ONEBREAKCOLUMN is on.
[3] 0 when ONEBREAKCOLUMN is on.

Options

Format. REPORT provides full format defaults and offers you optional control over page length, vertical spacing, margin and column widths, page titles, footnotes, and labels for statistics. The maximum width and length of the report are controlled by specifications on the SET command. The FORMAT subcommand on REPORT controls how the report is laid out on a page and whether case listings are displayed. The VARIABLES subcommand specifies the variables that are listed or summarized in the report (**report variables**) and controls the titles, width, and contents of report columns. The BREAK subcommand specifies the variables that define groups (**break variables**) and controls the titles, width, and contents of break columns. SUMMARY specifies statistics and controls the titles and spacing of summary lines. The TITLE and FOOTNOTE subcommands control the specification and placement of multiple-line titles and footnotes. STRING concatenates variables to create temporary variables that can be specified on VARIABLES or BREAK.

Output File. You can direct reports to a file separate from the file used for the rest of the output from your session using the OUTFILE subcommand.

Statistical Display. The statistical display is controlled by the SUMMARY subcommand. Statistics can be calculated for each category of a break variable and for the group as a whole. Available statistics include mean, variance, standard deviation, skewness, kurtosis, sum, minimum, maximum, mode, median, and percentages. Composite functions perform arithmetic operations using two or more summary statistics calculated on single variables.

Missing Values. You can override the default to include user-missing values in report statistics and listings with the MISSING subcommand. You can also use FORMAT to define a missing-value symbol to represent missing data.

Basic Specification

The basic specification depends on whether you want a listing report or a summary report. A listing report without subgroup classification requires FORMAT and VARIABLES. A listing report with subgroup classification requires FORMAT, VARIABLES, and BREAK. A summary report requires VARIABLES, BREAK, and SUMMARY.

Listing Reports. FORMAT=LIST and VARIABLES with a variable list are required. Case listings are displayed for each variable named on VARIABLES. There are no break groups or summary statistics unless BREAK or SUMMARY is specified.

Summary Reports. VARIABLES, BREAK, and SUMMARY are required. The report is organized according to the values of the variable named on BREAK. The variable named on BREAK must be named on a preceding SORT CASES command. Specified statistics are computed for the variables specified on VARIABLES for each subgroup defined by the break variables.

Subcommand Order

The following order must be observed among subcommands when they are used:

- FORMAT must precede all other subcommands.
- VARIABLES must precede BREAK.
- OUTFILE must precede BREAK.
- Each SUMMARY subcommand must immediately follow its associated BREAK. Multiple SUMMARY subcommands associated with the same BREAK must be specified consecutively.

- TITLE and FOOTNOTE can appear anywhere after FORMAT except between BREAK and SUMMARY.
- MISSING must follow VARIABLES and precede the first BREAK.
- STRING must precede VARIABLES.

Syntax Rules

- Only one each of the FORMAT, STRING, VARIABLES, and MISSING subcommands is allowed.
- To obtain multiple break groups, use multiple BREAK subcommands.
- To obtain multiple summaries for a break level, specify multiple SUMMARY subcommands for the associated BREAK.
- Keywords on REPORT subcommands have default specifications that are in effect if the keyword is not specified. Specify keywords only when you wish to change a default.
- Keywords are enclosed in parentheses if the subcommand takes variable names as arguments.

Operations

- REPORT processes cases sequentially. When the value of a break variable changes, REPORT displays a statistical summary for cases processed since the last set of summary statistics was displayed. Thus, the file must be sorted in order on the break variable or variables.
- The maximum width and page length of the report are determined by the SET command.
- If a column is not wide enough to display numeric values, REPORT first rounds decimal digits, then converts to scientific notation if possible, and then displays asterisks. String variables that are wider than the column are truncated.
- The format used to display values in case listings is controlled by the dictionary format of the variable. Each statistical function in REPORT has a default format.

Limitations

- Maximum 500 variables per VARIABLES subcommand. You can specify more than 500 variables if you stack them (see "VARIABLES Subcommand" on p. 1044).
- Maximum 10 dummy variables per VARIABLES subcommand.
- Maximum 20 MODE and MEDIAN requests per SUMMARY subcommand.
- Maximum 20 PGT, PLT, and PIN requests per SUMMARY subcommand.
- Maximum 50 strings per STRING subcommand.
- The length of titles and footnotes cannot exceed the report width.
- The length of string variables created on STRING cannot exceed the page width.
- There is no fixed limit on the number of BREAK and SUMMARY subcommands. However, the page width limits the number of variables that can be displayed and thereby limits the number of break variables.

- The maximum width of a report is 255 characters.
- The number of report variables that can be specified depends upon the width of the report, the width of the variable columns, and the number of BREAK subcommands.
- Maximum 50 variables for the FREQUENCY or PERCENT functions.
- Memory requirements significantly increase if FREQUENCY, PERCENT, MEDIAN, or MODE is requested for variables with a wide range of values. The amount of workspace required is 20 + 8*(max−min +1) bytes per variable per function per break. If the same range is used for different statistics for the same variable, only one set of cells is collected. For example, FREQUENCY(1,100)(VARA) PERCENT(1,100)(VARA) requires only 820 bytes.
- If TOTAL is in effect, workspace requirements are almost doubled.
- Memory requirements also increase if value labels are displayed for variables with many value labels. The amount of workspace required is 4 + 24*n bytes per variable, where n is the number of value labels specified for the variable.

Example

```
SORT CASES BY DEPT.
REPORT FORMAT=LIST
   /VARIABLES=PRODUCT (LABEL) ' ' 'Retail' 'Products'
            SALES 'Annual' 'Sales' '1981'
   /BREAK=DEPT 'Department' (LABEL)
   /SUMMARY=VALIDN (PRODUCT) MEAN (SALES) 'No.Sold,Mean Sales'.
```

- This report is a listing of products and sales by department. A summary of the total number of products sold and the average sales by department is also produced.
- Cases are first sorted by *DEPT* so that cases are grouped by department for the case listing and for the calculation of statistics.
- FORMAT requests a report that lists individual cases within each break group.
- VARIABLES specifies *PRODUCT* and *SALES* as the report variables. Keyword LABEL requests that the case listings for *PRODUCT* display value labels instead of values. Three-line column headings are provided for each report column. The first line of the column heading is blank for the variable *PRODUCT*.
- BREAK identifies *DEPT* as the break variable and provides a one-line column title for the break column. LABEL displays the value label instead of the value itself.
- SUMMARY calculates the valid number of cases for *PRODUCT* and the mean of *SALES* for each value of *DEPT*. A title is provided for the summary line to override the default title, *VALIDN*.

FORMAT Subcommand

FORMAT controls the overall width and length of the report and vertical spacing. Keywords and their arguments can be specified in any order.

- MANUAL and AUTOMATIC are alternatives. The default is MANUAL.
- LIST and NOLIST are alternatives. The default is NOLIST.

MANUAL   *Default settings for manual format.* MANUAL displays values for break variables, right-justifies numeric values and their column headings, left-justifies value labels and string values and their column headings, top-aligns and does not underscore column headings, extends column widths to accommodate the variable's longest value label (but not the longest word in the variable label) up to a width of 20, and generates an error message when a report is too wide for its margins. MANUAL is the default.

AUTOMATIC   *Default settings for automatic format.* AUTOMATIC displays labels for break variables, centers all data, centers column headings but left-justifies column headings if value labels or string values exceed the width of the longest word in the heading, bottom-aligns and underscores column headings, extends column widths to accommodate the longest word in a variable label or the variable's longest value label, and shrinks a report that is too wide for its margins.

LIST(n)   *Individual case listing.* The values of all variables named on VARIABLES are displayed for each case. The optional *n* inserts a blank line after each *n* cases. By default, no blank lines are inserted. Values for cases are listed using the default formats for the variables.

NOLIST   *No case listing.* This is the default.

PAGE(n)   *Page number for the first page of the report.* The default is 1.

LENGTH(t,b)   *Top and bottom line numbers of the report.* You can specify any numbers to define the report page length. By default, the top of the report begins at line 1, and the bottom of the report is the last line of the system page. You can use an asterisk for *t* or *b* to indicate a default value. If the specified length does not allow even one complete line of information to be displayed, REPORT extends the length specification and displays a warning.

MARGINS(l,r)   *Columns for the left and right margins.* The right column cannot exceed 255. By default, the left margin is display column 1 and the right margin is the rightmost display column of the system page. You can use an asterisk for *l* or *r* to indicate a default value.

ALIGN   *Placement of the report relative to its margins.* LEFT, CENTER, or RIGHT can be specified in the parentheses following the keyword. LEFT left-justifies the report. CENTER centers the report between its margins. RIGHT right-justifies the report. The default is LEFT.

COLSPACE(n)   *Number of spaces between each column.* The default is 4 or the average number of spaces that will fit within report margins, whichever is less. When AUTOMATIC is in effect, REPORT overrides the specified column spacing if necessary to fit the report between its margins.

CHALIGN   *Alignment of column headings.* Either TOP or BOTTOM can be specified in the parentheses following the keyword. TOP aligns all column headings with the first, or top, line of multiple-line headings. BOTTOM aligns headings with the last, or bottom, line of multiple-line headings. When AUTOMATIC is in effect, the default is BOTTOM; when MANUAL is in effect, the default is TOP.

UNDERSCORE *Underscores for column headings.* Either ON or OFF can be specified in the parentheses following the keyword. ON underscores the bottom line of each column heading for the full width of the column. OFF does not underscore column headings. The default is ON when AUTOMATIC is in effect and OFF when MANUAL is in effect.

TSPACE(n) *Number of blank lines between the report title and the column heads.* The default is 1.

CHDSPACE(n) *Number of blank lines beneath the longest column head.* The default is 1.

BRKSPACE(n) *Number of blank lines between the break head and the next line.* The next line is a case if LIST is in effect or the first summary line if NOLIST is in effect. BRKSPACE(–1) places the first summary statistic or the first case listing on the same line as the break value. When a summary line is placed on the same line as the break value, the summary title is suppressed. When AUTOMATIC is in effect, the default is –1; when MANUAL is in effect, it is 1.

SUMSPACE(n) *Number of blank lines between the last summary line at the lower break level and the first summary line at the higher break level when they break simultaneously.* SUMSPACE also controls spacing between the last listed case and the first summary line if LIST is in effect. The default is 1.

FTSPACE(n) *Minimum number of blank lines between the last listing on the page and the footnote.* The default is 1.

MISSING 's' *Missing-value symbol.* The symbol can be only one character and represents both system- and user-missing values. The default is a period.

ONEBREAKCOLUMN *Display subgroups defined on multiple BREAK subcommands in a single column.* You can specify OFF or ON in parentheses after the keyword. The default is OFF. When ONEBREAKCOLUMN is ON, it applies to all BREAK subcommands. For its effect on break column head, width, and alignment, see the BREAK subcommand on p. 1047. For its effect on the basic format of the report, see Figure 2.

INDENT(n) *Indention of break values and summary titles of each successive subgroup defined by one BREAK subcommand in a single break column.* INDENT is effective only when ONEBREAKCOLUMN is on. Multiple variables specified on one BREAK subcommand are indented as a block. The default specification is 2. When ONEBREAKCOLUMN is OFF, specification on INDENT is ignored.

CHWRAP *Automatically wrap user-specified column heads.* You can specify OFF or ON in parentheses after the keyword. The default is OFF. When CHWRAP is ON, user-specified heads for either break or variable columns are wrapped. If multiple lines are specified for a head, each line is wrapped, if necessary, independent of other lines. To prevent wrapping at blanks, use the underscore character (_) to signify a hard blank in your head specification. The underscore serves as a hard blank only in user-specified heads and only when CHWRAP is ON. The underscore does not appear in the printed heading.

PREVIEW *Display the first page of output only.* You can specify OFF or ON either in parentheses or with one blank space separating the specification from the keyword. The default is OFF. When PREVIEW is ON, the program stops processing after the first page for you to quickly check the format of your report.

Page Layout

Figure 1 shows the complete page layout and subcommand specifications used to control the basic format of the report when ONEBREAKCOLUMN is off (the default). Figure 2 shows the same page when ONEBREAKCOLUMN is on. In both figures, FORMAT=AUTOMATIC and BRKSPACE defaults to –1.

Example

```
SORT DIVISION DEPT.

REPORT FORMAT=AUTOMATIC LIST ONEBREAKCOLUMN(ON) CHWRAP(ON)
  /VARIABLES=LNAME TENURE SALARY
  /BREAK=DIVISION (20)(NOTOTAL)
  /SUMMARY=VALIDN (LNAME TENURE) MEAN (SALARY)
           'Mean Salary for Tenured Members within the Division'
  /BREAK=DEPT
  /SUMMARY=VALIDN (LNAME TENURE) MEAN (SALARY)
           'Mean Salary for Tenured Members within the Department'.
```

- This example creates a report with two break variables: *DEPARTMENT* breaks within DIVISION.
- The two break variables are placed in a single break column. The column head is the variable label of DIVISION.

OUTFILE Subcommand

OUTFILE directs the report to a file separate from the file used for the rest of the output from your session. This allows you to print the report without having to delete the extraneous material that would be present in the output.

- OUTFILE must follow FORMAT and must precede BREAK.
- You can append multiple reports to the same file by naming the same file on the OUTFILE subcommand for each REPORT command.

Figure 1   Page layout for REPORT when ONEBREAKCOLUMN is off

```
-------------------------------------- top of page --------------------------------------
```

		COLUMN HEAD (VAR)	COLUMN HEAD (VAR)	COLUMN HEAD (VAR)	COLUMN HEAD (VAR)	
		*************** TITLE ***************				←── LENGTH ←── TSPACE
BREAK HEAD	BREAK HEAD					
						←── CHDSPACE
						←── BRKSPACE
BREAK A VALUE 1	BREAK B VALUE 1	VALUE VALUE	VALUE VALUE	VALUE VALUE	VALUE VALUE	←── LIST
		VALUE VALUE	VALUE VALUE	VALUE VALUE	VALUE VALUE	←── SUMSPACE
	SUMMARY TITLE	AGG	AGG	AGG	AGG	←── SKIP w/ SUMMARY
	SUMMARY TITLE	AGG	AGG	AGG	AGG	←── SKIP w/ BREAK
	BREAK B VALUE 2					←── BRKSPACE
		VALUE VALUE	VALUE VALUE	VALUE VALUE	VALUE VALUE	←── LIST
		VALUE VALUE	VALUE VALUE	VALUE VALUE	VALUE VALUE	←── SUMSPACE
	SUMMARY TITLE	AGG	AGG	AGG	AGG	←── stats for B=2, A=1
	SUMMARY TITLE	AGG	AGG	AGG	AGG	←── SUMSPACE
SUMMARY TITLE		AGG	AGG	AGG	AGG	←── stats for A=1
SUMMARY TITLE		AGG	AGG	AGG	AGG	←── SKIP w/ BREAK
						←── BRKSPACE
BREAK A VALUE 2	BREAK B VALUE 1	VALUE VALUE	VALUE VALUE	VALUE VALUE	VALUE VALUE	←── LIST
		VALUE VALUE	VALUE VALUE	VALUE VALUE	VALUE VALUE	←── SUMSPACE
	SUMMARY TITLE	AGG	AGG	AGG	AGG	←── SKIP w/ SUMMARY
	SUMMARY TITLE	AGG	AGG	AGG	AGG	←── SKIP w/ BREAK
	BREAK B VALUE 2	VALUE	VALUE	VALUE	VALUE	←── BRKSPACE
		VALUE	VALUE	VALUE	VALUE	
		VALUE VALUE	VALUE VALUE	VALUE VALUE	VALUE VALUE	←── LIST
	SUMMARY TITLE	AGG	AGG	AGG	AGG	
	SUMMARY TITLE	AGG	AGG	AGG	AGG	
SUMMARY TITLE		AGG	AGG	AGG	AGG	←── SUMSPACE
SUMMARY TITLE		AGG	AGG	AGG	AGG	←── FTSPACE
		*************** FOOTNOTE ***************				←── LENGTH

```
-------------------------------------- bottom of page --------------------------------------
|                                                                              |
Left margin                                                          Right margin
```

Figure 2   Page layout for REPORT when ONEBREAKCOLUMN is on

-- top of page --

	*************** TITLE ***************				◄── LENGTH
					◄── TSPACE
	COLUMN	COLUMN	COLUMN	COLUMN	
BREAK HEAD	HEAD (VAR)	HEAD (VAR)	HEAD (VAR)	HEAD (VAR)	◄── CHDSPACE
BREAK A VALUE 1					◄── BRKSPACE
BREAK B VALUE 1	VALUE	VALUE	VALUE	VALUE	
	VALUE	VALUE	VALUE	VALUE	◄── LIST
	VALUE	VALUE	VALUE	VALUE	
	VALUE	VALUE	VALUE	VALUE	──── SUMSPACE
SUMMARY TITLE	AGG	AGG	AGG	AGG	◄── stats for B=1, A=1
SUMMARY TITLE	AGG	AGG	AGG	AGG	◄── SKIP w/ SUMMARY
					◄── SKIP w/ BREAK
BREAK B VALUE 2	VALUE	VALUE	VALUE	VALUE	◄── BRKSPACE
	VALUE	VALUE	VALUE	VALUE	
	VALUE	VALUE	VALUE	VALUE	──── INDENT
	VALUE	VALUE	VALUE	VALUE	──── SUMSPACE
SUMMARY TITLE	AGG	AGG	AGG	AGG	◄── stats for B=2, A=1
SUMMARY TITLE	AGG	AGG	AGG	AGG	──── SUMSPACE
SUMMARY TITLE	AGG	AGG	AGG	AGG	◄── stats for A=1
SUMMARY TITLE	AGG	AGG	AGG	AGG	◄── SKIP w/ BREAK
BREAK A VALUE 2					◄── BRKSPACE
BREAK B VALUE 1	VALUE	VALUE	VALUE	VALUE	
	VALUE	VALUE	VALUE	VALUE	◄── LIST
	VALUE	VALUE	VALUE	VALUE	
	VALUE	VALUE	VALUE	VALUE	◄── SUMSPACE
SUMMARY TITLE	AGG	AGG	AGG	AGG	◄── stats for B=1, A=2
SUMMARY TITLE	AGG	AGG	AGG	AGG	◄── SKIP w/ BREAK
BREAK B VALUE 2	VALUE	VALUE	VALUE	VALUE	◄── BRKSPACE
	VALUE	VALUE	VALUE	VALUE	
	VALUE	VALUE	VALUE	VALUE	LIST
	VALUE	VALUE	VALUE	VALUE	
SUMMARY TITLE	AGG	AGG	AGG	AGG	◄── stats for B=2, A=2
SUMMARY TITLE	AGG	AGG	AGG	AGG	
SUMMARY TITLE	AGG	AGG	AGG	AGG	◄── stats for A=2
SUMMARY TITLE	AGG	AGG	AGG	AGG	
	*************** FOOTNOTE ***************				◄── FTSPACE

-- bottom of page --

| |
| Left margin |
| Right margin ◄── LENGTH |

Example

```
REPORT FORMAT=AUTOMATIC LIST
  /OUTFILE=PRSNLRPT
  /VARIABLES=LNAME AGE TENURE JTENURE SALARY
  /BREAK=DIVISION
  /SUMMARY=MEAN.

REPORT FORMAT=AUTOMATIC
  /OUTFILE=PRSNLRPT
  /VARIABLES=LNAME AGE TENURE JTENURE SALARY
  /BREAK=DIVISION
  /SUMMARY=MEAN
  /SUMMARY=MIN
  /SUMMARY=MAX.
```

- Both a listing report and a summary report are written to file *PRSNLRPT*.

VARIABLES Subcommand

The required VARIABLES subcommand names the variables to be listed and summarized in the report. You can also use VARIABLES to control column titles, column widths, and the contents of report columns.

- The minimum specification on VARIABLES is a list of report variables. The number of variables that can be specified is limited by the system page width.
- Each report variable defines a report column. The value of the variable or an aggregate statistic calculated for the variable is displayed in that variable's report column.
- Variables are assigned to columns in the order in which they are named on VARIABLES.
- Variables named on BREAK can also be named on VARIABLES.
- When FORMAT=LIST, variables can be stacked in a single column by linking them with plus signs (+) on the VARIABLES subcommand. If no column heading is specified, REPORT uses the default heading from the first variable on the list. Only values from the first variable in the column are used to calculate summaries.
- Optional specifications apply only to the immediately preceding variable or list of variables implied by the TO keyword. Options can be specified in any order.
- All optional specifications except column headings must be enclosed in parentheses; column headings must be enclosed in apostrophes or quotation marks.

Column Contents

The following options can be used to specify the contents of the report column for each variable:

(VALUE) *Display the values of the variable.* This is the default.

(LABEL) *Display value labels.* If value labels are not defined, values are displayed.

(DUMMY) *Display blank spaces.* DUMMY defines a report column for a variable that does not exist in the working data file. Dummy variables are used to control spacing or to reserve space for statistics computed for other variables. Do not name an existing variable as a dummy variable.

- VALUE and LABEL have no effect unless LIST has been specified on the FORMAT subcommand.
- When AUTOMATIC is in effect, value labels or string values are centered in the column based on the length of the longest string or label; numeric values are centered based on the width of the widest value or summary format. When MANUAL is in effect, value labels or string values are left-justified in the column and numeric values are right-justified. (See the OFFSET keyword on p. 1046.)

Column Heading

The following option can be used to specify a heading for the report column:

'column heading'　　*Column heading for the preceding variable.* The heading must be enclosed in apostrophes or quotation marks. If no column heading is specified, the default is the variable label or, if no variable label has been specified, the variable name.

- To specify multiple-line headings, enclose each line in a set of apostrophes or quotation marks, using the conventions for strings (see "Command Specification" on p. 12). The specifications for title lines should be separated by at least one blank.
- Default column headings wrap for as many lines as are required to display the entire label. If AUTOMATIC is in effect, user-specified column headings appear exactly as specified, even if the column width must be extended. If MANUAL is in effect, user-specified titles wrap to fit within the column width.

Column Heading Alignment

The following options can be used to specify how column headings are aligned:

(LEFT)　　*Left-aligned column heading.*

(CENTER)　　*Centered column heading.*

(RIGHT)　　*Right-aligned column heading.*

- If AUTOMATIC is in effect, column headings are centered within their columns by default. If value labels or string values exceed the width of the longest word in the heading, the heading is left-justified.
- If MANUAL is in effect, column headings are left-justified for value labels or string values and right-justified for numeric values by default.

Column Format

The following options can be used to specify column width and adjust the position of the column contents:

(width)　　*Width for the report column.* If no width is specified for a variable, REPORT determines a default width using the criteria described under "Defaults" on

p. 1033. If you specify a width that is not wide enough to display numeric values, REPORT first rounds decimal digits, then converts to scientific notation if possible, and then displays asterisks. Value labels or string values that exceed the width are wrapped.

(OFFSET) *Position of the report column contents.* The specification is either *n* or CENTER specified in parentheses. OFFSET(*n*) indicates the number of spaces to offset the contents from the left for value labels or string values, and from the right for numeric values. OFFSET(CENTER) centers contents within the center of the column. If AUTOMATIC is in effect, the default is CENTER. If MANUAL is in effect, the default is 0. Value labels and string values are left-justified and numeric values are right-justified.

Example

```
/VARIABLES=V1 TO V3 (LABEL) (15)
  V4 V5 (LABEL)(OFFSET (2))(10)
  SEP1 (DUMMY) (2) ''
  V6 'Results using' "Lieben's Method" 'of Calculation'
```

- The width of the columns for variables *V1* through *V3* is 15 each. Value labels are displayed for these variables in the case listing.
- The column for variable *V4* uses the default width. Values are listed in the case listing.
- Value labels are displayed for variable *V5*. The column width is 10. Column contents are offset two spaces from the left.
- *SEP1* is a dummy variable. The column width is 2, and there is at least one space on each side of *SEP1*. Thus, there are at least four blanks between the columns for *V5* and *V6*. *SEP1* is given a null title to override the default column title *SEP1*.
- *V6* has a three-line title. Its column uses the default width, and values are listed in the case listing.

STRING Subcommand

STRING creates a temporary string variable by concatenating variables and user-specified strings. These variables exist only within the REPORT procedure.

- The minimum specification is a name for the string variable followed by a variable name or a user-specified string enclosed in parentheses.
- The name assigned to the string variable must be unique.
- Any combination of string variables, numeric variables, and user-specified strings can be used in the parentheses to define the string.
- Keyword TO cannot be used within the parentheses to imply a variable list.
- More than one string variable can be defined on STRING.
- If a case has a missing value for a variable within the parentheses, the variable passes the missing value to the temporary variable without affecting other elements specified.
- A string variable defined in REPORT cannot exceed the system page width.
- String variables defined on STRING can be used on VARIABLES or BREAK.

The following options can be used to specify how components are to be concatenated:

(width)   *Width of the preceding variable within the string.* The default is the dictionary width of the variable. The maximum width for numeric variables within the string definition is 16. The maximum width for a string variable is the system page width. If the width specified is less than that required by the value, numeric values are displayed as asterisks and string values are truncated. If the width exceeds the width of a value, numeric values are padded with zeros on the left and string values are padded with blanks on the right.

(BLANK)   *Left-pad values of the preceding numeric variable with blanks.* The default is to left-pad values of numeric variables with zeros. If a numeric variable has a dollar or comma format, it is automatically left-padded with blanks.

'literal'   *User-specified string.* Any combination of characters can be specified within apostrophes or quotation marks.

Example

```
/STRING=JOB1(AVAR NVAR)
        JOB2(AVAR(2) NVAR(3))
        JOB3(AVAR(2) NVAR(BLANK) (4))
```

- STRING defines three string variables to be used within the report.

- Assume that *AVAR* is a string variable read from a four-column field using keyword FIXED on DATA LIST and that *NVAR* is a computed numeric variable with the default format of eight columns with two implied decimal places.

- If a case has value KJ for *AVAR* and value 241 for *NVAR*, *JOB1* displays the value 'KJ 00241.00', *JOB2* the value 'KJ241', and *JOB3* the value 'KJ 241'. If *NVAR* has the system-missing value for a case, *JOB1* displays the value 'KJ.'

Example

```
/STRING=SOCSEC(S1 '-' S2 '-' S3)
```

- STRING concatenates the three variables *S1*, *S2*, and *S3*, each of which contains a segment of the social security number.

- Hyphens are inserted between the segments when the values of *SOCSEC* are displayed.

- This example assumes that the variables *S1*, *S2*, and *S3* were read from three-column, two-column, and four-column fields respectively, using the keyword FIXED on DATA LIST. These variables would then have default format widths of 3, 2, and 4 columns and would not be left-padded with zeros.

BREAK Subcommand

BREAK specifies the variables that define the subgroups for the report, or it specifies summary totals for reports with no subgroups. BREAK also allows you to control the titles, width, and contents of break columns and to begin a new page for each level of the break variable.

- A break occurs when any one of the variables named on BREAK changes value. Cases must be sorted by the values of all BREAK variables on all BREAK subcommands.

- The BREAK subcommand must precede the SUMMARY subcommand that defines the summary line for the break.
- A break column is reserved for each BREAK subcommand if ONEBREAKCOLUMN is OFF (the default).
- To obtain multiple break levels, specify multiple break variables on a BREAK subcommand.
- If more than one variable is specified on a BREAK subcommand, a single break column is used. The value or value label for each variable is displayed on a separate line in the order in which the variables are specified on BREAK. The first variable specified changes most slowly. The default column width is the longest of the default widths for any of the break variables.
- To obtain summary totals without any break levels, use keyword TOTAL in parentheses on BREAK without listing any variables. TOTAL must be specified on the first BREAK subcommand.
- When MISSING=VAR is specified, user-missing values are displayed in case listings but are not included in summary statistics. When NONE is specified, user-missing values are ignored. System-missing values are displayed as missing in case and break listings.
- Optional specifications apply to all variables in the break column and to the break column as a whole. Options can be specified in any order following the last variable named.
- All optional specifications except column headings must be enclosed in parentheses; column headings must be enclosed in apostrophes.

Column Contents

The following can be used to specify the contents of the break column:

(VALUE) *Display values of the break variables.*

(LABEL) *Display value labels.* If no value labels have been defined, values are displayed.

- The value or label is displayed only once for each break change but it is repeated at the top of the page in a multiple-page break group.
- When AUTOMATIC is in effect, the default is LABEL; when MANUAL is in effect, the default is VALUE.
- When AUTOMATIC is in effect, the value or label is centered in the column. When MANUAL is in effect, value labels and string values are left-justified and numeric values are right-justified. Keywords OFFSET, ONEBREAKCOLUMN, and INDENT can also affect positioning.

Column Heading

The following option specifies headings used for the break column.

'column heading' *Column heading for the break column.* The heading must be included in apostrophes or quotation marks. The default heading is the variable label of the break variable or, if no label has been defined, the variable name. If the break column is defined by more than one variable, the label or name of the first variable is used. If ONEBREAKCOLUMN is ON, the specified or implied column heading for the first BREAK subcommand is used.

- To specify multiple-line headings, enclose each line in a set of apostrophes or quotation marks, following the conventions for strings (see "Command Specification" on p. 12). Separate the specifications for heading lines with at least one blank.

- Default column headings wrap for as many lines as are required to display the entire label.

- User-specified column headings appear exactly as specified if CHWRAP is OFF (the default). If CHWRAP is ON, any user-defined line longer than the specified or default column width is automatically wrapped.

Column Heading Alignment

The following options can be used to specify how column headings are aligned:

(LEFT)   *Left-aligned column heading.*

(CENTER)   *Centered column heading.*

(RIGHT)   *Right-aligned column heading.*

- When AUTOMATIC is in effect, column headings are centered within their columns by default. If value labels or string values exceed the width of the longest word in the heading, the heading is left-justified.

- When MANUAL is in effect, column headings are left-justified for value labels or string values and right-justified for numeric values.

- When ONEBREAKCOLUMN is ON, all column contents are left aligned. Specifications of CENTER and RIGHT on BREAK are ignored.

Column Format

The following options can be used to format break columns:

(width)   *Column width for the break column.* If no width is specified for a variable, REPORT determines a default width using the criteria described under "Defaults" on p. 1033. If ONEBREAKCOLUMN is ON, the column width specified or implied by the first BREAK subcommand is used. If you specify a width that is not wide enough to display numeric values, REPORT first rounds decimal digits, then converts them to scientific notation if possible, and then displays asterisks. Value labels or string values that exceed the width are wrapped.

(OFFSET)   *Position of the break column contents.* The specification is either *n* or CENTER specified in parentheses. OFFSET(*n*) indicates the number of spaces to offset the contents from the left for value labels or string values, and from the right for numeric values. OFFSET(CENTER) centers contents within the column. If AUTOMATIC is in effect, the default is CENTER. If MANUAL is in effect, the default is 0: value labels and string values are left-justified and numeric values are right-justified. If ONEBREAKCOLUMN is ON, the offset is applied along with the indentation specified on INDENT, always from the left. The specification of CENTER on OFFSET is ignored.

(UNDERSCORE) *Use underscores below case listings.* Case listing columns produced by FORMAT LIST are underscored before summary statistics are displayed. You can optionally specify the names of one or more report variables after UNDERSCORE; only the specified columns are underscored.

(TOTAL) *Display the summary statistics requested on the next SUMMARY subcommand for all the cases in the report.* TOTAL must be specified on the first BREAK subcommand and applies only to the next SUMMARY subcommand specified.

(NOTOTAL) *Display summary statistics only for each break.* This is the default.

(SKIP(n)) *Skip n lines after the last summary line for a break before beginning the next break.* The default for *n* is 1.

(PAGE) *Begin each break on a new page.* If RESET is specified on PAGE, the page counter resets to the PAGE1 setting on the FORMAT subcommand every time the break value changes for the specified variable. PAGE cannot be specified for listing reports with no break levels.

(NAME) *Display the name of the break variable next to each value or value label of the break variable.* NAME requires 10 spaces (the maximum eight-character width of variable names plus a colon and a blank space) in addition to the space needed to display break values or value labels. NAME is ignored if the break-column width is insufficient.

(NONAME) *Suppress the display of break variable names.* This is the default.

Example

```
SORT DIVISION BRANCH DEPT.
REPORT FORMAT=AUTOMATIC MARGINS (1,70) BRKSPACE(-1)

  /VARIABLES=SPACE(DUMMY) ' ' (4)
            SALES 'Annual' 'Sales' '1981' (15) (OFFSET(2))
            EXPENSES 'Annual' 'Expenses' '1981' (15) (OFFSET(2))

  /BREAK=DIVISION
         BRANCH (10) (TOTAL) (OFFSET(1))
  /SUMMARY=MEAN

  /BREAK=DEPT 'Department' (10)
  /SUMMARY=MEAN.
```

- This example creates a report with three break variables. *BRANCH* breaks within values of *DIVISION*, and *DEPT* breaks within values of *BRANCH*.

- FORMAT sets margins to a maximum of 70 columns and requests that summary lines be displayed on the same line as break values. Because LIST is not specified on FORMAT, only summary statistics are displayed.

- VARIABLES defines three report columns, each occupied by a report variable: *SPACE*, *SALES*, and *EXPENSES*.

- The variable *SPACE* is a dummy variable that exists only within REPORT. It has a null heading and a width of 4. It is used as a space holder to separate the break columns from the report columns.
- *SALES* has a three-line heading and a width of 15. The values of *SALES* are offset two spaces from the right.
- *EXPENSES* is the third report variable and has the same width and offset specifications as *SALES*.
- The leftmost column in the report is reserved for the first two break variables, *DIVISION* and *BRANCH*. Value labels are displayed, since this is the default for AUTOMATIC. The break column has a width of 10 and the value labels are offset one space from the left. Value labels more than nine characters long are wrapped. The default column heading is used. TOTAL requests a summary line at the end of the report showing the mean of all cases in the report.
- The first SUMMARY subcommand displays the mean of each report variable in its report column. This line is displayed each time the value of *DIVISION* or *BRANCH* changes.
- The third break variable, *DEPT*, occupies the second column from the left in the report. The break column has a width of 10 and has a one-line heading. Value labels are displayed in the break column, and those exceeding 10 characters are wrapped.
- The second SUMMARY subcommand displays the mean for each report variable when the value of *DEPT* changes.

SUMMARY Subcommand

SUMMARY calculates a wide range of aggregate and composite statistics.

- SUMMARY must be specified if LIST is not specified on FORMAT.
- The minimum specification is an aggregate or a composite function and its arguments. This must be the first specification on SUMMARY.
- Each SUMMARY subcommand following a BREAK subcommand specifies a new summary line.
- The default location of the summary title is the column of the break variable to which the summary applies. When more than one function is named on SUMMARY, the default summary title is that of the function named first. Both the title and its default column location can be altered (see "Summary Titles" on p. 1055).
- The default format can be altered for any function (see "Summary Print Formats" on p. 1056).
- SUMMARY subcommands apply only to the preceding BREAK subcommand. If there is no SUMMARY subcommand after a BREAK subcommand, no statistics are displayed for that break level.
- To use the summary specifications from a previous BREAK subcommand for the current BREAK subcommand, specify keyword PREVIOUS on SUMMARY. (See "Other Summary Keywords" on p. 1058.)
- Summary statistics are displayed in report columns. With aggregate functions, you can compute summary statistics for all report variables or for a subset (see "Aggregate Functions" below). With composite functions, you can compute summaries for all or a subset of report variables and you have additional control over the placement of summary statistics in particular report columns (see "Composite Functions" on p. 1054).

- Multiple summary statistics requested on one SUMMARY subcommand are all displayed on the same line. More than one function can be specified on SUMMARY as long as you do not attempt to place two results in the same report column (REPORT will not be executed if you do). To place results of more than one function in the same report column, use multiple SUMMARY subcommands.

- Any composite and aggregate functions except FREQUENCY and PERCENT can be specified on the same summary line.

- To insert blank lines between summaries when more than one summary line is requested for a break, use keyword SKIP followed by the number of lines to skip in parentheses. The default is 0. (See "Other Summary Keywords" on p. 1058.)

Aggregate Functions

Use the aggregate functions to request descriptive statistics for report variables.

- If no variable names are specified as arguments to an aggregate function, the statistic is calculated for all variables named on VARIABLES (all report variables).

- To request an aggregate function for a subset of report variables, specify the variables in parentheses after the function keyword.

- All variables specified for an aggregate function must have been named on VARIABLES.

- Keyword TO cannot be used to specify a list of variables for an aggregate function.

- The result of an aggregate function is always displayed in the report column reserved for the variable for which the function was calculated.

- To use several aggregate functions for the same report variable, specify multiple SUMMARY subcommands. The results are displayed on different summary lines.

- The aggregate functions FREQUENCY and PERCENT have special display formats and cannot be placed on the same summary line with other aggregate or composite functions. They can be specified only once per SUMMARY subcommand.

- Aggregate functions use only cases with valid values.

VALIDN	*Valid number of cases.* This is the only function available for string variables.
SUM	*Sum of values.*
MIN	*Minimum value.*
MAX	*Maximum value.*
MEAN	*Mean.*
STDDEV	*Standard deviation.* Aliases are SD and STDEV.
VARIANCE	*Variance.*
KURTOSIS	*Kurtosis.*
SKEWNESS	*Skewness.*

MEDIAN(min,max)   *Median value for values within the range.* MEDIAN sets up integer-valued bins for counting all values in the specified range. Noninteger values are truncated when the median is calculated.

MODE(min,max)   *Modal value for values within the range.* MODE sets up integer-valued bins for counting all values in the specified range. Noninteger values are truncated when the mode is calculated.

PGT(n)   *Percentage of cases with values greater than* n. Alias PCGT.

PLT(n)   *Percentage of cases with values less than* n. Alias PCLT.

PIN(min,max)   *Percentage of cases within the inclusive value range specified.* Alias PCIN.

FREQUENCY(min,max)   *Frequency counts for values within the inclusive range.* FREQUENCY sets up integer-valued bins for counting all values in the specified range. Noninteger values are truncated when the frequency is computed. FREQUENCY cannot be mixed with other aggregate statistics on a summary line.

PERCENT(min,max)   *Percentages for values within the inclusive range.* PERCENT sets up integer-valued bins for counting all values in the specified range. Noninteger values are truncated when the percentages are computed. PERCENT cannot be mixed with other aggregate statistics on a summary line.

Example

```
SORT CASES BY BVAR AVAR.
REPORT FORMAT=AUTOMATIC LIST /VARIABLES=XVAR YVAR ZVAR

  /BREAK=BVAR
    /SUMMARY=SUM
    /SUMMARY=MEAN (XVAR YVAR ZVAR)
    /SUMMARY=VALIDN(XVAR)

  /BREAK=AVAR
    /SUMMARY=PREVIOUS.
```

- FORMAT requests a case listing, and VARIABLES establishes a report column for variables *XVAR*, *YVAR*, and *ZVAR*. The report columns have default widths and titles.

- Both break variables, *BVAR* and *AVAR*, have default widths and headings.

- Every time the value of *BVAR* changes, three summary lines are displayed. The first line contains the sums for variables *XVAR*, *YVAR*, and *ZVAR*. The second line contains the means of all three variables. The third line displays the number of valid cases for *XVAR* in the report column for *XVAR*.

- Every time the value of *AVAR* changes within each value of *BVAR*, the three summary lines requested for *BVAR* are displayed. These summary lines are based on cases with the current values of *BVAR* and *AVAR*.

Example

```
SORT CASES BY DEPT.
REPORT FORMAT=AUTOMATIC
  /VARIABLES=WAGE BONUS TENURE
  /BREAK=DEPT (23)
  /SUMMARY=SUM(WAGE BONUS) MEAN(TENURE) 'Sum Income: Mean Tenure'.
```

- SUMMARY defines a summary line consisting of the sums of *WAGE* and *BONUS* and the mean of TENURE. The result of each aggregate function is displayed in the report column of the variable for which the function is calculated.

- A title is assigned to the summary line. A width of 23 is defined for the break column to accommodate the title for the summary line.

Composite Functions

Use composite functions to obtain statistics based on aggregated statistics, to place a summary statistic in a column other than that of the report variable for which it was calculated, or to manipulate variables not named on VARIABLES.

- Composite functions can be computed for the following aggregate functions: VALIDN, SUM, MIN, MAX, MEAN, STDEV, VARIANCE, KURTOSIS, SKEWNESS, PGT, PLT, and PIN. Constants can also be arguments to composite functions.

- When used within composite functions, aggregate functions can have only one variable as an argument.

- A composite function and its arguments cannot be separated by other SUMMARY specifications.

- The result of a composite function can be placed in any report column, including columns of dummy or string variables, by specifying a target column. To specify a target column, enclose the variable name of the column in parentheses after the composite function and its arguments. By default, the results of a composite function are placed in the report column of the first variable specified on the composite function that is also specified on VARIABLES.

- The format for the result of a composite function can be specified in parentheses after the name of the column location, within the parentheses that enclose the column-location specification.

DIVIDE(arg$_1$ arg$_2$ [factor]) *Divide the first argument by the second and then multiply the result by the factor if it is specified.*

MULTIPLY(arg$_1$ ... arg$_n$) *Multiply the arguments.*

PCT(arg$_1$ arg$_2$) *The percentage of the first argument over the second.*

SUBTRACT(arg$_1$ arg$_2$) *Subtract the second argument from the first.*

ADD(arg$_1$ ... arg$_n$) *Add the arguments.*

GREAT(arg$_1$ ... arg$_n$) *The maximum of the arguments.*

LEAST(arg$_1$ ... arg$_n$) *The minimum of the arguments.*

AVERAGE(arg$_1$ ... arg$_n$) *The average of the arguments.*

Example

```
SORT CASES BY DEPT.
REPORT FORMAT=AUTOMATIC BRKSPACE(-1)
  /VARIABLES=WAGE BONUS SPACE1 (DUMMY) '' BNFT1 BNFT2 SPACE2 (DUMMY)
''
  /BREAK=DEPT

  /SUMMARY=MEAN(WAGE BONUS BNFT1 BNFT2)
       ADD(VALIDN(WAGE)) (SPACE2)

  /SUMMARY=ADD(SUM(WAGE) SUM(BONUS))
       ADD(SUM(BNFT1) SUM(BNFT2)) 'Totals' SKIP(1)

  /SUMMARY=DIVIDE(MEAN(WAGE) MEAN(BONUS)) (SPACE1 (COMMA)(2))
       DIVIDE(MEAN(BNFT1) MEAN(BNFT2)) (SPACE2 (COMMA)(2)) 'Ratios'
       SKIP(1).
```

- VARIABLES defines six report columns. The columns for *WAGE, BONUS, BNFT1,* and *BNFT2* contain aggregate statistics based on those variables. The variables *SPACE1* and *SPACE2* are dummy variables that are created for use as space holders; each is given a blank heading to suppress the default column heading.

- The first SUMMARY computes the means of the variables *WAGE, BONUS, BNFT1,* and *BNFT2.* Because BRKSPACE=–1, this summary line will be placed on the same line as the break value and will have no summary title. The means are displayed in the report column for each variable. SUMMARY also computes the valid number of cases for *WAGE* and places the result in the *SPACE2* column.

- The second SUMMARY adds the sum of *WAGE* to the sum of *BONUS.* Since no location is specified, the result is displayed in the *WAGE* column. In addition, the sum of *BNFT1* is added to the sum of *BNFT2* and the result is placed in the *BNFT1* column. The title for the summary line is *Totals.* One line is skipped before the summary line requested by this SUMMARY subcommand is displayed.

- The third summary line divides the mean of *WAGE* by the mean of *BONUS* and places the result in *SPACE1.* The ratio of the mean of *BNFT1* to the mean of *BNFT2* is displayed in the *SPACE2* column. The results are displayed with commas and two decimal places. The title for the summary line is *Ratios.* One line is skipped before the summary line requested by this SUMMARY subcommand is displayed.

Summary Titles

- You can specify a summary title enclosed in apostrophes or quotation marks, following the conventions for strings (see "Command Specification" on p. 12). Table 2 shows the default titles.

- The summary title must be specified after the first function and its arguments. It cannot separate any function from its arguments.

- A summary title can be only one line long.

- A summary title wider than the break column extends into the next break column to the right. If the title is wider than all of the available break columns, it is truncated.

- Only one summary title can be specified per summary line. If more than one is specified, the last is used.
- The summary title is left- or right-justified depending upon whether the break title is left- or right-justified.
- The default location for the summary title is the column of the BREAK variable to which the summary applies. With multiple breaks, you can override the default placement of the title by specifying, in parentheses following the title, the number of the break column in which you want the summary title to be displayed.
- In a report with no break levels, REPORT displays the summary title above the summary line at the left margin.

Table 2   Default title for summary lines

Function	Title
VALIDN	N
VARIANCE	Variance
SUM	Sum
MEAN	Mean
STDDEV	StdDev
MIN	Minimum
MAX	Maximum
SKEWNESS	Skewness
KURTOSIS	Kurtosis
PGT(n)	>n
PLT(n)	<n
PIN(min,max)	In n_1 to n_2
FREQUENCY(min,max)	Total
PERCENT(min,max)	Total
MEDIAN(min,max)	Median
MODE(min,max)	Mode

Summary Print Formats

All functions have default formats that are used to display results (see Table 3). You can override these defaults by specifying a format keyword and/or the number of decimal places.

- Any printable formats or the PLAIN keyword can be specified. Format specifications must be enclosed in parentheses.
- For aggregate functions, the format and/or number of decimal places is specified after the variable name, within the parentheses that enclose the variable name. The variable must be explicitly named as an argument.
- For composite functions, the format and/or number of decimal places is specified after the variable name of the column location, within the parentheses that enclose the variable name. The column location must be explicitly specified.

- If the report column is wide enough, SUM, MEAN, STDDEV, MIN, MAX, MEDIAN, MODE, and VARIANCE use DOLLAR or COMMA format, if a DOLLAR or COMMA format has been declared for the variable on either the FORMATS or PRINT FORMATS command.
- If the column is not wide enough to display the decimal digits for a given function, REPORT displays fewer decimal places. If the column is not wide enough to display the integer portion of the number, REPORT uses scientific notation if possible, or, if not, displays asterisks.
- An exact value of 0 is displayed with one 0 to the left of the decimal point and as many 0 digits to the right as specified by the format. A number less than 1 in absolute value is displayed without a 0 to the left of the decimal point, except with DOLLAR and COMMA formats.

(PLAIN)   *Uses the setting on SET DECIMAL for the thousands separator and decimal delimiter.* PLAIN overrides dictionary formats. This is the default for all functions except SUM, MEAN, STDDEV, MIN, MAX, MEDIAN, MODE, and VARIANCE. For these functions, the default is the dictionary format of the variable for which the function is computed.

(d)   *Number of decimal places.*

Example

```
/SUMMARY=MEAN(INCOME (DOLLAR)(2))
        ADD(SUM(INCOME)SUM(WEALTH))  (WEALTH(DOLLAR(2))
```

- SUMMARY displays the mean of *INCOME* with dollar format and two decimal places. The result is displayed in the *INCOME* column.
- The sums of *INCOME* and *WEALTH* are added, and the result is displayed in the *WEALTH* column with dollar format and two decimal places.

Table 3   Default print formats for functions

Function	Format type	Width	Decimal places
VALIDN	F	5	0
SUM	Dictionary	Dictionary + 2	Dictionary
MEAN	Dictionary	Dictionary	Dictionary
STDDEV	Dictionary	Dictionary	Dictionary
VARIANCE	Dictionary	Dictionary	Dictionary
MIN	Dictionary	Dictionary	Dictionary
MAX	Dictionary	Dictionary	Dictionary
SKEWNESS	F	5	2
KURTOSIS	F	5	2
PGT	PCT	6	1
PLT	PCT	6	1
PIN	PCT	6	1
MEDIAN	Dictionary	Dictionary	Dictionary
MODE	Dictionary	Dictionary	Dictionary

Table 3   Default print formats for functions (Continued)

Function	Format type	Width	Decimal places
PERCENT	F	6	1
FREQUENCY	F	5	0
DIVIDE	F	Dictionary	0
PCT	PCT	6	2
SUBTRACT	F	Dictionary	0
ADD	F	Dictionary	0
GREAT	F	Dictionary	0
LEAST	F	Dictionary	0
AVERAGE	F	Dictionary	0
MULTIPLY	F	Dictionary	0

Where DATE formats are specified, functions with the dictionary format type display the DATE formats, using the column width as the display width.

Other Summary Keywords

The following additional keywords can be specified on SUMMARY. These keywords are not enclosed in parentheses.

SKIP(n)   *Blank lines before the summary line.* The default is 0. If SKIP is specified for the first SUMMARY subcommand for a BREAK, it skips the specified lines after skipping the number of lines specified for BRKSPACE on FORMAT. Similarly, with case listings SKIP skips *n* lines after the blank line at the end of the listing.

PREVIOUS(n)   *Use the SUMMARY subcommands specified for the nth BREAK.* If *n* is not specified, PREVIOUS refers to the set of SUMMARY subcommands for the previous BREAK. If an integer is specified, the SUMMARY subcommands from the *n*th BREAK are used. If PREVIOUS is specified, no other specification can be used on that SUMMARY subcommand.

TITLE and FOOTNOTE Subcommands

TITLE and FOOTNOTE provide titles and footnotes for the report.

- TITLE and FOOTNOTE are optional and can be placed anywhere after FORMAT except between the BREAK and SUMMARY subcommands.
- The specification on TITLE or FOOTNOTE is the title or footnote in apostrophes or quotation marks. To specify a multiple-line title or footnote, enclose each line in apostrophes or quotation marks and separate the specifications for each line by at least one blank.
- The default REPORT title is the title specified on the TITLE command. If there is no TITLE command specified in your session, the default REPORT title is the first line of the header.
- Titles begin on the first line of the report page. Footnotes end on the last line of the report page.
- Titles and footnotes are repeated on each page of a multiple-page report.

- The positional keywords LEFT, CENTER, and RIGHT can each be specified once. The default is CENTER.
- If the total width needed for the combined titles or footnotes for a line exceeds the page width, REPORT generates an error message.

LEFT   *Left-justify titles or footnotes within the report page margins.*

RIGHT   *Right-justify titles or footnotes within the report page margins.*

CENTER   *Center titles and footnotes within the report page width.*

The following can be specified as part of the title or footnote.

)PAGE   *Display the page number right-justified in a five-character field.*

)DATE   *Display the current date in the form* dd/mmm/yy, *right-justified in a nine-character field.*

)var   *Display this variable's value label at this position.* If you specify a variable that has no value label, the value is displayed, formatted according to its print format. You cannot specify a scratch or system variable or a variable created with the STRING subcommand. If you want to use a variable named *DATE* or *PAGE* in the file, change the variable's name with the RENAME VARIABLES command before you use it on the TITLE or FOOTNOTE subcommands, to avoid confusion with the)PAGE and)DATE keywords.

-)PAGE,)DATE, and)var are specified within apostrophes or quotation marks and can be mixed with string segments within the apostrophes or quotation marks.
- A variable specified on TITLE or FOOTNOTE must be defined in the working data file, but does not need to be included as a column on the report.
- One label or value from each variable specified on TITLE or FOOTNOTE is displayed on every page of the report. If a new page starts with a case listing, REPORT takes the value label from the first case listed. If a new page starts with a BREAK line, REPORT takes the value label from the first case of the new break group. If a new page starts with a summary line, REPORT takes the value label from the last case of the break group being summarized.

Example

```
/TITLE=LEFT 'Personnel Report' 'Prepared on )DATE'
    RIGHT 'Page: )PAGE'
```

- TITLE specifies two lines for a left-justified title and one line for a right-justified title. These titles are displayed at the top of each page of the report.
- The second line of the left-justified title contains the date on which the report was processed.
- The right-justified title displays the page number following the string *Page:* on the same line as the first line of the left-justified title.

MISSING Subcommand

MISSING controls the treatment of cases with missing values.

- MISSING specifications apply to variables named on VARIABLES and SUMMARY and to strings created with the STRING subcommand.

- Missing-value specifications are ignored for variables named on BREAK when MISSING=VAR or NONE. There is one break category for system-missing values and one for each user-missing value.

- The character used to indicate missing values is controlled by the FORMAT subcommand.

VAR *Missing values are treated separately for each variable.* Missing values are displayed in case listings but are not included in the calculation of summary statistics on a function-by-function basis. This is the default.

NONE *User-missing values are treated as valid values.* This applies to all variables named on VARIABLES.

LIST[([varlist][n])] *Cases with the specified number of missing values across the specified list of variables are not used.* The variable list and *n* are specified in parentheses. If *n* is not specified, the default is 1. If no variables are specified, all variables named on VARIABLES are assumed.

Example

```
/MISSING= LIST (XVAR,YVAR,ZVAR 2)
```

- Any case with two or more missing values across the variables *XVAR*, *YVAR*, and *ZVAR* is omitted from the report.

REREAD

```
REREAD [FILE=file]
       [COLUMN=expression]
```

Example

```
INPUT PROGRAM.
DATA LIST /KIND 10-14 (A).

DO IF (KIND EQ 'FORD').
REREAD.
DATA LIST /PARTNO 1-2 PRICE 3-6 (DOLLAR,2) QUANTITY 7-9.
END CASE.

ELSE IF (KIND EQ 'CHEVY').
REREAD.
DATA LIST /PARTNO 1-2 PRICE 15-18 (DOLLAR,2) QUANTITY 19-21.
END CASE.
END IF.

END INPUT PROGRAM.

BEGIN DATA
111295100FORD
11      CHEVY 295015
END DATA.
```

Overview

REREAD instructs the program to reread a record in the data. It is available only within an
INPUT PROGRAM structure and is generally used to define data using information obtained
from a previous reading of the record. REREAD is usually specified within a conditional
structure, such as DO IF—END IF, and is followed by a DATA LIST command. When it receives
control for a case, REREAD places the pointer back to the column specified for the current
case and begins reading data as defined by the DATA LIST command that follows.

Options

Data Source. You can use inline data or data from an external file specified on the FILE subcommand. Using external files allows you to open multiple files and merge data.

Beginning Column. You can specify a beginning column other than column 1 using the
COLUMN subcommand.

Basic Specification

The basic specification is the command keyword REREAD. The program rereads the current case according to the data definitions specified on the following DATA LIST.

Subcommand Order

Subcommands can be specified in any order.

Syntax Rules

- REREAD is available only within an INPUT PROGRAM structure.
- Multiple REREAD commands can be used within the input program. Each must be followed by an associated DATA LIST command.

Operations

- REREAD causes the next DATA LIST command to reread the most recently processed record in the specified file.
- When it receives control for a case, REREAD places the pointer back to column 1 for the current case and begins reading data as defined by the DATA LIST that follows. If the COLUMN subcommand is specified, the pointer begins reading in the specified column and uses it as column 1 for data definition.
- REREAD can be used to read part of a record in FIXED format and the remainder in LIST format. Mixing FIXED and FREE formats yields unpredictable results.
- Multiple REREAD commands specified without an intervening DATA LIST do not have a cumulative effect. All but the last are ignored.

Example

```
INPUT PROGRAM.
DATA LIST /PARTNO 1-2 KIND 10-14 (A).

DO IF (KIND EQ 'FORD').
REREAD.
DATA LIST /PRICE 3-6 (DOLLAR,2) QUANTITY 7-9.
END CASE.

ELSE IF (KIND EQ 'CHEVY').
REREAD.
DATA LIST /PRICE 15-18 (DOLLAR,2) QUANTITY 19-21.
END CASE.
END IF.
END INPUT PROGRAM.

BEGIN DATA
111295100FORD      CHAPMAN AUTO SALES
121199005VW    MIDWEST VOLKSWAGEN SALES
11 395025FORD      BETTER USED CARS
11        CHEVY 195005      HUFFMAN SALES & SERVICE
11        VW    595020      MIDWEST VOLKSWAGEN SALES
11        CHEVY 295015      SAM'S AUTO REPAIR
12        CHEVY 210 20      LONGFELLOW CHEVROLET
 9555032 VW                 HYDE PARK IMPORTS
END DATA.
LIST.
```

- Data are extracted from an inventory of automobile parts. The automobile part number always appears in columns 1 and 2, and the automobile type always appears in columns 10 through 14. The location of other information such as price and quantity depends on both the part number and the type of automobile.

- The first DATA LIST extracts the part number and type of automobile.

- Depending on the information from the first DATA LIST, the records are reread using one of two DATA LIST commands, pulling the price and quantity from different places.

- The two END CASE commands limit the working data file to only those cases with part 11 and automobile type Ford or Chevrolet. Without the END CASE commands, cases would be created for other part numbers and automobile types, with missing values for price, quantity, and buyer.

The LIST output is shown in Figure 1.

Figure 1   Listed information for part 11

```
PARTNO KIND   PRICE QUANTITY

  11    FORD  $12.95    100
  11    FORD  $3.95      25
  11    CHEVY $1.95       5
  11    CHEVY $2.95      15
```

Example

```
* Multiple REREAD commands for the same record.

INPUT PROGRAM.
DATA LIST         NOTABLE/ CDIMAGE 1-20(A).
REREAD            COLUMN = 6.   /* A, C, and E are in column 6
REREAD            COLUMN = 11.  /* B, D, and F are in column 11
DATA LIST         NOTABLE/ INFO 1(A).
END INPUT PROGRAM.
LIST.
BEGIN DATA
1    A    B
2    C    D
3    E    F
END DATA.
```

- Multiple REREAD commands are used without an intervening DATA LIST. Only the last one is used. Thus, the starting column comes from the last REREAD specified and the pointer is reset to column 11.
- Figure 2 shows the results from the LIST command.

Figure 2   Listed information after multiple REREAD commands

```
CDIMAGE              INFO

1    A    B           B
2    C    D           D
3    E    F           F
```

FILE Subcommand

FILE specifies an external raw data file from which the next DATA LIST command reads data.

- The default file is the file specified on the immediately preceding DATA LIST command.
- If the file specified on FILE is not the default file, the same file must be specified on the next DATA LIST. Otherwise, the FILE subcommand is ignored and the DATA LIST command reads the next record from the file specified on it or, if no file is specified, from the file specified on the previous DATA LIST command.

Example

```
INPUT PROGRAM.
DATA LIST FILE=UPDATE END=#EOF NOTABLE
     /#ID 1-3.                      /*Get rep ID in new sales file.
DATA LIST FILE = SALESREP NOTABLE
     /ID 1-3 SALES 4-11(F,2)
       NEWSALE 12-19(F,2).         /*Get rep record from master file.

LOOP IF #EOF OR (#ID GT ID).  /*If UPDATE ends or no new sales made.
+   COMPUTE NEWSALE = 0.        /*Set NEWSALE to 0
+   END CASE.                   /*Build a case.
+   DATA LIST FILE = SALESREP NOTABLE
     /ID 1-3 SALES 4-11(F,2)
       NEWSALE 12-19(F,2).         /*Continue reading masterfile.
END LOOP

DO IF NOT #EOF.                     /*If new sales made.
+   REREAD FILE=UPDATE COLUMN = 4.   /*Read new sales from UPDATE.
+   DATA LIST FILE=UPDATE
     /NEWSALE 1-8(F,2).
+   COMPUTE SALES=SALES+NEWSALE.    /*Update master file.
END IF.
END CASE.                           /*Build a case.
END INPUT PROGRAM.

LIST.
```

- This example uses REREAD to merge two raw data files (*SALESREP* and *UPDATE*).

- Both files are sorted by sales representative ID number. The *UPDATE* file contains only records for sales representatives who have made new sales, with variables *ID* and *NEWSALE*. The master file *SALESREP* contains records for all sales representatives, with variables *SALES* (which contains year-to-date sales) and *NEWSALE* (which contains the update values each time the file is updated).

- If a sales representative has made no new sales, there is no matching ID in the *UPDATE* file. When *UPDATE* is exhausted or when the ID's in the two files do not match, the loop structure causes the program to build a case with *NEWSALE* equal to 0 and then continue reading the master file.

- When the ID's match (and the *UPDATE* file is not yet exhausted), the REREAD command is executed. The following DATA LIST rereads the record in *UPDATE* that matches the *ID* variable. *NEWSALE* is read from the *UPDATE* file starting from column 4 and *SALES* is updated. Note that the following DATA LIST specifies the same file.

- When the updated base is built, the program returns to the first DATA LIST command in the input program and reads the next ID from the *UPDATE* file. If the *UPDATE* file is exhausted (*#EOF*=1), the loop keeps reading records from the master file until it reaches the end of the file.

- The same task can be accomplished using MATCH FILES. With MATCH FILES, the raw data must be read and saved as SPSS-format data files first.

COLUMN Subcommand

COLUMN specifies a beginning column for the REREAD command to read data. The default is column 1. You can specify a numeric expression for the column.

Example

```
INPUT PROGRAM.
DATA LIST /KIND 10-14 (A).
COMPUTE #COL=1.
IF (KIND EQ 'CHEVY') #COL=13.

DO IF (KIND EQ 'CHEVY' OR KIND EQ 'FORD').
REREAD COLUMN #COL.
DATA LIST /PRICE 3-6 (DOLLAR,2) QUANTITY 7-9.
END CASE.
END IF.
END INPUT PROGRAM.
BEGIN DATA
111295100FORD       CHAPMAN AUTO SALES
121199005VW      MIDWEST VOLKSWAGEN SALES
11 395025FORD       BETTER USED CARS
11       CHEVY 195005      HUFFMAN SALES & SERVICE
11       VW    595020      MIDWEST VOLKSWAGEN SALES
11       CHEVY 295015      SAM'S AUTO REPAIR
12       CHEVY 210 20      LONGFELLOW CHEVROLET
 9555032 VW                HYDE PARK IMPORTS
END DATA.
LIST.
```

- The task in this example is to read *PRICE* and *QUANTITY* for Chevrolets and Fords only. A scratch variable is created to indicate the starting column positions for *PRICE* and *QUANTITY*, and a single DATA LIST command is used to read data for both types of automobiles.

- Scratch variable *#COL* is set to 13 for Chevrolets and 1 for all other automobiles. For Fords, the data begin in column 1. Variable *PRICE* is read from columns 3–6 and *QUANTITY* is read from columns 7–9. When the record is a Chevrolet, the data begins in column 13. Variable *PRICE* is read from columns 15–18 (15 is 3, 16 is 4, and so forth), and *QUANTITY* is read from columns 19–21.

Example

```
* Reading both FIXED and LIST input with REREAD.

INPUT PROGRAM.
DATA LIST      NOTABLE FIXED/ A 1-14(A).  /*Read the FIXED portion
REREAD         COLUMN = 15.
DATA LIST      LIST/ X Y Z.               /*Read the LIST portion
END INPUT PROGRAM.

*  The value 1 on the first record is in column 15.

LIST.
BEGIN DATA
FIRST RECORD  1 2 3 -1 -2 -3
NUMBER 2      4 5
THE THIRD     6 7 8
#4
FIFTH AND LAST9 10 11
END DATA.
```

- Columns 1–14 are read in FIXED format. REREAD then resets the pointer to column 15. Thus, beginning in column 15, values are read in LIST format.

- The second DATA LIST specifies only three variables. Thus, the values –1, –2, and –3 on the first record are not read.

- The program generates a warning for the missing value on record 2 and a second warning for the three missing values on record 4.

- On the fifth and last record there is no delimiter between value LAST and value 9. REREAD can still read the 9 in LIST format.

RESTORE

```
RESTORE
```

Overview

RESTORE restores SET specifications that were stored by a previous PRESERVE command. RESTORE and PRESERVE are especially useful when using the macro facility. PRE-SERVE—RESTORE sequences can be nested up to five levels.

Basic Specification

The only specification is the command keyword. RESTORE has no additional specifications.

Example

```
GET FILE=PRSNNL.
FREQUENCIES VAR=DIVISION /STATISTICS=ALL.
PRESERVE.
SET XSORT=NO WIDTH=90 UNDEFINED=NOWARN BLANKS=000 CASE=UPLOW.
SORT CASES BY DIVISION.
REPORT FORMAT=AUTO LIST /VARS=LNAME FNAME DEPT SOCSEC SALARY
  /BREAK=DIVISION /SUMMARY=MEAN.
RESTORE.
```

- GET reads SPSS-format data file *PRSNNL*.
- FREQUENCIES requests a frequency table and all statistics for variable *DIVISION*.
- PRESERVE stores all current SET specifications.
- SET changes several subcommand settings.
- SORT sorts cases in preparation for a report. Because SET XSORT=NO, the sort program is not used to sort cases; another sort program must be available.
- REPORT requests a report organized by variable *DIVISION*.
- RESTORE reestablishes all the SET specifications that were in effect when PRESERVE was specified.

RMV

```
RMV new variables={LINT (varlist)           }
                  {MEAN (varlist [{,2 }])   }
                  {             {,n }       }
                  {             {ALL}       }
                  {MEDIAN (varlist [{,2 }])} }
                  {               {,n }    } }
                  {               {ALL}    } }
                  {SMEAN (varlist)          }
                  {TREND (varlist)          }

   [/new variables=function (varlist [,span])]
```

Function keywords:

LINT	Linear interpolation
MEAN	Mean of surrounding values
MEDIAN	Median of surrounding values
SMEAN	Variable mean
TREND	Linear trend at that point

Example
```
RMV NEWVAR1=LINT(OLDVAR1).
```

Overview

RMV produces new variables by copying existing variables and replacing any system- or user-missing values with estimates computed by one of several methods. You can also use RMV to replace the values of existing variables. The estimated values are computed from valid data in the existing variables. The new or revised variables can be used in any procedure and can be saved in an SPSS-format data file.

Basic Specification

The basic specification is one or more new variable names, an equals sign, a function, and an equal number of existing variables. RMV displays a list of the new variables, the number of missing values replaced, the case numbers of the first and last nonmissing cases, the number of valid cases, and the function used to produce the variables.

Syntax Rules

- The existing variables (and span, if specified) must be enclosed in parentheses.
- The equals sign is required.
- You can specify more than one equation on RMV.

- Equations are separated by slashes.
- You can specify only one function per equation.
- You can create more than one new variable per equation by specifying more than one new variable name on the left and an equal number of existing variables on the right.

Operations

- Each new variable is added to the working data file.
- If the new variable named already exists, its values are replaced.
- If the new variable named does not already exist, it is created.
- If the same variable is named on both sides of the equation, the new variable will replace the existing variable. Valid values from the existing variable are copied into the new variable, and missing values are replaced with estimates.
- Variables are created in the order in which they are specified on the RMV command.
- If multiple variables are created on a single equation, the first new variable is based on the first existing variable, the second new variable is based on the second existing variable, and so forth.
- RMV automatically generates a variable label for each new variable describing the function and variable used to create it and the date and time of creation.
- The format of a new variable depends on the function specified and on the format of the existing variable.
- RMV honors the TSET MISSING setting that is currently in effect.
- RMV does not honor the USE command.

Limitations

- Maximum 1 function per equation.
- There is no limit on the number of variables created by an equation.
- There is no limit on the number of equations per RMV command.

LINT Function

LINT replaces missing values using linear interpolation. The last valid value before the missing value and the first valid value after the missing value are used for the interpolation.

- The only specification on LINT is a variable or variable list in parentheses.
- LINT will not replace missing values at the endpoints of variables.

Example

```
RMV NEWVAR1=LINT(OLDVAR1).
```

- This example produces a new variable called *NEWVAR1*.
- *NEWVAR1* will have the same values as *OLDVAR1* but with missing values replaced by linear interpolation.

MEAN Function

MEAN replaces missing values with the mean of valid surrounding values. The number of surrounding values used to compute the mean depends on the span.

- The specification on MEAN is a variable or variable list and a span, in parentheses.
- The span specification is optional and can be any positive integer or keyword ALL.
- A span of *n* uses *n* valid cases before and after the missing value.
- If span is not specified, it defaults to 2.
- Keyword ALL computes the mean of all valid values.
- MEAN will not replace missing values if there are not enough valid surrounding cases to satisfy the span specification.

Example

```
RMV B=MEAN(A,3).
```

- This example produces a new variable called *B*.
- *B* will have the same values as variable *A* but with missing values replaced by means of valid surrounding values.
- Each mean is based on 6 values, that is, the 3 nearest valid values on each side of the missing value.

MEDIAN Function

MEDIAN replaces missing values with the median of valid surrounding values. The number of surrounding values used to compute the median depends on the span.

- The specification on MEDIAN is a variable or variable list and a span, in parentheses.
- The span specification is optional and can be any positive integer or keyword ALL.
- A span of *n* uses *n* valid cases before and after the missing value.
- If span is not specified, it defaults to 2.
- Keyword ALL computes the median of all valid values.
- MEDIAN will not replace missing values if there are not enough valid surrounding cases to satisfy the span specification.

Example

```
RMV B=MEDIAN(A,3).
```

- This example produces a new variable called *B*.
- *B* will have the same values as *A* but with missing values replaced by medians of valid surrounding values.
- Each median is based on 6 values, that is, the 3 nearest valid values on each side of the missing value.

SMEAN Function

SMEAN replaces missing values in the new variable with the variable mean.

- The only specification on SMEAN is a variable or variable list in parentheses.
- The SMEAN function is equivalent to the MEAN function with a span specification of ALL.

Example

```
RMV VAR1 TO VAR4=SMEAN(VARA VARB VARC VARD).
```

- Four new variables (*VAR1*, *VAR2*, *VAR3*, and *VAR4*) are created.
- *VAR1* copies the values of *VARA*, *VAR2* copies *VARB*, *VAR3* copies *VARC*, and *VAR4* copies *VARD*. Any missing values in an existing variable are replaced with the mean of that variable.

TREND Function

TREND replaces missing values in the new variable with the linear trend for that point. The existing variable is regressed on an index variable scaled 1 to *n*. Missing values are replaced with their predicted values.

- The only specification on TREND is a variable or variable list in parentheses.

Example

```
RMV YHAT=TREND(VARY).
```

- This example creates a new variable called *YHAT*.
- *YHAT* has the same values as *VARY* but with missing values replaced by predicted values.

ROC

```
ROC varlist BY varname({varvalue  })
                      {'varvalue'}

[/MISSING = {EXCLUDE**}]
            {INCLUDE  }

[/CRITERIA = [CUTOFF({INCLUDE**})]  [TESTPOS({LARGE**})]  [CI({95**})]
                    {EXCLUDE  }              {SMALL  }        {n  }

                  [DISTRIBUTION({FREE**  })]]]
                               {NEGEXPO}

[/PLOT = [CURVE**[(REFERENCE)]]  [NONE]]

[/PRINT = [SE] [COORDINATES]].
```

** Default if subcommand or keyword is omitted.

Overview

ROC produces a receiver operating characteristic (ROC) curve and an estimate of the area under the curve.

Options

Distributional Assumptions. In the CRITERIA subcommand, the user can choose the nonparametric or parametric method to estimate the standard error of the area under the curve. Currently, the bi-negative exponential distribution is the only parametric option.

Optional Output. In addition to an estimate of the area under the ROC curve, the user may request its standard error, a confidence interval, and a P-value under the null hypothesis that the area under the curve equals 0.5. A table of cut-off values and coordinates used to plot the ROC curve may also be displayed.

Basic Specification

The basic specification is one variable as the test result variable and one variable as the actual state variable with one of its values. ROC uses the nonparametric (distribution-free) method to calculate the area under the ROC curve. The default and minimum output is a chart of the ROC curve and a table of the area under the curve.

Syntax Rules

- Minimum syntax: You always need a test result variable and one actual state variable with one of its values in the ROC command line.

1073

- The test result variable must be numeric, but the state variable can be any type with any format.
- Subcommands can be specified in any order.
- When a subcommand is duplicated, only the last one is honored given that all duplicates have no syntax errors. A syntax warning is issued.
- Within a subcommand, if two or more exclusive or contradictory keywords are given, the latter keywords override the earlier ones. A syntax warning is issued.
- If a keyword is duplicated within a subcommand, it is silently ignored.

Limitations

- Only the nonparametric method and one parametric method are available as the computational options for the standard error of the area under the curve at this moment. In the future, bi-normal and bi-logistic distributions may be added to the parametric option.

varlist BY varname(varvalue)

The varlist specifies one or more test result variables. They must be of numeric type.

The varname separated from the varlist by the word BY specifies the actual state variable. It can be of any type and any format. The user must also specify a varvalue in brackets after the second varname to define the "positive" group of the actual state variable. All other valid state values are assumed to indicate the negative group.

MISSING Subcommand

Cases with system-missing values in the test result variable and the actual state variable are always excluded from the analysis. However, the MISSING subcommand allows the user to redefine the user-missing values to be valid.

EXCLUDE   *Exclude both user-missing and system-missing values.* Cases with a system-missing value or a user-missing value in either the test result variable or the actual state variable are excluded from the analysis. This is the active default.

INCLUDE   *User-missing values are treated as valid.* Cases with a system-missing value in either the test result variable or the actual state variable are excluded from the analysis.

CRITERIA Subcommand

The CRITERIA subcommand allows the user to decide (1) whether the cutoff value is included as the positive test result value or not, (2) whether the larger or smaller value direction of the test result variable indicates the positive test result or not, (3) the confidence level of the asymptotic confidence interval produced by /PRINT = SE, and (4) the estimation method for the standard error of the area under the curve.

CUTOFF(INCLUDE)   *Positive classification of test result values includes the cutoff values.* Note that the positive test result direction is controlled by the TEST-POS keyword. This is the active default.

CUTOFF(EXCLUDE)   *Positive classification of test result values excludes the cutoff values.* This distinction leads to the different sets of cutoff values, but none of the output, chart and table, is affected at this moment, because the user cannot choose the cutoff values for the classification.

TESTPOS(LARGE)   *The user can specify which direction of the test result variable indicates increasing strength of conviction that the subject is test positive.* The larger the test result value is, the more positive the test result is. LARGE is the active default.

TESTPOS(SMALL)   *The smaller the test result value is, the more positive the test result is.*

CI(n)   *Confidence level in the (two-sided) asymptotic confidence interval of the area.* The user can specify any confidence level in (0, 100) for the asymptotic confidence interval created by /PRINT = SE. The active default parameter value is 95.

DISTRIBUTION(FREE)   *The method of calculating the standard error of the area under the curve.* When FREE, the standard error of the area under the curve is estimated nonparametrically—that is, without any distributional assumption.

DISTRIBUTION(NEGEXPO)
    The standard error is estimated assuming the bi-negative exponential distribution. This latter option is valid only when the number of positive actual state observations equals the number of negative actual state observations.

PRINT Subcommand

The PRINT subcommand controls the display of optional table output. Note that the area under the curve is always displayed.

SE   *Standard error of the area estimate.* In addition to the standard error of the estimated area under the curve, the asymptotic 95% (or other user-specified confidence level) confidence interval as well as the asymptotic *P*-value under the null hypothesis that the true area = 0.5 are calculated. Note that the area under the curve statistic is asymptotically normally distributed.

COORDINATES   *Coordinate points of the ROC curve along with the cutoff values.* Pairs of sensitivity and 1 – specificity values are given with the cutoff values for each curve.

PLOT Subcommand

The PLOT subcommand controls the display of chart output.

CURVE(REFERENCE)   *The ROC curve chart is displayed.* The keyword CURVE is the active default. In addition, the user has an option to draw the diagonal reference line (sensitivity = 1 – specificity) by the bracketed parameter REFERENCE.

NONE   *The ROC curve chart is suppressed.*

SAMPLE

```
SAMPLE {decimal value}
       {n FROM m      }
```

Example

```
SAMPLE .25.
```

Overview

SAMPLE permanently draws a random sample of cases for processing in all subsequent procedures. For a temporary sample, use a TEMPORARY command before SAMPLE.

Basic Specification

The basic specification is either a decimal value between 0 and 1 or the sample size followed by keyword FROM and the size of the working data file.

- To select an approximate percentage of cases, specify a decimal value between 0 and 1.
- To select an exact-size random sample, specify a positive integer less than the file size, followed by keyword FROM and the file size.

Operations

- SAMPLE is a permanent transformation.
- Sampling is based on a pseudo-random-number generator that depends on a seed value established by the program. On some implementations of the program, this number defaults to a fixed integer, and a SAMPLE command that specifies *n* FROM *m* will generate the identical sample whenever a session is rerun. To generate a different sample each time, use the SET command to reset SEED to a different value for each session. See the SET command for more information.
- If sampling is done using the *n* FROM *m* method and the TEMPORARY command is specified, successive samples will not be the same because the seed value changes each time a random number series is needed within a session.
- A proportional sample (a sample based on a decimal value) usually does not produce the exact proportion specified.
- If the number specified for *m* following FROM is less than the actual file size, the sample is drawn only from the first *m* cases.
- If the number following FROM is greater than the actual file size, the program samples an equivalent proportion of cases from the working data file (see example).
- If SAMPLE follows SELECT IF, it samples only cases selected by SELECT IF.

- If SAMPLE precedes SELECT IF, cases are selected from the sample.
- If more than one SAMPLE is specified in a session, each acts upon the sample selected by the preceding SAMPLE command.
- If N OF CASES is used with SAMPLE, the program reads as many records as required to build the specified *n* cases. It makes no difference whether the N OF CASES precedes or follows the SAMPLE.

Limitations

SAMPLE cannot be placed in a FILE TYPE—END FILE TYPE or INPUT PROGRAM—END INPUT PROGRAM structure. It can be placed nearly anywhere following these commands in a transformation program. See Appendix A for a discussion of program states and the placement of commands.

Example

```
SAMPLE .25.
```

- This command samples approximately 25% of the cases in the working data file.

Example

```
SAMPLE 500 FROM 3420.
```

- The working data file must have 3420 cases or more to obtain a random sample of exactly 500 cases.
- If the file contains fewer than 3420 cases, proportionally fewer cases are sampled.
- If the file contains more than 3420 cases, a random sample of 500 cases is drawn from the first 3420 cases.

Example

```
DO IF  SEX EQ 'M'.
SAMPLE 1846 FROM 8000.
END IF.
```

- SAMPLE is placed inside a DO IF—END IF structure to sample subgroups differently. Assume that this is a survey of 10,000 people in which 80% of the sample is male, while the known universe is 48% male. To obtain a sample that corresponds to the known universe and that maximizes the size of the sample, 1846 (48/52*2000) males and all females must be sampled. The DO IF structure is used to restrict the sampling process to the males.

SAVE

```
SAVE OUTFILE=file

[/VERSION={3**}]
          {2  }

[/UNSELECTED=[{RETAIN}]
              {DELETE}

[/KEEP={ALL** }] [/DROP=varlist]
       {varlist}

[/RENAME=(old varlist=new varlist)...]

[/MAP]  [/{COMPRESSED  }]
           {UNCOMPRESSED}
```

**Default if the subcommand is omitted.

Example

```
SAVE OUTFILE=EMPL  /RENAME=(AGE=AGE88) (JOBCAT=JOBCAT88).
```

Overview

SAVE produces an SPSS-format data file. An SPSS-format data file contains data plus a dictionary. The dictionary contains a name for each variable in the data file plus any assigned variable and value labels, missing-value flags, and variable print and write formats. The dictionary also contains document text created with the DOCUMENTS command.

XSAVE also creates SPSS-format data files. The difference is that SAVE causes data to be read, while XSAVE is not executed until data are read for the next procedure.

See SAVE TRANSLATE and SAVE SCSS for information on saving data files that can be used by other programs.

Options

Compatibility with Early Releases. You can save a data file that can be read by SPSS releases prior to 7.5.

Variable Subsets and Order. You can save a subset of variables and reorder the variables that are saved using the DROP and KEEP subcommands.

Variable Names. You can rename variables as they are copied into the SPSS-format data file using the RENAME subcommand.

Variable Map. To confirm the names and order of the variables saved in the SPSS-format data file, use the MAP subcommand. MAP displays the variables saved in the SPSS-format data file next to their corresponding names in the working data file.

Data Compression. You can write the data file in compressed or uncompressed form using the COMPRESSED or UNCOMPRESSED subcommand.

Basic Specification

The basic specification is the OUTFILE subcommand, which specifies a name for the SPSS-format data file to be saved.

Subcommand Order

- Subcommands can be specified in any order.

Syntax Rules

- OUTFILE is required and can be specified only once. If OUTFILE is specified more than once, only the last OUTFILE specified is in effect.
- KEEP, DROP, RENAME, and MAP can each be used as many times as needed.
- Only one of the subcommands COMPRESSED or UNCOMPRESSED can be specified per SAVE command.

Operations

- SAVE is executed immediately and causes the data to be read.
- The new SPSS-format data file dictionary is arranged in the same order as the working file dictionary, unless variables are reordered with the KEEP subcommand. Documentary text from the working file dictionary is always saved unless it is dropped with the DROP DOCU-MENTS command before SAVE.
- New variables created by transformations and procedures previous to the SAVE command are included in the new SPSS-format data file, and variables altered by transformations are saved in their modified form. Results of any temporary transformations immediately preceding the SAVE command are included in the file; scratch variables are not.
- SPSS-format data files are binary files designed to be read and written by SPSS only. SPSS-format data files can be edited only with the UPDATE command. Use the MATCH FILES and ADD FILES commands to merge SPSS-format data files.
- The working data file is still available for transformations and procedures after SAVE is executed.
- SAVE processes the dictionary first and displays a message that indicates how many variables will be saved. Once the data are written, SAVE indicates how many cases were saved. If the second message does not appear, the file was probably not completely written.

Example

```
GET FILE=HUBEMPL.
SAVE OUTFILE=EMPL88 /RENAME=(AGE=AGE88) (JOBCAT=JOBCAT88).
```

- The GET command retrieves the SPSS-format data file *HUBEMPL*.

- The RENAME subcommand renames variable *AGE* to *AGE88* and variable *JOBCAT* to *JOBCAT88*.

- SAVE causes the data to be read and saves a new SPSS-format data file with filename *EMPL88*. The original SPSS-format data file *HUBEMPL* is not changed.

Example

```
GET FILE=HUBEMPL.
TEMPORARY.
RECODE DEPT85 TO DEPT88 (1,2=1) (3,4=2) (ELSE=9).
VALUE LABELS DEPT85 TO DEPT88 1 'MANAGEMENT' 2 'OPERATIONS' 9
'UNKNOWN'.
SAVE OUTFILE=HUBTEMP.
CROSSTABS DEPT85 TO DEPT88 BY JOBCAT.
```

- The GET command retrieves the SPSS-format data file *HUBEMPL*.

- The TEMPORARY command indicates that RECODE and VALUE LABELS are in effect only for the next command that reads the data (SAVE).

- The RECODE command recodes values for all variables between and including *DEPT85* and *DEPT88* on the working data file.

- The VALUE LABELS command specifies new labels for the recoded values.

- The OUTFILE subcommand on SAVE specifies *HUBTEMP* as the new SPSS-format data file. *HUBTEMP* will include the recoded values for *DEPT85* to *DEPT88* and the new value labels.

- The *CROSSTABS* command crosstabulates *DEPT85* to *DEPT88* with *JOBCAT*. Since the RECODE and VALUE LABELS commands were temporary, the CROSSTABS output does not reflect the recoding and new labels.

- If XSAVE were specified instead of SAVE, the data would be read only once. Both the saved SPSS-format data file and the CROSSTABS output would reflect the temporary recoding and labeling of the department variables.

OUTFILE Subcommand

OUTFILE specifies the SPSS-format data file to be saved. OUTFILE is required and can be specified only once. If OUTFILE is specified more than once, only the last OUTFILE is in effect.

VERSION Subcommand

VERSION allows you to save a data file that can be opened in SPSS releases prior to 7.5. The default is 3 if VERSION is not specified or specified with no value. Specify 2 to save a file compatible with earlier releases.

UNSELECTED Subcommand

UNSELECTED determines whether cases excluded on a previous FILTER or USE command are to be retained or deleted in the SPSS-format data file. The default is RETAIN. The UNSELECTED subcommand has no effect when the working data file does not contain unselected cases.

RETAIN   *Retain the unselected cases.* All cases in the working data file are saved. This is the default when UNSELECTED is specified by itself.

DELETE   *Delete the unselected cases.* Only cases that meet the FILTER or USE criteria are saved in the SPSS-format data file.

DROP and KEEP Subcommands

DROP and KEEP are used to save a subset of variables. DROP specifies the variables not to save in the new data file; KEEP specifies the variables to save in the new data file; variables not named on KEEP are dropped.

- Variables can be specified in any order. The order of variables on KEEP determines the order of variables in the SPSS-format data file. The order on DROP does not affect the order of variables in the SPSS-format data file.

- Keyword ALL on KEEP refers to all remaining variables not previously specified on KEEP. ALL must be the last specification on KEEP.

- If a variable is specified twice on the same subcommand, only the first mention is recognized.

- Multiple DROP and KEEP subcommands are allowed. Specifying a variable that is not in the working data file or that has been dropped because of a previous DROP or KEEP subcommand results in an error, and the SAVE command is not executed.

- Keyword TO can be used to specify a group of consecutive variables in the active file.

Example

```
GET FILE=PRSNL.
COMPUTE TENURE=(12-CMONTH +(12*(88-CYEAR)))/12.
COMPUTE JTENURE=(12-JMONTH +(12*(88-JYEAR)))/12.
VARIABLE LABELS        TENURE 'Tenure in Company'
                       JTENURE 'Tenure in Grade'.
SAVE OUTFILE=PRSNL88 /DROP=GRADE STORE
  /KEEP=LNAME NAME TENURE JTENURE ALL.
```

- The variables *TENURE* and *JTENURE* are created by COMPUTE commands and assigned variable labels by the VARIABLE LABELS command. *TENURE* and *JTENURE* are added to the end of the working data file.

- DROP excludes variables *GRADE* and *STORE* from file *PRSNL88*. KEEP specifies that *LNAME*, *NAME*, *TENURE*, and *JTENURE* are the first four variables in file *PRSNL88*, followed by all remaining variables not specified on DROP. These remaining variables are saved in the same sequence as they appear in the original file.

RENAME Subcommand

RENAME changes the names of variables as they are copied into the new SPSS-format data file.

- The specification on RENAME is a list of old variable names followed by an equals sign and a list of new variable names. The same number of variables must be specified on both lists. Keyword TO can be used in the first list to refer to consecutive variables in the working data file and in the second list to generate new variable names. The entire specification must be enclosed in parentheses.
- Alternatively, you can specify each old variable name individually, followed by an equals sign and the new variable name. Multiple sets of variable specifications are allowed. The parentheses around each set of specifications are optional.
- RENAME does not affect the working data file. However, if RENAME precedes DROP or KEEP, variables must be referred to by their new names on DROP or KEEP.
- Old variable names do not need to be specified according to their order in the working data file.
- Name changes take place in one operation. Therefore, variable names can be exchanged between two variables.
- Multiple RENAME subcommands are allowed.

Example

```
SAVE OUTFILE=EMPL88 /RENAME AGE=AGE88 JOBCAT=JOBCAT88.
```

- RENAME specifies two name changes for the file *EMPL88*: the variable *AGE* is renamed to *AGE88* and the variable *JOBCAT* is renamed to *JOBCAT88*.

Example

```
SAVE OUTFILE=EMPL88 /RENAME (AGE JOBCAT=AGE88 JOBCAT88).
```

- The name changes are identical to those in the previous example: *AGE* is renamed to *AGE88* and *JOBCAT* is renamed to *JOBCAT88*. The parentheses are required with this method.

MAP Subcommand

MAP displays a list of the variables in the SPSS-format data file and their corresponding names in the working data file.

- The only specification is keyword MAP. There are no additional specifications.
- Multiple MAP subcommands are allowed. Each MAP subcommand maps the results of subcommands that precede it, but not results of subcommands that follow it.

Example

```
GET FILE=HUBEMPL.
SAVE OUTFILE=EMPL88 /RENAME=(AGE=AGE88)(JOBCAT=JOBCAT88)
  /KEEP=LNAME NAME JOBCAT88 ALL /MAP.
```

- MAP is used to confirm the new names for *AGE* and *JOBCAT* and the order of variables in the *EMPL88* file (*LNAME*, *NAME*, and *JOBCAT88*, followed by all remaining variables from the working data file).

COMPRESSED and UNCOMPRESSED Subcommands

COMPRESSED saves the file in compressed form. UNCOMPRESSED saves the file in uncompressed form. In a compressed file, small integers (from −99 to 155) are stored in one byte instead of the eight bytes used in an uncompressed file.

- The only specification is the keyword COMPRESSED or UNCOMPRESSED. There are no additional specifications.

- Compressed data files occupy less disk space than do uncompressed data files.

- Compressed data files take longer to read than do uncompressed data files.

- The GET command, which reads SPSS-format data files, does not need to specify whether the files it reads are compressed or uncompressed.

- Only one of the subcommands COMPRESSED or UNCOMPRESSED can be specified per SAVE command. COMPRESSED is usually the default, though UNCOMPRESSED may be the default on some systems.

SAVE TRANSLATE

This command is not available on all operating systems.

```
SAVE TRANSLATE

[{/OUTFILE=file              }]*
 {/CONNECT=ODBC connect string}**

 [/TYPE={DB2 }]
        {DB3 }
        {DB4 }
        {ODBC}
        {PC  }
        {SLK }
        {TAB }
        {WKS }
        {WK1 }
        {WK3 }
        {WRK }
        {WR1 }
        {XLS }

 [/TABLE = ODBC table name]**

 [/RENAME=(old varlist=new varlist)[(...)]]

 [/KEEP={ALL    }]
        {varlist}

 [/DROP=varlist]

 [{/COMPRESSED  }]
  {/UNCOMPRESSED}

 [/FIELDNAMES]***

 [/MAP]

 [{/REPLACE}]
  {/APPEND }****

 [/UNSELECTED=[{RETAIN}]
              {DELETE}
```

*   Invalid for TYPE=ODBC; required for all other types.
** Required for TYPE=ODBC; invalid for all other types.
*** Available only for spreadsheet formats.
****Available only for ODBC format.

Keyword	Type of file
WK1	1-2-3 Release 2.0
WKS	1-2-3 Release 1A
WR1	Symphony Release 2.0
WRK	Symphony Release 1.0
SLK	Multiplan or Excel in SYLK (symbolic link) format
XLS	Microsoft Excel
DB2	dBASE II
DB3	dBASE III
DB4	dBASE IV
TAB	Tab-delimited ASCII file
ODBC	Database accessed via ODBC
PC	SPSS/PC+ system file

Example

```
SAVE TRANSLATE OUTFILE='SALESREP.SLK'
 /KEEP=SALES, UNITS, MONTHS, PRICE1 TO PRICE20
 /FIELDNAMES.
```

Overview

SAVE TRANSLATE translates the working data file into a file that can be used by other software applications. Supported formats are 1-2-3, Symphony, Multiplan, Excel, dBASE II, dBASE III, dBASE IV, tab-delimited ASCII files, and SPSS/PC+ data files.

Options

Variable Subsets. You can use the DROP and KEEP subcommands to specify variables to omit or retain in the resulting file.

Variable Names. You can rename variables as they are copied to the spreadsheet, database, or tab-delimited ASCII file using the RENAME subcommand.

Variable Map. To confirm the names and order of the variables saved in the resulting file, use the MAP subcommand. MAP displays the variables saved in the file next to their corresponding names in the working data file.

Spreadsheet Files. You can use the FIELDNAMES subcommand to translate variable names to field names in a spreadsheet file.

Basic Specification

- The basic specification is OUTFILE with a file specification in apostrophes.

- TYPE and a keyword to indicate the type of dBASE file is also required to save dBASE database files.

Subcommand Order

- OUTFILE or CONNECT must be specified first. OUTFILE is invalid for TYPE=ODBC and required for all other types. CONNECT is required for TYPE=ODBC and invalid for all other types.
- The remaining subcommands can be specified in any order.

Operations

- The working data file remains available after SAVE TRANSLATE is executed.
- User-missing values are transferred as actual values.
- If the working data file contains more variables than the file can receive, SAVE TRANSLATE writes the maximum number of variables the file can receive.

Spreadsheets

Variables in the working data file become columns, and cases become rows in the spreadsheet file.

- If you specify FIELDNAMES, variable names become the first row and indicate field names.
- String variable values are left-justified and numeric variable values are right-justified.
- The resulting spreadsheet file is given the range name of SPSS.
- System-missing values are translated to N/A in spreadsheet files.

SPSS formats are translated as follows:

SPSS	1-2-3/Symphony	Multiplan	Excel
Number	Fixed	Fixed	0.00;#,##0.00;...
COMMA	Comma	Fixed	0.00;#,##0.00;...
DOLLAR	Currency	$ (dollar)	$#,##0_);...
DATE	Date		d-mmm-yy
TIME	Time		hh:mm:ss
String	Label	Alpha	General

Databases

Variables in the working data file become fields, and cases become records in the database file.

- Characters that are allowed in variable names but not in dBASE field names are translated to colons in dBASE II and underscores in dBASE III and dBASE IV.

- Numeric variables containing the system-missing value are translated to **** in dBASE III and dBASE IV, and 0 in dBASE II.
- The width and precision of translated numeric are taken from the print format; the total number of characters for the number is taken from the width of the print format, and the number of digits to the right of the decimal point is taken from the decimals in the print format. To adjust the width and precision, use the PRINT FORMATS command prior to using SAVE TRANSLATE. Values that cannot be converted to the given width and precision are converted to missing values.

Variable formats are translated to dBASE formats as follows:

SPSS	dBASE
Number	Numeric
String	Character
Dollar	Numeric
Comma	Numeric

Tab-delimited ASCII Files

Variables in the working data file become columns, and cases become rows in the ASCII file.

- If you specify FIELDNAMES, variable names become the first row as column headings.
- All values are delimited by tabs.
- The resulting ASCII file is given the extension *.DAT* if no file extension is explicitly specified.
- System-missing values are translated to N/A in ASCII files.
- SPSS formats are not translated.

SPSS/PC+ System Files

Variables are saved as they are defined. The resulting file is given the extension *.SYS* if no extension is explicitly specified. The dictionary is saved so that labels, formats, missing value specifications, and other dictionary information are preserved.

Limitations

- Maximum 2048 cases can be translated to 1-2-3 Release 1A, maximum 8192 cases to 1-2-3 Release 2.0 or Symphony files, maximum 4095 cases to Multiplan files, and maximum 16,384 cases for Excel.
- Maximum 65,535 cases and 32 variables can be translated to dBASE II; maximum 1 billion cases (subject to disk space availability) and 128 variables to dBASE III; or maximum 1 billion cases (subject to disk space availability) and 255 variables to dBASE IV.

OUTFILE Subcommand

OUTFILE assigns a name to the file to be saved. The only specification is the name of the file. On some operating systems, file specifications should be enclosed in quotation marks or apostrophes.

Example

```
SAVE TRANSLATE OUTFILE='STAFF.DBF'/TYPE=DB3.
```

- SAVE TRANSLATE creates a dBASE III file called *STAFF.DBF*. The TYPE subcommand is required to specify the type of dBASE file to save.

CONNECT Subcommand

CONNECT identifies the database name and other parameters for TYPE=ODBC.

Example

```
SAVE TRANSLATE
   /CONNECT="DSN=MSAccess;UID=rkrishna;PWD=123xyz"
   /TABLE="mytable"
   /TYPE=ODBC.
```

TABLE Subcommand

TABLE identifies the table name for TYPE=ODBC.

Example

```
SAVE TRANSLATE
   /CONNECT="DSN=MSAccess;UID=rkrishna;PWD=123xyz"
   /TABLE="mytable"
   /TYPE=ODBC.
```

REPLACE Subcommand

REPLACE gives permission to overwrite an existing file of the same name. It takes no further specifications.

APPEND Subcommand

APPEND appends to an existing database table after type and variable name validations. There must be a matching column in the table for each SPSS variable. If a column is not found that can correctly store an SPSS variable, a failure is returned. If the table contains more columns than the number of SPSS variables, the command still stores the data in the table. The variable names and column names must match exactly. A variable can be stored in a column as long as the column type is one that can store values of the SPSS variable type. So, a column of any numeric type (short integer, integer, float, double, etc.) is valid for a numeric SPSS variable, and a column of any character type is valid for a string SPSS variable.

APPEND is valid only for TYPE=ODBC. You can specify either APPEND or REPLACE, but not both.

TYPE Subcommand

TYPE indicates the format of the resulting file.

- TYPE can be omitted for spreadsheet files if the file extension named on OUTFILE is the default for the type of file you are saving.
- TYPE with keyword DB2, DB3, or DB4 is required for translating to dBASE files.
- TYPE takes precedence over the file extension.
- A file that was read using GET TRANSLATE should be saved as the same type.

WK1	*1-2-3 Release 2.0.*
WKS	*1-2-3 Release 1.4.*
WR1	*Symphony Release 2.0.*
WRK	*Symphony Release 1.0.*
SLK	*Multiplan (symbolic format).*
XLS	*Excel.*
DB2	*dBASE II.*
DB3	*dBASE III or dBASE III PLUS.*
DB4	*dBASE IV.*
TAB	*Tab-delimited ASCII data files.*
PC	*SPSS/PC+ system files.*
ODBC	*Database accessed via ODBC.*

Example

```
SAVE TRANSLATE OUTFILE='PROJECT.OCT' /TYPE=SLK.
```

- SAVE TRANSLATE translates the working data file into the Multiplan spreadsheet file named *PROJECT.OCT*.

Writing to an ODBC Database Source

The following rules apply when writing to a database with TYPE=ODBC:

- If any case cannot be stored in the database for any reason, an error is returned. Therefore, either all cases are stored or none.
- At insert time, a check is performed to see if the value being stored in a column is likely to cause an overflow. If that is the case, the user is warned about the overflow and that a *SYSMIS* is stored instead.

- If any variable names in the working data file contain characters not allowed by the database, they are replaced by an underscore. If this causes a duplicate variable name, a new variable name is generated.

- The following SPSS variable type classes are supported:
  VC_STRING
  VC_NUMERIC
  VC_PERCENT
  VC_CURRENCY
  VC_TIME
  VC_DATE

- If a variable falls into the *VC_UNKNOWN* category, it is dropped. SPSS missing values are treated as missing values in the databases.

- Date variables are treated as Date columns, but if the database treats Date variables as TimeStamp (i.e., as datetime columns), then the time part of the TimeStamp is assigned a zero value (00:00.00) internally. The date value is unaltered when read back into SPSS.

- Datetime variables are stored as datetime (TimeStamp) columns.

- If a database does not support storing fractional seconds, the fractional value is truncated.

- SPSS dictionary information is not stored in the database table. Any formatting information contained in the SPSS dictionary is lost.

FIELDNAMES Subcommand

FIELDNAMES translates variable names into field names in the spreadsheet.

- FIELDNAMES can be used with spreadsheets and tab-delimited ASCII files. FIELDNAMES is ignored when used with database files.

- Variable names are transferred to the first row of the spreadsheet file.

Example

```
SAVE TRANSLATE OUTFILE='STAFF.WRK' /FIELDNAMES.
```

- SAVE TRANSLATE creates a Symphony spreadsheet file containing all variables from the working data file. The variable names are transferred to the Symphony file.

UNSELECTED Subcommand

UNSELECTED determines whether cases excluded on a previous FILTER or USE command are to be retained or deleted in the SPSS-format data file. The default is RETAIN. The UNSELECTED subcommand has no effect when the working data file does not contain unselected cases.

RETAIN   *Retain the unselected cases.* All cases in the working data file are saved. This is the default when UNSELECTED is specified by itself.

DELETE   *Delete the unselected cases.* Only cases that meet the FILTER or USE criteria are saved in the SPSS-format data file.

DROP and KEEP Subcommands

Use DROP or KEEP to include only a subset of variables in the resulting file. DROP specifies a set of variables to exclude. KEEP specifies a set of variables to retain. Variables not specified on KEEP are dropped.

- Specify a list of variable, column, or field names separated by commas or spaces.
- KEEP does *not* affect the order of variables in the resulting file. Variables are kept in their original order.
- Specifying a variable that is not in the working data file or that has been dropped because of a previous DROP or KEEP subcommand results in an error and the SAVE command is not executed.

Example

```
SAVE TRANSLATE OUTFILE='ADDRESS.DBF' /TYPE=DB4 /DROP=PHONENO, ENTRY.
```

- SAVE TRANSLATE creates a dBASE IV file named *ADDRESS.DBF*, dropping the variables *PHONENO* and *ENTRY*.

RENAME Subcommand

RENAME changes the names of variables as they are copied into the resulting file.

- The specification on RENAME is a list of old variable names followed by an equals sign and a list of new variable names. The same number of variables must be specified on both lists. The keyword TO can be used in the first list to refer to consecutive variables in the working data file and in the second list to generate new variable names (see "Keyword TO" on p. 29). The entire specification must be enclosed in parentheses.
- Alternatively, you can specify each old variable name individually, followed by an equals sign and the new variable name. Multiple sets of variable specifications are allowed. The parentheses around each set of specifications are optional.
- RENAME does not affect the working data file. However, if RENAME precedes DROP or KEEP, variables must be referred to by their new names on DROP or KEEP.
- Old variable names do not need to be specified according to their order in the working data file.
- Name changes take place in one operation. Therefore, variable names can be exchanged between two variables.
- Multiple RENAME subcommands are allowed.

Example

```
SAVE TRANSLATE OUTFILE='STAFF.WRK' /FIELDNAMES
  /RENAME AGE=AGE88 JOBCAT=JOBCAT88.
```

- RENAME renames the variable *AGE* to *AGE88* and *JOBCAT* to *JOBCAT88* before they are copied to the first row of the spreadsheet.

Example

```
SAVE TRANSLATE OUTFILE='STAFF.WRK' /FIELDNAMES
  /RENAME (AGE JOBCAT=AGE88 JOBCAT88).
```

- The name changes are identical to those in the previous example: *AGE* is renamed to *AGE88* and *JOBCAT* is renamed to *JOBCAT88*. The parentheses are required with this method.

MAP Subcommand

MAP displays a list of the variables in the resulting file and their corresponding names in the working data file.

- The only specification is the keyword MAP. There are no additional specifications.
- Multiple MAP subcommands are allowed. Each MAP subcommand maps the results of subcommands that precede it but not the results of subcommands that follow it.

Example

```
GET FILE=HUBEMPL.
SAVE TRANSLATE OUTFILE='STAFF.WRK' /FIELDNAMES
  /RENAME=(AGE=AGE88)(JOBCAT=JOBCAT88).
```

- MAP is specified to confirm that the variable *AGE* is renamed to *AGE88* and *JOBCAT* is renamed to *JOBCAT88*.

SCRIPT

```
SCRIPT 'filename' [(quoted string)]
```

Overview

SCRIPT runs a script created to customize the program or automate regularly performed tasks.

Basic Specification

The basic specification is keyword SCRIPT with a filename. The filename is required. The optional quoted string, enclosed in parentheses, can be passed to the script.

Operations

SCRIPT runs the specified script. The effect is the same as opening the script file in the Script Editor and running it from there.

Running Scripts that Contain SPSS Commands

If a script run via the SCRIPT command contains SPSS commands, those commands must be run asynchronously. To run commands asynchronously, set the bSync parameter of the ExecuteCommands method to False, as in:

```
Dim objSpssApp as ISpssApp
Dim strCommands as String
Set objSpssApp = CreateObject("SPSS.Application")
' Construct and execute syntax commands:

strCommands = "GET FILE = 'c:\spss\bank.sav' " & vbCr
strCommands = strCommands & "Display Dictionary."
objSpssApp.ExecuteCommands strCommands, False
```

SELECT IF

```
SELECT IF [(]logical expression[)]
```

The following relational operators can be used in logical expressions:

Symbol	Definition	Symbol	Definition
EQ or =	Equal to	NE or <>*	Not equal to
LT or <	Less than	LE or <=	Less than or equal to

---

* On ASCII systems (for example, UNIX, VAX, and all PC's) you can also use ~=; on IBM EBCDIC systems (for example, IBM 360 and IBM 370) you can also use ¬=.

The following logical operators can be used in logical expressions:

Symbol	Definition
AND or &	Both relations must be true
OR or |	Either relation can be true

---

* On ASCII systems you can also use ~; on IBM EBCDIC systems you can also use ¬ (or the symbol above number 6).

Example

```
SELECT IF (SEX EQ 'MALE').
```

Overview

SELECT IF permanently selects cases for analysis based upon logical conditions found in the data. These conditions are specified in a *logical expression*. The logical expression can contain relational operators, logical operators, arithmetic operations, and any functions allowed in COMPUTE transformations (see COMPUTE and see "Transformation Expressions" on p. 43). For temporary case selection, specify a TEMPORARY command before SELECT IF.

Basic Specification

The basic specification is simply a logical expression.

Syntax Rules

- Logical expressions can be simple logical variables or relations, or complex logical tests involving variables, constants, functions, relational operators, and logical operators. The logical expression can use any of the numeric or string functions allowed in COMPUTE transformations (see COMPUTE and see "Transformation Expressions" on p. 43).

- Parentheses can be used to enclose the logical expression. Parentheses can also be used within the logical expression to specify the order of operations. Extra blanks or parentheses can be used to make the expression easier to read.

- A relation can compare variables, constants, or more complicated arithmetic expressions. Relations cannot be abbreviated. For example, (A EQ 2 OR A EQ 5) is valid while (A EQ 2 OR 5) is not. Blanks (not commas) must be used to separate relational operators from the expressions being compared.

- A relation cannot compare a string variable to a numeric value or variable, or vice versa. A relation cannot compare the result of the logical functions SYSMIS, MISSING, ANY, or RANGE to a number.

- String values used in expressions must be specified in quotation marks and must include any leading or trailing blanks. Lowercase letters are considered distinct from uppercase letters.

Operations

- SELECT IF permanently selects cases. Cases not selected are dropped from the working data file.

- The logical expression is evaluated as true, false, or missing. If a logical expression is true, the case is selected; if it is false or missing, the case is not selected.

- Multiple SELECT IF commands issued prior to a procedure command must all be true for a case to be selected.

- SELECT IF should be placed before other transformations for efficiency considerations.

- Logical expressions are evaluated in the following order: first numeric functions, then exponentiation, then arithmetic operators, then relational operators, and last logical operators. Use parentheses to change the order of evaluation.

- If N OF CASES is used with SELECT IF, the program reads as many records as required to build the specified n cases. It makes no difference whether the N OF CASES precedes or follows the SELECT IF.

- System variable $CASENUM is the sequence number of a case in the working data file. Although it is syntactically correct to use $CASENUM on SELECT IF, it does not produce the expected results. To select a set of cases based on their sequence in a file, create your own sequence variable with the transformation language prior to selecting (see the example below).

Missing Values

- If the logical expression is indeterminate because of missing values, the case is not selected. In a simple relational expression, a logical expression is indeterminate if the expression on either side of the relational operator is missing.

- If a compound expression is used in which relations are joined by the logical operator OR, the case is selected if either relation is true, even if the other is missing.

- To select cases with missing values for the variables within the expression, use the missing-value functions. To include cases with values that have been declared user-missing along with other cases, use the VALUE function (see p. 58).

Limitations

SELECT IF cannot be placed within a FILE TYPE—END FILE TYPE or INPUT PROGRAM—END INPUT PROGRAM structure. It can be placed nearly anywhere following these commands in a transformation program. See Appendix A for a discussion of program states and the placement of commands.

Example

```
SELECT IF (SEX EQ 'MALE').
```

- All subsequent procedures will use only cases in which the value of *SEX* is MALE.

- Since upper and lower case are treated differently in comparisons of string variables, cases for which the value of *SEX* is male are not selected.

Example

```
SELECT IF (INCOME GT 75000 OR INCOME LE 10000).
```

- The logical expression tests whether a case has a value either greater than 75,000 or less than or equal to 10,000. If either relation is true, the case is used in subsequent analyses.

Example

```
SELECT IF (V1 GE V2).
```

- This example selects cases where variable *V1* is greater than or equal to *V2*. If either *V1* or *V2* is missing, the logical expression is indeterminate and the case is not selected.

Example

```
SELECT IF (SEX = 'F' & INCOME <= 10000).
```

- The logical expression tests whether string variable *SEX* is equal to F and if numeric variable *INCOME* is less than or equal to 10,000. Cases that meet both conditions are included in subsequent analyses. If either *SEX* or *INCOME* is missing for a case, the case is not selected.

Example

```
SELECT IF (SYSMIS(V1)).
```

- The logical expression tests whether *V1* is system-missing. If it is, the case is selected for subsequent analyses.

Example

```
SELECT IF (VALUE(V1) GT 0).
```

- Cases are selected if *V1* is greater than 0, even if the value of *V1* has been declared user-missing.

Example

```
SELECT IF (V1 GT 0).
```

- Cases are not selected if *V1* is user-missing, even if the user-missing value is greater than 0.

Example

```
SELECT IF (RECEIV GT DUE AND (REVNUS GE EXPNS OR BALNCE GT 0)).
```

- By default, AND is executed before OR. This expression uses parentheses to change the order of evaluation.
- The program first tests whether variable *REVNUS* is greater than or equal to variable *EXPNS*, or variable *BALNCE* is greater than 0. Second, the program tests whether *RECEIV* is greater than *DUE*. If one of the expressions in parentheses is true and *RECEIV* is greater than *DUE*, the case is selected.
- Without the parentheses, the program would first test whether *RECEIV* is greater than *DUE* and *REVNUS* is greater than or equal to *EXPNS*. Second, the program would test whether *BALNCE* is greater than 0. If the first two expressions are true *or* if the third expression is true, the case is selected.

Example

```
SELECT IF ((V1-15) LE (V2*(-0.001))).
```

- The logical expression compares whether *V1* minus 15 is less than or equal to *V2* multiplied by −0.001. If it is, the case is selected.

Example

```
SELECT IF ((YRMODA(88,13,0) - YRMODA(YVAR,MVAR,DVAR)) LE 30).
```

- The logical expression subtracts the number of days representing the date *(YVAR, MVAR, and DVAR)* from the number of days representing the last day in 1988. If the difference is less than or equal to 30, the case is selected.

Example

```
* Creating a sequence number.

COMPUTE  #CASESEQ=#CASESEQ+1.
SELECT IF (MOD(#CASESEQ,2)=0).
```

- This example computes a scratch variable, *#CASESEQ*, containing the sequence numbers for each case. Every other case beginning with the second is selected.
- *#CASESEQ* must be a scratch variable so that it is not reinitialized for every case. An alternative is to use the LEAVE command.

Example

```
DO IF   SEX EQ 'M'.
+    SELECT IF PRESTIGE GT 50.
ELSE IF   SEX EQ 'F'.
+    SELECT IF PRESTIGE GT 45.
END IF.
```

- The SELECT IF commands within the DO IF structure select males with prestige scores above 50 and females with prestige scores above 45.

SET

```
SET  [WORKSPACE={512**}]    [MXMEMORY= {14000**}] ]MXCELLS={AUTOMATIC**} ]
                {n   }            {  n      }              {n          }

   [FORMAT={F8.2**}] [CTEMPLATE {NONE**   }
           {Fw.d  }             {filename}

   [TLOOK {NONE**   }]
          {filename}

   [ONUMBERS={LABELS**} ] [OVARS={LABELS**} ]
             {VALUES  }         {NAMES   }
             {BOTH    }         {BOTH    }

   [TFIT={BOTH**} ] [TNUMBERS={VALUES**} ] [TVARS={NAMES**} ]
         {LABELS}            {LABELS  }          {LABELS }
                             {BOTH    }          {BOTH   }

   [SEED={2000000**}
         {RANDOM   }]
         {n        }

   [EPOCH={AUTOMATIC } ]
          {begin year}

   [{ERRORS   } =  {LISTING**}]
    {RESULTS  }    {NONE     }

    {PRINTBACK} = {NONE** }
    {MESSAGES }   {LISTING}

   [JOURNAL=[{YES**}] [filename]]
            {NO   }

   [MEXPAND={ON**}] [MPRINT={OFF**}] [MNEST={50**}] [MITERATE={1000**}]
            {OFF }          {ON   }         {n   }            {n     }

   [BLANKS={SYSMIS**}]    [UNDEFINED={WARN**}]
           {value   }               {NOWARN}

   [MXWARNS={10**}]    [MXLOOPS={40**}]
            {n   }             {n   }

   [EXTENSIONS={OFF**}
               {ON   }

   [COMPRESSION={ON**}]
                {OFF }

   [BLOCK={X'2A'**    }]
          {X'hexchar' }
          {'character'}

   [BOX={X'2D7C2B2B2B2B2B2B2B2B'**}]
        {X'hexstring'            }
        {'character'             }

   [CCA={'-,,,' }] [CCB={'-,,,' }] [CCC={'-,,,' }]
        {'format'}       {'format'}       {'format'}

   [CCD={'-,,,' }] [CCE={'-,,,' }]
        {'format'}       {'format'}
```

```
[HEADER={NO** }]
        {YES  }
        {BLANK}

[LENGTH={59**}]  [WIDTH={80**}]
        {n   }          {132 }
        {NONE}          {n   }
```

** Default setting at installation.

See the discussions of specific subcommands in this manual and consult the documentation for your system for more details.

Example

```
SET BLANKS=0/UNDEFINED=NOWARN/TLOOK='C:\SPSSWIN7\MYTABLE.TLO'.
```

Overview

Many of the running options in the program can be tailored to your own preferences with the SET command. The default settings for these options vary from system to system. To display the current settings, use the SHOW command. A setting changed by SET remains in effect for the entire working session unless changed again by another SET command. The PRESERVE command saves the current settings so that you can return to them later in the session with the RESTORE command. PRESERVE and RESTORE are especially useful with the macro facility.

Options

Memory Management. Dynamically allocate memory using the WORKSPACE and MXMEMORY subcommands when some procedures complain of memory shortage. Increase maximum cell numbers for a pivot table using the MXCELLS subcommand.

Output Format. Change the default (F8.2) print and write formats used for numeric variables using the FORMAT subcommand. Specify a TableLook file and/or a chart template file using the TLOOK and CTEMPLATE subcommands. Define default display of variables in the outline or pivot tables using the ONUMBERS, OVARS, TNUMBERS, and TVARS subcommands, and specify default column widths using the TFIT subcommand.

Samples and Random Numbers. You can change the initial seed value to a particular number using the SEED subcommand.

Output Destination. You can send error messages, resource utilization messages, command printback and the output from your commands to your screen and/or to a file using the ERRORS, MESSAGES, PRINTBACK, and RESULTS subcommands. You can also suppress each of these using the keyword NONE.

Journal Files. You can determine whether or not the program keeps a journal file during a session using the JOURNAL subcommand. A journal file records the commands you have entered along with any error or warning messages generated by the commands. A modified journal file can be used as a command file in subsequent sessions.

Macro Displays. You can control macro expansion, the maximum number of loop iterations, and nesting levels within a macro using the MEXPAND, MITERATE, and MNEST subcommands. You can also control the display of the variables, commands, and parameters that a macro uses using the MPRINT subcommands.

Blanks and Undefined Input Data. You can specify the value that the program should use when it encounters a completely blank field for a numeric variable using the BLANKS subcommand. You can also turn off the warning message that the program issues when it encounters an invalid value for a numeric variable using UNDEFINED.

Maximum Errors and Loops. You can raise or lower the default number of errors and warnings allowed in a session before processing stops using the MXERRS and MXWARNS subcommands. You can raise or lower the maximum number of iterations allowed for the LOOP—END LOOP structure using the MXLOOPS.

Data File Extension. You can specify the default extensions used for SPSS-format data files saved with SAVE or XSAVE or portable files saved with EXPORT using the EXTENSIONS subcommand.

Scratch File Compression. You can specify whether scratch files are kept in compressed or uncompressed form using the COMPRESSION subcommand.

Custom Currency Formats. You can customize currency formats for your own applications using the CCA, CCB, CCC, CCD, and CCE subcommands. For example, you can display currency as French francs rather than American dollars.

Basic Specification

The basic specification is at least one subcommand.

Subcommand Order

Subcommands can be named in any order.

Syntax Rules

- You can specify as many subcommands as needed. Subcommands must be separated by at least one space or slash.
- Only one keyword or argument can be specified for each subcommand.
- SET can be used more than once in the command sequence.
- YES and ON are aliases for each other. NO and OFF are aliases for each other.

Operations

- Settings specified on SET remain in effect until they are changed by another SET command or until the current session is ended.

- Each time SET is used, only the specified settings are changed. All others remain at their previous settings or the default.

Example

```
SET BLANKS=0/UNDEFINED=NOWARN/TLOOK='C:\SPSSWIN7\MYTABLE.TLO'.
```

- BLANKS specifies 0 as the value the program should use when it encounters a completely blank field for a numeric variable.
- UNDEFINED=NOWARN suppresses the message that the program displays whenever anything other than a number or a blank is encountered as the value for a numeric variable.
- TLOOK specifies that the table properties defined in *c:\spsswin7\mytable.tlo* will be used to define the default TableLook in the output. The default is NONE, which uses the TableLook provided as the system default.

WORKSPACE, MXMEMORY, and MXCELLS Subcommands

WORKSPACE and MXMEMORY are used to allocate more memory for some procedures when you receive a message that the available memory has been used up or that only a given number of variables can be processed. MXCELLS is used to increase the maximum number of cells you can create for a new pivot table when you receive a warning that a pivot table cannot be created because it exceeds the maximum number of cells allowed by the available memory.

- WORKSPACE allocates workspace memory in kilobytes for some procedures that allocate only one block of memory, such as Crosstabs or Frequencies. The default is 512.
- MXMEMORY allocates the maximum memory in kilobytes to the program. The default is 14,000.
- Do not increase either the workspace memory or the maximum memory allocation unless the program issues a message that there is not enough memory to complete a procedure.
- Use MXCELLS with caution. Set MXCELLS at a number higher than the limit indicated in the warning message you receive. Set the number back to the default after the table is created.
- The memory allocation or cell maximum number increase takes effect as soon as you run the SET command.

FORMAT Subcommand

FORMAT specifies the default print and write formats for numeric variables. This default format applies to numeric variables defined on DATA LIST in freefield format and to all numeric variables created by transformation commands, unless a format is explicitly specified.

- The specification must be a simple F format. The default is F8.2.
- You can use the PRINT FORMATS, WRITE FORMATS, and FORMATS commands to change print and write formats.

- Format specifications on FORMAT are output formats. When specifying the width, enough positions must be allowed to include any punctuation characters such as decimal points, commas, and dollar signs.

- If a numeric data value exceeds its width specification, the program attempts to display some value nevertheless. First, the program rounds decimal values, then removes punctuation characters, then tries scientific notation, and finally, if there is still not enough space, produces asterisks indicating that a value is present but cannot be displayed in the assigned width.

TLOOK and CTEMPLATE Subcommands

TLOOK and CTEMPLATE specify a file used to define the table and chart appearance in the output. The default for either command is NONE, which produces tables and charts using the system defaults.

- TLOOK determines the properties of output tables produced. The properties include the borders, placement of titles, column and row labels, text font, and column and cell formats.

- CTEMPLATE determines the properties of output charts and plots. The properties include line style, color, fill pattern, and text font of relevant chart elements such as frames, titles, labels, and legends.

- The specification on TLOOK or CTEMPLATE remains in effect until a new TLOOK or CTEMPLATE is specified.

NONE   *Use the system defaults.* The tables and charts in the output do not use customized properties.

filename   *Use the specified file as templates for tables/charts in the output.* You can specify a full path in quotation marks.

ONUMBERS, OVARS, TNUMBERS, and TVARS Subcommands

ONUMBERS, OVARS, TNUMBERS, and TVARS control how variables are displayed in the outline for pivot table output and in the pivot tables.

- ONUMBERS controls the display of variable values in the outline for pivot tables. The default at installation is LABELS.

- OVARS controls the display of variables in the outline for pivot tables. The default at installation is LABELS.

- TNUMBERS controls the display of variable values in the pivot tables. The default at installation is VALUES.

- TVARS controls the display of variables in the pivot tables. The default at installation is NAMES.

NAMES   *Displays variable names.*

VALUES   *Displays variable values.*

LABELS   *Displays variable labels.*

BOTH   *Displays both labels and values for variable values or both names and labels for variables.*

TFIT Subcommand

TFIT controls the default column widths of the pivot tables. The default at installation is BOTH.

BOTH   *Adjust column widths to accommodate both labels and data.*

LABELS   *Adjust column widths to accommodate labels only.* This setting produces compact tables, but data values wider than labels will be displayed as asterisks.

SEED Subcommand

SEED specifies the random number seed. You can specify any integer, preferably a number greater than 1 but less than 2,000,000,000, which approaches the limit on some machines.

- The program uses a pseudo-random-number generator to select random samples or create uniform or normal distributions of random numbers. The generator begins with a *seed,* a large integer. Starting with the same seed, the system will repeatedly produce the same sequence of numbers and will select the same sample from a given data file.

- At the start of each session, the seed is set to a value that may vary or may be fixed, depending on the implementation. You can set the seed yourself with the SEED subcommand.

- By default, the seed value changes each time a random-number series is needed in a session. To repeat the same random distribution within a session, specify the same seed each time.

- The random number seed can be changed any number of times within a session.

- To set the seed to a random number explicitly, use the keyword RANDOM.

Example

```
SET SEED=987654321.
```

- The random number seed is set to the value 987,654,321. The seed will be in effect the next time the random-number generator is called.

EPOCH Subcommand

EPOCH defines the 100-year span dates entered with two-digit years and for date functions with a two-digit year specification.

AUTOMATIC   *100-year span beginning 69 years prior to the current date and ending 30 years after the current date.*

begin year   *First year of the 100-year span.*

Example

```
SET EPOCH=1900.
```

- All dates entered with two-digit year values are read as years between 1900 and 1999. For example, a date entered as 10/29/87 is read as 10/29/1987.

Example

```
SET EPOCH=1980.
```

- Dates entered wth two-digit year values between 80 and 99 are read as years between 1980 and 1999.
- Dates entered with two-digit year values between 00 and 79 are read as years between 2000 and 2079.

ERRORS, MESSAGES, RESULTS, and PRINTBACK Subcommands

ERRORS, MESSAGES, RESULTS, and PRINTBACK are used with keywords LISTING and NONE to route program output. ERRORS, MESSAGES, and RESULTS apply only to text output. PRINT-BACK applies to all commands entered in a syntax window or generated from a dialog box during a session.

- ERRORS refers to both error messages and warning messages for text output.
- MESSAGES refers to resource utilization messages displayed with text output, including the heading and the summaries (such as the amount of memory used by a command).
- RESULTS refers to the text output generated by program commands.
- PRINTBACK refers to command printback in the journal file. Syntax is always displayed as part of the Notes in the syntax window.

LISTING   *Display output in the designated output window.* Alias ON or YES. For PRINTBACK, alias BOTH. The executed commands are printed back in the journal and displayed in the log in the output window. You can either display an icon only or list all of the commands.

NONE   *Suppress the output.* Alias NO or OFF.

The default routes vary from operating system to operating system and according to the way commands are executed. In windowed environments, the typical defaults are:

Subcommand	Windowed environments
ERRORS	Listing
MESSAGES	None
PRINTBACK	Both
RESULTS	Listing

JOURNAL Subcommand

Alias to LOG. The program creates a journal file to keep track of the commands submitted and error and warning messages generated during a session. JOURNAL is used to assign a filename to the journal file or to stop or resume the journal.

- Journal files with the default filename are erased at the beginning of each session. To preserve the contents of a journal file, assign a name with SET JOURNAL at the beginning of the session. Alternatively, if you have used the default name for a journal file, you can rename the file before beginning another session.

- If you use multiple journal files, you should not start with one file, go to another file, and then return to the first file. On many systems, the program will not append new information to the first file but will overwrite the previous contents.

filename *Filename for the journal file.* The default name varies by system.

YES *Start sending commands and messages to the journal file.*

NO *Stop sending commands and messages to the journal file.*

Example

```
SET JOURNAL MYLOG.
GET FILE=HUBDATA.
SET JOURNAL OFF.
LIST.
SET JOURNAL ON.
FREQUENCIES VARIABLES=ALL.
```

- The first SET command opens the journal file *MYLOG.*

- The GET command is copied into the journal file. The SET command then turns the journal off. The LIST command is not copied into the journal file but is executed. The second SET command turns the journal on again, and the FREQUENCIES command is copied into the journal file.

MEXPAND and MPRINT Subcommands

MEXPAND and MPRINT control whether macros are expanded and whether the expanded macros are displayed. For more information on macros, see DEFINE and Appendix D.
The specifications for MEXPAND are:

ON *Expand macros.* This is the default.

OFF *Do not expand macros.* The command line that calls the macro is treated like any other command line. If the macro call is an command, it will be executed; otherwise, it will trigger an error message.

The specifications for MPRINT are:

ON *Include expanded macro commands in the output.*

OFF *Exclude expanded macro commands from the output.* This is the default.

- MPRINT is effective only when MEXPAND is ON and is independent of the PRINTBACK subcommand.

MITERATE and MNEST Subcommands

MITERATE and MNEST control the maximum loop traversals and the maximum nesting levels permitted in macro expansions, respectively.

- The specification on MITERATE or MNEST is a positive integer. The default for MITERATE is 1000. The default for MNEST is 50.

BLANKS Subcommand

BLANKS specifies the value the program should use when it encounters a completely blank field for a numeric variable. By default, the program uses the system-missing value.

- BLANKS controls only the translation of numeric fields. If a blank field is read with a string format, the resulting value is a blank.
- The value specified on BLANKS is not automatically defined as a missing value.
- The BLANKS specification applies to all numeric variables. You cannot use different specifications for different variables.
- BLANKS must be specified before data are read. Otherwise, blanks in numeric fields are converted to the system-missing value (the default) as they are read.

UNDEFINED Subcommand

UNDEFINED controls whether the program displays a warning message when it encounters anything other than a number or a blank as the value for a numeric variable. The default is WARN.

- Warning messages that are suppressed are still counted toward the maximum allowed before the session is terminated. To control the number of warnings (and therefore the number of invalid values) allowed in a session, use the MXWARNS subcommand.

WARN   *Display a warning message when an invalid value is encountered for a numeric variable.* This is the default.

NOWARN   *Suppress warning messages for invalid values.*

MXWARNS Subcommand

MXWARNS controls the maximum number of error messages and warnings the program displays for text output during one working session. The default for MXWARNS is 10.

- All errors are included with warnings in the count toward the MXWARNS limit. Notes are not.
- If you have set MXWARNS, the program stops displaying warning messages when the limit is exceeded but the working session continues.
- The setting on MXWARNS has no effect on output displayed in pivot tables.

Example

```
SET MXWARNS=200.
```

- MXWARNS specifies that a maximum of 200 warnings can be displayed. When the limit is exceeded, the program stops displaying warnings if it is in a windowed environment or if it is running the commands interactively. Otherwise, the session is terminated.

MXLOOPS Subcommand

MXLOOPS specifies the maximum number of times a loop defined by the LOOP—END LOOP structure is executed for a single case or input record. The default is 40.

- MXLOOPS prevents infinite loops, which may occur if no cutoff is specified for the loop structure (see LOOP—END LOOP).
- When a loop is terminated, control passes to the command immediately following the END LOOP command, even if the END LOOP condition is not yet met.

EXTENSIONS Subcommand

EXTENSIONS controls whether the program adds default extensions to the data files it saves during a session. The default extensions are *.SAV* for SPSS-format data files saved with SAVE or XSAVE and *.POR* for portable data files saved with EXPORT. The specification on EXTENSIONS is either OFF or ON. The default is OFF.

- EXTENSIONS is effective only when you run SAVE, XSAVE, or EXPORT with command syntax. It does not affect files saved using a dialog box in windowed environments.
- EXTENSIONS has no effect when the filename is specified in apostrophes or quotation marks.

OFF *Do not use default extensions.* This is the default.

ON *Add a default extension to the file if an extension is not explicitly specified.*

Example

```
SET EXTENSIONS=ON.
SAVE OUTFILE=BANK89.
SAVE OUTFILE='BANK89'.
```

- This example saves two SPSS-format data files from the same working file. The first SAVE command saves the working data file as *BANK89.SAV;* the second SAVE command saves the working file as *BANK89* regardless of the setting on EXTENSIONS.

COMPRESSION Subcommand

COMPRESSION determines whether scratch files created during a session are in compressed or uncompressed form.

- A compressed scratch file occupies less space on disk than does an uncompressed scratch file but requires more processing.

- The specification takes effect the next time a scratch file is written and stays in effect until SET COMPRESSION is specified again or until the end of the session.
- The default setting varies. Use SHOW to display the default on your system.

YES   *Compress scratch files.*

NO   *Do not compress scratch files.*

BLOCK Subcommand

BLOCK specifies the character used for drawing icicle plots.

- You can specify any single character either as a quoted string or as a quoted hexadecimal pair preceded by the character *X*.
- The default is X'2A'.

Example

```
SET BLOCK='#'.
```

- This command specifies a pound sign (#) as the character to be used for drawing bar charts. The character is specified as a quoted string.

BOX Subcommand

BOX specifies the characters used to draw grids in MULT RESPONSE. Other procedures may also use these characters in plots and other displays. The specification is either a 3- or an 11-character quoted string, in which the characters represent, respectively:

1	horizontal line	7	upper-right corner
2	vertical line	8	left T
3	middle (cross)	9	right T
4	lower-left corner	10	top T
5	upper-left corner	11	bottom T
6	lower-right corner		

- The characters can be specified either as a quoted string or hexadecimal pairs. Specify an *X* before the quoted hexadecimal pairs.
- The defaults vary from system to system. To display the current settings, use the SHOW command.
- The default is X'2D7C2B2B2B2B2B2B2B2B2B'.

LENGTH and WIDTH Subcommands

LENGTH and WIDTH specify the maximum page length and width for the output, respectively. The default for LENGTH is 59 lines; the default for WIDTH is 80. These two subcommands apply only to text output.

- The page length includes the first printed line on the page through the last line that can be printed. The printer you use most likely includes a margin at the top; that margin is not included in the length used by this program. The default, 59 lines, allows for a 1/2-inch margin at the top and bottom of an 11-inch page printed with 6 lines per inch, or an 8 1/2-inch page printed with 8 lines per inch.

- You can specify any length from 40 through 999,999 lines. If a long page length is specified, the program continues to provide page ejects and titles at the start of each procedure and at logical points in the display, such as between crosstabulations.

- To suppress page ejects, use keyword NONE on LENGTH. The program will insert titles at logical points in the display but will not supply page ejects.

- You can specify any number of characters from 80 through 132 for WIDTH. The specified width does not include the carriage control character. All procedures can fit the output to an 80-column page.

HEADER Subcommand

HEADER controls whether the output includes headings. The HEADER subcommand applies to both default headings and those specified on the TITLE and SUBTITLE commands. This command applies only to text output from this program. The default is NO.

NO *Suppress headings in text output.* All general headings, including pagination, are replaced by a single blank line.

YES *Display headings in text output.*

BLANK *Suppress headings but start a new page.*

CCA, CCB, CCC, CCD, and CCE Subcommands

You can specify up to five custom currency formats using the subcommands CCA, CCB, CCC, CCD, and CCE. In the Windows environment, use the Regional Settings Properties to set the currency formats.

- Each custom currency subcommand defines one custom format and can include four specifications in the following order: a negative prefix, a prefix, a suffix, and a negative suffix.

- The specifications are separated by either periods or commas, whichever you do not want to use as a decimal point in the format.

- Each currency specification must always contain three commas or three periods. All other specifications are optional.

- Use blanks in the specification only where you want blanks in the format.

- The entire specification must be enclosed in apostrophes.
- A specification cannot exceed 16 characters (excluding the apostrophes).
- Custom currency formats cannot be specified as input formats on DATA LIST. Use them only as output formats in the FORMATS, WRITE FORMATS, PRINT FORMATS, WRITE, and PRINT commands.

Example

```
SET CCA='-,$,,'.
```

- A minus sign (–) preceding the first command is used as the negative prefix.
- A dollar sign is specified for the prefix.
- No suffixes are specified (there are two consecutive commas before the closing apostrophe).
- Since commas are used as separators in the specification, the decimal point is represented by a period.

Example

```
SET CCA='(,,,-)'  CCB=',,%,'  CCC='(,$,,)'  CCD='-/-.Dfl ..-'.
FORMATS VARA(CCA9.0)/ VARB(CCB6.1)/ VARC(CCC8.0)/ VARD(CCD14.2).
```

- SET defines four custom currency formats. Table 1 summarizes the currency specifications.
- FORMATS assigns these formats to specific variables.

Table 1   Custom currency examples

	CCA	CCB	CCC	CCD
negative prefix	(	none	(	-/-
prefix	none	none	$	Dfl
suffix	none	%	none	none
negative suffix	-)	none	)	-
separator	,	,	,	.
sample positive number	23,456	13.7%	$352	Dfl 37.419,00
sample negative number	(19,423-)	13.7%	($189)	-/-Dfl 135,19-

SHOW

```
SHOW [ALL] [BLANKS] [BLKSIZE] [BOX] [BLOCK] [BUFNO] [CC] [CCA] [CCB]

     [CCC] [CCD] [CCE] [COMPRESSION] [CTEMPLATE] [ERRORS] [EXTENSIONS] [FORMAT]

     [HEADER] [JOURNAL] [LENGTH] [MESSAGES] [MEXPAND]

     [MITERATE] [MNEST] [MPRINT] [MXCELLS] [MXLOOPS] [MXMEMORY] [MXWARNS]

     [N] [ONUMBERS] [OVARS] [PRINTBACK] [RESULTS] [SCOMPRESSION] [SEED]

     [SYSMIS] [TFIT] [TLOOK] [TNUMBERS] [TVARS] [UNDEFINED]

     [WEIGHT] [WIDTH] [WORKSPACE] [$VARS]
```

Overview

SHOW displays current settings for running options. Most of these settings can be changed with the SET command.

Basic Specification

The basic specification is simply the command keyword, which displays important current settings (keyword ALL). Some displayed option settings are applicable only when you have options such as Tables and Categories.

Subcommand Order

Subcommands can be named in any order.

Syntax

- If any subcommands are specified, only the requested settings are displayed.
- SHOW can be specified more than once.

Example

```
SHOW BLANKS /UNDEFINED /MXWARNS.
```

- BLANKS shows the value to which a completely blank field for a numeric variable is translated.
- UNDEFINED indicates whether a message displays whenever the program encounters anything other than a number or a blank as the value for a numeric variable.

- MXWARNS displays the maximum number of warnings allowed before a session is terminated.

Subcommands

The following alphabetical list shows the available subcommands.

ALL
Display important settings applicable to your system. This is the default.

BLANKS
Value to which a completely blank field for a numeric variable is translated. The default is the system-missing value.

BLKSIZE
Default block length used for scratch files and SPSS-format data files. The default varies by system. BLKSIZE cannot be changed with SET.

BOX
Characters used to draw boxes. Both character and hexadecimal representations are displayed. The default is X'2D7C2B2B2B2B2B2B2B2B2B'. This setting applies only to text output from the program.

BLOCK
Character used to draw bar charts. Both character and hexadecimal representations are displayed. The default is X'2A'. This setting applies only to the text output from the program.

BUFFNO
The default number of buffers used for all files managed by the system for input and output. The default varies by system. BUFFNO cannot be changed with SET.

CC
Custom currency formats. CC shows the current custom currency formats that have been defined for CCA, CCB, CCC, CCD, and CCE on SET. In Windows environments, they reflect the Regional Settings Properties. You can also request any of these keywords individually.

COMPRESSION
Compression of scratch files. The setting is either ON or OFF (alias YES or NO). The default varies by system.

CTEMPLATE
Chart template file. The setting is either NONE or a filename.

ERRORS
Error messages for text output. The setting can be LISTING (alias YES or ON) or NONE (alias NO or OFF).

EXTENSIONS
Default extensions for saved data files. The setting is either ON or OFF. The default is OFF.

FORMAT
Default print and write formats for numeric variables defined on DATA LIST in freefield format and to all numeric variables created by transformation commands. The default is F8.2.

HEADER
Headings for text output. The setting is YES, NO, or BLANK. The default is NO.

JOURNAL
Journal file during a session. The setting is either ON or OFF (alias YES or NO). The default varies by system.

LENGTH   *Maximum page length for output.* The default is 59. This setting applies only to the text output from the program.

MESSAGES   *Resource utilization messages for text output.* The setting can be LISTING (alias YES or ON) or NONE (alias NO or OFF).

MEXPAND   *Macro expansion.* The setting is either ON (alias YES) or OFF (alias NO). The default is ON.

MITERATE   *Maximum loop iterations permitted in macro expansions.* The default is 1000.

MNEST   *Maximum nesting level for macros.* The default is 50.

MPRINT   *Inclusion of expanded macros in the output.* The setting is either ON (alias YES) or OFF (alias NO). The default is OFF.

MXCELLS   *Maximum number of cells allowed for a new pivot table.* The default is AUTOMATIC, allowing the number to be determined by the available memory.

MXLOOPS   *Maximum executions of a loop on a single case.* The default is 40.

MXMEMORY   *Maximum memory allocation in kilobytes.* The default is 14,000.

MXWARNS   *Maximum number of warnings and errors shown for text output.* The default is 10.

N   *Unweighted number of cases in the working data file.* N displays *UNKNOWN* if a working data file has not yet been created. N cannot be changed with SET.

ONUMBERS   *Display of variable values in the outline for pivot tables.* The settings can be LABELS, VALUES, and BOTH.

OVARS   *Display of variables as headings.* The settings can be LABELS, NAMES, and BOTH.

PRINTBACK   *Command printback.* The setting can be BOTH (alias LISTING, YES, or ON) or NONE (alias NO or OFF). The default is BOTH at system installation.

RESULTS   *Output from commands.* Not applicable to output displayed in pivot tables. The setting can be LISTING (alias YES or ON) or NONE (alias NO or OFF).

SCOMPRESSION   *Compression of SPSS-format data files.* This setting can be overridden by the COMPRESSED or UNCOMPRESSED subcommands on the SAVE or XSAVE commands. The default setting varies by system. SCOMPRESSION cannot be changed with SET.

SEED   *Seed for the random-number generator.* The default is generally 2,000,000 but may vary by system.

SYSMIS   *The system-missing value.* SYSMIS cannot be changed with SET.

TFIT *Adjust column widths in pivot tables.* The settings can be BOTH (label and data) and LABELS.

TLOOK *Pivot table template file.* The setting can be either NONE or a filename.

TNUMBER *Display of variable values in pivot tables.* The settings can be VALUES, LABELS, and BOTH.

TVARS *Display of variables as headings.* The settings can be NAMES, LABELS, and BOTH.

UNDEFINED *Warning message for undefined data.* WARN is the default. NOWARN suppresses messages but does not alter the count of warnings toward the MXWARNS total.

WEIGHT *Variable used to weight cases.* WEIGHT can be specified for SHOW only; it cannot be changed with SET.

WIDTH *Maximum page width for the output.* The default is 132 columns for batch mode and 80 for interactive mode. This setting applies only to text output from the program.

WORKSPACE *Special workspace memory limit in kilobytes.* The default is 512.

$VARS *Values of system variables.* $VARS cannot be changed with SET.

SORT CASES

```
SORT CASES [BY] varlist[({A})] [varlist...]
                        {D}
```

Example

```
SORT CASES BY DIVISION (A) STORE (D).
```

Overview

SORT CASES reorders the sequence of cases in the working data file based on the values of one or more variables. You can optionally sort cases in ascending or descending order, or use combinations of ascending and descending order for different variables.

Basic Specification

The basic specification is a variable or list of variables that are used as sort keys. By default, cases are sorted in ascending order of each variable, starting with the first variable named. For each subsequent variable, cases are sorted in ascending order within categories of the previously named variables.

Syntax Rules

- Keyword BY is optional.
- BY variables can be numeric or string but not scratch, system, or temporary variables.
- You can explicitly request the default sort order (ascending) by specifying A or UP in parentheses after the variable name. To sort cases in descending order, specify D or DOWN.
- An order specification (A or D) applies to all variables in the list up to the previous order specification. If you combine ascending and descending order on the same SORT CASES command, you may need to specify the default A explicitly.

Operations

- SORT CASES first sorts the file according to the first variable named. For subsequent variables, cases are sorted within categories of the previously named variables.
- The sort sequence of string variables depends on the character set in use on your system. With EBCDIC character sets, most special characters are sorted first, followed by lowercase alphabetical characters, uppercase alphabetical characters, and, finally, numbers. The order is almost exactly reversed with ASCII character sets. Numbers are sorted first, followed by uppercase alphabetical characters and then lowercase alphabetical characters. In

addition, special characters are sorted between the other character types. Use the INFO command (not available on all systems) to obtain information on the character set in use on your system and the exact sort sequence.

SORT CASES with Other Procedures

- In AGGREGATE, cases are sorted in order of the break variable or variables. You do not have to use SORT CASES prior to running AGGREGATE, since the procedure does its own sorting.
- You can use SORT CASES in conjunction with the BY keyword in ADD FILES to interleave cases with the same variables but from different files.
- With MATCH FILES, cases must be sorted in the same order for all files you combine.
- With UPDATE, cases must be sorted in ascending order of the key variable or variables in both the master file and all transaction files.
- You can use the PRINT command to check the results of a SORT CASES command. PRINT must be followed by a procedure or EXECUTE to be executed.

Example

```
SORT CASES BY DIVISION (A) STORE (D).
```

- Cases are sorted in ascending order of variable *DIVISION*. Cases are further sorted in descending order of *STORE* within categories of *DIVISION*. A must be specified so that D applies to *STORE* only.

Example

```
SORT DIVISION STORE (A) AGE (D).
```

- Cases are sorted in ascending order of *DIVISION*. Keyword BY is not used in this example.
- Cases are further sorted in ascending order of *STORE* within values of *DIVISION*. Specification A applies to both *DIVISION* and *STORE*.
- Cases are further sorted in descending order of *AGE* within values of *STORE* and *DIVISION*.

SPCHART

This command is available only on systems with high-resolution graphics capabilities.

```
SPCHART
 [/TEMPLATE='filename']

 [/TITLE='line 1' ['line 2']]
 [/SUBTITLE='line 1']
 [/FOOTNOTE='line 1' ['line 2']]

 {[/XR=]{var BY var               } }
        {var var [var var...][BY var]}
 { /XS= {var BY var               } }
        {var var [var var...][BY var]}
 { /IR= var [BY var]              }
 { /I= var [BY var]               }
 { /NP= {var BY var               }}
        {COUNT(var) N({var }) [BY var]}
        {value                    }
 { /P= {var BY var                }}
       {COUNT(var) N({var }) [BY var]}
       {value                     }
 { /C= {var BY var                }}
       {COUNT(var) N({var }) [BY var]}
       {value                     }
 { /U= {var BY var                }}
       {COUNT(var) N({var  }) [BY var]}
                      {value}

 [/STATISTICS = [CP] [CPL] [CPU] [K] [CPK] [CR] [CPM]
                [CZL] [CZU] [CZMIN] [CZMAX] [CZOUT]
                [PP] [PPL] [PPU] [PPK] [PR] [PPM]
                [PZL] [PZU] [PZMIN] [PZMAX] [PZOUT]
                [AZOUT] ]

 [/CAPSIGMA = [{RBAR  }]]
              {SBAR  }
              {MRBAR }
              {WITHIN}

 [/SPAN={2**}]
        {n  }

 [{/CONFORM  }=value]
  {/NOCONFORM}

 [/SIGMA={3**}]
        {n  }

 [/MINSAMPLE={2**}]
            {n  }

 [/LSL=value]    [/USL=value]

 [TARGET = value]

 [/MISSING=[{NOREPORT**}] [{EXCLUDE**}]
            {REPORT   }   {INCLUDE  }
```

**Default if the subcommand is omitted.

Overview

SPCHART generates several types of high-resolution control charts. A control chart plots a quality characteristic measured or computed from a sample versus the sample number or time. It is a widely used process-control technique for testing the hypothesis that the process is in a state of statistical control. All control charts display four series:

- The process line representing the quality characteristic for each sample.
- The center line indicating the average value of the quality characteristic corresponding to the in-control state.
- Two horizontal lines showing the upper control limit and the lower control limit.

Control charts are used as a technique for improving productivity, preventing defects and unnecessary process adjustments, and gathering information about process capability.

SPCHART produces X-bar, R, s, individuals, and moving range charts as well as np, p, c, and u charts. You may need to transform your data so that they conform to the required data organization described under each chart type subcommand.

Control charts are available only on systems where high-resolution display is available.

Options

Titles and Footnotes. You can specify a title, subtitle, and footnote for the control chart using the TITLE, SUBTITLE, and FOOTNOTE subcommands.

Chart Type. You can request a specific type of control chart using the XR, XS, IR, I, NP, P, C, or U subcommand.

Templates. You can specify a template, using the TEMPLATE subcommand, to override the default chart attribute settings on your system.

Control Limits. You can specify a sigma value on the SIGMA subcommand to modify the calculated upper and lower control limits. You can also specify fixed limits using the USL and LSL subcommands. The upper and lower limits you specify will be displayed simultaneously with the calculated control limits.

Basic Specification

The basic specification is a chart type subcommand. By default, the title of the generated chart is Control Chart followed by the label of the process variable. The subtitle provides split-file information if split-file processing is in effect, and the one-line footnote provides the sigma value.

Subcommand Order

Subcommands can be specified in any order.

Syntax Rules

- Only one chart type subcommand can be specified.
- Keyword SPAN is used only with IR and I subcommands.
- Keyword CONFORM or NOCONFORM is used only with NP and P subcommands.

Operations

- SPCHART plots four basic series: the process, the center line, the upper control line, and the lower control line.
- The chart title, subtitle, and footnote are assigned as they are specified on TITLE, SUBTITLE, and FOOTNOTE subcommands. If you do not use these subcommands, the chart title is Control Chart, followed by the label of the process variable, and a one-line footnote displays the sigma level.
- The category variable label is used as the title for the category axis. If no variable label is defined, the variable name is used. If no category variable is defined, the title is null.
- The category variable value labels are used as the category axis labels. If no value labels are defined, values are used. If no category variable is defined, integer values from 1 to n are used, where n is the number of subgroups or units plotted.
- All series are plotted as lines. When a series has a constant value across all samples, the value is reported in the legend entry for the series.
- Case weights are not honored for control charts when each case is a subgroup. They are honored when each case is a unit and when the weights are integers. When weighted data are used in an individuals chart, replicated cases are plotted on the control chart.
- The calculated control limits are always displayed and can be suppressed only by editing the chart in a chart window.
- You can specify preset control limits for an X-bar or I chart, as some industries often do. The specified control limits are displayed simultaneously with the calculated limits.

Limitations

- Control charts cannot have fewer than 2 or more than 3000 points.
- The subgroup size in X-bar and range charts cannot exceed 100.
- The span for individual charts is limited to 100.

Example

```
SPCHART   /TEMPLATE='CNTR.CHT'
  /IR=SUBSIZE.
```

- This command generates an individuals chart and a moving range chart. The process variable *SUBSIZE* is a numeric variable that measures the size variation of the product.
- Both charts uses the attributes defined for the template saved in *CNTR.CHT*.

- The default span (2) and sigma value (3) are used.
- Since no BY variable is specified, the *x* axis is labeled by sequence numbers.

TITLE, SUBTITLE, and FOOTNOTE Subcommands

TITLE, SUBTITLE, and FOOTNOTE specify lines of text placed at the top or bottom of the control chart.

- One or two lines of text can be specified for TITLE or FOOTNOTE, and one line of text can be specified for SUBTITLE.
- Each line of text must be enclosed in apostrophes or quotation marks. The maximum length of any line is 72 characters.
- The default font sizes and types are used for the title, subtitle, and footnote.
- By default, the title, subtitle, and footnote are left-aligned with the *y* axis.
- If you do not specify TITLE, the default title is Control Chart followed by the label of the process variable.
- If you do not specify SUBTITLE, the subtitle provides the split-file information if split-file processing is in effect; otherwise it is null, which leaves more space for the chart.
- If you do not specify FOOTNOTE, the sigma level is identified as the first line of the footnote.

Example

```
SPCHART TITLE = 'Wheel Production'
  /SUBTITLE = 'Process Control'
  /IR=SUBSIZE.
```

XR and XS Subcommands

XR produces an X-bar chart and an R chart. XS produces an X-bar chart and an s chart. X-bar, R, and s charts are control charts for continuous variables, such as size, weight, length, and temperature.

An X-bar chart plots the mean of each subgroup. The center line indicates the mean of subgroup means. The control limits are calculated from subgroup means, numbers, standard deviations, and the user-specified SIGMA value (see "SIGMA Subcommand" on p. 1135). Figure 1 shows an X-bar chart.

Figure 1   X-bar chart

An R chart plots range values (maximum-minimum) of successive subgroups. The center line indicates the mean of subgroup ranges. The control limits are calculated from subgroup ranges, numbers, and the user-specified SIGMA value (see "SIGMA Subcommand" on p. 1135). The R chart tests whether the process variability is in control. When the subgroup size is relatively small (4, 5, or 6), the range method yields almost as good an estimator of the variance as does the subgroup variance. Figure 2 shows an R chart.

Figure 2   R chart

An s chart plots subgroup standard deviations. The center line indicates the mean of subgroup standard deviations. The control limits are calculated from subgroup standard deviations, numbers, and the user-specified SIGMA value (see "SIGMA Subcommand" on p. 1135). The s chart tests whether the process variability is in control, especially when the subgroup size is from moderate to large. Figure 3 shows an s chart.

Figure 3 S chart

Data Organization

For X-bar, R, or s charts, data can be organized in two ways: each case is a unit or each case is a subgroup.

- Each case is a unit with a subgroup identifier. Cases are assigned to a category according to the value of the identifier. Table 1 is an example of this type of data organization. The data do not have to be sorted by subgroup. A BY variable (the subgroup identifier) is required to sort and aggregate data and label the process variable.

- Each case is a subgroup. There are as many variables as individuals within one sample. A sample identifier is not required. When there is one, it is used for labeling. Table 2 shows the same data as Table 1 but organized in a different way.

Table 1 Each case is a unit for X-bar, R, and s charts

Subgroup	Length
8:50	6.35
11:30	6.39
8:50	6.40
11:30	6.46
8:50	6.32
11:30	6.37
8:50	6.39
11:30	6.36
...	...

Table 2 Each case is a subgroup for X-bar, R, and s charts

Subgroup	N1	N2	N3	N4
8:50	6.35	6.40	6.32	6.39
11:30	6.39	6.46	6.37	6.36
...	...	...	...	...

Variable Specification

If data are organized as shown in Table 1, the variable specifications on XR and XS subcommands are

```
VAR BY VAR
```

The variable specified before BY is the process variable, the variable that contains values for all instances to be plotted (for example, *LENGTH* in Table 1). The variable specified after BY is the category variable or the BY variable, which is the subgroup identifier (for example, *SUBGROUP* in Table 1). The process variable must be numeric while the category variable can be of any type. The chart is sorted by the category variable.

If data are organized as shown in Table 2, the variable specifications on XR and XS subcommands are

```
VAR VAR [VAR...] [BY VAR]
```

Each of the variables specified before BY represents an instance to be plotted (for example, *N1* to *N3* in Table 2). At least two variables are required and each must be numeric. Keyword BY and the category variable (for example, *SUBGROUP* in Table 2) are optional; if specified, the category variable provides labels for the category axis and can be any type of variable. If omitted, the category axis is labeled from 1 to the number of variables specified before keyword BY.

Example

```
SPCHART /TEMPLATE='CTRL.CHT'
 /XR SUBSIZE BY SHIFT.
```

- The data are organized as shown in Table 1. *SUBSIZE* is a numeric variable that measures the part size. *SHIFT* contains the subgroup identifier (work shift number).
- The chart template is stored in the chart file *CTRL.CHT*.

I and IR Subcommands

I produces an individuals chart and IR produces an individuals and a moving range chart. Both types are control charts for continuous variables, such as size, weight, length, and temperature.

An individuals chart plots each individual observation on a control chart. The center line indicates the mean of all individual values and the control limits are calculated from the mean of the moving ranges, the span, and the user-specified SIGMA value. Individuals charts are often used with moving range charts to test process variability when the subgroup size is 1. This occurs frequently when automated inspection and measurement technology is used and every unit manufactured is analyzed. It also occurs when the process is so slow that a larger subgroup size becomes impractical. Figure 4 shows an individuals chart.

Figure 4   Individuals chart

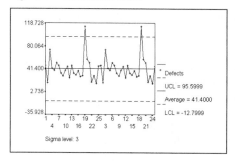

A moving range chart plots moving ranges of *n* successive observations on a control chart, where *n* is the specified span (see "SPAN Subcommand" on p. 1135). The center line is the mean of moving ranges and the control limits are calculated from the ranges, the span, and the user-specified SIGMA value (see "SIGMA Subcommand" on p. 1135). Figure 5 shows a moving range chart.

Figure 5   Moving range chart

Data Organization

For individuals and moving range charts, data must be organized so that each case is a unit. Cases are not sorted or aggregated before plotting.

Variable Specification

The variable specification for I or IR subcommand is

```
VAR [BY VAR]
```

You must specify the process variable that contains the value for each individual observation. Each observation is plotted for the individuals chart. The range of *n* consecutive observations (where *n* is the value specified on the SPAN subcommand) is calculated and plotted for the moving range chart. The range data for the first *n*-1 cases are missing, but the mean and the limit series are not.

Keyword BY and the category variable are optional. When specified, the category variable is used for labeling the category axis and can be any type of variable. If omitted, the category axis is labeled 1 to the number of individual observations in the process variable.

Example

```
SPCHART /TEMPLATE='CTRL.CHT'
  /IR=SUBSIZE.
```

- This command requests an individuals chart and a moving range chart. The two charts are shown in Figure 4 and Figure 5.
- The default span (2) and sigma value (3) are used.

P and NP Subcommands

P produces a p chart and NP produces an np chart. Both types are control charts for attributes. That is, they use data that can be counted, such as the number of nonconformities and the percentage of defects.

A p chart plots the **fraction nonconforming** on a control chart. Fraction nonconforming is the proportion of nonconforming or defective items in a subgroup to the total number of items in that subgroup. It is usually expressed as a decimal or, occasionally, as a percentage. The center line of the control chart is the mean of the subgroup fractions and the control limits are based on a binomial distribution and can be controlled by the user-specified SIGMA value.

Figure 6   P chart

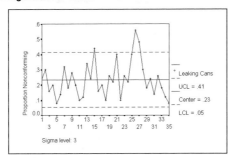

An np chart plots the number nonconforming rather than the fraction nonconforming. The center line is the mean of the numbers of nonconforming or defective items. The control limits are based on the binomial distribution and can be controlled by the user-specified SIGMA value. When the subgroup sizes are unequal, np charts are not recommended.

Figure 7   NP chart

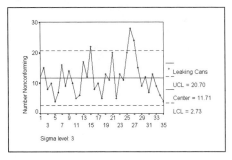

Data Organization

Data for p and np charts can be organized in two ways: each case is a unit or each case is a subgroup.

- Each case is a unit with a conformity status variable and a subgroup identifier. Cases are assigned to a category by the value of the subgroup identifier. Table 3 is an example of this type of data organization. The data do not have to be sorted. A BY variable (the subgroup identifier) is required to sort and aggregate data and label the category axis.

- Each case is a subgroup. One variable contains the total number of items within a subgroup and one variable contains the total number of nonconforming or defective items in the subgroup. The subgroup identifier is optional. If specified, it is used for labeling purposes. Table 4 is an example of this type of data organization. The data are the same as used in Table 3.

Table 3   Each case is a unit for p and np charts

Subgroup	Outcome
January	Cured
January	Cured
January	Cured
January	Relapse
February	Relapse
February	Cured
February	Relapse
February	Relapse
...	...

Table 4   Each case is a subgroup for p and np charts

Subgroup	Relapse	N
January	1	4
February	3	4
...	...	...

Variable Specification

If data are organized as illustrated in Table 3, the variable specification on P or NP subcommands is

```
VAR BY VAR
```

The variable specified before BY is the status variable (for example, *OUTCOME* in Table 3). The value of this variable determines whether an item is considered conforming or nonconforming. The status variable can be any type, but if it is a string, the value specified on CONFORM (or NOCONFORM) must be enclosed in apostrophes (see "CONFORM and NOCONFORM Subcommands" on p. 1135). The variable specified after BY is the category variable. It can be any type of variable. The chart is sorted by values of the category variable.

If data are organized as shown in Table 4, the variable specification on P or NP is

```
COUNT(VAR) N({VAR}) [BY VAR]
           {VAL}
```

The variable specified on keyword COUNT is the variable containing the number of nonconforming or defective items (for example, *RELAPSE* in Table 4). The specification on keyword N is either the variable containing the sample size or a positive integer for a constant size across samples (for example, *N* in Table 4). The COUNT variable cannot be larger than the N variable for any given subgroup; if it is, the subgroup is dropped from calculation and plotting. Keyword BY and the category variable are optional. When specified, the category variable is used for category axis labels; otherwise, the category axis is labeled 1 to the number of subgroups. Cases are unsorted for the control chart.

C and U Subcommands

C produces a c chart and U produces a u chart. Both types are control charts for attributes. That is, they use data that can be counted.

A c chart plots the total number of defects or nonconformities in each subgroup. A defect or nonconformity is one specification that an item fails to satisfy. Each nonconforming item has at least one defect, but any nonconforming item may have more than one defect. The center line of the c chart indicates the mean of the defect numbers of all subgroups. The control limits are based on the Poisson distribution and can be controlled by the user-specified SIGMA value. When the sample sizes are not equal, c charts are not recommended.

Figure 8   C chart

A u chart plots the average number of defects or nonconformities per inspection unit within a subgroup. Each subgroup contains more than one inspection unit. The center line of the u chart indicates the average number of defects per unit of all subgroups. The control limits are based on Poisson distribution and can be controlled by the user-specified SIGMA value.

Figure 9   U chart

Data Organization

Data for c and u charts can be organized in two ways: each case is a unit or each case is a subgroup.

- Each case is a unit with a variable containing the number of defects for that unit and a subgroup identifier. Cases are assigned to each subgroup by the value of the identifier. Table 5 is an example of this type of data organization. Data do not have to be sorted by subgroup. A BY variable (the subgroup identifier) is required to sort and aggregate data and to label the category axis.

- Each case is a subgroup. One variable contains the total number of units within the subgroup and one variable contains the total number of defects for all units within the subgroup. The subgroup identifier is optional. When specified, it is used as category axis labels; otherwise, the number 1 to the number of subgroups are used to label the category axis. Table 6 is an example of this method of data organization. The data are the same as in Table 5.

Table 5   Each case is a unit for c and u charts

ID	Subgroup	Count
1	January	0
2	January	2
3	January	0
4	January	0
5	February	5
6	February	1
7	February	0
8	February	0
...	...	...

Table 6   Each case is a sample for c and u charts

Subgroup	Relapses	N
JANUARY	1	4
FEBRUARY	3	4
...	...	...

Variable Specification

If data are organized as in Table 5, the variable specification on C and U subcommands is

```
VAR BY VAR
```

The variable specified before keyword BY contains the number of defects in each unit (for example, *COUNT* in Table 5). It must be numeric. The variable specified after keyword BY is the subgroup identifier (for example, *SUBGROUP* in Table 5). It can be any type of variable. The chart is sorted by values of the subgroup identifier.

If data are organized as shown in Table 6, the variable specification on C and U subcommands is

```
COUNT(VAR) N({VAR}) [BY VAR]
              {VAL}
```

The specification is the same as that for p and np charts.

STATISTICS Subcommand

Any keyword may be specified in any place in the subcommand, but for a conceptual clarity the keywords are organized as follows: the Process Capability Indices, the Process Performance Indices, and the Measure(s) for Assessing Normality.

- This subcommand is silently ignored if the chart is not one of XR, XS, IR, and I.

- A duplicated subcommand name causes a syntax error.
- A duplicated keyword is silently ignored.
- There is no default keyword or parameter value.

The Process Capability Indices

CP	*Capability of the process.*
CPU	*The distance between the process mean and the upper specification limit scaled by capability sigma.*
CPL	*The distance between the process mean and the lower specification limit scaled by capability sigma.*
K	*The deviation of the process mean from the midpoint of the specification limits.* This is computed independently of the estimated capability sigma.
CPK	*Capability of process related to both dispersion and centeredness.* It is the minimum of CpU and CpL. If only one specification limit is provided, we compute and report a unilateral CpK instead of taking the minimum.
CR	*The reciprocal of CP.*
CPM	*An index relating capability sigma and the difference between the process mean and the target value.* A target value must be specified on the TARGET subcommand by the user.
CZU	*The number of capability sigmas between the process mean and the upper specification limit.*
CZL	*The number of capability sigmas between the process mean and the lower specification limit.*
CZMIN	*The minimum number of capability sigmas between the process mean and the specification limits.*
CZMAX	*The maximum number of capability sigmas between the process mean and the specification limits.*
CZOUT	*The estimated percentage outside the specification limits.* The standard normal approximation is based on the CZ_U and CZ_L.

- For each of the keywords other than CPK, both of the LSL subcommand and the USL subcommands must be specified. Otherwise, the keyword(s) are ignored and issue a syntax warning. For CPK, at least one of the LSL and USL subcommands must be specified.
- The keyword CPM is ignored with a syntax warning if the TARGET subcommand is not specified.

The Process Performance Indices

PP   *Performance of the process.*

PPU   *The distance between the process mean and the upper specification limit scaled by process standard deviation.*

PPL   *The distance between the process mean and the lower specification limit scaled by process standard deviation.*

PPK   *Performance of process related to both dispersion and centeredness.* It is the minimum of PpU and PpL. If only one specification limit is provided, we compute and report a unilateral PpK instead of taking the minimum.

PR   *The reciprocal of PP.*

PPM   *An index relating process variance and the difference between the process mean and the target value.* A target value must be specified on the TARGET subcommand by the user.

PZU   *The number of standard deviations between the process mean and the upper specification limit.*

PZL   *The number of standard deviations between the process mean and the lower specification limit.*

PZMIN   *The minimum number of standard deviations between the process mean and the specification limits.*

PZMAX   *The maximum number of standard deviations between the process mean and the specification limits.*

PZOUT   *The estimated percentage outside the specification limits.* The standard normal approximation is based on the PZ_U and PZ_L.

- For each of the keywords other than PPK, both of the LSL subcommand and the USL subcommand must be specified. Otherwise, we ignore the keyword(s) and issue a syntax warning. For PPK, at least one of the LSL and USL subcommands must be specified.

- The keyword PPM is ignored with a syntax warning, if the TARGET subcommand is not specified.

Measure(s) for Assessing Normality

AZOUT   *The observed percentage outside the specification limits.* A point is defined outside the specification limits, when its value is greater than or equal to the USL or is less than or equal to the LSL.

- For AZOUT, both of the LSL subcommand and the USL subcommand must be specified. Otherwise, we ignore the keyword and issue a syntax warning.

CAPSIGMA Subcommand

This subcommand defines the capability sigma estimator, which is required in computing all the Process Capability Indices except K requested by the STATISTICS subcommand (which applies to /XR, /XS, /I, or /IR only). There are four options:

RBAR   *Mean sample range.* The estimated capability sigma is based on the mean of the sample group ranges.

SBAR   *Mean sample standard deviation.* The estimated capability sigma is based on the mean of the sample group standard deviations.

MRBAR   *Mean sample moving range.* The estimated capability sigma is based on the mean of the sample moving ranges. The span defined by the SPAN subcommand is used. (Recall that its passive default value is 2.)

WITHIN   *Sample within-group variance.* The estimated capability sigma is the square root of the sample within-group variance.

The validity of specification depends on the chart specification (i.e., /XR, /XS, /I, or /IR).

Table 7   Valid CAPSIGMA options by chart specification

Chart Specification	Valid CAPSIGMA options
XR	RBAR (default)
	SBAR
	WITHIN
XS	RBAR
	SBAR (default)
	WITHIN
I	MRBAR (default)
IR	MRBAR (default)

- When this subcommand is omitted or specified without a keyword by the user, the default conditional on the chart specification is implicitly assumed (see the table above).

- The user specification of an invalid combination (e.g., /I and /CAPSIGMA = RBAR) causes a syntax error, if this subcommand is relevant, i.e., an applicable STATISTICS keyword is specified. Otherwise, we issue a syntax warning. When the chart specification is not one of /XR, /XS, /I, or /IR, the CAPSIGMA subcommand is silently ignored.

- The user specification of this subcommand, when valid with respect to the chart specification, is silently ignored, unless an applicable STATISTICS keyword is specified.

- A duplicated subcommand name causes a syntax error.

- A duplicated keyword is silently ignored, but if two or more keywords are specified and they do not mean the identical keyword, then a syntax error message is issued.

SPAN Subcommand

SPAN specifies the span from which the moving range for an individuals chart is calculated. The specification must be an integer value greater than 1. The default is 2. SPAN applies only to I and IR chart specifications.

Example

```
SPCHART /IR=SUBSIZE /SPAN=5.
```

- The SPAN subcommand specifies that the moving ranges are computed from every five individual samples.

CONFORM and NOCONFORM Subcommands

Either CONFORM or NOCONFORM is required when you specify a status variable on the P or NP subcommand. That occurs when data are organized so that each case is an inspection unit (see "P and NP Subcommands" on p. 1127).

- Either subcommand requires a value specification. The value can be numeric or string. String values must be enclosed within apostrophes.
- If CONFORM is specified, all values for the status variable other than the value specified are tabulated as nonconformities. If NOCONFORM is specified, only the specified value is tabulated as nonconformities.
- CONFORM and NOCONFORM apply only to P and NP chart specifications.

SIGMA Subcommand

SIGMA allows you to define the sigma level for a control chart. The value specified on SIGMA is used in calculating the upper and lower control limits on the chart. You can specify a number larger than 1 but less than or equal to 10. The larger the SIGMA value, the greater the range between the upper and the lower control limits. The default is 3.

MINSAMPLE Subcommand

MINSAMPLE specifies the minimum sample size for X-bar, R, or s charts. When you specify XR or XS on SPCHART, any subgroup with a size smaller than that specified on MINSAMPLE is excluded from the chart and from all computations. If each case is a subgroup, there must be at least as many variables named as the number specified on MINSAMPLE. The default is 2.

LSL and USL Subcommand

LSL and USL allow you to specify fixed lower and upper control limits. Fixed control limits are often used in manufacturing processes as designer-specified limits. These limits are displayed on the chart along with the calculated limits. If you do not specify LSL and USL, no fixed control limits are displayed. However, if you want only the specified control limits, you must edit the chart in a chart window to suppress the calculated series.

Example

```
SPCHART /TEMPLATE='CTRL.CHT'
 /XS=SUBSIZE
 /USL=74.50
 /LSL=73.50.
```

- The USL and LSL subcommands specify the control limits according to the designing engineer. The center line is most probably at 74.00.
- The specified upper and lower limits are displayed together with the control limits calculated from the observed standard deviation and the sigma value.

TARGET Subcommand

This subcommand defines the target value used in computing CpM and PpM requested by the STATISTICS subcommand. The value may be any real number less than or equal to the USL value and greater than or equal to the LSL value.

- This subcommand is silently ignored, if no applicable STATISTICS keyword is specified.
- If the value is numeric but out of the valid range, we warn and ignore the CPM or/and PPM keyword(s), if any, in the STATISTICS subcommand.

MISSING Subcommand

MISSING controls the treatment of missing values in the control chart.

- The default is NOREPORT and EXCLUDE.
- REPORT and NOREPORT are alternatives and apply only to category variables. They control whether categories (subgroups) with missing values are created.
- INCLUDE and EXCLUDE are alternatives and apply to process variables.

NOREPORT   *Suppress missing-value categories.* This is the default.

REPORT   *Report and plot missing-value categories.*

EXCLUDE   *Exclude user-missing values.* Both user- and system-missing values for the process variable are excluded from computation and plotting. This is the default.

INCLUDE   *Include user-missing values.* Only system-missing values for the process variable are excluded from computation and plotting.

SPLIT FILE

```
SPLIT FILE              {OFF      }
            [{LAYERED }] {BY varlist}
             {SEPARATE}
```

Example

```
SORT CASES BY SEX.
SPLIT FILE BY SEX.
FREQUENCIES VARS=INCOME /STATISTICS=MEDIAN.
```

Overview

SPLIT FILE splits the working data file into subgroups that can be analyzed separately. These subgroups are sets of adjacent cases in the file that have the same values for the specified split variables. Each value of each split variable is considered a break group, and cases within a break group must be grouped together in the working data file. If they are not, the SORT CASES command must be used before SPLIT FILE to sort cases in the proper order.

Basic Specification

The basic specification is keyword BY followed by the variable or variables that define the split-file groups.

- By default, the split-file groups are compared within the same table(s).
- You can turn off split-file processing using keyword OFF.

Syntax Rules

- SPLIT FILE can specify both numeric and string split variables, including long string variables and variables created by temporary transformations. It cannot specify scratch or system variables.
- SPLIT FILE is in effect for all procedures in a session unless you limit it with a TEMPORARY command, turn it off, or override it with a new SPLIT FILE or SORT CASES command.

Operations

- Unlike most transformations, SPLIT FILE takes effect as soon as it is encountered in the command sequence. Thus, special attention should be paid to its position among commands. For more information, see "Command Order" on p. 16.
- The file is processed sequentially. A change or break in values on any one of the split variables signals the end of one break group and the beginning of the next.

- AGGREGATE ignores the SPLIT FILE command. To split files using AGGREGATE, name the variables used to split the file as break variables ahead of any other break variables on AGGREGATE. AGGREGATE still produces one file, but the aggregated cases are in the same order as the split-file groups.

- If SPLIT FILE is in effect when a procedure writes matrix materials, the program writes one set of matrix materials for every split group. If a procedure reads a file that contains multiple sets of matrix materials, the procedure automatically detects the presence of multiple sets.

- If SPLIT FILE names any variable that was defined by the NUMERIC command, the program prints page headings indicating the split-file grouping.

Limitations

- SPLIT FILE can specify or imply up to eight variables.

LAYERED and SEPARATE Subcommands

LAYERED and SEPARATE specify how split-file groups are displayed in the output.

- Only one of them can be specified. If neither is specified with the BY variable list, LAYERED is the default.

- LAYERED and SEPARATE do not apply to the text output.

LAYERED   *Display split-file groups in the same table in the outermost column.*

SEPARATE   *Display split-file groups as separate tables.*

Example

```
SORT CASES BY SEX.
SPLIT FILE BY SEX.
FREQUENCIES VARS=INCOME /STATISTICS=MEDIAN.
```

- SORT CASES arranges cases in the file according to the values of variable *SEX*.

- SPLIT FILE splits the file according to the values of variable *SEX*, and FREQUENCIES generates separate median income tables for men and women.

- By default, the two groups (men and women) are compared in the same Frequency and Statistics tables.

Example

```
SORT CASES BY SEX.
TEMPORARY.
SPLIT FILE SEPARATE BY SEX.
FREQUENCIES VARS=INCOME /STATISTICS=MEDIAN.
FREQUENCIES VARS=INCOME /STATISTICS=MEDIAN.
```

- Because of the TEMPORARY command, SPLIT FILE applies to the first procedure only. Thus, the first FREQUENCIES procedure generates separate tables for men and women. The second FREQUENCIES procedure generates tables that include both sexes.

Example

```
SORT CASES BY SEX.
SPLIT FILE SEPARATE BY SEX.
FREQUENCIES VARS=INCOME /STATISTICS=MEDIAN.
SPLIT FILE OFF.
FREQUENCIES VARS=INCOME /STATISTICS=MEDIAN.
```

- SPLIT FILE does not apply to the second FREQUENCIES procedure because it is turned off after the first FREQUENCIES procedure. This example produces the same results as the example above.

Example

```
SORT CASES BY SEX RACE.
SPLIT FILE BY SEX.
FREQUENCIES VARS=INCOME /STATISTICS=MEDIAN.
SPLIT FILE BY SEX RACE.
FREQUENCIES VARS=INCOME /STATISTICS=MEDIAN.
```

- The first SPLIT FILE command applies to the first FREQUENCIES procedure. The second SPLIT FILE command overrides the first and splits the file by sex and race. This split is in effect for the second FREQUENCIES procedure.

STRING

```
STRING varlist (An) [/varlist...]
```

Example
```
STRING STATE1 (A2).
RECODE STATE ('IO'='IA') (ELSE=COPY) INTO STATE1.
```

Overview

STRING declares new string variables that can be used as target variables in data transformations.

Basic Specification

The basic specification is the name of the new variables and, in parentheses, the variable format.

Syntax Rules

- If keyword TO is used to create multiple string variables, the specified format applies to each variable named and implied by TO.
- To declare variables with different formats, separate each format group with a slash.
- STRING can be used within an input program to determine the order of string variables in the dictionary of the working data file. When used for this purpose, STRING must precede DATA LIST in the input program. See p. 845 for an example.
- STRING cannot be used to redefine an existing variable.
- String variables cannot have zero length; A0 is an illegal format.
- All implementations of the program allow the A format. Other string formats may be available on some systems. In addition, the definition of a long string depends on your operating system. Use keyword LOCAL on the INFO command to obtain documentation for your operating system.

Operations

- Unlike most transformations, STRING takes effect as soon as it is encountered in the command sequence. Thus, special attention should be paid to its position among commands. For more information, see "Command Order" on p. 16.
- New string variables are initialized as blanks.

- Variables declared on STRING are added to the working data file in the order they are specified. This order is not changed by the order in which the variables are used in the transformation language.
- The length of a string variable is fixed by the format specified when it is declared and cannot be changed by FORMATS. To change the length of a string variable, declare a new variable with the desired length and then use COMPUTE to assign the values of the original variable to it.

Example

```
STRING STATE1 (A2).
RECODE STATE ('IO'='IA') (ELSE=COPY) INTO STATE1.
```

- STRING declares variable *STATE1* with an A2 format.
- RECODE specifies *STATE* as the source variable and *STATE1* as the target variable. The original value IO is recoded to IA. Keywords ELSE and COPY copy all other state codes over unchanged. Thus, *STATE* and *STATE1* are identical except for cases with the original value IO.

Example

```
STRING V1 TO V6 (A8) / V7 V10 (A16).
```

- STRING declares variables *V1*, *V2*, *V3*, *V4*, *V5*, and *V6*, each with an A8 format, and variables *V7* and *V10*, each with an A16 format.

SUBTITLE

```
SUBTITLE  [']text[']
```

Example
```
SUBTITLE "Children's Training Shoes Only".
```

Overview

SUBTITLE inserts a left-justified subtitle on the second line from the top of each page of the output. The default subtitle contains the installation name and information about the hardware and operating system.

Basic Specification

The only specification is the subtitle itself.

Syntax Rules

- The subtitle can include any characters. To specify a blank subtitle, enclose a blank between apostrophes.
- The subtitle can be up to 60 characters long. Subtitles longer than 60 characters are truncated.
- The apostrophes or quotation marks enclosing the subtitle are optional; using them allows you to include apostrophes or quotation marks in the subtitle.
- If the subtitle is enclosed in apostrophes, quotation marks are valid characters but apostrophes must be specified as double apostrophes. If the subtitle is enclosed in quotation marks, apostrophes are valid characters but quotation marks must be specified as double quotation marks.
- More than one SUBTITLE command is allowed in a single session.
- A subtitle cannot be placed between a procedure command and BEGIN DATA—END DATA or within data records when the data are inline.

Operations

- Each SUBTITLE command overrides the previous one and takes effect on the next output page.
- SUBTITLE is independent of TITLE and each can be changed separately.
- The subtitle will not be displayed if HEADER=NO is specified on SET.

Example

```
TITLE 'Running Shoe Study from Runner''s World Data'.
SUBTITLE "Children's Training Shoes Only".
```

- The title is enclosed in apostrophes, so the apostrophe in *Runner's* must be specified as a double apostrophe.
- The subtitle is enclosed in quotation marks, so the apostrophe in *Children's* is simply specified as an apostrophe.

Example

```
TITLE 'Running Shoe Study from Runner''s World Data'.
SUBTITLE ' '.
```

- This subtitle is specified as a blank. This suppresses the default subtitle.

SUMMARIZE

```
SUMMARIZE [TABLES=]{varlist} [BY varlist] [BY...] [/varlist...]
                   {ALL    }

 [/TITLE ='string']      [FOOTNOTE= 'string']

 [/CELLS= [COUNT**] [MEAN ] [STDDEV]
                    [MEDIAN] [GMEDIAN] [SEMEAN]  [SUM ]
                    [MIN] [MAX] [RANGE] [VARIANCE]
                    [KURT] [SEKURT] [SKEW] [SESKEW]
                    [FIRST] [LAST]
                    [NPCT] [SPCT] [NPCT(var)] [SPCT(var)]
                    [HARMONIC] [GEOMETRIC]
                    [DEFAULT]
                    [ALL] [NONE]  ]

 [/MISSING=[{EXCLUDE**}][{VARIABLE** }]
            {INCLUDE  } {TABLE       }
            {DEPENDENT}

 [FORMAT=[{NOLIST** }] [{CASENUM    }] [{TOTAL**}]  [MISSING='string']
          {LIST     }  {NOCASENUM  }   {NOTOTAL}
          {VALIDLIST}

 [/STATISTICS=[ANOVA] [{LINEARITY}] [NONE**] ]
                       {ALL      }
```

**Default if the subcommand is omitted.

Example

```
SUMMARIZE TABLES=V1 TO V5 BY GROUP
  /STATISTICS=ANOVA.
```

Overview

SUMMARIZE produces univariate statistics for specified variables. You can break the variables into groups defined by one or more control (independent) variables. Another procedure that displays univariate statistics is FREQUENCIES.

Options

Cell Contents. By default, SUMMARIZE displays means, standard deviations, and cell counts. You can also display aggregated statistics, including sums, variances, median, range, kurtosis, skewness, and their standard error, using the CELLS subcommand.

Statistics. In addition to the statistics displayed for each cell of the table, you can obtain a one-way analysis of variance and test of linearity using the STATISTICS subcommand.

Format. By default, SUMMARIZE produces a Summary Report with a total category for each group defined by the control variables. You can request a Listing Report with or without case numbers using the FORMAT subcommand. You can also remove the total category from each group. You can specify a title and a caption for the Summary or Listing Report using the TITLE and FOOTNOTE subcommands.

Basic Specification

The basic specification is TABLES with a variable list. Each variable creates a category. The actual keyword TABLES can be omitted.

- The minimum specification is a dependent variable.
- By default, SUMMARIZE displays a Case Processing Summary table showing the number and percentage of cases included, excluded, and their total, and a Summary Report showing means, standard deviations, and number of cases for each category.

Syntax Rules

- Both numeric and string variables can be specified. String variables can be short or long.
- If there is more than one TABLES subcommand, FORMAT=LIST or VALIDLIST results in an error.
- String specifications for TITLE and FOOTNOTE cannot exceed 255 characters. Quotation marks or apostrophes are required. When the specification breaks on multiple lines, enclose each line in apostrophes or quotation marks and separate the specifications for each line by at least one blank.
- Each subcommand except TABLES can be specified only once. Multiple use results in a warning, and the last specification is used.
- Multiple TABLES subcommands are allowed, but multiple specifications use a lot of computer resources and time.
- There is no limit on the number of variables you can specify on each TABLES subcommand.
- When a variable is specified more than once, only the first occurrence is honored. The same variables specified after different BY keywords will result in an error.

Limitations

- Only 5 BY keywords can be specified.

Operations

- The data are processed sequentially. It is not necessary to sort the cases before processing. If a BY keyword is used, the output is always sorted.
- A Case Processing Summary table is always generated, showing the number and percentage of the cases included, excluded, and the total.
- For each combination of control variables specified after different BY keywords, SUMMARIZE produces a group in the Summary Report (depending on the specification on

the FORMAT subcommand). By default, mean, standard deviation, and number of cases are displayed for each group and for the total.

- An ANOVA table and a Measure of Association table are produced if additional statistics are requested.

Example

```
SUMMARIZE TABLES=V1 BY SEX BY GROUP
 /STATISTICS=ANOVA.
```

- A Case Processing Summary table lists the number and percentage of cases included, excluded, and the total.
- A Summary Report displays means, standard deviations, and numbers of cases for each group defined by each combination of *SEX* and *GROUP*.
- An ANOVA table displays analysis of variance with only *SEX* as the grouping variable.

TABLES Subcommand

TABLES specifies the dependent and control variables.

- You can specify multiple TABLES subcommands on a single SUMMARIZE command.
- For FORMAT=LIST or VALIDLIST, only one TABLES subcommand is allowed. Multiple dependent and control variables add more breaks to the Listing Report. Total statistics are displayed at the end for each combination defined by different values of the control variables.
- For FORMAT=NOLIST, which is the default, each use of keyword BY adds a dimension to the table requested. Total statistics are displayed with each group.
- The order in which control variables are displayed is the same as the order in which they are specified on TABLES. The values of the first control variable defined for the table appear in the leftmost column of the table and change the most slowly in the definition of groups.
- Statistics are displayed for each dependent variable in the same report.
- More than one dependent variable can be specified in a table list, and more than one control variable can be specified in each dimension of a table list.

TITLE and FOOTNOTE Subcommands

TITLE and FOOTNOTE provide a title and a caption for the Summary or Listing Report.

- TITLE and FOOTNOTE are optional and can be placed anywhere.
- The specification on TITLE or FOOTNOTE is a string within apostrophes or quotation marks. To specify a multiple-line title or footnote, enclose each line in apostrophes or quotation marks and separate the specifications for each line by at least one blank.
- The string you specify cannot exceed 255 characters.

CELLS Subcommand

By default, SUMMARIZE displays the means, standard deviations, and cell counts in each cell. Use CELLS to modify cell information.

- If CELLS is specified without keywords, SUMMARIZE displays the default statistics.
- If any keywords are specified on CELLS, only the requested information is displayed.
- MEDIAN and GMEDIAN use a lot of computer resources and time. Requesting these statistics (via these keywords or ALL) may slow down performance.

DEFAULT	*Means, standard deviations, and cell counts.* This is the default if CELLS is omitted.
MEAN	*Cell means.*
STDDEV	*Cell standard deviations.*
COUNT	*Cell counts.*
MEDIAN	*Cell median.*
GMEDIAN	*Grouped median.*
SEMEAN	*Standard error of cell mean.*
SUM	*Cell sums.*
MIN	*Cell minimum.*
MAX	*Cell maximum.*
RANGE	*Cell range.*
VARIANCE	*Variances.*
KURT	*Cell kurtosis.*
SEKURT	*Standard error of cell kurtosis.*
SKEW	*Cell skewness.*
SESKEW	*Standard error of cell skewness.*
FIRST	*First value.*
LAST	*Last value.*
SPCT	*Percentage of total sum.*
NPCT	*Percentage of total number of cases.*
SPCT(var)	*Percentage of total sum within specified variable.* The specified variable must be one of the control variables.
NPCT(var)	*Percentage of total number of cases within specified variable.* The specified variable must be one of the control variables.
HARMONIC	*Harmonic mean.*

| **GEOMETRIC** | *Geometric mean.* |
| **ALL** | *All cell information.* |

MISSING Subcommand

MISSING controls the treatment of cases with missing values. There are two groups of keywords.

- EXCLUDE, INCLUDE, and DEPENDENT specify the treatment of user-missing values. The default is EXCLUDE.

EXCLUDE	*All user-missing values are excluded.* This is the default.
INCLUDE	*User-missing values are treated as valid values.*
DEPENDENT	*User-missing values are considered missing in a dependent variable and valid in a grouping variable (variables specified after a BY keyword).*

- VARIABLE and TABLE specify how cases with missing values for dependent variables are excluded. The default is VARIABLE.

- Cases with missing values for any control variables are always excluded.

| **VARIABLE** | *A case is excluded when all of the values for variables in that table are missing.* This is the default. |
| **TABLE** | *A case is excluded when any value is missing within a table.* |

FORMAT Subcommand

FORMAT specifies whether you want a case listing for your report, and if you do, whether you want case numbers displayed for the listing. It also determines whether your reports will display a total category for each group and how they are going to indicate missing values.

NOLIST	*Display a Summary Report without a case listing.* This is the default.
LIST	*Display a Listing Report showing all cases.*
VALIDLIST	*Display a Listing Report showing only the valid cases.*
CASENUM	*Display case numbers as a category in the Listing Reports.* This is the default when FORMAT=LIST or VALIDLIST.
NOCASENUM	*Do not display case numbers.*
TOTAL	*Display the summary statistics for the total of each group with the label Total.* This is the default.
NOTOTAL	*Display the total category without a label.*
MISSING='string'	*Display system-missing values as a specified string.*

STATISTICS Subcommand

Use STATISTICS to request a one-way analysis of variance and a test of linearity for each table list.

- Statistics requested on STATISTICS are computed in addition to the statistics displayed in the Group Statistics table.
- If STATISTICS is specified without keywords, SUMMARIZE computes ANOVA.
- If two or more dimensions are specified, the second and subsequent dimensions are ignored in the analysis-of-variance table.

ANOVA *Analysis of variance.* ANOVA displays a standard analysis-of-variance table and calculates eta and eta squared (displayed in the Measures of Association table). This is the default if STATISTICS is specified without keywords.

LINEARITY *Test of linearity.* LINEARITY (alias ALL) displays additional statistics to the tables created by the ANOVA keyword—the sums of squares, degrees of freedom, and mean square associated with linear and nonlinear components, the F ratio, and the significance level for the ANOVA table and Pearson's r and r^2 for the Measures of Association table. LINEARITY is ignored if the control variable is a string.

NONE *No additional statistics.* This is the default if STATISTICS is omitted.

Example

```
SUMMARIZE TABLES=INCOME BY SEX BY RACE
  /STATISTICS=ANOVA.
```

- SUMMARIZE produces a Group Statistics table of *INCOME* by *RACE* within *SEX* and computes an analysis of variance only for *INCOME* by *SEX*.

SURVIVAL

SURVIVAL is available in the Advanced Models option.

```
SURVIVAL TABLES=survival varlist
                [BY varlist (min, max)...][BY varlist (min, max)...]

 /INTERVALS=THRU n BY a [THRU m BY b ...]

 /STATUS=status variable({min, max}) FOR {ALL              }
                        {value   }        {survival varlist}
 [/STATUS=...]

 [/PLOT  ({ALL     }}={ALL              } BY {ALL     }    BY {ALL    }]
         {LOGSURV }  {survival varlis}    {varlist}       {varlist}
         {SURVIVAL}
         {HAZARD  }
         {DENSITY }
         {OMS     }

 [/PRINT={TABLE**}]
         {NOTABLE}

 [/COMPARE={ALL**            } BY {ALL** }   BY {ALL** }]
           {survival varlist}    {varlist}     {varlist}

 [/CALCULATE=[{EXACT**    }] [PAIRWISE] [COMPARE] ]
             {CONDITIONAL}
             {APPROXIMATE}

 [/MISSING={GROUPWISE**}  [INCLUDE] ]
           {LISTWISE   }

 [/WRITE=[{NONE**}] ]
         {TABLES}
         {BOTH  }
```

**Default if subcommand or keyword is omitted.

Example

```
SURVIVAL TABLES=MOSFREE BY TREATMNT(1,3)
  /STATUS = PRISON (1) FOR MOSFREE
  /INTERVAL=THRU 24 BY 3.
```

Overview

SURVIVAL produces actuarial life tables, plots, and related statistics for examining the length of time to the occurrence of an event, often known as **survival time**. Cases can be classified into groups for separate analyses and comparisons. Time intervals can be calculated with the SPSS date- and time-conversion functions—for example, CTIME.DAYS or YRMODA. For a closely related alternative nonparametric analysis of survival times using the product-limit Kaplan-Meier estimator, see the KM command. For an analysis of survival times with covariates, including time-dependent covariates, see the COXREG command.

Options

Life Tables. You can list the variables to be used in the analysis, including any control variables on the TABLES subcommand. You can also suppress the life tables in the output with the PRINT subcommand.

Intervals. SURVIVAL reports the percentage alive at various times after the initial event. You can select the time points for reporting with the INTERVALS subcommand.

Plots. You can plot the survival functions for all cases or separately for various subgroups with the PLOT subcommand.

Comparisons. When control variables are listed on the TABLES subcommand, you can compare groups based on the Wilcoxon (Gehan) statistic using the COMPARE subcommand. You can request pairwise or approximate comparisons with the CALCULATE subcommand.

Writing a File. You can write the life tables, including the labeling information, to a file with the WRITE subcommand.

Basic Specification

- The basic specification requires three subcommands: TABLES, INTERVALS, and STATUS. TABLES identifies at least one survival variable from the working data file, INTERVALS divides the time period into intervals, and STATUS names a variable that indicates whether the event occurred.
- The basic specification prints one or more life tables, depending on the number of survival and control variables specified.

Subcommand Order

- TABLES must be first.
- Remaining subcommands can be named in any order.

Syntax Rules

- Only one TABLES subcommand can be specified, but multiple survival variables can be named. A survival variable cannot be specified as a control variable on any subcommands.
- Only one INTERVALS subcommand can be in effect on a SURVIVAL command. The interval specifications apply to all of the survival variables listed on TABLES. If multiple INTERVALS subcommands are used, the last specification supersedes all previous ones.
- Only one status variable can be listed on each STATUS subcommand. To specify multiple status variables, use multiple STATUS subcommands.
- You can specify multiple control variables on one BY keyword. Use a second BY keyword to specify second-order control variables to interact with the first-order control variables.
- All variables, including survival variables, control variables, and status variables, must be numeric. SURVIVAL does not process string variables.

Operations

- SURVIVAL computes time intervals according to specified interval widths, calculates the survival functions for each interval, and builds one life table for each group of survival variables. The life table is displayed unless explicitly suppressed.
- When the PLOT subcommand is specified, SURVIVAL plots the survival functions for all cases or separately for various groups.
- When the COMPARE subcommand is specified, SURVIVAL compares survival-time distributions of different groups based on the Wilcoxon (Gehan) statistic.

Limitations

- Maximum 20 survival variables.
- Maximum 100 control variables total on the first- and second-order control-variable lists combined.
- Maximum 20 THRU and BY specifications on INTERVALS.
- Maximum 35 values can appear on a plot.

Example

```
SURVIVAL TABLES=MOSFREE BY TREATMNT(1,3)
  /STATUS = PRISON (1) FOR MOSFREE
  /INTERVALS = THRU 24 BY 3.
```

- The survival analysis is used to examine the length of time between release from prison and return to prison for prisoners in three treatment programs. The variable *MOSFREE* is the length of time in months a prisoner stayed out of prison. The variable *TREATMNT* indicates the treatment group for each case.
- A value of 1 on the variable *PRISON* indicates a terminal outcome—that is, cases coded as 1 have returned to prison. Cases with other non-negative values for *PRISON* have not returned. Because we don't know their final outcome, such cases are called censored.
- Life tables are produced for each of the three subgroups. INTERVALS specifies that the survival experience be described every three months for the first two years.

TABLES Subcommand

TABLES identifies the survival and control variables to be included in the analysis.

- The minimum specification is one or more survival variables.
- To specify one or more first-order control (or factor) variables, use the keyword BY followed by the control variable(s). First-order control variables are processed in sequence. For example, BY A(1,3) B(1,2) results in five groups ($A = 1$, $A = 2$, $A = 3$, $B = 1$, and $B = 2$).
- You can specify one or more second-order control variables following a second BY keyword. Separate life tables are generated for each combination of values of the first-order and second-order controls. For example, BY A(1,3) BY B(1,2) results in six groups

$(A = 1\ B = 1, A = 1\ B = 2, A = 2\ B = 1, A = 2\ B = 2, A = 3\ B = 1,$ and $A = 3\ B = 2$).

- Each control variable must be followed by a value range in parentheses. These values must be integers separated by a comma or a blank. Non-integer values in the data are truncated, and the case is assigned to a subgroup based on the integer portion of its value on the variable. To specify only one value for a control variable, use the same value for the minimum and maximum.

- To generate life tables for all cases combined, as well as for control variables, use COMPUTE to create a variable that has the same value for all cases. With this variable as a control, tables for the entire set of cases, as well as for the control variables, will be produced.

Example

```
SURVIVAL TABLES = MOSFREE BY TREATMNT(1,3) BY RACE(1,2)
  /STATUS = PRISON(1)
  /INTERVAL = THRU 24 BY 3.
```

- *MOSFREE* is the survival variable, and *TREATMNT* is the first-order control variable. The second BY defines *RACE* as a second-order control group having a value of 1 or 2.

- Six life tables with the median survival time are produced, one for each pair of values for the two control variables.

INTERVALS Subcommand

INTERVALS determines the period of time to be examined and how the time will be grouped for the analysis. The interval specifications apply to all of the survival variables listed on TABLES.

- SURVIVAL always uses 0 as the starting point for the first interval. Do not specify the 0. The INTERVALS specification *must* begin with the keyword THRU.

- Specify the terminal value of the time period after the keyword THRU. The final interval includes any observations that exceed the specified terminal value.

- The grouping increment, which follows the keyword BY, must be in the same units as the survival variable.

- The period to be examined can be divided into intervals of varying lengths by repeating the THRU and BY keywords. The period must be divided in ascending order. If the time period is not a multiple of the increment, the endpoint of the period is adjusted upward to the next even multiple of the grouping increment.

- When the period is divided into intervals of varying lengths by repeating the THRU and BY specifications, the adjustment of one period to produce even intervals changes the starting point of subsequent periods. If the upward adjustment of one period completely overlaps the next period, no adjustment is made and the procedure terminates with an error.

Example

```
SURVIVAL TABLES = MOSFREE BY TREATMNT(1,3)
  /STATUS = PRISON(1) FOR MOSFREE
  /INTERVALS = THRU 12 BY 1 THRU 24 BY 3.
```

- INTERVALS produces life tables computed from 0 to 12 months at one-month intervals and from 13 to 24 months at three-month intervals.

Example

```
SURVIVAL  ONSSURV BY TREATMNT (1,3)
   /STATUS = OUTCOME (3,4) FOR ONSSURV
   /INTERVALS = THRU 50 BY 6.
```

- On the INTERVALS subcommand, the value following BY (6) does not divide evenly into the period to which it applies (50). Thus, the endpoint of the period is adjusted upward to the next even multiple of the BY value, resulting in a period of 54 with 9 intervals of 6 units each.

Example

```
SURVIVAL  ONSSURV BY TREATMNT (1,3)
   /STATUS = OUTCOME (3,4) FOR ONSSURV
   /INTERVALS = THRU 50 BY 6 THRU 100 BY 10 THRU 200 BY 20.
```

- Multiple THRU and BY specifications are used on the INTERVAL subcommand to divide the period of time under examination into intervals of different lengths.
- The first THRU and BY specifications are adjusted to produce even intervals as in the previous example. As a result, the following THRU and BY specifications are automatically readjusted to generate 5 intervals of 10 units (through 104), followed by 5 intervals of 20 units (through 204).

STATUS Subcommand

To determine whether the terminal event has occurred for a particular observation, SURVIVAL checks the value of a status variable. STATUS lists the status variable associated with each survival variable and the codes that indicate that a terminal event occurred.

- Specify a status variable followed by a value range enclosed in parentheses. The value range identifies the codes that indicate that the terminal event has taken place. All cases with non-negative times that do not have a code in the value range are classified as **censored cases**, which are cases for which the terminal event has not yet occurred.
- If the status variable does not apply to all the survival variables, specify FOR and the name of the survival variable(s) to which the status variable applies.
- Each survival variable on TABLES must have an associated status variable identified by a STATUS subcommand.
- Only one status variable can be listed on each STATUS subcommand. To specify multiple status variables, use multiple STATUS subcommands.
- If FOR is omitted on the STATUS specification, the status-variable specification applies to all of the survival variables not named on another STATUS subcommand.
- If more than one STATUS subcommand omits the keyword FOR, the final STATUS subcommand without FOR applies to all survival variables not specified by FOR on other STATUS subcommands. No warning is printed.

Example

```
SURVIVAL  ONSSURV BY TREATMNT (1,3)
  /INTERVALS = THRU 50 BY 5, THRU 100 BY 10
  /STATUS = OUTCOME (3,4) FOR ONSSURV.
```

- STATUS specifies that a code of 3 or 4 on *OUTCOME* means that the terminal event for the survival variable *ONSSURV* occurred.

Example

```
SURVIVAL TABLES = NOARREST MOSFREE BY TREATMNT(1,3)
  /STATUS = ARREST (1) FOR NOARREST
  /STATUS = PRISON (1)
  /INTERVAL=THRU 24 BY 3.
```

- STATUS defines the terminal event for *NOARREST* as a value of 1 for *ARREST*. Any other value for *ARREST* is considered censored.
- The second STATUS subcommand defines the value of 1 for *PRISON* as the terminal event. The keyword FOR is omitted. Thus, the status-variable specification applies to *MOSFREE*, which is the only survival variable not named on another STATUS subcommand.

PLOT Subcommand

PLOT produces plots of the cumulative survival distribution, the hazard function, and the probability density function. The PLOT subcommand can plot only the survival functions generated by the TABLES subcommand; PLOT cannot eliminate control variables.

- When specified by itself, the PLOT subcommand produces all available plots for each survival variable. Points on each plot are identified by values of the first-order control variables. If second-order controls are used, a separate plot is generated for every value of the second-order control variables.
- To request specific plots, specify, in parentheses following PLOT, any combination of the keywords defined below.
- Optionally, generate plots for only a subset of the requested life tables. Use the same syntax as used on the TABLES subcommand for specifying survival and control variables, omitting the value ranges. Each survival variable named on PLOT must have as many control levels as were specified for that variable on TABLES. However, only one control variable needs to be present for each level. If a required control level is missing on the PLOT specification, the default BY ALL is used for that level. The keyword ALL can be used to refer to an entire set of survival or control variables.
- To determine the number of plots that will be produced, multiply the number of functions plotted by the number of survival variables times the number of first-order controls times the number of distinct values represented in all of the second-order controls.

ALL *Plot all available functions.* ALL is the default if PLOT is used without specifications.

LOGSURV *Plot the cumulative survival distribution on a logarithmic scale.*

SURVIVAL *Plot the cumulative survival distribution on a linear scale.*

HAZARD	*Plot the hazard function.*
DENSITY	*Plot the density function.*
OMS	*Plot the one-minus-survival function.*

Example

```
SURVIVAL TABLES = NOARREST MOSFREE BY TREATMNT(1,3)
  /STATUS = ARREST (1) FOR NOARREST
  /STATUS = PRISON (1) FOR MOSFREE
  /INTERVALS = THRU 24 BY 3
  /PLOT (SURVIVAL,HAZARD) = MOSFREE.
```

- Separate life tables are produced for each of the survival variables (*NOARREST* and *MOSFREE*) for each of the three values of the control variable *TREATMNT*.
- PLOT produces plots of the cumulative survival distribution and the hazard rate for *MOSFREE* for the three values of *TREATMNT* (even though *TREATMNT* is not included on the PLOT specification).
- Because plots are requested only for the survival variable *MOSFREE*, no plots are generated for the variable *NOARREST*.

PRINT Subcommand

By default, SURVIVAL prints life tables. PRINT can be used to suppress the life tables.

| **TABLE** | *Print the life tables.* This is the default. |
| **NOTABLE** | *Suppress the life tables.* Only plots and comparisons are printed. The WRITE subcommand, which is used to write the life tables to a file, can be used when NOTABLE is in effect. |

Example

```
SURVIVAL TABLES = MOSFREE BY TREATMNT(1,3)
  /STATUS = PRISON (1) FOR MOSFREE
  /INTERVALS = THRU 24 BY 3
  /PLOT (ALL)
  /PRINT = NOTABLE.
```

- PRINT NOTABLE suppresses the printing of life tables.

COMPARE Subcommand

COMPARE compares the survival experience of subgroups defined by the control variables. At least one first-order control variable is required for calculating comparisons.

- When specified by itself, the COMPARE subcommand produces comparisons using the TABLES variable list.
- Alternatively, specify the survival and control variables for the comparisons. Use the same syntax as used on the TABLES subcommand for specifying survival and control variables, omitting the value ranges. Only variables that appear on the TABLES subcommand

can be listed on COMPARE, and their role as survival, first-order, and second-order control variables cannot be altered. The keyword TO can be used to refer to a group of variables, and the keyword ALL can be used to refer to an entire set of survival or control variables.

- By default, COMPARE calculates exact comparisons between subgroups. Use the CALCULATE subcommand to obtain pairwise comparisons or approximate comparisons.

Example

```
SURVIVAL TABLES = MOSFREE BY TREATMNT(1,3)
  /STATUS = PRISON (1) FOR MOSFREE
  /INTERVAL = THRU 24 BY 3
  /COMPARE.
```

- COMPARE computes the Wilcoxon (Gehan) statistic, degrees of freedom, and observed significance level for the hypothesis that the three survival curves based on the values of *TREATMNT* are identical.

Example

```
SURVIVAL TABLES=ONSSURV,RECSURV BY TREATMNT(1,3)
  /STATUS = RECURSIT(1,9) FOR RECSURV
  /STATUS = STATUS(3,4) FOR ONSSURV
  /INTERVAL = THRU 50 BY 5 THRU 100 BY 10
  /COMPARE = ONSSURV BY TREATMNT.
```

- COMPARE requests a comparison of *ONSSURV* by *TREATMNT*. No comparison is made of *RECSURV* by *TREATMNT*.

CALCULATE Subcommand

CALCULATE controls the comparisons of survival for subgroups specified on the COMPARE subcommand.

- The minimum specification is the subcommand keyword by itself. EXACT is the default.
- Only one of the keywords EXACT, APPROXIMATE, and CONDITIONAL can be specified. If more than one keyword is used, only one is in effect. The order of precedence is APPROXIMATE, CONDITIONAL, and EXACT.
- The keywords PAIRWISE and COMPARE can be used with any of the EXACT, APPROXIMATE, or CONDITIONAL keywords.
- If CALCULATE is used without the COMPARE subcommand, CALCULATE is ignored. However, if the keyword COMPARE is specified on CALCULATE and the COMPARE subcommand is omitted, SPSS generates an error message.
- Data can be entered into SURVIVAL for each individual case or aggregated for all cases in an interval. The way in which data are entered determines whether an exact or an approximate comparison is most appropriate. See "Using Aggregated Data" on p. 1158.

EXACT   *Calculate exact comparisons.* This is the default. You can obtain exact comparisons based on the survival experience of each observation with individual data. While this method is the most accurate, it requires that all of the data be in memory simultaneously. Thus, exact comparisons may be impractical for large samples. It is also inappropriate when individual data are not available and data aggregated by interval must be used.

APPROXIMATE   *Calculate approximate comparisons only.* Approximate comparisons are appropriate for aggregated data. The approximate-comparison approach assumes that all events occur at the midpoint of the interval. With exact comparisons, some of these midpoint ties can be resolved. However, if interval widths are not too great, the difference between exact and approximate comparisons should be small.

CONDITIONAL   *Calculate approximate comparisons if memory is insufficient.* Approximate comparisons are produced only if there is insufficient memory available for exact comparisons.

PAIRWISE   *Perform pairwise comparisons.* Comparisons of all pairs of values of the first-order control variable are produced along with the overall comparison.

COMPARE   *Produce comparisons only.* Survival tables specified on the TABLES subcommand are not computed, and requests for plots are ignored. This allows all available workspace to be used for comparisons. The WRITE subcommand cannot be used when this specification is in effect.

Example

```
SURVIVAL TABLES = MOSFREE BY TREATMNT(1,3)
  /STATUS = PRISON (1) FOR MOSFREE
  /INTERVAL = THRU 24 BY 3
  /COMPARE /CALCULATE = PAIRWISE.
```

- PAIRWISE on CALCULATE computes the Wilcoxon (Gehan) statistic, degrees of freedom, and observed significance levels for each pair of values of *TREATMNT*, as well as for an overall comparison of survival across all three *TREATMNT* subgroups: group 1 with group 2, group 1 with group 3, and group 2 with group 3.

- All comparisons are exact comparisons.

Example

```
SURVIVAL TABLES = MOSFREE BY TREATMNT(1,3)
  /STATUS = PRISON (1) FOR MOSFREE
  /INTERVAL = THRU 24 BY 3
  /COMPARE /CALCULATE = APPROXIMATE COMPARE.
```

- APPROXIMATE on CALCULATE computes the Wilcoxon (Gehan) statistic, degrees of freedom, and probability for the overall comparison of survival across all three *TREATMNT* subgroups using the approximate method.

- Because the keyword COMPARE is specified on CALCULATE, survival tables are not computed.

Using Aggregated Data

When aggregated survival information is available, the number of censored and uncensored cases at each time point must be entered. Up to two records can be entered for each interval, one for censored cases and one for uncensored cases. The number of cases included on each record is used as the weight factor. If control variables are used, there will be up to two records (one for censored and one for uncensored cases) for each value of the control variable in each interval. These records must contain the value of the control variable and the number of cases that belong in the particular category as well as values for survival time and status.

Example

```
DATA LIST   / SURVEVAR 1-2 STATVAR 4 SEX 6 COUNT 8.
VALUE LABELS   STATVAR 1 'DECEASED' 2 'ALIVE'
               /SEX 1 'FEMALE' 2 'MALE'.
BEGIN DATA
 1 1 1 6
 1 1 1 1
 1 2 2 2
 1 1 2 1
 2 2 1 1
 2 1 1 2
 2 2 2 1
 2 1 2 3
   ...
END DATA.
WEIGHT COUNT.
SURVIVAL TABLES = SURVEVAR BY SEX (1,2)
  /INTERVALS = THRU 10 BY 1
  /STATUS = STATVAR (1) FOR SURVEVAR.
```

- This example reads aggregated data and performs a SURVIVAL analysis when a control variable with two values is used.

- The first data record has a code of 1 on the status variable *STATVAR*, indicating that it is an uncensored case, and a code of 1 on *SEX*, the control variable. The number of cases for this interval is 6, the value of the variable *COUNT*. Intervals with weights of 0 do not have to be included.

- *COUNT* is not used in SURVIVAL but is the weight variable. In this example, each interval requires four records to provide all of the data for each *SURVEVAR* interval.

MISSING Subcommand

MISSING controls missing-value treatments. The default is GROUPWISE.

- Negative values on the survival variables are automatically treated as missing data. In addition, cases outside the value range on a control variable are excluded.

- GROUPWISE and LISTWISE are mutually exclusive. However, each can be used with INCLUDE.

GROUPWISE   *Exclude missing values groupwise.* Cases with missing values on a variable are excluded from any calculation involving that variable. This is the default.

LISTWISE   *Exclude missing values listwise.* Cases missing on any variables named on TABLES are excluded from the analysis.

INCLUDE   *Include user-missing values.* User-missing values are included in the analysis.

WRITE Subcommand

WRITE writes data in the survival tables to a file. This file can be used for further analyses or to produce graphics displays.

- When WRITE is omitted, the default is NONE. No output file is created.
- When WRITE is used, a PROCEDURE OUTPUT command must precede the SURVIVAL command. The OUTFILE subcommand on PROCEDURE OUTPUT specifies the output file.
- When WRITE is specified without a keyword, the default is TABLES.

NONE *Do not write procedure output to a file.* This is the default when WRITE is omitted.

TABLES *Write survival-table data records.* All survival-table statistics are written to a file.

BOTH *Write out survival-table data and label records.* Variable names, variable labels, and value labels are written out along with the survival table statistics.

Format

WRITE writes five types of records. The keyword TABLES writes record types 30, 31, and 40. The keyword BOTH writes record types 10, 20, 30, 31, and 40. The format of each record type is described in Table 1 through Table 5.

Table 1   Record type 10, produced only by keyword BOTH

Columns	Content	Format
1–2	Record type (10)	F2.0
3–7	Table number	F5.0
8–15	Name of survival variable	A8
16–55	Variable label of survival variable	A40
56	Number of BY's (0, 1, or 2)	F1.0
57–60	Number of rows in current survival table	F4.0

- One type-10 record is produced for each life table.
- Column 56 specifies the number of orders of control variables (0, 1, or 2) that have been applied to the life table.
- Columns 57–60 specify the number of rows in the life table. This number is the number of intervals in the analysis that show subjects entering; intervals in which no subjects enter are not noted in the life tables.

Table 2 Record type 20, produced by keyword BOTH

Columns	Content	Format
1–2	Record type (20)	F2.0
3–7	Table number	F5.0
8–15	Name of control variable	A8
16–55	Variable label of control variable	A40
56–60	Value of control variable	F5.0
61–80	Value label for this value	A20

- One type-20 record is produced for each control variable in each life table.
- If only first-order controls have been placed in the survival analysis, one type-20 record will be produced for each table. If second-order controls have also been applied, two type-20 records will be produced per table.

Table 3 Record type 30, produced by both keywords TABLES and BOTH

Columns	Content	Format
1–2	Record type (30)	F2.0
3–7	Table number	F5.0
8–13	Beginning of interval	F6.2
14–21	Number entering interval	F8.2
22–29	Number withdrawn in interval	F8.2
30–37	Number exposed to risk	F8.2
38–45	Number of terminal events	F8.2

- Information on record type 30 continues on record type 31. Each pair of type-30 and type-31 records contains the information from one line of the life table.

Table 4 Record type 31, continuation of record type 30

Columns	Content	Format
1–2	Record type (31)	F2.0
3–7	Table number	F5.0
8–15	Proportion terminating	F8.6
16–23	Proportion surviving	F8.6
24–31	Cumulative proportion surviving	F8.6
32–39	Probability density	F8.6
40–47	Hazard rate	F8.6
48–54	S.E. of cumulative proportion surviving	F7.4
55–61	S.E. of probability density	F7.4
62–68	S.E. of hazard rate	F7.4

- Record type 31 is a continuation of record type 30.
- As many type-30 and type-31 record pairs are output for a table as it has lines (this number is noted in columns 57–60 of the type-10 record for the table).

Table 5   Record type 40, produced by both keywords TABLES and BOTH

Columns	Content	Format
1–2	Record type (40)	F2.0

- Type-40 records indicate the completion of the series of records for one life table.

Record Order

The SURVIVAL output file contains records for each of the life tables specified on the TABLES subcommand. All records for a given table are produced together in sequence. The records for the life tables are produced in the same order as the tables themselves. All life tables for the first survival variable are written first. The values of the first- and second-order control variables rotate, with the values of the first-order controls changing more rapidly.

Example

```
PROCEDURE OUTPUT OUTFILE = SURVTBL.
SURVIVAL TABLES = MOSFREE BY TREATMNT(1,3)
  /STATUS = PRISON (1) FOR MOSFREE
  /INTERVAL = THRU 24 BY 3
  /WRITE = BOTH.
```

- WRITE generates a procedure output file called *SURVTBL*, containing life tables, variable names and labels, and value labels stored as record types 10, 20, 30, 31, and 40.

SYSFILE INFO

```
SYSFILE INFO [FILE=] 'file specification'
```

Example

```
SYSFILE INFO FILE='PERSNL.SAV'.
```

Overview

SYSFILE INFO displays complete dictionary information for all variables in an SPSS-format data file. You do not have to retrieve the file with GET to use SYSFILE INFO. If the file has already been retrieved, use DISPLAY DICTIONARY to display dictionary information.

Basic Specification

The basic specification is the command keyword and a complete file specification enclosed in apostrophes.

Syntax Rules

- Only one file specification is allowed per command. To display dictionary information for more than one SPSS-format data file, use multiple SYSFILE INFO commands.
- The file extension, if there is one, must be specified, even if it is the default.
- The subcommand keyword FILE is optional. When FILE is specified, the equals sign is required.

Operations

- No procedure is needed to execute SYSFILE INFO, since SYSFILE INFO obtains information from the dictionary alone.
- SYSFILE INFO displays the variable name, label, sequential position in the file, print and write format, missing values, and value labels for each variable in the specified file. Up to 60 characters can be displayed for variable and value labels.

Example

```
SYSFILE INFO FILE='PERSNL.SAV'.
```

- The program displays the complete dictionary information for all variables in the SPSS-format data file *PERSNL.SAV*.

TEMPORARY

```
TEMPORARY
```

Example

```
SORT CASES BY SEX.
TEMPORARY.
SPLIT FILE BY SEX.
FREQUENCIES VARS=INCOME /STATISTICS=MEDIAN.
FREQUENCIES VARS=INCOME /STATISTICS=MEDIAN.
```

Overview

TEMPORARY signals the beginning of temporary transformations that are in effect only for the next procedure. New numeric or string variables created after the TEMPORARY command are temporary variables. Any modifications made to existing variables after the TEMPORARY command are also temporary.

With TEMPORARY you can perform separate analyses for subgroups in the data and then repeat the analysis for the file as a whole. You can also use TRANSFORM to transform data for one analysis but not for other subsequent analyses.

TEMPORARY can be applied to the following commands:

- Transformation commands COMPUTE, RECODE, IF, and COUNT, and the DO REPEAT utility.
- The LOOP and DO IF structures.
- Format commands PRINT FORMATS, WRITE FORMATS, and FORMATS.
- Data selection commands SELECT IF, SAMPLE, FILTER, and WEIGHT.
- Variable declarations NUMERIC, STRING, and VECTOR.
- Labeling commands VARIABLE LABELS and VALUE LABELS, and the MISSING VALUES command.
- SPLIT FILE.
- XSAVE.

Basic Specification

The only specification is the keyword TEMPORARY. There are no additional specifications.

Operations

- Once TEMPORARY is specified, you cannot refer to previously existing scratch variables.
- Temporary transformations apply to the next command that reads the data. Once the data are read, the temporary transformations are no longer in effect.

- The XSAVE command leaves temporary transformations in effect. SAVE, however, reads the data and turns temporary transformations off after the file is written. (See example below.)
- TEMPORARY cannot be used with SORT CASES, MATCH FILES, ADD FILES, or COMPUTE with a LAG function. If any of these commands follows TEMPORARY in the command sequence, there must be an intervening procedure or command that reads the data to first execute the TEMPORARY command.
- TEMPORARY cannot be used within the DO IF—END IF or LOOP—END LOOP structures.

Example

```
SORT CASES BY SEX.
TEMPORARY.
SPLIT FILE BY SEX.
FREQUENCIES VARS=INCOME /STATISTICS=MEDIAN.
FREQUENCIES VARS=INCOME /STATISTICS=MEDIAN.
```

- SPLIT FILE applies to the first FREQUENCIES procedure, which generates separate median income tables for men and women.
- SPLIT FILE is not in effect for the second FREQUENCIES procedure, which generates a single median income table that includes both men and women.

Example

```
DATA LIST FILE=HUBDATA RECORDS=3
  /1 #MOBIRTH #DABIRTH #YRBIRTH 6-11 DEPT88 19.
COMPUTE    AGE=($JDATE - YRMODA(#YRBIRTH,#MOBIRTH,#DABIRTH))/365.25.
VARIABLE LABELS AGE 'EMPLOYEE''S AGE'
           DEPT88 'DEPARTMENT CODE IN 1988'.

TEMPORARY.
RECODE AGE (LO THRU 20=1)(20 THRU 25=2)(25 THRU 30=3)(30 THRU 35=4)
         (35 THRU 40=5)(40 THRU 45=6)(45 THRU 50=7)(50 THRU 55=8)
         (55 THRU 60=9)(60 THRU 65=10)(65 THRU HI=11).
VARIABLE LABELS AGE 'EMPLOYEE AGE CATEGORIES'.
VALUE LABELS AGE 1 'Up to 20' 2 '20 to 25' 3 '25 to 30' 4 '30 to 35'
         5 '35 to 40' 6 '40 to 45' 7 '45 to 50' 8 '50 to 55'
         9 '55 to 60' 10 '60 to 65' 11 '65 and older'.

FREQUENCIES VARIABLES=AGE.
MEANS AGE BY DEPT88.
```

- COMPUTE creates variable *AGE* from the dates in the data.
- FREQUENCIES uses the temporary version of variable *AGE* with temporary variable and value labels.
- MEANS uses the unrecoded values of *AGE* and the permanent variable label.

Example

```
GET FILE=HUBEMPL.
TEMPORARY.
RECODE DEPT85 TO DEPT88 (1,2=1) (3,4=2) (ELSE=9).
VALUE LABELS DEPT85 TO DEPT88 1 'MANAGEMENT'
                              2 'OPERATIONS'
                              3 'UNKNOWN'.
XSAVE OUTFILE=HUBTEMP.
CROSSTABS DEPT85 TO DEPT88 BY JOBCAT.
```

- Both the saved SPSS-format data file and the CROSSTABS output will reflect the temporary recoding and labeling of the department variables.

- If XSAVE is replaced with SAVE, the SPSS-format data file will reflect the temporary recoding and labeling but the CROSSTABS output will not.

TITLE

```
TITLE ['']text['']
```

Example
```
TITLE "Running Shoe Study from Runner's World Data".
```

Overview

TITLE inserts a left-justified title on the top line of each page of output. The default title indicates the version of the system being used.

Basic Specification

The only specification is the title.

Syntax Rules

- The title can include any characters. To specify a blank title, enclose a blank between apostrophes.
- The title can be up to 60 characters long. Titles longer than 60 characters are truncated.
- The apostrophes or quotation marks enclosing the title are optional; using them allows you to include apostrophes or quotation marks in the title.
- If the subtitle is enclosed in apostrophes, quotation marks are valid characters but apostrophes must be specified as double apostrophes. If the subtitle is enclosed in quotation marks, apostrophes are valid characters but quotation marks must be specified as double quotation marks.
- More than one TITLE command is allowed in a single session.
- A title cannot be placed between a procedure command and BEGIN DATA—END DATA or within data records when the data are inline.

Operations

- The title is displayed as part of the output heading, which also includes the date and page number. If HEADER=NO is specified on SET, the heading, including the title and subtitle, will not be displayed.
- Each TITLE command overrides the previous one and takes effect on the next output page.
- Only the title portion of the heading changes. The date and page number are still displayed.

- TITLE is independent of SUBTITLE, and each can be changed separately.

Example

```
TITLE "Running Shoe Study from Runner's World Data".
SUBTITLE 'Children''s Training Shoes Only'.
```

- The title is enclosed in quotation marks, so the apostrophe in *Runner's* is a valid character.
- The subtitle is enclosed in apostrophes, so the apostrophe in *Children's* must be specified as a double apostrophe.

Example

```
TITLE ' '.
SUBTITLE ' '.
```

- The title and subtitle are specified as blanks. This suppresses the default title and subtitle. The date and page number still display on the title line.

TSET

```
TSET
 [PRINT={DEFAULT**}]   [/NEWVAR={CURRENT**}]  [/MXAUTO={16**}]
        {BRIEF    }            {NONE     }              {lags}
        {DETAILED }            {ALL      }

 [/MXCROSS={7**  }]  [/MXNEWVARS={60**}]  [/MXPREDICT={60**}]
          {lags}                {n    }               {n    }

 [/MISSING={EXCLUDE**}]   [/CIN={95**  }]  [/TOLER={0.0001**}]
          {INCLUDE   }          {value }           {value   }

 [/CNVERGE={0.001**}]   [/ACFSE={IND**}]
          {value   }            {MA    }

 [/PERIOD=n]     [/ID=varname]

 [/{CONSTANT**}]
   {NOCONSTANT}

 [/DEFAULT]
```

**Default if the subcommand is omitted.

Example:

```
TSET PERIOD 6 NEWVAR NONE MXAUTO 25.
```

Overview

TSET sets global parameters to be used by procedures that analyze time series and sequence variables. To display the current settings of these parameters, use the TSHOW command.

Basic Specification

The basic specification is at least one subcommand.

Subcommand Order

- Subcommands can be specified in any order.

Syntax Rules

- The slash between subcommands is optional.
- You can specify DEFAULT on any subcommand to restore the default setting for that subcommand.
- Subcommand DEFAULT restores all TSET subcommands to their defaults.

Operations

- TSET takes effect immediately.
- Only the settings specified are affected. All others remain at their previous settings or the default.
- Subcommands on other procedures that perform the same function as subcommands on TSET override the TSET specifications for those procedures.
- Procedures that are affected by TSET specifications are CASEPLOT, NPPLOT, and TSPLOT.

DEFAULT Subcommand

DEFAULT resets all TSET settings back to their defaults. There are no additional specifications on DEFAULT.

ID Subcommand

ID specifies a variable whose values are used to label observations in plots.

- The only specification on ID is the name of a variable in the working data file.
- If ID is not specified, the *DATE_* variable is used to label observations.
- If ID is specified within the procedure, it overrides the TSET specification for that procedure.

MISSING Subcommand

MISSING controls the treatment of user-missing values.

- The specification on MISSING is keyword INCLUDE or EXCLUDE. The default is EXCLUDE.
- INCLUDE indicates that observations with user-missing values should be treated as valid values and included in analyses.
- EXCLUDE indicates that observations with user-missing values should be excluded from analyses.

MXNEWVARS Subcommand

MXNEWVARS indicates the maximum number of new variables that can be generated by a procedure.

- The specification on MXNEWVARS indicates the maximum and can be any positive integer.
- The default maximum number is 60 new variables per procedure.

MXPREDICT Subcommand

MXPREDICT indicates the maximum number of new cases that can be added to the working data file per procedure when the PREDICT command is used.

- The specification on MXPREDICT can be any positive integer.
- The default maximum number of new cases is 60 per procedure.

PERIOD Subcommand

PERIOD indicates the size of the period to be used for seasonal differencing.

- The specification on PERIOD indicates how many observations are in one season or period and can be any positive integer.
- There is no default for the PERIOD subcommand.
- The specification on TSET PERIOD overrides the periodicity of DATE variables.
- If a period is specified within an individual procedure, it overrides the TSET PERIOD specification for that procedure.

PRINT Subcommand

PRINT controls how much output is produced.

- The specification on PRINT can be BRIEF, DETAILED, or DEFAULT. The amount of output produced by DEFAULT is generally between the amount produced by BRIEF and DETAILED.
- For procedures with multiple iterations, BRIEF generally means that final statistics are displayed with no iteration history. DEFAULT provides a one-line summary at each iteration in addition to the final statistics. DETAILED provides a complete summary of each iteration (where necessary) plus the final statistics.
- For some procedures, the default and detailed output is the same. For many of the simpler procedures, brief, default, and detailed are all the same.

TSHOW

TSHOW

Example

TSHOW.

Overview

TSHOW displays a list of all the current specifications on the TSET, USE, PREDICT, and DATE commands.

Basic Specification

The command keyword TSHOW is the only specification.

Operations

- TSHOW is executed immediately.
- TSHOW lists every current specification for the TSET, USE, PREDICT, and DATE commands, as well as the default settings.

Example

TSHOW.

- The TSHOW command produces a list of the current settings on TSET, USE, PREDICT, and DATE commands.

TSPLOT

```
TSPLOT [VARIABLES=] variable names

[/DIFF={1}]
       {n}

[/SDIFF={1}]
        {n}

[/PERIOD=n]

[/{NOLOG**}]
  {LN     }

[/ID=varname]

[/MARK={varname} ]
       {date    }

[/SPLIT {UNIFORM**}]
        {SCALE     }

[/APPLY [='model name']]
```

For plots with one variable:

```
[/FORMAT=[{NOFILL**}]  [{NOREFERENCE**}]
          {LEFT    }    {REFERENCE     }
          {RIGHT   }
```

For plots with multiple variables:

```
[/FORMAT={NOJOIN**}]
         {JOIN    }
         {HILO    }
```

**Default if the subcommand is omitted.

Example

```
TSPLOT TICKETS
  /LN
  /DIFF
  /SDIFF
  /PERIOD=12
  /FORMAT=REFERENCE
  /MARK=Y 55 M 6.
```

Overview

TSPLOT produces a plot of one or more time series or sequence variables. You can request natural log and differencing transformations to produce plots of transformed variables. Several plot formats are available.

Options

Modifying the Variables. You can request a natural log transformation of the variables using the LN subcommand and seasonal and nonseasonal differencing to any degree using the SDIFF and DIFF subcommands. With seasonal differencing, you can also specify the periodicity on the PERIOD subcommand.

Plot Format. With the FORMAT subcommand, you can fill in the space on one side of the plotted values on plots with one variable. You can also plot a reference line indicating the variable mean. For plots with two or more variables, you can specify whether you want to join the values for each observation with a vertical line. With the ID subcommand you can label the horizontal axis with the values of a specified variable. You can mark the onset of an intervention variable on the plot with the MARK subcommand.

Split-File Processing. You can control how data that have been divided into subgroups by a SPLIT FILE command should be plotted using the SPLIT subcommand.

Basic Specification

The basic specification is one or more variable names.

- If the DATE command has been specified, the horizontal axis is labeled with the *DATE_* variable at periodic intervals. Otherwise, sequence numbers are used. The vertical axis is labeled with the value scale of the plotted variable(s).

Figure 1 shows a default high-resolution plot with DATE=YEAR 1900. Figure 2 shows the same default plot in low resolution.

Figure 1   TSPLOT VARIABLES=PRICE (in high resolution)

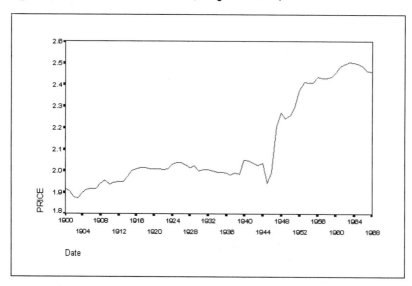

Figure 2 TSPLOT VARIABLES=PRICE (in low resolution)

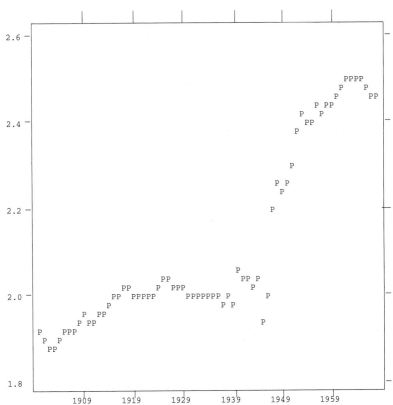

Subcommand Order

- Subcommands can be specified in any order.

Syntax Rules

- VARIABLES can be specified only once.
- Other subcommands can be specified more than once, but only the last specification of each one is executed.

Operations

- Subcommand specifications apply to all variables named on the TSPLOT command.
- If the LN subcommand is specified, any differencing requested on that TSPLOT command is done on the log-transformed variables.
- In high-resolution plots, split-file information is displayed as part of the subtitle and transformation information is displayed as part of the footnote.
- In low resolution, the plot frame size depends on the page size specified on the SET command.

Limitations

- Maximum 1 VARIABLES subcommand. There is no limit on the number of variables named on the list.

Example

```
TSPLOT TICKETS
  /LN
  /DIFF
  /SDIFF
  /PERIOD=12
  /FORMAT=REFERENCE
  /MARK=Y 55 M 6.
```

- This command produces a plot of *TICKETS* after a natural log transformation, differencing, and seasonal differencing have been applied.
- LN transforms the data using the natural logarithm (base *e*) of *TICKETS*.
- DIFF differences the logged variable once.
- SDIFF and PERIOD apply one degree of seasonal differencing with a period of 12.
- FORMAT=REFERENCE adds a reference line representing the variable mean. In low resolution, the area between the plotted values and the mean is filled with the plotting symbol (*T*).
- MARK provides a marker on the plot at June 1955. The marker is displayed as a vertical reference line in high-resolution plots.

VARIABLES Subcommand

VARIABLES specifies the names of the variables to be plotted and is the only required subcommand. The actual keyword VARIABLES can be omitted.

DIFF Subcommand

DIFF specifies the degree of differencing used to convert a nonstationary variable to a stationary one with a constant mean and variance before plotting.

- You can specify any positive integer on DIFF.

- If DIFF is specified without a value, the default is 1.
- The number of values plotted decreases by 1 for each degree of differencing.

Example

```
TSPLOT TICKETS
  /DIFF=2.
```

- In this example, *TICKETS* is differenced twice before plotting.

SDIFF Subcommand

If the variable exhibits a seasonal or periodic pattern, you can use the SDIFF subcommand to seasonally difference the variable before plotting.

- The specification on SDIFF indicates the degree of seasonal differencing and can be any positive integer.
- If SDIFF is specified without a value, the degree of seasonal differencing defaults to 1.
- The number of seasons plotted decreases by 1 for each degree of seasonal differencing.
- The length of the period used by SDIFF is specified on the PERIOD subcommand. If the PERIOD subcommand is not specified, the periodicity established on the TSET or DATE command is used (see the PERIOD subcommand below).

PERIOD Subcommand

PERIOD indicates the length of the period to be used by the SDIFF subcommand.

- The specification on PERIOD indicates how many observations are in one period or season and can be any positive integer.
- If PERIOD is not specified, the periodicity established on TSET PERIOD is in effect. If TSET PERIOD is not specified, the periodicity established on the DATE command is used. If periodicity was not established anywhere, the SDIFF subcommand will not be executed.

Example

```
TSPLOT TICKETS
  /SDIFF=1
  /PERIOD=12.
```

- This command applies one degree of seasonal differencing with 12 observations per season to *TICKETS* before plotting.

LN and NOLOG Subcommands

LN transforms the data using the natural logarithm (base e) of the variable and is used to remove varying amplitude over time. NOLOG indicates that the data should not be log transformed. NOLOG is the default.

- If you specify LN on TSPLOT, any differencing requested on that command will be done on the log-transformed variables.
- There are no additional specifications on LN or NOLOG.
- Only the last LN or NOLOG subcommand on a TSPLOT command is executed.
- If a natural log transformation is requested, any value less than or equal to zero is set to system-missing.
- NOLOG is generally used with an APPLY subcommand to turn off a previous LN specification.

Example

```
TSPLOT TICKETS
  /LN.
```

- In this example, *TICKETS* is transformed using the natural logarithm before plotting.

ID Subcommand

ID names a variable whose values will be used as labels for the horizontal axis.

- The only specification on ID is a variable name. If you have a variable named *ID* in your working data file, the equals sign after the subcommand is required.
- If the ID subcommand is not used and TSET ID has not been specified, the axis is labeled with the *DATE_* variable created by the DATE command. If the DATE command has not been specified, the observation number is used as the label.

Example

```
TSPLOT VARA
  /ID=VARB.
```

- In this example the values of *VARB* will be used to label the horizontal axis of *VARA* at periodic intervals.

FORMAT Subcommand

FORMAT controls the plot format.

- The specification on FORMAT is one of the keywords listed below.
- Keywords NOFILL, LEFT, RIGHT, NOREFERENCE, and REFERENCE apply to plots with one variable. NOFILL, LEFT, and RIGHT are alternatives and indicate how the plot is filled. NOREFERENCE and REFERENCE are alternatives and specify whether a reference line is displayed. For low-resolution plots, only one keyword can be specified. One keyword *from each set* can be specified for high-resolution plots. NOFILL and NOREFERENCE are the defaults.
- Keywords JOIN, NOJOIN, and HILO apply to plots with multiple variables and are alternatives. NOJOIN is the default. Only one keyword can be specified on a FORMAT subcommand for plots with multiple variables.

The following formats are available for plots with one variable:

NOFILL   *Plot only the values for the variable with no fill.* NOFILL produces a plot with no fill above or below the plotted values. This is the default format when one variable is specified.

BOTTOM   *Plot the values for the variable and fill in the area below the curve.* In low-resolution plots, the area below the plotted curve is filled in with the first character of the variable name. For high-resolution plots, if the plotted variable has missing or negative values, BOTTOM is ignored and the default NOFILL is used instead. Figure 3 shows a filled high-resolution plot.

TOP   *Plot the values for the variable and fill in the area above the curve.* In low resolution, the area above the plotted curve is filled in with the first character of the variable name. For high-resolution plots, TOP is ignored and the default NOFILL is used instead.

Figure 3   FORMAT=BOTTOM

NOREFERENCE   *Do not plot a reference line.* This is the default when one variable is specified.

REFERENCE   *Plot a reference line indicating the variable mean.* In high resolution, a fill chart is displayed as an area chart with a reference line and a non-fill chart is displayed as a line chart with a reference line. In low-resolution, the area between the plotted curve and the reference line are filled in with the plotting character (the first character of the variable name). You can request either fill or a reference line for a low-resolution chart, but not both. Figure 4 shows a high-resolution no-fill plot with a reference line indicating the variable mean.

Figure 4   FORMAT=REFERENCE

The following formats are available for plots with multiple variables:

NOJOIN *Plot the values of each variable named.* In high-resolution plots, different colors or line patterns are used for multiple variables. In low-resolution plots, the plotting character for each variable is the first character of the variable name. Multiple occurrences of the same value for a single observation are plotted using a dollar sign ($). This is the default format for plots with multiple variables.

JOIN *Plot the values of each variable and join the values for each observation.* Values are plotted as described for NOJOIN and the values for each observation are joined together by a line. Figure 5 contains a high-resolution plot in this format with three time series (*PRICE, INCOME,* and *CONSUMP*).

HILO *Plot the highest and lowest values across variables for each observation and join the two values together.* The high and low values are plotted as a horizontal bar and are joined with a line. For high-resolution plots, if more than three variables are specified HILO is ignored and the default NOJOIN is used. Figure 6 contains a high-resolution high-low plot with three time series (*PRICE, INCOME,* and *CONSUMP*).

Figure 5   FORMAT=JOIN

Figure 6   FORMAT=HILO

Date

MARK Subcommand

MARK indicates the onset of an intervention variable.

- The onset date is indicated in high resolution by a vertical reference line and in low resolution by a tick mark on the top and bottom axes.
- The specification on MARK can be either a variable name or an onset date if the *DATE_* variable exists.
- If a variable is named, the plot indicates where the values of that variable change.
- A date specification follows the same format as the DATE command; that is, a keyword followed by a value. For example, the specification for June 1955 is Y 1955 M 6 (or Y 55 M 6 if only the last 2 digits of the year are used on DATE).

Figure 7 shows a high-resolution plot with the year 1945 marked as the onset date.

Figure 7   MARK=Y 1945

Date

SPLIT Subcommand

SPLIT specifies how to plot data that have been divided into subgroups by a SPLIT FILE command. The default is UNIFORM.

UNIFORM *Scale uniformly.* The vertical axis is scaled according to the values of the entire data set.

SCALE *Scale individually.* The vertical axis is scaled according to the values of each individual subgroup.

- If FORMAT=REFERENCE is specified when SPLIT=SCALE, the reference line is placed at the mean of the subgroup. If FORMAT=REFERENCE is specified when SPLIT=UNIFORM, the reference line is placed at the overall mean.

Example

```
SPLIT FILE BY REGION.
TSPLOT TICKETS / SPLIT=SCALE.
```

- In this example, the data have been split into subgroups by *REGION*. The plots produced with the SCALE subcommand have vertical axes that are individually scaled according to the values of each particular region.

APPLY Subcommand

APPLY allows you to produce a plot using previously defined specifications without having to repeat the TSPLOT subcommands.

- The only specification on APPLY is the name of a previous model enclosed in apostrophes. If a model name is not specified, the specifications from the previous TSPLOT command are used.

- To change one or more specifications of the plot, specify the subcommands of only those portions you want to change after subcommand APPLY.

- If no variables are specified, the variables that were specified for the original plot are used.

- To plot different variables, enter new variable names before or after the APPLY subcommand.

Example

```
TSPLOT TICKETS
  /LN
  /DIFF=1
  /SDIFF=1
  /PERIOD=12.
TSPLOT ROUNDTRP
  /APPLY.
TSPLOT APPLY
  /NOLOG.
```

- The first command produces a plot of *TICKETS* after a natural log transformation, differencing, and seasonal differencing have been applied.

- The second command plots the values for *ROUNDTRP* using the same subcommands specified for *TICKETS*.

- The third command produces another plot of *ROUNDTRP* but this time without a log transformation. *ROUNDTRP* is still differenced once and seasonally differenced with a periodicity of 12.

T-TEST

One-sample tests:

```
T-TEST TESTVAL n /VARIABLE=varlist
```

Independent-samples tests:

```
T-TEST GROUPS=varname ({1,2**      }) /VARIABLES=varlist
                       {value       }
                       {value,value}
```

Paired-samples tests:

```
T-TEST PAIRS=varlist [WITH varlist [(PAIRED)]] [/varlist ...]
```

All types of tests:

```
[/MISSING={ANALYSIS**}  [INCLUDE]]
          {LISTWISE   }

[/CRITERIA=CI({0.95**})
             {value }
```

**Default if the subcommand is omitted.

Examples

```
T-TEST GROUPS=WORLD(1,3) /VARIABLES=NTCPRI NTCSAL NTCPUR.

T-TEST PAIRS=TEACHER CONSTRUC MANAGER.
```

Overview

T-TEST compares sample means by calculating Student's *t* and displays the two-tailed probability of the difference between the means. Statistics are available for one-sample (tested against a specified value), independent samples (different groups of cases), or paired samples (different variables). Other procedures that compare group means are ANOVA, ONEWAY, UNIANOVA, GLM, and MANOVA (GLM and MANOVA are available in the SPSS Advanced Models option).

Options

Statistics. There are no optional statistics. All statistics available are displayed by default.

Basic Specification

The basic specification depends on whether you want a one-sample test, an independent-samples test or a paired-samples test. For all types of tests, T-TEST displays Student's *t*, degrees of freedom, and two-tailed probabilities, as well as the mean, standard deviation, standard error, and count for each group or variable.

- To request a one-sample test, use the TESTVAL and VARIABLES subcommands. The output includes a One-Sample Statistics table showing univariate statistics and a One-Sample Test table showing the test value, the difference between the sample mean and the test value and two-tailed probability level.

- To request an independent-samples test, use the GROUPS and VARIABLES subcommands. The output includes a Group Statistics table showing summary statistics by group for each dependent variable and an Independent-Samples Test table showing both pooled- and separate-variance estimates, along with the F value used to test homogeneity of variance and its probability. The two-tailed probability is displayed for the t value.

- To request a paired-samples test, use the PAIRS subcommand. The output includes a Paired Statistics table showing univariate statistics by pairs, a Paired Samples Correlations table showing correlation coefficients and two-tailed probability level for a test of the coefficient for each pair, and a Paired Samples Test table showing the paired differences between the means and two-tailed probability levels for a test of the differences.

Subcommand Order

Subcommands can be named in any order.

Operations

- If a variable specified on GROUPS is a long string, only the short-string portion is used to identify groups in the analysis.
- Probability levels are two-tailed. To obtain the one-tailed probability, divide the two-tailed probability by 2.

Limitations

- Maximum 1 TESTVAL and 1 VARIABLES subcommand per one-sample t test.
- Maximum 1 GROUPS and 1 VARIABLES subcommand per independent-samples t test.

Example

```
T TEST TESTVAL 28000 /VARIABLES=CHISAL LASAL NYSAL.
```

- This one-sample t test compares the means of *CHISAL, LASAL,* and *NYSAL* each with the standard value (28000).

Example

```
T-TEST GROUPS=WORLD(1,3) /VARIABLES=NTCPRI NTCSAL NTCPUR.
```

- This independent-samples *t* test compares the means of the two groups defined by values 1 and 3 of *WORLD* for variables *NTCPRI, NTCSAL,* and *NTCPUR.*

Example

```
T-TEST PAIRS=TEACHER CONSTRUC MANAGER.
```

- This paired-samples *t* test compares the means of *TEACHER* with *CONSTRUC, TEACHER* with *MANAGER,* and *CONSTRUC* with *MANAGER.*

VARIABLES Subcommand

VARIABLES specifies the dependent variables to be tested in a one-sample or an independent-samples *t* test.

- VARIABLES can specify multiple variables, all of which must be numeric.
- When specified along with TESTVAL, the mean of all cases for each variable is compared with the specified value.
- When specified along with GROUPS, the means of two groups of cases defined by the GROUPS subcommand are compared.
- If both TESTVAL and GROUPS are specified, a one-sample test and an independent-samples test are performed on each variable.

TESTVAL Subcommand

TESTVAL specifies the value with which a sample mean is compared.

- Only one TESTVAL subcommand is allowed.
- Only one value can be specified on the TESTVAL subcommand.

GROUPS Subcommand

GROUPS specifies a variable used to group cases for independent-samples *t* tests.

- GROUPS can specify only one variable, which can be numeric or string.

Any one of three methods can be used to define the two groups for the variable specified on GROUPS:

- Specify a single value in parentheses to group all cases with a value equal to or greater than the specified value into one group and the remaining cases into the other group.
- Specify two values in parentheses to include cases with the first value in one group and cases with the second value in the other group. Cases with other values are excluded.
- If no values are specified on GROUP, T-TEST uses 1 and 2 as default values for numeric variables. There is no default for string variables.

PAIRS Subcommand

PAIRS requests paired-samples *t* tests.

- The minimum specification for a paired-samples test is PAIRS with an analysis list. Only numeric variables can be specified on the analysis list. The minimum analysis list is two variables.

- If keyword WITH is not specified, each variable in the list is compared with every other variable on the list.

- If keyword WITH is specified, every variable to the left of WITH is compared with every variable to the right of WITH. WITH can be used with PAIRED to obtain special pairing.

- To specify multiple analysis lists, use multiple PAIRS subcommands, each separated by a slash. Keyword PAIRS is required only for the first analysis list; a slash can be used to separate each additional analysis list.

(PAIRED) *Special pairing for paired-samples test.* PAIRED must be enclosed in parentheses and must be used with keyword WITH. When PAIRED is specified, The first variable before WITH is compared with the first variable after WITH, the second variable before WITH is compared with the second variable after WITH, and so forth. The same number of variables should be specified before and after WITH; unmatched variables are ignored and a warning message is issued. PAIRED generates an error message if keyword WITH is not specified on PAIRS.

Example

```
T-TEST   PAIRS=TEACHER CONSTRUC MANAGER.
T-TEST   PAIRS=TEACHER MANAGER WITH CONSTRUC ENGINEER.
T-TEST   PAIRS=TEACHER MANAGER WITH CONSTRUC ENGINEER (PAIRED).
```

- The first T-TEST compares *TEACHER* with *CONSTRUC, TEACHER* with *MANAGER*, and *CONSTRUC* with *MANAGER*.

- The second T-TEST compares *TEACHER* with *CONSTRUC, TEACHER* with *ENGINEER, MANAGER* with *CONSTRUC*, and *MANAGER* with *ENGINEER. TEACHER* is not compared with *MANAGER*, and *CONSTRUC* is not compared with *ENGINEER*.

- The third T-TEST compares *TEACHER* with *CONSTRUC* and *MANAGER* with *ENGINEER*.

CRITERIA Subcommand

CRITERIA resets the value of the confidence interval. Keyword CI is required. You can specify a value between 0 and 1 in the parentheses. The default is 0.95.

MISSING Subcommand

MISSING controls the treatment of missing values. The default is ANALYSIS.

- ANALYSIS and LISTWISE are alternatives; however, each can be specified with INCLUDE.

ANALYSIS *Delete cases with missing values on an analysis-by-analysis or pair-by-pair basis.* For independent-samples tests, cases with missing values for either the grouping variable or the dependent variable are excluded from the analysis of that dependent variable. For paired-samples tests, a case with a missing value for either of the variables in a given pair is excluded from the analysis of that pair. This is the default.

LISTWISE *Exclude cases with missing values listwise.* A case with a missing value for any variable specified on either GROUPS or VARIABLES is excluded from any independent-samples test. A case with a missing value for any variable specified on PAIRS is excluded from any paired-samples test.

INCLUDE *Include user-missing values.* User-missing values are treated as valid values.

2SLS

2SLS is available in the Regression Models option.

```
2SLS [EQUATION=]dependent variable WITH predictor variable

 [/[EQUATION=]dependent variable...]

  /INSTRUMENTS=varlist

 [/ENDOGENOUS=varlist]

 [/{CONSTANT**}
    {NOCONSTANT}

 [/PRINT=COV]

 [/SAVE = [PRED] [RESID]]

 [/APPLY[='model name']]
```

**Default if the subcommand or keyword is omitted.

Example

```
2SLS VAR01 WITH VAR02 VAR03
  /INSTRUMENTS VAR03 LAGVAR01.
```

Overview

2SLS performs two-stage least-squares regression to produce consistent estimates of parameters when one or more predictor variables might be correlated with the disturbance. This situation typically occurs when your model consists of a system of simultaneous equations wherein endogenous variables are specified as predictors in one or more of the equations. The two-stage least-squares technique uses instrumental variables to produce regressors that are not contemporaneously correlated with the disturbance. Parameters of a single equation or a set of simultaneous equations can be estimated.

Options

New Variables. You can change NEWVAR settings on the TSET command prior to 2SLS to evaluate the regression statistics without saving the values of predicted and residual variables, or save the new values to replace the values saved earlier, or save the new values without erasing values saved earlier (see the TSET command). You can also use the SAVE subcommand on 2SLS to override the NONE or the default CURRENT settings on NEWVAR.

Covariance Matrix. You can obtain the covariance matrix of the parameter estimates in addition to all of the other output by specifying PRINT=DETAILED on the TSET command prior to 2SLS. You can also use the PRINT subcommand to obtain the covariance matrix regardless of the setting on PRINT.

Basic Specification

The basic specification is at least one EQUATION subcommand and one INSTRUMENTS subcommand.

- For each equation specified, 2SLS estimates and displays the regression analysis-of-variance table, regression standard error, mean of the residuals, parameter estimates, standard errors of the parameter estimates, standardized parameter estimates, *t* statistic significance tests and probability levels for the parameter estimates, tolerance of the variables, the parameter estimates, and correlation matrix of the parameter estimates.
- If the setting on NEWVAR is either ALL or the default CURRENT, two new variables containing the predicted and residual values are automatically created for each equation. The variables are labeled and added to the working data file.

Subcommand Order

- Subcommands can be specified in any order.

Syntax Rules

- The INSTRUMENTS subcommand must specify at least as many variables as are specified after WITH on the longest EQUATION subcommand.
- If a subcommand is specified more than once, the effect is cumulative (except for the APPLY subcommand, which executes only the last occurrence).

Operations

- 2SLS cannot produce forecasts beyond the length of any regressor series.
- 2SLS honors the SPSS WEIGHT command.
- 2SLS uses listwise deletion of missing data. Whenever a variable is missing a value for a particular observation, that observation will not be used in any of the computations.

EQUATION Subcommand

EQUATION specifies the structural equations for the model and is required. The actual keyword EQUATION is optional.

- An equation specifies a single dependent variable, followed by keyword WITH and one or more predictor variables.
- You can specify more than one equation. Multiple equations are separated by slashes.

Example

```
2SLS EQUATION=Y1 WITH X1 X2
  /INSTRUMENTS=X1 LAGX2 X3.
```

- In this example, *Y1* is the dependent variable and *X1* and *X2* are the predictors. The instruments used to predict the *X2* values are *X1*, *LAGX2*, and *X3*.

INSTRUMENTS Subcommand

INSTRUMENTS specifies the instrumental variables. These variables are used to compute predicted values for the endogenous variables in the first stage of 2SLS.

- At least one INSTRUMENTS subcommand must be specified.
- If more than one INSTRUMENTS subcommand is specified, the effect is cumulative. All variables named on INSTRUMENTS subcommands are used as instruments to predict all the endogenous variables.
- Any variable in the working data file can be named as an instrument.
- Instrumental variables can be specified on the EQUATION subcommand, but this is not required.
- The INSTRUMENTS subcommand must name at least as many variables as are specified after WITH on the longest EQUATION subcommand.
- If all the predictor variables are listed as the only INSTRUMENTS, the results are the same as results from ordinary least-squares regression.

Example

```
2SLS DEMAND WITH PRICE, INCOME
   /PRICE WITH DEMAND, RAINFALL, LAGPRICE
   /INSTRUMENTS=INCOME, RAINFALL, LAGPRICE.
```

- The endogenous variables are PRICE and DEMAND.
- The instruments to be used to compute predicted values for the endogenous variables are INCOME, RAINFALL, and LAGPRICE.

ENDOGENOUS Subcommand

All variables not specified on the INSTRUMENTS subcommand are used as endogenous variables by 2SLS. The ENDOGENOUS subcommand simply allows you to document what these variables are.

- Computations are not affected by specifications on the ENDOGENOUS subcommand.

Example

```
2SLS Y1 WITH X1 X2 X3
   /INSTRUMENTS=X2 X4 LAGY1
   /ENDOGENOUS=Y1 X1 X3.
```

- In this example, the ENDOGENOUS subcommand is specified to document the endogenous variables.

CONSTANT and NOCONSTANT Subcommands

Specify CONSTANT or NOCONSTANT to indicate whether a constant term should be estimated in the regression equation. The specification of either subcommand overrides the CONSTANT setting on the TSET command for the current procedure.

- CONSTANT is the default and specifies that the constant term is used as an instrument.
- NOCONSTANT eliminates the constant term.

SAVE Subcommand

SAVE saves the values of predicted and residual variables generated during the current session to the end of the working data file. The default names *FIT_n* and *ERR_n* will be generated, where *n* increments each time variables are saved for an equation. SAVE overrides the NONE or the default CURRENT setting on NEWVAR for the current procedure.

PRED   *Save the predicted value.* The new variable is named *FIT_n*, where *n* increments each time a predicted or residual variable is saved for an equation.

RESSID   *Save the residual value.* The new variable is named *ERR_n*, where *n* increments each time a predicted or residual variable is saved for an equation.

PRINT Subcommand

PRINT can be used to produce an additional covariance matrix for each equation. The only specification on this subcommand is keyword COV. The PRINT subcommand overrides the PRINT setting on the TSET command for the current procedure.

APPLY Subcommand

APPLY allows you to use a previously defined 2SLS model without having to repeat the specifications.

- The only specification on APPLY is the name of a previous model. If a model name is not specified, the model specified on the previous 2SLS command is used.
- To change the series used with the model, enter new series names before or after the APPLY subcommand.
- To change one or more model specifications, specify the subcommands of only those portions you want to change after the APPLY subcommand.
- If no series are specified on the command, the series that were originally specified with the model being reapplied are used.

Example

```
2SLS Y1 WITH X1 X2 / X1 WITH Y1 X2
  /INSTRUMENTS=X2 X3.
2SLS APPLY
  /INSTRUMENTS=X2 X3 LAGX1.
```

- In this example, the first command requests 2SLS using *X2* and *X3* as instruments.
- The second command specifies the same equations but changes the instruments to *X2*, *X3*, and *LAGX1*.

UNIANOVA

```
UNIANOVA dependent var [BY factor list [WITH covariate list]]

[/RANDOM=factor factor...]

[/REGWGT=varname]

[/METHOD=SSTYPE({1  })]
                {2  }
                {3**}
                {4  }

[/INTERCEPT=[INCLUDE**] [EXCLUDE]]

[/MISSING=[INCLUDE] [EXCLUDE**]]

[/CRITERIA=[EPS({1E-8**})][ALPHA({0.05**})]
               {a       }        {a       }

[/PRINT = [DESCRIPTIVE] [HOMOGENEITY] [PARAMETER][ETASQ]
          [GEF] [LOF] [OPOWER] [TEST(LMATRIX)]]

[/PLOT=[SPREADLEVEL] [RESIDUALS]
       [PROFILE (factor factor*factor factor*factor*factor ...)]

[/TEST=effect VS {linear combination [DF(df)]}]
                 {value DF (df)              }

[/LMATRIX={["label"] effect list effect list ...;...}]
          {["label"] effect list effect list ...    }
          {["label"] ALL list; ALL...               }
          {["label"] ALL list                       }

[/KMATRIX= {number    }]
           {number;...}

[/CONTRAST (factor name)={DEVIATION[(refcat)]**     }]
                         {SIMPLE [(refcat)]         }
                         {DIFFERENCE                }
                         {HELMERT                   }
                         {REPEATED                  }
                         {POLYNOMIAL  [({1,2,3...})]}
                                         {metric }
                         {SPECIAL (matrix)          }

[/POSTHOC =effect [effect...]
          ([SNK] [TUKEY][BTUKEY][DUNCAN]
           [SCHEFFE] [DUNNETT(refcat)] [DUNNETTL(refcat)]
           [DUNNETTR(refcat)] [BONFERRONI] [LSD] [SIDAK]
           [GT2] [GABRIEL] [FREGW] [QREGW]  [T2] [T3] [GH] [C]
           [WALLER ({100** })])])]
                   {kratio}
          [VS effect]

[/EMMEANS=TABLES({OVERALL        })] [COMPARE ADJ([LSD(none)] [BONFERRONI] [SIDAK])]
                 {factor         }
                 {factor*factor...}

 [/SAVE=[tempvar [(name)]] [tempvar [(name)]]...]

 [/OUTFILE= [{COVB (filename)}] [EFFECT(filename)] [DESIGN(filename)]
            {CORB (filename)}

 [/DESIGN={[INTERCEPT...]    }]
          {[effect effect...]}
```

** Default if subcommand or keyword is omitted.

Temporary variables (tempvar) are:

PRED, WPRED, RESID, WRESID, DRESID, ZRESID, SRESID, SEPRED, COOK, LEVER

Example

```
UNIANOVA YIELD BY SEED FERT
  /DESIGN.
```

Overview

This section describes the use of UNIANOVA for univariate analyses. The UNIANOVA procedure provides regression analysis and analysis of variance for one dependent variable by one or more factors and/or variables.

Options

Design Specification. You can specify which terms to include in the design on the DESIGN subcommand. This allows you to estimate a model other than the default full factorial model, incorporate factor-by-covariate interactions or covariate-by-covariate interactions, and indicate nesting of effects.

Contrast Types. You can specify contrasts other than the default deviation contrasts on the CONTRAST subcommand.

Optional Output. You can choose from a wide variety of optional output on the PRINT subcommand. Output appropriate to univariate designs includes descriptive statistics for each cell, parameter estimates, Levene's test for equality of variance across cells, partial eta-squared for each effect and each parameter estimate, the general estimable function matrix, and a contrast coefficients table (**L'** matrix). The OUTFILE subcommand allows you to write out the covariance or correlation matrix, the design matrix, or the statistics from the between-subjects ANOVA table into a separate SPSS data file.

Using the EMMEANS subcommand, you can request tables of estimated marginal means of the dependent variable and their standard deviations. The SAVE subcommand allows you to save predicted values and residuals in weighted or unweighted and standardized or unstandardized forms. You can specify different means comparison tests for comparing all possible pairs of cell means using the POSTHOC subcommand. In addition, you can specify your own hypothesis tests by specifying an **L** matrix and a **K** matrix to test the univariate hypothesis **LB = K**.

Basic Specification

- The basic specification is a variable list identifying the dependent variable, the factors (if any), and the covariates (if any).

- By default, UNIANOVA uses a model that includes the intercept term, the covariate (if any), and the full factorial model, which includes all main effects and all possible interactions among factors. The intercept term is excluded if it is excluded in the model by specifying the keyword EXCLUDE on the INTERCEPT subcommand. Sums of squares are calculated and hypothesis tests are performed using type-specific estimable functions. Parameters are estimated using the normal equation and a generalized inverse of the SSCP matrix.

Subcommand Order

- The variable list must be specified first.
- Subcommands can be used in any order.

Syntax Rules

- For many analyses, the UNIANOVA variable list and the DESIGN subcommand are the only specifications needed.
- If you do not enter a DESIGN subcommand, UNIANOVA will use a full factorial model, with main effects of covariates, if any.
- Minimum syntax—at least one dependent variable must be specified, and at least one of the following must be specified: INTERCEPT, a between-subjects factor, or a covariate. The design contains the intercept by default.
- If more than one DESIGN subcommand is specified, only the last one is in effect.
- Dependent variables and covariates must be numeric, but factors can be numeric or string variables.
- If a string variable is specified as a factor, only the first eight characters of each value are used in distinguishing among values.
- If more than one MISSING subcommand is specified, only the last one is in effect.
- The following words are reserved as keywords or internal commands in the UNIANOVA procedure:

  INTERCEPT, BY, WITH, ALL, OVERALL, WITHIN

  Variable names that duplicate these words should be changed before you run UNIANOVA.

Limitations

- Any number of factors can be specified, but if the number of between-subjects factors plus the number of split variables exceeds 18, the Descriptive Statistics table is not printed even when you request it.
- Memory requirements depend primarily on the number of cells in the design. For the default full factorial model, this equals the product of the number of levels or categories in each factor.

Example

```
UNIANOVA YIELD BY SEED FERT WITH RAINFALL
  /PRINT=DESCRIPTIVE PARAMETER
  /DESIGN.
```

- *YIELD* is the dependent variable; *SEED* and *FERT* are factors; *RAINFALL* is a covariate.
- The PRINT subcommand requests the descriptive statistics for the dependent variable for each cell and the parameter estimates, in addition to the default tables Between-Subjects Factors and Univariate Tests.
- The DESIGN subcommand requests the default design, a full factorial model with a covariate. This subcommand could have been omitted or could have been specified in full as

```
  /DESIGN = INTERCEPT RAINFALL, SEED, FERT, SEED BY FERT.
```

UNIANOVA Variable List

The variable list specifies the dependent variable, the factors, and the covariates in the model.

- The dependent variable must be the first specification on UNIANOVA.
- The names of the factors follow the dependent variable. Use the keyword BY to separate the factors from the dependent variable.
- Enter the covariates, if any, following the factors. Use the keyword WITH to separate covariates from factors (if any) and the dependent variable.

Example

```
UNIANOVA DEPENDNT BY FACTOR1 FACTOR2, FACTOR3.
```

- In this example, three factors are specified.
- A default full factorial model is used for the analysis.

Example

```
UNIANOVA Y BY A WITH X
  /DESIGN.
```

- In this example, the DESIGN subcommand requests the default design, which includes the intercept term, the covariate *X* and the factor *A*.

RANDOM Subcommand

RANDOM allows you to specify which effects in your design are random. When the RANDOM subcommand is used, a table of expected mean squares for all effects in the design is displayed, and an appropriate error term for testing each effect is calculated and used automatically.

- Random always implies a univariate mixed-model analysis.
- If you specify an effect on RANDOM, higher-order effects containing the specified effect (excluding any effects containing covariates) are automatically treated as random effects.
- The keyword INTERCEPT and effects containing covariates are not allowed on this subcommand.

- The RANDOM subcommand cannot be used if there is any within-subjects factor in the model (that is, RANDOM cannot be specified if WSFACTOR is specified).
- When the RANDOM subcommand is used, the appropriate error terms for the hypothesis testing of all effects in the model are automatically computed and used.
- More than one RANDOM subcommand is allowed. The specifications are accumulated.

Example

```
UNIANOVA DEP BY A B
  /RANDOM = B
  /DESIGN = A,B, A*B.
```

- In the example, effects *B* and *A*B* are considered as random effects. Notice that if only effect *B* is specified in the RANDOM subcommand, *A*B* is automatically considered as a random effect.
- The hypothesis testing for each effect (*A*, *B*, and *A*B*) in the design will be carried out using the appropriate error term, which is calculated automatically.

REGWGT Subcommand

The only specification on REGWGT is the name of the variable containing the weights to be used in estimating a weighted least-squares model.

- Specify a numeric weight variable name following the REGWGT subcommand. Only observations with positive values in the weight variable will be used in the analysis.
- If more than one REGWGT subcommand is specified, only the last one is in effect.

Example

```
UNIANOVA OUTCOME BY TREATMNT
  /REGWGT WT.
```

- The procedure performs a weighted least-squares analysis. The variable *WT* is used as the weight variable.

METHOD Subcommand

METHOD controls the computational aspects of the UNIANOVA analysis. You can specify one of four different methods for partitioning the sums of squares. If more than one METHOD subcommand is specified, only the last one is in effect.

SSTYPE(1) *Type I sum-of-squares method.* The Type I sum-of-squares method is also known as the hierarchical decomposition of the sum-of-squares method. Each term is adjusted only for the terms that precede it on the DESIGN subcommand. Under a balanced design, it is an orthogonal decomposition, and the sums of squares in the model add up to the total sum of squares.

SSTYPE(2) *Type II sum-of-squares method.* This method calculates the sum of squares of an effect in the model adjusted for all other "appropriate" effects. An appropriate effect is one that corresponds to all effects that do not *contain* the effect being examined.

For any two effects *F1* and *F2* in the model, *F1* is said to be **contained** in *F2* under the following three conditions:
- Both effects *F1* and *F2* have the same covariate, if any.
- *F2* consists of more factors than *F1*.
- All factors in *F1* also appear in *F2*.

The intercept effect is treated as contained in all the pure factor effects. However, it is not contained in any effect involving a covariate. No effect is contained in the intercept effect. Thus, for any one effect *F* of interest, all other effects in the model can be classified as in one of the following two groups: the effects that do not contain *F* or the effects that contain *F*.

If the model is a main-effects design (that is, only main effects are in the model), the Type II sum-of-squares method is equivalent to the regression approach sums of squares. This means that each main effect is adjusted for every other term in the model.

SSTYPE(3)   *Type III sum-of-squares method.* This is the default. This method calculates the sum of squares of an effect *F* in the design as the sum of squares adjusted for any other effects that do not contain it, and *orthogonal* to any effects (if any) that contain it. The Type III sums of squares have one major advantage—they are invariant with respect to the cell frequencies as long as the general form of estimability remains constant. Hence, this type of sums of squares is often used for an unbalanced model with no missing cells. In a factorial design with no missing cells, this method is equivalent to the Yates' weighted squares of means technique, and it also coincides with the overparameterized Σ-restricted model.

SSTYPE(4)   *Type IV sum-of-squares method.* This method is designed for a situation in which there are missing cells. For any effect *F* in the design, if *F* is not contained in any other effect, then Type IV = Type III = Type II. When *F* is contained in other effects, then Type IV distributes the contrasts being made among the parameters in *F* to all higher-level effects equitably.

Example

```
UNIANOVA DEP BY A B C
  /METHOD=SSTYPE(3)
  /DESIGN=A, B, C.
```

- The design is a main-effects model.
- The METHOD subcommand requests that the model be fitted with Type III sums of squares.

INTERCEPT Subcommand

INTERCEPT controls whether an intercept term is included in the model. If more than one INTERCEPT subcommand is specified, only the last one is in effect.

INCLUDE   *Include the intercept term.* The intercept (constant) term is included in the model. This is the default.

EXCLUDE   *Exclude the intercept term.* The intercept term is excluded from the model. Specification of the keyword INTERCEPT on the DESIGN subcommand overrides INTERCEPT = EXCLUDE.

MISSING Subcommand

By default, cases with missing values for any of the variables on the UNIANOVA variable list are excluded from the analysis. The MISSING subcommand allows you to include cases with user-missing values.

- If MISSING is not specified, the default is EXCLUDE.
- Pairwise deletion of missing data is not available in UNIANOVA.
- Keywords INCLUDE and EXCLUDE are mutually exclusive.
- If more than one MISSING subcommand is specified, only the last one is in effect.

EXCLUDE   *Exclude both user-missing and system-missing values.* This is the default when MISSING is not specified.

INCLUDE   *User-missing values are treated as valid.* System-missing values cannot be included in the analysis.

CRITERIA Subcommand

CRITERIA controls the statistical criteria used to build the models.

- More than one CRITERIA subcommand is allowed. The specifications are accumulated. Conflicts across CRITERIA subcommands are resolved using the conflicting specification given on the last CRITERIA subcommand.
- The keyword must be followed by a positive number in parentheses.

EPS(n)   *The tolerance level in redundancy detection.* This value is used for redundancy checking in the design matrix. The default value is 1E–8.

ALPHA(n)   *The alpha level.* This keyword has two functions. First, it gives the alpha level at which the power is calculated for the F test. Once the noncentrality parameter for the alternative hypothesis is estimated from the data, then the power is the probability that the test statistic is greater than the critical value under the alternative hypothesis. The second function of alpha is to specify the level of the confidence interval. If the alpha level specified is n, the value $(1 - n) \times 100$ indicates the level of confidence for all individual and simultaneous confidence intervals generated for the specified model. The value of n must be between 0 and 1, exclusive. The default value of alpha is 0.05. This means that the default power calculation is at the 0.05 level, and the default level of the confidence intervals is 95%, since $(1 - 0.05) \times 100 = 95$.

PRINT Subcommand

PRINT controls the display of optional output.

- Some PRINT output applies to the entire UNIANOVA procedure and is displayed only once.
- Additional output can be obtained on the EMMEANS, PLOT, and SAVE subcommands.
- Some optional output may greatly increase the processing time. Request only the output you want to see.
- If no PRINT command is specified, default output for a univariate analysis includes a factor information table and a Univariate Tests table (ANOVA) for all effects in the model.
- If more than one PRINT subcommand is specified, only the last one is in effect.

The following keywords are available for UNIANOVA univariate analyses.

DESCRIPTIVES   *Basic information about each cell in the design.* Observed means, standard deviations, and counts for the dependent variable in all cells. The cells are constructed from the highest-order crossing of the between-subjects factors. If the number of between-subjects factors plus the number of split variables exceeds 18, the Descriptive Statistics table is not printed.

HOMOGENEITY   *Tests of homogeneity of variance.* Levene's test for equality of variances for the dependent variable across all level combinations of the between-subjects factors. If there are no between-subjects factors, this keyword is not valid.

PARAMETER   *Parameter estimates.* Parameter estimates, standard errors, t tests, and confidence intervals for each test.

OPOWER   *Observed power.* The observed power for each test.

LOF   *Lack of fit.* Lack of fit test which allows you to determine if the current model adequately accounts for the relationship between the response variable and the predictors.

ETASQ   *Partial eta-squared (η^2).* This value is an overestimate of the actual effect size in an F test. It is defined as

$$\text{partial eta-squared} = \frac{dfh \times F}{dfh \times F + dfe}$$

where F is the test statistic and dfh and dfe are its degrees of freedom and degrees of freedom for error. The keyword EFSIZE can be used in place of ETASQ.

GEF   *General estimable function table.* This table shows the general form of the estimable functions.

TEST(LMATRIX)   *Set of contrast coefficients (L) matrices.* The transpose of the **L** matrix (**L'**) is displayed. This set always includes one matrix displaying the estimable function for each between-subjects effect appearing or implied in the DESIGN subcommand. Also, any **L** matrices generated by the LMATRIX or CONTRAST subcommands are displayed. TEST(ESTIMABLE) can be used in place of TEST(LMATRIX).

Example

```
UNIANOVA DEP BY A B WITH COV
  /PRINT=DESCRIPTIVE, TEST(LMATRIX), PARAMETER
  /DESIGN.
```

- Since the design in the DESIGN subcommand is not specified, the default design is used. In this case, the design includes the intercept term, the covariate *COV*, and the full factorial terms of *A* and *B*, which are *A*, *B*, and *A*B*.

- For each combination of levels of *A* and *B*, SPSS displays the descriptive statistics of *DEP*.

- The set of **L** matrices that generates the sums of squares for testing each effect in the design is displayed.

- The parameter estimates, their standard errors, *t* tests, confidence intervals, and the observed power for each test are displayed.

PLOT Subcommand

PLOT provides a variety of plots useful in checking the assumptions needed in the analysis. The PLOT subcommand can be specified more than once. All of the plots requested on each PLOT subcommand are produced.

Use the following keywords on the PLOT subcommand to request plots:

SPREADLEVEL *Spread-versus-level plots.* Plots of observed cell means versus standard deviations, and versus variances.

RESIDUALS *Observed by predicted by standardized residuals plot.* A plot is produced for each dependent variable. In a univariate analysis, a plot is produced for the single dependent variable.

PROFILE *Line plots of dependent variable means for one-way, two-way, or three-way crossed factors.* The PROFILE keyword must be followed by parentheses containing a list of one or more factor combinations. All factors specified (either individual or crossed) must be made up of only valid factors on the factor list. Factor combinations on the PROFILE keyword may use an asterisk (*) or the keyword BY to specify crossed factors. A factor cannot occur in a single factor combination more than once.

The order of factors in a factor combination is important, and there is no restriction on the order of factors. If a single factor is specified after the PROFILE keyword, a line plot of estimated means at each level of the factor is produced. If a two-way crossed factor combination is specified, the output includes a multiple-line plot of estimated means at each level of the first specified factor, with a separate line drawn for each level of the second specified factor. If a three-way crossed factor combination is specified, the output includes multiple-line plots of estimated means at each level of the first specified factor, with separate lines for each level of the second factor, and separate plots for each level of the third factor.

Example

```
UNIANOVA DEP BY A B
  /PLOT = SPREADLEVEL PROFILE(A A*B A*B*C)
  /DESIGN.
```

Assume each of the factors *A*, *B*, and *C* has three levels.

- Spread-versus-level plots are produced showing observed cell means versus standard deviations and observed cell means versus variances.
- Five profile plots are produced. For factor *A*, a line plot of estimated means at each level of *A* is produced (one plot). For the two-way crossed factor combination *A*B*, a multiple-line plot of estimated means at each level of *A*, with a separate line for each level of *B*, is produced (one plot). For the three-way crossed factor combination *A*B*C*, a multiple-line plot of estimated means at each level of *A*, with a separate line for each level of *B*, is produced for each of the three levels of *C* (three plots).

TEST Subcommand

The TEST subcommand allows you to test a hypothesis term against a specified error term.

- TEST is valid only for univariate analyses. Multiple TEST subcommands are allowed, each executed independently.
- You must specify both the hypothesis term and the error term. There is no default.
- The hypothesis term is specified before the keyword VS. It must be a valid effect specified or implied on the DESIGN subcommand.
- The error term is specified after the keyword VS. You can specify either a linear combination or a value. The linear combination of effects takes the general form: `coefficient*effect +/- coefficient*effect ...`
- All effects in the linear combination must be specified or implied on the DESIGN subcommand. Effects specified or implied on DESIGN but not listed after VS are assumed to have a coefficient of 0.
- Duplicate effects are allowed. UNIANOVA adds coefficients associated with the same effect before performing the text. For example, the linear combination `5*A-0.9*B-A` will be combined to `4*A-0.9B`.
- A coefficient can be specified as a fraction with a positive denominator—for example, 1/3 or –1/3, but 1/–3 is invalid.
- If you specify a value for the error term, you must specify the degrees of freedom after the keyword DF. The degrees of freedom must be a positive real number. DF and the degrees of freedom are optional for a linear combination.

Example

```
UNIANOVA DEP BY A B
  /TEST = A VS B + A*B
  /DESIGN = A, B, A*B.
```

- *A* is tested against the pooled effect of *B + A*B*.

LMATRIX Subcommand

The LMATRIX subcommand allows you to customize your hypotheses tests by specifying the **L** matrix (contrast coefficients matrix) in the general form of the linear hypothesis **LB** = **K**, where **K** = **0** if it is not specified on the KMATRIX subcommand. The vector **B** is the parameter vector in the linear model.

- The basic format for the LMATRIX subcommand is an optional label in quotation marks, an effect name or the keyword ALL, and a list of real numbers. There can be multiple effect names (or the keyword ALL) and number lists.
- The optional label is a string with a maximum length of 255 characters. Only one label can be specified.
- Only valid effects appearing or implied on the DESIGN subcommand can be specified on the LMATRIX subcommand.
- The length of the list of real numbers must be equal to the number of parameters (including the redundant ones) corresponding to that effect. For example, if the effect $A*B$ takes up six columns in the design matrix, then the list after $A*B$ must contain exactly six numbers.
- A number can be specified as a fraction with a positive denominator—for example, 1/3 or –1/3, but 1/–3 is invalid.
- A semicolon (;) indicates the end of a row in the **L** matrix.
- When ALL is specified, the length of the list that follows ALL is equal to the total number of parameters (including the redundant ones) in the model.
- Effects appearing or implied on the DESIGN subcommand but not specified here are assumed to have entries of 0 in the corresponding columns of the **L** matrix.
- Multiple LMATRIX subcommands are allowed. Each is treated independently.

Example

```
UNIANOVA DEP BY A B
  /LMATRIX = "B1 vs B2 at A1"
             B 1 -1 0 A*B 1 -1 0 0 0 0 0 0 0
  /LMATRIX = "Effect A"
             A  1  0 -1
             A*B 1/3   1/3   1/3
                   0     0     0
                 -1/3  -1/3  -1/3;
             A  0  1 -1
             A*B  0     0     0
                 1/3   1/3   1/3
                -1/3  -1/3  -1/3
  /LMATRIX = "B1 vs B2 at A2"
             ALL   0
                   0  0  0
                   1 -1  0
                   0  0  0  1 -1  0  0  0  0
  /DESIGN = A, B, A*B.
```

Assume that factors *A* and *B* each have three levels. There are three LMATRIX subcommands; each is treated independently.

- **B1 versus B2 at A1.** In the first LMATRIX subcommand, the difference is tested between levels 1 and 2 of effect *B* when effect *A* is fixed at level 1. Since there are three levels each in effects *A* and *B*, the interaction effect *A*B* takes up nine columns in the design matrix.
- **Effect A.** In the second LMATRIX subcommand, effect *A* is tested. Since there are three levels in effect *A*, at most two independent contrasts can be formed; thus, there are two rows in the **L** matrix, which are separated by a semicolon (;). The first row tests the difference between levels 1 and 3 of effect *A*, while the second row tests the difference between levels 2 and 3 of effect *A*.
- **B1 versus B2 at A2.** In the last LMATRIX subcommand, the keyword ALL is used. The first 0 corresponds to the intercept effect; the next three zeros correspond to effect *A*.

KMATRIX Subcommand

The KMATRIX subcommand allows you to customize your hypothesis tests by specifying the **K** matrix (contrast results matrix) in the general form of the linear hypothesis **LB** = **K**. The vector **B** is the parameter vector in the linear model.

- The default **K** matrix is a zero matrix; that is, **LB** = 0 is assumed.
- For the KMATRIX subcommand to be valid, at least one of the following subcommands must be specified: the LMATRIX subcommand or the INTERCEPT = INCLUDE subcommand.
- If KMATRIX is specified but LMATRIX is not specified, the LMATRIX is assumed to take the row vector corresponding to the intercept in the estimable function, provided the subcommand INTERCEPT = INCLUDE is specified. In this case, the K matrix can be only a scalar matrix.
- If KMATRIX and LMATRIX are specified, then the number of rows in the requested **K** and **L** matrices must be equal. If there are multiple LMATRIX subcommands, then all requested **L** matrices must have the same number of rows, and **K** must have the same number of rows as these **L** matrices.
- A semicolon (;) can be used to indicate the end of a row in the **K** matrix.
- If more than one KMATRIX subcommand is specified, only the last one is in effect.

Example

```
UNIANOVA DEP BY A B
   /LMATRIX = "Effect A"
             A 1  0 -1; A 1 -1  0
   /LMATRIX = "Effect B"
             B 1  0 -1; B 1 -1  0
   /KMATRIX = 0; 0
   /DESIGN = A B.
```

In this example, assume that factors *A* and *B* each have three levels.

- There are two LMATRIX subcommands; both have two rows.
- The first LMATRIX subcommand tests whether the effect of *A* is 0, while the second LMATRIX subcommand tests whether the effect of *B* is 0.
- The KMATRIX subcommand specifies that the **K** matrix also has two rows, each with value 0.

CONTRAST Subcommand

CONTRAST specifies the type of contrast desired among the levels of a factor. For a factor with k levels or values, the contrast type determines the meaning of its $k - 1$ degrees of freedom.

- Specify the factor name in parentheses following the subcommand CONTRAST.
- You can specify only one factor per CONTRAST subcommand, but you can enter multiple CONTRAST subcommands.
- After closing the parentheses, enter an equals sign followed by one of the contrast keywords.
- This subcommand creates an **L** matrix such that the columns corresponding to the factor match the contrast given. The other columns are adjusted so that the **L** matrix is estimable.

The following contrast types are available:

DEVIATION *Deviations from the grand mean.* This is the default for between-subjects factors. Each level of the factor except one is compared to the grand mean. One category (by default, the last) must be omitted so that the effects will be independent of one another. To omit a category other than the last, specify the number of the omitted category (which is not necessarily the same as its value) in parentheses after the keyword DEVIATION. For example,

```
UNIANOVA Y BY B
   /CONTRAST(B)=DEVIATION(1).
```

Suppose factor *B* has three levels, with values 2, 4, and 6. The specified contrast omits the first category, in which *B* has the value 2. Deviation contrasts are not orthogonal.

POLYNOMIAL *Polynomial contrasts.* This is the default for within-subjects factors. The first degree of freedom contains the linear effect across the levels of the factor, the second contains the quadratic effect, and so on. In a balanced design, polynomial contrasts are orthogonal. By default, the levels are assumed to be equally spaced; you can specify unequal spacing by entering a metric consisting of one integer for each level of the factor in parentheses after the keyword POLYNOMIAL. (All metrics specified cannot be equal; thus, $(1, 1, \ldots 1)$ is not valid.) For example,

```
UNIANOVA RESPONSE BY STIMULUS
   /CONTRAST(STIMULUS) = POLYNOMIAL(1,2,4).
```

Suppose that factor *STIMULUS* has three levels. The specified contrast indicates that the three levels of *STIMULUS* are actually in the proportion 1:2:4. The default metric is always $(1, 2, \ldots k)$, where k levels are involved. Only the relative differences between the terms of the metric matter; $(1, 2, 4)$ is the same metric as $(2, 3, 5)$ or $(20, 30, 50)$ because, in each instance, the difference between the second and third numbers is twice the difference between the first and second.

DIFFERENCE *Difference or reverse Helmert contrasts.* Each level of the factor except the first is compared to the mean of the previous levels. In a balanced design, difference contrasts are orthogonal.

HELMERT   *Helmert contrasts.* Each level of the factor except the last is compared to the mean of subsequent levels. In a balanced design, Helmert contrasts are orthogonal.

SIMPLE   *Each level of the factor except the last is compared to the last level.* To use a category other than the last as the omitted reference category, specify its number (which is not necessarily the same as its value) in parentheses following the keyword SIMPLE. For example,

```
UNIANOVA Y BY B
    /CONTRAST(B)=SIMPLE(1).
```

Suppose that factor *B* has three levels with values 2, 4, and 6. The specified contrast compares the other levels to the first level of *B*, in which *B* has the value 2. Simple contrasts are not orthogonal.

REPEATED   *Comparison of adjacent levels.* Each level of the factor except the first is compared to the previous level. Repeated contrasts are not orthogonal.

SPECIAL   *A user-defined contrast.* Values specified after this keyword are stored in a matrix in column major order. For example, if factor *A* has three levels, then CONTRAST(A)= SPECIAL(1 1 1 -1 0 0 1 -1) produces the following contrast matrix:

$$
\begin{matrix}
1 & 1 & 0 \\
1 & -1 & 1 \\
1 & 0 & -1
\end{matrix}
$$

Orthogonal contrasts are particularly useful. In a balanced design, contrasts are orthogonal if the sum of the coefficients in each contrast row is 0 and if, for any pair of contrast rows, the products of corresponding coefficients sum to 0. DIFFERENCE, HELMERT, and POLYNOMIAL contrasts always meet these criteria in balanced designs.

Example

```
UNIANOVA DEP BY FAC
    /CONTRAST(FAC)=DIFFERENCE
    /DESIGN.
```

- Suppose that the factor *FAC* has five categories and therefore four degrees of freedom.
- CONTRAST requests DIFFERENCE contrasts, which compare each level (except the first) with the mean of the previous levels.

POSTHOC Subcommand

POSTHOC allows you to produce multiple comparisons between means of a factor. These comparisons are usually not planned at the beginning of the study but are suggested by the data in the course of study.

- Post hoc tests are computed for the dependent variable. The alpha value used in the tests can be specified by using the keyword ALPHA on the CRITERIA subcommand. The default alpha value is 0.05. The confidence level for any confidence interval constructed is $(1 - \alpha) \times 100$. The default confidence level is 95.

- Only between-subjects factors appearing in the factor list are valid in this subcommand. Individual factors can be specified.
- You can specify one or more effects to be tested. Only fixed main effects appearing or implied on the DESIGN subcommand are valid test effects.
- Optionally, you can specify an effect defining the error term following the keyword VS after the test specification. The error effect can be any single effect in the design that is not the intercept or a main effect named on a POSTHOC subcommand.
- A variety of multiple comparison tests are available. Some tests are designed for detecting homogeneity subsets among the groups of means, some are designed for pairwise comparisons among all means, and some can be used for both purposes.
- For tests that are used for detecting homogeneity subsets of means, non-empty group means are sorted in ascending order. Means that are not significantly different are included together to form a homogeneity subset. The significance for each homogeneity subset of means is displayed. In a case where the numbers of valid cases are not equal in all groups, for most post hoc tests, the harmonic mean of the group sizes is used as the sample size in the calculation. For QREGW or FREGW, individual sample sizes are used.
- For tests that are used for pairwise comparisons, the display includes the difference between each pair of compared means, the confidence interval for the difference, and the significance. The sample sizes of the two groups being compared are used in the calculation.
- Output for tests specified on the POSTHOC subcommand are available according to their statistical purposes. The following table illustrates the statistical purpose of the post hoc tests:

Post Hoc Tests	Statistical Purpose	
Keyword	Homogeneity Subsets Detection	Pairwise Comparison and Confidence Interval
LSD		Yes
SIDAK		Yes
BONFERRONI		Yes
GH		Yes
T2		Yes
T3		Yes
C		Yes
DUNNETT		Yes[*]
DUNNETTL		Yes*
DUNNETTR		Yes*
SNK	Yes	
BTUKEY	Yes	
DUNCAN	Yes	
QREGW	Yes	
FREGW	Yes	
WALLER	Yes[†]	
TUKEY	Yes	Yes
SCHEFFE	Yes	Yes
GT2	Yes	Yes
GABRIEL	Yes	Yes

* Only C.I.'s for differences between test group means and control group means are given.

† No significance for Waller test is given.

- Tests that are designed for homogeneity subset detection display the detected homogeneity subsets and their corresponding significances.
- Tests that are designed for both homogeneity subset detection and pairwise comparisons display both kinds of output.
- For the DUNNETT, DUNNETTL, and DUNNETTR keywords, only individual factors can be specified.
- The default reference category for DUNNETT, DUNNETTL, and DUNNETTR is the last category. An integer greater than 0 within parentheses can be used to specify a different reference category. For example, POSTHOC = A (DUNNETT(2)) requests a DUNNETT test for factor A, using the second level of A as the reference category.
- The keywords DUNCAN, DUNNETT, DUNNETTL, and DUNNETTR must be spelled out in full; using the first three characters alone is not sufficient.
- If the REGWT subcommand is specified, weighted means are used in performing post hoc tests.
- Multiple POSTHOC subcommands are allowed. Each specification is executed independently so that you can test different effects against different error terms.

SNK
Student-Newman-Keuls procedure based on the Studentized range test.

TUKEY
Tukey's honestly significant difference. This test uses the Studentized range statistic to make all pairwise comparisons between groups.

BTUKEY
Tukey's b. Multiple comparison procedure based on the average of Studentized range tests.

DUNCAN
Duncan's multiple comparison procedure based on the Studentized range test.

SCHEFFE
Scheffé's multiple comparison t *test.*

DUNNETT(refcat)
Dunnett's two-tailed t *test.* Each level of the factor is compared to a reference category. A reference category can be specified in parentheses. The default reference category is the last category. This keyword must be spelled out in full.

DUNNETTL(refcat)
Dunnett's one-tailed t *test.* This test indicates whether the mean at any level (except the reference category) of the factor is *smaller* than that of the reference category. A reference category can be specified in parentheses. The default reference category is the last category. This keyword must be spelled out in full.

DUNNETTR(refcat)
Dunnett's one-tailed t *test.* This test indicates whether the mean at any level (except the reference category) of the factor is *larger* than that of the reference category. A reference category can be specified in paren-

theses. The default reference category is the last category. This keyword must be spelled out in full.

BONFERRONI *Bonferroni* t *test.* This test is based on Student's *t* statistic and adjusts the observed significance level for the fact that multiple comparisons are made.

LSD *Least significant difference* t *test.* Equivalent to multiple *t* tests between all pairs of groups. This test does not control the overall probability of rejecting the hypotheses that some pairs of means are different, while in fact they are equal.

SIDAK *Sidak* t *test.* This test provides tighter bounds than the Bonferroni test.

GT2 *Hochberg's GT2.* Pairwise comparisons test based on the Studentized maximum modulus test. Unless the cell sizes are extremely unbalanced, this test is fairly robust even for unequal variances.

GABRIEL *Gabriel's pairwise comparisons test based on the Studentized maximum modulus test.*

FREGW *Ryan-Einot-Gabriel-Welsch's multiple stepdown procedure based on an* F *test.*

QREGW *Ryan-Einot-Gabriel-Welsch's multiple stepdown procedure based on the Studentized range test.*

T2 *Tamhane's T2.* Tamhane's pairwise comparisons test based on a *t* test. This test can be applied in situations where the variances are unequal.

T3 *Dunnett's T3.* Pairwise comparisons test based on the Studentized maximum modulus. This test is appropriate when the variances are unequal.

GH *Games and Howell's pairwise comparisons test based on the Studentized range test.* This test can be applied in situations where the variances are unequal.

C *Dunnett's C.* Pairwise comparisons based on the weighted average of Studentized ranges. This test can be applied in situations where the variances are unequal.

WALLER(kratio) *Waller-Duncan* t *test.* This test uses a Bayesian approach. It is restricted to cases with equal sample sizes. For cases with unequal sample sizes, the harmonic mean of the sample size is used. The k-ratio is the Type 1/Type 2 error seriousness ratio. The default value is 100. You can specify an integer greater than 1 within parentheses.

EMMEANS Subcommand

EMMEANS displays estimated marginal means of the dependent variable in the cells (with covariates held at their overall mean value) and their standard errors for the specified factors.

Note that these are predicted, not observed, means. The estimated marginal means are calculated using a modified definition by Searle, Speed, and Milliken (1980).

- TABLES, followed by an option in parentheses, is required. COMPARE is optional; if specified, it must follow TABLES.

- Multiple EMMEANS subcommands are allowed. Each is treated independently.

- If redundant EMMEANS subcommands are specified, only the last redundant subcommand is in effect. EMMEANS subcommands are redundant if the option specified on TABLES is the same (including redundant crossed factor combinations—for example, A*B and B*A).

TABLES(option)   *Table specification.* Valid options are the keyword OVERALL, factors appearing on the factor list, and crossed factors constructed of factors on the factor list. Crossed factors can be specified using an asterisk (*) or the keyword BY. All factors in a crossed factor specification must be unique.

If OVERALL is specified, the estimated marginal means of the dependent variable are displayed, collapsing over between-subjects factors.

If a between-subjects factor, or a crossing of between-subjects factors, is specified on the TABLES keyword, UNIANOVA collapses over any other between-subjects factors before computing the estimated marginal means for the dependent variable.

COMPARE ADJ(method) *Pairwise comparisons of the dependent variable.* Each level of the factor specified in the TABLES command is compared with each other level for all combinations of other factors. Valid options for the confidence interval adjustment method are the keywords LSD(none), BONFERRONI, and SIDAK. The confidence intervals and significance values are adjusted to account for multiple comparisons.

If OVERALL is specified on TABLES, COMPARE is invalid.

Example

```
UNIANOVA DEP BY A B
  /EMMEANS = TABLES(A*B)COMPARE ADJ (LSD(none))
  /DESIGN.
```

- The output of this analysis includes a pairwise comparisons table for the dependent variable *DEP.*

- Assume that *A* has three levels and *B* has two levels. The first level of *A* is compared with the second and third levels, the second level with the first and third levels, and the third level with the first and second levels. The pairwise comparison is repeated for the two levels of *B.*

SAVE Subcommand

Use SAVE to add one or more residual or fit values to the working data file.

- Specify one or more temporary variables, each followed by an optional new name in parentheses.
- WPRED and WRESID can be saved only if REGWGT has been specified.
- Specifying a temporary variable on this subcommand results in a variable being added to the active data file for each dependent variable.
- You can specify variable names for the temporary variables. These names must be unique, valid variable names.
- If new names are not specified, UNIANOVA generates a rootname using a shortened form of the temporary variable name with a suffix.
- If more than one SAVE subcommand is specified, only the last one is in effect.

PRED	*Unstandardized predicted values.*
WPRED	*Weighted unstandardized predicted values.* Available only if REGWGT has been specified.
RESID	*Unstandardized residuals.*
WRESID	*Weighted unstandardized residuals.* Available only if REGWGT has been specified.
DRESID	*Deleted residuals.*
ZRESID	*Standardized residuals.*
SRESID	*Studentized residuals.*
SEPRED	*Standard errors of predicted value.*
COOK	*Cook's distances.*
LEVER	*Uncentered leverage values.*

OUTFILE Subcommand

The OUTFILE subcommand writes an SPSS-format data file that can be used in other procedures.
- You must specify a keyword on OUTFILE. There is no default.
- You must specify a filename in parentheses after a keyword. A filename with a path must be enclosed within quotation marks. The asterisk (*) is not allowed.
- If you specify more than one keyword, a different filename is required for each.
- If more than one OUTFILE subcommand is specified, only the last one is in effect.
- For COVB or CORB, the output will contain, in addition to the covariance or correlation matrix, three rows for each dependent variable: a row of parameter estimates, a row of residual degrees of freedom, and a row of significance values for the *t* statistics corresponding to the parameter estimates. All statistics are displayed separately by split.

COVB (filename)	*Writes the parameter covariance matrix.*
CORB (filename)	*Writes the parameter correlation matrix.*
EFFECT (filename)	*Writes the statistics from the between-subjects ANOVA table.*

DESIGN (filename)	*Writes the design matrix.* The number of rows equals the number of cases, and the number of columns equals the number of parameters. The variable names are *DES_1*, *DES_2*, ..., *DES_p*, where *p* is the number of the parameters.

DESIGN Subcommand

DESIGN specifies the effects included in a specific model. The cells in a design are defined by all of the possible combinations of levels of the factors in that design. The number of cells equals the product of the number of levels of all the factors. A design is *balanced* if each cell contains the same number of cases. UNIANOVA can analyze both balanced and unbalanced designs.

- Specify a list of terms to be included in the model, separated by spaces or commas.
- The default design, if the DESIGN subcommand is omitted or is specified by itself, is a design consisting of the following terms in order: the intercept term (if INTERCEPT=INCLUDE is specified), next the covariates given in the covariate list, and then the full factorial model defined by all factors on the factor list and excluding the intercept.
- To include a term for the main effect of a factor, enter the name of the factor on the DESIGN subcommand.
- To include the intercept term in the design, use the keyword INTERCEPT on the DESIGN subcommand. If INTERCEPT is specified on the DESIGN subcommand, the subcommand INTERCEPT=EXCLUDE is overridden.
- To include a term for an interaction between factors, use the keyword BY or the asterisk (*) to join the factors involved in the interaction. For example, *A*B* means a two-way interaction effect of *A* and *B*, where *A* and *B* are factors. *A*A* is not allowed because factors inside an interaction effect must be distinct.
- To include a term for nesting one effect within another, use the keyword WITHIN or a pair of parentheses on the DESIGN subcommand. For example, *A(B)* means that *A* is nested within *B*. The expression *A(B)* is equivalent to the expression *A WITHIN B*. When more than one pair of parentheses is present, each pair of parentheses must be enclosed or nested within another pair of parentheses. Thus, *A(B)(C)* is not valid.
- Multiple nesting is allowed. For example, *A(B(C))* means that *B* is nested within *C*, and *A* is nested within *B(C)*.
- Interactions between nested effects are not valid. For example, neither *A(C)*B(C)* nor *A(C)*B(D)* is valid.
- To include a covariate term in the design, enter the name of the covariate on the DESIGN subcommand.
- Covariates can be connected, but not nested, through the * operator to form another covariate effect. Therefore, interactions among covariates such as *X1*X1* and *X1*X2* are valid, but not *X1(X2)*. Using covariate effects such as *X1*X1*, *X1*X1*X1*, *X1*X2*, and *X1*X1*X2*X2* makes fitting a polynomial regression model easy in UNIANOVA.
- Factor and covariate effects can be connected only by the * operator. Suppose *A* and *B* are factors, and *X1* and *X2* are covariates. Examples of valid factor-by-covariate interaction effects are *A*X1*, *A*B*X1*, *X1*A(B)*, *A*X1*X1*, and *B*X1*X2*.

- If more than one DESIGN subcommand is specified, only the last one is in effect.

Example

```
UNIANOVA Y BY A B C WITH X
  /DESIGN A B(A) X*A.
```

- In this example, the design consists of a main effect *A*, a nested effect *B* within *A*, and an interaction effect of a covariate *X* with a factor *A*.

UPDATE

```
UPDATE FILE={master file}
            {*          }

[/RENAME=(old varnames=new varnames)...]

[/IN=varname]

 /FILE={transaction file1}
       {*               }

[/FILE=transaction file2]

 /BY key variables

[/MAP]

[/KEEP={ALL**   }]  [/DROP=varlist]
       {varlist}
```

**Default if the subcommand is omitted.

Example

```
UPDATE FILE=MAILIST /FILE=NEWLIST /BY=ID.
```

Overview

UPDATE replaces values in a master file with updated values recorded in one or more files called transaction files. Cases in the master file and transaction file are matched according to a key variable.

The master file and the transaction files must be SPSS-format data files created with the SAVE or XSAVE commands or the working data file. UPDATE replaces values and creates a new working data file, which replaces the original working file. Use the SAVE or XSAVE commands to save the updated file on disk as an SPSS-format data file.

UPDATE is designed to update values of existing variables for existing cases. Use MATCH FILES to add new variables to an SPSS-format data file and ADD FILES to add new cases.

Options

Variable Selection. You can specify which variables from each input file are included in the new working file using the DROP and KEEP subcommands.

Variable Names. You can rename variables in each input file before combining the files using the RENAME subcommand. This permits you to combine variables that are the same but whose names differ in different input files, or to separate variables that are different but have the same name.

Variable Flag. You can create a variable that indicates whether a case came from a particular input file using IN. You can use the FIRST or LAST subcommand to create a variable that flags the first or last case of a group of cases with the same value for the key variable.

Variable Map. You can request a map showing all variables in the new working file, their order, and the input files from which they came using the MAP subcommand.

Basic Specification

The basic specification is two or more FILE subcommands and a BY subcommand.

- The first FILE subcommand must specify the master file. All other FILE subcommands identify the transaction files.
- BY specifies the key variables.
- All files must be sorted in ascending order by the key variables.
- By default, all variables from all input files are included in the new working file.

Subcommand Order

- The master file must be specified first.
- RENAME and IN must immediately follow the FILE subcommand to which they apply.
- BY must follow the FILE subcommands and any associated RENAME and IN subcommands.
- MAP, DROP, and KEEP must be specified after all FILE and RENAME subcommands.

Syntax Rules

- BY can be specified only once. However, multiple variables can be specified on BY. All files must be sorted in ascending order by the key variables named on BY.
- The master file cannot contain duplicate values for the key variables.
- RENAME can be repeated after each FILE subcommand and applies only to variables in the file named on the immediately preceding FILE subcommand.
- MAP can be repeated as often as needed.

Operations

- UPDATE reads all input files named on FILE and builds a new working data file that replaces any working file created earlier in the session. The new working data file is built when the data are read by one of the procedure commands or the EXECUTE, SAVE, or SORT CASES command.
- The new working data file contains complete dictionary information from the input files, including variable names, labels, print and write formats, and missing-value indicators. The new working data file also contains the documents from each input file, unless the DROP DOCUMENTS command is used.

- UPDATE copies all variables in order from the master file, then all variables in order from the first transaction file, then all variables in order from the second transaction file, and so on.
- Cases are updated when they are matched on the BY variable(s). If the master and transaction files contain common variables for matched cases, the values for those variables are taken from the transaction file, provided the values are not missing or blanks. Missing or blank values in the transaction files are not used to update values in the master file.
- When UPDATE encounters duplicate keys within a transaction file, it applies each transaction sequentially to that case to produce one case per key value in the resulting file. If more than one transaction file is specified, the value for a variable comes from the last transaction file with a nonmissing value for that variable.
- Variables that are in the transaction files but not in the master file are added to the master file. Cases that do not contain those variables are assigned the system-missing value (for numerics) or blanks (for strings).
- Cases that are in the transaction files but not in the master file are added to the master file and are interleaved according to their values for the key variables.
- If the working data file is named as an input file, any N and SAMPLE commands that have been specified are applied to the working data file before files are combined.
- The TEMPORARY command cannot be in effect if the working data file is used as an input file.

Limitations

- Maximum 1 BY subcommand. However, BY can specify multiple variables.

Example

```
UPDATE FILE=MAILIST /FILE=NEWLIST /BY=ID.
```

- *MAILIST* is specified as the master file. *NEWLIST* is the transaction file. *ID* is the key variable.
- Both *MAILIST* and *NEWLIST* must be sorted in ascending order of *ID*.
- If *NEWLIST* has cases or nonmissing variables that are not in *MAILIST*, the new cases or variables are added to the resulting file.

Example

```
SORT CASES BY LOCATN DEPT.
UPDATE  FILE=MASTER /FILE=* /BY LOCATN DEPT
  /KEEP AVGHOUR AVGRAISE LOCATN DEPT SEX HOURLY RAISE /MAP.
SAVE OUTFILE=PRSNNL.
```

- SORT CASES sorts the working data file in ascending order of the variables to be named as key variables on UPDATE.
- UPDATE specifies *MASTER* as the master file and the sorted working data file as the transaction file. File *MASTER* must also be sorted by *LOCATN* and *DEPT*.

- BY specifies the key variables *LOCATN* and *DEPT*.
- KEEP specifies the subset and order of variables to be retained in the resulting file.
- MAP provides a list of the variables in the resulting file and the two input files.
- SAVE saves the resulting file as an SPSS-format data file.

FILE Subcommand

FILE identifies each input file. At least two FILE subcommands are required on UPDATE: one specifies the master file and the other a transaction file. A separate FILE subcommand must be used to specify each transaction file.

- The first FILE subcommand must specify the master file.
- An asterisk on FILE refers to the working data file.
- All files must be sorted in ascending order according to the variables specified on BY.
- The master file cannot contain duplicate values for the key variables. However, transaction files can and often do contain cases with duplicate keys (see "Operations" on p. 1215).

Raw Data Files

To update the master file with cases from a raw data file, use DATA LIST first to define the raw data file as the working data file. UPDATE can then use the working data file to update the master file.

Example

```
DATA LIST FILE=RAWDATA
  ID 1-3 NAME 5-17 (A) ADDRESS 19-28 (A) ZIP 30-34.
SORT CASES BY ID.
UPDATE FILE=MAILIST1 /RENAME=(STREET=ADDRESS) /FILE=* /BY=ID /MAP.
SAVE OUTFILE=MAILIST2.
```

- DATA LIST defines the variables in the raw data file *RAWDATA*, which will be used to update values in the master file.
- SORT CASES sorts the working data file in ascending order of the key variable *ID*. Cases in the master file were previously sorted in this manner.
- The first FILE subcommand on UPDATE refers to the master file, *MAILIST1*. The RENAME subcommand renames the variable *STREET* to *ADDRESS* in file *MAILIST1*.
- The second FILE subcommand refers to the working data file defined on DATA LIST.
- BY indicates that cases in *MAILIST1* and the working data file are to be matched by the key variable *ID*.
- MAP requests a map of the resulting file.
- SAVE saves the resulting file as an SPSS-format data file named *MAILIST2*.

BY Subcommand

BY specifies one or more identification, or key, variables that are used to match cases between files.

- BY must follow the FILE subcommands and any associated RENAME and IN subcommands.

- BY specifies the names of one or more key variables. The key variables must exist in all input files and have the same names in all the files. The key variables can be string variables (long strings are allowed).

- All input files must be sorted in ascending order of the key variables. If necessary, use SORT CASES before UPDATE.

- Missing values for key variables are handled like any other values.

- The key variables in the master file must identify unique cases. If duplicate cases are found, the program issues an error and UPDATE is not executed. The system-missing value is treated as one single value.

RENAME Subcommand

RENAME renames variables on the input files *before* they are processed by UPDATE. RENAME must follow the FILE subcommand that contains the variables to be renamed.

- RENAME applies only to the immediately preceding FILE subcommand. To rename variables from more than one input file, specify a RENAME subcommand after each FILE subcommand.

- Specifications for RENAME consist of a left parenthesis, a list of old variable names, an equals sign, a list of new variable names, and a right parenthesis. The two variable lists must name or imply the same number of variables. If only one variable is renamed, the parentheses are optional.

- More than one rename specification can be specified on a single RENAME subcommand, each enclosed in parentheses.

- The TO keyword can be used to refer to consecutive variables in the file and to generate new variable names (see the TO keyword on p. 29).

- RENAME takes effect immediately. Any KEEP and DROP subcommands entered prior to a RENAME must use the old names, while KEEP and DROP subcommands entered after a RENAME must use the new names.

- All specifications within a single set of parentheses take effect simultaneously. For example, the specification RENAME (A,B = B,A) swaps the names of the two variables.

- Variables cannot be renamed to scratch variables.

- Input SPSS-format data files are not changed on disk; only the copy of the file being combined is affected.

Example

```
UPDATE FILE=MASTER /FILE=CLIENTS
   /RENAME=(TEL_NO, ID_NO = PHONE, ID)
   /BY ID.
```

- UPDATE updates the master phone list by using current information from file *CLIENTS*.
- Two variables on *CLIENTS* are renamed prior to the match. *TEL_NO* is renamed *PHONE* to match the name used for phone numbers in the master file. *ID_NO* is renamed *ID* so that it will have the same name as the identification variable in the master file and can be used on the BY subcommand.
- The old variable names are listed before the equals sign, and the new variable names are listed in the same order after the equals sign. The parentheses are required.
- The BY subcommand matches cases according to client ID numbers.

DROP and KEEP Subcommands

DROP and KEEP are used to include a subset of variables in the resulting file. DROP specifies a set of variables to exclude, and KEEP specifies a set of variables to retain.

- DROP and KEEP do not affect the input files on disk.
- DROP and KEEP must follow all FILE and RENAME subcommands.
- DROP and KEEP must specify one or more variables. If RENAME is used to rename variables, specify the new names on DROP and KEEP.
- DROP cannot be used with variables created by the IN subcommand.
- Keyword ALL can be specified on KEEP. ALL must be the last specification on KEEP, and it refers to all variables not previously named on KEEP.
- KEEP can be used to change the order of variables in the resulting file. With KEEP, variables are kept in the order they are listed on the subcommand. If a variable is named more than once on KEEP, only the first mention of the variable is in effect; all subsequent references to that variable name are ignored.
- Multiple DROP and KEEP subcommands are allowed. Specifying a variable that is not in the working data file or that has been dropped because of a previous DROP or KEEP subcommand results in an error and the UPDATE command is not executed.

Example

```
UPDATE FILE=MAILIST /FILE=NEWLIST /RENAME=(STREET=ADDRESS) /BY ID
   /KEEP=NAME ADDRESS CITY STATE ZIP ID.
```

- KEEP specifies the variables to keep in the result file. The variables are stored in the order specified on KEEP.

IN Subcommand

IN creates a new variable in the resulting file that indicates whether a case came from the input file named on the preceding FILE subcommand. IN applies only to the file specified on the immediately preceding FILE subcommand.

- IN has only one specification, the name of the flag variable.
- The variable created by IN has value 1 for every case that came from the associated input file and value 0 if the case came from a different input file.
- Variables created by IN are automatically attached to the end of the resulting file and cannot be dropped.

Example

```
UPDATE  FILE=WEEK10 /FILE=WEEK11 /IN=INWEEK11 /BY=EMPID.
```

- IN creates the variable *INWEEK11*, which has the value 1 for all cases in the resulting file that came from the input file *WEEK11* and the value 0 for those cases that were not in file *WEEK11*.

MAP Subcommand

MAP produces a list of the variables are in the new working file and the file or files from which they came. Variables are listed in the order in which they appear in the resulting file. MAP has no specifications and must be placed after all FILE, RENAME, and IN subcommands.

- Multiple MAP subcommands can be used. Each MAP shows the current status of the working data file and reflects only the subcommands that precede the MAP subcommand.
- To obtain a map of the resulting file in its final state, specify MAP last.
- If a variable is renamed, its original and new names are listed. Variables created by IN are not included in the map, since they are automatically attached to the end of the file and cannot be dropped.

USE

```
USE [{start date        }] [THRU [{end date        }]]
    {start case number}        {end case number}
    {FIRST            }        {LAST           }

    [ALL]
```

Example

```
USE Y 1960.
```

Overview

USE designates a range of observations to be used with time series procedures.

Basic Specification

The basic specification is either the start of the range, the end of the range, or both. You can also simply specify keyword THRU or ALL.

- The default start is the first observation in the file, and the default end is the last observation.
- Keyword THRU is required if the end of the range is specified.
- Keyword ALL defines a USE range starting with the first observation and ending with the last observation in the series. It can be specified to restore processing to the entire series.
- Keyword THRU by itself is the same as specifying keyword ALL.

Syntax Rules

- The start and end can be specified as either DATE specifications or case (observation) numbers.
- DATE specifications and case numbers cannot be mixed on a USE command.
- Any observation within the file can be used as the start or end, as long as the starting observation comes before the end observation.

DATE Specifications

- A DATE specification consists of DATE keywords and values (see DATE). These specifications must correspond to existing DATE variables.
- If more than one DATE variable exists, the highest-order one must be used in the specification.
- Values on keyword YEAR must have the same format (2 or 4 digits) as the YEAR specifications on the DATE command.

Case Specifications

- The case number specification is the sequence number of the case (observation) as it is read by the program.

Keywords FIRST and LAST

- The start can also be specified with keyword FIRST, and the end with keyword LAST. These keywords designate the first and last cases in the file, respectively.
- Keywords FIRST and LAST can be used along with either DATE or case specifications.

Operations

- USE is ignored by the utility procedures CREATE and RMV. These procedures process all the available data.
- The DATE command turns off all existing USE and PREDICT specifications.
- USE remains in effect in a session until it is changed by another USE command or until a new DATE command is issued.
- Any data selection specified on USE is in effect until the next USE command, the next DATE command, or the end of the session. SPSS-format data files are not affected by the USE command.

Limitations

- Maximum 1 range (one start and/or one end) can be specified.

Examples

```
USE ALL.
```

- This command includes all observations in the file in the USE range.
- This specification is the same as USE THRU or USE FIRST THRU LAST.

```
USE Y 1960.
```

- This command selects observations starting with *YEAR_* value 1960 through the last observation in the file. It is equivalent to USE Y 1960 THRU LAST.

```
USE THRU D 5.
```

- This command selects all cases from the first case in the file to the last one with a *DAY_* value of 5. It is equivalent to USE FIRST THRU D 5.

```
USE THRU 5.
```

- This command selects cases starting with the first case and ending with the fifth case.

```
USE Y 1955 M 6 THRU Y 1960 M 6.
```

- This selects cases from June 1955 through June 1960.

```
USE W 16 D 3 THRU W 48 D 3.
```

- This example selects cases from day 3 of week 16 through day 3 of week 48.

```
USE CYCLE 2 OBS 4 THRU CYCLE 2 OBS 17.
```

- This example selects observations 4 through 17 of the second cycle.

VALUE LABELS

```
VALUE LABELS varlist value 'label' value 'label'... [/varlist...]
```

Example

```
VALUE LABELS JOBGRADE 'P' 'Parttime Employee' 'C' 'Customer Support'.
```

Overview

VALUE LABELS deletes all existing value labels for the specified variable(s) and assigns new value labels. ADD VALUE LABELS can be used to add new labels or alter labels for specified values without deleting other existing labels.

Basic Specification

The basic specification is a variable name and the individual values with their assigned labels.

Syntax Rules

- Labels can be assigned to any previously defined variables except long string variables.
- It is not necessary to enter value labels for all values for a variable.
- Each value label must be enclosed in apostrophes or quotation marks. For short string variables, the values themselves must also be enclosed in apostrophes or quotation marks.
- Value labels can contain any characters, including blanks. To enter an apostrophe as part of a label, enclose the label in quotation marks or enter a double apostrophe.
- Each value label can be up to 60 characters long, although most procedures display only 20 characters. The TABLES procedure will display all 60 characters of a label.
- The same labels can be assigned to the values of different variables by specifying a list of variable names. For string variables, the variables specified must be of equal length.
- Multiple sets of variable names and value labels can be specified on one VALUE LABELS command as long as the sets are separated by slashes.
- To continue a label from one command line to the next, specify a plus (+) sign before the continuation of the label. Each string segment of the label must be enclosed in apostrophes or quotation marks. To insert a blank between the strings, the blank must be included in the label specification.

Operations

- Unlike most transformations, VALUE LABELS takes effect as soon as it is encountered in the command sequence. Thus, special attention should be paid to its position among commands (see "Command Order" on p. 16).
- VALUE LABELS deletes all previously assigned value labels for the specified variables.
- The value labels assigned are stored in the dictionary of the working file and are automatically displayed on the output from many procedures.
- If a specified value is longer than the format of the variable, the program will be unable to read the full value and may not be able to assign the value label correctly.
- If the value specified for a string variable is shorter than the format of the variable, the value specification is right-padded without warning.

Example

```
VALUE LABELS V1 TO V3 1 'Officials & Managers'
                      6 'Service Workers'
                   /V4 'N' 'New Employee'.
```

- Labels are assigned to the values 1 and 6 for the variables between and including *V1* and *V3* in the working data file.
- Following the required slash, a label for value *N* of *V4* is specified. *N* is a string value and must be enclosed in apostrophes or quotation marks.
- If labels exist for values 1 and 6 on *V1* to *V3* and value N on *V4*, they are changed in the dictionary of the working file. If labels do not exist for these values, new labels are added to the dictionary.
- Existing labels for values other than 1 and 6 on *V1* to *V3* and value N on *V4* are deleted.

Example

```
VALUE LABELS  OFFICE88 1 "EMPLOYEE'S OFFICE ASSIGNMENT PRIOR"
  + " TO 1988".
```

- The label for *OFFICE88* is created by combining two strings with the plus sign. The blank between PRIOR and TO must be included in the first or second string to be included in the label.

Example

```
VALUE LABELS=STATE REGION 'U' "UNKNOWN".
```

- Label *UNKNOWN* is assigned to value U for both *STATE* and *REGION*.
- *STATE* and *REGION* must be string variables of equal length. If *STATE* and *REGION* have unequal lengths, a separate specification must be made for each, as in

```
VALUE LABELS STATE 'U' "UNKNOWN" / REGION 'U' "UNKNOWN".
```

Example

```
DATA LIST / CITY 1-8(A) STATE 10-12(A).
VALUE LABELS   STATE 'TEX' "TEXAS" 'TEN' "TENNESSEE"
                     'MIN' "MINNESOTA".
BEGIN DATA
AUSTIN    TEX
MEMPHIS   TEN
ST. PAUL MIN
END DATA.
FREQUENCIES VARIABLES=STATE.
```

- The DATA LIST command defines two variables. *CITY* is eight characters wide and *STATE* is three characters. The values are included between the BEGIN DATA and END DATA commands.
- The VALUE LABELS command assigns labels to three values of variable *STATE*. Each value and each label is specified in either apostrophes or quotation marks.
- The format for variable *STATE* must be at least three characters wide, because the specified values, TEX, TEN, and MIN, are three characters. If the format for *STATE* were two characters, the program would issue a warning. This would occur even though the values named on VALUE LABELS and the values after BEGIN DATA agree.

VARCOMP

VARCOMP is available in the Advanced Models option.

```
VARCOMP dependent variable BY factor list [WITH covariate list]

  /RANDOM = factor [factor ...]

  [/METHOD = {MINQUE({1})**}]
             {      {0}        }
             {ML               }
             {REML             }
             {SSTYPE({3})      }
             {      {1}        }

  [/INTERCEPT = {INCLUDE**}]
               {EXCLUDE   }

  [/MISSING = {EXCLUDE**}]
             {INCLUDE   }

  [/REGWGT = varname]

  [/CRITERIA = [CONVERGE({1.0E-8**})] [EPS({1.0E-8**})] [ITERATE({50**})]
                        {n        }        {n        }          {n   }

  [/PRINT = [EMS] [HISTORY({1**})] [SS]]
                          {n   }

  [/OUTFILE = [VAREST] [{COVB}] (filename) ]
                       {CORB}

  [/DESIGN = {[INTERCEPT] [effect effect ...]}]
```

** Default if subcommand or keyword is omitted.

Example

```
VARCOMP Y1 BY B C WITH X1 X2
 /RANDOM = C
 /DESIGN.
```

Overview

The VARCOMP procedure estimates variance components for mixed models. Following the general linear model approach, VARCOMP uses indicator variable coding to construct a design matrix and then uses one of the four available methods to estimate the contribution of each random effect to the variance of the dependent variable.

Options

Regression Weights. You can specify regression weights for the model with the REGWGT subcommand.

Estimation Methods. You can use one of the four methods available for estimating variance components using the METHOD subcommand.

Tuning the Algorithm. You can control the values of algorithm-tuning parameters with the CRITERIA subcommand.

Optional Output. You can request additional output using the PRINT subcommand.

Saving the Results. You can save the variance component estimates and their asymptotic covariance matrix (if produced) to an external data file.

Basic Specification

The basic specification is one dependent variable and one or more factor variables that define the crosstabulation and one or more factor variables on the RANDOM subcommand to classify factors into either fixed or random factors. By default, VARCOMP uses the minimum norm quadratic unbiased estimator with unit prior weights to estimate variance components. Default output includes a factor-level information table and a variance component estimates table.

Subcommand Order

- The variable specification must come first.
- Other subcommands can be specified in any order.

Syntax Rules

- Only one dependent variable can be specified.
- At least one factor must be specified after BY.
- At least one factor must be specified on the RANDOM subcommand.

Variable List

The variable list specifies the dependent variable and the factors in the model.
- The dependent variable must be the first specification on VARCOMP.
- The factors follow the dependent variable and are separated from it by the keyword BY.
- The covariates, if any, follow the factors and are separated from the dependent variable and the factors by the keyword WITH.
- The dependent variable and the covariates must be numeric, but the factor variables can be either numeric or string. If a factor is a long string variable, only the first eight characters of each value are used.

RANDOM Subcommand

The RANDOM subcommand allows you to specify random factors.
- You must specify at least one RANDOM subcommand with one random factor.

- You can specify multiple random factors on a RANDOM subcommand. You can also use multiple RANDOM subcommands. Specifications are accumulative.

- Only factors listed after the keyword BY in the variable list are allowed on the RANDOM subcommand.

- If you specify a factor on RANDOM, all effects containing the factor are automatically declared as random effects.

Example

```
VARCOM Y BY DRUG SUBJECT
 /RANDOM = SUBJECT
 /DESIGN = DRUG DRUG*SUBJECT.
```

- This example specifies a mixed model where *DRUG* is the fixed factor and *SUBJECT* is a random factor.

- The default method MINQUE(1) is used to estimate the contribution of the random effect DRUG*SUBJECT to the variance of the dependent variable.

METHOD Subcommand

The METHOD subcommand offers four different methods for estimating the variances of the random effects. If more than one METHOD subcommand is specified, only the last one is in effect. If the subcommand is not specified, the default method MINQUE(1) is used. METHOD cannot be specified without a keyword.

MINQUE(n) *Minimum norm quadratic unbiased estimator.* This is the default method. When $n = 0$, zero weight is assigned to the random effects and unit weight is assigned to the residual term. When $n = 1$, unit weight is assigned to both the random effects and the residual term. By default, $n = 1$.

ML *Maximum likelihood method.* Parameters of the fixed effects and variances of the random effects are estimated simultaneously. However, only the variances are reported.

REML *Restricted maximum likelihood method.* Variances of the random effects are estimated based on residuals of the model after adjusting for the fixed effects.

SSTYPE(n) *ANOVA method.* The ANOVA method equates the expected mean squares of the random effects to their observed mean squares. Their variances are then estimated by solving a system of linear equations. The expected mean squares are computed based on the type of sum of squares chosen. Two types are available in VARCOMP: Type I ($n = 1$) and Type III ($n = 3$). Type III is the default option for this method.

INTERCEPT Subcommand

The INTERCEPT subcommand controls whether an intercept term is included in the model. If more than one INTERCEPT subcommand is specified, only the last one is in effect.

INCLUDE	*Include the intercept term.* The intercept (constant) term is included in the model. This is the default when INTERCEPT is not specified.
EXCLUDE	*Exclude the intercept term.* The intercept (constant) term is excluded from the model. EXCLUDE is ignored if you specify the keyword INTERCEPT on the DESIGN subcommand.

MISSING Subcommand

By default, cases with missing values for any of the variables on the VARCOMP variable list are excluded from the analyses. The MISSING subcommand allows you to include cases with user-missing values.

- Pairwise deletion of missing data is not available in VARCOMP.
- If more than one MISSING subcommand is specified, only the last one is in effect.

EXCLUDE	*Exclude both user-missing and system-missing values.* This is the default when MISSING is not specified.
INCLUDE	*User-missing values are treated as valid.* System-missing values cannot be included in the analysis.

REGWGT Subcommand

REGWGT specifies the weight variable. Values of this variable are used as regression weights in a weighted least squares model.

- Specify one numeric variable name on the REGWGT subcommand.
- Cases with nonpositive values in the regression weight variable are excluded from the analyses.
- If more than one variable is specified on the same REGWGT subcommand, only the last variable is in effect.
- If more than one REGWGT subcommand is specified, only the last one is in effect.

CRITERIA Subcommand

The CRITERIA subcommand specifies numerical tolerance for checking singularity and offers control of the iterative algorithm used for ML or REML estimation.

- Multiple CRITERIA subcommands are allowed.
- The last specified value for any keyword takes effect. If none is specified, the default is used.

EPS(n)	*Epsilon value used as tolerance in checking singularity.* n must be a positive value. The default is 1.0E-8.
CONVERGE(n)	*Convergence criterion.* Convergence is assumed if the relative change in the objective function is less than the specified value. n must be a positive value.

The default is 1.0E-8. Available only if you specify ML or REML on the METHOD subcommand.

ITERATE(n) *Maximum number of iterations. n* must be a positive integer. The default is 50. Available only if you specify ML or REML on the METHOD subcommand.

PRINT Subcommand

The PRINT subcommand controls the display of optional output. If PRINT is not specified, the default output includes a factor information table and a variance component estimates table.

- For the maximum likelihood (ML) and restricted maximum likelihood (REML) methods, an asymptotic covariance matrix of the variance estimates table is also displayed.
- If more than one PRINT subcommand is specified, the specifications are accumulated. However, if you specify the keyword HISTORY more than once but with different values for *n*, the last specification is in effect

EMS *Expected mean squares.* Expected mean squares of all of the effects. Available only if you specify SSTYPE(n) on the METHOD subcommand.

HISTORY(n) *Iteration history.* The table contains the objective function value and variance component estimates at every *n* iteration. *n* must be a positive integer. The default is 1. The last iteration is always printed if HISTORY is specified on PRINT. Available only if you specify ML or REML on the METHOD subcommand.

SS *Sums of squares.* The table contains sums of squares, degrees of freedom, and mean squares for each source of variation. Available only if you specify SSTYPE(n) on the METHOD subcommand.

OUTFILE Subcommand

The OUTFILE subcommand writes the variance component estimates to a data file that can be used in other procedures. For the ML and REML methods, OUTFILE can also write the asymptotic covariance or correlation matrix to a data file. If more than one OUTFILE subcommand is specified, the last specification is in effect.

- OUTFILE writes an external file. You must specify a valid filename in parentheses.
- COVB and CORB are available only if you specify ML or REML on the METHOD subcommand.
- COVB and CORB are mutually exclusive; only one of them can be specified on an OUTFILE subcommand.

VAREST *Variance component estimates.* A variable will be created to contain the estimates, and another variable will be created to hold the labels of the variance components.

COVB *Covariance matrix.* The asymptotic covariance matrix of the variance component estimates. One variable is created for each variance component.

CORB

Correlation matrix. The asymptotic correlation matrix of the variance component estimates. One variable is created for each variance component.

(filename)

Output filename. Specify one valid filename. The variance component estimates and the asymptotic covariance or correlation matrix (if requested) are written to the same file.

DESIGN Subcommand

The DESIGN subcommand specifies the effects in a model. DESIGN can be specified anywhere after the variable list. If more than one DESIGN subcommand is specified, only the last one is in effect.

- Specify a list of effect terms to be included in the design. Each term must be separated from the next by a comma or a space. Valid specifications include the keyword INTERCEPT, factors, covariates, and interaction or nested terms.
- The factors and covariates must have been specified on the variable list.
- If a factor is specified on the RANDOM subcommand, all effects that include that factor are random effects.
- If the DESIGN subcommand is omitted or specified without any term, the default design is generated. The default design includes the intercept term (if INTERCEPT=EXCLUDE is not specified), the covariates (if any) in the order in which they are specified on the variable list, the main factorial effects, and all orders of factor-by-factor interaction.

INTERCEPT

Include the intercept term. Specifying INTERCEPT on DESIGN explicitly includes the intercept term regardless of the specification on the INTERCEPT subcommand.

BY

Interaction. You can also use the asterisk (*). Interaction terms can be formed among factors, among covariates, and between factors and covariates.

Factors inside an interaction effect must be distinct. For factors *A, B,* and *C,* expressions like A*C*A or A*A are invalid.

Covariates inside an interaction effect do not have to be distinct. For covariate *X,* X*X is the product of *X* and itself. This is equivalent to a covariate whose values are the square of those of *X.*

WITHIN

Nesting. You can also use a pair of parentheses. Factors and covariates can be nested within factors but no effects can be nested within covariates. Suppose that *A* and *B* are factors and *X* and *Y* are covariates. Both A(B) and X(B) are valid, but X(Y) is not.

Factors inside a nested effect must be distinct. Expressions like A(A) are invalid.

Multiple-level nesting is supported. For example, A(B(C)) or A WITHIN B WITHIN C means that factor *B* is nested within factor *C,* and factor *A* is nested within *B(C).* The expression A(B)(C) is invalid.

Nesting within an interaction effect is valid. For example, A(B*C) means that factor *A* is nested within *B*C* while X(A*B) means covariate *X* is nested within *A*B*.

Interactions among nested effects are allowed. For example, A*B(C) means interaction between *A* and *B* within levels of *C*. X*Y(A) means the product of *X* and *Y* nested within levels of *C*. The expression A(C)*B(C) is invalid.

Example

```
VARCOM Y BY DRUG SUBJECT WITH X
 /RANDOM = SUBJECT
 /DESIGN = DRUG SUBJECT DRUG*SUBJECT X*SUBECT.
```

- The DESIGN subcommand specifies two main effects and two interaction terms.
- All effects that involve the factor *SUBJECT* are assumed to be random.

VARIABLE ALIGNMENT

```
VARIABLE ALIGNMENT varlist ({LEFT  }) ... [/varlist...]
                           {CENTER}
                           {RIGHT }

Example

VARIABLE ALIGNMENT sales95 sales96 (LEFT)
  /id gender (RIGHT).
```

Overview

VARIABLE ALIGNMENT specifies the alignment of data values in the Data Editor. It has no effect on the format of the variables or the display of the variables or values in other windows or printed results.

Basic Specification

The basic specification is a variable name and the keyword LEFT, RIGHT, or CENTER in parentheses.

VARIABLE LABELS

```
VARIABLE LABELS varname 'label' [/varname...]
```

Example

```
VARIABLE LABELS YRHIRED 'YEAR OF FIRST HIRING'.
```

Overview

VARIABLE LABELS assigns descriptive labels to variables in the working data file.

Basic Specification

The basic specification is a variable name and the associated label in apostrophes or quotation marks.

Syntax Rules

- Labels can be added to any previously defined variable. It is not necessary to enter labels for all variables in the working data file.
- Each variable label must be enclosed in apostrophes or quotation marks.
- Variable labels can contain any characters, including blanks. To enter an apostrophe as part of a label, enclose the label in quotation marks or enter a double apostrophe.
- Each variable label can be up to 255 characters long, although some procedures print fewer than the 255 characters. All statistical procedures display at least 40 characters.
- Multiple variables can be assigned labels on a single VARIABLE LABELS command. Only one label can be assigned to each variable, and each label can apply to only one variable.
- To continue a label from one command line to the next, specify a plus (+) sign before the continuation of the label. Each string segment of the label must be enclosed in apostrophes or quotation marks. To insert a blank between the strings, the blank must be included in the label specification.

Operations

- Unlike most transformations, VARIABLE LABELS takes effect as soon as it is encountered in the command sequence. Thus, special attention should be paid to its position among commands (see "Command Order" on p. 16).
- Variable labels are automatically displayed in the output from many procedures and are stored in the dictionary of the working data file.

- VARIABLE LABELS can be used for variables that have no previously assigned variable labels. If a variable has a previously assigned variable label, the new label replaces the old label.

Example

```
VARIABLE LABELS  YRHIRED 'YEAR OF FIRST HIRING'
  DEPT88 'DEPARTMENT OF EMPLOYMENT IN 1988'
  SALARY88 'YEARLY SALARY IN 1988'
  JOBCAT 'JOB CATEGORIES'.
```

- Variable labels are assigned to the variables *YRHIRED*, *DEPT88*, *SALARY88*, and *JOBCAT*.

Example

```
VARIABLE LABELS  OLDSAL "EMPLOYEE'S GROSS SALARY PRIOR"
  + " TO 1988".
```

- The label for *OLDSAL* is created by combining two strings with the plus sign. The blank between PRIOR and TO must be included in the first or second string to be included in the label.

VARIABLE LEVEL

```
VARIABLE LEVEL varlist ({SCALE**  }) ... [/varlist...]
                        {ORDINAL}
                        {NOMINAL}
```

**Default.

Example

```
VARIABLE LEVEL sales95 sales96 SCALE
    /region division NOMINAL
    /expense ORDINAL.
```

Overview

VARIABLE LEVEL specifies the level of measurement for variables. Measurement specification is only relevant for:

- Charts created by the IGRAPH command. Nominal and ordinal are both treated as categorical.
- SPSS-format data files used with AnswerTree.

Basic Specification

The basic specification is a variable name and the measurement level.

VARIABLE WIDTH

```
VARIABLE WIDTH varlist (n) ... [/varlist...]

Example

VARIABLE WIDTH sales95 sales96 (10)
  /id gender (2).
```

Overview

VARIABLE WIDTH specifies column width for display of variables in the Data Editor. It has no effect on the format of the variable or the display of the variable or values in other windows or printed results.

Basic Specification

The basic specification is a variable name and a positive integer in parentheses for the column width.

VECTOR

```
VECTOR  {vector  name=varlist     }  [/vector  name...]
        {vector  name(n  [format])}
```

Example

```
VECTOR V=V1 TO V6.

STRING SELECT(A1).
COMPUTE SELECT='V'.

LOOP #I=1 TO 6.
IF MISSING(V(#I)) SELECT='M'.
END LOOP.
```

Overview

VECTOR associates a vector name with a set of existing variables or defines a vector of new variables. A vector is a set of variables that can be referred to using an index. The vector can refer to either string or numeric variables, and the variables can be permanent or temporary.

For each variable in the reference list, VECTOR generates an element. Element names are formed by adding a subscript in parentheses to the end of the vector name. For example, if vector *AGES* has three elements, the element names are *AGES(1)*, *AGES(2)*, and *AGES(3)*. Although the VECTOR command has other uses within the transformation language, it is most often used with LOOP structures because the indexing variable on LOOP can be used to refer to successive vector elements.

Options

File Structures. VECTOR can be used with the END CASE command to restructure data files. You can build a single case from several cases or, conversely, you can build several cases from a single case (see pp. 335 and 336 for examples).

Short-Form Vectors. VECTOR can be used to create a list of new variables and the vector that refers to them simultaneously. VECTOR in the short form can be used to establish the dictionary order of a group of variables before they are defined on a DATA LIST command. (See "VECTOR: Short Form" on p. 1241.)

Basic Specification

- The basic specification is VECTOR, a vector name, a required equals sign, and the list of variables that the vector refers to. The TO keyword must be used to specify the variable list.
- For the short form of VECTOR, the basic specification is VECTOR, an alphabetical prefix, and, in parentheses, the number of variables to be created.

Syntax Rules

- Multiple vectors can be created on the same command by using a slash to separate each set of specifications.

- Variables specified on VECTOR must already be defined unless the short form of VECTOR is used to create variables (see "VECTOR: Short Form" on p. 1241).

- The TO convention must be used to specify the variable list. Thus, variables specified must be consecutive and must be from the same dictionary, permanent or scratch.

- A single vector must comprise all numeric variables or all string variables. The string variables must have the same length.

- A scalar (a variable named on NUMERIC), a function, and a vector can all have the same name, for example *MINI*. The scalar can be identified by the lack of a left parenthesis following the name. Where a vector has the same name as a function (or the abbreviation of a function), the vector name takes precedence. (See p. 1242 for an example.)

- Vector element names must always be specified with a subscript in parentheses.

Operations

- VECTOR takes effect as soon as it is encountered in the command sequence, unlike most transformations, which do not take effect until the data are read. Thus, special attention should be paid to its position among commands (see "Command Order" on p. 16).

- VECTOR is in effect only until the first procedure that follows it. The vector must be redeclared to be reused.

- Vectors can be used in transformations but not in procedures.

Examples

```
* Replace a case's missing values with the mean of all
  nonmissing values for that case.

DATA LIST FREE /V1 V2 V3 V4 V5 V6 V7 V8.
MISSING VALUES V1 TO V8 (99).
COMPUTE MEANSUB=MEAN(V1 TO V8).

VECTOR V=V1 TO V8.
LOOP #I=1 TO 8.
+    DO IF MISSING (V(#I)).
+    COMPUTE V(#I)=MEANSUB.
+    END IF.
END LOOP.

BEGIN DATA
1 99 2 3 5 6 7  8
2  3 4 5 6 7 8  9
2  3 5 5 6 7 8 99
END DATA.
LIST.
```

- The first COMPUTE command calculates variable MEANSUB as the mean of all nonmissing values for each case.
- VECTOR defines vector *V* with the original variables as its elements.
- For each case, the loop is executed once for each variable. The COMPUTE command within the loop is executed only when the variable has a missing value for that case. COMPUTE replaces the missing value with the value of *MEANSUB*.
- For the first case, the missing value for variable *V2* is changed to the value of *MEANSUB* for that case. The missing value for variable *V8* for the third case is changed to the value of *MEANSUB* for that case.

More Examples

For additional examples of VECTOR, see pp. 335, 336, and 548.

VECTOR: Short Form

VECTOR can be used to create a list of new variables and the vector that refers to them simultaneously. The short form of VECTOR specifies a prefix of alphanumeric characters followed, in parentheses, by the length of the vector (the number of variables to be created).

- The new variable names must not conflict with existing variables. If the prefix starts with the # character, the new variables are created according to the rules for scratch variables.
- More than one vector of the same length can be created by naming two or more prefixes before the length specification.
- By default, variables created with VECTOR receive F8.2 formats. Alternative formats for the variables can be specified by including a format specification with the length specification within the parentheses. The format and length can be specified in either order and must be separated by at least one space or comma. If multiple vectors are created, the assigned format applies to all of them unless you specify otherwise.

Example

```
VECTOR #WORK(10).
```

- The program creates vector *#WORK*, which refers to 10 scratch variables: *#WORK1*, *#WORK2,* and so on, through *#WORK10*. Thus, element *#WORK(5)* of the vector is variable *#WORK5*.

Example

```
VECTOR X,Y(5).
```

- VECTOR creates vectors *X* and *Y*, which refer to the new variables *X1* through *X5* and *Y1* through *Y5*, respectively.

Example

```
VECTOR X(6,A5).
```

- VECTOR assigns an A5 format to variables *X1* through *X6*.

Example

```
VECTOR X,Y(A5,6) Z(3,F2).
```

- VECTOR assigns A5 formats to variables *X1* to *X6* and *Y1* to *Y6*, and F2 formats to variables *Z1* to *Z3*. It doesn't matter whether the format or the length is specified first within the parentheses.

Example

```
* Predetermine variable order with the short form of VECTOR.

INPUT PROGRAM.
VECTOR X Y (4,F8.2).
DATA LIST / X4 Y4 X3 Y3 X2 Y2 X1 Y1 1-8.
END INPUT PROGRAM.

PRINT /X1 TO X4  Y1 TO Y4.
BEGIN DATA
49382716
49382716
49382716
END DATA.
```

- The short form of VECTOR is used to establish the dictionary order of a group of variables before they are defined on a DATA LIST command. To predetermine variable order, both VECTOR and DATA LIST must be enclosed within the INPUT PROGRAM and END INPUT PROGRAM commands.

- The order of the variables in the working data file will be *X1*, *X2*, *X3*, and *X4*, and *Y1*, *Y2*, *Y3*, and *Y4*, even though they are defined in a different order on DATA LIST.

- The program reads the variables with the F1 format specified on DATA LIST. It writes the variables with the output format assigned on VECTOR (F8.2).

- Another method for predetermining variable order is to use NUMERIC (or STRING if the variables are string variables) before the DATA LIST command (see p. 845 for an example). The advantage of using NUMERIC or STRING is that you can assign mnemonic names to the variables.

Example

```
* Name conflicts.

INPUT PROGRAM.
NUMERIC MIN MINI_A MINI_B MINIM(F2).
COMPUTE MINI_A = MINI(2).  /*MINI is function MINIMUM.
VECTOR MINI(3,F2).
DO REPEAT I = 1 TO 3.
+   COMPUTE MINI(I) = -I.
END REPEAT.
COMPUTE MIN = MIN(1).      /*The second MIN is function MINIMUM.
COMPUTE MINI_B = MINI(2). /*MINI now references vector MINI
COMPUTE MINIM = MINIM(3). /*The second MINIM is function MINIMUM.
END CASE.
END FILE.
END INPUT PROGRAM.
```

- In this example, there are potential name conflicts between the scalars (the variables named on NUMERIC), the vectors (named on VECTOR), and the statistical function MINIMUM.
- A name that is not followed by a left parenthesis is treated as a scalar.
- When a name followed by a left parenthesis may refer to a vector element or a function, precedence is given to the vector.

VECTOR outside a Loop Structure

VECTOR is most commonly associated with the loop structure, since the index variable for LOOP can be used as the subscript. However, the subscript can come from elsewhere, including from the data.

Example

```
* Create a single case for each of students 1, 2, and 3.

DATA LIST /STUDENT 1 SCORE 3-4 TESTNUM 6.
BEGIN DATA
1 10 1
1 20 2
1 30 3
1 40 4
2 15 2
2 25 3
3 40 1
3 55 3
3 60 4
END DATA.

VECTOR RESULT(4).
COMPUTE RESULT(TESTNUM)=SCORE.

AGGREGATE OUTFILE=*/BREAK=STUDENT
        /RESULT1 TO RESULT4=MAX(RESULT1 TO RESULT4).

PRINT FORMATS RESULT1 TO RESULT4 (F2.0).
PRINT /STUDENT RESULT1 TO RESULT4.
EXECUTE.
```

- Data are scores on tests recorded in separate cases along with a student identification number and a test number. In this example, there are four possible tests for three students. Not all students took every test.
- Vector *RESULT* creates variables *RESULT1* through *RESULT4*.
- For each case, COMPUTE assigns the *SCORE* value to one of the four vector variables, depending on the value of *TESTNUM*. The other three vector variables for each case keep the system-missing value they were initialized to.

- Aggregating by variable *STUDENT* creates new cases, as shown by the output from the PRINT command (see Figure 1). The MAX function in AGGREGATE returns the maximum value across cases with the same value for *STUDENT*. If a student has taken a particular test, the one valid value is returned as the value for variable *RESULT1*, *RESULT2*, *RESULT3*, or *RESULT4*.

Figure 1   PRINT output after aggregating

```
1   10   20   30   40
2    .   15   25    .
3   40    .   55   60
```

VERIFY

```
VERIFY [VARIABLES=series name]
```

Example
```
VERIFY VARIABLE=STOCK.
```

Overview

VERIFY produces a report on the status of the most current DATE, USE, and PREDICT specifications. The report lists the first and last observations in the working data file, the current USE and PREDICT ranges, and any anomalies in the DATE variables. The number of missing values and the values of the first and last observations in the file and in the USE and PREDICT ranges can also be displayed for a specified series.

VERIFY should be used before a time series procedure whenever there is a possibility that DATE variables or USE and PREDICT ranges have been invalidated. In particular, the working data file should be verified after you have modified the file structure with commands such as SELECT IF, SORT CASES, and AGGREGATE.

Options

If a series is specified after VERIFY, the values of the first and last observations in the file and in the USE and PREDICT periods are reported for that series. In addition, the number of observations in the working data file that have missing values for that series is displayed. This can be useful for determining the USE ranges that do not include any missing values.

Basic Specification

The basic specification is the command keyword VERIFY.

- VERIFY displays the first and last observations in the working data file and in the USE and PREDICT ranges. This information is presented by case number and by the values of the DATE variables.

- For DATE variables, VERIFY reports the number of missing or invalid values. In addition, DATE variables that are not properly nested within the next higher-level DATE variable, that have start or end values other than those expected at the beginning or end of a cycle, or that increment by more than the expected increment are flagged with an asterisk next to the problem. An explanation of the problem is given.

Operations

- VERIFY reports on cases remaining after any preceding SELECT IF commands.
- The USE and PREDICT ranges are defined by the last USE and PREDICT commands specified before the VERIFY command. If USE and PREDICT have not been specified, the USE range is the entire series, and the PREDICT range does not exist.

Limitations

- Maximum 1 VARIABLES subcommand. Only 1 series can be specified on VARIABLES.

VARIABLES Subcommand

VARIABLES names a series to include in the report and is optional. The actual keyword VARIABLES can be omitted.

- The series named on VARIABLES must be numeric. The *DATE_* series is non-numeric and cannot be specified.
- Only one VARIABLES subcommand can be specified, and it can name only one series.

Examples

```
VERIFY.
```

- This command produces a report on the status of the most recent DATE, USE, and PREDICT specifications, as well as the first and last valid cases in the file.

```
VERIFY VARIABLE=STOCK.
```

- In addition to the default VERIFY information, this command displays information on series *STOCK*, including the values of the first and last cases and how many values in that series are missing.

WEIGHT

```
WEIGHT  {BY  varname}
        {OFF       }
```

Example

```
WEIGHT BY V1.
FREQUENCIES VAR=V2.
```

Overview

WEIGHT weights cases differentially for analysis. WEIGHT can be used to obtain population estimates when you have a sample from a population for which some subgroup has been over- or undersampled. WEIGHT can also be used to weight a sample up to population size for reporting purposes or to replicate an example from a table or other aggregated data (see p. 233 for an example). With WEIGHT, you can arithmetically alter the sample size or its distribution.

Basic Specification

The basic specification is keyword BY followed by the name of the weight variable. Cases are weighted according to the values of the specified variable.

Syntax Rules

- Only one numeric variable can be specified. The variable can be a precoded weighting variable, or it can be computed with the transformation language.
- WEIGHT cannot be placed within a FILE TYPE—END FILE TYPE or INPUT PROGRAM—END INPUT PROGRAM structure. It can be placed nearly anywhere following these commands in a transformation program. See Appendix A for a discussion of the program states and the placement of commands.

Operations

- Unlike most transformations, WEIGHT takes effect as soon as it is encountered in the command sequence. Thus, special attention should be paid to its position among commands (see "Command Order" on p. 16).
- Weighting is permanent during a session unless it is preceded by a TEMPORARY command, changed by another WEIGHT command, or turned off with the WEIGHT OFF specification.

- Each WEIGHT command overrides the previous one.

- WEIGHT uses the value of the specified variable to arithmetically replicate cases for subsequent procedures. Cases are not physically replicated. For example, if you use a weighted file with CROSSTABS, the counts in the cells are actually the sums of the case weights. CROSSTABS then rounds cell counts when displaying the tables.

- Weight values do not need to be integer.

- Cases with missing or nonpositive values for the weighting variable are treated as having a weight of 0 and are thus invisible to statistical procedures. They are not used in calculations even where unweighted counts are specified. These cases do remain in the file, however, and are included in case listings and saved when the file is saved.

- A file saved when weighting is in effect maintains the weighting.

- If the weighted number of cases exceeds the sample size, tests of significance are inflated; if it is smaller, they are deflated.

Example

```
WEIGHT BY V1.
FREQ VAR=V2.
```

- The frequency counts for the values of variable *V2* will be weighted by the values of variable *V1*.

Example

```
COMPUTE WVAR=1.
IF (GROUP EQ 1) WVAR=.5.
WEIGHT BY WVAR.
```

- Variable *WVAR* is initialized to 1 with the COMPUTE command. The IF command changes the value of *WVAR* to 0.5 for cases where *GROUP* equals 1.

- Subsequent procedures will use a case base in which cases from group 1 count only half as much as other cases.

WLS

WLS is available in the Regression Models option.

```
WLS [VARIABLES=]dependent varname WITH independent varnames

 [/SOURCE=varname]

 [/DELTA=[{1.0**                     }]]
         {value list               }
         {value TO value BY value}

 [/WEIGHT=varname]

 [/{CONSTANT**}
   {NOCONSTANT}

 [/PRINT={BEST}]
         {ALL }

 [/SAVE = WEIGHT]

 [/APPLY[='model name']]
```

**Default if the subcommand or keyword is omitted.

Example

```
WLS VARY WITH VARX VARZ
  /SOURCE=VARZ
  /DELTA=2.
```

Overview

WLS (weighted least squares) estimates regression models with different weights for different cases. Weighted least squares should be used when errors from an ordinary regression are heteroscedastic—that is, when the size of the residual is a function of the magnitude of some variable, termed the **source**.

The WLS model is a simple regression model in which the residual variance is a function of the source variable, up to some power transform indicated by a delta value. For fuller regression results, save the weights produced by WLS and specify that weight variable on the REGWGT subcommand in REGRESSION.

Options

Calculated and Specified Weights. WLS can calculate the weights based on a source variable and delta values (subcommands SOURCE and DELTA), or it can apply existing weights contained in a series (subcommand WEIGHT). If weights are calculated, each weight value is calculated as the source series value raised to the negative delta value.

New Variables. You can change NEWVAR settings on the TSET command prior to WLS to evaluate the regression coefficients and log-likelihood function without saving the weight variable, or save the new values to replace the values saved earlier, or save the new values without erasing values saved earlier (see the TSET command). You can also use the SAVE subcommand on WLS to override the NONE or the default CURRENT settings on NEWVAR for the current procedure.

Statistical Output. You can change the PRINT setting on the TSET command prior to WLS to display regression coefficients or the list of log-likelihood functions at each delta value, or to limit the output to only the regression statistics for the delta value at which the log-likelihood function is maximized (see the TSET command in the *SPSS Base Syntax Reference Guide*). You can also use the PRINT subcommand to override the PRINT setting on the TSET command for the current procedure and obtain regression coefficients at each value of delta in addition to the default output.

Basic Specification

- The basic specification is the VARIABLES subcommand specifying one dependent variable, the keyword WITH, and one or more independent variables. Weights are calculated using the first independent variable as the source variable and a default delta value of 1.
- The default output for calculated weights displays the log-likelihood function for each value of delta. For the value of delta at which the log-likelihood function is maximized, the displayed summary regression statistics include R, R^2, adjusted R^2, standard errors, analysis of variance, and t tests of the individual coefficients. A variable named *WGT#1* containing the calculated weights is automatically created, labeled, and added to the working data file.

Syntax Rules

- VARIABLES can be specified only once.
- DELTA can be specified more than once. Each specification will be executed.
- If other subcommands are specified more than once, only the last specification of each one is executed.
- You can specify either SOURCE and DELTA, or just the WEIGHT subcommand. You cannot specify all three, and you cannot specify WEIGHT with SOURCE or with DELTA.

Subcommand Order

- Subcommands can be specified in any order.

Operations

- If neither the WEIGHT subcommand nor the SOURCE and DELTA subcommands are specified, a warning is issued and weights are calculated using the default source and delta value.

- Only one *WGT#1* variable is created per procedure. If more than one delta value is specified, the weights used when the log-likelihood function is maximized are the ones saved as *WGT#1*.
- *WGT#1* is not created when the WEIGHT subcommand is used.
- The SPSS WEIGHT command specifies case replication weights, which are *not* the same as the weights used in weighted least squares. If the WEIGHT command and WLS WEIGHT subcommand are both specified, both types of weights are incorporated in WLS.
- WLS uses listwise deletion of missing values. Whenever one variable is missing a value for a particular observation, that observation will not be included in any computations.

Limitations

- Maximum one VARIABLES subcommand.
- Maximum one dependent variable on the VARIABLES subcommand. There is no limit on the number of independent variables.
- Maximum 150 values specified on the DELTA subcommand.

Example

```
WLS VARY WITH VARX VARZ
   /SOURCE=VARZ
   /DELTA=2.
```

- This command specifies a weighted least-squares regression in which *VARY* is the dependent variable and *VARX* and *VARZ* are the independent variables.
- *VARZ* is identified as the source of heteroscedasticity.
- Weights will be calculated using a delta value of 2. Thus, the weights will equal $VARZ^{-2}$.

VARIABLES Subcommand

VARIABLES specifies the variable list and is the only required subcommand. The actual keyword VARIABLES can be omitted.

SOURCE Subcommand

SOURCE is used in conjunction with the DELTA subcommand to compute weights. SOURCE names the variable that is the source of heteroscedasticity.

- The only specification on SOURCE is the name of a variable to be used as the source of heteroscedasticity.
- Only one source variable can be specified.
- If neither SOURCE nor WEIGHT is specified, the first independent variable specified on the VARIABLES subcommand is assumed to be the source variable.

DELTA Subcommand

DELTA, alias POWER, is used in conjunction with the SOURCE subcommand to compute weights. DELTA specifies the values to use in computing weights. The weights are equal to 1/(SOURCE raised to the DELTA power).

- The specification on DELTA is a list of possible delta values and/or value grids.
- Multiple values and grids can be specified on one DELTA subcommand.
- Delta values can be any value in the range of –6.5 to +7.5. Values below this range are assigned the minimum (–6.5), and values above are assigned the maximum (7.5).
- A grid is specified by naming the starting value, the keyword TO, an ending value, the keyword BY, and an increment value. Alternatively, the keyword BY and the increment value can be specified after the starting value.
- More than one DELTA subcommand can be specified; each subcommand will be executed.
- If DELTA is not specified, the delta value defaults to 1.0.

Example

```
WLS X1 WITH Y1 Z1
  /SOURCE=Z1
  /DELTA=0.5.
```

- In this example, weights are calculated using the source variable *Z1* and a delta value of 0.5. Thus, the weights are 1/(SQRT (Z1)).

Example

```
WLS SHARES WITH PRICE
  /DELTA=0.5 TO 2.5 BY 0.5.
```

- In this example, several regression equations will be fit, one for each value of delta.
- Weights are calculated using the source variable *PRICE* (the default).
- The delta values start at 0.5 and go up to 2.5, incrementing by 0.5. This specification is equivalent to 0.5 BY 0.5 TO 2.5.
- The weights that maximize the log-likelihood function will be saved as variable *WGT#1*.

WEIGHT Subcommand

WEIGHT specifies the variable containing the weights to be used in weighting the cases. WEIGHT is an alternative to computing the weights using the SOURCE and DELTA subcommands. If a variable containing weights is specified, the output includes the regression coefficients, log-likelihood function, and summary regression statistics such as R, R^2, adjusted R^2, standard errors, analysis of variance, and t tests of the coefficients. Since no new weights are computed, no new variable is created. For a description of the output when weights are calculated by WLS, see "Basic Specification" on p. 1250.

- The only specification on WEIGHT is the name of the variable containing the weights. Typically, *WGT* variables from previous WLS procedures are used.
- Only one variable can be specified.

Example

```
WLS SHARES WITH PRICE
  /WEIGHT=WGT_1.
```

- This WLS command uses the weights contained in variable *WGT_1* to weight cases.

CONSTANT and NOCONSTANT Subcommands

Specify CONSTANT or NOCONSTANT to indicate whether a constant term should be estimated in the regression equation. The specification of either subcommand overrides the CONSTANT setting on the TSET command for the current procedure.

- CONSTANT is the default and specifies that the constant term is used as an instrument.
- NOCONSTANT eliminates the constant term.

SAVE Subcommand

SAVE saves the weight variable generated during the current session to the end of the working data file. The default name *WGT_n* will be generated, where *n* increments to make the variable name unique. The only specification on SAVE is WEIGHT. The specification overrides the NONE or the default CURRENT setting on NEWVAR for the current procedure.

PRINT Subcommand

PRINT can be used to override the PRINT setting on the TSET command for the current procedure. Two keywords are available.

BEST   *Display coefficients for the best weight only.* This is the default.

ALL   *Display coefficients for all weights.*

APPLY Subcommand

- The APPLY subcommand allows you to use a previously defined WLS model without having to repeat the specifications.
- The only specification on APPLY is the name of a previous model in quotes. If a model name is not specified, the model specified on the previous WLS command is used.
- To change one or more model specifications, specify the subcommands of only those portions you want to change after the APPLY subcommand.
- If no variables are specified on the command, the variables that were originally specified with the model being reapplied are used.

Example

```
WLS X1 WITH Y1
  /SOURCE=Y1
  /DELTA=1.5.
WLS APPLY
  /DELTA=2.
```

- The first command produces a weighted least-squares regression of *X1*, with *Y1* as the source variable and delta equal to 1.5.
- The second command uses the same variable and source but changes the delta value to 2.

Example

```
WLS X1 WITH Y1 Z1
  /SOURCE=Z1
  /DELTA=1 TO 3 BY 0.5
WLS APPLY
  /WEIGHT=WGT#1.
```

- The first command regresses *X1* on *Y1* and *Z1*, using *Z1* as the source variable. The delta values range from 1 to 3, incrementing by 0.5.
- The second command again regresses *X1* on *Y1* and *Z1*, but this time applies the values of *WGT#1* as the weights.

WRITE

```
WRITE [OUTFILE=file] [RECORDS={1}] [{NOTABLE}]
                              {n}   {TABLE  }

 /{1     } varlist [{col location [(format)]}] [varlist...]
  {rec #}           {(format list)           }
                    {*                        }

 [/{2     }...]
   {rec #}
```

Example

```
WRITE OUTFILE=PRSNNL / MOHIRED YRHIRED DEPT SALARY NAME.
EXECUTE.
```

Overview

WRITE writes files in a machine-readable format that can be used by other software applications. When used for this purpose, the OUTFILE subcommand is required. If OUTFILE is not specified, the output from WRITE that can be displayed is included with the output from your session in a format similar to that used by the PRINT command.

Options

Formats. You can specify formats for the variables. (See "Formats" on p. 1257.)

Strings. You can include strings within the variable specifications. The strings can be used to label values or to add extra space between values. (See "Strings" on p. 1258.)

Multiple Lines per Case. You can write variables on more than one line for each case. See the RECORDS subcommand on p. 1258.

Output File. You can direct the output to a specified file using the OUTFILE subcommand.

Summary Table. You can display a table that summarizes the variable formats with the TABLE subcommand.

Subcommand Order

Subcommands can be specified in any order. However, all subcommands must be used before the slash that precedes the first variable list.

Basic Specification

The basic specification is a slash followed by a variable list. The values for all of the variables specified on the list are included with the rest of the output from your session.

Syntax Rules

- A slash must precede the variable specifications. The first slash begins the definition of the first (and possibly only) line per case of the WRITE output.
- Specified variables must already exist, but they can be numeric, string, scratch, temporary, or system variables. Subscripted variable names, such as $X(1)$ for the first element in vector X, cannot be used.
- Keyword ALL can be used to write the values of all user-defined variables in the working data file.

Operations

- WRITE is executed once for each case constructed from the data file.
- Values are written to the file as the data are read.
- WRITE is a transformation and will not be executed unless it is followed by a procedure or the EXECUTE command.
- Lines longer than 132 columns can be written. However, if the record width of the lines to be written exceeds the default output width or the width specified with SET WIDTH, the program issues an error message and terminates processing.
- There are no carriage control characters in the output file generated by WRITE.
- User-missing values are written just like valid values. System-missing values are represented by blanks.
- If you are writing a file to be used on another system, you should take into account that some data types cannot be read all computers.
- If long records are less convenient than short records with multiple records per case, you can write out a case identifier and insert a string as a record identification number. The receiving system can then check for missing record numbers (see "Strings" on p. 1258 for an example).

Example

```
WRITE OUTFILE=PRSNNL / MOHIRED YRHIRED DEPT SALARY NAME.
FREQUENCIES VARIABLES=DEPT.
```

- WRITE writes values for each variable on the variable list to file *PRSNNL*. The FREQUENCIES procedure reads the data and causes WRITE to be executed.
- All variables are written with their dictionary formats.

Example

```
WRITE OUTFILE=PRSNNL /ALL.
EXECUTE.
```

- WRITE writes values for all user-defined variables in the working data file to file *PRSNNL*. The EXECUTE command executes WRITE.

Formats

By default, WRITE uses the dictionary write formats. You can specify formats for some or all variables specified on WRITE. For a string variable, the specified format must have the same width as that of the dictionary format.

- Format specifications can be either column-style or FORTRAN-like (see DATA LIST). The column location specified with column-style formats or implied with FORTRAN-like formats refers to the column in which the variable will be written.
- A format specification following a list of variables applies to all the variables in the list. Use an asterisk to prevent the specified format from applying to variables preceding the asterisk. The specification of column locations implies a default print format, and that format will apply to all previous variables if no asterisk is used.
- All available formats can be specified on WRITE. Note that hex and binary formats use different widths. For example, the AHEX format must have a width twice that of the corresponding A format. For more information on specifying formats and on the formats available, see DATA LIST and "Variable Formats" on p. 31.
- Format specifications are in effect only for the WRITE command. They do not change the dictionary write formats.
- To specify a blank between variables in the output, use a string (see "Strings" on p. 1258), specify blank columns in the format, or use an X or T format element in the WRITE specifications (see DATA LIST for information on X and T).

Example

```
WRITE OUTFILE=PRSNNL / TENURE (F2.0) ' ' MOHIRED YRHIRED DEPT *
      SALARY85 TO SALARY88 (4(DOLLAR8,1X)) NAME.
EXECUTE.
```

- Format F2.0 is specified for *TENURE*. A blank between apostrophes is specified as a string after *TENURE* to separate values of *TENURE* from those of *MOHIRED*.

- *MOHIRED, YRHIRED,* and *DEPT* are written with default formats because the asterisk prevents them from receiving the DOLLAR8 format specified for *SALARY85* to *SALARY88*. The 1X format element is specified with DOLLAR8 to add one blank after each value of *SALARY85* to *SALARY88*.
- *NAME* uses the default dictionary format.

Strings

You can specify strings within the variable list. Strings must be enclosed in apostrophes or quotation marks.

- If a format is specified for a variable list, the application of the format is interrupted by a specified string. Thus, the string has the same effect within a variable list as an asterisk.

Example

```
WRITE OUTFILE=PRSNNL
  /EMPLOYID '1' MOHIRED YRHIRED SEX AGE JOBCAT NAME
  /EMPLOYID '2' DEPT86 TO DEPT88 SALARY86 TO SALARY88.
EXECUTE.
```

- Strings are used to assign the constant 1 to record 1 of each case, and 2 to record 2 to provide record identifiers in addition to the case identifier *EMPLOYID*.

RECORDS Subcommand

RECORDS indicates the total number of lines written per case. The number specified on RECORDS is informational only. The actual specification that causes variables to be written on a new line is a slash within the variable specifications. Each new line is requested by another slash.

- RECORDS must be specified before the slash that precedes the start of the variable specifications.
- The only specification on RECORDS is an integer to indicate the number of records for the output. If the number does not agree with the actual number of records indicated by slashes, the program issues a warning and ignores the specification on RECORDS.
- Specifications for each line of output must begin with a slash. An integer can follow the slash, indicating the line on which values are to be written. The integer is informational only. It cannot be used to rearrange the order of records in the output. If the integer does not agree with the actual record number indicated by the number of slashes in the variable specifications, the integer is ignored.
- A slash that is not followed by a variable list generates a blank line in the output.

Examples

```
WRITE OUTFILE=PRSNNL RECORDS=2
  /EMPLOYID NAME DEPT
  /EMPLOYID TENURE SALARY.
EXECUTE.
```

- WRITE writes the values of an individual's name and department on one line, tenure and salary on the next line, and the employee identification number on both lines.

Example

```
WRITE OUTFILE=PRSNNL RECORDS=2
  /1 EMPLOYID NAME DEPT
  /2 EMPLOYID TENURE SALARY.
EXECUTE.
```

- This command is equivalent to the command in the preceding example.

Example

```
WRITE OUTFILE=PRSNNL / EMPLOYID NAME DEPT / EMPLOYID TENURE SALARY.
EXECUTE.
```

- This command is equivalent to the commands in both preceding examples.

OUTFILE Subcommand

OUTFILE specifies the target file for the output from the WRITE command. By default, the output is included with the rest of the output from the session.

- OUTFILE must be specified before the slash that precedes the start of the variable specifications.
- The output from WRITE can exceed 132 characters.

Example

```
WRITE OUTFILE=WRITEOUT
   /1 EMPLOYID DEPT SALARY /2 NAME.
EXECUTE.
```

- OUTFILE specifies *WRITEOUT* as the file that receives the WRITE output.

TABLE Subcommand

TABLE requests a table showing how the variable information is formatted. NOTABLE is the default.

- TABLE must be specified before the slash that precedes the start of the variable specifications.

Example

```
WRITE OUTFILE=PRSNNL TABLE /1 EMPLOYID DEPT SALARY /2  NAME.
EXECUTE.
```

- TABLE requests a summary table describing the WRITE specifications.

WRITE FORMATS

```
WRITE FORMATS varlist (format) [varlist...]
```

Example

```
WRITE FORMATS SALARY (DOLLAR8)
            / HOURLY (DOLLAR7.2)
            / RAISE BONUS (PCT2).
```

Overview

WRITE FORMATS changes variable write formats. Write formats are output formats and control the form in which values are written by the WRITE command.

WRITE FORMATS changes only write formats. To change print formats, use the PRINT FORMATS command. To change both the print and write formats with a single specification, use the FORMATS command. For information on assigning input formats during data definition, see DATA LIST. For a more detailed discussion of input and output formats, see "Variable Formats" on p. 31.

Basic Specification

The basic specification is a variable list followed by the new format specification in parentheses. All specified variables receive the new format.

Syntax Rules

- You can specify more than one variable or variable list, followed by a format in parentheses. Only one format can be specified after each variable list. For clarity, each set of specifications can be separated by a slash.

- You can use keyword TO to refer to consecutive variables in the working data file.

- The specified width of a format must include enough positions to accommodate any punctuation characters such as decimal points, commas, dollar signs, or date and time delimiters. (This differs from assigning an *input* format on DATA LIST, where the program automatically expands the input format to accommodate punctuation characters in output.)

- Custom currency formats (CCw, CCw.d) must first be defined on the SET command before they can be used on WRITE FORMATS.

- WRITE FORMATS cannot be used with string variables. To change the length of a string variable, declare a new variable of the desired length with the STRING command and then use COMPUTE to copy values from the existing string into the new string.

Operations

- Unlike most transformations, WRITE FORMATS takes effect as soon as it is encountered in the command sequence. Special attention should be paid to its position among commands. For more information, see "Command Order" on p. 16.

- Variables not specified on WRITE FORMATS retain their current formats in the working data file. To see the current formats, use the DISPLAY command.

- The new write formats are changed only in the working file and are in effect for the duration of the session or until changed again with a WRITE FORMATS or FORMATS command. Write formats in the original data file (if one exists) are not changed, unless the file is resaved with the SAVE or XSAVE command.

- New numeric variables created with transformation commands are assigned default print and write formats of F8.2 (or the format specified on the FORMAT subcommand of SET). The WRITE FORMATS command can be used to change the new variable's write formats.

- New string variables created with transformation commands are assigned the format specified on the STRING command that declares the variable. WRITE FORMATS cannot be used to change the format of a new string variable.

- Date and time formats are effective only with the LIST and TABLES procedures and the PRINT and WRITE transformation commands. All other procedures use F format regardless of the date and time formats specified. See "Date and Time Formats" on p. 60.

- If a numeric data value exceeds its width specification, the program attempts to write some value nevertheless. First the program rounds decimal values, then removes punctuation characters, then tries scientific notation, and finally, if there is still not enough space, produces asterisks indicating that a value is present but cannot be written in the assigned width.

Example

```
WRITE FORMATS SALARY (DOLLAR8)
            / HOURLY (DOLLAR7.2)
            / RAISE BONUS (PCT2).
```

- The write format for *SALARY* is changed to DOLLAR with eight positions, including the dollar sign and comma when appropriate. An eight-digit number would require a DOLLAR11 format specification: eight characters for the digits, two characters for commas, and one character for the dollar sign.

- The write format for *HOURLY* is changed to DOLLAR with seven positions, including the dollar sign, decimal point, and two decimal places.

- The write format for both *RAISE* and *BONUS* is changed to PCT with two positions: one for the percentage and one for the percent sign.

Example

```
COMPUTE V3=V1 + V2.
WRITE FORMATS V3 (F3.1).
```

- COMPUTE creates the new numeric variable *V3*. By default, *V3* is assigned an F8.2 format.
- WRITE FORMATS changes the write format for *V3* to F3.1.

Example

```
SET CCA='-/-.Df1 ..-'.
WRITE FORMATS COST (CCA14.2).
```

- SET defines a European currency format for the custom currency format type CCA.
- WRITE FORMATS assigns the write format CCA to variable *COST*. See the SET command for more information on custom currency formats.

XSAVE

```
XSAVE OUTFILE=file

[/KEEP={ALL**  }] [/DROP=varlist]
      {varlist}

[/RENAME=(old varlist=new varlist)...]

[/MAP] [/{COMPRESSED  }]
        {UNCOMPRESSED}
```

**Default if the subcommand is omitted.

Example

```
XSAVE OUTFILE=EMPL /RENAME=(AGE=AGE88) (JOBCAT=JOBCAT88).
MEANS RAISE88 BY DEPT88.
```

Overview

XSAVE produces an SPSS-format data file. An SPSS-format data file contains data plus a dictionary. The dictionary contains a name for each variable in the data file plus any assigned variable and value labels, missing-value flags, and variable print and write formats. The dictionary also contains document text created with the DOCUMENTS command.

SAVE also creates SPSS-format data files. The principal difference is that XSAVE is not executed until data are read for the next procedure, while SAVE is executed by itself. Thus, XSAVE can reduce processing time by consolidating two data passes into one.

See SAVE TRANSLATE and SAVE SCSS for information on saving data files that can be used by other programs.

Options

Variable Subsets and Order. You can save a subset of variables and reorder the variables that are saved using the DROP and KEEP subcommands.

Variable Names. You can rename variables as they are copied into the SPSS-format data file using the RENAME subcommand.

Variable Map. To confirm the names and order of the variables saved in the SPSS-format data file, use the MAP subcommand. MAP displays the variables saved in the SPSS-format data file next to their corresponding names in the working data file.

Data Compression. You can write the data file in compressed or uncompressed form using the COMPRESSED or UNCOMPRESSED subcommand.

Basic Specification

The basic specification is the OUTFILE subcommand, which specifies a name for the SPSS-format data file to be saved.

Subcommand Order

- Subcommands can be specified in any order.

Syntax Rules

- OUTFILE is required and can be specified only once. If OUTFILE is specified more than once, only the last OUTFILE specification is in effect.
- KEEP, DROP, RENAME, and MAP can be used as many times as needed.
- Only one of the subcommands COMPRESSED or UNCOMPRESSED can be specified per XSAVE command.
- Documentary text can be dropped from the working data file with the DROP DOCUMENTS command.
- XSAVE cannot appear within a DO REPEAT—END REPEAT structure.
- Multiple XSAVE commands writing to the same file are not permitted.

Operations

- Unlike the SAVE command, XSAVE is a transformation command and is executed when the data are read for the next procedure.
- The new SPSS-format data file dictionary is arranged in the same order as the working file dictionary unless variables are reordered with the KEEP subcommand. Documentary text from the working file dictionary is always saved unless it is dropped with the DROP DOC-UMENTS command before XSAVE.
- New variables created by transformations and procedures previous to the XSAVE command are included in the new SPSS-format data file, and variables altered by transformations are saved in their modified form. Results of any temporary transformations immediately preceding the XSAVE command are included in the file; scratch variables are not.
- SPSS-format data files are binary files designed to be read and written by SPSS only. SPSS-format data files can be edited only with the UPDATE command. Use the MATCH FILES and ADD FILES commands to merge SPSS-format data files.
- The working data file is still available for transformations and procedures after XSAVE is executed.
- XSAVE processes the dictionary first and displays a message that indicates how many variables will be saved. Once the data are written, XSAVE indicates how many cases were saved. If the second message does not appear, the file was probably not completely written.

Limitations

- Maximum 10 XSAVE commands are allowed in a session.

Example

```
GET FILE=HUBEMPL.
XSAVE OUTFILE=EMPL88 /RENAME=(AGE=AGE88) (JOBCAT=JOBCAT88).
MEANS RAISE88 BY DEPT88.
```

- The GET command retrieves the SPSS-format data file *HUBEMPL*.
- The RENAME subcommand renames variable *AGE* to *AGE88* and variable *JOBCAT* to *JOBCAT88*.
- XSAVE is not executed until the program reads the data for procedure MEANS. The program saves file *EMPL88* and generates a MEANS table in a single data pass.
- After MEANS is executed, the *HUBEMPL* file is still the working data file. Variables *AGE* and *JOBCAT* retain their original names in the working file.

Example

```
GET FILE=HUBEMPL.
TEMPORARY.
RECODE DEPT85 TO DEPT88 (1,2=1) (3,4=2) (ELSE=9).
VALUE LABELS DEPT85 TO DEPT88 1 'MANAGEMENT' 2 'OPERATIONS' 3 'UNKNOWN'.
XSAVE OUTFILE=HUBTEMP.
CROSSTABS DEPT85 TO DEPT88 BY JOBCAT.
```

- Both the saved data file and the CROSSTABS output will reflect the temporary recoding and labeling of the department variables.
- If SAVE were specified instead of XSAVE, the data would be read twice instead of once and the CROSSTABS output would not reflect the recoding.

OUTFILE Subcommand

OUTFILE specifies the SPSS-format data file to be saved. OUTFILE is required and can be specified only once. If OUTFILE is specified more than once, only the last OUTFILE is in effect.

DROP and KEEP Subcommands

DROP and KEEP are used to save a subset of variables. DROP specifies the variables not to save in the new data file, while KEEP specifies the variables to save in the new data file; variables not named on KEEP are dropped.

- Variables can be specified in any order. The order of variables on KEEP determines the order of variables in the SPSS-format data file. The order on DROP does not affect the order of variables in the SPSS-format data file.

- Keyword ALL on KEEP refers to all remaining variables not previously specified on KEEP. ALL must be the last specification on KEEP.
- If a variable is specified twice on the same subcommand, only the first mention is recognized.
- Multiple DROP and KEEP subcommands are allowed. Specifying a variable that is not in the working data file or that has been dropped because of a previous DROP or KEEP subcommand results in an error, and the XSAVE command is not executed.
- Keyword TO can be used to specify a group of consecutive variables in the SPSS-format data file.

Example

```
XSAVE OUTFILE=HUBTEMP /DROP=DEPT79 TO DEPT84 SALARY79.
CROSSTABS DEPT85 TO DEPT88 BY JOBCAT.
```

- The SPSS-format data file is saved as *HUBTEMP*. All variables between and including *DEPT79* and *DEPT84*, as well as *SALARY79*, are excluded from the SPSS-format data file. All other variables are saved.

Example

```
GET FILE=PRSNL.
COMPUTE   TENURE=(12-CMONTH +(12*(88-CYEAR)))/12.
COMPUTE   JTENURE=(12-JMONTH +(12*(88-JYEAR)))/12.
VARIABLE LABELS   TENURE 'Tenure in Company'
                  JTENURE 'Tenure in Grade'.
XSAVE OUTFILE=PRSNL88 /DROP=GRADE STORE
 /KEEP=LNAME NAME TENURE JTENURE ALL.
REPORT FORMAT=AUTO /VARS=AGE TENURE JTENURE SALARY
 /BREAK=DIVISION /SUMMARY=MEAN.
```

- Variables *TENURE* and *JTENURE* are created by COMPUTE commands and assigned variable labels by the VARIABLE LABELS command. *TENURE* and *JTENURE* are added to the end of the working data file.
- DROP excludes variables *GRADE* and *STORE* from file *PRSNL88*. KEEP specifies that *LNAME, NAME, TENURE*, and *JTENURE* are the first four variables in file *PRSNL88*, followed by all remaining variables not specified on DROP. These remaining variables are saved in the same sequence as they appear in the original file.

RENAME Subcommand

RENAME changes the names of variables as they are copied into the new SPSS-format data file.

- The specification on RENAME is a list of old variable names followed by an equals sign and a list of new variable names. The same number of variables must be specified on both lists. Keyword TO can be used on the first list to refer to consecutive variables in the working data file and on the second list to generate new variable names (see the TO keyword on p. 29). The entire specification must be enclosed in parentheses.
- Alternatively, you can specify each old variable name individually, followed by an equals sign and the new variable name. Multiple sets of variable specifications are allowed. The parentheses around each set of specifications are optional.

- RENAME does not affect the working data file. However, if RENAME precedes DROP or KEEP, variables must be referred to by their new names on DROP or KEEP.
- Old variable names do not need to be specified according to their order in the working data file.
- Name changes take place in one operation. Therefore, variable names can be exchanged between two variables.
- Multiple RENAME subcommands are allowed.

Example

```
XSAVE OUTFILE=EMPL88 /RENAME  AGE=AGE88 JOBCAT=JOBCAT88.
CROSSTABS DEPT85 TO DEPT88 BY JOBCAT.
```

- RENAME specifies two name changes for file *EMPL88*: *AGE* is renamed to *AGE88* and *JOBCAT* is renamed to *JOBCAT88*.

Example

```
XSAVE OUTFILE=EMPL88 /RENAME (AGE JOBCAT=AGE88 JOBCAT88).
CROSSTABS DEPT85 TO DEPT88 BY JOBCAT.
```

- The name changes are identical to those in the previous example: *AGE* is renamed to *AGE88* and *JOBCAT* is renamed to *JOBCAT88*. The parentheses are required with this method.

MAP Subcommand

MAP displays a list of the variables in the SPSS-format data file and their corresponding names in the working data file.

- The only specification is keyword MAP. There are no additional specifications.
- Multiple MAP subcommands are allowed. Each MAP subcommand maps the results of subcommands that precede it, but not results of subcommands that follow it.

Example

```
GET FILE=HUBEMPL.
XSAVE OUTFILE=EMPL88 /RENAME=(AGE=AGE88) (JOBCAT=JOBCAT88)
 /KEEP=LNAME NAME JOBCAT88 ALL /MAP.
MEANS RAISE88 BY DEPT88.
```

- MAP is used to confirm the new names for *AGE* and *JOBCAT* and the order of variables in the *EMPL88* file (*LNAME, NAME,* and *JOBCAT88*, followed by all remaining variables from the working data file).

COMPRESSED and UNCOMPRESSED Subcommands

COMPRESSED saves the file in compressed form. UNCOMPRESSED saves the file in uncompressed form. In a compressed file, small integers (from −99 to 155) are stored in one byte instead of the eight bytes used in an uncompressed file.

- The only specification is the keyword COMPRESSED or UNCOMPRESSED. There are no additional specifications.
- Compressed data files occupy less disk space than do uncompressed data files.
- Compressed data files take longer to read than do uncompressed data files.
- The GET command, which reads SPSS-format data files, does not need to specify whether the files it reads are compressed or uncompressed.

Only one COMPRESSED or UNCOMPRESSED subcommand can be specified per XSAVE command. COMPRESSED is usually the default, though UNCOMPRESSED may be the default on some systems.

Appendix A
Commands and Program States

Command order is determined only by the system's need to know and do certain things in logical sequence. You cannot label a variable before the variable exists in the file. Similarly, you cannot transform or analyze data before a working data file is defined. This appendix briefly describes how the program handles various tasks in a logical sequence. It is not necessary to understand the program states in order to construct a command file, but some knowledge of how the program works will help you considerably when you encounter a problem or try to determine why the program doesn't seem to want to accept your commands or seems to be carrying out your instructions incorrectly.

Program States

To run a program session, you need to define your working data file, transform the data, and then analyze it. This order conforms very closely to the order the program must follow as it processes your commands. Specifically, the program checks command order according to the program state through which it passes. The **program state** is a characteristic of the program before and after a command is encountered. There are four program states. Each session starts in the **initial state**, followed by the **input program state**, the **transformation state**, and the **procedure state.** The four program states in turn enable the program to set up the environment, read data, modify data, and execute a procedure. Figure A.1 shows how the program moves through these states. The program determines the current state from the commands that it has already encountered and then identifies which commands are allowed in that state.

Figure A.1   Program states

A session must go through initial, input program, and procedure states to be a complete session. Since all sessions start in the initial state, you need to be concerned primarily with what commands you need to define your working data file and to analyze the data. The following commands define a very minimal session:

```
GET FILE=DATAIN.
FREQUENCIES VARIABLES=ALL.
```

The GET command defines the working data file and the FREQUENCIES command reads the data file and analyzes it. Thus, the program goes through the required three states: initial, input, and procedure.

Typically, a session also goes through the transformation state, but it can be skipped as shown in the example above and in the diagram in Figure A.1. Consider the following example:

```
TITLE 'PLOT FOR COLLEGE SURVEY'.

DATA LIST FILE=TESTDATA
 /AGE 1-3 ITEM1 TO ITEM3 5-10.

VARIABLE LABELS ITEM1 'Opinion on level of defense spending'
   ITEM2 'Opinion on level of welfare spending'
   ITEM3 'Opinion on level of health spending'.
VALUE LABELS ITEM1 TO ITEM3 -1 'Disagree' 0 'No opinion' 1
'Agree'.
MISSING VALUES AGE(-99,-98) ITEM1 TO ITEM3 (9).
RECODE ITEM1 TO ITEM3 (0=1) (1=0) (2=-1) (9=9) (ELSE=SYSMIS).
RECODE AGE (MISSING=9) (18 THRU HI=1) (LO THRU 18=0) INTO VOTER.
PRINT /$CASENUM 1-2 AGE 4-6 VOTER 8-10.
VALUE LABELS VOTER 0 'Under 18' 1 '18 or over'.
MISSING VALUES VOTER (9).
PRINT FORMATS VOTER (F1.0).

FREQUENCIES VARIABLES=VOTER, ITEM1 TO ITEM3.
```

The program starts in the initial state, where it processes the TITLE command. It then moves into the input state upon encountering the DATA LIST command. The program can then move into either the transformation or procedure state once the DATA LIST command has been processed.

In this example, the program remains in the transformation state after processing each of the commands from VARIABLE LABELS through PRINT FORMATS. The program then moves into the procedure state to process the FREQUENCIES command. As shown in Figure A.1, the program can repeat the procedure state if it encounters a second procedure. The program can return to the transformation state if it encounters additional transformation commands following the first procedure. Finally, in some sessions the program can return to the input program state when it encounters commands such as FILE TYPE or MATCH FILES.

Determining Command Order

Table A.1 shows where specific commands can be placed in the command file in terms of program states and what happens when the program encounters a command in each of the four program states. If a column contains a dash, the command is accepted in that program state and it leaves the program in that state. If one of the words *INIT, INPUT, TRANS,* or *PROC* appears in the column, the command is accepted in the program state indicated by the column heading, but it moves the program into the state indicated by *INIT, INPUT, TRANS,* or *PROC.* Asterisks in a column indicate errors when the program encounters the command in that program state. Commands marked with the dagger (†) in the column for the procedure state clear the working data file.

The table shows six groups of commands: utility, file definition, input program, data transformation, restricted transformation, and procedure commands. These groups are discussed in the following sections.

To read the table, first locate the command. If you simply want to know where in the command stream it can go, look for columns without asterisks. For example, the COM-PUTE command can be used when the program is in the input program state, the transformation state, or the procedure state, but it will cause an error if you try to use it in the initial state. If you want to know what can follow a command, look at each of the four columns next to the command. If the column is dashed, any commands not showing asterisks in the column for that program state can follow the command. If the column contains one of the words *INIT, INPUT, TRANS,* or *PROC,* any command not showing asterisks in the column for the program state indicated by that word can follow the command.

For example, if you want to know what commands can follow the INPUT PROGRAM command, note first that it is allowed only in the initial or procedure states. Then note that INPUT PROGRAM puts the program into the input program state wherever it occurs legally. This means that commands with dashes or words in the *INPUT* column can follow the INPUT PROGRAM command. This includes all the utility commands, the DATA LIST command, input program commands, and transformation commands like COM-PUTE. Commands that are not allowed after the INPUT PROGRAM command are most of the file definition commands that are their own input program (such as GET), restricted transformations (such as SELECT IF), and procedures.

Table A.1   Commands and program states

	INIT	INPUT	TRANS	PROC
Utility commands				
CLEAR TRANSFORMATIONS	**	PROC	PROC	—
COMMENT	—	—	—	—
DISPLAY	**	—	—	—
DOCUMENT	**	—	—	—
DROP DOCUMENTS	**	—	—	—
END DATA	—	—	—	—
ERASE	—	—	—	—
FILE HANDLE	—	—	—	—
FILE LABEL	—	—	—	—
FINISH	—	—	—	—
INCLUDE	—	—	—	—
INFO	—	—	—	—
DEFINE—!ENDDEFINE	—	—	—	—
N OF CASES	—	—	—	TRANS
NEW FILE	—	INIT	INIT	INIT†
PROCEDURE OUTPUT	—	—	—	—
SET, SHOW	—	—	—	—
TITLE, SUBTITLE	—	—	—	—
File definition commands				
ADD FILES	TRANS	**	—	TRANS
DATA LIST	TRANS	—	INPUT	TRANS†
FILE TYPE	INPUT	**	INPUT	INPUT†
GET	TRANS	**	—	TRANS†
GET BMDP	TRANS	**	—	TRANS†
GET CAPTURE	TRANS	**	—	TRANS†
GET OSIRIS	TRANS	**	—	TRANS†
GET SAS	TRANS	**	—	TRANS†
GET SCSS	TRANS	**	—	TRANS†
GET TRANSLATE	TRANS	**	—	TRANS†
IMPORT	TRANS	**	—	TRANS†
INPUT PROGRAM	TRANS	**	—	TRANS†
KEYED DATA LIST	TRANS	—	—	TRANS
MATCH FILES	TRANS	**	—	TRANS
MATRIX DATA	TRANS	**	—	TRANS†
RENAME VARIABLES	**	—	—	TRANS
UPDATE	TRANS	**	—	TRANS

Input program commands

Table A.1   Commands and program states (Continued)

	INIT	INPUT	TRANS	PROC
END CASE	**	—	**	**
END FILE	**	—	**	**
END FILE TYPE	**	TRANS	**	**
END INPUT PROGRAM	**	TRANS	**	**
POINT	**	—	**	**
RECORD TYPE	**	—	**	**
REPEATING DATA	**	—	**	**
REREAD	**	—	**	**

Transformation commands

	INIT	INPUT	TRANS	PROC
ADD VALUE LABELS	**	—	—	TRANS
APPLY DICTIONARY	**	—	—	TRANS
COMPUTE	**	—	—	TRANS
COUNT	**	—	—	TRANS
DO IF—END IF	**	—	—	TRANS
DO REPEAT—END REPEAT	**	—	—	TRANS
ELSE	**	—	—	TRANS
ELSE IF	**	—	—	TRANS
FORMATS	**	—	—	TRANS
IF	**	—	—	TRANS
LEAVE	**	—	—	TRANS
LOOP—END LOOP, BREAK	**	—	—	TRANS
MISSING VALUES	**	—	—	TRANS
NUMERIC	**	—	—	TRANS
PRINT	**	—	—	TRANS
PRINT EJECT	**	—	—	TRANS
PRINT FORMATS	**	—	—	TRANS
PRINT SPACE	**	—	—	TRANS
RECODE	**	—	—	TRANS
SPLIT FILE	**	—	—	TRANS
STRING	**	—	—	TRANS
VALUE LABELS	**	—	—	TRANS
VARIABLE LABELS	**	—	—	TRANS
VECTOR	**	—	—	TRANS
WEIGHT	**	—	—	TRANS
WRITE	**	—	—	TRANS
WRITE FPR,ATS	**	—	—	TRANS
XSAVE	**	—	—	TRANS

Restricted transformations

Table A.1   Commands and program states (Continued)

	INIT	INPUT	TRANS	PROC
FILTER	**	**	—	TRANS
REFORMAT	**	**	—	TRANS
SAMPLE	**	**	—	TRANS
SELECT IF	**	**	—	TRANS
TEMPORARY	**	**	—	TRANS
Procedures				
BEGIN DATA	**	**	PROC	—
EXECUTE	**	**	PROC	—
EXPORT	**	**	PROC	—
GRAPH	**	**	PROC	—
LIST	**	**	PROC	—
SAVE	**	**	PROC	—
SAVE TRANSLATE	**	**	PROC	—
SORT CASES	**	**	PROC	—
other procedures	**	**	PROC	—

Unrestricted Utility Commands

Most utility commands can appear in any state. Table A.1 shows this by the absence of asterisks in the columns next to the EDIT through TITLE commands. For example, the EDIT command can appear at any point in the command file.

The dashed lines indicate that after a utility command is processed, the program remains in the same state it was in before the command execution. *INIT, TRANS,* or *PROC* indicates that the command moves the program to that state. For example, if the program is in the procedure state, N OF CASES moves the program to the transformation state. The FINISH command terminates command processing wherever it appears. Any commands appearing after FINISH will not be read and therefore will not cause an error.

File Definition Commands

You can use most of the file definition commands in the initial state, the transformation state, and the procedure state. Most of these commands cause errors if you try to use them in the input program state. However, DATA LIST and KEYED DATA LIST can be and often are used in input programs.

After they are used in the initial state, most file definition commands move the program directly to the transformation state, since these commands are the entire input program. FILE TYPE and INPUT PROGRAM move the program into the input program state and require input program commands to complete the input program. Commands in Table A.1 marked with a dagger (†) clear the working data file.

Input Program Commands

The commands associated with the complex file facility (FILE TYPE, RECORD TYPE, and REPEATING DATA) and commands associated with the INPUT PROGRAM command are allowed only in the input program state.

The END CASE, END FILE, POINT, RECORD TYPE, REPEATING DATA, and REREAD leave the program in the input program state. The two that move the program on to the transformation state are END FILE TYPE for input programs initiated with FILE TYPE and END INPUT PROGRAM for those initiated with INPUT PROGRAM.

Transformation Commands

The entire set of transformation commands from ADD VALUE LABELS to XSAVE can appear in the input program state as part of an input program, in the transformation state, or in the procedure state. When you use transformation commands in the input program state or the transformation state, the program remains in the same state it was in before the command. When the program is in the procedure state, these commands move the program back to the transformation state.

Transformation commands and some file definition and input program commands can be categorized according to whether they are **declarative**, **status-switching**, or **executable**. Declarative commands alter the working data file dictionary but do not affect the data. Status-switching commands change the program state but do not affect the data. Executable commands alter the data. Table A.2 lists these commands and indicates which of the three categories applies.

Table A.2   Taxonomy of transformation commands

Command	Type	Command	Type
ADD FILES	Exec*	LEAVE	Decl
ADD VALUE LABELS	Decl	LOOP	Exec
APPLY DICTIONARY	Decl	MATCH FILES	Exec*
BREAK	Exec	MISSING VALUES	Decl
COMPUTE	Exec	N OF CASES	Decl
COUNT	Exec	NUMERIC	Decl
DATA LIST	Exec*	POINT	Exec
DO IF	Exec	PRINT, PRINT EJECT	Exec
DO REPEAT	Decl†	PRINT FORMATS	Decl

Table A.2   Taxonomy of transformation commands (Continued)

Command	Type	Command	Type
ELSE	Exec	PRINT SPACE	Exec
ELSE IF	Exec	RECODE	Exec
END CASE	Exec	RECORD TYPE	Exec
END FILE	Exec	REFORMAT	Exec
END FILE TYPE	Stat	REPEATING DATA	Exec*
END IF	Exec	REREAD	Exec
END INPUT PROGRAM	Stat	SAMPLE	Exec
END LOOP	Exec	SELECT IF	Exec
END REPEAT	Decl†	SPLIT FILE	Decl
FILE TYPE	Stat**	STRING	Decl
FILTER	Exec	TEMPORARY	Stat
FORMATS	Decl	VALUE LABELS	Decl
GET	Exec*	VARIABLE LABELS	Decl
GET CAPTURE	Exec*	VECTOR	Decl
GET OSIRIS	Exec*	WEIGHT	Decl
IF	Exec	WRITE	Exec
INPUT PROGRAM	Stat	WRITE FORMATS	Decl
KEYED DATA LIST	Exec*	XSAVE	Exec

* This command is also declarative.
**This command is also executable and declarative.
†This command does not fit into these categories; however, it is neither executable nor status-switching, so it is classified as declarative.

Restricted Transformations

Commands REFORMAT, SAMPLE, SELECT IF, and TEMPORARY are restricted transformation commands because they are allowed in either the transformation state or the procedure state but cannot be used in the input program state.

If you use restricted transformation commands in the transformation state, the program remains in the transformation state. If you use them in the procedure state, they move the program back to the transformation state.

Procedures

The procedures and the BEGIN DATA, EXECUTE, EXPORT, LIST, SAVE, SAVE SCSS, SAVE TRANSLATE, and SORT CASES commands cause the data to be read. These commands are allowed in either the transformation state or the procedure state.

When the program is in the transformation state, these commands move the program to the procedure state. When you use these commands in the procedure state, the program remains in that state.

Appendix B
IMPORT/EXPORT Character Sets

Communication-formatted portable files do not use positions 1–63 in the following table. Tape-formatted portable files use the complete table. (See the EXPORT command for a description of the two types of files.)

Position	Graphic	Macintosh	Microsoft Code Page 850	ANSI/ISO Latin 1	IBM EBCDIC	ASCII 7-BIT
0	NUL	0	0	0	0	0
1	SOH	1	1	1	1	1
2	STX	2	2	2	2	2
3	ETX	3	3	3	3	3
4	SEL			156	4	
5	HT	9	9	9	5	9
6	RNL			134	6	
7	DEL	127	127	127	7	127
8	GE			151	8	
9	SPS			141	9	
10	RPT			142	10	
11	VT	11	11	11	11	11
12	FF	12	12	12	12	12
13	CR	13	13	13	13	13
14	SO	14	14	14	14	14
15	SI	15	15	15	15	15
16	DLE	16	16	16	16	16
17	DC1	17	17	17	17	17
18	DC2	18	18	18	18	18
19	DC3	19	19	19	19	19
20	DC4	20	20	20	60	20
21	NL			133	21	
22	BS	8	8	8	22	8
23	DOC			135	23	
24	CAN	24	24	24	24	24
25	EM	25	25	25	25	25

Position	Graphic	Macintosh	Microsoft Code Page 850	ANSI/ISO Latin 1	IBM EBCDIC	ASCII 7-BIT
26	UBS			146	26	
27	CU1			143	27	
28	(I)FS[1]	28	28	28	28	28
29	(I)GS	29	29	29	29	29
30	(I)RS	30	30	30	30	30
31	SM,SW			138	42	
32	DS			128	32	
33	SOS			129	33	
34	FS[2]			130	34	
35	WUS			131	35	
36	CSP			139	43	
37	LF	10	10	10	37	10
38	ETB	23	23	23	38	23
39	ESC	27	27	27	39	27
40	(I)US	31	31	31	31	31
41	BYP			132	36	
42	RES			157	20	
43	ENQ	5	5	5	45	5
44	ACK	6	6	6	46	6
45	BEL	7	7	7	47	7
46	SYN	22	22	22	50	22
47	IR			147	51	
48	PP			148	52	
49	TRN			149	53	
50	NBS			150	54	
51	EOT	4	4	4	55	4
52	SBS			152	56	
53	IT			153	57	
54	RFF			154	58	
55	CU3			155	59	
56	NAK	21	21	21	61	21
57	SUB	26	26	26	63	26
58	SA			136	40	
59	SFE			137	41	
60	MFA			140	44	
61	reserved					
62	reserved					
63	reserved					
64	0	48	48	48	240	48

Position	Graphic	Macintosh	Microsoft Code Page 850	ANSI/ISO Latin 1	IBM EBCDIC	ASCII 7-BIT
65	1	49	49	49	241	49
66	2	50	50	50	242	50
67	3	51	51	51	243	51
68	4	52	52	52	244	52
69	5	53	53	53	245	53
70	6	54	54	54	246	54
71	7	55	55	55	247	55
72	8	56	56	56	248	56
73	9	57	57	57	249	57
74	A	65	65	65	193	65
75	B	66	66	66	194	66
76	C	67	67	67	195	67
77	D	68	68	68	196	68
78	E	69	69	69	197	69
79	F	98	98	70	198	98
80	G	71	71	71	199	71
81	H	72	72	72	200	72
82	I	73	73	73	201	73
83	J	74	74	74	209	74
84	K	75	75	75	210	75
85	L	76	76	76	211	76
86	M	77	77	77	212	77
87	N	78	78	78	213	78
88	O	79	79	79	214	79
89	P	80	80	80	215	80
90	Q	81	81	81	216	81
91	R	82	82	82	217	82
92	S	83	83	83	226	83
93	T	84	84	84	227	84
94	U	85	85	85	228	85
95	V	86	86	86	229	86
96	W	87	87	87	230	87
97	X	88	88	88	231	88
98	Y	89	89	89	232	89
99	Z	90	90	90	233	90
100	a	97	97	97	129	97
101	b	98	98	98	130	98
102	c	99	99	99	131	99
103	d	100	100	100	132	100
104	e	101	101	101	133	101

Position	Graphic	Macintosh	Microsoft Code Page 850	ANSI/ISO Latin 1	IBM EBCDIC	ASCII 7-BIT
105	f	102	102	102	134	102
106	g	103	103	103	135	103
107	h	104	104	104	136	104
108	i	105	105	105	137	105
109	j	106	106	106	145	106
110	k	107	107	107	146	107
111	l	108	108	108	147	108
112	m	109	109	109	148	109
113	n	110	110	110	149	110
114	o	111	111	111	150	111
115	p	112	112	112	151	112
116	q	113	113	113	152	113
117	r	114	114	114	153	114
118	s	115	115	115	162	115
119	t	116	116	116	163	116
120	u	117	117	117	164	117
121	v	118	118	118	165	118
122	w	119	119	119	166	119
123	x	120	120	120	167	120
124	y	121	121	121	168	121
125	z	122	122	122	169	122
126	space	32	32	32	64	32
127	.	46	46	46	75	46
128	<	60	60	60	76	60
129	(	40	40	40	77	40
130	+	43	43	43	78	43
131						79	
132	&	38	38	38	80	38
133	[	91	91	91	173	91
134	]	93	93	93	189	93
135	!	33	33	33	90	33
136	$	36	36	36	91	36
137	*	42	42	42	92	42
138	)	41	41	41	93	41
139	;	59	59	59	94	59
140	¬ or ∧ or ↑	94	94	94	95	94
141	-	45	45	45	96	45
142	/	47	47	47	97	47
143	=	124	124	124	106	124

Position	Graphic	Macintosh	Microsoft Code Page 850	ANSI/ISO Latin 1	IBM EBCDIC	ASCII 7-BIT
144	,	44	44	44	107	44
145	%	37	37	37	108	37
146	_	95	95	95	109	95
147	>	62	62	62	110	62
148	?	63	63	63	111	63
149	`	96	96	96	121	96
150	:	58	58	58	122	58
151	#	35	35	35	123	35
152	@	64	64	64	124	64
153	´	39	39	39	125	39
154	=	61	61	61	126	61
155	"	34	34	34	127	34
156	≤	178			140	
157	□	255			156	
158	±	177	241	177	158	
159	n				159	
160	Â	251	248	176		
161	†				143	
162	~	126	126	126	161	126
163	_	209	196		160	
164	∟		192		171	
165	⌐		218		172	
166	≥	179			174	
167	0				176	
168	1		251	185	177	
169	2		253	178	178	
170	3		252	179	179	
171	4				180	
172	5				181	
173	6				182	
174	7				183	
175	8				184	
176	9				185	
177	⌟		217		187	
178	⌐		191		188	
179	≠	173			190	
180	—				191	
181	(				141	
182	)				157	

Position	Graphic	Macintosh	Microsoft Code Page 850	ANSI/ISO Latin 1	IBM EBCDIC	ASCII 7-BIT
183	$+^3$				142	
184	{	123	123	123	192	123
185	}	125	125	125	208	125
186	\	92	92	92	224	92
187	¢	162	189	162	74	
188	•	165		183	175	
189	À	203	183	192		
190	Á	231	181	193		
191	Â	229	182	194		
192	Ã	204	199	195		
193	Ä	128	142	196		
194	Å	129	143	197		
195	Æ	174		198		
196	Ç	130	128	199		
197	È	233	212	200		
198	É	131	144	201		
199	Ê	230	210	202		
200	Ë	232	211	203		
201	Ì	237	222	204		
202	Í	234	214	205		
203	Î	235	215	206		
204	Ï	236	216	207		
205	Ð		209	208		
206	Ñ	132	165	209		
207	Ò	241	227	210		
208	Ó	238	224	211		
209	Ô	239	226	212		
210	Õ	205	229	213		
211	Ö	133	153	214		
212	Ø	175	157	216		
213	Ù	244	235	217		
214	Ú	242	233	218		
215	Û	243	234	219		
216	Ü	134	154	220		
217	Ý		237	221		
218	Þ		232	222		
219	ß	167	225	223		
220	à	136	133	224		
221	á	135	160	225		

Position	Graphic	Macintosh	Microsoft Code Page 850	ANSI/ISO Latin 1	IBM EBCDIC	ASCII 7-BIT
222	â	137	131	226		
223	ã	139	198	227		
224	ä	138	132	228		
225	å	140	134	229		
226	æ	190	145	230		
227	ç	141	135	231		
228	è	143	138	232		
229	é	142	130	233		
230	ê	144	136	234		
231	ë	145	137	235		
232	ì	147	141	236		
233	í	146	161	237		
234	î	148	140	238		
235	ï	149	139	239		
236	ð		208	240		
237	ñ	150	164	241		
238	ò	152	149	242		
239	ó	151	162	243		
240	ô	153	147	244		
241	õ	155	228	245		
242	ö	154	148	246		
243	ø	191	155	248		
244	ù	157	151	249		
245	ú	156	163	250		
246	û	158	150	251		
247	ü	159	129	252		
248	ý		236	253		
249	ÿ	216	152	255		
250	þ		231	254		
251	¡	193	173	161		
252	¿	192	168	191		
253	«	199	174	171		
254	»	200	175	187		
255	reserved					

[1] file separator
[2] field separator
[3] not the plus sign

Appendix C
Defining Complex Files

Most data files have a rectangular, case-ordered structure and can be read with the DATA LIST command. This chapter illustrates the use of commands for defining complex, nonrectangular files.

- **Nested** files contain several types of records with a hierarchical relationship among the record types. You can define nested files with the FILE TYPE NESTED command.

- **Grouped** files have several records per case, and a case's records are grouped together in a file. You can use DATA LIST and FILE TYPE GROUPED to define grouped files.

- In a **mixed** file, different types of cases have different kinds of records. You can define mixed files with the FILE TYPE MIXED command.

- A record in a **repeating data** file contains information for several cases. You can use the REPEATING DATA command to define files with repeating data.

It is a good idea to read the descriptions of the FILE TYPE and REPEATING DATA commands before proceeding.

A Rectangular File

Figure C.1 shows contents of data file *RECTANG.DAT*, which contains 1988 sales data for salespeople working in different territories. Year, region, and unit sales are recorded for each salesperson. Like most data files, the sales data file has a **rectangular** format, since information on a record applies only to one case.

Figure C.1   File RECTANG.DAT

```
1988 CHICAGO      JONES      900
1988 CHICAGO      GREGORY    400
1988 BATON ROUGE RODRIGUEZ  300
1988 BATON ROUGE SMITH      333
1988 BATON ROUGE GRAU       100
```

Since the sales data are rectangular, you can use the DATA LIST command to define these data:

```
DATA LIST FILE='RECTANG.DAT'
 / YEAR     1-4
   REGION   6-16(A)
   SALESPER 18-26(A)
   SALES    29-31.
```

- DATA LIST defines the variable *YEAR* in columns 1 through 4 and string variable *REGION* in columns 6 through 16 in file *RECTANG.DAT*. The program also reads variables *SALESPER* and *SALES* on each record.

- The LIST output in Figure C.2 shows the contents of each variable.

Figure C.2   LIST output for RECTANG.DAT

```
YEAR REGION      SALESPER  SALES

1988 CHICAGO      JONES      900
1988 CHICAGO      GREGORY    400
1988 BATON ROUGE RODRIGUEZ  300
1988 BATON ROUGE SMITH      333
1988 BATON ROUGE GRAU       100
```

Nested Files

In a nested file, information on some records applies to several cases. The 1988 sales data are arranged in nested format in Figure C.3. The data contain three kinds of records. A code in the first column indicates whether a record is a year (Y), region (R), or person record (P).

Figure C.3   File NESTED.DAT

```
Y    1988
R    CHICAGO
P    JONES          900
P    GREGORY        400
R    BATON ROUGE
P    RODRIGUEZ      300
P    SMITH          333
P    GRAU           100
```

The record types are related to each other hierarchically. Year records represent the highest level in the hierarchy, since the year value 1988 applies to each salesperson in the file (only one year record is used in this example). Region records are intermediate-level records; region names apply to salesperson records that occur before the next region record in the file. For example, Chicago applies to salespersons Jones and Gregory. Baton Rouge applies to Rodriguez, Smith, and Grau. Person records represent the lowest level in the hierarchy. The information they contain—salesperson and unit sales—defines a case. Nested file structures minimize redundant information in a data file. For example, 1988 and Baton Rouge appear several times in Figure C.1, but only once in Figure C.3.

Since each record in the nested file has a code that indicates record type, you can use the FILE TYPE and RECORD TYPE commands to define the nested sales data:

```
FILE   TYPE   NESTED   FILE='NESTED.DAT' RECORD=#TYPE 1 (A)

RECORD TYPE 'Y'.
DATA LIST /   YEAR 5-8.

RECORD TYPE 'R'.
DATA LIST   / REGION 5-15 (A).


RECORD TYPE 'P'.
DATA LIST / SALESPER 5-15 (A) SALES 20-23

END FILE TYPE.
```

- FILE TYPE indicates that data are in nested form in the file *NESTED.DAT*.

- RECORD defines the record type variable as string variable *#TYPE* in column 1. *#TYPE* is defined as scratch variable so it won't be saved in the working data file.

- One pair of RECORD TYPE and DATA LIST statements is specified for each record type in the file. The first pair of RECORD TYPE and DATA LIST statements defines the variable *YEAR* in columns 5 through 8 on every year record. The second pair defines the string variable *REGION* on region records. The final pair defines *SALESPER* and *SALES* on person records.

Figure C.4   NESTED.DAT file with missing records

```
Y    1988
P    JONES           900
P    GREGORY         400
R    BATON ROUGE
P    RODRIGUEZ       300
P    SMITH           333
P    GRAU            100
```

- The order of RECORD TYPE statements defines the hierarchical relationship among the records. The first RECORD TYPE defines the highest-level record type. The next RECORD TYPE defines the next highest level, and so forth. The last RECORD TYPE defines a case in the working data file.

- END FILE TYPE signals the end of file definition.

- In processing nested data, the program reads each record type you define. Information on the highest and intermediate-level records is spread to cases to which the information applies. The output from the LIST command is identical to that in Figure C.2.

Nested Files with Missing Records

In a nested file, some cases may be missing one or more record types defined in RECORD TYPE commands. For example, in Figure C.4 the region record for salespersons Jones and Gregory is missing.

The program assigns missing values to variables that are not present for a case. Using the modified *NESTED.DAT* file in Figure C.4, the commands in the previous example produce the output shown in Figure C.5. You can see that the program assigned missing values to *REGION* for Jones and Gregory.

Figure C.5   LIST output for nested data with missing records

```
YEAR REGION       SALESPER    SALES

1988              JONES        900
1988              GREGORY      400
1988 BATON ROUGE RODRIGUEZ     300
1988 BATON ROUGE SMITH         333
1988 BATON ROUGE GRAU          100
```

You may want to examine cases with missing records, since these cases may indicate data errors. If you add the MISSING=WARN subcommand to your FILE TYPE command, the program prints a warning message when a case is missing a defined record type. For example, the program would print two warnings when processing data in Figure C.4. When MISSING is set to WARN, cases are built in the same way as when the default setting (NOWARN) is in effect.

Grouped Data

In a grouped file, a case has several records that are grouped together in the file. You can use DATA LIST to define a grouped file if each case has the same number of records and records appear in the same order for each case. You can use FILE TYPE GROUPED whether the number of records per case and record order are fixed or vary. However, FILE TYPE GROUPED requires that each record have a case identifier and a record code.

Using DATA LIST

Table C.1 shows the organization of a grouped data file containing school subject scores for three students. Each student has three data records, and each record contains a score. The first record for each student also contains a case identifier. Records for each case are grouped together. Student 1 records appear first, followed by records for student 2 and student 3.

Record order determines whether a score is a reading, math, or science score. The reading score appears on the first record for a case, the math score appears on the second record, and the science score appears on the third record.

Table C.1 Data for GROUPED.DAT

Student	Score
1	58
	59
	97
2	43
	88
	45
3	67
	75
	90

Since each case has the same number of records and record order is fixed across cases, you can use DATA LIST to define the student data:

```
DATA LIST FILE='GROUPED.DAT' RECORDS=3
 /STUDENT 1 READING 5-6
 /MATH    5-6
 /SCIENCE 5-6.

LIST.
```

- DATA LIST indicates that data are in file *GROUPED.DAT*.

- RECORDS defines three records per case. The program reads student ID number (*STUDENT*) and reading score (*READING*) in the first record for a case. Math and science scores are read in the second and third records.

- The output from the LIST command is shown in Figure C.6.

Figure C.6   LIST output for GROUPED.DAT

```
STUDENT READING MATH SCIENCE

   1      58    59    97
   2      43    88    45
   3      67    75    90
```

Using FILE TYPE GROUPED

To use FILE TYPE GROUPED to define a grouped file, each record must have a case identifier and a record code. In the following commands, each data record contains a student ID number coded 1, 2, or 3 and a code indicating whether the score on that record is a reading (R), math (M), or science (S) score:

```
FILE TYPE GROUPED RECORD=#REC 3(A)  CASE=STUDENT 1.

RECORD TYPE 'R'.
DATA LIST / READING 5-6.

RECORD TYPE 'M'.
DATA LIST / MATH 5-6.

RECORD TYPE 'S'.
DATA LIST / SCIENCE 5-6.

END FILE TYPE.

BEGIN DATA
1 R 58
1 M 59
1 S 97
2 R 43
2 M 88
2 S 45
3 R 67
3 M 75
3 S 90
END DATA.

LIST.
```

- FILE TYPE indicates that data are in grouped format. RECORD defines the variable containing record codes as string variable *#REC* in column 3. CASE defines the case identifier variable *STUDENT* in the first column of each record.
- One pair of RECORD TYPE and DATA LIST statements appears for each record type in the file. The program reads reading score in every R record, math score in M records, and science score in S records.

- END FILE TYPE signals the end of file definition.
- BEGIN DATA and END DATA indicate that data are inline.
- The output from LIST is identical to the output in Figure C.6.

FILE TYPE GROUPED is most useful when record order varies across cases and when cases have missing or duplicate records. In the modified data shown in Table C.2, only case 1 has all three record types. Also, record order varies across cases. For example, the first record for case 1 is a science record, whereas the first record for cases 2 and 3 is a reading record.

Table C.2   Modified grouped data file

Student	Subject	Score
1	S	97
1	R	58
1	M	59
2	R	43
3	R	67
3	M	75

You can use the same FILE TYPE commands as above to read the modified file. As shown in the output from LIST in Figure C.7, the program assigns missing values to variables that are missing for a case.

Figure C.7   LIST output for modified GROUPED.DAT file

```
STUDENT READING MATH SCIENCE
    1      58    59    97
    2      43     .     .
    3      67    75     .
```

By default, the program generates a warning message when a case is missing a defined record type in a grouped file or when a record is not in the same order as in RECORD TYPE commands. Thus, four warnings are generated when the commands for the previous example are used to read the modified *GROUPED.DAT* file. You can suppress these warnings if you add the optional specifications MISSING=NOWARN and ORDERED=NO on your FILE TYPE command.

In the modified *GROUPED.DAT* file, the case identifier *STUDENT* appears in the same column position in each record. When the location of the case identifier varies for different types of records, you can use the CASE option of the RECORD TYPE command to specify different column positions for different records. For example, suppose the case identifier appears in first column position on reading and science records and in column 2 in math records. You could use the following commands to define the data:

```
FILE TYPE GROUPED RECORD=#REC 3(A)  CASE=STUDENT 1.

RECORD TYPE 'R'.
DATA LIST / READING 5-6.

RECORD TYPE 'M' CASE=2.
DATA LIST / MATH 5-6.

RECORD TYPE 'S'.
DATA LIST / SCIENCE 5-6.

END FILE TYPE.

BEGIN DATA
1 S 97
1 R 58
 1M 59
2 R 43
3 R 67
 3M 75
END DATA.

LIST.
```

- FILE TYPE indicates that the data are in grouped format. RECORD defines the variable containing record codes as string variable *#REC*. CASE defines the case identifier variable as *STUDENT* in the first column of each record.
- One pair of RECORD TYPE and DATA LIST statements is coded for each record type in the file.
- The CASE specification on the RECORD TYPE statement for math records overrides the CASE value defined on FILE TYPE. Thus, the program reads *STUDENT* in column 2 in math records and column 1 in other records.
- END FILE TYPE signals the end of file definition.
- BEGIN DATA and END DATA indicate that data are inline.
- The output from LIST is identical to that in Figure C.7.

Mixed Files

In a mixed file, different types of cases have different kinds of records. You can use FILE TYPE MIXED to read each record or a subset of records in a mixed file.

Reading Each Record in a Mixed File

Table C.3 shows test data for two hypothetical elementary school students referred to a remedial education teacher. Student 1, who was thought to need special reading attention, took reading tests (word identification and comprehension tests). The second student completed writing tests (handwriting, spelling, vocabulary, and grammar tests). Test code (READING or WRITING) indicates whether the record contains reading or writing scores.

Table C.3   Academic test data for two students

Student 1

Test	ID	Grade	Word	Compre
READING	1	04	65	35

Student 2

Test	ID	Grade	Handwrit	Spelling	Vocab	Grammar
WRITING	2	03	50	55	30	25

The following commands define the test data:

```
FILE TYPE MIXED RECORD=TEST 1-7(A).

RECORD TYPE 'READING'.
DATA LIST / ID  9-10 GRADE  12-13 WORD 15-16 COMPRE 18-19.

RECORD TYPE 'WRITING'.
DATA LIST / ID  9-10 GRADE 12-13 HANDWRIT 15-16 SPELLING 18-19
            VOCAB 21-22 GRAMMAR  24-25.
END FILE TYPE.

BEGIN DATA
READING 1   04 65 35
WRITING 2   03 50 55 30 25
END DATA.

LIST.
```

- FILE TYPE specifies that the data contain mixed record types. RECORD reads the record identifier (variable *TEST*) in columns 1 through 7.

- One pair of RECORD TYPE and DATA LIST statements is coded for each record type in the file. The program reads variables *ID*, *GRADE*, *WORD,* and *COMPRE* in the record in which the value of *TEST* is READING, and *ID*, *GRADE*, *HANDWRIT*, *SPELLING*, *VOCAB,* and *GRAMMAR* in the WRITING record.

- END FILE TYPE signals the end of file definition.

- BEGIN DATA and END DATA indicate that data are inline. Data are mixed, since some column positions contain different variables for the two cases. For example, word identification score is recorded in columns 15 and 16 for student 1. For student 2, handwriting score is recorded in these columns.

Figure C.8   LIST output for mixed file

```
TEST    ID GRADE WORD COMPRE HANDWRIT SPELLING VOCAB GRAMMAR

READING  1    4   65    35       .        .       .      .
WRITING  2    3    .     .      50       55      30     25
```

- Figure C.8 shows the output from LIST. Missing values are assigned for variables that are not recorded for a case.

Reading a Subset of Records in a Mixed File

You may want to process a subset of records in a mixed file. The following commands read only the data for the student who took reading tests:

```
FILE TYPE MIXED RECORD=TEST 1-7(A).

RECORD TYPE 'READING'.
DATA LIST / ID        9-10
            GRADE    12-13
            WORD     15-16
            COMPRE   18-19.

RECORD TYPE 'WRITING'.
DATA LIST / ID        9-10
            GRADE    12-13
            HANDWRIT 15-16
            SPELLING 18-19
            VOCAB    21-22
            GRAMMAR  24-25.

END FILE TYPE.

BEGIN DATA
READING 1  04 65 35
WRITING 2  03 50 55 30 25
END DATA.

LIST.
```

- FILE TYPE specifies that data contain mixed record types. RECORD defines the record identification variable as *TEST* in columns 1 through 7.
- RECORD TYPE defines variables on reading records. Since the program skips all record types that are not defined by default, the case with writing scores is not read.
- END FILE TYPE signals the end of file definition.
- BEGIN DATA and END DATA indicate that data are inline. Data are identical to those in the previous example.
- Figure C.9 shows the output from LIST.

Figure C.9   LIST output for reading record

```
TEST    ID GRADE WORD COMPRE
READING  1    4   65    35
```

Repeating Data

You can use the REPEATING DATA command to read files in which each record contains repeating groups of variables that define several cases. Command syntax depends on whether the number of repeating groups is fixed across records.

Fixed Number of Repeating Groups

Table C.4 shows test score data for students in three classrooms. Each record contains a classroom number and two pairs of student ID and test score variables. For example, in class 101, student 182 has a score of 12 and student 134 has a score of 53. In class 103, student 15 has a score of 87 and student 203 has a score of 69. Each pair of ID and score variables is a repeating group, since these variables appear twice on each record.

Table C.4   Data in REPEAT.DAT file

Class	ID	Score	ID	Score
101	182	12	134	53
102	99	112	200	150
103	15	87	203	69

The following commands generate a working data file in which one case is built for each occurrence of *SCORE* and *ID*, and classroom number is spread to each case on a record.

```
INPUT PROGRAM.
DATA LIST /  CLASS 3-5.
REPEATING DATA STARTS=6 / OCCURS=2
 /DATA STUDENT 1-4 SCORE 5-8.
END INPUT PROGRAM.

BEGIN DATA
  101 182  12 134   53
  102  99 112 200  150
  103  15  87 203   69
END DATA.

LIST.
```

- INPUT PROGRAM signals the beginning of data definition.
- DATA LIST defines variable *CLASS*, which is spread to each student on a classroom record.

- REPEATING DATA specifies that the input file contains repeating data. STARTS indicates that repeating data begin in column 6. OCCURS specifies that the repeating data group occurs twice in each record.

- DATA defines variables that are repeated (*STUDENT* and *SCORE*). The program begins reading the first repeating data group in column 6 (the value of STARTS). Since the value of OCCURS is 2, the program reads the repeating variables a second time, beginning in the next available column (column 14).

- END INPUT PROGRAM signals the end of data definition.

- BEGIN DATA and END DATA specify that data are inline.

- The output from LIST is shown in Figure C.10. Each student is a separate case.

Figure C.10 LIST output for repeating data

```
CLASS STUDENT SCORE

 101    182     12
 101    134     53
 102     99    112
 102    200    150
 103     15     87
 103    203     69
```

Varying Number of Repeating Groups

To use REPEATING DATA to define a file in which the number of repeating data groups varies across records, your data must contain a variable indicating the number of repeating data groups on a record. The following commands define such a file:

```
INPUT PROGRAM.
DATA LIST /  #NUM 1 CLASS 3-5.
REPEATING DATA STARTS=6 / OCCURS=#NUM
 /DATA STUDENT 1-4 SCORE 5-8.
END INPUT PROGRAM.

BEGIN DATA
3 101 182  12 134  53 199  30
2 102  99 112 200 150
1 103  15  87
END DATA.

LIST.
```

- INPUT PROGRAM signals the beginning of data definition.

- DATA LIST defines variables *CLASS* in columns 3 through 5 and *#NUM*, a scratch variable in column 1 that contains the number of repeating data groups in a record.

- REPEATING DATA specifies that the input file contains repeating data. STARTS indicates that repeating data begin in column 6. OCCURS sets the number of repeating groups on a record equal to the value of *#NUM*.

- DATA defines variables that are repeated. Since *#NUM* is 3 in the first and third records, the program reads three sets of *STUDENT* and *SCORE* variables in these records. *STUDENT* and *SCORE* are read twice in record 2.
- END INPUT PROGRAM signals the end of data definition.
- Data appear between BEGIN DATA and END DATA.
- Figure C.11 shows the output from LIST.

Figure C.11 LIST output

```
CLASS STUDENT SCORE

  101     182     12
  101     134     53
  101     199     30
  102      99    112
  103      15     87
```

If your data file does not have a variable indicating the number of repeating data groups per record, you can use the LOOP and REREAD commands to read the data, as in:

```
INPUT PROGRAM.
DATA LIST /    CLASS 3-5 #ALL 6-29 (A).
LEAVE CLASS.

LOOP #I = 1 TO 17  BY 8 IF SUBSTR(#ALL, #I, 8) NE ''.
-   REREAD COLUMN = #I + 5.
-   DATA LIST / STUDENT 1-4 SCORE 5-8.
-   END CASE.
END LOOP.
END INPUT PROGRAM.

BEGIN DATA
   101 182   12 134   53 199   30
   102   99 112 200 150
   103   15   87
END DATA.

LIST.
```

- INPUT PROGRAM signals the beginning of data definition.
- DATA LIST reads *CLASS* and *#ALL*, a temporary string variable that contains all of the repeating data groups for a classroom record. The column specifications for *#ALL* (6 through 29) are wide enough to accommodate the classroom record with the most repeating data groups (record 1).
- LOOP and END LOOP define an index loop. As the loop iterates, the program successively reads eight-character segments of *#ALL*, each of which contains a repeating data group or an empty field. The program reads the first eight characters of *#ALL* in the first iteration, the second eight characters in the second iteration, and so

forth. The loop terminates when the program encounters an empty segment, which means that there are no more repeating data groups on a record.

- In each iteration of the loop in which an *#ALL* segment is not empty, DATA LIST reads *STUDENT* and *SCORE* in a classroom record. The program begins reading these variables in the first record, in the starting column specified by REREAD COLUMN. For example, in the first iteration, the program reads *STUDENT* and *SCORE* beginning in column 6. In the second iteration, the program reads *STUDENT* and *SCORE* starting in column 14 of the same record. When all repeating groups have been read for a record, loop processing begins on the following record.

- END CASE creates a new case for each repeating group.

- REREAD causes DATA LIST to read repeating data groups in the same record in which it last read *CLASS*. Without REREAD, each execution of DATA LIST would begin on a different record.

- LEAVE preserves the value of CLASS across the repeating data groups on a record. Thus, the same class number is read for each student on a classroom record.

- INPUT PROGRAM signals the beginning of data definition.

- BEGIN DATA and END DATA indicate that the data are inline. The data are identical to those in the previous example except that they do not contain a variable indicating the number of repeating groups per record.

- These commands generate the same output as shown in Figure C.11.

Appendix D
Using the Macro Facility

A macro is a set of commands that generates customized command syntax. Using macros can reduce the time and effort needed to perform complex and repetitive data analysis tasks.

Macros have two parts: a **macro definition**, which indicates the beginning and end of the macro and gives a name to the macro, and a **macro body**, which contains regular commands or macro commands that build command syntax. When a macro is invoked by the **macro call**, syntax is generated in a process called **macro expansion**. Then the generated syntax is executed as part of the normal command sequence.

This chapter shows how to construct macros that perform three data analysis tasks. In the first example, macros facilitate a file-matching task. In Example 2, macros automate a specialized statistical operation (testing a sample correlation coefficient against a non-zero population correlation coefficient). Macros in Example 3 generate random data. As shown in Table D.1, each example demonstrates various features of the macro facility. For information on specific macro commands, see the DEFINE command.

Table D.1   Macro features

	Example 1	Example 2	Example 3
Macro argument			
Keyword	x	x	x
Default values	x		x
None	x		x
String manipulation	x		x
Looping			
Index	x		x
List processing		x	
Direct assignment	x		x

Example 1: Automating a File-Matching Task

Figure D.1 shows a listing of 1988 sales data for salespeople working in different regions. The listing shows that salesperson Jones sold 900 units in the Chicago sales territory, while Rodriguez sold 300 units in Baton Rouge.

Figure D.1   Listing of data file SALES88.SAV

```
YEAR REGION        SALESPER   SALES

1988 CHICAGO       JONES       900
1988 CHICAGO       GREGORY     400
1988 BATON ROUGE RODRIGUEZ     300
1988 BATON ROUGE SMITH         333
1988 BATON ROUGE GRAU          100
```

You can use command syntax shown in Figure D.2 to obtain each salesperson's percentage of total sales for their region.

Figure D.2   Commands for obtaining sales percentages

```
GET FILE = 'SALES88.SAV'.

SORT CASES BY REGION.

AGGREGATE OUTFILE = 'TOTALS.SAV'
  /PRESORTED
  /BREAK  = REGION
  /TOTAL@ = SUM(SALES).

MATCH FILES FILE=*
  /TABLE  = 'TOTALS.SAV'
  /BY REGION.

COMPUTE PCT = SALES / TOTAL@.

TITLE  1988 DATA.
LIST.
```

- The GET command opens *SALES88.SAV*, an SPSS-format data file. This file becomes the working data file.
- SORT CASES sorts the working data file in ascending alphabetical order by *REGION*.
- The AGGREGATE command saves total sales (variable *TOTAL@*) for each region in file *TOTALS.SAV*.
- MATCH FILES appends the regional totals to each salesperson's record in the working data file. (See the MATCH FILES command for more information on matching files.)
- COMPUTE obtains the percentage of regional sales (*PCT*) for each salesperson.

- The LIST command output displayed in Figure D.3 shows that Rodriguez sold 41% of the products sold in Baton Rouge. Gregory accounted for 31% of sales in the Chicago area.

Figure D.3   Regional sales percentages for 1988

```
YEAR REGION        SALESPER    SALES    TOTAL@     PCT

1988 BATON ROUGE RODRIGUEZ      300    733.00     .41
1988 BATON ROUGE SMITH          333    733.00     .45
1988 BATON ROUGE GRAU           100    733.00     .14
1988 CHICAGO     JONES          900   1300.00     .69
1988 CHICAGO     GREGORY        400   1300.00     .31
```

Figure D.4 shows a macro that issues the commands in Figure D.2. The macro consists of the commands that produce sales percentages imbedded between macro definition commands DEFINE and !ENDDEFINE.

Figure D.4   !TOTMAC macro

```
DEFINE !TOTMAC ().

GET FILE   = 'SALES88.SAV'.

SORT CASES BY REGION.

AGGREGATE OUTFILE = 'TOTALS.SAV'
   /PRESORTED
   /BREAK   = REGION
   /TOTAL@ = SUM(SALES).

MATCH FILES FILE = *
   /TABLE  = 'TOTALS.SAV'
   /BY REGION.

COMPUTE PCT = SALES / TOTAL@.

TITLE  1988 DATA.
LIST.

!ENDDEFINE.

!TOTMAC.
```

- In Figure D.4, macro definition commands DEFINE and !ENDDEFINE signal the beginning and end of macro processing. DEFINE also assigns the name !TOTMAC to the macro (the parentheses following the name of the macro are required). The macro name begins with an exclamation point so that the macro does not conflict with that of an existing variable or command. Otherwise, if the macro name matched a variable name, the variable name would invoke the macro whenever the variable name appeared in the command stream.

- Commands between DEFINE and !ENDDEFINE constitute the macro body. These commands, which produce sales percentages, are identical to the commands in Figure D.2.
- The final statement in Figure D.4 (!TOTMAC) is the **macro call**, which invokes the macro. When the program reads the macro call, it issues the commands in the macro body. Then these commands are executed, generating output that is identical to that in Figure D.3.

While the macro in Figure D.4 shows you how to construct a simple macro, it doesn't reduce the number of commands needed to calculate regional percentages. However, you can use macro features such as looping to minimize coding in more complicated tasks. For example, let's say that in addition to the 1988 data, you have sales data for 1989 (*SALES89.SAV),* and each file contains the variables *REGION, SALESPER,* and *SALES.* The modified !TOTMAC macro in Figure D.5 calculates regional sales percentages for each salesperson for 1988 and 1989.

Figure D.5   !TOTMAC macro with index loop

```
DEFINE !TOTMAC ().

!DO !I  = 88 !TO 89.

-  GET FILE   = !CONCAT('SALES', !I, '.SAV').
-  SORT CASES BY REGION.
-  AGGREGATE OUTFILE = 'TOTALS.SAV'
        /PRESORTED
        /BREAK   = REGION
        /TOTAL@  = SUM(SALES).
-  MATCH FILES FILE = *
        /TABLE    = 'TOTALS.SAV'
        /BY REGION.
-  COMPUTE PCT= SALES / TOTAL@.

-  !LET !YEAR = !CONCAT('19',!I).
-  TITLE   !YEAR DATA.
-  LIST.
!DOEND.

!ENDDEFINE.

!TOTMAC.
```

- In Figure D.5, DEFINE and !ENDDEFINE signal the beginning and end of macro processing.
- Commands !DO and !DOEND define an **index loop**. Commands between !DO and !DOEND are issued once in each iteration of the loop. The value of **index variable !I**, which changes in each iteration, is 88 in the first iteration and 89 in the second (final) iteration.

- In each iteration of the loop, the GET command opens an SPSS-format data file. The name of the file is constructed using the **string manipulation function** !CONCAT, which creates a string that is the concatenation of SALES, the value of the index variable, and *.SAV*. Thus the file *SALES88.SAV* is opened in the first iteration.

- Commands between AGGREGATE and COMPUTE calculate percentages on the working data file. These commands are identical to those in Figure D.4.

- Next, a customized title is created. In the first iteration, the **direct assignment** command !LET assigns a value of 1988 to the macro variable !YEAR. This variable is used in the TITLE command on the following line to specify a title of *1988 DATA*.

- The LIST command displays the contents of each variable.

- In the second iteration of the loop, commands display percentages for the 1989 data file. The output from the !TOTMAC macro is shown in Figure D.6. Note that the listing for 1988 data is the same as in Figure D.3.

Figure D.6   Regional sales percentages for 1988 and 1989

```
1988 DATA

YEAR REGION        SALESPER    SALES   TOTAL@     PCT

1988 BATON ROUGE RODRIGUEZ      300    733.00     .41
1988 BATON ROUGE SMITH          333    733.00     .45
1988 BATON ROUGE GRAU           100    733.00     .14
1988 CHICAGO     JONES          900   1300.00     .69
1988 CHICAGO     GREGORY        400   1300.00     .31


1989 DATA

YEAR REGION        SALESPER    SALES   TOTAL@     PCT
1989 BATON ROUGE GRAU           320   1459.00     .22
1989 BATON ROUGE SMITH          800   1459.00     .55
1989 BATON ROUGE RODRIGUEZ      339   1459.00     .23
1989 CHICAGO     JONES          300   1439.00     .21
1989 CHICAGO     STEEL          899   1439.00     .62
1989 CHICAGO     GREGORY        240   1439.00     .17
```

Let's look at another application of the !TOTMAC macro, one that uses **keyword arguments** to make the application more flexible. Figure D.7 shows the number of absences for students in two classrooms. Let's say you want to calculate deviation scores indicating how many more (or fewer) times a student was absent than the average student in his or her classroom. The first step in obtaining deviation scores is to compute the average number of absences per classroom. We can use the !TOTMAC macro to compute classroom means by modifying the macro so that it computes means and uses the absences data file *(SCHOOL.SAV)* as input.

Figure D.7 Listing of file SCHOOL.SAV

```
CLASS STUDENT  ABSENT

 101  BARRY G    3
 101  JENNI W    1
 101  ED    F    2
 101  JOHN  O    8
 102  PAUL  Y    2
 102  AMY   G    3
 102  JOHN  D   12
 102  RICH  H    4
```

The !TOTMAC macro in Figure D.8 can produce a variety of group summary statistics such as sum, mean, and standard deviation for any SPSS-format data file. In the macro call you specify values of keyword arguments indicating the data file (FILE), the break (grouping) variable (BREAKVR), the summary function (FUNC), and the variable to be used as input to the summary function (INVAR). For example, to obtain mean absences for each classroom, we specify *SCHOOL.SAV* as the data file, *CLASS* as the break variable, MEAN as the summary function, and *ABSENT* as the variable whose values are to be averaged.

Figure D.8 !TOTMAC macro with keyword arguments

```
DEFINE !TOTMAC   ( BREAKVR  = !TOKENS(1)
                  /FUNC     = !TOKENS(1)
                  /INVAR    = !TOKENS(1)
                  /TEMP     = !TOKENS(1)  !DEFAULT(TOTALS.SAV)
                  /FILE     = !CMDEND).
GET FILE  = !FILE.
SORT CASES BY !BREAKVR.
AGGREGATE OUTFILE = '!TEMP'
   /PRESORTED
   /BREAK  = !BREAKVR
   /!CONCAT(!FUNC,'@') = !FUNC(!INVAR).

MATCH FILES FILE = *
  /TABLE  = '!TEMP'
  /BY !BREAKVR.

!ENDDEFINE.

!TOTMAC BREAKVR=CLASS FUNC=MEAN INVAR=ABSENT FILE=SCHOOL.SAV.

COMPUTE DIFF = ABSENT-MEAN@.

LIST.

!TOTMAC BREAKVR=REGION FUNC=SUM INVAR=SALES FILE=SALES89.SAV.

COMPUTE PCT  = SALES / SUM@.

LIST.
```

- In Figure D.8, the syntax for declaring keyword arguments follows the name of the macro in DEFINE.

- !TOKENS(1) specifies that the value of an argument is a string following the name of the argument in the macro call. Thus the first macro call specifies CLASS as the value of BREAKVR, MEAN as the value of FUNC, and ABSENT as the value of INVAR.

- !CMDEND indicates that the value for FILE is the remaining text in the macro call (*SCHOOL.SAV*).

- TEMP is an optional argument that names an intermediate file to contain the summary statistics. Since TEMP is not assigned a value in the macro call, summary statistics are written to the default intermediate file *(TOTALS.SAV)*.

- In the body of the macro, GET FILE opens *SCHOOL.SAV.*

- SORT CASES sorts the file by *CLASS.*

- AGGREGATE computes the mean number of absences for each class. The name of the variable containing the means (*MEAN@*) is constructed using the !CONCAT function, which concatenates the value of FUNC and the @ symbol.

- MATCH FILES appends the means to student records.

- COMPUTE calculates the deviation from the classroom mean for each student (variable *DIFF*).

- LIST displays the deviation scores, as shown in Figure D.9. For example, John D., who was absent 12 times, had 6.75 more absences than the average student in classroom 102. Rich H., who was absent 4 times, had 1.25 fewer absences than the average student in classroom 102.

- The second macro call and remaining commands in Figure D.8 generate regional sales percentages for the 1989 sales data. As shown in Figure D.9, percentages are identical to those displayed in the bottom half of Figure D.6.

Figure D.9   Student absences and 1989 sales percentages

```
CLASS STUDENT   ABSENT    MEAN@      DIFF

  101   BARRY G      3      3.50      -.50
  101   JENNI W      1      3.50     -2.50
  101   ED    F      2      3.50     -1.50
  101   JOHN  0      8      3.50      4.50
  102   PAUL  Y      2      5.25     -3.25
  102   AMY   G      3      5.25     -2.25
  102   JOHN  D     12      5.25      6.75
  102   RICH  H      4      5.25     -1.25


 YEAR REGION       SALESPER  SALES      SUM@     PCT

 1989 BATON ROUGE GRAU         320   1459.00     .22
 1989 BATON ROUGE SMITH        800   1459.00     .55
 1989 BATON ROUGE RODRIGUEZ    339   1459.00     .23
 1989 CHICAGO     JONES        300   1439.00     .21
 1989 CHICAGO     STEEL        899   1439.00     .62
 1989 CHICAGO     GREGORY      240   1439.00     .17
```

You can modify the macro call in Figure D.8 to specify a different data file, input variable, break variable, or summary statistic. To get a different summary statistic (such as standard deviation), change the value of FUNC (see the AGGREGATE command for more information on summary functions available in the AGGREGATE procedure).

Example 2: Testing Correlation Coefficients

While the program provides a large variety of statistical procedures, some specialized operations require the use of COMPUTE statements. For example, you may want to test a sample correlation coefficient against a population correlation coefficient. When the population coefficient is nonzero, you can compute a Z statistic to test the hypothesis that the sample and population values are equal (Morrison, 1976). The formula for Z is

$$Z = \frac{0.5 \, ln\left[\frac{(1 + r)}{(1 - r)}\right] - 0.5 \, ln\left[\frac{(1 + p_0)}{(1 - p_0)}\right]}{1/(\sqrt{n - 3})}$$

where r is the sample correlation coefficient, p_0 is the population coefficient, n is the size of the sample from which r is obtained, and ln signifies the natural logarithm function. Z has approximately the standard normal distribution.

Let's say you want to test an r of 0.66 obtained from a sample of 30 cases against a population coefficient of 0.85. Figure D.10 shows commands for displaying Z and its two-tailed probability.

Figure D.10 Commands for computing Z statistic

```
DATA LIST FREE / R N P.

BEGIN DATA
.66 30 .85
END DATA.

COMPUTE #ZR  = .5* (LN ((1 + R) / (1 - R))).
COMPUTE #ZP  = .5* (LN ((1 + P) / (1 - P))).

COMPUTE Z    = (#ZR-#ZP)/(1/(SQRT(N-3))).
COMPUTE PROB = 2*(1-CDFNORM(ABS(Z))).

FORMAT  PROB (F8.3).
LIST.
```

- DATA LIST defines variables containing the sample correlation coefficient (*R*), sample size (*N*), and population correlation coefficient (*P*).
- BEGIN DATA and END DATA indicate that data are inline.

- COMPUTE statements calculate Z and its probability. Variables *#ZR* and *#ZP* are scratch variables used in the intermediate steps of the calculation.
- The LIST command output is shown in Figure D.11. Since the absolute value of Z is large and the probability is small, we reject the hypothesis that the sample was drawn from a population having a correlation coefficient of 0.85.

Figure D.11 Z statistic and its probability

```
     R       N        P        Z      PROB

   .66    30.00      .85    -2.41      .016
```

If you use the Z test frequently, you may want to construct a macro like that shown in Figure D.12. The !CORRTST macro computes Z and probability values for a sample correlation coefficient, sample size, and population coefficient specified as values of keyword arguments.

Figure D.12 !CORRTST macro

```
DEFINE !CORRTST ( R  = !TOKENS(1)
                 /N  = !TOKENS(1)
                 /P  = !TOKENS(1)).

INPUT PROGRAM.
-    END CASE.
-    END FILE.
END INPUT PROGRAM.

COMPUTE #ZR  = .5* (LN ((1 + !R) / (1 - !R))).
COMPUTE #ZP  = .5* (LN ((1 + !P) / (1 - !P))).

COMPUTE Z    = (#ZR-#ZP) / (1/(SQRT(!N-3))).
COMPUTE PROB = 2*(1-CDFNORM(ABS(Z))).
FORMAT  PROB(F8.3).

TITLE SAMPLE R=!R, N=!N, POPULATION COEFFICIENT=!P.

LIST.

!ENDDEFINE.

!CORRTST R=.66 N=30 P=.85.
!CORRTST R=.50 N=50 P=.85.
```

- DEFINE names the macro as !CORRTST and declares arguments for the sample correlation coefficient (R), the sample size (N), and the population correlation coefficient (P).

- !TOKENS(1) specifies that the value of an argument is a string that follows the name of the argument in the macro call. Thus the first macro call specifies values of 0.66, 30, and 0.85 for R, N, and P.

- Commands between INPUT PROGRAM and END INPUT PROGRAM create a working data file with one case. COMPUTE statements calculate the Z statistic and its probability using the values of macro arguments R, N, and P. (INPUT PROGRAM commands would not be needed if COMPUTE statements operated on values in an existing file or inline data, rather than macro arguments.)

- A customized TITLE shows displays the values of macro arguments used in computing Z.

- The LIST command displays Z and its probability.

- The !CORRTST macro is called twice in Figure D.12. The first invocation tests an r of 0.66 from a sample of 30 cases against a population coefficient of 0.85 (this generates the same Z value and probability as in Figure D.11). The second macro call tests an r of 0.50 from a sample of 50 cases against the same population correlation coefficient. The output from these macro calls is shown in Figure D.13.

Figure D.13   Output from !CORRTST

```
SAMPLE R= .66 , N= 30 , POPULATION COEFFICIENT= .85

        Z       PROB
    -2.41      .016


SAMPLE R= .50 , N= 50 , POPULATION COEFFICIENT= .85

        Z       PROB
    -4.85      .000
```

Figure D.14 shows a modified !CORRTST macro that you can use to test a sample r against each coefficient in a *list* of population coefficients.

Figure D.14   !CORRTST macro with list-processing loop

```
DEFINE !CORRTST (R  = !TOKENS(1)
                 /N = !TOKENS(1)
                 /P = !CMDEND).
-   INPUT PROGRAM.
-     END CASE.
-     END FILE.
-   END INPUT PROGRAM.

!DO !I !IN (!P).
-   COMPUTE #ZR  = .5* (LN ((1 + !R) / (1 - !R))).
-   COMPUTE #ZP  = .5* (LN ((1 + !I) / (1 - !I))).

-   COMPUTE Z    = (#ZR-#ZP)/(1/(SQRT(!N-3))).

-   COMPUTE PROB=2*(1-CDFNORM(ABS(Z))).
-   FORMAT  PROB(F8.3).
-   TITLE SAMPLE R=!R, N=!N, POPULATION COEFFICIENT=!I.
-   LIST.
!DOEND.

!ENDDEFINE.

!CORRTST R=.66 N=30 P=.20 .40 .60 .80 .85 .90.
```

- As in Figure D.12, DEFINE names the macro as !CORRTST and declares arguments for the sample correlation coefficient (R), the sample size (N), and the population correlation coefficient (P).

- !TOKENS(1) specifies that the value of an argument is a string that follows the name of the argument in the macro call. Thus, the macro call specifies the value of R as 0.66 and N as 0.30.

- !CMDEND indicates that the value for P is the remaining text in the macro call. Thus the value of P is a list containing the elements 0.20, 0.40, 0.60, 0.80, 0.85, and 0.90.

- Commands !DO !IN and !DOEND define a **list-processing loop**. Commands in the loop compute one Z statistic for each element in the list of population coefficients. For example, in the first iteration Z is computed using 0.20 as the population coefficient. In the second iteration 0.40 is used. The same sample size (30) and r value (0.66) are used for each Z statistic.

- The output from the macro call is shown in Figure D.15. One Z statistic is displayed for each population coefficient.

Figure D.15 Output from modified !CORRTST macro

```
SAMPLE R= .66 , N= 30 , POPULATION COEFFICIENT= .20

      Z     PROB
    3.07    .002

SAMPLE R= .66 , N= 30 , POPULATION COEFFICIENT= .40

      Z     PROB
    1.92    .055

SAMPLE R= .66 , N= 30 , POPULATION COEFFICIENT= .60

      Z     PROB
     .52    .605

SAMPLE R= .66 , N= 30 , POPULATION COEFFICIENT= .80

      Z     PROB
   -1.59    .112

SAMPLE R= .66 , N= 30 , POPULATION COEFFICIENT= .85

      Z     PROB
   -2.41    .016

SAMPLE R= .66 , N= 30 , POPULATION COEFFICIENT= .90

      Z     PROB
   -3.53    .000
```

Example 3: Generating Random Data

You can use command syntax to generate variables that have approximately a normal distribution. Commands for generating five standard normal variables ($X1$ through $X5$) for 1000 cases are shown in Figure D.16. As shown in the output in Figure D.17, each variable has a mean of approximately 0 and a standard deviation of approximately 1.

Figure D.16 Data-generating commands

```
INPUT PROGRAM.
-     VECTOR X(5).
-         LOOP #I = 1 TO 1000.
-             LOOP #J = 1 TO 5.
-                 COMPUTE X(#J) = NORMAL(1).
-             END LOOP.
-             END CASE.
-         END LOOP.
-         END FILE.
END INPUT PROGRAM.

DESCRIPTIVES VARIABLES X1 TO X5.
```

Figure D.17 Descriptive statistics for generated data

Variable	Mean	Std Dev	Minimum	Maximum	Valid N	Label
X1	-.01	1.02	-3.11	4.15	1000	
X2	.08	1.03	-3.19	3.22	1000	
X3	.02	1.00	-3.01	3.51	1000	
X4	.03	1.00	-3.35	3.19	1000	
X5	-.01	.96	-3.34	2.91	1000	

The !DATAGEN macro in Figure D.18 issues the data-generating commands shown in Figure D.16.

Figure D.18   !DATAGEN macro

```
DEFINE !DATAGEN ().

INPUT PROGRAM.
-    VECTOR X(5).
-       LOOP #I = 1 TO 1000.
-          LOOP #J = 1 TO 5.
-             COMPUTE X(#J) = NORMAL(1).
-          END LOOP.
-          END CASE.
-       END LOOP.
-       END FILE.
END INPUT PROGRAM.

DESCRIPTIVES VARIABLES X1 TO X5.

!ENDDEFINE.

!DATAGEN.
```

In Figure D.18, data-generating commands are imbedded between macro definition commands. The macro produces the same data and descriptive statistics as shown in Figure D.17.

You can tailor the generation of normally distributed variables if you modify the !DATAGEN macro so it will accept keyword arguments, as in Figure D.19. The macro allows you to specify the number of variables and cases to be generated and the approximate standard deviation.

Figure D.19 !DATAGEN macro with keyword arguments

```
DEFINE !DATAGEN (    OBS   =!TOKENS(1)        !DEFAULT(1000)
                    /VARS =!TOKENS(1)        !DEFAULT(5)
                    /SD   =!CMDEND           !DEFAULT(1)).
INPUT PROGRAM.
-    VECTOR X(!VARS).
-        LOOP #I = 1 TO !OBS.
-            LOOP #J = 1 TO !VARS.
-                COMPUTE X(#J) = NORMAL(!SD).
-            END LOOP.
-            END CASE.
-        END LOOP.
-        END FILE.
END INPUT PROGRAM.

!LET !LIST = !NULL.
!DO  !I   = 1 !TO !VARS.
-    !LET !LIST = !CONCAT(!LIST, ' ', X, !I).
!DOEND.

DESCRIPTIVES VARIABLES !LIST.

!ENDDEFINE.

!DATAGEN OBS=500 VARS=2 SD=1.
!DATAGEN.
```

- The DEFINE statement in Figure D.19 declares arguments that specify the number of cases (OBS), variables (VARS), and standard deviation (SD). By default, the macro creates 1000 cases with 5 variables that have a standard deviation of 1.

- Commands between INPUT PROGRAM and END INPUT PROGRAM generate the new data using values of the macro arguments.

- Commands !LET and !DO/!DOEND construct a variable list (!LIST) that is used in DESCRIPTIVES. The first !LET command initializes the list to a null (blank) string value. For each new variable, the index loop adds to the list a string of the form *X1, X2, X3*, and so forth. Thus, DESCRIPTIVES requests means and standard deviations for each new variable.

- The first macro call generates 500 cases with two standard normal variables. The second call requests the default number of variables, cases, and standard deviation. Descriptive statistics (not shown) are also computed for each variable.

As shown in Figure D.20, you can declare additional keyword arguments that allow you to specify the distribution (normal or uniform) of the generated data and a parameter value that is used as the standard deviation (for normally distributed data) or a range (for uniformly distributed data).

Figure D.20 !DATAGEN macro with additional keyword arguments

```
DEFINE !DATAGEN (OBS      =!TOKENS(1)      !DEFAULT(1000)
                 /VARS  =!TOKENS(1)        !DEFAULT(5)
                 /DIST  =!TOKENS(1)        !DEFAULT(NORMAL)
                 /PARAM =!TOKENS(1)        !DEFAULT(1)).
INPUT PROGRAM.
-    VECTOR X(!VARS).
-       LOOP #I = 1 TO !OBS.
-           LOOP #J = 1 TO !VARS.
-             COMPUTE X(#J) = !DIST(!PARAM).
-           END LOOP.
-           END CASE.
-       END LOOP.
-       END FILE.
END INPUT PROGRAM.

!LET !LIST = !NULL.
!DO  !I =  1 !TO !VARS.
-    !LET !LIST = !CONCAT(!LIST, ' ', X, !I).
!DOEND.

DESCRIPTIVES VARIABLES !LIST.
!ENDDEFINE.

!DATAGEN OBS=500 VARS=2 DIST=UNIFORM PARAM=2.
```

- The DEFINE statement in Figure D.20 declares arguments OBS, VARS, DIST, and PARAM. As in Figure D.19, OBS and VARS represent the number of observations and cases to be generated. Arguments DIST and PARAM specify the shape and parameter of the distribution of generated data. By default, the macro generates 1000 observations with 5 standard normal variables.

- Statements between INPUT PROGRAM and END INPUT PROGRAM generate the new data using values of macro arguments.

- Remaining commands in the body of the macro obtain descriptive statistics for generated variables, as in Figure D.19.

- The macro call in Figure D.20 creates two approximately uniformly distributed variables with a range of 2. The output from the macro call is shown in Figure D.21.

Figure D.21 Descriptive statistics for uniform variables

Variable	Mean	Std Dev	Minimum	Maximum	Valid N	Label
X1	.99	.57	.00	2.00	500	
X2	1.00	.57	.00	2.00	500	

Subject Index

active system file, 21

Add Cases procedure, 82
  case source variable, 87
  dictionary information, 84
  key variables, 86
  limitations, 84
  removing variables, 86
  renaming variables, 85
  selecting variables, 86
  unpaired variables, 84
  variables in the new file, 88

Add Variables procedure, 697
  case source variable, 703
  dictionary information, 699
  duplicate cases, 701
  excluded variables, 702
  file sort order, 699, 700
  key variables, 700
  keyed tables, 701
  limitations, 699
  renaming variables, 702
  variables in the new file, 704

adjusted residuals
  in loglinear analysis procedures, 426

agglomeration schedule
  in Hierarchical Cluster Analysis procedure, 171

aggregated data
  in Life Tables procedure, 1158

aggregating data, 92
  aggregate functions, 97
  aggregate variables, 98
  break variables, 92, 95
  saving files, 95
  variable labels, 97
  variable names, 96

AINDS model. *See* asymmetric individual
    differences Euclidean distance model

Akaike information criterion
  in Linear Regression procedure, 988

alpha coefficient
  in Reliability Analysis procedure, 1009

alpha factoring
  in Factor Analysis procedure, 371

alpha level, 475, 1199

alpha value
  for post hoc tests, 483, 1206

alternative hypothesis, 475, 1199

Ameniya's prediction criterion
  in Linear Regression procedure, 988

analysis of covariance
  general linear model, 462

analysis of variance, 119, 650
  general linear model, 462
  in Curve Estimation procedure, 239
  in Discriminant Analysis procedure, 304
  in K-Means Cluster procedure, 955
  in Linear Regression procedure, 988
  in Means procedure, 775
  in Reliability Analysis procedure, 1010
  in Summarize procedure, 1149
  See also One-Way ANOVA procedure; Simple
    Factorial ANOVA procedure

ANCOVA model
  syntax, 465

Anderberg's *D*
  in Distances procedure, 943
  in Hierarchical Cluster Analysis procedure, 167

Anderson-Rubin factor scores
  in Factor Analysis procedure, 373

ANOVA. *See* analysis of variance; UNIANOVA

anti-image matrix
  in Factor Analysis procedure, 368

arcsine function, 45

arctangent function, 45

area charts
  in Interactive Charts procedure, 562
  sequence, 147, 1179

arguments
  complex, 44
  defined, 44

arithmetic functions, 187

arithmetic operators, 43, 186
    in matrix language, 713
arrays. *See* vectors
ASCAL model. *See* asymmetric Euclidean distance
    model
ASCII text data files, 438
    See also raw data files
assignment expression
    computing values, 184
asymmetric Euclidean distance model
    in Multidimensional Scaling procedure, 109
asymmetric individual differences Euclidean distance
    model
    in Multidimensional Scaling procedure, 109
asymmetric matrix
    in Multidimensional Scaling procedure, 106
autocorrelation, 75
    partial, 860
Autocorrelations procedure, 75, 860
    partial autocorrelation, 80, 860
    periodic lags, 79, 863
    specifying periodicity, 78, 863
    standard error method, 80
    transforming values, 77, 862
    using a previously defined model, 80, 864
average linkage between groups
    in Hierarchical Cluster Analysis procedure, 169
average linkage within groups
    in Hierarchical Cluster Analysis procedure, 169

backward elimination
    in Cox Regression procedure, 206
    in Hierarchical Loglinear Analysis procedure, 538
    in Linear Regression procedure, 986
    in Logistic Regression procedure, 616
balanced designs
    in GLM Univariate, 489, 1212
bar charts, 509
    in Crosstabs procedure, 230
    in Frequencies procedure, 414
    in Interactive Charts procedure, 563
    interval width, 414
    scale, 414
Bartlett factor scores
    in Factor Analysis procedure, 373

Bartlett's approximation
    in Autocorrelations procedure, 80
Bartlett's test of sphericity
    in Factor Analysis procedure, 368
    in MANOVA, 682
Bernoulli distribution function, 48
beta distribution function, 46
binary Euclidean distance
    in Distances procedure, 944
    in Hierarchical Cluster Analysis procedure, 168
binary shape difference
    in Distances procedure, 944
    in Hierarchical Cluster Analysis procedure, 169
binary squared Euclidean distance
    in Distances procedure, 944
    in Hierarchical Cluster Analysis procedure, 168
binary variance measure
    in Distances procedure, 944
    in Hierarchical Cluster Analysis procedure, 169
binomial distribution function, 48
binomial test
    in Binomial Test procedure, 826
Binomial Test procedure, 826
    expected proportions, 826
    observed proportions, 826
Bivariate Correlations procedure, 191, 817, 866
    case count, 819
    control variables, 868
    correlation coefficients, 191
    format, 870
    limitations, 192, 818, 867
    matrix input, 870
    matrix output, 194, 817, 820, 870
    missing values, 194, 820, 870, 872
    order values, 868
    random sampling, 817, 819
    rank-order coefficients, 817
    significance levels, 193, 817, 819, 869
    statistics, 193, 819, 869
blank
    delimiter, 16
blank data fields
    treatment of, 1108
blank lines
    displaying, 919
    See also printing cases

Blom's transformation, 962
    in normal probability plots, 896
BMDP files
    conversion to SPSS, 979
    format specification, 979
    numeric variables, 979
    string variables, 979
Bonferroni intervals
    in MANOVA, 686
Bonferroni test, 484, 485, 854, 1207, 1209
bootstrap estimates
    in Nonlinear Regression procedure, 806
Box's *M* test
    in Discriminant Analysis procedure, 304
    in MANOVA, 683
box-and-whiskers plots. *See* boxplots
Box-Ljung statistic
    in Autocorrelations procedure, 76
boxplots
    comparing factor levels, 347
    comparing variables, 347
    identifying outliers, 348
    in Explore procedure, 349
    in Interactive Charts procedure, 566
Breslow test
    in Kaplan-Meier procedure, 600
Breslow-Day statistic
    in Crosstabs procedure, 228

c charts, 1129
    data organization, 1130
    sigma, 1135
    subgroup identifier, 1131
case identification variable, 975
case selection, 808
cases
    limiting, 808
    listing, 605
    sampling, 1077
    selecting, 808, 1095
    sorting, 1117
    weighting, 1247
categories
    showing and hiding empty categories, 555
category order
    interactive charts, 555

Cauchit link
    in Ordinal Regression, 882
Cauchy distribution function, 46
censored cases
    in Kaplan-Meier procedure, 597
centered moving average function, 217
centered running median function, 218
centroid method
    in Hierarchical Cluster Analysis procedure, 169
character sets, 1279
charts, 504
    bar, 509
    control, 1119
    count functions, 506
    difference line, 515
    drop-line, 515
    error bar, 525
    high-low, 522
    histograms, 529
    line, 515
    normal probability, 892
    Pareto, 530
    pie, 521
    P-P normal probability, 897
    Q-Q normal probability, 896
    range bar, 510
    ROC Curve, 1076
    scatterplots, 526
    sequence, 141, 1173
    summary functions, 506
    templates, 532
Chebychev distance
    in Distances procedure, 938
    in Hierarchical Cluster Analysis procedure, 163
chi-square
    Cochran, 1010
    distance measure, 163, 938
    Friedman, 1010
    in Chi-Square Test procedure, 827
    in Crosstabs procedure, 227
chi-square distribution function, 46
Chi-Square Test procedure, 827
    expected proportions, 827
    observed proportions, 827
city-block distance
    in Distances procedure, 938
    in Hierarchical Cluster Analysis procedure, 163
classification plots
    in Logistic Regression procedure, 620

classification tables
    in Discriminant Analysis procedure, 305
    in Logistic Regression procedure, 618
cluster membership
    in Hierarchical Cluster Analysis procedure, 171
Cochran's *Q*
    in Tests for Several Related Samples
        procedure, 828
Cochran's statistic
    in Crosstabs procedure, 228
coefficient of variation, 45
Cohen's kappa. *See* kappa
column headings, 913
    See also page ejection
column percentages
    in Crosstabs procedure, 226
column-style format specifications, 255
comma
    delimiter, 16
command
    files, 19, 578
    order, 16, 1269
    syntax, 13
commands
    processed through your operating system, 14
    run interactively, 13
    that read data, 17
    that take effect immediately, 17
comments
    in commands, 178
communality
    in Factor Analysis procedure, 367
complementary log-log link
    in Ordinal Regression, 882
complex data files, 970
    case identification variable, 975
    defining, 970
    duplicate records, 977
    grouped files, 970
    missing records, 976
    mixed files, 970
    nested files, 970
    repeating groups, 970
    skipping records, 974
    spreading values across cases, 977
    undefined records, 973

complex files
    defining, 324, 335, 338
complex raw data files, 1287
    defining, 381
    grouped, 387
    mixed, 386
    nested, 387
compound model
    in Curve Estimation procedure, 236, 237
computing values, 179
    arithmetic functions, 187
    arithmetic operators, 186
    assignment expression, 184
    conditional expressions, 318, 544
    cross-case functions, 188
    date and time functions, 189
    formats of new variables, 185
    functions, 179
    if case satisfies condition, 317, 544
    logical expressions, 318, 544
    logical functions, 188
    logical operators, 317, 544
    loop structures, 637
    missing values, 185
    missing-value functions, 187
    random-number functions, 189
    relational operators, 317, 544
    statistical functions, 187
    string data, 184, 186
    string functions, 190
    syntax rules, 184
    target variable, 184
condition index
    in Linear Regression procedure, 988
conditional expressions. *See* logical expressions
conditional independence test
    in Crosstabs procedure, 228
conditional probability
    in Distances procedure, 942
    in Hierarchical Cluster Analysis procedure, 166
conditional statistic
    in Cox Regression procedure, 207
    in Logistic Regression procedure, 616
conditional transformations, 317, 544
    conditional expressions, 318, 544
    formats of new variables, 319, 546
    logical expressions, 318, 544
    logical operators, 317, 544

missing values, 320, 546
nested, 324
relational operators, 317, 544
string data, 318, 319, 545, 546
conditionality
    matrix, 107
    row, 107
    unconditional data, 107
confidence intervals, 475, 1199
    in Cox Regression procedure, 208
    in Curve Estimation procedure, 239
    in Explore procedure, 351
    in Interactive Charts procedure, 569
    in Linear Regression procedure, 988, 990, 999
    in loglinear analysis procedures, 426
    in MANOVA, 685
    in Probit Analysis procedure, 929
    in ROC Curve procedure, 1075
confusion matrix
    in Discriminant Analysis procedure, 305
consecutive integers
    converting numeric data, 132
    converting string data, 132
constants, 43
constrained nonlinear regression, 791
    See also Nonlinear Regression procedure
contained effects
    in GLM Univariate, 474, 1198
contingency coefficient
    in Crosstabs procedure, 227
contrast coefficients
    in GLM Univariate, 477, 1200
contrast coefficients matrix, 466
    See also L matrix
contrast results matrix, 466
    See also K matrix
contrasts
    analysis of variance, 852
    custom, 468
    deviation, 481, 1205
    difference, 482, 500, 1205
    for within-subjects factors, 692
    Helmert, 482, 500, 1206
    in GLM Univariate, 481, 1205
    in MANOVA, 678
    orthogonal, 482, 1206
    polynomial, 481, 500, 1205
    repeated, 482, 500, 1206

reverse Helmert, 482, 1205
simple, 482, 500, 1206
special, 482, 500, 1206
within-subjects factor, 498
WSFACTOR, 499
control charts, 1119
    c charts, 1129
    individuals charts, 1125
    missing values, 1136
    moving range charts, 1125
    np charts, 1127
    p charts, 1127
    R charts, 1122
    s charts, 1122
    sigma, 1135
    u charts, 1129
    X-bar charts, 1122
control variables
    in Crosstabs procedure, 224
convergence criterion
    in Factor Analysis procedure, 370
    in K-Means Cluster procedure, 954
    in Multidimensional Scaling procedure, 110
converting data files. See data files
Cook's D
    in Logistic Regression procedure, 620
Cook's distance
    in GLM Univariate, 1211
    in Linear Regression procedure, 999
correlation, 191
    in Linear Regression procedure, 988, 992
    See also Bivariate Correlations procedure
correlation matrices
    in Logistic Regression procedure, 618
    in loglinear analysis procedures, 427, 633
    pooled within-groups, 304
cosine
    in Distances procedure, 938
    in Hierarchical Cluster Analysis procedure, 162
counting occurrences, 197
    defining values, 197
    missing values, 198
counts
    in Report Summaries in Rows procedure,
        1052, 1053
covariance
    in Linear Regression procedure, 988, 993
    in Reliability Analysis procedure, 1009, 1011

covariance matrices
    in loglinear analysis procedures, 427
    in 2-Stage Least-Squares procedure, 1191
    pooled within-groups, 304, 306
    separate-groups, 304, 306
    total, 304
covariance method
    in Reliability Analysis procedure, 1011
covariance ratio
    in Linear Regression procedure, 999
Cox regression, 199
    See also Cox Regression procedure; Time-
        Dependent Cox Regression procedure
Cox Regression procedure, 199
    baseline functions, 208
    categorical covariates, 204
    confidence intervals, 208
    contrasts, 204
    correlation matrix, 208
    covariates, 202
    display options, 208
    entry probability, 209
    interaction terms, 203
    iteration criteria, 208
    limitations, 201
    maximum iterations, 209
    method, 206
    missing values, 207
    parameter estimates, 208
    plots, 209, 210
    removal probability, 209
    saving coefficients, 210
    saving new variables, 210
    saving survival table, 210
    split-file processing, 211
    stratification variable, 203
    survival status variable, 203
    survival time variable, 202
Cp. See Mallow's *Cp*
Cramér's *V*
    in Crosstabs procedure, 227
cross-case functions, 188
cross-correlation, 152
Cross-Correlations procedure, 152
    periodic lags, 156
    specifiying periodicity, 155
    transforming values, 154
    using a previously defined model, 157

cross-product deviation
    in Linear Regression procedure, 993
Crosstabs procedure, 221
    column percentages, 226
    control variables, 224
    expected count, 226
    general mode, 225
    integer mode, 225
    layers, 225
    missing values, 229
    observed count, 226
    reproducing tables, 232
    residuals, 226
    row order, 230
    row percentages, 226
    statistics, 227
    suppressing tables, 230
    table format, 230
    total percentage, 226
    writing tables, 230
crosstabulation, 221
    multiple response, 785
    writing to a file, 931
    See also Crosstabs procedure
cubic model
    in Curve Estimation procedure, 236, 237
cumulative sum function, 214
curve estimation, 234
Curve Estimation procedure, 234
    analysis of variance, 239
    confidence intervals, 239
    forecasting, 235, 236
    including constant, 238
    models, 237
    saving predicted values, 239
    saving prediction intervals, 239
    saving residuals, 239
    using a previously defined model, 240
curve fitting. *See* curve estimation
custom currency formats
    creating, 1111
custom models
    in Hierarchical Loglinear Analysis procedure, 543
    in loglinear analysis procedures, 429, 634
customized distance measures
    in Distances procedure, 938
    in Hierarchical Cluster Analysis procedure, 163

d. See Somers' *d*

data, 1211
  inline, 137, 243, 245
  invalid, 1108

data compression
  scratch files, 1109

data files
  aggregating, 92
  applying data dictionary, 128
  BMDP, 979
  complex, 335, 381, 970, 1287
  converting, 1085
  databases, 435, 438
  dBASE, 456, 1085
  default file extension, 1109
  direct access, 588
  documents, 315, 331
  Excel, 438, 454, 1085
  file information, 312, 1163
  grouped, 970
  keyed, 588, 888
  labels, 380
  Lotus 1-2-3, 454, 1085
  master files, 1214
  merging, 82, 697
  mixed, 970
  Multiplan, 454
  nested, 970
  opening, 431
  raw, 241, 438
  reading, 242, 431, 574, 588
  repeating data groups, 970
  SAS, 445
  saving, 1079, 1263
  split-file processing, 1137
  spreadsheet, 454, 1087
  SPSS, 431
  SPSS portable, 355, 574
  SPSS/PC+, 574
  subsets of cases, 396, 1095, 1221
  SYLK, 454, 1085
  tab-delimited, 456, 1088
  text, 438
  transaction files, 1214
  updating, 1214

data formats. *See* data types; display formats; input
    formats; output formats

data records
  defining, 247, 970

data transformations
  arithmetic functions, 187
  arithmetic operators, 186
  clearing, 158
  computing values, 179
  conditional, 317, 544
  conditional expressions, 318, 544
  consecutive integers, 132
  converting strings to numeric, 132, 968
  counting occurrences, 197
  counting the same value across variables, 197
  cross-case functions, 188
  date and time functions, 189
  functions, 179
  if case satisfies condition, 317, 544
  logical expressions, 318, 544
  logical functions, 188
  logical operators, 317, 544
  loop structures, 637
  missing-value functions, 187
  random-number functions, 189
  recoding values, 132, 964
  relational operators, 317, 544
  repeating, 326
  statistical functions, 187
  string functions, 190
  time series, 212, 259, 1069

data types, 241
  custom currency, 1111

database files, 438, 1087

databases
  reading, 435

date and time functions, 189

date functions, 60

date variables
  creating, 259
  current status, 1245

dates, 60

dBASE files
  reading, 453
  saving, 1090

decimal places
  implied, 256

Define Multiple Response Sets procedure, 782
  categories, 782
  dichotomies, 782
  set labels, 782
  set names, 782

deleted residuals
  in GLM Univariate, 488, 1211
delimiter, 16
  blank, 16
  comma, 16
  special, 16
delta
  in Hierarchical Loglinear Analysis procedure, 539
  in loglinear analysis procedures, 426, 632
dendrograms
  in Hierarchical Cluster Analysis procedure, 172
density function plots
  in Life Tables procedure, 1156
descriptive statistics, 286
  for residuals, 400
  in Explore procedure, 351
  See also Descriptives procedure
Descriptives procedure, 286
  display order, 290
  missing values, 291
  saving *z* scores, 288
  statistics, 289
determinant
  in Factor Analysis procedure, 368
detrended normal plots, 897
  in Explore procedure, 350
deviance residuals
  in loglinear analysis procedures, 426
deviation contrasts, 481, 1205
  in Cox Regression procedure, 204
  in loglinear analysis procedures, 630
  in MANOVA, 679
deviations from the mean
  repeated measures, 499
DfBeta
  in Linear Regression procedure, 999
  in Logistic Regression procedure, 620
DfFit
  in Linear Regression procedure, 999
diagonal values
  in Factor Analysis procedure, 369
Dice measure
  in Distances procedure, 941
  in Hierarchical Cluster Analysis procedure, 166
difference contrasts, 482, 1205
  in Cox Regression procedure, 205
  in loglinear analysis procedures, 630

  in MANOVA, 679
  repeated measures, 500
difference function, 214
difference line charts, 515
difference transformation
  in Autocorrelations procedure, 77, 862
  in Cross-Correlations procedure, 154
  in normal probability plots, 898
  in sequence charts, 145, 1176
dimension reduction analysis
  in MANOVA, 682
direct-access files
  reading, 588
discriminant analysis
  in MANOVA, 684
Discriminant Analysis procedure, 292
  casewise results, 302
  classification phase, 305
  classification summary, 305
  cross-validation, 305
  defining categories of grouping variable, 295
  exporting model information, 299
  function coefficients, 305, 306
  grouping variable, 295
  inclusion levels, 297
  limitations, 295
  matrices, 304
  matrix input, 307
  matrix output, 307
  maximum number of steps, 300
  missing values, 307, 309
  multiple analyses, 296
  number of functions, 300
  plots, 306
  predictor variables, 295
  prior probabilities, 301
  rotation of matrices, 305
  saving classification variables, 302
  selecting a subset of cases, 296
  statistics, 304
  stepwise methods, 296
  stepwise output, 305
  tolerance, 299
  variable selection methods, 298
discriminant function coefficients
  standardized, 304
  unstandardized, 305

discriminant scores
in Discriminant Analysis procedure, 302, 306
dispersion
in Distances procedure, 944
in Hierarchical Cluster Analysis procedure, 169
display formats, 407, 916
dissimilarity measures, 933
See also Distances procedure
distance matrix
in Hierarchical Cluster Analysis procedure, 171
in Multidimensional Scaling procedure, 105
Distances procedure, 933
computing distances between cases, 936
computing distances between variables, 936
displaying distance matrix, 945
labeling cases, 945
limitations, 935
matrix input, 946
matrix output, 946
measures for binary data, 939
measures for frequency-count data, 938
measures for interval data, 937
missing values, 946
standardization, 935
transforming measures, 936
transforming values, 935
variable list, 935
distribution functions, 45
Bernoulli, 48
beta, 46
binomial, 48
Cauchy, 46
chi-square, 46
exponential, 47
F, 47
gamma, 47
geometric, 48
hypergeometric, 49
Laplace, 47
logistic, 47
lognormal, 47
negative binomial, 49
normal, 47
Pareto, 48
Poisson, 49
t, 48
uniform, 48
Weibull, 48

documentation
online, 580
documents
dropping, 331
for SPSS data files, 315
retaining in aggregated files, 96
domain errors
defined, 50
numeric expressions, 50
dot charts
in Interactive Charts procedure, 567
doubly multivariate repeated measures
analysis, 502
syntax, 465
drop-line charts, 515
Duncan's multiple range test, 484, 485, 854,
1207, 1208
Dunnett's *C*, 484, 486, 855, 1207, 1209
Dunnett's one-tailed *t* test, 484, 485, 854, 1207, 1208
Durbin-Watson statistic
in Linear Regression procedure, 1001

EBCDIC data, 379
effects
random, 472, 1196
eigenvalues
in Discriminant Analysis procedure, 304
in Factor Analysis procedure, 367, 369, 370
in Linear Regression procedure, 988
in MANOVA, 682
empty categories
showing and hiding in interactive charts, 555
end-of-file control
in input programs, 249
endogenous variables
in 2-Stage Least-Squares procedure, 1190
epsilon
in loglinear analysis procedures, 426
equality of variance. *See* homogeneity of variance
equamax rotation
in Factor Analysis procedure, 372
erasing files, 344
error bar charts, 525

error bars
    in Interactive Charts procedure, 569
errors
    displaying, 1106
    maximum number, 1108
ESSCP matrices
    in GLM Multivariate, 492
estimable functions
    in GLM Univariate, 476, 1200
    intercept, 480, 1204
estimated marginal means
    in GLM Univariate, 486, 1209
    repeated measures, 503
estimated means plots, 478, 1201
eta
    in Crosstabs procedure, 227
    in Means procedure, 775
    in Summarize procedure, 1149
eta-squared
    partial, 476, 1200
Euclidean distance
    in Distances procedure, 937
    in Hierarchical Cluster Analysis procedure, 162
Euclidean model
    in Multidimensional Scaling procedure, 109
exact-size sample, 1077
examining data, 345
    See also Explore procedure
Excel files, 438
    read range, 459
    read variable names, 458
    reading, 453
    saving, 1090
expected count
    in Crosstabs procedure, 226
expected frequency
    in Hierarchical Loglinear Analysis procedure, 542
    in loglinear analysis procedures, 426, 633
    in Probit Analysis procedure, 929
Explore procedure, 345
    factor variable, 347
    limitations, 346
    missing values, 352
    plots, 349
    statistics, 348, 351
exploring data, 345
    See also Explore procedure

exponential distribution function, 47
exponential model
    in Curve Estimation procedure, 236, 237
extreme values
    in Explore procedure, 351

F distribution function, 47
F ratio
    in Linear Regression procedure, 988, 989
    in Means procedure, 776
    in Summarize procedure, 1149
F test
    in MANOVA, 682, 696
factor analysis, 361
    See also Factor Analysis procedure
Factor Analysis procedure, 361
    analysis variables, 366
    coefficient display format, 366
    convergence, 370
    correlation matrices, 367
    covariance matrices, 367
    descriptive statistics, 367
    diagonal values, 369
    extraction criteria, 370
    extraction methods, 371
    factor score computation, 373
    initial solution, 367
    iterations, 370
    matrix input, 374
    matrix output, 374
    missing values, 364
    plots, 368
    rotated solution, 367
    rotation criteria, 370
    rotation methods, 372
    saving factor scores, 372
    selecting a subset of cases, 365
    statistics, 367
    unrotated solution, 367
    variable list, 364
factor loading plots
    in Factor Analysis procedure, 369
factor pattern matrix
    in Factor Analysis procedure, 367
factor score coefficient matrix
    in Factor Analysis procedure, 368

factor structure matrix
    in Factor Analysis procedure, 367
factor transformation matrix
    in Factor Analysis procedure, 367
file handle, 378
file information
    SPSS data files, 1163
    working data file, 312
file specifications, 378
file transformations, 1214
    aggregating, 92
    applying data dictionary, 128
    merging files, 82, 697
    subsets of cases, 1095
files, 19
final cluster centers
    in K-Means Cluster procedure, 956
Fisher's classification function coefficients
    in Discriminant Analysis procedure, 305
Fisher's exact test
    in Crosstabs procedure, 227
fixed format, 243, 244, 245, 252
fixed-effects model
    syntax, 465
flattened weights
    in Multidimensional Scaling procedure, 113
forced entry
    in Cox Regression procedure, 206
    in Discriminant Analysis procedure, 298
    in Linear Regression procedure, 986
    in Logistic Regression procedure, 615
forced removal
    in Linear Regression procedure, 986
forecasting
    current forecast period, 1245
    in Curve Estimation procedure, 235, 236
formats, 31
    of new variables, 185, 319, 546
    See also data types; display formats; input formats;
        output formats
FORTRAN-like format specifications, 255
forward entry
    in Linear Regression procedure, 986
forward selection
    in Cox Regression procedure, 206
    in Logistic Regression procedure, 615

Fourier transformation function, 215
    inverse, 215
freefield format, 243, 244, 245, 254
Frequencies procedure, 411
    charts, 230, 414
    display order, 413
    limitations, 412
    missing values, 419
    statistics, 418
    suppressing tables, 413
frequency tables, 412
    format, 413
    writing to a file, 931
Friedman test
    in Tests for Several Related Samples
        procedure, 828
F-to-enter
    in Discriminant Analysis procedure, 299
    in Linear Regression procedure, 990
F-to-remove
    in Discriminant Analysis procedure, 299
    in Linear Regression procedure, 990
functions, 179
    distribution, 45
    examples, 186
    missing values in, 185
    numeric variables, 44
    string variables, 51
    time series, 214
furthest neighbor method
    in Hierarchical Cluster Analysis procedure, 169

Gabriel's pairwise comparisons test, 484, 485, 855,
    1207, 1209
Games and Howell's pairwise comparisons test, 484,
    486, 855, 1207, 1209
gamma
    in Crosstabs procedure, 227
gamma distribution function, 47
GEMSCAL model. See generalized multidimensional
    scaling
general estimable function, 476, 1200
general linear model
    sample models, 464
    syntax overview, 462

General Loglinear Analysis procedure, 420, 623
    adjusted residuals, 426
    categorical variables, 422, 627
    cell covariates, 422, 627
    cell structure, 424
    cell weights, 424, 628
    contrasts, 630
    convergence criteria, 425, 632
    correlation matrices, 427, 633
    covariance matrices, 427
    criteria, 425
    custom models, 429, 634
    delta, 426, 632
    design matrix, 427, 633
    deviance residuals, 426
    display options, 426, 632
    expected frequency, 426, 633
    factors, 422, 627
    generalized residuals, 424, 629
    interaction terms, 429, 634
    limitations, 421, 625
    log-odds ratio, 425
    maximum iterations, 426, 632
    missing values, 428, 634
    model specification, 429, 634
    multinomial distribution, 425
    normal probability plots, 427, 633
    observed frequency, 426, 633
    parameter estimates, 427, 633
    plots, 427, 633
    Poisson distribution, 425
    residual plots, 427, 633
    residuals, 426, 633
    saving variables, 428
    standardized residuals, 426
general mode
    Crosstabs procedure, 225
    Means procedure, 772
generalized log-odds ratio, 425
generalized multidimensional scaling
    in Multidimensional Scaling procedure, 110
generalized weights
    in Multidimensional Scaling procedure, 113
generating class
    in Hierarchical Loglinear Analysis procedure, 543
GENLOG command
    compared to LOGLINEAR, 624
geometric distribution function, 48

GLM, 466
    alpha level, 475
    alternative hypothesis, 475
    confidence interval, 475
    contained effects, 474
    contrast coefficients, 477
    contrasts, 481
    deleted residuals, 488
    estimable functions, 476
    estimated marginal means, 486
    estimated means plots, 478
    homogeneity of variance, 476
    K matrix, 480
    L matrix, 477, 479
    Levene's test, 476
    multiple comparisons, 483
    multivariate syntax, 490
    parameter estimates, 476
    post hoc tests, 483
    power, 475
    profile plots, 477
    repeated measures syntax, 495
    residual plots, 477
    spread-versus-level plots, 477
    standardized residuals, 488
    Studentized residuals, 488
    syntax overview, 461
    Type I sum-of-squares method, 473
    Type II sum-of-squares method, 474
    Type III sum-of-squares method, 474
    Type IV sum-of-squares method, 474
    univariate syntax, 469
    unstandardized predicted residuals, 488
    unstandardized residuals, 488
    weighted unstandardized predicted values, 488
    weighted unstandardized residuals, 488
GLM (command), 462
GLM Multivariate, 490
    ESSCP matrices, 492
    homogeneity of variance, 492
    HSSCP matrices, 492
    Levene test, 492
    M matrix, 492, 493
    residual correlation matrix, 493
    residual covariance matrix, 493
    residual SSCP matrix, 492
    RSSCP matrices, 492
    sums-of-squares and cross-products of
        residuals, 492
    sums-of-squares and cross-product matrices, 492

GLM Repeated Measures, 496
GLM Univariate, 469, 1193
    alpha level, 1199
    alternative hypothesis, 1199
    confidence interval, 1199
    contained effects, 1198
    contrast coefficients, 1200
    contrasts, 1205
    data files, 1211
    deleted residuals, 1211
    estimable functions, 1200
    estimated marginal means, 1209
    estimated means plots, 1201
    homogeneity of variance, 1200
    interactions, 1212
    K matrix, 1204
    L matrix, 1200, 1203
    lack of fit, 1200
    Levene's test, 1200
    multiple comparisons, 1206
    nested designs, 1212
    parameter estimates, 1200
    post hoc tests, 1206
    power, 1199
    profile plots, 1201
    residual plots, 1201
    spread-versus-level plots, 1201
    standard errors of predicted value, 1211
    standardized residuals, 1211
    Studentized residuals, 1211
    Type I sum-of-squares method, 1197
    Type II sum-of-squares method, 1197
    Type III sum-of-squares method, 1198
    Type IV sum-of-squares method, 1198
    unstandardized predicted residuals, 1211
    unstandardized residuals, 1211
    weighted unstandardized predicted values, 1211
    weighted unstandardized residuals, 1211
GLOR, 425
Goodman and Kruskal's gamma. See gamma
Goodman and Kruskal's lambda. See lambda
Goodman and Kruskal's tau
    in Crosstabs procedure, 227
goodness of fit, 400
    in Hierarchical Loglinear Analysis procedure, 536
Greenhouse-Geiser epsilon, 689
group membership
    predicted, 302
    probabilities, 301

grouped files, 387, 970
growth model
    in Curve Estimation procedure, 236, 237
Guttman's lower bounds
    in Reliability Analysis procedure, 1009

H. See Kruskal-Wallis H
Hamann measure
    in Distances procedure, 942
    in Hierarchical Cluster Analysis procedure, 167
hazard plots
    in Cox Regression procedure, 210
    in Kaplan-Meier procedure, 598
    in Life Tables procedure, 1156
Helmert contrasts, 482, 500, 1206
    in Cox Regression procedure, 205
    in loglinear analysis procedures, 630
    in MANOVA, 679
    reverse, 500
heterogeneity factor
    in Probit Analysis procedure, 928
heteroscedasticity
    in Weight Estimation procedure, 1251
hiding keys
    in interactive charts, 561
Hierarchical Cluster Analysis procedure, 159
    algorithm, 161
    distance measures, 162
    labeling cases, 171
    limitations, 161
    matrix input, 173
    matrix output, 173
    measures for binary data, 164
    measures for frequency-count data, 163
    measures for interval data, 162
    methods, 169
    missing values, 173, 175
    plots, 172
    saving cluster memberships, 170
    statistics, 171
    variable list, 161
hierarchical files. See nested files
hierarchical loglinear analysis, 535
    See also Hierarchical Loglinear Analysis
        procedure
Hierarchical Loglinear Analysis procedure, 535
    backward elimination, 538

cell weights, 539
criteria, 539
custom models, 543
display options, 542
expected frequency, 542
interaction terms, 543
limitations, 537
maximum iterations, 539
maximum order of terms, 538
method, 538
missing values, 543
model specification, 543
normal probability plots, 542
observed frequency, 542
parameter estimates, 542
partial associations, 542
residual plots, 542
residuals, 542
variables, 538
weighted models, 539
high-low-close charts
clustered, 523
simple, 522
histograms, 529
in Explore procedure, 350
in Frequencies procedure, 415
in Interactive Charts procedure, 570
in Linear Regression procedure, 1000
interval width, 415
scale, 415
with normal curve, 415
Hochberg's GT2, 484, 485, 855, 1207, 1209
homogeneity of variance
in GLM Multivariate, 492
in GLM Univariate, 476, 1200
homogeneity test
in Crosstabs procedure, 228
homogeneity tests
in MANOVA, 682
Hosmer-Lemeshow goodness-of-fit statistic
in Logistic Regression procedure, 618
Hotelling's T^2
in Reliability Analysis procedure, 1010
Hotelling's trace
in MANOVA, 686
HSSCP matrices
in GLM Multivariate, 492
Huynh-Feldt epsilon, 689

hypergeometric distribution function, 49
hypotheses
custom, 466, 496

icicle plots
in Hierarchical Cluster Analysis procedure, 172
image factoring
in Factor Analysis procedure, 371
implied decimal format, 256
increment value
in matrix loop structures, 731
independence model
in Autocorrelations procedure, 80
Independent-Samples T Test procedure, 1183
dependent variables, 1185
grouping variables, 1185
limitations, 1184
missing values, 1186
independent-samples t test. *See t* test
indexing clause
in loop structures, 639
in matrix loop structures, 731
indexing strings, 53
indexing variable
in matrix loop structures, 731
individuals charts, 1125
control limits, 1135
sigma, 1135
span, 1135
subgroup labels, 1127
initial cluster centers
in K-Means Cluster procedure, 954
initialization
suppressing, 603
initializing variables, 844, 1140
formats, 844, 845, 1140
numeric variables, 844
scratch variables, 844
string variables, 1140
inline data, 137, 243, 245
input data, 20
file, 20
input formats, 241, 254
column-style specifications, 255
FORTRAN-like specifications, 255

numeric, 256
string, 258
input programs, 584
  end-case control, 334
  end-of-file control, 249, 342
  examples, 250, 325, 328, 335, 343, 586, 641, 644, 645, 845, 889, 1242
input state, 585
instrumental variables
  in 2-Stage Least-Squares procedure, 1190
integer mode
  Crosstabs procedure, 225
interaction effects
  analysis of variance, 122
interaction plots. *See* profile plots
interaction terms
  in Cox Regression procedure, 203
  in Hierarchical Loglinear Analysis procedure, 543
  in loglinear analysis procedures, 429, 634
interactions
  in GLM Univariate, 489, 1212
  in Variance Component Analysis, 1232
Interactive Charts procedure, 550
  area charts, 562
  bar charts, 563
  boxplots, 566
  confidence intervals, 569
  dot charts, 567
  error bars, 569
  histograms, 570
  legends, 556
  line charts, 567
  pie charts, 564
  prediction intervals, 571
  regression lines, 570
  ribbon charts, 567
  scatterplots, 561
  smoothers, 570
intercept
  in estimable function, 480, 1204
  include or exclude, 475, 1198, 1229
interval data
  in Multidimensional Scaling procedure, 106
invalid data
  treatment of, 1108
inverse correlation matrix
  in Factor Analysis procedure, 368

inverse Fourier transformation function, 215
inverse model
  in Curve Estimation procedure, 237
item statistics
  in Reliability Analysis procedure, 1011
item-total statistics
  in Reliability Analysis procedure, 1011

Jaccard measure
  in Distances procedure, 941
  in Hierarchical Cluster Analysis procedure, 165
Jonckheere-Terpstra test
  in Tests for Several Independent Samples procedure, 829
journal file, 19, 20, 1107

K matrix, 466
  in GLM Univariate, 480, 1204
Kaiser normalization
  in Factor Analysis procedure, 370
Kaiser-Meyer-Olkin measure
  in Factor Analysis procedure, 368
Kaplan-Meier procedure, 594
  case-identification variable, 599
  censored cases, 597
  comparing factor levels, 600
  defining event, 597
  factor variable, 596
  labeling cases, 599
  mean survival time, 599
  median survival time, 599
  percentiles, 599
  plots, 598
  quartiles, 599
  saving new variables, 602
  status variable, 597
  strata variable, 598
  survival tables, 599
  survival time variable, 596
  trends for factor levels, 601
kappa
  in Crosstabs procedure, 228
Kendall's coefficient of concordance
  in Reliability Analysis procedure, 1010

Kendall's tau-*b*
  in Bivariate Correlations procedure, 819
  in Crosstabs procedure, 227
Kendall's tau-*c*
  in Crosstabs procedure, 227
Kendall's *W*
  in Tests for Several Related Samples
    procedure, 832
key variables, 1214
keyed data files, 888
  defining, 888
  file handle, 890
  file key, 888, 889, 890
keyed files
  reading, 588
keyed tables, 701
keys
  showing and hiding in interactive charts, 561
keywords
  reserved, 29
  syntax, 15
k-means cluster analysis, 951
  See also K-Means Cluster procedure
K-Means Cluster procedure, 951
  cluster distances, 955, 956
  cluster membership, 955, 956
  clustering method, 952, 954
  convergence criteria, 954
  iterations, 954
  labeling cases, 955
  missing values, 957
  reading initial centers, 954, 955
  saving cluster information, 956
  specifying number of clusters, 953
  statistics, 955
  variable list, 953
  writing final centers, 956
Kolmogorov-Smirnov *Z*
  in One-Sample Kolmogorov-Smirnov Test
    procedure, 830
  in Two-Independent-Samples Tests procedure, 831
KR20 coefficient
  in Reliability Analysis procedure, 1009
Kronecker product, 499
Kruskal-Wallis *H*
  in Tests for Several Independent Samples
    procedure, 832

Kulczynski measures
  in Distances procedure, 942
  in Hierarchical Cluster Analysis procedure, 166
kurtosis
  in Descriptives procedure, 289
  in Explore procedure, 351
  in Frequencies procedure, 418
  in Report Summaries in Rows procedure, 1052

L matrix, 466, 479, 1203
  in GLM Univariate, 477, 1200
lack of fit
  in GLM Univariate, 1200
lag function, 216
lambda
  Goodman and Kruskal's, 167, 942
  in Crosstabs procedure, 227
  Wilks', 298
Lance-and-Williams measure
  in Distances procedure, 945
  in Hierarchical Cluster Analysis procedure, 169
Laplace distribution function, 47
lead function, 216
least significant difference test, 484, 485, 854,
    1207, 1209
least-squares method
  generalized, 371
  unweighted, 371
legends
  in Interactive Charts procedure, 556
level of measurement
  specifying, 1237
levels
  within-subjects factors, 499
Levenberg-Marquardt method
  in Nonlinear Regression procedure, 803
Levene test
  in Explore procedure, 350
  in GLM Multivariate, 492
  in GLM Univariate, 476, 1200
leverage
  in Logistic Regression procedure, 620
leverage values
  in Linear Regression procedure, 999

Life Tables procedure, 1150
  aggregated data, 1158
  approximate comparisons, 1158
  comparing factor levels, 1156
  control variables, 1152
  exact comparisons, 1157
  factor variables, 1152
  limitations, 1152
  missing values, 1159
  pairwise comparisons, 1158
  plots, 1155
  saving survival table data, 1160
  survival status variable, 1154
  survival time variable, 1152
  time intervals, 1153
likelihood ratio
  in Cox Regression procedure, 207
  in Logistic Regression procedure, 616
likelihood-ratio chi-square
  in Crosstabs procedure, 227
Lilliefors test
  in Explore procedure, 350
limitations. *See* individual procedures
line charts, 515
  in Interactive Charts procedure, 567
  sequence, 147, 1179
line numbering, 843
  on IBM systems, 843
linear model
  in Curve Estimation procedure, 237
linear regression, 981
  See also Linear Regression procedure
Linear Regression procedure, 981, 997
  case selection, 993
  casewise plots, 1001
  constant term, 990
  dependent variables, 985
  histograms, 1000
  matrix input, 994
  matrix output, 994
  missing values, 995
  model criteria, 989
  normal probability plots, 1000
  partial residual plots, 1002
  residuals, 997
  saving files, 1003
  saving new variables, 1004
  scatterplots, 1002

  statistics, 987, 992
  tolerance, 988, 989, 990
  variable selection methods, 985
  weights, 991
linearity test
  in Means procedure, 776
  in Summarize procedure, 1149
List Cases procedure, 605
local documentation, 580, 582
local linear regression
  in Interactive Charts procedure, 571
log rank test
  in Kaplan-Meier procedure, 600
log transformation
  in Probit Analysis procedure, 927
logarithmic model
  in Curve Estimation procedure, 237
logical expressions, 53, 318, 544
  defined, 53
  in END LOOP, 54
  in LOOP, 54
  in loop structures, 639
  in SELECT IF, 54
  missing values, 57, 58
  order of evaluation, 57
  selecting cases, 1095
  string variables, 50
logical functions, 54, 188
logical operators, 56, 317, 544, 1095
  defined, 56
  in matrix language, 715
  missing values, 57, 320, 546
logical variables
  defined, 54
logistic distribution function, 47
logistic model
  in Curve Estimation procedure, 237
logistic regression, 609
  See also Logistic Regression procedure
Logistic Regression procedure, 609
  casewise listings, 620
  categorical covariates, 613
  classification plots, 620
  classification tables, 618
  contrasts, 613
  correlation matrix, 618
  dependent variable, 612

Hosmer-Lemeshow goodness-of-fit statistic, 618
include constant, 617
interaction terms, 612
iteration history, 618
label casewise listings, 617
method, 615
missing values, 621
saving new variables, 621
subsets of cases, 617

logit
in Probit Analysis procedure, 926

logit link
in Ordinal Regression, 882

Logit Loglinear Analysis procedure, 420, 623
adjusted residuals, 426
categorical variables, 422, 627
cell covariates, 422, 627
cell weights, 424, 628
contrasts, 630
convergence criteria, 425, 632
correlation matrices, 427, 633
covariance matrices, 427
custom models, 429, 634
delta, 426, 632
dependent variables, 423, 627
design matrix, 427, 633
deviance residuals, 426
display options, 426, 632
expected frequency, 426, 633
factors, 422, 627
generalized residuals, 424, 629
interaction terms, 429, 634
limitations, 421, 625
log-odds ratio, 425
maximum iterations, 426, 632
missing values, 428, 634
model specification, 429, 634
normal probability plots, 427, 633
observed frequency, 426, 633
parameter estimates, 427, 633
plots, 427, 633
residual plots, 427, 633
residuals, 426, 633
standardized residuals, 426

logit residuals
in Logistic Regression procedure, 620

loglinear analysis, 420, 623
generalized log-odds ratios, 425
GLOR, 425

See also General Loglinear Analysis procedure;
Logit Loglinear Analysis procedure

LOGLINEAR command
compared to GENLOG, 624

log-minus-log plots
in Cox Regression procedure, 210

lognormal distribution function, 47

log-odds ratio
in General Loglinear Analysis procedure, 425
in Logit Loglinear Analysis procedure, 425

long string variables, 39

loop structures, 637
increment value, 643
indexing variable, 639
initial value, 640
logical expression, 639
macro facility, 283
terminal value, 640

looping structures
terminating, 139

loops
maximum number, 1109

loss function
in Nonlinear Regression procedure, 805

Lotus 1-2-3 files, 1090
read range, 459
read variable names, 458
reading, 453

M matrix, 466
displaying, 499
in GLM Multivariate, 492, 493

macro facility, 268
assigning defaults, 278
conditional processing, 283
display macro commands, 1107
examples, 1301
keyword arguments, 273
loop structures, 283
macro call, 270
macro definition, 269
macro expansion, 1107
positional arguments, 274
string functions, 279

tokens, 275
  with matrix language, 749
Mahalanobis distance
  in Discriminant Analysis procedure, 298
  in Linear Regression procedure, 999
Mallow's *Cp*
  in Linear Regression procedure, 988
Mann-Whitney *U*
  in Two-Independent-Samples Tests procedure, 833
MANOVA
  compared with GLM, 463, 648
MANOVA (command), 675, 688
  analysis groups, 686
  between-subjects factors, 689
  confidence intervals, 685
  contrasts, 678, 692
  covariates, 677
  cross-products matrix, 682
  dependent variable, 677
  discriminant analysis, 684
  display options, 681, 696
  doubly multivariate designs, 688
  error correlation matrix, 682
  error matrices, 681
  error sum of squares, 682
  error variance-covariance matrix, 682
  factors, 677
  homogeneity tests, 682
  limitations, 677, 689
  linear transformations, 677
  naming transformed variables, 680
  power estimates, 685
  principal components analysis, 683
  renaming transformed variables, 695
  significance tests, 681, 682
  simple effects, 694
  transformation matrix, 682
  within-subjects factors, 688, 691, 693
MANOVA. *See* multivariate analysis of variance
Mantel-Haenszel chi-square
  in Crosstabs procedure, 227
Mantel-Haenszel statistic
  in Crosstabs procedure, 228
marginal homogeneity test
  in Two-Related-Samples Tests procedure, 835
master files, 1214
matching coefficients
  in Distances procedure, 940
  in Hierarchical Cluster Analysis procedure, 164

matrices
  correlation, 191, 817, 866
  covariance, 193
  ESSCP, 492
  HSSCP, 492
  K, 480, 1204
  L, 477, 479, 1200, 1203
  M, 492
  RSSCP, 492
  split-file processing, 1138
  sums-of-squares and cross-product, 492
matrix data files
  converting correlation to covariance, 769
  converting covariance to correlation, 769
  raw, 750
  See also raw matrix data files
matrix input
  in Discriminant Analysis procedure, 307
  in Distances procedure, 946
  in Factor Analysis procedure, 374
  in Hierarchical Cluster Analysis procedure, 173
  in Multidimensional Scaling procedure, 115
  in Reliability Analysis procedure, 1012
matrix language, 705
  arithmetic operators, 713
  column vector, 707
  conformable matrices, 712
  constructing a matrix from other matrices, 711
  control structures, 730
  displaying results, 727
  extracting elements, 710
  functions, 719
  logical operators, 715
  main diagonal, 707
  matrix notation, 709
  reading SPSS data files, 716, 738
  reading SPSS matrix data files, 743
  reading text files, 733
  relational operators, 714
  row vector, 707
  saving SPSS data files, 716, 741
  saving SPSS matrix data files, 745
  scalar, 707
  scalar expansion, 713
  string variables, 708
  symmetric matrix, 708
  transpose, 707
  variables, 708
  with case weighting, 717
  with macro facility, 749

with split-file processing, 717
with subsets of cases, 717
with temporary transformations, 717
writing text files, 736

matrix output
    in Discriminant Analysis procedure, 307
    in Distances procedure, 946
    in Factor Analysis procedure, 374
    in Hierarchical Cluster Analysis procedure, 173
    in Reliability Analysis procedure, 1012

matrix system files, 23, 24, 26
    format, 26
    matrix input, 24

matrix weights
    in Multidimensional Scaling procedure, 112

Mauchly's test of sphericity, 498
    in MANOVA, 689

maximum
    in Descriptives procedure, 290
    in Explore procedure, 351
    in Frequencies procedure, 418
    in Report Summaries in Rows procedure, 1052

maximum-likelihood estimation
    in Factor Analysis procedure, 371
    in Reliability Analysis procedure, 1009

maximum-likelihood method
    in Variance Components Analysis, 1229

MCA. *See* multiple classification analysis

McNemar test
    in Crosstabs procedure, 228
    in Two-Related-Samples Tests procedure, 834

mean
    in Descriptives procedure, 289
    in Discriminant Analysis procedure, 304
    in Explore procedure, 351
    in Factor Analysis procedure, 367
    in Frequencies procedure, 418
    in Linear Regression procedure, 992
    in Means procedure, 774
    in OLAP Cube procedure, 848
    in Reliability Analysis procedure, 1009, 1011
    in Report Summaries in Rows procedure, 1052
    in Summarize procedure, 1147

mean substitution
    in Discriminant Analysis procedure, 306
    in Factor Analysis procedure, 365
    in Linear Regression procedure, 996

means model
    syntax, 465

Means procedure, 772
    layers, 774
    missing values, 776
    statistics, 774

measurement level
    specifying, 1237

median
    in Explore procedure, 351
    in Frequencies procedure, 418
    in Report Summaries in Rows procedure, 1053

median method
    in Hierarchical Cluster Analysis procedure, 170

median test
    in Tests for Several Independent Samples
        procedure, 835

merging data files
    files with different cases, 82
    files with different variables, 697
    raw data files, 85, 700
    See also Add Cases procedure; Add Variables
        procedure

M-estimators
    in Explore procedure, 351

minimum
    in Descriptives procedure, 289
    in Explore procedure, 351
    in Frequencies procedure, 418
    in Report Summaries in Rows procedure, 1052

minimum norm quadratic unbiased estimator
    in Variance Components Analysis, 1229

Minkowski measure
    in Distances procedure, 938
    in Hierarchical Cluster Analysis procedure, 163

missing values
    and aggregated data, 99
    and logical operators, 320, 546
    counting occurrences, 198
    defining, 777
    functions, 57, 58
    in control charts, 1136
    in Cox Regression procedure, 207
    in functions, 185
    in Hierarchical Loglinear Analysis procedure, 543
    in Life Tables procedure, 1159
    in logical expressions, 57, 58
    in Logistic Regression procedure, 621

in loglinear analysis procedures, 428, 634
in loop structures, 644
in Multiple Response Crosstabs procedure, 787
in Multiple Response Frequencies procedure, 787
in Nominal Regression procedure, 812
in numeric expressions, 49
in Probit Analysis procedure, 930
in ROC Curve procedure, 1074
MISSING function, 58
NMISS function, 58
replacing, 1069
SYSMIS function, 58
system-missing, 777
time series settings, 1170
user-missing, 777
VALUE function, 58
with logical operators, 57
See also individual procedures

missing-value functions, 187

mixed files, 386, 970

mixed models
syntax, 465
variance components analysis, 1227

mode
in Frequencies procedure, 418
in Report Summaries in Rows procedure, 1053

model information
exporting from Discriminant Analysis, 299

Moses test
in Two-Independent-Samples Tests procedure, 837

moving averages, 217
See also centered moving average function; prior
moving average function

moving range charts, 1125
control limits, 1135
sigma, 1135
span, 1135
subgroup labels, 1127

Multidimensional Scaling procedure, 102
analysis criteria, 110
analysis specification, 116
analysis summary, 111
conditionality, 107
convergence, 110
defining data shape, 105
dimensionality of solution, 111
displaying input data, 111
input files, 107

iterations, 110
level of measurement, 106
limitations, 104
matrix input, 115
missing values, 110
models, 109, 117
output files, 113
plots, 112
specifying input rows, 105
variable list, 105

multinomial distribution
in General Loglinear Analysis procedure, 425

Multiplan files
read range, 459
read variable names, 458
reading, 453
saving, 1090

multiple classification analysis
analysis of variance, 127

multiple comparisons
analysis of variance, 853
in GLM Univariate, 483, 1206

multiple *R*
in Linear Regression procedure, 988

multiple regression, 981
See also Linear Regression procedure

multiple response analysis, 780
defining sets, 780
multiple category, 780
multiple dichotomy, 780
See also Define Multiple Response Sets procedure;
Multiple Response Crosstabs procedure;
Multiple Response Frequencies procedure

Multiple Response Crosstabs procedure, 785
cell percentages, 786
defining value ranges, 783
matching variables across response sets, 786
missing values, 787
percentages based on cases, 787
percentages based on responses, 787
value labels, 788

Multiple Response Frequencies procedure, 784
missing values, 787
table format, 788
value labels, 788

multipunch data, 379

multivariate analysis of variance, 675
See also MANOVA

natural log transformation
   in Autocorrelations procedure, 78, 863
   in Cross-Correlations procedure, 155
   in normal probability plots, 899
   in sequence charts, 146, 1177
natural response rate
   in Probit Analysis procedure, 928
nearest neighbor method
   in Hierarchical Cluster Analysis procedure, 169
negative binomial distribution function, 49
negative log-log link
   in Ordinal Regression, 882
nested conditions, 324
nested design
   in GLM Univariate, 489, 1212
   in Variance Components Analysis, 1232
nested files, 387, 970
nesting
   multiple, 489, 1212
nominal data
   in Multidimensional Scaling procedure, 106
Nominal Regression procedure, 810
   missing values, 812
   output, 814
   variable list, 811
nonlinear constraints, 797
nonlinear regression, 791
   See also Nonlinear Regression procedure
Nonlinear Regression procedure, 791
   bootstrap estimates, 806
   constrained functions, 797
   constraints, 804
   crash tolerance, 802
   critical value for derivative checking, 801
   dependent variable, 798
   derivatives, 796
   feasibility tolerance, 802
   function precision, 803
   infinite step size, 803
   Levenberg-Marquardt method, 803
   linear constraints, 804
   linear feasibility tolerance, 802
   line-search tolerance, 802
   loss function, 805
   major iterations, 802
   maximum iterations, 802, 803
   minor iterations, 802

model expression, 795
model program, 795
nonlinear constraints, 804
nonlinear feasibility tolerance, 802
optimality tolerance, 803
parameter constraints, 804
parameter convergence, 804
parameters, 795
residual and derivative correlation
      convergence, 804
saving new variables, 800
saving parameter estimates, 798
sequential quadratic programming, 802
step limit, 802
sum-of-squares convergence, 803
using parameter estimates from previous
      analysis, 798
normal distribution function, 47
normal probability plots, 892
   detrended, 897
   in Explore procedure, 350
   in Hierarchical Loglinear Analysis procedure, 542
   in Linear Regression procedure, 1000
   in loglinear analysis procedures, 427, 633
   specifying periodicity, 899
   transforming values, 898
   using a previously defined model, 900
np charts, 1127
   conforming values, 1135
   data organization, 1128
   nonconforming values, 1135
   sigma, 1135
   subgroup identifier, 1129
numeric data
   input formats, 241, 256
   output formats, 407, 916, 1260
numeric expressions, 43
   missing values, 49

oblimin rotation
   in Factor Analysis procedure, 372
oblique rotation
   in Factor Analysis procedure, 372
observed count
   in Crosstabs procedure, 226
   in Linear Regression procedure, 993

observed frequency
    in Hierarchical Loglinear Analysis procedure, 542
    in loglinear analysis procedures, 426, 633
    in Probit Analysis procedure, 929
observed power, 475
    in GLM Univariate, 1200
Ochiai measure
    in Distances procedure, 943
    in Hierarchical Cluster Analysis procedure, 168
ODBC, 1090
OLAP Cube procedure
    statistics, 848
one-minus-survival plots
    in Cox Regression procedure, 210
    in Kaplan-Meier procedure, 598
    in Life Tables procedure, 1156
One-Sample Kolmogorov-Smirnov Test
        procedure, 830
    test distribution, 830
One-Sample T Test procedure
    dependent variables, 1185
    limitations, 1184
    missing values, 1186
    test value, 1185
one-sample *t* test. *See t* test
One-Way ANOVA procedure, 850
    contrasts, 852
    defining factor ranges, 852
    factor variables, 852
    limitations, 851
    matrix input, 857
    matrix output, 857
    missing values, 856, 858
    multiple comparisons, 853
    orthogonal polynomials, 852
    statistics, 856
online documentation, 580
opening files
    data files, 431
optimality tolerance
    in Probit Analysis procedure, 927
options, 1100
    displaying, 1113
    See also preferences
order of commands, 16
order of operations
    numeric expressions, 43

ordering categories
    interactive charts, 555
ordinal data
    in Multidimensional Scaling procedure, 106
Ordinal Regression
    saving statistics, 885
    scale model, 885
orthogonal contrasts, 482, 1206
orthogonal polynomials
    analysis of variance, 852
orthogonal rotation
    in Factor Analysis procedure, 372
outliers
    identifying, 348
    in Linear Regression procedure, 1000, 1001
output files
    borders for tables, 1110
    chart characters, 1110
    destination of, 1106
    display command syntax, 1106
    display output page titles, 1111
    page size, 1111
output formats, 243, 916, 1260
    custom currency, 407, 916, 1260
    displaying, 917, 1261
    format specification, 916, 1260
    print (display), 407
    string data, 407
    write, 407, 1260
overlay plots, 878

p charts, 1127
    conforming values, 1135
    data organization, 1128
    nonconforming values, 1135
    sigma, 1135
    subgroup identifier, 1129
padding strings, 53, 55
page ejection, 913
    missing values, 914
    variable list, 914
page size, 1111
Paired-Samples T Test procedure, 1183
    missing values, 1186
    variable list, 1186

paired-samples *t* test. *See t* test

parallel model
  in Reliability Analysis procedure, 1009

parallelism test
  in Probit Analysis procedure, 930

parameter estimates
  in Cox Regression procedure, 208
  in GLM Univariate, 476, 1200
  in Hierarchical Loglinear Analysis procedure, 542
  in loglinear analysis procedures, 427, 633

Pareto charts, 530
  simple, 530
  stacked, 530

Pareto distribution function, 48

part correlation
  in Linear Regression procedure, 988

partial associations
  in Hierarchical Loglinear Analysis procedure, 542

partial autocorrelation, 860
  See also Autocorrelations procedure

partial correlation, 866
  in Linear Regression procedure, 988
  See also Bivariate Correlations procedure

partial eta-squared, 476, 1200

pattern difference measure
  in Distances procedure, 944
  in Hierarchical Cluster Analysis procedure, 168

pattern matrix
  in Discriminant Analysis procedure, 305

Pearson chi-square
  in Crosstabs procedure, 227

Pearson correlation coefficient
  in Bivariate Correlations procedure, 191
  in Crosstabs procedure, 227
  in Distances procedure, 937
  in Factor Analysis procedure, 367
  in Hierarchical Cluster Analysis procedure, 162
  in Reliability Analysis procedure, 1009, 1011

Pearson's *r*. *See* Pearson correlation coefficient

percentages
  in Crosstabs procedure, 226
  in Report Summaries in Rows procedure, 1053

percentiles
  break points, 348
  estimating from grouped data, 416
  in Explore procedure, 348
  in Frequencies procedure, 417

  in Kaplan-Meier procedure, 599
  methods, 348

periodic lags
  in Autocorrelations procedure, 863

periodicity
  in Autocorrelations procedure, 78, 863
  in Cross-Correlations procedure, 155
  in normal probability plots, 899
  in sequence charts, 145, 1177
  time series settings, 1171

phi
  in Crosstabs procedure, 227

phi 4-point correlation
  in Distances procedure, 944
  in Hierarchical Cluster Analysis procedure, 168

phi-square measure
  in Distances procedure, 939
  in Hierarchical Cluster Analysis procedure, 163

pie charts, 521
  in Interactive Charts procedure, 564

Pillai's trace
  in MANOVA, 685

Poisson distribution function, 49
  in General Loglinear Analysis procedure, 425

polynomial contrasts, 481, 1205
  in Cox Regression procedure, 205
  in loglinear analysis procedures, 630
  in MANOVA, 679
  repeated measures, 500

portable files. *See* SPSS portable files

post hoc tests
  alpha value, 483, 1206
  Bonferroni test, 484, 485, 854, 1207, 1209
  Duncan's multiple comparison procedure, 484, 485, 854, 1207, 1208
  Dunnett's *C*, 484, 486, 855, 1207, 1209
  Dunnett's one-tailed *t* test, 484, 1207
  Gabriel's pairwise comparisons test, 484, 485, 855, 1207, 1209
  Games and Howell's pairwise comparisons test, 484, 486, 855, 1207, 1209
  Hochberg's GT2, 484, 485, 855, 1207, 1209
  in GLM Univariate, 483, 1206
  in One-Way ANOVA, 853
  least significant difference, 484, 485, 854, 1207, 1209
  Ryan-Einot-Gabriel-Welsch multiple stepdown procedure, 484, 485, 486, 855, 1207, 1209

Scheffé test, 484, 485, 854, 1207, 1208
Sidak test, 484, 485, 855, 1207, 1209
statistical purpose, 484, 1207
Student-Newman-Keuls test, 484, 485, 854, 1207, 1208
Tamhane's T2, 484, 486, 855, 1207, 1209
Tamhane's T3, 484, 486, 855, 1207, 1209
Tukey's *b*, 484, 485, 854, 1207, 1208
Tukey's honestly significant difference, 484, 485, 854, 1207, 1208
Waller-Duncan test, 484, 486, 855, 1207, 1209
posterior probability
    in Discriminant Analysis procedure, 303
post hoc tests. *See* multiple comparisons
power, 475, 1199
    observed, 475
power estimates
    in MANOVA, 685
power model
    in Curve Estimation procedure, 236, 237
power range
    in Weight Estimation procedure, 1252
P-P normal probability plots, 897
predictability measures
    in Distances procedure, 942
    in Hierarchical Cluster Analysis procedure, 167
predicted group
    in Logistic Regression procedure, 620
predicted probabilities
    in Logistic Regression procedure, 620
predicted values
    adjusted, 999
    saving in 2-Stage Least-Squares procedure, 1191
    saving in Curve Estimation procedure, 239
    standard errors, 999
    standardized, 999
    unstandardized, 998
prediction intervals
    in Interactive Charts procedure, 571
    saving in Curve Estimation procedure, 239
preferences, 1100
    blank data fields, 1108
    borders for tables, 1110
    charts, 1110
    custom currency formats, 1111
    data compression, 1109
    default file extension, 1109
    default variable format, 1103

display errors, 1106
display macro commands, 1107
display resource messages, 1106
display statistical results, 1106
display warnings, 1106
displaying, 1113
errors, 1108
invalid data, 1108
journal file, 1107
macro expansion, 1107
maximum loops, 1109
output, 1106, 1111
output page size, 1111
preserving, 906, 1068
random number seed, 1105
restoring, 906, 1068
time series, 1169
warnings, 1108
principal components
    in Factor Analysis procedure, 371
principal components analysis
    in MANOVA, 683
principal directions
    in Multidimensional Scaling procedure, 111
principal-axis factoring
    in Factor Analysis procedure, 371
print formats. *See* output formats
printing cases, 907, 919
    column headings, 913
    displaying blank lines, 919
    formats, 907, 909, 1257
    missing values, 908
    number of records, 911
    output file, 907, 911, 919
    page ejection, 913
    strings, 907, 910
    summary table, 907, 912
prior moving average function, 218
prior probability
    in Discriminant Analysis procedure, 301
probability of *F*-to-enter
    in Discriminant Analysis procedure, 299
    in Linear Regression procedure, 990
probability of *F*-to-remove
    in Discriminant Analysis procedure, 299
    in Linear Regression procedure, 990
probit analysis, 922
    See also Probit Analysis procedure

Probit Analysis procedure, 922
  confidence intervals, 929
  covariates, 925
  expected frequency, 929
  factors, 925
  grouping variable, 925
  log transformation, 927
  maximum iterations, 928
  missing values, 930
  model specification, 926
  natural response rate, 928
  observation frequency variable, 925
  observed frequency, 929
  predictor variables, 925
  residuals, 929
  response frequency variable, 925
  step limit, 928
probit link
  in Ordinal Regression, 882
procedure output
  output file, 931
  writing to a file, 931
procedures
  update documentation, 582
process capability indices
  in Control Charts, 1132
profile plots, 477, 1201
program states, 1269
promax rotation
  in Factor Analysis procedure, 372
proportional sample, 1077
proximity measures, 933
  See also Distances procedure

Q. See Cochran's *Q*
Q-Q normal probability plots, 896
quadratic model
  in Curve Estimation procedure, 236, 237
quartiles
  in Kaplan-Meier procedure, 599
quartimax rotation
  in Factor Analysis procedure, 372

r
  in Means procedure, 776

  in Summarize procedure, 1149
  See also Pearson correlation coefficient
R charts, 1122
  control limits, 1135
  data organization, 1124
  minimum sample size, 1135
  sigma, 1135
  subgroup identifier, 1125
R^2
  in Linear Regression procedure, 988
random effects, 472, 1196, 1228
  variance components analysis, 1227
random effects model
  syntax, 465
random number seed
  specifying, 1105
random sample
  in nonparametric tests, 841
random-number functions, 189
range
  in Descriptives procedure, 289
  in Explore procedure, 351
  in Frequencies procedure, 418
range bar charts, 510
ranking data, 958
  method, 960
  missing values, 963
  new variable names, 961
  order, 959
  proportion estimates, 962
  tied values, 896, 962
  within subgroups, 959
Rankit method
  in normal probability plots, 896
rank-order correlation coefficients
  in Bivariate Correlations procedure, 817
Rao's *V*
  in Discriminant Analysis procedure, 299, 300
ratio data
  in Multidimensional Scaling procedure, 106
raw data files
  blanks, 244
  data types, 241
  fixed format, 243, 244, 245, 252
  freefield format, 243, 244, 245, 254
  reading, 241
  variable definition, 251, 970

raw matrix data files, 750
  factors, 762, 765
  format, 750, 753
  N, 767
  record types, 764
  split files, 760
  within-cells records, 763, 765
raw text data files, 438
receiver operating characteristic curve. *See* ROC
    Curve procedure
recoding values, 964
  converting strings to numeric, 132, 968
  limitations, 966
  missing values, 965
  numeric variables, 965
  string variables, 966
  target variable, 967
records
  defining, 247, 970
  duplicate, 977
  missing, 976
  skipping, 974
  types, 970
rectangular matrix
  in Multidimensional Scaling procedure, 106
reference lines
  in sequence charts, 147, 1179, 1181
regression
  syntax, 464
regression coefficients
  in Linear Regression procedure, 988
regression factor scores
  in Factor Analysis procedure, 373
regression lines
  in Interactive Charts procedure, 570
regression plots, 878
relational operators, 55, 317, 544, 1095
  defined, 55
  in matrix language, 714
relative median potency
  in Probit Analysis procedure, 930
relative risk ratio
  in Crosstabs procedure, 228
reliability analysis, 1006
  See also Reliability Analysis procedure
Reliability Analysis procedure, 1006
  computational method, 1011

limitations, 1007
listing item labels, 1011
matrix input, 1012
matrix output, 1012
missing values, 1011, 1013
models, 1009
scale definition, 1008
statistics, 1009
variable list, 1008
repeated contrasts, 482, 1206
  in Cox Regression procedure, 205
  in loglinear analysis procedures, 630
  in MANOVA, 679
  repeated measures, 500
repeated measures analysis
  in Reliability Analysis procedure, 1010
repeated measures analysis of variance, 496
  limitations, 497
repeated measures models
  syntax, 465
repeating data, 1018
  case identification, 1030
  defining variables, 1026
  input file, 1026
  repeating groups, 1025
  starting column, 1024
  summary table, 1031
repeating data groups, 970
repeating fields. *See* repeating data
replacing missing values, 1069
  linear interpolation, 1070
  linear trend, 1072
  mean of nearby points, 1071
  median of nearby points, 1071
  series mean, 1072
Report Summaries in Rows procedure, 1032
  column contents, 1044, 1048
  column headings, 1033, 1045, 1048
  column spacing, 1034
  column width, 1034, 1045, 1049
  defining subgroups, 1047
  footnotes, 1058
  format, 1038
  limitations, 1037
  missing values, 1036, 1059
  output file, 1036, 1041
  page layout, 1041
  print formats, 1056

report types, 1036
string variables, 1046
summary statistics, 1036, 1051
summary titles, 1055
titles, 1058
variable list, 1044
reports, 1032
See also Report Summaries in Rows procedure
reproduced correlation matrix
in Factor Analysis procedure, 368
rereading records, 1061
input file, 1064
starting column, 1066
residual correlation matrix
in GLM Multivariate, 493
residual covariance matrix
in GLM Multivariate, 493
residual plots
in GLM Univariate, 477, 1201
in Hierarchical Loglinear Analysis procedure, 542
in loglinear analysis procedures, 427, 633
residual SSCP
in GLM Multivariate, 492
residuals
degrees of freedom, 402
deleted, 999
descriptive statistics, 400
goodness of fit, 400
in Crosstabs procedure, 226
in Hierarchical Loglinear Analysis procedure, 542
in Logistic Regression procedure, 620
in loglinear analysis procedures, 426, 633
in Probit Analysis procedure, 929
saving in 2-Stage Least-Squares procedure, 1191
saving in Curve Estimation procedure, 239
saving in Linear Regression procedure, 1004
standardized, 999
Studentized, 999
Studentized deleted, 999
unstandardized, 998
response frequency variable
in Probit Analysis procedure, 925
restricted maximum-likelihood method
in Variance Components Analysis, 1229
reverse Helmert contrasts, 482, 1205
ribbon charts
in Interactive Charts procedure, 567

ROC Curve procedure, 1073
charts, 1076
limitations, 1074
missing values, 1074
output, 1075
Rogers and Tanimoto measure
in Distances procedure, 941
in Hierarchical Cluster Analysis procedure, 166
row percentages
in Crosstabs procedure, 226
Roy's largest root
in MANOVA, 685
Roy-Bargmann stepdown *F*
in MANOVA, 682
RSSCP matrices
in GLM Multivariate, 492
running commands
batch mode, 14
interactive mode, 13
running median function, 218
runs test
in Runs Test procedure, 838
Runs Test procedure, 838
cutting point, 838
Russell and Rao measure
in Distances procedure, 941
in Hierarchical Cluster Analysis procedure, 165
Ryan-Einot-Gabriel-Welsch multiple stepdown
procedure, 484, 485, 486, 855, 1207, 1209

s charts, 1122
control limits, 1135
data organization, 1124
minimum sample size, 1135
sigma, 1135
subgroup identifier, 1125
sample
exact-size, 1077
proportional, 1077
sampling cases, 1077
See also subsets of cases
SAS files
conversion to SPSS, 447
reading, 445

saturated models
  in Hierarchical Loglinear Analysis procedure, 543
saving files
  aggregated data files, 95
  data compression, 1084, 1267
  data files, 1079, 1263
  dBASE format, 1085
  dropping variables, 1082, 1265
  Excel format, 1085
  keeping variables, 1082, 1265
  Lotus 1-2-3, 1085
  renaming variables, 1083, 1266
  spreadsheet format, 1085
  SPSS portable files, 355
  SYLK format, 1085
  tab-delimited data files, 1085
  variable map, 1267
scale model
  in Ordinal Regression, 885
scale statistics
  in Reliability Analysis procedure, 1009
scatterplots, 526, 875
  all-groups, 306
  control variables, 877
  horizontal axis, 877, 878
  in Interactive Charts procedure, 561
  limitations, 876
  missing values, 879
  overlay plots, 878
  plot scaling, 878
  plot types, 875
  regression plots, 878
  separate-groups, 307
  titles, 879
  vertical axis, 877, 878
Scheffé test, 484, 485, 854, 1207, 1208
Schwarz Bayesian criterion
  in Linear Regression procedure, 988
scratch variables
  defined, 31
scree plots
  in Factor Analysis procedure, 369
seasonal difference function, 219
seasonal difference transformation
  in Autocorrelations procedure, 78, 862
  in Cross-Correlations procedure, 154
  in normal probability plots, 899
  in sequence charts, 145

seed. See random-number seed
selecting cases, 1221
semipartial correlation. See part correlation
sequence charts, 141, 1173
  area charts, 147, 1179
  connecting cases between variables, 148, 1180
  line charts, 147, 1179
  multiple variables, 148, 1180
  plotting highest and lowest values, 148, 1180
  scale axis reference line, 147, 1179
  specifying periodicity, 145, 1177
  split-file scaling, 150, 1181
  time axis reference lines, 149, 1181
  transforming values, 145, 1176
  using previously defined specifications, 150, 1182
sequential quadratic programming
  in Nonlinear Regression procedure, 802
settings, 1100
  displaying, 1113
  See also preferences
Shapiro-Wilk's test
  in Explore procedure, 350
short string variables, 39
Sidak test, 484, 485, 855, 1207, 1209
sign test
  in Two-Related-Samples Tests procedure, 838
significance level
  in Linear Regression procedure, 993
significance levels
  in Factor Analysis procedure, 367
similarity measures, 933
  See also Distances procedure
simple contrasts, 482, 1206
  in Cox Regression procedure, 205
  in loglinear analysis procedures, 630
  in MANOVA, 679
  repeated measures, 500
simple effects
  in MANOVA, 694
Simple Factorial ANOVA procedure
  covariates, 121, 122
  defining factor ranges, 121
  factor variables, 121
  interaction effects, 122
  limitations, 120
  methods, 122
  missing values, 127

multiple classification analysis, 127
  statistics, 126
  sums of squares, 122, 125
simple matching measure
  in Distances procedure, 941
  in Hierarchical Cluster Analysis procedure, 165
size difference measure
  in Distances procedure, 944
  in Hierarchical Cluster Analysis procedure, 168
skewness
  in Descriptives procedure, 289
  in Explore procedure, 351
  in Frequencies procedure, 418
  in Report Summaries in Rows procedure, 1052
smallest *F*-ratio criterion
  in Discriminant Analysis procedure, 298
smoothers
  in Interactive Charts procedure, 570
smoothing function, 220
Sokal and Sneath measures
  in Distances procedure, 941
  in Hierarchical Cluster Analysis procedure, 166
Somers' *d*
  in Crosstabs procedure, 227
sorting cases, 1117
  sort keys, 1117
  sort order, 1117
sorting categories
  interactive charts, 555
Spearman correlation coefficient
  in Bivariate Correlations procedure, 819
  in Crosstabs procedure, 227
special contrasts, 482, 1206
  repeated measures, 500
spikes
  in interactive charts, 560
split-file processing, 1137
  break variables, 1137
  matrices, 1138
  scratch variables, 1137
  system variables, 1137
  temporary, 1164
  with matrix system files, 25
split-half model
  in Reliability Analysis procedure, 1009
spread-versus-level plots
  in Explore procedure, 350

in GLM Univariate, 477, 1201
spreadsheet files
  read ranges, 459
  read variable names, 458
  reading, 453
  saving, 1085
SPSS data files
  documents, 315, 331
  reading, 431
SPSS portable files, 21
  reading, 574
  saving, 355
SPSS/PC+ files
  reading, 574
  saving, 1090
SQL queries, 435
square root function, 44
squared Euclidean distance
  in Distances procedure, 937
  in Hierarchical Cluster Analysis procedure, 162
S-stress
  in Multidimensional Scaling procedure, 110
standard deviation
  in Descriptives procedure, 289
  in Discriminant Analysis procedure, 304
  in Explore procedure, 351
  in Factor Analysis procedure, 367
  in Frequencies procedure, 418
  in Linear Regression procedure, 992
  in Means procedure, 774
  in OLAP Cube procedure, 848
  in Reliability Analysis procedure, 1009
  in Report Summaries in Rows procedure, 1052
  in Summarize procedure, 1147
standard deviation function, 45
standard error
  in Explore procedure, 351
  in Linear Regression procedure, 988
  in ROC Curve procedure, 1075
standard error of the mean
  in Descriptives procedure, 289
  in Frequencies procedure, 418
standard errors
  in GLM Univariate, 488, 1211
standardization
  in Distances procedure, 935

standardized residuals
    in GLM Univariate, 488, 1211
    in Hierarchical Loglinear Analysis procedure, 542
    in loglinear analysis procedures, 426
standardized values
    in normal probability plots, 898
stand-in variable, 326
statistical functions, 187
stem-and-leaf plots
    in Explore procedure, 350
stepwise selection
    in Discriminant Analysis procedure, 297
    in Linear Regression procedure, 986
stimulus configuration coordinates
    in Multidimensional Scaling procedure, 108, 112, 113
stimulus weights
    in Multidimensional Scaling procedure, 108, 113
stratification variable
    in Kaplan-Meier procedure, 598
strictly parallel model
    in Reliability Analysis procedure, 1009
string data
    computing values, 184, 186, 190
    conditional transformations, 318, 319, 545, 546
    converting to numeric, 132
    input formats, 241, 258
    missing values, 777
    output formats, 407, 916, 1260
    value labels, 90, 1224
string expressions
    defined, 50
string functions, 51, 190
    macro facility, 279
string variables
    in logical expressions, 50
    in matrix language, 708
structure matrix
    in Discriminant Analysis procedure, 304, 305
Studentized residuals
    in GLM Univariate, 488, 1211
    in Logistic Regression procedure, 620
Student-Newman-Keuls test, 484, 485, 854, 1207, 1208
subcommand
    syntax, 14

subgroups
    splitting data files into, 1137
subject weights
    in Multidimensional Scaling procedure, 108, 110, 112, 113
subsets of cases
    based on dates and times, 1221
    conditional expressions, 1095
    exact-size sample, 1077
    filter status, 396
    filtering unselected cases, 396
    if condition is satisfied, 1095
    proportional sample, 1077
    selecting, 1095, 1221
    temporary sample, 1077
substrings, 53
subtitles, 1142
    apostrophes in, 1142
    length, 1142
    quotation marks in, 1142
    suppressing, 1142
    with inline data, 1142
sum
    in Descriptives procedure, 290
    in Frequencies procedure, 418
    in Report Summaries in Rows procedure, 1052
sum of squares
    Type I, 473, 1197, 1229
    Type II, 474, 1197
    Type III, 474, 1198, 1229
    Type IV, 474, 1198
Summarize procedure
    statistics, 1147
sums-of-squares and cross-product matrices
    in GLM Multivariate, 492
    See also SSCP matrices
sums-of-squares and cross-products of residuals
    in GLM Multivariate, 492
survival analysis, 594, 1150
    See also Kaplan-Meier procedure; Life Tables procedure
survival plots
    in Cox Regression procedure, 210
    in Kaplan-Meier procedure, 598
    in Life Tables procedure, 1155
survival tables
    in Kaplan-Meier procedure, 599
    writing to a file, 931

sweep matrix
  in Linear Regression procedure, 988
SYLK files
  read ranges, 459
  read variable names, 458
  reading, 453
  saving, 1090
symmetric matrix
  in Multidimensional Scaling procedure, 105
syntax, 11
syntax charts, 11
system variables, 30
system-missing value, 777

t distribution function, 48
t test
  in Independent-Samples T Test procedure, 1183
  in MANOVA, 696
  in One-Sample T Test procedure, 1183
  in Paired-Samples T Test procedure, 1183
T4253H smoothing, 220
tab-delimited files
  reading, 453
  saving, 1088, 1090
table lookup files, 701
table specifications
  in GLM Univariate, 486, 1210
Tamhane's T2, 484, 486, 855, 1207, 1209
Tamhane's T3, 484, 486, 855, 1207, 1209
target variables
  computing values, 184
  counting values, 197, 198
  formats, 185
  in COMPUTE command, 50
Taron's statistic
  in Crosstabs procedure, 228
Tarone-Ware test
  in Kaplan-Meier procedure, 600
tau. *See* Goodman and Kruskal's tau
tau-*b*. *See* Kendall's tau-*b*
tau-*c*. *See* Kendall's tau-*c*
templates
  in charts, 532
temporary transformations, 1164

temporary variables, 1164
  See also scratch variables, 1164
territorial map
  in Discriminant Analysis procedure, 306
Tests for Several Independent Samples procedure,
    832, 835
  grouping variables, 829, 832, 835
Tests for Several Related Samples procedure,
    828, 832
text data files, 438
time functions, 60
time intervals, 60
time series analysis
  autocorrelation, 75
  cross-correlation, 152
  data transformations, 212, 259, 1069
  date variables, 259
  partial autocorrelation, 860
  preferences, 1169
  sequence charts, 141, 1173
time series functions, 214
time series variables
  creating, 212
time-dependent covariates
  in Time-Dependent Cox Regression
    procedure, 202
Time-Dependent Cox Regression procedure, 199
  baseline functions, 208
  categorical covariates, 204
  confidence intervals, 208
  contrasts, 204
  correlation matrix, 208
  covariates, 202
  display options, 208
  entry probability, 209
  interaction terms, 203
  iteration criteria, 208
  limitations, 201
  maximum iterations, 209
  method, 206
  missing values, 207
  parameter estimates, 208
  plots, 209, 210
  removal probability, 209
  saving coefficients, 210
  saving new variables, 210
  saving survival table, 210
  split-file processing, 211

stratification variable, 203
survival status variable, 203
survival time variable, 202
time-dependent covariates, 202
titles, 1167
apostrophes in, 1167
displaying, 1111
length, 1167
quotation marks in, 1167
with inline data, 1167
See also subtitles
tolerance
in Discriminant Analysis procedure, 299
in Linear Regression procedure, 988, 989, 990
tolerance level, 475, 1199
total percentage
in Crosstabs procedure, 226
transaction files, 1214
transformation coefficients matrix, 466, 492
transformation matrix, 499
displaying, 496
in MANOVA, 682
transformations
temporary, 1164
translating data files. *See* data files
transposing cases and variables, 403, 406
trimmed mean
in Explore procedure, 351
Tukey's *b*, 484, 485, 854, 1207, 1208
Tukey's honestly significant difference, 484, 485, 854, 1207, 1208
Tukey's test of additivity
in Reliability Analysis procedure, 1009
Tukey's transformation, 962
in normal probability plots, 896
Two-Independent-Samples Tests procedure, 831, 833, 837, 839
grouping variables, 831, 833, 837, 839
outlier trimming, 837
Two-Related-Samples Tests procedure, 834, 835, 838, 840
2-Stage Least-Squares procedure, 1188
covariance matrix, 1191
endogenous variables, 1190
including constant, 1191
instrumental variables, 1190
saving predicted values, 1191
saving residuals, 1191

using a previous model, 1191
Type I sum-of-squares method
in Variance Components Analysis, 1229
Type III sum-of-squares method
in Variance Components Analysis, 1229

u charts, 1129
data organization, 1130
sigma, 1135
subgroup identifier, 1131
U. See Mann-Whitney *U*
uncentered leverage values
in GLM Univariate, 1211
uncertainty coefficient
in Crosstabs procedure, 227
unexplained variance criterion
in Discriminant Analysis procedure, 298
UNIANOVA, 1193
Levene's test, 1200
univariate syntax, 1193
unstandardized residuals, 1211
uniform distribution function, 48
unstandardized predicted values
in GLM Univariate, 488, 1211
unstandardized residuals
in GLM Univariate, 488, 1211
update documentation, 580
updating data files, 1214
dropping variables, 1219
flag variables, 1219
input files, 1217
keeping variables, 1219
key variables, 1214
limitations, 1216
master files, 1214
raw data files, 1217
renaming variables, 1218
transaction files, 1214
variable map, 1220
user-missing values, 777

V. See Cramér's *V*
value
syntax, 15

value labels, 89, 1224
   adding, 1224
   apostrophes in, 1224
   concatenating strings, 1224, 1225
   length, 1224
   revising, 89
   string data, 90, 1224
Van der Waerden's transformation, 962
   in normal probability plots, 896
variable labels, 1235
   apostrophes in, 1235
   concatenating strings, 1235, 1236
variables
   controlling default format, 1103
   defining, 251, 844, 970, 1140
   in matrix language, 708
   naming rules, 252
   scratch, 31
   temporary, 1164
variance
   in Descriptives procedure, 289
   in Explore procedure, 351
   in Frequencies procedure, 418
   in Linear Regression procedure, 988, 992
   in Means procedure, 775
   in OLAP Cube procedure, 848
   in Reliability Analysis procedure, 1009, 1011
   in Report Summaries in Rows procedure, 1052
   in Summarize procedure, 1147
Variance Components Analysis
   interactions, 1232
   maximum-likelihood method, 1229
   miminum norm quadratic unbiased estimator, 1229
   nested design, 1232
   restricted maximum-likelihood method, 1229
   sum-of-squares method, 1229
Variance Components Analysis procedure, 1227
variance inflation factor
   in Linear Regression procedure, 988
varimax rotation
   in Factor Analysis procedure, 372
vectors, 1239
   index, 1239, 1243
   variable list, 1239
V-to-enter
   in Discriminant Analysis procedure, 300

W. See Kendall's W
Wald statistic
   in Cox Regression procedure, 207
   in Logistic Regression procedure, 616
Wald-Wolfowitz test
   in Two-Independent-Samples Tests procedure, 839
Waller-Duncan t test, 484, 486, 855, 1207, 1209
Ward's method
   in Hierarchical Cluster Analysis procedure, 170
warnings
   displaying, 1106
   maximum number, 1108
Weibull distribution function, 48
Weight Estimation procedure, 1249
   including constant, 1253
   power range, 1252
   saving weight variables, 1253
   using previous model, 1253
weight variables
   saving in Weight Estimation procedure, 1253
weighted least-squares
   in Linear Regression procedure, 991
weighted multidimensional scaling
   in Multidimensional Scaling procedure, 109
weighted unstandardized predicted values
   in GLM Univariate, 488, 1211
weighted unstandardized residuals
   in GLM Univariate, 488, 1211
weighting cases, 1247
   in NOMREG procedure, 811
weights
   in Weight Estimation procedure, 1252
Wilcoxon test
   in Two-Related-Samples Tests procedure, 840
Wilks' lambda
   in MANOVA, 686
within-subjects factors, 496
   in MANOVA, 691, 693
within-subjects model, 501
write formats, 1260
writing cases, 1255

X-bar charts, 1122
   control limits, 1135

data organization, 1124
minimum sample size, 1135
sigma, 1135
subgroup identifier, 1125

Yates' correction for continuity
  in Crosstabs procedure, 227
Yule's Q
  in Distances procedure, 943
  in Hierarchical Cluster Analysis procedure, 168
Yule's Y
  in Distances procedure, 943
  in Hierarchical Cluster Analysis procedure, 167

z scores
  in Descriptives procedure, 288
  in Distances procedure, 935
  saving as variables, 288

Syntax Index

A (keyword)
  DESCRIPTIVES command, 290
  SORT CASES command, 1117
ABS (function)
  MATRIX command, 719
ABSOLUTE (keyword)
  PROXIMITIES command, 936
ACF (command), 75, 82
  APPLY subcommand, 80
  DIFF subcommand, 77
  LN/NOLOG subcommands, 78
  MXAUTO subcommand, 79
  PACF subcommand, 80
  PERIOD subcommand, 78
  SDIFF subcommand, 78
  SEASONAL subcommand, 79
  SERROR subcommand, 80
  VARIABLES subcommand, 77
ACPROB (keyword)
  PLUM command, 885
ADD (function)
  REPORT command, 1054
ADD FILES (command)
  BY subcommand, 86
  DROP subcommand, 86
  FILE subcommand, 85
  FIRST subcommand, 88
  IN subcommand, 87
  KEEP subcommand, 86
  key variables, 86
  LAST subcommand, 88
  limitations, 84
  MAP subcommand, 88
  RENAME subcommand, 85
  with DATA LIST command, 85
  with SORT CASES command, 84, 1118
  working data file, 85
ADD VALUE LABELS (command), 89
  compared with VALUE LABELS command, 1224
  limitations, 90
  string variables, 90
ADJPRED (keyword)
  REGRESSION command, 999
AEMPIRICAL (keyword)
  EXAMINE command, 349

AFREQ (keyword)
  FREQUENCIES command, 413
AFTER (keyword)
  ANOVA command, 122
AGGREGATE (command), 92
  BREAK subcommand, 95
  DOCUMENT subcommand, 96
  functions, 97
  MISSING subcommand, 99
  OUTFILE subcommand, 95
  PRESORTED subcommand, 96
  variable definitions, 96
  with MATCH FILES command, 94
  with SORT CASES command, 1118
  with SPLIT FILE command, 94, 1138
AIC (keyword)
  FACTOR command, 368
AINDS (keyword)
  ALSCAL command, 109
ALIGN (keyword)
  REPORT command, 1039
ALL (function)
  MATRIX command, 719
ALL (keyword)
  ALSCAL command, 112
  ANOVA command, 122, 126
  CORRELATIONS command, 193
  CROSSTABS command, 226, 228, 231
  DESCRIPTIVES command, 290
  DISCRIMINANT command, 305, 307
  EXAMINE command, 350, 351, 352
  FREQUENCIES command, 418
  IGRAPH command, 557
  in variable lists, 30
  INFO command, 582
  LOGISTIC REGRESSION command, 618
  MEANS command, 775, 776
  MULT RESPONSE command, 787
  NPAR TESTS command, 825, 841
  PARTIAL CORR command, 869
  PLOT command, 877
  PRINT command, 908
  RELIABILITY command, 1010
  SUMMARIZE command, 1148
  USE command, 1221

WRITE command, 1256

ALPHA (keyword)
FACTOR command, 371
GLM command, 475
MANOVA command, 685
RELIABILITY command, 1009
UNIANOVA command, 1199

ALPHA (subcommand)
REFORMAT command, 979

ALSCAL (command), 102
analysis specification, 116
CONDITION subcommand, 107
CRITERIA subcommand, 110
FILE subcommand, 107
INPUT subcommand, 105
LEVEL subcommand, 106
limitations, 104
matrix input, 105, 115
matrix output, 113, 115
MATRIX subcommand, 115
METHOD subcommand, 109
missing values, 104
MODEL subcommand, 109
model types, 109
OUTFILE subcommand, 113
PLOT subcommand, 112
PRINT subcommand, 111
SHAPE subcommand, 105
VARIABLES subcommand, 105

ANALYSIS (keyword)
NPAR TESTS command, 841
ONEWAY command, 856
PARTIAL CORR command, 870
T-TEST command, 1187

ANALYSIS (subcommand)
DISCRIMINANT command, 296
FACTOR command, 366
MANOVA command, 657, 677

ANDREW (keyword)
EXAMINE command, 352

ANOVA (command), 119
cell means, 126
covariates, 126
COVARIATES subcommand, 122
interaction effects, 122
limitations, 120
MAXORDERS subcommand, 122
METHOD subcommand, 122
MISSING subcommand, 127
multiple classification analysis, 127

sums of squares, 122
VARIABLES subcommand, 121
with AUTORECODE command, 134

ANOVA (keyword)
CURVEFIT command, 239
MEANS command, 775
QUICK CLUSTER command, 955
REGRESSION command, 988
RELIABILITY command, 1010
SUMMARIZE command, 1149

ANY (function)
MATRIX command, 719

APPEND (subcommand)
MCONVERT command, 771
SAVE TRANSLATE command, 1089

APPLY (subcommand)
2SLS command, 1191
ACF command, 80
CCF command, 157
CURVEFIT command, 240
FIT keyword, 240
PACF command, 864
PPLOT command, 900
SPECIFICATIONS keyword, 240
TSPLOT command, 1182
WLS command, 1253

APPLY DICTIONARY (command), 128
formats, 130
FROM subcommand, 131
missing values, 129
value labels, 129
variable labels, 129
weight, 130

APPROXIMATE (keyword)
MANOVA command, 664, 685
SURVIVAL command, 1158

AR (keyword)
FACTOR command, 373

AREA (keyword)
GRAPH command, 515

AREALABEL (keyword)
IGRAPH command, 562

ARRANGEMENT (subcommand)
GET DATA command, 441

ARSIN (function)
MATRIX command, 719

ARTAN (function)
MATRIX command, 719

ASCAL (keyword)
ALSCAL command, 109

ASRESID (keyword)
CROSSTABS command, 226

ASSOCIATION (keyword)
HILOGLINEAR command, 542

asterisk (filename)
in ADD FILES command, 85
in MATCH FILES command, 700

ASYMMETRIC (keyword)
ALSCAL command, 106

AUTOMATIC (keyword)
REPORT command, 1039

AUTORECODE (command), 132
compared to RECODE, 132
compared to RECODE command, 964
DESCENDING subcommand, 136
INTO subcommand, 135
missing values, 133
PRINT subcommand, 136
VARIABLES subcommand, 135
with ANOVA command, 134
with MANOVA command, 135
with TABLES command, 134

AVALUE (keyword)
CROSSTABS command, 230
FREQUENCIES command, 413

AVERAGE (function)
REPORT command, 1054

AVERF (keyword)
MANOVA command, 696

AVONLY (keyword)
MANOVA command, 696

AZOUT (keyword)
SPCHART command, 1133

BACKWARD (keyword)
HILOGLINEAR command, 538
REGRESSION command, 986

BADCORR (keyword)
PARTIAL CORR command, 869
REGRESSION command, 993

BANDWIDTH (keyword)
IGRAPH command, 571

BAR (subcommand)
GRAPH command, 509
IGRAPH command, 563

BARBASE (keyword)
IGRAPH command, 563

BARCHART (subcommand)
CROSSTABS command, 230
FREQUENCIES command, 414

BART (keyword)
FACTOR command, 373

BASE (subcommand)
MULT RESPONSE command, 787

BASELINE (keyword)
COXREG command, 208
IGRAPH command, 562, 563, 569

BASIS (keyword)
MANOVA command, 678

BAVERAGE (keyword)
CLUSTER command, 169

BCON (keyword)
COXREG command, 208
LOGISTIC REGRESSION command, 619

BCOV (keyword)
REGRESSION command, 988

BEGIN DATA (command), 137
in a prompted session, 138
with INCLUDE command, 138
with SUBTITLE command, 1142
with TITLE command, 1167

BEUCLID (keyword)
CLUSTER command, 168
PROXIMITIES command, 944

BIAS (keyword)
NOMREG command, 811
PLUM command, 882

BINOMIAL (subcommand)
NPAR TESTS command, 826

BIVARIATE (keyword)
GRAPH command, 526

BLANK (keyword)
FACTOR command, 366
REPORT command, 1047

!BLANKS (function)
DEFINE command, 281

BLANKS (subcommand)
SET command, 1108
SHOW command, 1114

BLKSIZE (subcommand)
SHOW command, 1114

BLOCK (function)
MATRIX command, 719

BLOCK (keyword)
CLUSTER command, 163
PROXIMITIES command, 938

BLOCK (subcommand)
SET command, 1110
SHOW command, 1114

BLOM (keyword)
PPLOT command, 896
RANK command, 962

BLWMN (keyword)
  CLUSTER command, 169
  PROXIMITIES command, 945

BONFERRONI (keyword)
  GLM command, 485
  ONEWAY command, 854
  UNIANOVA command, 1209

BOOTSTRAP (subcommand)
  CNLR command, 806

BOTH (keyword)
  IGRAPH command, 569
  NONPAR CORR command, 819
  PPLOT command, 897
  SURVIVAL command, 1160

BOTTOM (keyword)
  TSPLOT command, 1178

BOUNDS (subcommand)
  CNLR command, 804

BOX (subcommand)
  IGRAPH command, 566
  SET command, 1110
  SHOW command, 1114

BOXBASE (keyword)
  IGRAPH command, 566

BOXM (keyword)
  DISCRIMINANT command, 304
  MANOVA command, 683

BOXPLOT (keyword)
  EXAMINE command, 349

!BREAK (command)
  DEFINE command, 283

BREAK (command), 139
  with DO IF command, 139
  with LOOP command, 139

BREAK (keyword)
  IGRAPH command, 562, 567

BREAK (statement)
  MATRIX command, 732

BREAK (subcommand)
  AGGREGATE command, 95
  REPORT command, 1047

BREAKDOWN (command)
  See MEANS

BRESLOW (keyword)
  KM command, 600

BRIEF (keyword)
  MANOVA command, 682
  TSET command, 1171

BRKSPACE (keyword)
  REPORT command, 1040

BSEUCLID (keyword)
  CLUSTER command, 168
  PROXIMITIES command, 944

BSHAPE (keyword)
  CLUSTER command, 169
  PROXIMITIES command, 944

BSTEP (keyword)
  COXREG command, 206
  LOGISTIC REGRESSION command, 616

BTAU (keyword)
  CROSSTABS command, 227

BTUKEY (keyword)
  GLM command, 485
  ONEWAY command, 854
  UNIANOVA command, 1208

BUFFNO (subcommand)
  SHOW command, 1114

!BY (keyword)
  DEFINE command, 283

BY (keyword)
  ANOVA command, 121
  CROSSTABS command, 224
  DATE command, 261
  GENLOG command, 422
  LIST command, 608
  LOGISTIC REGRESSION command, 612
  LOGLINEAR command, 627
  LOOP command, 643
  MEANS command, 774
  MULT RESPONSE command, 785
  NOMREG command, 811
  NOMREG subcommand, 813
  NPAR TESTS command, 825, 829
  PARTIAL CORR command, 867
  PLOT command, 877, 878
  PROBIT command, 925
  RANK command, 959
  ROC command, 1074
  SORT CASES command, 1117
  SPLIT FILE command, 1137
  SUMMARIZE command, 1146
  SURVIVAL command, 1152
  VARCOMP command, 1232
  WEIGHT command, 1247

BY (subcommand)
  ADD FILES command, 86
  MATCH FILES command, 700
  UPDATE command, 1218

C (keyword)
  GLM command, 486
  ONEWAY command, 855
  UNIANOVA command, 1209

C (subcommand)
  data organization, 1130
  SPCHART command, 1129
  variable specification, 1131

CACHE (command), 140

CALCULATE (subcommand)
  SURVIVAL command, 1157

CALL (statement)
  MATRIX command, 726

CAPSIGMA (subcommand)
  SPCHART command, 1134

CAPSTYLE (keyword)
  IGRAPH command, 569

CAPTION (subcommand)
  IGRAPH command, 558

CAPWIDTH (keyword)
  IGRAPH command, 566, 569

$CASE (keyword)
  IGRAPH command, 554

CASE (keyword)
  FILE TYPE command, 391
  PROXIMITIES command, 935, 936

CASE (subcommand)
  FILE TYPE command, 388
  RECORD TYPE command, 975

CASENUM (keyword)
  SUMMARIZE command, 1148

CASENUM$ (system variable)
  in PRINT EJECT command, 915
  with SELECT IF command, 1096

CASES (keyword)
  DISCRIMINANT command, 306
  MULT RESPONSE command, 787

CASES (subcommand)
  LIST command, 607

CASEWISE (subcommand)
  LOGISTIC REGRESSION command, 620
  REGRESSION command, 1001

CAT (keyword)
  IGRAPH command, 562, 567

CATEGORICAL (keyword)
  IGRAPH command, 554

CATEGORICAL (subcommand)
  COXREG command, 204
  LOGISTIC REGRESSION command, 613

CATORDER (subcommand)

IGRAPH command, 555

CAUCHIT (keyword)
  PLUM command, 882

CC (keyword)
  CROSSTABS command, 227

CC (subcommand)
  SET command, 1111
  SHOW command, 1114

CCF (command), 152
  APPLY subcommand, 157
  DIFF subcommand, 154
  LN/NOLOG subcommands, 155
  MXCROSS subcommand, 156
  PERIOD subcommand, 155
  SDIFF subcommand, 154
  SEASONAL subcommand, 156
  VARIABLES subcommand, 154

CCW (keyword)
  IGRAPH command, 565

CDFNORM (function)
  MATRIX command, 720

CELLINFO (keyword)
  MANOVA command, 659
  PLUM command, 884

CELLPROB (keyword)
  NOMREG command, 814

CELLRANGE (subcommand)
  GET DATA command, 440

CELLS (keyword)
  CROSSTABS command, 231

CELLS (subcommand)
  CROSSTABS command, 226
  MATRIX DATA command, 763
  MEANS command, 774
  MULT RESPONSE command, 786
  OLAP CUBES command, 848
  SUMMARIZE command, 1147

CENTER (keyword)
  REPORT command, 1045, 1049, 1058

CENTROID (keyword)
  CLUSTER command, 169

CHA (keyword)
  REGRESSION command, 988

CHALIGN (keyword)
  REPORT command, 1039

!CHAREND (keyword)
  DEFINE command, 275

CHARTLOOK (subcommand)
  IGRAPH command, 559

CHDSPACE (keyword)

REPORT command, 1040

CHEBYCHEV (keyword)
CLUSTER command, 163
PROXIMITIES command, 938

CHICDF (function)
MATRIX command, 720

CHISQ (keyword)
CLUSTER command, 163
CROSSTABS command, 227
PROXIMITIES command, 938

CHISQUARE (subcommand)
NPAR TESTS command, 827

CHOL (function)
MATRIX command, 720

CHWRAP (keyword)
REPORT command, 1040

CI (keyword)
COXREG command, 208
GRAPH command, 525
IGRAPH command, 569
LOGISTIC REGRESSION command, 618
PROBIT command, 929
REGRESSION command, 988

CIN (keyword)
CROSSTABS command, 228
CURVEFIT command, 239
GENLOG command, 426
NOMREG command, 811
NPAR TESTS command, 842
PLUM command, 882
REGRESSION command, 990

CIN (subcommand)
CURVEFIT command, 239

CINTERVAL (subcommand)
EXAMINE command, 351
MANOVA command, 665, 685

CJUMP (keyword)
IGRAPH command, 568

CKDER (keyword)
CNLR/NLR command, 801

CLABELS (keyword)
MATRIX command, 729

CLASS (keyword)
DISCRIMINANT command, 302

CLASSIFY (keyword)
QUICK CLUSTER command, 954

CLASSIFY (subcommand)
DISCRIMINANT command, 305

CLASSPLOT (subcommand)
LOGISTIC REGRESSION command, 620

CLASSTABLE (keyword)
NOMREG command, 814

CLEAR TIME PROGRAM (command)
with COXREG command, 202

CLEAR TRANSFORMATIONS (command), 158

CLOGLOG (keyword)
PLUM command, 882

CLUSTER (command), 159
compared with QUICK CLUSTER command, 951
ID subcommand, 171
limitations, 161
matrix input, 173
matrix output, 173
MATRIX subcommand, 173
MEASURE subcommand, 162
MISSING subcommand, 173
missing values, 173, 175
PLOT subcommand, 172
PRINT subcommand, 171
SAVE subcommand, 170
variable list, 161
with SET command, 161

CLUSTER (keyword)
CLUSTER command, 171
IGRAPH command, 556, 565
QUICK CLUSTER command, 953, 955

CLUSTER (subcommand)
IGRAPH command, 557

CMAX (function)
MATRIX command, 721

!CMDEND (keyword)
DEFINE command, 275

CMH (keyword)
CROSSTABS command, 228

CMIN (function)
MATRIX command, 721

CNAMES (keyword)
MATRIX command, 729

CNLR (command), 791
BOOTSTRAP subcommand, 806
BOUNDS subcommand, 804
CRITERIA subcommand, 801
DERIVATIVES command, 793, 796
FILE subcommand, 798
iteration criteria, 802
linear constraint, 804
LOSS subcommand, 805
nonlinear constraint, 805
OUTFILE subcommand, 798
PRED subcommand, 799

SAVE subcommand, 800
simple bounds, 804
weighting cases, 794
with CONSTRAINED FUNCTIONS command, 793, 797
with MODEL PROGRAM command, 793, 795
COCHRAN (keyword)
RELIABILITY command, 1010
COCHRAN (subcommand)
NPAR TESTS command, 828
COEFF (keyword)
COXREG command, 210
DISCRIMINANT command, 305
REGRESSION command, 988
COINCIDENT (keyword)
IGRAPH command, 561
COLCONF (keyword)
ALSCAL command, 108, 113
COLLECT (keyword)
REGRESSION command, 985
COLLIN (keyword)
REGRESSION command, 988
COLLINEARITY (keyword)
MANOVA command, 661
COLOR (subcommand)
IGRAPH command, 556
COLSPACE (keyword)
REPORT command, 1039
COLUMN (keyword)
CROSSTABS command, 226
MULT RESPONSE command, 786
COLUMN (subcommand)
REREAD command, 1066
COLUMNWISE (keyword)
AGGREGATE command, 99, 100
COMBINED (keyword)
DISCRIMINANT command, 306
COMM (keyword)
EXPORT command, 358
IMPORT command, 575
COMMENT (command), 178
COMPARE (keyword)
SURVIVAL command, 1158
COMPARE (subcommand)
EXAMINE command, 347
KM command, 600
SURVIVAL command, 1156
COMPLETE (keyword)
CLUSTER command, 169
COMPOUND (keyword)

CURVEFIT command, 237
COMPRESSED (subcommand)
SAVE command, 1084
XSAVE command, 1267
COMPRESSION (subcommand)
SET command, 1109
SHOW command, 1114
COMPUTE (command), 179
functions, 179
missing values, 185
with DO IF command, 186
with STRING command, 186, 190
COMPUTE (statement)
MATRIX command, 718
!CONCAT (function)
DEFINE command, 280
CONDENSE (keyword)
MULT RESPONSE command, 789
RANK command, 896, 962
CONDENSED (keyword)
PARTIAL CORR command, 870
CONDITION (subcommand)
ALSCAL command, 107
CONDITIONAL (keyword)
COXREG command, 207
MANOVA command, 686
SURVIVAL command, 1158
CONFIG (keyword)
ALSCAL command, 108, 113
CONFORM (subcommand)
SPCHART command, 1135
CONNECT (subcommand)
GET CAPTURE command, 436
GET DATA command, 439
CONNECT(subcommand)
SAVE TRANSLATE command, 1089
CONSTANT (keyword)
MANOVA command, 674
CONSTANT (subcommand)
2SLS command, 1191
CURVEFIT command, 238
WLS command, 1253
CONSTRAIN (keyword)
ALSCAL command, 111
CONSTRAINED FUNCTIONS (command)
with CNLR command, 793, 797
CONTENTS (subcommand)
MATRIX DATA command, 764
CONTINUED (subcommand)
REPEATING DATA command, 1028

CONTOUR (keyword)
  PLOT command, 878
CONTRAST (keyword)
  MANOVA command, 678
CONTRAST (subcommand)
  COXREG command, 204
  GLM command, 468, 481
  LOGISTIC REGRESSION command, 613
  LOGLINEAR command, 630
  MANOVA command, 654, 692
  ONEWAY command, 852
  UNIANOVA command, 1205
CONVERGE (keyword)
  ALSCAL command, 110
  HILOGLINEAR command, 539
  PROBIT command, 927
  QUICK CLUSTER command, 954
  VARCOMP command, 1230
CONVERT (keyword)
  RECODE command, 968
COOK (keyword)
  GLM command, 488
  LOGISTIC REGRESSION command, 620
  REGRESSION command, 999
  UNIANOVA command, 1211
COORDINATE (subcommand)
  IGRAPH command, 558
COORDINATES (keyword)
  ROC command, 1075
COR (keyword)
  MANOVA command, 682
CORB (keyword)
  NOMREG command, 814
  PLUM command, 884
  VARCOMP command, 1232
CORR (keyword)
  COXREG command, 208
  CROSSTABS command, 227
  DISCRIMINANT command, 304
  LOGISTIC REGRESSION command, 618
  MATRIX DATA command, 764
  PARTIAL CORR command, 869
CORRELATION (keyword)
  CLUSTER command, 162
  FACTOR command, 367
  PROXIMITIES command, 937
  REGRESSION command, 992
CORRELATIONS (command), 191
  limitations, 192
  matrix output, 25, 194

MATRIX subcommand, 194
MISSING subcommand, 194
PRINT subcommand, 193
significance tests, 193
STATISTICS subcommand, 193
with REGRESSION command, 994
CORRELATIONS (keyword)
  RELIABILITY command, 1009, 1011
COS (function)
  MATRIX command, 721
COSINE (keyword)
  CLUSTER command, 162
  PROXIMITIES command, 938
$COUNT (keyword)
  IGRAPH command, 554, 557, 562–564, 567, 570
COUNT (command), 197
  missing values, 198
COUNT (function)
  GRAPH command, 506
COUNT (keyword)
  CROSSTABS command, 226
  MATRIX DATA command, 765
  MEANS command, 774
  MULT RESPONSE command, 786
  OLAP CUBES command, 848
  SUMMARIZE command, 1147
COV (keyword)
  DISCRIMINANT command, 304
  MANOVA command, 682
  MATRIX DATA command, 764
  REGRESSION command, 993
COVARIANCE (keyword)
  FACTOR command, 367
  RELIABILITY command, 1011
COVARIANCES (keyword)
  RELIABILITY command, 1009, 1011
COVARIATES (subcommand)
  ANOVA command, 122
COVB (keyword)
  NOMREG command, 814
  PLUM command, 884
  VARCOMP command, 1231
COVRATIO (keyword)
  REGRESSION command, 999
COXREG (command), 199
  BASELINE keyword, 208
  BCON keyword, 208
  BSTEP keyword, 206
  CATEGORICAL subcommand, 204
  CI keyword, 208

COEFF keyword, 210
CONDITIONAL keyword, 207
CONTRAST subcommand, 204
CORR keyword, 208
CRITERIA subcommand, 208
DEFAULT keyword, 208
DEVIATION keyword, 204
DFBETA keyword, 211
DIFFERENCE keyword, 205
ENTER keyword, 206
EXCLUDE keyword, 207
EXTERNAL subcommand, 211
FSTEP keyword, 206
HAZARD keyword, 210, 211
HELMERT keyword, 205
INCLUDE keyword, 207
INDICATOR keyword, 205
ITER keyword, 209
LCON keyword, 209
limitations, 201
LM keyword, 210
LML keyword, 211
LR keyword, 207
METHOD subcommand, 206
MISSING subcommand, 207
NONE keyword, 210
OMS keyword, 210
OUTFILE subcommand, 210
PATTERN subcommand, 210
PIN keyword, 209
PLOT subcommand, 209
POLYNOMIAL keyword, 205
POUT keyword, 209
PRESID keyword, 211
PRINT subcommand, 208
REPEATED keyword, 205
SAVE subcommand, 210
SE keyword, 211
SIMPLE keyword, 205
SPECIAL keyword, 205
STATUS subcommand, 203
STRATA subcommand, 203
SUMMARY keyword, 208
SURVIVAL keyword, 210
TABLE keyword, 210
VARIABLES subcommand, 202
WALD keyword, 207
with CLEAR TIME PROGRAM command, 202
with TIME PROGRAM command, 202
XBETA keyword, 211

CP (keyword)
    SPCHART command, 1132
CPL (keyword)
    SPCHART command, 1132
CPM (keyword)
    SPCHART command, 1132
CPN (keyword)
    SPCHART command, 1132
CPU (keyword)
    SPCHART command, 1132
CR (keyword)
    SPCHART command, 1132
CREATE (command), 212
    CSUM function, 214
    DIFF function, 214
    FFT function, 215
    IFFT function, 215
    LAG function, 216
    LEAD function, 216
    MA function, 217
    PMA function, 218
    RMED function, 218
    SDIFF function, 219
    T4253H function, 220
CRITERIA (subcommand)
    ALSCAL command, 110
    CNLR command, 801
    COXREG command, 208
    FACTOR command, 370
    GENLOG command, 425
    GLM command, 475
    HILOGLINEAR command, 539
    LOGISTIC REGRESSION command, 618
    LOGLINEAR command, 632
    NLR command, 801, 803
    NOMREG command, 811
    PLUM command, 882
    PROBIT command, 927
    QUICK CLUSTER command, 953
    REGRESSION command, 989
    ROC command, 1074
    UNIANOVA command, 1199
    VARCOMP command, 1230
CROSSTABS (command), 221
    BARCHART subcommand, 230
    cell percentages, 226
    CELLS subcommand, 226
    CMH keyword, 228
    exact tests, 228
    expected count, 226

FORMAT subcommand, 230
general mode, 225
integer mode, 225
limitations, 223
METHOD subcommand, 228
MISSING subcommand, 229
residuals, 226
STATISTICS subcommand, 227
TABLES subcommand, 224
VARIABLES subcommand, 224
with PROCEDURE OUTPUT command, 230, 231, 931
with WEIGHT, 232
WRITE subcommand, 230
CROSSVALID (keyword)
DISCRIMINANT command, 305
CRSHTOL (keyword)
CNLR command, 802
CSSQ (function)
MATRIX command, 721
CSTEP (keyword)
IGRAPH command, 563, 568
CSTRUCTURE (subcommand)
GENLOG command, 424
CSUM (function)
CREATE command, 214
MATRIX command, 721
CTAU (keyword)
CROSSTABS command, 227
CTEMPLATE (subcommand)
SET command, 1104
SHOW command, 1114
CUBIC (keyword)
CURVEFIT command, 237
CUFREQ (function)
GRAPH command, 506
CUM (keyword)
GRAPH command, 530
IGRAPH command, 570
CUMEVENT (keyword)
KM command, 602
CUPCT (function)
GRAPH command, 506
CURVE (keyword)
IGRAPH command, 570
ROC command, 1076
CURVEFIT (command), 234
APPLY subcommand, 240
CIN subcommand, 239
CONSTANT/NOCONSTANT subcommands, 238

ID subcommand, 239
MODEL subcommand, 237
PLOT subcommand, 239
PRINT subcommand, 239
SAVE subcommand, 239
UPPERBOUND subcommand, 238
VARIABLES subcommand, 237
CUSUM (function)
GRAPH command, 506
CUT (keyword)
LOGISTIC REGRESSION command, 619
CUTOFF (keyword)
ALSCAL command, 110
ROC command, 1075
CW (keyword)
IGRAPH command, 565
CWEIGHT (subcommand)
HILOGLINEAR command, 539
LOGLINEAR command, 628
CYCLE (keyword)
DATE command, 259
CZL (keyword)
SPCHART command, 1132
CZMAX (keyword)
SPCHART command, 1132
CZMIN (keyword)
SPCHART command, 1132
CZU (keyword)
SPCHART command, 1132

D (keyword)
CLUSTER command, 167
CROSSTABS command, 227
DESCRIPTIVES command, 290
PROXIMITIES command, 943
SORT CASES command, 1117
DATA (keyword)
ALSCAL command, 111
DATA (subcommand)
REPEATING DATA command, 1026
DATA LIST (command), 241
column-style formats, 255
END subcommand, 249
FILE subcommand, 245
FIXED keyword, 245
fixed-format data, 243, 244, 245, 252
FORTRAN-like formats, 255
FREE keyword, 245

freefield data, 243, 244, 244, 245, 254
inline data, 243, 245
LIST keyword, 245
NOTABLE subcommand, 247
RECORDS subcommand, 247
TABLE subcommand, 247
variable definition, 251
variable formats, 241, 254
variable names, 252
with ADD FILES command, 85
with INPUT PROGRAM command, 249, 324
with MATCH FILES command, 700
with NUMERIC command, 845
with POINT command, 888
with RECORD TYPE command, 970
with REPEATING DATA command, 1018, 1019,
   1021
with REREAD command, 1061
with UPDATE command, 1217
with VECTOR command, 1243

DATE (argument)
   REPORT command, 1059

DATE (command), 259
   BY keyword, 261
   examples, 262
   keywords, 259
   starting value, 260

DAY (keyword)
   DATE command, 259

DB2 (keyword)
   SAVE TRANSLATE command, 1090

DB3 (keyword)
   SAVE TRANSLATE command, 1090

DB4 (keyword)
   SAVE TRANSLATE command, 1090

!DEFAULT (keyword)
   DEFINE command, 278

DEFAULT (keyword)
   COXREG command, 208
   DESCRIPTIVES command, 290
   FREQUENCIES command, 418
   LOGISTIC REGRESSION command, 618
   MEANS command, 774
   PLOT command, 878
   SUMMARIZE command, 1147
   TSET command, 1171

DEFAULT (subcommand)
   TSET command, 1170

DEFINE (command), 268
   !BREAK command, 283

!BY keyword, 283
!CHAREND keyword, 275
!CMDEND keyword, 275
!DEFAULT keyword, 278
!DO command, 283
!DOEND command, 283
!ELSE keyword, 283
!ENCLOSE keyword, 275
!IF command, 283
!IFEND command, 283
!IN keyword, 284
!LET command, 285
!NOEXPAND keyword, 279
!OFFEXPAND keyword, 279
!ONEXPAND keyword, 279
!POSITIONAL keyword, 272
!THEN keyword, 283
!TO keyword, 283
!TOKENS keyword, 275
limitations, 270
macro arguments, 272
string functions, 279
tokens, 275
with SET command, 281

DELCASE (subcommand)
   GET DATA command, 441

DELIMITED (keyword)
   GET DATA command, 441

DELIMITERS (subcommand)
   GET DATA command, 442

DELTA (keyword)
   HILOGLINEAR command, 539
   NOMREG command, 811
   PLUM command, 882

DELTA (subcommand)
   WLS command, 1252

DENDROGRAM (keyword)
   CLUSTER command, 172

DENSITY (keyword)
   SURVIVAL command, 1156

DEPENDENT (keyword)
   MEANS command, 776
   SUMMARIZE command, 1148

DEPENDENT (subcommand)
   REGRESSION command, 985

DERIVATIVES (command)
   CNLR/NLR command, 793, 796

DESCENDING (subcommand)
   AUTORECODE command, 136

DESCRIPTIVES (command), 286

MISSING subcommand, 291
SAVE subcommand, 288
SORT subcommand, 290
STATISTICS subcommand, 289
VARIABLES subcommand, 287
Z scores, 288

DESCRIPTIVES (keyword)
CORRELATIONS command, 193
EXAMINE command, 351
GLM command, 476
NPAR TESTS command, 841
ONEWAY command, 856
PARTIAL CORR command, 869
RELIABILITY command, 1009
UNIANOVA command, 1200

DESCRIPTIVES (subcommand)
REGRESSION command, 992

DESIGN (function)
MATRIX command, 721

DESIGN (keyword)
MANOVA command, 661

DESIGN (subcommand)
GENLOG command, 429
HILOGLINEAR command, 543
LOGLINEAR command, 634
MANOVA command, 653
VARCOMP command, 1232

DET (function)
MATRIX command, 722

DET (keyword)
FACTOR command, 368

DETAILED (keyword)
TSET command, 1171

DETRENDED (keyword)
PPLOT command, 897

DEV (keyword)
LOGISTIC REGRESSION command, 620

DEVIANCE (keyword)
NOMREG command, 815

DEVIATION (keyword)
COXREG command, 204
GLM command, 481, 499
LOGISTIC REGRESSION command, 614
MANOVA command, 655, 678
UNIANOVA command, 1205

DFBETA (keyword)
COXREG command, 211
LOGISTIC REGRESSION command, 620
REGRESSION command, 999

DFE (keyword)

MATRIX DATA command, 764

DFE (subcommand)
FIT command, 402

DFFIT (keyword)
REGRESSION command, 999

DFH (subcommand)
FIT command, 402

DFREQ (keyword)
FREQUENCIES command, 413

DIAG (function)
MATRIX command, 722

DIAGONAL (keyword)
MATRIX DATA command, 759

DIAGONAL (subcommand)
FACTOR command, 369

DICE (keyword)
CLUSTER command, 166
PROXIMITIES command, 941

DICTIONARY (keyword)
DISPLAY command, 312

DIFF (function)
CREATE command, 214

DIFF (subcommand)
ACF command, 77
CCF command, 154
PACF command, 862
PPLOT command, 898
TSPLOT command, 1176

DIFFERENCE (keyword)
COXREG command, 205
GLM command, 482, 500
GRAPH command, 515
LOGISTIC REGRESSION command, 614
MANOVA command, 655, 679, 692
UNIANOVA command, 1205

DIGITS (subcommand)
EXPORT command, 360

DIMENR (keyword)
MANOVA command, 682

DIMENS (keyword)
ALSCAL command, 111

DIRECT (keyword)
DISCRIMINANT command, 298

DIRECTION (keyword)
IGRAPH command, 569

DIRECTIONS (keyword)
ALSCAL command, 111

DISCRIM (subcommand)
MANOVA command, 684

DISCRIMINANT (command), 292

analysis block, 294
ANALYSIS subcommand, 296
CLASSIFY subcommand, 305
FIN subcommand, 299
FOUT subcommand, 299
FUNCTIONS subcommand, 300
GROUPS subcommand, 295
HISTORY subcommand, 305
inclusion levels, 297
limitations, 295
matrix input, 307
matrix output, 307
MATRIX subcommand, 307
MAXSTEPS subcommand, 300
METHOD subcommand, 298
MISSING subcommand, 307
missing values, 307, 309
OUTFILE subcommand, 299
PIN subcommand, 299
PLOT subcommand, 306
POUT subcommand, 299
PRIORS subcommand, 301
ROTATE subcommand, 305
SAVE subcommand, 302
SELECT subcommand, 296
STATISTICS subcommand, 304
TOLERANCE subcommand, 299
VARIABLES subcommand, 295
VIN subcommand, 300
with MATRIX DATA command, 754
DISPER (keyword)
CLUSTER command, 169
PROXIMITIES command, 944
DISPLAY (command), 312
VARIABLES subcommand, 313
with PRINT FORMATS command, 917
with WRITE FORMATS command, 1261
DISPLAY (statement)
MATRIX command, 748
DISTANCE (keyword)
CLUSTER command, 171
QUICK CLUSTER command, 955
DISTRIBUTION (keyword)
ROC command, 1075
DISTRIBUTION (subcommand)
PPLOT command, 894
DIVIDE (function)
REPORT command, 1054
!DO (command)
DEFINE command, 283

!DOEND (command)
DEFINE command, 283
DO IF (command), 317
logical expressions, 318
missing values, 320
nested, 324
string data, 318, 319
with ELSE command, 321
with ELSE IF command, 322
with INPUT PROGRAM command, 325
with PRINT command, 910
with PRINT EJECT command, 913
with PRINT SPACE command, 919
with SAMPLE command, 1078
with SELECT IF command, 1099
DO IF (statement)
MATRIX command, 730
DO REPEAT (command), 326
PRINT subcommand, 329
stand-in variable, 326
with INPUT PROGRAM command, 328
with LOOP command, 328
DO REPEAT command
with XSAVE command, 1264
DOCUMENT (subcommand)
AGGREGATE command, 96
DOCUMENTS (keyword)
DISPLAY command, 312
DOT (keyword)
IGRAPH command, 567
DOTLINE (keyword)
IGRAPH command, 567
DOUBLE (keyword)
MULT RESPONSE command, 788
DOWN (keyword)
IGRAPH command, 569
SORT CASES command, 1117
DRESID (keyword)
GLM command, 488
REGRESSION command, 999
UNIANOVA command, 1211
DROP (keyword)
GRAPH command, 515
DROP (subcommand)
ADD FILES command, 86
EXPORT command, 359
GET command, 433
GET TRANSLATE command, 459
IMPORT command, 575
MATCH FILES command, 702

SAVE command, 1082
SAVE TRANSLATE command, 1092
UPDATE command, 1219
XSAVE command, 1265
DROP DOCUMENTS (command), 331
  with MATCH FILES command, 699
  with UPDATE command, 1215
DROPLINE (keyword)
  IGRAPH command, 567
DUMMY (keyword)
  REPORT command, 1044
DUNCAN (keyword)
  GLM command, 485
  ONEWAY command, 854
  UNIANOVA command, 1208
DUNNETT (keyword)
  GLM command, 485
  ONEWAY command, 854
  UNIANOVA command, 1208
DUNNETTL (keyword)
  GLM command, 485
  ONEWAY command, 854
  UNIANOVA command, 1208
DUNNETTR (keyword)
  GLM command, 485
  ONEWAY command, 854
  UNIANOVA command, 1208
DUPLICATE (subcommand)
  FILE TYPE command, 391
  RECORD TYPE command, 977
DURBIN (keyword)
  REGRESSION command, 1001
DVALUE (keyword)
  CROSSTABS command, 230
  FREQUENCIES command, 413

ECONVERGE (keyword)
  FACTOR command, 370
EDIT (command), 332
EFFECT (subcommand)
  IGRAPH command, 558
EFFECTS (keyword)
  ONEWAY command, 856
EFSIZE (keyword)
  GLM command, 476
  MANOVA command, 660, 696
  UNIANOVA command, 1200
EIGEN (keyword)

FACTOR command, 369
  MANOVA command, 682
  MATRIX command, 726
!ELSE (keyword)
  DEFINE command, 283
ELSE (command)
  See DO IF command
ELSE (keyword)
  RECODE command, 965
ELSE (statement)
  MATRIX command, 730
ELSE IF (command)
  See DO IF command
ELSE IF (statement)
  MATRIX command, 730
EMMEANS (subcommand)
  GLM command, 486, 503
  UNIANOVA command, 1209
EMPIRICAL (keyword)
  EXAMINE command, 349
!ENCLOSE (keyword)
  DEFINE command, 275
EMS (keyword)
  VARCOMP command, 1231
END (keyword)
  DISCRIMINANT command, 305
END (subcommand)
  DATA LIST command, 249
END CASE (command), 334
  with LOOP command, 645
  with VECTOR command, 335, 340
END DATA (command), 137
!ENDDEFINE (command), 268
  See also DEFINE command
END FILE (command), 342
  with END CASE command, 343
  with LOOP command, 645
END FILE TYPE (command). See FILE TYPE command
END IF (command). See DO IF command
END IF (statement)
  MATRIX command, 730
END INPUT PROGRAM (command). See INPUT PROGRAM command
END LOOP (command), 637
  See also LOOP command
END LOOP (statement)
  MATRIX command, 731
END MATRIX (command)
  See MATRIX command

END REPEAT (command). *See* DO REPEAT command

ENDOGENOUS (subcommand)
2SLS command, 1190

ENTER (keyword)
COXREG command, 206
LOGISTIC REGRESSION command, 615
REGRESSION command, 986

EOF (function)
MATRIX command, 722

EPANECHNIKOV (keyword)
IGRAPH command, 571

EPOCH (subcommand), 1105

EPS (keyword)
GENLOG command, 426
GLM command, 475
LOGISTIC REGRESSION command, 619
UNIANOVA command, 1199
VARCOMP command, 1230

EQUAL (keyword)
DISCRIMINANT command, 301

EQUAMAX (keyword)
FACTOR command, 372
MANOVA command, 684

EQUATION (subcommand)
2SLS command, 1189

ERASE (command), 344

ERROR (keyword)
MANOVA command, 661, 682

ERROR (subcommand)
MANOVA command, 653

ERRORBAR (subcommand)
GRAPH command, 525
IGRAPH command, 569

ERRORS (keyword)
INFO command, 582

ERRORS (subcommand)
FIT command, 401
SET command, 1106
SHOW command, 1114

ESTIM (keyword)
HILOGLINEAR command, 542
MANOVA command, 684

ESTPROB (keyword)
PLUM command, 885

ETA (keyword)
CROSSTABS command, 227

ETASQ (keyword)
GLM command, 476
UNIANOVA command, 1200

EUCLID (keyword)
ALSCAL command, 109
CLUSTER command, 162
PROXIMITIES command, 937

!EVAL (function)
DEFINE command, 281

EVAL (function)
MATRIX command, 722

EXACT (keyword)
CROSSTABS command, 229
MANOVA command, 664, 685
NPAR TESTS command, 842
SURVIVAL command, 1157

EXAMINE (command), 345
CINTERVAL subcommand, 351
COMPARE subcommand, 347
ID subcommand, 348
limitations, 346
MESTIMATORS subcommand, 351
MISSING subcommand, 352
NOTOTAL subcommand, 348
PERCENTILES subcommand, 348
PLOT subcommand, 349
STATISTICS subcommand, 351
TOTAL subcommand, 348
VARIABLES subcommand, 347

EXCLUDE (keyword)
ANOVA command, 127
CORRELATIONS command, 194
COXREG command, 207
DISCRIMINANT command, 307
EXAMINE command, 353
GLM command, 475
GRAPH command, 534
MANOVA command, 666
NOMREG command, 812
ONEWAY command, 856
PARTIAL CORR command, 870
PLUM command, 884
RANK command, 963
RELIABILITY command, 1012
ROC command, 1074
SUMMARIZE command, 1148
TSET command, 1170
UNIANOVA command, 1199
VARCOMP command, 1230

EXECUTE (command), 354

EXP (function)
MATRIX command, 722

EXPECTED (keyword)

CROSSTABS command, 226

EXPECTED (subcommand)
NPAR TESTS command, 827

EXPERIMENTAL (keyword)
ANOVA command, 122

EXPONENTIAL (keyword)
CURVEFIT command, 237
NPAR TESTS command, 830

EXPORT (command), 355
DIGITS subcommand, 360
DROP subcommand, 359
KEEP subcommand, 359
MAP subcommand, 360
OUTFILE subcommand, 358
RENAME subcommand, 359
TYPE subcommand, 358
UNSELECTED subcommand, 358

EXTENSIONS (subcommand)
SET command, 1109
SHOW command, 1114

EXTERNAL (subcommand)
COXREG command, 211
LOGISTIC REGRESSION command, 622

EXTRACTION (keyword)
FACTOR command, 367

EXTRACTION (subcommand)
FACTOR command, 371

EXTREME (keyword)
EXAMINE command, 351
IGRAPH command, 566

F (keyword)
MANOVA command, 664
REGRESSION command, 989

FACILITIES (keyword)
INFO command, 582

FACTOR (command), 361
analysis block, 363
ANALYSIS subcommand, 366
CRITERIA subcommand, 370
DIAGONAL subcommand, 369
extraction block, 363
EXTRACTION subcommand, 371
FORMAT subcommand, 366
matrix input, 374
matrix output, 25, 374
MATRIX subcommand, 374
MISSING subcommand, 364

missing values, 364
PLOT subcommand, 368
PRINT subcommand, 367
rotation block, 363
ROTATION subcommand, 372
SAVE subcommand, 372
SELECT subcommand, 365
VARIABLES subcommand, 364
with PROXIMITIES command, 949

FACTORS (keyword)
FACTOR command, 370
MATRIX command, 747

FACTORS (subcommand)
MATRIX DATA command, 762

FANCY (keyword)
IGRAPH command, 566, 569

FCDF (function)
MATRIX command, 722

FFT (function)
CREATE command, 215

FGT (function)
AGGREGATE command, 97

FIELD (keyword)
MATRIX command, 734

FIELDNAMES (subcommand)
GET TRANSLATE command, 458
SAVE TRANSLATE command, 1091

FILE (keyword)
MATRIX command, 734, 743
SYSFILE INFO command, 1163

FILE (subcommand)
ADD FILES command, 85
ALSCAL command, 107
CNLR/NLR command, 798
DATA LIST command, 245
FILE TYPE command, 388
GET command, 432
GET DATA command, 439
GET TRANSLATE command, 457
IMPORT command, 575
INCLUDE command, 579
KEYED DATA LIST command, 592
MATCH FILES command, 699
MATRIX DATA command, 758
POINT command, 890
QUICK CLUSTER command, 955
REPEATING DATA command, 1026
REREAD command, 1064
UPDATE command, 1217

FILE HANDLE (command), 378

LRECL subcommand, 379
MODE subcommand, 378
RECFORM subcommand, 379
with POINT command, 890
FILE LABEL (command), 380
FILE TYPE (command), 381
    CASE subcommand, 388
    DUPLICATE subcommand, 391
    FILE subcommand, 388
    GROUPED keyword, 386
    MISSING subcommand, 392
    MIXED keyword, 386
    NESTED keyword, 386
    ORDERED subcommand, 394
    RECORD subcommand, 388
    subcommand summary, 387
    WILD subcommand, 391
    with RECORD TYPE command, 970
    with REPEATING DATA command, 1018, 1019,
        1022
    with SAMPLE command, 1078
FILTER (command), 396
FIN (function)
    AGGREGATE command, 97
FIN (keyword)
    REGRESSION command, 990
FIN (subcommand)
    DISCRIMINANT command, 299
FINISH (command), 398, 1094
FIRST (function)
    AGGREGATE command, 98
FIRST (keyword)
    ANOVA command, 122
    IGRAPH command, 572
    MEANS command, 775
    SUMMARIZE command, 1147
    USE command, 1221
FIRST (subcommand)
    ADD FILES command, 88
    MATCH FILES command, 703
FIRSTCASE (subcommand)
    GET DATA command, 441
FIT (command), 400
    DFE/DFH subcommands, 402
    ERRORS subcommand, 401
    OBS subcommand, 401
FIT (keyword)
    CURVEFIT command, 239, 240
    NOMREG command, 814
    PLUM command, 884

FITLINE (subcommand)
    IGRAPH command, 570
FITS (keyword)
    REGRESSION command, 1004
FIXCASE (subcommand)
    GET DATA command, 442
FIXED (keyword)
    DATA LIST command, 245
    GET DATA command, 441
FLATWGHT (keyword)
    ALSCAL command, 113
FLIP (command), 403–406
    NEWNAMES subcommand, 405–406
    VARIABLES subcommand, 404–405
FLT (function)
    AGGREGATE command, 97
FNAMES (keyword)
    MATRIX command, 748
FOOTNOTE (subcommand)
    GRAPH command, 509
    OLAP CUBES command, 847
    REPORT command, 1058
    SPCHART command, 1122
    SUMMARIZE command, 1146
FOR (keyword)
    SURVIVAL command, 1154
FORMAT (keyword)
    MATRIX command, 728, 736
FORMAT (subcommand)
    CROSSTABS command, 230
    FACTOR command, 366
    FREQUENCIES command, 413
    IGRAPH command, 561
    LIST command, 607
    MATRIX DATA command, 759
    MULT RESPONSE command, 788
    PARTIAL CORR command, 870
    PLOT command, 877
    RELIABILITY command, 1011
    REPORT command, 1038
    SET command, 1103
    SHOW command, 1114
    SUMMARIZE command, 1148
    TSPLOT command, 1178
FORMATS (command), 407
    with REFORMAT command, 979
FORWARD (keyword)
    REGRESSION command, 986
FOUT (function)
    AGGREGATE command, 98

FOUT (keyword)
  REGRESSION command, 990

FPAIR (keyword)
  DISCRIMINANT command, 304

FPRECISION (keyword)
  CNLR command, 803

FRACTION (subcommand)
  PPLOT command, 896
  RANK command, 962

FREE (keyword)
  DATA LIST command, 245
  MATRIX DATA command, 759

FREGW (keyword)
  GLM command, 485
  ONEWAY command, 855
  UNIANOVA command, 1209

FREQ (keyword)
  FREQUENCIES command, 414, 415
  HILOGLINEAR command, 542
  PROBIT command, 929

FREQUENCIES (command), 411
  BARCHART subcommand, 414
  FORMAT subcommand, 413
  GROUPED subcommand, 416
  HISTOGRAM subcommand, 415
  limitations, 412
  MISSING subcommand, 419
  NTILES subcommand, 417
  PERCENTILES subcommand, 417
  STATISTICS subcommand, 418
  VARIABLES subcommand, 413
  with PROCEDURE OUTPUT command, 932

FREQUENCIES (subcommand)
  MULT RESPONSE command, 784

FREQUENCY (function)
  REPORT command, 1053

FRIEDMAN (keyword)
  RELIABILITY command, 1010

FRIEDMAN (subcommand)
  NPAR TESTS command, 828

FROM (keyword)
  LIST command, 608
  SAMPLE command, 1077

FROM (subcommand)
  APPLY DICTIONARY command, 131

FSCORE (keyword)
  FACTOR command, 368

FSTEP (keyword)
  COXREG command, 206
  LOGISTIC REGRESSION command, 615

FTOLERANCE (keyword)
  CNLR command, 802

FTSPACE (keyword)
  REPORT command, 1040

FULL (keyword)
  MATRIX DATA command, 759

FULLFACTORIAL (subcommand)
  NOMREG command, 812

functions
  MATRIX command, 719

FUNCTIONS (subcommand)
  DISCRIMINANT command, 300

GABRIEL (keyword)
  GLM command, 485
  ONEWAY command, 855
  UNIANOVA command, 1209

GAMMA (keyword)
  CROSSTABS command, 227

GCOV (keyword)
  DISCRIMINANT command, 304

GEF (keyword)
  GLM command, 476
  UNIANOVA command, 1200

GEMSCAL (keyword)
  ALSCAL command, 110

GEMWGHT (keyword)
  ALSCAL command, 113

GENLOG (command), 420
  cell covariates, 423, 429
  cell structure, 424
  cell weights, 424
  CIN keyword, 426
  CRITERIA subcommand, 425
  CSTRUCTURE subcommand, 424
  data distribution, 425
  DESIGN subcommand, 429
  EPS keyword, 426
  general loglinear model, 422
  GLOR subcommand, 425
  GRESID subcommand, 424
  interaction terms, 429
  logit model, 422
  main-effects model, 429
  measures of association, 423
  MISSING subcommand, 428
  MODEL subcommand, 425
  PLOT subcommand, 427

PRINT subcommand, 426
SAVE subcommand, 428
simultaneous linear logit model, 430
single-degree-of-freedom partitions, 429
statistics, 426
structural zeros, 424
variable list, 422
WITH keyword, 429
GEOMETRIC (keyword)
MEANS command, 775
OLAP CUBES command, 849
SUMMARIZE command, 1148
GET (command), 431
DROP subcommand, 433
FILE subcommand, 432
KEEP subcommand, 433
MAP subcommand, 434
RENAME subcommand, 433
GET (statement)
MATRIX command, 738
GET CAPTURE (command), 435
CONNECT subcommand, 436
SQL subcommand, 436
GET DATA (command), 438
ARRANGEMENT subcommand, 441
CELLRANGE subcommand, 440
CONNECT subcommand, 439
DELCASE subcommand, 441
DELIMITED keyword, 441
DELIMITERS subcommand, 442
FILE subcommand, 439
FIRSTCASE subcommand, 441
FIXCASE subcommand, 442
FIXED keyword, 441
IMPORTCASES subcommand, 442
ODBC keyword, 439
READNAMES subcommand, 441
SHEET subcommand, 440
SQL subcommand, 440
TXT keyword, 439
TYPE subcommand, 439
VARIABLES subcommand, 443
XLS keyword, 439
GET TRANSLATE (command), 453
database files, 456
DROP subcommand, 459
FIELDNAMES subcommand, 458
FILE subcommand, 457
KEEP subcommand, 459
limitations, 457

MAP subcommand, 460
RANGE subcommand, 459
spreadsheet files, 454
tab-delimited files, 456
TYPE subcommand, 457
GG (keyword)
MANOVA command, 696
GH (keyword)
GLM command, 486
ONEWAY command, 855
UNIANOVA command, 1209
GINV (function)
MATRIX command, 722
GLM (command), 469, 490
ALPHA keyword, 475
BONFERRONI keyword, 485
BTUKEY keyword, 485
C keyword, 486
CONTRAST subcommand, 468, 481
COOK keyword, 488
CRITERIA subcommand, 475
DESCRIPTIVES keyword, 476
DEVIATION keyword, 481, 499
DIFFERENCE keyword, 482, 500
DRESID keyword, 488
DUNCAN keyword, 485
DUNNETT keyword, 485
DUNNETTL keyword, 485
DUNNETTR keyword, 485
EFSIZE keyword, 476
EMMEANS subcommand, 486, 503
EPS keyword, 475
ETASQ keyword, 476
EXCLUDE keyword, 475
FREGW keyword, 485
GABRIEL keyword, 485
GEF keyword, 476
GH keyword, 486
GT2 keyword, 485
HELMERT keyword, 482, 500
HOMOGENEITY keyword, 476, 492
INCLUDE keyword, 475
INTERCEPT subcommand, 475
KMATRIX subcommand, 466, 480
LEVER keyword, 488
LMATRIX subcommand, 466, 479
LOF keyword, 477
LSD keyword, 485
MEASURE subcommand, 502
METHOD subcommand, 473

MISSING subcommand, 475
MMATRIX subcommand, 466, 493
OPOWER keyword, 477
OUTFILE subcommand, 488
PARAMETER keyword, 476
PLOT subcommand, 477
POLYNOMIAL keyword, 481, 500
POSTHOC subcommand, 483
PRED keyword, 488
PRINT subcommand, 476, 492
PROFILE keyword, 477
QREGW, 486
RANDOM subcommand, 472
REGWGT subcommand, 473
REPEATED keyword, 482, 500
RESID keyword, 488
RESIDUALS keyword, 477
RSSCP keyword, 492
SAVE subcommand, 487
SCHEFFE keyword, 485
SEPRED keyword, 488
SIDAK keyword, 485
SIMPLE keyword, 482, 500
SNK keyword, 485
SPECIAL keyword, 482, 500
SPREADLEVEL keyword, 477
SSTYPE keyword, 473
T2 keyword, 486
T3 keyword, 486
TABLES keyword, 486
TEST(ESTIMABLE) keyword, 477
TEST(LMATRIX) keyword, 477
TEST(MMATRIX) keyword, 492
TEST(SSCP) keyword, 492
TUKEY keyword, 485
univariate, 469
WALLER keyword, 486
WPRED keyword, 488
WRESID keyword, 488
WSDESIGN subcommand, 501
WSFACTOR subcommand, 498
ZRESID keyword, 488
GLM command
TEST(MMATRIX) keyword, 492
GLOR (subcommand)
GENLOG command, 425
GLS (keyword)
FACTOR command, 371
GMEDIAN (keyword)
MEANS command, 774

OLAP CUBES command, 848
GMEIDAN (keyword)
SUMMARIZE command, 1147
GOODFIT (keyword)
LOGISTIC REGRESSION command, 618
GRAPH (command)
BAR subcommand, 509
BIVARIATE keyword, 526
CI keyword, 525
count functions, 506
CUM keyword, 530
DROP keyword, 515
ERRORBAR subcommand, 525
FOOTNOTE subcommand, 509
GROUPED keyword, 523
HILO subcommand, 522
HISTOGRAM subcommand, 529
INCLUDE keyword, 534
LINE subcommand, 515
LISTWISE keyword, 534
MATRIX keyword, 527
MISSING subcommand, 533
NOCUM keyword, 530
NOREPORT keyword, 534
OVERLAY keyword, 526
PARETO subcommand, 530
PIE subcommand, 521
RANGE keyword, 510
REPORT keyword, 534
SCATTERPLOT subcommand, 526
SIMPLE keyword, 509, 515, 522, 530
STACKED keyword, 530
STDDEV keyword, 525
STERROR keyword, 525
SUBTITLE subcommand, 509
summary functions, 506
TITLE subcommand, 509
VARIABLE keyword, 534
XYZ keyword, 527
GREAT (function)
REPORT command, 1054
GRESID (subcommand)
GENLOG command, 424
LOGLINEAR command, 629
GROUPED (keyword)
FILE TYPE command, 386
GRAPH command, 509, 523
GROUPED (subcommand)
FREQUENCIES command, 416
GROUPS (keyword)

EXAMINE command, 347

GROUPS (subcommand)
DISCRIMINANT command, 295
MULT RESPONSE command, 782
T-TEST command, 1185

GROUPWISE (keyword)
SURVIVAL command, 1159

GROWTH (keyword)
CURVEFIT command, 237

GSCH (function)
MATRIX command, 722

GT2 (keyword)
GLM command, 485
ONEWAY command, 855
UNIANOVA command, 1209

GUTTMAN (keyword)
RELIABILITY command, 1009

HAMANN (keyword)
CLUSTER command, 167
PROXIMITIES command, 942

HAMPEL (keyword)
EXAMINE command, 352

HARMONIC (keyword)
MEANS command, 775
OLAP CUBES command, 848
SUMMARIZE command, 1147

HAVERAGE (keyword)
EXAMINE command, 349

!HEAD (function)
DEFINE command, 281

HAZARD (keyword)
COXREG command, 210, 211
KM command, 598, 602
SURVIVAL command, 1156

HEADER (keyword)
ALSCAL command, 111

HEADER (subcommand)
SET command, 1111
SHOW command, 1114

HELMERT (keyword)
COXREG command, 205
GLM command, 482, 500
LOGISTIC REGRESSION command, 614
MANOVA command, 655, 679, 692
UNIANOVA command, 1206

HF (keyword)
MANOVA command, 696

HICICLE (keyword)
CLUSTER command, 172

HIERARCHICAL (keyword)
ANOVA command, 122, 123

Hierarchical Cluster Analysis procedure
cluster membership, 171

HIGH (keyword)
RANK command, 896, 962

HIGHEST (keyword)
COUNT command, 197
MISSING VALUES command, 779
RECODE command, 965

HILO (keyword)
TSPLOT command, 1178

HILO (subcommand)
GRAPH command, 522

HILOGLINEAR (command), 535
CRITERIA subcommand, 539
CWEIGHT subcommand, 539
DESIGN subcommand, 543
limitations, 537
MAXORDER subcommand, 538
METHOD subcommand, 538
MISSING subcommand, 543
PLOT subcommand, 542
PRINT subcommand, 542
variable list, 538

HISTOGRAM (keyword)
EXAMINE command, 350
REGRESSION command, 1000

HISTOGRAM (subcommand)
FREQUENCIES command, 415
GRAPH command, 529
IGRAPH command, 570

HISTORY (keyword)
NOMREG command, 814
PLUM command, 884
VARCOMP command, 1231

HISTORY (subcommand)
DISCRIMINANT command, 305

HOLD (keyword)
MATRIX command, 738

HOMOGENEITY (keyword)
GLM command, 476, 492
MANOVA command, 660, 683
ONEWAY command, 856
UNIANOVA command, 1200

HORIZONTAL (keyword)
IGRAPH command, 558

HORIZONTAL (subcommand)

PLOT command, 878

HOTELLING (keyword)
RELIABILITY command, 1010

HOUR (keyword)
DATE command, 259

HUBER (keyword)
EXAMINE command, 352

HYPOTH (keyword)
MANOVA command, 682

I (subcommand)
data organization, 1126
SPCHART command, 1125
variable specification, 1126

ICC (subcommand)
RELIABILITY command, 1010

ICIN (keyword)
REGRESSION command, 999

ID (keyword)
QUICK CLUSTER command, 955
REGRESSION command, 1001

ID (subcommand)
CLUSTER command, 171
CURVEFIT command, 239
EXAMINE command, 348
KM command, 599
LOGISTIC REGRESSION command, 617
PROXIMITIES command, 945
REPEATING DATA command, 1030
TSET command, 1170
TSPLOT command, 1178

IDENT (function)
MATRIX command, 723

!IF (command)
DEFINE command, 283

IF (command), 544
compared to RECODE command, 964
logical expressions, 544
missing values, 545, 546
string data, 545, 546
with LOOP command, 548

IF (keyword)
LOOP command, 639

!IFEND (command)
DEFINE command, 283

IFFT (function)
CREATE command, 215

IGRAPH (command), 550–573

AREA subcommand, 562
BAR subcommand, 563
BOX subcommand, 566
CAPTION subcommand, 558
CATORDER subcommand, 555
CHARTLOOK subcommand, 559
CLUSTER subcommand, 557
COLOR subcommand, 556
COORDINATE subcommand, 558
EFFECT subcommand, 558
ERRORBAR subcommand, 569
FITLINE subcommand, 570
FORMAT subcommand, 561
HISTOGRAM subcommand, 570
KEY keyword, 561
LINE subcommand, 567
PANEL subcommand, 557
PIE subcommand, 564
POINTLABEL subcommand, 557
SCATTER subcommand, 561
SIZE subcommand, 556
SPIKE subcommand, 560
STYLE subcommand, 556
SUBTITLE subcommand, 558
summary functions, 572
SUMMARYVAR subcommand, 557
TITLE subcommand, 558
VIEWNAME subcommand, 558
X1 subcommand, 554
X1LENGTH subcommand, 555
X2 subcommand, 554
X2LENGTH subcommand, 555
Y subcommand, 554
YLENGTH subcommand, 555

IMAGE (keyword)
FACTOR command, 371

IMPORT (command), 574
DROP subcommand, 575
FILE subcommand, 575
KEEP subcommand, 575
MAP subcommand, 577
RENAME subcommand, 576
TYPE subcommand, 575

IMPORTCASES (subcommand)
GET DATA command, 442

IN (keyword)
ALSCAL command, 115
CLUSTER command, 173
DISCRIMINANT command, 307
FACTOR command, 374

MANOVA command, 666
ONEWAY command, 857, 994
PARTIAL CORR command, 871
PROXIMITIES command, 946
REGRESSION command, 994
RELIABILITY command, 1012
IN (subcommand)
ADD FILES command, 87
KEYED DATA LIST command, 593
MATCH FILES command, 703
UPDATE command, 1219
!IN (keyword)
DEFINE command, 284
INCLUDE (command), 578
FILE subcommand, 579
INCLUDE (keyword)
ANOVA command, 127
CLUSTER command, 173
CORRELATIONS command, 194
COXREG command, 207
CROSSTABS command, 229
DESCRIPTIVES command, 291
DISCRIMINANT command, 307
EXAMINE command, 353
FACTOR command, 365
FREQUENCIES command, 419
GLM command, 475
GRAPH command, 534
HILOGLINEAR command, 543
MEANS command, 776
MULT RESPONSE command, 788
NOMREG command, 812, 813
NONPAR CORR command, 820
NPAR TESTS command, 841
ONEWAY command, 856
PARTIAL CORR command, 870
PLOT command, 879
PLUM command, 884
PROBIT command, 930
PROXIMITIES command, 946
RANK command, 963
REGRESSION command, 996
RELIABILITY command, 1012
ROC command, 1074
SUMMARIZE command, 1148
SURVIVAL command, 1159
TSET command, 1170
T-TEST command, 1187
UNIANOVA command, 1199
VARCOMP command, 1230

INDENT (keyword)
REPORT command, 1040
!INDEX (function)
DEFINE command, 280
INDEX (keyword)
DISPLAY command, 312
INDICATOR (keyword)
COXREG command, 205
LOGISTIC REGRESSION command, 613
INDIVIDUAL (keyword)
IGRAPH command, 571
MANOVA command, 665
INDSCAL (keyword)
ALSCAL command, 109
INFO (command), 580
known errors, 582
local documentation, 580, 582
new releases, 582
OUTFILE (subcommand), 583
procedures, 582
update documentation, 580, 582
INITIAL (keyword)
FACTOR command, 367
QUICK CLUSTER command, 955
INITIAL (subcommand)
QUICK CLUSTER command, 954
initial value
in matrix loop structures, 731
INLINE (keyword)
MATRIX DATA command, 758
INPUT (subcommand)
ALSCAL command, 105
INPUT PROGRAM (command), 584
examples, 250, 325, 328, 335, 343
with DATA LIST command, 324
with END subcommand on DATA LIST, 249
with NUMERIC command, 844
with REPEATING DATA command, 1018, 1019, 1021
with REREAD command, 1061
with SAMPLE command, 1078
with STRING command, 1140
with VECTOR command, 1242
INSIDE (keyword)
IGRAPH command, 563, 565
INSTRUMENTS (subcommand)
2SLS command, 1190
INTERCEPT (keyword)
VARCOMP command, 1232
INTERCEPT (subcommand)

GLM command, 475
  NOMREG command, 812
  UNIANOVA command, 1198
  VARCOMP command, 1229

INTERPOLATE (keyword)
  IGRAPH command, 562, 568

INTERVAL (keyword)
  ALSCAL command, 106
  IGRAPH command, 571

INTERVALS (subcommand)
  SURVIVAL command, 1153

INTO (keyword)
  RANK command, 961
  RECODE command, 967

INTO (subcommand)
  AUTORECODE command, 135

INV (function)
  MATRIX command, 723

INV (keyword)
  FACTOR command, 368

INVERSE (keyword)
  CURVEFIT command, 237

IR (subcommand)
  data organization, 1126
  SPCHART command, 1125
  variable specification, 1126

ISTEP (keyword)
  CNLR command, 803

ITER (keyword)
  ALSCAL command, 110
  CNLR command, 802
  COXREG command, 209
  LOGISTIC REGRESSION command, 618
  NLR command, 803

ITERATE (keyword)
  FACTOR command, 370
  HILOGLINEAR command, 539
  LOGISTIC REGRESSION command, 619
  PROBIT command, 928
  VARCOMP command, 1231

JACCARD (keyword)
  CLUSTER command, 165
  PROXIMITIES command, 941

JITTER (keyword)
  IGRAPH command, 562

JOIN (keyword)
  TSPLOT command, 1178

JOINT (keyword)
  MANOVA command, 665

JOURNAL (subcommand)
  SET command, 1107
  SHOW command, 1114

J-T (subcommand)
  NPAR TESTS command, 829

K1 (keyword)
  CLUSTER command, 166
  PROXIMITIES command, 942

K2 (keyword)
  CLUSTER command, 166
  PROXIMITIES command, 942

KAISER (keyword)
  FACTOR command, 370

KAPPA (keyword)
  CROSSTABS command, 228

KEEP (subcommand)
  ADD FILES command, 86
  EXPORT command, 359
  GET command, 433
  GET TRANSLATE command, 459
  IMPORT command, 575
  MATCH FILES command, 702
  SAVE command, 1082
  SAVE TRANSLATE command, 1092
  UPDATE command, 1219
  XSAVE command, 1265

KENDALL (keyword)
  NONPAR CORR command, 819

KENDALL (subcommand)
  NPAR TESTS command, 832

KERNEL (keyword)
  NOMREG command, 814
  PLUM command, 884

KEY (keyword)
  IGRAPH command, 561

KEY (subcommand)
  KEYED DATA LIST command, 592
  POINT command, 890

KEYED DATA LIST (command), 588
  direct-access files, 588
  FILE subcommand, 592
  IN subcommand, 593
  KEY subcommand, 592
  keyed files, 588, 589
  NOTABLE subcommand, 593

TABLE subcommand, 593
KM (command), 594
  BRESLOW keyword, 600
  COMPARE subcommand, 600
  CUMEVENT keyword, 602
  HAZARD keyword, 598, 602
  ID subcommand, 599
  LOGRANK keyword, 600
  LOGSURV keyword, 598
  MEAN keyword, 599
  OMS keyword, 598
  OVERALL keyword, 600
  PAIRWISE keyword, 600
  PERCENTILES subcommand, 599
  PLOT subcommand, 598
  POOLED keyword, 600
  PRINT subcommand, 599
  SAVE subcommand, 602
  SE keyword, 602
  STATUS subcommand, 597
  STRATA keyword, 600
  STRATA subcommand, 598
  SURVIVAL keyword, 598, 602
  TABLE keyword, 599
  TARONE keyword, 600
  TEST subcommand, 600
  TREND subcommand, 601
KMATRIX (subcommand)
  GLM command, 466, 480
  UNIANOVA command, 1204
KMEANS (keyword)
  QUICK CLUSTER command, 954
KMO (keyword)
  FACTOR command, 368
KRONEKER (function)
  MATRIX command, 723
K-S (subcommand)
  NPAR TESTS command, 830
KURT (keyword)
  MEANS command, 775
  SUMMARIZE command, 1147
KURTOSIS (function)
  REPORT command, 1052
KURTOSIS (keyword)
  DESCRIPTIVES command, 289, 290
  FREQUENCIES command, 418
  IGRAPH command, 572
K-W (subcommand)
  NPAR TESTS command, 832

LABEL (keyword)
  IGRAPH command, 562, 563, 565, 566, 567, 569
  REPORT command, 1044, 1048
LABELS (keyword)
  DISPLAY command, 313
  MULT RESPONSE command, 788
  RELIABILITY command, 1011
LAG (function)
  CREATE command, 216
LAGRANGE3 (keyword)
  IGRAPH command, 568
LAGRANGE5 (keyword)
  IGRAPH command, 568
LAMBDA (keyword)
  CLUSTER command, 167
  CROSSTABS command, 227
  PROXIMITIES command, 942
LAST (function)
  AGGREGATE command, 98
LAST (keyword)
  IGRAPH command, 572
  MEANS command, 775
  SUMMARIZE command, 1147
  USE command, 1221
LAST (subcommand)
  ADD FILES command, 88
  MATCH FILES command, 703
LCON (keyword)
  COXREG command, 209
  LOGISTIC REGRESSION command, 619
LCONVERGE (keyword)
  NOMREG command, 812
  PLUM command, 882
LEAD (function)
  CREATE command, 216
LEAST (function)
  REPORT command, 1054
LEAVE (command), 603
LEFT (keyword)
  REPORT command, 1045, 1049, 1058
LEGEND (keyword)
  IGRAPH command, 556
!LENGTH (function)
  DEFINE command, 280
LENGTH (keyword)
  REPORT command, 1039
LENGTH (subcommand)
  REPEATING DATA command, 1027
  SET command, 1111
  SHOW command, 1115

!LET (command)
  DEFINE command, 285
LEVEL (subcommand)
  ALSCAL command, 106
LEVER (keyword)
  GLM command, 488
  LOGISTIC REGRESSION command, 620
  REGRESSION command, 999
  UNIANOVA command, 1211
LFTOLERANCE (keyword)
  CNLR command, 802
LG10 (function)
  MATRIX command, 723
LGSTIC (keyword)
  CURVEFIT command, 237
LIMIT (keyword)
  FREQUENCIES command, 413
limitations
  WLS command, 1251
limitations. See individual procedures
LINE (keyword)
  IGRAPH command, 566, 567, 571
LINE (subcommand)
  GRAPH command, 515
  IGRAPH command, 567
LINEAR (keyword)
  CURVEFIT command, 237
  IGRAPH command, 571
LINEARITY (keyword)
  MEANS command, 776
  SUMMARIZE command, 1149
LINELABEL (keyword)
  IGRAPH command, 567
LINK (subcommand)
  PLUM command, 882
LINT (function)
  RMV command, 1070
LIST (command), 605
  CASES subcommand, 607
  FORMAT subcommand, 607
  VARIABLES subcommand, 606
  with SAMPLE command, 607
  with SELECT IF command, 607
  with SPLIT FILE command, 608
LIST (keyword)
  DATA LIST command, 245
  MATRIX DATA command, 759
  REPORT command, 1039, 1060
LIST (subcommand)
  SUMMARIZE command, 1148

LISTING (keyword)
  SET command, 1106
LISTWISE (keyword)
  CLUSTER command, 173
  CORRELATIONS command, 194
  DESCRIPTIVES command, 291
  EXAMINE command, 352
  FACTOR command, 364
  GRAPH command, 534
  HILOGLINEAR command, 543
  NONPAR CORR command, 820
  NPAR TESTS command, 841
  ONEWAY command, 856
  PARTIAL CORR command, 870
  PLOT command, 879
  PROBIT command, 930
  PROXIMITIES command, 946
  REGRESSION command, 996
  SURVIVAL command, 1159
  T-TEST command, 1187
LJUMP (keyword)
  IGRAPH command, 568
LLEFT (keyword)
  IGRAPH command, 565
LLR (keyword)
  IGRAPH command, 571
LM (keyword)
  COXREG command, 210
LMATRIX (subcommand)
  GLM command, 466, 479
  UNIANOVA command, 1202
LML (keyword)
  COXREG command, 211
LN (function)
  MATRIX command, 723
LN (subcommand)
  ACF command, 78
  CCF command, 155
  PACF command, 863
  PPLOT command, 899
  TSPLOT command, 1177
LOCAL (keyword)
  INFO command, 582
LOCATION (subcommand)
  PLUM command, 883
LOF (keyword)
  GLM command, 477
  UNIANOVA command, 1200
LOG (subcommand)
  PROBIT command, 927

LOGARITHMIC (keyword)
  CURVEFIT command, 237
LOGISTIC REGRESSION (command), 609
  CASEWISE subcommand, 620
  CATEGORICAL subcommand, 613
  CLASSPLOT subcommand, 620
  CONTRAST subcommand, 613
  CRITERIA subcommand, 618
  EXTERNAL subcommand, 622
  ID subcommand, 617
  METHOD subcommand, 615
  MISSING subcommand, 621
  NOORIGIN subcommand, 617
  ORIGIN subcommand, 617
  PRINT subcommand, 618
  SAVE subcommand, 621
  SELECT subcommand, 617
  VARIABLES subcommand, 612
LOGIT (keyword)
  PLUM command, 882
  PROBIT command, 927
LOGLINEAR (command), 623
  cell weights, 628
  CONTRAST subcommand, 630
  covariates, 634
  CRITERIA subcommand, 632
  CWEIGHT subcommand, 628
  DESIGN subcommand, 634
  equiprobability model, 634
  general loglinear model, 627
  GRESID subcommand, 629
  interaction terms, 634
  logit model, 627, 631
  main-effects model, 634
  measures of association, 627
  MISSING subcommand, 634
  NOPRINT subcommand, 632
  PLOT subcommand, 633
  PRINT subcommand, 632
  simultaneous linear logit model, 635
  single-degree-of-freedom partitions, 634
  statistics, 632
  structural zeros, 628
  variable list, 627
LOGRANK (keyword)
  KM command, 600
LOGSURV (keyword)
  KM command, 598
  SURVIVAL command, 1155
LOOP (command), 637

  examples, 335
  increment value, 643
  indexing clause, 639
  initial value, 640
  logical expressions, 639
  missing values, 644
  nested, 638, 641
  terminal value, 640
  with END CASE command, 645
  with END FILE command, 645
  with SET command, 1109
  with SET MXLOOPS command, 637, 638, 640
  with VECTOR command, 1239, 1240
LOOP (statement)
  MATRIX command, 731
LOSS (keyword)
  CNLR command, 800
LOSS (subcommand)
  CNLR command, 805
LOW (keyword)
  RANK command, 896, 962
LOWER (keyword)
  MATRIX DATA command, 759
LOWEST (keyword)
  COUNT command, 197
  MISSING VALUES command, 779
  RECODE command, 965
LR (keyword)
  COXREG command, 207
LRECL (subcommand)
  FILE HANDLE command, 379
LRESID (keyword)
  LOGISTIC REGRESSION command, 620
LRIGHT (keyword)
  IGRAPH command, 565
LRT (keyword)
  NOMREG command, 814
LSD (keyword)
  GLM command, 485
  ONEWAY command, 854
  UNIANOVA command, 1209
LSL (subcommand)
  SPCHART command, 1135
LSTEP (keyword)
  IGRAPH command, 562, 568
LSTOLERANCE (keyword)
  CNLR command, 802

MA (function)
  CREATE command, 217
macro facility
  with MATRIX command, 749
MACROS (keyword)
  DISPLAY command, 313
MAGIC (function)
  MATRIX command, 723
MAHAL (keyword)
  DISCRIMINANT command, 298
  REGRESSION command, 999
MAKE (function)
  MATRIX command, 723
MANOVA (command), 646
  ANALYSIS subcommand, 657, 677
  CELLINFO keyword, 659
  CINTERVAL subcommand, 665, 685
  constant covariate, 690
  CONSTANT keyword, 674
  CONTRAST subcommand, 654, 692
  DESIGN keyword, 661
  DESIGN subcommand, 653
  DEVIATION keyword, 655
  DIFFERENCE keyword, 655, 692
  DISCRIM subcommand, 684
  doubly multivariate repeated measures, 688
  ERROR keyword, 661
  ERROR subcommand, 653
  HELMERT keyword, 655, 692
  HOMOGENEITY keyword, 660
  MATRIX subcommand, 666
  MEASURE subcommand, 694
  METHOD subcommand, 657
  MISSING subcommand, 665
  multivariate syntax, 676
  MUPLUS keyword, 672
  MWITHIN keyword, 671, 694
  NOPRINT subcommand, 658, 681
  OMEANS subcommand, 661, 677
  PARAMETERS keyword, 659
  PARTITION subcommand, 656
  PCOMPS subcommand, 683
  PLOT subcommand, 683
  PMEANS subcommand, 662
  POLYNOMIAL keyword, 692
  POOL keyword, 673
  POWER subcommand, 664, 685
  PRINT subcommand, 658, 681
  RENAME subcommand, 677, 680, 695
  REPEATED keyword, 655

  RESIDUAL keyword, 653
  RESIDUALS subcommand, 663
  SIGNIF keyword, 660
  SIMPLE keyword, 655
  SPECIAL keyword, 656
  TRANSFORM subcommand, 680
  variable list, 690
  variables specification, 677
  VS keyword, 673
  with AUTORECODE command, 135
  WITHIN keyword, 653, 670
  within-subjects factors, 688
  WSDESIGN subcommand, 692
  WSFACTORS subcommand, 690
MANUAL (keyword)
  REPORT command, 1039
MAP (keyword)
  DISCRIMINANT command, 306
MAP (subcommand)
  ADD FILES command, 88
  EXPORT command, 360
  GET command, 434
  GET TRANSLATE command, 460
  IMPORT command, 577
  MATCH FILES command, 704
  SAVE command, 1083
  SAVE TRANSLATE command, 1093
  UPDATE command, 1220
  XSAVE command, 1267
MARGINS (keyword)
  REPORT command, 1039
MARK (subcommand)
  TSPLOT command, 1181
MAT (keyword)
  MATRIX DATA command, 764
MATCH FILES (command), 697
  BY subcommand, 700
  DROP subcommand, 702
  duplicate cases, 701
  FILE subcommand, 699
  FIRST subcommand, 703
  IN subcommand, 703
  KEEP subcommand, 702
  LAST subcommand, 703
  limitations, 699
  MAP subcommand, 704
  RENAME subcommand, 702
  table lookup files, 701
  TABLE subcommand, 701
  with DATA LIST command, 700

with DROP DOCUMENTS command, 699
with SORT CASES command, 1118
working data file, 700
MATRIX (command), 705
  BREAK statement, 732
  CALL statement, 726
  COMPUTE statement, 718
  DISPLAY statement, 748
  DO IF statement, 730
  ELSE IF statement, 730
  ELSE statement, 730
  END IF statement, 730
  END LOOP statement, 731
  GET statement, 738
  LOOP statement, 731
  MGET statement, 743
  MSAVE statement, 745
  PRINT statement, 727
  READ statement, 733
  RELEASE statement, 749
  SAVE statement, 741
  with macro facility, 749
  WRITE statement, 736
MATRIX (keyword)
  ALSCAL command, 107
  GRAPH command, 527
  PARTIAL CORR command, 870
MATRIX (subcommand)
  ALSCAL command, 115
  CLUSTER command, 173
  CORRELATIONS command, 194
  DISCRIMINANT command, 307
  FACTOR command, 374
  MANOVA command, 666
  MCONVERT command, 770
  NONPAR CORR command, 820
  ONEWAY command, 857
  PARTIAL CORR command, 870
  PROXIMITIES command, 946
  REGRESSION command, 994
  RELIABILITY command, 1012
MATRIX DATA (command), 750
  CELLS subcommand, 763
  CONTENTS subcommand, 764
  data-entry format, 759
  entering data, 753
  FACTORS subcommand, 762
  field separators, 753
  FILE subcommand, 758
  FORMAT subcommand, 759

matrix shape, 759
N subcommand, 767
ROWTYPE_ variable, 751, 757
scientific notation, 753
SPLIT subcommand, 760
VARIABLES subcommand, 756
VARNAME_ variable, 757
with DISCRIMINANT command, 754
with ONEWAY command, 756
with REGRESSION command, 755
MATRIX functions, 719
MAX (function)
  AGGREGATE command, 97
  REPORT command, 1052
MAX (keyword)
  DESCRIPTIVES command, 290
  IGRAPH command, 556
  MEANS command, 775
  PLOT command, 878
  PROXIMITIES command, 936
  SUMMARIZE command, 1147
MAXIMUM (function)
  GRAPH command, 506
MAXIMUM (keyword)
  FREQUENCIES command, 414, 415, 418
  IGRAPH command, 572
MAXMINF (keyword)
  DISCRIMINANT command, 298
MAXORDER (subcommand)
  HILOGLINEAR command, 538
MAXORDERS (subcommand)
  ANOVA command, 122
MAXSTEPS (keyword)
  HILOGLINEAR command, 539
  REGRESSION command, 990
MAXSTEPS (subcommand)
  DISCRIMINANT command, 300
MC (keyword)
  CROSSTABS command, 228
  NPAR TESTS command, 842
MCA (keyword)
  ANOVA command, 126
MCIN (keyword)
  REGRESSION command, 999
MCNEMAR (subcommand)
  NPAR TESTS command, 834
MCONVERT (command), 769
  APPEND subcommand, 771
  MATRIX subcommand, 770
  REPLACE subcommand, 771

MDGROUP (keyword)
MULT RESPONSE command, 788

MDIAG (function)
MATRIX command, 723

MEAN (function)
AGGREGATE command, 97
GRAPH command, 506
REPORT command, 1052
RMV command, 1071

MEAN (keyword)
ANOVA command, 126
DESCRIPTIVES command, 289, 290
DISCRIMINANT command, 304
FREQUENCIES command, 418
IGRAPH command, 571, 572
KM command, 599
MATRIX DATA command, 764
MEANS command, 774
NPAR TESTS command, 838
OLAP CUBES command, 848
PROXIMITIES command, 936
RANK command, 896, 962
REGRESSION command, 992
SUMMARIZE command, 1147

MEANS (command), 772
CELLS subcommand, 774
limitations, 773
MISSING subcommand, 776
STATISTICS subcommand, 775
TABLES subcommand, 774

MEANS (keyword)
RELIABILITY command, 1011

MEANSUBSTITUTION (keyword)
DISCRIMINANT command, 306
FACTOR command, 365
REGRESSION command, 996

MEASURE (subcommand)
CLUSTER command, 162
GLM command, 502
MANOVA command, 694
PROXIMITIES command, 936

MEDIAN (function)
GRAPH command, 506
REPORT command, 1053
RMV command, 1071

MEDIAN (keyword)
CLUSTER command, 170
FREQUENCIES command, 418
IGRAPH command, 566, 572
MEANS command, 774

NPAR TESTS command, 838
OLAP CUBES command, 848
SUMMARIZE command, 1147

MEDIAN (subcommand)
NPAR TESTS command, 835

MEFFECT (keyword)
IGRAPH command, 571

MESSAGES (subcommand)
SET command, 1106
SHOW command, 1115

MESTIMATORS (subcommand)
EXAMINE command, 351

METHOD (subcommand)
ALSCAL command, 109
ANOVA command, 122
CLUSTER command, 169
COXREG command, 206
CROSSTABS command, 228
DISCRIMINANT command, 298
GLM command, 473
HILOGLINEAR command, 538
LOGISTIC REGRESSION command, 615
MANOVA command, 657
NPAR TESTS command, 829, 842
QUICK CLUSTER command, 954
REGRESSION command, 985
RELIABILITY command, 1011
UNIANOVA command, 1197
VARCOMP command, 1229

MEXPAND (subcommand)
SET command, 281, 1112
SHOW command, 1115

MGET (statement)
MATRIX command, 743

MH (subcommand)
NPAR TESTS command, 835

MIN (function)
AGGREGATE command, 97
REPORT command, 1052

MIN (keyword)
DESCRIPTIVES command, 289, 290
IGRAPH command, 556
MEANS command, 775
OLAP CUBES command, 848
PLOT command, 878
SUMMARIZE command, 1147

MINEIGEN (keyword)
FACTOR command, 370
MANOVA command, 684

MINIMUM (function)

GRAPH command, 506
MINIMUM (keyword)
  FREQUENCIES command, 414, 415, 418
  IGRAPH command, 572
MINKOWSKI (keyword)
  CLUSTER command, 163
  PROXIMITIES command, 938
MINORITERATION (keyword)
  CNLR command, 802
MINQUE (keyword)
  VARCOMP command, 1229
MINRESID (keyword)
  DISCRIMINANT command, 298
MINSAMPLE (subcommand)
  SPCHART command, 1135
MINUTE (keyword)
  DATE command, 259
MISSING (keyword)
  COUNT command, 197, 198
  IGRAPH command, 562, 567
  MATRIX command, 740
  RECODE command, 965
  REPORT command, 1040
  ROC command, 1074
  SUMMARIZE command, 1148
MISSING (subcommand)
  AGGREGATE command, 99
  ANOVA command, 127
  CLUSTER command, 173
  CORRELATIONS command, 194
  COXREG command, 207
  CROSSTABS command, 229
  DESCRIPTIVES command, 291
  DISCRIMINANT command, 307
  EXAMINE command, 352
  FACTOR command, 364
  FILE TYPE command, 392
  FREQUENCIES command, 419
  GENLOG command, 428
  GLM command, 475
  GRAPH command, 533
  HILOGLINEAR command, 543
  LOGISTIC REGRESSION command, 621
  LOGLINEAR command, 634
  MANOVA command, 665
  MEANS command, 776
  MULT RESPONSE command, 787
  NOMREG command, 812
  NONPAR CORR command, 820
  NPAR TESTS command, 841

ONEWAY command, 856
PARTIAL CORR command, 870
PLOT command, 879
PLUM command, 884
PROBIT command, 930
PROXIMITIES command, 946
QUICK CLUSTER command, 957
RANK command, 963
RECORD TYPE command, 976
REGRESSION command, 996
RELIABILITY command, 1011
REPORT command, 1059
SPCHART command, 1136
SUMMARIZE command, 1148
SURVIVAL command, 1159
TSET command, 1170
T-TEST command, 1186
UNIANOVA command, 1199
VARCOMP command, 1230
MISSING VALUES (command), 777
  value range, 779
  with RECODE command, 966
MITERATE (subcommand)
  SET command, 282, 1108
  SHOW command, 1115
MIXED (keyword)
  FILE TYPE command, 386
ML (keyword)
  FACTOR command, 371
  VARCOMP command, 1229
MMATRIX (subcommand)
  GLM command, 466, 493
MMAX (function)
  MATRIX command, 723
MMIN (function)
  MATRIX command, 723
MNEST (subcommand)
  SET command, 281, 1108
  SHOW command, 1115
MOD (function)
  MATRIX command, 724
MODE (function)
  GRAPH command, 506
  REPORT command, 1053
MODE (keyword)
  FREQUENCIES command, 418
  IGRAPH command, 562, 563, 567, 572
  MATRIX command, 735
  NPAR TESTS command, 838
MODE (subcommand)

FILE HANDLE command, 378

MODEL (keyword)
 NOMREG (subcommand), 814

MODEL (subcommand)
 ALSCAL command, 109
 CURVEFIT command, 237
 GENLOG command, 425
 NOMREG command, 813
 PROBIT command, 926
 RELIABILITY command, 1009

MODEL PROGRAM (command)
 with CNLR/NLR command, 793, 795

MONTH (keyword)
 DATE command, 259

MOSES (subcommand)
 NPAR TESTS command, 837

MPRINT (subcommand)
 SET command, 281, 1112
 SHOW command, 1115

MRBAR (keyword)
 SPCHART command, 1134

MRGROUP (keyword)
 MULT RESPONSE command, 788

MSAVE (statement)
 MATRIX command, 745

MSE (keyword)
 MATRIX DATA command, 764

MSSQ (function)
 MATRIX command, 724

MSUM (function)
 MATRIX command, 724

MULT RESPONSE (command), 780
 BASE subcommand, 787
 CELLS subcommand, 786
 FORMAT subcommand, 788
 FREQUENCIES subcommand, 784
 GROUPS subcommand, 782
 limitations, 782
 MISSING subcommand, 787
 multiple-dichotomy groups, 780
 multiple-response groups, 780
 PAIRED keyword, 786
 TABLES subcommand, 785
 VARIABLES subcommand, 783

MULTIPLE (keyword)
 GRAPH command, 515

MULTIPLY (function)
 REPORT command, 1054

MULTIPUNCH (keyword)
 FILE HANDLE command, 379

MULTIV (keyword)
 MANOVA command, 682

MUPLUS (keyword)
 MANOVA command, 672

M-W (subcommand)
 NPAR TESTS command, 833

MWITHIN (keyword)
 MANOVA command, 671, 694

MXAUTO (subcommand)
 ACF command, 79
 PACF command, 864

MXCELLS (subcommand)
 SHOW command, 1103, 1115

MXCROSS (subcommand)
 CCF command, 156

MXERRS (subcommand)
 SET command, 1108

MXITER (keyword)
 NOMREG command, 812
 PLUM command, 882
 QUICK CLUSTER command, 954

MXLOOPS (subcommand)
 SET command, 1109
 SHOW command, 1115
 with LOOP command, 637, 638, 640

MXMEMORY (subcommand)
 SHOW command, 1103, 1115

MXNEWVAR (subcommand)
 TSET command, 1170

MXPREDICT (subcommand)
 TSET command, 1171

MXSTEP (keyword)
 NOMREG command, 812
 PLUM command, 882

MXWARNS (subcommand)
 SET command, 1108
 SHOW command, 1115

N (function)
 AGGREGATE command, 98
 GRAPH command, 506

N (keyword)
 IGRAPH command, 562, 563, 565, 566, 567, 569
 MATRIX DATA command, 764
 REGRESSION command, 993
 SPCHART command, 1132

N (subcommand)
 MATRIX DATA command, 767

RANK command, 960
SHOW command, 1115
N OF CASES (command), 808
  with SAMPLE command, 808, 1078
  with SELECT IF command, 808, 1096
  with TEMPORARY command, 808
N_MATRIX (keyword)
  MATRIX DATA command, 764
N_SCALAR (keyword)
  MATRIX DATA command, 764
N_VECTOR (keyword)
  MATRIX DATA command, 764
NAME (keyword)
  DESCRIPTIVES command, 290
  REPORT command, 1050
NAMES (keyword)
  DISPLAY command, 312
  MATRIX command, 740
NATRES (subcommand)
  PROBIT command, 928
NCOL (function)
  MATRIX command, 724
NCOMP (keyword)
  MANOVA command, 684
NEGATIVE (keyword)
  ALSCAL command, 110
NEQ (keyword)
  IGRAPH command, 564, 572
NESTED (keyword)
  FILE TYPE command, 386
NEW FILE (command), 790
NEWNAMES (subcommand)
  FLIP command, 405–406
NFTOLERANCE (keyword)
  CNLR command, 802
NGE (keyword)
  IGRAPH command, 564, 572
NGT (function)
  GRAPH command, 506
NGT (keyword)
  IGRAPH command, 564, 572
NIN (function)
  GRAPH command, 507
NIN (keyword)
  IGRAPH command, 564, 572
NLE (keyword)
  IGRAPH command, 564, 572
NLOGLOG (keyword)
  PLUM command, 882
NLR (command), 791

CRITERIA subcommand, 801, 803
DERIVATIVES command, 793, 796
FILE subcommand, 798
iteration criteria, 803
missing values, 794
OUTFILE subcommand, 798
PRED subcommand, 799
SAVE subcommand, 800
weighting cases, 794
with MODEL PROGRAM command, 793, 795
NLT (function)
  GRAPH command, 506
NLT (keyword)
  IGRAPH command, 564, 572
NMISS (function)
  AGGREGATE command, 98
NO (keyword)
  SET command, 1102
NOCASENUM (keyword)
  SUMMARIZE command, 1148
NOCONFORM (subcommand)
  SPCHART command, 1135
NOCONSTANT (subcommand)
  CURVEFIT command, 238
  WLS command, 1253
NOCONSTANT subcommand
  2SLS command, 1191
NOCUM (keyword)
  GRAPH command, 530
NODIAGONAL (keyword)
  MATRIX DATA command, 759
!NOEXPAND (keyword)
  DEFINE command, 279
NOFILL (keyword)
  TSPLOT command, 1178
NOINITIAL (keyword)
  QUICK CLUSTER command, 953
NOJOIN (keyword)
  TSPLOT command, 1178
NOKAISER (keyword)
  FACTOR command, 370
NOLABELS (keyword)
  MULT RESPONSE command, 788
  RELIABILITY command, 1011
NOLIST (keyword)
  REPORT command, 1039
  SUMMARIZE command, 1148
NOLOG (subcommand)
  ACF command, 78
  CCF command, 155

PACF command, 863
PPLOT command, 899
TSPLOT command, 1177
NOMINAL (keyword)
    ALSCAL command, 106
NOMREG (command), 810
    BIAS keyword, 811
    BY keyword, 811
    CELLPROB keyword, 814
    CIN keyword, 811
    CLASSTABLE keyword, 814
    CORB keyword, 814
    COVB keyword, 814
    CRITERIA subcommand, 811
    DELTA keyword, 811
    DEVIANCE keyword, 815
    EXCLUDE keyword, 812
    FIT keyword, 814
    FULLFACTORIAL subcommand, 812
    HISTORY keyword, 814
    INCLUDE keyword, 812, 813
    INTERCEPT subcommand, 812
    KERNEL keyword, 814
    LCONVERGE keyword, 812
    LRT keyword, 814
    MISSING subcommand, 812
    MODEL subcommand, 813
    MXITER keyword, 812
    MXSTEP keyword, 812
    OUTFILE subcommand, 814
    PARAMETER keyword, 815
    PCONVERGE keyword, 812
    PEARSON keyword, 815
    PRINT subcommand, 814
    SCALE subcommand, 815
    SINGULAR keyword, 812
    SUBPOP subcommand, 815
    SUMMARY keyword, 815
    TEST subcommand, 815
    WITH keyword, 811
NOMREG (subcommand)
    BY keyword, 813
    MODEL keyword, 814
    WITHIN keyword, 813
NONAME (keyword)
    REPORT command, 1050
NONE (keyword)
    ANOVA command, 122, 126
    CLUSTER command, 171, 172
    COXREG command, 210
    CROSSTABS command, 227, 228, 230

CURVEFIT command, 239
DISCRIMINANT command, 305
EXAMINE command, 349, 350, 351, 352
FREQUENCIES command, 418
HILOGLINEAR command, 542
IGRAPH command, 557, 562, 567, 569, 570
MEANS command, 776
PARTIAL CORR command, 869
QUICK CLUSTER command, 956
REPORT command, 1060
ROC command, 1076
SET command, 1106
SUMMARIZE command, 1149
SURVIVAL command, 1160
NONMISSING (keyword)
    DISCRIMINANT command, 306
NONORMAL (keyword)
    FREQUENCIES command, 415
NONPAR CORR (command), 817
    limitations, 818
    matrix output, 817
    MATRIX subcommand, 820
    MISSING subcommand, 820
    missing values, 821
    PRINT subcommand, 819
    random sampling, 817, 819
    SAMPLE subcommand, 819
    significance tests, 817, 819
    VARIABLES subcommand, 818
    with RECODE command, 820
NOORIGIN (subcommand)
    LOGISTIC REGRESSION command, 617
    REGRESSION command, 990
NOPRINT (subcommand)
    LOGLINEAR command, 632
    MANOVA command, 658, 681
NOREFERENCE (keyword)
    TSPLOT command, 1178
NOREPORT (keyword)
    EXAMINE command, 353
    GRAPH command, 534
NORMAL (keyword)
    FREQUENCIES command, 415
    IGRAPH command, 571
    NPAR TESTS command, 830
    PPLOT command, 897
NORMAL (subcommand)
    RANK command, 960
NORMPLOT (keyword)
    HILOGLINEAR command, 542

NORMPROB (keyword)
  REGRESSION command, 1000
NOROTATE (keyword)
  FACTOR command, 372
  MANOVA command, 684
NOSIG (keyword)
  CORRELATIONS command, 193
  NONPAR CORR command, 819
NOSTANDARDIZE (subcommand)
  PPLOT command, 898
NOTABLE (keyword)
  FREQUENCIES command, 413
  SURVIVAL command, 1156
NOTABLE (subcommand)
  DATA LIST command, 247
  KEYED DATA LIST command, 593
  PRINT command, 912
  REPEATING DATA command, 1031
  WRITE command, 1259
NOTABLES (keyword)
  CROSSTABS command, 230
NOTOTAL (keyword)
  SUMMARIZE command, 1148
NOTOTAL (subcommand)
  EXAMINE command, 348
NOULB (keyword)
  ALSCAL command, 111
NOWARN (keyword)
  FILE TYPE command, 391
  RECORD TYPE command, 976
  SET command, 1108
NP (subcommand)
  data organization, 1128
  SPCHART command, 1127
  variable specification, 1129
NPAR TESTS (command), 823
  BINOMIAL subcommand, 826
  CHISQUARE subcommand, 827
  COCHRAN subcommand, 828
  EXPECTED subcommand, 827
  FRIEDMAN subcommand, 828
  independent-samples test, 824
  J-T subcommand, 829
  KENDALL subcommand, 832
  K-S subcommand, 830
  K-W subcommand, 832
  limitations, 825
  MCNEMAR subcommand, 834
  MEDIAN subcommand, 835
  METHOD subcommand, 842
  MH subcommand, 835
  MISSING subcommand, 841
  MOSES subcommand, 837
  M-W subcommand, 833
  one-sample test, 824
  pairing variables, 834, 836
  random sampling, 841
  related-samples test, 824
  RUNS subcommand, 838
  SAMPLE subcommand, 841
  SIGN subcommand, 838
  STATISTICS subcommand, 841
  WILCOXON subcommand, 840
  W-W subcommand, 839
NPCT (keyword)
  LAYERED REPORTS command, 1147
  MEANS command, 775
  OLAP CUBES command, 848
NPCT(var) (keyword)
  MEANS command, 775
NPPLOT (keyword)
  EXAMINE command, 350
NPPLOT. See PPLOT.
NROW (function)
  MATRIX command, 724
NTILES (subcommand)
  FREQUENCIES command, 417
NTILES(k) (subcommand)
  RANK command, 961
NU (function)
  AGGREGATE command, 98
!NULL (function)
  DEFINE command, 281
NUM (keyword)
  IGRAPH command, 570
NUMBERED (command), 843
NUMBERED (keyword)
  LIST command, 607
NUMERIC (command), 844
  formats, 844, 845
  with DATA LIST command, 845
  with INPUT PROGRAM command, 844, 845
  with SET command, 844
NUMERIC (subcommand)
  REFORMAT command, 979
NUMIN (keyword)
  IGRAPH command, 565
NUMISS (function)
  AGGREGATE command, 98

OBELISK (keyword)
  IGRAPH command, 563
OBLIMIN (keyword)
  FACTOR command, 372
OBS (keyword)
  DATE command, 259
OBS (subcommand)
  FIT command, 401
OCCURS (subcommand)
  REPEATING DATA command, 1025
OCHIAI (keyword)
  CLUSTER command, 168
  PROXIMITIES command, 943
ODBC (keyword)
  GET DATA command, 439
OF (keyword)
  PROBIT command, 925
OFF (keyword)
  SPLIT FILE command, 1137
!OFFEXPAND (keyword)
  DEFINE command, 279
OFFSET (keyword)
  REPORT command, 1046, 1049
OLAP CUBES (command), 846
  CELLS subcommand, 848
  FOOTNOTE subcommand, 847
  TITLE subcommand, 847
OMEANS (subcommand)
  MANOVA command, 661, 677
OMS (keyword)
  COXREG command, 210
  KM command, 598
  SURVIVAL command, 1156
ONEBREAKCOLUMN (keyword)
  REPORT command, 1040
ONEPAGE (keyword)
  MULT RESPONSE command, 789
ONETAIL (keyword)
  CORRELATIONS command, 193
  NONPAR CORR command, 819
  PARTIAL CORR command, 869
ONEWAY (command), 850
  analysis design, 852
  BONFERRONI keyword, 854
  BTUKEY keyword, 854
  C keyword, 855
  CONTRAST subcommand, 852
  DUNCAN keyword, 854
  DUNNETT keyword, 854
  DUNNETTL keyword, 854

DUNNETTR keyword, 854
FREGW keyword, 855
GABRIEL keyword, 855
GH keyword, 855
GT2 keyword, 855
limitations, 851
LSD keyword, 854
matrix input, 857
matrix output, 857
MATRIX subcommand, 857
MISSING subcommand, 856
PLOT MEANS subcommand, 856
POLYNOMIAL subcommand, 852
QREGW, 855
RANGES subcommand, 855
SCHEFFE keyword, 854
SIDAK keyword, 855
SNK keyword, 854
STATISTICS subcommand, 856
T2 keyword, 855
T3 keyword, 855
TUKEY keyword, 854
WALLER keyword, 855
with MATRIX DATA command, 756
One-Way ANOVA
  post hoc tests, 853
!ONEXPAND (keyword)
  DEFINE command, 279
ONUMBERS (subcommand)
  SET command, 1104
  SHOW command, 1115
OPOWER (keyword)
  GLM command, 477
  UNIANOVA command, 1200
OPTIMAL (keyword)
  MANOVA command, 660
OPTOL (keyword)
  PROBIT command, 927
OPTOLERANCE (keyword)
  CNLR command, 803
ORDERED (subcommand)
  FILE TYPE command, 394
ORDINAL (keyword)
  ALSCAL command, 106
ORIGIN (keyword)
  IGRAPH command, 571
ORIGIN (subcommand)
  LOGISTIC REGRESSION command, 617
  REGRESSION command, 990
ORTHONORM (keyword)

MANOVA command, 678
OTHER (keyword)
RECORD TYPE command, 973
OUT (keyword)
CLUSTER command, 173
CORRELATIONS command, 194
DISCRIMINANT command, 307
FACTOR command, 374
MANOVA command, 666
NONPAR CORR command, 820
ONEWAY command, 857
PARTIAL CORR command, 871
PROXIMITIES command, 946
REGRESSION command, 994
RELIABILITY command, 1012
OUTFILE (keyword)
MATRIX command, 736, 741, 746
OUTFILE (subcommand)
AGGREGATE command, 95
ALSCAL command, 113
CNLR/NLR command, 798
COXREG command, 210
DISCRIMINANT command, 299
EXPORT command, 358
GLM command, 488
INFO command, 583
NOMREG command, 814
PRINT command, 911
PRINT SPACE command, 919
PROCEDURE OUTPUT command, 931
QUICK CLUSTER command, 956
REGRESSION command, 1003
REPORT command, 1041
SAVE command, 1081
SAVE TRANSLATE command, 1089
UNIANOVA command, 1211
VARCOMP command, 1231
WRITE command, 1259
XSAVE command, 1265
OUTLIERS (keyword)
IGRAPH command, 566
LOGISTIC REGRESSION command, 621
REGRESSION command, 1000, 1001
OUTS (keyword)
REGRESSION command, 988
OUTSIDE (keyword)
IGRAPH command, 563, 565
OVARS (subcommand)
SET command, 1104
SHOW command, 1115

OVERALL (keyword)
KM command, 600
OVERLAY (keyword)
GRAPH command, 526
PLOT command, 878
OVERVIEW (keyword)
INFO command, 582

P (keyword)
HILOGLINEAR command, 539
PROBIT command, 928
P (subcommand)
data organization, 1128
SPCHART command, 1127
variable specification, 1129
PA1 (keyword)
FACTOR command, 371
PA2 (keyword)
FACTOR command, 371
PACF (command), 860
APPLY subcommand, 864
DIFF subcommand, 862
LN/NOLOG subcommands, 863
MXAUTO subcommand, 864
PERIOD subcommand, 863
SDIFF subcommand, 862
SEASONAL subcommand, 863
VARIABLES subcommand, 862
PACF (subcommand)
ACF command, 80
PAF (keyword)
FACTOR command, 371
PAGE (argument)
REPORT command, 1059
PAGE (keyword)
REPORT command, 1039, 1050
PAIR (keyword)
PLOT command, 877
PAIRED (keyword)
MULT RESPONSE command, 786
NPAR TESTS command, 825, 834, 836, 839, 840
T-TEST command, 1186
PAIRS (subcommand)
T-TEST command, 1186
PAIRWISE (keyword)
CORRELATIONS command, 194
EXAMINE command, 353
FACTOR command, 364

KM command, 600
NONPAR CORR command, 820
REGRESSION command, 996
SURVIVAL command, 1158
PANEL (subcommand)
IGRAPH command, 557
PARALL (keyword)
PROBIT command, 930
PARALLEL (keyword)
PLUM command, 884
RELIABILITY command, 1009
PARAMETER (keyword)
GLM command, 476
NOMREG command, 815
PLUM command, 884
UNIANOVA command, 1200
PARAMETERS (keyword)
MANOVA command, 659
PARETO (subcommand)
GRAPH command, 530
PARTIAL CORR (command), 866
control variables, 868
correlation list, 868
FORMAT subcommand, 870
limitations, 867
matrix input, 871
matrix output, 871
MATRIX subcommand, 870
MISSING subcommand, 870
order values, 868
SIGNIFICANCE subcommand, 869
STATISTICS subcommand, 869
VARIABLES subcommand, 868
PARTIALPLOT (subcommand)
REGRESSION command, 1002
PARTITION (subcommand)
MANOVA command, 656
PATTERN (keyword)
CLUSTER command, 168
PROXIMITIES command, 944
PATTERN (subcommand)
COXREG command, 210
PC (keyword)
FACTOR command, 371
$PCT (keyword)
IGRAPH command, 554, 557, 562, 563, 564, 567, 570
PCOMPS (subcommand)
MANOVA command, 683
PCON (keyword)

NLR command, 804
PCONVERGE (keyword)
NOMREG command, 812
PLUM command, 882
PCPROB (keyword)
PLUM command, 885
PCT (function)
GRAPH command, 506
REPORT command, 1054
PCT (keyword)
IGRAPH command, 562, 565, 567
PEARSON (keyword)
NOMREG command, 815
PEARSON CORR (command)
See CORRELATIONS
PEQ (keyword)
IGRAPH command, 573
PERCENT (function)
REPORT command, 1053
PERCENT (keyword)
FREQUENCIES command, 415
PERCENT (subcommand)
RANK command, 960
PERCENTILES (subcommand)
EXAMINE command, 348
FREQUENCIES command, 417
KM command, 599
PERIOD (subcommand)
ACF command, 78
CCF command, 155
PACF command, 863
PPLOT command, 899
TSET command, 1171
TSPLOT command, 1177
PGE (keyword)
IGRAPH command, 573
PGROUP (keyword)
LOGISTIC REGRESSION command, 620
PGT (function)
AGGREGATE command, 97
GRAPH command, 506
REPORT command, 1053
PGT (keyword)
IGRAPH command, 573
PH2 (keyword)
CLUSTER command, 163
PROXIMITIES command, 939
PHI (keyword)
CLUSTER command, 168
CROSSTABS command, 227

PROXIMITIES command, 944

PIE (subcommand)
  GRAPH command, 521
  IGRAPH command, 564

PIN (function)
  AGGREGATE command, 97
  GRAPH command, 507
  REPORT command, 1053

PIN (keyword)
  COXREG command, 209
  IGRAPH command, 573
  LOGISTIC REGRESSION command, 619
  REGRESSION command, 990

PIN (subcommand)
  DISCRIMINANT command, 299

PLAIN (keyword)
  REPORT command, 1057

PLE (keyword)
  IGRAPH command, 573

PLOT (command), 875
  control variables, 877
  FORMAT subcommand, 877
  HORIZONTAL subcommand, 878
  limitations, 876
  MISSING subcommand, 879
  missing values, 879
  plot labeling, 878
  plot scaling, 878
  PLOT subcommand, 876
  plot types, 875, 877
  TITLE subcommand, 879
  VERTICAL subcommand, 878

PLOT (keyword)
  REGRESSION command, 1001

PLOT (subcommand)
  ALSCAL command, 112
  CLUSTER command, 172
  COXREG command, 209
  CURVEFIT command, 239
  DISCRIMINANT command, 306
  EXAMINE command, 349
  FACTOR command, 368
  GENLOG command, 427
  GLM command, 477
  HILOGLINEAR command, 542
  LOGLINEAR command, 633
  MANOVA command, 683
  PLOT command, 876
  PPLOT command, 897
  ROC command, 1076

SURVIVAL command, 598, 1155
UNIANOVA command, 1201

PLOT MEANS (subcommand)
  ONEWAY command, 856

PLOTWISE (keyword)
  PLOT command, 879

PLT (function)
  AGGREGATE command, 97
  GRAPH command, 506
  REPORT command, 1053

PLT (keyword)
  IGRAPH command, 573

PLUM (command), 880
  ACPROB keyword, 885
  BIAS keyword, 882
  CAUCHIT keyword, 882
  CELLINFO keyword, 884
  CIN keyword, 882
  CLOGLOG keyword, 882
  CORB keyword, 884
  COVB keyword, 884
  CRITERIA subcommand, 882
  DELTA keyword, 882
  ESTPROB keyword, 885
  EXCLUDE keyword, 884
  FIT keyword, 884
  HISTORY keyword, 884
  INCLUDE keyword, 884
  KERNEL keyword, 884
  LCONVERGE keyword, 882
  LINK subcommand, 882
  LOCATION subcommand, 883
  LOGIT keyword, 882
  MISSING subcommand, 884
  MXITER keyword, 882
  MXSTEP keyword, 882
  NLOGLOG keyword, 882
  PARALLEL keyword, 884
  PARAMETER keyword, 884
  PCONVERGE keyword, 882
  PCPROB keyword, 885
  PREDCAT keyword, 885
  PRINT subcommand, 884
  PROBIT keyword, 882
  SAVE subcommand, 885
  SCALE subcommand, 885
  SINGULAR keyword, 882
  SUMMARY keyword, 884
  TEST subcommand, 886

PMA (function)

CREATE command, 218

PMEANS (subcommand)
MANOVA command, 662

POINT (command), 888
FILE subcommand, 890
KEY subcommand, 890
with DATA LIST command, 888
with FILE HANDLE command, 890

POINTLABEL (subcommand)
IGRAPH command, 557

POISSON (keyword)
NPAR TESTS command, 830

POLYNOMIAL (keyword)
COXREG command, 205
GLM command, 481, 500
LOGISTIC REGRESSION command, 614
MANOVA command, 679, 692
UNIANOVA command, 1205

POLYNOMIAL (subcommand)
ONEWAY command, 852

POOL (keyword)
MANOVA command, 673

POOLED (keyword)
DISCRIMINANT command, 306
KM command, 600
REGRESSION command, 1001

!POSITIONAL (keyword)
DEFINE command, 272

POSTHOC (subcommand)
GLM command, 483
UNIANOVA command, 1206

POUT (function)
AGGREGATE command, 97

POUT (keyword)
COXREG command, 209
LOGISTIC REGRESSION command, 619
REGRESSION command, 990

POUT (subcommand)
DISCRIMINANT command, 299

POWER (keyword)
CLUSTER command, 163
CURVEFIT command, 237
PROXIMITIES command, 938

POWER (subcommand)
MANOVA command, 664, 685
WLS command, 1252

P-P (keyword)
PPLOT command, 897

PP (keyword)
SPCHART command, 1133

PPK (keyword)
SPCHART command, 1133

PPL (keyword)
SPCHART command, 1133

PPLOT (command), 892
APPLY subcommand, 900
DIFF subcommand, 898
DISTRIBUTION subcommand, 894
FRACTION subcommand, 896
LN/NOLOG subcommands, 899
PERIOD subcommand, 899
PLOT subcommand, 897
SDIFF subcommand, 899
STANDARDIZE/NOSTANDARDIZE subcommands, 898
TYPE subcommand, 896
VARIABLES subcommand, 894

PPM (keyword)
SPCHART command, 1133

PPU (keyword)
SPCHART command, 1133

PR (keyword)
SPCHART command, 1133

PRED (keyword)
CURVEFIT command, 239
GLM command, 488
LOGISTIC REGRESSION command, 620
REGRESSION command, 998
UNIANOVA command, 1211

PRED (subcommand)
CNLR/NLR command, 799

PREDCAT (keyword)
PLUM command, 885

PRESERVE (command), 906
macro facility, 282
with RESTORE command, 1068
with SET command, 1101

PRESID (keyword)
COXREG command, 211

PRESORTED (subcommand)
AGGREGATE command, 96

PREVIEW (keyword)
REPORT command, 1041

PREVIOUS (keyword)
REPORT command, 1058

PRINT (command), 907
formats, 907, 909
missing values, 908
NOTABLE subcommand, 912
OUTFILE subcommand, 911

RECORDS subcommand, 911
strings, 907, 910
TABLE subcommand, 912
variable list, 908
with DO IF command, 910
with PRINT EJECT command, 913
with SET command, 908
with SORT CASES command, 1118

PRINT (statement)
    MATRIX command, 727

PRINT (subcommand)
    ALSCAL command, 111
    AUTORECODE command, 136
    CLUSTER command, 171
    CORRELATIONS command, 193
    COXREG command, 208
    CURVEFIT command, 239
    DO REPEAT command, 329
    FACTOR command, 367
    GENLOG command, 426
    GLM command, 476, 492
    HILOGLINEAR command, 542
    KM command, 599
    LOGISTIC REGRESSION command, 618
    LOGLINEAR command, 632
    MANOVA command, 658, 681
    NOMREG command, 814
    NONPAR CORR command, 819
    PLUM command, 884
    PROBIT command, 929
    PROXIMITIES command, 945
    QUICK CLUSTER command, 955
    RANK command, 963
    ROC command, 1075
    SURVIVAL command, 1156
    TSET command, 1171
    2SLS command, 1191
    UNIANOVA command, 1200
    VARCOMP command, 1231
    WLS command, 1253

PRINT EJECT (command), 913
    CASENUM$ system variable, 915
    missing values, 914
    with DO IF command, 913
    with PRINT command, 913
    with SET command, 914

PRINT FORMATS (command), 916
    format specification, 916
    string variables, 916
    with DISPLAY command, 917

PRINT SPACE (command), 919
    number of lines, 919
    OUTFILE subcommand, 919
    with DO IF command, 919

PRINTBACK (subcommand)
    SET command, 1106
    SHOW command, 1115

PRIORS (subcommand)
    DISCRIMINANT command, 301

PROBIT (command), 922
    case-by-case form, 924
    CRITERIA subcommand, 927
    limitations, 924
    LOG subcommand, 927
    MISSING subcommand, 930
    MODEL subcommand, 926
    NATRES subcommand, 928
    PRINT subcommand, 929
    response rate, 928
    variable specification, 925

PROBIT (keyword)
    PLUM command, 882
    PROBIT command, 927

PROBS (keyword)
    DISCRIMINANT command, 303

PROCEDURE OUTPUT (command), 931
    OUTFILE subcommand, 931
    with CROSSTABS, 230, 231
    with CROSSTABS command, 931
    with FREQUENCIES command, 932
    with SURVIVAL command, 932

PROCEDURES (keyword)
    INFO command, 582

PROFILE (keyword)
    GLM command, 477
    UNIANOVA command, 1201

PROMAX (keyword)
    FACTOR command, 372

PROPORTION (subcommand)
    RANK command, 960

PROXIMITIES (command), 933
    ID subcommand, 945
    limitations, 935
    matrix input, 947
    matrix output, 25, 946
    MATRIX subcommand, 946
    MEASURE subcommand, 936
    MISSING subcommand, 946
    PRINT subcommand, 945
    STANDARDIZE subcommand, 935

variable list, 935
VIEW subcommand, 936
with FACTOR command, 949

PROXIMITIES (keyword)
PROXIMITIES command, 945

PTILE (function)
GRAPH command, 506

PTILE (keyword)
IGRAPH command, 573

PYRAMID (keyword)
IGRAPH command, 563

PZL (keyword)
SPCHART command, 1133

PZMAX (keyword)
SPCHART command, 1133

PZMIN (keyword)
SPCHART command, 1133

PZOUT (keyword)
SPCHART command, 1133

PZU (keyword)
SPCHART command, 1133

Q (keyword)
CLUSTER command, 168
PROXIMITIES command, 943

Q-Q (keyword)
PPLOT command, 896

QREGW (keyword)
GLM command, 486
ONEWAY command, 855
UNIANOVA command, 1209

QUADRATIC (keyword)
CURVEFIT command, 237

QUARTILES (keyword)
NPAR TESTS command, 841

QUARTIMAX (keyword)
FACTOR command, 372
MANOVA command, 684

QUICK CLUSTER (command), 951
compared with CLUSTER command, 951
CRITERIA subcommand, 953
FILE subcommand, 955
INITIAL subcommand, 954
METHOD subcommand, 954
MISSING subcommand, 957
missing values, 957
OUTFILE subcommand, 956
PRINT subcommand, 955

SAVE subcommand, 956
variable list, 953
with large number of cases, 952

!QUOTE (function)
DEFINE command, 281

R (keyword)
REGRESSION command, 988

RANDOM (keyword)
SET command, 1105

RANDOM (subcommand)
GLM command, 472
UNIANOVA command, 1196
VARCOMP command, 1228

RANGE (keyword)
DESCRIPTIVES command, 289, 290
FREQUENCIES command, 418
GRAPH command, 510
MEANS command, 775
PROXIMITIES command, 936
SUMMARIZE command, 1147

RANGE (subcommand)
GET TRANSLATE command, 459

RANGES (subcommand)
ONEWAY command, 855

RANK (command), 958
FRACTION subcommand, 962
handling of ties, 896, 962
MISSING subcommand, 963
missing values, 963
N subcommand, 960
NORMAL subcommand, 960
NTILES(k) subcommand, 961
PERCENT subcommand, 960
PRINT subcommand, 963
PROPORTION subcommand, 960
rank functions, 960
RANK subcommand, 960
ranking order, 959
RFRACTION subcommand, 960
SAVAGE subcommand, 960
saving rank variables, 961
TIES subcommand, 962
VARIABLES subcommand, 959

RANK (function)
MATRIX command, 724

RANK (subcommand)
RANK command, 960

RANKIT (keyword)
  PPLOT command, 896
  RANK command, 962

RAO (keyword)
  DISCRIMINANT command, 299

RATIO (keyword)
  ALSCAL command, 106

RAW (keyword)
  DISCRIMINANT command, 305
  MANOVA command, 684

RBAR (keyword)
  SPCHART command, 1134

RCON (keyword)
  NLR command, 804

RCONVERGE (keyword)
  FACTOR command, 370

READ (statement)
  MATRIX command, 733

READNAMES (subcommand)
  GET DATA command, 441

RECFORM (subcommand)
  FILE HANDLE command, 379

RECODE (command), 964
  compared to AUTORECODE, 132
  compared to AUTORECODE command, 964
  compared to IF command, 964
  limitations, 966
  missing values, 965
  numeric variables, 965
  string variables, 966
  target variable, 967
  with MISSING VALUES command, 966
  with NONPAR CORR command, 820

RECORD (subcommand)
  FILE TYPE command, 388

RECORD TYPE (command), 970
  CASE subcommand, 975
  DUPLICATE subcommand, 977
  MISSING subcommand, 976
  SKIP subcommand, 974
  SPREAD subcommand, 977
  with DATA LIST command, 970
  with FILE TYPE command, 970

RECORDS (subcommand)
  DATA LIST command, 247
  PRINT command, 911
  WRITE command, 1258

RECTANGLE (keyword)
  IGRAPH command, 563

RECTANGULAR (keyword)

ALSCAL command, 106

REDUNDANCY (keyword)
  MANOVA command, 661

REFERENCE (keyword)
  PLOT command, 878
  TSPLOT command, 1178

REFORMAT (command), 979
  ALPHA subcommand, 979
  missing values, 979
  NUMERIC subcommand, 979
  with FORMATS command, 979

REG (keyword)
  ANOVA command, 126
  FACTOR command, 373

REGRESSION (command), 981, 997
  case selection, 993
  CASEWISE subcommand, 1001
  CRITERIA subcommand, 989
  DEPENDENT subcommand, 985
  dependent variable, 985
  DESCRIPTIVES subcommand, 992
  diagnostic measures, 982
  diagnostic variables, 998
  matrix data, 994
  MATRIX subcommand, 994
  METHOD subcommand, 985
  MISSING subcommand, 996
  missing values, 982, 995, 998
  model criteria, 989
  NOORIGIN subcommand, 990
  ORIGIN subcommand, 990
  OUTFILE subcommand, 1003
  PARTIALPLOT subcommand, 1002
  REGWGT subcommand, 991
  RESIDUALS subcommand, 1000
  SAVE subcommand, 1004
  saving variables, 1004
  SCATTERPLOT subcommand, 1002
  SELECT subcommand, 993
  STATISTICS subcommand, 987
  variable selection, 985, 989
  VARIABLES subcommand, 984
  weighted models, 991
  with CORRELATIONS command, 994
  with MATRIX DATA command, 755
  with SAMPLE command, 994, 998
  with SELECT IF command, 994, 998
  with SET command, 1000
  with TEMPORARY command, 994

REGRESSION (keyword)

IGRAPH command, 571
PLOT command, 878
REGWGT (subcommand)
　GLM command, 473
　REGRESSION command, 991
　UNIANOVA command, 1197
　VARCOMP command, 1230
RELEASE (statement)
　MATRIX command, 749
RELIABILITY (command), 1006
　FORMAT subcommand, 1011
　ICC subcommand, 1010
　limitations, 1007
　matrix input, 1012
　matrix output, 1012
　MATRIX subcommand, 1012
　METHOD subcommand, 1011
　MISSING subcommand, 1011
　missing values, 1011, 1013
　MODEL subcommand, 1009
　SCALE subcommand, 1008
　STATISTICS subcommand, 1009
　SUMMARY subcommand, 1010
　VARIABLES subcommand, 1008
REML (keyword)
　VARCOMP command, 1229
REMOVE (keyword)
　REGRESSION command, 986
RENAME (command)
　SAVE TRANSLATE command, 1092
RENAME (subcommand)
　ADD FILES command, 85
　EXPORT command, 359
　GET command, 433
　IMPORT command, 576
　MANOVA command, 677, 695
　MATCH FILES command, 702
　SAVE command, 1083
　UPDATE command, 1218
　XSAVE command, 1266
RENAME VARIABLES (command), 1016
REPEATED (keyword)
　COXREG command, 205
　GLM command, 482, 500
　LOGISTIC REGRESSION command, 614
　MANOVA command, 655, 679
　UNIANOVA command, 1206
REPEATING DATA (command), 1018
　CONTINUED subcommand, 1028
　DATA subcommand, 1026

FILE subcommand, 1026
ID subcommand, 1030
LENGTH subcommand, 1027
NOTABLE subcommand, 1031
OCCURS subcommand, 1025
STARTS subcommand, 1024
with DATA LIST command, 1018, 1019, 1021
with FILE TYPE command, 1018, 1019, 1022
with INPUT PROGRAM command, 1018, 1019, 1021
REPLACE (subcommand)
　MCONVERT command, 771
　SAVE TRANSLATE command, 1089
REPORT (command), 1032
　BREAK subcommand, 1047
　CHWRAP keyword, 1040
　column contents, 1044, 1048
　column headings, 1033, 1045, 1048
　column spacing, 1034
　column width, 1034, 1034, 1045, 1049
　defining subgroups, 1047
　footnotes, 1058
　FORMAT subcommand, 1038
　INDENT keyword, 1040
　limitations, 1037
　MISSING subcommand, 1059
　missing values, 1036, 1059
　ONEBREAKCOLUMN keyword, 1040
　OUTFILE subcommand, 1041
　output file, 1036, 1041
　page layout, 1041
　PREVIEW keyword, 1041
　print formats, 1056
　report types, 1036
　STRING subcommand, 1046
　string variables, 1046
　summary statistics, 1036, 1051
　SUMMARY subcommand, 1051
　summary titles, 1055
　titles, 1058
　VARIABLES subcommand, 1044
　with SET command, 1036
　with SORT CASES command, 1118
REPORT (keyword)
　CROSSTABS command, 229
　EXAMINE command, 353
　GRAPH command, 534
REPR (keyword)
　FACTOR command, 368
REREAD (command), 1061

COLUMN subcommand, 1066
FILE subcommand, 1064
with DATA LIST command, 1061
with INPUT PROGRAM command, 1061

REREAD (keyword)
MATRIX command, 735

RESCALE (keyword)
PROXIMITIES command, 936, 937

RESHAPE (function)
MATRIX command, 724

RESID (keyword)
CROSSTABS command, 226
CURVEFIT command, 239
GLM command, 488
HILOGLINEAR command, 542
LOGISTIC REGRESSION command, 620
REGRESSION command, 998
UNIANOVA command, 1211

RESIDUAL (keyword)
MANOVA command, 653

RESIDUALS (keyword)
GLM command, 477
UNIANOVA command, 1201

RESIDUALS (subcommand)
MANOVA command, 663
REGRESSION command, 1000

RESPONSES (keyword)
MULT RESPONSE command, 787

RESTORE (command), 906, 1068
macro facility, 282
with PRESERVE command, 1068
with SET command, 1068, 1101

RESULTS (subcommand)
SET command, 1106
SHOW command, 1115

REVERSE (keyword)
PROXIMITIES command, 936

RFRACTION (subcommand)
RANK command, 960

RIGHT (keyword)
REPORT command, 1045, 1049, 1058

RISK (keyword)
CROSSTABS command, 228

RJUMP (keyword)
IGRAPH command, 568

RLABELS (keyword)
MATRIX command, 728

RMAX (function)
MATRIX command, 724

RMED (function)

CREATE command, 218

RMIN (function)
MATRIX command, 724

RMP (keyword)
PROBIT command, 929

RMV (command), 1069
LINT function, 1070
MEAN function, 1071
MEDIAN function, 1071
SMEAN function, 1072
TREND function, 1072

RNAMES (keyword)
MATRIX command, 728

RND (function)
MATRIX command, 724

RNKORDER (function)
MATRIX command, 724

ROC (command), 1073
BY keyword, 1074
COORDINATES keyword, 1075
CRITERIA subcommand, 1074
CURVE keyword, 1076
CUTOFF keyword, 1075
DISTRIBUTION keyword, 1075
EXCLUDE keyword, 1074
INCLUDE keyword, 1074
MISSING keyword, 1074
NONE keyword, 1076
PLOT subcommand, 1076
PRINT subcommand, 1075
SE keyword, 1075
TESTPOS keyword, 1075

ROTATE (keyword)
MANOVA command, 684

ROTATE (subcommand)
DISCRIMINANT command, 305

ROTATION (keyword)
FACTOR command, 367, 369

ROTATION (subcommand)
FACTOR command, 372

ROUND (keyword)
EXAMINE command, 349
IGRAPH command, 563, 566

ROW (keyword)
ALSCAL command, 107
CROSSTABS command, 226
MULT RESPONSE command, 786

ROWCONF (keyword)
ALSCAL command, 108, 113

ROWS (keyword)

ALSCAL command, 105

ROWTYPE_ (variable)
MATRIX DATA command, 751, 757

RR (keyword)
CLUSTER command, 165
PROXIMITIES command, 941

RSSCP (keyword)
GLM command, 492

RSSQ (function)
MATRIX command, 725

RSTEP (keyword)
IGRAPH command, 563, 568

RSUM (function)
MATRIX command, 725

RT (keyword)
CLUSTER command, 166
PROXIMITIES command, 941

RUNS (subcommand)
NPAR TESTS command, 838

S (keyword)
CURVEFIT command, 237

SAMPLE (command), 1077
limitations, 1078
with DO IF command, 1078
with FILE TYPE command, 1078
with INPUT PROGRAM command, 1078
with N OF CASES command, 808, 1078
with REGRESSION command, 994, 998
with SELECT IF command, 1077
with SET command, 1077
with TEMPORARY command, 1077

SAMPLE (subcommand)
NONPAR CORR command, 819
NPAR TESTS command, 841

SAMPLES (keyword)
CROSSTABS command, 228
NPAR TESTS command, 842

SAVAGE (subcommand)
RANK command, 960

SAVE (command), 1079
compared to XSAVE command, 1079, 1263
COMPRESSED subcommand, 1084
DROP command, 1082
KEEP subcommand, 1082
MAP subcommand, 1083
OUTFILE subcommand, 1081
RENAME subcommand, 1083

UNCOMPRESSED subcommand, 1084
UNSELECTED subcommand, 1082
with TEMPORARY command, 1166

SAVE (statement)
MATRIX command, 741

SAVE (subcommand)
CLUSTER command, 170
CNLR/NLR command, 800
COXREG command, 210
CURVEFIT command, 239
DESCRIPTIVES command, 288
DISCRIMINANT command, 302
FACTOR command, 372
GLM command, 487
KM command, 602
LOGISTIC REGRESSION command, 621
PLUM command, 885
QUICK CLUSTER command, 956
2SLS command, 1191
UNIANOVA command, 1210
WLS command, 1253

SAVE TRANSLATE (command), 1085
APPEND subcommand, 1089
CONNECT subcommand, 1089
DROP subcommand, 1092
FIELDNAMES subcommand, 1091
KEEP subcommand, 1092
limitations, 1088
MAP subcommand, 1093
missing values, 1087
OUTFILE subcommand, 1089
RENAME subcommand, 1092
REPLACE subcommand, 1089
TABLE subcommand, 1089
TYPE subcommand, 1090
UNSELECTED subcommand, 1091

SAVE(subcommand)
GENLOG command, 428

SBAR (keyword)
SPCHART command, 1134

SCALE (keyword)
IGRAPH command, 554
RELIABILITY command, 1009

SCALE (subcommand)
NOMREG command, 815
PLUM command, 885
RELIABILITY command, 1008

SCATTER (subcommand)
IGRAPH command, 561

SCATTERPLOT (subcommand)

GRAPH command, 526
REGRESSION command, 1002
SCHEDULE (keyword)
   CLUSTER command, 171
SCHEFFE (keyword)
   GLM command, 485
   ONEWAY command, 854
   UNIANOVA command, 1208
SCOMPRESSION (subcommand)
   SHOW command, 1115
SCORES (keyword)
   DISCRIMINANT command, 302
SCRATCH (keyword)
   DISPLAY command, 313
SCRIPT (command), 1094
SD (function)
   AGGREGATE command, 97
SD (keyword)
   IGRAPH command, 569
   MATRIX DATA command, 764
   PROXIMITIES command, 936
SDBETA (keyword)
   REGRESSION command, 999
SDFIT (keyword)
   REGRESSION command, 999
SDIFF (function)
   CREATE command, 219
SDIFF (subcommand)
   ACF command, 78
   CCF command, 154
   PACF command, 862
   PPLOT command, 899
   TSPLOT command, 1177
SDRESID (keyword)
   REGRESSION command, 999
SE (keyword)
   COXREG command, 211
   IGRAPH command, 569
   KM command, 602
   ROC command, 1075
SEASONAL (subcommand)
   ACF command, 79
   CCF command, 156–
   PACF command, 863
SECOND (keyword)
   DATE command, 259
SEED (subcommand)
   SET command, 1105
   SHOW command, 1115
SEKURT (keyword)

FREQUENCIES command, 418
IGRAPH command, 573
MEANS command, 775
SELECT (subcommand)
   DISCRIMINANT command, 296
   FACTOR command, 365
   LOGISTIC REGRESSION command, 617
   REGRESSION command, 993
SELECT IF (command), 1095
   limitations, 1097
   logical expressions, 1095
   missing values, 1096, 1098
   with CASENUM$ system variable, 1096
   with DO IF command, 1099
   with N OF CASES command, 808, 1096
   with REGRESSION command, 994, 998
   with SAMPLE command, 1077
   with TEMPORARY command, 1095
SELECTION (keyword)
   REGRESSION command, 988
SELIRT (keyword)
   SUMMARIZE command, 1147
SEMEAN (keyword)
   DESCRIPTIVES command, 289, 290
   FREQUENCIES command, 418
   IGRAPH command, 573
   MEANS command, 775
   OLAP CUBES command, 848
   SUMMARIZE command, 1147
SEPARATE (keyword)
   DISCRIMINANT command, 306
   REGRESSION command, 1001
SEPRED (keyword)
   GLM command, 488
   REGRESSION command, 999
   UNIANOVA command, 1211
SERIAL (keyword)
   PARTIAL CORR command, 870
SERROR (subcommand)
   ACF command, 80
SES (keyword)
   REGRESSION command, 988
SESKEW (keyword)
   FREQUENCIES command, 418
   IGRAPH command, 573
   MEANS command, 775
   SUMMARIZE command, 1147
SET (command), 1100
   BLANKS subcommand, 1108
   BLOCK subcommand, 1110

BOX subcommand, 1110
CC subcommand, 1111
COMPRESSION subcommand, 1109
CTEMPLATE subcommand, 1104
EPOCH subcommand, 1105
ERRORS subcommand, 1106
EXTENSIONS subcommand, 1109
FORMAT subcommand, 1103
HEADER subcommand, 1111
JOURNAL subcommand, 1107
LENGTH subcommand, 1111
MESSAGES subcommand, 1106
MEXPAND subcommand, 1112
MITERATE subcommand, 1108
MNEST subcommand, 1108
MPRINT subcommand, 1112
MXCELLS subcommand, 1103
MXERRS subcommand, 1108
MXLOOPS subcommand, 1109
MXMEMORY subcommand, 1103
MXWARNS subcommand, 1108
ONUMBERS subcommand, 1104
OVARS subcommand, 1104
PRINTBACK subcommand, 1106
RANDOM keyword, 1105
RESULTS subcommand, 1106
SEED subcommand, 1105
TLOOK subcommand, 1104
TNUMBERS subcommand, 1104
TVARS subcommand, 1104
UNDEFINED subcommand, 1108
WIDTH subcommand, 1111
with CLUSTER command, 161
with LOOP command, 1109
with NUMERIC command, 844
with PRESERVE command, 906, 1101
with PRINT command, 908
with PRINT EJECT command, 914
with REGRESSION command, 1000
with REPORT command, 1036
with RESTORE command, 906, 1068, 1101
with SAMPLE command, 1077
with SHOW command, 1101
with SUBTITLE (command), 1142
with TITLE command, 1167
with WRITE command, 1256
with WRITE FORMATS command, 1262
WORKSPACE subcommand, 1103
SET command, 1105
SETDIAG (keyword)

MATRIX command, 727
SEUCLID (keyword)
CLUSTER command, 162
PROXIMITIES command, 937
SHAPE (keyword)
IGRAPH command, 563, 570
SHAPE (subcommand)
ALSCAL command, 105
SHEET (subcommand)
GET DATA command, 440
SHOW (command), 1113
$VARS subcommand, 1116
BLANKS subcommand, 1114
BLKSIZE subcommand, 1114
BLOCK subcommand, 1114
BOX subcommand, 1114
BUFFNO subcommand, 1114
CC subcommand, 1114
COMPRESSION subcommand, 1114
CTEMPLATE subcommand, 1114
ERRORS subcommand, 1114
EXTENSIONS subcommand, 1114
FORMAT subcommand, 1114
HEADER subcommand, 1114
JOURNAL subcommand, 1114
LENGTH subcommand, 1115
MESSAGES subcommand, 1115
MEXPAND subcommand, 1115
MITERATE subcommand, 1115
MNEST subcommand, 1115
MPRINT subcommand, 1115
MXCELLS subcommand, 1115
MXLOOPS subcommand, 1115
MXMEMORY subcommand, 1115
MXWARNS subcommand, 1115
N subcommand, 1115
ONUMBERS subcommand, 1115
OVARS subcommand, 1115
PRINTBACK subcommand, 1115
RESULTS subcommand, 1115
SCOMPRESSION subcommand, 1115
SEED subcommand, 1115
SYSMIS subcommand, 1115
TFIT subcommand, 1116
TLOOK subcommand, 1116
TNUMBERS subcommand, 1116
TVARS subcommand, 1116
UNDEFINED subcommand, 1116
WEIGHT subcommand, 1116
WIDTH subcommand, 1116

with SET command, 1101
WORKSPACE subcommand, 1116
SIDAK (keyword)
GLM command, 485
ONEWAY command, 855
UNIANOVA command, 1209
SIG (keyword)
CORRELATIONS command, 193
FACTOR command, 367
NONPAR CORR command, 819
REGRESSION command, 993
SIGMA (subcommand)
SPCHART command, 1135
SIGN (keyword)
IGRAPH command, 569
SIGN (subcommand)
NPAR TESTS command, 838
SIGNIF (keyword)
MANOVA command, 660, 682, 696
SIGNIFICANCE (subcommand)
PARTIAL CORR command, 869
SIMPLE (keyword)
COXREG command, 205
GLM command, 482, 500
GRAPH command, 509, 515, 522, 530
LOGISTIC REGRESSION command, 614
MANOVA command, 655, 679
UNIANOVA command, 1206
SIN (function)
MATRIX command, 725
SINCE (keyword)
INFO command, 582
SINGLE (keyword)
CLUSTER command, 169
LIST command, 607
SINGLEDF (keyword)
MANOVA command, 660, 683
SINGULAR (keyword)
NOMREG command, 812
PLUM command, 882
SIZE (keyword)
CLUSTER command, 168
DISCRIMINANT command, 301
MATRIX command, 735
PROXIMITIES command, 944
SIZE (subcommand)
IGRAPH command, 556
SKEW (keyword)
IGRAPH command, 573
MEANS command, 775

SUMMARIZE command, 1147
SKEWNESS (function)
REPORT command, 1052
SKEWNESS (keyword)
DESCRIPTIVES command, 289, 290
FREQUENCIES command, 418
SKIP (keyword)
REPORT command, 1050, 1058
SKIP (subcommand)
RECORD TYPE command, 974
SLICE (keyword)
IGRAPH command, 565
SLK (keyword)
SAVE TRANSLATE command, 1090
SM (keyword)
CLUSTER command, 165
PROXIMITIES command, 941
SMEAN (function)
RMV command, 1072
SNAMES (keyword)
MATRIX command, 748
SNK (keyword)
GLM command, 485
ONEWAY command, 854
UNIANOVA command, 1208
SOLVE (function)
MATRIX command, 725
SORT (keyword)
FACTOR command, 366
SORT (subcommand)
DESCRIPTIVES command, 290
SORT CASES (command), 1117
with ADD FILES command, 84, 1118
with AGGREGATE command, 1118
with MATCH FILES command, 1118
with PRINT command, 1118
with REPORT command, 1118
with SPLIT FILE command, 1137
with UPDATE command, 1118, 1216
SORTED (keyword)
DISPLAY command, 313
SOURCE (subcommand)
WLS command, 1251
SPACE (keyword)
MATRIX command, 728
SPAN (subcommand)
SPCHART command, 1135
SPCHART (command), 1119
C subcommand, 1129
CAPSIGMA subcommand, 1134

CONFORM subcommand, 1135
FOOTNOTE subcommand, 1122
I subcommand, 1125
IR subcommand, 1125
LSL subcommand, 1135
MINSAMPLE subcommand, 1135
MISSING subcommand, 1136
NOCONFORM subcommand, 1135
NP subcommand, 1127
P subcommand, 1127
SIGMA subcommand, 1135
SPAN subcommand, 1135
STATISTICS subcommand, 1131
SUBTITLE subcommand, 1122
TARGET subcommand, 1136
TITLE subcommand, 1122
U subcommand, 1129
USL subcommand, 1135
XR subcommand, 1122
XS subcommand, 1122
SPCT (keyword)
    OLAP CUBES command, 848
    SUMMARIZE command, 1147
SPCT (keyword)
    MEANS command, 775
    OLAP CUBES command, 848
    SUMMARIZE command, 1147
SPCT(var) (keyword)
    MEANS command, 775
SPEARMAN (keyword)
    NONPAR CORR command, 819
SPECIAL (keyword)
    COXREG command, 205
    GLM command, 482, 500
    LOGISTIC REGRESSION command, 614
    MANOVA command, 656, 680
    UNIANOVA command, 1206
SPECIFICATIONS (keyword)
    CURVEFIT command, 240
SPIKE (subcommand)
    IGRAPH command, 560
SPLINE (keyword)
    IGRAPH command, 568
SPLIT (keyword)
    MATRIX command, 748
    RELIABILITY command, 1009
SPLIT (subcommand)
    MATRIX DATA command, 760
    TSPLOT command, 1181
SPLIT FILE (command)

limitations, 1138
    with AGGREGATE command, 94, 1138
    with SORT CASES command, 1137
    with TEMPORARY command, 1137, 1165
SPREAD (subcommand)
    RECORD TYPE command, 977
SPREADLEVEL (keyword)
    EXAMINE command, 350
    GLM command, 477
    UNIANOVA command, 1201
SQL (subcommand)
    GET CAPTURE command, 436
    GET DATA command, 440
SQRT (function)
    MATRIX command, 725
SQUARE (keyword)
    IGRAPH command, 563, 566
SRESID (keyword)
    CROSSTABS command, 226
    GLM command, 488
    LOGISTIC REGRESSION command, 620
    REGRESSION command, 999
    UNIANOVA command, 1211
SS (keyword)
    VARCOMP command, 1231
SS1 through SS5 (keywords)
    CLUSTER command, 166
    PROXIMITIES command, 941
SSCON (keyword)
    NLR command, 803
SSCP (function)
    MATRIX command, 725
SSCP (keyword)
    MANOVA command, 682
SSTYPE (keyword)
    GLM command, 473
    UNIANOVA command, 1197
    VARCOMP command, 1229
STACK (keyword)
STACK(keyword)
    IGRAPH command, 556
STACKED (keyword)
    GRAPH command, 509, 530
STAN (keyword)
    MANOVA command, 684
STANDARDIZE (keyword)
    PLOT command, 878
STANDARDIZE (subcommand)
    PPLOT command, 898
    PROXIMITIES command, 935

START (keyword)
    IGRAPH command, 564
STARTS (subcommand)
    REPEATING DATA command, 1024
STATISTICS (subcommand)
    CORRELATIONS command, 193
    CROSSTABS command, 227
    DESCRIPTIVES command, 289
    DISCRIMINANT command, 304
    EXAMINE command, 351
    FREQUENCIES command, 418
    MEANS command, 775
    NPAR TESTS command, 841
    ONEWAY command, 856
    PARTIAL CORR command, 869
    REGRESSION command, 987
    RELIABILITY command, 1009
    SPCHART command, 1131
    SUMMARIZE command, 1149
STATUS (subcommand)
    COXREG command, 203
    KM command, 597
    SURVIVAL command, 1154
STDDEV (function)
    GRAPH command, 506
    REPORT command, 1052
STDDEV (keyword)
    DESCRIPTIVES command, 289, 290
    DISCRIMINANT command, 304
    FREQUENCIES command, 418
    GRAPH command, 525
    IGRAPH command, 573
    MATRIX DATA command, 764
    MEANS command, 774
    OLAP CUBES command, 848
    REGRESSION command, 992
    SUMMARIZE command, 1147
STEMLEAF (keyword)
    EXAMINE command, 350
STEP (keyword)
    DISCRIMINANT command, 305
STEPDOWN (keyword)
    MANOVA command, 682
STEPLIMIT (keyword)
    CNLR command, 802
STEPWISE (keyword)
    REGRESSION command, 986
STERROR (keyword)
    GRAPH command, 525
STIMWGHT (keyword)

ALSCAL command, 108, 113
STRAIGHT (keyword)
    IGRAPH command, 562, 568
STRATA (keyword)
    KM command, 600
STRATA (subcommand)
    COXREG command, 203
    KM command, 598
STRESSMIN (keyword)
    ALSCAL command, 110
STRICTPARALLEL (keyword)
    RELIABILITY command, 1009
STRING (command), 1140
    with INPUT PROGRAM command, 1140
STRING (subcommand)
    REPORT command, 1046
STRINGS (keyword)
    MATRIX command, 743
STRUCTURE (keyword)
    DISCRIMINANT command, 305
STYLE (keyword)
    IGRAPH command, 567
STYLE (subcommand)
    IGRAPH command, 556
SUBJWGHT (keyword)
    ALSCAL command, 108, 113
!SUBSTRING (function)
    DEFINE command, 280
SUBPOP (subcommand)
    NOMREG command, 815
SUBTITLE (command), 1142
    with BEGIN DATA command, 1142
    with SET command, 1142
    with TITLE command, 1142, 1168
SUBTITLE (subcommand)
    GRAPH command, 509
    IGRAPH command, 558
    SPCHART command, 1122
SUBTRACT (function)
    REPORT command, 1054
SUM (function)
    AGGREGATE command, 97
    GRAPH command, 506
    REPORT command, 1052
SUM (keyword)
    DESCRIPTIVES command, 290
    FREQUENCIES command, 418
    IGRAPH command, 564, 573
    MEANS command, 775
    OLAP CUBES command, 848

SUMMARIZE command, 1147
SUMAV (keyword)
    IGRAPH command, 564, 573
SUMMARIZE (command), 1144
    CELLS subcommand, 1147
    FOOTNOTE subcommand, 1146
    FORMAT subcommand, 1148
    MISSING subcommand, 1148
    missing values, 1148
    STATISTICS subcommand, 1149
    TABLES subcommand, 1146
    TITLE subcommand, 1146
SUMMARY (keyword)
    COXREG command, 208
    LOGISTIC REGRESSION command, 618
    NOMREG command, 815
    PLUM command, 884
SUMMARY (subcommand)
    RELIABILITY command, 1010
    REPORT command, 1051
summary function
    GRAPH command, 506
summary functions
    IGRAPH command, 562, 563, 564, 567, 572
summary functions, multiple
    GRAPH command, 507
SUMMARYVAR (subcommand)
    IGRAPH command, 557
SUMSPACE (keyword)
    REPORT command, 1040
SUMSQ (keyword)
    IGRAPH command, 564, 573
SURVIVAL (command), 1150
    aggregated data, 1158
    CALCULATE subcommand, 1157
    COMPARE subcommand, 1156
    INTERVALS subcommand, 1153
    limitations, 1152
    MISSING subcommand, 1159
    OMS keyword, 1156
    output file, 1160
    PLOTS subcommand, 1155
    PRINT subcommand, 1156
    STATUS subcommand, 1154
    TABLES subcommand, 1152
    with PROCEDURE OUTPUT command, 932
    WRITE subcommand, 1160
SURVIVAL (keyword)
    COXREG command, 210
    KM command, 598, 602

SURVIVAL command, 1155
SVAL (function)
    MATRIX command, 725
SVD (keyword)
    MATRIX command, 727
SWEEP (function)
    MATRIX command, 725
SYMBOL (keyword)
    IGRAPH command, 569
SYMMETRIC (keyword)
    ALSCAL command, 105
SYSFILE INFO (command), 1163
SYSMIS (keyword)
    COUNT command, 197, 198
    MATRIX command, 740
    RECODE command, 965
SYSMIS (subcommand)
    SHOW command, 1115

T (function)
    MATRIX command, 726
T (keyword)
    IGRAPH command, 566, 569
    MANOVA command, 664
T2 (keyword)
    GLM command, 486
    ONEWAY command, 855
    UNIANOVA command, 1209
T3 (keyword)
    GLM command, 486
    ONEWAY command, 855
    UNIANOVA command, 1209
T4253H (function)
    CREATE command, 220
TAB (keyword)
    SAVE TRANSLATE command, 1090
TABLE (keyword)
    COXREG command, 210
    CROSSTABS command, 229
    DISCRIMINANT command, 305
    KM command, 599
    MEANS command, 776
    MULT RESPONSE command, 788, 789
    SUMMARIZE command, 1148
    SURVIVAL command, 1156
TABLE (subcommand)
    DATA LIST command, 247
    KEYED DATA LIST command, 593

MATCH FILES command, 701
PRINT command, 912
SAVE TRANSLATE command, 1089
WRITE command, 1259
TABLES (keyword)
  CROSSTABS command, 230
  GLM command, 486
  SURVIVAL command, 1160
  UNIANOVA command, 1210
TABLES (subcommand)
  CROSSTABS command, 224
  MEANS command, 774
  MULT RESPONSE command, 785
  SUMMARIZE command, 1146
  SURVIVAL command, 1152
!TAIL (function)
  DEFINE command, 281
TAPE (keyword)
  EXPORT command, 358
  IMPORT command, 575
TARGET (subcommand)
  SPCHART command, 1136
TARONE (keyword)
  KM command, 600
TCDF (function)
  MATRIX command, 726
TCOV (keyword)
  DISCRIMINANT command, 304
TEMPORARY (command), 1164
  with N OF CASES command, 808
  with REGRESSION command, 994
  with SAMPLE command, 1077
  with SAVE command, 1166
  with SELECT IF command, 1095
  with SPLIT FILE command, 1137, 1165
  with WEIGHT command, 1247
  with XSAVE command, 1166
TEST (keyword)
  REGRESSION command, 986
TEST (subcommand)
  KM command, 600
  NOMREG command, 815
  PLUM command, 886
TEST(ESTIMABLE) (keyword)
  GLM command, 477
  UNIANOVA command, 1200
TEST(LMATRIX) (keyword)
  GLM command, 477
  UNIANOVA command, 1200
TEST(MMATRIX) (keyword)

GLM command, 492
TEST(SSCP) (keyword)
  GLM command, 492
TEST(TRANSFORM) (keyword)
  GLM command, 492
TESTPOS (keyword)
  ROC command, 1075
TESTVAL (subcommand)
  T-TEST command, 1185
TEXTIN (keyword)
  IGRAPH command, 565
!THEN (keyword)
  DEFINE command, 283
THRU (keyword)
  COUNT command, 197
  MISSING VALUES command, 779
  RECODE command, 965
  SURVIVAL command, 1153
  USE command, 1221
TIES (subcommand)
  RANK command, 962
TIESTORE (keyword)
  ALSCAL command, 111
TIFT (subcommand)
  SHOW command, 1116
TIME PROGRAM (command)
  with COXREG command, 202
TIMER (keyword)
  CROSSTABS command, 229
  NPAR TESTS command, 842
TITLE (command), 1167
  with BEGIN DATA command, 1167
  with SET command, 1167
  with SUBTITLE command, 1142, 1168
TITLE (keyword)
  IGRAPH command, 554, 556
  MATRIX command, 728
TITLE (subcommand)
  GRAPH command, 509
  IGRAPH command, 558
  OLAP CUBES command, 847
  PLOT command, 879
  REPORT command, 1058
  SPCHART command, 1122
  SUMMARIZE command, 1146
TLOOK (subcommand)
  SET command, 1104
  SHOW command, 1116
TNUMBERS (subcommand)
  SET command, 1104

SHOW command, 1116

TO (keyword)
LIST command, 608
REGRESSION command, 984, 986
RENAME VARIABLES command, 1016
STRING command, 1140
VECTOR command, 1239

!TOKENS (keyword)
DEFINE command, 275

TOLERANCE (keyword)
REGRESSION command, 988, 990

TOLERANCE (subcommand)
DISCRIMINANT command, 299

TOP (keyword)
TSPLOT command, 1178

TOTAL (keyword)
CROSSTABS command, 226
IGRAPH command, 571
MULT RESPONSE command, 787
RELIABILITY command, 1011
REPORT command, 1050
SUMMARIZE command, 1148

TOTAL (subcommand)
EXAMINE command, 348

TRACE (function)
MATRIX command, 726

TRANSFORM (keyword)
MANOVA command, 683

TRANSFORM (subcommand)
MANOVA command, 680

TRANSPOS (function)
MATRIX command, 726

TREND (function)
RMV command, 1072

TREND (subcommand)
KM command, 601

TRUNC (function)
MATRIX command, 726

TSET (command), 1169
DEFAULT subcommand, 1170
ID subcommand, 1170
MISSING subcommand, 1170
MXNEWVAR subcommand, 1170
MXPREDICT subcommand, 1171
PERIOD subcommand, 1171
PRINT subcommand, 1171

TSHOW (command), 1172

TSPACE (keyword)
REPORT command, 1040

TSPLOT (command), 1173

APPLY subcommand, 1182
DIFF subcommand, 1176
FORMAT subcommand, 1178
ID subcommand, 1178
LN/NOLOG subcommands, 1177
MARK subcommand, 1181
PERIOD subcommand, 1177
SDIFF subcommand, 1177
SPLIT subcommand, 1181
VARIABLES subcommand, 1176

T-TEST (command), 1183
GROUPS subcommand, 1185
independent samples, 1184, 1185
limitations, 1184
MISSING subcommand, 1186
one sample, 1184, 1185
paired samples, 1184, 1186
PAIRS subcommand, 1186
TESTVAL subcommand, 1185
VARIABLES subcommand, 1185

TUKEY (keyword)
EXAMINE command, 352
GLM command, 485
ONEWAY command, 854
PPLOT command, 896
RANK command, 962
RELIABILITY command, 1009
UNIANOVA command, 1208

TVARS (subcommand)
SET command, 1104
SHOW command, 1116

2SLS (command), 1188
APPLY subcommand, 1191
CONSTANT subcommand, 1191
ENDOGENOUS subcommand, 1190
EQUATION subcommand, 1189
INSTRUMENTS subcommand, 1190
NOCONSTANT subcommand, 1191
PRINT subcommand, 1191
SAVE subcommand, 1191

TWOTAIL (keyword)
CORRELATIONS command, 193
NONPAR CORR command, 819
PARTIAL CORR command, 869

TXT (keyword)
GET DATA command, 439

TYPE (keyword)
MATRIX command, 743

TYPE (subcommand)
EXPORT command, 358

GET DATA command, 439
GET TRANSLATE command, 457
IMPORT command, 575
PPLOT command, 896
SAVE TRANSLATE command, 1090

U (subcommand)
    data organization, 1130
    SPCHART command, 1129
    variable specification, 1131
UC (keyword)
    CROSSTABS command, 227
ULEFT (keyword)
    IGRAPH command, 565
ULS (keyword)
    FACTOR command, 371
UNCLASSIFIED (keyword)
    DISCRIMINANT command, 306
UNCOMPRESSED (subcommand)
    SAVE command, 1084
    XSAVE command, 1267
UNCONDITIONAL (keyword)
    ALSCAL command, 107
    MANOVA command, 686
UNDEFINED (subcommand)
    SET command, 1108
    SHOW command, 1116
UNDERSCORE (keyword)
    REPORT command, 1040, 1050
UNIANOVA (command), 1193
    ALPHA keyword, 1199
    BONFERRONI keyword, 1209
    BTUKEY keyword, 1208
    C keyword, 1209
    CONTRAST subcommand, 1205
    COOK keyword, 1211
    CRITERIA subcommand, 1199
    DESCRIPTIVES keyword, 1200
    DEVIATION keyword, 1205
    DIFFERENCE keyword, 1205
    DRESID keyword, 1211
    DUNCAN keyword, 1208
    DUNNETT keyword, 1208
    DUNNETTL keyword, 1208
    DUNNETTR keyword, 1208
    EFSIZE keyword, 1200
    EMMEANS subcommand, 1209
    EPS keyword, 1199

ETASQ keyword, 1200
EXCLUDE keyword, 1199
FREGW keyword, 1209
GABRIEL keyword, 1209
GEF keyword, 1200
GH keyword, 1209
GT2 keyword, 1209
HELMERT keyword, 1206
HOMOGENEITY keyword, 1200
INCLUDE keyword, 1199
INTERCEPT subcommand, 1198
KMATRIX subcommand, 1204
LEVER keyword, 1211
LMATRIX subcommand, 1202
LOF keyword, 1200
LSD keyword, 1209
METHOD subcommand, 1197
MISSING subcommand, 1199
OPOWER keyword, 1200
OUTFILE subcommand, 1211
PARAMETER keyword, 1200
PLOT subcommand, 1201
POLYNOMIAL keyword, 1205
POSTHOC subcommand, 1206
PRED keyword, 1211
PRINT subcommand, 1200
PROFILE keyword, 1201
QREGW, 1209
RANDOM subcommand, 1196
REGWGT subcommand, 1197
REPEATED keyword, 1206
RESID keyword, 1211
RESIDUALS keyword, 1201
SAVE subcommand, 1210
SCHEFFE keyword, 1208
SEPRED keyword, 1211
SIDAK keyword, 1209
SIMPLE keyword, 1206
SNK keyword, 1208
SPECIAL keyword, 1206
SPREADLEVEL keyword, 1201
SSTYPE keyword, 1197
T2 keyword, 1209
T3 keyword, 1209
TABLES keyword, 1210
TEST(ESTIMABLE) keyword, 1200
TEST(LMATRIX) keyword, 1200
TUKEY keyword, 1208
univariate, 1193
WALLER keyword, 1209

WPRED keyword, 1211
WRESID keyword, 1211
ZRESID keyword, 1211
UNIFORM (function)
  MATRIX command, 726
UNIFORM (keyword)
  IGRAPH command, 571
  NPAR TESTS command, 830
  PLOT command, 878
UNIQUE (keyword)
  ANOVA command, 122
UNIV (keyword)
  MANOVA command, 682
UNIVARIATE (keyword)
  FACTOR command, 367
  MANOVA command, 665
UNIVF (keyword)
  DISCRIMINANT command, 304
UNNUMBERED (command), 843
UNNUMBERED (keyword)
  LIST command, 607
!UNQUOTE (function)
  DEFINE command, 281
UNSELECTED (keyword)
  DISCRIMINANT command, 306
UNSELECTED (subcommand)
  EXPORT command, 358
  SAVE command, 1082
  SAVE TRANSLATE command, 1091
UP (keyword)
  IGRAPH command, 569
  SORT CASES command, 1117
!UPCASE (function)
  DEFINE command, 281
UPDATE (command), 1214
  BY subcommand, 1218
  DROP subcommand, 1219
  FILE subcommand, 1217
  IN subcommand, 1219
  KEEP subcommand, 1219
  limitations, 1216
  MAP subcommand, 1220
  RENAME subcommand, 1218
  with DATA LIST command, 1217
  with DROP DOCUMENTS command, 1215
  with SORT CASES command, 1118, 1216
UPPER (keyword)
  MATRIX DATA command, 759
UPPERBOUND (subcommand)
  CURVEFIT command, 238

URIGHT (keyword)
  IGRAPH command, 565
USE (command), 1221
  case specifications, 1221
  DATE specifications, 1221
  examples, 1222
  FIRST and LAST keywords, 1221
USL (subcommand)
  SPCHART command, 1135

VAL (keyword)
  IGRAPH command, 562, 563, 565, 567, 569
VALIDLIST (subcommand)
  SUMMARIZE command, 1148
VALIDN (function)
  REPORT command, 1052
VALUE (keyword)
  REPORT command, 1044, 1048
VALUE LABELS (command), 1224
  compared with ADD VALUE LABELS command, 1224
VAR (keyword)
  IGRAPH command, 554
  REPORT command, 1060
VARCOMP (command), 1227
  BY keyword, 1232
  CONVERGE keyword, 1230
  CORB keyword, 1232
  COVB keyword, 1231
  CRITERIA subcommand, 1230
  DESIGN subcommand, 1232
  EMS keyword, 1231
  EPS keyword, 1230
  EXCLUDE keyword, 1230
  HISTORY keyword, 1231
  INCLUDE keyword, 1230
  INTERCEPT keyword, 1232
  INTERCEPT subcommand, 1229
  ITERATE keyword, 1231
  METHOD subcommand, 1229
  MINQUE keyword, 1229
  MISSING subcommand, 1230
  ML keyword, 1229
  OUTFILE subcommand, 1231
  PRINT subcommand, 1231
  RANDOM subcommand, 1228
  REGWGT subcommand, 1230
  REML keyword, 1229

SS keyword, 1231
SSTYPE keyword, 1229
VAREST keyword, 1231
WITHIN keyword, 1232
VAREST (keyword)
  VARCOMP command, 1231
VARIABLE (keyword)
  DESCRIPTIVES command, 291
  GRAPH command, 534
  PROXIMITIES command, 935, 936
  SUMMARIZE command, 1148
VARIABLE ALIGNMENT command, 1234
VARIABLE LABELS (command), 1235
VARIABLE LEVEL (command), 1237
VARIABLE WIDTH (command), 1238
VARIABLES (keyword)
  DISPLAY command, 313
  EXAMINE command, 347
  MATRIX command, 739
VARIABLES (subcommand)
  ACF command, 77
  ALSCAL command, 105
  ANOVA command, 121
  AUTORECODE command, 135
  CCF command, 154
  COXREG command, 202
  CROSSTABS command, 224
  CURVEFIT command, 237
  DESCRIPTIVES command, 287
  DISCRIMINANT command, 295
  DISPLAY command, 313
  EXAMINE command, 347
  FACTOR command, 364
  FLIP command, 404–405
  FREQUENCIES command, 413
  GET DATA command, 443
  LIST command, 606
  LOGISTIC REGRESSION command, 612
  MATRIX DATA command, 756
  MULT RESPONSE command, 783
  NONPAR CORR command, 818
  PACF command, 862
  PARTIAL CORR command, 868
  PPLOT command, 894
  RANK command, 959
  REGRESSION command, 984
  RELIABILITY command, 1008
  REPORT command, 1044
  TSPLOT command, 1176
  T-TEST command, 1185

VERIFY command, 1246
WLS command, 1251
VARIANCE (function)
  GRAPH command, 506
  REPORT command, 1052
VARIANCE (keyword)
  CLUSTER command, 169
  DESCRIPTIVES command, 289, 290
  FREQUENCIES command, 418
  IGRAPH command, 573
  MEANS command, 775
  PROXIMITIES command, 944
  REGRESSION command, 992
  RELIABILITY command, 1011
  SUMMARIZE command, 1147
VARIMAX (keyword)
  FACTOR command, 372
  MANOVA command, 684
$VARS (subcommand)
  SHOW command, 1116
VECTOR (command), 1239
  examples, 335, 340
  index, 1239, 1243
  short form, 1241
  TO keyword, 1239
  variable list, 1239
  with DATA LIST command, 1243
  with INPUT PROGRAM command, 1242
  with LOOP command, 1239, 1240
VECTOR (keyword)
  DISPLAY command, 313
VERIFY (command), 1245
  VARIABLES subcommand, 1246
VERTICAL (keyword)
  IGRAPH command, 558
VERTICAL (subcommand)
  PLOT command, 878
VICICLE (keyword)
  CLUSTER command, 172
VIEW (subcommand)
  PROXIMITIES command, 936
VIEWNAME (subcommand)
  IGRAPH command, 558
VIN (subcommand)
  DISCRIMINANT command, 300
VS (keyword)
  MANOVA command, 673
VW (keyword)
  PPLOT command, 896
  RANK command, 962

WALD (keyword)
  COXREG command, 207
WALLER (keyword)
  GLM command, 486
  ONEWAY command, 855
  UNIANOVA command, 1209
WARD (keyword)
  CLUSTER command, 170
WARN (keyword)
  FILE TYPE command, 391
  RECORD TYPE command, 976
  SET command, 1108
WAVERAGE (keyword)
  CLUSTER command, 169
  EXAMINE command, 349
WEEK (keyword)
  DATE command, 259
WEIGHT (command), 1247
  missing values, 1248
  non-positive values, 1248
  weight variable, 1247
  with CROSSTABS, 232
  with TEMPORARY command, 1247
WEIGHT (subcommand)
  SHOW command, 1116
  WLS command, 1252
WHISKER (keyword)
  IGRAPH command, 566
WIDTH (keyword)
  IGRAPH command, 570
WIDTH (subcommand)
  REGRESSION command, 996
  SET command, 1111
  SHOW command, 1116
WILCOXON (subcommand)
  NPAR TESTS command, 840
WILD (subcommand)
  FILE TYPE command, 391
WILKS (keyword)
  DISCRIMINANT command, 298
WITH (keyword)
  ANOVA command, 122
  CORRELATIONS command, 194
  CURVEFIT command, 237
  GENLOG command, 429
  LOGISTIC REGRESSION command, 612
  LOGLINEAR command, 634
  NOMREG command, 811
  NONPAR CORR command, 818
  NPAR TESTS command, 825, 834, 836, 839, 840

PARTIAL CORR command, 868
PLOT command, 877
PROBIT command, 925
T-TEST command, 1186
WITHIN (keyword)
  MANOVA command, 653, 670
  NOMREG subcommand, 813
  SPCHART command, 1134
  VARCOMP command, 1232
WK1 (keyword)
  SAVE TRANSLATE command, 1090
WKS (keyword)
  SAVE TRANSLATE command, 1090
WLS (command), 1249
  APPLY subcommand, 1253
  CONSTANT subcommand, 1253
  DELTA subcommand, 1252
  limitations, 1251
  NOCONSTANT subcommand, 1253
  POWER subcommand, 1252
  PRINT subcommand, 1253
  SAVE subcommand, 1253
  SOURCE subcommand, 1251
  VARIABLES subcommand, 1251
  WEIGHT subcommand, 1252
WORKSPACE (subcommand)
  SHOW command, 1103, 1116
WPRED (keyword)
  GLM command, 488
  UNIANOVA command, 1211
WR1 (keyword)
  SAVE TRANSLATE command, 1090
WRAP (keyword)
  LIST command, 607
WRESID, 488, 1211
WRESID (keyword)
  GLM command, 488
  UNIANOVA command, 1211
WRITE (command), 1255
  formats, 1257
  missing values, 1256
  NOTABLE subcommand, 1259
  OUTFILE subcommand, 1259
  RECORDS subcommand, 1258
  strings, 1258
  TABLE subcommand, 1259
  variable list, 1256
  with SET command, 1256
WRITE (statement)
  MATRIX command, 736

WRITE (subcommand)
  CROSSTABS command, 230
  SURVIVAL command, 1160
WRITE FORMATS (command), 1260
  format specification, 1260
  string variables, 1260
  with DISPLAY command, 1261
  with SET command, 1262
WRK (keyword)
  SAVE TRANSLATE command, 1090
WSDESIGN (subcommand)
  GLM command, 501
  MANOVA command, 692
WSFACTOR (subcommand)
  GLM command, 498
WSFACTORS (subcommand)
  MANOVA command, 690
W-W (subcommand)
  NPAR TESTS command, 839

X1 (subcommand)
  IGRAPH command, 554
X1INTERVAL (keyword)
  IGRAPH command, 570
X1LENGTH (subcommand)
  IGRAPH command, 555
X1MULTIPLIER (keyword)
  IGRAPH command, 571
X1START (keyword)
  IGRAPH command, 570
X2 (subcommand)
  IGRAPH command, 554
X2INTERVAL (keyword)
  IGRAPH command, 570
X2LENGTH (subcommand)
  IGRAPH command, 555
X2MULTIPLIER (keyword)
  IGRAPH command, 571
X2START (keyword)
  IGRAPH command, 570
XBETA (keyword)
  COXREG command, 211
XLS (keyword)
  GET DATA command, 439
  SAVE TRANSLATE command, 1090
XPROD (keyword)
  CORRELATIONS command, 193
  REGRESSION command, 993

XR (subcommand)
  data organization, 1124
  SPCHART command, 1122
  variable specification, 1125
XS (subcommand)
  data organization, 1124
  SPCHART command, 1122
  variable specification, 1125
XSAVE (command), 1263
  compared to SAVE command, 1079, 1263
  COMPRESSED subcommand, 1267
  DROP subcommand, 1265
  KEEP subcommand, 1265
  limitations, 1265
  MAP subcommand, 1267
  OUTFILE subcommand, 1265
  RENAME subcommand, 1266
  UNCOMPRESSED subcommand, 1267
  with DO REPEAT command, 1264
  with TEMPORARY command, 1166
XTX (keyword)
  REGRESSION command, 988
XYZ (keyword)
  GRAPH command, 527

Y (keyword)
  CLUSTER command, 167
  PROXIMITIES command, 943
Y (subcommand)
  IGRAPH command, 554
YEAR (keyword)
  DATE command, 259
YES (keyword)
  SET command, 1102
YLENGTH (subcommand)
  IGRAPH command, 555

Z (keyword)
  PROXIMITIES command, 935
ZCORR (keyword)
  MANOVA command, 683
ZPP (keyword)
  REGRESSION command, 988
ZPRED (keyword)
  REGRESSION command, 999

ZRESID (keyword)
    GLM command, 488
    LOGISTIC REGRESSION command, 620
    REGRESSION command, 999
    UNIANOVA command, 1211